THE

NEW

ANNUAL ARMY LIST,

WITH AN INDEX.

CORRECTED TO 7TH FEBRUARY,

1840.

BY

H. G. HART, LIEUT. 49TH REGT.

LONDON:
JOHN MURRAY, ALBEMARLE STREET.
1840.

EXPLANATIONS.

K.G	Knight of the Order of the Garter.
K.T.	Knight of the Order of the Thistle.
K.P.	Knight of the Order of St. Patrick.
G.C.B.	Knight *Grand Cross* of the Order of the Bath.
K.C.B.	Knight *Commander* of the Order of the Bath.
C.B.	*Companion* of the Order of the Bath.
G.C.M.G.	Knight *Grand Cross* of the Order of St. Michael and St. George.
K.C.M.G.	Knight *Commander* of ditto ditto
C.M.G.	*Companion* of ditto ditto
G.C.H.	Knight *Grand Cross* of the Royal Hanoverian Guelphic Order.
K.C.H.	Knight *Commander* of ditto ditto
K.H.	Knight of ditto ditto
K.C.	Knight of the Crescent.
ℂ	Before the Name, denotes that the Officer was at the Battle of *Trafalgar*.
ℙ	Before the Name, denotes that the Officer served in the *Peninsula*, or the South of France.
🅆	Waterloo Medal. { Officers actually present in either of the actions of the 16th, 17th, or 18th June, 1815.*
p	Before the Date, indicates that the Commission was *Purchased*.†
*	Before the Name, or date of Commission, denotes Temporary Rank only.

N. B. In the List of General and Field Officers, the Names printed in Italic are those of Officers retired from the Army, who have been specially allowed to retain their Rank, but without receiving Pay or progressive Promotion.

* Officers present in either of these actions are allowed two years' additional service.
† This bears reference to the commissions of Officers on Full-pay only.

CONTENTS.

	page		page
Actions or Battles	448	Gibraltar Garrison	444
Adjutant-General's Department	*114	Gravesend and Tilbury Fort	444
Adjutants of Recruiting Districts	*115, 263	Great Britain Staff	*114
African Colonial Corps	259	Guernsey, Island of	444
Aides-de-Camp to the Queen	108	Half-pay List	315
Alderney, Island of	443	Hibernian Military School	447
American Staff	*115	Honorary Distinctions	448
Artillery, Royal	264	Horse Guards, Royal Regiment of	120
Bath, Officers of the Order of	463	Hull Garrison	444
Battles or Actions	448	Jamaica Staff	*116
Belfast Garrison	443	Jersey, Island of	444
Berwick Garrison	443	Index	478
Brigadier Generals	115	Inspecting Field Officers	263
Cadets, Company of Gentlemen	271	Inverness Garrison	444
Canada Staff	*115	Ionian Islands, Staff	*115
Cape Breton Garrison	443	Ireland, Staff in	*115
Cape Mounted Riflemen	260	Kinsale Garrison	443
Cape of Good Hope Staff	*116	Land-Guard Fort	444
Captains Local Rank	70	Lieutenant-Generals	10
Carlisle Garrison	443	Lieutenant-Colonels	53
Carrickfergus Garrison	443	Life-Guards	118, 119
Ceylon Rifle Regiment	257	Light Dragoons	130
Ceylon Staff	*116	Local Rank	115
Chaplains Department	416	Londonderry and Culmore Garrison	444
Chatham Depôt Staff	*114	Maidstone Depôt Staff	*114
Chelsea Hospital	446	Major Generals	16
Chester Garrison	443	Majors	83
Colonels	32	Malta Fencibles	262
Commissariat Department	205, 405	Malta Garrison	444
Dartmouth Garrison	443	Marines, Royal	292
Depôt Staff	*114	Mauritius Staff	*116
Dragoon Guards	121	Medical Department	309, 407
Dragoons	128	Medical Department of Ordnance	287
Dublin Garrison	443	Milford Haven Garrison	444
Dumbarton Castle	443	Military Departments	305, 405
Duncannon Fort	443	Military College	446
Edinburgh Castle	444	Military Asylum	447
Engineers, Royal	282	Montreal Garrison	444
Field Marshals	5	New Brunswick Garrison	445
Foot Guards	144	Newfoundland Veteran Companies	161
Foot (Numbered Regiments)	151	New Geneva Garrison	445
Foreign Corps on Half-pay	432	North America Staff	*115
Foreign Orders	468	Nova Scotia Staff	*116
Foreign Stations, Staff on	*115	Order of the Garter	462
Fort William	446	———— Thistle	462
Galway Garrison	444	———— St. Patrick	462
Garrisons	443	———— Bath	463
Garter, Order of	462	———— St. Michael and St. George	468
Generals	6	Orders, Foreign	468
General Officers receiving Rewards for Distinguished Services	447	Ordnance Department	264
German Legion	432	Paymasters of Recruiting Districts	*115, 263

Contents.

	page		page
Permanent Assistant Quarter-Masters-General	*114	St. Mawe's Garrison	445
Placentia Garrison	445	St. Michael and St. George, Order of	468
Plymouth Garrison	445	St. Patrick, Order of	462
Portsmouth Garrison	445	Sappers and Miners	286
Prince Edward's Island	*116, 445	Scarborough Castle	445
Provisional Battalion at Chatham	261	Sheerness Garrison	445
Quarter-Master-General's Department	*114	Staff at Head Quarters	117
Quebec Garrison	445	Staff and Miscellaneous Appointments (held by Commission)	*114
Recruiting Staff	*115, 263	Stirling Castle	445
Retired Officers on Full Pay	315	Thistle, Order of	462
Rewards for Distinguished Services, Officers receiving	108	Tower of London	446
Rifle Brigade	252	Tynemouth and Cliff Fort	446
Riding Establishment, Ordnance	273	Western Australia, Staff of	*116
St. Helena Garrison	445	West India Regiments	254
St. John's Newfoundland	445	West India Staff	*116
		Wight, Isle of	446

THE NEW ANNUAL ARMY LIST.

1840.

FIELD MARSHALS.

𝔓 𝔚 *HIS GRACE* ARTHUR, *DUKE OF* WELLINGTON, KG. GCB. GCH.
   Ensign, 7 March, 1787; *Lieut.* 25 Dec. 87; *Captain*, 30 June, 91; *Major*, 30 April, 93; *Lieut.-Colonel*, 30 Sept. 93; *Colonel*, 3 May, 96; *Major-General*, 29 April, 02; *Lieut.-General*, 25 April, 08; *General* (in Spain and Portugal), 31 July, 11; *Field Marshal*, 21 June, 13. Colonel of the Grenadier Regiment of Foot Guards, 22 Jan. 1827; Colonel-in-Chief of the Rifle Brigade, 19th Feb. 1820; Constable of the Tower of London, 29 Dec. 1826; and Lord Warden of the Cinque Ports, 27 Dec. 1828.

HIS MAJESTY THE KING OF HANOVER, KG. KP. GCB. *Lieut.-General,* 18 May, 1798; *General,* 25 Sept. 1803; *Field Marshal,* 26 Nov. 1813.

HIS ROYAL HIGHNESS ADOLPHUS FREDERICK, *DUKE OF* CAMBRIDGE, KG. GCB. GCMG. GCH. *Lieut.-General,* 24 Aug. 1798; *General,* 25 Sept. 1803; *Field Marshal,* 26 Nov. 1813. Colonel of the Coldstream Regiment of Foot Guards, 5 Sept. 1805; and Colonel-in-Chief of the 60th (or the King's Royal Rifle Corps), 22 Jan. 1827.

HIS MAJESTY THE KING OF THE BELGIANS, KG. GCB. GCH. *General,* 2 May, 1816; *Field Marshal,* 24 May, 1816.

HIS ROYAL HIGHNESS FRANCIS ALBERT AUGUSTUS CHARLES EMANUEL, *DUKE OF* SAXE, *PRINCE OF* SAXE COBOURG AND GOTHA, KG. 8 Feb. 1840.

GENERALS.

	CORNET, 2d LIEUT. or ENSIGN.	LIEUT.	CAPTAIN.	MAJOR.	LIEUT.-COLONEL.	COLONEL.	MAJOR-GENERAL.	LIEUT.-GENERAL.	GENERAL.	
Wm. *Earl* Cathcart, KT.	2 June 77	14 Nov. 77	10 Dec. 77	13 April 79	2 Feb. 81	18 Nov. 90	3 Oct. 94	1 Jan. 01	1 Jan. 12	{ 2 Life Gds. *Gov. of Hull.*
Sir Henry Pigot, GCMG.	23 Jan. 69	24 Sept. 72	16 Mar. 75	4 April 81	6 May 83	20 Dec. 93	26 Feb. 95	29 April 02	do	38 *Foot.*
Sir George Nugent, *Bart.* GCB.	5 July 73	23 Nov. 75	28 April 78	9 May 82	8 Sept. 83	1 Mar. 94	3 May 96	25 Sept. 03	4 June 13	{ 6 Foot, *Capt. of St. Mawes.*
Rt. Hon. Sir G. Hewett, *Bt.* GCB.	27 April 62	20 April 64	2 June 75	31 Dec. 81	12 Oct. 87	do	do	do	do	61 *Foot.*
Edward Morrison	20 Jan. 77	never	15 Sept. 80	never	13 Jan. 90	26 Feb. 95	1 Jan. 98	1 Jan. 05	4 June 14	{ 13 Foot, *Gov. of Chester.*
Geo. James *Earl* Ludlow, GCB.	17 May 78	never	16 Mar. 81	never	24 Nov. 90	21 Aug. 95	18 June 98	30 Oct. 05	do	Scots Fus. Guards.
Hon. Frederick St. John¹	31 Aug. 79	7 Feb. 80	12 Dec. 80	8 April 83	23 Feb. 91	do	do	do	do	
His Roy. Highness W. F. H. the Hered. *Prince of* Orange, GCB.²										
Hon. Edward Finch	never	never	never	never	11 June 11	17 Oct. 11	13 Dec. 13	8 July 14	25 July 14	
Isaac Gascoyne	27 Dec. 78	7 Oct. 79	5 Feb. 83	never	3 Oct. 92	3 May 96	1 Jan. 01	25 April 08	12 Aug. 19	22 *Foot.*
Thomas Grosvenor	8 Feb. 79	never	18 Aug. 84	never	5 Dec. 92	do	do	do	do	54 *Foot.*
James, *Lord* Forbes	1 Oct. 79	never	20 Oct. 84	never	25 April 93	do	29 April 02	do	do	65 *Foot.*
Henry, *Marq. of* Anglesey, KG. GCB. GCH.	13 June 81	never	21 April 86	never	23 Aug. 93	do	do	do	do	21 *Foot.*
Sir George Cockburn, G.C.H.³	never	11 Mar. 95	30 Mar. 95	20 May 95	12 Sept. 93	do	do	do	do	{ 7 Hussars, *Capt. of Cowes Castle.*
Edward Dunne⁴	9 May 81	never	4 Feb. 84	30 Nov. 90	31 Dec. 93	26 Jan. 97	25 Sept. 03	25 July 10	19 July 21	
Sir Alex. Mackenzie, *Bt.* GCH⁵	9 Sept. 80	24 May 84	28 Feb. 85	30 Sept. 91	do	do	do	do	do	From 36 Foot.
Thos. *Lord* Lynedoch, GCB.	30 June 87	23 Feb. 91	22 Feb. 93	25 July 93	10 Feb. 94	22 July 95	do	do	do	{ 1 F. *Gov. of Dumbarton Castle.*
GCMG.	never	never	never	never						

Generals.

	CORNET, ETC.	LIEUT.	CAPTAIN.	MAJOR.	LIEUT.-COLONEL.	COLONEL.	MAJ.-GEN.	LIEUT.-GENERAL.	GENERAL.	
Francis Fuller	26 Jan. 78	1 June 78	9 April 81	21 Dec. 85	1 Mar. 94	1 Jan. 98	1 Jan. 05	4 June 11	27 May 25	2 W. I. Regt.
Sir Gordon Drummond, GCB.	21 Sept. 89	31 Mar. 91	31 Jan. 92	28 Feb. 94	do	do	do	do	do	49 Foot.
James Wharton	29 June 82	31 May 90	31 July 92	28 Feb. 94	do	do	do	do	do	From 21 Dragoons.
Hon. Edward Bligh	28 Nov. 87	never	24 Jan. 91	1 Mar. 94	5 Mar. 94	do	do	do	do	
Edmund, Earl of Cork, KP.[6]	13 April 85	7 Dec. 85	24 Jan. 91		29 Mar. 94	do	do	do	do	13 Dragoons.
Hon. Sir H. G. Grey, GCB. GCH.	17 Oct. 79	28 July 81	31 May 87	23 Oct. 93	21 April 94	do	do	do	do	{ 28 Foot, Gov. of Chelsea Hosp.
Hon. Sir Edward Paget, GCB.	23 Mar. 92		7 Dec. 92	14 Nov. 93	30 April 94	do	do	do	do	1 L. G. Gov. of Sheerness.
Stapleton, Visc. Combermere, GCB. GCH.	26 Feb. 90	16 Mar. 91	28 Feb. 93	28 April 94	9 Mar. 94	1 Jan. 00	30 Oct. 05	1 Jan. 12	do	{ R. H. G. Gov. of Plymouth. Gen. Com. in Chief
Rowland, Lord Hill, GCB. GCH. KC.	31 July 90	24 Jan. 91	23 Mar. 93	10 Feb. 94	13 May 94	do	do	do	do	58 Foot.
Sir George Pigot, Bart.	5 June 87	30 July 91	31 Aug. 93	15 Jan. 94	12 June 94	do	do	do	do	
Frederick Maitland	1 Sept. 79	19 Sept. 82	2 Dec. 89	21 Aug. 93	2 July 94	do	do	do	do	{ From 104 F. Gov. of Stirling Cas.
Sir Martin Hunter, GCMG. GCH.[7]	30 Aug. 71	18 June 75	21 Nov. 77	30 Oct. 93	19 July 94	do	do	do	do	16 Foot Gov. of Jersey.
Wm. Carr, Visc. Beresford, GCB. GCH.	27 Aug. 85	25 June 89	24 Jan. 91	1 Mar. 94	11 Aug. 94	do	25 April 08	do	do	
Thomas Baker	23 July 74	never	3 April 79	1 Mar. 94	22 Aug. 94	do	do	4 June 13	22 July 30	
Henry Williams	25 Dec. 78	16 Feb. 80	31 May 88	8 May 94	22 Aug. 94	do	do	do	do	
Sir John Fraser, GCH.[8]	never	29 Sept. 78	21 Apr. 83	1 Mar. 94	28 Aug. 94	do	do	do	do	{ From R. Y. Rang. Lt. Gov. Chester.
Peter Heron	14 Apr. 90	2 Sept. 93	13 Feb. 94	12 Sept. 94	28 Aug. 94	do	do	do	do	From Chass. Brit.
John Ramsay	1 Nov. 82	14 June 83	22 June 85	never	16 Sept. 94	do	do	do	do	63 Foot.
Sir J. Delves Broughton, Bart.	20 Apr. 85	25 Dec. 87	24 Jan. 91	17 May 94	18 Sept. 94	do	do	do	do	79 Foot.
William Dyott	4 Mar. 81	9 May 82	25 Apr. 93	19 May 94	18 Sept. 94	do	do	do	do	32 Foot.
Sir R. Craufurd Ferguson, GCB.	3 April 90	31 May 91	19 Feb. 93	31 May 94	19 Sept. 94	do	do	do	do	
Sir R. Macfarlane, KCB., GCH.	26 May 89	22 May 93	25 Sept. 93	12 Nov. 94	19 Sept. 94	do	do	do	do	
Sir John Gustavus Crosbie, GCH.	29 June 80	30 April 81	1 May 83	31 Dec. 93	28 Sept. 94	do	do	do	do	
Hon. John Brodrick[9]	6 Nov. 82	never	3 Mar. 90	never	5 Oct. 94	1 Jan. 01	do	do	do	
James Durham	28 June 69	13 Mar. 79	11 Mar. 79	1 Sept. 94	20 Oct. 94	do	do	do	do	
John Manners Kerr	21 Feb. 85	24 Sept. 87	10 Nov. 90	29 June 94	25 Oct. 94	do	do	do	do	{ From 5 Royal Vet. Battalion.
Thomas Scott[10]	20 May 61	7 June 65	14 July 77	13 Nov. 93	27 Oct. 94	do	do	do	do	From 94 Foot.

Generals.

	CORNET, ETC.		LIEUT.		CAPTAIN.		MAJOR.		LIEUT. COLONEL.		COLONEL.		MAJOR GENERAL.		LIEUT. GENERAL.		GENERAL.	
Sir Hilgrove Turner, G C H., KC.	20 Feb.	82	never		13 Oct.	89	never		12 Nov.	94	1 Jan.	01	25 Apr.	08	4 June	13	22 July	30	19 Foot.
Hon. Wm. Mordaunt Maitland[11]	20 Oct.	79	22 May	82	5 Apr.	83	1 Mar.	94	15 Nov.	94	do		do		do		do		27 F. Gov. Grav. and Tilbury Ft.
Hon. Sir G. Lowry Cole, GCB.	31 Mar.	87	31 May	91	30 Nov.	92	31 Oct.	93	26 Nov.	94	do		do		do		do		
Francis Moore	30 Sept.	87	31 Aug.	91	22 June	91	20 July	94	20 Dec.	94	do		do		do		do		
Robert, Viscount Lorton[12]	30 June	93	28 Feb.	93	3 Dec.	93	7 Mar.	94	20 Dec.	94	do		do		do		do		55 Foot.
Sir Wm. Henry Clinton, GCB.	22 Dec.	84	7 Mar.	87	9 June	90	never		29 Dec.	94	do		do		do		do		Lieut.-Gov. of Edin. Castle.
Francis Thomas Hammond, GCH.	24 Aug.	80	2 Jan.	82	23 Feb.	82	3 Mar.	94	3 Feb.	95	29 Apr.	02	25 Oct.	09	4 June	14	10 Jan.	37	
Robert Dudley Blake	8 Mar.	93	29 June	93	21 May	93	18 Sept.	94	28 Feb.	95	do		do		do		do		
Hon. Robert Meade	7 Nov.	87	15 May	93	23 Sept.	93	30 Oct.	94	10 Mar.	95	do		do		do		do		12 Foot.
Sir W. Houstoun, Bart., GCB., G C H.																			
George Michell[13]	18 July	81	2 Apr.	82	13 Mar.	83	1 Mar.	94	18 Mar.	95	do		do		do		do		20 Foot.
Sir T. Hislop, Bart., GCB.	6 Feb.	76	20 May	79	27 Oct.	84	1 Mar.	94	25 Mar.	95	do		do		do		do		
Thomas, Earl of Elgin, KC.	28 Dec.	78	28 Jan.	83	28 Jan.	85	16 Aug.	94	25 Mar.	95	do		do		do		do		48 Foot.
David Hunter	6 April	85	never		9 May	89	30 Nov.	94	17 Apr.	95	do		do		do		do		
Sir John Slade, Bart., G C H.	6 June	88	24 Jan.	91	2 Apr.	93	16 April	95	17 Apr.	95	do		do		do		do		5 Dragoon Guards.
Sir Fred. A. Wetherall, GCH.	11 May	80	28 Apr.	83	24 Oct.	87	1 Mar.	94	29 Apr.	95	do		do		do		do		17 Foot.
Hon. Sir W. Lumley, GCH.	23 Aug.	75	27 Aug.	76	17 May	81	1 Mar.	94	20 May	95	do		do		do		do		6 Dragoons.
Sir Moore Disney, KCB	24 Oct.	87	19 May	90	4 Dec.	85	10 Mar.	95	25 May	95	do		do		do		do		15 Foot.
John McKenzie[14]	17 Apr.	83	never		3 June	91	never		12 June	95	do		do		do		do		
Alexander Graham Stirling	18 Mar.	82	1 Jan.	78	13 Feb.	82	1 Mar.	94	15 July	95	do		do		do		do		
John Michell[15]	7 Feb.	81	11 Feb.	85	30 June	90	28 Feb.	95	12 Aug.	95	do		do		do		do		
Sir Wm. Wilkinson, GCMG.[16]	20 May	80	25 June	85	31 July	90	30 Nov.	92	24 Aug.	95	do		do		do		do		
John Hodgson	13 July	91	10 Apr.	73	17 Nov.	75	1 Mar.	94	1 Sept.	95	25 Sept.	03	25 July	10	do		do		From 30 Foot.
Richard Thomas Nelson	never		22 Feb.	91	30 Apr.	80	14 May	94	do		do		do		do		do		4 Foot.
James Robertson[17]	6 Feb.	82	23 Dec.	77	24 Sept.	87	18 Sept.	94	4 Nov.	95	do		do		do		do		
Edward Wm. Leyborne Popham	24 Sept.	87	7 June	93	19 July	82	1 Mar.	95	11 Nov.	95	do		do		do		do		
Sir Fitzroy J. G. Maclean, Bart	20 Sept.	86	19 June	88	31 May	83	19 Aug.	95	18 Nov.	95	do		do		do		do		84 Foot.
Sir H. F. Campbell, KCB GCH.			never		15 July	93	Mar.	95	6 April	96	do		do		do		do		25 Foot.
Cha. Wm. Marq. of Londonderry, KCB. GCH.	11 Oct.	94	30 Oct.	94	25 April	93	never												
Lewis Bayly Wallis	28 Dec.	91	7 Mar.	93	12 Nov.	94	31 July	95	1 Jan.	97	do		do		do		do		10 Hussars.
John Sullivan Wood[18]	30 May	87	20 April	91	7 Mar.	93	18 Nov.	94	2 Feb.	96	1 Jan.	05	12 Aug.	19	do		do		From 8 Drag., Lieut. of the Tower of London
Hon. Sir Charles Colville, GCB. GCH.	6 Dec.	81	30 Sept.	87	24 Jan.	91	2 Sept.	95	26 Aug.	96	do		do		do		do		5 Foot.

Generals.

	CORNET, ETC.	LIEUT.	CAPTAIN.	MAJOR.	LIEUT. COLONEL.	COLONEL.	MAJOR GENERAL.	LIEUT. GENERAL.	GENERAL.	
Frederick Charles White [19]	19 Feb. 81	30 Dec. 82	6 May 83	1 Jan. 94	5 Sept. 96	1 Jan. 05	25 July 10	12 Aug. 19	10 Jan. 37	From Gren. Gds.
Gore Browne	5 July 80	3 Mar. 89	8 June 93	15 June 94	30 Nov. 96	do	do	do	do	44 Foot.
🜚 *Sir* Henry Fane, GCB.	31 May 92	29 Sept. 92	3 April 93	24 Aug. 95	1 Jan. 97	do	do	do	do	1 Dragoon Guards.
🜚 *Sir* George Anson, GCB.	3 May 86	16 Mar. 91	9 Sept. 92	25 Dec. 94	21 Dec. 97	do	do	do	do	4 Dragoon Guards.
🜚 Kenneth Alex. *Earl of Effingham*, GCB.	21 April 86	never	25 April 93	never	30 Dec. 97	do	do	do	do	3 Foot.
Thomas R. Charleton	17 June 72	7 July 79	1 Dec. 82	1 Mar. 94	1 Jan. 98	28 June 05	4 June 11	do	do	From Royal Art. { From S. Fu.Gds. Lt.-Gov.Quebec
🜚 William Thomas Dilkes [20]	4 Dec. 79	1 Sept. 81	25 April 92	never	4 Feb. 97	30 Oct. 05	do	do	do	35 Foot.
🜚 *Sir* J. Oswald, GCB. GCMG.	1 Feb. 88	29 Jan. 89	24 Jan. 91	1 Sept. 95	30 Mar. 97	do	do	do	do	From 69 Foot.
Pinson Bonham [21]	24 April 89	26 Jan. 91	9 June 93	4 Nov. 95	9 Sept. 97	do	do	do	do	47 Foot.
🜚 *Sir* Wm. Anson, *Bart.*, KCB.	13 June 89	never	25 April 93	never	28 Sept. 97	do	do	do	do	
Sir Thomas Saunarez [22]	25 Jan. 76	22 Nov. 77	13 Sept. 79	1 Mar. 94	1 Jan. 98	25 April 08	do	19 July 21	28 June 38	From 88 Foot.
Campbell Callendar	29 Mar. 75	5 Mar. 77	17 May 81	do	do	do	do	do	do	From Roy.Marines
James Meredith	16 Jan. 76	17 Mar. 78	4 Sept. 82	do	do	do	do	do	do	From 61 Foot.
🜚 John Stratford Saunders [23]	26 May 79	2 Dec. 79	12 Sept. 82	do	do	do	do	do	do	From R. Inval.Art.
George Wilson	15 Mar. 71	7 July 79	1 Dec. 82	do	do	do	do	do	do	From Coldst. Gds
🜚 *Sir* W. M. Peacocke, KCH. KC.ᴿ [21]	12 Dec. 80	22 May 82	14 April 83	do	do	do	do	do	do	33 Foot.
Sir Charles Wale, KCB.	June 79	13 April 80	25 June 83	do	do	do	do	do	do	
🜚 🜚 *Sir* John Ormsby Vandeleur, GCB.	29 Dec. 81	21 July 83	7 Mar. 92	do	do	do	do	do	do	16 Dragoons.
Charles Pye Douglas	31 Dec. 82	9 June 86	24 Aug. 92	do	do	do	do	do	do	From 3 Dragoons.
Robert Browne Clayton, KC.	1 Sept. 84	30 April 90	31 Mar. 93	do	do	do	do	do	do	12 Dragoons.
🜚 Alexander John Goldie [25]	8 Jan. 88	11 May 91	30 April 94	1 Jan. 97	17 Feb. 98	do	do	do	do	From 6 Drag .Gds.
Sir Roger Hale Sheaffe, *Bart.*	1 May 78	27 Dec. 80	6 May 95	13 Dec. 97	22 Mar. 98	do	do	do	do	36 Foot.
Hon. *Sir* Alex. Duff, GCH.	23 May 93	15 Jan. 94	16 Jan. 98	28 Nov. 94	14 April 98	do	do	do	do	37 Foot.
🜚 *Sir* R. Shaw Donkin, KCB. GCH.	21 Mar. 78	9 Sept. 79	31 May 93	1 Sept. 95	24 May 98	do	do	do	do	{ 11 Foot, Surv.- Gen.of the Ord.
William Eden [26]	26 Aug. 86	31 May 90	3 June 95	16 Dec. 95	15 Aug. 98	do	do	do	do	From 84 Foot.
🜚 *Sir* G. T. Walker, *Bart.*, GCB.	4 Mar. 82	13 Mar. 83	13 Mar. 89	28 Aug. 94	6 Sept. 98	do	do	do	do	{ 50 Ft. *Lt. Gov. of Chelsea Hosp.*
Sir J. Hamilton Dalrymple, *Bart.*	28 Feb. 90	30 April 92	26 April 93	never	6 Dec. 98	do	do	do	do	92 Foot.

LIEUTENANT-GENERALS.

	CORNET, 2nd LIEUT., or ENSIGN.	LIEUT.	CAPTAIN.	MAJOR.	LIEUT.-COLONEL.	COLONEL.	MAJOR-GENERAL.	LIEUT.-GENERAL.	
William Thornton[27]	6 Nov. 78	never	18 Mar. 82	never	25 April 93	3 May 96	29 April 02	25 April 08	Late of 1 Foot Guards.
Richard Northey Hopkins	1 Sept. 73	29 Mar. 76	12 Nov. 78	29 Aug. 93	5 Nov. 93	26 Jan. 97	25 Sept. 03	25 Oct. 09	Late of 32 Foot.
William Thomas[28]	31 Mar. 77	19 Feb. 79	31 Oct. 81	31 Dec. 93	20 Aug. 95	29 April 02	25 Oct. 09	4 June 14	{ Lt. Gov. of Tynemouth Cliff and Fort.
Frederick, Count, von der Decken, GCH.	never	never	never	never	2 June 03	28 July 03	25 July 03	do	Half-pay German Legion.
George Meyrick	21 April 84	30 June 87	8 April 93	14 June 94	19 Mar. 96	1 Jan. 05	do	12 Aug. 19	
Terence O'Loghlin[29]	14 Dec. 92	13 Mar. 93	1 April 95	19 Feb. 99	14 Aug. 01	1 Sept. 08	1 Jan. 10	27 May 25	Late of 27 Foot.
Right Hon. Sir George Murray, GCB. GCH.	12 Mar. 89	never	16 Jan. 94	never	5 Aug. 99	9 Mar. 09	do	do	{ 42 Foot, Gov. of Fort George.
Right Hon. Sir J. Kempt, GCB. GCH.	31 Mar. 83	18 Aug. 84	30 May 94	18 Sept. 94	28 Aug. 99	9 Mar. 09	do	do	{ 2 Foot, Lieut. Gov. of Fort William.
Sir Evan Lloyd, KCH.	25 Nov. 80	5 Feb. 87	25 Oct. 93	1 Sept. 95	11 Feb. 99	25 Oct. 09	do	do	7 Dragoon Guards.
Matthew Sharpe	18 Feb. 91	19 Feb. 93	25 Mar. 95	27 Feb. 96	5 Aug. 99	do	do	do	
Richard Blunt	31 Jan. 87	23 Feb. 93	12 July 98	17 May 96	23 Aug. 99	do	do	do	66 Foot.
Sir Henry Bayly, GCH.	12 April 83	never	28 Aug. 93	never	5 Sept. 99	do	do	do	8 Foot.
Francis Slater Rebow[30]	14 Nov. 87	14 Oct. 89	18 Sept. 92	20 Feb. 96	25 Sept. 99	do	do	do	From 1 Life Guards.
Sir Wm. Henry Pringle, GCB.	6 July 92	24 Feb. 93	15 Oct. 94	19 Sept. 94	5 Dec. 99	do	do	do	45 Foot.
Gerard Gosselin[31]	29 Nov. 80	26 Jan. 91	6 June 94	15 June 94	1 Jan. 00	25 July 10	4 June 13	do	
Sir Fred. Philipse Robinson, GCB.	11 Sept. 78	1 Sept. 79	3 July 94	1 Sept. 94	do	do	do	do	59 Foot.
Arthur Richard Dillon[32]	31 May 91	31 May 92	18 May 93	18 Sept. 94	do	do	do	do	
Duncan Darroch[33]	31 Mar. 92	31 Dec. 93	1 April 94	1 Nov. 94	do	do	do	do	From 36 Foot.
John Murray	6 Feb. 91	8 Mar. 93	28 May 94	1 Nov. 94	do	do	do	do	From late 96 Foot.
Sir Phineas Riall, KCH.	31 Jan. 92	28 Feb. 94	31 May 94	8 Dec. 94	do	do	do	do	74 Foot.
William Brooke	29 June 93	7 Oct. 93	14 Dec. 93	13 Dec. 94	do	do	do	do	From 5 Dragoon Guards.

Lieutenant-Generals.

	2D LIEUT. ETC.	LIEUT.	CAPTAIN.	MAJOR.	LIEUT.-COLONEL.	COLONEL.	MAJOR-GENERAL.	LIEUT.-GENERAL.	
Sir Thomas Molyneux, Bart.[34]	27 Sept. 86	16 Nov. 91	30 April 94	19 Dec. 94	1 Jan. 00	25 July 10	4 June 13	27 May 25	From 80 Foot.
Benjamin Gordon[35]	never	22 Aug. 79	1 Sept. 91	12 Mar. 95	do	do	do	do	69 Foot.
John Vincent	16 July 81	3 Aug. 82	26 Oct. 86	6 May 95	do	do	do	do	From late R. Irish Art.
Joseph Walker	1 Sept. 81	5 Feb. 84	31 Oct. 92	20 May 95	do	do	do	do	From 48 Foot, *Gov. of Carrickfergus.*
⊕ Sir William Hutchinson, KCH.[36]	1 June 81	26 Jan. 83	7 Nov. 92	20 May 95	do	do	do	do	29 F. *Gov. of Londonderry and Culmore.*
⊕ ⊞ John, Lord Strafford, GCB. GCH.	30 Sept. 93	1 Dec. 93	24 May 94	Dec. 99	14 Mar. 00	do	do	do	34 Foot.
⊕ Sir T. M. Brisbane, Bt. GCB. GCH.[37]	10 Jan. 89	30 July 91	12 April 93	5 Aug. 95	4 April 00	do	do	do	From late 104 Foot.
Sir Alcxander Halkett, KCH.	31 Mar. 90	31 Mar. 93	25 Mar. 94	27 Nov. 99	25 Aug. 00	do	do	do	2 Dragoons.
Sir Wm. Keir Grant, KCB. GCH.	30 May 92	18 Feb. 93	6 July 93	6 Jan. 96	3 Dec. 00	do	do	do	4 Dragoons.
⊕ ⊞ Lord R. E. H. Somerset, GCB.	4 Feb. 93	4 Dec. 93	28 Aug. 94	22 Nov. 99	25 Dec. 00	do	do	do	
Hon. Arthur Annesley	7 Aug. 90	24 Sept. 94	30 Oct. 94	10 July 95	1 Jan. 01	do	do	do	From 56 Foot.
Boyle Travers	31 July 90	28 Feb. 93	19 July 94	19 Aug. 95	do	do	do	do	Late of Coldstream Gds.
Frederick William Buller[38]	20 Jan. 90	14 Dec. 93	30 Mar. 93	1 Sept. 95	do	do	do	do	30 Foot.
⊕ Sir Thos. Bradford, GCB. GCH.	20 Oct. 93	9 Dec. 93	15 April 94	9 Sept. 95	do	do	do	do	
John Granby Clay[39]	6 Nov. 82	30 April 88	18 April 94	16 Sept. 95	do	do	do	do	70 Foot.
Gage John Hall	29 May 83	13 Dec. 83	16 Dec. 94	23 Dec. 95	do	do	do	do	
Hon. William De Blaquiere	31 Aug. 87	12 April 93	1 Aug. 93	1 Feb. 98	22 Jan. 01	do	do	do	10 Foot.
Sir Thomas Browne, KCH.	24 Sept. 86	26 Sept. 89	3 Sept. 95	23 Aug. 99	29 Mar. 01	do	do	do	From 69 Foot.
⊕ ⊞ Sir John Lambert, GCB.	27 Jan. 91	never	9 Oct. 93	never	14 May 01	do	do	do	10 Foot.
⊕ Sir J. W. Gordon, Bart. GCB. GCH.	17 Oct. 83	5 Mar. 89	2 Sept. 95	9 Nov. 97	21 May 01	do	do	do	23 F. Qr. Master General.
⊕ Sir Joseph Fuller, GCH.	29 Sept. 90	never	22 Jan. 94	never	18 June 01	do	do	do	75 Foot.
Sir Thos. Gage Montresor, KCH.	12 Mar. 83	4 April 83	17 June 94	12 April 99	27 June 01	do	do	do	2 Dragoon Guards.
⊕ Sir Ralph Darling, GCH.	15 May 93	2 Sept. 93	6 Sept. 95	2 Feb. 00	17 July 01	do	do	do	41 Foot.
George Horsford	15 Aug. 87	14 Oct. 93	16 July 94	4 June 96	28 Aug. 01	do	do	do	From 18 Foot.
⊕ Sir Robert Thomas Wilson	April 94	21 Sept. 94	21 Sept. 96	28 June 00	27 Feb. 02	do	do	do	15 Hussars.
Matthew, Lord Aylmer, GCB.	19 Oct. 87	26 Oct. 91	8 Aug. 94	9 Oct. 00	25 Mar. 02	4 June 11	4 June 14	22 July 30	18 Foot.
Sir Charles Imhoff	83 June 83	29 Mar. 99	4 April 99	20 Nov. 00	25 Feb. 02	do	do	do	
Gabriel Gordon	24 June 81	26 Nov. 84	10 July 89	16 May 00	9 Mar. 02	do	do	do	91 Foot.
Edward Webber	19 April 81	never	11 April 83	3 May 96	29 April 02	do	do	do	
Thomas L'Estrange[40]	26 Oct. 75	18 Aug. 78	23 April 88	3 May 96	do	do	do	do	
Charles Craven	31 Jan. 90	30 Nov. 92	30 May 94	17 May 96	do	do	do	do	
Joseph Foveaux	26 May 89	5 June 89	6 April 91	10 June 96	do	do	do	do	

11

Lieutenant-Generals.

	CORNET, ETC.	LIEUT.	CAPTAIN.	MAJOR.	LIEUT.-COLONEL.	COLONEL.	MAJOR-GENERAL.	LIEUT.-GENERAL.	
Birkenhead Glegg [41]	30 April 90	31 Oct. 92	24 Nov. 94	17 Aug. 97	29 April 02	4 June 11	4 June 14	22 July 30	24 Foot.
⊕ ✠ *Sir* James Lyon, KCB. GCH.	4 Aug. 91	26 April 93	5 April 95	21 Feb. 99	13 May 02	do	do	do	From late 99 Foot.
James Orde	28 Sept. 94	Jan. 95	6 Feb. 95	June 02	13 Aug. 02	do	do	do	89 Foot.
⊕ *Sir* C. B. Egerton, GCMG. KCH.	16 Nov. 91	21 Mar. 93	22 April 95	1 June 98	14 Nov. 02	do	do	do	12 Lancers.
⊕ *Sir* Henry John Cumming, KCH.	12 May 90	9 Feb. 93	21 Feb. 94	25 Oct. 98	17 Feb. 03	1 Jan. 12	do	do	From 44 Foot.
Sir Charles Phillips [42]	24 June 83	31 Aug. 93	2 Sept. 95	14 Jan. 02	9 Mar. 03	do	do	do	{ From Quarter-Master General's Department.
Thomas Birch Reynardson [43]	28 Feb. 93	28 Mar. 93	26 April 94	1 June 99	27 April 03	do	do	do	From Grenadier Guards.
⊕ ✠ John, *Earl of Carysfort* [44]	3 June 95	3 Sept. 95	28 Feb. 98	25 Mar. 02	27 April 03	do	do	do	From Grenadier Guards.
⊕ ✠ *Sir* Peregrine Maitland, KCB.	20 June 92	never	30 April 94	never	25 June 03	do	do	do	76 Foot.
⊕ *Hon.* Thomas Edward Capel [45]	10 April 93	never	4 Oct. 94	never	25 June 03	do	do	do	From Grenadier Guards.
Godfrey Basil Mundy [46]	24 Aug. 95	23 Dec. 95	24 Aug. 97	27 Aug. 02	2 July 03	do	do	22 July 30	From 2 Foot.
⊕ *Hon. Sir* R. W. O'Callaghan, GCB.	29 Nov. 94	6 Dec. 94	31 Jan. 95	17 Feb. 03	16 July 03	do	do	do	39 Foot.
⊕ John, *Lord* Keane, GCB. GCH.	1793	28 April 03	12 Nov. 94	27 May 02	20 Aug. 03	do	do	do	43 Foot.
Henry Eustace	never	never	8 May 90	2 Sept. 98	25 Sept. 03	do	do	do	Late of R. Engineers.
⊕ ✠ *Sir* Colin Halkett, KCB. GCH.	3 June 95	never	never	3 Oct. 98	17 Nov. 03	do	do	do	31 Foot.
Sir Henry Edw. Bunbury, *Bt.* KCB.	14 Jan. 95	never	16 Aug. 97	11 Mar. 02	31 Dec. 03	do	do	do	Late of R. New. Fencibles.
Sir Hudson Lowe, KCB. GCMG.	25 Sept. 87	16 Nov. 91	6 Sept. 95	5 July 00	25 June 04	do	do	do	56 Foot.
⊕ ✠ *Rt. Hon. Sir* Fred. Adam, KCB. GCMG.	4 Nov. 95	2 Feb. 96	30 Aug. 99	9 July 03	28 Aug. 04	20 Feb. 12	do	do	57 Foot.
⊕ ✠ *Rt. Hon. Sir* R. Hussey Vivian, *Bt.* GCB. GCH.	31 July 93	20 Oct. 93	7 May 94	9 Mar. 03	28 Sept. 04	do	do	do	1 Dragoons.
Benj. *Lord* Bloomfield, GCB. GCH.	24 May 81	21 Nov. 87	9 Sept. 94	1 Jan. 05	3 Dec. 06	do	do	do	Royal Artillery.
Sir Henry Sheehy Keating, KCB.	31 Aug. 81	31 Jan. 94	8 Sept. 96	8 Sept. 00	1 Aug. 04	4 June 13	12 Aug. 19	10 Jan. 37	90 Foot.
Sir Lewis Grant, KCH.	14 Feb. 94	15 Feb. 94	11 June 96	8 Sept. 02	16 April 04	do	do	do	96 Foot.
⊕ *Sir* Arthur Brooke, KCB.	31 Oct. 92	26 Nov. 93	19 Sept. 95	26 Dec. 02	15 June 04	do	do	do	86 Foot.
Peter Carey	9 Dec. 95	21 June 97	14 Aug. 01	9 July 03	29 June 04	do	do	do	From 84 Foot.
Henry Shrapnel	9 July 79	3 Dec. 81	15 Aug. 93	29 April 02	20 July 04	do	do	do	Royal Artillery.
John M'Nair [47]	May 94	13 June 94	8 Aug. 94	5 April 01	1 Aug. 04	do	do	do	From 90 Foot.
⊕ *Sir* John Alex. Wallace, *Bt.* KCB.	28 Dec. 87	6 April 90	8 June 96	9 July 03	28 Aug. 04	do	do	do	88 Foot.
Hastings Fraser, CB.	9 April 88	3 Nov. 90	7 Dec. 97	28 July 02	7 Sept. 04	do	do	do	83 Foot.
Sebright Mawby [48]	20 June 87	18 May 91	2 Sept. 95	1 June 99	5 Oct. 04	do	do	do	From 53 Foot.
John Montagu Mainwaring [49]	31 May 84	11 Nov. 89	8 Oct. 94	22 June 01	23 Nov. 04	do	do	do	From 26 Foot.
⊕ *Hon.* John Meade, CB. [50]	30 Oct. 94	12 Nov. 94	29 Aug. 99	4 June 01	1 Dec. 04	do	do	do	From 45 Foot.

Lieutenant-Generals.

Name	ENSIGN, ETC.	LIEUT.	CAPTAIN.	MAJOR.	LIEUT.-COLONEL.	COLONEL.	MAJOR-GENERAL.	LIEUT.-GENERAL.	
Sir Geo. Pownoll Adams, KCH....	5 Oct. 95	12 Mar. 96	11 Oct. 97	5 Feb. 02	8 Dec. 04	4 June 13	12 Aug. 19	10 Jan. 37	From late 25 Dragoons.
Sir John Macleod, CB. KCH......	9 Mar. 93	2 May 94	24 June 95	9 June 99	1 Jan. 05	do	do	do	77 Foot.
Henry Elliot[51]	22 Mar. 86	14 Mar. 89	1 Aug. 94	9 Aug. 99	do	do	do	do	From late 5 R. Vet. Bat.
Sir Benj. D'Urban, KCB. KCH.	April 94	1 July 94	2 July 94	21 Nov. 99	do	do	do	do	51 Foot.
George Wulff	9 July 79	14 Feb. 82	25 Sept. 93	29 April 02	28 Jan. 05	do	do	do	Royal Artillery.
Sir John Taylor, KCB.	Nov. 94	6 Dec. 94	9 Sept. 95	2 Sept. 01	28 Feb. 05	do	do	do	80 Foot.
Sir Samuel Trevor Dickens, KCH.	16 June 89	2 Mar. 89	29 Oct. 94	never	1 Mar. 05	do	do	do	Royal Engineers.
Sir Wiltshire Wilson, KCH.	9 July 79	28 Feb. 82	1 Nov. 93	29 April 02	10 Mar. 05	do	do	do	Royal Artillery.
Sir Thos. Reynell, Bart. KCB	30 Sept. 93	3 Dec. 94	29 July 97	3 Aug. 04	10 Mar. 05	do	do	do	87 Foot.
Sir Loftus Wm. Otway, CB.[52]	17 May 96	2 Sept. 96	27 Oct. 98	24 Feb. 05	28 Mar. 05	do	do	do	From 26 Foot.
Sir Wm. Nicolay, CB. KCH.	28 May 90	15 Aug. 93	29 Aug. 98	26 June 01	4 April 05	do	do	do	1 West India Regiment.
Sir E. Kerrison, Bt. CB. GCH.	23 June 96	1 Feb. 98	18 Oct. 98	12 May 03	4 April 05	do	do	do	14 Dragoons.
Sir Lionel Smith, Bt. KCB. GCH.	Mar. 95	28 Oct. 95	22 May 01	22 April 02	6 June 05	do	do	do	40 Foot, Gov. of the Mauritius.
Sir Robert Barton, KCH.[53] ...	April 94	14 May 94	5 April 96	17 Feb. 03	14 June 05	do	do	do	From 7 Foot, Captain of Carisbrook Castle.
Sir Wm. Paterson, KCH.[54] ...	27 Jan. 86	24 Jan. 91	2 Sept. 95	11 Dec. 02	20 June 05	do	do	do	From Scots Fusilier Gds.
Sir John Wright Guise, Bt. KCB.[55]	4 Nov. 94	never	25 Oct. 98	never	25 July 05	do	do	do	From late 10 R. Vet. Bat.
Sir Charles W. Doyle, CB. GCH.[56]	28 April 83	12 Feb. 93	21 June 94	9 July 03	22 Aug. 05	4 June 13	do	do	From late 1 Argyll Fen. Gov. of Berwick.
Sir James Bathurst, KCB.[57]	10 May 94	16 Nov. 94	25 Dec. 99	1 Oct. 03	10 Oct. 05	do	do	do	78 Foot.
Paul Anderson, CB...........	31 Mar. 88	13 Mar. 91	1 July 95	25 June 01	17 Oct. 05	do	do	do	Rifle Brigade.
Sir A. F. Barnard, KCB. GCH.	26 Aug. 94	Sept. 94	13 Nov. 94	1 Jan. 05	28 Jan. 08	do	do	do	
Richard Pigot	4 Sept. 93	16 Sept. 93	21 Dec. 93	29 April 02	1 May 06	4 June 14	19 July 21	do	From 21 Dragoons.
Sir James Watson, KCB........	24 June 83	18 April 92	11 Mar. 95	3 Dec. 02	15 May 06	do	do	do	14 Foot.
Spencer Claudius Parry	3 Nov. 80	4 Mar. 86	14 Aug. 94	1 Jan. 05	1 June 06	do	do	do	Royal Artillery.
Sir Augustus De Butts, KCH. ...	22 Aug. 87	21 Nov. 92	3 Mar. 97	never	1 July 06	do	do	do	Royal Engineers.
Sir Richard Bourke, KCB.	22 Nov. 98	never	25 Nov. 99	27 Aug. 05	16 Sept. 06	do	do	do	64 Foot.
Hon. Patrick Stuart..........	26 Sept. 93	6 June 94	12 April 96	1 Feb. 03	25 Sept. 06	do	do	do	60 Foot.
George William Phipps........	21 April 79	20 Dec. 86	21 Nov. 92	1 Jan. 00	9 Oct. 06	do	do	do	From Royal Military Academy at Woolwich.
Hon. Henry Otway Trevor, CB.[58]	27 April 93	never	23 June 95	never	25 Oct. 06	do	do	do	From Coldstream Gds.
Sir James Stevenson Barns, KCB.	11 July 92	2 Jan. 94	27 Feb. 96	17 Sept. 02	6 Nov. 06	do	do	do	Rifle Brigade.
W. G. Lord Harris, CB. KCH.	24 May 95	3 Jan. 96	16 Oct. 00	15 June 04	29 Dec. 08	do	do	do	73 Foot.

Lieutenant-Generals.

	CORNET, ETC.	LIEUT.	CAPTAIN.	MAJOR.	LIEUT.-COLONEL.	COLONEL.	MAJOR-GENERAL.	LIEUT.-GENERAL.	
⚑ *Sir* H. Douglas, *Bt.* CB. GCMG. [59]	1 Jan. 94	30 May 94	2 Oct. 99	12 Oct. 04	31 Dec. 06	4 June 14	19 July 21	10 Jan. 37	{ Lord High Commissioner, and Commander of the Troops in the Ionian Islands.
Montagu Burrows	31 Jan. 93	26 Nov. 93	19 Mar. 94	29 April 02	14 May 07	do	do	do	From 64 Foot.
⚑ *Hon.* Arthur Percy Upton, CB. [60]	28 April 93	never	2 Dec. 95	never	14 May 07	do	do	do	From Grenadier Guards.
⚑ *Sir* John Cameron, KCB.	25 Sept. 87	30 Sept. 90	11 July 94	9 Oct. 00	28 May 07	do	do	do	9 Foot.
Samuel Huskisson [61]	17 May 99	27 Jan. 01	24 Feb. 03	4 July 05	28 May 07	do	do	do	From 67 Foot.
George Salmon	24 May 81	6 June 88	9 Sept. 94	1 Jan. 05	18 June 07	do	do	do	Royal Artillery.
Henry Monckton	5 Mar. 95	29 April 96	20 April 96	24 July 02	18 June 07	do	do	do	From 72 Foot.
⚑ John Maister [62]	13 Nov. 93	14 Jan. 94	30 Mar. 95	20 June 01	20 Aug. 07	do	do	do	{ From 34 F. Comm. the Troops in the Windward and Leeward Islands.
⚑ *Hon.* George Murray [63]	2 Dec. 95	24 Jan. 98	4 Mar. 00	never	20 Aug. 07	do	do	do	From 2 Life Guards.
⚑ ⚑ *Sir* Henry Askew, CB. [64]	19 June 93	never	18 Mar. 95	never	27 Aug. 07	do	do	do	From Grenadier Guards.
⚑ *Sir* Jasper Nicolls, KCB.	24 May 93	25 Nov. 94	12 Sept. 99	6 July 04	29 Oct. 07	do	do	do	{ 93 F. General and Commander-in-Chief in the East Indies.
⚑ Samuel Brown [65]	15 Mar. 98	18 April 00	2 May 00	10 Nov. 04	16 Jan. 08	do	27 May 25	28 June 38	{ From late York Light Infantry Volunteers.
Dennis Herbert [66]	Jan. 94	4 Sept. 94	21 Feb. 99	30 Jan. 00	28 Jan. 08	do	do	do	46 Foot.
John Ross, CB.	2 June 93	8 May 96	11 Jan. 00	15 Aug. 04	do	do	do	do	85 Foot.
Sir William Thornton, KCB.	31 Mar. 96	1 Mar. 97	25 June 03	13 Nov. 06	do	do	do	do	Royal Artillery.
Richard Dickinson	29 June 81	17 May 90	6 Mar. 95	15 Sept. 06	1 Feb. 08	do	do	do	67 Foot, *Adjutant General*
Sir John Macdonald, KCB.	April 95	2 Feb. 96	22 Oct. 02	28 Feb. 05	17 Mar. 08	do	do	do	From Coldstream Guards.
Hon. John Bruce Richard O'Neill	10 Oct. 99	never	8 May 00	30 July 07	21 April 08	do	do	do	
Anthony Salvin [67]	15 Feb. 76	1 Oct. 77	24 April 81	1 Mar. 94	25 April 08	do	do	do	
Sir William Johnston, KCB.	3 June 91	7 Jan. 94	4 April 95	27 Feb. 00	do	do	do	do	68 Foot.
Francis Newbery [68]	12 Mar. 94	28 Mar. 94	29 Mar. 94	20 Mar. 00	do	do	do	do	From 16 Dragoons.
Alexander Armstrong	7 July 83	31 Oct. 92	16 Dec. 93	24 July 00	do	do	do	do	Late R. Irish Artillery.
Daniel Francis Blommart [69]	15 Jan. 94	13 Feb. 94	28 Feb. 95	17 July 01	do	do	do	do	8 Hussars.
⚑ ⚑ *Sir* Joseph Straton, CB. KCH.	Dec. 94	2 Dec. 95	2 Mar. 97	14 Aug. 01	do	do	do	do	
⚑ *Rt. Hon. Sir* E. Blakeney, KCB. GCH.	28 Feb. 94	24 Sept. 94	24 Dec. 94	17 Sept. 01	do	do	do	do	{ 7 F. Comm. the Troops in Ireland.

14

Lieutenant-Generals.

	2D LIEUT. ETC.	LIEUT.	CAPTAIN.	MAJOR.	LIEUT.-COLONEL.	COLONEL.	MAJOR-GENERAL.	LIEUT.-GENERAL.	
Sir James Charles Dalbiac, KCH.	4 July 93	24 Feb. 94	11 Oct. 98	15 Oct. 01	25 April 08	4 June 14	27 May 25	28 June 38	3 Dragoon Guards.
Sir John Maclean, KCB.	30 April 94	1 May 94	15 June 97	2 Aug. 04	9 June 08	do	do	do	60 Foot.
Sir Richard Downes Jackson, KCB.	9 July 94	never	24 May 98	never	4 Aug. 08	do	do	do	{84 F. Com. of the Forces in North America.
Sir Thomas Hawker, KCH.	12 May 95	5 April 96	10 July 99	23 Nov. 04	2 Sept. 08	do	do	do	6 Dragoon Guards.
Sir G. A. Quentin, CB. KCH.[70]	25 Feb. 93	1 Oct. 94	17 May 96	14 Feb. 05	13 Oct. 08	do	do	do	{72 Foot, Lieut. Gov. of Nova Scotia.
Sir Colin Campbell, KCB.	3 Oct. 99	21 Aug. 01	9 Jan. 05	2 Sept. 08	3 May 10	do	do	do	82 Foot.
Sir John Wilson, KCB.	26 Mar. 94	12 Aug. 95	18 Jan. 99	27 May 02	22 Dec. 08	do	do	do	71 Foot.
Sir S. F. Whittingham, KCB. KCH.	20 Jan. 03	25 Feb. 03	14 Feb. 05	12 Mar. 10	30 May 11	do	do	do	26 Foot.
J. Lord Seaton, GCB. GCH.	10 July 94	4 Sept. 95	12 Jan. 00	21 Jan. 08	2 Feb. 09	do	do	do	62 Foot.
Sir Arch. Campbell, Bart. GCB.	28 Dec. 78	26 April 91	17 Nov. 99	14 Sept. 04	16 Feb. 09	do	do	do	94 Foot.
Sir Thos. McMahon, Bart. KCB.	2 Feb. 97	24 Oct. 99	8 Oct. 03	6 Nov. 06	4 May 09	do	do	do	{From Coldstream Gds. Governor of Gibraltar.
Sir Alex. Woodford, KCB. GCMG.[71]	6 Dec. 94	15 July 95	11 Dec. 99	never	8 Mar. 10	do	do	do	52 Foot.
Sir Thomas Arbuthnot, KCB.	23 Nov. 95	1 May 96	25 June 98	7 April 08	24 May 10	do	do	do	{From Coldstream Gds. Governor of Malta.
Sir H. F. Bouverie, KCB. GCMG.[72]	5 Aug. 90	never	19 Nov. 00	never	28 June 10	do	do	do	From 63 Foot.
J. Lord Burghersh, KCB. GCH.	Dec. 03	5 Jan. 04	3 May 05	20 Dec. 10	12 Dec. 11	do	do	do	{53 F. Military Sec. to the General Commanding in Chief.
Lord Fitz Roy James Henry Somerset, KCB.	9 June 04	30 May 05	5 May 08	9 June 11	27 April 12	28 Aug. 15	do	do	Royal Engineers.
Henry Evatt	11 July 88	16 Jan. 93	29 Aug. 98	never	24 June 09	16 Nov. 16	do	do	{R. Engineers, Inspector Gen. of Fortifications.
Sir Fredl. Wm. Mulcaster, KCH.	14 June 92	27 Nov. 93	11 Sept. 98	25 July 10	1 May 11	7 Feb. 17	do	do	
Lord C. Somerset Manners, KCB.	7 Feb. 98	1 June 99	21 Aug. 00	13 Oct. 08	1 Aug. 11	6 Nov. 17	do	do	3 Dragoons.

15

MAJOR-GENERALS.

	CORNET, 2nd LIEUT. or ENSIGN.	LIEUT.	CAPTAIN.	MAJOR.	LIEUT.-COLONEL.	COLONEL.	MAJOR GENERAL.	
William Goodday Strutt[73]	23 May 78	Nov. 79	7 Dec. 79	9 Aug. 88	18 Nov. 90	21 Aug. 95	18 June 98	*Governor of Quebec.*
Lawrence Bradshaw, KC.[74]	25 Sept. 80	3 Sept. 81	30 April 90	11 Sept. 94	1 Sept. 95	25 Sept. 03	25 July 10	Late of 1 Life Guards.
⚜ Siegesmund C. G. Baron Low, KCB. KCH.[75]	never	never	never	never	never	20 Dec. 04	do	Half-pay German Legion.
⚜ ⚜ Chas. *Count* Alten, GCB. GCH.[76]	never	never	never	never	never	22 Dec. 04	do	do.
Edward Scott[77]	29 June 80	4 Aug. 81	30 June 90	1 Sept. 95	1 Jan. 01	25 July 10	4 June 13	Late of 96 Foot.
William Henry Beckwith[78]	19 Oct. 78	28 Jan. 82	31 May 94	26 May 99	17 Sept. 03	1 Jan. 12	4 June 14	do.
Alex. Mark Kerr Hamilton	24 May 86	10 Sept. 88	15 July 94	14 July 00	28 Aug. 04	4 June 13	12 Aug. 19	Late 4 Royal Veteran Battalion.
William Nedham	24 Sept. 87	28 Oct. 89	23 April 95	12 Mar. 00	11 April 05	do	do	Late 2 do.
Sir George Leith, *Bart.*[79]	13 Oct. 80	13 Nov. 80	1 Nov. 92	1 Jan. 00	13 June 05	do	do	Late 9 do.
George Duncan Robertson, CB.[80] ...	3 July 82	30 June 88	25 Aug. 94	1 Jan. 05	5 Feb. 07	4 June 14	19 July 21	Late of 89 Foot.
⚜ Louis Wm. Viscount de Chabot, KCH.[81]	30 April 93	19 Dec. 93	23 July 99	24 Oct. 02	12 Feb. 07	do	do	Late of 50 Foot.
⚜ Sir Patrick Ross, GCMG. KCH.[82]	10 May 94	12 May 94	14 May 94	25 Sept. 03	9 April 07	do	do	Late of 75 Foot.
⚜ David Walker[83]	30 June 87	16 Feb. 91	1 Oct. 94	7 Feb. 00	16 April 07	do	do	Late of 58 Foot.
Henry Charles Darling[84]	15 Oct. 94	4 Sept. 95	25 April 99	19 Dec. 01	28 Jan. 08	do	do	Late of Nova Scotia Fencibles.
⚜ Charles Palmer[85]	17 May 96	29 Mar. 97	17 May 99	22 Aug. 05	3 May 10	do	27 May do	
Robert Ellice	8 Nov. 98	5 Jan. 99	4 May 01	12 May 06	16 Mar.	do	do	
⚜ Sir John Buchan, KCB.	29 July 95	21 Oct. 95	15 Mar. 02	30 June 04	30 Mar. 09	12 Aug. 19	22 July 30	
Edward Pritchard	1 July 82	27 Oct. 90	6 May 94	18 June 07	30 April 09	do	do	95 Foot.
Sir Maurice Chas. O'Connell, KCH.[86]	never	never	1 Oct. 94	1 Jan. 05	4 May 09	do	do	Royal Artillery.
Sir James Viney, CB. KCH	1 July 82	24 Mar. 91	1 Oct. 95	1 Feb. 08	20 June 09	do	do	From 73 Foot.
Cosmo Gordon[87]	6 Dec. 92	28 Oct. 94	23 Oct. 00	12 Feb. 07	20 July 09	do	do	From Royal Artillery.
George Elliot Vinicombe	28 Aug. 79	20 Aug. 79	9 June 94	25 Sept. 03	25 July 09	do	do	
⚜ Sir Hugh Gough, KCB.	7 Aug. 94	11 Oct. 94	25 June 03	8 Aug. 05	29 July 09	do	do	From Royal Marines.
⚜ ⚜ Sir Jas. Macdonell, KCB. KCH.[88]	Jan. 96	2 Feb. 96	10 Sept. 03	17 April 04	7 Sept. 09	do	do	99 Foot.
Sir Andrew Pilkington, KCB.[89]	7 Mar. 83	24 Jan. 91	2 Mar. 95	31 Mar. 04	5 Oct. 09	do	do	From Coldstream Guards.
Alexander Bethune[90]	14 Mar. 89	13 June 92	12 April 98	29 April 02	25 Oct. 09	do	do	Half-pay (Major) 16 Gar. Batt.
⚜ Sir John Gardiner, KCB.[91]	23 Nov. 91	12 July 93	17 May 96	18 Dec. 06	29 Oct. 09	do	do	From 6 Foot, Dep. Adjt. General.
⚜ George Middlemore, CB.[92]	Jan. 93	5 April 93	15 Oct. 94	14 Sept. 04	2 Nov. 09	do	do	*Governor of St. Helena.*
James Lomax	never	2 July 96	15 June 98	20 April 03	16 Nov. 09	do	do	From 60 Foot.
⚜ ⚜ Jas. Wallace Sleigh, CB.	Feb.	95 29 April 95	25 Oct. 98	14 June 05	14 Dec. 09	do	do	9 Dragoons.

Major-Generals.

Name	2D LIEUT. ETC.	LIEUT.	CAPTAIN.	MAJOR.	LIEUT.-COLONEL.	COLONEL.	MAJOR-GENERAL.	
Alexander Nesbitt	4 Dec. 94	23 Feb. 96	1 Dec. 99	25 Mar. 05	21 Dec. 09	12 Aug. 19	22 July 30	
☙ *Sir* Wm. Gabriel Davy, CB. KCH.[93]	Mar. 97	22 May 97	1 Jan. 02	5 Feb. 07	28 Dec. 08	do	do	
Sir Chas. Wm. Maxwell, CB. KCH.[94]	1 July 95	1 Dec. 96	1 Nov. 07	15 June 08	29 Dec. 09	do	do	Royal Artillery.
☙ Robert Beevor[95]	12 July 88	1 July 91	3 Oct. 95	1 Feb. 08	22 Jan. 10	do	do	
Mark Napier[95]	7 Feb. 94	13 Mar. 94	26 Jan. 96	2 Aug. 06	4 29 Mar. 10	do	do	
☙ John Wardlaw[96]	27 April 96	5 Oct. 96	24 May 98	16 Jan. 06	10 May 10	do	do	From late 3 Ceylon Regt.
Wm. Augustus Johnson	18 Sept. 93	2 Jan. 94	23 April 94	2 April 08	17 May 10	do	do	
Jonathan Yates[97]	14 Feb. 99	21 Feb. 99	11 Dec. 01	18 Dec. 06	19 July 10	do	do	
☙ *Sir* James Kearney, KCH.[98]	28 Feb. 88	9 May 94	31 May 95	27 May 02	25 July 10	do	do	From 2 Dragoon Guards.
Edward James O'Brien	31 Jan. 88	13 Nov. 93	28 Oct. 95	3 June 02	do	do	do	
Thomas Foster	4 Nov. 95	2 Sept. 96	3 July 01	24 July 02	do	do	do	
John Le Mesurier		28 Aug. 93	31 Aug. 06	14 Nov. 02	do	do	do	Half-pay (Major) 17 Foot.
Hon. John Ramsay	27 Mar. 93	6 June 93	14 Feb. 94	9 July 03	do	do	do	
Robert Owen[99]	3 July 82	28 Aug. 83	11 July 94	27 Aug. 03	do	do	do	From 20 Foot.
☙ *Sir* John Forster FitzGerald, KCB.[100]	29 Oct. 93	31 Jan. 94	9 May 94	25 Sept. 03	do	do	do	{ From R. Irish Artillery. (Captain on retired full pay.)
James Shortall[101]	12 Feb. 93	7 Aug. 93	16 June 94	do	do	do	do	{ From R. I. Art. and h.-p. 73 F. (Captain on retired full pay.)
Robert Crawford	never	do	17 June 94	do	do	do	do	17 Dragoons.
☙ ☙ *Sir* Arth. Benj. Clifton, KCB.KCH.	6 June 94	7 Aug. 94	27 Feb. 99	17 Dec. 03	do	do	do	From 3 Foot.
William Stewart[102]	10 Mar. 94	1 Sept. 94	25 Jan. 99	14 Mar. 05	16 Aug. 10	do	do	
Sir Wm. C. Eustace, CB. KCH.[103]	never	27 Sept. 83	24 Dec. 02	17 Mar. 08	23 Aug. 10	do	do	
☙ ☙ *Charles Murray, Lord Greenock,* KCB.[104]	May 90	10 Aug. 99	3 Feb. 03	14 May 07	30 Aug. 10	do	do	*Governor of Edinburgh Castle.*
Effingham Lindsay[105]	22 Aug. 88	30 June 92	11 June 95	30 Oct. 07	8 Dec. 10	do	do	
Philip Philpot	26 Dec. 87	23 Nov. 88	10 Jan. 97	1 Nov. 07	24 Jan. 11	19 July 21	do	11 Dragoons.
☙ *Sir* Alexander Leith, KCB.[106]	8 Aug. 92	Oct.	27 Nov. 94	1 Aug. 04	7 Feb. 11	do	do	
Count Francis Rivarola, KCH.[107]	4 April 95	21 Feb. 98	18 Mar. 04	6 Feb. 07	7 Mar. 11	do	do	Royal Malta Fencible Regiment.
☙ *Sir* John Browne, KCH.[107]	27 May 95	17 May 96	1 June 97	16 Feb. 09	14 Mar. 11	do	do	From 13 Dragoons.
☙ *Sir* Rob. L. Dundas, KCB.[108]	1 Dec. 97	2 May 00	6 Aug. 02	14 July 04	11 April 11	do	do	
☙ *Hon. Sir* Hugh Arbuthnott, CB.[109]	18 May 96	15 Sept. 96	20 Mar. 99	23 Nov. 04	9 May 11	do	do	
☙ *Sir* Robert Arbuthnot, KCB.[110]	1 Jan. 97	1 June 97	20 Aug. 02	13 April 09	22 May 11	do	do	
☙ Geo. Guy Carleton L'Estrange, CB.[111]	1 April 98	24 Nov. 98	13 Mar. 04	22 May 09	30 May 11	do	do	
☙ *Sir* Tho. Pearson, CB. KCH.[112]	2 Oct. 96	25 April 99	7 Aug. 00	8 Dec. 04	do	do	do	From 23 Foot.

17

Major-Generals.

	ENSIGN, ETC.	LIEUT.	CAPTAIN.	MAJOR.	LIEUT.-COLONEL.	COLONEL.	MAJOR-GENERAL.	
❀ *Sir* Dugald Little Gilmour, KCB.[113]	10 July 94	20 Aug. 94	13 May 95	23 May 05	30 May 11	19 July 21	22 July 30	
❀ *Sir* Greg. Holman Bromley Way, CB.[114]	24 Aug. 97	3 Nov. 99	13 Aug. 02	25 Feb. 08	do	do	do	*Lieut.-Governor of Guernsey.*
❀ *Sir* James Douglas, KCB.[115]	10 July 99	19 June 00	16 Sept. 02	16 Feb. 09	do	do	do	Captain of Yarmouth Castle.
❀ ✠ *Sir* John Waters, KCB.[116]	2 Aug. 97	15 Feb. 99	24 Sept. 03	do	do	do	do	
❀ *Sir* William Macbean, KCB.[117]	20 Feb. 96	1 Oct. 96	25 Oct. 04	do	do	do	do	From 18 Foot.
❀ ✠ *Rt. Hon. Sir* Hen. Hardinge, KCB.[118]	8 Oct. 98	29 Nov. 94	9 July 03	13 April 09	do	do	do	97 Foot.
❀ *Sir* Wm. Parker Carrol, CB. KCH.[118]	31 Oct. 98	25 Mar. 02	7 April 04	13 April 09	do	do	do	98 Foot.
❀ *Sir* Willoughby Cotton, KCB. KCH.	26 Dec. 98	never	25 Nov. 99	never	12 June 12	25 July 21	do	
❀ *Sir* Henry W. Rooke, CB. KCH.[119]	19 Dec. 99	never	14 Mar. 00	1 Jan. 00	28 Feb. 12	do	do	From Scots Fusilier Guards.
❀ John Clitherow[120]	30 July 99	never	24 Feb. 03	never	8 Oct. 12	do	do	From Grenadier Guards.
Sir John Hanbury, KCH.	9 July 03	26 Sept. 99	3 June 03	never	20 Dec. 12	do	do	From 1 Life Guards.
❀ *Hon.* Henry Beauchamp Lygon[121]	1 June 03	24 May 04	15 Jan. 07	14 May 12	18 June 15	24 Mar. 22	10 Jan. 37	From 2 Life Guards.
❀ ✠ *Hon.* Edw. Pyndar Lygon, CB.[122]	23 May 00	7 Nov. 05	15 Feb. 08	never	27 April 15	27 April 22	do	From Grenadier Guards.
❀ ✠ *Sir* J. G. Woodford, KCB. KCH.[123]	24 April 93	never	13 Nov. 04	never	1 July 13	20 Nov. 23	do	Royal Engineers.
❀ *Sir* Howard Elphinstone, *Bart.*	24 April 93	5 Feb. 96	1 July 00	1 Jan. 00	21 July 13	2 Dec. 24	do	From Royal Engineers.
Elias Walker Durnford	18 Sept. 93	5 Feb. 96	11 Feb. 01	4 June 13	do	23 Mar. 25	do	do.
Sir George Whitmore, KCH.	23 May 97	26 Aug. 98	28 Feb. 01	do	do	23 Mar. 25	do	
Henry Shadforth		31 July 94	21 Mar. 99	25 Feb. 00	4 June 04	27 May 25	do	
Arthur Lloyd		8 July 94	31 Aug. 95	22 May 95	do	do	do	
❀ ✠ John Millet Hamerton, CB.[124]	31 Oct. 92	31 Jan. 94	28 Oct. 96	15 June 96	do	do	do	
John Pringle	17 Mar. 94	2 Sept. 95	29 June 97	1 Aug. 97	do	do	do	
Parry Jones Parry, KH.	April 94	15 Oct. 94	30 Oct. 94	28 Aug. 94	do	do	do	
❀ *Sir* David Ximenes, KCH.[125]	19 May 93	18 June 94	27 Nov. 94	28 Aug. 95	do	do	do	From 16 Foot.
❀ Daniel Colquhoun[126]	13 Sept. 91	26 Oct. 93	4 Sept. 95	1 Sept. 04	do	do	do	
Sir Jas. Kyrle Money, *Bart.*	2 Nov. 94	8 Mar. 98	18 Aug. 95	28 Sept. 04	do	do	do	{ Half-pay (Major) Armstrong's Recruiting Corps.
John Stafford	15 Mar. 98	4 July 98	23 April 00	29 Dec. 04	do	do	do	
❀ Charles Nicol, CB.[127]	June 95	31 Aug. 95	30 Nov. 95	3 April 06	13 June 06	do	do	
❀ *Sir* William Tuyll, KCH.[128]	22 Oct. 99	18 July 01	7 April 04	20 Nov. 06	do	do	do	From 66 Foot.
❀ *Sir* G. H. Fred. Berkeley, KCB.[129]	21 Jan. 02	27 Aug. 03	1 May 05	28 Jan. 08	do	do	do	
Sackville Hamilton Berkeley[130]	1 May 00	25 Nov. 00	25 Dec. 04	18 Feb. 08	20 June	do	do	
❀ *Sir* Charles James Napier, KCB.[131]	31 Jan. 94	8 May 94	22 Dec. 03	29 May 06	27 June	do	do	
Helier Touzel	20 Feb. 95	9 Dec. 95	4 Aug. 04	14 July 08	11 July	do	do	
❀ ✠ *Sir* Jeremiah Dickson, KCB.[132]	25 Oct. 98	6 Aug. 99	2 Mar. 03	16 Sept. 06	1 Aug.	do	do	

Major-Generals.

	CORNET, ETC.	LIEUT.	CAPTAIN.	MAJOR.	LIEUT.-COLONEL.	COLONEL.	MAJOR-GENERAL.	
Sir Octavius Carey, KCH.	Mar. 01	5 June 01	27 Aug. 04	2 Nov. 00	30 Sept. 00	27 May 25	10 Jan. 37	Lieut.-Governor of Hull.
Sir Charles Wade Thornton, KCH.[133]	9 July 79	8 May 82	1 Nov. 93	23 Feb. 97	4 Nov. 07	do	do	Lieut.-Governor of Heligoland.
Sir Henry King, CB. KCH.[134]	25 Mar. 94	12 Aug. 95	3 May 00	5 Feb. 07	31 Dec. 07	do	do	Gov. of the Windward Islands.
Sir E.J.M.MacGregor, Bt.KCB. KCH.[135]	Dec. 91	Feb. 92	4 Aug. 04	19 April 10	14 Jan. 12	do	do	Lieut.-Governor of Jersey.
Sir Edward Gibbs, KCB.[136]	14 Nov. 98	28 Nov. 99	24 Feb. 03	4 Feb. 08	6 Feb. do	do	do	Gov. of the Cape of Good Hope.
Sir George Thomas Napier, KCB.[137]	25 Jan. 00	18 June 00	5 Jan. 04	30 May 11	do	do	do	{ Director General Field Train
Sir Charles Broke Vere, KCB.[138]	23 June 96	7 Dec. 96	21 Feb. 99	4 June 08	27 April 08	do	do	Depart. and Dep. Adjt. Gen.
Hon.Sir Hercules R. Pakenham, KCB.[139]	23 July 03	3 Mar. 04	2 Aug. 05	30 Aug. 10	do	do	do	R. Artillery. }
Sir Alex. Dickson, GCB. KCH.	6 Nov. 94	6 Mar. 95	14 Oct. 01	6 Feb. 05	do	do	do	From Royal Engineers.
Sir John Thomas Jones, Bart. KCB.[140]	30 Aug. 98	14 Sept. 98	1 Mar. 05	6 Feb. 12	do	do	do	Lieut.-Gov. of New Brunswick.
Sir John Harvey, KCB. KCH.[141]	18 Sept. 94	15 July 95	8 Jan. 00	4 Jan. 08	25 June do	do	do	From 45 Foot.
Sir Leonard Greenwell, KCB.[142]	7 Aug. 98	16 Sept. 98	31 July 04	25 Oct. 10	17 Aug. do	do	do	Gov. of the R. Military College.
Sir George Scovell, KCB.[143]	20 June 98	4 May 00	10 Mar. 04	30 May 11	5 Sept. 12	do	do	
Ulysses, Lord Downes.[144]	31 Mar. 04	12 Nov. 04	4 Sept. 06	31 Mar. 11	8 Oct. do	do	do	
Sir Rob. Hen. Dick, KCB. KCH.[145]	22 Nov. 00	27 June 02	17 April 04	24 April 08	8 Oct. do	do	do	
Sir Neil Douglas, KCB. KCH.[146]	28 Jan. 01	16 July 02	19 April 04	31 Jan. 11	3 Dec. 12	do	do	From Royal Artillery.
George Marq. of Tweeddale, CB. KT.[147]	24 April 93	11 Sept. 93	1 Nov. 97	22 Jan. 10	17 Dec. do	do	do	Half-pay (Lieut.-Col.) 100 Foot.
William Keith Elphinstone, CB.	04 June 04	12 Oct. 04	14 May 06	14 May 12	21 June 13	do	do	{ Half-pay Permanent Assistant-
Sir Frederick William Trench, KCH.[148]	24 Mar. 04	4 Aug. 04	18 June 06	2 May 11	30 Sept. do	do	do	Quarter-Master-General. }
Alexander Lord Saltoun, CB. GCH.	12 Nov. 03	never	12 Nov. 07	1 Aug. 11	25 Nov. do	do	do	From Grenadier Guards.
Henry Wyndham[148]	28 April 02	2 Sept. 02	7 Sept. 04	never	25 Dec. 13	do	do	
Frederick Rennell Thackeray, CB.	27 April 06	never	8 June 09	9 Aug. 13	20 Jan. 14	2 June 25	do	From Royal Engineers.
Sir John Boscawen Savage, CB. KCH.[149]	18 Sept. 98	18 June 98	18 April 96	19 May 01	21 July 10	20 June 25	do	From Royal Marines.
Sir Steph.Remnant Chapman,CB.KCH.	27 April 96	1 Jan. 80	24 April 95	15 Aug. 05	1 Jan. 12	29 July 25	do	From Royal Engineers.
John Francis Birch, CB.	18 Sept. 93	20 Nov. 96	18 April 01	30 Sept. 10	26 April 12	do	do	do.
Gustavus Nicolls	do	do	do	6 Mar. 11	21 July 13	do	do	do.
Sir Joseph Hugh Carncross, KCB.	6 Nov. 94	3 Mar. 97	30 Mar. 02	4 June 13	1 Sept. 14	do	do	Royal Artillery.
Alexander Watson	15 June 92	17 Jan. 93	28 Oct. 96	25 Feb. 08	14 Feb. do	do	do	From Royal Artillery.
Edward Vaughan Worsley	19 June 92	do	9 Jan. 97	20 June 09	1 May 14	do	do	do.
Cornelius Mann	23 Jan. 93	15 Aug. 93	1 April 97	4 Sept. 08	4 June 14	do	do	From Royal Engineers.
	22 April 95	29 Aug. 98	1 Dec. 02	4 June 13	30 Sept. 14	do	do	

Major-Generals.

	CORNET, ETC.	LIEUT.	CAPTAIN.	MAJOR.	LIEUT.-COLONEL.	COLONEL.	MAJOR-GENERAL.	
10 Henry Evelegh	24 April 93	1 Jan. 94	3 Nov. 97	25 July 10	20 Dec. 14	29 July 25	10 Jan. 37	From Royal Artillery.
Peter Fyers, CB.	do	do	16 July 99	4 June 11	do	do	do	do.
Hon. William Henry Gardner	18 Sept. 93	do	do	do	do	do	do	do.
George Wright	15 Aug. 96	29 Aug. 98	3 April 04	4 June 11	do	do	do	From Royal Engineers.
Frederick Walker	18 Sept. 93	1 Jan. 94	16 July 99	4 June 11	3 July 15	do	do	From Royal Artillery.
10 Sir Edward Bowater, KCH.[150]	1 Jan. 94	14 Aug. 94	2 Oct. 93	do	2 Jan. 14	29 Aug. 25	do	do.
10 Clement Hill[151]	31 Mar. 04	never	23 Aug. 09	never	25 July 14	12 Oct. 26	do	From Scots Fusilier Guards.
10 Percy Drummond, CB.	22 Aug. 05	4 April 06	4 April 11	19 Dec. 11	30 Dec. 13	21 June 27	do	From Royal Horse Guards.
Joseph Webbe Tobin	1 Jan. 94	14 Aug. 94	7 Oct. 99	4 June 12	19 July 19	13 Oct. 27	do	From Royal Artillery.
10 Sir William M. Gomm, KCB.[152]	24 May 94	16 Nov. 94	25 June 03	1 Jan. 00	17 Aug. 21	31 Dec. 29	do	do.
10 Henry D'Oyly[153]	2 Aug. 97	never	25 Nov. 99	10 Oct. 00	27 May 13	16 May 30	28 June 38	From Coldstream Guards.
				4 June 11		12 Feb.		From Grenadier Guards.
Foster Coulson	16 Dec. 93	16 Dec. 93	1 July 94	1 Jan. 05	1 Jan. 12	22 July do	do	{ Late of Royal Irish Artillery. (Captain on Retired Full-pay.)
Richard Uniacke	16 Feb. 80	do	do	do	do	do	do	do.
George Irving	21 Nov. 92	4 April 82	25 July 94	do	do	do	do	do.
William Gray[154]	31 May 98	30 April 94	10 Nov. 94	do	do	do	do	do.
10 Edward Darley[155]	9 Feb. 91	6 Mar. 98	3 Dec. 94	do	do	do	do	Half-pay (Captain) 1 Foot.
Christopher Hamilton, CB.[156]	16 May 00	29 June 03	25 June 03	do	do	do	do	From 61 Foot.
George James Reeves, CB. KH.[157]	26 April 98	11 June 99	21 Dec. 97	10 Oct. 05	2 Jan. 12	do	do	From 97 Foot.
10 Hon. Henry Murray, CB.[158]	18 July 98	7 Feb. 00	24 Aug. 01	26 Mar. 07	2 Jan. 12	do	do	Lieut.-Governor of Placentia.
10 Lincoln Stanhope, CB.[158]	22 Oct. 99	8 May 99	25 Oct. 02	11 June 07	6 Feb. 12	do	do	
John Grey, CB.[159]	12 Dec. 98	6 Sept. 00	31 Oct. 03	27 Nov. 06	27 April 12	do	do	
10 Sir Alexander Cameron, KCB.[160]	6 Mar. 95	31 Dec. 98	6 May 05	30 May 11	do	do	do	Half-pay (Major) 5 Foot.
Sir James Wilson, KCB.[161]	29 Aug. 98	27 May 99	18 April 03	20 June 11	do	do	do	Deputy Governor of St. Mawes.
Sir John May, KCB. KCH.	22 May 97	7 Oct. 95	1 Mar. 05	6 Feb. 12	do	do	do	
10 Sir John Fox Burgoyne, KCB.	6 May 95	1 July 00	23 Oct. 04	6 Feb. 12	do	do	do	From Royal Artillery.
Sir Thomas Dalmer, CB.[162]	26 Nov. 96	12 June 99	25 June 02	10 Dec. 04	17 Aug. 07	do	do	From Royal Engineers.
Sir Henry Watson, KH.[163]	3 Dec. 94	10 Feb. 95	25 June 02	18 Jan. 10	1 Oct. 12	do	do	
Edward Walker, KH.[163]		14 Sept. 96	26 Jan. 02	4 Dec. 06				
Thomas Evans, CB.[164]		1 Oct. 94	19 Nov. 03	6 Feb. 12	13 Oct. 12	do	do	From 70 Foot.

Notes to General Officers, not being Colonels of Regiments.

1 General Hon. Fred. St. John served throughout the rebellion in Ireland in 1798. Served also the two campaigns against the Mahrattas, as second in command under Lord Lake, including seven sieges and two general actions.
2 His Royal Highness the Prince of Orange served in the Peninsula, from 1811 to the end of the war, and has received a cross and two clasps for Ciudad Rodrigo, Badajoz, Salamanca, Vittoria, Pyrenees, and Nivelle. Severely wounded by a musket-ball through the left shoulder at Waterloo.
3 Sir George Cockburn served at Gibraltar during the siege in 1782, as aide-de-camp to Lord Heathfield.
4 General Dunne served in Ireland during the rebellion in 1798.
5 Sir Alex. Mackenzie served with Lord Moira's army in the expedition to the relief of Ostend in 1793. Was second in command at the capture of the Cape of Good Hope in 1795. Commanded a division of the expedition against Naples, and afterwards the army in the two Calabrias.
6 Lord Cork served in Flanders in 1793, and was present at the sieges of Valenciennes and Dunkirk, at the former of which he was in the storming party. In 1794 he accompanied the expedition under Lord Moira; was present at the battle of Alost, and made prisoner at the capitulation of Bergen-op-Zoom. Served with the Guards in Holland in 1799. Commanded the first battalion of the Coldstream Guards in Egypt in 1801, and was present at the taking of Alexandria, and in the different engagements with the army under Sir Eyre Coote to the westward of Alexandria.
7 Sir Martin Hunter served in the first American war, including the battles of Bunker's Hill, Brooklyn, and Brandywine; storming the heights of Fort Washington; and the night attack on General Wayne's brigade, where he was wounded. Served afterwards in the East Indies, and commanded the 52nd regiment at the sieges of Cannanore (commanded a corps of light infantry that stormed the breach), Pollighautcherry, and Bangalore; battle near Seringapatam, and storming of the fort of Savandroog; the night attack on Tippoo's intrenched camp under the walls of Seringapatam, and was wounded in the body and arm. In 1797 he commanded a brigade at the capture of Trinidad, and at the siege of Porto Rico; and at the blockade of Malta in 1800 he commanded the 48th regiment.
8 Sir John Fraser served on board the *Defence*, under Sir George Rodney, which ship, in the general action of the 16th Jan. 1780, engaged and made prize the Spanish Admiral's ship *Phœnix*, of superior force. Served afterwards at Gibraltar during the siege of 1780, 1, and 2, and received two severe wounds, one by a splinter, and the other by a cannon shot which carried off his right leg. In 1804, when in command on the coast of Africa, he was attacked by a very superior force, and obliged to capitulate: the enemy's loss in killed on this occasion exceeded the British force at the commencement of the action.
9 General Hon. John Brodrick served at the siege of Dunkirk in Sept. 1793; and in 1794 in the actions of the 17th and 18th May, and at the taking of Fort St. André. Served in the Peninsula in 1808 and the early part of 1809.
10 General Scott's services:—Campaign of 1762 in Germany under Prince Ferdinand of Brunswick; and carried the colours of the 24th regiment in the action of Willimstall, and the attack of the British piquets on the Fulda. First American war in 1776 and 77, under General Burgoyne and Sir Henry Clinton, during which period he was frequently engaged with the enemy, and was in danger of being hanged as a spy. Campaigns of 1793 and 4 in Flanders, under the Duke of York, including the action at Famars; sieges of Valenciennes, Dunkirk, and Newport; attack on the village of Premont; and action of the 24th May, at which last he was wounded in the right thigh by a musket-ball. Commanded a brigade during the campaign of 1799 in Mysore, and was present at the siege and capture of Seringapatam, for which he has received a medal.
11 General Hon. Wm. M. Maitland served in the East Indies, and was present at the storming of Tippoo's lines, and siege of Seringapatam, at which last he was wounded.
12 Lord Lorton served at the taking of Martinique, St. Lucia, and Guadaloupe, and was engaged in the different actions of that campaign, and received a contusion at Point-a-Petre.
13 General George Mitchell served in Flanders in 1793, 4, and 5, including the actions

Notes to the General Officers.

from Tournay to Bremen; sieges of Valenciennes and Dunkirk; and the actions at Famars, Cateau, Thuyl, and Geldermalsen.

14 General M'Kenzie served the campaigns of 1794 on the Continent, including the several actions between the Wael and Rhine; forcing the enemy from St. André; sortie from Nimeguen; and the actions at Thuyl and Geldermalsen. Served also on the eastern coast of Spain under Sir Wm. Henry Clinton.

15 General John Michel served at the siege of Fort St. Philip, in Minorca, and was taken prisoner on its surrender.

16 Sir Wm. Wilkinson served in South Carolina at the latter end of the first American war. At the commencement of the French Revolution he served in the Mediterranean as a marine officer, landed at Toulon, where he acted as Town Major. Served also in Corsica; in the rebellion in Ireland; in Malta; in Egypt (under Sir Ralph Abercromby); and in the East Indies.

17 General Robertson's services:—Taking of Goree. In every action in India under Sir Eyre Coote and Lord Cornwallis. With the storming parties at Nundy Droog, Bangalore, and Savandroog. Siege and capture of Pondicherry in 1793. Storming of the French lines before Cuddalore.

18 General Wood served as a Major-General on the staff in the East Indies, and was actively employed in the Nepaul war.

19 General White served the campaigns in Flanders, including the sieges of Valenciennes and Dunkirk; and the action and storming of Lincelles.

20 General Dilkes's services:—Campaigns of 1793, 4, and 5 on the Continent, including the different actions. Rebellion in Ireland in 1798. Expedition to the Helder in 1799, including the different actions. Served in the Peninsula during 1810 and part of 1811, and was second in command at the battle of Barrosa, for which he has received a medal.

21 General Bonham served upwards of 22 years in the West Indies, and acted as chief of the Quarter-Master-General's department on the two expeditions against St. Lucie and Tobago, and Demerara and Berbice; on the latter he was second in command. He was also present at the storming of Morne Fortunée, St. Lucie, on the night of the 2nd June, 1803.

22 Sir Thomas Saumarez served in the first American war from 1775 to its termination, and was present in several of the principal actions, and at the sieges of Charlestown, and Yorktown, at which last he was made prisoner.

23 General Saunders has seen a great deal of service in the West Indies, and was actively employed against Demerara, St. Eustatia, and St. Vincent. During two years' service in Martinique and St. Lucie he was present in the engagements of the Vigie, Gros Islet, Cul de Sac, and Carnagie. Accompanied General Baird's army to Egypt in 1801. Proceeded to the Peninsula in June, 1809, and commanded the 61st regiment at the battle of Talavera, for which he has received a medal.

24 Sir Warren M. Peacocke served during the rebellion in Ireland, and was present at the affair at Antrim, and at the battle of Ballynahinch. Served in Egypt in 1801. Accompanied the expedition to Hanover in 1805; and that to Copenhagen in 1807. Embarked for the Peninsula, Dec. 1808; and in June, 1809, he was appointed by Lord Wellington to command a brigade, and subsequently to the command of Lisbon.

25 General Goldie served during the rebellion in Ireland in 1798. Served also in the Peninsula for a few months in 1812.

26 General Eden served in Flanders in 1794, and in Holland in 1795. Served also at the capture of Java in 1811, for which he has received a medal.

27 Lieut.-General Thornton served with the Guards in Flanders, Holland, and Germany, in 1794 and 5.

28 Lieut.-General Thomas served in the first American war, and was present at the several landings on Staten, Long, and York Islands; the battle of the 27th Aug. 1776 on Long Island; capture of Forts Lee and Washington; battles of Brandywine and Germantown, at which last he received two balls in his head. Proceeded to the West Indies in 1778, and was present at the capture of St. Lucie, and in the battle of the Vigie. Served on board the *Cornwall* in the action off Grenada, between Admiral Byron and the Comte d'Estaignes 6th July, 1779; also on board the *Conqueror* in the action between Admiral Parker and La Motte Picquet, in Fort Royal Bay, Martinique, 19th Dec. 1779; and in the successive actions between Rear Admiral Rowley with the Comte de Guichen off Martinique, 17th April following. Present at the capture of Port-au-Prince, 4th June, 1794. Served also in Ireland during the Rebellion in 1798.

29 Lieut.-General O'Loghlin served the campaign of 1794, in Flanders, and was wounded at the battle near Tournay. Commanded the brigade of Life Guards in the Peninsula.

30 Lieut.-General Rebow was at the taking of Martinique, St. Lucia and Guadaloupe in 1794, at which last he was severely wounded through both thighs. Served in the Peninsula in 1812.

Notes to the General Officers.

31 Lieut.-General Gosselin served in the expedition against Genoa under Lord Wm. Bentinck, and subsequently in the American war.

32 Lieut.-General Dillon served in Ireland during the rebellion in 1798.

33 Lieut.-General Darroch's services:—Rebellion in Ireland, 1798. Expedition to Hanover, 1805. Expedition to South America, 1807. Peninsular campaigns of 1808, 9, 10, and 11, including the affair near Carvalhos, passage of the Douro, and attack of Soult's rear-guard at Salamonde.

34 Sir Thomas Molyneux served at the taking of Martinique, St. Lucia, and Guadaloupe in 1794.

35 Lieut.-General Benj. Gordon served in India for twenty years, between 1788 and 1811, and was present in most of the battles, sieges, and assaults which took place, including the storming of Seringapatam.

36 Sir Wm. Hutchinson was actively employed in the West Indies in 1793 and 4, including the taking of Jeronomie, Cape St. Nichola Mole, Cape Tiberoun, and storming of Fort L'Acul, at which last he was wounded. Served in the expedition to the Helder in 1799, and was severely wounded at the battle of Egmont-op-Zee. Accompanied the expedition to Copenhagen, under Lord Nelson, 1801. Served a short period on the staff in the Peninsula in 1812.

37 Sir Alexander Halkett's services:—Capture of Martinique, St. Lucia, and Guadaloupe, 1794. Ostend, under Sir Eyre Coote, where he was taken prisoner. Expedition to the Helder in 1799, where he was twice wounded. Capture of the Cape of Good Hope in 1806.

38 Lieut.-Gen. Buller served the campaigns of 1793 and 94 in Flanders, and subsequently in the West Indies, including the siege of St. Lucia, and reduction of Grenada.

39 General Clay was at the taking of Martinique and St. Lucia in 1794, including the storming of Morne de Pierre (led the forlorn hope), siege and reduction of Forts Louis and Bourbon. Accompanied the expedition under Sir James Pulteney to Belle Isle, Ferrol, and Vigo Bay. Served in Egypt in 1801, and was present in the actions of the 13th and 21st March, the siege of Alexandria, and other affairs of less importance. Medal for services in Egypt.

40 Lieut.-General T. L'Estrange served in the first American war.

41 Lieut.-General Glegg served at the taking of Martinique, St. Lucia, and Guadaloupe in 1794.

42 Sir Charles Phillips was at the taking of Martinique, St. Lucia, and Guadaloupe in 1794, including the siege of Fort Bourbon. Served in Egypt in 1801, and has received the Egyptian medal.

43 Lieut.-General Reynardson served in Egypt in 1801, and at Walcheren in 1809. Medal for services in Egypt.

44 Lord Carysfort's services: Campaign of 1796 in Germany under the Archduke Charles, including the siege of Kehl. Rebellion in Ireland, 1798. Employed afterwards on the Continent, and was present with the Russian army at the battle of Zurich. Campaign in Egypt, as Aide-de-camp to Sir Ralph Abercromby and Lord Hutchinson. Expedition to Sweden, and afterwards to Spain under Sir John Moore, including the battle of Corunna. Embarked for Walcheren July 1809, and served in the reserve in South Beveland. Accompanied the Guards to Spain in 1811, and served there until 1813, including the defence of Tarifa. Campaign of 1814, in Holland, including the attack on Bergen-op-Zoom, on which occasion he commanded a brigade of Guards.

45 Lieut.-General Hon. T. E. Capel served the campaigns in Flanders under the Duke of York. Employed on the staff at Cadiz in 1811.

46 Lieut.-General Mundy served in Ireland during the rebellion in 1798.

46* Sir Henry Edw. Bunbury served in Holland in 1799, including the battles of the 19th Sept., 2d and 6th October. Served also in the expedition to Naples and Calabria in 1805 and 6, and was present at the battle of Maida, for which he has received a medal.

47 General M'Nair served on the coast of France and in the Mediterranean in 1795; capture of Malta, 1798; expedition to Cadiz, 1800; Egyptian campaign, 1801 (medal); capture of Martinique in 1809, for which he has also received a medal.

48 Lieut.-General Mawby served at Toulon in 1793, and at Corsica in 1794, including the siege of Calvi, and storming of the Mozelle Fort.

49 Lieut.-General Mainwaring served at the reduction of Martinique in 1794. Accompanied the 51st regiment to Corunna in 1808. Expedition to Walcheren, 1809, where he took two eight-pounders, and many prisoners. Served in the Peninsula in 1811, and was present at the battle of Fuentes d'Onor and the second siege of Badajoz.

50 Lieut.-General Hon. John Meade served in Holland under the Duke of York. Accompanied the expeditions to the Ferrol and to Portugal, 1800. Served also in the Peninsula, and commanded the 45th regiment at the battle of Busaco, for which he has received a medal.

Notes to the General Officers.

51 Lieut.-General Elliot served at the taking of the French colonies in the West Indies in 1794, and of the Danish colonies in 1808.

52 Sir Loftus W. Otway served in Ireland during the rebellion in 1798, and was present in the action at Vinegar Hill. Proceeded to the Peninsula in 1808 as a Major in the 18th Hussars, and on the 13th of Dec., at Rueda, he surprised and captured the whole of the French Cavalry out-lying piquet. On the 16th following, near to Valladolid, whilst *en decouvert*, he encountered Colonel Antignac, commandant of the 22d Chasseurs à Cheval, at the head of a strong force; charged and routed him; took the Colonel prisoner, and more of his Chasseurs than he had Dragoons to guard them, and brought them all into Head Quarters, horses, men, arms, and baggage. At Benevente, whilst commanding the out-lying piquet, he was opposed to Lieut.-General Le Fevre (for nearly an hour) at the head of six squadrons of the Imperial Guard; charged and broke his advanced-guard, whose commanding officer was killed, and whose sword he took. In the affair of Campo Mayor he gained the rear of the enemy, and captured between five and six hundred men and their entire battering train (sixteen 24-pounders), and brought them part of the way back, but was obliged to abandon his capture with the exception of sixteen prisoners and one tumbril, the enemy being in possession of the road by which he was to return. At Albuhera he commanded the three regiments of Portuguese Cavalry, which covered the left flank of the army.

53 Sir Robert Barton served the campaign of 1799 in Holland, and was present in the actions of the 8th, 10th, and 19th September. Accompanied the Life Guards to the Peninsula, where he served for a short period.

54 Sir Wm. Paterson served at the taking of the French West India Islands in 1794. Served also in the last American war, and was present at several operations in the Chesapeake, and with the expedition against New Orleans, where he was severely wounded.

55 Sir John W. Guise served in Egypt in 1801, and has received the Egyptian medal. Proceeded with the expedition to Hanover in 1805. Served afterwards in the Peninsula, and commanded the 3d Foot Guards at the battles of Fuentes d'Onor, Salamanca, Vittoria, and the Nive, for which he has received a cross.

56 Sir Charles Wm. Doyle served in Holland in 1793 and 94, including the actions at Famars and Lannoy. Expedition to the Texel, 1796. Actively employed in the West Indies in 1796, 97, and 98. Egyptian campaign of 1801; wounded in the action of the 21st March. Employed in the Peninsula with the Spanish armies, and was wounded in the shoulder at the siege of Tarragona. Medal for services in Egypt.

57 Sir James Bathurst was at the capture of Surinam under Sir Tho. Trigge. Egyptian campaign of 1801 (medal). Expedition to Hanover, 1805. Served in Poland with the Russian and Prussian armies, and was present in several of the principal actions. Sieges of Stralsund and Copenhagen, 1807. Proceeded to the Peninsula in 1808, and was present at the battles of Roleia, Vimiera, Corunna, Talavera, and Busaco, for which he has received a cross.

58 Lieut.-General Hon. H. O. Trevor commanded the Coldstream Guards at the battle of Salamanca, for which he has received a medal.

59 Sir Howard Douglas served in Portugal and Spain in 1808 and 9, and was present at the battle of Corunna. Served afterwards at Walcheren, including the siege and bombardment of Flushing.

60 Lieut.-General A. P. Upton served in the Peninsula as an Assistant Quarter-Master General, and has received a medal and one clasp for the battles of Vittoria and the Nive.

61 Lieut.-General Huskisson served in the field in India under Lord Lake, and subsequently at the siege of Ryghur, and at the capture of several towns and forts. In October, 1818, commanded at Candeish, at the taking of Behauderpore and Amulneir.

62 Lieut.-General Maister served with the expedition to the Helder in 1799, and was present in the actions of the 10th Sept., 2nd and 6th Oct. at which last he received four wounds.

63 Lieut.-General Hon. George Murray served the Peninsular campaigns of 1813 and 14 in command of the 2nd Life Guards.

64 Sir Henry Askew served in Holland and Flanders in 1794 and 95. Expedition to Walcheren, 1809. Peninsula from Sept. 1812, to the end of the war (medal for the battle of the Nive). Campaign of 1815, and wounded at Quatre Bras.

65 Lieut.-General S. Brown served in Egypt in 1801. Employed in Portugal in 1801, and was present as a volunteer at the battle of Roleia.

66 Lieut.-General Herbert served on the Continent with the army under Lord Moira, and the Duke of York. Engaged during the Carib war in St. Vincent's; at Port-au-Prince in St. Domingo; and at Fort Irvis during the siege. Served also at the siege of Copenhagen in 1807.

67 Lieut.-General Salvin served in the first American war, and was present at the battles of Brandywine and German Town, siege of Charlestown, battle of Guilford Court House (wounded), and siege of York Town, in Virginia.

68 Lieut.-General Newbery served in Ireland during the rebellion in 1798.

Notes to the General Officers.

69 Lieut.-General Blommart served in the West Indies, and was present at the surrender of Demerara and Berbice. Served also with the expedition to the Helder in 1799, including the actions of the 2nd, 3rd, and 6th October.

70 Sir George A. Quentin served in the Peninsula in command of the 10th Hussars, and has received a medal and one clasp for the battles of Orthes and Toulouse. Served also the campaign of 1815, and was severely wounded at Waterloo.

71 Sir Alexander Woodford served in the Peninsula, and has received a medal and two clasps for the battles of Salamanca, Vittoria, and the Nive. Served also the campaign of 1815, and was present at Waterloo.

72 Sir Henry Fred. Bouverie served in the Peninsula as an Assistant Adjutant-General, and has received a cross and one clasp for Salamanca, Vittoria, San Sebastian, Nive, and Orthes.

73 Major-General Strutt served at Gibraltar, from March, 1782, to the termination of the siege. On the Continent during the campaigns of 1794 and 95. Actively employed in the island of St. Vincent during the latter part of 1795 and early part of 1796; in the action of the 8th Jan. he received three wounds, viz: in the mouth, in the breast by a buck-shot, and above the right knee by a musket-ball, which buried itself in the bone, and occasioned amputation of the right leg.

74 Major-General Bradshaw was actively employed in St. Domingo in 1793, 94, and 95, and commanded at St. Mare's and Tiburon, when those posts were attacked by the enemy. Served in Ireland during the rebellion in 1798. Expedition to the Ferrol, 1800, Egyptian campaign of 1801, including the actions of the 8th, 13th, and 21st March. Medal for services in Egypt.

75 Baron Low has received a medal and one clasp for the battles of Talavera and Salamanca.

76 Count Alten served on the Continent during the campaigns of 1793, 94, and 95, including the battles of Famars, Houdschooten and Hoogleede; sieges of Valenciennes and Menin; and attack near Nimeguen. Accompained the expedition to the North of Germany, 1805; to Copenhagen, 1807; to Gottenburg, 1808, and afterwards to Portugal and Spain under Sir John Moore. Proceeded with the expedition to Walcheren in 1809, and was present at the siege of Flushing. Served afterwards in the Peninsula, from February, 1811, to the end of the war, and has received a cross and three clasps for the battles of Albuhera, Salamanca, Vittoria, Nivelle, Nive, Orthes, and Toulouse. Independent of the above, Count Alten was personally engaged in a great many actions of less importance. Served also the campaign of 1815, including the battles of Quatre Bras and Waterloo, at which last he was severely and dangerously wounded.

77 Major-General Scott served in St. Domingo in 1794 and 95. Rebellion in Ireland, 1798. Expedition to the Ferrol and Cadiz, under Sir James Pulteney. Egyptian campaign of 1801, including the actions of the 8th, 13th, and 21st March, in which last he was severely contused on the breast by a musket-ball. Medal for services in Egypt.

78 Major-General Wm. H. Beckwith was at the siege of Fort Matilda and capture of Guadaloupe in 1794. Served also the campaign of 1799 in Holland.

79 Sir George Leith served in India under Sir Wm. Meadows and Lord Cornwallis, including the sieges of Bangalore and Savandroog, storming of Tippoo's lines, 6th Feb. 1792, and the subsequent siege of Seringapatam.

80 Major-General Robertson was at the reduction of the French West India Islands by Sir Charles Grey in 1794, including the taking of Forts Bourbon and Royal; also at Morne Fortunée, the storming of Fleur d'Epée, attack of Point Petre, and siege of Fort Matilda. Served in Holland, and was severely wounded near Alkmaar. Proceeded with the expedition to Naples and Calabria, and was present at the battle of Maida, for which he has received a medal. In 1812 he took the islands of Lagosta and Cuzzola. Joined the Austrian army under the command of Count Nugent, and was present at the capture of Trieste, and the affairs at Ferrara, Reggio, and Parma.

81 Viscount de Chabot served in Holland in 1799; in Spain under Sir John Moore; with the expedition to Walcheren; and subsequently in the Peninsula until 1810.

82 Sir Patrick Ross served the Mysore campaign under Lord Harris, including the battle of Mallavelly and siege of Seringapatam; with the divisions under Sir Arthur Wellesley in the campaign of 1801 against the Mahratta chief Dhoondiah; from Feb. 1802 to 1804, in the Mahratta country, and at the reduction of the ceded provinces. Served also in the Peninsula as Lieut.-Colonel of the 48th regiment, and in command of Lord Hill's brigade of British Infantry until 1810.

83 Major-General D. Walker's services :—St. Domingo in 1794 and 95, including the engagement at Tiburon, reduction of Port-au-Prince, and action near Bizotan. Campaign of 1799 in Holland, including the actions of the 10th Sept., 2nd and 9th Oct. Egyptian campaign of 1801, including the attack on the green hill to the east of Alexandria, and the driving in of the enemy's piquet in August. Battle of Maida, 1806. Capture of the island

Notes to the General Officers.

of Ischia, June, 1809. Peninsula, from 1812 to the end of the war, including the battle of Castella, at which he commanded a brigade.

84 Major-General Palmer served in the Peninsula with the 10th Hussars.

85 Major-General Ellice served with the expedition to South America, and was present at the capture of Buenos Ayres.

86 Sir Maurice O'Connell served at Dominica, and commanded the Light Company of the 46th regiment at Roseau, 22nd Feb. 1805, and successfully resisted the repeated attacks of a very superior French force.

87 Major-General Gordon was at the siege of Pondicherry, battle of Argaum, sieges of Asseerghur, Gawilghur, and various other hill forts. Served also at Walcheren, 1809.

88 Sir James Macdonell served with the expedition to Naples and Calabria in 1805 and 6, including the battle of Maida, for which he has received a medal. Served afterwards in Portugal, Spain, France, and Flanders.

89 Sir Andrew Pilkington served on board the Channel Fleet in 1793 and 94 ; commanded a company of the Queen's Royals on board the *Royal George*, in Lord Howe's action of 1st June, 1794, and received two splinter wounds. Employed in the West Indies in 1795, 6, and 7, including the capture of Trinidad. Rebellion in Ireland, 1798. Expeditions to the Helder, 1799, and 1805. In 1814, commanded a brigade at the reduction of the islands in Passamaquoddy Bay. On passage to India in 1800, he was severely wounded in the defence of the *Kent* East Indiaman against a large French privateer.

90 Major-General Bethune served in Holland in 1799, and was severely wounded in the lungs at the battle of Alkmaar. Served on board the *Bellona* at Copenhagen, under Lord Nelson, and received a wound from a cannon-shot, which lacerated his lower jaw.

91 Sir John Gardiner served in Lord Moira's expedition in Flanders and Holland in 1794 and 95. Actively employed in the West Indies, from 1795 to 1802. Accompanied the expedition to Walcheren in 1809. Served in the Peninsula during 1813 and 14, and commanded a brigade at the battles of the Nivelle and Orthes, for which he has received a medal and a clasp. Commanded the Infantry Brigade that took possession of Bourdeaux, and in the various operations which took place in the neighbourhood of that town, until the embarkation of the army for America.

92 Major-General Middlemore served in the Peninsula with the 48th regiment, and has received a medal for the battle of Talavera.

93 Sir Wm. G. Davy commanded the 5th battalion of the 60th regiment at the battles of Roleia, Vimiera, and Talavera, and has received a medal and a clasp.

94 Sir Charles Wm. Maxwell served on the Western Coast of Africa in 1809, and reduced the French colony of Senegal.

95 Major-General Mark Napier served on the coast of France in 1794 and 95. Six years in the Mediterranean ; at Minorca and in Egypt present with his regiment in action. In the West Indies several years, and commanded the 90th regiment at the capture of Guadaloupe, for which he has received a medal.

96 Major-General Wardlaw commanded the 76th regiment at the battle of the Nive, for which he has received a medal.

97 Major-General Yates served in Egypt in 1801, and has received the Egyptian medal.

98 Sir James Kearney served at Walcheren in 1809.

99 Major-General Owen's services :— Capture of Martinique, St. Lucia, and Guadaloupe in 1794 ; at the repulse of the enemy's attack at Berville, in Guadaloupe, he was severely wounded. Rebellion in Ireland, 1798. Campaign of 1799 in Holland.

100 Sir John F. Fitz Gerald commanded a light battalion and a brigade in the Peninsula, and has received a cross for Badajoz, Salamanca, Vittoria, and the Pyrenees.

101 Major-General Shortall served on the Continent under the Duke of York, in 1794 and 95.

102 Major-General Wm. Stewart served in the Peninsula, and has received a medal for the battle of Albuhera.

103 Sir Wm. C. Eustace commanded the Chasseurs Brittaniques at the battles of Fuentes d'Onor and Salamanca, and has received a medal and a clasp.

104 Lord Greenock served in the Helder expedition, 1799 ; in Naples and Sicily, 1805 and 6; at Walcheren, including the siege of Flushing, 1809 ; in the Peninsula, including the battles of Barrosa, Salamanca, and Vittoria, for which he has received a medal and two clasps ; and in the Netherlands and France, in 1815, including the battle of Waterloo.

105 Major-General Effingham Lindsay was actively employed at St. Domingo in 1793 and 94. Served the campaigns of 1803, 4, and 5 in India under Lord Lake ; commanded the column which captured by assault the fort of Deig, where he was wounded ; and commanded the right column of attack against Bhurtpore, and was severely wounded.

106 Sir Alexander Leith served in Holland in 1799, and was severely wounded and lost

Notes to the General Officers.

an eye. Commanded the 31st regiment in the battles of Vittoria, Pyrenees, Nivelle, Nive, and Orthes, for which he has received a cross and a clasp.

107 Sir John Browne served in the Peninsula with the Portuguese army, and received five wounds in action with the enemy on the 18th Feb. 1811.

108 The Hon. Sir R. L. Dundas served in the Peninsula with the Royal Staff Corps, and has received a cross and three clasps for the battles of Talavera, Salamanca, Vittoria, Pyrenees, Nivelle, Nive, and Toulouse.

109 Major-General Hon. Hugh Arbuthnott served at the Helder, 1799. Expedition to the Baltic, and battle of Copenhagen, 1801; and again with the second expedition in 1807. Served with the expedition to Sweden, and in Portugal and Spain under Sir John Moore, and subsequently in the Peninsula under the Duke of Wellington. Medal for the battle of Busaco, where he commanded the 52nd Foot.

110 Sir Robert Arbuthnot served in Ireland during the rebellion in 1798, including the battle of Ballynahinch. Capture of the Cape of Good Hope, 1806. Expedition to South America, 1807 (taken prisoner). Served in the Peninsula, from 1808 to the end of the war (with the exception of the first part of 1813), and has received a cross and three clasps for Busaco, Albuhera, Badajoz, Nivelle, Nive, Orthes, and Toulouse. Independent of the above, he was personally engaged at the battle of Corunna, the siege and storming of Ciudad Rodrigo, and in a great many operations of less importance. Served also the campaign of 1815, and was present at the battle of Waterloo.

111 Major-General L'Estrange commanded the 31st regiment at the battle of Albuhera, and has received a medal.

112 Sir Thomas Pearson served at the Helder in 1799, including the actions of the 27th Aug., 2nd and 6th October. Expedition to the Ferrol, 1800. Egyptian campaign of 1801, including the storming of the heights of Aboukir (severely wounded in the thigh), and actions of the 13th and 21st March. Siege and capture of Copenhagen, 1807. Capture of Martinique, 1809. Peninsular campaigns during the latter part of 1810 and 1811, including the first siege of Badajoz, battle of Albuhera, and action at Fuentes Guinaldo, at which last he received a severe wound which shattered the thigh-bone. Served also throughout the American war, including the action at Chrystler's Farm, attack and capture of Oswego, actions at Chippewa and Lundy's Lane (wounded in the arm). Siege of Fort Erie, where he was dangerously wounded by a rifle-ball in the head, in an attack made by the Americans on the British position. Medal and a clasp for the battles of Albuhera and Chrystler's Farm.

113 Sir Dugald Gilmour's services:—Expedition to Quiberon Bay, 1795. Taking of the colonies of Demerara, Esequibo and Berbice, 1796. Campaign of 1799 in Holland, under the Duke of York, including the battles of Bergen, and on the 2nd and 6th Oct. at Castricum, where he was severely wounded in the head, and taken prisoner. In May, 1805, he was promoted to a Majority in the 95th (Rifle Brigade), and served with it at the investment of Copenhagen, the battle of Keog, and the march through Zealand, until the surrender of the town. Went in command of three companies of the 1st battalion Rifle Brigade under Sir John Moore, to Sweden; from whence he joined Sir Arthur Wellesley's army near Vimiera, shortly after the battle. On the retreat from Salamanca he was on the rear-guard the whole way, almost constantly engaged with the enemy, and at Calcavellas lost out of a picquet of 300 men one officer and one serjeant-major killed, and nearly ninety men taken prisoners or killed. At the battle of Corunna he commanded the left wing of his regiment on the right of our line. In June, 1809, he returned to Portugal with the 1st battalion of the Rifle Brigade, and arrived at Talavera early in the morning of the day the enemy retired, and was engaged with his skirmishers. In 1810 marched to Almeida, and was with the advanced guard on the Coa and Agueda, during the siege of Ciudad Rodrigo by Massena, from which period he commanded his regiment. On the rear-guard at the passage of the Coa near Almeida, on the retreat, when the regiment suffered a severe loss in defending the bridge. Skirmishes before and battle of Busaco, and from thence to the Lines. In the retreat of Massena in 1811, he was engaged in the different skirmishes at Pombal, Redinha, Sabugal, Foz d'Aronce, battle of Fuentes d'Onor, and Guinaldo. Rejoined his regiment in Aug. 1813 at Lesacca, in the Pyrenees (having been sent to England by a board of health), and was engaged in the different skirmishes in the mountains; the passages of the Bidassoa, Nivelle, Nive, and the vicinity of Bayonne; actions at Vic Bigorre, and Tarbes, and, finally, at the battle of Toulouse. Sir Dugald has received a cross for the battles of Busaco, Fuentes d'Onor, Nive, and Toulouse.

114 Sir Gregory Way embarked with the expedition to Hanover in 1805; was shipwrecked on the Dutch coast and taken prisoner. Proceeded with the expedition to South America, and commanded the right wing of the Infantry Brigade at the storming of Buenos Ayres. Served under Sir Brent Spencer off Cadiz, and from thence joined the army under the Duke of Wellington; present at the battle of Roleia, actions of the 10th, 11th, and 12th

Notes to the General Officers.

May, at and near Oporto, passage of the Douro, battles of Talavera, and Albuhera, at which last he commanded the 29th regiment, and has received a medal.

115 Sir James Douglas served in the Peninsula with the Portuguese army, and has received a cross and three clasps for the battles of Busaco, Salamanca, Pyrenees, Nivelle, Nive, Orthes, and Toulouse.

116 Sir John Waters has received a medal and a clasp for Badajoz and Salamanca. Served the campaign of 1815, and was slightly wounded at Waterloo.

117 Sir Wm. Macbean served in Ireland during the rebellion in 1798, including the action at Vinegar Hill and capture of Wexford. Landed with the army in Portugal in Aug. 1808, and served throughout the Peninsular war, including the battles of Roleia, Vimiera, Corunna, Busaco, and Salamanca. Siege, assault, and capture of San Sebastian, passages of the Bidassoa, Nivelle, and Nive, and investment of Bayonne, at which last he was severely wounded, as also in opposing a French division on its advance to Lamego in 1810. Sir William has received a cross for Busaco, Salamanca, San Sebastian, and the Nive.

118 Sir Wm. Parker Carrol served in Holland in 1796; and with the expedition to South America in 1807, including the storming of Buenos Ayres. Served with the Spanish army from 1808 to the end of the war; was personally engaged in twenty-four actions, and wounded at Durango, 31st Oct. 1808, and again on the 28th Nov. 1809 in action with the enemy's cavalry on the Tormes. Medal for the battle of Albuhera.

119 Sir Henry W. Rooke served in Holland in 1799, including the actions of the 27th Aug., 10th and 19th Sept., 2nd and 6th October. Served also the campaigns of 1814 and 15 in Holland, Flanders, and France, including the bombardment of the French fleet at Antwerp, attack on Bergen-op-Zoom, and actions at Quatre Bras and Waterloo.

120 Major-General Clitherow served at Walcheren in 1809; proceeded to the Peninsula in 1810, and was severely wounded at the battle of Fuentes d'Onor, and again at the siege of Burgos.

121 Major-General the Hon. Henry B. Lygon served in the Peninsula, from March, 1809 to Sept. 1810, and again from Feb. 1814 to the end of the war, including the capture of Oporto, battle of Talavera, and passage of the Coa. Severely wounded in the neck, 28th Aug. 1810, in Massena's advance to the battle of Busaco.

122 Major-General the Hon. Edward P. Lygon served in the Peninsula, from Nov. 1812, to the end of the war, including the battle of Vittoria. Served also the campaign of 1815, and was present at the battle of Waterloo.

123 Sir John Geo. Woodford served in the Peninsula as an Assistant-Quarter-Master-General, and has received a cross for the battles of Nivelle, Nive, Orthes, and Toulouse. Served also the campaign of 1815, including the battle of Waterloo.

124 Major-General Hamilton served on the Continent under the Duke of York in 1794. Embarked for the West Indies in 1795, and was at the capture of St. Lucia the following year. Served in Egypt in 1801. Commanded the 44th regiment at the battle of Waterloo, and was wounded.

125 Sir David Ximenes commanded the 62nd regiment at the capture of Genoa, under Lord Wm. Bentinck, in 1814; and afterwards at Castine, in America, under Sir John Sherbrook.

126 Major-General Colquhoun served in Flanders under the Duke of York, and was wounded and taken prisoner in 1795. Employed in Ireland during the rebellion, 1798. Served also, for a short period, in Portugal.

127 Major-General Nicol has received a medal for the battle of the Nive.

128 Sir Wm. Tuyll served at the Helder in 1799; and in Portugal, Spain, and Walcheren, in 1808 and 9, as aide-de-camp to the present Marquis of Anglesey.

129 Sir George H. F. Berkeley served in Egypt in 1807. In 1809 he was appointed Assistant-Adjutant-General to the army in Portugal, and was present in the actions of the 10th, 11th, and 12th May, 1809, passage of the Douro, battles of Talavera, Busaco, Fuentes d'Onor, Salamanca, Vittoria, and the Nive; and sieges of Badajoz and San Sebastian. Served also the campaign of 1815, including the battle of Waterloo. He has received a cross and three clasps.

130 Major-General S. H. Berkeley served at the capture of Surinam, 1804; the Danish Islands of St. John, and St. Croix, 1807; and of Martinique in 1809, including the siege of Fort Bourbon.

131 Sir Charles Napier has a medal for the battle of Corunna, where he was made prisoner, after receiving five wounds. Also severely wounded at the battle of Busaco.

132 Sir Jeremiah Dickson served in the Peninsula as an Assistant-Quarter-Master-General, and has received a cross and a clasp for the battles of Vittoria, the Pyrenees, Nivelle, Orthes, and Toulouse. Served also the campaign of 1815, including the battle of Waterloo.

133 Sir Charles Wade Thornton served on the Continent under the Duke of York, and lost an arm by a cannon-shot at Lannoi.

Notes to the General Officers.

134 Sir Henry King was at the siege of Porto Rico, and capture of Trinidad in 1797. Whilst quartered at Marin, to windward of Martinique, he was ordered to proceed in a small vessel to St. Pierre, with a detachment of twenty-six men, to form a guard for the governor, Sir Wm. Keppel; encountered a French privateer off the Diamond Rock, mounting four long nines, with seventy men on board, which after a sharp action of twenty minutes, was beaten off with a loss of ten men killed and fifteen wounded, Sir Henry having only one man killed, and himself wounded in the shoulder. Served the Egyptian campaign of 1801, including the action at the landing at Aboukir Bay, siege of the castle, and actions of the 21st March, and 9th May at Rahmanie, at which latter he commanded a squadron of the 26th Light Dragoons, and lost his right leg. Expedition to Walcheren, and siege of Flushing, 1809. Appointed Commandant of Tarifa in 1810, and for his services at its defence his commission as Lieut.-Col. was antedated to the day of the assault, 31 Dec. 1811. Joined Lord Wellington's army a few days after the battle of Salamanca; commanded the 82nd at the battle of Vittoria, and towards the close of the action the command of the brigade devolved on him. Sir Henry has received the Egyptian medal, and a medal for the battle of Vittoria.

135 Sir Evan J. M. MacGregor served at Cadiz, the latter part of 1810 and beginning of 1811, as Assistant-Adjutant-General, and subsequently in the East Indies in the same department, and was severely wounded in the operations of the army under Sir Thos. Hislop, 27th Feb. 1818.

136 Sir Edward Gibbs commanded the 52nd regiment at Ciudad Rodrigo, Badajoz, and Vittoria, and has received a medal and two clasps.

137 Sir George Napier has received a medal and a clasp for Martinique and Ciudad Rodrigo, at which latter he led the storming party of the Light Division, and was severely wounded (right arm amputated) in ascending the breach. Also severely wounded at Cazal Nova, and slightly at Busaco.

138 Sir Charles Broke Vere served at the Helder, 1799; with the expedition to Hanover, 1805; to South America, 1807, including the attack on Buenos Ayres; and subsequently in the Peninsula, and has received a cross and five clasps for Albuhera, Badajoz, Salamanca, Vittoria, Pyrenees, Nivelle, Nive, Orthes, and Toulouse. Served also the campaign of 1815, including the battle of Waterloo.

139 The Hon. Sir Hercules Pakenham served in the Peninsula as an Assistant-Adjutant-General, and has received a cross for Busaco, Fuentes d'Onor, Ciudad Rodrigo, and Badajoz.

140 Sir John Harvey served in Holland in 1794 and 95; at the capture of the Cape of Good Hope, 1796; in Egypt, 1801; campaigns in India, under Lord Lake, including the siege of Bhurtpore, and the subsequent operations against the Mahratta chief, Holkar. Served in the American war during the campaigns of 1813 and 14, and was wounded before Fort Erie, 6th Aug. 1814. Medal for Chrystler's Farm.

141 Sir Leonard Greenwell accompanied the expedition to South America, and was present at the attack on Buenos Ayres, where he was severely wounded. Landed in Portugal, Aug. 1808, and served throughout the Peninsular war (except on two occasions when absent in consequence of wounds) including the battle of Fuentes d'Onor, storm and capture of Badajoz, battles of Salamanca, and Orthes. Sir Leonard has been shot through the neck, the body, both arms, and wounded in one leg. Medal and two clasps.

142 Sir George Scovell served in the Peninsula as an Assistant-Quarter-Master-General, and from 1813 in command of the Staff Corps of Cavalry. Served also the campaign of 1815, and was present at the battle of Waterloo. Sir George has received a cross and one clasp for the battles of Vittoria, the Pyrenees, Nivelle, Nive, and Toulouse.

143 Lord Downes served throughout the Peninsular war as an aide-de-camp to Sir John Cradock, and afterwards to the Duke of Wellington. His lordship has received a cross and a clasp for the battles of Vittoria, the Pyrenees, Nivelle, Nive, and Toulouse; and was wounded at Talavera.

144 Sir Robert Henry Dick commanded the 42nd Highlanders in the battles of Busaco, Fuentes d'Onor, and Salamanca, for which he has received a medal and two clasps. Served also the campaign of 1815, and was severely wounded at Quatre Bras.

145 Sir Neil Douglas served at the siege of Copenhagen in 1807; expedition to Sweden in 1808, and subsequently to Portugal and Spain, including the battle of Corunna; expedition to Walcheren, and siege of Flushing, 1809; in the Peninsula from Dec. 1809 to Jan. 1811, and again from April, 1813, to the end of the war, including the siege of Cadiz, and battles of Busaco (wounded through the left shoulder-joint by a ball, and by another in the left arm), the Pyrenees, Nivelle, Nive, and Toulouse. Served also the campaign of 1815, and was severely wounded through the knee by a ball, and contused from a ball hitting a button, at Quatre Bras. Sir Neil has received a cross for the battles of the Pyrenees, Nivelle, Nive, and Toulouse.

146 Lord Tweeddale served in the Peninsula as an Assistant-Quarter-Master-General, and has received a medal for the battle of Vittoria, and was slightly wounded at Busaco. Served also in the American war, and was wounded.

Notes to the General Officers.

147 Sir Fred. Wm. Trench served at Walcheren, 1809; in the Peninsula in 1811; and in Holland in 1814.

148 Major-General Wyndham served the Peninsular campaigns of 1808, 9, 11, and 13, including the actions of Roliça, Vimiera, Benevente, Albuhera, Usagne, Morales de Toro, Vittoria, and the Pyrenees. Served also the campaign of 1815, and was severely wounded at Waterloo.

149 Sir John B. Savage joined H. M. S. *Bedford* in 1780, and sailed with the Channel Fleet under the command of Sir George Rodney to the relief of Gibraltar; on the passage captured a Spanish 64, and a frigate with a convoy. Engaged the Spanish fleet under Don Langaro; captured six sail of the line, and drove two on shore. On return to England captured one French ship of the line and two frigates. In 1795 embarked in H. M. S. *Orion*, and joined the squadron under the command of Sir John Jarvis. On the 14th Feb. 1797, engaged the Spanish fleet off Cape St. Vincent, and captured four sail of the line. Blockaded Cadiz until June, 1798; then went up the Mediterranean with Sir Horatio Nelson; engaged the French squadron off the mouth of the Nile; took and destroyed eleven sail of the line and two frigates—in this action he was severely wounded. In 1801 joined H. M. S. *Ganges*; went with the fleet to the Baltic; was in the next ship to Lord Nelson in the action of Copenhagen, 2nd April, 1801; took and destroyed six sail of the line, and all the vessels opposed to our squadron.

150 Sir Edward Bowater served at the siege and taking of Copenhagen in 1807, and subsequently in the Peninsula, from Dec. 1808 to Nov. 1809, and again from Dec. 1811, to the end of the war, including the passage of the Douro and taking of Oporto, battles of Talavera and Salamanca, capture of Madrid, siege of Burgos, battle of Vittoria, siege of San Sebastian, passage of the Bidassoa, and battle of the Nive, (Mayor's house.) Served also the campaign of 1815, including the battles of Quatre Bras and Waterloo. Wounded at Talavera, and again at Waterloo.

151 Major-General Hill landed in Portugal, Aug. 1808, and served throughout the Peninsular war as aide-de-camp to Lord Hill. Served also the campaign of 1815. Slightly wounded at Oporto on the passage of the Douro, and severely at Waterloo.

152 Sir Wm. M. Gomm served in the Peninsula as an Assistant-Quarter-Master-General, and has received a cross and a clasp for Badajoz, Salamanca, Vittoria, San Sebastian, and Nive. Served also the campaign of 1815, including the battle of Waterloo.

153 Major-General D'Oyly served in the Peninsula as an Assistant-Adjutant-General. Served also the campaign of 1815, and was severely wounded at Waterloo.

154 Major-General Wm. Gray commanded a detachment on board the *Fortitude*, in Lord Howe's action after the relief of Gibraltar, 20th Oct. 1782. Served with his company as marines under Admiral Milbank, in the North Sea; removed with detachment on board the *Boyne*, and served in the Channel Fleet under Lord Howe; on this service the *Boyne* captured a French 20-gun ship. Proceeded on board the *Boyne* to the West Indies, and was present at the taking of Martinique, St. Lucia, and Guadaloupe, where he was wounded in the knee. Served the campaign of 1799 in Holland. Wounded in the arm in the action of the 2nd Oct., and on the 6th following he led the left wing of his regiment (the 2nd Foot) into action. Served the Egyptian campaign of 1801, and was present in the several engagements. Medal for services in Egypt.

155 Major-General Darley was at the sieges of Port-au-Prince, in St. Domingo, and of Morne Fortunée, in St. Lucia. Served in Egypt in 1807; and in the Peninsula, from Aug. 1813 to the end of the war, including the battle of the Nivelle, and before Bayonne, 9th, 10th, and 11th Dec. 1813.

156 Major-General Hamilton served in Holland in 1799, and was severely wounded at the battle of Crabbenham on the Zuyper Sluis, 10th Sept. 1799 (leg amputated). Served also in the American war; commanded the 100th regiment at the capture of Fort George, and at the capture by assault of Fort Niagara; and commanded the militia of Upper Canada at the battle of Lundy's Lane.

157 Major-General Reeves was at the capture of the French West India Islands, under Sir Charles Grey, and was wounded. Rebellion in Ireland, 1798, including the battle of Vinegar Hill. Commanded the 8th regiment during the Egyptian campaign of 1801, and present at the taking of Ischia and Procida, 1809; and served afterwards in the Peninsula, from 1811 to 1813, including the taking of Alcoy, and the battles of Biar (in command of division), Castalla, and Ordal; severely wounded, and sent home for recovery. Medal for services in Egypt.

158 Major-General the Hon. Lincoln Stanhope commanded the 16th Light Dragoons at the battle of Talavera, for which he has received a medal.

159 Major-General John Grey served in the East Indies in the campaign against Tippoo Sultan, including the battle of Mallavelly, the attack of the Toap and Sultan pettah before Seringapatam, siege of Seringapatam, and on the storming party at the assault (medal for this service.) Served in the Peninsula with the 5th regiment, and was a major in the 2nd

Notes to the General Officers.

battalion when the French and Polish Lancers attacked that regiment at El Bodon; present at the siege of Ciudad Rodrigo, also at the scaling of the *fausse braye* on the night of the storm, and at the storming of the great breach, which was carried by the 2nd battalion of the 5th regiment. Twice wounded during the siege of Ciudad Rodrigo.

160 Sir Alexander Cameron served the campaign of 1799 in Holland. Expedition to the Ferrol, 1800. Egyptian campaign of 1801; severely wounded in the arm and side at the battle of Alexandria. Expedition to Germany under Lord Cathcart, 1805; and to Copenhagen, 1807, including the battle of Keog. Landed in Portugal in 1808, and was present at the battle of Vimiera, with the rear-guard during the retreat, affair of Calcavellas, and battle of Corunna. Proceeded again to the Peninsula in May, 1809, and was present at the battle of Fuentes d'Onor, sieges and assaults of Ciudad Rodrigo and Badajoz, battles of Salamanca and Vittoria, besides a great many minor actions and other desultory services, until obliged to return to England, owing to a severe wound received at Vittoria. Served also the campaigns of 1814 and 15 in Holland, Flanders, and France, including the action at Merxem, operations before Antwerp, and battles of Quatre Bras and Waterloo, at which last he was severely wounded. Sir Alexander has received a medal for services in Egypt, and a medal and two clasps for Ciudad Rodrigo, Badajoz, and Salamanca.

161 Sir James Wilson has received a cross and a clasp for Albuhera, Badajoz, Salamanca, Vittoria, and Toulouse.

162 Major-General Dalmer commanded a light battalion at the battles of Salamanca and Vittoria, and has received a medal and a clasp. Served the campaign of 1815, including the battle of Waterloo.

163 Sir Henry Watson commanded the 1st Portuguese cavalry at the battle of Salamanca, and has received a medal.

164 Major-General Thomas Evans served in Egypt in 1801, and has received the medal. Served also in the American war, and was wounded in three places at Sackett's Harbour; contused at Fort Erie, and horse killed.

COLONELS.

	CORNET, 2nd LIEUT. or ENSIGN.	LIEUT.	CAPTAIN.	MAJOR.	LIEUT.-COLONEL.	COLONEL.	WHEN PLACED ON HALF PAY.	REGIMENTAL RANK.	
Sir David Cunynghame, Bart.[1]	14 Nov. 81	5 Feb. 83	20 Mar. 83	never	15 Jan. 94	26 Jan. 97			Late of 82 Foot.
William Stewart	24 Feb. 75	14 Mar. 76	14 July 77	1 Mar. 94	17 May 94	1 Jan. 00			Late of 89 Foot.
Henry Mordaunt Clavering	7 Feb. 94	12 Feb. 94	13 Feb. 94	30 July 94	19 Aug. 95	29 April 02			Late of 98 Foot.
* Sir John Burke, Bart.	never	never	never	never		22 May 04			Late of 98 Foot.
Hon. Francis Wm. Grant	July 93	31 July 93	14 Feb. 94	29 Nov. 94	23 Jan. 99	25 Oct. 00			Late of 2 Argyll Fencibles.
William Say	22 Feb. 86	16 Mar. 91	10 Feb. 94	15 Nov. 94	1 Jan. 00	25 July 10			Late of 99 Foot.
Hugh Baillie	12 April 93	27 Nov. 93	13 Feb. 94	29 Dec. 94	do	do			Late of Surrey Rangers.
Henry Cuyler	1 Dec. 82	3 Sept. 88	18 Dec. 93	9 Sept. 97	16 May 01	do			Late of 46 Foot.
John Richard Broadhead	24 Oct. 89	Nov. 93	9 Dec. 93	9 Sept. 95	1 Jan. 01	do			Late of 121 Foot.
* Sir Arch. Christie, KCH.	3 Mar. 80	26 Aug. 82	16 May 94	25 Sept. 03	21 May 07	13 July 11			Late Comm. at Chatham.
John Dick Burnaby	1 Feb. 92	never	5 Mar. 94	never	25 June 03	1 Jan. 12			Late of Grenadier Gds.
Hon. Fulke Greville Howard	28 April 93	never	15 Oct. 94	never	16 April 04	4 June 13			Late of 9 Garrison Batt.
Edward Drummond		4 Feb. 95	8 Nov. 98	11 June 01	29 Dec. 04	do			Late of 86 Foot.
Launcelot Holland	27 Oct. 98	never	25 Nov. 99	1 Nov. 04	16 Sept. 06	4 June 14			Late of 134 Foot.
John Goulston Price Tucker[2]	29 April 95	25 May 96	31 Aug. 01	13 Jan. 05	17 April 07	do			Late of 5 W. India Regt.
Charles, Earl of Harrington	2 Dec. 95	never	21 Nov. 99	24 Jan. 03	25 June 07	do	13 Aug. 12	Lieut.-Col.	Half-pay 3 W. India Regt.
⊕ ❋ Hon. Alex. Abercromby, CB.[3]	16 Aug. 99	19 Mar. 00	21 May 00	17 July 06	28 Jan. 08	do			Late of Coldstream Gds.
Francis Sherlock, KH.[4]	31 Aug. 98	19 Dec. 93	22 Dec. 93	4 June 01	do	do			Late of 4 Dragoon Gds.
Benjamin Wynne Ottley[5]	1 Oct. 94		1 July 95	25 July 01	do	do			Late of 70 Foot.
James Home	21 Nov. 76	18 Aug. 78	30 April 93	29 April 02	27 July 08	do		Lieut.-Col.	Late of Royal Marines.
⊕ ❋ John, Earl of Portarlington[6]	Mar. 98	20 Dec. 98	24 Mar. 00	25 Nov. 06	1 Sept. 08	do			Late of 23 Light Dragoons.
Augustus Rottiger	never	never	never	24 Dec.	25 Nov. 08	do			Late of German Legion.
⊕ ❋ Sir Robt. Chambre Hill, CB.[7]	May 93	15 Oct. 93	11 April 00	14 Nov. 05	1 Jan. 12	1 Jan. 19			Late of R. Horse Guards.
Robert Moncrieffe	28 Nov. 76	24 Aug. 78	3 May 93	29 April 02	15 Feb. 09	12 Aug. 19			Late of Royal Marines.
⊕ Sir William Cox[8]	1 Oct. 94	3 Sept. 95	7 Aug. 00	19 June 06	16 Feb. 11	do			Late of Portuguese Serv.
Thomas Francklin	1 July 82	24 Mar. 91	6 Mar. 95	27 June 07	1 May 12	do			Late of Royal Artillery.
John Potter Hamilton, KH.	April 94	13 Aug. 94	16 Aug. 99	27 Feb. 02	25 Oct.	do			Late of Scots Fus. Gds.

32

Colonels.

Name	2D LIEUT. ETC.	LIEUT.	CAPTAIN.	MAJOR.	LIEUT.-COLONEL.	COLONEL.	WHEN PLACED ON HALF PAY.	REGIMENTAL RANK.	
Bohun Shore	2 Feb. 84	5 Dec. 87	17 Feb. 98	29 April 02	25 Oct. 09	12 Aug. 19			Late of 4 Dragoons.
Cavendish Sturt	5 June 89	24 Jan. 91	24 July 93	do	do	do			Late of 39 Foot.
Francis Dunne	31 Jan. 92	never	26 Aug. 93	do	do	do			Late of 7 Dragoon Gds.
Hn. H. G. P. Townshend, KCH.[9]	23 Sept. 95	never	20 Sept. 99	never	26 Oct.	do	12 Feb. 30	Lieut.-Col.	Unattached.
Sir Horace St. Paul, Bart.	14 Feb.	3 Jan. 94	16 April 98	24 Oct. 02	25 July 03	do			Late of 5 Foot.
John Fred. Browne, CB.[10]	15 Sept. 81	31 Jan. 88	2 Sept. 95	9 July 03	do 10	do			Late of 28 Foot.
Frederick Griffiths	5 June 89	1 July 91	7 Oct. 95	1 Feb. 06	27 Sept. 10	do			Late of Royal Artillery. Late 1 R. Vct. Bn. Dep. Gov. of Stirling Castle.
Sir Arch. Christie, KCH.	3 Mar. 80	26 Aug. 82	16 May 94	25 Sept. 03	21 May 07	1 Nov. 19		Colonel.	Late of 6 Foot.
John Castle		1 Sept. 95	14 Aug. 00	13 June 05	10 Jan. 11	19 July 21			Late of 67 Foot.
Nathaniel Burslem, KH.[11]	2 Dec. 89	16 Aug. 93	4 April 95	7 Mar. 05	1 Mar.	do			Late of Scots Fus. Gds.
Benjamin Ansley, KC.	21 Mar. 98	never	25 Nov. 99	never	28 Mar.	do			Late of R. Invalid Engin.
William Gravatt	18 June 92	27 Nov. 93	1 July 97	never	1 May	do			Late of 62 Foot.
George Gauntlett[12]	2 Mar. 91	12 Feb. 94	9 Feb. 97	1 Aug. 04	2 May	do			Late of 60 Foot.
William Woodgate, CB.[13]	21 Mar. 00	19 Nov. 00	6 April 03	13 Aug. 07	30 May	do			Late of 43 Foot.
Christopher C. Patrickson, CB.[14]	31 Aug. 93	25 Mar. 94	25 Mar. 94	28 Sept. 09	10 Dec. 12	25 July 21			Late of Scots Fus. Gds.
James Johnstone Cochrane	26 Dec. 99	never	5 Jan. 04	never	4 June 11	27 May 25			Late of 96 Foot.
Michael White Lee	24 Feb. 95	3 Sept. 95	1 July 96	21 April 04	4 June 11	27 May 25			Late of 25 Foot.
Alex. Whatley Light	11 Dec. 93	12 Jan. 94	3 Oct. 99	1 Aug. 04	do	do			Late of 9 Foot.
David Campbell[15]	27 Oct. 90	29 Jan. 94	1 Sept. 95	do	do	do			Late of 82 Foot.
Henry Thornton, CB.[16]	8 Oct. 94	24 June 95	23 Nov. 96	do	do	do			Late of 2 Dragoon Gds.
William Spearman	15 Oct. 94	6 Jan. 95	20 July 96	29 Aug.	do	do	29 May 06	Major	Half-pay 14 Garrison Bn.
Thomas Weston	18 July 80	25 Dec. 87	1 Sept. 95	1 Sept. 95	do	do			Late of Scots Fus. Gds.
Sir Fred. Hankey, GCMG.	10 June 95	22 June 96	24 Jan. 01	1 Nov.	15 Aug. 11	do			Late of 15 Foot.
Sir John Milley Doyle, KCB.[17]	31 May 94	21 June 94	3 Dec. 02	22 Sept. 08	26 Sept.	do			Late of 12 Garrison Bn.
John Hamilton	21 Nov. 99	never	9 July 01	16 Feb. 09	30 Jan. 12	do			Late of Coldstream Gds.
William Henly Raikes	9 May 00	10 May 00	13 May 01	never	3 June 13	do			Late of Coldstream Gds.
Charles Gold, CB.	1 June 90	17 Jan. 93	26 April 02	25 April 08	17 Dec.	29 July 25			Late of Royal Artillery.
Wm. Augustus Keate[18]	28 Aug. 00	never	1 Oct.	never	9 Aug.	15 Sept. 25			Late of Scots Fus. Gds.
John Richard Ward, CB.[19]			24 May 04	25 April 08	1 Jan. 12	22 July 30			Late of 2 Dragoons.
George Grogan			8 Dec. 94	1 Jan. 05	do	do	25 April 17	Captain	Half-pay Corsican Regt.
John Daniell	6 Jan. 96	20 Jan. 96	24 Dec. 02	28 Feb. 05	do	do			Late of 49 Foot.
Wm. Williams Blake, CB.[20]	26 April 97	31 Oct. 99	18 Feb. 02	21 Mar. 05	do	do			Late of 11 Dragoons.

33

Colonels.

	CORNET, ETC.	LIEUT.	CAPTAIN.	MAJOR.	LIEUT.-COLONEL.	COLONEL.	WHEN PLACED ON HALF PAY.	REGIMENTAL RANK.	
Sir *Edward Miles*, CB.[21]	13 Aug. 94	8 July 95	25 Oct. 02	21 Mar. 05	1 Jan. 12	22 July 30			Late of 89 Foot.
John Shedden	9 Feb. 97	22 Mar. 98	25 July 99	20 June 05		do	21 Jan. 13	Major	Late of 89 Foot.
Wm. H. Knight Erskine, CB.[22]		3 Sept. 89	19 Dec. 95	12 Sept. 05	do	do	25 Dec. 18	Lieut.-Col.	Half-pay Bradshaw's Levy
Matthew Mahon	31 Dec. 89	11 May 91	9 Sept. 98	28 Nov. 05	do	do	25 Mar. 19	do	Half-pay R. York Rang.
John Mathias Everard	5 Dec. 96	28 Dec. 96	18 Dec. 99	10 July 06	23 Jan. 13	do	25 June 16	do	Half-pay 77 Foot.
George Wyndham	31 Mar. 03	Apr. 05	19 Sept. 05	31 Jan. 11	13 Mar. do		30 July 29	Lieut.-Col.	Half-pay 20 Dragoons.
Sir Archibald Maclaine, CB.[23]	16 April 94	20 April 95	22 Dec. 04	4 Oct. 06	10 Mar. do		27 Oct. 37	do	Unattached.
Sir James Hay, CB.[24]	10 June 95	26 April 98	28 Feb. 05	2 Jan. 07	12 Feb. do		11 May 15	do	Half-pay 41 Foot.
William Wood, CB. KH.	27 Jan. 97	27 Dec. 97	3 Dec. 02	14 May 07	8 April do		1 April 37	do	Unat. *Comm. at Chatham*.
Sir William Warre, CB.[25]	5 Nov. 03	2 June 04	25 April 06	30 May 11	13 May do		25 Mar. 16	Major	Half-pay Greek Light Inf.
Chas. Ashe A'Court, CB. KH.	Dec. 01	2 Sept. 02	25 July 04	26 Feb. 11	19 May do				{ Unat. *Dep.-Adj.-Gen. in Ireland.*
Geo. Charles D'Aguilar, CB.[26]	24 Sept. 99	1 Dec. 99	30 Mar. 08	1 April 13	20 May do		13 Sept. 21	Lieut.-Col.	
Charles Wm. Pasley, CB.	1 Dec. 97	28 Aug. 99	1 Mar. 95	5 Feb. 12	27 May do			do	Royal Engineers.
Jacob Glen Cuyler	26 Oct. 99	11 June 01	9 July 03	26 Jan. 06	4 June do		25 May 17	Major	Half-pay Cape Regiment.
Sir George O'Malley, CB.[27]	23 Feb. 00	2 June 01	25 April 05	21 Aug. 06	4 June do		9 Aug. 39	Lieut.-Col.	Unattached.
Peter D'Arcy	Nov.	26 Nov. 93	23 Sept. 99	26 Nov. 06	do	do	25 Mar. 10	Major	Half-pay 7 Garrison Batt.
Edwin Row. Joseph Cotton[28]	22 May 97	11 Oct. 97	9 July 03	4 Mar. 07	do	do	25 Feb. 12	Captain	Half-pay 10 Foot.
Charles Turner[29]	29 April 95	5 Mar. 96	22 Nov. 98	9 April do		do	7 May 12	Lieut.-Col.	Unat. *Assist. Ad.-Gen. in Ire.*
Wm. Fra. Bentinck Loftus	30 Aug. 99	16 July 00	20 April 04	5 30 April 07	do	do	25 Dec. 14	Major	Half-pay 38 Foot. [*Ire.*
George Burrell	4 Feb. 97	3 May 97	15 Aug. 00	2 4 June do		do	12 Jan. 26	Lieut.-Col.	18 Foot.
James Ogilvie, CB.[30]	21 Mar. 00	22 Aug. 00	5 April 02	4 June do		do		do	Unattached.
James Farrer	17 Mar. 94	29 July 95	5 April 96	2 July do		do	14 Sept. 20	Major	Half-pay Greek Light Inf.
Thomas Brabazon Aylmer[31]	9 Aug. 97	15 Aug. 98	31 May 00	2 Sept. do		do	25 Feb. 16	do	Half-pay 9 Foot.
Henry James Riddell, KH.	Mar. 98	19 April 98	24 Dec. 02	10 Dec. do		do		Lieut.-Col.	Assist. Qr. Mas.-Gen. in
Richard Goodall Elrington, CB.	4 Dec. 90	19 Feb. 94	1 June 95	25 April 08	do	do		do	47 Foot. [*Ireland.*
Henry Chas. Edw. Vernon, CB.[32]	28 Nov. 98	26 Sept. 99	17 July 01	13 June 11	do	do	25 Feb. 28	do	Unattached.
John Ready			20 Aug.	30 Aug. 10	10 June do		6 Feb. 15	do	{ Half-pay 1 Garr. Batt. Lt.-Gov. of Isle of Man.
Chas. Albert Vigoureux, CB.[33]	10 May 93	2 Dec. 93	4 April 95	25 April 08	21 June 13	do	12 July 39	Lieut.-Col.	Half-pay 45 Foot.
Sir James Arch. Hope, KCB.[34]	12 Jan. 00	3 June 00	18 Feb. 06	6 Mar. 11	do	do	1 Nov. 39	do	Unattached.
Sir Robert John Harvey, CB.[35]	8 Oct. 03	24 Mar. 04	2 Jan. 06	25 July 11	do	do	25 Oct. 15	do	Unattached.
Sir H. Dalrymple Ross, KCB.	6 Mar. 95	10 May 96	1 Sept. 03	31 Dec. 11	do	do		Colonel	Half-pay Portuguese Ser. Royal Artillery.
Sir Dudley St. Leger Hill, CB.[36]	27 Aug. 04	10 Oct. 05	16 Aug. 10	27 April 12	do	do	19 Jan. 26	Major	Unattached.

Colonels.

	ENSIGN, ETC.	LIEUT.	CAPTAIN.	MAJOR.	LIEUT.-COLONEL.	COLONEL.	WHEN PLACED ON HALF PAY.	REGIMENTAL RANK.	
҉ *Sir* Edm. K. Williams, KCB.	30 Aug. 99	18 April 00	25 Sept. 07	8 Oct. 12	21 June 13	22 July 30		Lieut.-Col.	9th Foot.
Henry Sullivan, CB.	17 May 98	20 Sept. 98	18 July 01	21 Jan. 08	1 July 13	do		do	6th Foot.
҉ Burges Carnac		29 May 03	18 Aug. 08	11 June 11	29 July 13	do	29 June 28	Captain	Unattached.
Robert M'Douall, CB.	31 Aug. 96	1 Nov. 97	24 Oct. 04	24 June 13	29 July 13	do	4 Dec. 16	Major	Half-pay Glengarry Fen.
҉ Henry Freke, CB.	3 Dec. 93		26 Sept. 95	25 April 08	9 Aug. 13	do			Late of 51 Foot.
҉ *Sir* Richard Armstrong, CB.[37]	23 June 96	5 Nov. 99	9 July 07	30 May 11	26 Aug. 13	do	13 Feb. 35	Lieut.-Col.	Unattached.
҉ *Sir* Fred. Stovin, KCB. KCMG.[38]	22 Mar. 00	7 Jan. 01	24 June 02	27 April 12	do	do	23 April 20	do	Unattached.
									{ Do. *Dep. Quar.-Mast.-* *in Ireland.*
҉ ҉ *Sir* Guy Campbell, *Bart*. CB.[39]	9 Dec. 94	4 April 96	14 Sept. 04	1 April 13	do	do	26 Feb. 16	do	Unattached.
Richard Goddard Hare, CB.[40]	6 July 96	1 Nov. 96	9 July 03	1 July 13	16 Sept. 13	do	27 Aug. 25	Colonel	Royal Engineers.
҉ *Sir* Charles Felix Smith, CB.	2 July 01	1 Oct. 02	18 Nov. 07	31 Dec. 11	21 Sept. 13	do		Captain	Half-pay 98 Foot.
҉ Alexander Thomson, CB.[41]	23 Sept. 03	29 Feb. 08	14 May 09	9 April 12	do	do	1 April 19	Colonel	Royal Engineers.
Charles Grene Ellicombe, CB.	never	1 July 01	1 July 06	27 April 12	do	do		do	Royal Engineers.
Henry Goldfinch, CB.	1 Mar. 98	11 June 00	1 Mar. 05	17 Dec. 12	do	do		do	Royal Artillery.
҉ ҉ James Webber Smith, CB.	6 Mar. 95	3 Oct. 95	25 Nov. 02	4 June 06	do	do			Half-pay Can. Voltigeurs.
Fred. George Heriot, CB.[42]	28 Aug. 01	9 Oct. 01	20 Nov. 06	10 June 10	11 Nov. 13	do			
҉ William Crosse, CB.[43]	2 Dec. 99	28 Feb. 00	25 Feb. 02	8 Dec. 08	22 Nov. 13	do	29 April 24	Lieut.-Col.	Unattached.
҉ ҉ Samuel Rice, CB, KH.[44]	12 Feb. 93	5 May 94	18 June 98	13 July 09	do	do	5 July 31	Major	Half-pay 43 Foot.
҉ Wm. Fra. Patrick Napier, CB.[45]	14 June 00	18 April 01	2 June 04	30 May 11	22 Nov. 13	do	17 June 19	Lieut.-Col.	Half-pay 43 Foot.
John Duffy, CB.[46]	21 Oct. 95	6 Jan. 96	12 Aug. 04	6 Feb. 12	do	do	20 Mar. 28	do	Unattached.
Martin Lindsay, CB.[47]	July 94	22 Aug. 94	22 Nov. 01	4 Jan. 10	25 Nov. 13	do			Late of 78 Foot.
Henry Daubeney, KH.[48]	8 July 95	21 Oct. 95	7 Sept. 97	26 May 08	11 Dec. 13	do	21 Nov. 22	Lieut.-Col.	Half-pay 83 Foot.
҉ ҉ Douglas Mercer, CB.[49]	24 Mar. 03	never	20 Mar. 06	never	20 Dec. 13	do	11 Aug. 37	do	Unattached.
Francis Miles Milman,[50]	3 Dec. 00	never	28 April 04	never	25 Dec. 13	do	8 Aug. 37	do	Unattached.
҉ ҉ John Reeve.	23 Oct. 00	never	11 April 05	never	do	do	14 April 25	do	Unattached.
҉ ҉ Jacob Tonson,[51]	9 Feb. 91	19 Mar. 93	13 Sept. 95	26 May 08	26 Dec. 13	do	12 Aug. 24	Captain	Half-pay 37 Foot.
Wm. Alex. Gordon, CB.[52]	2 Oct. 94	29 Dec. 94	8 Jan. 01	4 June 13	do	do	26 Nov. 18	do	Half-pay 95 Foot.
҉ ҉ S. Arthur Goodman, CB. KH.	13 Oct. 94	5 Sept. 95	9 July 03	do	do	do	1814	Major	Half-pay 48 Foot.
Thomas Kenah, CB.	14 Aug. 99	9 May 00	3 Mar. 04	5 Nov. 12	27 Dec. 13	do	3 April 17	do	Half-pay 58 Foot.
҉ ҉ *Sir* R. Gardiner, KCB. KCH.	7 April 97	16 July 99	12 Oct. 04	27 April 12	3 Mar. 14	do		Colonel	{ R. Artillery, *Aide-de-Camp to the Queen.*
Samuel Lambert	5 Nov. 03	never	27 Aug. 07	never	16 Mar. 14	do		Lieut.-Col.	Grenadier Guards.
҉ ҉ John Fremantle, CB.[53]	17 Oct. 05	never	2 Aug. 10	21 June 13	21 Mar. 14	do	31 Dec. 39	do	{ Unattached, *Aide-de-Camp to the Queen.*

Colonels.

	CORNET, ETC.	LIEUT.	CAPTAIN.	MAJOR.	LIEUT.-COLONEL.	COLONEL.	WHEN PLACED ON HALF PAY.	REGIMENTAL RANK.	
↯ Lord Geo. Wm. Russell, GCB.[54]	5 Feb. 06	11 Sept. 06	25 Mar. 08	4 Feb. 13	12 April 14	22 July 30	17 May 31	Lieut.-Col.	Unattached, Aide-de-Camp to the Queen.
↯ Edward Wynyard, CB.	17 Dec. 03	never	7 Jan. 08	25 Mar. 13	28 May 14	do	17 Feb. 37	do	Unattached, do.
↯ James Fergusson, CB.[55]	20 Aug. 01	9 Feb. 04	1 Dec. 06	3 Dec. 12	16 May 14	do	10 May 39	do	H.p. Coldst. Gds.
↯ Thomas Wm. Brotherton, CB.	24 Jan. 00	never	27 July 01	28 Nov. 11	19 May 14	do		do	16 Dr. Com. Can. Dep. do.
↯ Sir Adolphus J. Dalrymple, Bart.[56]	25 Oct. 99	12 June 00	7 Jan. 03	15 Sept. 08	1 June 14	do	Dec. 14	do	H. p. 2 Gar. Bat.
↯ Sir James Henry Reynett, KCH.[56]	25 Nov. 99	14 Mar. 00	24 Mar. 04	8 April 13	do	do	20 Mar. 17	Major	H. p. 52 Foot.
William Smelt, CB.	16 Mar. 98	11 Dec. 99	21 Mar. 05	28 Jan. 08	4 June 14	do		Lieut.-Col.	37 Foot,
Thomas Abernethie, KH.	12 Oct. 78	1 June 81	18 Mar. 95	25 April 08	do	do		Col. Comm.	Late of R. Marines.
↯ Andrew Creagh, CB.[57]	never	1 Oct. 94	26 Aug. 96	do		do			Late of 81 Foot.
James Robertson Arnold, KH.	1 Mar. 98	11 June 00	1 Mar. 05	never	20 Dec. 14	do		Colonel	{ R. Engineers, Aide-de-Camp to the Queen.
↯ William Wemys	3 July 03	12 Sept. 05	18 Aug. 08	27 May 13	16 Mar. 15	do	25 Feb. 16	Lieut.-Col.	Half-pay 93 Foot, do.
↯ George, Earl of Munster[58]	5 Feb. 07	9 Mar. 09	2 Aug. 11	16 June 18	21 Jan. 19	do	24 Dec. 28	do	{ Unatt. Gov. and Capt. of Winds. Castle, Aide-de-Camp to the Queen.
Robert Pym, CB.	30 May 94	14 Aug. 94	3 Dec. 00	1 Jan. 12	19 July 21	do		Colonel	Royal Artillery.
Walter Tremenheere, KH.	2 Jan. 79	12 Jan. 82	28 Jan. 96	25 April 08	4 June 14	28 Dec. 30		Col-Com.	Late of Royal Marines.
Harry Percival Lewis	28 Feb. 79	15 Sept. 82	21 Mar. 96	do	do	do		do	Late of Royal Marines.
↯ Archibald Campbell, CB.[59]	9 Nov. 97	20 June 98	22 Dec. 03	3 Sept. 12	17 Feb. 14	6 May 31			Late of 46 Foot.
↯ John Bell, CB.[60]	15 Aug. 05	1 Oct. 07	12 Mar. 12	21 June 13	12 April 14	do	10 Nov. 14	Lieut.-Col.	{ H.-pay Assist. Qr.-Mas. Gen. Extra Aide-de-Camp to the Queen.
↯ Samuel Benj. Auchmuty, CB.[61]	15 Oct. 97	13 Mar. 00	14 Nov. 05	26 Aug. 13	do	do	1 Aug. 22	Major	Half-pay 8 Gar. Bn.
↯ Thomas Lightfoot, CB.[62]	Aug. 99	14 Mar. 00	15 Dec. 04	21 June 13	19 May 14	do	25 Dec. 14	do	Half-pay 45 Foot, do.
↯ Alured Dodsworth Faunce, CB.	2 Dec. 95	13 Oct. 96	6 Aug. 03	14 Feb. 11	29 Sept. 14	do		do	Insp. F. Offic. Rec. Dis. do.
George Brown, CB. KH.	23 Jan. 06	18 Sept. 06	20 June 11	26 May 14	29 Sept. 14	do		do	Rifle Brigade, do.
Lord Fred. Fitz Clarence, GCH.	never	12 May 14	23 Feb. 20	10 Jan. 22	1 April 24	do	24 Aug. 32	do	Unattached, do.
↯ George Prescott Wingrove.[63]	3 May 93	17 Dec. 94	1 Nov. 01	4 June 13	26 Aug. 26	do		Col. Comm.	Late of Royal Marines.
Richard Seeker Brough	never	2 Sept. 94	1 Jan. 98	25 July 10	12 Aug. 19	21 Nov. 33		Colonel	Royal Artillery.
↯ Andrew Bredin	never	9 Sept. 94	6 July 98	25 July 10	do	20 July 34		do	Royal Artillery.
James Power	never	30 Sept. 94	22 Feb. 99	4 June 11	do	5 June 35		do	Royal Artillery.
Charles Younghusband	9 Oct. 94	29 Sept. 94	18 April 01	4 June 13	25 Jan. 25	12 June 35		do	Royal Artillery.
↯ George Crawford	9 Oct. 94	31 Oct. 94	do	do	2 Mar. 25	27 April 36		do	Royal Artillery.

Colonels.

	ENSIGN, ETC.	LIEUT.	CAPTAIN.	MAJOR.	LIEUT.-COLONEL.	COLONEL.	WHEN PLACED ON HALF PAY.	REGIMENTAL RANK.	
John Aitchison	25 Oct. 05	never	22 Nov. 10	never	15 Dec. 14	20 May 36	1 Jan. 33	Lieut.-Col.	Scots Fusilier Guards.
Chas. Edward Conyers, CB.[64]	13 Sept. 94	2 Sept. 95	25 June 02	16 Feb. 09	3 Mar. 14	10 Jan. 37	10 Feb. 17	do	Half-pay Insp. F. Officer.
Geo. Aug. Henderson, KH.[65]	1 Sept. 93	1 Mar. 95	20 Aug. 01	4 June 13	12 April 14	do	27 July 26	do	Half-pay Insp. F. Officer.
Richard Roberts, KH.	8 June 96	2 Mar. 97	31 Jan. 99	11 April 11	19 April 14	do	25 Nov. 28	do	Unattached.
Roger Parke[66]	30 June 95	1 Oct. 95	9 Oct. 00	25 Feb. 08	4 June 14	10 Jan. 37	28 Nov. 16	Major	Half-pay 71 Foot.
Robt. Bar. Macpherson, CB. KH.[67]	3 June 95	22 July 95	3 Dec. 00	17 Mar. 08	do	do	25 Dec. 15	Captain	Half-pay 71 Foot.
George Hamilton Gordon	2 April 94	17 Sept. 94	13 Jan. 95	25 April do	do	do	22 Feb. 21	Major	Half-pay 25 Dragoons.
Philip Hay		31 Oct. 93	22 July do				25 June 17	do	{ Late R. Irish Artillery, { (Capt.) and h.p. 35 F.
John Slessor		14 June 94	25 July do	do	do	do	do	Captain	Late Roy. Irish Artillery.
Hans Allen	never	29 July 94	do	do	do	do	do	do	Late Roy. Irish Artillery.
James Irving	never	3 Aug. 94	do	do	do	do	do	do	Late Roy. Irish Artillery.
John Carr	never	21 July 95	31 July do	do	do	do	do		Late of 17 Foot.
David Williams	19 May 94	14 Jan. 95	25 May 98	16 June 00	do	do	25 Feb. 16	Major	Half-pay 27 Foot.
Patrick Nicolson	3 Nov. 96	14 Dec. 96	11 April 00	15 Oct. 03	do	do	30 July 18	Lieut.-Col.	Half-pay 50 Foot.
Cha. Philip de Bossett, CB. KH.[66]	Aug. 96	25 Sept. 98	22 Oct. 99	20 July 09	do	do	do	do	57 Foot.
James Allan, CB.	1 Jan. 95	18 May 95	10 Sept. 99	14 Dec. 09	do	do	24 June 19	Major	Half-pay 60 Foot.
Archibald Money, C.B.	April 94	13 May 94	3 May 01	4 Mar. 13	14 July 14	do	5 Jan. 36	Lieut.-Col.	{ Half-pay 38 Foot, Adj. { Gen. in East Indies.
Robert Torrens, CB.[69]	30 Sept. 96	25 Jan. 01	18 May 06	never	25 July do	do	31 Aug. 26	do	Late of Grenadier Gds.
Henry Edmund Joddrell	29 Dec. 03	never	7 April 08	never	25 July do	do	14 Sept. 17	do	Unattached.
Henry Dawkins[70]	10 Mar. 04	never	25 June 08	29 Aug. 11	28 July do	do		do	Half-pay 78 Foot.
David Forbes, CB.[71]	13 Mar. 93	3 May 94	25 June 03	29 Oct. 12	15 Sept. do	do	26 Nov. 18	Major	Insp. Fd. Offic. Rec. Dist.
John Fred. Ewart, CB.	1 Nov. 03	10 Mar. 04	17 April 06	30 April 12	17 Sept. do	do	17 Sept. 23	Captain	Half-pay 6 Foot.
Henry Adolphus Proctor, CB.[72]	14 Jan. 01	25 Mar. 02	16 May 05	19 Dec. 12	22 Sept. do	do	22 July 30	Lieut.-Col.	Half-pay 53 Foot.
William Jervois, KH.	7 April 04	4 Aug. do	14 July 08	23 July 13	13 Oct. do	do	25 Oct. 18	Captain	Unattached.
Thomas Fenn Addison[74]	6 Dec. 98	27 Nov. 99	23 July 03	4 June 14	do	do		Lieut.-Col.	Half-pay 99 Foot.
Francis Cockburn	4 May 00	17 Dec. 02	24 Dec. 03	27 June 11	27 Oct. do	do	1 June 29	Lieut.-Col.	{ 2 W. India Regt. Lt.- { Gov. of the Bahamas.
Thomas Steele	16 Oct. 00	6 April 03	3 Mar. 04	29 Dec. do	do	do	25 Dec. 16	Major	Unattached.
Carlo Joseph Doyle[75]	17 Mar. 04	never	1 June 09	23 Jan. 12	8 Mar. 15	do	24 July 16	do	{ H.-p. 2 Gar. Bat. Lieut. { Governor of Grenada.
Thomas Charretie[76]	28 July 03	never	13 Mar. do	6 Jan. 12	do	do			Half-pay 7 W. India Reg.
	9 June 04	6 Feb. 05	25 Dec. 07	27 April 15	21 May 15	do		do	F

Colonels.

	CORNET, ETC.	LIEUT.	CAPTAIN.	MAJOR.	LIEUT.-COLONEL.	COLONEL.	WHEN PLACED ON HALF PAY.	REGIMENTAL RANK.	
Sir George Arthur, KCH.	25 Aug. 04	24 June 05	5 May 08	5 Nov. 12	1 June 15	10 Jan. 37	25 Oct. 19	Lieut.-Col.	{ H.-p. York Chasseurs, Lt.-Gov.of Upper Can.
Colley Lygon Lucas Foster	1 Dec. 9	16 Mar. 00	5 Aug. 04	19 Dec. 13	10 June 15	do	25 June 14	Major	Unattached.
𝔚 𝔊𝔄 Edward Parkinson, CB.[77]	27 Feb. 96	12 Jan. 00	7 Mar. 05	27 Oct. 10	18 June 15	do	11 Sept. 17	do	Half-pay 11 Foot.
𝔚 𝔊𝔄 Thomas Hunter Blair, CB.[78]	24 July 02	14 Sept. 02	28 Mar. 04	30 May 11	do	do	25 Feb. 31	Lieut.-Col.	Unattached.
𝔚 𝔊𝔄 Edward Cheney, CB...........	Sept. 94	32 Oct. 94	3 May 00	1 Jan. 12	do	do	17 Sept. 18	Major	Half-pay Watteville's Reg.
𝔚 𝔊𝔄 Richard Lluellyn, CB.[79]	24 July 03	7 April 04	28 Feb. 05	23 April 12	do	do	25 Feb. 17	Captain	Half-pay 98 Foot.
𝔚 𝔊𝔄 Peter Aug. Lautour, CB.KH.	31 Mar. 04	4 July 05	8 May 06	20 May 13	do	do	25 Jan. 18	Major	Half-pay 23 Dragoons.
𝔚 𝔊𝔄 John Hare, CB.KH..........	29 Oct. 99	17 May 00	9 Sept. 05	17 June 13	do	do		Lieut.-Col.	{ 27 Ft. Lieut.-Gov. of the Eastern District of the Cape of Good Hope.
𝔚 Peter Brown	7 Dec. 99	18 Dec. 02	21 Mar. 05	21 June 13	do	do	5 Sept. 16	Major	Half-pay 14 Foot.
𝔚 𝔊𝔄 Thomas Francis Wade, CB.[80]	21 Feb. 05	31 July 06	13 July 09	do	do	do	20 April 32	Lieut.-Col.	Unattached.
𝔚 𝔊𝔄 Richard Egerton, CB.	1 Dec. 98	29 Mar. 98	28 Sept. 00	26 Aug. 13	do	do	16 Dec. 19	Major	Half-pay 57 Foot.
𝔚 𝔊𝔄 William Chalmers, CB.KH.[81]	9 July 03	25 Oct. 03	27 Aug. 07	26 Aug. 13	do	do	2 Oct. 17	Lieut.-Col.	Unattached.
𝔚 𝔊𝔄 Francis Dalmer	10 Mar. 04	18 April 04	10 Dec. 05	do 07	do	do	20 July 26	Lieut.-Col.	Royal Artillery.
𝔚 𝔊𝔄 John Boteler Parker, CB.....	1 April 02	1 Sept. 03	5 June 08	21 Sept. 13	do	do		do	{ 31 Foot, Quar.-Mast.-General East Indies.
𝔚 𝔊𝔄 Chatham Hor. Churchill, CB.	19 June 06	never	27 Aug. 12	22 Nov. 13	do	do		do	Unattached.
𝔚 𝔊𝔄 George Miller, CB.[82]	18 July 04	8 May 05	21 Jan. 08	3 Mar. 14	do	do	25 May 26	do	Half-pay Rifle Brigade.
𝔚 𝔊𝔄 Charles Beckwith, CB.[83] ...	2 June 03	29 Aug. 04	28 July 08	do	do	do	27 Jan. 20	Captain	Late of 22 Foot.
𝔚 𝔊𝔄 John Campbell, CB.[84]	June	19 Sept. 04	3 Dec. 07	12 April 14	do	do		Captain	Half-pay 22 Dragoons.
𝔚 𝔊𝔄 William Campbell, CB.	4 May 04	18 April 05	23 June 08	do	do	do	25 Oct. 21	Major	{ Half-pay 23 Foot, Gov. of Scarborough Castle.
𝔚 𝔊𝔄 James Claud. Bourchier	28 Sept. 97	6 Aug. 99	20 Jan. 03	4 June 14	do	do	25 Sept. 20	Captain	Half-pay Rifle Brigade.
𝔚 𝔊𝔄 James Grant, CB.	22 Mar. 97	22 Jan. 01	9 July 03	do	do	do	10 June 19	Major	Lieut.-Gov. R. Mil. Col.
𝔚 𝔊𝔄 Fielding Browne, CB.[85]	7 Mar. 00	1 Oct. 02	22 Dec. 04	4 June 14	do	do	22 June 20	Captain	Half-pay 1 Foot.
𝔚 𝔊𝔄 Thomas Wm. Taylor, CB.[86]	14 July 04	12 June 05	22 Jan. 07	7 July 14	do	do	7 Nov. 16	Lieut.-Col.	Late of 6 Dragoons.
𝔚 𝔊𝔄 Lawrence Arguimbau, CB.[87]	9 Oct. 01	26 Oct. 03	9 Mar. 09	11 Aug. 14	do	do		do	{ Unatt. Dep.Quar.Mas.Gen.Cape of Gd. Hope.
𝔚 𝔊𝔄 Michael Childers, CB.[88] ...	25 Feb. 05	25 Aug. 05	14 June 08	25 Aug. 14	do	do	19 Dec. 26	Lieut.-Col.	Unattached.
𝔚 𝔊𝔄 Henry George Smith, CB.[89]	8 May 05	15 Aug. 05	28 Feb. 12	29 Sept. 14	do	do	25 Sept. 26	do	
𝔚 𝔊𝔄 Felix Calvert, CB.	1 Oct. 07	15 Sept. 08	27 June 11	27 Oct. 14	do	do			

Colonels.

	CORNET, ETC.	LIEUT.	CAPTAIN.	MAJOR.	LIEUT.-COLONEL.	COLONEL.	WHEN PLACED ON HALF PAY.	REGIMENTAL RANK.	
William Staveley, CB.	14 July 04	21 April 08	6 May 13	15 Dec. 14	18 June 15	10 Jan. 37	29 Sept. 25	Major	Unattach. Dep.-Quar.-Mast.-Gen. Mauritius.
Sir De Lacy Evans, KCB.[90]	1 Feb. 07	1 Dec. 08	12 Jan. 15	11 May 15	do	do	25 April 17	Captain	Half-p. 5 West India Reg.
Hon. Leicester Stanhope, CB.	25 Sept. 99	20 Oct. 03	31 Mar. 03	4 June 14	20 June 14	do	26 June 23	Lieut.-Col.	Unattached.
Alexander Higginson	26 Jan. 04	never	14 Sept. 09	never	1 July	do		Major&Col.	Grenadier Guards.
Thos. Henry Hastings Davies	2 June 04	31 Jan. 05	4 Feb. 08	never	3 July	do	12 April 27	Lieut.-Col.	Late of 6 Dragoon Gds.
Charles Allix	28 April 04	never	13 Dec. 10	never	4 July	do			Unattached.
Thomas Brooke	7 Mar. 05	never	14 Feb. 11	never	5 July	do			Late of Grenadier Gds.
William Henry Scott[91]	27 Oct. 05	never	28 Mar. 11	never	5 July	do	1 Nov. 39	Major&Col.	Scots Fusilier Guards.
Hugh Percy Davison	25 Oct. 05	11 Nov. 06	26 Nov. 07	19 Mar.	24 Aug.	do	5 Feb. 18	do	Half-p. 5 West India Reg.
Sir Thomas Reade, CB.[92]	Aug. 99	18 May 00	8 Sept. 05	3 Jan.	11 19 Oct.	do	27 May 24	Captain	Half-pay 24 Foot.
Sir J. Morillyon Wilson, CB. KH.[93]	1 Sept.	4 28 Feb.	05 1 Jan.	07 5 July	14 27 Nov.	do	25 July 22		H.-p. 77 Foot, Adjt. of Chelsea Hospital.
Sir Thomas Willshire, KCB.	June 95	5 Sept. 95	28 Aug. 04	21 Sept. 13	4 Dec.	do		Lieut.-Col.	2 Foot.
Henry Oglander, CB.	20 Aug. 06	8 Sept. 08	2 April 12	14 Oct. 13	14 Dec.	do		do	26 Foot.
Matthew Stewart	1 Mar. 04	1 Mar.	05 4 May 09	8 Dec. 14	1 Feb. 16	do	8 Jan. 24	do	Half-pay Portuguese Serv.
George Evatt	26 Aug. 94	18 Nov. 95	20 April 02	4 June 13	25 May	do	21 May 18	Major	Unatt. Comm. R. Mil. Asylum at Southampt.
Hon. Henry Edward Butler	15 Feb. 00	21 June 00	22 May 11	30 May 11	4 July	do	25 Dec. 16	Lieut.-Col.	Half-pay 2 Garrison Batt.
William Drummond	20 Mar. 06	never	24 Oct. 11	18 June 15	4 July 16	do		Major&Col	Scots Fusilier Guards.
Edward Fleming, CB. KCH	24 June 02	6 July 04	30 May 07	1 April 13	18 July	do		Lieut.-Col.	Insp. Fld. Officer R. Dist.
Sir William Gosset, CB. KCH.	20 Dec. 98	18 April 01	1 Mar. 05	2 Feb. 14	3 Oct.	do		Colonel.	Royal Engineers.
Alex. Anderson, CB.[94]	9 Oct. 99	9 April 01	8 Feb. 09	21 June 13	2 Nov.	do	29 Aug. 26	Lieut.-Col.	Unattached.
John Rolt, CB.[95]	7 Mar. 00	1 June 01	5 Sept. 05	25 Nov. 13	do	do	9 Feb. 26	do	Unattached.
George Carlew	20 Dec. 98	18 April 01	1 Mar. 05	never	26 Nov.	do		Colonel	Royal Engineers.
Turner Grant	13 June 05	never	20 Feb. 11	never	26 Nov.	do		Major&Col.	Grenadier Guards.
Sir Chas. Webb Dance, KH.[96]	7 Sept. 04	5 Sept. 05	9 April 07	20 June 16	27 Mar. 17	do	1 Aug. 22	Major	H.-p. R. York Rangers.
James Hughes, CB.[97]	4 April 00	16 Sept. 02	22 Sept. 09	24 Sept. 12	21 June	do	10 Nov. 21	H.-p. 18 Dragoons.
Philip Bainbrigge, CB.[98]	30 June 00	13 Nov. 00	17 Oct. 05	15 Oct. 12	do	do		Lieut.-Col.	Assist. Quar. Mast. Gen.
Wm. Greenshields Power, CB. KH.[KH]	31 May 00	11 Feb. 02	13 June 07	21 Sept. 13	do	do	25 Dec. 16	do	Royal Artillery.
Kenneth Snodgrass, CB.[99]	22 Oct. 00	9 Aug. 04	20 Oct. 08	do	do	do	1 June 26	do	Late Unattached.
William Balvaird, CB.[100]	24 Mar. 03	17 April 04	16 May 05	22 Nov.	do	do		do	Unattached.
Sempronius Stretton, CB.[101]	Nov. 00	18 July 01	11 Sept. 06	do	do	do	19 Feb. 24	Major	Half-pay 84 Foot.

Colonels.

	2D LIEUT., ETC.	LIEUT.	CAPTAIN.	MAJOR.	LIEUT.-COLONEL.	COLONEL.	WHEN PLACED ON HALF PAY.	REGIMENTAL RANK.	
⊕ Thomas Erskine Napier, CB.	3 July 05	1 May 06	27 Oct. 08	26 Dec. 13	21 June 17	10 Jan. 37	1814	Captain	{ H.-p. Chas. Brit. Assist. Adj.-Gen. in Ireland.
⊕ Nathaniel Thorn, CB. KH.	15 Oct. 02	25 Jan. 03	4 Jan. 10	3 Mar. 14	do	do		Lieut.-Col.	Assist.-Qua.-Mast.-Gen.
⊕ William Henry Sewell, CB.	27 Mar. 06	26 Feb. 07	12 Mar. 12	3 Mar.	do	do		do	{ 6 Ft. Dep.-Qua.-Mast.-Gen. East Indies.
⊕ ⊞ William Lindsay Darling[102]	13 Dec. 01	23 June 02	13 June 08	14 April	do	do	7 Dec. 14	Major	H.-p. 2 Garrison Batt.
⊕ ⊞ Sir Jos. Thackwell, KCB. KH.	23 April 00	13 June 01	9 April 07	18 June 15	do	do		Lieut.-Col.	3 Dragoons.
⊕ ⊞ Alexander Macdonald, CB.	3 Dec. 03	1 May 04	1 Oct. 12	do	do	do		Captain	Royal Artillery.
⊕ Sir W. Lewis Herries, CB. KCH.[103]	23 Jan. 01	17 Mar. 03	19 Oct. 09	2 June 14	31 July	do	31 July 17	Lieut.-Col.	Unattached.
⊕ John M'Donald, CB.	17 Dec.	21 Mar. 05	7 Sept. 09	26 Aug. 13	4 Sept.	do		do	92 Foot.
⊕ Tho. Staunton St. Clair, CB. KH.[104]	12 Aug. 03	6 Aug. 04	30 Sept. 07	2 June 14	do	do	9 Dec. 28	Major	Unattached.
⊕ George Wm. Paty, CB. KII.	28 April 04	7 May 05	28 April 08	do	do	do		do	94 Foot.
⊕ Geo. Henry Zululeke, CB.[105]	30 Dec. 97	6 Aug. 00	11 Jan. 10	2 June 14	do	do	25 Dec. 16	Major	H.-p. Portuguese Service.
George Warren Walker	17 May 99	18 June 01	5 April 09	15 April 17	5 Mar. 18	do		Lieut.-Col.	21 Foot.
Thos. Hatherton Dawes, CB.	23 Jan. 06	6 Aug. 07	8 Feb. 10	never	26 Mar.	do	26 Nov. 30	do	Unattached.
Harry Buiteel Harris, KH.		5 Feb.	30 Oct. 01	2 Jan. 12	7 Nov.	do	25 Sept. 20	Major	Half-pay 22 Dragoons.
Thos. James Wemyss, CB.	17 Mar. 04	29 Dec.	4 15 Jan. 07	27 Oct. 14	17 Jan. 19	do			Late of 93 Foot.
Robert Burd Gabriel, CB. KH.	9 June 03	1 Mar.	30 Nov. 06	21 June	21 Jan.	do	10 Feb. 20	Major	Half-pay 99 Foot.
Henry Thomas, CB.	28 Sept. 97	3 May 00	9 May	26 Aug. 13	do	do	10 Jan. 22	Captain	Half-pay 22 Dragoons.
⊕ ⊞ William Rowan, CB.[106]	1 April 98	29 Dec.	98 10 Sept. 05	do	do	do		Lieut.-Col.	20 Foot.
⊕ ⊞ James Shaw Kennedy, CB.	4 Nov. 03	15 June	4 19 Oct. 08	3 Mar. 14	do	do	22 July 30	do	Unattached.
⊕ ⊞ Arth. A. W. M. Lord Sandys[107]	18 April 05	23 Jan.	6 16 July 12	18 June 15	do	do	25 Mar. 17	Major	Unattached.
⊕ Sir Thos. Henry Browne, KCH.[108]	27 July 09	19 July	10 25 Aug. 13	27 July 15	do	do	29 Dec. 37	Lieut.-Col.	Half-pay 23 Foot.
Richard W. H. Howard Vyse	28 Oct. 05	18 Sept.	6 15 April 13	21 June 17	do	do	25 Dec. 14	Captain	Unattached.
Gideon Gorrequer, KH.	5 May 00	17 June	1 24 June 02	4 June	13 May	do	10 Sept. 25	Lieut.-Col.	Unattached.
Thomas Watkin Forster[109]	1 June 97	20 June	98 14 Sept. 04	4 June	4 Aug.	do			Late of 4 Foot.
Thos. Phipps Howard, KH.[110]	31 July 93	2 Feb.	95 16 July 98	22 Feb.	10 12 Aug.	do	9 Nov. 15	Major	Half-pay 24 Foot.
Archibald Maclachlan		1793	25 Sept. 94	1 Dec. 98	15 Mar.	do	25 Jan. 18	do	Half-pay 23 Dragoons.
Robert William Mills	6 May 95	7 July	96 1 Dec. 97	25 July	do	do	25 Nov. 16	do	Half-pay 69 Foot.
Frederick Ashworth	June	95 12 Aug.	95 19 July 98	do	do	do	25 Jan. 15	Captain	Half-pay 9 Foot.
⊕ Robert Bryce Fearon, CB.	6 July 99	23 April	00 18 Oct. 02	22 Nov.	do	do	20 Feb. 17	Major	Half-pay 58 Foot.
	June 95	4 Sept.	95 21 April 14	20 Dec.	do	do		Lieut.-Col.	{ 40 Foot, Dep. Adj. Gen. East Indies.
⊕ Henry Balneavis, CMG. KH.	3 Jan. 97	5 Nov.	99 11 Sept. 05	30 May 11	do	do	1 June 26	do	Unatt. Town Maj. Malta.

40

Colonels.

	ENSIGN, ETC.	LIEUT.	CAPTAIN.	MAJOR.	LIEUT.-COLONEL.	COLONEL.	WHEN PLACED ON HALF PAY.	REGIMENTAL RANK.	
Vincent Edward Eyre	21 May 94	27 May 95	15 Mar. 99	4 June 11	12 Aug. 19	10 Jan. 37	1811	Lt. & Capt.	Late Horse Grenad. Gds.
ⓟ Patrick Burke		31 Jan. 95	5 Dec. 99	4 June	do	do		Captain	Half-p. 96 Foot.
John Whetham[111]		6 Dec. 94	23 July 03	13 June	do	do	13 Mar. 15	Major	Half-p. 1 Garrison Batt.
ⓟ Thos. Thornbury Wooldridge, KH.	17 Mar. 93	5 July 94	25 Nov. 02	20 June	do	do	1811	do	Half-p. 91 Foot.
ⓟ Geo. Leigh Goldie, CB.	3 Sept. 03	14 Mar. 05	4 Dec. 06	do	do	do		Lieut.-Col.	11 Foot.
Gustavus Rochfort	14 July 98	2 Nov. 99	25 Nov. 00	10 July	do	do	23 May 18	Major	Half-p. 100 Foot.
ⓟ ⓡⓜ Thomas Wildman[112]	5 Mar. 07	29 Sept. 08	18 Feb. 13	18 July	23 Dec. 19	do	23 Dec. 19	Lieut.-Col.	Half-p. 9 Dragoons.
Hon. Frederick Cathcart	12 Jan. 05	1 May 07	17 Sept. 07	28 July	24 Feb. 20	do	18 May 20	Captain	Half-p. 92 Foot.
William Henry Meyrick	28 Feb. 05	30 May 05	11 Aug. 08	24 Feb.	17 29 June	do	24 Aug. 32	Lieut.-Col.	Unattached.
ⓟ Geo. Powell Higginson	6 Nov. 05	never	3 April 11	never	26 Oct.	do	11 April 34	do	Unattached.
Sir John Macra, KCH.	17 April 05	5 Sept. 05	23 Dec. 12	2 June	15 24 June	do	4 May 26	Major	Unattached.
ⓟ ⓡⓜ George Bowles	20 Dec. 04	never	1 Feb. 05	10 July	24 June	do		Cpt.&Lt.Cl.	Coldstream Guards.
Thomas Bunbury, KH.	25 Mar. 04	22 Dec. 04	3 Nov. 08	14 April	14 5 July	do		Lieut.-Col.	67 Foot.
ⓟ Hon. Henry Fred. C. Cavendish	never	26 May	6 June 08	2 April	18 12 July	do	18 Dec. 23	Lt.Cl.&Col.	1 Life Guards.
Thomas Younghusband	31 May 93	19 Dec. 93	3 May 00	1 Jan.	12 19 July	do	25 Feb. 16	Captain	Half-p. 4 Dragoon Gds.
Henry Standish	21 Oct. 95	20 Jan. 96	24 July 00	do	do	do	12 Mar. 12	Major	Half-p. 39 Foot.
Philip Ray	1 June 96	29 Nov. 98	30 July 00	do	do	do	25 Dec. 18	Lt. & Capt.	Half-p. Scots Fus. Gds.
John Williams Aldred		17 Aug. 97	19 Nov. 97	do	do	do	15 July 16	Major	Half-p. 60 Foot.
ⓟ Lord John T. H. Somerset	4 Aug. 04	14 Aug. 05	15 April 08	18 June	do	do	23 Jan. 35	Lieut.-Col.	Unattached.
ⓟ George Couper, CB. KH.	2 Nov. 97	2 Nov. 99	14 April 08	21 June	13 23 July	do	25 June 27	do	Unattached.
ⓟ Henry Godwin, CB.	30 Oct. 99	19 Aug. 03	28 Mar. 08	26 May	14 26 July	do		do	Half-p. 87 Foot.
ⓟ Philip Wodehouse	7 Aug. 06	3 Sept. 07	14 June 11	6 Mar.	17 30 Aug.	do		do	Late of 1 Life Guards.
ⓟ ⓡⓜ Thomas Wm. Robbins[113]	26 Sept. 05	25 May 08	25 May 09	24 Dec.	18 24 Oct.	do	24 Oct. 21	Lieut.- Col.	Half-p. 18 Foot.
ⓟ ⓡⓜ Roderick Macneil	17 Mar. 08	9 May 09	1 Dec. 14	9 Aug.	21 25 Jan. 22	do	17 June 28	do	Unattached.
George Dean Pitt, KH.	4 June 05	5 Dec. 08	10 Aug. 05	13 Jan.	18 April	do		do	Insp. F. Officer Rec. Dist.
William Sutherland	15 Dec.	1 July 06	18 Aug. 14	25 Sept.	17 16 May 22	do		do	5 Foot.
Henry Rainy, CB. KH.	24 Aug. 04	1 Nov. 09	13 April 09	21 June	17 15 Aug.	do	4 May 26	Major	Unattached.
ⓟ ⓡⓜ Hon. Charles Gore, CB. KH.	21 Oct. 08	4 Jan. 10	13 Mar. 15	21 Jan.	19 Sept.	do	20 Aug. 25	do	{ Unatt. Dep. Quar. Mas. General in Canada.
ⓟ Robert Dalyell	22 Mar. 98	23 Jan. 01	26 Aug. 04	12 April	14 31 Dec.	do	31 Dec. 22	Lt.-Col.	Unattached.
ⓟ ⓡⓜ Wm. Lovelace Walton	8 May 06	never	7 Mar. 11	never	20 Feb. 23	do		Maj. & Col.	Coldstream Guards.
ⓟ William Richardson	27 Feb. 06	20 Aug. 07	26 Dec. 11	24 July	24 July 23	do		Lt.-Col.	Royal Horse Guards.
ⓟ Thomas Fyers	2 May 06	18 April 01	21 Aug. 05	12 Aug.	19 23 Mar. 25	do		Colonel	Royal Engineers.
ⓟ Edward Fanshawe, CB.		1 July 06	1 July 01	do	do	do		do	Royal Engineers.

41

Colonels.

	CORNET, ETC.	LIEUT.	CAPTAIN.	MAJOR.	LIEUT.-COLONEL.	COLONEL.	WHEN PLACED ON HALF PAY.	REGIMENTAL RANK.	
Thomas Cunningham	2 July 01	30 Mar. 02	24 July 06	12 Aug. 19	9 April 25	10 Jan. 37		Colonel	Royal Engineers.
Thomas John Forbes	6 Mar. 95	13 Apr. 95	9 Sept. 02	4 June 13	29 July	do		do	Royal Artillery.
Alexander Munro, KH.	do	27 Jan. 96	2 May 03	4 June 14	do	do		do	Royal Artillery.
Thomas Colby	do	do	17 May 03	do 21	do	do		do	Royal Artillery.
James Pattison Cockburn	2 July 01	6 Aug. 02	1 July 07	19 July	do 26	do		do	Royal Engineers.
Robert Henry Birch	9 Mar. 95	25 July 95	12 Sept. 03	4 June 14	12 Dec.	do		do	Royal Artillery.
Charles Richard Fox	29 June 15	5 Nov. 18	9 Aug. 20	6 Nov. 24	14 Aug. 27	do	11 Nov. 36	Lt.-Col.	{ Unatt. Extra Aide-de-Camp to the Queen.
James Armstrong	9 Mar. 95	31 July 95	12 Sept. 03	4 June 14	13 Oct.	do		Colonel	Royal Artillery.
Thomas Paterson	1 Dec. 95	3 June 97	6 Dec. 03	do	6 Nov.	do		do	Royal Artillery.
Nathaniel Wilmot Oliver	2 June 96	13 Feb. 98	2 Mar. 04	do	do	do		do	Royal Artillery.
Richard John James Lacy	8 Aug. 96	17 Mar. 98	20 July 04	do	31 Dec.	23 June 37		do	Royal Artillery.
George Lewis, CB.114	25 April 93	6 Oct. 94	1 Oct. 01	4 June 13	28 Sept.	10 July 37		Col. Comm.	Late of Royal Marines.
Elias Lawrence, CB.	8 May 93	14 Feb. 95	3 Dec. 01	do	15 Nov. 26	do		do	{ Commandant of Royal Marines at Chatham.
Edward Carter Hornby	13 June 93	24 April 95	12 July 03	4 June	5 Nov. 29	do		do	Late of Royal Marines.
George Jones	19 June 93	24 April 95	16 July 03	4 June 14	22 July	30 July 37		do	Com. of R. Mar. at Ports.
Thomas Adair, CB.	1 Dec.	24 April 95	20 Sept. 03	do	do	do		do	Com. of R. Mar. at Plym.
James Montagu Bevians	27 Mar. 95	27 Jan. 96	1 Aug. 05	12 Aug. 19	16 April 32	do		do	Late of R. Marines.
William Connolly	8 May 95	7 April 96	15 Aug. 05	do	do	do		do	Com. of R. Mar. Wooln.
Charles Augustus Shawe	26 May 08	never	23 April 12	never	28 April 25	8 Aug. 37		Major & Col.	Coldstream Guards.
His Royal Highness Prince George W. F. C. of Cambridge, KG.	never	never	never	never	never	3 Nov. 37			
George Beatty	16 May 95	20 Nov. 96	15 Aug. 05	12 Aug. 19	16 April 32	27 Dec. 37		Col. Comm.	R. Marines.
Robert Ellison	17 Dec. 07	never	20 Dec.	12 18 June	15 April 24	9 Jan. 38		Major & Col.	Grenadier Guards.
George Greenwood	23 June 17	26 Jan. 19	1 Jan.	24 26 Nov. 30	2 Jan.	31 12 Jan. 38		Lieut.-Col.	2 Life Guards.
Thos. Adams Parke, CB.	19 May 95	23 Nov. 96	15 Aug. 05	12 Aug. 19	31 Dec.	32 26 April 38		Col. Comm.	{ R. Marines, Aide-de-Camp to the Queen.
Frederick Campbell	12 Jan. 97	16 July 99	29 July 04	4 June 14	23 Nov.	28 11 June 38		Colonel	R. Artillery.
John Alexander Mein	14 Nov. 99	5 April 01	29 Feb. 04	11 Nov.	13 20 Mar.	23 28 June 38		Lieut.-Col.	74 Foot.
Peter Dumas115	1 June 97	5 Nov. 99	26 Nov. 06	22 June 15	1 May	do	17 Aug. 32	do	{ H.-p. 4 W. I. Reg. Lt.-Go. Gravesend Tilb.Ft.
Mildmay Fane	11 June 12	25 Sept. 13	28 July 14	2 Mar. 20	12 June	do		do	54 Foot.
John Martin	30 July 07	16 May 09	8 Feb. 13	10 Jan. 22	do	do	12 June 23	do	Unattached.

Colonels.

	CORNET, ETC.	LIEUT.	CAPTAIN.	MAJOR.	LIEUT.-COLONEL.	COLONEL.	WHEN PLACED ON HALF PAY.	REGIMENTAL RANK.	
George Henry Hewett	12 June 06	18 Dec. 06	12 April 10	18 June 12	26 June 23	28 June 38	28 June 27	Lieut.-Col.	Unattached.
Charles Wyndham	17 Oct. 11	5 Nov. 12	24 Feb. 17	20 Dec. 21	do	do	15 May 27	do	Late of 76 Foot.
Henry, Earl of Uxbridge	14 July 14	21 July 14	27 Feb. 17	never	5 Aug.	do	21 Apr. 25	do	Unattached.
Hon. Henry Hely Hutchinson	28 July 08	21 Mar. 11	22 July 13	5 July 21	4 Sept.	do		do	5 Dragoon Guards.
Sir Jas. Maxwell Wallace, KH.	14 Aug. 05	5 June 06	22 Oct. 07	1 Jan. 17	25 Sept.	do		do	Half-p. Chasseurs Britt.
Edward Wildman, KH.[116]	8 May 06	14 May 07	17 Dec. 14	24 Sept. 18	do	do	1 Mar. 39	do	Unattached.
Hon. John Finch, CB.[117]	5 Oct. 09	20 Dec. 10	17 Feb. 14	5 Mar. 18	25 Oct.	do	12 Dec. 30	do	Unattached.
James Lindsay	16 Dec. 07	never	10 Dec. 12	never	20 Nov.	do	19 Nov. 30	do	Unattached.
Wm. George Moore	18 April 11	10 Sept. 12	14 April 14	21 Jan. 19	12 Feb. 24	do	16 Sept. 26	do	Unattached.
Sir Aug. Fred. d'Este, KCH.[118]	never	26 Sept. 11	14 Mar. 15	11 July 22	1 July	do	1 July 24	do	95 Foot.
James Campbell, KH.	17 Sept. 03	25 Aug. 08	31 Mar. 08	3 June 19	10 July	do		do	Unatt. *Assist.-Adj.-Gen*.
William Cochrane[119]	13 Feb. 05	29 May 06	11 Aug. 12	17 Mar. 23	15 July	do	10 July 37	do	Cape Mounted Riflemen.
Henry Somerset, KH.	5 Dec. 11	30 Dec. 12	6 Oct. 15	25 Mar. 21	17 Sept.	do		do	50 Foot.
Nicholas Wodehouse	3 Jan. 07	31 Aug. 07	26 Sept. 11	18 Oct. 21	2 Sept.	do	9 Sept. 24	do	Unattached.
Hector Maclaine[120]	24 Sept. 03	25 Sept. 04	1 Dec. 06	19 May 14	9 Sept.	do	6 July 26	do	Unattached.
Henry, Earl of Darlington	6 July 15	22 May 17	22 Oct. 18	3 July 23	23 Sept.	do		do	1 Foot.
Geo. Aug. Wetherall, CB. KH.	never	29 July 95	13 May 12	12 Aug. 19	11 Dec.	do		do	9 Foot.
John M'Caskill, KH.	10 Mar. 97	14 May 01	6 Mar. 06	do 25	17 Feb.	do		do	1 Foot.
John Carter, KH.	June 96	2 July 96	31 Dec. 06	11 Dec. 13	3 Mar.	do	27 Jan. 29	do	Half-pay Royal Engineers.
William Douglas	1 July 01	12 Oct. 01	1 July 12	12 Aug. 19	23 Mar.	do	31 May 39	do	Unattached.
James Simpson[121]	3 April 11	never	25 Dec. 13	never 15	28 April	do		do	73 Foot.
Hon. George Anson	26 Oct. 04	5 June 05	11 July 16	1 April 24	5 May	do	19 May 25	Lieut.-Col.	Unattached.
Duncan M'Gregor[122]	8 Jan. 14	never	20 Jan. 17	25 Nov. 13	19 May	do	27 July 38	Major	Half-pay 26 Foot.
Edward Warner	12 July 00	31 Aug. 99	17 April 04	25 Nov. 13	26 May	do	25 Dec. 14	do	Half-pay 88 Foot.
Wm. Cardon Seton, CB.[123]	22 Nov. 98	5 Aug. 99	14 Sept. 03	30 Jan. 12	27 May	do	25 Feb. 16	Lieut.-Col.	*Insp. F. Officer Recr. Dis.*
Nicholas Hamilton, KH.	11 Oct. 96	25 Oct. 97	9 July 03	30 April 08	do	do		Major	Half-pay 50 Foot.
Herman Stapleton	15 June 96	9 Dec. 96	25 June 03	18 June 06	do	do	1814	Lieut.-Col.	3 Foot.
James Dennis	19 Nov. 02	7 Aug. 04	4 Sept. 08	19 June 19	do	do		do	Half-pay Cape Regiment.
Matthew Gregory Blake	2 Sept. 96	12 April 97	6 Aug. 03	13 Oct. 08	do	do	25 Feb. 17	Captain	Half-pay 96 Foot.
Thomas Kennedy	20 Feb. 96	4 May 00	3 Feb. 04	12 Nov. 08	do	do		do	Coldstream Guards.
Cha. Anth. Ferdinand Bentinck	never	4 Dec. 05	18 Feb. 08	3 Dec. 15	do	do	1811	Cpt.Lt-Col.	13 Foot
Sir Robert Henry Sale, KCB.	16 Nov. 95	12 April 97	24 Sept. 12	18 June 13	2 June 25	do	9 June 25	Lieut.-Col.	Unattached.
Henry Lane	4 Dec. 11	3 Sept. 12	25 Dec. 18	5 Aug. 24	9 June	do		do	

43

Colonels.

	CORNET, ETC.	LIEUT.	CAPTAIN.	MAJOR.	LIEUT.-COLONEL.	COLONEL.	WHEN PLACED ON HALF PAY.	REGIMENTAL RANK.	
John Gregory Baumgardt.........	1 Aug. 98	20 Mar. 01	10 Jan. 10	21 Oct. 24	9 June 25	28 June 38		Lieut.-Col.	2 Foot.
⊕ Robert Nickle, KH.[124].........	22 Jan. 01	26 Jan. 02	1 June 09	21 Jan. 19	30 June	do		do	Particular Service.
Daniel Falla	8 Mar. 98	26 April 98	1 Dec. 04	4 June 14	25 July	do	25 July 22	Major	{ Unattach. Town Major of Gibraltar.
⊕ Griffith Geo. Lewis, CB.	15 Mar. 03	2 July 03	18 Nov. 07	21 Sept. 13	29 July	do		Lieut.-Col.	Royal Engineers.
⊕ Sir Geo. Chas. Hoste, CB.	20 Dec. 02	21 Dec. 02	do	17 Mar. 14	do	do		do	Royal Engineers.
Geo. Judd Harding, CB.	1 Oct. 02	1 Dec. 02	do	19 July 21	do	do		do	Royal Engineers.
John Ross Wright	1 Mar. 03	1 April 03	do	do	do	do		do	Royal Engineers.
⊕ Sir Henry Geo. Macleod, KH. ...	3 Nov. 07	15 July 08	29 Sept. 13	21 June 17	18 Aug.	do	4 May 26	Major	Unatt. Lt. Gov. of Trinid.
⊕ ⊕ Sampson Stawell	15 Jan. 01	9 July 02	28 Feb. 05	18 June 15	1 Oct.	do		Lt.-Col.	12 Dragoons.
Chas. Geo. Jas. Arbuthnot	never	26 Dec.	16 Mar. 20	3 July 23	do	do		do	72 Foot.
Thomas Valiant, KH.	31 Mar. 04	21 June	21 Aug. 05	24 Oct. 21	8 Oct.	do		do	40 Foot.
Chest. Grant Falconar, KH.	1 Sept. 95	1 Nov. 99	26 Dec. 05	12 Aug. 19	22 Oct.	do		do	Insp. F. Officer Recr. Dis.
⊕ John Grey..................	16 Mar. 05	26 Sept. 05	6 April 09	11 Oct. 21	25 Oct.	do		do	Late of 88 Foot.
⊕ Richard England, KH..........	25 Feb. 08	1 June 09	11 June 11	4 Sept. 23	29 Oct.	do		Lieut.-Col.	41 Foot.
Charles Middleton [125]	19 Sept. 04	28 April 06	18 July 15	8 Feb. 19	19 Nov.	do	19 Nov. 25	do	{ Unatt. Assist. Comm. Cavalry Depôt.
⊕ Alex. Fisher Macintosh, KH.[126]	31 Oct. 11	11 June 12	6 June 16	18 Sept. 23	15 Dec.	do	18 Jan. 39	do	Unattached.
⊕ ⊕ Beaumont, Lord Hotham....	27 June 10	never	25 Dec. 13	21 Jan. 19	24 Dec.	do	24 Dec. 25	do	Unattached.
⊕ Joseph Paterson	17 May 99	7 Feb. 01	23 Oct. 06	29 Sept. 14	31 Dec.	do	6 Feb. 39	do	Unattached.
⊕ George Turner, CB...........	14 Jan. 97	16 July 99	29 July 04	4 June 14	25 Nov. 28	do		Colonel	Royal Artillery.
Richard Francis Cleaveland	24 Feb. 97	do	9 Oct. 04	do	9 Dec. 28	10 Aug. 39		do	Royal Artillery.
⊕ John Owen, CB. KH.	1 Mar. 96	22 Oct. 98	4 May 07	19 July 21	10 Jan. 37	26 Aug. 39		do	{ Dep. Adjt. Gen. R. Mar. Aide-de-C. to the Qn.
John Wright, KH.............	21 April 96	10 June 99	27 July 08	16 Sept. 16	do	do		do	R. Marines.
Thompson Aslett	1 June 96	2 May 00	do	27 May 25	10 July 37	do		do	R. Marines.

44

Notes to the Colonels.

1 Sir David Cunynghame served the campaign of 1793, including the actions at Famars, St. Amand, and Lincelles (severely wounded), and the siege of Valenciennes. Taken prisoner in the action at Ostend, May, 1798.
2 Colonel Tucker served at the taking of the Cape of Good Hope in 1795; in South America, in 1807, and received a bayonet wound in the arm at the assault of Monte Video.
3 Colonel the Hon. Alex. Abercromby served in Holland in 1799; with the expedition to the Ferrol, 1800; and subsequently in the Peninsula, including the battles of Albuhera, Vittoria, Pyrenees, and Orthes, for which he has received a cross. Served also the campaign of 1815, including the battle of Waterloo.
4 Colonel Sherlock served the campaigns of 1794 and 95 in Holland.
5 Colonel Ottley was actively employed in the Carib war of 1795 and 96 in St. Vincent. Served in Portugal and Spain in 1808 and 9, including the battles of Roleia, Vimiera, and Corunna; in the expedition to the Scheldt, 1809; campaigns of 1813 and 14 in Germany and Holland, including the storming of Bergen-op-Zoom, where he led one of the columns of attack, and was severely wounded.
6 Lord Portarlington served in Holland in 1799; with the expedition to Hanover, 1805; Peninsular campaign of 1809, including the battle of Talavera; campaign of 1815, including the actions at Quatre Bras and Waterloo.
7 Sir Robert Chambre Hill served in the Peninsula, and commanded a brigade of cavalry at the battle of Vittoria, for which he has received a medal. Served also the campaign of 1815, and was severely wounded at Waterloo.
8 Sir Wm. Cox was at the retaking of Grenada in 1796. Served in Egypt in 1801. Employed on a particular service in Spain in 1808, and was present in the action at Lugo, and battle of Corunna. Commanded the fortress of Almeida, from April, 1809 to the 27th Aug. 1810, when, by the unfortunate explosion of its magazines, he was obliged to surrender it to the army under Massena.
9 Sir Horatio G. P. Townshend served in the Peninsula, France, and Flanders, with the Grenadier Guards, and was severely wounded at Quatre Bras.
10 Colonel John Fred. Browne served in Flanders in 1793, 94, and 95, including the siege of Nimeguen, and sortie from thence. Present at the taking of St. Lucia in 1796. Served in Egypt in 1801, including the actions of the 8th, 13th, and 31st March; with the expedition to Hanover, 1805; campaign in Zealand, 1807; expedition to Sweden, 1808; and to Walcheren, 1809. Served afterwards in the Peninsula, and commanded the 28th regiment at the battle of Barrosa, for which he has received a medal.
11 Colonel Burslem served at the capture of the Isle of France, and at the attack and conquest of Java, for which latter he has received a medal.
12 Colonel Gauntlett was actively employed against the Maroons in the West Indies. Served also in Egypt.
13 Colonel Woodgate has received a medal for the battle of Fuentes d'Onor, and was wounded.
14 Colonel Patrickson served in the Peninsula with the 43d Light Infantry, and has received a medal for the battle of Toulouse, on which occasion he commanded the regiment.
15 Colonel David Campbell was actively employed in the West Indies, and was present at the siege of Fort Bourbon. Served at the Helder in 1799, and afterwards at the Ferrol. Proceeded to Portugal in 1808, and was present at the battle of Vimiera.
16 Colonel Thornton served in the Peninsula, and commanded the 40th regiment at the battles of Talavera, Nivelle, Orthes, and Toulouse, for which he has received a cross.
17 Sir John Milley Doyle served the Egyptian campaign of 1801, including the actions of the 8th, 13th, and 21st March. Served also in the Peninsula, and commanded the 19th Portuguese at Fuentes d'Onor, Ciudad Rodrigo, Vittoria, the Pyrenees, and Orthes, for which he has received a cross and a clasp. He has also received a medal for services in Egypt.
18 Colonel Keate served in the Peninsula from Dec. 1808, to Jan. 1813, including the passage of the Douro, battle of Busaco, siege of Ciudad Rodrigo, battle of Salamanca, and siege of Burgos.

Notes to the Colonels.

19 Colonel Ward served in the Peninsula, and has received a medal and two clasps for Salamanca, Badajoz, and the Pyrenees.

20 Colonel Wm. W. Blake served at the taking of the Cape of Good Hope in 1806; and afterwards in South America, including the affair of San Carlos, and siege of Monte Video. Served also in the Peninsula, including the battles of Roleia, and Vimiera; the passage of the Douro; battle of Castalla, and the affair of Villa Franca. Medal for Roleia and Vimiera.

21 Sir Edward Miles served on the Continent in 1794 and 95, including the battle of Lincelles, action at the bridge of Wallam, storming of Fort Nook, siege of Nimeguen, and defence of the Emms River. Actively employed in the West Indies in 1796 and 97, and was present at the sieges of St. Lucia and Grenada, and capture of Trinidad. Served in Ireland during the rebellion in 1798. Embarked for the Peninsula in 1808, and was present at the battles of Roleia, Vimiera, action at Lugo, and battle of Corunna. Proceeded with the expedition to Walcheren, 1809. Served afterwards in the Peninsula, from June, 1812, to the end of the war, including the battle of Salamanca (severely and dangerously wounded), action at Villa Moriel, battles of Vittoria and the Pyrenees, siege and storming of San Sebastian (dangerously wounded at the assault), passage of the Bidassoa, battles of Nivelle, and Nive (9th to 13th Dec.) Proceeded to Ava in command of a brigade, and was engaged in all the operations against the enemy in that country from June to 17th Aug. 1824; embarked for the eastward, and commanded the force at the storm and capture of Mergui, 6th Oct.; returned to Rangoon in Nov. and served there during its investment in Dec. 1824, and commanded the Madras force in several assaults on the enemy. Sir Edward has received a medal and a clasp for Salamanca and San Sebastian.

22 Colonel Knight Erskine commanded the 27th regt. at Badajoz, and has received a medal.

23 Sir Archibald Maclaine's services :—Mysore campaign of 1799 against Tippoo Sultan, including the battle of Mallavelly, siege and storming of Seringapatam, where he received three wounds, from the effects of which he was confined in hospital for upwards of a year. Capture of the Danish settlement of Tranquebar; and the Paligar war in 1801, including the battle of Ardingy, and affair of Serungapore, where he was wounded. Mahratta war of 1802, 3, and 4 against Scindia, Holcar, and the Bera Rajah, including the storm of Jalnaghur, siege and storming of Gawilghur, siege of Asseerghur (wounded), and battle of Argaum. Ordered home in 1804 in consequence of severe wounds received in the different actions from 1799 to 1804. Peninsular campaigns 1810, 11, 12, including the siege of Cadiz; the defence of Matagorda (an outwork of Cadiz, and a ruined redoubt when taken possession of from the enemy) from 22nd Feb. to 22nd April, 1810, during which long period Sir Archibald (then a captain in the old 94th regiment) with a very small force under his command, most gallantly kept at bay 8,000 of the enemy under Marshal Soult, who conducted the siege, and did not evacuate until ordered to do so by Lieut.-General Sir Thos. Graham, his men being nearly all either killed or wounded. Served also at the battle of Barrosa (dangerously wounded, and his horse killed), and capture of Seville.

24 Colonel James Hay served in the Peninsula, France, and Flanders, with the 16th Light Dragoons, and was severely wounded at Waterloo. Medal and a clasp for the battles of Vittoria and the Nive.

25 Sir William Warre served in the Peninsula from 1808 to 1813, including the battles of Roleia, Vimiera, and Corunna; the passage of the Douro; 1st siege of Badajoz, sieges and assaults of Ciudad Rodrigo and Badajoz; and battle of Salamanca, besides various minor affairs.

26 Colonel D'Aguilar served in India under Lord Lake, and was present at the reduction of several forts, and at the assault on Bhurtpore. Proceeded to Walcheren, June, 1809. Served also on the eastern coast of Spain under Sir John Murray and Sir Henry Clinton.

27 Colonel O'Malley served in Ireland during the rebellion in 1798; with the expedition to the Ferrol, 1800; the Egyptian campaign of 1801, wounded in the action of the 13th March. Served also the campaign of 1815, including the actions at Quatre Bras and Waterloo, at which latter he was twice wounded, and had two horses shot under him, but did not quit the field.

28 Colonel Cotton served at the Helder, including the actions of the 2nd and 6th Oct. 1799. Proceeded to the Peninsula in 1808, and served with the Spanish army.

29 Colonel Charles Turner served the Egyptian campaign of 1801, including the actions of the 8th and 13th March, and was taken prisoner in a skirmish near Lake Mareotis, 18th March. Served also at the capture of Martinique in 1809. Medal for services in Egypt.

30 Colonel Ogilvie served in the American war, and was severely wounded at Stoney Creek.

31 Colonel Aylmer served at the Helder in 1799, including the action of the 18th Sept. Egyptian campaign of 1801; in Spain and Portugal in 1808 and 9, including the battles of Roleia, Vimiera, and Corunna; with the expedition to Walcheren, 1809.

Notes to the Colonels.

32 Colonel Vernon served in the Peninsula, and was present at the battle of Talavera, siege of the forts at and battle of Salamanca (severely wounded), and siege of Burgos.

33 Colonel Vigoureux's services :—Campaigns in Holland in 1794, 95, and 99 ; besieged in Nimeguen, 1794, and was present at the battle of the 19th Sept. 1799. Peninsular campaigns of 1810, 11, 12, and 13, including the battles of Fuentes d'Onor, Salamanca, and Vittoria. Campaigns of 1814 and 15 in Holland and Flanders, and severely wounded at Waterloo. Medal and a clasp for the battles of Fuentes d'Onor and Vittoria.

34 Sir James A. Hope served with the expedition to Hanover, in 1805 ; to Zealand, 1807, including the siege of Copenhagen ; to Sweden, 1808 ; Portugal and Spain, 1808 and 9, including the action at Lugo and battle of Corunna ; expedition to Walcheren, 1809 ; and in the Peninsula from 1810 to the end of the war, including the battle of Barrosa, siege of Ciudad Rodrigo, covering the siege of Badajoz, affairs in front of Salamanca and at Osma, battle of Vittoria, siege of San Sebastian, passages of the Bidassoa, Gave d'Oleron, and Gave de Pau, and battles of the Nivelle, Nive, Orthes, and Toulouse. Sir James has received a cross and a clasp for the battles of Vittoria, Nivelle, Nive, Orthes and Toulouse.

35 Sir Robert John Harvey served in the Peninsula as an Assistant-Quarter-Master-General to the Portuguese army, and has received a medal for the battle of Orthes.

36 Sir Dudley Hill served with the expedition to South America in 1806, including the storming of Monte Video (with the Forlorn Hope), battle of Colonia, and attack on Buenos Ayres, where he was wounded in the thigh, and taken prisoner. Served afterwards in the Peninsula, and was present at the battle of Roleia (wounded in the leg), action at Benevente, retreat to Corunna, battle of Talavera, action of the Coa, battles of Busaco and Fuentes d'Onor, siege and storming of Badajoz, battle of Salamanca (severely wounded in the breast and through the arm), siege of Burgos, defence of the river Carrion (wounded and taken prisoner), siege of San Sebastian (twice wounded), investment of Bayonne, and repulse of the sortie from thence. Sir Dudley has received a cross and a clasp for Fuentes d'Onor, Badajoz, Salamanca, Vittoria, and San Sebastian.

37 Sir Richard Armstrong served in the Peninsula from August, 1808, to the end of the war, including the capture of Oporto ; battle of Busaco ; actions at Pombal, and Redinha ; defence of Alba de Tormes ; battles of Vittoria, the Pyrenees, (severely wounded through the arm), and Toulouse, besides a great many minor actions and skirmishes. Served also the campaigns of 1825 and 26 in Burmah, as a brigadier ; stormed and carried stockades near Prome, on the 1st and 5th Dec. 1825. Sir Richard has received a medal and two clasps for the battles of Busaco, Vittoria, and the Pyrenees.

38 Sir Frederick Stovin served at the Ferrol in 1800 ; in Germany, 1805 ; at the siege and capture of Copenhagen, 1807 ; with the expedition to Sweden, 1808 ; in Spain and Portugal in 1808 and 9, including the retreat to, and battle of Corunna ; expedition to Walcheren and capture of Flushing, 1809 ; and subsequently in the Peninsula, including the sieges and captures of Ciudad Rodrigo, and Badajoz, battles of Salamanca, Vittoria, Pyrenees, Nivelle, Orthes, and Toulouse. Served also at New Orleans, where he was wounded. Sir Frederick has received a cross and two clasps for the six above-mentioned battles.

39 Sir Guy Campbell commanded the 6th regiment at the battle of the Pyrenees, for which he has received a medal. Served also the campaign of 1815, including the battle of Waterloo.

40 Colonel Richard G. Hare served in the Peninsula as an Assistant-Adjutant-General, and has received a medal and a clasp for the battles of Nivelle, and Nive.

41 Colonel Alexander Thomson served as an assistant engineer at San Sebastian, and has received a medal.

42 Colonel Heriot served in the American war, and commanded the Canadian Voltigeurs in the action at Chrystler's Farm, for which he has received a medal.

43 Colonel Wm. Crosse accompanied the expedition to Hanover in 1805 ; to South America in 1806, and was present at the storming of Buenos Ayres. Served also in the Peninsula with the 36th regiment, and was present at the battles of Roleia, Vimiera, Fuentes d'Onor, Nivelle, Nive, Orthes, and Toulouse, besides various minor actions and skirmishes. He has received a cross for the four last-mentioned battles.

44 Colonel Rice served in Corsica in 1794, and was present at the sieges of Bastia and Calvi ; the attack upon Elba by Lord Nelson. Served also in Portugal, Spain, France, and Flanders, including the battles of Corunna, Fuentes d'Onor, Salamanca, Nivelle (including the heights of St. Pé), Orthes, and Waterloo. Medal for the battle of Nivelle.

45 Colonel Wm. F. P. Napier was an actor in many of the soul-stirring scenes which he has described with so much ability in his admirable history of the Peninsular war, and was severely wounded in the action of Casal Nova, 14th March, 1811. He commanded the 43rd Light Infantry at the battles of Salamanca, Nivelle, and Nive, for which he has received a medal and two clasps.

Notes to the Colonels.

46 Colonel Duffy served in the Peninsula with the 43rd Light Infantry; the command of the regiment devolved on him at the assault and capture of Badajoz after Colonel Macleod was killed; he has received the medal.

47 Colonel Martin Lindsay served the campaign in Java in 1811, including the actions of the 22nd August and 16th Sept., in which latter he commanded eight companies of the 78th Highlanders, and has received the medal. Served also the campaign of 1814 in Holland, including the actions at Merxem, and bombardment of Antwerp.

48 Colonel Daubeney served at Walcheren in 1809.

49 Colonel Mercer accompanied the expedition to Hanover in 1805, and that to Walcheren in 1809. Served in the Peninsula from March, 1810, to May, 1811, and again from July, 1811, to March, 1814, including the affair at Sobral (wounded), battle of Barrosa (wounded), siege of Ciudad Rodrigo, battle of Salamanca, capture of Madrid, siege of Burgos, passage of the Bidassoa, and battle of the Nivelle. Served also the campaign of 1815, including the battles of Quatre Bras and Waterloo, and capture of Paris.

50 Colonel Milman served in the Peninsula with the Coldstream Guards, and was wounded at the battle of Talavera.

51 Colonel Tonson served at the capture of Martinique in 1794; and was wounded and taken prisoner at St. Vincent's the following year. Actively employed in Ireland during the rebellion in 1798; and in Holland in 1799; and at Walcheren in 1809. Served in the Peninsula from July, 1813, including the battle of the Nive, for which he has received a medal.

52 Colonel Wm. Alex. Gordon served in Holland in 1799; at Walcheren in 1809; and in the Peninsula from 1810 to the end of the war, including the battle of Fuentes d'Onor, action at Aroya de Molino, battles of Vittoria and the Nive, besides various minor affairs. Severely wounded in the left arm at Vittoria, and again in the right foot in forcing the enemy's lines at Haspaine, 14th Feb. 1814. Medal for the Nive.

53 Colonel Fremantle served in Germany under Lord Cathcart in 1806; in South America under General Whitelock, 1807; afterwards throughout the Peninsular war. Served also the campaign of 1815, including the battle of Waterloo. Medal for the battle of Orthes.

54 Lord George Wm. Russell served at the siege of Copenhagen in 1807, and subsequently in the Peninsula, including the battles of Talavera (wounded), Barrosa, and Toulouse, for which last he has received a medal.

55 Colonel James Fergusson's services:—Campaigns in Portugal and Spain in 1808 and 9, including the battles of Vimiera and Corunna. Expedition to Walcheren, 1809. Peninsular campaigns, from March 1810 to the end of the war, including the passage of the Coa near Almeida, battle of Busaco, actions at Pombal, Redinha, Miranda de Corva, Foz d'Aronce, Sabugal, battle of Fuentes d'Onor, sieges and assaults of Ciudad Rodrigo and Badajoz, battle of Salamanca, affair of San Munos, passage of the Bidassoa, battles of the Nivelle and Nive, and investment of Bayonne. Col. Fergusson has received five wounds, viz.: at Vimiera, slightly; at the storming of Ciudad Rodrigo, severely in the body, and slightly in the foot; at Badajoz, slightly in the side by a splinter of a shell in the trenches, and in the head at the assault. Medal for Badajoz.

56 Sir James H. Reynett was on the expedition against Ferrol in 1800, and was present at the action before that place. Appointed to the Quarter-Master-General's staff upon the army entering Spain in Nov. 1808, and was present at Lugo, the affairs upon the retreat to, and at the battle of Corunna. Re-appointed to the Quarter-Master-General's staff in Portugal, in April, 1809; present at the affairs previous to, and at the passage of the Douro, and capture of Oporto; affair of Salamonde; battles of Talavera, and Busaco; affairs upon the retreat to the lines before Lisbon, and subsequently in 1811 at those upon the advance from thence, at Pombal, Redinha, Sabugal, and Foz d'Aronce; and at the battle of Fuentes d'Onor.

57 Colonel Creagh was actively employed in St. Domingo in 1797 and 98; in Holland in 1799, including the actions of the 27th Aug., 19th Sept., 2nd and 6th Oct. Served in Portugal and Spain in 1808, and was present at the battles of Roleia and Vimiera, for which he has received a medal. Served also at New Orleans, including the engagements of the 25th Dec. 1814, and 1st and 8th Jan. 1815. Severely wounded at Vimiera.

58 Lord Munster served in the Peninsula, and was severely wounded at the battle of Toulouse.

59 Colonel Archibald Campbell was at Dominica when it was attacked by the French, 22nd Feb. 1805. Served also in the Peninsula, from Sept. 1811 to 1814, including the battles of Salamanca, and Vittoria (severely wounded); capture of San Sebastian; crossing the Bidassoa; forcing the enemy's lines, 10th Nov.; battle of the Nive, 9th, 10th, and 11th Dec. 1813. Medal for the Nive.

60 Colonel John Bell served in the Peninsula as an Assistant-Quarter-Master-General, and has received a cross for the battles of the Pyrenees, Nivelle, Orthes, and Toulouse.

Notes to the Colonels.

61 Colonel Auchmuty served in the Peninsula, and has received a medal and a clasp for the battles of Orthes and Toulouse.

62 Colonel Lightfoot served in the Peninsula with the 45th regiment, and was present at the battles of Roleia, Vimiera, Talavera, Busaco, and Fuentes d'Onor; first siege of Badajoz; sieges and assaults of Ciudad Rodrigo and Badajoz (slightly wounded), including the storming of Fort Picurina (slightly wounded); battles of Salamanca, Vittoria, Pyrenees, Orthes and Toulouse (severely wounded), besides various minor actions and skirmishes. Medal and two clasps for Vittoria, Pyrenees, and Toulouse.

63 Colonel Wingrove served at the taking of the Cape of Good Hope in 1795; battle of Trafalgar; taking of Genoa, 1814; on board the *Boyne* when that ship singly engaged three French ships of the line and three frigates off Toulon in 1814; and on board the *Hercule* in a single action off Cape Nichola Mole.

64 Colonel Conyers served in the Peninsula, and has received a medal for Orthes.

65 Colonel Henderson served in Ireland during the rebellion in 1798; at the Helder in 1799, and was present at the first landing, and battles of the 19th Sept., 2nd and 6th Oct. Expedition to Egypt under Sir Ralph Abercromby, 1801. Landed in Portugal in 1808, and was present at the battle of Vimiera, retreat to, and battle of Corunna. Expedition to the Scheldt and siege of Flushing, 1809. Served afterwards in the Peninsula, from 1811 to the end of the war, and commanded the Queen's at the battle of Toulouse.

66 Colonel Roger Parke served in the Peninsula with the 39th regiment, and was present at the battles of Albuhera, and Barrosa.

67 Colonel Macpherson commanded the 88th regiment at the battles of Vittoria and Orthes, for which he has received a medal and a clasp.

68 Colonel C. P. de Bosset served with the expedition to Hanover in 1805; expedition to Zealand, siege and surrender of Copenhagen, 1807; expedition to Sweden, and subsequently to Portugal, 1808; siege of Santa Maura, 1810.

69 Colonel Torrens was actively employed in the East Indies, from 1801 to 1807, including the assault and capture of the city of Ahmednuggur, battles of Assaye, and Argaum, and various other minor operations. Served in the Peninsula from Nov. 1813, to the end of the war; and also the campaign of 1815, including the battle of Waterloo.

70 Colonel Henry Dawkins served in the Peninsula, from Jan. 1810, to the end of the war, including the sieges of Ciudad Rodrigo, and Burgos; battles of Fuentes d'Onor, Salamanca, Vittoria, Nivelle, and Nive; passage of the Adour; blockade of Bayonne, and repulse of the sortie from thence, on which occasion he was severely wounded. Served also the campaign of 1815, including the battle of Waterloo.

71 Colonel Forbes has received a medal for the capture of Java.

72 Colonel Proctor served with the expedition to Walcheren, 1809, and was present at the siege of Flushing. At Gibraltar, Tarifa, and in the Peninsula, from 1810 to Dec. 1812, and subsequently in the Peninsula and South of France, from April to July, 1814, including the affair of Posts near Malaga, battle of Barrosa (contusion on the body), and retreat from Madrid. Embarked from Bourdeaux for Canada, and commanded the 82nd regiment before Fort Erie, from 2nd Sept., and throughout the successive operations of the war.

73 Colonel Wm. Riddall was actively employed with the 62nd regiment in Sicily, Egypt, Calabria, Italy, Spain, and America, from 1806 to the end of the war.

74 Colonel Addison served in the American war, on the staff of Sir J. Sherbrooke.

75 Colonel C. J. Doyle served in the Peninsula, and was present at the passage of the Douro, capture of Oporto, battle of Talavera, action at Campo Mayor, and battle of Fuentes d'Onor.

76 Colonel Charretie served in the Peninsula, from 1812 to the end of the war, including the battles of Vittoria and Toulouse.

77 Colonel Parkinson served at the capture of the Island of Bourbon, on the staff of Sir H. S. Keating. Served also the campaigns of 1814 and 15 in the Netherlands and France, including the attack on Merxem, operations before Antwerp and Bergen-op-Zoom, and battle of Quatre Bras, where he was slightly wounded.

78 Colonel Tho. Hunter Blair served in Portugal and Spain, from August, 1808, to Jan. 1809, including the affair of Obidos, battles of Roleia and Vimiera, action at Lugo, and battle of Corunna. Proceeded again to the Peninsula in August, 1809, and was present at the capture of Oporto, affair of Salamonde, and battle of Talavera, at which last he was severely wounded, and made prisoner in hospital. Served also the campaign of 1815, and was severely wounded at Waterloo. Commanded a brigade in Ava, including the capture of Melloon.

79 Colonel Lluellyn served in the Peninsula with the 28th regiment, from 1809 to the end of the war; also the campaign of 1815, including the battles of Quatre Bras and Waterloo, at which latter he was severely wounded.

80 Colonel Wade served in the Peninsula as aide-de-camp to Sir Lowry Cole, and was severely wounded at the battle of Albuhera.

Notes to the Colonels.

81 Colonel Wm. Chalmers served in Sicily, in 1807. The campaigns of 1808 and 9 in Portugal and Spain. Expedition to Walcheren, 1809. At Cadiz in 1810 and 11, and the subsequent campaigns, including the battle of Barrosa, attack of the enemy on the heights near Moresco, battles of Salamanca, Vittoria, attack at Maya, battle of Pampeluna, and a great many minor actions and skirmishes. Served also in the Netherlands in 1814 and 15, including the battle of Waterloo, and subsequent operations in France. He was severely wounded in the Pyrenees, and has had nine horses killed or wounded under him in action, three of them at Waterloo.

82 Colonel Miller served in the Peninsula, France, and Flanders, with the Rifle Brigade, and has received a medal for the battle of the Nivelle.

83 Colonel Beckwith served in the Peninsula, France, and Flanders, and has received a medal for the battle of Toulouse. Severely wounded at Waterloo.

84 Colonel John Campbell served in the Peninsula, France, and Flanders, and has received a medal and a clasp for the battles of Orthes and Toulouse.

85 Colonel Fielding Browne served in the Peninsula with the 40th regiment, and has received a medal for the assault and capture of Badajoz.

86 Colonel T. W. Taylor served at the capture of Java, including the attack of the outpost near Weltevreden, and the storming of the lines of Cornielis. Served also the campaign of 1815, including the battle of Waterloo.

87 Colonel Arguimbau served in the Peninsular with the 3rd battalion of the Royals, and lost an arm at San Sebastian. Served also the campaign of 1815, and was slightly wounded at Quatre Bras, and also at Waterloo.

88 Colonel Childers served at the Helder in 1799; and in the Peninsula, France, and Flanders, from May, 1811, to the end of the war. Commanded a brigade of cavalry at the siege of Bhurtpore, under Lord Combermere.

89 Colonel H. G. Smith served in the Peninsula with the Rifle Brigade, and on the staff of Major-General Skerrett; and at New Orleans and the subsequent campaign in Flanders and France on the staff of Major-General Lambert.

90 Sir De Lacy Evans served in the Peninsula from 1812 to the end of the war, and subsequently in the American war, including the operations against Washington, Baltimore, and New Orleans. Served also the campaign of 1815, including the battle of Waterloo. Wounded at New Orleans.

91 Colonel Wm. H. Scott proceeded to the Peninsula in 1809, and was present at the capture of Oporto, subsequent pursuit of Soult's army, and battle of Talavera, where he was wounded through the body, and afterwards made prisoner, being left in hospital upon the retreat of the army.

92 Sir Thomas Reade served in Sicily as an Assistant-Quarter-Master-General, and commanded a flotilla of gun-boats in and near the straits of Messina during the attempted invasion of Sicily by the French forces in 1810.

93 Sir John Morillyon Wilson prior to entering the army served six years in the Royal Navy, including the expedition to the Helder in 1799 (wounded), and that to Egypt in 1801, and received the thanks of the Captain Pacha, and a medal for saving the lives of the crew of a Turkish man-of-war's boat. Accompanied the expedition to Walcheren in 1809, and was twice wounded at the siege of Flushing, one ball having passed through his body. Served in the Peninsula, from the latter end of 1809 to 1812, including the battles of Busaco, and Fuentes d'Onor, and all the various actions which were fought during that period. Joined the 1st battalion of the Royal Scots in Canada in the winter of 1812, and in 1813 and 14 he was in the various attacks made on Sackett's Harbour, Great Sodus (received a severe bayonet wound during a night attack), Fort Niagara, Black Rock, and Buffaloe, and battle of Chippewa, on which occasion he was left for dead on the field of battle, and fell into the hands of the enemy, having received seven wounds, viz.: three in the left arm, in which one ball is still lodged, a fourth ball passed through his left thigh, a fifth entered his left thigh and was extracted, a sixth fractured and greatly injured his hip-bone, and the seventh ball penetrated his left groin, passing upwards and backwards to the region of the spinal column, where it is still lodged. Sir John has thus received thirteen wounds during his professional career in the navy and the army, and he has two musket-balls still lodged in his body.

94 Sir Alexander Anderson commanded the 11th Portuguese regiment in the Peninsular war, and has received a cross and three clasps for the assault and capture of Badajoz, and the battles of Salamanca, Vittoria, Pyrenees, Nivelle, Orthes, and Toulouse.

95 Colonel Rolt served in Egypt in 1801, and was wounded through the body in the action at the landing (medal). Served also in the Peninsula, from 1809 to the end of the war, and commanded the 17th Portuguese regiment at the battles of Vittoria, Nivelle, Nive, Orthes, and Toulouse.

96 Sir Charles Webb Dance served in the Peninsula, France, and Flanders, and was slightly wounded at Waterloo.

Notes to the Colonels.

97 Colonel Hughes served in Portugal and Spain under Sir John Moore, and was present in the cavalry actions at Mayorga and Benevente. Served afterwards in the Peninsula, from Feb. 1813, to the end of the war, including the action at Morales, and battles of Vittoria, Orthes, and Toulouse, for which he has received a medal and two clasps. Severely wounded near Ellite in the south of France.

98 Colonel Bainbrigge served in the Peninsula from 1810 to the end of the war, as an Assistant-Quarter-Master-General.

99 Colonel Kenneth Snodgrass served in Portugal and Spain under Sir John Moore, including the retreat to and battle of Corunna. Served afterwards in the Peninsula, including the assaults and captures of Badajoz and San Sebastian; and battles of Fuentes d'Onor, Vittoria, Nivelle, Nive, and Orthes, besides various minor actions and other desultory services. Wounded at San Sebastian, the Nive, and at Orthes very severely in the head. Colonel Snodgrass has received a cross for San Sebastian, Nivelle, Nive, and Orthes.

100 Colonel Balvaird served in the Peninsula with the Rifle Brigade, and has received a medal and a clasp for the battles of Nivelle and Nive.

101 Colonel Stretton served in the Peninsula from 1812 to the end of the war, including the battles of Vittoria, Pyrenees, Nivelle, Nive, Orthes, and Toulouse, besides various minor actions and skirmishes. Served afterwards at New Orleans, and the subsequent campaign of 1815, including the battle of Waterloo. Medal for the battle of Toulouse.

102 Colonel Darling served at the reduction of Guadaloupe in 1810, and was severely wounded in the left knee by a musket-shot in storming the heights of Matauba. Proceeded to the Peninsula, and joined the 51st Light Infantry in May 1812 at Castello Branco; engaged on the heights of San Christoval; the battle of Salamanca; surrender of the Retiro, Madrid; and siege of Burgos: after the retreat from thence he was attacked by typhus fever, and sent to England for recovery in May 1812. Rejoined the army on the heights of Echellar in September following, and was present at the battle of Nivelle, and the subsequent attack of the heights of St. Pé. Appointed Major of Brigade Dec. 1813, and attached to Major-General Hay's brigade in the 5th division, and was employed throughout the blockade and operations before Bayonne. Appointed Assistant-Adjutant-General to the 5th division in April 1814, and remained in charge of that department until the embarkation of the division in August 1814. On the renewal of the war in 1815, he was re-appointed to the staff as Assist.-Adjt.-General and attached to the 4th division, under Sir Charles Colville; employed with his division in the operations connected with the battle of Waterloo, the storming of Cambray, and capitulation of Paris.

103 Sir Wm. Lewis Herries proceeded with the expedition to South America in 1807; to Walcheren in 1809, including the siege and capture of Flushing. Served in the Peninsula from 1812 to the end of the war, and was severely wounded (leg amputated) and taken prisoner at the repulse of the sortie from Bayonne.

104 Colonel St. Clair served at Walcheren in 1809, and in the Peninsula from March 1810 to the end of the war, including the battles of Busaco and Fuentes d'Onor, first siege of Badajoz, battle of the Nive, and investment of Bayonne. Medal for the Nive.

105 Colonel Zuhlcke served throughout the whole of the Peninsular war, including the battles of Roleia and Vimiera; capture of Oporto; battles of Talavera (severely wounded), and Fuentes d'Onor; sieges of Badajoz and Ciudad Rodrigo; battles of Salamanca, Vittoria, the Pyrenees, Nivelle, Nive, and Orthes, besides various minor actions and skirmishes. Medal and two clasps.

106 Colonel Wm. Rowan served in Portugal and Spain under Sir John Moore; with the expedition to Walcheren 1809; in the Peninsula from January to June 1811, and again from January 1813 to the end of the war, including the battles of Vittoria, the Bidassoa, Nivelle, Nive, Orthes, and Toulouse. Served also the campaign of 1815, including the battle of Waterloo.

107 Lord Sandys served in the Peninsula, France, and Flanders, from 1812 to the end of the war, including the action at Morales, and battles of Vittoria, Pampeluna, and Waterloo.

108 Sir Thomas Henry Browne served at the siege of Copenhagen in 1807; at the capture of Martinique, 1809 (wounded). Served afterwards in the Peninsula as a Deputy-Assistant-Adjutant-General at the head-quarters of the Duke of Wellington; and, subsequently, at the head-quarters of the Austrian, Russian, and Prussian armies, as aide-de-camp to Lord Stewart. During the Peninsular war he was present at every action, from the battle of Salamanca to that of Toulouse, and received a sabre cut on the head at the battle of Vittoria.

109 Colonel Tho. W. Forster acted as major of brigade at the capture of the Cape of Good Hope in 1806. Senior officer on board the *Astell*, Indiaman, when that ship and two others were for some hours engaged with two French frigates and a corvette in July, 1810.

110 Colonel Howard served on the Continent in 1793 and 94; in St Domingo and the West India Islands, from 1795 to 1799. Served also in the Peninsula, and was most severely wounded at the battle of Talavera, 27th July, 1809, and made prisoner.

Notes to the Colonels.

111 Colonel Whetham served with the expedition to South America, and was severely wounded (right leg amputated) at the assault of Monte Video.

112 Colonel Thomas Wildman served with the 7th Hússars in the campaign of 1808 and 9 under Sir John Moore, and was present in the cavalry engagements at Mayorga, Benevente, and throughout the retreat to Corunna. Served also the Peninsular campaigns of 1813 and 14, including the investment and surrender of Pampeluna, the battle of Orthes, and intermediate affairs. Served the campaign of 1815 as aide-de-camp to the Earl of Uxbridge, including the action at Quatre Bras, retreat on the 17th, and battle of Waterloo, at which last he was slightly wounded.

113 Colonel Robbins served in the Peninsula, France, and Flanders with the 7th Hussars, and was severely wounded at Waterloo.

114 Colonel George Lewis served in Sir Richard Strachan's action 4th Nov. 1805. Commanded a Battalion of Marines in the American war, including the action at Bladensburg, attack on Baltimore, and various skirmishes in the Chesapeak.

115 Colonel Dumas served at the blockade of Malta in 1799, in Egypt in 1801, and again in 1807; and at the battle of Maida. Medal for services in Egypt.

116 Colonel Edward Wildman served in the Peninsula, from April, 1809, to Sept. 1811, and again from July, 1812, to the end of the war, including the battles of Talavera and Busaco, action at Redinha, battle of Albuhera, retreat from Salamanca to Portugal, battles of Vittoria, Pyrenees, Tarbes and Toulouse. Served also the campaign of 1815, and had three horses killed under him at Waterloo. Received two severe sabre wounds in the head and arm, and made prisoner at the battle of Albuhera.

117 Colonel the Hon. John Finch served in the Peninsula, from Nov. 1812 to the end of the war, and received a sabre wound at the battle of Vittoria.

118 Sir Augustus d'Este served at New Orleans on the staff of Sir John Lambert, and behaved with great gallantry.

119 Colonel Cochrane landed with the first army in Portugal on the 3d Aug. 1808, and served in the Peninsula during the campaigns of 1808, 9, 10, 11, and part of 1812, including the battles and sieges of Roliça, Vimiera, Talavera, Busaco, Redinha, Olivença, Badajoz (1st siege), and Ciudad Rodrigo. Served nearly two years in Canada during the American war, as aide-de-camp to the Governor-General and Commander of the Forces, Lieut.-General Sir George Prevost.

120 Colonel Hector Maclaine served in the Peninsula, and has received a medal for the battle of Nivelle.

121 Colonel Simpson served in the Peninsula from May 1812 to May 1813, including the latter part of the siege of Cadiz, and the attack on Seville. Served also the campaign of 1815, and was severely wounded at Quatre Bras.

122 Colonel Duncan M'Gregor was actively employed in Sicily and Italy in 1806, including the skirmish at St. Euphemie, battle of Maida, attack on Scylla Castle, and capture of Catrone. Campaign of 1807 in Egypt, including the attacks in the Desert, and siege of Rosetta. Campaign in Holland in 1809, including the attacks and captures of Ter Vere, and Flushing. Campaigns in the Peninsula during part of 1813 and 14. Capture of Corsica in May 1814. Wounded through the right shoulder by a musket-shot at the battle of Maida.

123 Colonel Seton served the Egyptian campaign of 1801 (medal); in South America in 1807; and subsequently in the Peninsula, including the battles and sieges of Talavera, Busaco, Fuentes d'Onor, Ciudad Rodrigo, Badajoz, and Salamanca. Wounded at the attack on Buenos Ayres. Medal and a clasp for the assault and capture of Badajoz, and battle of Salamanca.

124 Colonel Nickle served in South America in 1807, including the actions of the 2nd and 5th July, and was severely wounded. In the Peninsula from 1808 to the end of the war, including the battles of Talavera, Busaco, Vittoria, Pyrenees, Nivelle, Nive, Orthes, and Toulouse (severely wounded); and the second siege of Badajoz. Served subsequently in the American war, and was present at the action at Plattsburg (wounded), and various other affairs.

125 Colonel Middleton served at the capture of Java, 1811; throughout the Mahratta war in 1817 and 18, and was severely wounded in the battle of Challapore.

126 Colonel Macintosh served in the Peninsula, from August, 1812, to the end of the war, including the actions at Alba de Tormes, and San Munos; passage of the Tormes above Salamanca, and attack on the French rear-guard under General Villate; battle of Vittoria, investment of Pampeluna; affair at Tarbes, and battle of Toulouse.

LIEUTENANT-COLONELS.

	CORNET, 2nd LIEUT. or ENSIGN.	LIEUT.	CAPTAIN.	MAJOR.	LIEUT.-COLONEL.	WHEN PLACED ON HALF PAY.	REGIMENTAL RANK.	
John Drinkwater Bethune[1]	22 Dec. 77	5 April 80	8 Sept. 83	1 Mar. 94	1 Sept. 95	1798	Captain	Half-pay Commissary General.
Thomas Frederick	26 Jan. 79	Nov. 80	14 Oct. 81	do	1 Jan. 98		Major	Half-pay 84 Foot.
Wm. *Earl of* Lonsdale, KG.	6 Mar. 04	8 Mar. 94	17 May 94	22 Aug. 94	1 Jan. 00	12 Nov. 94	do	Half-pay 84 Foot.
Philip Walsh	never	never	never	1 Oct.	do		do	Half-pay Irish Brigade.
John Grey[2]	11 June 78	20 Sept. 79	31 Aug. 91	30 Sept. 95	1 Jan. 01	3 Dec. 02	Lt.-Col.	Half-pay York Fencible Infantry.
Robert Walker	22 Sept. 75	20 Apr. 78	13 July 91	1 Jan. 98	25 Sept. 03			Late 9 R.Vet. Bn. *Lt.-Gov. of Sheern.* {Late 1 Royal Vet. Batt. *Lt.-Gov.* *of Landguard Fort.*
Charles Augustus West[3]	20 Mar. 94	never	4 Feb. 97	never	5 May 04		do	Late 5 R. Vet. Bn. *Maj. of Chel. Hos.*
Henry Le Blanc	9 July 92	22 May 95	1 June 99	12 June 06	5 Feb. 07		do	Half-pay Roll's Reg.
Charles De Vogelsang	never	never	9 Dec. 94	25 Sept. 02	25 July 10	25 July 16	Major	Half-pay Macdonald's Rec. Corps.
Samuel Dales, KH.	18 July 82	24 Sept. 87	15 July 95	9 July 03	do		do	Half-pay German Legion.
John, *Baron* Bulow, CB. KH.[4]	never	never	3 Sept. 03	*30 June 05	1 Aug. 05	24 Feb. 16	Lt.-Col.	Half-pay German Legion.
John Wm. de Ulmenstein	never	never	never	*12 Jan. 05	23 Oct. 10	24 May 16	do	Half-pay German Legion.
Colin James Milnes, CB.	15 Mar. 93	1 Oct. 94	1 Feb. 98	2 Oct. 06	4 June 11			Late of 65 Foot.
Luke Alen, CB.[5]	never	1 Oct. 94	18 Jan. 98	16 May 05	11 July 11			Late of 55 Foot.
Richard Harvey Cooke, CB.[6]	20 Feb. 98	24 Sept. 99	25 Nov. 99	never	7 Nov. 11			Late of Grenadier Guards.
Francis Plunkett	July 94	24 Sept. 94	26 Nov. 94	1 Jan. 05	1 Jan. 12		Captain	Late 5 Royal Veteran Battalion.
John Mansel, CB.[7]	Mar. 95	3 Sept. 95	4 April 00	28 Feb. 05	do			Late of 53 Foot.
Hugh Halkett, CB. KCH.[8]	never	never	never	1 July 05	do			Late of German Legion.
Russell Manners, CB.[9]	1 Sept. 91	9 June 94	3 May 01	1 Mar. 08	6 Feb. 12			Late of 74 Foot.
Raymond Pelly, CB.[10]	2 May 00	3 July 01	6 Aug. 02	1 Nov. 10	23 April 12			Late of 56 Foot.
John Philip Hunt, CB.[11]	8 Mar. 99	29 Nov. 99	17 Dec. 02	8 Sept. 08	27 April 12			Late of 11 Foot.
Charles Rowan, CB.[12]	15 May 97	15 Mar. 99	25 June 03	9 May 11	do			Late of 52 Foot.
Harcourt Fort Holcombe, CB.[13]	6 Mar. 95	1 July 96	12 Sept. 03	6 Feb. 12	do			Late of Royal Artillery.
Rodolphe de May	never	never	1 May 01	13 Nov. 06	21 May 12	24 Oct. 16	Lt.-Col.	Half-pay Watteville's Regt.
John Bacon Harrison, CB.[14]	Jan. 95	10 June 95	1 June 97	23 Feb. 09	19 June 12			Late of 50 Foot.
Charles Cother, CB.[15]	Jan. 00	16 July 00	25 Mar. 03	9 Mar. 09	do			Late of 83 Foot.

53   H

Lieutenant-Colonels.

	CORNET, ETC.	LIEUT.	CAPTAIN.	MAJOR.	LIEUT.-COLONEL.	WHEN PLACED ON HALF PAY.	REGIMENTAL RANK.	
ⓟ ⓦⓜ Sir J. Hartmann, KCB. KCH.[16]	never	never	*9 Nov. 03	*12 Apr. 06	17 Aug. 12	24 Feb. 16	Major	Half-pay German Foot.
ⓟ Gustavus Brown, CB.[17]	never	never	30 Dec. 97	25 July 10	do			Late of 95 Foot.
James Williamson	never	never	never	never	17 Sept. 12			*Comm. Royal Military Asylum.*
Sir Richard Church, CB. GCH.[18]	3 July 00	13 Jan. 03	7 Jan. 06	25 Feb. 11	19 Nov. 12			Late of Greek Light Infantry.
Robert Oswald, CB.	20 Dec. 99	7 Feb. 00	8 Sept. 02	19 Apr. 10	18 May 13			Late of Greek Light Infantry.
Sir James Malcolm, KCB.	29 Nov. 79	18 April 93	1 Jan. 97	7 Feb. 06	4 June 13			Late of Royal Marines.
Charles Plenderleath, CB.[19]	29 May 96	6 Mar. 97	3 July 99	16 Oct. 06	do			Late of 49 Foot.
*Thomas Armstrong	never	never	never	never	19 June 13			Late of Coldstream Guards.
John P. Hawkins, CB.[20]	20 Dec. 99	23 May 00	24 Aug. 04	17 Sept. 12	21 June 13			Late of 68 Foot.
Wm. Grove White, CB.[21]	14 April 95	21 Oct. 95	14 April 04	25 Nov. 09	26 Aug. 13			Late of 94 Foot.
George Feud, CB.	19 Dec. 99	never	3 Dec. 03	never	13 Dec. 13			Late of Grenadier Guards.
George Macdonell, CB.[22]	15 Sept. 96	4 May 98	4 Sept. 03	6 Feb. 12	24 Feb. 14			Late of 79 Foot.
John Galiffe, CB.[23]	never	1 July 95	31 Oct. 96	25 April 08	3 Mar. 14			Late of 60 Foot.
William Covell, CB.[24]	1 April 97	1 June 97	8 Dec. 01	16 Mar. 09	do			Late of 42 Foot.
Wm. Lewis Herford, CB.[25]	1 June 97	7 Mar. 00	25 Oct. 04	16 Aug. 12	do			Late of 23 Foot.
George Muttlebury, CB.	Jan. 95	3 Sept. 95	21 Feb. 98	25 July 10	17 Mar. 14			Late of 69 Foot.
Charles Newhouse[26]	29 Sept. 89	1 July 91	26 Jan. 96	1 Feb. 08	4 June 14		Major	Late Royal Invalid Artillery.
George Wilkins, CB. KH.[27]	14 Sept. 94	7 Jan. 95	30 Apr. 95	25 April 08	do			Late of Rifle Brigade.
Morris Wm. Bailey, CB.[28]	26 May 95	10 Sept. 95	21 Feb. 98	17 Jan. 09	do			Late of 64 Foot.
Fiennes S. Miller, CB.[29]	19 Dec. 99	25 June 03	5 Oct. 04	25 May 09	do			Late of 6 Dragoons.
Philip Dorville, CB.	4 Sept. 94	27 May 95	21 July 97	25 Oct. 09	do	8 Mar. 27	Major	Unattached.
Sir Henry Pynn, CB.[30]	Oct. 95	28 Nov. 99	30 May 05	15 Nov. 09	do			Late of Portuguese Service.
* Meyrick Shawe	never	never	never	never	9 June 14			Late of 76 Foot.
Patrick Campbell[31]	6 Mar. 95	3 Oct. 95	20 Mar. 03	14 Oct. 13	1 June 15		Lieut.-Col.	Late of Royal Artillery.
Wm. von Robertson, CB. KCH.[32]	never	never	*25 Oct. 03	27 Jan. 11	18 June 15	24 Feb. 16	Major	Half-pay German Legion.
Geo. Baron von Krauchenberg, CB. KCH.								
James Paul Bridger, CB.	14 Mar. 00	14 Aug. 02	28 Jan. 04	30 May 11	do	do	do	Half-pay German Legion.
G. Baron von Baring, CB. KCH.	never	never	20 Aug. 02	10 Dec. 12	do			Late of 12 Dragoons.
Jonathan Leach, CB.	15 Aug. 01	15 Oct. 01	10 Nov. 03	21 June 13	do	24 Feb. 16	do	Half-pay German Legion.
Geo. Davis Wilson, CB.[33]	27 April 97	7 Aug. 99	7 April 04	21 June 13	do			Late of Rifle Brigade.
Leslie Walker, CB. KH.[34]	22 Aug. 99	23 Aug. 99	28 Aug. 04	26 Dec. 13	do			Late of 4 Foot.
Hon. G. L. Dawson Damer, CB.	4 Dec. 06	31 Dec. 07	31 Dec. 12	10 Mar. 14	31 Aug. 15			Late of 25 Foot.
Arthur Helsham Gordon	25 April 96	6 July 98	8 April 99	4 June 11	8 Feb. 16	6 May 24	Lieut.-Col.	Late of 89 Foot. Unattached.

Lieutenant-Colonels.

Name	2D LIEUT. ETC.	LIEUT.	CAPTAIN.	MAJOR.	LIEUT.-COLONEL.	WHEN PLACED ON HALF PAY.	REGIMENTAL RANK.	
Geo. Francis Macleod, CB.	never	1 July 01	1 July 06	6 Feb. 12	21 June 17			Late of Royal Engineers.
Robert Lisle, CB.	27 Mar. 91	25 Dec. 95	23 Jan. 01	4 June 13	do		Lieut.-Col.	Late of 13 Dragoons.
Gabriel Burer	never	30 Dec. 97	24 Nov. 03	1 July 13	3 July 17	22 Mar. 27		Unattached.
Samuel South	22 May 97	10 Aug. 99	13 Feb. 05	21 Oct. 13	17 Dec. 18	21 Dec. 20	do	Half-pay 8 Foot.
Nathan Wilson, KH.[35]	20 Jan. 95	30 Sept. 96	23 Feb. 03	22 Feb. 10	12 Aug. 19	15 Nov. 33	do	Unattached.
Henry Richardson			20 Oct. 02	17 May 10	do	25 Dec. 14	Major	Half-pay 32 Foot.
Edward Nicolls[36]	24 Mar. 95	27 Jan. 96	25 July 05	8 Aug. 10	do	1811	do	Late of Royal Marines.
Geo. Ralph Payne Jarvis	8 Feb. 92	19 Dec. 93	14 Nov. 99	20 Dec. 10	do		do	Half-pay 36 Foot.
John Wm. O'Donoghue, CB.[37]	1 Oct. 94	23 April 00	12 June 06	31 Dec. 11	do			Late Unattached.
James Payler[38]	2 Nov. 03	24 Mar. 04	30 Nov. 06	13 Jan. 14	31 July 23	17 May 33	Lt.-Col.	Unattached.
Geo. Edw. Pratt Barlow[39]	24 Apr. 03	25 Dec. 14	14 Oct. 05	26 Mar. 12	4 Dec. 23	24 Aug. 32	do	Unattached.
Hon. Robert Moore[40]	21 Mar. 11	never	2 June 14	never	1 April 24	1 April 24	Cpt.&Lt.Cl.	Half-pay Coldstream Guards.
Sir Henry Floyd, Bart.	7 July 08	15 Mar. 10	2 Dec. 13	16 Nov. 20	6 May 24	6 May 24	Lt.-Col.	Unattached.
Edward Keane[41]	1 Dec. 03	21 Nov. 04	1 Dec. 06	18 June 18	17 May 24	29 Mar. 33	do	Unattached.
Charles Purvis[42]	3 June 96	31 Dec. 98	26 Feb. 01	7 May 12	27 May 25	11 June 18	Major	Half-pay Canadian Fencibles.
Robert Macdonald, CB.[43]	6 Jan. 95	6 Mar. 95	6 Apr. 02	17 Aug. 12	do			Late of Royal Artillery.
Benjamin Graves	April	19 Sept. 95	26 Aug. 96	24 Sept. 12	25 Jan. 18		Major	Half-pay 12 Foot.
Henry Madox, KH.[44]	14 May 03	23 July 08	18 June 18	31 Dec. 15	25 8 June 38	8 June 38	Lt.-Col.	Unattached.
Francis Fuller, CB.[45]	9 July 03	5 Sept. 04	5 Oct. 09	17 July 17	19 Jan. 26			Late of 59 Foot.
Mathias Everard, CB. KH.	28 Sept. 04	21 Mar. 05	23 April 07	19 July 21	do		Lt.-Col.	14 Foot.
Cecil Bisshopp, CB.	10 Dec. 99	14 Oct. 00	23 June 08	27 May 25	do		Major	11 Foot.
Charles Parker Ellis[46]	28 Jan. 11	never	25 Dec. 13	never	16 Feb. 26	10 May 31	Lt.-Col.	Half-pay Roll's Regiment.
Warner Westenra Higgins, KH.	4 Mar. 98	4 May 00	28 Feb. 05	16 June 14	25 Feb. 26	25 Feb. 26	do	Unattached.
Sir Wm. Rob. Clayton, Bart.[47]	28 Sept. 04	14 Nov. 05	27 April 09	21 Dec. 15	8 April 26	8 April 26	do	Unattached.
Francis Henry Dawkins	25 June 12	never	28 Apr. 14	never	do	8 April 26	do	Unatt. Dep.-Quarter-Must.-Gen. Ionian Islands.
William Macadam, KH.[48]	14 Jan. 08	10 Aug. 08	17 Nov. 14	23 Sept. 24	22 April 26	22 April 26	do	Unattached.
Hon. George Cathcart	10 May 10	1 July 11	24 Dec. 18	8 April 26	13 May 26		do	1 Dragoon Guards.
John Spink, KH.[49]	2 Sept. 06	9 May 07	13 Oct. 12	13 May 24	20 May 26	20 May 26	do	Unattached.
James Jackson, KH.	9 Oct. 06	25 Jan. 08	25 June 13	18 June 15	25 May 26		do	6 Dragoon Guards.
Robt. Christopher Mansel, KH.	29 Jan. 07	27 Jan. 08	4 Feb. 13	5 July 21	10 June 26	10 June 26	do	Unatt. Assist.-Adjt.-Gen.in Ireland.
Geo. Paris Bradshaw, KH.	2 Oct. 06	16 June 08	23 May 16	26 Dec. 22	do		do	77 Foot.
William Hay	4 Aug. 06	11 Sept. 05	11 Nov. 13	3 Feb. 25	do	10 do	do	Unattached.
Thomas Dobbin	April 06	7 Aug. 07	10 April 13	3 Nov. 25	do		Lieut.-Col.	Unattached.

Lieutenant-Colonels.

	ENSIGN, ETC.	LIEUT.	CAPTAIN.	MAJOR.	LIEUT.-COLONEL.	WHEN PLACED ON HALF PAY.	REGIMENTAL RANK.	
John Drummond	22 Nov. 10	never	26 May 14	never	22 June 26	13 April 32	Lieut.-Col.	Unattached.
⊕ Robert Fran. Melville Browne [50]	22 Oct. 99	24 June 02	27 Aug. 04	13 Jan. 14	11 July 26	11 July 26	do	Unattached.
⊕ James Freeth, KH.	25 Dec. 06	30 May 09	21 April 14	21 Jan. 19	do	25 June 30	Major	H.-p. R. Staff Corps, *Asst. Qr. M. Gen.*
⊕ ⊞ Francis Le Blanc	30 May 07	16 Mar. 09	28 Sept. 13	31 Dec. 22	do	28 Feb. 28	Lieut.-Col.	Unattached.
⊕ ⊞ George Wm. Horton	22 Feb. 10	25 July 11	5 Oct. 20	17 Aug. 21	1 Aug. 26	13 July 26	do	Unattached.
Sir Chas. Routledge O'Donnell	19 Jan. 09	4 April 11	20 July 15	never	do	1 Aug. 26	do	Unattached.
⊕ John Buck Riddlesden	9 Sept. 13	7 Sept. 15	11 July 22	14 Jan. 26	15 Aug. 26	15 Aug. 26	do	Unattached.
⊕ Thomas Chaplin	18 April 11	never	6 Oct. 14	never	do	do	Cpt. & Lt. Cl.	Coldstream Guards.
John Leslie, KH.	7 Aug. 06	2 June 08	30 Nov. 09	1 Jan. 19	20 Aug. 26	5 July 39	Lieut.-Col.	4 Foot.
⊕ Robert Bartlett Coles	20 Aug. 03	1 May 05	8 Sept. 08	24 Oct. 21	19 Sept. 26	19 Sept. 26	do	Unattached.
James Fleming	4 Aug. 00	25 June 03	10 Feb. 14	26 June 23	do	do	do	Unattached.
⊕ ⊞ Edward Clive	4 July 11	never	25 Dec. 13	never	do	do	Cpt. & Lt. Cl.	Grenadier Guards.
⊕ ⊞ Edward Pery Buckley	10 Sept. 12	never	23 Mar. 14	19 July 21	26 Sept. 26	9 Nov. 30	Lieut.-Col.	Unattached.
Richard Doherty	10 Sept. 08	22 Nov. 04	21 May 12	16 Sept. 24	do	26 Sept. 26	do	Royal African Colonial Corps.
⊕ ⊞ Edward Byam [51]	14 Nov. 11	29 April 13	26 Aug. 19	16 June 25	do	do	do	Unattached.
William Rogers	24 June 09	20 Feb. 06	4 Mar. 13	23 June 25	do	do	do	Unattached.
⊕ Chas. O'Neil Prendergast [52]	26 Aug. 09	never	13 Dec. 13	never	26 Oct. 26	5 July 39	do	Unattached.
George *Earl of Lucan*	29 Aug. 16	24 Dec. 18	16 May 22	23 June 25	9 Nov. 26	14 April 26	do	Unattached.
⊕ Thomas Drake, CMG. [53]	23 May 05	15 May 07	6 Feb. 28	22 April 13	16 Nov. 26	16 July 26	do	Unattached.
⊕ ⊞ Charles Yorke	29 Jan. 07	18 Feb. 08	24 Dec. 13	9 June 25	30 Nov. 26	9 June 26	do	Unattached.
⊕ Edward Jackson, KH.	8 Aug. 99	28 Feb. 03	20 Aug. 07	11 June 18	12 Dec. 26	12 Dec. 26	Major	Unattached.
⊕ John Hogge, KH.	3 Sept. 03	1 Aug. 05	9 Mar. 09	17 Dec. 18	do	do	do	Unattached.
⊕ Holman Custance	20 Oct. 08	22 Feb. 10	26 May 14	2 Sept. 24	do	do	Lieut.-Col.	Unattached.
John Henry Richardson	16 Aug. 09	3 Nov. 08	4 Dec. 17	14 July 25	do	do	do	10 Foot.
⊕ *Sir* John Row. Eustace, KH.	June 08	3 Nov. 08	17 Mar. 14	9 Nov. 21	10 Dec. 26	do	Cpt. & Lt. Cl.	Grenadier Guards.
Henry Stisted	8 Dec. 03	24 Jan. 05	5 Jan. 09	25 Sept. 23	do	19 Dec. 26	Lieut.-Col.	Unattached.
⊞ Berkeley Drummond	5 Mar. 12	never	4 July 15	never	21 Dec. 26	do	Cpt. & Lt. Cl.	Scots Fusilier Guards.
⊕ ⊞ John James Snodgrass [54]	9 May 12	7 April 13	22 Dec. 25	14 Nov. 26	25 Dec. 26	28 June 33	Lieut.-Col.	{ Unattached, *Deputy Quar. Mast. Gen. Nova Scotia.* }
⊕ *Hon. Sir* Edward Cust, KCH.	15 Mar. 10	27 Dec. 10	9 Dec. 13	24 Nov. 26	26 Dec. 26	26 Dec. 26	do	Unattached.
Dennis Daly	28 Aug. 00	15 Jan. 01	13 May 07	19 July 21	30 Dec. 26	30 Dec. 26	do	Unattached.
William Chamberlayne	19 Aug. 06	18 Dec. 06	9 May 11	1 July 24	do	do	do	Unattached.
William Leader Maberly	never	23 Mar. 15	14 May 18	19 May 25	9 Mar. 26	9 Mar. 32	do	Unattached.
Henry Salwey	13 June 11	never	20 July 15	never	do	6 Aug. 29	do	Unattached,

Lieutenant-Colonels.

	CORNET, ETC.	LIEUT.	CAPTAIN.	MAJOR.	LIEUT.-COLONEL.	WHEN PLACED ON HALF PAY.	REGIMENTAL RANK.	
Henry Dwyer...........	11 Feb. 13	10 Nov. 14	13 June 19	10 Sept. 25	10 Jan. 27	10 Sept. 25	Major	Unattached.
John Gurwood, CB.[55]	30 Mar. 08	3 Aug. 08	6 Feb. 12	6 Mar. 17	15 Mar. 27	20 July 30	do	Unatt. *Deputy Lieut. of the Tower.*
Jeremiah Taylor[56]....	28 Feb. 05	1 Oct. 07	2 Oct. 17	1 April 24	22 Mar. 27	31 May 31	Lieut.-Col.	Unattached.
John Elliott Cairnes, KH.	2 Oct. 03	22 Nov. 04	1 Feb. 12	26 May 25	29 Mar. 27	29 Mar. 27	do	Unattached.
Francis John Davies...	3 Feb. 08	26 Jan. 09	12 Aug. 13	never	30 April 27		Cpt.&Lt.Cl	Grenadier Guards.
John Home........	19 Jan. 13	never	30 June 15	never	10 May 27		do	Grenadier Guards.
Sir Henry Robartes Wyatt[57]	22 Sept. 12	22 Nov. 13	11 Nov. 19	never	21 May 27	26 Dec. 37	Lieut.-Col.	Unattached.
John Fraser[58].........	19 April 09	12 Sept. 11	28 Jan. 13	31 Oct. 18	24 May 27	16 Aug. 27	Major	{ Half-pay 1 Royal Vet. Bn. Dep. Quar. Mast. Gen. Ceylon.
John Frederick Crewe	27 June 05	13 Feb. 06	7 July 14	never	5 June 27	5 June 27	Lieut.-Col.	Unattached.
Jonathan Peel	15 June 15	3 Dec. 18	13 Dec. 21	19 May 25	7 June 27	9 Aug. 27	do	Unattached.
Geo. Douglas Standen	19 Mar. 12	never	6 July 15	never	12 July 27		Cpt.&Lt.Cl.	Scots Fusilier Guards.
John Peddie, KH.	26 Sept. 05	26 Aug. 07	23 Sept. 13	16 June 25	8 Aug. 27		Lieut.-Col.	90 Foot.
John Shelton ...	21 Nov. 05	26 Aug. 07	17 June 13	6 Feb. 25	6 Sept. 27		do	44 Foot.
Thomas Bell, CB.	13 Nov. 99	17 Jan. 01	12 Sept. 05	26 Aug. 13	20 Sept. 27		do	48 Foot.
Charles King, KH.	9 May 05	30 Jan. 06	18 Feb. 13	2 June 25	27 Oct. 27		do	Insp. Field Officer Rec. District.
William Roberts[59]	1 Dec. 95	22 April 97	24 Oct. 03	4 June 14	6 Nov. 27		do	Late of Royal Artillery.
Sir Henry Fairfax, *Bart.*	21 April 08	23 Nov. 09	22 July 13	17 July 23	do		do	Unattached.
Marcus Beresford	4 Sept. 17	1 Feb. 21	16 Sept. 24	26 Sept. 26	do		do	3 Foot.
James Chas. Chatterton, KH.	23 Nov. 09	6 June 11	26 Mar. 18	22 July 24	18 Dec. 27	6 Nov. 27	do	4 Dragoon Guards.
John Vandeleur	6 July 09	30 May 11	28 Feb. 22	1 Oct. 25	do		do	10 Dragoons.
Robert Douglas, CB.[61]	1 Nov. 96	13 July 15	22 Oct. 18	4 June 25	25 Dec. 27	9 June 25	Major	Late of Royal Artillery.
James M'Alphine	4 May 15	1 Sept. 18	30 July 04	4 June 14	31 Dec. 27		Lieut.-Col.	Unattached.
Hon. Geo. Berkeley Molyneux	15 May 15	16 Nov. 15	31 Oct. 22	15 Aug. 26	do	31 Dec. 27	do	8 Dragoons.
James Alex. *Earl of* Rosslyn	25 Feb. 19	19 July 20	16 Nov. 16	28 Sept. 26	do		do	9 Dragoons.
Wm. Thomas Knollys	9 Dec. 13	never	25 Mar. 23	12 Dec. 26	do		Cpt.&Lt.Cl	Scots Fusilier Guards.
Walter Fred. O'Reilly, CB.	17 Oct. 11	6 Jan. 13	25 Sept. 17	never	18 Jan. 28	29 Jan. 29	Lieut.-Col.	Half-pay Royal African Corps.
Charles F. R. Lascelles.	10 Sept. 12	never	3 May 13	21 June 25	21 Feb. 28		Cpt.&Lt.Cl	Grenadier Guards.
Wm. Cuth. Elph. Holloway, CB.	1 Jan. 04	1 Mar. 05	9 June 14	never	17 Feb. 28		Lieut.-Col.	Royal Engineers.
Edward Studd	22 Feb. 16	17 July 17	24 June 09	21 June 17	26 Feb. 28	31 Aug. 38	do	Unattached.
Chas. Stuart Campbell, CB.[62]	7 Dec. 96	14 May 97	7 Aug. 23	26 Sept. 26	do		do	Half-pay 1 Foot.
Robert Bartley	28 Feb. 06	7 Oct. 10	15 May 04	21 April 14	25 April 28	27 Oct. 31	do	49 Foot.
George Thornhill, CB.[63]	24 Nov. 96	20 July 98	12 June 05	12 Aug. 15	5 Feb. 24		do	Late of 14 Foot.
					19 Aug. 28			
					1 May 28			

57

Lieutenant-Colonels.

Name	2D LIEUT. ETC.	LIEUT.	CAPTAIN.	MAJOR.	LIEUT.-COLONEL.	WHEN PLACED ON HALF PAY.	REGIMENTAL RANK.	
Henry Robert Ferguson	18 Mar. 18	25 Feb. 19	26 Sept. 22	19 Dec. 26	8 May 28		Cpt.&Lt.Cl.	Grenadier Guards.
Ernest Fred. Gascoigne	2 May 11	13 May 13	6 July 15	19 May 25	3 June 28	25 Feb. 39	Lt.-Col.	Unattached.
Dugald Campbell[64]	6 Dec. 96	16 July 99	29 July 04	4 June 14	17 June 28		do	Late of Royal Artillery.
James Considine, KH.[65]	18 May 09	27 Dec. 10	29 Aug. 10	11 July 26	1 July 28	6 May 36	do	Unattached.
George Hillier	23 Mar. 09	10 May 10	9 July 12	21 June 17	24 July 28		do	62 Foot.
Henry Craig	31 Dec. 99	5 Sept. 01	11 Feb. 08	27 May 25	do	15 Mar. 18	Captain	Half-pay 100 Foot.
Richard Beauchamp	14 Mar. 11	19 Feb. 12	6 July 20	13 Aug. 25	5 Aug. 28	9 Mar. 32	Lt.-Col.	Unattached.
Lovell Benj. Badcock, KH.	18 Dec. 05	19 May 08	12 Dec. 11	21 Jan. 19	21 Nov. 28		do	15 Dragoons.
Hon. Geo. Ralph Abercromby	never	26 June 17	14 Mar. 22	8 April 26	do	21 Nov. 28	do	Unattached.
Henry Armytage	27 Nov. 12	never	5 Mar. 18	never	do	24 Jan. 40	do	Half-pay, 22 Dragoons.
Hon. Arch. Montgomery Maxwell, KH.	1 July 01	17 May 03	1 Feb. 08	27 May 25	25 Nov. 28		do	36 Foot.
Hon. Augustus Fred. Ellis	10 April 17	17 Dec. 18	24 Oct. 21	12 Nov. 25	18 Dec. 28		do	60 Foot.
Peter Margetson Wallace	10 May 97	16 July 99	15 Nov. 04	4 June 14	30 Dec. 28		do	Royal Artillery.
St. John Augustus Clerke, KH.[66]	13 Oct. 08	6 June 11	11 Mar. 19	26 May 25	do	30 Dec. 28	do	Unattached.
Hugh William Barton	12 Nov. 12	7 July 15	5 Dec. 21	never	do	21 Mar. 29	Major	Royal Artillery.
Richard Jones	12 May 97	16 July 99	5 Dec. 04	4 June 14	31 Dec. 28		Lt.-Col.	Royal Artillery.
John Edward Jones	12 July 97	do	20 Dec. 04	do	do		do	Royal Artillery.
Henry Du Vernet	22 Dec. 03	12 Sept. 09	30 May 09	2 June 25	1 July 29		do	Half-pay Royal Staff Corps.
Robert Wallace, KH.	4 Dec. 06	25 Mar. 08	20 Oct. 14	5 Nov. 25	1 Dec. 29		do	Unattached.
Frederick Wm. Mann	9 Feb. 04	25 June 06	17 Dec. 12	17 Aug. 26	24 Sept. 29	31 Dec. 28	do	Half-pay Royal Staff Corps.
Henry Wm. Vavasour	1 Feb. 04	1 Mar. 05	24 June 09	never	do		do	Royal Engineers.
Thos. Perronet Thompson	23 Jan. 06	21 Jan. 08	7 July 14	9 June 25	28 Jan. 29	24 Feb. 29	do	Unattached.
Alexander Findlay, KH.	27 July 14	1 Feb. 16	24 Oct. 21	28 Dec. 26	19 Mar. 29	19 Mar. 29	do	Half-pay Royal African Corps.
James Holmes Schoedde	May 00	1 Oct. 01	19 Sept. 05	21 June 13	20 Mar. 29		do	55 Foot.
Hon. Henry Rich. Molyneux	22 May 17	24 Oct. 21	9 May 23	29 Aug. 26	9 April 29		do	60 Foot.
Hon. Standish O'Grady	21 Mar. 11	6 Aug. 12	20 July 15	29 Oct. 25	16 April 29		do	Unattached.
John Townsend	24 Jan. 05	8 Mar. 06	6 June 11	21 Jan. 19	14 April 29	14 April 29	do	14 Dragoons.
Henry John Wm. Bentinck	25 Mar. 13	never	18 Jan. 20	never	16 May 29		Cpt.&Lt.Cl.	Coldstream Guards.
William Bush, KH.	7 Jan. 08	29 June 09	22 July 13	8 April 26	22 May 29		Lieut.-Col.	1 West India Regiment.
George Graydon, KH.	1 June 04	1 Mar. 05	2 Dec. 09	never	do		do	Royal Engineers.
Frederick Thomas Buller	never	30 Dec. 13	6 Sept. 21	never	4 June 29	3 Feb. 32	do	Unattached.
James Dunbar Tovey	26 Oct. 99	3 July 00	9 Oct. 07	24 Jan. 19	11 Aug. 29	30 May 34	do	Unattached.
Bellingham John Smith	25 June 04	15 Feb. 05	15 June 11	27 May 19	do	11 Aug. 29	do	Unattached.
Thomas Reed	26 Aug. 13	2 May 15	19 Feb. 24	15 June 26	do		do	62 Foot.

Lieutenant-Colonels.

	CORNET, ETC.	LIEUT.	CAPTAIN.	MAJOR.	LIEUT.-COLONEL.	WHEN PLACED ON HALF PAY.	REGIMENTAL RANK.	
Henry Despard	25 Oct. 99	25 June 08	19 Nov. 06	12 Aug. 19	13 Aug. 29		Lient.-Col.	Insp. Field Officer Recruit. Dist.
⊕ ⚔ *Robert Macdonald*, CB. ...	10 Feb. 03	28 Oct. 08	8 Feb. 10	21 Sept. 13	25 Aug. 29		do	Late of 35 Foot.
⊕ Thos. Alston Brandreth, CB. ...	19 July 97	16 July 99	20 Dec. 04	4 June 14	27 Oct. 29		do	Royal Artillery.
Hon. Henry Dundas, CB.	never	18 Nov. 19	1 April 24	11 July 26	3 Dec. 29		do	83 Foot.
David Story	1 Sept. 97	18 July 99	1 Mar. 05	12 Aug. 19	10 Dec. 29		do	Royal Artillery.
⊕ ⚔ Joseph Logan	20 Dec. 99	8 Aug. 01	2 Feb. 09	18 June 15	17 Dec. 29		do	63 Foot.
⊕ Robert Thomson	1 Nov. 04	1 Mar. 05	10 July 10	never	26 Dec. 29		do	Royal Engineers.
Benj. Chapman Browne	17 June 13	2 Jan. 17	18 July 22	29 Aug. 26	16 Mar. 30	16 Mar. 30	do	Unattached.
Sir John Mark Fred. Smith, KH.	1 Dec. 05	1 May 06	11 May	never	do		do	Royal Engineers.
⊕ Rice Jones, KH.	1 Feb. 06	1 July 06	do	never	8 June 30		do	Royal Engineers.
⊕ ⚔ A. K. Clarke Kennedy, CB. KH.	8 Sept. 08	25 Dec. 13	13 Dec. 10	26 May 25	11 June 30		do	7 Dragoon Guards.
⊕ Saumarez Brock, KH.⁶⁷	1803	14 April 04	28 Mar. 05	12 Oct. 15	12 June 30	13 May 35	do	Half-pay 48th Foot.
⊕ Thomas Mackrell	19 Sept. 04	25 May 07	11 June 18	12 Nov. 25	25 June 30		do	44 Foot.
⊕ Henry Booth, KH.	6 Mar. 06	11 June 07	25 June 12	29 Aug. 22	29 June 30		do	43 Foot.
⊕ Edward Wells Bell	never	16 May 11	20 June 22	19 Dec. 26	do	29 June 30	do	Unattached.
Henry Colvile	29 Dec. 13	never	6 Nov. 17	never	6 July 30		Cpt.&Lt.Cl.	Scots Fusilier Guards.
Alexander Campbell, KH	24 Aug. 06	4 Sept. 13	13 Aug. 12	9 Aug. 21	16 July 30		Major	9 Dragoons.
⊕ Horatio George Broke	29 May 06	15 Feb. 08	18 Mar. 13	28 July 14	20 July 30	20 July 30	do	Unattached.
⊕ John Reed	26 Mar. 99	21 Mar. 00	12 May 08	27 May 25	do		Lient.-Col.	54 Foot.
John Moore, KH.⁶⁸	April 96	6 May 96	4 Aug. 04	4 Feb. 13	22 July 30	16 Jan. 35	do	Unattached.
⊕ James Jones, KH.	6 Nov. 01	23 Nov. 05	17 Aug. 08	14 April 13	do	31 Aug. 15	Captain	Half-pay 15 Dragoons.
Charles Milner	28 Mar. 05	19 Dec. 05	18 Jan. 10	do	do	24 Feb. 20	do	Half-pay 3 Foot.
William Fawcett	8 June 96	1 Nov. 96	7 Sept. 04	22 April 13	do	24 Feb. 18	Major	Half-pay 14 Foot.
Joseph Phillott ⁶⁹	12 Jan. 96	9 Nov. 96	9 July 03	27 May 13	do	25 June 17	do	Half-pay 35 Foot.
Sir Wm. M. Geo. Colebrooke, KH.	17 Aug. 03	12 Sept. 04	27 Sept. 10	1 June 13	do		Lieut.-Col.	R. Art. *Gov. of the Leeward Islands.*
Thomas Tisdal	never	10 Oct. 94	18 April 01	4 June 13	do		1st Lieut.	Late Royal Irish Artillery.
Maxwell Close	6 Dec. 98	8 Aug. 99	24 April 01	do	do	6 Dec. 14	Captain	Half-pay 1 Garrison Battalion.
William Henry Taynton	27 Feb. 94	1 April 95	4 July 01	do	do	7 Dec. 15	do	Half-pay 31 Foot.
Fountain Elwin	Apr. 98	10 May 98	14 Jan. 02	do	do	25 Mar. 16	Major	Half-pay 44 Foot.
Wm. Mansfield Morrison	10 July 99	14 Aug. 01	24 Aug. 02	do	do	8 Aug. 22	Captain	Half-pay 23 Dragoons.
Hugh John Cameron	27 Nov. 95	25 Nov. 96	1 Aug. 04	do	do	12 Aug. 24	Major	Half-pay York Chasseurs.
Edward Carlyon	24 Mar. 03	9 Feb. 05	25 July 05	do	do	25 Nov. 17	do	Half-pay 66 Foot.
⊕ ⚔ Patrick Campbell, CB.⁷⁰ ...	31 Aug. 97	1 Mar. 00	16 Aug. 04	21 June 13	do	14 May 18	Captain	Half-pay 52 Foot.
⊕ Thomas Weare, KH.	14 Sept. 04	25 June 05	19 April 10	do	do		Lieut.-Col.	Provisional Battalion *at Chatham*.

Lieutenant-Colonels.

Name	CORNET, ETC.	LIEUT.	CAPTAIN.	MAJOR.	LIEUT.-COLONEL.	WHEN PLACED ON HALF PAY.	REGIMENTAL RANK.	
Thomas Burke	1 Oct. 94	25 Oct. 99	12 Aug. 04	22 July 13	22 July 13	25 Feb. 16	Major	Half-pay 4 Foot.
Alexander Tod	5 Dec. 63	14 July 06	21 April 08	26 Aug. 13	do	25 Mar. 16	Captain	Half-pay 2 Garrison Bn.
Joseph Creighton	1 Jan. 01	17 Mar. 03	6 Nov. 06	23 Sept. 13	do	20 Sept. 19	Major	Half-pay 59 Foot.
Bayntun Stone[71]	25 Nov. 99	21 May 00	1 Dec. 04	22 Nov. 13	do	25 Dec. 18	Captain	Half-pay 58 Foot.
Thos. Samuel Trafford[72]	Nov. 03	7 Sept. 04	20 Mar. 06	do	do	27 May 24	Major	Half-pay 24 Foot.
Chas. Hamilton Smith, KH.	never	30 Dec. 97	18 Jan. 06	13 Dec. 13	do	25 Oct. 21	Captain	Half-pay 15 Foot.
James Lewis Basden, CB.	12 Jan. 00	17 Mar. 01	4 Sept. 06	30 Dec. 13				89 Foot.
Donald Campbell	24 July 00	22 Oct. 03	19 April 04	13 Jan. 14	do	25 Feb. 16	Major	Half-pay 79 Foot.
Henry Bristow	14 Feb. 05	30 Sept. 05	1 Sept. 08	20 Jan. 14	do	27 April 15	do	Half-pay 88 Foot.
James Poole Oates, KH.[73]	3 Mar. 97	12 May 97	19 Oct. 04	3 Mar. 14	do	26 Mar. 18	Captain	Half-pay 88 Foot.
Edw. Thos. Fitz Gerald, KH.[74]	13 June 06	16 May 06	28 Aug. 06	17 Mar. 14	do	25 Jan. 18	do	Half-pay 12 Foot.
Thomas Michell, CB.	8 Sept. 13	13 Sept. 13	11 Aug. 11	do	do		Lt.-Col	Royal Artillery.
Charles Pratt	10 Oct. 05	25 Aug. 07	28 Sept. 00	24 Mar. 14	do	1814	Major	Half-pay 96 Foot.
George Spottiswoode	4 Jan. 99	15 Aug. 99	19 June 06	31 Mar. 14	do	25 Feb. 16	do	Half-pay 71 Foot.
James Harvey, KH.	28 Feb. 03	7 Oct. 03	12 Oct. 08	12 April 14	do	1814	do	Half-pay 92 Foot.
Charles Campbell	27 Sept. 04	17 Mar. 04	14 July 08	do	do	25 Dec. 18	do	Half-pay 94 Foot.
Hamlet Obins	15 Aug. 04	25 Dec. 04	22 Dec. 08	do	do	29 Mar. 21	Captain	Half-pay 53 Foot.
William Cator	7 May 03	12 Sept. 03	1 May 09	do	do		Lt.-Col.	Royal Artillery.
George Tovey[75]	8 Nov. 05	21 Nov. 05	9 Nov. 09	do	do	7 Dec. 38	Major	Unattached.
James Horton	5 Aug. 99	16 May 01	23 July 07	18 May 14	do	30 Sept. 19	do	Half-pay Meuron's Regiment.
James Laing	Oct. 96	23 Nov. 96	7 Mar. 05	19 May 14	do	1814	do	Half-pay 61 Foot.
Edw. Anthony Angelo, KH.	9 July 03	28 Aug. 04	1 Dec. 06	2 June 14	do		Captain	Unattached.
John Bradish		3 Nov. 94	2 June 03	4 June 14	do	12 Dec. 34	do	Half-pay 2 Ceylon Regiment.
Geo. Saunders Thwaites	12 Sept. 95	23 Dec. 95	2 July 03	do	do	25 Nov. 21	do	Half-pay 57 Foot.
William Sall, KH.	30 Oct. 94	26 Nov. 94	9 July 03	do	do	6 Feb. 17	do	R. Newfoundland Vet. Companies.
Lord Robert Kerr, KH.	6 Sept. 98	29 Jan. 00	9 July 08	do	do		do	{ Half-pay 6 Garrison Bn. *Assist. Adjt. Gen. in North Britain.*
Nathaniel Hamilton English	14 Nov. 93	24 April 95	25 July 95	do	do		Lt.-Col.	Late of Royal Marines.
Richard Bunce[76]	27 Nov. 93	24 April 95	28 July 95	do	do	5 Aug. 33	do	Half-pay Royal Marines
John M'Mahon	25 Mar. 00	16 July 02	20 Aug. 02	do	do	29 Mar. 33	Major	Unattached.
Daniel O'Donoghue	never	1 Oct. 94	27 Aug. 94	do	do	6 Dec. 14	Captain	Half-pay 1 Garrison Bn.
Joseph Jerrard	13 May 95	1 June 97	8 Oct. 97	do	do	4 Feb. 15	do	Half-pay 6 Garrison Bn.
Robert Terry	Sept. 99	7 Mar. 00	8 Oct. 08	do	do	18 Aug. 25	do	H.-p. 31 Ft, *Town Adjt. of Malta.*
Colin Pringle	never	never	17 Nov.	do	do	25 Dec. 16	Major	Half-pay German Legion.

Lieutenant-Colonels.

	ENSIGN, ETC.	LIEUT.	CAPTAIN.	MAJOR.	LIEUT.-COLONEL.	WHEN PLACED ON HALF PAY.	REGIMENTAL RANK.	
John Thomas Whelan	29 Nov. 98	31 May 93	24 Nov. 03	4 June 14	22 July 30	25 June 16	Captain	H.-p. R. Newfoundland Fencibles.
※ Arthur Morris	30 May 94	23 Feb. 00	3 Dec. 04	do	do	8 Mar. 21	do	Half-pay 14 Foot.
※ Charles Süsted, KH.[77]	1 Mar. 98	6 Feb. 95	25 Feb. do	do	do	19 May 37	Lt.-Col.	Unattached.
※ John Michell, CB.	do	2 Oct. 99	20 Sept. 05	29 Sept. 14	do		do	Royal Artillery.
※ ⚜ Edw. Chas. Whinyates, CB. KH.		do	8 July 05	18 July 15	do		do	Royal Artillery.
※ ⚜ Thomas Hutchesson	1 Dec. 97	do	10 April 05	12 Aug. 19	do		do	Royal Artillery.
※ ⚜ Lonsdale Boldero	15 Sept. 09	never	20 Oct. 13	never			Cpt.&Lt.Cl.	Grenadier Guards.
※ ⚜ John Linton[78]	8 Sept. 08	25 Jan. 09	15 May 17	21 July 25	31 Aug. do	31 Aug. 30	Lt.-Col.	Unattached.
Courtenay Chambers	10 June 13	never	6 July 15	29 Oct. 25	do		do	25 Foot.
Charles Rowley	15 Jan. 18	27 May 19	13 June 22	22 April 26	do	31 Aug. 30	do	Unattached.
John Scott, CB.	4 May 15	26 Oct. 15	28 June 21	9 Nov. 26	do		do	4 Dragoons.
William Graham	29 May 17	13 Dec. 21	30 Jan. 23	18 Dec. 27	do	31 Aug. 30	do	Unattached.
	Aug. 00	25 Jan. 07	30 Aug. 10	21 Jan. 19	10 Sept.		do	33 Foot.
※ Charles Knight	12 Dec. 11	never	4 July 15	never	28 Sept.		Cpt.&Lt.Cl.	Grenadier Guards.
John Ord Honeyman	9 July 03	1 Aug. 04	16 May 09	25 Nov. 19	9 Nov.		Lt.-Col.	75 Foot.
※ Charles Barker Turner, KH.[79]	11 Sept. 06	12 Mar. 07	15 Oct. 12	16 Mar. 26	9 Nov.		Lieut.-Col.	Particular Service.
Thomas Moody	1 April 06	1 July 00	1 May 11	23 May 16	2 Dec.		do	Royal Engineers.
Jas. Thos. *Earl of* Cardigan	6 May 24	13 Jan. 25	9 June 26	3 Aug. 30	3 Dec.		do	11 Dragoons.
Godfrey Thornton	20 Jan. 14	never	11 Oct. 21	never	do		Cpt.&Lt.Cl.	Grenadier Guards.
※ William Cowper Coles[80]	31 Oct. 05	8 Feb. 07	19 Nov. 12	9 June 25	10 Dec.	20 Jan. 32	Lieut.-Col.	Unattached.
Sir Michael Creagh, KH.	9 May 02	28 Feb. 04	25 Nov. 09	24 Oct. 21	31 Dec.		do	86 Foot.
John Eden, CB.[81]	14 Feb. 07	14 Aug. 07	26 Dec. 18	9 Nov. 25	do	31 Dec. 30	do	Unatt. *Dep. Adjt. Gen. in Canada.*
Hon. Fra. Henry Needham	8 April 13	9 Dec. 13	24 Oct. 21	never 26	do		Cpt.&Lt.Cl.	Grenadier Guards.
※ ⚜ Richard Brunton	10 Oct. 08	12 Dec. 10	10 Nov. 13	2 Mar. 26	8 Feb.	31 14 Sept. 38	Lieut.-Col.	13 Dragoons.
※ Edmund Richard Story[82]	6 Oct. 15	11 Mar. 21	6 Dec. 21	15 April 22	do		do	Unattached.
※ ⚜ John Cross, KH.	9 July 05	29 May 06	31 Dec. 12	28 June 25	do	8 Feb. 31	do	68 Foot.
※ William Fraser[83]	10 June 13	19 July 15	23 Sept. 24	13 July 26	8 Mar.	8 Mar. 31	do	Unattached.
Robert Burdett	22 Oct. 18	7 June 19	4 Oct. 21	7 Nov. 26	8 Mar.	5 April	do	Unattached.
※ Charles Shee[84]	never	3 Sept. 07	18 Nov. 13	20 May 26	5 April	31 Dec. 33	do	H.-p. *Insp. Fld. Officer of Militia.*
George Teulon	17 Aug. 09	14 July 11	13 Mar. 17	17 Oct. 27	12 April	4 Sept. 35	do	Unattached.
※ Humphrey Robert Hartley[85]	8 Oct. 12	2 Sept. 13	29 Nov. 21	8 Nov. 27	26 April	26 April 31	do	Unattached.
Lord Edward Hay	31 Oct. 16	24 Oct. 21	29 Jan. 24	19 Sept. 26	26 April		Cpt.&Lt.Cl.	Grenadier Guards.
Henry William Barnard	9 June 14	never	15 Aug. 22	never	17 May		Lieut.-Col.	Royal Artillery.
※ Hamelin Trelawney	28 April 98	2 Oct. 99	28 Dec. 05	12 Aug. 19	27 May			

I

Lieutenant-Colonels.

	ENSIGN, ETC.	LIEUT.	CAPTAIN.	MAJOR.	LIEUT.-COLONEL.	WHEN PLACED ON HALF PAY.	REGIMENTAL RANK.	
Hugh Piper	29 Mar. 99	18 Nov. 06	13 June 11	10 June 28	28 May 31		Lieut.-Col.	38 Foot.
🞉 🞊 James Campbell, KH.[86]	12 June 99	25 Dec. 00	1 Aug. 05	12 Aug. 19	12 July 31		do	Unattached.
Charles Chichester	5 Mar. 11	4 Nov. 12	23 Dec. 24	29 Aug. 26	do		do	81 Foot.
Hon. Charles Grey	16 Nov. 20	10 April 23	16 June 25	19 Feb. 28	do		do	71 Foot.
🞊 Henry Webster	27 Mar. 10	13 June 11	14 Dec. 15	22 April 26	9 Aug. 26	22 April 26	Major	Unattached.
🞉 John Chester[87]	28 April 98	6 Oct. 99	29 Dec. 05	12 Aug. 19	3 Sept. 19	26 Oct. 31	Lieut.-Col.	Half-pay Royal Artillery.
William, Lord de Ros	29 Mar. 19	24 Aug. 21	23 Oct. 24	5 June 27	8 Sept. 27	5 June 31	Major	Unattached.
Manley Dixon[88]	3 Jan. 00	12 July 00	20 Oct. 05	12 Aug. 19	27 Sept. 19	27 Sept. 31	Lieut.-Col.	Unattached.
🞉 Arthur Hunt	11 Nov. 98	18 April 01	1 June 06	12 April 26	26 Sept. 26		do	Royal Artillery.
🞉 John Geddes, KH.[89]	Aug. 04	25 Oct. 05	1 Dec. 08	24 Feb. 25	11 Nov. 30	11 Nov. 31	do	Unattached.
🞉 🞊 John Oldfield, KH.	2 Mar. 06	1 July 06	1 May 11	22 July 30	2 Nov. 30		do	Royal Engineers.
🞉 🞊 Robert Anderson, KH.	9 July 03	12 Oct. 04	30 April 12	23 Sept. 24	2 Dec. 24		do	91 Foot.
William Henry Cornwall	never	10 Aug. 15	6 Nov. 24	never	10 Feb. 32		Cpt.&Lt.Cl.	Coldstream Guards.
George Alexander Reid	7 Mar. 18	20 Mar. 21	11 Nov. 24	23 July 31	17 Feb.		Ma.&Lt.Cl.	2 Life Guards.
Charles Fitz Roy Maclean	never	16 Aug. 16	18 Oct. 21	1 Aug. 26	16 Mar.	25 Oct. 39	Cpt.&Lt.Cl.	Unattached.
Philip Spencer Stanhope	30 Mar. 15	never	17 July 23	never	do		Cpt.&Lt.Cl.	Grenadier Guards.
Charles Collins Blane	never	4 July 15	31 July 23	19 Sept. 26	20 April	20 April 32	Lieut.-Col.	Unattached.
Brinckman Broadhead	never	11 Sept. 17	28 Apr. 25	never	do		Cpt.&Lt.Cl.	Coldstream Guards.
William Nesbitt Burrowes	12 Mar. 18	29 Dec. 21	17 Feb. 25	31 Dec. 27	27 April	27 April 32	Lieut.-Col.	Unattached.
Philip Dundas	24 July 23	17 Sept. 25	11 July 26	3 Dec. 30	27 June	do	do	Unattached.
🞉 Alexander Maclachlan	3 Dec. 03	6 Dec. 03	17 June 12	22 July 30	1 June		Captain	Royal Artillery.
🞉 Edward French Boys	17 Nov. 08	3 April 10	8 June 15	3 Feb. 29	21 June		Lieut.-Col.	45 Foot.
Charles Murray Hay	20 April 20	1 Nov. 21	24 Dec. 25	never	22 June		Cpt.&Lt.Cl.	Coldstream Guards.
William H. Dennie, C.B.	1 Jan. 00	4 Aug. 04	4 Oct. 10	19 Apr. 21	6 July		Lieut.-Col.	13 Foot.
🞉 William Elliot, KH.[90]	26 Nov. 07	28 Jan. 08	9 Oct. 11	2 May 22	13 July	13 July 32	Major	Unattached.
John Lyster	27 April 15	never	6 Nov. 23	never	2 July		Cpt.&Lt.Cl.	Grenadier Guards.
Frederick Farquharson	17 Sept. 13	25 May 14	23 Sept. 19	29 June 30	7 Sept.		Lt.-Col.	7 Foot.
Edmund Henry Bridgeman	never	30 June 15	24 Oct. 21	23 June 25	14 Sept.	23 June 25	Major	Unattached.
🞉 Charles Gilmour[91]	21 April 14	3 Dec. 23	1 June 23	never	21 Sept.		Cpt.&Lt.Cl.	Scots Fusilier Guards.
🞉 Hon. Henry Montagu	20 Dec. 98	28 June 09	12 June 06	12 Aug. 10	27 Sept.		Lt.-Col.	Late of Royal Artillery.
Colin Campbell	26 May 08	never	9 Nov. 13	26 Nov. 25	26 Oct.		do	98 Foot.
🞉 Henry Gooch	23 July 12	28 Oct. 19	28 Oct. 19	never	26 Nov.		Cpt.&Lt.Cl.	Coldstream Guards.
🞉 🞊 Everard Wm. Bouverie	2 April 12	15 Oct. 12	9 Sept. 19	6 May 31	4 Dec.		Major	Royal Horse Guards.
🞉 William Fendall	20 Sept. 08	3 Oct. 09	3 Feb. 20	2 June 25	24 Dec.		Lt.Col.	4 Dragoons.

Lieutenant-Colonels.

	ENSIGN, ETC.	LIEUT.	CAPTAIN.	MAJOR.	LIEUT.-COLONEL.	WHEN PLACED ON HALF PAY.	REGIMENTAL RANK.	
⚔ ⚜ Joseph Thomas Pidgeon[92]	17 Mar. 04	22 April 05	1 Dec. 08	21 Jan. 19	28 Dec. 32	30 Aug. 32	Lieut.-Col.	Unattached.
⚔ Charles Leslie, KH.[93]	18 Dec. 06	10 Feb. 08	5 Nov. 13	18 Dec. 28	do	28 Dec. 32	do	Unattached.
Henry Edward Porter	3 July 17	23 Dec. 19	14 July 25	4 Oct. 31	1 Feb. 33	1 Feb. 33	do	Unattached.
Lord Thomas Cecil	24 Oct. 16	30 Mar. 20	24 Oct. 22	28 June 27	5 April 33	15 June 38	do	Unattached.
Charles John Hill	12 Sept. 16	29 Mar. 21	29 July 20	24 Dec. 27	do	29 Oct. 37	do	Late of R. Marines.
John Wolrig[93*]	29 Oct. 95	30 Aug. 97	26 Nov. 05	12 Aug. 19	5 Aug.		Cpt.&Lt.Cl.	Scots Fusilier Guards.
Hon. John Craven Westenra	4 May 14	never	23 Sept. 24	never	9 Aug.		Lt.-Col.	63 Foot.
James W. Fairtlough	20 Aug. 02	24 May 04	14 Mar. 14	19 Sept.			do	Unattached.
⚔ ⚜ Charles Cadell, KH.[94]	7 Sept. 04	1 Aug. 05	9 Mar. 09	14 Dec. 26	27 Sept.	27 Sept. 33	do	87 Foot.
Henry C. Streatfield	Oct. 01	13 Nov. 01	7 Nov. 05	12 Aug. 19	4 Oct.		do	57 Foot.
George E. Jones, KH.	16 June 06	16 April 07	8 Oct. 12	22 July 30	8 Nov.		do	Unattached.
John Dawson Rawlon	12 Dec. 22	30 Jan. 26	10 June 26	never	15 Nov.		Cpt.&Lt.Cl.	Coldstream Guards.
William Persse, CB.	10 Jan. 06	27 Nov. 06	23 Jan. 12	25 May 22	6 Dec.	6 Dec. 33	do	16 Dragoons.
⚔ ⚜ William Beckwith, KH.[95]	1 July 15	12 May 15	9 May 22	14 Feb. 28	6 Dec.		Lieut.-Col.	Unattached.
Ferrars Loftus	13 Aug. 04	20 Nov. 23	never	never	27 Dec.		Cpt.&Lt.Cl.	Grenadier Guards.
James Macdonald Robertson[96]	28 May 06	7 Nov. 05	2 Mar. 20	14 Nov. 26	31 Dec.	31 Dec. 33	Lieut.-Col.	Unattached.
⚔ Henry Edward Robinson	3 May 21	9 Feb. 08	26 July 22	20 Sept. 27	1 Jan. 34		-do	30 Foot.
George Todd	22 Nov. 98	24 July 23	17 Sept. 25	22 Mar. 33	31 Jan.	31 Jan. 34	do	Unattached.
Adam Gordon Campbell	never	14 Oct. 00	29 Sept. 04	4 June 14	8 Feb.		do	16 Foot.
Hon. Edw. Gordon Douglas	11 July 31	31 Aug. 15	13 May 24	never	18 April	25 April 34	Cpt.&Lt.Cl.	Grenadier Guards.
Francis Venables Harcourt	18 July 22	26 Mar. 17	8 July 24	2 May	2 May		Lieut.-Col.	Unattached.
Hon. Henry Sutton Fane	never	27 Nov. 22	23 Nov. 25	18 Dec. 28	9 May	9 Feb. 38	Cpt.&Lt.Cl.	Grenadier Guards.
William Greenwood	16 Mar. 15	18 April 27	18 Nov. 24	never	do		Lieut.-Col.	4 Foot.
Henry William Breton	4 Aug. 10	27 July 20	21 July 25	31 Dec. 28	11 July		do	13 Dragoons.
⚔ ⚜ Allan T. Maclean	1 Aug. 99	11 July 31	23 Dec. 18	29 Oct. 30	do		do	Royal Artillery.
Stephen Kirby	18 Feb. 08	28 Dec. 09	1 June 00	12 Aug. 19	20 July			} Unatt. Dep.-Qr.-Mast.-Gen. in the Windward & Leeward Islands.
⚔ ⚜ John Tyler, KH.[97]	20 Mar. 23	1 July 27	11 Feb. 14	18 June 15	12 Aug.	12 Aug. 34	Major	Unattached.
Arthur *Marquis of* Douro	4 Oct. 10	12 May 12	8 May 28	2 Nov. 30	do	do	Lieut.-Col.	Unattached.
⚔ ⚜ George Gawler, KH.[98]	16 Jan. 06	11 Oct. 07	9 June 25	8 Feb. 31	do	do	do	Unatt. *Gov. of South Australia.*
Francis Fuller	never	9 April 18	13 Feb. 07	22 July 30	22 Aug.		do	59 Foot.
John Julius Wm. Angerstein	25 June 25	15 Sept. 04	2 April 25	12 Sept.	12 Sept.		Cpt.&Lt.Cl.	Grenadier Guards.
⚔ Alexander Cairncross, KH.	6 May 13	28 Dec. 15	7 June 10	10 June 26	19 Sept.		Lieut.-Col.	96 Foot.
Henry Senior			24 April 28	12 Mar. 29	do		do	65 Foot.

63

Lieutenant-Colonels.

	ENSIGN, ETC.	LIEUT.	CAPTAIN.	MAJOR.	LIEUT.-COLONEL.	WHEN PLACED ON HALF PAY.	REGIMENTAL RANK.	
George Cobbe	9 Oct. 99	7 Sept. 01	2 June 06	12 Aug. 19	20 Nov. 34		Lt.-Col.	Royal Artillery.
Peter Edmonstone Craigie	3 June 13	29 Sept. 14	24 Oct. 21	10 Aug. 26	21 Nov.		do	55 Foot.
⊕ Cudbert French, KH.	3 Sept. 12	1 Apr. 14	10 June 24	22 June 32	19 Dec.		do	28 Foot.
William Burke Nicolls	10 June 95	4 April 98	3 Aug. 04	4 June 14	12 Jan.		do	2 West India Regiment.
Thomas Fletcher	28 July 03	13 Mar. 05	12 Mar. 10	6 Dec. 27	27 Feb.		do	Ceylon Rifle Regiment.
Robert Ferguson	24 Feb. 20	2 Jan. 23	7 July 25	31 Aug. 30	13 Mar.		do	79 Foot.
⊕ James Macpherson	1 Mar. 08	28 Feb. 10	25 April 15	6 July 32	27 Mar.		Cpt.&Lt.Cl.	Ceylon Rifle Regiment.
Hon. Thomas Ashburnham	never	30 Jan. 23	22 June 26	never	do		Lt.-Col.	Coldstream Guards.
John Wilson Kettlewell 99	13 Dec. 99	14 Oct. 01	24 Oct. 06	12 Aug. 19	6 May		do	Late of Royal Artillery.
⊕ Thomas Marten, KH	20 Nov. 13	23 June 17	4 May 22	12 Dec. 26	29 May		do	1 Dragoons.
Alex. Cavalie Mercer	20 Dec. 99	1 Dec. 01	3 Dec. 06	12 Aug. 19	5 June		do	Royal Artillery.
Sir John Montagu Burgoyne, Bart.	17 Oct. 16	1 Oct. 18	28 April 25	never	do		Cpt.&Lt.Cl.	Grenadier Guards.
Matthew Charles Dixon	2 April 06	1 July 06	1 May 11	22 July 30	25 June		Lt.-Col.	Royal Engineers.
Patrick Doul Calder	1 Aug. 06	1 Dec. 06	13 May 11	do	do		do	Royal Engineers.
George Marshall 100	8 Nov. 95	30 Aug. 97	1 Jan. 06	12 Aug. 19	17 July		do	Late of Royal Marines.
Philip James Yorke	5 May 14	never	24 Feb. 25	never	7 Aug.		Cpt.&Lt.Cl.	Scots Fusilier Guards.
⊕ Joseph Jones	31 Jan. 11	5 Feb. 14	25 Sept. 23	8 Oct. 30	28 Aug.		Lt.-Col.	12 Foot.
⊕ Brooke Firman 101	8 Aug. 99	29 Nov. 99	28 Nov. 05	12 Aug. 19	25 Sept.	25 Sept. 35	do	Unattached.
⊕ Thomas Gerrard Ball	17 Sept. 07	1 Dec. 08	27 April 14	24 June 24	2 Oct.		do	8 Foot.
⊕ Eaton Monins	1 Dec. 14	9 Sept. 19	23 June 25	19 Nov. 30	do		do	(63) Foot.
Charles Hughes	25 May 96	11 May 97	28 Aug. 04	4 June 14	10 Oct.		do	24 Foot.
⊕ Samuel Bolton	5 Feb. 07	6 April 09	24 Oct. 22	14 June 33	24 Nov.		do	31 Foot.
⊕ ⊕ John Charles Hope, KH.	8 Jan. 07	2 Feb. 09	9 Nov. 20	22 July 30	4 Dec.		do	Rifle Brigade.
William James	8 Dec. 03	23 Nov. 04	5 Nov. 12	25 April 28	25 Dec.		do	26 Foot.
Guy Carleton Coffin	1 July 00	11 Feb. 02	18 June 07	19 July 21	4 Feb.	36	do	Late of Royal Artillery.
⊕ William Cox, KH.102	6 June 05	19 Nov. 07	16 Sept. 13	1 Aug. 26	5 Feb.		do	Particular Service.
William Croker	27 Mar. 03	2 June 04	20 Nov. 12	12 Aug. 19	1 April		do	17 Foot.
Henry Capadose	24 Mar. 96	30 Oct. 99	24 Mar. 04	4 June 14	22 April		do	1 W. India Regt.
James Stokes Bastard	15 Nov. 00	12 May 02	1 Feb. 08	27 May 25	27 April		do	Royal Artillery.
Richard Frederick Hill	24 June 19	12 June 23	27 Aug. 25	11 June 30	13 May		do	53 Foot.
George Morton Eden	18 July 22	10 Sept. 25	12 Dec. 26	11 Oct. 31	20 May		Cpt.&Lt.Cl.	Scots Fusilier Guards.
George Dixon	never	20 Jan. 20	8 April 26	never	do		do	Scots Fusilier Guards.
⊕ Frederick Maunsell	16 Mar. 12	28 Jan. 13	24 June 19	14 Aug. 27	23 May		Lt.-Col.	85 Foot.
Thomas Cubitt	20 Dec. 00	11 June 02	1 Feb. 08	27 May 25	25 May		do	Royal Artillery.

Lieutenant-Colonels.

	CORNET, ETC.	LIEUT.	CAPTAIN.	MAJOR.	LIEUT.-COLONEL.	WHEN PLACED ON HALF PAY.	REGIMENTAL RANK.	
⊕ ⊕⊕ George Baker	6 July 09	15 Aug. 11	19 Oct. 20	18 July 26	3 June 36	18 July 26	Major	Unattached.
Cyprian Bridge	20 Dec. 00	8 Aug. 02	1 Feb. 08	27 May 25	4 June		Lt.-Col.	Royal Artillery.
Edw. Kent. S. Butler	27 Aug. 18	7 April 25	8 April 26	29 Mar. 33	17 June		do	35 Foot.
⊕⊕ Thomas Gore Browne	23 Feb. 01	12 Nov. 02	1 Feb. 08	27 May 25	1 July		do	Royal Artillery.
George William Eyres	never	3 Dec.	18 26 May	never	do		Cpt.&Lt.Cl.	Grenadier Guards.
William John Codrington	22 Feb. 21	24 April 23	20 July 26	never	8 July		do	Coldstream Guards.
Duncan Grant	23 Feb. 01	23 Nov. 02	1 Feb. 08	27 May 25	12 July		Lt.-Col.	Royal Artillery.
Francis Copland	10 Aug. 20	27 Sept. 21	7 July 25	12 April 33	15 July	15 July 36	do	Unattached.
Henry Alexander Scott	28 April 01	20 April 03	1 Feb. 08	27 May 25	10 Aug.		do	Royal Artillery.
⊕ William Wylde	8 Sept. 03	6 Dec. 03	16 Mar. 12	16 July 30	19 Aug.		do	Royal Artillery.
John Cade Petley	1 Oct. 01	13 June 03	1 Feb. 08	27 May 25	11 Nov.		do	Royal Artillery.
⊕ ⊕⊕ William Turnor 103	15 Aug. 04	23 May 05	15 Aug. 11	19 Dec. 26	22 Nov.	22 Nov. 36	Major	Unatt. Dep. Adjt. Gen. in Jamaica.
Edmund Morris	21 June 10	21 April 13	1 Dec. 25	13 Sept. 33	do		Lt.-Col.	49 Foot.
William Fludyer	30 Dec. 19	25 Oct. 21	7 July 25	never	2 Dec.		Cpt.&Lt.Cl.	Grenadier Guards.
⊕ ⊕⊕ John Ross 104	1 July 03	1 Nov. 05	15 April 13	5 Nov. 25	9 Dec.	9 Dec. 36	Lieut.-Col.	Unattached.
John Wharton Frith	17 July 04	27 Feb. 05	29 Jan. 12	22 July 30	16 Dec.		do	58 Foot.
Thomas Falls	21 Mar. 05	4 Dec. 06	23 Sept. 13	29 Sept. 14	23 Dec.	23 Dec. 36	Major	Unatt. Dep.-Adjt-Gen. Windward and Leeward Islands.
Ambrose Lane	1783	15 Sept. 94	18 Feb. 04	4 June 14	10 Jan. 37	25 Jan. 21	Captain	Half-pay 44 Foot.
Anthony Lyster	24 Sept. 94	15 Dec.	24 Feb.	do	do	1 June 26	Major	Unattached.
John Charles Smith	31 Aug. 99	19 June 00	24 April	do	do	16 July 30	do	Unatt. Assist.-Adjt.-Gen.in Ireland.
Nathaniel Bean	25 Nov. 99	10 Sept. 01	2 June	do	do	16 Feb. 15	Captain	Half pay 49 Foot.
John Austen, K.H. 105	28 June 96	19 Jan. 97	4 Aug.	do	do	4 May 26	Major	Unattached.
Jacob Watson	15 Feb. 98	30 Aug. 99	5 Aug.	do	do	do	do	Unattached.
Henry Nooth	never	27 July 99	22 Aug.	do	do	26 Mar. 18	Captain	Half-pay 14 Foot.
James M'Haffie	7 Sept. 97	1 Feb. 98	24 Aug.	do	do	26 Nov. 18	do	Half-pay 60 Foot.
Joseph Dacre Lacy	5 Aug. 99	17 Dec. 99	27 Aug.	do	do	25 Dec. 16	do	Half-pay 2 Garrison Battalion.
Alexander Daniel	18 April 96	28 Jan. 97	19 Sept.	do	do	1814	do	Half-pay 63 Foot.
John Blackmore	15 April 94	1 Sept. 95	23 Oct.	do	do	25 Feb. 16	Major	Half-pay 8 Foot.
George Dods	1 Sept. 95	2 July 97	25 Oct.	do	do	20 June 16	Captain	Half-pay 1 Foot.
George Jackman Rogers	5 Mar. 95	9 July 03	26 Oct.	do	do	11 May 26	Major	Unattached.
Robert Blake Lynch	1 Nov. 96	1 April 97	23 Nov.	do	do	26 Feb. 28	do	Unattached.
Charles Cranstoun Dixon	16 Dec. 95	24 Aug. 97	6 Dec.	do	do	do	do	Superintend. of Hosps. at Chatham.
Henry Blake	1 Mar. 00	30 Oct. 00	Dec.	do	do	4 Feb. 15	Captain	Half-pay 6 Garrison Batt.

Lieutenant-Colonels.

	ENSIGN, ETC.	LIEUT.	CAPTAIN.	MAJOR.	LIEUT.-COLONEL.	WHEN PLACED ON HALF PAY.	REGIMENTAL RANK.	
Eyre Evans Kenny	13 Jan. 96	13 Dec. 96	24 Dec. 04	4 June 14	10 Jan. 37	27 July 26	Major	Unattached.
William Burton Tylden	19 Nov. 06	1 May 07	15 April 12	23 June	do	11 May 26	Lieut.-Col.	Royal Engineers.
Francis Campbell	15 Mar. 99	30 Nov. 01	21 Nov. 05	25 July	do	25 Feb. 16	Major	Unattached.
Colin Campbell Mackay	9 July 03	4 Nov. 03	9 July 05	11 Aug.	do	25 June 16	do	Half-pay 78 Foot.
Wm. Brewse Kersteman	31 Dec. 00	24 July 02	24 Jan. 05	18 Aug.	do		Captain	Half-pay 10 Foot.
✪ Thomas Blanshard, CB. [106]	28 Sept. 07	1 Apr. 08	21 July 13	29 Sept.	do		Lieut.-Col.	Royal Engineers.
John Falconer Briggs, KH. [106]	9 July 03	31 Oct. 05	18 Jan. 10	8 Dec.	do	25 Dec. 14	Major	Half-pay 28 Foot.
✪ Robert Simson, KH.	8 Dec. 03	9 June 04	17 Aug. 09	8 Jan.	do	11 Jan. 21	Captain	Half-pay 18 Ft. *Town Maj. of Hull*
William Moore	25 July 00	16 May 02	29 May 06	23 Mar. 15	do	31 Oct. 19	do	Half-pay 14 Foot.
Peter Mathewson	9 Feb. 03	4 May 04	15 June 08	27 April	do	25 Dec. 18	do	Half-pay Royal York Rang.
Archibald Cameron	14 July 96	3 Nov. 99	9 May 05	4 May	do	28 Mar. 16	do	Half-pay 5 Foot.
Hon. Edward Cadogan	4 Dec. 06	26 Feb. 08	4 Jan. 10	25 May	do	19 Dec. 16	do	Half-pay 8 West India Regiment.
✪ Edward Knight [107]	22 Dec. 03	18 Sept. 06	21 June 10	6 June	do	25 Dec. 16	Captain	Half-pay Portuguese Service.
✪ Cassius Matthew Clanchy [108]	2 Dec. 02	5 July 04	20 June 11	do	do	do	Major	Half-pay Portuguese Service.
✪ Samuel Reed	5 Feb. 01	24 July 03	29 Nov. 06	18 June	do	25 Oct. 21	Lieut.-Col.	Royal Artillery.
✪ Thomas Dyneley, CB.	1 Dec. 03	1 July 06	28 May 08	do	do		Captain	*Royal Military College.*
✪ Charles Diggle, KH. [109]	31 Aug. 04	14 Feb. 05	24 May 10	9 July	do	16 Nov. 20	do	Half-pay Portuguese Service.
✪ Richard Croker	27 June 05	2 Jan. 06	9 July 12	do	do	18 May 26	Major	Unattached.
✪ Robert Kennedy	25 May 03	14 Sept. 04	1 Sept. 13	do	do	5 July 31	do	Unattached.
Adam Giffard Downing	24 July 03	1 Aug. 05	11 July 11	4 Dec.	do	25 Feb. 16	do	Half-pay 81 Foot.
John Blake Lynch	26 June 99	7 Mar. 00	26 Dec. 05	21 Dec. 16	do	1 June 26	do	Unattached.
John Murray Belshes	21 Oct. 95	26 Oct. 99	21 Aug. 05	23 May	do	4 May 26	do	Unattached.
✪ William Reid, CB.	14 Nov. 04	29 Aug. 05	4 Sept. 12	20 Mar. 17	do		Captain	Royal Engineers, *Gov. of Bermuda.*
Edward Knox	10 Feb. 06	23 April 10	20 Dec. 14	do	do	10 April 23	do	Half-pay 2 Garrison Bn.
✪ John Babington	26 Oct. 04	14 Mar. 05	5 Nov. 07	21 June	do	21 Mar. 22	do	Half-pay 24 Dragoons.
Sir John Scott Lillie, CB. [110]	25 June 02	19 July 04	27 Dec. 09	do	do	27 Mar. 28	do	Half-pay 31 Foot.
Sir Frederick Watson	3 Mar. 07	29 Mar. 10	11 Nov. 13	do	do	25 Dec. 16	do	Half-pay Portuguese Service.
Sir Edward Brackenbury	9 July 03	7 Sept. 04	7 May 12	4 Sept.	do	10 Nov. 38	Major	Unattached.
✪ Benjamin Orlando Jones [111]	July 03	8 Dec. 03	23 July 12	do	do	6 July 26	do	Unattached.
✪ Thomas Peacocke	29 May 05	23 Oct. 06	9 Sept. 12	do	do	25 Dec. 16	Captain	Half-pay Portuguese Service.
✪ James De Lancey [112]	3 April 06	26 Aug. 08	26 Aug. 13	do	do	7 Dec. 38	Major	Unattached.
William Hulme	24 Jan. 05	18 Sept. 08	26 Feb. 13	24 Oct.	do		do	Half-pay Portuguese Service.
Bissell Harvey, KH.	25 Sept. 03	26 June 05	26 Aug. 13	23 Dec.	do		Captain	96 Foot. [*District.*
	9 Nov. 97	24 Feb. 04	11 April 11	16 May 18	do	25 Oct. 21	Captain	*Insp. Field Officer of a Recruiting*

Lieutenant-Colonels.

	2D LIEUT., ETC.	LIEUT.	CAPTAIN.	MAJOR.	LIEUT.-COLONEL.	WHEN PLACED ON HALF PAY.	REGIMENTAL RANK.	
❦ Wm. Leighton Wood, KH.	19 Nov. 03	24 April 04	1 Jan. 07	21 Jan. 19	10 Jan. 19	29 April 19	Captain	Half-pay 21 Foot.
❦ ❦ Henry Baynes, KH.[113]	23 Feb. 01	1 Sept. 02	1 Feb. 08	do	do	12 Dec. 26	Major	Half-pay Royal Artillery.
❦ ❦ Alexander Barton, KH.	1 Aug. 05	7 May 07	17 Jan. 11	do	do	do	do	12 Dragoons.
❦ Wm. Bolden Dundas, CB.	8 Sept. 03	12 Sept. 03	11 July 11	do	do	do	Lieut.-Col.	Royal Artillery.
❦ William Mackay	24 Nov. 04	25 May 04	9 Jan. 12	do	do	12 April 21	Captain	Half-pay 60 Foot.
❦ ❦ William Tomkinson	9 July 07	6 Oct. 08	12 Mar. 12	do	do	8 Nov. 21	do	Half-pay 24 Dragoons.
❦ ❦ William Webber[114]	8 Sept. 03	6 Dec. 03	17 April 12	do	do	28 Aug. 26	Major	Half-pay Royal Artillery.
❦ John Neave Wells, CB.	6 Nov. 06	1 May 07	20 May 12	do	do	do	Lieut.-Col.	Royal Engineers.
❦ ❦ Sir Digby Mackworth, Bt. KH.	never	9 July 07	16 July 12	do	do	13 Aug. 30	Major	Unattached.
❦ ❦ John Browne[115]	21 Oct. 04	28 Feb. 05	25 May 15	do	do	10 Feb. 37	do	Unattached.
❦ ❦ William Brereton, CB. KH.	10 May 05	1 June 06	30 Sept. 16	do	do	do	Captain	Royal Artillery.
William Bennett	22 Oct. 99	23 Jan. 00	14 Feb. 05	12 Aug. 19	do	1 June 26	Major	Unattached.
Samuel Fox	5 April 01	25 June 03	28 Mar.	do	do	11 May 26	do	Unattached.
❦ ❦ John Crowe, KH.[116]	30 May 00	2 April 03	30 May	do	do	4 May 26	Captain	2 West India Regiment.
Thomas Maling	9 July 98	7 Sept. 04	11 July	do	do	do	do	Half-pay 3 West India Regiment.
James Ross	1 June 98	1 Feb. 00	23 Aug.	do	do	19 Oct. 19	Major	Unattached.
John Bazalgette	29 July 96	26 April 99	17 Oct.	do	do	13 Aug. 30	do	Half-pay 84 Foot.
Charles Collis	23 Jan. 00	24 June 02	31 Oct. 05	do	do	9 Dec. 19	Captain	Unattached. 98 Foot.
Peter Tripp	2 Sept. 02	3 Sept. 03	6 Nov. 06	do	do	25 Oct. 21	do	Half-pay 27 Foot.
❦ Charles Pepper	26 May 03	5 Jan. 04	2 Jan.	do	do	25 Aug. 21	do	Half-pay 32 Foot.
❦ Carlisle Spedding	12 June 99	7 Aug. 00	17 July	do	do	19 Sept. 26	Major	Unattached.
William Green, KH.	16 Feb. 97	25 July 99	26 July	do	do	1 June 26	do	Unattached.
Daniel Baby	9 Nov. 97	10 May 99	6 Aug.	do	do	25 Dec. 21	Captain	Half-pay 63 Foot.
Hugh M'Gregor	9 Feb. 04	25 Mar. 05	17 Aug.	do	do	7 July 25	do	Half-pay 16 Foot.
Charles Lionel FitzGerald	2 Jan. 04	23 Aug. 06	23 Aug.	do	do	20 July 26	Major	Unattached.
James Anton	7 Nov. 00	25 July 03	6 Sept.	do	do	1 June 26	do	Unattached.
Dunlop Digby	20 Sept. 98	17 July 00	16 Sept.	do	do	13 Aug. 30	do	Unattached.
❦ ❦ Thomas Cox Kirby[117]	1 Mar. 00	26 May 03	25 Sept. 06	do	do	17 Aug. 26	do	Unattached.
Richard Cole	23 Dec. 95	27 Feb. 96	25 Nov.	do	do	18 May 26	do	Unattached.
Joshua Crosse	30 Nov. 99	25 June 03	1 Dec.	do	do	do	Captain	Half-pay Malta Regiment.
John George Nathaniel Gibbes	15 Feb. 04	28 Mar. 05	2 Dec.	24 Aug.	do	20 Jan. 20	Major	Half-pay 98 Foot.
Thomas Buck	11 Oct. 98	18 Sept. 00	16 June 03	17 Feb.	do	20 June 22	Captain	Half-pay 74 Foot.
James Ballard Gardiner	3 Aug. 03	4 Jan.	20 July 09	17	20	do	do	
Thomas Jones	18 April 01	4 April 05	3 May 10	8 July	do	8 July 20	Major	Half-pay 21 Dragoons.

67

Lieutenant-Colonels.

	ENSIGN, ETC.	LIEUT.	CAPTAIN.	MAJOR.	LIEUT.-COLONEL.	WHEN PLACED ON HALF PAY.	REGIMENTAL RANK.	
George Nicholls	26 June 99	25 May 03	23 Feb. 09	5 July 21	10 Jan. 37	11 May 26	Major	Unattached.
Anthony Emmett	16 Feb. 08	24 June 09	21 July 13	do	do		Lt.-Col.	Royal Engineers.
William Crokat	9 April 07	30 June 08	31 Mar. 14	do	do	7 Nov. 26	Major	Unattached.
Daniel Wright	12 Nov. 02	3 Sept. 03	26 Feb. 07	19 July	do	4 May 26	do	Unattached.
Robert Bateman[118]	10 Mar. 04	3 July 05	5 Mar. 07	do	do	13 Aug. 30	do	Unattached.
Peter Dudgeon	4 April 00	3 Sept. 01	19 Mar. 07	do	do	4 May 26	do	Unattached.
Gerard Quill[119]	9 April 00	5 Feb. 01	12 April 07	do	do	29 July 36	do	Unattached.
William Hanbury Davies[120]	9 Sept. 99	18 May 00	16 July 07	do	do	20 July 30	do	Unattached.
John Mitchell	9 July 03	5 Dec. 04	1 Oct. 08	do	do	1 June 26	do	Unattached.
Stephen Cuppage	5 Nov. 03	30 June 04	15 Oct. 08	do	do	25 May 26	du	Unattached.
James Thomson[121]	1 Sept. 04	27 June 05	22 Oct. 08	do	do	15 May 27	do	Unattached.
Peter Jones	15 Mar. 96	20 Jan. 99	18 Nov. 09	do	do		do	Late of Royal Marines.
Charles Wright, KH.	never	never	Dec.	do	do		Captain	*Royal Military College.*
Noreliffe Noreliffe, KH.[122]	5 Feb. 07	25 April 08	29 Feb. 16	9 Aug.	do	22 May 23	Major	Half-pay 18 Dragoons.
Sir William Davison, KH.	never	never	25 Dec. 13	20 Oct.	do	25 Sept. 14	Captain	Half-pay 2 Foot.
Robert Martin Leake	2 Oct. 05	11 Dec. 06	14 Feb. 11	18 July 22	do	26 Feb. 24	Major	Unattached.
Edmund Yeamans Walcott	20 Dec. 02	12 Sept. 03	23 Mar. 09	15 Aug.	do		Lt.-Col.	Royal Artillery.
Abraham Josias Cloete, KH.	29 June 09	17 May 10	5 Nov. 12	21 Nov.	do	16 Mar. 20	Captain	Half-pay 21 Dragoons.
Charles Christopher Johnson	5 May 04	12 Sept. 05	18 Aug. 14	26 Dec.	do	30 Oct. 23	Major	Half-pay 10 Foot.
Henry Charles Russel	1 April 02	12 Sept. 03	15 July 08	27 May 25	do		Lt.-Col.	Royal Artillery.
Joseph Darby	1 July 02	do	22 Mar. 00	22 July 30	do		do	Royal Artillery.
Samuel Rudyerd	15 Mar. 03	do	24 Mar. 09	do	do		do	Royal Artillery.
Chas. Cornwallis Dansey, CB.	19 July 03	do	1 Oct. 09	do	do		do	Royal Artillery.
Daniel Bissett	do	do	22 Jan. 10	do	do		do	Royal Artillery.
Adam Fife Crawford	17 Aug. 03	do	3 Aug. do	do	do		do	Royal Artillery.
Henry William Gordon	do	do	do	do	do		do	Royal Artillery.
Richard Thomas King	8 Sept. 03	do	8 May 11	do	do		do	Royal Artillery.
William Daniel Jones	do	do	do	do	do		do	Royal Artillery.
Charles Dixon	7 Oct. 06	1 Dec. 06	1 May 11	do	do		do	Late of Royal Engineers.
William Henry Slade	1 Nov. 06	1 May 07	4 Mar. 12	do	do		do	Royal Engineers.
George Macdonald	5 Sept. 05	25 July 06	17 Aug. 15	13 Aug.	do		do	16 Foot.
Richard Zachary Mudge	4 May 07	14 July 07	21 July 13	never	do		do	Royal Engineers.
Archibald Walker	21 July 07	1 Mar. 08	do	never	do		do	Royal Engineers.
Sherburne Williams[123]	25 July 07	do	do	never	do		do	Late of Royal Engineers.

68

Lieutenant-Colonels.

	CORNET, ETC.	LIEUT.	CAPTAIN.	MAJOR.	LIEUT.-COLONEL.	WHEN PLACED ON HALF PAY.	REGIMENTAL RANK.	
ᛃ Frederick English	8 Sept. 07	1 April 08	21 July 13	never	10 Jan. 37		Lieut.-Col.	Royal Engineers.
Alexander Brown		1 Aug. 08	do	never	do		do	Royal Engineers.
ᛃ Philip Joshua Perceval	2 July 03	15 Aug. 05	10 Mar. 14	never	do		Cpt.&Lt.Cl.	Grenadier Guards.
ᛃ ᛃᛃ Wm. Frederick Johnston	12 D ec.1	never	16 Mar. 14	never	do		do	Grenadier Guards.
Ely Duodecimus Wigram	never	29 May 23	1 Aug. 26	never	13 Jan.		do	Coldstream Guards.
ᛃ ᛃᛃ John Cox, KH.124	16 Mar. 08	8 June 09	23 Dec. 19	19 Aug. 28	17 Feb.	17 Feb. 37	Lieut.-Col.	Unattached.
James Robertson Craufurd	14 June 21	29 Aug. 22	19 Sept. 26	never	18 Feb.		Cpt.&Lt.Cl.	Grenadier Guards.
William Stewart Balfour	8 Feb. 21	12 May 25	17 June 26	never	24 Feb.		do	Coldstream Guards.
ᛃᛃᛃ Joseph Wakefield	26 May 14	29 Aug. 15	29 July 19	27 May 34	10 Mar.		Lieut.-Col.	39 Foot.
ᛃᛃᛃ William Ross	7 Sept. 04	5 June 06	16 Dec. 13	29 Aug. 26	24 Mar.		do	23 Foot.
Narborough Baker	17 April 06	10 Mar. 08	18 Nov. 19	25 May 32	do		do	80 Foot.
Henry N. Douglas	23 Sept. 03	23 May 05	14 Dec. 11	22 Oct. 25	28 April		do	78 Foot.
Hon. Chas. Beaumont Phipps	never	17 Aug. 20	12 Oct. 26	never	26 May		Cpt.&Lt.Cl.	Scots Fusilier Guards.
Charles Cyril Taylor, CB.	26 May 23	26 May 25	11 July 26	27 Sept. 31	16 June		Lieut.-Col.	Particular Service.
George Gustavus Tuite	23 June 14	19 Oct. 20	5 May 25	25 Nov. 28	30 June	11 Oct. 39	do	Unattached.
ᛃ *Sir* Fra. Geary Gardner Lee	19 July 96	15 Jan. 01	2 Feb. 10	22 July 30	10 July		do	Royal Marines.
Edward Smith Mercer	25 Mar. 97	17 July 03	22 Sept. 10	do	do		do	Royal Marines.
William Walker	2 Sept. 97	3 Aug. 03	8 Jan. 12	do	do		do	Royal Marines.
John M'Callum	29 Jan. 96	18 Oct. 03	12 May 12	do	do		do	Commanding Royal Marine Artillery.
ᛃ Charles Menzies, KH.	17 Feb. 96	21 Dec. 03	13 April 13	10 Jan. 37	do		do	Royal Marines.
ᛃ Henry John Murton	1 May 98	18 Feb. 04	20 Oct. 13	do	do		do	Royal Marines.
William Fergusson	10 Sept. 98	29 April 04	23 Feb. 14	do	do		do	41 Foot.
William Booth	5 May 06	25 Mar. 09	3 May 21	28 June 27	11 July		do	Unattached.
James England	5 Aug. 19	12 Aug. 24	8 April 26	11 July 34	do	25 Jan. 39	Cpt.&Lt.Cl.	Coldstream Guards.
Hon. James Hope	never	8 April 24	30 Dec. 26	never	8 Aug.		do	Scots Fusilier Guards.
John George Robinson	never	23 Jan. 17	5 June 27	never	12 Aug.		Major	Unattached.
Richard Greaves 125	25 June 12	16 July 12	28 Oct. 24	8 May 28	29 Sept.	21 Jan. 37	Lieut.-Col.	Half-pay 11 Dragoons.
Henry Fane	30 May 22	15 May 23	30 Dec. 26	24 April 35	17 Oct.	19 Jan. 38	do	7 Dragoons.
John James Whyte	21 Aug. 23	22 Dec. 25	31 Dec. 27	5 April 33	21 Oct.		do	2 Dragoon Guards.
Charles Kearney	10 Sept. 12	8 Sept. 14	19 June 17	30 Dec. 26	28 Oct.		do	88 Foot.
ᛃ Robert O'Hara	29 Aug. 05	3 Dec. 07	4 April 11	14 May 29	10 Nov.	1 Dec. 37	Major	Unatt. *Dep.-Adj.-Gen. in Ceylon.*
ᛃ Edward Charleton, KH.126	26 Oct. 04	25 Sept. 06	22 June 09	22 July 30	17 Nov.		Lieut.-Col.	Unattached.
Alexander Maclean Fraser	8 Nov. 04	17 July 05	25 June 24	29 July 36	27 Nov.	10 Aug. 38	do	Unattached.
James Edward Freeth	19 May 13	23 April 14	17 April 17	24 Dec. 29	1 Dec.		do	64 Foot.

K

Lieutenant-Colonels.

	CORNET, ETC.	LIEUT.	CAPTAIN.	MAJOR.	LIEUT.-COLONEL.	WHEN PLACED ON HALF PAY.	REGIMENTAL RANK.	
William Cuthbert Ward	10 May 08	24 June 09	21 July 13	10 Jan. 37	9 Dec. 37		Lieut.-Col.	Royal Engineers.
Frederick Arabin	8 Sept. 03	12 Sept. 03	11 July 11	22 July 30	18 Dec.		do	Royal Artillery.
John Hall	12 June 17	24 July 22	2 Aug.	8 Sept. 31	27 Dec.		Maj.&Lt.Cl	Life Guards.
Richard Swale	24 Sept. 98	5 June 04	27 July	10 Jan. 37	do		Lieut.-Col.	Royal Marines.
*Marq. Guiseppe de Piro, CMG.	never	never	never	25 April 25	29 Dec.		do	Royal Malta Fencible Regiment.
Lord Charles Wellesley	16 Jan.	21 Nov. 24	26 Feb. 28	8 Sept. 30	31 do		do	15 Foot.
Charles Wyndham	13 May 13	4 May	15 24 June	14 12 Dec.	26 30 Dec.		do	2 Dragoons.
Joseph Walker	8 Dec. 98	18 Aug.	04 19 July	21 10 Jan.	37 1 Jan.		do	Royal Marines.
Frederick Clinton	never	19 Nov.	23 10 May	27 never	12 Jan.		Cpt.&Lt.Cl.	Grenadier Guards.
Richard Airey	15 Mar. 21	4 Dec.	23 22 Oct.	25 9 May	34 10 Feb.		Lieut.-Col.	34 Foot.
James Gordon	11 July 08	24 June	09 1 Sept.	13 10 Jan.	37 31 Mar.		do	Royal Engineers.
Sir Wm. Alexander Maxwell, Bart.	14 Dec. 09	15 Aug.	11 2 Feb.	15 31 Dec.	28 6 April	6 April 38	do	Unattached.
Thomas Peebles	12 June 99	18 Aug.	04 19 Dec.	22 10 Jan.	37 26 April		do	Royal Marines.
Francis Rawdon Chesney	9 Nov. 20	Sept.	05 20 June	15 2 Dec.	36 27 April		Captain	Royal Artillery.
Jeremiah Ratcliffe, KH.	11 April 11	11 Mar.	12 22 Feb.	27 27 July	32 9 June		Lieut.-Col.	6 Dragoons.
Thomas Hall	26 Sept.	06 29 Aug.	07 16 Sept.	13 19 Jan.	26 23 June		do	17 Foot.
Wm. Henry Elliott, KH.	6 Dec.	09 13 Aug.	12 9 Nov.	20 12 July	31 27 June		do	51 Foot.
David Graham	5 May	04 21 Nov.	05 11 Jan.	10 22 May	23 38 June	2 June 25	Major	Half-pay 56 Foot.
Peter Edwards	1 Oct. 07	3 June	09 17 Mar.	11 13 May	24 do	11 May 26	do	Unattached.
William Freke Williams, KH.	30 Aug. 10	10 June	11 31 Oct.	14 9 April	25 do		do	Particular Service.
William Cartwright [127]	2 July	12 6 Jan.	14 16 Nov.	20 19 May	do	19 May 25	do	Unattached.
John Garland, KH. [128]	14 Mar. 05	4 Nov.	06 26 Nov.	13 26 May	do	26 May 25	do	Unattached.
Robert Fraser, KH.	4 Aug.	00 21 Jan.	01 1 Jan.	08 27 May	do	20 Mar. 23	Captain	H.-p. 93 Foot, Fort-Maj. of Jersey.
Richard Weld Hartstonge	26 Mar. 99	17 May	00 7 Jan.	do	do	7 Nov. 26	Major	Unattached.
William Miller, KH.	1 Oct.	01 13 June	03 1 Feb.	do	do	29 Aug.	do	Half-pay Royal Artillery.
John Campbell	9 July	03 17 Mar.	04 5 May	do	do		Lieut.-Col.	97 Foot.
Hardress Robert Saunderson	15 June	04 18 Feb.	06 do	do	do	30 Sept. 26	Major	Unattached.
William Parry Yale [129]	24 Sept.	05 16 Dec.	06 17 May	do	do	1 June 26	do	Unattached.
Donald Urquhart	25 Mar.	01 17 Sept.	03 21 May	do	do		do	39 Foot.
Charles Hervey Smith	7 May	05 26 Dec.	05 26 May	do	do	25 Feb. 26	Captain	Half-pay 40 Foot.
William Henry Newton, KH.	20 June	00 25 Dec.	00 25 June	do	do	11 May 26	Major	Unattached.
Nicholas Lawson Darrah	16 Aug. 04	2 April	05 30 June	do	do		do	97 Foot.
Melville Glenie	23 Oct.	00 30 June	03 4 July	do	do		Captain	60 Foot.
Arthur Gore [130]	22 Dec.	04 10 Oct.	05 14 July 08	do	do	4 May 26	Major	Unattached.

Lieutenant-Colonels.

	2D LIEUT. ETC.	LIEUT.	CAPTAIN.	MAJOR.	LIEUT.-COLONEL.	WHEN PLACED ON HALF PAY.	REGIMENTAL RANK.	
William Wilkinson	12 Dec. 99	4 Mar. 01	1 Sept. 08	27 May 25	28 June 38		Captain	49 Foot.
George Marshall, KH.	6 Dec. 99	15 Aug. 04	27 Oct. 08	do	do		Lieut.-Col.	82 Foot.
David Goodsman	12 Aug. 99	23 Mar. 00	28 Nov.	do	do	1 June 26	Major	Unattached.
Loftus Owen	22 Dec. 99	1 Nov. 02	8 Dec.	do	do	10 June 26	do	Unattached.
Pringle Taylor, KH.[131]	15 Aug. 11	2 July 12	2 Jan.	20 16 June	do	4 July 34	do	Unattached.
James Alfred Schreiber [132]	Mar.	06 29 May	06 19 Nov.	12 23 June	do	23 June 25	do	92 Foot.
Robert Winchester, KH.	18 Sept. 05	6 Feb.	08 19 July	15 16 Aug.	do		do	Unattached.
Henry Dundas Campbell	27 June	18 27 June	18 24 Oct.	21 27 Aug.	do	27 Aug.	do	Unattached.
Thomas Robert Swinburne	24 June 13	never	20 Dec.	16 10 Sept.	do	10 Sept.	do	Unattached.
Robert Smith Webb	7 Nov. 11	25 Mar. 12	7 Nov.	16 22 Oct.	do	22 Oct.	do	Unattached.
George Whichcote	10 Jan. 11	8 July	12 22 Jan.	18 29 Oct.	do	29 Oct.	do	Unattached.
James Wood	29 Dec. 13	23 Nov. 15	8 June	20 do	do	do	do	Unattached.
James Arthur Butler	23 June 13	never	18 April 16	19 Nov.	do	19 Nov.	do	Unattached.
William Frederick Tinling	27 Jan. 14	never	26 Dec.	21 10 Dec.	do	10 Dec.	do	Unattached.
Andrew Clarke, KH.	22 Aug. 06	29 July	08 4 Feb.	13 15 Dec.	do		Lieut.-Col.	46 Foot.
Henry Herbert Manners, KH.	23 April 07	1 Feb.	09 9 Sept.	19 25 Dec.	do		do	37 Foot.
Charles Forbes	16 July	06 11 Mar.	10 24 Oct.	28 15 Aug. 26	do		- do	61 Foot.
Joseph Kelsall	17 Dec. 03	21 Feb.	05 11 Nov.	13 23 Nov. 32	do		do	70 Foot.
John Luard	25 May 09	3 June	11 13 Dec.	21 17 Oct. 34	do		Major	21 Foot.
George Smith	5 Nov.	12 18 Nov.	13 22 June	20 10 Jan. 37	do		Captain	Royal Horse Guards.
Courtney Cruttenden	8 Sept.	03 24 Oct.	03 11 Aug.	11 22 July 30	7 July		Lieut.-Col.	Royal Artillery.
Richard William Astell	never	20 Nov.	23 13 Sept.	27 never	13 July		Cpt.Lt-Col.	Grenadier Guards.
Ranald Macdonald, CB. KH.	25 Mar. 07	5 May	08 3 Dec.	18 24 Jan. 37	28 13 July		Major	4 Foot, Dep.-Adjt.-Gen. at Bombay.
George Knox	15 May	23 15 June	25 20 May	26 never	27 July		Cpt.&Lt.Cl.	Coldstream Guards.
Robert Spark	May	07 3 Sept.	07 17 Feb.	20 25 Dec.	35 28 July		Lieut.-Col.	98 Foot.
Thomas Butler	never	20 Aug.	18 9 June	25 11 Aug.	29 31 Aug.	31 Aug. 38	do	Unattached.
Lord William Thynne	17 Aug.	20 6 June	22 24 Feb.	25 31 Aug.	30 do	do	do	Unattached.
George Maunsell	13 Mar.	06 25 Dec.	06 18 July	11 21 Nov.	28 15 Sept.		do	3 Dragoon Guards.
Frederick MacBean, KH.	9 June	03 6 May	05 24 Dec.	12 18 July	26 2 Nov.		do	84 Foot.
Walter Powell	31 Jan.	00 21 Sept.	04 14 Nov.	23 18 Mar. 37	7 Nov.		do	Royal Marines.
Pat. Fitzroy Wellesley Campbell	13 Jan.	25 14 July	25 3 July	29 never	never		Cpt.&Lt.Cl.	Scots Fusilier Guards.
George Deare	30 Oct.	17 8 July	22 30 Dec.	24 26 Oct.	32 28 Dec.		Lieut.-Col.	21 Foot.
Thomas Henry Johnston	21 Feb.	22 1 Oct.	25 24 Oct.	26 20 May	36 do		do	66 Foot.
Thomas Hamilton	15 July	13 9 June	14 3 Nov.	25 23 Jan. 37	do		do	19 Foot.

71

Lieutenant-Colonels.

	CORNET, ETC.	LIEUT.	CAPTAIN.	MAJOR.	LIEUT.-COLONEL.	WHEN PLACED ON HALF PAY.	REGIMENTAL RANK.	
Thomas Henry Wingfield	never	11 Nov. 13	12 Sept. 22	3 June 28	19 Jan. 39		Lt.-Col.	32 Foot.
Henry Aitchison Hankey	26 June 23	10 Mar. 25	15 Aug. 26	27 Sept. 33	1 Mar.		do	Unattached.
John Campbell	23 Jan. 12	28 Mar. 14	2 April 18	22 April 26	29 Mar.		Major	Particular Service.
Plomer Young, KH.	8 May 05	3 Sept. 08	20 April 15	12 Feb. 28	do		do	Particular Service.
Lewis Carmichael [133]	8 June 09	7 Mar. 12	5 Dec. 20	26 Nov. 30	do		do	Particular Service.
Henry Dive Townshend	16 July 13	14 Sept. 15	1 Nov. 21	10 Oct. 35	29 Mar. 39		do	24 Foot.
James B. Bucknall Estcourt	13 July 20	9 Dec. 24	5 Nov. 25	21 Oct. 36	do		do	43 Foot.
George Phillpotts	1 May 11	7 June 11	23 Mar. 25	28 June 38	do		Captain	Royal Engineers.
Thomas Wright	17 Dec. 12	22 Apr. 14	14 July 25	10 Mar. 37	24 April 39		Lieut.-Col.	39 Foot.
Frederick Charles Griffiths	17 June 24	16 Feb. 26	5 April 31	28 Oct. 37	3 May	3 May 39	do	Unattached.
William Blois	3 May 15	30 Aug. 21	12 Aug. 25	12 Aug. 34	11 May		do	52 Foot.
Sir Walter Scott, Bart.	10 June 19	24 Oct. 21	16 June 25	26 Feb. 28	31 May		do	15 Dragoons.
Thomas William Nicholson, KH. [134]	28 Aug. 04	11 Oct. 05	14 Oct. 13	12 June 30	28 June	28 June 39	do	Unattached.
Thomas Wood	16 Nov. 20	12 June 23	25 June 25	28 June 38	do		Cpt.&Lt.Cl.	Grenadier Guards.
Hon. Charles A. Wrottesley	21 Dec. 15	5 July 21	16 June 25	5 April 31	3 July		Lieut.-Col.	29 Foot.
Charles Robert Cureton	24 Feb. 04	27 June 16	12 Nov. 21	6 Dec. 33	23 July		do	16 Dragoons.
John Pennycuick, KH.	31 Aug. 07	15 Jan. 12	14 June 21	25 April 34	do		Major	17 Foot.
Edward T. Tronson	28 Nov. 06	26 Jan. 08	2 Sept. 19	27 Mar. 35	do		do	13 Foot.
Fra. Dermot Daly	5 Dec. 11	26 Nov. 13	26 June 24	27 Oct. 35	do		do	4 Dragoons.
Richard Carruthers	19 May 14	25 Jan. 16	April 25	19 Feb. 36	do		do	2 Foot.
George James M'Dowell	4 April 16	4 Dec. 17	14 Nov. 27	4 Aug. 37	do		do	16 Dragoons.
William Hassall Eden	31 Mar. 14	22 June 20	31 July 23	29 Aug. 26	10 Aug.		do	56 Foot.
Peter Faddy	8 Sept. 03	1 Nov. 03	5 Sept. 11	22 July 30	do		do	Royal Artillery.
Henry George Jackson	22 Dec. 03	1 May 04	31 Dec. 12	do	16 Aug.		do	Royal Artillery.
Forbes Macbean	15 Sept. 04	20 May 05	20 Dec. 14	10 Jan. 37	do		Captain	Royal Artillery.
George Johnstone	5 Aug. 19	9 Nov. 21	17 Nov. 25	3 Oct. 26	23 Aug.		do	42 Foot.
Wm. Moulden Burton	4 Aug. 00	21 Dec. 04	8 April 24	28 June 38	26 Aug.		Lieut.-Col.	Royal Marines.
Abraham Henry Gordon	5 Jan. 01	18 July 05	18 Dec. 24	do	do		do	Royal Marines.
Hugh Henry Rose	8 June 20	24 Oct. 21	22 July 24	30 Dec. 26	17 Sept.	17 Sept. 39	do	Unattached.
Joseph Clarke	22 Mar. 10	10 June 13	24 Feb. 25	26 June 33	do		do	76 Foot.
John Lysaght Pennefather	14 Jan. 18	20 Feb. 23	5 Nov. 25	22 Mar. 31	18 Oct. 39		do	22 Foot.
Sir John Gaspard Le Marchant	26 Oct. 20	24 Oct. 21	30 June 25	14 Dec. 32	do		do	99 Foot.
Henry Pratt	17 April 00	30 June 01	12 Oct. 09	22 July 30	22 Oct		do	18 Foot.

Lieutenant-Colonels.

	CORNET, ETC.	LIEUT.	CAPTAIN.	MAJOR.	LIEUT.-COLONEL.	WHEN PLACED ON HALF PAY.	REGIMENTAL RANK.	
Charles Gascoyne	7 Dec. 20	30 Jan. 23	31 Dec. 25	23 Aug. 31	22 Oct. 39		Lieut.-Col.	94 Foot.
William Frederick Snell	never	13 Aug.	4 July 25	29 13 Aug. 31	1 Nov.		Cpt.&Lt.Cl.	Scots Fusilier Guards.
Brownlow Wm. Knox	8 Jan. 24	13 Aug.	15 June 30	never	do		do	Scots Fusilier Guards.
Charles Edward Gordon	8 Sept. 03	6 Dec.	17 Mar. 03	12 22 July 30	24 Nov.		Lieut.-Col.	{ R. Artillery, *Assist.-Adjt.-Gen. in Ireland.*
Michael White	15 Aug. 04	14 May 05	7 Nov. 15	10 Jan. 37	13 Dec.		do	3 Dragoons.
Sam. Robinson Warren	21 April 08	23 Oct. 09	1 May 23	28 June 38	20 Dec.		Captain	{ 65 Foot, *Dep. Qr.-Mas.-Gen. in Jamaica.*
Matthew C. D. St. Quintin	29 June 20	8 Jan. 24	9 Nov. 26	15 April 37	31 Dec.		Lieut.-Col.	17 Dragoons.
Hon. Arthur Upton	never	10 Feb. 25	16 May 29	never	do		Cpt.&Lt.Cl.	Coldstream Guards.
Frederick Paget	20 Mar. 23	24 Feb. 25	4 June 29	never	24 Jan. 40		do	Coldstream Guards.
George Moncrieffe	never	8 April 26	6 July 30	never	do		do	Scots Fusilier Guards.
Marcus J. Slade	15 July 19	12 May 25	22 April 26	27 Sept. 31	7 Feb.	7 Feb. 40	Lieut.-Col.	Unattached.
J. T. Goldie Taubman	8 April 26	10 June 26	20 July 30	never	14 Feb.		Cpt.&Lt.Cl.	Scots Fusilier Guards.

Notes to Lieutenant-Colonels.

1 Lieut.-Colonel Drinkwater Bethune served at Gibraltar during the memorable siege.

2 Lieut.-Col. John Grey has seen a great deal of active service in the West Indies, including the battles of the 26th and 27th May, 1782, between the British and French fleets under Sir Samuel Hood and Count De Grasse; the captures of Martinique and St. Lucia in 1794, and subsequent campaign in St. Domingo, where he was wounded in the right arm in storming the enemy's camp near Fort Bigolon.

3 Lieut.-Col. West served in Holland from Nov., 1794, to May, 1796, and was present when the French attacked the British after crossing the Waal; also the campaign of 1799 in Holland, including the actions of the 27th Aug., 10th and 19th Sept. and 2d October, storming of Oude Carspel; bayonet-wound in the thigh at Castacum, and again severely wounded in action on falling back upon Limma. Proceeded with the expedition to Hanover, 1805; to Zealand, 1807, and was present at the siege of Copenhagen. Embarked for the Peninsula in 1808, and was present at the passage of the Douro, capture of Oporto, action at Salamonde, and battle of Talavera.

4 Baron Bulow served in the Peninsula, France, and Flanders, and has received a medal and two clasps for the battles of Salamanca, Vittoria, and Toulouse.

5 Lieut.-Col. Luke Alen served at the captures of Martinique and the Saintes in 1809, and Guadaloupe in 1810.

6 Lieut.-Col. R. H. Cooke served in the Peninsula, France, and Flanders, and was severely wounded at Waterloo. Medal for the assault and capture of San Sebastian.

7 Lieut.-Col. John Mansel has seen a great deal of active service in the West Indies, including the captures of St. Lucia and Trinidad. Served in the Peninsula from Aug., 1811, to Nov., 1812, and again from March, 1814, to the end of the war, including the reduction of the Forts at Salamanca, and battles of Salamanca and Toulouse, for which he has received a medal and a clasp.

8 Lieut.-Col. Halkett served in the Peninsula, France, and Flanders, and has received a medal and a clasp for the battles of Albuhera and Salamanca.

9 Lieut.-Col. Russell Manners served the second Mysore campaign, including Seringapatam and siege of Pondicherry. Served also in the Peninsula; and has received a cross for Fuentes d'Onor, Ciudad Rodrigo, Badajos, and Orthes.

10 Lieut.-Col. Pelly served the Egyptian campaign of 1801, including the 8th, 13th, and 21st March. Served also in the Peninsula during the campaigns of 1809, 10, 11, and 12, including the battles of Oporto, Talavera, Busaco, and Fuentes d'Onor, besides various skirmishes. Wounded and taken prisoner on the retreat from Burgos.

11 Lieut.-Col. J. P. Hunt served with the expedition to the Ferrol in 1800; and in Sweden, Portugal, and Spain in 1808 and 9, under Sir John Moore. Expedition to Walcheren, 1809. Served in the Peninsula from Jan., 1811, until disabled by severe wounds at the assault of San Sebastian; and was present in the action of Sabugal, battle of Fuentes d'Onor, siege and assault of Badajoz, battle of Salamanca. action at San Munos, and in the Pyrenees, and siege and assault of San Sebastian, where he received two severe wounds. Medal and two clasps for Badajoz, Salamanca, aad San Sebastian.

12 Lieut.-Col. Charles Rowan served in the Peninsula, France, and Flanders, and was slightly wounded at Waterloo. Medal and two clasps for Ciudad Rodrigo, Badajoz, and Salamanca.

13 Lieut.-Col. Holcombe served in the Peninsula, and has received a medal for the assault and capture of Badajoz.

14 Lieut.-Col. J. B. Harrison served in the Peninsula, and has received a medal and two ;asps for the battles of the Pyrenees, Nive, and Orthes.

15 Lieut.-Col. Cother served at the capture of the Cape of Good Hope in 1806, and the subsequent campaign in South America. Served afterwards in the Peninsula, including the battles of Roleia, Vimiera, Corunna, and Vittoria, for which last he has received a medal.

16 Sir Julius Hartmann served in the Peninsula, France, and Flanders; and has received a cross and two clasps for Talavera, Albuhera, Salamanca, Vittoria, San Sebastian, and the Nive.

17 Lieut.-Col. Gustavus Brown has seen a great deal of active service in the West Indies from 1796 to 1804 inclusive, and was present at the attacks and captures of several

Notes to Lieutenant-Colonels.

islands. Served also in the Peninsula from 1809 to the end of the war, and has received a cross for the battles of Salamanca, Pyrenees, Nivelle, and Nive.

18 Sir Richard Church served at the Ferrol in 1800; the Egyptian campaign of 1801, including the actions of the 8th, 13th, and 21st March, and taking of Alexandria. Present at the battle of Maida, and defence of Capri, at which last he was wounded in the head; present also at the capture of Ischia, 1809; in the expedition to the Ionian Isles, and at the taking of Zante and Cephalonia. Severely wounded in the arm in an attack on Stellaura.

19 Lieut.-Col. Plenderleath served with the 49th Regiment in the American war, and was severely wounded in action with the enemy near Lake Ontario, 6th June, 1813. Medal for the action at Chrystler's farm.

20 Lieut.-Col. J. P. Hawkins served in the Peninsula with the 68th regiment, and has received a medal and two clasps for the battles of Vittoria, the Pyrenees, and Nivelle.

21 Lieut.-Col. Wm. G. White served in the Peninsula with the 48th regiment, and has received a medal and a clasp for the battles of Vittoria and the Pyrenees.

22 Lieut.-Col. George Macdonell served in the American war, and has received a medal for the action at Chateauguay.

23 Lieut.-Col. Galiffe served in the Peninsula; was slightly wounded at the battle of Talavera, and has received a cross for the battles of Vittoria, Nivelle, Orthes, and Toulouse.

24 Lieut.-Col. Wm. Cowell served the Egyptian campaign of 1801, and has received the medal. Served also in the Peninsula, and has received a medal and a clasp for the battles of Nivelle and Orthes.

25 Lieut.-Col. Herford served in the Peninsula with the 23rd Fusiliers, and has received a medal and a clasp for the battles of Orthes and Toulouse.

26 Lieut.-Col. Newhouse served at Toulon in 1794; at Corsica, in 1795, including the several operations at St. Fiorenzo, Bastia, and Calvi. Commanded a detachment of artillery in the successful operation against the Isle of Caprarjo. Served also the Egyptian campaign of 1801; and with the expedition to Copenhagen in 1807, and was present in the battle of Kiog. Medal for services in Egypt.

27 Lieut.-Col. Wilkins served in the Peninsula, France, and Flanders, with the Rifle Brigade, and was severely wounded at Waterloo. Medal for the battle of Salamanca.

28 Lieut.-Col. M. Wm. Bailey was severely wounded at Waterloo.

29 Lieut.-Col. F. S. Miller was severely wounded at Waterloo.

30 Sir Henry Pynn served in the Peninsula, and was severely wounded in the Pyrenees. Medal and two clasps for the battles of Fuentes d'Onor, the Pyrenees, and Orthes.

31 Lieut.-Col. Patrick Campbell (R. Artillery) was at the capture of St. Lucia in 1796, and subsequently in the Carib war in St. Vincent. Served also in the Peninsula from Jan. 1809 to the end of the war, including the battles of Talavera and Castalla.

32 Lieut.-Col. Von Robertson was severely wounded at Waterloo.

33 Lieut.-Col. G. D. Wilson served in Holland in 1799; at the siege of Copenhagen in 1807; expedition to Sweden, and afterwards to Portugal and Spain under Sir John Moore; expedition to Walcheren, 1809; Peninsular campaigns from 1810 to the end of the war; also the campaign of 1815. Slightly wounded at Corunna, severely at Badajoz, and slightly at Waterloo. Medal for the assault and capture of Badajoz.

34 Lieut.-Col. Leslie Walker served with the 71st regiment in the Peninsula, France, and Flanders, and was wounded in the Pyrenees.

35 Lieut.-Col. Nathan Wilson served the campaign of 1799 in Mysore, including the battle of Malavelly and siege of Seringapatam. Campaign of 1800, in pursuit of Dhoondia Waugh; campaign of 1803, against the Mahrattas. Present at the quelling of the mutiny at Vellore. Severely wounded at the battle of Assaye, right arm shattered by a grape-shot, and two slighter wounds. Medal for Seringapatam.

36 Lieut.-Col. Edward Nicolls has served in every quarter of the globe, and has been several times severely wounded.

37 Lieut.-Col. John Wm. O'Donoghue was at the attack on Ferrol, 26th Aug. 1800; at the siege and capture of Monte Video, in 1807; at the defence of Cadiz, and Tarifa, in 1810 and 11, including the defeat of the French in the assault on Tarifa in Dec. 1811. Served the Mahratta campaigns of 1817 and 18; and in the Burmese war in 1824 and 25. Slightly wounded at Tarifa.

38 Lieut.-Col. Payler served in the Peninsula under Sir John Moore in 1808 and 1809, and subsequently under the Duke of Wellington, including the battle of Fuentes d'Onor, siege of Ciudad Rodrigo, and battles of Nivelle and Nive.

39 Lieut.-Col. Barlow served in India under Lord Lake during the campaigns of 1803, 4 and 5, and was present at the siege of Deig, battle of Futtyghur, siege of Bhurtpore, and battle of Afzalgurh. Served also at the captures of Bourbon and the Isle of France, in 1810.

40 Lieut.-Col. the Hon. Robert Moore was severely wounded at Waterloo.

Notes to Lieutenant-Colonels.

41 Lieut.-Col. Edward Keane served with the expedition to the north of Germany in 1805; in Portugal and Spain under Sir John Moore, including the retreat to and battle of Corunna; and subsequently under the Duke of Wellington, from Nov. 1813 to the end of the war, including the battles of Orthes and Toulouse. Served also the campaign of 1815, and was present at the battle of Waterloo.

42 Lieut.-Col. Purvis served in the Peninsula with the Royal Dragoons, and has received a medal for the battle of Vittoria.

43 Lieut.-Col. Robert Macdonald has received a medal for the battle of Salamanca.

44 Lieut.-Col. Madox served the campaign of 1815, and was present at the battle of Waterloo.

45 Lieut.-Col. Fuller served at the capture of the Cape of Good Hope in 1806. Peninsular campaigns from Dec. 1812 to Feb. 1814, including the battle of Vittoria, siege of San Sebastian, and battle of the Nive, where he was wounded in the shoulder and thigh. Campaign of 1815, including the battle of Waterloo, storming of Cambray, and capture of Paris. Served also at Bhurtpore under Lord Combermere in 1826, and was slightly wounded in the arm.

46 Lieut.-Col. C. P. Ellis served the campaigns of 1813, 14, and 15, including the passage of the Bidassoa, and battles of Nivelle, Nive, before Bayonne, and Waterloo, at which last he was slightly wounded.

47 Sir Wm. Robert Clayton accompanied his regiment (the Royal Horse Guards) to the Peninsula in Oct. 1812, and commanded a squadron at the battles of Vittoria, the Pyrenees, and at the period when Marshal Soult attempted to relieve Pampeluna. In 1815 again accompanied his regiment to the Netherlands, and was at the battles of Quatre Bras, Genappe, and Waterloo.

48 Lieut.-Col. Macadam landed in Portugal 1st Aug. 1808, with the 9th Regiment, and served throughout the whole of the Peninsular war, including the battles of Roleia, and Vimiera; passage of the Douro; defence of Tarifa; affairs on the retreat from Burgos in 1812; siege and storming of San Sebastian (twice wounded, and commanded the false attack on the breach on the 31st Aug. the day of the capture); passages of the Bidassoa (shot through the body), and Adour; several affairs connected with the investment of Bayonne, and also the repulse of the sortie from thence; besides a variety of minor affairs, and other desultory services during the Peninsular war.

49 Lieut.-Col. Spink served with the Light Company of the 12th Regiment in several actions in the Travancore war, East Indies. Severely wounded through the leg when leading a night attack against the enemy's position at St. Mary's, Bourbon. Present also at the capture of the Isle of France, his company forming the advance on landing, and repeatedly engaged previous to its capture.

50 Lieut.-Col. R. F. Melville Browne served as Aide-de-Camp to Sir Brent Spencer in the battles of Roliça, Vimiera, Busaco, Fuentes d'Onor, and the different affairs during the retreat of Massena from Portugal. Also at the siege of Flushing in 1809, as Aide-de-camp to General Gore Browne.

51 Lieut.-Col. Byam served the campaigns of 1812, 13, 14, and 15, including the battles of Salamanca, Vittoria, Orthes, Toulouse, and Waterloo, besides minor affairs. Severely wounded by a grape-shot when carrying the regimental colour of the 38th at Salamanca, and slightly wounded at Waterloo.

52 Lieut.-Col. Prendergast served in the Peninsula from Dec. 1811 to March 1814, including the battles of Salamanca and Vittoria, and sieges of Badajoz and San Sebastian.

53 Lieut.-Col. Drake served with the army on the Elbe, under Lord Cathcart, in 1805 and 6; in Portugal and Spain, under Sir John Moore, in 1808 and 9; with the expedition to Walcheren, 1809; in the Peninsula in 1810 and 11, as Aide-de-camp to Sir Brent Spencer; and in 1812 and 13 on the staff of the Quarter-Master General in the Peninsula.

54 Lieut.-Col. J. J. Snodgrass served in the Peninsula, France, and Flanders, from June 1812 to the end of the war, including the battles and affairs of Vittoria, the Pyrenees, Vera, Nivelle, Nive, Orthes, Tarbes, Toulouse, and Waterloo. Served also during the whole of the Burmese war.

55 Lieut.-Col. Gurwood served in the Peninsula, France, and Flanders, and was slightly wounded at the assault of Ciudad Rodrigo, and severely at Waterloo.

56 Lieut.-Col. Jeremiah Taylor served in the Peninsula from Aug. 1808 to Feb. 1813, and again from Oct. 1813 to the end of the war, including the battles of Vimiera (wounded); Busaco, and Salamanca, retreat from Burgos, combat at Villa Murial (wounded), and repulse of the sortie from Bayonne.

57 Sir Henry R. Wyatt served the campaign of 1814, including the battle of Toulouse.

58 Major John Fraser served in the Peninsula from June 1809 to June 1813, including the battles of Busaco and Fuentes d'Onor, siege of Ciudad Rodrigo, battle of Salamanca, and siege of Burgos, where he was at the taking of the Horn Work 19th Sept., and led the

Notes to the Lieutenant-Colonels.

storming party to the breach formed by the mine on the 14th Oct. 1812. Employed in the field throughout the whole of the Kandyan rebellion in Ceylon, in 1817 and 18.

59 Lieut.-Col. Wm. Roberts served in the Peninsula from May 1810 to Oct. 1812, and again from May 1813 to Sept. 1814, including the defence of Cadiz, battle of Barrosa, and capture of Seville. Medal for Barrosa.

60 Lord Howden served as Aide-de-camp to his Grace the Duke of Wellington during the years 1817 and 18, to the close of the occupation in France. Employed by Government on a special mission, and present at the battle of Navarin in 1827 (wounded and mentioned in Commander-in-Chief's despatch); siege of Antwerp in 1832 (wounded); campaign in Spain, in Navarre and Basque Provinces, in 1834.

61 Lieut.-Col. Robert Douglas served at the capture of the Danish and Swedish West India Islands in 1801; expedition to the north of Germany in 1805 and 6. Peninsular campaigns from Feb. 1812 to March 1814, including the battles of Salamanca, Vittoria, and the Pyrenees (27th to 31st July), siege of San Sebastian (24th Aug. to 8th Sept.), and battle of Nivelle. He has received a cross for Salamanca, Vittoria, Pyrenees, and Nivelle.

62 Lieut.-Col. Chas. Stuart Campbell served in Egypt in 1801; in Portugal and Spain in 1808 and 9, including the battle of Corunna; expedition to Walcheren, and siege of Flushing, 1809; Peninsular campaigns from 1811 to 1814, including the battle of Vittoria, siege and assault of San Sebastian, at which latter he was severely wounded in the thigh, and where the ball still remains. Medal and a clasp.

63 Lieut.-Col. Thornhill served in Egypt in 1801; at the captures of Martinique and Guadaloupe in 1809 and 10; and in the Burmese war under Sir Archibald Campbell. Severely wounded in the attack on the Burmese lines 25th Dec. 1824, and at the assault of the island of Cheduba.

64 Lieut.-Col. Dugald Campbell served at the Ferrol in 1800; in Egypt in 1801, including the battles of the 8th, 13th, and 21st March; and again in 1807, including the bombardment of Rosetta. Present at the battle of Maida, 4th July, 1806; and at the capture of the islands of Ischia and Procida in 1809. Severely wounded in the battle of the 21st March 1801, in Egypt. Medal for services in Egypt.

65 Lieut.-Col. Considine served in the Peninsula from May 1810 to Feb. 1814, including the combat of the Coa; battle of Busaco; combats of Redinha, Condeixa, and Sabugal; sieges and assaults of Ciudad Rodrigo, and Badajoz; battle of Salamanca; passage of the Bidassoa, and battle of Nivelle, besides various skirmishes. Served also at the attack on New Orleans 8th Jan. 1815. Severely wounded at the assault of Badajoz, and again at the battle of Nivelle.

66 Lieut.-Col. St. John Augustus Clerke served with the old 94th regiment at the defence of Cadiz, and also until the retreat from Santarem was closed at Fuentes d'Onor, having been present in the actions at Redinha, Foz d'Aronce, and Sabugal. Joined the 77th regiment (also in the Peninsula) on promotion, and served with it in the action at El Bodon, sieges and assaults of Ciudad Rodrigo and Badajoz, including the storming of Fort Picurina. Severely wounded in the leg at the storming of the castle of Badajoz.

67 Lieut.-Col. Brock served in the Peninsula with the 43rd Light Infantry from Aug. to Nov. 1808, June to Dec. 1811, and from Nov. 1812 to the end of the war, including the following battles and affairs, viz. :—Vimiera, Vittoria, Vera, Nivelle, Nive, Tarbes, Arcangues, and Toulouse, besides various skirmishes and affairs of out-posts. Also in the attack on New Orleans, and the capture of Paris. Served in the Coorg campaign in India, where a portion of his regiment (the 48th) bore a conspicuous and distinguished part.

68 Lieut.-Col. John Moore served at the capture of Martinique in 1809, and Guadaloupe in 1810.

69 Lieut.-Col. Phillott served at the Helder in 1799; at the blockade and capture of Malta, 1800; battle of Maida, 1806; expedition to Egypt in 1807, including the siege and capture of Alexandria, blockade of Rosetta, and subsequent retreat. Served also with the expedition from Sicily to the bay of Naples, and was present at the capture of Ischia and Procida.

70 Lieut.-Col. Patrick Campbell (h. p. 52nd regiment) served with the 52nd regiment in the expedition to Ferrol and Cadiz, 1800; expedition to Gottenburg, 1808, and subsequently in the Peninsula, France, and Flanders, during the whole of the war, including the retreat to Corunna, action of the Coa, battle of Busaco, retreat to the lines of Torres Vedras, and all the actions in the advance to Sabugal, where he was severely wounded, and sent to England for recovery. Rejoined the army in the advance to Madrid, and served in the subsequent retreat to Portugal, battle of Vittoria, attack on the heights of Vera (twice wounded at the head of his regiment, the 52nd), battles of the Pyrenees, Nivelle (the 88th French regiment surrendered to the 52nd on this occasion), Nive, Orthes (wounded), Toulouse, and Waterloo. Medal and a clasp for the battles of Nivelle and Nive.

71 Lieut.-Col. Stone has received a medal for the battle of Nivelle.

72 Lieut.-Col. Trafford served in the Peninsula, and was present at the battles of Tala-

vera (wounded), Albuhera, Busaco, Vittoria, Pyrenees, Nivelle, Nive, Orthes, and Toulouse.

73 Lieut.-Col. Oates, during eight years' active service in the West Indies, was frequently engaged with the enemy, and twice severely wounded, viz., in the right side by a musket-ball at Cote de Fer, and in the left ankle in an attack near Port au Prince. Served also five years in the East Indies and in Egypt, and crossed the Desert under Sir David Baird. Expedition to South America in 1807; and subsequently throughout the whole of the Peninsular war, including the battles of Talavera (severely wounded on the head by the bursting of a shell), Busaco, Fuentes d'Onor; 2nd and 3rd sieges of Badajoz (severely wounded at the storming of Fort Picurina); battles of Vittoria, Nivelle, and Orthes, where he was severely wounded through the right thigh. Medal for services in Egypt.

74 Lieut.-Col. Edw. Thos. Fitzgerald served the campaign of 1815 on the staff of the Quarter-Master General, and was slightly wounded at Waterloo.

75 Lieut.-Col. George Tovey served in Calabria, and was present at the battle of Maida. Served also in the Peninsula from July 1808 to Nov. 1809, and again from Oct. 1812 to the end of the war, including the battles of Vimiera, Talavera, Vittoria, Pyrenees (25th July to 2nd Aug.); siege of San Sebastian; and battles of Nivelle, Nive, and Orthes.

76 Lieut.-Col. Bunce served on board H.M.S. *Bedford* at the battle of Camperdown, under Lord Duncan, and capture of the Dutch fleet, 11th Oct. 1797. In 1799 landed from the fleet under Lord Nelson at the siege and capitulation of St. Elmo at Naples, surrender of the castles of Uovo and Nuovo, and the siege and fall of Capua. Served in Egypt in 1801. In May 1806 he commanded the seamen and marines landed from the squadron under Sir Sydney Smith, at the attack and capture of the island of Capri, and was afterwards at the fall of Gaeta. Commanded the battalion of marines, landed from the fleet under Sir Robert Stopford during the attack and capture of Java in 1811, including the storming the intrenched lines and fortifications of Corneilis, the fall of Gresil and Saurabaya. Independent of the above, he has been frequently engaged in boat actions. Medal for Java.

77 Lieut.-Col. Charles Stisted served the Peninsular campaign of 1810, with the 13th Light Dragoons.

78 Lieut.-Col. Linton served the campaign of 1815, and was present at the battle of Waterloo.

79 Lieut.-Col. C. B. Turner served in the Peninsula from Aug. 1809 to Jan. 1814, including the battles of Busaco, and Fuentes d'Onor; second siege of Badajoz; siege and storming of Ciudad Rodrigo; battle of Salamanca; siege of Burgos; investment of Pampeluna; battles of the Pyrenees (28th, 29th, and 30th July), and Nivelle, besides being engaged in twenty-eight different affairs and skirmishes. Severely wounded in the shoulder by a musket-shot whilst pressing the rear-guard of the enemy after the battle of Nivelle.

80 Lieut.-Col. Coles served in South America in 1807, including the operations previous to, and storming of Monte Video. Served afterwards in the Peninsula from Aug. 1808 to Nov. 1811, and again from April 1813 to the end of the war, including the battles of Roleia, Vimiera, Talavera, Busaco, and Albuhera; cavalry action at Usagre; and passages of the Bidassoa, Nive, and Adour.

81 Lieut.-Col. John Eden served the campaign in Java in 1811, including the actions on the 10th and 26th Aug. Present also at the battle of Maheidpore, in the East Indies, 21st Dec. 1817.

82 Lieut.-Col. Story served in the Peninsula from Aug. 1809 to the end of the war, including the following battles, sieges, &c., viz. :—Busaco, Redinha, Campo Mayor, Los Santos, Albuhera, Usagre, Ciudad Rodrigo, Badajoz (2 operations), Vittoria, Pampeluna, and Toulouse.

83 Lieut.-Col. Wm. Fraser served the campaign of 1815, and was slightly wounded at Quatre Bras.

84 Lieut.-Col. Shee served the early part of the compaign of 1809 in Portugal; and the latter end of 1809 and the years 1810 and 11 with the Sicilian army. Served also the Peninsular campaigns of 1812, 13, and 14, with the Portuguese army.

85 Lieut.-Col. Hartley served in the Peninsula from Dec. 1813 to the end of the war, and was present at the battle of Nivelle.

86 Lieut.-Col. James Campbell served at the capture of Kandy in Ceylon in 1803 ; campaign in Spain, and battle of Corunna ; campaigns of 1811, 12, 13, 14, and 15, under the Duke of Wellington, including the second siege of Badajoz, battles of Vittoria, the Pyrenees, Nivelle and St. Pé, Orthes, and Waterloo, and storming of Cambray.

87 Lieut.-Col. Chester served in Holland in 1799, and was present in the action near Bergen, 2nd Oct. Served also the campaign in Spain from Sept. 1808 to Jan. 1809, including the actions at Benevente, Villa Franca, and Lugo, and retreat to Corunna.

88 Lieut.-Col. Manley Dixon served at the capture of various islands in the West Indies, in 1801, under Sir Thomas Trigge.

89 Lieut.-Col. Geddes served in Calabria in 1806 ; capture of Procida 1809 ; in Sicily in

Notes to the Lieutenant-Colonels.

1810; and subsequently in the Peninsula, including the battles of Nivelle, Nive, Orthes, and Toulouse, at which last he received a severe wound, which broke the left thigh-bone near the hip-joint.

90 Lieut.-Col. Wm. Elliot served in the Peninsula, and was present at the battles of Vimiera, Talavera, Busaco, and Albuhera.

91 Lieut.-Col. Gilmour served at the capture of Ischia, Zante, and Cephalonia, in 1809, and of Santa Maura in 1810. Served afterwards on the eastern coast of Spain, and was present at the battle of Castalla; engaged with the enemy on several occasions covering the retreat; and employed in the batteries against Tarragona. After leaving Spain, he went to Genoa, under Lord Wm. Bentinck.

92 Lieut.-Col. Pidgeon served in Portugal and Spain from Aug. 1808 to Jan. 1809, including the battles of Roleia, Vimiera, and Corunna; expedition to Walcheren, including the capture of Ter Vere and Flushing; Peninsular campaigns from Nov. 1812 to the end of the war, including the battles of Vittoria (slightly wounded), the Pyrenees, Nivelle, Nive, Orthes, and Toulouse; besides various other affairs of less importance. Served also the campaign of 1815, and was present at the battle of Waterloo.

93 Lieut.-Col. Charles Leslie served in the Peninsula at various periods, and was present at the battles of Roleia and Vimiera, capture of Oporto, battle of Talavera, first siege of Badajoz, and battle of Albuhera, besides skirmishes and affrays at out-posts. At the battle of Talavera he was severely wounded in the right leg, where the ball still remains.

93* Lieut.-Col. John Wolrige was present at the attack on New Orleans, 8th Jan. 1815.

94 Lieut.-Col. Cadell served at the siege of Copenhagen in 1807; expedition to Sweden, and afterwards to the Peninsula, including the battle of Corunna; expedition to Walcheren; Peninsular campaigns from 1811 to the end of the war, including the following battles, sieges, &c., viz.:—Barrosa (slightly wounded), Cadiz, Arroya de Molino, Almarez (reduction of forts), Vittoria, Pyrenees (25th to 31st July), Nivelle, Nive, St. Palais, Orthes, and Toulouse. Served also the campaign of 1815, and was present at the battle of Waterloo.

95 Lieut.-Col. Wm. Beckwith served in the Peninsula from July 1813 to the end of the war, including the battles of the Nivelle and Nive. Served also the campaign of 1815, and was present at the battle of Waterloo.

96 Lieut.-Col. J. M. Robertson served at the capture of Guadaloupe in 1810, and again in 1815.

97 Lieut.-Col. Tyler served in the Peninsula from Aug. 1808 to the end of the war, including the battles of Roleia, Vimiera, Oporto, Talavera and Busaco (wounded in the left shoulder); in the lines at Torres Vedras and pursuit of the enemy from thence; battle of Fuentes d'Onor; first siege of Badajoz; actions at El Bodon and Aldea de Ponte; sieges and captures of Ciudad Rodrigo and Badajoz; battles of Vittoria, Pyrenees, Nivelle, Orthes, and Toulouse. Served also the campaign of 1815, including the battles of Quatre Bras and Waterloo.

98 Lieut.-Col. Gawler served in the Peninsula from Nov. 1811 to the end of the war, including the siege and assault of Badajoz; battles of Vittoria, Nivelle, Orthes, and Toulouse, besides various minor affairs. Served also the campaign of 1815, and was present at the battle of Vittoria. Wounded below the right knee by a musket shot at the storming of Badajoz, 6th April 1812, and in the neck by a musket-shot, at San Munos, 17 Nov. following.

99 Lieut.-Col. Kettlewell served at Copenhagen in 1807; and in Ceylon during the rebellion in 1817 and 18.

100 Lieut.-Col. George Marshall served at the battle of Copenhagen.

101 Lieut.-Col. Firman served in the Peninsula in 1812 and 13, including the retreat from Madrid, battle of Vittoria, and the pass of Maya, at which last he was twice wounded.

102 Lieut.-Col. Wm. Cox served at Copenhagen in 1807, and in the Peninsula from June 1808 to Jan. 1809, May 1809 to Sept. 1810, and again from Sept. 1812 to May 1814, including the battles of Roleia, Vimiera, Talavera, Vittoria, Nivelle, Nive, and Orthes, and affair at Tarbes. Severely wounded through the right shoulder by a musket-shot at Vittoria; in the left side at Nivelle; and through the right leg at Tarbes.

103 Lieut.-Col. Wm. Turnor served in Hanover in 1805 and 06; battle of Corunna, expedition to Walcheren and siege of Flushing, 1809. Campaign of 1815, including the battle of Waterloo.

104 Lieut.-Col. John Ross served in the Peninsula under Sir John Moore, including the action at Lugo on the retreat, and battle of Corunna. Expedition to Walcheren, and siege of Flushing, 1809. Peninsular campaigns from Jan. 1811 to the end of the war, including the battle of Fuentes d'Onor; siege of Badajoz and storming of fort St. Christoval in 1811; covering the sieges of Ciudad Rodrigo, and Badajoz; battle of Salamanca; capture of the Retiro at Madrid; siege of Burgos, and retreat from thence; action at San Munos; battle of Nivelle, and carrying the heights of St. Pé, and battle of Orthes. Served also the cam-

Notes to the Lieutenant-Colonels.

paign of 1815, including the battle of Waterloo, and taking of Cambray. Wounded in action at Lasaca, 31st Aug. 1813.

105 Lieut.-Col. Austen was at the landing at the Helder in Aug. 1799, and severely wounded at the battle of Egmont-op-Zee, 2nd Oct. following. Served in Egypt in 1801, including the surrender of Alexandria. Present at the capture of Guadaloupe in 1810, and again in 1815.

106 Lieut.-Col. Briggs served at the siege and capture of Copenhagen in 1807; afterwards to Sweden under Sir John Moore; and subsequently to Portugal, where he landed with his regiment (the 28th) immediately after the battle of Vimiera, and was present at the passage of the Douro, battles of Talavera, Busaco, Albuhera, the Nivelle, Nive, Orthes, and Toulouse; the siege of Badajoz; and Lord Hill's action before Bayonne, 13 Dec. 1813, besides all the minor affairs connected with the above mentioned actions.

107 Lieut.-Col. Edward Knight commanded the 11th Portuguese regiment at the battle of Vittoria, and has received the medal.

108 Lieut.-Col. Clanchy served in Hanover under Lord Cathcart in 1805 and 6. Expedition to Madeira, 1807, and capture of the lines of Funchal. Peninsular campaigns from Sept. 1808 to the end of the war, including the battle of Busaco; retreat to the lines at Torres Vedras, and the subsequent advance; pursuit of the French army under Massena; actions at Pombal, Redinha, and Condeixa; scaling the heights of the Echellar; action at Sabugal; first siege of Almeida, and its subsequent blockade; battle of Fuentes d'Onor; and retreat from Burgos.

109 Lieut.-Col. Diggle was severely wounded at Waterloo.

110 Sir John Scott Lillie served in the 6th Regt., with the first expedition to Portugal in 1808, and was present at the battle of Vimiera, and capture of Lisbon. In 1809, as captain in the Lusitanian Legion, in various engagements for the defence of Portugal during the important interval between the embarkation at Corunna and the return of the second expedition to Lisbon. Campaign of 1810—battle of Busaco, and retreat to the lines of Torres Vedras. 1811—actions of Redinha and Pombal, capture of Campo Mayor, sieges of Olivença and Badajoz. 1812—battle of Salamanca, capture of Madrid, and retreat from Burgos. 1813—actions at Aldea de Ponte, Osma, and bridge of Subijana de Morellas (wounded), battle of Vittoria, blockade of Pampeluna, actions in the Pyrenees (24th, 25th, 26th, 28th, and 30th July), Irun and St. Martial, capture of San Sebastian, passage of the Bidassoa, battles of Nivelle (wounded) and Nive. 1814—battles of Orthes and Toulouse, at which last he was severely wounded and left for forty-eight hours on the field of battle, supposed to have been killed. Cross for the battles of the Pyrenees, Nivelle, Orthes, and Toulouse.

111 Lieut.-Col. B. Orlando Jones served in Hanover in 1805 and 6; and afterwards in the Peninsula from 1808 to the end of the war, including the battles of Roliça, Vimiera, Busaco, (lines of Lisbon), Fuentes d'Onor, Vittoria, Nivelle, near Bayonne 9th Dec., St. Jean de Luz 11th, 12th, and 13th Dec., investment of Bayonne, and repulse of the sortie; besides about thirteen other affairs of less note. Slightly wounded at the attack on Fort St. Gaitano, at Salamanca; and severely in the action of Tolosa in Biscay.

112 Lieut.-Col. De Lancey served at Walcheren in 1809; and in the Peninsula during parts of 1811, 12, and 13.

113 Lieut.-Col. Baynes served the campaign in Naples in 1805. Peninsular campaign from Jan. 1809 to Jan. 1813, and was wounded in the head at the battle of Talavera. Served also in Holland, the Netherlands, and France from Dec. 1813 to Nov. 1818, including the bombardment of the French fleet at Antwerp, and battle of Waterloo, where he was slightly wounded in the face and body. Medal for Talavera.

114 Lieut.-Col. Webber was employed in the expedition to, and in the capture of the colony of Surinam 1804. Campaign in the Peninsula under Sir John Moore; and subsequently under the Duke of Wellington, from May 1812 to the end of the war, including the battles of Vittoria, the Pyrenees, St. Palais, Orthes, and Toulouse, besides affairs of outposts. Campaign of 1814 in Canada under Sir George Prevost; and that of 1815 under the Duke of Wellington, including the battle of Waterloo, where he was wounded. Wounded also during the operations against the forts in the River Surinam, by the falling of a building in consequence of the explosion of a magazine.

115 Lieut.-Col. John Browne served in the Peninsula with the 4th Regt., including the lines at Torres Vedras, pursuit of Massena, action at Redinha, battle of Fuentes d'Onor, siege of Badajoz (wounded), siege and capture of Ciudad Rodrigo. Served also the campaign of 1815, including the battles of Quatre Bras and Waterloo, at which latter he was severely wounded.

116 Lieut.-Col. Crowe served in the Peninsula from July 1811 to the end of the war, including the support of the siege of Ciudad Rodrigo, and covering the siege of Badajoz, action at Usagre, siege and storming the fort at, and battle of Salamanca, siege of Burgos, actions before Bayonne, and battle of Orthes. Served also the campaign of 1815, and was severely wounded at Quatre Bras.

Notes to the Lieutenant-Colonels.

117 Lieut.-Col. T. C. Kirby served at the Ferrol in 1800. Egyptian campaign of 1801, including the actions of the 8th and 13th March (wounded), and 15th October. Served also in the campaigns in Holland, France, and Flanders, including the action at Merxem, bombardment of Antwerp, battle of Waterloo, taking of Cambray, and capture of Paris.

118 Lieut.-Col. Bateman served with the expedition to South America under General Crawford, and was in the attack on Buenos Ayres. Served in the Peninsula in 1810, 11, and 13, and was severely wounded at the battle of Vittoria. Served also in the American war in 1814, and was present at Plattsburg.

119 Lieut.-Col. Quill served at the captnre of the French West India Islands in 1815, under Sir James Leith.

120 Lieut.-Col. W. H. Davies served in South America in 1806; and subsequently in the Peninsula, including the sieges of Cadiz, Tarragona, and Tarifa.

121 Lieut.-Col. James Thomson was severely wounded at the battle of Orthes.

122 Lieut.-Col. Norcliffe served in the Peninsula with the 4th Dragoons, and was present at the battles of Talavera, Busaco, and Salamanca, in which last he was severely wounded and taken prisoner.

123 Lieut.-Col. Sherburne Williams served at the capture of Guadaloupe in 1815.

124 Lieut.-Col. John Cox, with the exception of a few months, served throughout the whole of the Peninsular war with the 95th (Rifle Brigade) commencing with the first affair, when his company formed part of the detachment which dislodged the French from the post of Obidos, 15th Aug. 1808. He was also engaged with the enemy in the following battles, sieges, affairs, &c. viz. Roleia, Vimiera, bridge of Benevente, in front of Talavera, Barba del Puerca, Galligos, Barquillo, Almeida, Mora Morta, Sista, Busaco, Alenquier, Arada, Santerim, Pombal, Redinha, Condeixa, Cazal Nova, Foz d'Aronce, Truxadas, Sabugal, Almeida (10th to 14th April 1811) Marcalva Bridge, Fuentes d'Onor, Nava d'Avar, Forcaylos, Ciudad Rodrigo (siege and storming), San Milan, Vittoria, Echarrianos, Pampeluna, heights of Santa Barbara, pass of Echellar, Vera, pass of Vera, Nivelle, Arcangues, and Tarbes. Served also the campaign of 1815, including the affairs of out-post on the 17th June, and the battle of Waterloo, 18th June. Wounded in the right shoulder by a musket-ball at Vimiera; compound fracture of the left arm by a musket-shot at the storming of Ciudad Rodrigo; left leg badly fractured by a musket-shot at Tarbes, ball still lodged.

125 Lieut.-Col. Greaves was present in the attack on New Orleans, 8th Jan. 1815.

126 Lieut.-Col. Charleton served in the Peninsula, and has received a medal for the battle of Toulouse, where he was severely wounded.

127 Lieut.-Col. Cartwright served the campaigns of 1813, 14, and 15, including the battles of the Pyrenees, Nivelle, Nive, Orthes, Toulouse, and Waterloo.

128 Lieut.-Col. Garland was severely wounded at Waterloo.

129 Lieut.-Col. Yale has received a medal for the battle of Albuhera.

130 Lieut.-Col. Arthur Gore was slightly wounded at Waterloo.

131 Lieut.-Col. Pringle Taylor served the campaigns in the Deccan of 1817, 18, and 19, including the actions at Bucktowlie, Nagpore, and Ashta; siege and capture of Capauldroog, where he led the Forlorn Hope, and was shot through the lungs and body.

132 Lieut.-Col. Schreiber was slightly wounded at Waterloo.

133 Lieut.-Col. Carmichael served in the Peninsula, France, and Flanders, from Aug. 1812 to the end of the war, including the battle of Vittoria, siege and assault of San Sebastian, and battles of the Nivelle, Nive, and Waterloo. Received three wounds at the storming of San Sebastian, and at the battle of the Nive; served also in the Kandyan rebellion in Ceylon; and at Bhurtpore, under Lord Combermere.

134 Lieut.-Col. Nicholson served the campaign of 1814 in Holland, including the bombardment of Antwerp, and storming of Bergen-op-Zoom, where he was severely wounded.

MAJORS.

	CORNET, 2nd LIEUT. or ENSIGN.	LIEUT.	CAPTAIN.	MAJOR.	WHEN PLACED ON HALF PAY.	REGIMENTAL RANK.	
William West	7 Jan. 76	2 Dec. 77	27 Aug. 85	3 May 96		Captain	Late of Royal Invalids.
Edward Wood[1]	19 Aug. 78	12 July 80	14 Mar. 92	1 Jan. 00		do	Late of Royal Invalid Artillery.
Thomas Browne	Feb. 94	2 Apr. 94	25 Mar. 95	29 Jan. 02	16 Oct. 06	Major	Half-pay 9 Foot.
Henry Bowen	2 Aug. 79	25 Feb. 82	1 Mar. 94	25 Dec. 02		Captain	Late of Royal Invalids.
Hugh Goodwin	27 Dec. 78	4 May 80	13 Oct. 94	9 July 03			Late of 48 Foot.
William White	25 Mar. 80	24 Mar. 84	25 Oct. 94	1 Jan. 05		Major	Late of 5 Royal Veteran Battalion.
Alexander Rose	14 Mar. 93	1 Oct. 94	2 July 96	10 Dec. 07		do	Late of 6 Royal Veteran Battalion.
John Williams	9 Mar. 81	1 July 82	31 Jan. 96	25 April 08	16 Sept. 12	do	Half-pay Royal Marines.
George Wolfe[1]*	1 Jan. 81	18 April 93	18 April 98	25 July 10		Captain	Late of Royal Marines.
Benjamin Wm. M'Gibbon	22 Jan. 82	18 April 99	19 Aug. 99	4 June 11		do	Late of Royal Marines.
Richard Henry Tolson	7 Nov. 93	19 Jan. 95	3 May 00	1 Jan. 12	25 April 17	do	Half-pay 25 Foot.
❦ George Langlands[2]	2 Feb. 96	Dec. 02	23 Sept. 03	27 April 12		Major	Late 13 Royal Veteran Battalion.
Amand de Courten		never	1 May 01	4 June 13	1815	Captain	Half-pay Watteville's Regiment.
George Esdaile Elrington	28 Aug. 99	never	14 May	do		do	Late 5 Royal Veteran Battalion.
John Staunton		2 Sept. 95	3 Sept. 02	do		do	Late 1 Royal Veteran Battalion.
Thomas Sheppard	4 May 93	18 Dec. 94	1 Nov.	do	8 Mar. 26	do	Half-pay Royal Marines.
❦ William Onslow, KH[3]	12 Dec. 98	26 Feb. 01	29 Jan. 02	do	2 July 29	Major	Unattached.
Joseph Mignon May	16 May 93	24 Mar. 95	1 Mar.	do	16 Aug. 16	Captain	Half-pay Royal Marines.
Hon. Charles Murray	3 Oct. 98	3 April 01	22 May	do	4 May 15	do	Half-pay 17 Dragoons.
John Marjoram Close	6 Mar. 95	3 Oct.	25 Nov. 02	do	1 Sept. 19	Captain	Half-pay Royal Artillery.
Charles Emanuel May		25 Sept. 98	11 June 07	17 June	25 Sept. 16	Major	Half-pay Meuron's Regiment.
❦ William Campbell[4]	27 Oct. 99	1 Mar. 00	22 Dec.	4 26 Aug.	23 April 29	do	Unattached.
❦ *Sir* Victor von Arentsschildt, CB. KCH.[5]		never	4 Nov. 03	28 Aug.	24 May 16	do	Half-pay German Legion.
❦ James Lepper	20 Feb. 00	25 Jan.	22 June 05	25 Nov.	24 Feb. 16	Captain	Half-pay German Legion.
William Bernard		11 Mar.	25 June 09	3 Mar. 14	4 Dec. 17	do	Half-pay 27 Foot.
Richard Jones	never	8 July	25 June 03	4 June	25 Dec. 17	do	Late 5 Royal Veteran Battalion.
Alexander Alexander	27 Sept. 93	1 June 96	25 June	do		do	Half-pay 81 Foot.
Francis Wernyss	16 June 93	24 April 95	14 July	do		do	Late 5 Royal Veteran Battalion.
Joseph Beausire	never	never	20 July	do	1 Feb. 17	do	Late of Royal Marines.
Andrew Kinsman	12 Nov. 03	24 April 95	23 July	do	20 Jan. 21	do	Late Royal Foreign Artillery.
Francis Clarke	never	never	26 July	do	1 Mar. 17	do	Half-pay Royal Foreign Artillery.

Majors.

	CORNET, ETC.	LIEUT.	CAPTAIN.	MAJOR.	WHEN PLACED ON HALF PAY.	REGIMENTAL RANK.	
William Sladden............	16 Nov. 93	24 April 95	27 July 03	4 June 14	22 June 16	Captain	Half-pay Royal Marines.
John Philips	1 Feb. 94	24 April 95	20 Oct.	do	13 Dec. 14	do	Half-pay Royal Marines.
ⓓ Nicholas Philibert de Brem..	never	*1 May	25 Nov.	do	1811	do	Half-pay Chasseurs Britanniques.
ⓓ James William Wilson.....	6 May 95	28 Oct. 95	21 Dec.	do	18 Feb. 19	do	Half-pay 3 West India Regiment.
ⓓ Nicholas Muller...........	never	never	5 Jan. 04	do	1816	do	Half-pay Roll's Regiment.
Robert Hart................	4 Feb. 94	2 Aug. 95	8 May	do	30 Jan. 17	do	Half-pay Royal Marines.
William Milne	24 Aug. 99	May	4 22 May	do		do	Late 2 Royal Veteran Battalion.
George de Muller	never	never	16 June	do	25 June 14	do	Half-pay German Legion.
Francis Hawker	28 Feb. 96	25 June	25 July	do		do	Late 2 Royal Veteran Battalion.
John Field Holdham........	26 April 96	10 Feb. 97	4 Aug.	do		do	Late 8 Royal Veteran Battalion.
Alexander Stewart..........	28 Oct. 95	1 June 96	5 Aug.	do	18 June 18	do	Half-pay 4 Ceylon Regiment.
George Plastow Juxon.......	27 Nov. 94	22 May 97	6 Sept.	do		do	Late 10 Royal Veteran Battalion.
Henry William Dammers.....	never	never	14 Sept.	do	24 Feb. 16	Major	Half-pay German Legion.
Augustus Kuckuck	never	never	15 Sept.	do	do	do	Half-pay German Legion.
ⓓ Philip Henry Fred Mejer...	never	never	22 Sept.	do	do	do	Half-pay German Legion.
ⓓ John Lockhart Gallie	5 Mar. 96	12 July	27 Sept.	do	3 Feb. 20	Captain	Half-pay 83 Foot.
George Lovell Spinluff	1 Feb. 96	17 Nov. 99	1 Nov.	do		do	Late Veteran Company.
John Robyns, KH.[6]	13 Mar. 96	1 Jan. 99	19 June	07 27 Oct. 14		Major	Late of Royal Marines.
ⓓⓓ Wm. *Baron Decken*, KH.	never	*4 Feb. 04	13 Dec.	06 18 June 15	24 Feb. 16	Captain	Half-pay German Legion.
ⓓⓓ Lewis de Dreves.........	18 Dec. 06	19 May 06	18 Jan.	08	do	do	Half-pay German Legion.
Charles von Kronenfeldt, KH...	never	never	23 April	05 17 Aug.	do	Major	Half-pay German Legion.
Peregrine Francis Thorne, KH.[7]	16 July 07	1 Jan. 09	13 Aug.	13 24 Feb. 17	3 Aug. 20	do	Unattached.
Bennett Holgate	12 May 04	23 Nov.	23 June	08 13 Nov.	9 Feb. 26	do	Half-pay 40 Foot.
ⓓ William Meadows Hamerton	18 Dec. 06	19 Nov.	16 Jan.	12 21 Jan. 19	22 April 19	Captain	Half-pay 67 Foot.
Stopford Cane	20 Jan. 96	5 Nov. 99	14 Feb.	05 12 Aug.	22 July 24	do	Half-pay 18 Foot.
Charles de Havilland	27 Nov. 00	17 June 00	21 Mar.	do	28 Nov. 22	do	Half-pay 51 Foot.
William Macdonald	13 May 95	3 Oct.	15 Aug.	do	4 Feb. 23	do	Half-pay Royal Marines.
Archibald M'Intyre			17 Oct.	do		do	Late 2 Royal Veteran Battalion.
Thomas Wilson	Oct. 00	7 Jan. 01	14 Nov.	do	10 May 21	do	Half-pay 60 Foot.
Christopher Wilkinson[8] ...	27 Oct. 98	1 Aug. 00	24 April 06	do	1 July 25	do	Half-pay Royal Artillery.
ⓓ Charles Downes	1 Dec. 03	9 Feb.	25 April	do		do	Late 1 Royal Veteran Battalion.
ⓓⓓ Charles Freeman Sandham[9]	27 Oct. 98	7 Nov. 00	1 June	do	7 June 22	do	Half-pay Royal Artillery.
ⓓ James Lane	1 July 01	18 April 05	30 Nov.	do	20 Jan. 20	do	Half-pay West India Rangers.
Henry Ross Gore, CB.[10] ...	13 Nov. 00	16 Mar. 03	4 Dec.	do	17 April 35	do	Half-pay 3 Foot.

Majors.

	2D LIEUT. ETC.	LIEUT.	CAPTAIN.	MAJOR.	WHEN PLACED ON HALF PAY.	REGIMENTAL RANK.	
Robert Preston	22 Dec. 00	19 Feb. 06	1 Nov. 10	2 Sept. 19	28 June 21	Major	Half-pay 12 Foot.
Charles Teulon	14 Feb. 05	12 June 06	27 Sept. 10	7 Oct. 20	4 Aug. 25	do	Half-pay 42 Foot.
John Wm. Henderson, KH.	12 July 05	25 July 01	12 Mar. 07	19 July 21	5 May 25	Captain	Half-pay 41 Foot.
John Thornton	29 Aug. 04	26 June 05	26 Nov. 07	do	14 June 27	do	Half-pay Cape Corps.
Thomas Macky	26 May 03	22 Aug. 05	3 Dec. 07	do	14 July 25	do	Unattached.
Marcus Amesley [11]	16 Jan. 98	26 April 98	24 Dec. 07	do	5 July 33	Major	Unattached.
George Luard	24 June 02	5 Feb. 07	21 July 13	27 Sept.	8 April 26	do	Unattached.
Thomas Hutton [12]	16 Mar. 09	24 July 11	1 Dec. 14	15 May 23	19 April 31	do	Unattached.
Richard Staunton Sitwell	8 Oct. 02	3 April 05	22 Aug. 08	10 July	2 Aug. 26	do	Unattached.
John Paget Sweeny [13]	13 June 05	20 Aug. 06	9 Jan. 12	28 Aug.	3 June 24	do	Half-pay 2 Ceylon Regiment.
Timothy Davies	4 Aug. 04	26 June 05	1 Feb. 08	28 Oct.	24 Dec. 26	do	Unattached.
Thomas Greatly [14]	15 Nov. 00	12 April 02	1 Feb. 08	27 May	25 22 Nov. 28	Captain	Half-pay Royal Artillery.
Hon. Sir Fra. Cha. Stanhope	24 April 06	28 Aug. 06	7 Mar. 08	do	4 May 26	Major	Unattached.
George Pipon, KH.	17 April 10	4 Feb. 08	7 Mar. 14	10 Sept.	25 Dec. 28	do	Unattached.
George Hall [15]	3 May 10	9 May 12	30 Aug. 21	19 Nov.	7 April 35	do	Unattached.
Joseph Brooksbank	17 Mar. 08	22 June 09	12 Oct. 20	24 Dec.	24 Dec. 25	do	Unattached.
Charles Cornwallis Michell, KH. [16]	2 Oct. 09	16 Mar. 13	4 Sept. 5 Jan.	26	4 Sept. 17	Captain	Half-pay Portuguese Service.
Frederick Meade	26 Mar. 05	30 Mar. 09	7 April 25	19 Jan.	28 Aug. 27	Major	Unattached.
John Wildman	3 June 13	11 Nov. 14	30 Mar. 20	11 Feb.	11 Feb. 26	do	Unattached.
Joseph Anderson, KH.	27 June 05	6 Oct. 08	20 Jan. 14	16 Feb.		do	Unattached.
Wm. Frederick Forster, KH.	never	26 Nov. 13	26 June 17	18 Feb.	26 18 April 26	do	50 Foot.
William Beetham	5 Oct. 04	18 July 05	16 Jan. 12	8 April		do	Unattached, Assist. Adjt. Gen. in Ireland.
James Mill [17]	25 Jan. 10	7 Nov. 11	24 Mar. 16	do	7 May 29	do	54 Foot.
Frederick Johnston	4 April 10	18 Feb. 13	21 Aug. 17	do	26 Feb. 36	do	Unattached.
Thomas Atkins	16 July 00	16 Mar. 02	11 Oct. 10	22 April	10 May 27	do	Unattached.
Fred. Alex. Mackenzie Fraser	4 Mar. 13	6 Feb. 14	24 April 16	do		do	Unattached.
Forbes Champagne	29 Jan. 07	19 May 08	30 Mar. 14	4 May	26 Dec. 26	Captain	Half-pay 35 Foot.
William Bragge [18]	24 May 10	11 Oct. 10	24 June 13	10 June	10 June 26	Major	Unattached.
George Walter Prosser	30 May 11	20 Feb. 12	22 Feb. 16	do	do	do	Unattached.
Edward M'Arthur	6 Oct. 12	16 Sept. 13	24 Jan. 18	do	do	do	Unattached.
Edward Jones [19]	27 Oct. 08	6 July 09	8 Feb. 21	do	do	do	Unattached.
John Cole	26 Aug. 07	15 Nov. 10	7 Feb. 22	26 June	28 Dec. 32	do	Unattached.
John Whitehill Parsons, CMG.	14 Feb. 05	5 June 05	28 Feb. 11	26 June	2 April 29	do	Unattached.
		3 Dec. 05	21 Sept. 15	11 July	11 July 26	do	Unattached.

Majors.

	CORNET, ETC.	LIEUT.	CAPTAIN.	MAJOR.	WHEN PLACED ON HALF PAY.	REGIMENTAL RANK.	
Day Hort Macdowall	15 April 13	10 Mar. 14	11 Sept. 17	18 July 26		Major	44 Foot.
⚜ James Price Hely, KH.	4 April 35	9 July 03	15 Feb. 10	1 Aug.	1 Aug. 26	do	Unattached.
Jasper Taylor Hall	never	1 June 15	13 Nov. 23	do	do	do	Unattached.
⚜ Sir Henry Bayly, KH.	30 April 07	6 May 09	24 April 17	15 Aug.	15 Aug.	do	Unattached.
⚜ ☒ Charles Robert Bowers [20]	18 Jan. 10	18 Oct. 18	8 Dec. 18	do	do	do	Unattached.
Robert Vandeleur	22 May 15	19 Oct. 15	24 Oct. 21	do	do	do	Unattached.
Charles Lowrie	17 Dec. 02	14 July 04	11 June 12	29 Aug.	21 Nov. 28	do	Unattached.
⚜ George Browne [21]	10 July 06	17 June 07	26 Aug. 13	do	29 Aug. 26	do	Unattached.
⚜ John Arnaud, KH.	2 July 07	13 Nov. 08	13 Jan. 14	do	do	do	Unattached.
⚜ Percy Pratt [22]	24 Sept. 12	8 Sept. 14	26 Nov. 18	do	do	do	Unattached.
⚜ ☒ Frederick Towers	18 Nov. 13	18 April 15	8 July 20	do	do	do	Unattached.
⚜ Alexander Fraser [23]	31 Aug. 08	12 April 10	2 May 22	do	26 May 37	do	Unattached.
George Blomefield	11 May 15	1 Aug. 16	16 May 22	do	29 Aug. 26	do	Unattached.
⚜ Sir Thomas Livingston Mitchell [24]	24 July 11	16 Sept. 13	3 Oct. 22	do	do	do	Unattached.
William Wright Bampton	29 Nov. 03	13 Nov. 04	6 July 09	19 Sept.	19 Oct. 26	do	Unattached.
Joshua Wilson	28 Aug. 04	28 Mar. 05	7 Mar. 11	do	19 Sept. 26	do	Unattached.
⚜ James Price Gwynne Holford	13 July 09	5 July 11	17 Mar. 14	do	do	do	46 Foot.
⚜ Robert Garrett, KH.	6 Mar. 11	3 Sept. 12	7 July 14	do	do	do	Unattached.
Richard Connop	30 Dec. 13	15 Sept. 14	25 Sept. 17	do	19 Sept. 26	do	Unattached.
⚜ Tho. Molyneux Williams, KH.	14 Feb. 11	28 Feb. 12	16 Sept. 19	do	do	do	Unattached.
William Hodgson Cadogan	23 Jan. 12	10 Sept. 12	24 Oct. 21	do	do	do	Unattached.
⚜ ☒ Hon. John Massy	31 Mar. 14	23 Nov. 15	28 Nov. 22	do	do	do	Unattached.
Alex. Wilton Dashwood	23 April 18	1 Nov. 21	23 Oct. 23	do	do	do	Unattached.
Herbert Vaughan	4 July 18	20 July 20	13 Nov. 23	do	6 Aug. 29	do	Unattached.
Henry Stephen Olivier	27 Jan. 14	9 May 16	10 Oct. 22	10 Oct.	10 Oct. 26	do	Unattached.
⚜ ☒ Orlando Felix [25]	14 Aug. 10	10 Nov. 14	20 Nov. 24	31 Oct.	31 Oct. 26	do	Unattached.
George Green Nicolls	11 Aug. 14	2 Dec. 19	24 April 19	7 Nov.	7 Sept. 38	do	Unattached.
⚜ ☒ William Nepean	11 July 11	2 April 12	4 Oct. 21	14 Nov.	14 Nov. 26	do	Unattached.
⚜ William Harding	11 July 18	18 Nov. 13	13 Mar. 23	do	do	do	Unattached.
James Adair	7 Mar. 10	10 Oct. 11	25 Mar. 15	12 Dec.	1 Feb. 27	do	Unattached.
⚜ ☒ Arthur Hill Trevor, KH. [26]	1 April 09	1 Jan. 10	27 July 15	do	12 Dec. 26	do	Unattached.
Sir Grenville Temple Temple, Bart.	9 Sept. 19	31 Oct. 22	5 Aug. 24	do	do	do	Unattached.
Patrick Mac Dougall	2 Mar. 08	16 Feb. 11	28 Dec. 14	19 Dec.	do	do	48 Foot.
⚜ Robert Carlile Pollock	4 Mar. 08	11 July 11	5 Oct. 15	26 Dec.	26 Dec. 26	do	Unattached.

Majors.

	ENSIGN, ETC.	LIEUT.	CAPTAIN.	MAJOR.	WHEN PLACED ON HALF PAY.	REGIMENTAL RANK.	
Richard Rich Wilford Brett	23 Dec. 13	24 July 14	24 May 16	30 Dec. 26	20 Sept. 33	Major	Unattached.
Armine Simcoe Henry Mountain	20 July 15	3 Dec. 18	26 May 25	do	do	do	26 Foot.
Charles Maxwell Maclean	29 Oct. 07	21 Dec. 09	24 July 23	1 Feb. 27		do	72 Foot.
P Hon. Arthur Fra. Southwell	2 June 08	27 Dec. 09	16 June 14	20 Mar. 20 Mar. 27	do	Unattached.
William Holmes Dutton	never	4 May 15	15 Aug. 22	do	5 July 27	do	Unattached.
P Hon. Geo. Thomas Keppel	4 April 15	25 May 20	17 Feb. 25	do	20 Mar. 27	do	Unattached.
P Theodore Henry Elliot [27]	7 May 10	1 May 11	18 Nov. 20	do	do	do	Unattached.
John Anderson	2 Nov. 09	24 Jan. 11	16 Mar. 20	22 Mar.		do	2 West India Regiment.
Hon. James Sinclair	2 Feb. 14	9 Nov. 15	10 Sept. 25	do	19 Feb. 29	do	Unattached.
George Thomas Colomb	8 Dec. 08	18 Oct. 10	23 June 14	27 April	27 April 27	do	Unattached.
P John Henry Slade	7 May 12	25 Feb. 13	24 Oct. 21	5 June		do	1 Dragoon Guards.
P William Burney, KH.	28 April 08	1 May 10	2 June 14	6 Sept.		do	Cape Mounted Riflemen.
Fra. *Marq. of* Conyngham, KP. GCH.	24 Oct. 21	21 Sept. 20	12 June 23	2 Oct.	2 Oct. 27	do	Unattached.
Thomas Seward [28]	7 Aug. 90	1 Sept. 04	10 May 23	10 Nov.		Captain	Late of Royal Marines.
P Henry Arthur Magenis	1 Oct. 12	4 Mar. 13	9 Sept. 19	20 Nov.		Major	87 Foot.
P Joseph Mark Harty, KH.	23 April 07	1 May 07	11 Mar. 13	20 Dec.		do	33 Foot.
P William Bruce, KH.[29]	1 Dec. 06	17 Jan. 08	14 Mar. 11	31 Dec. 28		do	Unattached.
P John Singleton, KH.	11 Jan. 10	25 July 12	15 April 24	10 Jan.	27 Nov. 28	do	90 Foot.
P Peter Bishop, KH.	24 Nov. 03	1 Dec. 04	12 Mar. 17	17 Jan.	11 June 29	do	Unattached.
Sidney John Cotton	19 April 10	13 Feb. 12	1 Jan. 20	18 Jan.		do	28 Foot.
P Eyre John Crabbe, KH.	11 June 07	11 Mar. 08	19 May 14	31 Jan.		do	74 Foot.
William Maxwell Mills	25 Oct. 03	24 Oct. 04	18 April 11	24 April		do	1 West India Regiment.
Gerald Rochfort	28 Feb. 05	25 Sept. 05	1 July 12	1 May		do	3 Foot.
P James Leslie	4 April 05	15 May 06	3 Jan. 15	15 May	11 June 29	do	Unattached.
Arthur Richardson	24 Oct. 11	2 Dec. 13	2 May 22	3 June	3 June 28	do	Unattached.
Maurice Barlow	21 July 14	23 Mar. 15	20 Dec. 21	12 June		do	14 Foot.
P James Forlong, KH.	11 Mar. 13	22 Dec. 14	20 Sept. 21	1 July		do	43 Foot.
Wemyss Thomas Cockburn	22 May 17	10 Dec. 18	26 Dec. 22	25 Nov.		do	60 Foot.
Nicholas Wilson, KH.	31 Oct. 09	7 Oct. 13	24 Oct. 21	30 Dec.		do	77 Foot.
P Sir Trevor Wheler, *Bart*.[30]	17 Nov. 08	11 July 10	10 April 17	5 Feb.	29 30 Nov. 30	do	Unattached.
Philip Mair	never	7 April 14	17 Nov. 25	22 May	11 April 39	do	Unattached.
Harry Smith Ormond	8 Nov. 99	28 Aug. 12	24 Sept. 10	10 June		do	30 Foot.
P John Napper Jackson	1 July 05	1 Jan. 06	28 Feb. 12	11 June		do	99 Foot.
Agnew Champain	31 July 17	26 Dec. 22	16 June 25	16 July	17 April 35	do	Unattached.

Majors.

	ENSIGN, ETC.	LIEUT.	CAPTAIN.	MAJOR.	WHEN PLACED ON HALF PAY.	REGIMENTAL RANK.	
ɷ ❦ James Richard Rotton	27 June 11	9 Jan. 12	18 Sept. 17	11 Aug. 20	6 June 34	Major	11 Dragoons.
George Allan	17 Sept. 17	17 July 23	1 Oct. 25	1 Oct.		do	Unattached.
James William Bouverie	29 June 20	3 July 23	16 Aug. 25	26 Nov.		do	86 Foot.
Botel Trydell	19 Oct. 04	30 Oct. 06	17 Nov. 18	3 Dec.		do	83 Foot.
ɷ ❦ Hugh Andrew Fraser[31]	25 April 06	8 Feb. 09	12 Dec. 22	do	4 May 32	do	Unattached.
❦ ❦ John Clark, KH.	2 June 14	27 Nov. 21	29 Aug. 26	25 Dec.		do	54 Foot.
Frederick Hammond	14 Nov. 16	20 Mar. 23	14 July 25	16 Mar. 30	1 Feb. 33	do	Unattached.
John Gowdie	10 Nov. 14	9 April 18	1 Nov. 21	11 June	10 Oct. 34	do	Unattached.
Hon. James Yorke Scarlett	26 Mar. 18	24 Oct. 21	9 June 25	do		do	5 Dragoon Guards.
Edward Caulfield Arcler	3 May 12	30 Mar. 14	26 May 25	15 June	5 April 31	do	Unattached.
ɷ ❦ Thomas Wright[32]	5 May 04	3 Sept. 07	23 Dec. 13	25 June	5 Nov. 30	do	Half-pay R. Staff Corps.
William James King	16 May 05	29 May 09	17 Feb. 14	do	25 June 30	do	Half-pay R. Staff Corps.
Hon. Nath. Hen. Cha. Massy	7 Oct. 20	7 July 25	20 May 26	16 July	25 Feb. 31	do	Unattached.
Richard Parry	3 Aug. 96	16 Jan. 01	20 Jan. 09	22 July		Captain	Late of Royal Marines.
Robert White	4 Aug. 96	21 Sept. 01	20 Jan.	do		do	Late of Royal Marines.
John J. Hollis	9 July 03	1 Dec. 04	30 Mar.	do		do	25 Foot.
ɷ John Procter	3 Dec. 03	8 June 04	4 May	do		Major	30 Foot.
ɷ Robert Hunt	25 Jan. 98	6 Nov. 99	11 May	do	4 Jan. 39	Captain	57 Foot.
John Birch	21 Oct. 08	8 Dec. 03	14 May	do	9 Aug. 33	do	Half-pay Rifle Brigade.
Francis Louis Barralier[33]	14 Aug. 00	16 May 05	6 July	do		do	44 Foot.
Benjamin Halfhide	28 Oct. 99	7 April 04	25 Aug.	do		Major	1 Foot.
ɷ Robert Mullen, KH.	25 June 02	25 May 04	25 Aug.	do		Captain	41 Foot.
Archibald Hook	Feb. 00	28 Mar. 00	12 Oct.	do	28 Nov. 34	do	Unattached.
ɷ ❦ James Henderson, KH.[34]	9 Feb. 94	1 Oct. 94	19 Oct.	do		Major	57 Foot.
ɷ Harvey Welman	5 Aug. 02	18 Feb. 04	2 Nov.	do	10 May 33	do	Unattached.
Wm. Smith (*Quarter-Master*, 16 Nov. 1800)[35]	25 July 02	5 Aug. 04	12 Nov. 10	do		Major	56 Foot.
Peter Shadwell Norman	9 July 03	2 June 04	8 Mar.	do	22 April 36	do	Unattached.
Samuel Workman[36]	23 Oct. 03	23 July 04	22 Mar.	do		Captain	13 Foot.
Robert Joseph Debnam	25 June 03	10 June 04	1 April	do	20 Feb. 35	do	Unattached.
ɷ Walter Sweetman[37]	9 July 03	8 Aug. 03	5 April	do		do	Late of Royal Marines.
James Ryves Hore[38]	13 Mar. 97	9 July 97	30 June	do		do	Late of Royal Marines.
Thomas Lewis Lawrence[39]	15 Mar. 97	10 July 03	19 July	do		do	32 Foot.
ɷ John Swinburn	28 Aug. 04	16 May 05	15 Aug.	do	15 Jan. 29	do	Half-pay 40 Foot, *Fort-Maj. Dartmouth*.
ɷ Robert Kelly[40]	22 Feb. 99	17 Oct. 00	16 Aug.	do		do	

Majors.

	ENSIGN, ETC.	LIEUT.	CAPTAIN.	MAJOR.	WHEN PLACED ON HALF PAY.	REGIMENTAL RANK.	
⊕ Richard Steele Wilkinson [41]	1 June 97	20 July 03	24 Sept. 10	22 July 30	5 April 30	Captain	Half-pay Royal Marines.
James Winniett Nunn	7 April 04	6 May 05	13 Dec.	do		do	80 Foot.
George Stuart	1 Mar. 03	1 Sept. 04	21 Feb. 11	do		do	77 Foot.
Thomas Kelly [42]	10 Mar. 95	25 June 03	28 Feb.	do		do	Half-pay, Cheshire Fenc., Fort-Major of [Tilbury Fort.
John Tongue	9 July 03	24 May 04	7 Mar.	do		Major	30 Foot.
James Johnston	3 Dec. 03	5 Aug. 04	7 Mar.	do		Captain	44 Foot.
Thomas Mitchell	6 June 97	23 July 03	30 Mar.	do		do	Late of Royal Marines.
⊕ Richard Jebb	12 Sept. 05	4 Aug. 08	9 May	do		Major	40 Foot.
Pieare Lowen, KH.	19 May 99	25 July 05	13 June	do		Captain	Cape Mounted Riflemen.
Edward Goate	9 May 05	8 Jan. 07	27 June	do		do	35 Foot.
Archibald Smith	9 April 07	18 Oct. 07	25 July	do	19 April 33	do	Unattached.
Robert Hammill	3 Dec. 03	22 Jan. 06	29 July	do		do	18 Foot.
Malcolm Macgregor	24 June 02	24 June 04	7 Aug.	do	22 Feb. 33	do	Unattached.
⊕ Richard Burges Hunt [43]	8 Sept. 03	22 Sept. 03	11 Aug.	do	16 Oct. 32	do	Half-pay Royal Artillery.
Thomas Henry Shadwell Clerke, KH. [44]	30 July 05	12 Mar. 07	22 Aug.	do	1 July 33	do	Half-pay Depôt Staff.
Joseph Williams	2 July 97	28 July 03	27 Aug.	do		do	Late of Royal Marines.
John Kitson	25 April 06	15 Jan. 07	3 Oct.	do		do	44 Foot.
George Gibson	11 Aug. 00	2 June 03	9 Jan. 12	do	24 Nov. 35	do	Unattached.
⊕ Chas. Andrews Bayley, CMG.	25 Nov. 04	16 May 05	15 Jan.	do	5 Oct. 26	do	Unattached.
Anthony Alexander O'Reilly	30 June 95	25 Sept. 00	23 Jan.	do	16 Mar. 20	do	h. p. 21 Drag. *Maj. of Brig. Cape of Good* [*Hope.*
Frederick Waters	3 Nov. 97	6 Aug. 03	25 Feb.	do		do	Late of R. Marines.
David England Johnson	9 Feb. 04	29 Dec. 04	12 Mar.	do		Major	5 Foot.
Stephen Noel	8 Aug. 00	25 July 03	19 Mar.	do		Captain	92 Foot.
William Taylor	16 Jan. 98	10 Aug. 03	24 Mar.	do		do	Late of R. Marines.
⊕ Moyle Sherer [45]	Jan. 07	4 June 07	26 Mar.	do	6 July 32	do	Unattached.
⊕ William Eyles Maling [46]	8 Sept. 03	6 Dec. 03	9 April	do	16 Oct. 32	do	Half-pay Royal Artillery.
⊕ Samuel Thorpe, KH. [47]	2 April 07	14 Jan. 08	16 April	do	20 Feb. 35	do	Unattached.
Gillies Macpherson	9 July 03	22 May 04	7 May	do		do	99 Foot.
⊕ Thomas Stirling Begbie [48]	8 Oct. 07	10 Nov. 08	7 May	do	2 Nov. 32	do	Unattached.
Thomas Lemon	30 Jan. 98	19 Oct. 03	19 May	do		do	Late of Royal Marines.
Philip Warren Walker	3 Dec. 03	6 Dec. 03	1 June	do		do	Royal Artillery.
⊕ Charles Blachley	do	1 Mar. 04	21 June	do	6 Sept. 33	do	Royal Artillery.
⊕ John Macpherson [49]	23 Sept. 99	2 July 03	2 July	do	14 Dec. 32	do	Unattached.
Simson Kennedy [50]	16 Aug. 04	25 Dec. 04	8 Oct.	do		do	Unattached.

Majors.

	2D LIEUT. ETC.	LIEUT.	CAPTAIN.	MAJOR.	WHEN PLACED ON HALF PAY.	REGIMENTAL RANK.	
William Henry Hartman	9 July 03	28 Mar. 05	30 Oct. 12	22 July 30		Captain	9 Foot.
Perry Baylee	25 April 05	8 Aug. 05	5 Nov. 15	do		Major	63 Foot.
George Pinckney	17 Sept. 01	22 Nov. 04	19 Nov. 04	do		Captain	82 Foot.
Hassel Richard Moor	22 Dec. 03	1 May 04	1 Dec. 09	do		do	Royal Artillery.
Robert Edward Burrowes, KH.[51]	3 Jan. 06	23 Aug. 09	5 July 15	do		Major	Unattached.
Honeyman Mackay[52]	5 Aug. 07	30 June 08	30 May 16	do	6 Sept. 31	do	Unattached.
Thomas Ryan, KH.	10 Oct. 05	28 April 08	30 Sept. 19	13 Aug.	29 May 35	do	50 Foot.
William Henry Grote	20 April 15	18 Sept. 17	4 Dec. 23	10 Sept.		do	Unattached.
Lord William Paulet	1 Feb. 21	23 Aug. 22	12 Feb. 25	do	22 June 38	do	68 Foot.
Benjamin Everard	25 Feb. 13	10 Sept. 18	16 June 25	21 Sept.		do	1 Dragoons.
Thomas Gloster[53]	1 April 07	17 Mar. 08	7 April 25	8 Oct.	8 Oct. 30	do	Unattached.
William Miles Kington	7 April 14	25 April 16	5 July 23	17 Dec.	17 Dec. 30	do	Unattached.
Robert Pattison Holmes	11 Feb. 12	12 Dec. 11	4 Sept. 23	do		do	23 Foot.
William Havelock, KH.	12 July 10	12 May 12	19 Feb. 18	31 Dec.		do	4 Dragoons.
Thomas A. Drought	11 Nov. 13	16 Oct. 17	10 Oct. 22	do		do	15 Foot.
Cornwall Burne	4 Oct. 10	25 July 15	3 Feb. 25	8 Feb. 31		do	91 Foot.
Jos. Clavell Sladdon Slyfield, KH.	15 Oct. 12	30 Mar. 14	26 May 25	12 April		do	60 Foot.
Philip Aubin	14 Feb. 11	29 April 13	22 June 26	do		do	57 Foot.
Thomas George Harriott	28 May 07	11 Oct. 11	13 Mar. 23	19 April	19 April 31	do	Half-pay Royal Staff Corps.
Henry Piers	22 June 09	12 Oct. 11	17 Mar. 25	do	5 Nov. 31	do	Half-pay Royal Staff Corps.
William Hawkins Ball	27 Oct. 14	24 Oct. 16	26 May 25	26 April	26 April 31	do	Unattached.
William Mitchell	21 Mar. 22	28 July 25	8 April 26	do	13 June 34	do	Unattached.
Robert Brookes	16 May 11	23 Aug. 13	27 Aug. 25	3 May		do	69 Foot.
John Walter	15 July 06	3 Sept. 07	24 Mar. 13	26 May		do	95 Foot.
James Kerr Ross, KH.[54]	19 Mar. 07	4 May 08	22 Oct. 18	7 June	7 June 31	do	Unattached.
George Graham	27 April 20	28 Feb. 22	26 Jan. 25	do	7 June 31	do	Unattached.
Bardley Wilmot	11 Mar. 19	11 July 22	12 May 25	21 June	21 June 31	do	47 Foot.
Philip Dundas	22 Aug. 05	25 Aug. 07	16 Nov. 20	28 June		do	67 Foot.
Edward Basil Brooke	15 Dec. 17	9 April 25	11 July 26	5 July		do	Unattached.
Thos. Rich. Plumhe Tempest	9 Nov. 15	30 Nov. 20	25 Dec. 12	July	6 July 38	do	Unattached.
James Badham Thornhill, KH.[55]	6 Sept. 04	21 Nov. 05	4 July 16	13 July	10 May 33	do	Unattached.
Christian Frederick Lardy	12 Oct. 09	27 Sept. 10	7 July 25	19 July	19 July 31	do	Unattached.
Henry Robert Bullock[56]	30 Dec. 13	9 Oct. 17	26 Dec. 21	23 July		Captain	Half-pay 60 Foot.
Arthur Charles Gregory	24 Oct. 21	1 Oct. 25	15 Aug. 26	18 Oct.	28 April 37	Major	98 Foot.

Majors.

	2D LIEUT. ETC.	LIEUT.	CAPTAIN.	MAJOR.	WHEN PLACED ON HALF PAY.	REGIMENTAL RANK.	
ℬ 𝔐 Norman Lamont, KH	26 Aug. 13	3 Sept. 18	7 April 25	2 Dec. 31		Major	91 Foot.
ℬ 𝔐 Severus Wm. Lynam Stretton	11 June 12	6 Jan. 14	13 Aug. 25	do		do	64 Foot.
Henry Bennett Everest	22 Dec. 04	1 Mar. 07	22 June 20	23 Dec.		do	6 Foot.
Edw. Geo. Walpole Keppel	4 June 18	29 Aug. 22	1 Sept. 25	do	14 Oct. 36	do	Unattached.
ℬ Robert Henry Willcocks, KH.	12 Sept. 11	26 Aug. 13	21 July 25	16 Mar. 32		do	81 Foot.
ℬ 𝔐 John Fitz Maurice, KH. [57]	25 April 11	14 Jan. 13	16 June 25	30 Mar.	30 Mar. 32	do	Unattached.
Henry Dundas Maclean	never	5 Sept. 16	6 Nov. 24	20 April		do	95 Foot.
James Dudgeon Brown [58]	13 May 13	24 Aug. 15	29 July 24	18 May	18 May 32	do	Unattached.
Alexander Campbell	2 May 06	16 June 07	13 June 22	6 June	11 Oct. 39	do	Unattached.
John Campbell	30 Mar. 15	11 Jan. 21	26 May 25	15 June	15 June 32	do	Unattached.
Peter Farquharson	1 Sept. 07	1 May 10	2 June 25	24 Aug.		do	65 Foot.
ℬ 𝔐 George Dry Hall [59]	4 Oct. 10	28 Nov. 11	2 June 25	do	1 Jan. 39	do	Half-pay Royal Staff Corps.
ℬ William Seward [60]	26 Mar. 08	26 April 09	15 July 19	18 Oct. 32	12 Nov. 35	do	Unattached.
ℬ George Cairnes	15 Dec. 08	2 Jan. 12	4 Nov. 24	4 Dec.		do	36 Foot.
William Nelson Hutchinson	24 Feb. 20	25 Oct. 23	17 June 26	do		do	20 Foot.
Edward James White	30 Mar. 09	5 April 10	14 July 25	14 Dec.		do	70 Foot.
ℬ𝔐 Alex. Duke Hamilton	27 Oct. 14	21 Dec. 14	15 Sept. 25	28 Dec.	18 May 38	do	Unattached.
Walter Trevelyan	18 Nov. 17	25 Sept. 25	19 Sept. 26	do		do	60 Foot.
Bartholomew V. Derinzy, KH	26 May 06	16 Mar. 08	25 Oct. 14	4 Jan. 33		do	11 Foot.
Peter Crofton	5 April 10	9 Nov. 11	15 Dec. 25	2 Mar.		do	83 Foot.
Charles Head [61]	11 April 11	3 June 13	10 Feb. 25	22 Mar.	2 Sept. 39	do	Unattached.
ℬ James Butler, KH. [62]	13 Aug. 07	14 Dec. 00	7 April 25	do	22 Mar. 33	do	Unattached.
𝔐 J. C. Wallington	21 Oct. 13	27 Dec. 14	16 Dec. 24	5 April		do	10 Hussars.
Courtenay Philipps	26 Dec. 18	18 May 22	14 Jan. 26	do		do	15 Hussars.
Abr. Beresford Taylor, KH.	14 Feb. 11	24 Dec. 12	22 April 25	19 April		do	9 Foot.
ℬ John Blood [63]	3 Mar. 11	26 Mar. 25	6 Aug. 29	3 May	12 Oct. 38	do	Half-pay Royal Waggon Train.
Edward Allen	20 Dec. 08	24 Jan. 11	25 Nov. 19	24 May	28 Aug. 35	do	Unattached.
ℬ Thomas William Ogilvy McNiven [64]	23 July 12	31 Mar. 14	29 Oct. 25	do	24 May 33	do	Unattached.
John Westlake [65]	12 Sept. 05	15 Jan. 07	8 July 13	28 May	28 May	do	Unattached.
Charles Markham	28 June 21	23 June 25	29 Aug. 26	31 May		do	60 Foot.
ℬ Thomas Steplucus	28 Nov. 06	18 Aug. 08	23 Dec. 13	4 June		do	49 Foot.
ℬ John F. Mackay	14 Dec. 04	19 Feb. 07	16 Aug. 13	5 July		do	82 Foot.
Henry Robert Milner	7 Feb. 22	3 Dec. 25	12 Dec. 26	do		do	94 Foot.
ℬ Samuel Dillman Pritchard	4 May 09	11 April 11	7 April 25	30 Aug. 33	1 Jan. 39	do	Unattached.

Majors.

	ENSIGN, ETC.		LIEUT.		CAPTAIN.		MAJOR.		WHEN PLACED ON HALF PAY.		REGIMENTAL RANK.	
⊕ John Crawford Young [66]	16 Aug.	04	13 Aug.	05	6 Oct.	13	6 Sept.	33	10 May	39	Major	Unattached.
John Messiter	18 July	15	3 July	23	19 Sept.	26	27 Sept.				do	28 Foot.
Frederick Hope	11 July	26	24 Oct.	21	9 June	25	4 Oct.				do	72 Foot.
Lord Cha. Jas. Fox Russell	8 May	28	2 Aug.	26	23 Mar.	27	11 Oct.		11 Oct.	33	do	Unattached.
James Bowes	12 Sept.	11	1 April	13	23 Aug.	25	18 Oct.				do	87 Foot.
⊕ Lewis Alexander During [67]	25 Nov.	95	5 May	04	15 April	13	8 Nov.		13 Dec.		do	Unattached.
Walter Pearse	22 Aug.	05	9 Dec.	06	27 Mar.	19	24 Dec.				do	80 Foot.
Giles Vandeleur Creagh	6 Jan.		20	10 April	25	1 Aug.	26	27 Dec.			do	81 Foot.
James Robert Young	27 July		15	14 Dec.	18	13 May	26	31 Dec.			do	25 Foot.
Joshua Simmonds Smith	26 Dec.		21	25 May	22	19 April	27	do			do	5 Foot.
S. G. Carter	11 July		11	6 May	13	17 Sept.	25	7 Feb.	34	7 Feb.	34	do	Half-pay Royal Staff Corps.
Basil Jackson	23 Mar.		04	27 Mar.	05	25 Dec.	14	8 Feb.				do	16 Foot.
William Henry Sperling	14 April		14	4 May	15	15 July	28	7 Mar.		8 July	36	do	Unattached.
⊕ George Young	1 Nov.		10	28 Aug.	07	12 Feb.	18	25 27 April				do	38 Foot.
⊕ James Anderson	never			1 Aug.	07	1 Sept.	13	2 May				do	Ceylon Rifle Regiment.
⊕ Robert Bidwell Edwards, KH.	18 Aug.		08	5 Jan.	09	28 July	14	do		2 May	34	do	Unattached.
Duncan Gordon	30 July		07	9 June	08	20 April	15	4 July				do	59 Foot.
Aralander Tennant	20 Oct.		08	10 June	13	10 June	26	1 Aug.				do	35 Foot.
George Milne Stevenson	21 April		13	11 Jan.	15	24 Oct.	21	12 Aug.				do	Rifle Brigade.
Charles Crespigny Vivian	4 Feb.		25	8 April	26	14 April	29	do		2 June	37	Captain	Unattached.
William Nesbitt Orange	5 Feb.		14	10 Jan.	19	24 Oct.	21	15 Aug.	34			Major	67 Foot.
⊕ Nicholas Hovenden	6 April		09	12 Dec.	11	19 Jan.	26	22 Aug.				do	50 Foot.
⊕ Robert Law, KH.	8 June		09	27 May	11	18 Oct.	21	29 Aug.				do	Royal Newf. Vet. Companies.
Chas. Brownlow Cumberland	21 Dec.		20	15 Oct.	25	10 June	26	19 Sept.				do	96 Foot.
Samuel Walker	10 Oct.		22	12 May	25	1 Nov.	27	do				do	65 Foot.
John Patton	18 Sept.		17	1 Mar.	21	10 Sept.	25	31 Oct.				do	12 Foot.
⊕ John Jenkins	29 Jan.		07	31 Dec.	07	22 Dec.	14	13 Nov.				do	11 Dragoons.
⊕ Thomas Bunbury	7 Mar.		07	17 Aug.	09	25 Oct.	14	21 Nov.				do	80 Foot.
Charles Warren	24 Nov.		14	13 Nov.	18	1 Aug.	22	do				do	55 Foot.
Sir Jas. John Hamilton, *Bart.*	10 July		23	12 May	25	8 April	26	28 Nov.		28 Nov.	34	do	Unattached.
Gore Browne	14 Jan.		24	11 July	26	11 June	29	19 Dec.				do	41 Foot.
⊕ Duncan M'Pherson	19 Sept.		05	10 Nov.	06	25 Mar.	24	27 Dec.			35	do	27 Foot.
Thomas M'Pherson	8 Aug.		11	19 May	13	25 Dec.	23	12 Jan.				do	2 West India Reg.
Elliott Armstrong	25 Mar.		23	23 June	25	10 June	26	20 Feb.				do	45 Foot.

Majors.

	CORNET, ETC.	LIEUT.	CAPTAIN.	MAJOR.	WHEN PLACED ON HALF PAY.	REGIMENTAL RANK.	
Samuel Braybrooke	17 Dec. 12	29 April 18	6 Mar. 23	27 Feb. 35		Major	Ceylon Rifle Regiment.
ᚼ Charles Makepeace	13 April 15	14 Mar. 16	24 July 23	6 Mar.		do	4 Dragoon Guards.
Redmond Wm. Brough	10 Mar. 07	15 July 08	10 Jan. 22	29 May		do	2 Foot.
ᚼ Henry Fred. Lockyer, KH.	25 Mar. 13	19 Jan. 14	20 June 22	12 June		do	97 Foot.
Charles Deane, KH.	5 Sept. 04	6 July 06	5 Dec. 18	19 June		do	1 Foot.
ᚼ ᚼ Alexander Forbes[68]	28 Sept. 09	8 Aug. 11	17 Mar. 25	7 Aug.	25 May 38	do	Unattached.
Henry Arthur O'Neill	11 Oct. 21	10 Sept. 24	4 Feb. 26	28 Aug.		do	12 Foot.
Gervas Power	12 Sept. 16	7 April 25	8 April 26	4 Sept.		do	10 Foot.
Simcoe Baynes	24 June 12	28 Dec. 15	24 June 24	2 Oct.		do	8 Foot.
Walter Ogilvy[94]	29 Nov. 21	7 Nov. 23	8 April 26	do	20 Nov. 35	do	Unattached.
William James D'Urban	7 Oct. 19	25 Sept. 23	8 April 26	16 Oct.		do	25 Foot.
ᚼ James Macdougall	11 June 12	8 Sept. 13	10 Sept. 25	23 Oct.		do	42 Foot.
ᚼ Geo. Fitz Gerald Stack, KH.	13 June 05	4 Dec. 06	25 May 15	26 Oct.		do	24 Foot.
ᚼ George Hibbert	25 Feb. 13	14 June 15	6 Mar. 23	13 Nov.		do	40 Foot.
Thomas Skinner	25 Jan. 16	6 Aug. 19	9 Oct. 23	24 Nov.		do	31 Foot.
William Noel Hill	13 Nov. 17	24 Oct. 21	14 Nov. 26	do		do	60 Foot.
ᚼ ᚼ Alexander Grant, KH.[69]	16 Aug. 04	24 Mar. 06	15 April 13	25 Dec.	25 Dec. 35	do	Unattached.
Thomas Simson Pratt	2 Feb. 14	20 April 20	17 Sept. 25	do		do	26 Foot.
Henry Stones	28 Dec. 15	7 Nov. 18	25 Dec. 23	19 Feb. 36		do	13 Dragoons.
John Byrne	1 Oct. 08	21 Dec. 09	19 April 21	26 Feb.		Captain	31 Foot.
James Hunter	23 Mar. 15	24 June 19	20 Aug. 25	4 Mar.	4 Mar. 36	Major	Unattached.
Henry Clinton	22 Mar. 21	31 July 23	11 July 26	do	do	do	Unattached.
George James Romney[70]	Dec. 06	15 Jan. 07	19 Aug. 19	1 April	10 Nov. 37	do	Unattached.
John Cornell Chads	4 May 09	1 Dec. 14	27 Jan. 20	22 April		do	1 West India Regiment.
John Stuart	22 Jan. 20	26 Mar. 23	13 Aug. 25	6 May		do	7 Foot.
Philip Hill	11 Mar. 24	17 Sept. 25	29 Aug. 26	13 May		do	53 Foot.
ᚼ ᚼ Charles Stewart[71]	17 Mar. 08	29 Dec. 13	27 July 20	27 May	24 April 38	do	Unattached.
Forrester Owen Leighton	30 Dec. 13	7 April 25	29 Mar. 27	20 May		do	56 Foot.
Henry John French	27 Aug. 12	21 July 13	25 Sept. 23	23 May		do	85 Foot.
Benj. Fra. Dalton Wilson	27 Aug. 25	10 June 26	20 April 32	17 June		do	35 Foot.
ᚼ Fred. Chidley Irwin, KH.	25 Mar. 08	17 Aug. 09	27 Mar. 27	28 June		Captain	63 Ft. *Commandant of the Troops in [Western Australia.*
Robert Dampier Hallifax	22 July 23	8 April 26	11 June 30	8 July		Major	7 Dragoon Guards.
Henry C. Cowell[72]	31 July 23	23 June 25	8 April 26	30 July		do	75 Foot.
	25 Aug. 04	26 Mar. 05	21 July 13	16 Sept.	16 Sept. 36	do	Unattached.

Majors.

	CORNET, ETC.	LIEUT.	CAPTAIN.	MAJOR.	WHEN PLACED ON HALF PAY.	REGIMENTAL RANK.	
Saville Broom.............	28 Dec. 15	15 Jan. 20	10 Mar. 25	16 Sept. 36		Major	10 Foot.
Samuel Blyth..............	21 Feb. 11	28 April 13	25 April 28	22 Nov.		do	49 Foot.
⑩ James Nisbet Colquhoun	1 June 08	8 Sept. 10	6 Nov. 27	2 Dec.		Captain	Royal Artillery.
Samuel Brendram Boileau	4 Oct. 21	1 Aug. 26	25 Nov. 28	9 Dec.		Major	22 Foot.
Joseph Bradshaw	12 May 25	12 Dec. 26	2 Dec. 31	do		do	37 Foot.
⑩ ⑳ John Flamank[73]	2 Nov. 09	12 Dec. 11	17 Feb. 21	16 Dec.	30 June 37	do	Unattached.
William Firebrace	28 July 14	20 June 17	28 Mar. 22	do		do	58 Foot.
John Arthur	25 Dec. 13	2 Mar. 20	8 Dec. 25	30 June 37		do	98 Foot.
Edward Sabine............	22 Dec. 03	20 July 04	24 Jan. 13	10 Jan. 37		Captain	Royal Artillery.
Henry Cooper	3 Oct. 05	18 June 07	25 Mar.	do		do	35 Foot.
⑩ Henry Simmonds	21 Mar. 05	28 Nov. 05	21 Mar.	do		Major	61 Foot.
Thomas Reed	9 July 03	25 Sept. 04	27 May	do		do	70 Foot.
⑩ Vance Young Donaldson	14 Sept. 04	25 Dec. 05	24 June	do		Captain	57 Foot
⑩ William Dunn	22 Dec. 03	20 July 04	22 July 13	do		do	Royal Artillery.
⑩ Henry Owen Wood	6 July 04	25 Dec. 04	22 July	do		Captain	37 Foot.
Zachary Clutterbuck Bayly	22 Dec. 03	27 July 04	28 Aug.	do		do	Royal Artillery.
⑩ Henry Clements	7 April 05	26 Aug. 07	1 Sept.	do		Major	16 Foot.
⑩ George Barney	11 July 08	24 June 09	1 Sept.	do		Captain	Royal Engineers.
⑩ John Doyle	28 Sept. 04	13 Nov. 05	29 Sept.	do		do	72 Foot.
Edwin Cruttenden........	14 Jan. 04	29 July 04	25 Oct.	do		do	Royal Artillery.
⑩ Harry David Jones	17 Sept. 08	24 June 09	12 Nov.	do		do	Royal Engineers.
Charles Gregory..........	27 Feb. 05	2 Aug. 05	8 Dec.	do		do	49 Foot.
⑩ John Hankey Bainbrigge	25 Mar. 09	9 Mar. 09	9 Mar.	do	25 Dec. 14	do	H.-p. 41 Foot, *Fort-Maj.-&-Adj. Guernsey.*
Henry Crause.............	14 Nov. 05	12 Oct. 07	16 Dec.	do		do	Cape Mounted Riflemen.
Richard Henry Bonnycastle	28 Sept. 08	24 June 09	11 Feb.	do		do	Royal Engineers.
⑩ ⑳ James Sinclair	9 June 09	15 Nov. 04	14 Feb.	do		do	Royal Artillery.
⑩ Roche Meade, KH.[74]	3 Aug. 09	23 Oct. 11	17 Feb.	do	31 May 39	Major	Unattached, *Dep.-Assist.-Adjt.-General* Late of Royal Marines.
James Hull Harrison[75]	6 Sept. 98	16 April 04	23 Feb.	do		Captain	Royal Engineers.
⑩ Anthony Marshall......	1 Oct. 08	1 Aug. 09	28 Feb.	do		do	Royal Engineers.
George Forbes Thompson	30 June 04	9 May 05	1 Mar.	do		do	Unattached.
Henry Hutton Jacob[76]	10 Jan. 09	20 Dec. 04	10 Mar.	do	17 Sept. 39	Major	Royal Artillery.
James Gray...............	10 Jan. 09	1 Dec. 09	4 May	do		Captain	Royal Engineers.
⑩ Robert Sloper Piper	30 July 07	30 Mar. 09	16 May	do		do	Royal Engineers.
⑩ Charles Barnwell			19 May	do		do	9 Foot.

Majors.

	2D LIEUT. ETC.	LIEUT.	CAPTAIN.	MAJOR.	WHEN PLACED ON HALF PAY.	REGIMENTAL RANK.	
Henry Clinton Van Cortlandt	8 May 01	1 Nov. 03	5 July 14	10 Jan. 37		Major	31 Foot.
John Charles Griffiths	15 Oct. 07	20 July 09	7 July	do	25 Dec. 18	Captain	Half pay 94 Foot.
Julius Fleming	22 Sept. 98	8 May 04	27 July	do		do	Late of Royal Marines.
Sir George Gipps	11 Jan. 09	21 Dec. 09	30 Sept.	do		Captain	R. Engineers, *Gov. of New South Wales.*
Philip Barry	10 Feb. 09	1 Mar. 10	1 Oct.	do		do	Royal Engineers.
James Fogo	18 June 04	21 Dec. 04	4 Oct.	do		do	Royal Artillery.
Thomas Smith	1 Dec.	4 25 June	5 25 Oct.	do		do	97 Foot.
Geo. Henry Edw. Murphy	27 Nov. 05	2 July 07	25 Oct.	do		do	6 Foot.
Wm. Ranaldson Dickson	25 Dec. 06	28 Jan. 08	25 Oct.	do		do	Half-pay New Brunswick Fencibles.
John Macphail	2 Jan. 06	29 Sept. 08	25 Oct.	do		do	98 Foot, *Lieut.-Governor of Dominica.*
O'Hara Baynes	16 July 04	21 Dec. 04	28 Nov.	do	1 Aug. 27	do	h. p. R. Art. *Town Major of Alderney.*
Richard Wheeler Hooper	28 Aug. 07	4 Jan. 10	8 Dec.	do		do	69 Foot.
Hon. William Arbuthnott	16 July 04	21 Dec. 04	20 Dec.	do		do	Royal Artillery.
Henry Blachley	10 Aug. 04	18 Feb. 05	20 Dec.	do		do	Royal Artillery.
James Archibald Chalmer	10 Aug. 04	1 Mar. 05	20 Dec.	do		do	Royal Artillery.
William Redman Ord	25 April 09	29 May 10	20 Dec.	do		do	Royal Engineers.
Peter John Willats	31 Aug. 09	2 June 11	22 Dec.	do		Major	48 Foot.
John Costlcy	14 Feb. 05	1 Mar. 06	12 Jan. 15	do	15 Feb. 39	Captain	Unattached.
John Casimer Harold	25 Sept. 06	28 May 07	16 Feb.	do		do	74 Foot.
Charles Wallett	16 Aug. 04	9 Oct. 06	23 Mar.	do		do	Ceylon Rifle Regiment.
Wm. Henry Stopford	15 Sept. 04	2 July 05	1 April	do		do	Royal Artillery.
George Bolton[77]	27 Mar. 06	11 Dec. 06	4 April	do	27 Oct. 37	do	Half-pay 30 Foot.
Thomas Hewitt Baylie	14 Aug. 06	25 June 07	6 April	do		do	66 Foot.
Lloyd Dowse	29 Sept. 04	3 July 05	16 May	do		do	Royal Artillery.
George Denis Colman	29 Dec. 04	21 May 06	18 May	do		do	15 Foot.
George John Belson	29 Sept. 04	6 July 05	21 May	do		do	Royal Artillery.
Peter Desbrisay Stewart	29 Sept. 04	7 July 05	21 May	do		do	Royal Artillery.
Robert Franck Romer	9 Nov. 04	16 July 05	23 May	do		do	Royal Artillery.
Thomas Reid	2 July 05	20 June 06	16 June	do		Major	33 Foot.
Roger Kelsall	12 Feb. 09	1 May 11	16 June	do		Captain	Royal Engineers.
Richard Carr Molesworth	9 Nov. 04	17 July 05	20 June	do		do	Royal Artillery.
James Wm. Henry Walch[78]	10 May 97	27 Sept. 03	1 July	do	17 Feb. 37	Major	Unattached.
William Bell	23 Nov.	2 Dec. 05	3 July	do		Captain	Royal Artillery.
John Thoreau	26 Oct. 04	28 May 07	19 July	do		do	37 Foot.

Majors.

	2D LIEUT. ETC.	LIEUT.	CAPTAIN.	MAJOR.	WHEN PLACED ON HALF PAY.	REGIMENTAL RANK.	
‡ Oswald Pilling[79]........	30 Aug. 09	31 Jan. 10	27 July 15	10 Jan. 37	17 Jan. 34	Captain	Half-pay Portuguese Serv. Fort Major of [Sheerness.
George Brodie Fraser.....	14 Dec. 04	3 Dec. 05	1 Aug.	do		do	Royal Artillery.
William Cox	1 May 06	8 Aug. 07	21 Sept.	do		do	54 Foot.
‡ ¶¶ Matthew Louis	14 Dec.	28 Dec. 05	26 Oct.	do		do	Royal Artillery.
‡ Thomas Grantham	14 Dec.	29 Dec. 04	28 Oct.	do		do	Royal Artillery.
‡ Henry John Savage	30 Sept. 09	1 May 11	1 Dec.	do		do	Royal Engineers.
Samuel Charters[80].........	14 Dec.	13 Feb. 06	15 Jan. 16	do	2 Feb. 28	do	Half-pay Royal Artillery.
James Mason	11 July	5 Mar. 07	18 Jan.	do		do	77 Foot.
‡ Thomas Bennett Hickin .	2 May 05	31 Oct. 05	9 May	do		Major	29 Foot.
‡ ¶¶ William Irwin	10 Nov.	20 July 09	9 May	do		Captain	28 Foot.
Henry Lecky	25 July	19 Oct. 05	23 May	do		do	36 Foot.
Francis Haultain	14 Dec.	23 Feb. 06	7 June	do		do	Royal Artillery.
John Gordon	10 May	1 June 06	5 Aug.	do		do	Royal Artillery.
‡ ¶¶ Marcus Antonius Waters	30 Sept. 09	1 May 11	1 Nov.	do		do	Royal Engineers.
Robert Martin	15 Aug.	28 Mar. 05	21 Nov.	do		do	46 Foot.
Pennel Cole	1 Feb. 10	1 May 11	7 Feb. 17	do		do	Royal Engineers.
‡ Poole Vallancey England	10 May 05	1 June 06	11 Mar.	do		do	Royal Artillery.
Alexander Maclean	6 Sept.	16 Sept. 04	30 June	do		do	86 Foot.
Charles Boyd	15 Aug.	19 Dec. 05	12 July	do	3 May 39	do	Unattached.
‡ ¶¶ Edward Duncan	3 Sept.	28 Feb. 08	24 July	do		Captain	48 Foot.
Henry Burnside	8 Oct.	18 Feb. 07	13 Nov.	do		Major	61 Foot.
‡ ¶¶ Richard Handcock ...	10 Sept.	5 Nov. 05	30 July 18	do		Captain	46 Foot.
Irwine Whitty	12 July 05	1 June 06	23 Oct.	do		do	Royal Artillery.
William Greenville........	9 Mar. 09	12 Dec. 11	1 Jan. 19	do		do	2 Foot.
Edward Wm. Bray........	12 Jan.	20 April 05	6 April	do		do	31 Foot.
Henry Lewis Sweeting	9 Aug. 05	1 June 06	1 May	do		do	Royal Artillery.
Peter Sutherland	1 Sept.	15 Jan. 04	20 May	do		do	72 Foot.
David Hay	6 Oct.	31 Oct. 08	5 Aug.	do		* Major	6 Dragoon Guards.
‡ William Turner	9 April	26 Aug. 07	4 Nov.	do		Captain	50 Foot.
‡ George Cosby Harpour ..	20 April 96	29 Dec. 08	9 Dec.	do		do	67 Foot.
‡ William Johnstone	25 Feb.	30 Mar. 08	20 April 20	do		do	26 Foot.
‡ Frederick Wright	13 Sept. 05	1 June 06	22 April	do		do	Royal Artillery.
‡ James Humphreys Wood	13 Sept. 05	1 June	11 May	do		do	Royal Artillery.
Wm. James Sutherland ...	3 May 14	22 Sept. 14	20 June	do		do	21 Foot.

Majors.

	CORNET, ETC.	LIEUT.	CAPTAIN.	MAJOR.	WHEN PLACED ON HALF PAY.	REGIMENTAL RANK.	
William Ernst Jackson	13 Sept. 05	1 June 06	29 July 20	10 Jan. 37		Captain	Royal Artillery.
‡ Lewis Moore Bennett	25 Feb. 08	30 May 08	3 Aug.	do		do	64 Foot.
‡ John Patterson	27 Nov. 06	22 Dec.	19 Oct.	do	3 May 21	do	Half-pay York Chasseurs.
‡ Basil Robinson Heron	13 Sept. 05	1 June 06	6 Nov.	do		do	Royal Artillery.
Thomas Stewart[81]	April	30 Oct.	9 Nov.	do	27 July 38	do	Unattached.
George Topp Lindsay	21 Dec. 08	21 Sept. 09	27 Dec.	do		Major	94 Foot.
‡ Edward Matson	7 May 10	1 May	11 9 Jan. 21	do		Captain	Royal Engineers.
‡ John Crawfurd	14 May 12	17 Sept. 13	17 May	do		do	6 Foot.
Charles O'Neill	18 May 15	27 June	16 31 May	do		do	44 Foot.
‡ James Conway Victor	1 June	1 May	11 19 June	do		do	Royal Engineers.
‡ Crighton Grierson	1 June	1 May	11 1 July	do		do	Royal Engineers.
‡ Henry Reid[82]	17 Mar. 08	26 July	09 26 July	do	27 Sept. 39	Major	Half-pay 3 Ceylon Regiment.
George Durnford	1 Nov.	1 June	06 6 Aug.	do		Captain	R. Artillery.
‡‡‡ Wm. Warburton Huntley	16 June	14 23 Oct.	15 13 Sept.	do		do	3 Dragoon Guards.
‡ Tristram Charnley Squire	24 April	09 31 Jan.	10 18 Oct.	do		Major	13 Foot.
George Duff	6 Feb.	17 14 Oct.	19 9 Nov.	do		Captain	93 Foot.
‡‡‡ George Pringle[83]	9 July	11 1 June	06 24 Dec. 22	do		do	Late of Royal Artillery.
William Chambre	23 May	16 27 May	12 10 Jan.	do		do	11 Foot.
Hon. Arthur Charles Legge		27 Feb.	17 17 Jan.	do	23 June 37	do	Unattached.
*Francisco Bussiett	6 Oct. 08	14 June	10 31 Oct.	do		do	Royal Malta Fencibles Regt.
‡‡ William Long[64]	18 July	11 19 Mar.	12 7 Nov.	do	23 Mar. 38	do	Half-pay 9 Foot.
Wm. White Crawley	16 May	06 20 Nov.	07 14 Nov.	do		Major	74 Foot.
William Kemp	2 Dec.	07 24 May	10 5 Dec.	do		Captain	80 Foot.
‡ Edward Philip White	1 June	10 1 May	11 20 Dec.	do	22 Mar. 39	Major	Half-pay Royal Staff Corps.
‡ Richard John Barou	1 April	06 11 Feb.	08 26 Dec.	do		Captain	Royal Engineers.
Thomas Edwin Kelly	1 Mar.	06 1 June	06 30 Dec.	do		Major	Rifle Brigade.
Charles Dalton	21 Mar.	06 3 June	06 31 Dec.	do		Captain	Royal Artillery.
James Robert Colebrooke	9 Dec.	19 May	25 19 Sept.	26 17 Feb.	23 Mar. 38	do	Royal Artillery.
Melville Dalyell	28 Aug.	17 20 April	26 3 April	28		Major	Unattached.
Henry Eyre	15 Mar.	21 25 Aug.	23 3 Aug.	26 10 Mar.		do	1 Foot.
Richard Bennett	26 Nov.	07 10 Aug.	09 25 Nov.	23 7 April		do	98 Foot.
‡ Charles Jowett Van der Meulen	16 Dec.	13 5 Dec.	18 26 June	23 28 April		do	73 Foot.
Martin Geo. Thomas Lindsay	18 Sept. 17	6 Oct.	25 22 April	26 16 June		do	78 Foot.
Charles John Deshon						do	17 Foot.

Majors.

	2D LIEUT. ETC.	LIEUT.	CAPTAIN.	MAJOR.	WHEN PLACED ON HALF PAY.	REGIMENTAL RANK.	
Charles Cranfurd Hay	27 June	24 24 Dec.	25 19 Sept.	26 16 June 37		Major	19 Foot.
Hon. George Upton	24 April	23 29 Oct.	25 12 Dec.	do		do	62 Foot.
Edward St. Maur	22 June	15 16 Nov.	20 29 May	23 1 July		do	51 Foot.
Henry Houghton Irving	1 Feb.	14 26 Dec.	16 3 June	24 11 July		do	58 Foot.
Samuel Madden Francis Hall	21 Jan.	19 7 April	25 22 April	26 do		do	75 Foot.
George Gayton Palmer	20 Dec.	09 1 Oct.	13 26 Aug.	31 do		Captain	Royal Artillery.
George Ruxton	7 Nov.	22 24 Jan.	25 4 Mar.	26 4 Aug.		Major	34 Foot.
Joseph Simmons	16 April	12 23 Dec.	13 18 Feb.	27 22 Aug.		do	41 Foot.
George Lenox Davis	15 Sept.	08 15 Oct.	11 7 April	25 17 Oct.		do	9 Foot.
Thomas Matheson	17 Aug.	15 30 Oct.	23 2 Aug.	26 20 Oct.		do	23 Foot.
Arthur William Biggs	29 July	24 11 Feb.	26 14 May	29 21 Oct.		do	7 Dragoons.
D'Arcey Wentworth	21 Feb.	11 9 Aug.	12 7 April	25 3 Nov.	1 Dec. 37	do	Unattached.
Horatio Walpole	never	8 May	17 13 Jan.	17 Nov.		do	39 Foot.
Hon. Geo. Augustus Browne	27 April	20 28 Aug.	29 31 Dec.	1 Dec.		do	64 Foot.
Arthur Cunliffe Pole	7 Nov.	26 5 June	30 18 Oct.	33 1 Dec.		do	63 Foot.
Francis Perry	8 Oct.	12 18 Feb.	13 8 June	26 8 Dec.		do	Royal African Corps.
George Procter	25 Nov.	21 1 July	24 11 July	26 26 Dec.		Captain	*Adjutant Royal Military College.*
John Campbell	19 Feb.	18 11 Oct.	21 14 July	25 29 Dec.		Major	38 Foot.
John Fred. Sales Clarke	6 Jan.	19 26 May	25 25 Feb.	25 30 Dec.		do	2 Dragoons.
Charles St. Lo Malet	11 Oct.	21 27 Nov.	24 10 June	26 10 Jan. 38		do	8 Foot.
Clopton Lewis Wingfield	2 Apr.	07 4 May	09 25 Aug.	25 2 Feb.		do	66 Foot.
William Sadlier	25 May	09 25 July	11 17 Aug.	25 4 Feb.	16 Feb. 38	do	4 Foot.
George Simmons	23 Dec.	19 2 Oct.	23 19 Nov.	28 16 Feb.		do	Unattached.
Henry Deedes	30 May	22 7 April	25 19 Sept.	25 23 Feb.		do	34 Foot.
Ormsby Phibbs	12 April	25 28 Jan.	26 25 Nov.	26 16 Mar.		do	88 Foot.
John Gordon	10 Jan.	22 23 June	25 27 Sept.	31 24 Mar.		do	47 Foot.
William Denny	19 Jan.	14 13 April	20 15 April	33 24 April		do	71 Foot.
Jonathan Forbes	16 Nov.	09 23 July	12 19 Nov.	24 18 May 38		do	78 Foot.
Dugald M'Nicol	26 Oct.	20 17 Mar.	25 5 April	25 23 May		do	1 Foot.
Andrew Brown	10 Dec.	25 14 Feb.	28 22 Mar.	31 26 May		do	79 Foot.
Charles Barton	14 Oct.	24 22 July	25 24 April	33 1 June		do	14 Dragoons.
Raymond White	26 Oct.	20 17 Mar.	25 5 April	28 9 June		do	6 Dragoons.
George Browne	10 June	13 30 Sept.	19 10 Feb.	32 15 June		Captain	32 Foot.
James Oliphant Clunie	27 Aug.	13 1 Dec.	14 9 Feb.	26 23 June		Major	3 Foot.

Majors.

Name	2D LIEUT. ETC.	LIEUT.	CAPTAIN.	MAJOR.	WHEN PLACED ON HALF PAY.	REGIMENTAL RANK.	
John Picton Beete	7 Sept. 20	16 Sept. 24	6 Nov. 27	26 June 38		Major	21 Foot.
⚜ ✠ Frederick Mainwaring	5 April 10	15 April 13	4 Dec. 28	27 June do		do	51 Foot.
⚜ John Bonamy	19 Dec. 11	10 Feb. 14	24 Jan. 23	28 June do		Captain	6 Foot.
⚜ John Marshall	14 May 08	23 Nov. 09	20 Feb. do	do		do	91 Foot.
⚜ Thomas James Adair	25 May 09	20 Feb. 11	27 Mar. do	do		do	67 Foot.
⚜ Richard Manners	13 April 09	8 Feb. 10	22 May do	do		do	59 Foot.
James Tomlinson	5 Oct. 15	5 Nov. 18	5 June do	do		do	11 Dragoons.
Richard Burne Rawnsley	21 Mar. 06	22 Oct. 06	12 June do	do		do	Royal Artillery.
⚜ ✠ William Augustus Raynes	25 April 06	22 Oct. 06	26 June do	do		do	Royal Artillery.
⚜ ✠ Richard Hardinge, KH.	23 May 06	14 Jan. 07	17 July do	do		do	Royal Artillery.
Joseph Hanwell	21 Nov. 05	25 Dec. 06	4 Sept. do	do		do	18 Foot.
Jeremiah Cowper	15 Mar. 09	19 April 10	31 Dec. do	do		do	25 Foot.
✠ John Henry Cooke	30 Sept. 13	7 Aug. 17	1 April 24	do		do	11 Foot.
⚜ ✠ Henry Keane Bloomfield	8 April 13	22 June 15	5 May do	do		do	Unattached.
⚜ ✠ Barton Parker Browne[87]	25 May 09	1 Mar. 11	6 May do	do	10 May 39	do	3 Dragoons.
Henry Bond	14 April 13	14 Jan. 19	13 May do	do		Major	32 Foot.
⚜ ✠ John Birtwhistle	12 June 17	3 Feb. 20	24 June do	do		Captain	22 Foot.
Arthur Myers	13 Oct. 08	18 Feb. 12	18 Aug. do	do		do	87 Foot.
⚜ James T. Moore	16 May 13	2 Nov. 19	2 Sept. do	do		do	50 Foot.
James H. Serjeantson	13 May 13	19 Jan. 15	23 Sept. do	do	6 Dec. 39	do	Unattached.
Walter Harris	22 Nov. 10	28 Feb. 12	21 Oct. do	do		do	90 Foot.
⚜ Horace Suckling	15 Aug. 13	26 April 14	18 Nov. do	do		do	60 Foot.
Robert Andrews	1 July 06	15 Oct. 07	26 Nov. do	do		do	Royal Artillery.
Thomas Howard Fenwick	21 July 10	1 May 11	2 Dec. do	do		do	Royal Engineers.
⚜ William Fraser	8 April 13	19 Jan. 14	9 Dec. do	do		do	43 Foot.
Lewis Alexander Hall	21 July 10	1 May 11	12 Jan. 25	do		do	Royal Engineers.
⚜ John Clarke	14 July 08	3 Oct. 09	13 Jan. do	do		do	66 Foot.
*Giovanni Gouder			24 Jan. do	do		do	Royal Malta Fencibles Regt.
⚜ ✠ John Stoyte	21 Mar. 11	4 July 13	27 Jan. do	do		do	24 Foot.
James Spence	26 Nov. 08	20 Dec. 10	10 Feb. do	do		do	31 Foot.
⚜ James Algeo	2 Sept. 06	4 Sept. 06	24 Feb. do	do		do	77 Foot.
Edmund Sheppard	1 July 06	1 Feb. 08	2 Mar. do	do		do	Royal Artillery.
⚜ Andrew Snape Hamond Aplin	5 July 10	24 Sept. 12	9 Mar. do	do		Major	89 Foot.

Majors.

	CORNET, ETC.	LIEUT.	CAPTAIN.	MAJOR.	WHEN PLACED ON HALF PAY.	REGIMENTAL RANK.	
Patrick Yule	1 May 11	11 May 11	23 Mar. 25	28 June 38		Captain	Royal Engineers.
Charles Jasper Selwyn	1 May 11	18 July 11	23 Mar.	do		do	Royal Engineers.
James Hutchinson	14 Nov. 05	14 April 08	2 April	do	17 Aug. 38	do	Half-pay 5 Foot.
Francis Williams Dillon	5 Dec. 05	6 Mar. 07	7 April	do		do	18 Foot.
Isaac Richardson	5 Aug. 07	1 Oct. 08	do	do		do	11 Foot.
Robert Browne	12 May 08	8 June 09	do	do		do	16 Foot.
William Cannon	26 Aug. 07	7 June 10	do	do		do	97 Foot.
Richard Tatton	28 July 09	7 June 11	do	do		do	77 Foot.
James Jackson	2 Mar. 09	19 June 11	do	do		do	57 Foot.
James Creagh	1 Jan. 10	4 Mar. 12	do	do		Major	86 Foot.
William Graham	13 July 09	12 May 12	do	do		Captain	59 Foot.
William A. Riach	17 Oct. 11	17 June 13	do	do		do	79 Foot.
Thomas Nickoll	23 May 05	29 April 06	8 April	do		do	1 Foot.
George Ogilvy	Jan. 07	5 Nov. 07	do	do		do	31 Foot.
William Henry Arthure	19 Feb. 07	21 Jan. 08	do	do		do	56 Foot.
Thomas L'Estrange	9 Oct. 06	29 Feb. 08	do	do		Major	36 Foot.
William Bindon	21 Mar. 00	19 May	do	do		Captain	Royal Newf. Vet. Companies.
Fred. Campbell Montgomery	18 Mar. 07	14 July	do	do		do	50 Foot.
William Matthew Gosset	14 Dec. 11	1 July 12	9 April	do		do	Royal Engineers.
William Thomas Hunt	29 April 13	17 Nov. 14	26 May	do		Major	85 Foot.
Nicholas Palmer	11 Nov. 13	3 May 21	do	do		Captain	56 Foot.
Thomas L. L. Galloway	14 April 13	14 Nov. 22	2 June	do		do	10 Foot.
Joseph Robert Raines	19 Sept. 05	28 May 07	7 June	do		do	95 Foot.
Daniel Bolton	14 Dec. 11	1 July 12	9 June	do		do	Royal Engineers.
Henry Sykes Stephens	24 June 15	8 Nov. 15	do	do		do	86 Foot.
Charles Baillie Brisbane	21 Mar. 16	20 May 19	do	do		do	34 Foot.
John Lewis Black	22 April 13	10 Mar. 14	16 June	do		do	53 Foot.
Charles Douglas	never	19 May 14	do	do	16 Aug. 39	do	9 Foot.
Lawrence Greame	16 Mar. 15	13 Dec. 21	do	do		do	Unattached.
Charles Hastings Doyle	23 Dec. 19	27 Sept. 22	do	do		do	24 Foot.
Walter White	16 June 08	7 Aug. 09	23 June	do	23 June 25	do	Unattached, *Town Major of Dublin.*
Richard Westmore	28 May 12	1 April 13	do	do		do	33 Foot.
Thomas Bonnor	5 Oct.	24 Dec. 18	30 June	do		do	Ceylon Rifle Regiment.
Manley Power	24 June 19	17 April 23	do	do		do	85 Foot.

Majors.

	CORNET, ETC.	LIEUT.	CAPTAIN.	MAJOR.	WHEN PLACED ON HALF PAY.	REGIMENTAL RANK.	
William Henry Law	29 April 13	28 Nov. 16	14 July 25	28 June 38		Captain	83 Foot.
Charles Barry	23 Mar. 14	3 Feb. 15	21 July	do		do	73 Foot.
James M'Queen	31 Mar.	11 Feb. 19	do	do		do	15 Dragoons.
Lewis Shuldham Barrington Robertson[88]	1 July 06	1 Feb. 08	29 July	do		do	Late of Royal Artillery.
Walter Elphinstone Lock	do	do	2 Mar.	do		do	Royal Artillery.
Philip Sandilands	4 Oct. 06	do	do	do		do	Royal Artillery.
Browne Willis	do	do	do	do		do	Royal Artillery.
Benjamin Hutcheson Vaughan	do	do	do	do		do	Royal Artillery.
Thomas Gordon Higgins	do	do	do	do		do	Royal Artillery.
Frederick Wm. Whinyates	14 Dec. 11	1 July 12	29 July	do		do	Royal Engineers.
Alexander Watt Robe	do	do	do	do		do	Royal Engineers.
Ralph Carr Alderson	do	do	do	do		do	Royal Engineers.
Charles Wright	1 July 12	1 Mar. 13	do	do		do	Royal Engineers.
Charles Rivers	do	do	do	do		do	Royal Engineers.
Francis Ringler Thomson	do	21 July 13	do	do		do	Royal Engineers.
Amherst Wright	18 Dec. 06	1 Feb. 08	2 Mar.	do		do	Royal Artillery.
Hale Young Wortham	1 July 12	21 July 13	24 Sept.	do		do	Royal Artillery.
Charles Hall	21 May 18	27 Feb. 23	31 July	do		do	Royal Engineers.
Harman Jeffares	15 Feb. 10	4 Mar. 12	11 Aug.	do		do	1 Life Guards.
Edward Thorp	7 Mar. 11	28 Jan. 13	13 Aug.	do		do	Royal Newf. Veteran Companies.
Richard Hort	26 Jan. 19	4 May 22	27 Aug.	do		do	89 Foot.
John Lawrenson	12 Nov. 18	6 Dec. 21	27 Aug.	do		do	81 Foot.
Hunter Ward	1 Mar. 09	10 Sept. 12	1 Sept.	do		do	17 Dragoons.
John Dalzell	9 Sept. 19	31 Dec. 22	10 Sept.	do		do	16 Foot.
Alex. Boswell Armstrong	30 Jan. 12	5 Feb. 14	15 Sept.	do		do	48 Foot.
HarcourtMaster	30 July 18	6 Mar. 23	17 Sept.	do		do	Cape Mounted Riflemen.
Henry Winchcombe Hartley	10 Sept. 18	1 Oct. 20	1 Oct.	do		do	4 Dragoons.
Joseph Swinburne	16 Aug. 09	4 June 12	6 Oct.	do		do	8 Foot.
Samuel Waymouth	18 May 12	28 Mar. 13	13 Oct.	do		do	83 Foot.
James M'Douall	19 Feb.	2 Oct. 18	19 Oct.	do		do	30 Foot.
Edward Twopeny	27 Jan. 14	17 Aug. 20	22 Oct.	do		do	2 Life Guards.
George Montagu	8 Dec. 14	31 Oct. 22	22 Oct.	do		do	78 Foot.
George Carpenter	1 Oct. 18	1 Mar. 20	29 Oct.	do		do	42 Foot.
George Whannell	1 Mar. 11	16 Mar. 14	3 Nov.	do		do	41 Foot.
						do	33 Foot.

Majors.

	CORNET, ETC.	LIEUT.	CAPTAIN.	MAJOR.	WHEN PLACED ON HALF PAY.	REGIMENTAL RANK.	
Daniel Frazer	31 Oct. 11	13 June 16	5 Nov. 25	28 June 38		Captain	42 Foot.
Alexander Buchan 89	8 June 09	3 Oct. 11	10 Nov. 25	do	25 April 39	do	Unattached.
George Hogarth	22 May 17	13 Sept. 21	12 Nov. do	do		do	26 Foot.
訥 William Thain	13 May 13	15 Aug. 15	17 Nov. do	do		do	21 Foot.
John Crofton Peddie	4 May 14	29 June 20	26 Nov. do	do		do	21 Foot.
Richard Willington	1 Oct. 12	2 Oct. 14	3 Dec. do	do		Major	84 Foot.
William Snow	19 Dec. 15	19 Mar. 24	15 Dec. do	do		Captain	65 Foot.
Peter Cheape	25 May 13	3 Aug. 15	24 Dec. do	do		do	96 Foot.
John Alexander Forbes	5 Dec. 16	22 May 23	24 Dec. do	do		Major	92 Foot.
訥 Alexander M'Leod	3 Aug. 09	12 Dec. 11	31 Dec. do	do		Captain	61 Foot.
Charles Smith	20 Oct. 13	21 April 14	31 Dec. do	do		do	20 Foot.
Charles Highmore Potts	8 Feb. 16	13 Nov. 17	31 Dec. do	do		do	19 Foot.
Francis Westenra	31 July 17	24 Oct. 21	31 Dec. do	do		do	5 Dragoon Guards.
Edward Gage	never	26 Oct. 30	20 May 36	do		Lt. & Capt.	Scots Fusilier Guards.
Lord Arthur Lennox	24 June 23	22 Feb. 25	1 Aug. 26	6 July		Major	71 Foot.
Mont. Cholmley Johnstone	27 Feb. 23	16 Dec. 24	19 Sept.	27 July		do	27 Foot.
John Burgh	25 Nov. 19	7 April 25	19 Sept.	28 July		do	93 Foot.
Thomas Richard Baker	9 Dec. 19	1 April 24	18 Feb.	31 Aug.		do	7 Foot.
Harry Shakespear Phillips	8 Jan. 24	12 May 25	14 Feb. 28	do		do	53 Foot.
Thomas Arthur	23 June 25	19 Sept. 26	8 Feb. 31	15 Sept.		do	3 Dragoon Guards.
Richardson William Huey	26 Mar. 25	19 Dec. 26	11 June 30	13 Oct.		do	68 Foot.
William Hake	25 June 07	1 Nov. 10	7 May 27	23 Nov.		do	13 Dragoons.
Studholme John Hodgson	30 Dec. 19	3 Feb. 25	30 Dec. 26	28 Dec.		do	19 Foot.
Charles Franklyn	17 July 23	8 April 26	10 July 28	do		do	84 Foot.
Thomas Leigh Goldie	13 June 25	10 Dec. 25	24 Nov. 28	do		do	66 Foot.
Henry Williams Adams	31 July 23	31 Dec. 25	10 June 26	18 Jan. 39		do	18 Foot.
John Heneage Grubbe	20 Aug. 18	24 Feb. 25	13 May 26	19 Jan.		do	76 Foot.
Charles Stoddard	15 Mar. 23	9 Feb. 25	7 Feb. 34	1 Feb.	7 Feb. 34	Captain	Half-pay Royal Staff Corps
George Henry Lockwood	10 Mar. 25	10 Aug. 26	7 Sept. 32	6 Mar.		Major	3 Dragoons.
訥 George Bell	14 Mar. 11	17 Feb. 14	7 Aug. 28	29 Mar.		Captain	1 Foot.
Gustavus Charles Du Plat, KH.	1 Aug. 14	1 July 15	8 Feb. 36	do		do	Royal Engineers.
Thomas Foster	1 Sept. 15	7 Sept. 19	10 Jan. 37	do		do	Royal Engineers.
Alexander Murray Tulloch	9 April 26	30 Nov. 27	12 Mar. 38	do		do	Unattached.
訥 John Maclean	2 May 11	10 Dec. 12	25 Dec. 30	12 April	1 June 38	Major	20 Foot.

Majors.

	2D LIEUT. ETC.	LIEUT.	CAPTAIN.	MAJOR.	WHEN PLACED ON HALF PAY.	REGIMENTAL RANK.	
Richard French	9 June 25	30 Dec. 26	2 Mar. 32	11 May 39		Major	52 Foot.
Hon. Lauderdale Maule	24 Aug. 26	21 July 31	22 May 35	do		do	79 Foot.
Richard Irton	11 May 15	20 May 24	29 Aug. 26	31 May		do	Rifle Brigade.
Augustus Wathen	9 July 20	24 June 23	26 Sept. 26	do		do	15 Hussars.
John James Slater	20 May 14	7 Jan. 19	17 Aug. 26	21 June		do	82 Foot.
Wm. Robert Brudenell Smith	29 July 24	28 Jan. 26	20 Mar. 27	do		do	15 Foot.
William Eyre	17 April 23	5 Nov. 25	20 Mar. 27	19 July		do	73 Foot.
James Kershaw	13 Feb. 17	2 Dec. 24	11 Aug. 29	23 July		Captain	13 Foot.
Thomas Sidney Powell	13 May 26	31 May 31	13 Nov. 35	do		do	6 Foot.
🜚 Wm. Henry Rutherford [90]	1 Sept. 08	22 Nov. 10	14 May 29	10 Aug.	1 Nov. 39	Major	Unattached.
Arthur Charles Lowe	20 April 15	10 Aug. 15	3 April 27	21 Aug.		do	16 Dragoons.
Duncan Alexander Cameron	8 April 25	15 Aug. 26	21 June 33	23 Aug.		do	42 Foot.
Francis Octavius Montgomery	13 April 26	28 April 27	15 Nov. 30	6 Sept.		do	45 Foot.
Robert Fanshawe Martin	26 June 23	20 Aug. 25	10 June 26	17 Sept.		do	76 Foot.
🜚 Edgar Gibson [91]	5 Dec. 12	26 Mar. 14	24 May 31	20 Sept.	13 Dec. 39	do	Unattached.
Alexander Sharrock	7 Aug. 06	30 June 08	27 April 27	27 Sept.		do	29 Foot.
Frederick Markham	13 May 24	22 Oct. 25	16 April 29	28 Sept.		do	32 Foot.
Edw. Hungerford Delaval Elers Napier	11 Aug. 25	11 Oct. 26	21 June 31	11 Oct.		do	46 Foot.
Edward Last	13 Oct. 14	20 Nov. 24	22 May 30	18 do		do	99 Foot.
John H. Poole	24 Mar. 14	30 Sept. 19	1 Nov. 30	do		do	22 Foot.
Sir Wm. Payne Gallwey, Bart.	29 July 24	22 Sept. 25	21 Sept. 32	1 Nov.		do	88 Foot.
🜚 Edward Nevil Macready [92]	8 Sept. 13	20 July 14	16 July 29	22 Nov.	22 Nov. 39	do	Unattached.
John Peter Nelley	13 Aug. 25	10 June 26	11 Oct. 31	29 Nov.		do	77 Foot.
Richard Stack	24 Jan. 09	3 Mar. 11	12 Nov. 27	6 Dec.		Captain	45 Foot.
George Alexander Malcolm	31 Dec. 25	7 June 27	30 Dec. 31	13 Dec.		Major	3 Dragoons.
Henry Wilmot Charlton	23 June 25	30 Dec. 26	13 Nov. 32	do		do	2 Dragoon Guards.
Henry Samuel Davis	13 April 27	8 Oct. 30	17 July 35	do		do	52 Foot.
Godfrey Charles Mundy	25 Nov. 21	28 Aug. 23	13 May 26	31 Dec.	31 Dec. 39	do	Unattached.
🜚 Leonard Morse Cooper [93]	2 Mar. 20	28 Mar. 25	19 Aug. 28	do		do	Rifle Brigade.
James Watson	26 May 14	23 Jan. 17	25 Feb. 31	10 Jan.	10 Jan. 40	do	Unattached.
Samuel Lettsom	22 Mar. 21	25 Dec. 22	14 Dec. 32	do		do	14 Foot.
James Mac Call	6 Mar. 27	2 April 29	4 Oct. 33	17 Jan.		do	80 Foot.
Thomas Woodward Eyles	23 June 25	17 Oct. 26	3 Aug. 30	31 Jan.		do	8 Dragoons.
David Lynar Fawcett	30 Mar. 20	6 Nov. 24	15 Aug. 26	7 Feb.		do	90 Foot.
	6 April 26	21 Nov. 28	21 Nov. 34	do		do	55 Foot.

Notes to the Majors.

1 Major Edward Wood served the Egyptian campaign of 1801, and has received the medal.

1* Major Wolfe served the Egyptian campaign of 1801, and has received the medal.

2 Major Langlands served in the Peninsula with the 74th regiment, and has received a medal and a clasp for the assaults and captures of Ciudad Rodrigo and Badajoz: slightly wounded at the former, and severely at the latter.

3 Major Onslow served the campaign of 1799 in Holland, including the actions of the 10th and 19th Sept., 2nd and 6th October. Served also in the Peninsula from 1809 to the end of the war, including the battles of Talavera, Albuhera, Usagre, Busaco, Salamanca, Vittoria, and Toulouse, besides various skirmishes.

4 Major Wm. Campbell served in the Peninsula, and has received a medal and a clasp for the battles of the Pyrenees and Nivelle.

5 Sir Victor Von Arentsschildt served in the Peninsula, and has received a medal and two clasps for the battles of Busaco, Fuentes d'Onor, and Toulouse.

6 Major Robyns served in the American war.

7 Major Thorne served in the American war, and was present at the attack and capture of the fort and town of Castine, Bangor, and Machias, on the river Penobscot.

8 Major Christopher Wilkinson served the campaign of 1799 in Holland under the Duke of York. Accompanied the expedition to the north of Germany in 1805, under Lord Cathcart.

9 Major Sandham's services:—Campaign of 1799 in Holland, including the actions of the 27th Aug., 10th and 19th Sept., and 2nd Oct. Expedition to Copenhagen in 1807; to Sweden, and afterwards to Portugal and Spain, under Sir John Moore, 1808 and 9; and to Walcheren, 1809. Campaign in Holland, 1814; and in Flanders and France in 1815, including the battle of Waterloo.

10 Major Gore served in the American war, including the actions at Chrystler's Farm, and Niagara. Served also throughout the Burmese war, and commanded the 89th regiment five times in action during the war.

11 Major Annesley's services:—Campaign in Egypt, 1801; in Italy and Calabria, 1805 and 6, including the battle of Maida, and siege of Scylla Castle; in the Peninsula from Aug. 1811 to Feb. 1814, including the siege of the forts at, and battle of Salamanca, siege of Burgos, battles of the Pyrenees (28th July to 2nd Aug.), and Nivelle, at which last he was wounded in the ankle. Medal for the battle of Salamanca.

12 Major Hutton served in the Peninsula with the 4th Dragoons, from Aug. 1811 to May 1813.

13 Major Sweeny was severely wounded at Waterloo.

14 Major Greatly served in South America, under General Whitelock, in 1807; in Portugal and Spain in 1808 and 9, including the cavalry action at Benevente, and battle of Corunna. Served also at the attack and capture of Guadaloupe in 1810.

15 Major George Hall served in the Peninsula from Jan. 1811 to June 1812, and again from Oct. 1813 to the end of the war, including the following battles and sieges, viz.:—Fuentes d'Onor, Ciudad Rodrigo, Badajoz (severely wounded), Nive, Orthes, and Toulouse. Served also the campaign of 1815, and was present at the battle of Waterloo.

16 Major C. C. Michell served in the Peninsula, and has received a medal and a clasp for the battles of Vittoria, and Toulouse.

17 Major James Mill was slightly wounded at Waterloo.

18 Major Goldsmid served in the Peninsula from 1812 to the end of the war, including the cavalry affairs at Castrajon, Quintara de Puerta, and Monasterio, battles of Salamanca, and Vittoria, and siege of San Sebastian. Served also the campaign of 1815, and was present at the battle of Waterloo.

19 Major Edward Jones served at Walcheren in 1809; and in the Peninsula from July 1811 to the end of the war, including the action at El Bodon, and sieges and assaults of Ciudad Rodrigo, and Badajoz. Severely wounded at the storming of Ciudad Rodrigo.

20 Major Bowers was slightly wounded at Waterloo.

21 Major George Browne served in Portugal and Spain in 1808 and 9, including the retreat to, and battle of Corunna. Expedition to Walcheren, 1809. Peninsular campaigns of 1810, 11, 12, and 13, including the siege of Olivença, first investment of Badajoz, battle of Albuhera, affairs of Fuente Guinaldo and Aldea de Ponte, siege of Ciudad Rodrigo, siege

Notes to the Majors.

and assault of Badajoz, battle of Salamanca, retreat from Madrid, affair at Osma, and battles of Vittoria and the Pyrenees. Severely wounded at the assault of Badajoz, slightly at Salamanca, and severely at the Pass of Roncesvalles.

22 Major Percy Pratt joined the 2nd battalion of the 47th regiment in the Peninsula shortly after the fall of San Sebastian.

23 Major Alexander Fraser served at Walcheren in 1809, and afterwards in the Peninsula, including the following battles, sieges, &c. viz.: Busaco, Salamanca, Vittoria, San Sebastian, Bidassoa, Nivelle, and Nive.

24 Sir T. Livingston Mitchell served with his regiment the 95th (Rifle Brigade), at the sieges of Ciudad Rodrigo and Badajoz; and on the Quarter-Master-General's staff until the termination of the Peninsular war, when he was sent back to Spain and Portugal on a special mission to make surveys of the fields of battle and positions of the armies.

25 Major Felix was slightly wounded at Quatre Bras.

26 Major Trevor accompanied the 33rd regiment to the North of Germany in 1813; served with it in Holland in 1814, and was present at both attacks on Merxem, and the storming of Bergen-op-Zoom. Served also the campaign of 1815, including the actions at Quatre Bras and Waterloo, 16th, 17th, and 18th June.

27 Major T. H. Elliot served in the Peninsula from 1811 to Nov. 1813.

28 Major Thomas Seward was at the battle of Copenhagen in 1801; and at Navarin in 1827.

29 Major Wm. Bruce served in the Peninsula from 1812 to the end of the war, including the battles of the Pyrenees 28th, 29th, and 30th July, blockade of Pampeluna, battles of Nivelle 10th Nov., Nive 10th, 11th, 12th, and 13th Dec., investment of Bayonne, and battle of Toulouse. Served also the campaign of 1815, and was severely wounded at Waterloo.

30 Sir Trevor Wheler served in the Peninsula from June 1810 to the end of the war, including the actions of Pombal, Redinha, Foz d'Aronce, and Sabugal; battle of Fuentes d'Onor; affairs of Llerena, and Castrejon; battle of Salamanca; retreat from Burgos; battles of Vittoria, Nivelle, and near Bayonne on the 9th, 10th, 11th, and 12th Dec. 1813. Served also the campaign of 1815, including the battle of Waterloo.

31 Major H. A. Fraser served in Portugal and Spain in 1808 and 9, under Sir John Moore, including the battle of Corunna. Expedition to Walcheren 1809. Peninsular campaigns from 7th Aug. 1810 to Dec. 1812, and again from Feb. 1814 to the end of the war, including the battles of Busaco and Fuentes d'Onor, siege of Ciudad Rodrigo, battle of Salamanca, siege of Burgos (severely wounded through the body), and battle of Toulouse, where he was again severely wounded, a musket-ball having entered the right thigh. Served also the campaign of 1815, including the actions at Quatre Bras and Waterloo, at which latter he was slightly wounded.

32 Major Thomas Wright was slightly wounded at Waterloo.

33 Major Barralier served at the capture of Martinique in 1809, and of Guadaloupe in 1810, and again in 1815.

34 Major James Henderson served at the siege of Copenhagen and action at Keog in 1807. Expedition to Sweden, and afterwards to Portugal and Spain under Sir John Moore, 1808 and 9, including the action at Lugo and battle of Corunna. Expedition to Walcheren, 1809. Campaigns of 1814 and 15 in France and Flanders, including the affair at Tarbes, and battles of Toulouse and Waterloo, at which last he was severely wounded in the thigh by a grape-shot.

35 Major Wm. Smith served at the capture of Martinique in 1809.

36 Major Workman served at the capture of Martinique and the Saintes in 1809, and of Gaudaloupe in 1810, and again in 1815.

37 Major Sweetman served in Ireland during the rebellion in 1798; at the siege of Copenhagen in 1807; and afterwards in Portugal aud Spain, including the battles of Roleia, Vimiera, Corunna, capture of Oporto, and battle of Talavera.

38 Major Hore served in Egypt in 1801, and has received the medal.

39 Major Lawrence served in Egypt in 1801, and has received the medal.

40 Major Robert Kelly served in the Peninsula with the 5th battalion of the 60th regiment, and was severely wounded in action with the enemy 19th March 1814.

41 Major Wilkinson served on board H.M.S. *Dromeda* in Lord Duncan's fleet off Camperdown, blockading the Dutch fleet in the Texel in 1798; after which proceeded to India and fell in with a large body of Malay pirates off Batavia, which were completely destroyed. On board the *Leander* at the capture of the *Ville de Milan*, French frigate, and recapture of the *Cleopatra*, off Bermuda. Served also in the expedition on the north coast of Spain, under Sir James Malcolm, and Captain (now Colonel) Parke. Major Wilkinson has served in every quarter of the globe, and was taken prisoner by the Americans near Norfolk in Virginia while carrying despatches. Medal for services in Egypt.

42 Major Thomas Kelly served the Egyptian campaign of 1801, and has received the medal.

Notes to the Majors.

43 Major R. B. Hunt served at Hanover in 1805 and 6; at Copenhagen in 1807; and in the Peninsula from Sept. 1810 to May 1812, including the siege of Ciudad Rodrigo.

44 Major Shadwell Clerke served the Peninsular campaigns of 1808, 9, 10, and first part of 1811, including the battles of Roliça and Vimiera, retreat to Corunna, actions at Lugo and before Corunna, battle of Corunna (contused on the forehead by a musket-ball), operations on the Coa during the siege and battle of Almeida, battle of Busaco, retreat to the lines of Torres Vedras, affair near Leiria, and actions at Pombal and Redinha, at which last he was severely wounded in the right leg which was afterwards amputated.

45 Major Moyle Sherer served in the Peninsula from July 1809 to Dec. 1811, and from August 1812 to July 1813, including the actions at Busaco, Albuhera, Arroya de Molinos, Vittoria, and Maya in the Pyrenees.

46 Major Wm. E. Maling served at Copenhagen in 1807; and in the Peninsula in 1808.

47 Major Samuel Thorpe served in the Peninsula under Sir John Moore, including the affair at Lugo and battle of Corunna. Capture of Walcheren 1809. Subsequently in the Peninsula, including the sieges of Olivença and Badajoz, battles of Albuhera (twice wounded) and Toulouse, when he was again severely wounded. Served afterwards in the American war, and was present at Plattsburg.

48 Major Begbie served in the Peninsula from Aug. 1808 to Nov. 1809, including the capture of Oporto, and battle of Talavera.

49 Major John Macpherson served in Hanover in 1805 and 6; at Buenos Ayres in 1807; in Portugal and Spain from July 1808 to January 1809, including the battles of Roleia and Vimiera, action at Lugo, and battle of Corunna. Expedition to Walcheren and siege of Flushing where he was wounded. Peninsula from May to Dec. 1812, including the battle of Salamanca, where he was severely wounded.

50 Major Kennedy served at Walcheren and was present at the siege of Flushing.

51 Major Burrowes served at the capture of the Isle of France in 1810.

52 Major Honeyman Mackay served on the expedition to Walcheren, and at the capture of Flushing, 1809. Served also in the Peninsula from June 1811 to the end of the war, including the battle of Salamanca, retreat from Burgos, and battles of Vittoria (wounded in the head), Pyrenees, Nivelle and Orthes.

53 Major Gloster served in the Peninsula from Oct. 1809 to the end of the war, including the battles of Busaco and Fuentes d'Onor, siege of the forts at Salamanca, battles of Salamanca, the Pyrenees (28th July to 2nd Aug.), Nivelle, Nive, Orthes, and Toulouse. Wounded in the left arm at the battle of Salamanca, and through the right breast at Toulouse, the ball passing through the right lobe of the lungs and out at the back.

54 Major James Kerr Ross was slightly wounded at Waterloo.

55 Major Thornhill served at the capture of Gaudaloupe in 1809.

56 Major Bullock served the campaign of 1815, including the battle of Waterloo and capture of Paris.

57 Major Fitz Maurice served in the Peninsula from April 1811 to the end of the war, including the action at Sabugal, battle of Fuentes d'Onor, sieges and assaults of Ciudad Rodrigo and Badajoz, action at San Milan, battle of Vittoria, actions at the Bridge of Yanzi and Vera, battles of Nivelle and Nive, affair at Tarbes, and battle of Toulouse. Served also the campaign of 1815, including the battle of Quatre Bras. Leg broken at the storming of Badajoz, and severely wounded in the thigh by a musket-ball at Quatre Bras.

58 Major James Dudgeon Brown served the campaign of 1814 in Holland, and was present at the storming of Bergen-op-Zoom.

59 Major George Dry Hall was severely wounded at Waterloo.

60 Major Wm. Seward served in the Peninsula from Aug. 1808 to Jan. 1809, and was present at the battle of Vimiera. Expedition to Walcheren, 1809; and subsequently in the Peninsula, including Tarifa, Barrosa (wounded), Vittoria, and the Nive.

61 Major Charles Head served with the expedition to the southern states of America, and the campaign against New Orleans.

62 Major James Butler served in the Peninsula from Aug. 1808 to the end of the war, including the battles of Roleia, Vimiera, Talavera, Busaco, Vittoria, Pyrenees, Nivelle, Orthes, and Toulouse; sieges and captures of Olivença, Ciudad Rodrigo, and Badajoz, besides a great many minor actions and skirmishes. Wounded at Vimiera; severely through the left leg by a musket-shot in a sortie from Fort St. Christoval; and again severely in the left breast, shoulder, and back, at the storming of Badajoz.

63 Major Blood served in the Peninsula from Nov. 1813 to the end of the war, including the battle of Nivelle, and actions of the 9th, 10th, and 11th Dec. 1813, near Bidart. Slightly wounded at Nivelle.

64 Major M'Niven served the campaigns of 1813 and 14, including the investment of Bayonne in 1813, battle of Orthes, action at Aire, and battle of Toulouse, where he was

Notes to the Majors.

severely wounded near the groin by a musket-ball while carrying the regimental colour of the 42nd Highlanders.

65 Major Westlake served in the retreat to Corunna under Sir John Moore. Expedition to Walcheren and siege of Flushing, 1809. Peninsula from June 1811 to Aug. 1812. Slightly wounded at the siege of Flushing.

66 Major John Crawford Young served in the Peninsula from Aug. 1808 to Jan. 1809, including the battles of Roleia, Vimiera, Calcavellas, and Corunna. Expedition to Walcheren, 1809. Peninsular campaigns from Oct. 1812 to the end of the war, including the battles of Nivelle, Nive, Orthes, Tarbes, and Toulouse.

67 Major During served in the Peninsula during the Corunna campaign, and subsequently from the latter part of 1812 to the end of the war, including the battles of Corunna, Vittoria, Pyrenees, Nivelle, Nive, Orthes, and Toulouse.

68 Major Alexander Forbes served in the Peninsula from Aug. 1811 to July 1812, and again from Sept. 1813 to the end of the war, including the covering of the siege of Badajoz March and April 1812, and battles of Nivelle and Nive. Served also the campaign of 1815, including the actions of the 16th, 17th, and 18th June, at Quatre Bras and Waterloo, at which last he was wounded in the right leg by a musket-shot.

69 Major Alexander Grant served at the capture of the Cape of Good Hope, and was engaged on the 6th and 8th Jan. 1806. Proceeded with the expedition from thence to Buenos Ayres, and was present in the engagements of the 26th and 27th June, and 1st, 11th, and 12th Aug. 1806. Campaign in the Peninsula from Aug. 1808 to Jan. 1809, including the actions at Roleia, Vimiera, Lugo, and Corunna. Expedition to Walcheren, and engaged with the enemy on the 30th and 31st July, 1809. Peninsular campaigns from Sept 1810 to the end of the war, including the battles and affairs of Vittoria, the Pyrenees (4th, 6th, 25th, 30th, and 31st July), Cambo, Nive, Bayonne, Orthes, Aire, Tarbes, and Toulouse. Served also the campaign of 1815, including the battle of Waterloo. Wounded at Vittoria, Maya, and near Bayonne. In all, thirty-three times engaged, and three times wounded.

70 Major Romney served the Mahratta campaign of 1817, including the affair at Jubblepore, also at the siege and capture of Gounourie in 1807.

71 Major Charles Stewart served in the Peninsula from Sept. 1810 to June 1813, including the battle of Fuentes d'Onor (slightly wounded), and actions at Arroya de Molino and Almaraz. Served also the campaign of 1815, and was present at the battle of Waterloo.

72 Major Cowell served at the battle and storming of Nagpore in the East Indies in 1818.

73 Major Flamank served in the Peninsula from Jan. 1811 to the end of the war, including the battle of Fuentes d'Onor, 2nd siege of Badajoz, covering the sieges of Ciudad Rodrigo and Badajoz, affair of Moresco, battle of Salamanca, retreat from Burgos, battles of Vittoria and the Pyrenees, passage of the Bidassoa, battles of Nivelle and St. Pé, and Orthes. Served also the campaign of 1815, including the battle of Waterloo, and capture of Cambray.

74 Major Meade served in the Peninsula from Sept. 1810 to Oct. 1811 including the battle of Fuentes d'Onor, and other minor affairs. On the staff of General Count Wallmoden, in 1813, at the actions of Rastorf in Mecklenburg, and Goerde in Hanover. Assisted also at the defence of Rostock by the Swedes, where his horse was killed, and his left arm disabled. Served the campaign in Holland, in 1814, including the attack on Merxem, bombardment of Antwerp, and attack on Bergen-op-Zoom.

75 Major Harrison served in the American war.

76 Major Jacob served the Mahratta campaign of 1818. Present at the storming of Boodge, March 1819, captures of Ras-el-Khyma and Ziah, Dec. 1819; Dawarka and Bete, Dec. 1820; Beni-Boo-Alli, March 1821. Served in Arracan in 1825.

77 Major George Bolton served the campaign in Spain under Sir John Moore, including the battle of Corunna. Served on the expedition to Walcheren, and at the siege of Flushing in 1809.

78 Major Walch served the campaign in Travancore, East Indies, in 1809; and the campaigns in Ava in 1824 and 25.

79 Major Pilling served in South America in 1807, and was present in the attack on Buenos Ayres. Served also in the Peninsula from Aug. 1808 to Nov. 1809, including the battles of Roleia, Vimiera, and Talavera, at which latter he was wounded between the shoulders.

80 Major Charters served with the expedition to Hanover under Lord Cathcart in 1805; Walcheren expedition, 1809; and campaign in Holland under Lord Lynedoch, in 1814.

81 Major Thomas Stewart served at the reduction of Martinique, St. Martin's, and St. Eustatius, in 1809, and of Guadaloupe in 1810, and again in 1815.

82 Major Henry Reid served at Cadiz from March 1813 to the end of the war. Served also in the American war, including the affair at Hampden.

83 Major Pringle served at Walcheren in 1809. Also the campaigns of 1814 and 15 in

Notes to the Majors.

Holland, Flanders, and France, including the action at Merxem, bombardment of Antwerp, and battle of Waterloo.

84 Major Wm. Long served the campaigns from Sept. 1813 to the end of the war, including the following battles and affairs, viz. :—Cambo, Nive, before Bayonne (wounded), Orthes, Aire, Tarbes, Toulouse, and Waterloo.

85 Major Wentworth served in Ceylon during the Kandyan rebellion in 1817 and 18.

86 Major George Simmons served in the Peninsula with the 95th regiment (Rifle Brigade) from May 1809 to the end of the war. On piquet at Barba-del-Puerco when the enemy attacked at midnight and were repulsed. Present in the action of the Light Division at the bridge of Almeida; lines at Torres Vedras; actions of Pombal, Redinha, Casal Nova, Foz d'Aronce, and Sabugal; battle of Fuentes d'Onor; sieges and assaults of Ciudad Rodrigo, and Badajoz; battle of Salamanca; advance to, and capture of Madrid; affair of San Munos on the retreat from it; action at San Milan; battles of Vittoria, and Echellar; passage of the Bidassoa, and heights of Vera; actions of the Nivelle, Orthes, and Tarbes, besides various affairs of out-posts. Served also the campaign of 1815 including the actions of the 16th, 17th, and 18th June at Quatre Bras and Waterloo. Severely wounded through the thigh. at Almeida, by a musket-shot which injured the bone, and bruised in the leg by another ball; right knee-pan fractured by a musket-ball at Tarbes; and received a gun-shot wound in the right side at Waterloo, the ball in its course broke two ribs, passed through the liver, and was afterwards cut out of his breast.

87 Captain Barton Parker Browne served the campaign of 1815, and was present at the battle of Waterloo.

88 Major Lewis S. B. Robertson served with the expedition to Walcheren, and was present at the siege of Flushing. Served also at the taking of the Kandyan country in Ceylon under Sir Robert Brownrigg.

89 Major Buchan served the campaign of 1814 in Holland, including the reconnoitring of the position before Antwerp, action of Merxem, and bombardment of Antwerp.

90 Major Rutherford served in the Peninsula, and was present at the siege of Cadiz, action at Sabugal, battle of Fuentes d'Onor, first siege of Badajoz, and battles of Nivelle, Orthes and Toulouse. Served afterwards in the American war.

91 Major Gibson served in the Peninsula from Aug. 1813 to the end of the war, including the battles of the Pyrenees, siege of San Sebastian, passage of the Bidassoa (wounded), and the subsequent actions in which the left wing of the army was engaged. Served also the campaign of 1815, including the battle of Waterloo.

92 Major Macready served the campaigns of 1814 and 15 in Holland, Flanders, and France, and was present at Fort Frederick Hendrick, and at the actions of the 16th, 17th, and 18th June at Quatre Bras and Waterloo. Served afterwards in the East Indies and was present at the siege of Asseerghur, March and April 1819.

93 Major L. Morse-Cooper served the campaign of 1814, including the investment of Bayonne, and repulse of the sortie from thence. Also the campaign of 1815, including the battles of Quatre Bras and Waterloo. Served also at the siege and capture of Bhurtpore. Slightly wounded at Bayonne, and severely at Waterloo, where he received five wounds.

94 Major Walter Ogilvy served in the Burmese war, and was present at the taking of Arracan.

AIDES-DE-CAMP TO THE QUEEN.

Colonel *Sir* Rob. Gardiner, *KCB. & KCH.* R. Art.
―――― John Fremantle, *CB.* Coldst. Gds.
―――― *Lord* Geo. Wm. Russell, *GCB.* Unatt.
―――― Edward Wynyard, *CB.* do.
―――― James Fergusson, *CB.* h.p. Coldst. Gds.
―――― Thomas Wm. Brotherton, *CB.* 16 Dr.
―――― *Sir* A. J. Dalrymple, *Bt.* h.p. 2 Gar. Bn.
―――― *Sir* J. H. Reynett, *KCH.* h.p. 52 F.
―――― William Smelt, *CB.* 37 F.
―――― James Robertson Arnold, *KH.* R. Eng.
―――― William Wemys, h.p. 93 F.
―――― George, *Earl of* Munster, Unatt.
Gov. and Capt. of Windsor Castle.
Sir W. W. Wynn, *Bt.* R. Denbigh Mil.
G. *M. of* Huntly, *KT.* Aberdeen Mil.
T. Wood, Roy. East Middlesex Mil.
John Le Couteur, Jersey Militia.
John Guille, Guernsey Militia.

Ernest *Earl of* Mount Edgcumb, Duke of Cornwall's Rangers.
Thos. *Earl* de Grey, York Hussar Yeo. Cav.
Edward Baker, R. Wilts Yeo. Cav.
Colonel Thos. Adams Parke, *CB.* R. Mar.
Colonel John Owen, *CB. & KH.* R. Mar.

Extra.

Colonel John Bell, *CB.* h.p. Staff.
―――― S. B. Auchmuty, *CB.* h.p. 8 Gn. Bn.
―――― Thos. Lightfoot, *CB.* h.p. 45 F.
―――― A. D. Faunce, *CB. Insp. F. O. of Rec. Dist.*
―――― George Brown, *CB. & KH.* Rifle Brigade.
―――― *Lord* F. Fitzclarence, *GCH.* Unatt.
Cha. D. *of* Richmond, *KG.* Sussex Mil.
William, *Marq. of* Thomond, *KP.* Cork City Mil.
Colonel Cha. Rich. Fox, Unatt.

OFFICERS WITH LOCAL RANK.

GENERALS.

W. *Earl* Cathcart, *KT.*
13 Nov. 05 *Continent*
🆖 T. *Lord* Lynedoch,
GCB. & GCMG.
7 Dec. 13 *Holland, &c.*
🆖 *Hon. Sir* E. Paget, *GCB.*
29 Nov. 20 *East Ind.*
🆖 S. *Visc.* Combermere,
G.C.B. & G.C.H. do. do.
🆖 *Sir* Hen. Fane, *GCB.*
30 Jan. 35 *do.*
Robert Bell 10 Jan. 37 *do.*
Bennet Marley 28 June 38 *do*
Samuel Bradshaw do. *do.*
Sir H. Maclean,
KCB. do. *do.*
🆖 *Sir* Jasper Nicolls,
KCB. 18 Oct. 39 *do.*

LIEUT.-GENERALS.

Count Walmoden, *KCB.*
21 Jan. 13 *Continent.*
🆖 *Rt. Hon. Sir* G. Murray,
GCB.& GCH. 19 Dec. 14
N. Amer.
🆖 *Rt. Hon. Sir* G. Murray,
GCB.& GCH. 25 June 15
Continent
Sir H. Lowe, *KCB. &
GCMG.* 9 Nov. *St. Helena*
🆖 🆖 *Rt. Hon. Sir* J. Kempt,
GCB. & GCH. 28 Oct. 19
N. Amer.
🆖 🆖 *Rt. Hon. Sir* F. Adam,
KCB. & GCMG.
10 Feb. 24. *Ion. Isl.*
Alex. Cuppage do. *E. Ind.*
Chas. Rumley do. *do.*
Tredway Clarke do. *do.*
*W.H.*Blachford do. *do.*
Sir H. Lowe, *KCB. &
GCMG.* 29 Sept.
Continent
🆖 🆖 *Sir* James Lyon,
KCB. & GCH.
1 May 28 *Windw. &
Leew. Isl.*
🆖 🆖 *Sir* P. Maitland, *KCB.*
21 Aug. *N. Amer.*
St. Geo. Ashe 22 July 30
E. Ind.
🆖 🆖 John, *Lord* Seaton,
GCB. & GCH. 8 July, 36
*Upper and Lower
Canada.*
🆖 *Rt. Hon. Sir* Ed. Blakeney,
KCB. & GCH. 26 Aug. 36
Ireland.
🆖 *Sir* S. Ford Whittingham,
KCB.& GCH. 30 Sept. 36
Windw. & Leew. Isl.
J. Dighton, 10 Jan. 37 *E.Ind.*
Lambert Loveday do. *do.*
Sir John Doveton, *GCB.*
do. *do.*
Nath. Forbes do. *do.*
John W. Morris do. *do.*
Tho. Marriott do. *do.*
John Skelton do. *do.*
George Dick do. *do.*
J. Cuninghame 28 June 38
do.

MAJOR-GENERALS.

James Price 22 July 30
E. Ind.
Thomas Boles do. *do.*

Sir H. Worsley,
GCB. 22 July, 30 *E. Ind.*
Sir Hugh Fraser,
KCB. do. *do.*
Sir Hopetoun Stratford
Scott, *KCB.* do. *do.*
Sir J. Sinclair *Bt.*do. *do.*
🆖 *Sir* S. R. Chapman, *CB. &
KCH.* 28 Oct. 31
Bermuda
Sir Hen. Bethune, *Bt.*
21 Dec. 35 *Asia*
H. S. Osborne 10 Jan. 37
E. Ind.
Sir Jas. L. Caldwell,
KCB. do. *do.*
G. Carpenter do. *do.*
Sir Alex. Caldwell,
KCB. do. *do.*
Wm. Roome do. *do.*
J. L. Richardson do. *do.*
Sir Dav. Leighton,
KCB. do. *do.*
Sir Chas. Deacon,
KCB. do. *do.*
Jas. Welsh do. *do.*
Sir Thos. Corsellis,
KCB. do. *do.*
John N. Smith 10 Jan. 37
E. Ind.
Chas. Farran do. *do.*
Sir Jas. Russell,
KCB. do. *do.*
Sir Don. Macleod,
KCB. do. *do.*
Sir Jos. O'Halloran,
KCB. do. *do.*
Martin White do. *do.*
E. Boardman do. *do.*
Geo. Wahab do. *do.*
Dav. C. Kenny do. *do.*
Josiah Marshall do. *do.*
Rich. Podmore do. *do.*
Sir Rob. Houstoun,
KCB. do. *do.*
A. Molesworth do. *do.*
Jn. Greenstreet do. *do.*
Christ. Fagan do. *do.*
Sir Wm. Casement,
KCB. do. *do.*
Wm. Croxton do. *do.*
Jas. R Lumley do. *do.*
William Comyn do. *do.*
M. L. Pereira do. *do.*
T. Pollok, *CB.* do. *do.*
Sir John Rose,
KCB. do. *do.*
Wm. Munro do. *do.*
Geo. R. Kemp do. *do.*
Hen. Roome do. *do.*
John Munro do. *do.*
J. Cunningham do. *do.*
C. T. G. Bishop do. *do.*
J. A. P. Macgregor
do. *do.*
Alex. Limond do. *do.*
J. D. Greenhill,
CB. do. *do.*
Sir J. Prendergast do. *do.*
Sir Wm. Richards,
KCB. do. *do.*
Alex. Duncan do. *do.*
Sir T. Whitehead,
KCB. do. *do.*
Rob. J. Latter do. *do.*
Thos. Stewart do. *do.*
Jerry F. Dyson. do. *do.*
W. D. Cleiland do. *do.*
W. H. Perkins do. *do.*

Sir John Doveton,
KCB. 10 Jan. 37. *E.Ind.*
Alex. Fair, *CB.* do. *do.*
Sir David Foulis,
KCB. do. *do.*
D. M'Pherson do. *do.*
Wm. Hopper do. *do.*
Sir Thos. Anburey,
KCB. do. *do.*
Sir J. L. Lushington,
GCB. do. *do.*
B. W. D. Sealy do. *do.*
Wm. C. Fraser do. *do.*
Wm. Gilbert do. *do.*
Sir George Arthur,
KCH. 22 Dec.
Upper Canada.
Jas. Considine, *KH.*
25 May 38
Africa
Brackley Kennett
28 June *E.Ind.*
Wm. Innes do. *do.*
John P. Dunbar do. *do.*
And. Aitcheson do. *do.*
Adam Hogg do. *do.*
Christ. Hodgson do. *do.*
Rich. Whish do. *do.*
A. Andrews, *CB.* do. *do.*
Gab. R. Penny do. *do.*
James Ahmuty do. *do.*
James Cock do. *do.*
Wm. Hull, *CB.* do. *do.*
Sir Jas. Limond,
CB. do. *do.*
C. M'Leod, *CB.* do. *do.*
Thos. Garner do. *do.*
R. Pitman, *CB.* do. *do.*
C. Sull. Fagan, *CB.* do. *do.*
E. W. Shuldham do. *do.*
W. S. Heathcote do. *do.*
Rich. H. Yates do. *do.*
J. Mayne, *CB.* do. *do.*
W. Sandwith, *CB.* do. *do.*
Mossem Boyd do. *do.*
John M'Innes do. *do.*
J. F. Salter, *CB.* do. *do.*
Sir Eph. G. Stannus
CB. do. *do.*
Patrick Byers do. *do.*
Wm. Burgh do. *do.*
E. Cartwright do. *do.*
H. G. A. Taylor,
CB. do. *do.*
A. Richards, *CB.* do. *do.*
Sir J. Sutherland do. *do.*
Her. Bowen, *CB.* do. *do.*
Arch. Watson do. *do.*
W. Dickson, *CB.* do. *do.*
John Wells Fast do. *do.*
Wm. P. Price do. *do.*
Jas. Durant do. *do.*
Rob. Hampton do. *do.*
Brook Bridges Parlby, *CB.*
28 June 38. *E.Ind.*
Hen. Hodgson do. *do.*
Fretcheville Dykes
Ballantine do. *do.*
F. J. T. John-
stone, *CB.* do. *do.*
Wm. G. Pearse do. *do.*
Sir R. Hen. Cun-
liffe, *CB. Bt.* do. *do.*
Wm. Clapham do. *do.*
John Truscott do. *do.*
Edw. Edwards do. *do.*
Tho. Webster do. *do.*
Gilbert Waugh do. *do.*
Tho. Hat. Smith do. *do.*

E. Millian Gulli-
fer Showers
28 June 38 *E. Ind.*
W. Woodhouse do. *do.*
Hen. Faithful do. *do.*
F. W. Wilson, *CB.*do. *do.*
John Tombs do. *do.*
John H. Collett do. *do.*
Geo. L. Wahab do. *do.*
Patrick Cameron do. *do.*
John Carfrae do. *do.*
Rich. West do. *do.*
Geo. Jackson do. *do.*
S. Goodfellow do. *do.*
Cha. A. Walker do. *do.*
Rich. A. Willis do. *do.*
Fred. Bowes do. *do.*
Jas. S. Fraser do. *do.*
Isaac Kinnersley do. *do.*
P. De la Motte,
CB. do. *do.*
Hen. Huthwaite do. *do.*
T. Wilson, *CB.* do. *do.*
F. Vinc. Raper do. *do.*
Geo. Swiney do. *do.*
G. Pollock *CB.* do. *do.*
A. Lindsay, *CB.* do. *do.*
Jas. Alexander, do. *do.*
Vans Kennedy do. *do.*
W. R. Gilbert do. *do.*
Tho. P. Smith do. *do.*
E. Frederick, *CB.* do. *do.*
Geo. B. Brooks do. *do.*
Arch. Robertson do. *do.*
W. Clinton Bad-
deley, *CB.* do. *do.*
Hen. Bowdler do. *do.*
Peter Lodwick do. *do.*
Jas. F. Dundas
Jas. Morse do. *do.*
Ed. H. Simpson do. *do.*
Jas. Hackett do. *do.*
Tho. Newton do. *do.*
John A. Biggs do. *do.*
Ed. H. Bellasis do. *do.*
Wm. Nott do. *do.*
Geo. Cooper do. *do.*
Sueton. H. Todd do. *do.*
John Briggs do. *do.*
Harry Thomson do. *do.*
Sir Robt. Henry Sale, *KCB.*
23 July 39 *Affghanistan*

BRIGADIER-GENERAL.

Cha. Dallas, 14
Feb. 28 *St. Helena*
Lord Geo. Wm.
Russell, *GCB.*
27 May 32 *Portugal*

COLONELS.

A. *Disney* 25 July 10 *E. Ind.*
Strickl. Kingston do. *do.*
Sir Jas. H. Reynett,
KCH. 25 Jan. 21 *Continent*
Fran. Cockburn
3 Sept. 29 *Honduras*
A. Findlay, *KH.*
26 Oct. 30 *W. Coast
of Africa*
Fra. Raw. Chesney
27 Nov. 34 *Asia*
🆖 A. Macdonald
28 Oct. 36 *Honduras*
W. Wylde 10 Feb. 37 *Spain*
R. Doherty 5 May *W. Coast
of Africa*
🆖 E T. Michell, *CB. Spain*

STAFF APPOINTMENTS.

(*Held by Commission.*)

GREAT BRITAIN.

ADJUTANT-GENERAL TO THE FORCES.

🅱 Sir John Macdonald, *KCB*.　　　27 July 1830|Lt.-Gen. 28 June 1838
Deputy Adj.-Gen. 🅱 Sir John Gardiner, *KCB*.　4 Dec. 1830|M.-Gen. 22 July 1830

QUARTER-MASTER GENERAL TO THE FORCES.

🅱 Sir J. Willoughby Gordon, *Bt. GCB. GCH.*　10 Aug. 1811|Lt.-Gen. 27 May 1825
Assist. Quar. Mas. Gen. 🅱 James Freeth, *KH*.　　11 July 1826|Lt.-Col. 11 July 1826

PERMANENT ASSISTANT QUARTER-MASTERS GENERAL.

Lieut.-Colonel .. { 🅱 Henry James Riddell, *KH*.　3 July 1823|Col.　22 July 1830
　　　　　　　　　 🅱 Philip Bainbrigge, *CB*.　　2 Aug.　27| —　10 Jan.　37
　　　　　　　　　 🅱 Nathaniel Thorn, *CB. KH*.　14 Dec.　32| —　　do

DEPOTS.

Chatham. (*Infantry.*)

Superintendent } Chas. Cranstoun Dixon　24 Mar. 1837|Lt.-Col. 10 Jan. 1837
of Hospitals .
Captain .... 🅱 Henry Anderson¹　31 Mar. 1837|12 Feb. 1836
Paymaster ...... Charles Grimes²　　19 Feb. 1836|16 Apr. 1812
Paymaster of } James Macdonald　1 May 1832
Indian Depôts

Maidstone. (*Cavalry.*)

Paymaster ...... William Castle　　19 Feb. 1836 { 16 Feb. 1829
　　　　　　　　　　　　　　　　　　　　　　　　 Capt. 10 June 1826
Riding Master .. Lewis Chas. Aug. Meyer　1 May 1826|**Capt.*　1 May 1826
Acting Adjutant.. Fran. L'Estrange Shaw　26 Apr. 1839|**Cornet* 26 Apr. 1839
Quarter-Master .. John Swindley　　1 Nov. 1839
Vet. Surgeon .... Alexander Black　28 Aug. 1838|10 Nov. 1814

---

¹ Capt. Anderson served the campaigns of 1814 and 15 in Holland and the Netherlands, including the action at Merxem, bombardment of Antwerp, storming of Bergen-op-Zoom, and actions at Quatre Bras and Waterloo. Severely wounded at Waterloo by a musket-ball, which broke the left shoulder, passed through the lungs, and made its exit at the back, breaking the scapulæ.

² Paymaster Grimes served the campaigns of 1813, 14, and 15, in Lower Canada, under Sir George Prevost. Served also in the Burmese war.

Officers with Local Rank.

LIEUT.-COLONELS.

J. Thompson 1 Jan. 00 *E. Ind.*
F. A. Daniell 1 Jan. 12 *do.*
John Crosdill, *CB.*
    4 June 13 *do.*
Wm. Nicholl *do. do.*
H. Prince Reuss
    30 Dec. 13 *Continent*
A. Steiger 19 May 14 *do.*
W. Franklin 4 June *E. Ind.*
J. Johnson, *CB. do. do.*
Cha. Mandeville *do. do.*
Thomas Lyster
    16 Nov. 15 *St. Helena*
J. Utterton 7 Mar. 16
    Gibraltar
Bissell Harvey, *KH.*
    16 May 18 *Continent*
C. R. G. Hodson 12 Aug. 19
    St. Helena and Eastward
    of the Cape of Good Hope
Ed. Hay 5 Sept. 22 *Comm. at*
    the E. I. Dep. Chatham
Wm. Thorn, *KH.*
    13 Oct. 25 *Continent*
J. F. Fulton, *KH.* 24 N. *do.*
J. F. De Burgh
    12 Jan. 26 *Continent*
W. L. Watson, *CB.*
    19 *do. E. Ind.*
E. Hawkshaw
    15 June *Continent*
Anth. S. King 3 Aug. *do.*
J. M. A. Skerrett *do. do.*
Sir H. Wheatley,
    GCH. 14 Sept. *Continent*
Robert Nixon *do. do.*
Hen. Roberts 5 Oct. *do.*
Andrew Tilt 12 *do. do.*
T. G. Fitz Gerald
    19 *do. do.*
Aug. Meade *do. do.*
Hon. J. Walpole
    26 *do. do.*
Donald Mackay *do. do.*
J. L. Higgins 2 Nov. *do.*
Anth. Rumpler 9 *do. do.*
Jos. D'Arcy 16 *do. do.*
Wm. Ingleby *do. do.*
Andrew Geils *do. do.*
Wm. Thornhill *do. do.*
H. W. Espinasse
    30 *do. do.*
Fletcher Wilkie *do. do.*
J. S. Hawkshaw
    14 Dec. *do.*
L. A. Northey *do. do.*
Jas. Ormsby 28 *do. do.*
Hon. J. Browne *do. do.*
Wm. Verner *do. do.*
J. Carr. Smith *do. do.*
Sir T. S. Sorell,
    KH. 30 *do. do.*
D. Macpherson *do. do.*
J. R. Udney *do. do.*
J. H. Lord Howden, *KH.*
    31 July 27 *special Mission*
    abroad.
George Baker
    31 Aug. 29 *Greece*
J. G. Bonner 1 Sept. 31 *E. Ind.*
B. B. Shee 25 Apr. 36 *Persia*
Jas. Nisb. Colquhoun
    10 Feb. 37 *Spain*
Justin Sheil 2 June 37 *Persia*
Cha. Stoddart *do. do.*
Rich. Wilbraham *do. do.*
G. P. Cameron *do. do.*
Geo. Woodfall *do. do.*
Ralph Carr Alderson
    22 June 38 *Spain*
Sir Alex. Burnes 7 Aug.
    Affghanistan & Persia
G. C. Du Plat, *KH.*
    16 Aug. 39 *Spain*

MAJORS.

Hen. Bowen 26 Sept. 96
    Scilly Isls.
J. Leathart 25 Apr. 08 *E. In.*
J. Y. Bradford *do. do.*
Rob. Blackall *do. do.*

G. Fuller 25 July 10 *E. In.*
David Robertson *do. do.*
J. Loyd Jones 1 Jan. 12 *do.*
R. H. Fotheringham *do.*
J. D. Brown 4 June 13 *do.*
Sir W. Dick, *Bt. do. do.*
Hen. Yarde 4 June 14 *do.*
Charles Marriott *do. do.*
Major H. Court *do. do.*
Wm. H. Richards *do. do.*
W. J. Matthews *do. do.*
Skeff. Lutwidge *do. do.*
Ernest, *Baron de*
    Schmiedern, KH.
    20 Sept. *Continent*
John Norton, *alias Tey-*
    oninhokarawen, Capt.
    and Leader of the In-
    dians of the Five Nations.
    15 Feb. 16 *Canada*
Tho. Hall 12 Aug. 19 *E. Ind.*
H. E. Somerville 28 Sept. 20
    E. I. Dep. at Chatham
H. C. W. Smyth
    19 July 21 *E. Ind.*
Sir E. A. Camp-
    bell, *CB. do. do.*
R. W. Pogson *do. do.*
Arthur Wight *do. do.*
D. D. Anderson *do. do.*
R. Nich. Penny *do. do.*
T. C. Graham 8 Apr. *Contin.*
Sa. Sankey 10 Aug. *do.*
Cha. Irvine 21 Sept. *do.*
Cha. M. Graham *do. do.*
M. M'Pherson 6 Oct. *do.*
C. Bayley, *CMG.*
    5 Oct. *Mediterr.*
A. M. Bennett 12 Dec. *Contin.*
West. Hames 19 *do. do.*
Henry Light 12 *do. do.*
G. Tito Brice 9 Nov. *do.*
Thomas Dent *do. do.*
D. MacGregor *do. do.*
B. Lutyens *do. do.*
T. H. Morice, *KH. do.*
E. H. Garthwaite *do. do.*
Tho. Pipon 16 *do. do.*
Charles Wayth *do. do.*
Robert Abbey *do. do.*
P. D. Fellowes *do. do.*
Cha. Hames 30 *do. do.*
G. J. Wolseley 14 D. *do.*
J. Rainey *do. do.*
W. Phipps *do. do.*
W. D. Spooner 28 *do. do.*
Wm. Thomson *do. do.*
Ab. James 30 *do. do.*
John Gordon *do. do.*
Tho. Shaw *do. do.*
Wm. W. Swaine *do. do.*
Fra. B. Eliot *do. do.*
R. Axford, 16 Oct. 28 *Rec. for*
    E. In. Comp. at Liverpool
W. Ogilvie 10 Jan. 37 *do.*
Geo. W. Gibson *do. do.*
John Laurie *do. do.*
James Cocke *do. do.*
Cha. Andrews *do. do.*
Edw. Pettingal *do. do.*
John W. Watson *do. do.*
Robert Becher *do. do.*
John Brandon *do. do.*
John Cowslade *do. do.*
Wm. Hough *do. do.*
Fred. Geo. Lister *do. do.*
Hen. C. Barnard *do. do.*
William Cubitt *do. do.*
Robert Stewart *do. do.*
Robert Hawkes *do. do.*
John Mackenzie *do. do.*
G. Hutchinson *do. do.*
Geo. F. Holland *do. do.*
Hugh Sibbald *do. do.*
Stephen Moody *do. do.*
J. J. Farrington *do. do.*
Hen. Moberley *do. do.*
Geo. Brooke *do. do.*
Fred. H. Sandys *do. do.*
T. Lumsden, *CB. do. do.*
J. Oram Clarkson *do. do.*

Tho. Croxton
    28 June 31 *E. Ind.*
G. J. B. Johnston *do. do.*
Ben. R. Hitchens *do. do.*
Hugh R. Murray *do. do.*
Jas. R. Colnett *do. do.*
Peter Johnston *do. do.*
Charles Snell *do. do.*
Cha. Edw. Davis *do. do.*
Rich. Gardner *do. do.*
A. Macintosh *do. do.*
Theoph. Bolton *do. do.*
Hen. Fra. Caley *do. do.*
Rich. Bayldon *do. do.*
Charles Rogers *do. do.*
G. A. Kempland *do. do.*
W. Henderson *do. do.*
T. Timbrell, *CB. do. do.*
Robert Butler *do. do.*
William Stokoe *do. do.*
C. St. Jn. Grant *do. do.*
James Malton *do. do.*
Wm. Macleod *do. do.*
J. R. Wornum *do. do.*
Benjamin Ashe *do. do.*
James Steel *do. do.*
John Barclay *do. do.*
Fra. Farrant 2 June *Persia*
Elliott D. Todd *do. do.*
H. C. Rawlinson *do. do.*
John Laughten *do. do.*
Ed. Pat. Lynch 3 *do. do.*
*T. Ritherdon 16 F. 38 *E. I.*
    Sem. at Addiscombe
J. Wilson 28 June 38 *E. Ind.*
T. R. Macqueen *do. do.*
Francis Hugh M.
    Wheeler *do. do.*
John Wilson *do. do.*
Geo. Hicks *do. do.*
Jas. W. Douglas *do. do.*
Jas. Manson *do. do.*
John Ward *do. do.*
Stratford Powell *do. do.*
Wm. Burlton *do. do.*
S. L. Thornton *do. do.*
Hope Dick *do. do.*
David Hepburn *do. do.*
W. Simonds *do. do.*
J. H. Simmonds *do. do.*
H. Fisher Salter *do. do.*
John Angelo *do. do.*
J. G. Drummond *do. do.*
Tho. Williams *do. do.*
L. Saunders Bird *do. do.*
Geo. Blake *do. do.*
R. L. Anstruther *do. do.*
Edm. Herring *do. do.*
Rodk. Roberts *do. do.*
Geo. G. Denniss *do. do.*
Alex. Davidson *do. do.*
Eyre Ev. Bruce *do. do.*
John Hall *do. do.*
John Hailes *do. do.*
J. Sam. Marshall *do. do.*
Dan. A. Fenning *do. do.*
G. B. Aitcheson *do. do.*
Christ. Newport *do. do.*
Geo. Chapman *do. do.*
John Hicks *do. do.*
J. Landon Jones *do. do.*
Griffiths Holmes *do. do.*
John Rawlins *do. do.*
G. H. Woodrooffe *do. do.*
Rich. O. Meriton *do. do.*
J. H. Mackinlay *do. do.*
Owen Phillips *do. do.*
Wm. Bolton Gir-
    dlestone *do. do.*
Niel Campbell *do. do.*
Robert Kent *do. do.*
Wm. Hen. Earle *do. do.*
A. M'Kinnon *do. do.*
Wm. Sage *do. do.*
Andrew Goldie *do. do.*
Henry Carter *do. do.*
Wm. Ramsey *do. do.*
Cha. Thoresby *do. do.*
James Bedford *do. do.*
Wm. Edw. Blair
    Leadbeater *do. do.*
Jer. B. Nottidge *do. do.*
George Lee *do. do.*

D. Montgomerie
    28 June 38 *E. Ind.*
A. M. Campbell *do. do.*
Luc. Hor. Smith *do. do.*
Jn. Farquharson *do. do.*
John Worthy *do. do.*
John Forbes *do. do.*
Frederick Bond *do. do.*
Thomas Biddle *do. do.*
Wm. Mactier *do. do.*
H. Macfarquhar *do. do.*
John Howison *do. do.*
Hen. John Wood *do. do.*
George Dods *do. do.*
Jn. Morgan Ley *do. do.*
R. G. Polwhele *do. do.*
John Chisholm *do. do.*
Wm. Foquett *do. do.*
E. Parry Gowan *do. do.*
James Allen *do. do.*
John Hen. Irwin
John Cartwright *do. do.*
Fras. Frankland
    Whinyates *do. do.*
Wm. Hill Waterfield
George Fryer *do. do.*
Rich. Budd *do. do.*
Pat. Thomson *do. do.*
George Barker *do. do.*
Fras. Plowden *do. do.*
John Fitzgerald *do. do.*
James Oliphant *do. do.*
Francis Straton *do. do.*
J. J. Underwood *do. do.*
J. Monson Boyes *do. do.*
Wm. Fred. Steer *do. do.*
G. W. Bonham *do. do.*
Tho. Wilkinson *do. do.*
G. H. Robinson *do. do.*
Hugh C. Cotton *do. do.*
Cha. Smclair *do. do.*
Alex. Lawe *do. do.*
Charles Hosmer *do. do.*
R. Somner Seton *do. do.*
Alex. MacArthur *do. do.*
Wm. Prescott *do. do.*
John Thos. Croft *do. do.*
C. Waddington *do. do.*
W. H. Terraneau *do. do.*
Charles Wahab *do. do.*
Stuart Corbett *do. do.*
G. Fred. Penley *do. do.*
J. S. H. Weston *do. do.*
John Wynch *do. do.*
W. J. Thompson *do. do.*
Humphrey Hay *do. do.*
Malc. Nicolson *do. do.*
Hen. Monke *do. do.*
Henry Barkley
    Henderson *do. do.*
Tho. Best Jervis *do. do.*
Fred. S. Sotheby *do. do.*
Henry Liddell *do. do.*
Edw. Huthwaite *do. do.*
G. R. Crawfurd *do. do.*
Hen. Delafosse *do. do.*
J. R. Woodhouse *do. do.*
Robert Leech 7 Aug. *Aff-*
    ghanistan & Persia
Niel Campbell 28 July 39 *E. I.*
G. Thopson, *CB. do. do.*
Wm. Garden *do. do.*
John Hay *do. do.*
John Lloyd *do. do.*
Patrick Craigie *do. do.*
Alex. C. Peat *do. do.*
Wm. Alexander *do. do.*
Eldred Pottinger, *C.B.*
    23 July 39 *Affghanistan.*

CAPTAINS

Recruitng for the E. India
Company's Army.

James Murray *London*
Tho. Otho Travers *Cork*
Richard Geo. Grange *Dublin*
H. Vibart Glegg *Edinburgh*
G. D. Drummond
    22 Dec. 25 *Chatham*
Hen. Brown 10 Jan. 34. *E. I.*
    Depot at Chatham
Wm. Elsey 2 Dec. 30 *E. I.*

Staff Appointments.

RECRUITING DISTRICTS, &c.

Paymaster	Francis Wemys	25 May 1811		
	Nicholas Maunsell	21 Aug. 13		
	H. Benj. Briscoe Adams	16 Feb. 19		
	Edward Edmonds	16 Oct. 28	5 Sept. 1803	
	𝔅 Richard Jellicoe	do	24 Feb. 14	
	𝔅 John Woodgate	25 June 29	Capt. 20 Feb. 1812	
	Henry Balthaser Adams	19 Feb. 36	{ 30 Oct. 1828 { Capt. 17 Sept. 25	
	𝔅 Francis Edward Leech	26 do.	19 Nov. 1807	
	Hugh Percy Forster	30 June 37	{ 10 June 24 { Lieut. 14 Dec. 15	
Adjutant......	Thomas Shields	28 July 1803	Lieut.	3 Aug. 1801
	John Maguire	4 Aug. 09	——	9 Oct. 06
	Henry Bertles	3 June 13	——	3 June 13
	𝔅 ⚔ William Graham	25 Dec. 35	——	28 Mar. 34
	𝔅 ⚔ James Hope	29 Jan. 36	——	7 Jan. 13
	𝔅 James White	10 Feb. 37	——	7 Oct. 24
	Philip Henry Despard	24 do.	——	22 Nov. 27
	Robert M'Nair	14 July	——	24 Mar. 14
	𝔅 William O'Neill	15 Nov. 39	——	22 May 18
	Thomas Dagg	31 Dec.	——	31 Dec. 39

Principal Veterinary Surgeon { 𝔅 ⚔ Fred. Clifford Cherry* 17 Sept. 1839

IRELAND.

Dep. Adjutant Gen... 𝔅 Geo. Chas. D'Aguilar, *CB.* 22 July 1830 | Col. 22 July 1830
Dep. Quart.-Master { 𝔅 ⚔ *Sir* Guy Campbell,
General .... { *Bt. CB.* 22 July 1830 | Col. 22 July 1830
Provost Marshal .... *Lieut.* Robert Speedy 14 May 1804

FOREIGN STATIONS.

IONIAN ISLANDS.

Dep. Qr.-Mast. { 𝔅 ⚔ Francis Henry Dawkins 13 Jan. 1837 | Lt.-Col. 8 Apr. 1826
General ....

NORTH AMERICA.
Canada.

Commander of } 𝔅 *Sir* Richard Downes Jack-
the Forces .. } son, *KCB.* 16 Sept. 1839 | Lt.-Gen. 28 June 1838
Dep. Adj.-Gen. ... John Eden, *CB.* 14 Sept. 1832 | Lt.-Col. 31 Dec. 1830
Dep. Qr.-Master } 𝔅 ⚔ *Hon.* Charles Gore,
General .... } *CB. KH.* 20 Apr. 1826 | Col. 10 Jan. 1837

* Mr. Cherry served Sir John Moore's campaign in Spain, including the battle of Corunna. Expedition to Walcheren, 1809. Peninsula from Jan. 1812 to the end of the war. Also the campaign of 1815, including the battle of Waterloo.

Staff Appointments.

Nova Scotia.

Dep. Qr.-Master General	🅟 🅒🅑 John Jas. Snodgrass	12 Sept. 1834	Lt.-Col. 25 Dec. 1826

Prince Edward's Island.

Sub. Insp. and District Adj. of Mililia	🅟 Ambrose Lane	2 Aug. 1831	Lieut. 7 Mar. 1811 *Capt. 2 Aug. 1831
	Coun Douly Rankin	do.	Lieut. 2 Nov. 1811 *Capt. 2 Aug. 1831

LEEWARD AND WINDWARD ISLANDS.

Dep. Adj. Gen.	Thomas Falls	23 Dec. 1836	Lt.-Col. 23 Dec. 1836
Dep. Qr.-Master General	🅟 🅒🅑 John Tyler, *KH.*	12 Aug. 1834	Lt.-Col. 12 Aug. 1834

JAMAICA.

Dep. Adj.-Gen.	🅟 🅒🅑 William Turnor	22 Nov. 1836	Lt.-Col. 22 Nov. 1836
Dep. Qr.-Master General	Samuel Robinson Warren	20 Dec. 1839	Lt.-Col. 20 Dec. 1839

EAST INDIES.

Commander-in-Chief	🅟 *Sir* Jasper Nicolls, *KCB.*	13 Aug. 1839	Lt.-G. 10 Jan. 1837 General in India 18 Oct. 1839
Adjutant-General	🅟 🅒🅑 Robert Torrens, *CB.*	1 May 1828	Col. 10 Jan. 1837
Deputy do.	Robert Bryce Fearon, *CB.*	1 May 1828	Col. 10 Jan. 1837
Quarter-Master General	🅟 🅒🅑 Chatham Horace Churchill, *CB.*	11 Aug. 1837	Col. 10 Jan. 1837
Deputy do.	🅟 William Henry Sewell, *CB.*	24 Feb. 1828	Col. 10 Jan. 1837
Dep. Adj.-Gen. Bombay	🅟 🅒🅑 Ranald Macdonald, *CB. KH.*	13 July 1838	Lt.-Col. 13 July 1838

CAPE OF GOOD HOPE.

Dep. Qr.-Master General	🅟 🅒🅑 Henry Geo. Smith, *CB.*	24 July 1828	Col. 10 Jan. 1837

CEYLON.

Dep. Adj. Gen.	🅟 Edward Charleton, *KH.*	17 Nov. 1837	Lt.-Col. 17 Nov. 1837
Dep. Qr.-Master General	🅟 John Fraser	24 May 1827	Lt.-Col. 24 May 1827

MAURITIUS.

Dep. Qr.-Master General	🅟 🅒🅑 William Staveley, *CB.*	29 Sept. 1825	Col. 10 Jan. 1837

WESTERN AUSTRALIA.

Commandant	🅟 Frederick Chidley Irwin, *KH.*	28 June 1836	Major 28 June 1836

STAFF AT HEAD QUARTERS.

GENERAL COMMANDING IN CHIEF.

🅑 🅒 *Right Hon.* General *Lord* HILL, G.C.B., G.C.H., and K.C., Colonel of the Royal Regiment of Horse Guards.

Military Secretary.

🅑 🅒 Lieut.-General *Lord* Fitzroy Somerset, K.C.B., Colonel of the 53rd Regiment.

Assistant Military Secretary.

Lieut.-Colonel Maling, 2nd West India Regiment.

Aides-de-Camp.

🅑 🅒 Colonel Richard Egerton, Half-pay Unattached.
🅑 Colonel George Powell Higginson, ditto.
Captain Alfred Edward Hill, 68th Regiment.
Captain Edward Charles Fletcher, 1st Life Guards.

ADJUTANT-GENERAL.

🅑 Lieut.-General *Sir* John Macdonald, K.C.B., Colonel of the 67th Regiment.

Deputy Adjutant-General.

🅑 Major-General *Sir* John Gardiner, K.C.B.

Assistant Adjutants-General.

Colonel *Lord* Frederick Fitzclarence, G.C.H., Half-pay Unattached.
🅑 Colonel William Cochrane, Half-pay Unattached.

Deputy Assistant Adjutant-General.

🅑 Major Roche Meade, K.H., Half-pay Unattached.

Inspecting Field Officer.

🅑 Colonel Wm. Gordon Macgregor.

QUARTER-MASTER GENERAL.

🅑 Lieut.-General *Sir* James Willoughby Gordon, *Bart.*, G.C.B., and G.C.H., Colonel of the 23rd Royal Welsh Fusiliers.

Assistant Quarter-Master General.

🅑 Lieut.-Colonel James Freeth, K.H., Half-pay Royal Staff Corps.

Deputy Assistant Quarter-Master General.

🅑 🅒 Captain John Enoch, 23rd Royal Welsh Fusiliers.

1st Regiment of Life Guards.

"PENINSULA"—"WATERLOO."

Years' Serv.						
50		\[P\] Stapleton *Viscount* Combermere,[1] G.C.B. & G.C.H. 2nd Lieut. 26 Feb. 1790; Lieut. 16 March, 91; *Capt.* 28 Feb. 93; *Major*, 28 April, 94; *Lieut.-Col.* 9 March, 94; *Col.* 1 Jan. 1800; *Major-Gen.* 30 Oct. 05; *Lieut.-Gen.* 1 Jan. 12; *Gen.* 27 May, 25. Col. 1st Life-Guards, 16 Sept. 29.				
Full Pay.	Half Pay.					

Colonel.

Lieut.-Colonel and Colonel.

26	6	\[P\] Hon. H. F. C. Cavendish,[2] *Lieut.* 7th Fusiliers, P 26 May, 08; *Capt.* P 6 June, 11; *Major*, P 2 April, 18; *Lieut.-Col.* P 12 July, 21; *Col.* 10 Jan. 37.

Major and Lieut.-Colonel.

23	1/12	John Hall, *Cornet*, P 12 June, 17; *Lieut.* P 24 July, 17; *Capt.* P 2 Aug. 22; *Brevet-Major*, 8 Sept. 31; *Lieut.-Col.* P 27 Dec. 1837.

		CAPTAINS.	COR. AND SUB-LIEUT.	LIEUT.	CAPTAIN.	BREVET-MAJOR.
20	2 4/12	Charles Hall	P 21 May 18	P 27 Feb. 23	P 31 July 25	28 June 38
20	0	Edward Charles Fletcher.	P 30 Nov. 20	P 4 April 23	P 21 May 27	
18	0	Richard Parker	P 2 Aug. 22	P 31 July 25	P 30 June 28	
14	0	Thos. Middleton Biddulph	P 7 Oct. 26	P 23 Feb. 29	P 16 May 34	
12	0	Thomas Bulkeley	P 30 June 28	P 24 May 31	P 5 May 37	
11	0	Hon. J. W. B. Macdonald	P 1 Oct. 29	P 24 Jan. 34	P 24 June 37	
11	0	*Lord* F. A. Gordon	P 2 Aug. 29	18 June 34	P 1 Dec. 37	
11	0	*Lord* Wm. Beresford....	P 30 April 29	P 4 July 34	P 27 Dec. 37	
		LIEUTENANTS.				
8	0	Richard Brooke	P 18 Oct. 32	P 3 April 35		
8	0	George Rushout........	P 18 Jan. 33	P 10 Feb. 37		
7	0	*Lord* Chas. P. P. Clinton	P 24 Jan. 34	P 5 May 37		
6	0	*Lord* Thos. C. P. Clinton	P 16 May 34	P 24 June 37		
6	0	*Lord* G. Aug. Fred. Paget	P 25 July 34	P 1 Dec. 37		
6	0	\[W\] William Anderton ..	24 July 34	18 Dec. 37		
6	0	Caledon Du Pre Alexander	P 12 Sept. 34	P 27 Dec. 37		
5	0	Hon. Octavius Duncombe	P 3 April 35	P 19 July 39		
3	0	*Sir* Chas. Wm. Kent, *Bt.*	P 10 Feb. 37	P 16 Aug. 39		
		CORNETS AND SUB-LIEUTENANTS.				
4	0	Robert Bromley........	P 4 Nov. 36			
3	0	William Wells.........	P 24 June 37			
3	0	Seymour Phillips Allen..	P 1 Dec. 37			
3	0	Rt. Winterbottom, R. M.	18 Dec. 37			
3	0	John Farrer	P 27 Dec. 37			
2	0	Fulke Greville	P 13 April 38			
1	0	John Talbot Clifton	P 5 April 39			
1	0	Watkin Wms. Wynn....	P 19 July 39			
1	0	Francis Fred. Lovell	P 16 Aug. 39			
6	0	*Adjutant.*—\[W\] William Anderton, (*Lieut.*) 18 Dec. 37.				
4	0	*Quarter-Master.*—\[W\] Robert Falconer, 2 Sept. 36.				
27	0	*Surgeon.*—William Bromet, M.D. 6 Nov. 35; *Assist.-Surg.* 3 Nov. 14; *Hosp.-Assist.* 4 Oct. 13.				
5	0	*Assistant-Surgeon.*—Alexander Elliot Campbell, M.D. 27 Nov. 35.				
17	10 4/12	*Veterinary-Surgeon.*—\[P\] William Percivall,[3] 30 Nov. 12.				

Scarlet.—*Facings* Blue.—*Agent*, Mr. Collyer, Park-place, St. James's.
[*Returned from France, January,* 1816.]

1 Lord Combermere served in Flanders in 1793 and 4 under the Duke of York; from 1796 to 1800 in India in the Mysore war, including Seringapatam; in the Peninsula and South of France, in command of a brigade of cavalry, from 1808 to 1814, including the operations at Oporto; battle of Talavera, and various actions in covering the retreat from Almeida to Torres Vedras; battle of Busaco; cavalry action at Villa Garcia, Castrajon, Fuentes d'Onor, Salamanca, (severely wounded), El Bodon, the Pyrenees and Orthes; present at the siege and capture of Bhurtpore in 1825 and 6 as Commander-in-chief. His lordship has received a Cross and one Clasp.

2 Colonel Cavendish served in the Peninsula from July 1808 to January, 1809, as aid-de-camp to Lord Wm. Bentinck, and was wounded through the wrist at the battle of Corunna.

3 Mr. Percivall served in the Peninsula from September, 1813, to the end of the War, including the battle of Toulouse.

2d Regiment of Life Guards.

" PENINSULA"—"WATERLOO."

Colonel.

Years' Serv.		
63		William, *Earl* Cathcart, K.T. *Cornet*, 2 June, 1777 ; *Lieut.* 14 Nov. 77 ; *Capt.* 10 Dec. 77 ; *Major*, 13 April, 79 ; *Lieut.-Col.* 2 Feb. 81 ; *Col.* 18 Nov. 90 ; *Major-Gen.* 3 Oct. 94 ; *Lieut.-Gen.* 1 Jan. 1801 ; *Gen.* 1 Jan. 12 ; *Col.* 2nd Life-Guards, 7 Aug. 97.
Full Pay.	Half Pay.	

Lieut.-Colonel.

23	0	George Greenwood, *Cornet and Sub-Lieut.* P 23 June, 1817 ; *Lieut.* P 26 Jan. 19 ; *Capt.* P 1 Jan. 24 ; *Major*, P 26 Nov. 30 ; *Lieut.-Col.* 2 Jan. 31 ; *Col.* 12 Jan. 38.

Major and Lieut.-Colonel.

22	0	George Alexander Reid, *Cornet and Sub-Lieut.* P 7 Mar. 18 ; *Lieut.* 20 Mar. 21 ; *Capt.* P 11 Nov. 24 ; *Brevet-Major*, 23 July, 31 ; *Lieut. Col.* P 17 Feb. 32.

Full Pay.	Half Pay.	CAPTAINS.	COR. AND SUB-LIEUT.	LIEUT.	CAPTAIN.	BREVET-MAJOR
22	7/12	James M'Douall........	P 19 Feb. 18	P 2 Oct. 23	P 19 Oct. 25	28 June 38
20	0	Lewis Duncan Williams..	P 21 June 20	P 23 July 25	P 15 July 28	
16	2/12	Hon. W. E. Fitz Maurice	P 18 Nov. 24	P 24 Sept. 25	P 26 Feb. 28	
14	0	John Roche	P 27 Oct. 26	P 29 Jan. 30	P 25 Mar. 36	
13	0	Francis Mountjoy Martyn	P 27 Dec. 27	P 22 Mar. 31	P 22 April 36	
12	0	Thomas Gardnor	P 30 Dec. 28	P 9 Aug. 31	P 24 Mar. 37	
10	0	Geo. Howard Vyse.....	P 26 Nov. 30	P 17 April 35	P 1 Sept. 37	
9	0	Robert Blane	P 1 Nov. 31	P 25 Mar. 36	P 8 June 38	
		LIEUTENANTS.				
8	0	Hon. Major Henniker ..	P 8 Mar. 32	P 22 April 36		
8	0	Thomas Ogilvy	P 9 Mar. 32	P 29 April 36		
9	0	Thomas Naylor	P 30 Dec. 31	P 16 Mar. 33		
5	0	Fenton J. Evans Freke ..	P 24 Nov. 35	P 24 Mar. 37		
4	0	Henry George Boyce....	P 11 Mar. 36	P 28 April 37		
4	0	Wm. Aug. Tollemache ..	P 15 April 36	P 1 Sept. 37		
4	0	J. J. W. Peyton	P 28 April 36	P 8 June 38		
6	0	James King, R. M......	24 July 34	22 Aug. 38		
		CORNETS AND SUB-LIEUTENANTS.				
4	0	Edm. Vernon MacKinnon	P 29 April 36			
4	0	J. K. Wedderburn	P 7 July 36			
4	0	Robert Neville Lawley ..	P 8 July 36			
4	0	E. M. *Earl of* Longford	P 9 July 36			
6	0	Cha. H. Drummond, Lt.[1]	P 24 Mar. 37			
3	0	Charles J. Tottenham ...	P 28 April 37			
2	0	Richard Lucas	P 8 June 38			
2	0	A. W. *Visct.* Drumlanrig.	P 27 July 38			
1	0	Peter Sherwen	21 June 39			

1	0	*Adjutant.*—Peter Sherwen, (*Cornet & Sub-Lieut.*) 21 June, 39.
6	0	*Quarter-Master.*—William Allen, 25 July, 34.
22	4 5/12	*Surgeon.*—Jas. Bett,[2] 1 Sept. 37 ; *Assist.-Surg.* 9 Nov. 15 ; *Hosp.-Assist.* 6 Nov. 13.
5	0	*Assist.-Surgeon.*—Francis Wm. Grant Calder, 25 Sept. 35.
1	0	*Veterinary-Surgeon.*—James Horne, 31 May 39.

Scarlet—*Facings* Blue.—*Agent*, Messrs. Cox & Co.

[*Returned from France, February,* 1816.]

---

1 Cornet 15th Hussars, 18 July, 1834 ; Lieut. 30 April, 1836.
2 Dr. Bett was at the capture of Genoa 15th April, 1814, and capture of Castine in America 1st Sept. 1814.

Royal Regiment of Horse Guards.

"PENINSULA"—"WATERLOO."

Years' Serv.		
Full Pay	Half Pay	
50		*Colonel.* ₽ ⚔ Rowland *Lord* Hill,[1] G.C.B. G.C.H. & K.C. *Ens.* 31 July, 1790; *Lieut.* 24 Jan. 91; *Capt.* 23 March, 93; *Major*, 10 Feb. 94; *Lieut.-Col.* 13 May, 94; *Col.* 1 Jan. 1800; *Maj.-Gen.* 30 Oct. 05; *Lieut.-Gen.* 1 Jan. 12; *Gen.* 27 May, 25; *Col.* Royal Horse-Guards, 19 Nov. 30.
		Lieut.-Colonel.
34	0	₽ William Richardson, *Cornet*, ᴾ 27 Feb. 06; *Lieut.* ᴾ 20 Aug. 07; *Capt.* ᴾ 26 Dec. 11; *Lieut.-Col.* ᴾ 24 July, 23; *Col.* 10 Jan. 37.
		Major.
28	0	₽ ⚔ Everard W. Bouverie,[2] *Cornet*, ᴾ 2 April, 12; *Lieut.* 15 Oct. 12; *Capt.* ᴾ 9 Sept. 19; *Brev.-Maj.* 6 May, 31; *Lieut.-Col.* ᴾ 4 Dec. 32.

Full Pay	Half Pay	CAPTAINS.	CORNET.	LIEUT.	CAPTAIN.	BREVET-MAJOR.
28	0	₽ ⚔ George Smith[3] ..	5 Nov. 12	18 Nov. 13	ᴾ 22 June 20	10 Jan. 37
25	0	J. Constantine Trent	ᴾ 16 Nov. 15	ᴾ 22 June 20	ᴾ 2 Aug. 26	
16	0	*Hon.* G. C. Weld Forester	ᴾ 27 May 24	ᴾ 1 Aug. 26	ᴾ 6 July 32	
12	0	Vincent Corbet	ᴾ 4 June 28	ᴾ 30 Nov. 30	ᴾ 14 Mar. 34	
11	0	Wyndham Edw. Hanmer	ᴾ 26 Mar. 29	ᴾ 15 Mar. 31	ᴾ 9 Jan. 35	
10	0	*Hon.* Horace Pitt	ᴾ 27 Feb. 30	ᴾ 6 July 32	ᴾ 11 Nov. 36	
10	0	Richard Silver Oliver....	ᴾ 29 July 30	ᴾ 4 Dec. 32	ᴾ 16 Dec. 36	
10	0	Walter Rob. Tyrrell	ᴾ 19 Nov. 30	ᴾ 18 Jan. 33	ᴾ 30 June 37	
		LIEUTENANTS.				
28	0	Simeon Hirst	16 Oct. 12	10 Sept. 13		
18	3 9/12	Thomas Brunt, R.M.....	28 Jan. 19	31 July 26		
10	0	R. H. R. Howard Vyse ..	ᴾ 30 Nov. 30	ᴾ 31 May 33		
10	0	Alex. Thompson Munro..	11 Jan. 31	1 June 33		
9	0	Wm. Chas. Nethercote ..	ᴾ 22 Mar. 31	ᴾ 25 Oct. 33		
8	0	*Lord* Alfred Paget......	ᴾ 6 July 32	ᴾ 14 Mar. 34		
7	0	*Lord* Alg. P. B. St. Maur	ᴾ 31 May 33	ᴾ 11 Nov. 36		
7	0	*Hon.* Chas. Hen. Maynard	ᴾ 25 Oct. 33	ᴾ 16 Dec. 36		
7	0	Robert Oliver	ᴾ 17 Jan. 34	ᴾ 21 April 37		
6	0	*Hon.* Chas. Hen. Cust ..	ᴾ 14 Mar. 34	ᴾ 30 June 37		
5	0	Thomas B. Proctor......	ᴾ 16 Oct. 35	ᴾ 1 June 38		
		CORNETS.				
5	0	J. W. Hamilton Anson ..	ᴾ 25 Dec. 35			
4	0	Philip Perceval	ᴾ 23 Dec. 36			
3	0	J. P. P. Wade Bastard ..	ᴾ 21 April 37			
3	0	Alex. Bateman P. Hood .	ᴾ 30 June 37			
5	0	*Hon.* F. H. P. Methuen..	ᴾ 6 Mar. 35			
2	0	C. R. P. Morewood	ᴾ 1 June 38			
1	0	Chas. H. Gordon Lennox, *Earl of* March	ᴾ 24 May 39			

10	0	*Adjutant.*—Alexander Thompson Munro, (*Lieut.*) 18 Jan. 31.
10	0	*Quarter-Master.*—Herbert Turner, 1 Jan. 31.
28	0	*Surgeon.*—₽ Archibald Hair,[4] M.D. 12 Jan. 26; *Assist.-Surg.* 12 Nov. 12.
		Assistant-Surgeon.—George Gulliver, 12 June, 28; *Hospital-Assist.* 17 May, 27.
26	1 9/12	*Veterinary-Surgeon.*—⚔ John Siddall, 10 Oct. 12.

Blue—*Facings* Scarlet.—*Agent,* Messrs. Cox & Co.

[*Returned from France, February*, 1816.]

1 Lord Hill served the campaign of 1801 in Egypt, and was wounded 13th March. His Lordship has received a Cross and four Clasps for Roleia and Vimiera, Corunna, Talavera (wounded), Vittoria, Pyrenees, Nivelle, Nive and Orthes.

2 Colonel Bouverie served in the Peninsula from October, 1812, to the end of the war, including the battle of Vittoria; wounded 18th June at Waterloo.

3 Colonel Smith served the campaign of 1814 in the Peninsula; present at Waterloo on the 18th June. Brevet-lieut.-colonel 28th June, 38.

4 Dr. Hair was present at the battle of Vittoria, San Sebastian, August and September, 1813, battles of the Nivelle, Nive, and Orthes, and at the affairs of Vera; served in the last American war, and was present in the action in front of New Orleans.

Emb. for For. Service, 1838.] **1st (or the King's) Regiment of Dragoon Guards.** [Serving in Canada.

Years' Serv.		"WATERLOO."

48

Colonel.

Full Pay.	Half Pay.	
		⚔ Sir Henry Fane,[1] G.C.B. *Cornet*, 31 May, 1792; *Lieut.* 29 Sept. 92; *Capt.* 3 April, 93; *Major*, 24 Aug. 95; *Lieut.-Col.* 1 Jan. 97; *Col.* 1 Jan. 1805; *Major-Gen.* 25 July, 10; *Lieut.-Gen.* 12 Aug. 19; *Gen.* 10 Jan. 37; *Col. 1st Dragoon Guards*, 24 Feb. 27.

Lieut.Colonel.

| 25 | 5 | ⚔ Hon. George Cathcart,[2] *Cornet & Sub-Lieutenant*, 10 May, 10; *Lieut.* 1 July, 11; *Capt.* 24 Dec. 18; *Major*, ᴾ 8 April, 26; *Lieut.-Col.* ᴾ 13 May, 26. |

Major.

| 12 | 16⁵⁄₁₂ | ⚔ John Henry Slade, *Cornet*, 7 May, 12; *Lieut.* ᴾ 25 Feb. 13; *Capt.* ᴾ 24 Oct. 21; *Major*, ᴾ 5 June, 27. |

		CAPTAINS.	CORNET.	LIEUT.	CAPTAIN.	BREVET-MAJOR.
25	0	John Spencer Manning..	25 Oct. 15	ᴾ 7 Sept. 20	ᴾ 3 April 28	
25	0	Richard Martin	5 Oct. 15	ᴾ 2 Jan. 23	ᴾ 31 Dec. 28	
11	0	James Smith Schonswar	ᴾ 5 Mar. 29	ᴾ 17 Dec. 30	ᴾ 6 May 36	
9	0	Hastings David Sands ..	ᴾ 18 June 31	ᴾ 24 Dec. 33	ᴾ 18 May 38	
9	0	Alfred Scott	ᴾ 27 Sept. 31	ᴾ 11 July 34	ᴾ 8 Mar. 39	
8	0	Burrell Fuller..........	ᴾ 6 Apr. 32	ᴾ 17 Oct. 34	ᴾ 29 Mar. 39	
11	0	Henry Martin Turnor ..	ᴾ 20 Aug. 29	ᴾ 31 Dec. 33	ᴾ 14 June 39	
7	0	B. O'Neale *Visc.* Amiens	ᴾ 24 Dec. 33	ᴾ 6 May 36	ᴾ 27 Sept. 39	
		LIEUTENANTS.				
28	1	⚔ F. Hammersley,[3] R.M.	ᴾ 23 Jan. 12	ᴾ 9 April 12		
7	0	Stephen P. Groves......	ᴾ 12 July 33	ᴾ 23 Dec. 36		
6	0	Tho. Ommaney Pipon ..	ᴾ 17 Oct. 34	ᴾ 24 Feb. 37		
4	0	Edmund James Power ..	ᴾ 6 May 36	ᴾ 22 Aug. 37		
4	0	Manaton Pipon	ᴾ 20 May 36	ᴾ 29 Dec. 37		
4	0	⚔ Richard Hollis	1 July 36	12 Jan. 38		
4	0	Wm. Chas. Grant	ᴾ 23 Dec. 36	ᴾ 18 May 38		
3	0	Thomas Richard Mills ..	ᴾ 30 June 37	ᴾ 8 Mar. 39		
3	0	Henry Keown	ᴾ 22 Aug. 37	ᴾ 29 Mar. 39		
3	0	Bingham Newland......	ᴾ 29 Dec. 37	ᴾ 14 June 39		
2	0	John Blackburn Hawkes	ᴾ 2 Mar. 38	ᴾ 27 Sept. 39		
		CORNETS.				
4	0	Cornelius Powell	ᴾ 28 Oct. 36			
1	0	Geo. Wm. C. Jackson ..	ᴾ 29 Mar. 39			
1	0	Wm. Steele Wilkinson...	ᴾ 1 June 39			
3	0	John Borlase Maunsell...	ᴾ 17 Nov. 37			
1	0	James Peach Cleaver....	ᴾ 15 June 39			
1	0	Arth. Cecil Crewe Fleming	ᴾ 11 Oct. 39			

22	4⁷⁄₁₂	*Paymaster*.—⚔ David Scott Kin. Maclaurin,[4] 18 Sept. 23; *Deputy Assistant Commissary General*, 7 March, 14.
4	0	*Adjutant*.—⚔ Richard Hollis, (*Lieut.*) 8 July, 36.
2	0	*Quarter-Master*. —Joseph Missett, 30 March, 38.
28	1⁵⁄₁₂	*Surgeon*.—⚔ Thomas Lewis,[5] M.D. 19 Nov. 30; *Assist.-Surg.* 9 Sept. 13; *Hosp.-Assist.* 8 July 11.
14	0	*Assistant-Surgeon*.—Alex. Smith, M.D. 28 Sept. 26; *Hosp.-Assist.* 21 March, 26.
24	14⁹⁄₁₂	*Veterinary Surgeon*.—John Mellows, 6 Nov. 01.

Scarlet—*Facings* Blue.—*Agent*, Messrs. Cox & Co.

1 Sir Henry Fane has received a Cross and one Clasp for Roleia and Vimiera, Corunna, Talavera, Vittoria, Orthes.
2 Colonel *Hon.* G. Cathcart served the campaigns of 1813 and 14 in Germany as aid-de-camp to Lord Cathcart, and was engaged at Lutzen 3rd May, Boulzen 20th and 21st May, Dresden 28th August, Leipsic 16th, 18th, and 19th October, 1814, Brierme 1st February, Bar-sur-Aube, Areis 21st March, and Fere Champ 25th March, 14; served at Waterloo on the 16th and 18th June.
3 Lieut. Hammersley was present at the battles of Vittoria and Toulouse, and the investment of, and the Heights before Pampeluna; shot through the shoulder whilst protecting a house in the neighbourhood of Dublin, on duty, when in the Militia.
4 Paymaster Maclaurin served in the Peninsula during the campaign of 1813, and that in Holland in 1814, and subsequently at Waterloo, and with the army of occupation as Deputy Assistant Commissary General.
5 Doctor Lewis served in the Peninsula from July 1811 to June 1813.

2nd (or The Queen's) Regiment of Dragoon Guards.

Years' Serv.			
57		*Colonel.*	
Full Pay.	Half Pay.	Sir Thos. Gage Montresor,[1] K.C.H. *Ens.* 12 March, 1783; *Lieut.* 4 April, 83; *Capt.* 17 June, 94; *Major*, 12 April, 99; *Lieut.-Col.* 27 June, 1801; *Col.* 25 July, 10; *Major-Gen.* 4 June, 13; *Lieut.-Gen.* 27 May, 25; *Col.* 2nd Dragoon Guards, 20 Feb. 37.	
		Lieut.-Colonel.	
28	0	Charles Kearney, *Cornet*, p 10 Sept. 12; *Lieut.* p 8 Sept. 14; *Capt.* p 19 June, 17; *Major*, p 30 Dec. 26; *Lieut.-Col.* p 28 Oct. 37.	
		Major.	
15	0	Henry Wilmot Charlton, *Cornet*, p 23 June 25; *Lieut.* p 30 Dec. 26; *Capt.* p 13 Nov. 32; *Major*, p 13 Dec. 39.	

			CORNET.	LIEUT.	CAPTAIN.	BREVET-MAJOR.
		CAPTAINS.				
8	0	William Campbell	p 6 Jan. 32	p 12 Apr. 33	p 27 May 36	
8	0	Rich. Duckworth Dunn..	p 9 Mar. 32	p 13 Sept. 33	p 28 Oct. 37	
15	1 2/12	Power Le Poer Trench ..	p 12 Aug. 24	p 17 Dec. 25	p 30 Dec. 26	
12	0	Hen. St. John Mildmay..	p 20 Nov. 28	p 8 June 30	p 7 Apr. 37	
8	0	Geo. Henry Elliott......	p 27 July 32	p 13 June 34	p 22 June 38	
8	0	*Sir* Hen. Chas. Paulet, *Bt.*	p 13 Nov. 32	p 29 Aug. 34	p 13 Dec. 39	
		LIEUTENANTS.				
7	0	Egerton Leigh..........	p 12 April 33	p 19 June 35		
7	0	John Chichester Knox ..	p 13 Sept. 33	p 14 Aug. 35		
9	0	Hylton Briscoe	p 11 Oct. 31	p 25 July 34		
8	0	Edw. Lovett Robertson..	p 11 Jan. 33	p 14 Nov. 35		
5	0	George Arthur Ede	p 14 Aug. 35	p 17 Feb. 37		
8	0	William Wernham, R.M.	4 Dec. 32	p 15 July 36		
5	0	Francis Haviland	24 Nov. 35	20 Sept. 37		
7	0	William Persse	p 13 Sept. 33	p 27 Oct. 35		
4	4/12	Jackson V. Tuthill	p 30 Apr. 36	p 17 May 39		
3	0	Robt. Wm. Dallas	p 6 Oct. 37	p 13 Dec. 39		
		CORNETS.				
2	0	R. Dudley Ackland	p 22 June 38			
1	0	Fred. James Ibbetson....	p 17 May 39			
1	0	James Ley	p 13 Dec. 39			

14	0	*Paymaster.*—Henry Boys, 1 Aug. 37; *Ens.* 8 April, 26; *Lieut.* 13 Feb. 30; *Capt.* 6 Sept. 33.
5	0	*Adjutant.*—Francis Haviland, (*Lieut.*) 4 Dec. 35.
4	0	*Quarter-Master.*—John Haviland, 15 July, 36.
28	3/12	*Surgeon.*—D James Dawn,[2] 28 Dec. 26; *Assist.-Surg.* 28 Oct. 13; *Hosp.-Assist.* Aug. 12.
		Assistant-Surgeon.—Alexander George Home, M.D. 18 Jan. 27; *Hosp.-Assist.* 26 Oct. 26.
27	0	*Veterinary Surgeon.*—William Woodman, 25 Feb. 13.

Scarlet—*Facings* Black.—*Agents*, Messrs. Hopkinson, Barton, and Knyvett, Regent-street.

[*Returned from France, November*, 1818.]

1 Sir Tho. G. Montresor has been twenty-four years on regimental full-pay, during which period he served at Gibraltar in 1790 and 91; in Flanders and Holland in 1793, 4, and 5; the Egyptian campaign of 1801, and subsequently many years in India.
2 Dr. Dawn served in the Peninsula from September, 1812, to the end of the war, including the siege of San Sebastian, and battles of Nivelle, Nive, and Toulouse.

3rd or (*The Prince of Wales's*) Regt. of Dragoon Guards.

"TALAVERA" — "ALBUHERA" — "VITTORIA" — "PENINSULA."

Years' Serv.		
Full Pay	Half Pay	*Colonel.*
47		₿ Sir James Charles Dalbiac,¹ K.C.H. *Cornet*, 4 July, 1793; *Lieut.* 24 Feb. 94; *Capt.* 11 Oct. 98; *Major*, 15 Oct. 1801; *Lieut.-Col.* 25 April, 08; *Col.* 4 June, 14; *Major-Gen.* 27 May, 25; *Lieut.-Gen.* 28 June, 38; *Col.* 3rd Dragoon-Guards, 1 Jan. 39.

Lieut.-Colonel.

34	0	₿ George Maunsell,² *Cornet*, P 13 March, 1806; *Lieut.* P 25 Dec. 06; *Capt.* P 18 July, 11; *Major*, P 21 Nov. 28; *Lieut.-Col.* P 15 Sept. 38.

Major.

15	0	Thomas Arthur, *Cornet*, P 23 June, 1825; *Lieut.* P 19 Sept. 26; *Capt.* P 8 Feb. 31; *Major*, P 15 Sept. 38.

		CAPTAINS.	CORNET.	LIEUT.	CAPTAIN.	BREVET MAJOR.
14	11 9/12	₿ Wm. Warb. Huntley	P 16 June 14	23 Oct. 15	P 13 Sept. 21	10 Jan. 37
13	1 4/12	Christopher Teesdale	P 11 July 26	P 15 June 30	P 1 June 32	
11	0	Wm. Chas. Jas. Campbell	P 21 May 29	P 20 Jan. 32	P 2 May 34	
10	0	John Hopton	P 8 Feb. 31	P 9 Mar. 32	P 30 Oct. 35	
9	0	John Daniel Dyson	P 9 Dec. 31	P 22 Mar. 33	P 8 July 36	
8	0	John Nugent	P 17 Feb. 32	P 18 Oct. 33	P 15 Sept. 38	
		LIEUTENANTS.				
15	0	Aylmer L. Bourke, R.M.	7 July 25	18 Jan. 27		
9	0	J. Geo. Wm. Brydges	P 20 Jan. 32	P 2 May 34		
8	0	Francis Garratt	P 9 Mar. 32	P 30 Jan. 35		
9	0	Francis Watt	P 17 Aug. 31	P 8 July 36		
7	0	Edward Dyson	P 18 Oct. 33	P 27 Oct. 37		
6	0	John Rodon	P 30 Jan. 35	P 15 Sept. 38		
5	0	Isaac R. Warner	P 30 Oct. 35	16 May 39		
4	0	Matthew Thos. Forde	P 16 Sept. 36	P 17 May 39		
		CORNETS.				
3	0	William Squire	P 24 Mar. 37			
3	0	Edward D. Freeman	P 27 Oct. 37			
2	0	Henry H. Bacon	P 8 June 38			
2	0	Edward Bagwell	P 15 Sept. 38			
1	0	Manners M'Kay	P 17 May 39			

10	0	*Paymaster.*—Ernest Aug. Hawker, 19 Oct. 38; *Ens.* 30 Sept. 30; *Lieut.* 8 July, 36.
5	0	*Adjutant.*—Isaac Redston Warner, (*Lieut.*) 21 Sept. 38.
30	0	*Quarter-Master.*—₿ John Martin,³ 22 Feb. 10.
33	0	*Surgeon.*—₿ George Alex. Stephenson,⁴ 28 Oct. 13; *Assist. Surg.* 14 May, 07. *Assistant Surgeon.*—David Lister, 18 Oct. 27; *Hospital Assist.* 26 Oct. 26.
15	0	*Veterinary Surgeon.*—Isaac Timm, 17 Feb. 25.

Scarlet — *Facings* Yellow. — *Agent*, Messrs. Hopkinson, Barton, and Knyvett.

[*Returned from France, January*, 1816.]

---

1 Sir Charles Dalbiac served the Campaign of 1809 in the Peninsula, and was at the battles of Talavera the 27th and 28th July. Served the winter campaign of 1810 in the Lines of Lisbon. Served the campaign of 1811, and commanded his Regt. (always the 4th Dragoons) in the affair of Campo-Mayo, 25th March; and in the Cavalry affair of Los Santos, 16th April. Served the campaign of 1812, and was engaged in the affair at Llerena, 11th April, when Lord Combermere defeated Marshal Soult's rear-guard. Present at the battle of Salamanca, 22d July. Sir Charles published, with the approbation of His Royal Highness the late Duke of York, a military catechism for the use and instruction of young officers and non-commissioned officers of Cavalry.

2 Colonel Maunsell served in the Peninsula from April, 1809, to the end of the war, including the following battles and sieges, viz.:—Talavera, 27th, 28th July, 1809, Busaco, Albuhera, Usagre, Ciudad Rodrigo, January and February, 1812, Badajoz, March and April, 1812, Vittoria and Toulouse. Col. M. commanded a squadron at the brilliant cavalry affair of Usagre, where three French regiments were defeated by the 3rd Dragoon Guards.

3 Quarter-Master Martin served in the Peninsula from April, 1809, to the end of the war, including the following battles and sieges, viz.:—Talavera 27th and 28th July, Busaco, Albuhera, Usagre, Badajoz, March and April, 1812, Vittoria, Pampeluna, and Toulouse.

4 Dr. Stephenson served in the Peninsula from March, 1809, to the end of the war.

4th (or Royal Irish) Regiment of Dragoon Guards.

On the Standards and Appointments the HARP AND CROWN, and the Star of ST. PATRICK, with the motto "*Quis Separabit*"
"PENINSULA."

Years' Serv.			
54		*Colonel.*	
		₽ Sir George Anson,[1] G.C.B. *Cornet*, 3 May, 1786; *Lieut.* 16 March, 91; *Capt.* 9 Sept. 92; *Major*, 25 Dec. 94; *Lieut.-Col.* 21 Dec. 97; *Col.* 1 Jan. 05; *Maj.-Gen.* 25 July 10; *Lieut.-Gen.* 12 Aug. 19; *Gen.* 10 Jan 37; *Col.* 4th Dragoon-Guards, 24 Feb. 27.	
Full Pay.	Half Pay.		
25	6 1/12	*Lieut.-Colonel.*	
		₽ ₡₤ James Charles Chatterton,[2] K.H. *Cornet*, ᴾ 23 Nov. 09; *Lieut.* 6 June, 11; *Capt.* ᴾ 26 March, 18; *Major*, ᴾ 22 July, 24; *Lieut.-Col.* ᴾ 18 Dec. 27.	
24	1	*Major.*	
		₡₤ Charles Makepeace, *Ens.* ᴾ 13 April, 15; *Lieut.* ᴾ 14 March, 16; *Capt.* ᴾ 24 July, 23; *Major*, ᴾ 6 March, 35.	

		CAPTAINS.	CORNET.	LIEUT.	CAPTAIN.	BREVET MAJOR.
14	0	Edward Cooper Hodge ..	3 Aug. 26	ᴾ 3 July 28	ᴾ 19 Dec. 34	
12	3	George Wynell Mayow ..	ᴾ 9 June 25	ᴾ 12 Feb. 30	ᴾ 6 Mar. 35	
11	0	Clement Robert Archer..	ᴾ 21 May 29	ᴾ 13 Aug. 30	ᴾ 24 April 35	
10	0	Lionel Place	ᴾ 6 July 30	ᴾ 3 May 31	ᴾ 4 Sept. 35	
10	0	Alex. Duncan Tait	ᴾ 2 Nov. 30	ᴾ 31 Aug. 32	ᴾ 30 June 37	
8	0	William Hosken Harper	ᴾ 19 Oct. 32	ᴾ 17 Jan. 34	ᴾ 16 Aug. 39	
		LIEUTENANTS.				
7	0	Francis Meynell	ᴾ 17 Jan. 34	ᴾ 24 April 35		
5	0	Granville H. Eliot	ᴾ 6 Mar. 35	ᴾ 8 April 36		
8	0	Mildmay Clerk	ᴾ 4 May 32	ᴾ 7 Mar. 34		
5	0	Charles Parke Ibbetson..	ᴾ 24 April 35	ᴾ 30 June 37		
7	0	Ferdinand W. Arkwright	ᴾ 9 Aug. 33	ᴾ 2 June 37		
4	0	Gustavus Rochfort......	ᴾ 8 April 36	ᴾ 27 April 38	3 Captain Drawwater served in the Expedition to Copenhagen in 1807; the capture of Martinique; and subsequently in the Peninsula, including the battle of Busaco.	
3	0	Thos. Oliver W. Coster..	ᴾ 4 Aug. 37	ᴾ 23 Nov. 38		
2	0	George Thomson Jacob..	ᴾ 27 April 38	ᴾ 16 Aug. 39		
2	0	Edmund John Turner ..	ᴾ 23 Nov. 38	ᴾ 7 Feb. 40		
		CORNETS.			4 Dr. Flanagan served in the Peninsula, including the battles of the Pyrenees, Orthes, and subsequent affairs. Served also in the American war, including the siege and repulse of the sortie at Fort Erie, and the defeat of the Americans at Cook's Mills.	
5	0	Richard Souter, R.M. ..	25 Sept. 35			
1	0	Thos. Geo. Symons	ᴾ 3 May 39			
1	0	Milbourne Kemeys Tynte	ᴾ 16 Aug. 39			
1	0	Fra. Rowland Forster....	ᴾ 7 Feb. 40			

34	1 2/12	*Paymaster.*—₽ Aug. Chas. Drawwater,[3] 11 Nov. 19; *Ens.* 1 May, 05; *Lieut.* 20 March, 06; *Capt.* 15 Aug. 11.	
5	0	*Adjutant.*—Charles P. Ibbetson, (*Lieut.*) 27 April, 38.	
6	0	*Quarter-Master.*—John Andrews, 20 June, 34.	
33	10/12	*Surgeon.*—₽ John Bickerton Flanagan,[4] 21 Oct 13; *Assist.-Surg.* 12 March, 07; *Hosp.-Assist.* 6 May, 06.	
14	0	*Assist.Surgeon.*—Patrick O'Callaghan, M.B. 21 Feb. 28; *Hosp.-Assist.* 18 July, 26.	
12	0	*Veterinary Surgeon.*—James Rainsford, 25 Dec. 28.	

Scarlet — *Facings* Blue. — *Agent*, Mr. Collyer, Park-place, St. James's.

[*Returned from Portugal, May,* 1813.]

1 Sir George Anson has received a Medal and two Clasps for Talavera, Salamanca, and Vittoria.
2 Col. Chatterton served in the Peninsula, Flanders, and France, from 1811 to 1818, including the cavalry actions at Fuente Gurnaldo and Aldea de Ponte; sieges of Ciudad Rodrigo and Badajoz; actions at Usagne, Llerena, Salamanca, Heights of St. Christoval, Castrajon, to the battle of Salamanca; affairs at Valladolid, and to the investment of Burgos; combats at Monasterio, and at Hermoza upon the retreat from Burgos to Salamanca; affairs thence to Ciudad Rodrigo; upon the advance from Portugal; the out-post affairs and combat at Osma; battle of Vittoria; actions at Villa Franca and Tolosa; siege and capture of San Sebastian; actions on crossing the Bidassoa and carrying the enemy's fortified entrenchments; battle of the Nivelle and affairs at St. Jean de Luz, and in front of Bayonne, connected with the passage and battle of the Nive; passage of the Adour and investment of Bayonne; occupation of Bourdeaux; passage of the Garonne and affair upon the Dordoyne; battles of Quatre Bras and Waterloo, 16th, 17th, and 18th June; advance to, and capture of Paris; and with the army of occupation in France.

5th (or *Princess Charlotte of Wales's*) *Regt. of Dragoon Guards.*

The motto " *Vestigla nulla retrorsum.*" — " SALAMANCA " — " VITTORIA "— " TOULOUSE "— " PENINSULA."

Years' Serv.		
Full Pay.	Half Pay.	
60		*Colonel.* ⚐ Sir John Slade, Bt.[1] G.C.H., *Cornet*, 11 May, 1780; *Lieut.* 28 April, 83; *Capt.* 24 Oct. 87; *Major*, 1 March, 94; *Lieut.-Col.* 29 April, 95; *Col.* 29 April, 1802; *Major-Gen.* 25 Oct. 09; *Lieut.-Gen.* 4 June, 14; *Gen.* 10 Jan. 37; *Col.* 5th Dragoon Guards, 20 July 31.
32	2 8/12	*Lieut.-Colonel.* ⚐ Sir James Maxwell Wallace,[2] K.H. *Cornet*, P 14 Aug. 05; *Lieut.* P 5 June, 06; *Capt.* P 22 Oct. 07; *Major*, P 1 Jan. 17; *Lieut.-Col.* P 25 Sept. 23; *Col.* 28 June, 38.
21	1 9/12	*Major.* Hon. James Yorke Scarlett, *Cornet,* P 26 March, 18; *Lieut.* P 24 Oct. 21; *Capt.* P 9 June, 25; *Major,* P 11 June, 30.

			CORNET.	LIEUT.	CAPTAIN.	BREVET-MAJOR.
		CAPTAINS.				
20	3	Francis Westenra	P 31 July 17	P 24 Oct. 21	P 31 Dec. 25	28 June 38
15	0	John Wallace King......	P 24 Mar. 25	P 14 Feb. 28	P 28 Dec. 32	
15	0	Abraham Bolton........	P 12 Oct. 25	P 26 June 27	P 8 Mar. 33	
11	0	Francis Parnell Hovenden	P 12 Nov. 29	P 13 July 32	P 6 May 36	
10	0	Robert Meade..........	P 26 Oct. 30	P 14 Dec. 32	P 30 Dec. 36	
8	0	Robert Bell............	P 16 Nov. 32	P 27 June 34	P 9 Mar. 38	
		LIEUTENANTS.				
7	0	Goodwin C. Colquitt	P 2 Aug. 33	P 2 Oct. 35		
6	0	W. Beaumaris Knipe....	P 23 Jan. 35	P 6 May 36		
5	0	J. Ireland Blackburne ..	P 3 April 35	P 17 June 36		
7	0	Norman Cowley........	P 26 April 33	P 19 June 35		
4	0	Arch. Rowan Hamilton..	P 13 May 36	P 30 June 37		
4	0	James Conolly	P 17 June 36	P 28 Nov. 37		
4	0	James Charles Yorke....	P 13 Jan. 37	P 10 Aug. 38		
3	0	Arthur Prime.	P 30 June 37	P 5 April 39		
		CORNETS.				
16	0	⚐ J. Henley, R. M.[3]	6 Jan. 25			
9	0	Henry Ash	18 Oct. 31			
3	0	George Lloyd Robson....	P 28 Nov. 37			
2	0	W. Noel Algernon Hill ..	P 10 Aug. 38			
1	0	William Barnett........	P 5 April 39			

24	1 4/12	*Paymaster.*—Henry Aug. Jackson, 15 Dec. 37; *Ens.* 27 Aug. 15; *Lieut.* 8 April, 25; *Capt.* 18 Dec. 35.
9	0	*Adjutant.*—Henry Ash, (*Cornet,*) 18 Oct. 31.
5	0	*Quarter-Master.*—James Brand, 17 July, 35.
31	5 9/12	*Surgeon.*—James Barlow,[4] M.D. 29 July, 13; *Assist.-Surg.* 5 March, 07; *Hosp.-Assist.* 25 June, 03.
		Assistant-Surgeon.—Charles Hay Carnegy, M.D. 14 March, 34.
26	0	⚐ *Veterinary Surgeon.*—John Constant,[5] 3 March, 14.

Scarlet—*Facings* Green.—*Agent*, Messrs. Cox & Co.

[*Returned from Spain, July*, 1814.]

1 Sir John Slade served in Portugal and Spain, under Sir John Moore, in command of the Hussar Brigade, including the different operations terminating with the battle of Corunna. Placed again on the staff in the Peninsula, in Aug. 1809, where he served until June, 1813, in command of a brigade of cavalry. Sir John has received a Medal and one Clasp for the battles of Corunna, and Fuentes d'Onor.
2 Sir J. M. Wallace served at Waterloo on the 16th, 17th, and 18th June.
3 Cornet Henley served the campaign of 1814 in the Peninsula, including the battle of Toulouse.
4 Dr. Barlow's services :—Expedition to Copenhagen in 1807; capture of Martinique in 1809; campaign of 1815 in the Netherlands and France.
5 Mr. Constant served at Waterloo on the 16th, 17th, and 18th June.

6th Regiment of Dragoon Guards (or Carabineers.)

Years' Serv.		
Full Pay.	Half Pay.	
45		**Colonel.** P Sir Thomas Hawker,[1] K.C.H. *Cornet*, 12 May, 1795; *Lieut*. 5 April, 96; *Capt* 10 July, 99; *Major*, 23 Nov. 1804; *Lieut.-Col.* 2 Sept. 08; *Col.* 4 June, 14; *Major-Gen.* 27 May, 25; *Lieut-Gen.* 28 June, 38; *Col.* 6th Dragoon Guards, 7 June, 39.
34	0	**Lieut.-Colonel.** P ☘ James Jackson,[2] K.H. *Ens.* 9 Oct. 06; *Lieut.* 25 Jan. 08; *Capt.* P 25 June, 13; *Brevet-Major*, 18 June, 15; *Regtl.-Major*, P 26 April, 27; *Brevet-Lieut.-Col.* 25 May, 26; *Regtl.-Lieut.-Col.* P 2 March, 39.
32	0	**Major.** David Hay, *Cornet*, 6 Oct. 08; *Lieut.* P 31 Oct. 11; *Capt.* P 5 Aug. 19; *Brevet-Major*, 10 Jan. 37; *Regtl.-Major*, P 14 April, 37.

			CORNET.	LIEUT.	CAPTAIN.	BREVET-MAJOR.
		CAPTAINS.				
15	0	Henry Richmond Jones..	P 9 June 25	P 14 Nov. 26	P 12 June 30	
15	0	Joseph Deane Browne ..	P 10 Sept. 25	P 26 April 27	P 26 April 31	
14	0	Henry Hayhurst France	P 2 Nov. 26	P 10 Feb. 29	P 25 Jan. 33	
11	0	Thomas Edward Taylor..	P 10 Feb. 29	P 26 April 31	P 2 Nov. 38	
12	1 4/12	Brook John Knight	P 26 Oct. 26	8 June 30	P 26 June 35	
16	2 8/12	John Rowland Smyth[3] ..	P 5 July 21	P 26 May 25	P 29 Nov. 27	
		LIEUTENANTS.				
18	0	William S. Philips, R.M.	25 Oct. 22	16 Feb. 26		
10	0	James Johnston	P 12 June 30	P 6 April 32		
9	0	Hon. A. G. Fred. Jocelyn	P 26 April 31	P 6 July 32		
10	0	William Scott	P 12 Feb. 30	P 16 Jan. 35		
8	0	James Hen. Dickson	P 6 July 32	P 22 May 35		
5	0	Thomas Manders	P 30 July 35	6 Oct. 38		
3	0	Edward Lewis Pryse	P 17 Mar. 37	P 2 Nov. 38		
5	0	Robert F. *Lord* Gifford ..	P 4 Dec. 35	P 27 July 38		
4	0	Henry L. Cocksedge	P 1 April 36	P 24 Mar. 37		
3	0	Lindsey Zachariah Cox..	P 14 April 37	P 6 Sept. 39		
		CORNETS.				
2	0	Robert J. Knox	P 5 Oct. 38			
2	0	Ernle Warriner	P 2 Nov. 38			
1	0	Phillips Buchanan......	P 6 Sept. 39			

S Dr. Heriot served in the Peninsula from June, 1809, to the end of the war, including the battles of Talavera and Salamanca; siege of Burgos; and battles of Vittoria, the Pyrenees, and Orthes.

Paymaster.—

5	0	*Adjutant.*—Thomas Manders, (*Lieut.*) 31 July, 35.
5	0	*Quarter-Master.*—Thomas Smith, 26 June, 35.
30	5 11/12	*Surgeon.*—P John Heriot,[3] M.D. 16 April, 12; *Assistant-Surgeon*, 8 Nov. 04; *Hosp.-Assist.* 11 May, 04.
		Assistant-Surgeon.—Henry Carline, 28 Sept. 26; *Hospital-Assistant*, 31 Aug. 26.
7	19 6/12	*Veterinary Surgeon.*—Thomas Browne, 25 July, 34; *Ens.* 25 Dec. 13.

Scarlet—*Facings* White.—*Agent*, Messrs. Cox & Co.
[*Returned from Buenos Ayres*, 1808.]

1 Sir Thomas Hawker was present in the actions in North Holland, the Helder expedition, on the 10th, 19th September, 2nd and 6th October, 1799; and was present in command of the 20th Light Dragoons in every action in which the British troops were engaged on the eastern coast of Spain, in 1812 and 1813; he has subsequently served on the Staff, in India, as Major-General.

2 Colonel Jackson served in the Peninsula, from April, 1809, to the end of the war, including the battles of Oporto, Talavera, Busaco, Redinha, Fuentes d'Onor; first siege of Badajoz, from 29th May, to 16th June, 1811; action at Elbodon; siege and capture of Ciudad Rodrigo; second siege and capture of Badajoz, 6th April, 1812; battles of Salamanca, Vittoria, Maya Pass, Pampeluna, 15th July, Pyrenees, 30th July, Nivelle, Nive, and Bayonne. Present at Waterlooo, and with the army of occupation in France. Served in India and Arabia from 1819 to 1826, including the capture of Beni-Boo-Ali, as Military Secretary to Sir Lionel Smith, and, for which service, he was recommended by the Marquis of Hastings for the rank of Lieut.-Col.

3 Captain Smyth served in India with the 16th Lancers, and was at the siege of Bhurtpore under Lord Combermere.

7th (or the Princess Royal's) Regiment of Dragoon Guards.

Years' Serv.		
Full Pay	Half Pay	
60		**Colonel.** Sir Evan Lloyd,[1] K.C.H. *Cornet,* 25 Nov. 1780; *Lieut.* 5 Feb. 87; *Capt.* 25 Oct. 93; *Major,* 1 Sept. 95; *Lieut.-Col.* 11 Feb. 99; *Col.* 25 Oct. 1809; *Major-Gen.* 1 Jan. 12; *Lieut.-Gen.* 27 May, 25; *Col.* 7th Dragoon Guards, 18 March, 36.
38	0	**Lieut.-Colonel.** ᵽ ᴋʜ Alex. Kennedy Clark Kennedy,[2] CB. KH. *Cornet,* ᵖ8 Sept. 02; *Lieut.* ᵖ15 Dec. 04; *Capt.* ᵖ 13 Dec. 10; *Major,* ᵖ 26 May, 25; *Lieut.-Col.* ᵖ 11 June, 30.
16	0	**Major.** John Bolton, *Cornet,* ᵖ 22 July, 24; *Lieut.* ᵖ 8 April, 26; *Capt.* ᵖ 11 June, 30; *Major,* ᵖ 8 July, 36.

			CORNET.	LIEUT.	CAPTAIN.	BREVET-MAJOR.
		CAPTAINS.				
14	0	Robert Richardson......	ᵖ 8 June 26	ᵖ 9 April 29	ᵖ 16 Aug. 33	
13	0	Thomas Le Marchant....	ᵖ 14 June 27	ᵖ 11 June 30	ᵖ 17 Oct. 34	
10	1 2/12	G. A. F. Cunynghame ..	ᵖ 22 May 28	ᵖ 12 July 33	ᵖ 16 Jan. 35	
10	0	John Hope Gibsone	ᵖ 8 Oct. 30	ᵖ 16 Aug. 33	ᵖ 24 July 35	
10	0	James William Hunter ..	ᵖ 17 Dec. 30	ᵖ 17 Aug. 33	ᵖ 8 July 36	
10	0	William Sandilands	ᵖ 18 Jan. 31	ᵖ 27 Sept. 33	ᵖ 2 Sept. 36	
		LIEUTENANTS.				
9	0	C. H. Thompson, R.M...	ᵖ 16 Aug. 31	ᵖ 24 July 35		
7	0	Edward Codrington	ᵖ 17 Aug. 33	ᵖ 8 July 36		
7	0	William Henry Peters ..	ᵖ 27 Sept. 33	ᵖ 2 Sept. 36		
7	0	John Clark Kennedy....	ᵖ 25 Oct. 33	ᵖ 10 Mar. 37		
8	0	John Greene	ᵖ 24 Feb. 32	ᵖ 19 June 35		
6	0	John R. Heaton	19 Dec. 34	22 Aug. 37		
6	0	Geo. R. Stevenson......	4 July 34	ᵖ 5 July 39		
		CORNETS.				
6	0	John Campbell	ᵖ 16 Jan. 35			
5	0	Henry Schonswar	ᵖ 24 July 35			
6	0	Hon. Const. Aug. Dillon .	ᵖ 9 Jan. 35			
4	0	John Crofts............	ᵖ 8 July 36			
5	0	William Hogg..........	ᵖ 30 Oct. 35			
1	0	O'Neal Segrave	ᵖ 5 July 39			

18	0	*Paymaster.*—Nenon Armstrong, 28 Sept. 38; *Ens.* 8 Aug. 22; *Lieut.* 19 April, 26.
6	0	*Adjutant.*—John R. Heaton, (*Lieut.*) 11 Jan. 39.
15	0	*Quarter-Master.*—ᵽ Henry Higgins,[4] 14 April, 25.
32	0	*Surgeon.*—Martin Cathcart,[3] 27 April, 15; *Assist.-Surgeon,* 23 March, 09; *Hosp.-Assist.* 5 Jan. 08.
		Assist.-Surg.—Henry Marshall, 28 Sept. 26; *Hosp.-Assist.* 3 Aug. 26.
26	2 5/12	*Veterinary Surgeon.*—John Schroeder, 25 June, 12.
		Scarlet—*Facings* black.—*Agent,* Messrs. Cox & Co.
		[*Returned from Holland,* 1763.]

1 Sir Evan Llyod served on regimental full-pay from 1780 to 1812, the whole period in the 17th Light Dragoons, and was present with that corps in nearly all the actions and sieges in which it was engaged in India; he also served in South America in 1806 and 7, and was at the taking of Monte Video, and in the expedition to Buenos Ayres.

2 Colonel Clark Kennedy served in the Peninsula from Sept. 1809 to Sept. 1813, including the battles of Fuentes d'Onor and Vittoria, besides various affairs of out-posts; received two wounds at Waterloo. While leading his squadron in a successful charge against the Count D'Erlon's corps at Waterloo, perceiving an Eagle to the left, he changed the direction of his squadron, and ran the officer through the body who carried it, and which belonged to the 105th French Regiment of Infantry, and is now deposited in Whitehall.

3 Dr. Cathcart served at the capture of Martinique in 1809, and Guadaloupe in 1810. Also throughout the Burmese war, and was present in almost every action and storming party during the war.

4 Quarter-Master Higgins served at Walcheren in 1809, and in the Peninsula from July 1811 to the end of the war, including the battles of Salamanca, Vittoria, and Toulouse, and other minor actions in which the 3rd Light Dragoons was engaged.

1st (or Royal) Regiment of Dragoons.

On the Standard an Eagle.—"PENINSULA"—"WATERLOO."

Years' Serv.			
Full Pay.	Half Pay.		
47		₽ ꝂꝀ Rt. Hon. Sir Rich. Hussey Vivian,¹ Bt. G.C.B. and G.C.H. *Ens.* 31 July, 1793; *Lieut.* 20 Oct. 93; *Captain,* 7 May, 94; *Major,* 9 March, 1803; *Lieut.-Col.* 28 Sept. 04; *Col.* 20 Feb. 12; *Major-Gen.* 4 June, 14; *Lieut.-Gen.* 22 July, 30; *Col.* 1st Dragoons, 20 Jan. 37.	

Colonel.

Lieut.-Colonel.

| 27 | ¾ | ₽ ꝂꝀ Thomas Marten,² K.H. *Cornet & Sub-Lieut.* 22 Nov. 13; *Lieut.* ᴾ 23 June, 17; *Capt.* ᴾ 4 May, 22; *Major,* ᴾ 12 Dec. 26; *Lieut.-Col.* 29 May, 35. | |

Major.

| 26 | 1 4/12 | Benjamin Everard,³ *Ens.* 25 Feb. 13; *Lieut.* 10 Sept. 18; *Capt.* ᴾ 16 June, 25; *Major,* ᴾ 21 Sept. 30. | |

			CORNET.	LIEUT.	CAPTAIN.	BREVET-MAJOR.
		CAPTAINS.				
15	2 1/12	Wm. Mostyn Owen	ᴾ 25 Sept. 23	ᴾ 1 Dec. 25	ᴾ 14 Nov. 26	
15	1/12	Charles P. Ainslie	10 April 25	ᴾ 28 Jan. 26	ᴾ 16 Mar. 30	
14	0	William R. Sands	ᴾ 17 Aug. 26	ᴾ 21 Sept. 30	ᴾ 5 Dec. 34	
11	0	Edward Littledale	ᴾ 24 Dec. 29	ᴾ 21 Dec. 32	ᴾ 1 May 35	
10	0	John Dalton	ᴾ 21 Sept. 30	ᴾ 30 May 34	ᴾ 4 Sept. 35	
9	0	Thos. John Burke	ᴾ 27 Jan. 32	ᴾ 31 Oct. 34	ᴾ 20 July 38	
		LIEUTENANTS.				
8	0	John Yorke.............	ᴾ 21 Dec. 32	ᴾ 5 Dec. 34		
6	0	William Charles Yates ..	ᴾ 30 May 34	ᴾ 1 May 35		
8	0	John Chamberlain, R.M.	1 June 32	ᴾ 10 July 35		
10	0	Charles Field⁴.........	18 July 34	10 July 35		
6	0	Robt. Manners Croft....	ᴾ 7 Nov. 34	ᴾ 4 Sept. 35		
3	0	William Peel	ᴾ 3 Nov. 37	ᴾ 12 Jan. 39		
5	0	Lawrence Palk	ᴾ 1 May 35	ᴾ 6 Sept. 39		
		CORNETS.				
5	0	Robert Wardlaw........	ᴾ 5 June 35			
5	0	Evan H. Lloyd	ᴾ 4 Sept. 35			
4	0	Chas. C. Waldo Sibthorp	ᴾ 28 Oct. 36			
1	0	Walter B. Barttelot	ᴾ 1 Mar. 39			
1	0	Jonas Morris	ᴾ 23 April 39			
1	0	Aubrey Rickets	ᴾ 6 Sept. 39			

2 Col. Marten served the campaign of 1814, in the Peninsula, with the household brigade. Present at Waterloo.

4 Quarter-master, 9th November, 1830, from which date the period of service has been computed.

5 Dr. Bartley served in the Peninsula, and was present at the battle of Salamanca.

11	0	*Paymaster.*—Wm. Thos. Wodehouse, 5 April, 39; *Ens.* 8 Oct. 29; *Lieut.* 31 Dec. 33.
10	0	*Adjutant.*—Charles Field, (*Lieut.*) 18 July, 34.
6	0	*Quarter-Master.*—ꝂꝀ John Partridge, 18 July, 34.
29	3/12	*Surgeon.*—₽ John Metge Bartley,⁵ M.D. 31 Aug. 26; *Assist.-Surg.* 27 Dec. 10.
		Assist.-Surgeon.—William Renny, M.D. 29 June, 32.
3	0	*Veterinary Surgeon.*—Matthew Poett, 21 April, 19.

Scarlet—*Facings* Blue.—*Agent,* Messrs. Cox & Co.

[*Returned from France, January,* 1816.]

1 Sir Hussey Vivian served in Flanders and Holland, under the Duke of York, from June, 1794, until the return of the British army in 1795. Present in the sortie from Nimeguen, and was left with a picquet of the 28th regt., in conjunction with other picquets, to hold it after the retreat of the army. Present in the affair at Geldermalsen, in which his regt. (the 28th) suffered severely, and in other skirmishes. Also present in all the different battles which took place during the expedition to the Helder, excepting on the landing. Commanded the 7th Hussars in the campaigns under Sir John Moore, in 1808 and 9. Commanded a brigade of cavalry in the Peninsula, from Sept. 1813, until the return of the army, including the battles of Orthes, Nive, and Toulouse. Severely wounded in carrying the bridge of Croix d'Orade, near Toulouse. Served at the battle of Waterloo. Sir Hussey has received a medal and one clasp for Sahagun and Benevente, and Orthes.

3 Major Everard served in the Mahratta war in 1817.

2nd (or Royal North British) Regt. of Dragoons.

On the Standard an Eagle.—" WATERLOO."

Colonel.
Sir Wm. Kier Grant,[1] K.C.B. G.C.H. *Ens.* 30 May, 1792; *Lieut.* 18 Feb. 93; *Capt.* 6 July, 94; *Major*, 6 Jan. 96; *Lieut.-Col.* 3 Dec. 1800; *Col.* 25 July, 10; *Major-Gen.* 4 June, 13; *Lieut.-Gen.* 27 May, 25; *Col. 2d Dr.* 24 Aug. 39

Lieut.-Colonel.
Charles Wyndham,[2] *Cornet*, p 13 May, 13; *Lieut.* 4 May, 15; *Capt.* p 24 June, 19; *Major*, p 12 Dec. 26; *Lieut.-Col.* p 30 Dec. 37.

Major.
John Fred. Sales Clarke, *Cornet*, p 19 Feb. 18; *Lieut.* p 11 Oct. 21; *Capt.* p 14 July, 25; *Major*, p 30 Dec. 37.

Years' Serv.			CORNET.	LIEUT.	CAPTAIN.	BREVET-MAJOR.
Full Pay	Half Pay					
48						
27	3/12					
20	2 11/12					
		CAPTAINS.				
20	2 1/12	George Hobart	p 9 July 18	p 21 July 25	p 30 July 29	
14	0	Francis Charles Forde ..	p 10 June 26	p 8 June 30	p 10 July 35	
14	0	St. Vincent W. Ricketts	p 13 July 26	p 5 April 31	p 6 Nov. 35	
10	0	Lachlan Macquarie	p 18 Jan. 31	p 6 Nov. 35	p 23 Feb. 38	
15	0	Michael Goold Adams ..	p 21 July 25	p 30 July 29	p 28 Dec. 38	
11	3/12	Henry Darby Griffith ..	p 25 Nov. 28	p 25 Nov. 31	p 1 Aug. 34	
		LIEUTENANTS.				
12	0	Robert Stein Forlong....	p 21 Nov. 28	22 May 35		
6	0	Thos. Wm. Trafford	p 21 Feb. 34	p 10 Nov. 37		
6	0	G. A. F. J. Lord Glenlyon	p 21 Nov. 34	p 30 Dec. 37		
5	0	Donald John M. Macleod	p 10 July 35	p 23 Feb. 38		
5	0	John Campbell	p 6 Nov. 35	p 28 Dec. 38		
6	0	Lord W. F. A. M. Hill..	p 8 April 34	p 21 Oct. 36		
		CORNETS.				
5	0	Charles Craven	p 22 Jan. 36			
4	0	G. Aug. Filmer Sulivan..	p 29 July 36			
3	0	Mark W. Vane Milbank..	p 30 Dec. 37			
2	0	Edward Barnett........	p 23 Feb. 38			
2	0	George Reid	10 Aug. 38			
2	0	Hugh Mont. Campbell ..	p 1 Feb. 39			
1	0	Frederick Philips, R.M.	p 11 May 39			

25	0	*Paymaster.*—William Crawford, 24 March, 29; *Cornet*, 17 Aug. 15; *Lieut.* 25 June, 19.
2	0	*Adjutant.*—George Reid, (*Cornet*,) 10 Aug. 38.
5	0	*Quarter-Master.*—Michael Nelson, 25 Dec. 35; *Ens.* 4 Dec. 35.
31	0	*Surgeon.*—John Winterscale,[3] 12 June, 28; *Assist.-Surg.* 8 Feb. 10; *Hosp.-Assist.* 17 Sept. 09.
		Assistant-Surgeon.—James Munro, M.D. 2 Nov. 32.
1	0	*Veterinary Surgeon.*—Thomas Jex, 4 Oct. 39.

Scarlet—*Facings* Blue.—*Agent*, Messrs. Hopkinson, Barton, & Knyvett.—*Irish Agent*, Messrs. Borough, Armit & Co.

[*Returned from France, January*, 1816.]

---

1 Sir Wm. Kier Grant served in Flanders, and was present at Famars, siege of Valenciennes, &c. in 1793. In 1794 he was present in the actions of the 17th, 24th, and 26th of April, the 10th, 17th, 18th, and 22nd of May. Joined the Russian and Austrian army in Italy early in 1799, and served the campaigns of that and the two following years, including the battles of Novi, Rivoli, Mondovi, Saviliano, Marengo, &c.; the sieges of Alexandria, Sarranal, Tortona, Cunio, Savona, Genoa, &c. Sir Wm. served as Adjutant-General in the East Indies from 1806 to 1813; commanded a body of troops in the Persian Gulf.

2 Col. Wyndham received two severe wounds at Waterloo, on the 18th June.

3 Dr. Winterscale served at Walcheren, in 1809, and in the Peninsula, from Sept. 1810, to Dec. 1812, including the battle of Fuentes d'Onor. Present at Waterloo.

[Emb. for Foreign Service, 1837.] **3rd (or *King's Own*) Regt. Lt. Dragoons.** [Serving in the East Indies.]

The White Horse, within the Garter on the 2nd and 3rd Standards, with the Motto, "*Nec aspera terrent.*"—"SALAMANCA"–"VITTORIA"—"TOULOUSE"—"PENINSULA."

Colonel.

Years' Serv.		
43		**¶ Lord** Chas. Somerset Manners, K.C.B.[1] *Cornet,* 7 Feb. 98; *Lieut.* 1 June, 99; *Capt.* 21 Aug. 1800; *Major,* 13 Oct. 08; *Lieut.-Col.* 1 Aug. 11; *Col.* 6 Nov. 17; *Major-Gen.* 27 May, 25; *Lieut.-Gen.* 28 June, 38; *Col.* 3rd Dragoons, 8 Nov. 39.
Full Pay.	Half Pay.	
33	7	*Lieut.-Colonels.*—**¶** Sir Joseph Thackwell,[2] K.C.B. & K.H. *Cornet,* P 23 Apr. 00; *Lieut.* 13 June, 01; *Capt.* P 9 April, 07; *Major,* 18 June, 15; *Brevet-Lieut.-Col.* 21 June, 17; *Regtl.-Lieut.-Col.* 15 June, 20; *Col.* 10 Jan. 37.
36	1/12	Michael White,[3] *Cornet,* P 15 Aug. 04; *Lieut.* P 14 May, 05; *Capt.* P 7 Nov. 15; *Brevet-Major,* 10 Jan. 37; *Regtl.-Major,* 4 Jan. 39; *Lieut.-Col.* P 13 Dec. 39.
15	0	*Majors.*—Geo. Henry Lockwood, *Cornet,* P 10 Mar. 25; *Lieut.* P 10 Aug. 26; *Capt.* P 7 Sept. 32; *Major,* 6 March, 39.
13	1 3/12	Geo. Alex. Malcolm, *Cornet,* P 31 Dec. 25; *Lieut.* P 7 June 27; *Capt.* P 30 Dec. 31; *Major,* P 13 Dec. 39.

		CAPTAINS.	CORNET.	LIEUT.	CAPTAIN.	BREV.-MAJ.
15	0	Chas. W. Morley Balders	P 10 Nov. 25	P 25 Nov. 28	P 15 July 36	
31	3/12	Henry Bond[4]	P 25 May 09	1 Mar. 11	P 6 May 24	28 June 38
27	7/12	John Tritton[5]	14 Jan. 13	14 Aug. 15	7 Oct. 36	
27	1 4/12	William White[6]	28 May 12	1 Aug. 14	30 June 37	
14	0	John Wm. Yerbury	P 12 Dec. 26	P 5 July 33	1 July 37	
9	0	John Rich. Blagden Hale	P 7 June 31	P 16 May 34	P 10 July 37	
20	8/12	John Bloomfield Gough	24 Feb. 20	P 1 Oct. 25	P 1 Aug. 26	2 Sir J. Thackwell served the campaign in Galicia & Leon under Sir John Moore, and was engaged in several skirmishes, and present at the battle of Corunna; served in the Peninsula, including the battles of Vittoria, the Pyrenees in front of Pampeluna, 27th, 28th, 29th, and 30th July; blockade of Pampeluna, from 18th to the 31st Oct., when it surrendered; battle of Orthes, affair at Tarbes, and battle of Toulouse; besides many affairs of advanced guards, out-posts, &c.; contused on the right shoulder at Vittoria, and severely wounded at Waterloo (left arm amputated close to the shoulder) in charging a square of infantry; had also two horses shot under him.
13	0	Meyrick Jones	P 1 Mar. 27	P 31 Dec. 30	6 Mar. 39	
7	0	R. Algernon Smith	P 5 July 33	P 22 Nov. 36	P 13 Dec. 39	
		LIEUTENANTS.				
15	0	John Edward Dyer, R.M.	26 May 25	21 Dec. 26		
7	0	Walter Unett	P 23 Aug. 33	P 31 Mar. 37		
11	4 5/12	John Edward Codd	P 21 July 25	P 27 April 27		
13	0	Samuel Fisher[7]	15 June 27	P 16 Aug. 31		
13	0	Wm. Howe Hadfield	25 Oct. 27	P 20 Sept. 31		
12	0	George Newton	1 May 28	P 17 Aug. 32		
9	0	John Rose Holden Rose	P 19 July 31	P 11 Jan. 33		
10	0	George Forbes	10 Dec. 30	15 Feb. 34		3 Col. White served at the capture of Hattrass in 1817, and during the Mahratta campaigns of 1817 and 18; also at siege and capt. of Bhurtpore.
11	0	W. E. Fitz Edward Barnes	19 Nov. 29	P 24 July 35		
7	0	James Martin	P 6 Sept. 33	P 11 Mar. 36		
6	0	Edward Geo. Swinton	P 6 June 34	7 Oct. 36		
6	0	James Cowell	P 18 July 34	P 17 Mar. 37		4 Maj. Bond served at the taking of Anjar in Cutch in 1816; the Mahratta campaigns of 1817 and 18; and at the siege of Bhurtpore in 1825.
6	0	Rich. Tho. Montgomery	P 16 Jan. 35	1 July 37		
4	0	Rich. A. Moore	P 12 Feb. 36	P 10 July 37		
6	0	Hon. Charles Powys	P 28 Feb. 34	P 1 July 36		
4	0	John Wyld	P 15 July 36	6 Mar. 39		5 Capt. Tritton served at the siege and capture of Hattrass; the Mahratta campaigns of 1817 and 18; and the siege and capture of Bhurtpore.
5	0	James White	P 22 May 35	17 Apr. 39		
3	0	Hugh H. Bradshaw	P 26 May 37	P 13 Dec. 39		
3	0	John Sullivan	9 July 37	31 Dec. 39		
		CORNETS.				6 Capt. White served at the siege and capture of Hattrass; the Mahratta campaign of 1817; and the siege and capture of Bhurtpore.
3	0	Henry Wood	P 10 July 37			
3	0	Edmund Roche	P 11 July 37			
3	0	George Cookes	P 14 July 37			7 Lieut. Fisher served at Bhurtpore as a volunteer.
6	0	George Gladstone	19 Dec. 34			8 Capt. Cormick served the campaign in Portugal in 1808 and 9, and on the eastern coast of Spain, from Sept. 1812 to Sept. 1813, including the battle of Castalla.
1	0	Charles Bowles	P 16 Aug. 39			
1	0	Hon. Alfred A. Harbord	P 20 Sept. 39			
1	0	Alfred Fisher	P 29 Nov. 39			9 Dr. Henderson served at the capture of Guadaloupe in 1810; two years in the American war; and during the whole of the Burmese war.
25	9 1/12	*Paymaster.*—**¶** Edward Cormick,[8] 24 Jan. 28; *Cornet,* 4 Dec. 06; *Lieut.* 25 Sept. 07; *Capt.* 23 Sept. 13.				
3	0	*Adjutant.*—John Sullivan, (*Lieut.*) 9 July, 37.				
6	0	*Quarter-Master.*—Thomas Adams, 20 June, 34.				
31	0	*Surgeon.*—Jas. Henderson,[9] M.D. 20 April, 26; *Assist.-Surgeon,* 22 March, 10; *Hosp.-Assist.* 5 Aug. 09.				
		Assistant-Surgeons.—Geo. Knox, 23 June, 25; *Hospital-Assist.* 25 Dec. 15. Arthur Wood, M.D. 19 Nov. 36; *Hospital-Assist.* 22 Dec. 25.				
11	0	*Veterinary Surgeon.*—George Edlin, 17 Dec. 29.				

Scarlet—Facings Blue.—*Agents,* Messrs. Cox & Co.

1 Lord Chas. Manners served the campaign of 1808 in Spain, including the cavalry engagement at Benevente. Served at Walcheren as Aide-de-Camp to Lord Chatham, and was engaged at the siege of Flushing. His Lordship served subsequently in the Peninsula, and has received a medal and two clasps for Salamanca, Vittoria, and Toulouse.

Emb. for Foreign Service, 1821.] **4th (or Queen's Own) Regt. Light Dragoons.** [Serving in the East Indies.

"TALAVERA" "ALBUHERA" "SALAMANCA" "VITTORIA" "TOULOUSE" "PENINSULA."

Years' Serv.		
48		
Full Pay.	Half Pay.	
32	0	
21	4	
30	0	
28	11/12	

Colonel.
🎖 ⚔ Lord Robt. Edw. Henry Somerset,¹ G.C.B. *Cornet*, 4 Feb. 1793; *Lieut.* 4 Dec. 93; *Capt.* 28 Aug. 94; *Major*, 21 Nov. 99; *Lieut.-Col.* 25 Dec. 1800; *Colonel*, 25 July, 10; *Major-Gen.* 4 June, 13; *Lieut.-Gen.* 27 May, 25; *Col.* 4th Dragoons, 31 Mar. 36.

Lieut.-Colonels.—🎖 William Fendall,² *Cornet*, 29 Sept. 08; *Lieut.* 3 Oct. 09; *Capt.* P 3 Feb. 20; *Major*, 2 June, 25; *Lieut.-Col.* P 24 Dec. 32.
John Scott, C.B. *Cornet*, P 4 May, 15; *Lieut.* P 26 Oct. 15; *Capt.* P 28 June, 21; *Major*, P 9 Nov. 26; *Lieut.-Col.* 31 Aug. 30.

Majors.—🎖 ⚔ William Havelock,³ K. H. *Ens.* 12 July, 10; *Lieut.* 12 May, 12; *Capt.* P 19 Feb. 18; *Major*, P 31 Dec. 30.
🎖 Fra. Dermot Daly,⁴ *Ens.* 5 Dec. 11; *Lieut.* 26 Nov. 13; *Capt.* 26 June, 24; *Major*, P 27 Oct. 35; *Brev.-Lieut.-Col.* 23 July 39.

			CORNET.	LIEUT.	CAPTAIN.	BREV.-MAJ.
		CAPTAINS.				
21	7/12	Harcourt Master	P 30 July 18	P 6 Mar. 23	P 17 Sept. 25	28 June 38
24	1/12	William Parlby	P 3 Oct. 16	P 6 May 24	P 28 Sept. 26	
14	2¾/11	Alex. Houstoun	P 4 Dec. 23	P 19 Nov. 25	P 12 Dec. 26	
21	0	Sir Keith A. Jackson, *Bt.*	P 2 Dec. 19	P 19 Dec. 22	P 31 Dec. 30	
15	0	Bertram Newton Ogle ..	P 10 Aug. 25	P 14 Dec. 26	P 24 Dec. 32	
24	0	Chas. Lush. Cumberlege	P 12 Dec. 16	P 29 July 19	3 Oct. 34	
16	0	John Harrison	25 June 24	13 Aug. 25	P 27 Oct. 35	
14	0	Edward Scott..........	P 28 Dec. 26	P 8 June 30	P 31 Aug. 38	
29	0	George Gardine Shaw⁵ ..	P 30 May 11	21 Dec. 13	31 May 39	
		LIEUTENANTS.				
20	0	Arch. Edm. Bromwich ..	17 Feb. 20	12 Aug. 25		
13	2 8/12	Richard Fra. Poore	P 22 July 24	P 3 Dec. 25		
13	0	Thomas Lloyd..........	P 15 Mar. 27	P 12 Oct. 30		
12	0	George Chas. Dalbiac....	31 July 28	10 May 31		
7	0	J. H. T. Warde, R.M....	P 21 June 33	P 22 May 35		
7	0	Rob. Dennistown Campbell	P 22 Oct. 33	P 27 Mar. 35		
6	0	Philip Kemp	P 22 Aug. 34	P 2 Sept. 36		
8	0	Francis Fred. Janvrin ..	P 23 Mar. 32	3 June 35		
6	0	Thomas Wm. Geils	P 28 Nov. 34	P 28 April 37		
6	0	J. T. Douglas Halkett ..	P 23 Jan. 35	6 July 37		
5	0	Arthur Scudamore......	P 29 May 35	18 Feb. 37		
9	18 6/12	Edward Inge	11 Mar. 13	10 Mar. 14		
5	0	Alexander Low	P 2 Oct. 35	P 6 July 38		
5	0	William Drysdale	P 29 Dec. 35	P 31 Aug. 38		
5	0	W. W. W. Humbley	27 Mar. 35	15 Dec. 38		
4	0	Jos. Rogers J. Coles	P 2 Sept. 36	P 22 Mar. 39		
3	0	John F. Fitz Gerald	P 24 Mar. 37	31 May 39		
3	0	John August. Todd.....	P 28 April 37	P 14 June 39		
2	0	R. Buckley Prettejohn ..	P 23 Feb. 38	P 18 Oct. 39		
		CORNETS.				
2	0	Wm. Aug. Hyder	P 6 July 38			
2	0	Hen. Fred. Hodson	P 14 Sept. 38			
2	0	Martin Kirwan	P 23 Nov. 38			
1	0	Geo. Edw. Campion	P 22 Mar. 39			
1	0	Algernon G. Brenchley ..	P 29 Mar. 39			
1	0	Tho. John Francis	P 14 June 39			
1	0	Frederick Pipon	P 15 June 39			
1	0	William Kingston Fraser	P 18 Oct. 39			
33	4/21	*Paymaster.*—Henry Heyman, 30 Aug. 33; *Cornet*, 20 Aug. 07; *Lieut.* 1 July, 09; *Capt.* 24 June, 23.				
13	0	*Adjutant.*—Thomas Lloyd, (*Lieut.*) 6 Sept. 36.				
19	11¾/12	*Quarter-Master.*—Geo. H. Croad,⁶ 8 Jan. 29; *Ens.* 30 Nov. 09; *Lieut.* 14 Nov. 11.				
32	0	*Surgeon.*—🎖 ⚔ David Perston,⁷ M.D. 17 Feb. 25; *Assist.-Surg.* 1 Feb. 10; *Hosp.-Assist.* 19 Oct. 08.				
		Assist.-Surgs.—John Stewart Graves, 28 Sept. 26; *Hosp.-Assist.* 22 Feb. 26. Nelson Dartnell, 4 Dec. 32.				
2	0	*Veterinary Surgeon.*—John Byrne, 14 Dec. 38.				

Side notes (captains/lieutenants column):
2 Col. Fendall served in the Peninsula from 1809 to the end of the war, including the battles of Albuhera, Usagre, Vittoria, and Toulouse.
3 Major Havelock served in the Peninsula from July 1810 to the end of the war, including the battles of Busaco, Sabugal, Salamanca, and Vittoria; crossing the Bidassoa; battle of Nivelle; affairs near Bayonne; battles of Orthes and Toulouse; wounded at Quatre Bras.
4 Col. Daly served the campaigns of 1813 and 14 in the Peninsula, and was wounded at Bayonne; served also in the American war, and was engaged at the siege and battle of Plattsburgh.
5 Capt. Shaw served at the siege of Hattrass, and in the Mahratta campaigns of 1817 and 18.
6 Lieut. (Quarter-Master) Croad served in the American war.
7 Dr. Perston served in the Peninsula from Jan. 1809 to April 1812, including the battle of Salamanca, and siege of Burgos; present at Quatre Bras and Waterloo.

Scarlet— *Facings* Green.— *Agent*, Messrs. Hopkinson, Barton & Knyvett.

¹ Lord Edward Somerset served on the expedition to the Helder in 1799, as aide-de-camp to H. R. H. the Duke of York, and was present at the battles of the 19th Sept., 2nd and 6th Oct. Served in the campaigns in the Peninsula in command of the 4th Dragoons, (including the battle of Talavera, the cavalry action at Usagre, and the battles of Salamanca and Vittoria,) until he obtained the rank of Major-General in 1813: from that period till the end of the war, he commanded the Hussar Brigade, with which he was present at Orthes and Toulouse. Served at the battle of Waterloo in command of the Household Brigade of Cavalry, and subsequently upon the Staff of the Army of Occupation in France until its return to England. His lordship has received a cross and one clasp for Talavera, Salamanca, Vittoria, Orthes, and Toulouse.

6th (or Inniskilling) Regiment of Dragoons.

"WATERLOO."

Years' Serv.		
Full Pay	Half Pay	
53		*Colonel.* ₽ Hon. Sir William Lumley,¹ G.C.B. *Cornet*, 24 Oct. 1787; *Lieut.* 19 May 90; *Capt.* 4 Dec. 93; *Major*, 10 Mar. 95; *Lieut.-Col.* 25 May, 95; *Col.* 29 April, 1802; *Major-Gen.* 25 Oct. 09; *Lieut.-Gen.* 4 June, 14; *Gen.* 10 Jan. 37; *Col.* 6th Dragoons, 3 Nov. 37.
29	0	*Lieut.-Colonel.* ₽ Jeremiah Ratcliffe,² K.H. *Cornet*, P 11 April, 11; *Lieut.* 11 March, 12; *Capt.* 22 Feb. 27; *Major*, P 27 July, 32; *Lieut.-Col.* P 9 June, 38.
16	0	*Major.* Raymond White, *Cornet*, P 14 Oct. 24; *Lieut.* P 22 July, 25; *Capt.* P 24 April, 28; *Major*, P 9 June, 38.

			CORNET.	LIEUT.	CAPTAIN.	BREVET-MAJOR.
		CAPTAINS.				
15	5 2/12	Willoughby Moore	P 7 Sept. 20	P 17 July 23	P 4 Mar. 26	
15	0	Frederick Wollaston	P 22 July 25	P 10 June 26	P 23 Aug. 31	
14	0	Henry Crichton	P 8 April 26	P 19 July 27	P 1 Nov. 33	
13	0	Robt. Douglas Barbor	P 15 Mar. 27	P 9 April 29	P 28 April 37	
12	0	William Arkwright	P 24 July 28	P 25 June 30	P 11 May 38	
11	0	Thos. Westropp M'Mahon	24 Dec. 29	P 2 Dec. 31	P 9 June 38	
		LIEUTENANTS.				
26	0	William Armstrong, R.M.	23 June 14	P 29 May 17		
9	0	Fra. Ed. Winning. Ingram	P 23 Aug. 31	P 27 July 32		
9	0	Frederick Thompson	P 2 Dec. 31	P 1 Nov. 33		
10	0	Herbert Mansel	P 11 June 30	1 Jan. 34		
8	0	Mervyn Archdall	P 9 Mar. 32	9 Jan. 35		
8	0	John Kingston James	P 14 Dec. 32	P 17 April 35		
9	0	H. J. Denny	7 June 31	22 May 35		
8	0	Tonman Mosley	P 28 Dec. 32	P 23 Jan. 35		
3	0	Edward S. May	P 4 May 37	P 11 May 38		
3	0	James King	P 5 May 37	P 9 June 38		
2	0	Hen. Dalrymple White	P 11 May 38	P 8 Feb. 39		
		CORNETS.				
2	0	James Davidson	P 9 June 38			
3	0	James C. Strode	P 24 Mar. 37			

15	2/12	*Paymaster.*—Hen. Fowler Mackay, 1 Nov. 31; *Cornet*, 9 June, 25; *Lieut.* 12 Jan. 26; *Capt.* 12 Feb. 30.
9	0	*Adjutant.*—H. J. Denny, (*Lieut.*) 18 July, 34.
11	0	*Quarter-Master.*—₽ Frederick M'Dowell,³ 10 Dec. 29.
33	0	*Surgeon.*—William Daunt,⁴ M.D. 12 May, 14; *Assist.-Surg.* 3 Mar. 08; *Hosp.-Assist.* 12 Sept. 07.
		Assist.-Surg.—Charles R. Boyes, M.D. 22 Nov. 26; *Hosp.-Assist.* 17 Aug. 26.
10	0	*Veterinary Surgeon.*—Herbert Hallen, 3 Aug. 30.

Scarlet—*Facings* Yellow.—*Agent*, Messrs. Cox & Co.—*Irish Agent*, Messrs Borough, Armit & Co.

[*Returned from France, November*, 1818.]

1 Sir William Lumley was severely wounded through the ankle joint at Antrim, 7th June, 1798, and preserved the town from being burnt by the rebels. Sir William commanded the 22d Dragoons in Egypt; accompanied the expedition from the Cape to South America, and has received a medal for Albuhera.
2 Col. Ratcliffe served in the Peninsula from June 1811 to the end of the war, including the battles of Salamanca, Vittoria, Pyrenees, and Toulouse.
3 Quarter Master M'Dowell received a severe sabre wound in the head on the 18th June at Waterloo.
4 Dr. Daunt served at the capture of Madeira in 1807, and of Martinique in 1809. Served also in the Burmese war.

Emb. for For. Service, 1838.] **7th (or Queen's own) Regt. Lt. Dragoons (Hussars.)** [Serving in Canada.

"PENINSULA"—"WATERLOO."

Years' Serv.			CORNET.	LIEUT.	CAPTAIN.	BREVET-MAJOR.
47		*Colonel.* ₽ ᚛ Henry William, *Marquis of* Anglesey,[1] K.G. G.C.B. G.C.H. *Lieut.-Col.* 12 Sept. 1793; *Col.* 3 May, 96; *Major-Gen.* 29 April, 1802; *Lieut.-Gen.* 25 April, 08; *Gen.* 12 Aug. 19; *Col.* 7th Hussars, 16 May, 01.				
Full Pay.	Half Pay.					
17	0	*Lieut.-Colonel.* John James Whyte, *Cornet,* ᴾ 21 Aug. 23; *Lieut.* ᴾ 22 Dec. 25; *Capt.* ᴾ 31 Dec. 27; *Major,* ᴾ 5 April, 33; *Lieut.-Col.* ᴾ 21 Oct. 37.				
16	0	*Major.* Arthur William Biggs, *Cornet,* ᴾ 29 July, 24; *Lieut.* ᴾ 11 Feb. 26; *Capt.* ᴾ 14 May, 29; *Major,* ᴾ 21 Oct. 37.				
		CAPTAINS.				
14	8/12	Thos. Edm. Campbell ..	ᴾ 30 June 25	ᴾ 13 May 26	ᴾ 17 Feb. 32	
12	2/12	*Hon.* Henry Cole	ᴾ 17 Jan. 28	ᴾ 12 Feb. 30	ᴾ 6 Mar. 35	
10	0	Arthur Shirley	ᴾ 31 Aug. 30	ᴾ 1 Feb. 33	ᴾ 15 July 36	
10	4 8/12	Gervase P. Bushe	ᴾ 8 Apr. 26	ᴾ 26 Sept. 26	ᴾ 21 Sept. 32	
8	0	Charles Hagart	ᴾ 15 June 32	ᴾ 12 Aug. 34	ᴾ 21 Oct. 37	
8	0	Henry John Sutton	ᴾ 1 Feb. 33	ᴾ 9 Jan. 35	ᴾ 16 Mar. 38	
		LIEUTENANTS.				
11	0	₽ ᚛ Thomas Paterson [2]	ᴾ 10 Dec. 29	15 Mar. 33		
7	0	William Grasett........	ᴾ 5 Apr. 33	ᴾ 25 Dec. 35		
7	0	Albany B. Savile	ᴾ 31 May 33	ᴾ 22 Jan. 36		
6	0	Robert James	ᴾ 21 Mar. 34	ᴾ 15 July 36		
6	0	Fred. Thos. Farquharson	ᴾ 12 Aug. 34	ᴾ 14 Apr. 37		
6	0	Charles Hen. Wyndham	ᴾ 9 Jan. 35	ᴾ 26 May 37		
5	0	Thos. Hen. Preston	ᴾ 25 Dec. 35	ᴾ 21 Oct. 37		
5	0	Hugh Joceline Percy....	ᴾ 22 Jan. 36	ᴾ 16 Mar. 38		
		CORNETS.				
5	0	R. Bishop, R.M.........	16 Oct. 35			
4	0	Albert Helyar..........	ᴾ 15 July 36			
3	0	Geo. Fred. Wm. Miles ..	ᴾ 14 Apr. 37			
3	0	James Macaul Hagart ..	ᴾ 26 May 37			
3	0	*Hon.* W. H. Stap. Cotton	ᴾ 21 Oct. 37			
27	1	*Paymaster.*—Charles M'Carty, 2 Nov. 30; *Quarter-Master,* 14 May, 12; *Cornet,* 11 March, 13; *Lieut.* 20 Jan. 14; *Capt.* 14 Dec. 26.				
11	0	*Adjutant.*—₽ ᚛ Thomas Paterson, (*Lieut.*) 10 Dec. 29.				
1	0	*Quarter-Master.*—Henry Humphrys, 22 Feb. 39.				
		Surgeon.—James Low Warren, M.D. 17 April, 38; *Assist.-Surg.* 19 Feb. 24; *Hosp.-Assist.* 1 Feb. 16.				
		Assistant-Surgeon.—Thomas Beavan, 28 Sept. 26; *Hosp.-Assist.* 10 Nov. 25.				
3	0	*Veterinary Surgeon.*—George Johnston, 26 May, 37.				

Blue.—*Agent,* Messrs. Cox & Co.

---

1 Lord Anglesey has received a medal for Sahagun and Benevente, &c. Lost a leg at Waterloo.
2 Lieut. Paterson served in the Peninsula, from Oct. 1813 to the end of the war, including the battles of the Nive, 9th and 13th Dec. (wounded), Salvatore, Orthes, Aire and Toulouse. Served also at Waterloo.

8th (or King's Royal Irish) Regiment of Light Dragoons—(Hussars.)

Harp and Crown. *"Pristinæ virtutis memores."*—" LESWARREE "— "HINDOOSTAN."

Years' Serv.						
Full Pay.	Half Pay.					
46		*Colonel.* p ⊞ Sir Joseph Straton,¹ C.B. & K.C.H. *Cornet*, Dec. 1794; *Lieut.* 2 Dec. 95; *Capt.* 2 March, 97; *Major*, 14 Aug. 1801; *Lieut.-Col.* 25 Feb. 08; *Col.* 4 June, 14; *Major-Gen.* 27 May, 25; *Lieut.-Gen.* 28 June, 38; *Col.* 8th Hussars, 24 Aug. 1839.				
24	1	*Lieut.-Colonel.* Hon. George Berkeley Molyneux, *Cornet*, p 3 May, 15; *Lieut.* p 12 Sept. 16; *Capt.* p 11 April, 22; *Major*, p 28 Sept. 26; *Lieut.-Col.* p 31 Dec. 27.				
15	0	*Major.* James MacCall, *Cornet*, p 23 June 25: *Lieut.* p 17 Oct. 26; *Capt.* p 3 Aug. 30; *Major*, p 31 Jan. 40.				

		CAPTAINS.	CORNET.	LIEUT.	CAPTAIN.	BREVET-MAJOR.
13	0	Jas. Harrison Cholmeley	p 23 Aug. 27	p 17 Dec. 30	p 13 Feb. 35	
13	0	Frederick Geo. Shewell..	p 28 Aug. 27	6 Sept. 31	p 28 Apr. 37	
10	0	Rodolph de Salis	p 17 Dec. 30	p 28 June 33	p 13 July 38	
8	0	Thos. Wm. Selby Lowndes	p 15 June 32	p 12 July 33	p 2 Mar. 39	
13	0	Hon. Rich. Howe Browne	p 6 Nov. 27	p 10 Aug. 32	p 15 Nov. 39	
7	0	Magnus G. Laing Meason	p 28 June 33	p 13 Feb. 35	p 31 Jan. 40	
		LIEUTENANTS.				
7	0	Joseph Reilly, R.M.	p 26 Apr. 33	27 Mar. 34		
7	0	Edward Mostyn	p 12 July 33	p 3 Apr. 35		
9	0	George J. Huband	p 9 Aug. 31	3 Oct. 34		
6	0	George Brown	p 28 Mar. 34	31 Mar. 37		
12	0	Henry Rowles	p 9 Sept. 28	p 9 Aug. 33		
5	0	Carrington Smythe	p 3 Apr. 35	p 13 July 38		
6	0	Cha. Joseph Longmore	p 30 May 34	p 17 Aug. 38		
3	0	Fleet. Thos. Hugh Wilson	p 5 May 37	p 17 Sept. 39		
2	0	J. Craven Carden	p 13 July 38	p 15 Nov. 39		
1	0	Hon. Jas. Sandilands	p 2 Mar. 39	p 31 Jan. 40		
		CORNETS.				
1	0	Arth. Jas. *Lord* Killeen	p 17 Sept. 39			
1	0	Wm. Henry Cooper	p 15 Nov. 39			
1	0	Alex. Cruikshank Lindsay	p 31 Jan. 40			
32	3	*Paymaster.*—John Gibson Whitaker, 9 Jan. 17; *Cornet*, March. 05; *Lieut.* 31 Oct. 05.				
6	0	*Adjutant.*—George Brown, (*Lieut.*) 3 Feb. 37.				
1	0	*Quarter-Master.*—James Landers, 29 Nov. 39.				
24	1	*Surgeon.*—John Squair, M.D. 3 March, 37; *Assist.-Surg.* 30 June, 25; *Hosp.-Assist.* 16 June, 15.				
13	0	*Assistant-Surgeon.*—Tho. Coke Gaulter, M.D. 29 July. 30; *Hosp.-Assist.* 22 Mar. 27.				
29	1 10/12	*Veterinary Surgeon.*—Lawrence Bird, 29 June, 09.				

Blue.—*Agents*, Messrs. Cox & Co.; *Irish Agents*, Borough, Armit & Co.
[*Returned from the East Indies, May*, 1823.]

---

1 Sir Joseph Straton accompanied his regiment, the 13th Dragoons, to the Peninsula, in 1810, where he served three years. Sir Joseph was wounded at Waterloo, where he commanded the 6th Dragoons, until Sir Wm. Ponsonby fell, when the command of a Brigade devolved on him.

9th (or the Queen's Royal) Regiment of Light Dragoons—(Lancers).

"PENINSULA."

Years' Serv.	
Full Pay	Half Pay
45	

Colonel.

James Wallace Sleigh,[1] C.B., *Cornet,* Feb. 95; *Lieut.* 29 Apr. 95; *Capt.* 25 Oct. 98; *Major*, 14 June, 05; *Lieut.-Col.* 14 Dec. 09; *Col.* 12 Aug. 19; *Major-Gen.* 22 July, 30; *Col.* 9th Lancers, 24 Aug. 39.

Lieut.-Colonel.

20 | 1 8/12 — James Alex. *Earl of* Rosslyn, *Cornet*, p 25 Feb. 19; *Lieut.* p 9 July, 20; *Capt.* p 25 March, 23; *Major*, p 12 Dec. 26; *Lieut.-Col.* p 31 Dec. 27.

Major.

33 | 9/12 — Alexander Campbell,[2] K.H., *Cornet*, 24 Aug. 06; *Lieut.* p 4 Sept. 06; *Capt.* p 13 Aug. 12; *Major*, p 9 Aug. 21; *Brevet-Lieut.-Col.* 16 July, 30.

			CORNET.	LIEUT.	CAPTAIN.	BREVET-MAJOR.
		CAPTAINS.				
18	0	James Alex. Fullerton	p 1 Aug. 22	p 30 Dec. 24	p 19 Sept. 26	
15	0	Arthur Chas. Williams	p 16 June 25	p 29 Aug. 26	p 5 July 31	
14	0	J. Hope Grant	p 29 Aug. 26	p 26 Feb. 28	p 29 May 35	
9	0	Archibald Little	p 4 Oct. 31	p 31 Aug. 32	p 24 Feb. 37	
8	0	Thos. Palmer Whalley	p 4 May 32	p 12 April 33	p 17 Aug. 38	
7	0	Andrew Spottiswoode	p 10 May 33	p 29 April 36	p 11 Oct. 39	
		LIEUTENANTS.				
13	0	Robert Cooke[3]	p 27 April 27	5 April 31		
9	0	J. N. Macartney, R.M.	p 10 May 31	p 11 April 34		
4	0	John Anstruther Thomson	p 12 Feb. 36	p 24 Feb. 37		
4	0	John Wm. Gooch Spicer	p 29 April 36	p 5 May 37		
4	0	Frederick James Isacke	p 2 Sept. 36	p 17 Nov. 37		
4	0	Fra. Digby Willoughby	p 16 Sept. 36	p 9 Feb. 38		
3	0	Kingsmill Manley Power	p 24 Feb. 37	p 17 Aug. 38		
3	0	Phillip Haughton Clarke	p 5 May 37	p 11 Oct. 39		
3	0	John Sutherland	p 17 Nov. 37	p 31 Jan. 40		
		CORNETS.				
3	0	Gilbert T. Nicholson	p 9 Feb. 38			
2	0	J. Edward Madocks	p 17 Aug. 38			
1	0	Hon. Brownlow C. Berbie	p 11 Oct. 39			
1	0	Eustace Arkwright	p 31 Jan. 40			

31	3 10/12	*Paymaster.*—Henry Knight, 2 July, 05.
13	0	*Adjutant.*—Robert Cooke, (*Lieut.*) 27 April, 27.
2	0	*Quarter-Master.*—J. C. Williamson, 17 Aug. 38.
36	1 4/12	*Surgeon.*—Anth. Cæsar Colclough,[4] 14 April, 13; *Assist.-Surg.* 11 Nov. 02.
15	0	*Assistant-Surg.*—Wm. Irwin Breslin, 8 March, 27; *Hosp.-Assist.* 9 Feb. 26.
11	0	*Veterinary Surgeon.*—James Robertson, 24 Sept. 29.

Scarlet—Facings Blue.—*Agent*, Mr. Collyer.

[*Returned from Portugal, May,* 1813.]

---

1 General Sleigh served in Flanders in 1795; in the actions in North Holland and the Helder, 10th and 19th Sept., and 2d and 6th Oct. 1799. In the Peninsula in 1811 and 12. Commanded the 11th Dragoons at Waterloo, towards the close of which the command of the 4th Brigade devolved on him. In 1819 he accompanied his regiment to India, and commanded the Cavalry division at the siege of Bhurtpore in 1825 & 6.

2 Col. Campbell was present at the taking of the Cape of Good Hope, in 1806, and served subsequently in the East Indies.

3 Lieut. Cooke's services :—expedition to South America, and siege of Buenos Ayres. Expedition to Walcheren and siege of Flushing.

4 Dr. Colclough served in the Mahratta war from Aug. 1812 to Dec. 1813; Kandian campaign of 1815, including the capture of Kandy in the island of Ceylon. Deccan campaigns of 1818 and 19, including the storm and capture of Capaul Droog.

10th (or *Prince of Wales's own*) *Royal Regt. of Light Dragoons* (*Hussars.*)

"PENINSULA." — "WATERLOO."

Years' Serv.		
Full Pay	Half Pay	
46		*Colonel.* Ᵽ Charles W. *Marq.* of Londonderry,[1] G.C.B. G.C.H., *Ensign*, 11 Oct. 1794; *Lieut.* 30 Oct. 94; *Capt.* 12 Nov. 94; *Major*, 31 July, 95; *Lieut.-Col.* 1 Jan. 97; *Colonel*, 25 Sept. 1803; *Major-Gen.* 25 July, 10; *Lieut.-Gen.* 4 June, 14; *Gen.* 10 Jan. 37; *Col.* 10th Hussars, 3 Feb. 20.
21	10 6/12	*Lieut.-Colonel.* Ᵽ ᛭ John Vandeleur,[2] *Ensign*, 6 July, 09; *Lieut.* 30 May 11; *Capt.* ᴘ 28 Feb. 22; *Major*, ᴘ 1 Oct. 25; *Lieut.-Col.* ᴘ 18 Dec. 27.
27	0	*Major.* ᛭ J. C. Wallington,[3] *Cornet*, ᴘ 21 Oct. 13; *Lieut.* ᴘ 27 Dec. 14; *Capt.* ᴘ 16 Dec. 24; *Major*, ᴘ 5 April, 33.

		CAPTAINS.	CORNET.	LIEUT.	CAPTAIN.	BREVET-MAJOR.
17	0	George Lister Lister Kaye	ᴘ 25 Mar. 23	ᴘ 14 April 25	ᴘ 24 Aug. 26	
11	0	Henry Fred. Bonham	ᴘ 22 May 29	ᴘ 14 June 31	ᴘ 16 May 34	
11	0	John Rowley	ᴘ 3 Dec. 29	ᴘ 19 July 31	ᴘ 21 Aug. 35	
9	0	Geo. A. F. Quentin	ᴘ 14 June 31	ᴘ 1 June 32	ᴘ 12 Feb. 36	
9	0	Edw. D. C. Hilliard	ᴘ 19 July 31	ᴘ 5 April 33	ᴘ 1 Dec. 37	
9	0	Sir J. Gardiner Baird, *Bt.*	ᴘ 16 Aug. 31	ᴘ 30 Aug. 33	ᴘ 20 Sept. 39	
		LIEUTENANTS.				
12	0	Matt. M'Donough, R.M.	6 Mar. 28	ᴘ 14 Dec. 32		
7	0	William G. Cavendish	ᴘ 30 Aug. 33	ᴘ 30 Dec. 34		
6	0	William Tomline	ᴘ 2 May 34	ᴘ 24 July 35		
8	0	Newcombe E. Blackall	ᴘ 1 Feb. 33	ᴘ 21 Aug. 35		
6	0	Rob. Blucher Wood	ᴘ 30 Dec. 34	ᴘ 12 Feb. 36		
5	0	Arthur W. Williams	ᴘ 24 July 35	ᴘ 1 Dec. 37		
5	0	John Long	ᴘ 21 Aug. 35	ᴘ 11 May 38		
3	0	Robert Edw. Ward	ᴘ 1 Dec. 37	ᴘ 28 Aug. 38		
5	0	Andrew Cathcart	ᴘ 26 Jan. 36	ᴘ 5 April 39		
2	0	Henry Edward Surtees	ᴘ 23 Feb. 38	ᴘ 20 Sept. 39		
		CORNETS.				
2	0	John Wilkie	ᴘ 11 May 38			
2	0	Lord G. A. Beauclerk	ᴘ 28 Aug. 38			
1	0	George Webb	28 June 39			
24	5/12	*Paymaster.*—Ᵽ Samuel Wells,[4] 25 June, 26; *Cornet*, 8 Feb. 16; *Lieut.* 30 Dec. 19.				
1	0	*Adjutant.*—George Webb, 20 Sept. 39.				
18	3 9/12	*Quarter-Master.*—James Creighton M'Clellan,[5] 28 Jan. 19.				
29	0	*Surgeon.*—Ᵽ Wm. Reynolds Rogers,[6] 3 Aug. 26; *Assist.-Surg.* 7 Nov. 11; *Hosp.-Assist.* 22 Aug. 11.				
		Assistant-Surgeon.—Wm. Stewart, 28 Sept. 26; *Hosp.-Assist.* 24 Nov. 25.				
8	0	*Veterinary Surgeon.*—John Gloag, 29 June, 32.				

Blue.—*Agent*, Messrs. Cox & Co.
[*Returned from Portugal, March*, 1828.]

1 Lord Londonderry has received a cross and one clasp for Sahagun and Benevente, Talavera, Busaco, Fuentes d'Onor, and Badajoz, and was severely wounded in the head by a musket-ball in Holland, 10th Oct. 1799.
2 Lieut.-Col. Vandeleur was severely wounded at Fuentes d'Onor.
3 Major Wallington served at Waterloo on the 17th and 18th June.
4 Paymaster Wells served at Sahagun, Mayorca, Benevente and Corunna; and subsequently in the Peninsula from 1813 to the end of the war, including the battles of Moralles, Vittoria, Pyrenees, Orthes, Tarbes and Toulouse.
5 Quarter-Master M'Clellan served throughout the campaigns of 1813 and 14 on the Niagara Frontiers, including the action before Fort George, Blackrock, Buffalo, Chippewa, Lundy's Lane, Niagara, before Fort Erie, Cook's Mills, and pass of Grand River. Received a contusion in the head by a musket shot at the moment of passing through the enemy's line in the charge at Chippewa, 4th July, 1814.
6 Dr. Rogers served in the Peninsula from Jan. 1813 to the end of the war, including the action at Moralles, battles of Vittoria, Pyrenees, Orthes, and Toulouse.

11th *Regiment of Light Dragoons.*

The *Sphinx*, with the words, " EGYPT "— " PENINSULA "—
" WATERLOO "—" BHURTPORE."

Years' Serv		
Full Pay	Half Pay	
53		*Colonel.* Philip Philpot, *Ens.* 26 Dec. 87; *Lieut.* 23 Nov. 88; *Capt.* 10 Jan. 97; *Major*, 1 Nov, 07; *Lieut.-Col.* 24 Jan. 11; *Col.* 19 July 21; *Major.-Gen.* 22 July 30; *Col.* 11th Dragoons, 8 Nov. 39.
13	3 3/12	*Lieut.-Colonel.* James Thomas *Earl of* Cardigan, *Cornet*, P 6 May, 24; *Lieut.* P 13 Jan. 25; *Capt.* P 9 June, 26; *Major*, P 3 Aug. 30; *Lieut.-Col.* 3 Dec. 30.
		Majors.
29	1/12	𝔅 𝔚 James Rich. Rotton,¹ *Cornet*, 27 June, 11; *Lieut.* P 9 Jan. 12; *Capt.* P 18 Sept. 17; *Major,* P 11 Aug. 29.
33	0	𝔅 𝔚 John Jenkins,² *Cornet*, 29 Jan. 07; *Lieut.* P 31 Dec. 07; *Capt.* P 22 Dec. 14; *Major*, 13 Nov. 34.

		CAPTAINS.	CORNET.	LIEUT.	CAPTAIN.	BREVET-MAJOR.
25	0	James Tomlinson³	P 5 Oct. 15	5 Nov. 18	P 5 June 23	28 June 38
14	2/12	Rich. Anthony Reynolds	P 19 Jan. 26	25 June 29	P 17 Mar. 37	
12	0	Inigo Jones	P 8 April 28	P 17 Dec. 30	P 14 Apr. 37	
7	0	John Hen. Forrest	P 12 Apr. 33	P 25 Dec. 35	P 11 Oct. 39	
8	3	John Douglas	P 18 June 29	P 25 Oct. 33	P 11 May 39	
5	0	John Williams Reynolds	P 18 Sept. 35	P 2 Nov. 38	P 10 Jan. 40	
		LIEUTENANTS.				
20	0	𝔚 R. Bambrick,⁴ R.M.	14 Dec. 20	P 12 Oct. 25		
4	0	Wm. Chas. Forrest	P 11 Mar. 36	P 5 Jan. 39		
3	0	Hen. Gorges Moysey	P 17 Mar. 37	P 11 Jan. 39		
5	0	Frederick Sutton	P 24 Apr. 35	P 13 May 36		
4	0	T. Mathias Luz. Weguelin	P 23 Dec. 36	P 28 June 39		
3	0	John Wm. Brotherton	P 1 Dec. 37	P 16 Oct. 39		
2	0	Thos. Chaloner Smith	P 2 Nov. 38	P 22 Nov. 39		
2	0	Frederick Knowles⁵	23 Nov. 38	9 Jan. 40		
2	0	John Cunningham	P 11 Jan. 39	P 10 Jan. 40		
		CORNETS.				
1	0	Henry Grimstone Hale	P 28 June 39			
1	0	Broadley Harrison	P 11 Oct. 39			
1	0	William Grey Pitt	P 22 Nov. 39			
1	0	Peter Roe	P 31 Jan. 40			
13	1 9/12	*Paymaster.*—Wm. Devaynes Bedford, 28 April, 37; *Ens.* 6 April, 26; *Lieut.* 31 Jan. 27.				
2	0	*Adjutant.*—F. Knowles, (*Lieut.*) 5 Jan. 39.				
6	0	*Quarter-Master.*—Francis Collins, 6 Feb. 1834.				
		Surgeon.—B. L. Sandham, M.D. 28 July, 20; *Assist.-Surg.* 12 Nov. 07.				
7	0	*Assist-Surgeon.*—Andrew Maclean, M.D., 4 Oct. 33.				
5	0	*Veterinary Surgeon.*—Opie Smith, Cornet. 16 Feb. 35.				

Scarlet — *Facings* Buff. — *Agent*, Messrs. Cox & Co.
[*Returned from the East Indies, June* 1838.]

1 Major Rotton served in the Peninsula from April, 1812, to June, 1813, including the battle of Salamanca. Present at Waterloo on the 16th, 17th and 18th June. Served also at the siege and capture of Bhurtpore.
2 Major Jenkins served in the Peninsula from May, 1811, to the end of the war, and was engaged in front of Elvas; on the banks of the Aguoda; at Torre de Sillas; Castrajon; Badajoz (wounded); upon the Douro at Salamanca; Monestero; Burgos, and Torguanada. Present at Waterloo on the 16th and 17th June. Served also at the siege and capture of Bhurtpore.
3 Major Tomlinson served at the siege and capture of Bhurtpore.
4 Lieut. Bambrick served at Waterloo on the 18th June. Also at the siege and capture of Bhurtpore.
5 Lieut. Knowles served at the siege and capture of Bhurtpore.

12th (or the Prince of Wales's) Royal Regt. of Lancers.

The *Sphinx*, with the words, " EGYPT "— " PENINSULA " — " WATERLOO."

Years' Serv.	
Full Pay.	Half Pay.

Colonel.

| 50 | | ᛝ Sir Henry John Cumming,¹ K.C.H. *Cornet*, 12 May, 1790; *Lieut.* 9 Feb. 93; *Capt.* 21 Feb. 94; *Major*, 25 Oct. 98; *Lieut-Col.* 17 Feb. 1803; *Col.* 1 Jan. 12; *Major-Gen.* 4 June, 14; *Lieut.-Gen.* 22 July, 30; *Col.* 12th Lancers, 20 Jan. 37. |

Lieut-Colonels.

| 56 | 0 | Robert Browne Clayton,² K.C. *Ens.* 1 Sept. 84 ; *Lieut.* 30 April, 90; *Capt.* 31 March, 93 ; *Major*, 1 March, 94: *Lieut.-Col.* 1 Jan. 98 ; *Col.* 25 April, 1808 ; *Major-Gen.* 4 June, 11 ; *Lieut.-Gen.* 19 July, 21; *Gen.* 28 June, 38. |
| 37 | 2 3/12 | ᛝ ᛰ Sampson Stawell,³ *Ens.* ᴾ 15 Jan. 01; *Lieut.* ᴾ 9 July, 02 ; *Capt.* 28 Feb. 05 ; *Brevet-Major*, 18 June, 15 ; *Reg.-Major*, 16 Sept. 19 ; *Lieut.-Col.* ᴾ 1 Oct. 25 ; *Col.* 28 June, 28. |

Major.

| 35 | 0 | ᛝ ᛰ Alexander Barton,⁴ K.H. *Cornet*, ᴾ 1 Aug. 05 : *Lieut.* ᴾ 7 May, 07 ; *Capt.* ᴾ 17 Jan. 11 ; *Brevet-Major*, 21 Jan. 19 ; *Reg.-Major*, ᴾ 19 Feb. 24 ; *Brevet-Lieut.-Col.* 10 Jan. 37. |

		CAPTAINS.	CORNET.	LIEUT.	CAPTAIN.	BREVET-MAJOR.
17	0	Edward Vandeleur	22 Sept. 23	5 Jan. 26	ᴾ 3 Aug. 30	
15	0	Edward Pole	ᴾ 7 July 25	ᴾ 19 Sept. 26	ᴾ 18 Nov. 31	
13	0	Edward Sivewright	ᴾ 9 Aug. 27	ᴾ 12 Mar. 29	ᴾ 3 Aug. 32	
13	0	Baskerville Glegg	ᴾ 3 Jan. 28	ᴾ 30 Apr. 29	ᴾ 2 Nov. 32	
13	0	Hon. C. R. W. Forester	ᴾ 18 Dec. 27	ᴾ 3 Aug. 30	ᴾ 23 Aug. 33	
11	0	Jonathan Childe	ᴾ 30 April 29	ᴾ 4 Jan. 31	ᴾ 24 Apr. 35	
		LIEUTENANTS.				
10	0	Thomas W. D. Willan	ᴾ 8 June 30	ᴾ 17 Feb. 32		
8	0	J. Fitz R. H. L. Wellesley	ᴾ 3 Aug. 32	ᴾ 20 Sept. 33		
15	0	Joseph Philips, R.M.	18 Aug. 25	ᴾ 13 Dec. 33		
7	0	Hon. Robt. Needham	ᴾ 23 Aug. 33	ᴾ 12 Dec. 34		
7	0	Edward Morant	ᴾ 20 Sept. 33	ᴾ 24 Apr. 35		
7	0	W. Heathcote Tottenham	ᴾ 13 Dec. 33	ᴾ 23 Oct. 35		
5	0	Thomas Bernard	ᴾ 24 Apr. 35	ᴾ 26 Apr. 39		
5	0	Howard J. St. George	ᴾ 23 Oct. 35	ᴾ 24 May 39		
7	0	Sydney Aug. Capel⁵	7 July 37	25 May 39		
		CORNETS.				
2	0	Henry Arthur Scott	ᴾ 25 May 38			
2	0	Arthur Munro	ᴾ 28 Dec. 38			
1	0	Thos. Henry Clifton	ᴾ 26 Apr. 39			
2	0	Francis Delaval Gray	ᴾ 11 Jan. 39			

29	3/12	*Paymaster.*—L. M. M. Prior,⁶ 6 July, 20; *Ens.* 12 Sept. 11; *Lieut.* 9 Dec. 13.
7	0	*Adjutant.*—Sydney Augustus Capel, 7 July, 37 ; (*Lieut.*) 7 July 37.
3	0	*Quarter-Master.*—Charles Armstrong, 7 July, 37.
19	0	*Surgeon.*—ᛝ ᛰ Jas. Moffitt,⁷ M.D. 17 Jan. 28 ; *Assist. Surg.* 24 Oct. 11.
		Assistant-Surgeon.—Thomas Hunter, M.D. 18 April, 34.
7	0	*Veterinary Surgeon.*—Charles Brett, 8 March, 33.

Scarlet — *Facings* Blue. — *Agent*, Mr. Collyer.

[*Returned from Portugal, March* 1828.]

1 Sir Hen. John Cumming served in Flanders and Holland in 1793, 4, and 5; and again in Holland in 1799. Served also in the Peninsula, and commanded the 11th Light Dragoons at Salamanca, for which he has received a medal. He was wounded by a sabre cut in the arm in the action of the 25th Sept. 1811.

2 Sir Robert Browne Clayton served the Egyptian campaign of 1801, including the actions of the 8th, 13th, and 21st March. Served also at Walcheren in 1809, and was present at the siege of Flushing. Medal for serving in Egypt.

3 Col. Stawell served with the Walcheren expedition, and subsequently in the Peninsula from 1811 to 1814, including the sieges of Ciudad Rodrigo, and Badajoz ; the cavalry affair of La Rena ; destruction of the bridge of Almoras ; battle of Vittoria ; siege and capture of San Sebastian. Served also at Waterloo.

4 Col. Barton's services :— expedition to Walcheren ; Peninsula from April, 1812, to the end of the war, including the cavalry affairs at Castrajon, Quintana de Puenta, and Monastero ; battles of Salamanca and Vittoria ; and siege of San Sebastian. Served also at Waterloo.

5 Quarter-Master 11 Oct. 1833, from which date the period of service has been computed.

6 Paymaster Prior served the campaign of 1817 in the East Indies against the Pindarrees.

7 Dr. Moffitt served in the Peninsula from Aug. 1813 to the end of the war, including the battles of the Pyrenees, Orthes, and Toulouse. Present on the 16th, 17th and 18th June at Waterloo.

Emb. for Foreign Service, 1819.] **13th *Regiment of Light Dragoons*.** [Serving in the East Indies.

On the chacoes and appointments, the Motto, " *Vivet in Æternum*."—" PENINSULA"—" WATERLOO."

Years' Serv.		
Full Pay	Half Pay	**Colonel.**
61		Hon. Sir H. G. Grey, G.C.B. G.C.H. *Ens.* 17 Oct. 1779; *Lieut.* 28 July, 81; *Capt.* 31 May, 87; *Maj.* 23 Oct. 93; *Lieut.-Col.* 21 April, 94; *Col.* 1 Jan. 98; *Maj.-Gen.* 1 Jan. 1805; *Lieut.-Gen.* 4 June, 11; *Gen.* 27 May, 25; *Col.* 13th Dragoons, 30 Dec. 11.
31	1/12	*Lieut.-Cols.*— ⓟ ⓦ R. Brunton,[1] *Ens.* 10 Nov. 08; *Lieut.* 12 Dec. 09; *Capt.* 10 Nov. 13; *Maj.* ᴾ 2 March, 26; *Lieut.-Col.* ᴾ 31 Dec. 30.
31	0	ⓟ ⓦ Allan T. Maclean,[2] *Ens.* 4 Jan. 10; *Lieut.* ᴾ 11 July, 11; *Capt.* ᴾ 23 Dec. 18; *Maj.* 29 Oct. 30; *Lieut.-Col.* 11 July, 34.
25	0	*Majors.*—Henry Stones, *Cornet*, ᴾ 28 Dec. 15; *Lieut.* 7 Nov. 18; *Capt.* ᴾ 25 Dec. 18; *Maj.* ᴾ 19 Feb. 36.
31	2 6/12	William Hake,[3] *Ens.* 25 June, 1807; *Lieut.* 1 Nov. 10; *Capt.* 7 May, 27; *Maj.* 23 Nov. 38.

		CAPTAINS.	**CORNET.**	**LIEUT.**	**CAPTAIN.**	**BREV-MAJ.**
25	0	Wm. Digby Hamilton ..	25 May 15	9 Nov. 19	ᴾ 31 Dec. 30	
19	3	Robert Ellis............	23 April 18	5 Oct. 22	ᴾ 13 May 26	
22	0	ⓟ ⓦ Thomas Rosser[4]..	29 Oct. 18	24 June 19	8 Sept. 31	
15	3/12	James Sargeaunt........	ᴾ 9 June 25	ᴾ 30 Mar. 26	ᴾ 18 July 34	
18	5/12	George Weston	ᴾ 28 Dec. 21	ᴾ 19 May 25	ᴾ 16 Mar. 30	
14	3/12	William Knox..........	ᴾ 12 Jan. 26	ᴾ 20 Mar. 27	ᴾ 14 Dec. 32	
24	3	George Manners	13 May 13	8 Sept. 14	15 Sept. 37	
15	0	Bernard MacMahon	10 Nov. 25	ᴾ 30 Nov. 26	23 Nov. 38	
		LIEUTENANTS.				
14	0	Thomas John Parker	ᴾ 10 Aug. 26	14 Aug. 28	4 Captain Rosser acccompanied the 13th Light Dragoons to Portugal in 1810, and was present with it in every action in which it was engaged, without having been absent from it for a single day. Served also at Waterloo.	
17	10 7/12	James Boalth	ᴾ 24 Sept. 12	ᴾ 6 May 13		
13	0	John C. Campbell	25 Oct. 27	ᴾ 16 Mar. 32		
10	17	Denis Browne	3 May 13	ᴾ 15 Mar. 33		
11	0	Geo. Jas. Walker	8 Jan. 29	ᴾ 10 Jan. 34		
11	0	Wm. Mavor Julius	ᴾ 9 July 29	ᴾ 18 April 34		
10	0	Hen. Horatio Kitchener..	ᴾ 29 June 30	ᴾ 11 July 34	5 Lieut. Ready served at the siege and capture of Bhurtpore	
9	0	Edw. Rudston Read	ᴾ 18 Nov. 31	ᴾ 12 Dec. 34		
10	0	John A. De Balinhard ..	ᴾ 11 June 30	ᴾ 29 Mar. 33	6 Doctor Mouat served in the Burmese war.	
9	0	Charles Floyd	8 Sept. 31	16 Sept. 37		
5	0	Werner Cathrey	ᴾ 25 Dec. 35	ᴾ 30 June 37		
6	0	Jas. Allen Cameron	ᴾ 11 July 34	5 Oct. 38		
15	0	William Ready[5]	19 May 25	28 June 27		
6	0	Chas. C. Shute	ᴾ 19 July 34	ᴾ 10 May 39		
		CORNETS.				
6	0	Wm. Shute Wint	ᴾ 18 July 34			
6	0	Henry Hamilton	ᴾ 21 Dec. 34			
4	0	C. H. D. Donovan	ᴾ 16 Feb. 36			
3	0	Charles Deacon	ᴾ 14 April 37			
3	0	Thomas W. Smith......	ᴾ 7 July 37			
2	0	Alfred R. Hole	ᴾ 27 July 38			

17	10	*Paymaster.*—R. Storey, 5 Aug. 19; *Ens.* 15 Apr. 13; *Lieut.* 9 Feb. 15.
9	0	*Adjutant.*—Charles Floyd, (*Lieut.*) 8 Sept. 31.
12	0	*Quarter-Master.*—John O'Reilly, 25 Dec. 28.
28	0	*Surg.*—Jas. Mouat,[6] M.D. 15 Feb. 27; *Assist.-Surg.* 1 Oct. 12; *Hosp.-Assist.* 16 July, 12.
13	0	*Assist.-Sur.*—John Clark, M.D. 29 July. 30, *Hosp.-Assistant*, 4 Oct. 27. Patrick Nicolson, M.D. 31 Dec. 33.
10	0	*Veterinary Surg.*—John Legrew, 9 July, 30.

Scarlet—*Facings* Green.—*Agent*, Messrs. Cox & Co.

1 Col. Brunton served in the Peninsula from May 1809, to Feb. 1814, including the action at the bridge of Coa near Almeida, Busaco, Fuentes d'Onor, Arroyo de Molino, Almarez, Vittoria, Mayo Pass, Pyrenees, Nivelle, Nive. Slightly wounded at the battle of the Pyrenees 30th July, and severely at St. Pierre d'Arrubé near Bayonne 13th Dec. 1813. Served at Water oo on the 18th June.

2 Col. Maclean served with the 13th Light Dragoons in every action and affair in which it was engaged in the Peninsula from Dec. 1810 to the end of the war. Wounded and taken prisoner at Couches, 13th March, 1814. Served also at Waterloo.

3 Major Hake served the campaigns of 1810 and 11 against the Caffre tribes. Served also at the siege of Bhurtpore.

14th (or the King's) Regt. of Light Dragoons.

The "PRUSSIAN EAGLE"—"DOURO"—"TALAVERA"—"FUENTES D'ONOR"—"SALAMANCA"—"VITTORIA"—"ORTHES"—"PENINSULA."

Years' Serv.		
Full Pay.	Half Pay.	

Colonel.

44 — ẞ ₡₡ Sir **Edward Kerrison**, Bart.¹ C.B. & G.C.H. *Cornet*, 23 June, 1796; *Lieut.* 1 Feb. 98; *Capt.* 18 Oct. 98; *Major.* 12 May, 1803; *Lieut.-Col.* 4 April, 05; *Col.* 4 June, 13: *Major-Gen.* 12 Aug. 19; *Lieut.-Gen.* 10 Jan. 37; *Col.* 14th Dragoons, 18 June, 30.

Lieut.-Colonel.

36 | 0 | ẞ John Townsend,² *Cornet,* ᵖ 24 Jan. 05; *Lieut.* 8 Mar. 06; *Capt.* 6 June, 11; *Brevet-Major.* 21 Jan. 19; *Regtl.-Major,* ᵖ 13 Sept. 21; *Lieut.-Col.* ᵖ 16 April, 29.

Major.

15 | 0 | Charles Barton, *Cornet,* ᵖ 10 Dec. 25; *Lieut.* ᵖ 14 Feb. 28; *Capt.* ᵖ 22 March, 33; *Major.* ᵖ 1 June, 38.

		CAPTAINS.	CORNET.	LIEUT.	CAPTAIN.	BREV.-MAJ.
15	8/10	Edward Harvey³	ᵖ 24 Mar. 25	ᵖ 4 May 26	ᵖ 12 Oct. 30	
14	0	Fran. H. Stephens	ᵖ 23 Feb. 26	31 July 28	ᵖ 17 July 35	
10	0	John Henderson	ᵖ 25 Jan. 31	ᵖ 31 Dec. 33	ᵖ 4 Aug. 37	
8	0	Wm. Henry Archer	ᵖ 28 Dec. 32	ᵖ 17 July 35	ᵖ 1 June 38	
7	0	John B. Culpeper	ᵖ 13 Sept. 33	ᵖ 29 April 36	ᵖ 27 July 38	
7	0	Henry Edw. Doherty	ᵖ 31 Dec. 33	ᵖ 15 July 36	ᵖ 17 May 39	
		LIEUTENANTS.				
5	0	Charles E. Doherty	ᵖ 24 April 35	ᵖ 6 Jan. 37		
8	0	Geo. Main Fullerton	ᵖ 14 Dec. 32	ᵖ 30 Oct. 35		
5	0	Isaac Cornock	ᵖ 17 July 35	ᵖ 4 Aug. 37		
4	0	John Henry Tonge	ᵖ 29 April 36	ᵖ 1 June 38		
5	0	Charles T. Griffis R.M.	ᵖ 5 Feb. 36	ᵖ 27 July 38		
4	0	Archibald Robert Miller	ᵖ 6 Jan. 37	ᵖ 13 Dec. 39		
		CORNETS.				
3	0	William Faber	ᵖ 4 Aug. 37			
4	0	G. K. M. Dawson	ᵖ 30 July 36			
3	0	William Clarke⁴	24 April 38			
1	0	Rob. Hugh Smith Barry	ᵖ 17 May 39			
1	0	John Hesketh Goddard	ᵖ 26 July 39			
1	0	Wm. Warner Allen	ᵖ 29 Nov. 39			
1	0	J. W. M. G. Hughes	ᵖ 13 Dec. 39			
28	0	*Paymaster.*—ẞ Samuel Rofe,⁵ 3 Sept. 12.				
3	0	*Adjutant.*—William Clarke, (*Cornet,*) 24 Apr. 38.				
11	1	*Quarter-Master.*—ẞ ₡₡ Samuel Brodribb,⁶ 15 Jan. 29.				
30	0	*Surgeon.*—ẞ ₡₡ Patrick Henry Lavens,⁷ 3 Aug. 26: *Assist.-Surg.* 24 Oct. 11; *Hosp.-Assist.* 28 June, 10.				
		Assistant-Surgeon.—Jas. W. Moffat, 8 Feb. 27; *Hosp.-Assist.* 28 Sept. 26.				
2	0	*Veterinary Surgeon.*—J. G. Philips, 28 Aug. 38.				

Scarlet—*Facings* Blue.—*Agent,* Messrs. Cox. & Co.

[*Returned from Spain, July,* 1814.]

1 Sir Edward Kerrison served at the Helder in 1799; with Sir John Moore's army in Spain in 1808, and at Corunna. Served subsequently in the Peninsula, and commanded the 7th Hussars at Orthes, and at Waterloo, for which he has received medals. Sir Edward was severely wounded (his arm having been broken in two places) in Spain, 25 Dec. 1808, and slightly wounded at Waterloo.

2 Col. Townsend served in the Peninsula from Dec. 1808, until taken prisoner near the city of Pau in France, 8th March 1814, including the different affairs of the 10th and 11th, in crossing the Douro on the 12th May 1809; battle of Talavera; affair with the enemy's advanced posts 11th July 1810 in front of Ciudad Rodrigo when Col. Talbot who was killed; passage of the Coa; skirmishes of the enemy's retreat from the rear guard from Almeida to the lines of Torres Vedras in 1810; affairs in the enemy's retreat from Santarem to the frontiers of Spain from 6th March to 4th April 1811; battle of Fuentes d'Onor (wounded); affair with the enemy's lancers 25th Sept. 1811; siege of Badajoz; affairs with the enemy's cavalry at Usagre, Llerena, in front of Salamanca, and near Castrillos; battle of Salamanca; affair with the enemy's rear guard near Panerandos; several skirmishes from Madrid to near Ciudad Rodrigo, and from the 26th May near Salamanca to the battle of Vittoria; taking of a gun from the enemy near Pampeluna; and several engagements and skirmishes from the entrance of the British army into France, until the battle of Orthes. Embarked for America in Oct. 1814, and was present at the attack on New Orleans 8th Jan. 1815.

3 Capt. Harvey served at the investment of Kolapore in the East Indies in Sept. 1827.

4 Quarter-Master, 15 Sept. 1837, from which date the period of service has been computed.

5 Paymaster Rofe served in the Peninsula from October 1812 to the end of the war.

6 Quart.-Master Brodripp served in the Peninsula from Sept. 1813 to the end of the war; present at Waterloo.

7 Dr. Lavens served the campaigns of 1812, 13, and 14, in the Peninsula, and was attached to the light troops which attacked the castle of Mirabete near Almarez, on the night of the 19th May, 1812. Present at the battles of Vittoria, the Pyrenees, Nivelle; storming the Heights of Garris; and battle of Orthes. Present at Waterloo on the 16th and 18th June.

Emb. for For. Service, 1839.] **15th (*or the King's*) *Light Dragoons.*—(*Hussars*).** [Serving in the East Indies.

"EMSDORF"—"EGMONT-OP-ZEE"—"VILLIERS EN COUCHE"—"SAHAGUN"
"VITTORIA"—"PENINSULA"—"WATERLOO."

Years' Serv.						
46		*Colonel.*				
		ꝑ Sir Robert Thomas Wilson,[1] *Cornet*, Apr. 1794; *Lieut.* 31 Oct. 94; *Capt.* 21 Sept. 96; *Major*, 28 June, 1800; *Lieut.Col.* 27 Feb. 02; *Col.* 25 July, 10; *Major-Gen.* 4 June, 13; *Lieut.-Gen.* 27 May, 25; *Col.* 15th Hussars 29 Dec. 35.				
Full Pay.	Half Pay.					
29	5 4/12	*Lieut.-Colonel.*—ꝑ Lovell Benjamin Badcock,[2] K. H. *Cornet*, ꝑ 18 Dec. 05; *Lieut.* ꝑ 19 May, 08; *Capt.* ꝑ 12 Dec. 11; *Brevet-Major*, 21 Jan. 19; *Regtl.-Major*, ꝑ 28 Oct. 24; *Lieut.-Col.* ꝑ 21 Nov. 28.				
20	1 7/12	Sir Walter Scott, *Bart. Cornet*, ꝑ 10 June, 19; *Lieut.* ꝑ 24 Oct. 21; *Capt.* ꝑ 16 June, 25; *Major*, ꝑ 26 Feb. 28; *Lieut.-Col.* 31 May, 39.				
21	3/12	*Majors.*—Courtenay Phillipps, *Cornet & Sub.-Lieut.* ꝑ 26 Dec. 18; *Lieut.* 18 May, 21; *Capt.* ꝑ 14 Jan. 26; *Major*, ꝑ 5 Apr. 33.				
19	1 2/12	Augustus Wathen, *Cornet*, ꝑ 9 July, 20; *Lieut.* ꝑ 24 June, 23; *Capt.* ꝑ 26 Sept. 26; *Major*, 31 May, 39.				
		CAPTAINS.	CORNET.	LIEUT.	CAPTAIN.	BREV.-MAJ.
22	4 3/12	James M'Queen........	31 Mar. 14	ꝑ 11 Feb. 19	ꝑ 21 July 25	28 June 38
14	0	John P. Hickman......	ꝑ 19 Oct. 26	ꝑ 25 Feb. 31	ꝑ 1 Apr. 36	
9	0	George Wm. Key.....	ꝑ 5 July 31	25 Aug. 33	ꝑ 16 Sept. 37	
8	0	E. Tho. Harley Chambers.	ꝑ 14 Dec. 32	ꝑ 2 Aug. 33	ꝑ 28 Nov. 37	
10	0	Michael Wm. Smith....	19 Nov. 30	ꝑ 21 Feb. 34	ꝑ 23 Apr. 39	
22	3	Robt. Rollo Gillespie[3] ..	31 Aug. 15	ꝑ 9 Apr. 18	6 July 37	
20	0	William Penn.........	ꝑ 1 Sept. 20	29 June 26	5 Oct. 38	
29	0	ꝑ Tho. Coven. Brander	27 June 11	ꝑ 30 Mar. 14	1 June 39	
14	0	Charles H. T. Hecker.....	ꝑ 29 Aug. 26	ꝑ 3 Jan. 28	2 June 39	
		LIEUTENANTS.				
9	0	Justinian Vernon......	ꝑ 21 June 31	9 Feb. 34		
9	0	Richard Knox.........	ꝑ 28 June 31	20 Apr. 34		
10	7 8/12	Hugh B. Higgins.......	ꝑ 1 Aug. 22	15 Dec. 25		
8	0	John Bunce Pilgrim....	ꝑ 4 Dec. 32	ꝑ 16 Sept. 37		
5	0	John Surman, R. M.	12 June 35	ꝑ 9 Mar. 38		
8	0	Fra. Woodley Horne...	ꝑ 31 Aug. 32	ꝑ 6 Sept. 33		
6	0	John Brett............	ꝑ 10 Oct. 34	ꝑ 14 Apr. 37		
7	0	Rob. *Visc.* Jocelyn.....	ꝑ 24 May 33	4 Aug. 38		
2	0	Chas. Hugh Key......	ꝑ 9 Mar. 38	ꝑ 23 May. 39		
12	0	Geo. Aberc. Robertson[4]..	26 Apr. 28	13 May 31		
13	0	Octavius Geo. Perrott ..	26 May 27	11 Oct. 32		
12	0	P. D'Ormieux Von Streng	ꝑ 11 Nov. 28	17 Apr. 34		
9	0	Cha. Alex. Sinclair	13 Oct. 31	2 June 34		
7	0	John Macartney........	ꝑ 27 Sept. 33	ꝑ 19 Dec. 34		
7	0	Tho. Brooke Jackson....	ꝑ 10 Jan. 34	ꝑ 19 Feb. 36		
11	0	John Hamilton Gray....	ꝑ 24 Nov. 29	15 Sept. 37		
5	0	George Horne.........	ꝑ 19 June 35	ꝑ 28 Aug. 38		
2	0	John Gore Townsend....	ꝑ 28 Dec. 38	ꝑ 29 Nov. 39		
		CORNETS.				
2	0	Jos. Clayton Jennyns....	ꝑ 8 Feb. 39			
1	0	Lewis Edw. Nolan......	ꝑ 15 Mar. 39			
1	0	John Cocks............	14 June 39			
6	0	Tho. R. Crawley.......	19 Dec. 34			
1	0	Cha. Erskine Steuart....	ꝑ 20 June 39			
1	0	Henry Brett	ꝑ 21 June 39			
1	0	Blackwood Moutray Read	ꝑ 22 June 39			
1	0	Herbert Morgan........	ꝑ 23 June 39			
1	0	Charles Bill	ꝑ 29 Nov. 39			

[1] Sir Robert Wilson served in Flanders and Holland in 1793, 4, and 5; in the rebellion in Ireland in 1798; in Holland in 1799; the Egyptian campaign of 1801; capture of the Cape of Good Hope in 1806; raised and commanded the Lusitanian Legion in 1808 and 9 in Spain and Portugal. Served several campaigns with the Russian army in Russia, Poland, Germany, and France.

[2] Lieut.-Colonel Badcock was wounded at Fuentes d'Onor.

[3] Capt. Gillespie served in the Burmese war.

[4] Lieutenant Robertson was wounded in action at Coorg, Madras, April 1834.

[5] Dr. Chambers served in the American war, and was present in the actions before New Orleans.

9	0	*Paymaster.*—Henry Routh, 11 Oct. 39; *Ens.* 26 Apr. 31; *Lieut.* 27 Sept. 33.
1	0	*Adjutant.*—John Cocks, (*Cornet*) 14 June 39.
5	0	*Quarter-Master.*—William Betson, 1 Nov. 35.
31	0	*Surgeon.*—John Chambers,[5] 24 July, 35; *Assist.-Surg.* 29 April, 24; *Hosp.-Assist.* 27 Nov. 09.
3	0	*Assistant-Surgeons.*—Thomas Bisset, M.D., 10 Nov. 37.
1	0	Henry Cooper Reade, 31 May, 39
2	0	*Veterinary Surgeon.*—Thomas Hurford, 25 Jan. 39.

Blue—*Agent*, Messrs. Cox & Co.
[*Returned from France, May*, 1816.]

[Emb. for For. Service, 1822.] **16th (or Queen's) Regt. of Light Drags. (Lancers).** [Serving in Bengal.

"TALAVERA"—"FUENTES D'ONOR"—"SALAMANCA"—"VITTORIA"—"NIVE"
"PENINSULA"—"WATERLOO"—"BHURTPORE."

Years' Serv.			
Full Pay.	Half Pay.		
59		**Colonel.** P ✠ Sir Jn. Ormsby Vandeleur,[1] G. C. B. *Ens.* 29 Dec. 1781; *Lieut.* 21 July, 83; *Capt.* 7 Mar. 92; *Major*, 1 Mar. 94; *Lieut.-Col.* 1 Jan. 98; *Col.* 25 Apr. 1808; *Major-Gen.* 4 June, 11; *Lieut.-Gen.* 19 July, 21; *Gen.* 10 Jan. 38; *Col.* 16th Lancers 18 June 30.		
37	3 1/12	*Lieut.-Colonels.*—P Thos. Wm. Brotherton,[2] C. B. *Ens.* 24 Jan. 00; *Lieut.* & *Capt.* P 27 July, 01; *Major*, P 28 Nov. 11; *Brevet-Lieut.-Col.* 19 May, 14; *Lieut.-Col.* P 12 Oct. 20; *Col.* 22 July 30.		
35	0	P William Persse,[3] C.B. *Cornet*, 10 Jan. 06; *Lieut.* P 27 Nov. 06; *Capt.* 23 Jan. 12; *Major*, 25 May, 22; *Lieut.-Col.* P 6 Dec. 33.		
26	0	P Charles Robert Cureton,[4] *Ens.* 24 Feb. 14; *Lieut.* 27 June, 16; *Capt.* P 12 Nov. 25; *Major*, P 6 Dec. 33; *Brevet-Lt.-Col.* 23 July, 39; *Lieut.-Col.* 21 Aug. 39.		
24	0	*Majors.*—George James M'Dowell,[5] *Cornet*, P 4 April, 16; *Lieut.* P 4 Dec. 17; *Capt.* P 14 Nov. 27; *Major*, P 4 Aug. 37; *Brevet-Lieut.-Col.* 23 July, 39.		
20	5 9/12	Arthur Charles Lowe,[6] *Cornet*, 20 Apr. 15; *Lieut.* P 10 Aug. 15; *Capt.* P 3 Apr. 27; *Major*, 21 Aug. 39.		

		CAPTAINS.	CORNET.	LIEUT.	CAPTAIN.	BREV.-MAJ.
15	0	Thos. Hooke Pearson[7]	P 14 Mar. 25	P 1 Aug. 26	P 16 Aug. 31	
31	2 3/12	William Hilton[8]	5 Dec. 06	1 Jan. 09	25 Sept. 32	
20	0	George Mansel	7 Sept. 20	P 1 Dec. 25	P 6 Aug. 29	
15	0	Edw. Baker Bere	P 13 Aug. 25	P 29 Aug. 26	P 6 Dec. 33	
15	0	Peter T. Robinson	P 7 July 25	P 29 Mar. 27	P 31 Oct. 34	
13	0	G. O'Halloran Gavin	P 13 Nov. 27	P 14 Oct. 29	P 26 May 37	4 Col. Cureton served in the Peninsula from 1809 to the end of the war, including the battles of Talavera, Busaco, and Fuentes d'Onor; siege of Badajoz, April 1812; battle of Salamanca; capture of Madrid; battles of Vittoria, Orthes, Tarbes, and Toulouse; wounded in the right leg by a rifle ball in crossing the Mondego, near Coimbra, 1st Oct. 1810; received a severe sabre cut on the head (skull fractured), and another on the left hand at Fuentes d'Onor, 5th May, 1811; served also at the siege and capture of Bhurtpore.
14	0	Lawrence Fyler	P 7 Sept. 26	P 10 July 28	P 7 Feb. 34	
13	0	Pinson Bonham	P 10 Jan. 28	P 25 June 30	P 23 Mar. 38	
10	0	William Wilmer	P 15 June 30	11 Apr. 33	P 31 Dec. 39	
		LIEUTENANTS.				
19	0	Chas. Fred. Havelock[9]	P 13 Dec. 21	7 May 27		5 Colonel M'Dowell served at the siege and capture of Bhurtpore.
12	0	Edward James Pratt	14 Feb. 28	P 20 Jan. 32		6 Major Lowe was wounded at Bhurtpore.
11	0	Francis Thos. Meik	P 9 July 29	P 4 May 32		7 Capt. Pearson served at the siege of Bhurtpore, and was a volunteer for the dismounted cavalry storming party.
11	0	✠ Wm. Webster, R. M.[10]	P 14 Oct. 29	25 Sept. 32		
8	0	Charles Wm. Reynolds	P 29 June 32	27 Mar. 34		
8	0	Richard Pattinson	P 16 Nov. 32	P 18 Apr. 34		8 Capt. Hilton served at the capture of the Isle of France in 1810 and the campaigns of 1817 and 18 in the Deccan; and the siege and assault of Bhurtpore.
14	3/12	Charles B. Codrington	P 7 Oct. 26	P 22 July 29		
7	0	Wm. Petrie Waugh	P 1 Nov. 33	P 29 May 35		
7	0	Geo. Thos. W. Pipon	P 10 Jan. 34	P 3 July 35		
6	0	George Harriott	P 11 Apr. 34	P 8 July 36		
6	0	Thomas Pattle	P 13 June 34	P 23 Dec. 36		9 Lieut. Havelock served at Bhurtpore.
5	0	Rob. Abercromby Yule	P 3 July 35	P 26 May 37		10 Lieut. Webster served at Waterloo on the 17th and 18th June; also at the siege and capture of Bhurtpore; received a sabre cut on the right hand in an affair with the enemy in front of Bhurtpore, 10th Dec. 1825.
4	0	D. H. Mac Kinnon	P 1 July 36	P 23 Mar. 38		
4	0	Charles John Foster	P 8 Apr. 36	21 Dec. 38		
4	0	Wm. Simpson Mitchell	P 2 July 36	29 May 39		
4	0	John Percy Smith	P 8 July 36	21 Aug. 39		11 Paymaster Williams served the campaign of 1799 in Holland; served also at the siege and capture of Bhurtpore in 1825 and 6.
4	0	Henry Donl. Swetenham	P 3 Feb. 37	P 13 Oct. 39		
3	0	Marmaduke Gwynne	P 26 May 37	P 31 Dec. 39		
		CORNETS.				12 Dr. White expedition with the to Naples in 1809, and was present at the capture of Ischia and Procida; served also the campaigns of 1813 and 14 in the Peninsula, and was present at the sortie from Bayonne.
4	0	Randolph Routh	P 8 July 36			
3	0	Tho. Folliott Powell	P 27 May 37			
3	0	F. Courtney Trower	P 30 June 37			
2	0	J. Ross O'Conor	P 23 Mar. 38			
1	0	Patrick Dynon	29 May 39			
1	0	Henry Lee	P 12 Oct. 39			
1	0	Arthur Need	P 13 Oct. 39			
1	0	Dottin Maycock	P 31 Dec. 39			
35	0	*Paymast.*—W. Williams,[11] 2 Sept. 24; *Cornet* & *Adjt.* 16 Mar. 05; *Lieut.* 12 Feb. 06.				
19	0	*Adjutant.*—Chas. Fred. Havelock; (*Lieut.*) 6 Oct. 27.				
4	0	*Quarter-Master.*—George Rosser, 23 Sept. 36; *Ens.* 20 Aug. 36.				
35	0	*Surgeon.*—P W. Ramsay White,[12] 24 Feb. 14; *Assist. Surg.* 21 Nov. 05; *Hosp.-Assist.* 4 Nov. 05.				
		Ass.-Surgs.—M. J. Maclaine Ross, 15 Feb. 27; *Hosp. Assist.* 28 Sept. 26. John Strange Chapman, 28 Sept. 26; *Hosp. Assist.* 15 Dec. 25.				
5	0	*Veterinary Surgeon.*—Richard J. G. Hurford, 17 July, 35.				
		Scarlet—*Facings* Blue.—*Agent*, Messrs. Cox & Co.				

1 Sir J. Vandeleur has received a cross for Ciudad Rodrigo (wounded when leading his division to the breach), Salamanca, Vittoria, and Nive. Sir John has also performed most distinguished service in the East Indies in Lord Lake's campaigns.

2 Col. Brotherton was wounded at Salamanca.

3 Col. Persse served in the Peninsula from 1809 to the end of the war, and was severely wounded by a musket shot in the action of the 10th Dec. 1813, near Bayonne; served at New Orleans; also at the siege and capture of Bhurtpore.

17th Regiment of Light Dragoons.—(Lancers.)

On the Standards or Guidons, "*Death's Head,*" with the Motto, "*Or Glory.*"

Years' Serv.		
Full Pay.	Half Pay.	
46		**Colonel.** 🏵 ⚜ Sir Arthur Benjamin Clifton,[1] K.C.B. *Cornet,* 6 June, 1794; *Lieut.* 7 Aug. 1794; *Capt.* 27 Feb. 1799; *Major,* 17 Dec. 1803; *Lieut. Col.* 25 July, 1810; *Col.* 12 Aug. 1819; *Major Gen.* 22 July 30; *Col.* 17th Lancers, 25 Aug. 1839.
20	0	**Lieut.-Colonel.** Matthew C. D. St. Quintin, *2nd Lieut.* p 29 June, 20; *Lieut.* p 8 Jan. 24; *Capt.* p 9 Nov. 26; *Major,* p 15 April, 37; *Lieut.-Col.* p 31 Dec. 39.
20	1 5/12	**Major.** John Lawrenson, *Cornet,* 12 Nov. 18; *Lieut.* p 6 Dec. 21; *Capt.* p 27 Aug. 25; *Brevet-Major,* 28 June 38; *Regtl.-Maj.* p 31 Dec. 39.

		CAPTAINS.	CORNET.	LIEUT.	CAPTAIN.	BREVET-MAJOR.
14	0	William C. Douglas	p 20 May 26	p 6 Sept. 27	p 11 Aug. 35	
14	0	Lionel Ames	p 3 Oct. 26	p 6 Jan. 32	p 4 Mar. 36	
11	0	Walter Williams........	p 26 Mar. 29	p 21 Dec. 32	p 18 Mar. 37	
8	0	Edward Croker	p 7 Sept. 32	p 11 Aug. 35	p 1 Mar. 39	
8	0	Robt. Arthur Fitzharding Kingscote	p 2 Nov. 32	p 4 Mar. 36	p 1 Nov. 39	
5	0	Wallace Barrow	p 6 Mar. 35	p 9 Dec. 36	p 31 Dec. 39	
		LIEUTENANTS.				
5	0	John R. Palmer.........	p 7 Aug. 35	p 18 Mar. 37		
5	0	John B. Broadley	p 6 Nov. 35	p 15 Apr. 37		
6	0	Francis Burdett........	p 18 Apr. 34	p 14 Apr. 37		
4	0	John Davy Brett	p 4 Mar. 36	p 1 Mar. 39		
7	0	Archibald *Earl* of Cassilis	p 5 July 33	p 19 Oct. 38		
4	0	Aug. Saltren Willett	p 9 Dec. 36	p 31 Dec. 39		
4	0	*Hon.* Henry S. Blackwood	p 10 June 36	p 4 Jan. 39		
		CORNETS.				
2	0	Thomas Lindsay........	4 Jan. 39			
1	0	Edw. Calvert Scobell....	p 1 Mar. 39			
2	0	Henry Robert Boucherett	p 27 July 38			
1	0	Abraham Hamilton	p 1 Nov. 39			
2	0	Wm. Oxenden Hammond	p 3 Aug. 38			
1	0	Henry Roxby Benson ..	p 31 Jan. 40			

26	3 8/12	*Paymaster.*—George Chandler,[2] 25 Sept. 28 ; *Ens. & Adj.* 25 Feb. 11 ; *Lieut.* 26 March, 12; *Capt.* 25 March, 14.
2	0	*Adjutant.*—Thomas Lindsay, (*Cornet*) 8 Feb. 39.
9	0	*Quarter-Master.*—William Hall, 10 May, 31.
29	4	*Surgeon.*—🏵 ⚜ James Goodall Elkington,[3] 11 March, 13; *Assist.-Surg.* 7 July, 08; *Hosp.-Assist.* 8 Aug. 07.
		Assist.-Surgeon.—James Brown Gibson, M.D., 12 Jan. 29; *Hosp.-Assist.* 14 Dec. 26.
14	0	*Veterinary Surgeon.*—John Wilkinson, 27 April, 26.

Scarlet—*Facings* White.—*Agent,* Messrs. Cox & Co.—*Irish Agent,* Cane & Co.

[*Returned from the East Indies, May,* 1823.]

---

1 Sir Arthur Clifton served in the Peninsula, and has received a medal and one clasp for Fuentes d'Onor, and Vittoria. Served also at Waterloo.

2 Capt. Chandler's services :—Campaign of 1799 in Holland, including the actions of the 2nd and 6th Oct.; siege of Malta, and surrender of La Valetta; battle of Maida; expedition to Egypt in 1807; Ionian Islands in 1809, and siege and capture of Santa Maura in 1810; wounded before Rosetta in 1807.

3 Dr. Elkington served at the capture of Madeira in 1807, and in the Peninsula from April 1809 to Nov. 1812; present at the battle of Talavera; left prisoner with the wounded at that city, and marched into France; released in 1810, and rejoined the army in Portugal on its retreat from Busaco; present with it at the lines of Torres Vedras; battle of Fuentes d'Onor; sieges of Ciudad Rodrigo, and Badajoz; battle of Salamanca; capture of Madrid; and during the whole siege of Burgos in charge of the Hospital for receiving the wounded; in the retreat of the army he was left in charge of the English and French wounded, and again made prisoner; present at Waterloo, and the capture of Paris.

1st (or Grenadier) Regiment of Foot Guards.

"LINCELLES"—"CORUNNA"—"BARROSA"—"PENINSULA"— "WATERLOO."

Years' Serv		
Full Pay.	Half Pay.	
53	0	**Colonel.** 🛡️ 👑 Arthur, *Duke of* Wellington,[1] K.G. G.C.B. & G.C.H. *Ens.* 7 March, 87; *Lieut.* 25 Dec. 87; *Capt.* 30 June, 91; *Major*, 30 April, 93; *Lieut.-Col.* 30 Sept. 93; *Col.* 3 May, 96; *Major-Gen.* 29 April, 1802; *Lieut.-Gen.* 25 April, 08; *Gen.* (in Spain and Portugal) 31 July, 11; *Field Marshal*, 21 June, 13; *Col.* Grenadier Guards, 22 Jan. 27.
37	0	**Lieut.-Colonel.** 🛡️ Samuel Lambert,[2] *Ens.* P5 Nov. 03; *Lieut. & Capt.* 27 Aug. 07; *Capt. & Lieut.-Col.* 16 March, 14; *Major*, with rank of *Col.* 22 July, 30; *Lieut.-Col.* 28 June, 38.
35	0	**Majors.** 🛡️ Turner Grant,[3] *Ens.* P13 June, 05; *Lieut. & Capt.* P20 Feb. 11; *Capt. & Lieut.-Col.* 26 Dec. 16; *Brevet-Col.* 10 Jan. 37; *Major*, with rank of *Col.* P17 Feb. 37.
33	$\frac{1}{12}$	🛡️ 👑 Robert Ellison,[4] *Ens.* P17 Dec. 07; *Lieut. & Capt.* P20 Dec. 12; *Brevet-Major*, 18 June, 15; *Lieut.-Col.* P15 April, 24; *Major*, with rank of *Col.* P9 Jan. 38.
37	0	🛡️ Alexander Higginson,[5] *Ens.* 26 Jan. 04; *Lieut. & Capt.* 14 Sept. 09; *Capt. & Lieut.-Col.* 1 July, 15; *Brevet-Col.* 10 Jan. 37; *Major*, with rank of *Col.* 28 June, 38.
29	0	**Captains and Lieut.-Colonels.** 🛡️ 👑 Edward Clive,[6] *Ens.* P4 July, 11; *Lieut. & Capt.* 25 Dec. 13; *Lieut.-Col.* P19 Sept. 26.
33	0	🛡️ Francis John Davies,[7] *Ens.* P3 Feb. 08; *Lieut.* P26 Jan. 09; *Capt.* P12 Aug. 13; *Capt. & Lieut.-Col.* P30 April, 27.
28	0	John Home, *Ens.* P19 Jan. 13; *Lieut. & Capt.* P30 June, 15; *Capt. & Lieut.-Col.* P10 May, 27.
27	$5\frac{6}{12}$	🛡️ Sir John Rowland Eustace, K.H. *Cornet*, June, 08; *Lieut.* P3 Nov. 08; *Capt.* P17 March, 14; *Major*, P9 Nov. 21; *Lieut.-Col.* P19 Dec. 26.
28	0	🛡️ 👑 Cha. F. Rowley Lascelles,[8] *Ens.* P10 Sept. 12; *Lieut. & Capt.* 9 June, 14; *Capt. & Lieut.-Col.* P21 Feb. 28.
18	4	Henry Robert Ferguson, *Cornet*, P18 March, 18; *Lieut.* P25 Feb. 19; *Capt.* P26 Sept. 22; *Major*, P19 Dec. 26; *Lieut.-Col.* P8 May, 28.
31	0	🛡️ 👑 Lonsdale Boldero,[9] *Ens.* 15 Sept. 09; *Lieut. & Capt.* 20 Oct. 13; *Capt. & Lieut.-Col.* 22 July, 30.
29	0	John Ord Honeyman, *Cornet*, 12 Dec. 11; *Lieut. & Capt.* 4 July, 15; *Capt. & Lieut.-Col.* P28 Sept. 30.
26	0	Godfrey Thornton, *Ens.* P20 Jan. 14; *Lieut. & Capt.* P11 Oct. 21; *Capt. & Lieut.-Col.* P3 Dec. 30.
27	0	Hon. Francis Henry Needham, *Ens.* 8 April, 13; *Lieut.* P9 Dec. 13; *Lieut. & Capt.* P24 Oct. 21; *Capt. & Lieut.-Col.* P31 Dec. 30.
26	0	Henry William Barnard, *Ens.* 9 June, 14; *Capt.* P15 Aug. 22; *Capt. & Lieut.-Col.* P17 May, 31.
25	$\frac{2}{12}$	Philip Spencer Stanhope, *Ens.* 30 March, 15; *Lieut. & Capt.* P17 July, 23; *Capt. & Lieut.-Col.* P16 March, 32.
25	$\frac{1}{12}$	John Lyster, *Ens.* 27 April, 15; *Lieut. & Capt.* P6 Nov. 23; *Capt. & Lieut.-Col.* P27 July, 32.
25	$\frac{5}{12}$	Ferrars Loftus, *Ens.* 1 July, 15; *Lieut. & Capt.* P20 Nov. 23; *Capt. & Lieut.-Col.* P27 Dec. 33.
23	$\frac{8}{12}$	Francis Venables Harcourt, *Ens.* 11 July, 16; *Ens. & Lieut.* P26 March, 17; *Lieut. & Capt.* P8 July, 24; *Capt. & Lieut.-Col.* P2 May, 34.
23	$\frac{10}{12}$	William Greenwood, *Ens. & Lieut.* 18 April, 16; *Lieut. & Capt.* P18 Nov. 24; *Capt. & Lieut.-Col.* P9 May, 34.
20	$2\frac{1}{12}$	John Julius Wm. Angerstein, *Ens. & Lieut.* P9 April, 18; *Lieut. & Capt.* P2 April, 25; *Capt. & Lieut.-Col.* P12 Sept. 34.

1 For Notes, see page 146.

1st (or Grenadier) Regiment of Foot Guards.

Years' Serv.						
Full Pay.	Half Pay.					
21	2 10/12	Sir John Montague Burgoyne, *Bt. Ens.* 17 Oct. 16; *Ens. & Lieut.* 1 Oct. 18; *Lieut. & Capt.* p 28 April, 25; *Capt. & Lieut.-Col.* p 5 June, 35.				
19	2 6/12	George William Eyres, *Ens. & Lieut.* p 3 Dec. 18; *Lieut. & Capt.* p 26 May, 25; *Capt. & Lieut.-Col.* p 1 July, 36.				
21	0	William Fludyer, *Ens.* 30 Dec. 19; *Ens. & Lieut.* p 25 Oct. 21; *Lieut. & Capt.* p 7 July, 25; *Copt. & Lieut.-Col.* p 2 Dec. 36.				
37	0	𝔅 Philip Joshua Perceval,¹⁰ *2nd Lieut.* Royal Marines, 2 July, 03; *1st Lieut.* 15 Aug. 05; *Ens.* Grenadier Guards, 11 June, 11; *Lieut. & Capt.* 10 March, 14; *Capt. & Lieut.-Col.* 10 Jan. 37.				
29	0	𝔅 ᏟᏚ Wm. Fred. Johnston,¹¹ *Ens.* p 12 Dec. 11; *Lieut. & Capt.* 16 March, 14; *Capt. & Lieut.-Col.* 10 Jan. 37.				
18	10/12	Jas. Robertson Craufurd, *Ens.* 14 June, 21; *Ens. & Lieut.* p 29 Aug. 22; *Lieut. & Capt.* p 19 Sept. 26; *Capt. & Lieut.-Col.* p 18 Feb. 37.				
17	0	Fred. Clinton, *Ens. & Lieut.* p 19 Nov. 23; *Lieut. & Capt.* p 10 May, 27; *Capt. & Lieut.-Col.* p 12 Jan. 38.				
17	0	Richard Wm. Astell, *Ens. & Lieut.* p 20 Nov. 23; *Lieut. & Capt.* p 13 Sept. 27; *Capt. & Lieut.-Col.* p 7 July, 38.				
16	3 5/12	Thomas Wood, *Cornet,* p 16 Nov. 20; *Lieut.* p 12 June 23; *Capt.* p 25 June 25; *Brev.-Maj.* 28 June 38; *Capt. & Lieut.-Col.* p 28 June, 39.				

		LIEUTS. AND CAPTAINS.	COR. 2D LT. OR ENSIGN.	ENSIGN AND LIEUT.	LIEUT. AND CAPTAIN.	BREVET-MAJOR.
16	0	George M'Kinnon	29 June 24	p 4 Nov. 24	p 21 Feb. 28	
16	0	Charles Bagot..........	5 Aug. 24	24 Feb. 25	p 30 Dec. 28	
15	0	Geo. Aug. Fred. Houstoun	....	p 2 Apr. 25	p 11 June 30	
15	0	Arth. Wellesley Torrens	....	14 Apr. 25	12 June 30	
15	0	*Hon.* Ch. J. Fox. Stanley	....	p 27 Apr. 25	p 18 June 30	
15	0	Hugh Fitz Roy	....	p 7 July 25	20 Nov. 30	
15	0	John Dixon............	....	p 10 Dec. 25	p 1 Dec. 30	
14	0	William Thornton	....	p 8 Apr. 26	p 3 Dec. 30	
13	0	*Hon.* Fr. Grosvenor Hood	....	p 30 Apr. 27	p 31 Dec. 30	
12	0	Charles Wm. Ridley	....	p 21 Feb. 28	p 14 June 31	
12	0	*Hon.* Aug. Fred. Foley..	....	p 30 Dec. 28	p 16 Mar. 32	
14	0	Charles Stuart	p 30 Dec. 26	p 31 Dec. 28	p 26 July 32	
10	0	G. Herb. Fred. Campbell	....	p 11 June 30	p 27 July 32	
15	4/12	Henry Penleaze	p 23 June 25	p 20 May 26	p 12 Feb. 30	
11	0	Edw. Birch Reynardson	p 5 Nov. 29	p 12 June 30	p 12 Oct. 32	
10	0	*Hon.* Robert Bruce	....	p 18 June 30	p 22 Feb. 33	
15	0	Chris. Hamp. Nicholson..	p 3 Mar. 25	p 14 Jan. 26	p 5 July 31	
11	0	John Spottiswoode......	p 12 Mar. 29	p 29 June 30	p 4 Oct. 33	
10	0	Joseph Henry Hudson ..	....	6 July 30	p 29 Nov. 33	
10	0	Percy Aug. Evans Freke	....	p 28 Sept. 30	p 27 Dec. 33	
10	0	Wm. Fra. Joseph Lautour	....	p 26 Nov. 30	p 2 May 34	
10	0	Henry C. Compton	....	p 2 Dec. 30	p 9 May 34	
10	0	*Hon.* Wm. Leicester ...	....	p 3 Dec. 30	p 12 Sept. 34	
14	1	Chas. Algernon Lewis ..	p 13 Oct. 25	p 15 Aug. 26	p 12 Apr. 33	
9	0	Jas. Walker Drummond	....	p 31 May 31	p 1 July 36	
13	0	Rob. Blenkinsop Coulson	15 Nov. 27	p 14 June 31	p 29 July 36	
9	0	Fred. Wm. Hamilton....	....	12 July 31	1 Dec. 36	
8	0	*Hon.* James Lindsay....	....	p 16 Mar. 32	p 2 Dec. 36	
10	0	Francis Chas. Joddrell ..	p 11 June 30	p 11 May 32	p 18 Feb. 37	
8	0	Ar. W. Fitz Roy Somerset	....	18 May 32	p 24 Feb. 37	
8	0	Henry Cartwright......	....	p 26 July 32	p 2 June 37	
8	0	Augustus Cox..........	....	p 27 July 32	p 8 Aug. 37	
7	0	*Hon.* Geo. Cadogan	....	p 22 Feb. 33	p 9 Jan. 38	
7	0	Hen. Geo. Conroy......	....	p 21 June 33	p 12 Jan. 38	
7	0	Hugh And. Robt. Mitchell	....	p 4 Oct. 33	p 7 July 38	
7	0	John Home Purves	....	p 29 Nov. 33	p 13 July 38	
7	0	Edward Goulburn	....	p 27 Dec. 33	p 14 July 38	
8	0	*Hon.* Montagu P. Bertie	p 13 July 32	p 21 Mar. 34	p 28 June 39	

1st (or Grenadier) Regiment of Foot Guards.

Years' Serv					
Full Pay.	Half Pay.				

ENSIGNS AND LIEUTENANTS.

Full	Half				
6	0	Frederick William Allix	p 18 Apr. 34	George Grey Rous......	p 24 Feb. 37
6	0	Hon. Alexander Gordon	p 2 May 34	Hon. Rd. C. Neville....	p 2 June 37
6	0	G. J. Fr. *Visc.* Cantilupe	p 9 May 34	Robert Peel Dawson....	p 8 Aug. 37
5	0	Henry Torrens D'Aguilar	29 May 35	Edward G. Wynyard....	p 9 Jan. 38
5	0	Rt. Cav. Spencer Clifford	p 5 June 35	*Ens.* 69th Ft. 12 May, 37	
5	0	John Arthur Lambert ..	p 10 July 35	Edw. Wm. Pakenham ..	p 12 Jan. 38
10	0	Hervey Hopwood	p 24 July 35	Thomas Lloyd Fitzhugh	p 12 July 38
		Ens. 51st Ft. p 21 Sept. 30		Harry B. Trelawny	p 13 July 38
5	0	John Augustus Udny....	p 13 Nov. 35	*Hon.* R. W. Penn Curzon	p 14 July 38
4	0	*Hon.* Hen. H. M. Percy	p 1 July 36	Henry B. Powell	p 28 June 39
4	0	Charles *Lord* Blantyre ..	p 29 July 36	*Ens.* 10th Ft. 22 Sept. 37	
4	0	Richard Henry Glynn ..	p 2 Dec. 36	Sandford Graham.......	p 30 Aug. 39
3	0	John Temple West......	p 18 Feb. 37	Jas. Townsend Oswald ..	p 6 Dec. 39
3	0	*Hon.* H. T. Forester	23 Feb. 37	*Ens.* 35 Ft. 11 Jan. 39	
9	0	*Adjutants.*—F. W. Hamilton, (*Capt.*) 22 July, 36.			
13	0	Hon. F. G. Hood, (*Capt.*) 17 March, 37.			
8	0	Hon. J. Lindsay, (*Capt.*) 23 March, 38.			
25	0	*Quarter-Masters.*—p 1 John Payne, 31 Aug. 15.			
11	0	Richard France, 24 Dec. 29.			
10	0	John Lilley, 8 June, 30.			
31	0	*Surgeon-Major.*—p 1 John Harrison,[12] 17 March, 37 ; *Batt.-Surg.* 29 April, 24 ; *Assist.-Surg.* 29 June, 09.			
		Battalion-Surgeon.—Jas. Johnson, 13 March, 28 ; *Assist.-Surg.* 25 July, 13.			
16	0	Jas. Dennis Wright, 11 May, 32 ; *Assist.-Surg.* 11 Nov. 24.			
		Assistant-Surgeons.—			
		Wm. Bowes Daykin, 15 June, 26 ; *Hosp.-Assist.* 16 June, 25.			
		George Brown, 12 Jan. 26 ; *Hosp.-Assist.* 21 April, 25.			
		Fra. Cornelius Huthwaite, 10 Nov. 25 ; *Hosp.-Assist.* 16 Nov. 23.			
		George Eleazar Blenkins, 13 April, 38.			
		Solicitor.—John Parkinson, 19 July, 31.			
		1st *Battalion returned from Portugal,* 1828.			
		2d *Battalion embarked for Canada, April,* 1838.			
		3d *Battalion returned from France, Nov.* 1818.			
		Facings Blue.—*Agent,* Messrs. Cox & Co.			

War Office, 20th July, 1815.

THE PRINCE REGENT, as a mark of His Royal Approbation of the distinguished gallantry of the Brigade of Foot Guards in the Victory of Waterloo, has been pleased, in the name and on the behalf of His Majesty, to approve of all the Ensigns of the Three Regiments of Foot Guards having the Rank of Lieutenants, and that such Rank shall be attached to all the future Appointments to Ensigncies in the Foot Guards, in the same manner as the Lieutenants in those Regiments obtain the Rank of Captain.

His Royal Highness has also been pleased to approve of the First Regiment of Foot Guards being made a Regiment of Grenadiers, and styled " *The First, or Grenadier Regiment of Foot Guards,*" in commemoration of their having defeated the Grenadiers of the French Imperial Guards upon this memorable occasion.

1 The Duke of Wellington has received a cross and nine clasps for Roleia and Vimiera, Talavera, Busaco, Fuentes d'Onor, Ciudad Rodrigo, Badajoz, Salamanca, Vittoria, Pyrenees, Nivelle, Nive, Orthes, and Toulouse. To sketch an outline of the pre-eminent services of the greatest soldier of the age, would far exceed the limits of this work.

2 Col. Lambert served the campaign under Sir John Moore in 1809; expedition to Walcheren; Cadiz, 1810 and 11; Peninsula, 1812, 13, and 14; was Adjutant at Corunna and Barrosa.

3 Col. Grant served Sir John Moore's campaign in 1809, including battle of Corunna; expedition to Walcheren; Peninsula, 1812, 13, and 14.

4 Col. Ellison served at Cadiz in 1811; the Peninsula in 1812, 13, and 14; battles of Quatre Bras and Waterloo, and taking of Peronne, 26th June, 1815. Received the Brevet rank of Major for his conduct at Waterloo.

5 Col. Higginson served the campaign of 1809, including the battle of Corunna. Served in the Walcheren expedition, and in the Peninsula, in 1812, 13, and 14.

6 Col. Clive served in the Peninsula in 1814. Present at the battles of Quatre Bras, and Waterloo, and taking of Peronne.

7 Col. Davies was wounded at Badajoz.

8 Col. Lascelles served in the Peninsula in 1814. Present at the battles of Quatre Bras and Waterloo, and taking of Peronne.

9 Col. Boldero served at Cadiz in 1810 and 11; in the Peninsula in 1812 and 13; and in Holland in 1814. Was Adjutant at the battles of Quatre Bras, Waterloo, and taking of Peronne.

10 Col. Perceval served in the Peninsula in 1813 and 14, and was severely wounded at Bayonne, 14th April, 1814.

11 Col. Johnston served in the Peninsula in 1814. Was present at the battles of Quatre Bras and Waterloo, and taking of Peronne.

12 Doctor Harrison served in the Walcheren Expedition, 1809; at Cadiz and in the Peninsula in 1811, 12, and 13; expedition to Holland, 1814; Netherlands and France from 1814 till 1818. Present at the assault of Seville, bombardment of Antwerp, storming of Bergen-op-Zoom, battles of Quatre Bras and Waterloo, and taking of Peronne.

Coldstream Regiment of Foot Guards.

"LINCELLES."—The *Sphinx*, with the words "EGYPT"—"TALAVERA"—
"BARROSA"—"PENINSULA"—"WATERLOO."

Years' Serv.		
Full Pay.	Half Pay.	
42		*Colonel.* His Royal Highness A. F. *Duke of Cambridge*, K.G. G.C.B. G.C.M.G. G.C.H. *Lieut.-Gen.* 24 Aug. 1798; *Gen.* 25 Sept. 03; *Field-Marshal*, 26 Nov. 13; *Colonel*, Coldstream Guards, 5 Sept. 05.
		Lieut.-Colonel.
34	0	ᛃ ᛞᛒ Wm. LovelaceWalton,[1] *Ens.* p 8 May, 06; *Lieut. & Capt.* 7 Mar. 11; *Capt. & Lieut.-Col.* p 20 Feb. 23; *Major*, with rank of *Col.* 10 Jan. 37; *Lieut.-Col.* p 31 Dec. 39.
		Majors.
32	0	ᛃ Charles Augustus Shawe,[2] *Ens.* p 26 May, 08; *Lieut. & Capt.* p 23 April, 12; *Capt. & Lieut.-Col.* p 28 April, 25; *Major*, with rank of *Col.* p 8 Aug. 37.
36	0	ᛃ ᛞᛒ George Bowles,[3] *Ens.* p 20 Dec. 04; *Lieut. & Capt.* p 1 Feb. 10; *Brevet-Major*, 18 June, 15; *Brevet-Lieut.-Col.* 14 June, 21; *Capt. & Lieut.-Col.* 27May, 25; *Brevet-Col.* 10 Jan. 37; *Major* with rank of *Colonel* p 31 Dec. 39.
		Captains & Lieut.-Colonels.
32	0	ᛃ ᛞᛒ Chas. Ant. Fred. Bentinck,[4] *Ens.* 16 Nov. 08; *Lieut. & Capt.* 24 Sept. 12; *Brevet-Major*, 18 June, 15; *Capt. & Lieut.-Col.* 27 May, 25; *Col.* 28 June, 38.
29	0	ᛃ Thomas Chaplin,[5] *Ens.* p 18 April, 11; *Lieut. & Capt.* 6 Oct. 14; *Lieut.-Col.* p 15 Aug. 26.
27	0	Henry John Wm. Bentinck, *Ens.* 25 Mar. 13; *Lieut. & Capt.* 18 Jan. 20; *Capt. & Lieut.-Col.* p 16 May, 29.
23	1 10/12	Wm. Henry Cornwall, *Ens. & Lieut.* 10 Aug. 15; *Lieut. & Capt.* p 6 Nov. 24; *Capt. & Lieut.-Col.* p 10 Feb. 32.
20	2 8/12	Brinckman Broadhead, *Ens. & Lieut.* p 11 Sept. 17; *Lieut. & Capt.* p 28 April, 25; *Capt. & Lieut.-Col.* p 20 April, 32.
20	0	Chas. Murray Hay, *Ens.* p 20 April, 20; *Ens. & Lieut.* p 1 Nov. 21; *Lieut. & Capt.* p 24 Dec. 25; *Capt. & Lieut.-Col.* p 22 June, 32.
28	0	ᛞᛒ Henry Gooch,[6] *Ens.* 23 July, 12; *Lieut. & Capt.* p 28 Oct. 19; *Capt. & Lieut.-Col.* 26 Nov. 32.
18	0	John Dawson Rawdon, *Ens.* 12 Dec. 22; *Ens. & Lieut.* p 30 Jan. 23; *Lieut. & Capt.* p 10 June, 26; *Capt. & Lieut.-Col.* p 15 Nov. 33.
18	0	Hon. Thos. Ashburnham, *Ens. & Lieut.* p 30 Jan. 23; *Lieut. & Capt.* p 22 June, 26; *Capt. & Lieut.-Col.* p 27 Mar. 35.
18	1	Wm. John Codrington, *Ens.* p 22 Feb. 21; *Ens. & Lieut.* p 24 April, 23; *Lieut. & Capt.* p 20 July, 26; *Capt. & Lieut.-Col.* p 8 July, 36.
17	0	Ely Duodecimus Wigram, *Ens. & Lieut.* p 29 May, 23; *Lieut. & Capt.* p 1 Aug. 26; *Capt. & Lieut.-Col.* p 13 Jan. 37.
17	2 1/12	Wm. Stewart Balfour, *Ens.* p 8 Feb. 21; *Lieut.* p 12 May, 25; *Capt.* p 17 June, 26; *Capt. & Lieut.-Col.* p 24 Feb. 37.
16	0	Hon. James Hope, *Ens. & Lieut.* p 8 April, 24; *Lieut. & Capt.* p 30 Dec. 26; *Capt. & Lieut.-Col.* p 8 Aug. 37.
16	1 7/12	George Knox, *Cornet*, p 15 May, 23; *Lieut.* p 15 June, 25; *Capt.* p 20 May, 26; *Capt. & Lieut.-Col.* p 27 July, 38.
15	0	Hon. Arthur Upton *Ens. & Lieut.* p 10 Feb. 25; *Lieut. & Capt.* p 16 May, 29; *Capt. & Lieut.-Col.* p 31 Dec. 39.
17	0	Frederick Paget, *Ensign*, 20 Mar. 23; *Ens. & Lieut.* 24 Feb. 25; *Lieut. & Capt.* p 4 June 29; *Capt. & Lieut.-Col.* p 24 Jan. 40.

1 Col. Walton's services :—Siege of Copenhagen in 1807; campaigns of 1809, 1810, and the first part of 1811, in the Peninsula, including the Passage of the Douro, battles of Talavera and Busaco, retreat to the Lines of Torres Vedras, and the subsequent advance to the Spanish frontier. Served also in Holland, Belgium and France, from Nov. 1813 to Nov. 1818, including the battle of Waterloo.

2 Colonel Shawe served the campaigns of 1810, 1811, and part of 1812, in the Peninsula, including the battle of Busaco. Served also in Holland and Belgium from Nov. 1813 to Sept. 1814, and was severely wounded at Bergen-op-Zoom.

3 Colonel Bowles served in the north of Germany in 1805 & 6, under Lord Cathcart. Present at the siege and capture of Copenhagen in 1807. In the Peninsula from 1809 to 1814 (excepting the winters of 1810 and 11), and was present at the passage of the Douro; battles of Talavera, Salamanca, and Vittoria; sieges of Ciudad Rodrigo, Badajoz, Burgos, and San Sebastian; capture of Madrid; passages of the Bidassoa, Nivelle, Nive, and Adour; and the investment of Bayonne. Present at the battles of Quatre Bras and Waterloo, and at the capture of Paris.

4 Colonel Charles Bentinck was wounded at Barrosa.

5 Col. Chaplin was severely wounded at St. Sebastian.

6 Col. Gooch served in Holland in 1814, and commanded an advanced party in protection of the ladders at the attack on Bergen-op-Zoom. Present with the Light Companies of the second Brigade of Guards at the battle of Quatre Bras, and assisted in the defence of Hougoamont at the battle of Waterloo.

Coldstream Regiment of Foot Guards.

Years' Serv. Full Pay.	Years' Serv. Half Pay.	LIEUTENANTS AND CAPTAINS.	CORNET, 2D LIEUT. OR ENSIGN.	ENSIGN AND LIEUT.	LIEUT. AND CAPTAIN.	BREVET-MAJOR.
15	0	Hon. E. B. Wilbraham..	....	p 28 April 25	p 13 Aug. 29	
15	0	Lord M. W. Graham....	....	p 10 May 25	p 16 Mar. 30	
15	0	John Henry Pringle	....	p 24 Dec. 25	15 June 30	
15	0	John Christie Clitherow..	11 April 25	p 8 April 26	22 July 30	
14	0	Gordon Drummond	....	p 10 June 26	p 3 Aug. 30	
14	0	Lord Fred. Paulet......	....	11 June 26	p 21 Sept. 30	
14	0	Christ. Wilmot Horton..	....	p 29 June 26	p 27 Jan. 32	
15	0	John Forbes	p 20 Oct. 25	p 1 Aug. 26	p 10 Feb. 32	
14	0	Robert Vansittart	....	p 21 Sept. 26	26 Nov. 32	
14	0	Charles Ash Windham ..	....	p 30 Dec. 26	p 31 May 33	
12	0	Chas. Philip Wilbraham ..	....	p 21 Nov. 28	p 1 June 33	
11	0	James Loftus Elrington..	....	p 4 June 29	p 5 Dec. 34	
11	0	Henry Daniell..........	....	p 13 Aug. 29	p 27 Mar. 35	
13	6/12	Hon. Rob. Edw. Boyle..	p 14 Nov. 26	p 16 July 29	p 23 Aug. 33	
10	0	Frederick Halkett	....	p 11 June 30	p 8 July 36	
10	0	Rich. Samuel Hulse	....	p 21 Sept. 30	p 21 April 37	
9	0	Stephen Rowley Conroy	....	p 27 Jan. 32	p 8 Aug. 37	
9	0	Hon. F. W. C. Villiers ..	....	p 10 Feb. 32	p 27 July 38	
8	0	Henry Brand	....	p 20 April 32	p 25 Dec. 38	
7	0	J. Du Pre, *Earl of* Caledon	....	p 31 May 33	p 5 July 39	
7	0	George John Johnson ..	....	p 15 Nov. 33	p 19 July 39	
6	0	Wm. Samuel Newton	....	p 5 Dec. 34	p 31 Dec. 39	
6	0	Hon. Charles Grimston..	....	6 Dec. 34	p 24 Jan. 40	
		ENSIGNS AND LIEUTS.				
5	0	George V. Mundy	....	27 Feb. 35		
6	0	Peter James Bathurst ..	28 Nov. 34	p 27 Mar. 35		
5	0	Egerton C. W. M. Milman	....	p 24 April 35		
4	0	Hon. Louis Hope	....	p 8 July 36		
4	0	Spencer Perceval	....	p 13 Jan. 37		
4	0	Hon. A. E. Paget Graves	....	3 Feb. 37		
3	0	Matthew Edw. Tierney..	....	p 10 Mar. 37		
3	0	Wm. Capel Clayton	....	p 21 April 37		
3	0	Hon. T. Vesey Dawson ..	....	p 11 Aug. 37		
3	0	Thomas M. Steele	12 Jan. 38	p 20 July 38		
3	0	J. A. Vesey Kirkland....	p 22 Aug. 37	p 27 July 38		
2	0	Adolphus F. A. Woodford	....	p 25 Dec. 38		
1	0	Jas. Richard Wigram....	....	p 5 July 39		
1	0	John Wingfield S. Fraser	....	p 19 July 39		
2	0	Charles H. White	11 Jan. 39	p 31 Dec. 39		
1	0	Charles Lygon Cocks ..	....	p 24 Jan. 40		

Adjutants.
14	0	C. W. Horton, (*Captain*) 10 Feb. 32.
14	0	Lord Fred. Paulet (*Captain*) 25 Dec. 38.
4	0	*Quarter-Masters.*—William Morse, 2 June, 36.
3	0	Thomas Lee, 25 July, 37.
20	6 2/12	*Surgeon-Major.*— ᴘ ᴍ W. Hunter,[7] M.D. 16 Mar. 38 ; *Surg.* 4 Sept. 36 ; *Assist.-Surg.* 10 Feb. 14.
23	3 6/12	*Battalion-Surgeon.*—ᴍ F. Gilder. 16 Mar. 38 ; *Assist-Surg.* 9 June, 14.

Assistant-Surgeons.
4	0	James Wedderburn, 21 Oct. 36.
		Edw. Greatrex, 16 Nov. 26 ; *Hosp.-Assist.* 24 Nov. 25.
2	0	Wm. Thos. Chris. Robinson, 23 Mar. 38.
		Solicitor.—William George Carter, 29 Jan. 24.

Facings Blue—*Agent*, Messrs. Cox & Co.

[1st Battalion returned from France, *July*, 1814.]
[2d Battalion embarked for Canada *April*, 1838.]

7 Doctor Hunter served in the Peninsula, and was present during the blockade of Bayonne.

Scots Fusilier Guards.

"LINCELLES"—The "*Sphynx*," with the words, "EGYPT"—"TALAVERA"—"BARROSA" "PENINSULA"—"WATERLOO."

Years' Serv.		
Full Pay.	Half Pay.	
62		**Colonel.** George James, *Earl* Ludlow,[1] G.C.B. *Ens.* 17 May, 1778; *Lieut. & Capt.* 16 March, 81; *Capt. & Lieut.-Col.* 24 Nov. 90; *Col.* 21 Aug. 95; *Major-Gen.* 18 June, 98; *Lieut.-Gen.* 30 Oct. 1805; *Gen.* 4 June, 14; *Col.* Scots Fusilier Guards, 30 May, 36.
		Lieut.-Colonel.
35	0	ẞ John Aitchison,[2] *Ens.* p 25 Oct. 05; *Lieut. & Capt.* 22 Nov.10 : *Capt. & Lieut.-Col.* p 15 Dec. 14; *Major*, with rank of *Col.* p 20 May, 36; *Lieut.-Col.* p 11 Aug. 37.
		Majors.
35	0	ẞ Wm. Henry Scott,[4] *Ens.* 27 Oct. 05; *Lt. & Capt.* 28 Mar. 11; *Capt. & Lt.-Col.* 5 July, 15; *Brevet-Col.* 10 Jan. 37; *Major*, with rank of *Col.* p 11 Aug. 37.
34	0	ẞ ҉ William Drummond,[5] *Ens.* p 20 March, 06; *Lieut. & Capt.* 24 Oct. 11; *Brevet-Major*, 18 June, 15; *Capt. & Lieut.-Col.* p 4 July, 16; *Brevet-Col.* 10 Jan. 37; *Major*, with rank of *Col.* p 1 Nov. 39.
		Captains and Lieut.-Colonels.
28	0	҉ Berkeley Drummond,[6] *Ens.* 5 March, 12; *Lieut. & Capt.* 4 July, 15: *Capt. & Lieut.-Col.* p 21 Dec. 26.
28	0	҉ George Douglas Standen,[7] *Ens.* 19 March. 12; *Lieut. & Capt.* 6 July, 15; *Capt. & Lieut.-Col.* p 12 July, 27.
27	2/12	ẞ William Thomas Knollys,[8] *Ens.* 9 Dec. 13; *Lieut. & Capt.* 25 Sept. 17; *Capt. & Lieut.-Col.* p 31 Dec. 27.
27	2/12	Henry Colvile, *Ens.* p 29 Dec. 13; *Lieut. & Capt.* p 6 Nov. 17; *Capt. & Lieut.-Col.* p 6 July, 30.
28	3 4/12	ẞ Henry Robert Digby,[9] *Ens.* p 26 Jan. 09; *Lieut.* p 1 March, 10; *Capt.* p 2 Dec. 13; *Capt. & Lieut.-Col.* p 20 July, 30.
26	0	҉ *Hon.* Hen. Montagu,[11] *Ens.* 21 April, 14; *Lieut. & Capt.* p 12 June, 23 : *Capt. & Lieut.-Col.* p 21 Sept. 32.
26	0	*Hon.* J. Craven Westenra, *Ens.* 4 May, 14; *Capt.* p 23 Sept. 24; *Capt. & Lieut.-Col.* p 9 Aug. 33.
26	0	Philip James Yorke, *Ens.* 5 May, 14; *Lieut. & Capt.* p 24 Feb. 25 : *Capt. & Lieut.-Col.* p 7 Aug. 35.
21	0	George Dixon, *Ens. & Lieut.* p 20 Jan. 20; *Capt.* p 8 April, 26; *Capt. & Lieut.-Col.* p 20 May, 36.
20	0	*Hon.* C. Beaumont Phipps, *Ens. & Lieut.* p 17 Aug. 20; *Lieut. & Capt.* p 12 Oct. 26; *Capt. & Lieut.-Col.* p 26 May, 37.
18	5 2/12	John George Robinson, *Ens. & Lieut.* 23 Jan. 17; *Lieut. & Capt.* p 5 June, 27; *Capt. & Lieut.-Col.* p 12 Aug. 37.
16	0	Patrick Fitz Roy W. Campbell, *2nd Lieut.* 13 Jan. 25; *Ens. & Lieut.* p 14 July, 25; *Lieut. & Capt.* p 3 July, 29; *Capt. & Lieut.-Col.* p 9 Nov. 38.
18	5/12	George Morton Eden, *Ens.* p 18 July,22; *Lieut.* p 10 Sept. 25; *Capt.* p 12 Dec. 26; *Major*, p 11 Oct. 31; *Lieut.-Col.* p 20 May, 36.
15	0	Wm. Fred. Snell, *Ens. & Lieut.* p 13 Aug. 25; *Lieut. & Capt.* p 4 July, 29; *Brevet-Major*, 13 Aug. 31; *Capt. & Lieut.-Col.* p 1 Nov. 39.
17	0	Brownlow Wm. Knox, *Ens.* 8 Jan. 24; *Ens. & Lieut.* p 13 Aug. 25; *Lieut. & Capt.* p 15 June 30; *Capt. & Lieut.-Col.* p 1 Nov. 39.
14	0	George Moncrieffe, *Ens. & Lieut.* p 8 April, 26; *Lieut. & Capt.* p 6 July, 30; *Capt. & Lieut.-Col.* p 24 Jan. 40.

1 Lord Ludlow served in the American war, and was made prisoner at York Town. In 1793 he joined the army in Flanders, and served in the different actions of that and the following campaign until wounded, the 17th May, 1794, near Roubaix, when, having lost his left arm, he returned to England. Lord L. accompanied Sir James Pulteney to the Ferrol, took part in the Egyptian campaign in 1801; commanded a division in the expedition to Hanover in 1805; and was present at the capture of Copenhagen in 1807.

2 Col. Aitchison accompanied the expedition to Copenhagen in 1807. In 1808 proceeded with the army under Sir Arthur Wellesley to the Peninsula, and was present at the passage of the Douro, taking of Oporto, and subsequent pursuit of Soult's army. At Talavera he was wounded in the arm while carrying the King's colour, which was also shot through. He served in the campaigns of 1810, 12, 13, and 14, and was present at Busaco, Salamanca, capture of Madrid, siege of Burgos, battle of Vittoria, siege of San Sebastian, St. Jean de Luz, passage of the Adour, battle of the Nive, investment of and sortie from Bayonne.

4 Colonel Scott proceeded to the Peninsula in 1808, and was present at the passage of the Douro, capture of Oporto, and subsequent pursuit of Soult's army. Wounded through the body at Talavera, and being left there in hospital, was made prisoner by the enemy.

5 Colonel Wm. Drummond served in the Peninsula from 1809 to 1812, including the battles of Busaco, and Fuentes d'Onor, the retreat to the lines of Torres Vedras, and subsequent advance from thence. Served also the campaign of 1814 in Holland, including the bombardment of Antwerp, and storming of Bergen-op-Zoom. Present at Quatre Bras and Waterloo.

6 Colonel B. Drummond served the campaign of 1814 in Holland, including the storming of Bergen-op-Zoom. Present at Quatre Bras and Waterloo.

7 Colonel Standen served the campaign of 1814 in Holland, including the bombardment of Antwerp, and storming of Bergen-op-Zoom. Present at Quatre Bras and Waterloo.

Scots Fusilier Guards.

Years' Serv. Full Pay.	Years' Serv. Half Pay.	LIEUTENANTS AND CAPTAINS.	CORNET, 2D LIEUT. OR ENSIGN.	ENSIGN AND LIEUT.	LIEUT. AND CAPTAIN.	BREVET-MAJOR.
23	1 3/12	Fred. Henry Turner	....	4 July 15	p 26 Oct. 26	
14	0	J. T. Goldie Taubman ..	p 8 April 26	p 10 June 26	p 20 July 30	
14	0	Nathaniel Micklethwaite		p 12 Oct. 26	p 31 Dec. 30	
15	0	Henry Bathurst.........	p 17 Nov. 25	p 5 April 27	p 11 June 30	
14	0	Wm. Fred. Elrington....		p 14 Nov. 26	p 30 Aug. 31	
13	0	Edw. Walter Walker....		p 8 Mar. 27	p 18 Oct. 31	11 Col. Montagu was present at Quatre Bras and Waterloo.
13	0	Chas. John Jas. Hamilton		p 5 June 27	p 6 Jan. 32	
13	0	Fras. Hugh Geo. Seymour		p 12 July 27	24 Aug. 32	
13	0	Delmé Seymour Davies..		p 13 July 27	p 31 Aug. 32	
12	0	Hon. Geo. A. F. Liddell		p 27 Nov. 28	p 24 April 35	12 Quarter-Master Aston served the campaign of 1814 in Holland, including the bombardment of Antwerp, and storming of Bergen-op-Zoom. Presen at Quatre Bras and Waterloo.
11	0	Frederick Brandreth		p 4 July 29	p 5 June 35	
14	0	Frederick Romilly......	p 11 July 26	26 Mar. 29	p 6 June 34	
10	0	R. F. B. Rushbrooke....		p 20 July 30	p 12 Feb. 36	
10	0	Edward Gage*.........		p 26 Oct. 30	p 20 May 36	
9	0	Hon. Alex. Nelson Hood		p 30 Aug. 31	p 1 July 36	
8	0	John Binns Wall		p 31 Aug. 32	p 26 May 37	
10	0	Robert Moorsom	3 Aug. 30	p 21 Sept. 32	p 12 Aug. 37	
8	0	Arthur Edw. Onslow....		p 11 Jan. 33	p 10 Nov. 37	
12	1 3/12	Hon. David Hen. Murray	p 20 Mar. 27	p 9 Nov. 30	p 15 May 35	13 Qu.-Mast. Copeland served in the Peninsula, from March, 1813, to the end of the war, including the battle of Vittoria, siege of San Sebastian, passage of the Bidassoa, Nive, and the Adour, investment of and sortie from Bayonne. Present at Quatre Bras and Waterloo.
5	0	Jas. Hunter Blair......		p 24 April 35	p 9 Nov. 38	
5	0	Chas. Francis Seymour..		p 5 June 35	p 23 Nov. 38	
5	0	William John Ridley....		p 19 June 35	p 24 May 39	
4	0	Hon. C. Grantham Scott		p 12 Feb. 36	p 1 Nov. 39	
6	0	Chas. Tyrwhitt Jones ..	p 1 Aug. 34	p 26 Feb. 36	p 15 Nov. 39	
4	0	Mort. Percy Drummond		p 8 April 36	p 24 Jan. 40	
		ENSIGNS AND LIEUTS.				
4	0	Edward John Stracey ..		p 3 June 36		14 Dr. Good served with the expedition to Copenhagen in 1807; proceeded with the army to the Peninsula in 1808, and served there until the end of the war, including the passage of the Douro, taking of Oporto, battles of Busaco and Fuentes d'Onor, sieges of Ciudad Rodrigo and Badajoz, battle of Salamanca, capture of Madrid, siege of Burgos, battle of Vittoria, siege of San Sebastian, passage of the Bidassoa, the Nive, and the Adour, and investment of Bayonne. Present at Quatre Bras and Waterloo.
4	0	John Dalrymple.......		p 1 July 36		
4	0	Hon. Geo. Anson Byron		p 8 July 36		
3	0	Charles De Salis.......		21 April 37		
3	0	Hon. J. C. Plant Murray		p 26 May 37		
3	0	F. Chas. A. Stephenson.		25 July 37		
4	0	Chas. A. Fitz-H. Berkeley	p 27 May 36	p 12 Aug. 37		
4	0	Thomas Harcourt Powell		p 22 Aug. 37		
3	0	John H. E. Dalrymple..		p 10 Nov. 37		
2	0	Fras. Hastings Russell ..		p 28 Aug. 38		
2	0	Geo. Aug. Constantine, Earl of Mulgrave		p 9 Nov. 38		
2	0	Robt. Dennet Rodney ..		p 23 Nov. 38		
1	0	Hon. Spencer Lyttleton..		p 24 May 39		
1	0	Hen. Percival De Bathe		p 1 Nov. 39		
1	0	Sir A. K. Macdonald, Bt.	p 12 July 39	p 15 Nov. 39		
1	0	Lord Gerald Fitz Gerald		p 24 Jan. 40		
1	0	Geo. Henry Cavendish ..		31 Jan. 40		
13	0	Adjutants.—F. H. G. Seymour, (Captain) 17 Aug. 32.				
13	0	D. S. Davies, (Captain) 14 April, 37.				
7	0	Quarter-Masters.—🅟 🅒🅐 Joseph Aston,[12] 9 Aug. 33.				
3	0	🅟 🅒🅐 George Copeland,[13] 7 April, 37.				
34	0	Surgeon-Major.—🅟 🅒🅐 Samuel Good,[14] 24 Feb. 37; Surg. 25 Dec. 13; Assist.-Surg. 20 Feb. 06.				
		Battal.-Surgeon.—Wm. Henry Judd, 12 July, 27; Assist.-Surg. 1 Jan. 18.				
17	0	Assistant-Surgeons.—Thomas Richardson, 4 Dec. 23.				
13	0	John Bowling, 12 July, 27.				
		Solicitor.—Wilmer Wilmer, 27 Dec. 33.				

Facings Blue.—*Agent*, Messrs. Cox and Co.

[1st *Battalion embarked for the Peninsula Dec.* 1808, *and returned from France July,* 1814.]
[2d *Battalion embarked for the Netherlands Nov.* 1813, *and returned from France Jan.* 1816. *Served in Portugal from Dec.* 1826 *to March,* 1828.

8 Colonel Knollys was present at the Sortie from Bayonne, on which occasion Sir Henry Sullivan and ten officers of the Guards were killed or died of their wounds.

9 Colonel Digby served with the expedition to Walcheren in 1809, and subsequently in the Peninsula, including the siege of Ciudad Rodrigo, retreat from Burgos, battle of Vittoria, affairs at Tarbes and d'Oleron, battles of Orthes and Toulouse.

* Brevet-Major, 28th June, 1388.

1st (or the Royal) Regiment of Foot.

"Egmont-op-Zee."—"St Lucia."—*The Sphinx*, with the words, "Egypt"—"Corunna"—"Busaco"—"Salamanca"—"Vittoria"—"St. Sebastian"—"Nive"—"Peninsula"—"Niagara"—"Waterloo"—"Nagpore"—"Maheidpoor"—"Ava."

Years' Serv.		
Full Pay.	Half Pay.	
47		*Colonel.* 🅑 Thomas *Lord* Lynedoch,[1] G.C.B. & G.C.M.G. *Lieut.-Col.* 10 Feb. 1794; *Col.* 22 July, 95; *Major-Gen.* 25 Sept. 1803; *Lieut.-Gen.* 25 July 10; *Gen.* 19 July 21; *Col.* of the Royals, 12 Dec. 34.
		Lieut.-Colonels.
44	3/12	1 John Carter,[2] K.H. *Ens.* P June, 96; *Lieut.* P 2 July, 96; *Capt.* P 31 Dec. 06; *Major*, 11 Dec. 13; *Lieut.-Col.* P 3 March, 25; *Col.* 28 June, 38.
40	5	2 Geo. Augustus Wetherall,[3] C.B. & K.H. *Lieut.* 7th Fusiliers, 29 July, 95; *Capt.* 13 May, 05; *Brevet-Major*, 12 Aug. 19; *Regtl.-Major, Brevet-Lieut.-Col.* 11 Dec. 24; *Regtl.-Lieut.-Col.* P 7 Aug. 28; *Col.* 28 June, 38.
39	0	*Majors.*—1 🅑 Robert Mullen,[4] K.H. *Adj.* 2 Aug. 01; *Ens.* 25 June, 02; *Lieut.* 25 May, 04; *Capt.* 25 Aug. 09; *Brevet-Major*, 22 July, 30; *Regtl.-Major*, 8 Aug. 33.
33	3 4/12	1 Charles Deane,[5] K.H. *Cornet*, 5 Sept. 04; *Lieut.* P 6 July, 06; *Capt.* P 5 Dec. 18; *Major*, P 19 June, 35.
19	5/12	2 Richard Bennett,[6] *Ens.* 15 March, 21; *Lieut.* P 25 Aug. 23; *Capt.* P 3 Aug. 26; *Major*, P 10 March, 37.
23	7 3/12	2 Dugald M'Nicol, *Ens.* 16 Nov. 09; *Lieut.* 23 July, 12; *Capt.* P 19 Nov. 25; *Major*, 23 May, 38.

		CAPTAINS.	ENSIGN.	LIEUT.	CAPTAIN.	BREV. MAJ.
21	8 7/12	2 🅑 George Bell[8]	14 Mar. 11	17 Feb. 14	P 7 Aug. 28	29 Mar. 39
20	0	2 Burton Daveney	27 April 20	P 7 July 25	P 8 Nov. 27	
27	0	2 George Goodall[9]	P 9 Sept. 13	P 1 Aug. 22	18 May 32	
21	0	2 Ed. A. G. Muller[10]	3 Feb. 20	11 Aug. 25	P 11 Jan. 33	
25	0	1 🅑 R. Blacklin[11]	18 July 15	13 July 20	4 Aug. 33	
16	0	1 A. B. Montgomery	25 Nov. 24	30 Oct. 26	P 16 Aug. 33	
14	0	1 Thomas Graham	21 May 26	P 27 April 27	P 9 Aug. 33	
15	0	2 H. P. Raymond	9 April 25	P 17 May 27	P 21 Mar. 34	
28	7 2/12	1 Thomas Nickoll[12]	23 May 05	29 April 06	8 April 25	28 June 38
14	0	2 Richard Going	9 April 26	P 2 Feb. 27	P 19 June 35	
14	0	2 John Mayne	22 June 26	P 12 April 27	P 5 Feb. 36	
14	0	2 Henry Alex. Kerr	P 17 Aug. 26	22 Mar. 32	P 18 Mar. 36	
16	3	1 Wm. MacPherson	P 22 Nov. 26	22 Sept. 25	P 17 Sept. 36	
10	0	2 Trevor Davenport	8 June 30	P 22 Mar. 33	P 10 Mar. 37	
9	0	1 F. G. Urquhart	P 18 Nov. 31	P 16 Aug. 33	P 14 April 37	
10	0	1 David S. Cooper	P 29 June 30	P 10 May 33	P 2 Feb. 38	
9	0	2 A. A. Macnicol	P 23 Dec. 31	P 23 May 34	P 9 Feb. 38	
21	9	1 John Sampson[13]	29 Nov. 10	9 Dec. 13	23 May 38	
8	0	1 John Money Carter	18 May 32	P 7 Aug. 35	P 17 Sept. 39	
8	0	2 *Lord* Chas. Beauclerk	P 14 Dec. 32	P 5 Feb. 36	P 20 Dec. 39	

1 Lord Lynedoch has received a cross for Barrosa, Ciudad Rodrigo, Vittoria, and St. Sebastian.
2 Col. Carter was present in many of the actions of the Mahratta war, and commanded the Grenadiers of the 84th at the taking of the Isle of France.
3 Col. Wetherall was in action with a squadron of French frigates in the Mosambique channel in June 1810; in the attack of a squadron of French frigates in Port S. E. of the Isle of France in July 1810. At the attack and conquest of Java in 1811, as Aid-de-Camp to Major-General Wetherall.
4 Major Mullen was present at the capture of St. Martin and St. Thomas in 1801; nud of Demerara, Esquibo, and Berbice, in Sept. 1803; attack and capture of Guadaloupe in Feb. 1810, on which occasion, although a captain, and holding the staff appointment of Town Major of St. Ann's, he volunteered to proceed as a subaltern with a company of the 1st Battalion, which formed a part of the 1st Light Infantry Battalion upon that expedition, and resigned his staff appointment for that purpose. Present at the affair of the Pass of Osma in Spain on the 18th; and at the battle of Vittoria, 21st June, 1813; siege of St. Sebastian, and in the assault, 25th July, 1813, when the command of the 3rd Battalion devolved on him, all his seniors having been either killed or severely wounded. The loss sustained by the 3rd Battalion in this assault was 16 officers out of 21, and upwards of 300 non-commissioned officers and privates killed and wounded.
5 Major Deane served the campaign of 1809 against the Rajah of Lahore. Present at the siege of Hatrass and other forts in 1817. Served in the Burmese war in 1825 and 6.
6 Major Bennett served in the Burmese war, and was made prisoner 24th Nov. 1825, when returning sick from Prome to Rangoon, and taken by the enemy to Ava, the capital, and after having experienced the most barbarous treatment, he was given up to Sir Archibald Campbell 18th Feb. 1826. Received a wound over the left temple when taken.
8 Major Bell served in the Peninsula from July 1811 to Aug. 1814, including Arroyo de Molino, Vittoria, Pyrenees, 7th, 25th, 26th, 30th, and 31st July, 1813, Nivelle, Nive, Bayonne, Orthes, and Toulouse, besides a great many affairs and skirmishes. Served in the Burmese war. Actively employed during the rebellion in Canada, particularly at the capture of St. Charles, and St. Eustache; he afterwards commanded the Fort and garrison of Coteau-du-Lac, an important position on the Frontier, and received the thanks of Sir John Colborne for his exertions in recovering the guns and shot from the bottom of the River, and mounting them in position when it was reported impracticable; the guns were 24-pounders, sixteen of which and 4,000 round shot he recovered in the depth of winter, in the very face of the rebels.
9 Capt. Goodall served the campaign of 1814 in Holland, including the action at Merxem, operations before Antwerp, and attack on Bergen-op-Zoom, where he was severely wounded.
10 [For this and other notes, see next page.]

1st (or the Royal) Regiment of Foot.

Years' Serv.					
Full Pay.	Half Pay.	LIEUTENANTS.	ENSIGN.	LIEUT.	
20	0	2 James Richardson [14]	7 April 20	3 Nov. 25	10 Capt. Muller served in the Burmese war.
23	1 5/12	1 John Wells Butt	P 16 Jan. 16	2 Mar. 26	11 Capt. Blucklin, served with the 3rd Batt. Royals at Quatre Bras 16th June, the retreat on the 17th, at Waterloo on the 18th, (at which last he was wounded) and with the army of occupation in France in 1815 & 16. Embarked to join the 2nd battalion in the East Indies, and served with the army in the Deccan the campaigns of 1817, 18, & 19; the pursuit of the Nagpore Rajah; battle of Nagpore, and other minor actions and skirmishes. Served with Sir John Doveton's force in pursuit of the Peishwa; the siege of Asseerghur in 1819, and commanded the leading company at the assault. Served with the 1st Batt. in the West Indies.
20	0	1 John Mullen	13 July 20	3 Mar. 26	
16	0	2 Aug. H. Ormsby [15]	29 June 24	22 Mar. 26	
16	0	1 Tyrrell M. Byrne	30 June 24	23 Mar. 26	
16	0	1 Charles Curtis	10 Feb. 25	19 Feb. 27	
13	0	2 William Webster	20 Feb. 27	P 24 Aug. 32	
10	17 5/12	1 Geo. Rich. Campsie	5 Nov. 12	14 July 14	
10	0	2 Fred. Nicholson	13 June 30	P 24 April 35	
8	0	1 Henry R. Marindin	P 11 Jan. 33	P 18 Mar. 36	
7	0	1 Arch. C. Sanderson	P 15 Feb. 33	P 25 Mar. 36	
7	0	2 Don G. Angus Darroch	P 22 Mar. 33	P 26 Aug. 36	
7	0	2 Thomas Scott Hawkins	P 29 Mar. 33	P 17 Sept. 36	
7	0	1 William Little Stewart	P 12 April 33	13 Jan. 37	
7	0	2 Henry Draper Neville	P 16 Aug. 33	P 20 Jan. 37	
7	0	2 Hon. C. Dawson Plunkett....	P 11 Oct. 33	P 10 Mar. 37	
7	0	2 Frederick R. Mein	22 Oct. 33	P 14 April 37	12 Maj. Nickoll was at the taking of the Danish Islands of St. Croix and St. Thomas in 1807. Thanked in public order for driving away (with the light company of the 90th) an American privateer of large force from off Barbadoes in 1813. Served during the war in Canada in 1814.
6	0	2 Edw. Robert Wetherall	P 27 June 34	P 22 Aug. 37	
6	0	2 Daniel Lysons	P 26 Dec. 34	P 23 Aug. 37	
6	0	2 David Green	P 30 Dec. 34	P 2 Feb. 38	
5	0	2 John Edward Sharp	P 24 April 35	P 9 Feb. 38	
5	0	1 Fra. L. Whitmore	P 7 Aug. 35	10 May 39	
10	18 9/12	1 [?] Arthur Gray [16]	11 July 11	4 Feb. 16	
5	0	1 Arthur Cæsar Hawkins	P 5 Feb. 36	P 18 Sept. 39	13 Capt. Sampson served the campaign in Tuscany, and was in the action before Genoa, and at the capture of that city in 1814. Served in the expedition to the Chesapeak, and in the action of Bladensburgh, and at the capture of Washington, 24th Aug. 1814. Present in the action before Baltimore Sept. 1814. Served in Florida, and was in the action before New Orleans 8th Jan. 1815.
5	0	2 James P. Gore............	P 6 Feb. 36	P 20 Dec. 39	
		ENSIGNS.			
4	0	1 Thomas J. Parker	P 18 Mar. 36		
4	0	1 Edward C. Mullen	P 26 Aug. 36		
4	0	2 W. H. Courtenay..........	P 17 Sept. 36		
4	0	2 Walter Mitchelson	P 20 Jan. 37		14 Lt Richardson served in the Burmese war.
3	0	2 J. D. Windham	P 10 Mar. 37		15 Lieut. Ormsby served in the Burmese war from Sept. 1824 to Jan. 1826, and was present at the siege and capture of Aracan, and in the Talack expedition. Mentioned in Col. Wetherall's despatch for distinguished gallantry in action with the rebels at St. Eustache and St. Benoit, in Canada, 14th Dec. 1837.
3	0	1 Frederick Moor	P 14 April 37		
3	0	2 Edward V. Keane	P 23 Aug. 37		
3	0	1 Charles Y. Edgcombe	P 2 Feb. 38		
2	0	2 Edward S. Claremont	P 9 Feb. 38		
2	0	1 Alexander Gordon	6 April 38		16 Lieut. Gray served in the Peninsula from 1811 to the end of the war, including the battle of Salamanca; surrender of Retiro, Madrid; operations before, siege, and storming of the breaches at Burgos; battles of Vittoria, the Pyrenees, Nivelle, and Orthes, besides a great many affairs and skirmishes. Served the campaign of 1815 in Nepaul (including the battle of Hurripore); and the Mahratta campaigns of 1817 & 18.
2	0	1 John M'Court	13 July 38		
2	0	2 Andrew Anderson	P 19 Oct. 38		
1	0	Cha. Evered Poole	P 10 May 39		
1	0	Arthur Newland	P 18 Sept. 39		
1	0	John Henry Dickson	15 Nov. 39		17 Paymaster Mitchell accompanied his regiment to the Cape of Good Hope, Monte Video, Portugal, Spain, Sicily, Holland, Flanders, and Waterloo.
1	0	Grenville G. Wells	P 20 Dec. 39		

21	13 11/12	Paymasters. — { 1 [?] William Mitchell, [17] 13 Aug. 12; Assist.-Paym. 05.
13	0	{ 2 Wm. Granville Sharp, 1 April, 27.
6	0	Adjutants. — { 2 E. R. Wetherall, (Lieut.) 16 Feb. 38.
2	0	{ 1 John M'Court, (Ens.) 9 Nov. 38.

Quarter-Masters.

| 8 | 16 6/12 | 1 Alexander Imlach, 28 Dec. 32; Ens. 9 Nov. 15. |
| 11 | 15 2/12 | 2 Charles Pieters, 26 June, 35; Ens. 4 Aug. 14; Lieut. 9 Sept. 19. |

Surgeons.

2 G. R. Dartnell, 4 Jan. 39; Assist.-Surg. 20 Oct. 25; Hosp.-Assist. 30 Nov. 20.

| 17 | 8 5/12 | 1 John Hutchison, 6 Sept. 39; Asst.-Surg. 24 April, 17; Hosp.-Asst. 28 June,15. |

8	0	Assistant-Surgeons.- { 1 George Clerihew, M.D. 2 Nov. 32.
6	0	{ 2 Geo. Gordon Robertson, M.D. 12 Aug. 34.
7	0	{ 2 Alexander Knox, M.D. 12 April, 33.
2	0	{ 1 Cardinal Brewster, 30 Oct. 38.

Facings Blue—Agent, Messrs. Cox & Co.

[1st Battalion embarked for Foreign Service, 25 Nov. 39. Serving at Gibraltar.]

[2d Battalion embarked for Canada, 5 July, 36.]

Emb. for Foreign Service, 1825.] **2nd (or Queen's Royal) Regiment of Foot.** [Serving in the East Indies.

"*The Paschal Lamb*," with the mottos "*Pristinæ virtutis memor*," and "*Vel exuviæ triumphant*." The Queen's Cypher within the Garter, having the Crown over it. On the Grenadiers' Caps, the King's Crest and the Queen's Cypher and Crown; and on the Drums the Queen's Cypher. The Sphinx, with the words "EGYPT"—"VIMIERA"—"CORUNNA"—"SALAMANCA"—"VITTORIA"—"PYRENEES"—"NIVELLE"—"TOULOUSE"—"PENINSULA."

Marginal notes (left): Emb. for Foreign Service, 1825. — Serving in the East Indies. — *Captains Lyster and Sealy, Lieutenants Simmons and Holdsworth, were severely wounded in the assault and capture of the Fort of Khelat, in Affghanistan, 13th Nov. 1830; and Lieutenant Dickinson was slightly wounded.*

Years' Serv.		
Full Pay.	Half Pay.	**Colonel.**
57		🏅 Rt. Hon. Sir James Kempt,[1] G.C.B. G.C.H., *Ens.* 31 Mar. 1783; *Lieut.* 18 Aug. 84; *Capt.* 30 May, 94; *Major*, 18 Sept. 94; *Lieut.-Col.* 28 Aug. 99; *Col.* 9 March, 09; *Major-Gen.* 1 Jan. 12; *Lieut.-Gen.* 27 May, 25; *Col.* of the Queen's Royals, 23 Dec. 34.
		Lieut.-Colonels.—🏅 Sir Thos. Willshire,[2] K.C.B. *Ens.* June, 95; *Lieut.* 5 Sept. 95; *Capt.* 28 Aug. 04; *Brevet-Major*, 21 Sept. 13; *Brevet-Lieut.-Col.* 4 Dec. 15; *Regtl.-Major*, 10 Sept. 23; *Regtl.-Lieut.-Col.* 30 Aug. 27; *Col.* 10 Jan. 37.
45	0	
41	7/12	John Gregory Baumgardt,[3] *Ens.* 1 Aug. 98; *Lieut.* 20 March, 01; *Capt.* 10 Jan. 10; *Major*, P 21 Oct. 24; *Lieut.-Col.* P 9 June, 25; *Col.* 28 June, 38.
31	2 2/12	**Majors.**—Redmond Wm. Brough, *Ens.* 10 March, 07; *Lieut.* 15 July, 08; *Capt.* P 10 Jan. 22; *Major*, 29 May, 35.
26	0	Richard Carruthers, *Ens.* 19 May, 14; *Lieut.* 25 Jan. 25; *Capt.* P 16 April, 29; *Major*, P 19 Feb. 36; *Brevet-Lieut.-Col.* 23 July, 39.

		CAPTAINS.	**ENSIGN.**	**LIEUT.**	**CAPTAIN.**	**BREV.-MAJ.**
18	0	Geo. Dalhousie J. Raitt[4]	6 Feb. 23	12 May 25	P 7 June 31	
27	7/12	John Good S. Gilland ..	31 Dec. 12	19 Feb. 17	20 Aug. 31	
31	0	William Greenville	9 Mar. 09	12 Dec. 11	P 1 Jan. 19	10 Jan. 37
20	3 3/12	Wm. Martin Lyster	19 Feb. 17	14 June 21	P 22 Mar. 33	
26	1 5/12	Thomas Meldrum	P 22 July 13	27 Mar. 17	8 Mar. 34	
23	0	John Carney	20 Feb. 17	P 3 Jan. 22	29 May 35	
21	5 8/12	🏅 Mount S. H. Lloyd[5]	16 Dec. 13	2 Mar. 15	13 Sept. 35	
20	0	Oliver Robinson[4]	5 Oct. 20	24 Jan. 25	P 19 Feb. 36	
12	0	Thomas Sealy..........	P 27 Nov. 28	P 15 Mar. 31	P 16 June 37	
20	0	George Stirling	4 May 20	10 Feb. 25	5 Mar. 39	
		LIEUTENANTS.				
16	0	Wm. Nicol Ralph	26 Jan. 25	29 Aug. 26		
14	13	George V. Hamilton	2 Feb. 14	29 Oct. 29		
13	1 4/12	Peter Grehan	P 8 April 26	26 Nov. 30		
13	0	James Stirling	P 10 Jan. 28	21 Aug. 31		
14	1	Henry Reynolds........	P 8 Oct. 25	1 Mar. 33		
14	0	Thomas Wingate	P 13 May 26	17 May 30		
10	0	Medwin R. Pilfold......	1 Feb. 30	16 Mar. 34		
9	0	Hugh Halkett	P 23 Aug. 31	17 Mar. 34		
9	0	Jas. Egbert Simmons[4] ..	20 Jan. 32	29 May 35		
8	0	St. George Hen. Stock ..	P 20 April 32	13 Sept. 35		
10	0	Stanhope Wm. Jephson..	P 26 Nov. 30	P 19 Feb. 36		
7	0	Hon. Edw. Arth. W. Keane	15 Feb. 33	P 11 Mar. 36		
6	0	G. N. K. A. Yonge[4]	P 22 Aug. 34	29 June 37		
5	0	Godfrey Piercy	P 24 July 35	16 April 38		
9	0	J. Aug. Macdonald......	P 10 May 31	11 May 38		
7	0	Edward Honeywood	P 14 June 33	P 28 July 38		
5	0	Hen. Wm. Stisted[4]	P 4 Dec. 35	P 29 Sept. 38		
5	0	Thos. W. E. Holdsworth	P 15 Jan. 36	P 14 Dec. 38		
3	0	Douglas John Dickinson	P 30 June 37	30 Jan. 39		
3	0	Thomas Addison	15 Sept. 37	31 Jan. 39		
5	0	Henry Cole Faulkner....	P 13 Nov. 35	P 18 May 39		
2	0	Henry Piercy	P 9 Mar. 38	30 Dec. 39		
		ENSIGNS.				
2	0	J. Hardie Kippen	P 3 Aug. 38			
2	0	Frederick Connor	P 29 Sept. 38			
2	0	Robert Stephenson	P 23 Mar. 38			
2	0	Henry Cox	14 Dec. 39			
1	0	Louis J. M'Pherson	6 Sept. 39			
1	0	Charles Darby	6 Sept. 39			
1	0	Demetrius W. G. James..	P 31 Jan. 40			
13	0	*Paymaster.*—James Moore, 18 Aug. 37; *Ens.* 6 Feb. 27; *Lieut.* 20 Aug. 31.				
12	0	*Adjutant.*—Jas. Egbert Simmons, (*Lieut.*) 11 June, 36.				
15	0	*Quarter-Master.*—W. H. S. Hadley,[4] 12 Aug. 36; *Ens.* 10 Ap. 25; *Lt.* 24 Sept. 31.				
25	3 7/12	*Surg.*—🏅 Wm. H. Young,[7] 4 Sept. 28; *Assist.-S.* 4 Feb. 13; *H.A.* 19 Dec. 11.				
13	0	*Assist.-Surg.*—Rob. Hope Alston Hunter, 15 June, 30; *Hosp.-Asst.* 10 Jan. 27.				
1	0	James Jopp, M.D., 22 Feb. 39.				

Facings Blue.—**Agent,** Mr. Lawrie, Charles-street, St. James's.

Side notes (right):
[1] Sir James Kempt has received a Cross and three Clasps for Maida, Badajos, Vittoria, Nivelle, Nive, Orthes, and Toulouse, and was severely wounded at Waterloo.
[2] Sir T. Willshire's services: Battles of Roleia and Vimiera; campaign and battle of Corunna; expedition to Walcheren; Peninsula from June, 1812 to May, 1814, including battle of Salamanca (twice wounded); retreat from Burgos, and action at Villa Murilla 25th Oct. 1812; battle of Vittoria; first assault of San Sebastian; also second assault and capture; crossing the Bidassoa; Nivelle; Nive, 9th, 10th, and 11th Dec. 1813. Repulsed with 300 men the attack of 10,000 Caffres upon the open village of Graham's Town, on the frontiers of the Cape of Good Hope; capture of Kittoor, in the Dooab, E. Ind. Dec. 1824.
[3] Col. Baumgardt was present at every siege, battle, and in every campaign in which the 8th Hussars were eng. in India.
[4] Capt. Raitt, Lieuts. Simmons, Stisted, and Hadley were slightly wounded; Capt. Robinson, and Lieut. Yonge, severely, in the assault and capture of the fortress and citadel of Ghuznee, in Affghanistan, 23 July, 1839.
[5] Capt. Lloyd was at Waterloo 18th June; taking of Cambray, 24th June, 1815, and capture of Paris. Served one campaign latter part of 1826 against the Rajah of Kolapore.

6 Dr. Young served in the Peninsula, from March, 1811 to Feb. 1813, including the siege of Badajoz, April, 1812, and battle of Salamanca. Served also the campaigns of 1813 and 14 in Germany and Holland, including the attack on Bergen-op-Zoom. Present on the 18th June at Waterloo.

Emb. for For. Service, 1822.] **3d (or East Kent) Regiment of Foot (or Buffs.)** [Serving in the East Indies.

Years' Serv		
54		
Full Pay.	Half Pay.	
44	0	
16	7 3/12	
35	0	
23	3 6/12	

The *Dragon* "DOURO" "TALAVERA" "ALBUHERA" "PYRENEES" "NIVELLE" "NIVE" "PENINSULA."

Colonel.

₽ Kenneth Alexander, *Earl* of Effingham,¹ G.C.B., *Ens.* 21 April, 1786; *Capt.* 25 April, 93; *Lieut.-Col.* 30 Dec. 97; *Col.* 1 Jan. 1805; *Major-Gen.* 25 July, 10; *Lieut.-Gen.* 12 Aug. 19; *Gen.* 10 Jan. 37; *Col.* of the Buffs, 30 Jun. 32.

Lieut.-Colonels.—James Dennis,² *Ens.* 2 Sept. 96; *Lieut.* 12 April, 97; *Capt.* 6 Aug. 03; *Brevet-Major*, 13 Oct. 12; *Brevet-Lieut.-Col.* 27 May, 25; *Regtl.-Major*, 25 Apr. 28; *Regtl.-Lieut.-Col.* 4 June, 33; *Col.* 28 June, 38.

Marcus Beresford, *Second Lieut.* ₽ 4 Sept. 17; *Lieut.* 1 Feb. 21; *Capt.* ₽ 16 Sept. 24; *Major*, ₽ 26 Sept. 26; *Lieut.-Col.* ₽ 6 Nov. 27.

Majors.—Gerald Rochfort,³ *Ens.* ₽ 28 Feb. 05; *Lieut.* 25 Sept. 05; *Capt.* 1 July, 12; *Major*, ₽ 1 May, 28.

Jas. O. Clunie,⁴ *Ens.* 27 Aug. 13; *Lieut.* 1 Dec. 14; *Capt.* ₽ 9 Feb. 26; *Major*, ₽ 23 June, 38.

		CAPTAINS.	ENSIGN.	LIEUT.	CAPTAIN.	BREV.-MAJ.
20	6 5/12	Basil H. Burchell	25 Dec. 13	8 April 25	₽ 30 Dec. 26	
18	0	Gustavus L. Christie	₽ 20 June 22	25 Mar. 26	₽ 17 Jan. 28	
25	3 2/12	Patrick M'Kie⁵	3 Nov. 12	3 Nov. 14	₽ 3 Oct. 29	
15	0	Marcus Barr	₽ 24 Feb. 25	₽ 8 April 26	₽ 11 June 30	
17	2/12	John Michel	₽ 3 April 23	₽ 28 April 25	₽ 12 Dec. 26	
14	0	George Isaac Austin	₽ 12 Dec. 26	₽ 25 Nov. 28	₽ 26 June 35	
15	9 3/12	Donald Stewart	14 Dec. 15	26 Mar. 26	3 April 38	
15	0	Jas. Charles Rouse	₽ 30 June 25	₽ 17 May 27	₽ 7 April 38	
25	2 1/12	Peter Dore⁶	8 April 13	21 Aug. 19	29 Aug. 38	
17	9	Thomas Chatterton	29 Dec. 14	2 Jan. 17	21 Dec. 38	
		LIEUTENANTS.				
15	0	Lawrence Desborough	10 April 25	3 Aug. 27		
15	0	Henry Dacre Lacy	11 April 25	4 Aug. 27		
12	0	Donald M. Cameron	26 April 28	₽ 17 Mar. 30		
14	0	Philip G. Beers	₽ 11 July 26	₽ 15 June 30		
13	0	Harry Blair	9 Dec. 27	9 Nov. 31		
12	0	James Speedy	15 May 28	23 May 32		
11	0	George Bridge	16 April 29	21 Sept. 32		
9	0	Samuel Daniel	₽ 30 Dec. 31	₽ 26 July 33		
10	0	Jas. Talbot Airey	11 Feb. 30	₽ 3 May 33		
8	0	Wm. Jas. Hamilton	6 April 32	₽ 6 Sept. 33		
8	0	Richard N. Magrath	1 June 32	₽ 24 Dec. 33		
8	0	John C. Handfield	21 Sept. 32	₽ 2 May 34		
9	0	Allan Menzies	18 Oct. 31	16 Aug. 35		
7	0	Charles Sawyer	₽ 6 Sept. 33	₽ 8 April 36		
6	0	Hall P. Chamberlain	₽ 14 Feb. 34	₽ 3 June 36		
7	0	Alex. John Cameron	₽ 24 Dec. 34	25 Sept. 36		
7	0	Rob. Manners Sparks⁷	16 Aug. 33	30 April 37		
6	0	Wm. John Dorehill	₽ 16 Jan. 35	10 Mar. 38		
5	0	Peter Browne	₽ 20 Feb. 35	7 Dec. 38		
5	0	Richard Herbert Gall	₽ 3 July 35	7 Dec. 38		
5	0	Oct. H. St. Geo. Anson	27 Nov. 35	8 Dec. 38		
4	0	Kenneth M'Kenzie	₽ 3 June 36	₽ 31 May 39		
7	0	Stonehouse Geo. Bunbury	₽ 28 June 33	₽ 25 Dec. 38		
		ENSIGNS.				
4	0	Wm. Duncan Hilton	₽ 19 Feb. 36			
2	0	C. W. Green	₽ 7 April 38			
2	0	Wm. G. Meacham	7 Dec. 38			
2	0	Alex. Ham. Robson	₽ 25 Dec. 38			
2	0	Chas. A. Thompson	4 Jan. 39			
1	0	James Reid Hope	31 May 39			
1	0	Nicholas Henry Flood	4 Oct. 39			
1	0	Thomas Kains	₽ 29 Nov. 39			

1 Lord Effingham has received a medal and one clasp for Vittoria and Nive.
2 Col. Dennis accompanied the expedition to Copenhagen in 1801, and was wounded in both hands and contused. Served in the last American war, including battle of Queenstown (wounded); storming of Fort George; action at Stoney Creek, (wounded in two places); and action of the Rapids at Hooples Creek, contused by having his horse shot, which fell on him.
3 Major Rochfort was at the capture of the Isle of France in 1810, and of Java in 1811, including capture of Cornelis, storming of Serondola and Fort Djocjocarta; storming of redoubts at the island of Borneo; Nepaul campaign in 1814; siege and storm of Hutrass; Mahratta campaigns of 1817 and 18; siege and storm of Bhurtpore 1825 and 6.
4 Major Clunie served in the American war, and was at the siege and attack of Fort Erie in 1814.
5 Capt. M'Kie served in the Nepaulese war of 1814 and 15. Present at the siege and capture of Hatrass. Served the Mahratta and Pindarree campaign of 1817 and 18, and in the Burmese war, from June, 1824, until its conclusion in 1826. Wounded at the assault of Mergule 6th Oct. 1824.

30	0	*Paymaster.*—J. Lukis, 24 Dec. 29; *Ens.* 22 Feb. 10; *Lieut.* 6 Aug. 12.
15	0	*Adjutant.*—Lawrence Desborough, (*Lieut.*) 26 Sept. 38.
9	18	*Quarter-Master.*—Harry Williams, 14 Dec. 32; *Ens.* 12 Aug. 13.
28	0	*Surg.*—A. MacQueen,⁸ M.D. 24 Ap. 26; *Assist.-S.* 13 May, 13; *Hosp.-A.* 19 Jan. 13.
6	0	*Assistant-Surgeons.*—Robert Stevenson, M.D., 14 March, 34.
4	0	Samuel Currie, M.D., 14 Oct. 36.

Facings Buff.—*Agent*, Messrs. Cox & Co.

6 Capt. Dore served in the Nepaulese war in 1815 and 16, and in the Deccan campaign in 1817 and 18.
7 Lieut. Sparks was wounded in the Caffre war.
8 Dr. Mac Queen served the Kandian campaign in Ceylon during the Rebellion in 1817 and 18.

Embarked for Foreign Service, 1831. **4th (or King's Own) Regt. of Foot.** [Serving in the East Indies.

"*The Lion of England*"—"CORUNNA"—"BADAJOS"—"SALAMANCA"—"VITTORIA" "ST. SEBASTIAN"—"NIVE"—"PENINSULA"—"BLADENSBURG"—"WATERLOO."

Colonel.

Years' Serv.	Full Pay.	Half Pay.	
61			John Hodgson,[1] *Ens.* 20 May, 1779; *Lieut.* 27 Nov. 80; *Capt.* 24 Sept. 87; *Maj.* 14 May, 94; *Lieut.-Col.* 1 Sept. 95; *Col.* 25 Sept. 03; *Major-Gen.* 25 July, 10; *Lieut.-Gen.* 4 June, 14; *Gen.* 10 Jan. 37; *Col.* 4th Regt. 30 Sept. 35.
	25	0	**Lieutenant-Colonels.**—Henry Wm. Breton, *Ens.* 16 March, 15; *Lieut.* P 27 July, 20; *Capt.* P 21 July, 25; *Major,* P 31 Dec. 28; *Lieut.-Col.* P 11 July, 34.
	22	12 4/12	John Leslie,[2] K.H.; *Ens.* 7 Aug. 1806; *Lieut.* 2 June, 08; *Capt.* P 30 Nov. 09; *Major,* P 1 Jan. 19; *Lieut.-Col.* P 29 Aug. 26.
	26	7	**Majors.**—John Ranald Macdonald,[3] C.B. K.H. *Ens.* 25 March, 07; *Lieut.* 5 May, 08; *Capt.* P 3 Dec. 18; *Major,* P 24 Jan. 28; *Brevet-Lieut.-Col.* 13 July, 38.
	33	0	P William Sadlier,[4] *Ens.* 2 April, 07; *Lieut.* 4 May, 09; *Capt.* 25 Aug. 25; *Major,* 4 Feb. 38.

Years' Serv. Full	Half	CAPTAINS.	ENSIGN.	LIEUT.	CAPTAIN.	BREV.-MAJ.
20	0	Richard Chetwode	24 May 20	P 15 Aug. 22	P 20 Mar. 27	
18	0	Thomas Williams	P 12 Sept. 22	P 7 July 25	P 17 June 28	
13	0	Thomas Faunce	5 April 27	P 12 Nov. 29	P 23 June 37	
10	0	Farquhar M. Campbell ..	3 Aug. 30	P 6 Dec. 33	P 6 Oct. 37	
11	0	William Henry Mounsey .	P 28 May 29	P 4 Jan. 33	P 14 April 37	
7	0	Fred. Leopold Arthur...	P 6 Dec. 33	P 3 July 35	P 8 June 38	
8	0	John Hilton	P 21 Sept. 32	P 30 Jan. 35	P 14 Dec. 38	
15	5/12	Charles J. Otter[5]	20 Dec. 24	12 Nov. 27	9 Mar. 39	
7	0	George Kennedy........	P 24 Dec. 33	P 1 July 36	P 15 Mar. 39	
12	14 10/12	Thomas Gibson	17 May 13	2 Dec. 14	1 July 39	

LIEUTENANTS.

7	0	John Snodgrass	13 Dec. 33	1 Dec. 36	
6	0	George King	P 11 July 34	P 7 April 37	1 Gen. Hodgson was severely wounded at Egmont-op-Zee.
6	0	John Henry Hay Ruxton	P 19 July 34	P 23 June 37	2 Colonel Leslie was at the taking of Travancore in 1808; also at the capture of the Island of Bourbon, and the Isle of France; present in the engagements in Java, the 10th, 22nd, and 26th Aug. 1811. Served in the Pindarree war in 1817. Army of occupation in France.
18	0	Dennis A. Curtayne[6] ..	18 April 22	P 26 May 25	
15	1/12	Charles S. Teale........	7 April 25	10 Dec. 27	
17	0	Abraham C. Anderson ..	12 June 23	9 July 29	
11	0	Wm. Charles Sheppard..	11 June 29	10 Nov. 34	
9	0	W. H. M. Ogilvie	P 18 Nov. 31	P 29 May 35	
5	21 6/12	John Cameron..........	25 Dec. 13	7 July 37	
9	0	Robert Hawkes	P 2 Dec. 31	8 July 37	
5	0	Robert O'Neill	P 3 July 35	9 July 37	3 Lieut.-Col. Macdonald was severely wounded at Waterloo.
7	0	Jas. S. Shortt.........	3 May 33	10 July 37	
5	0	Chas. Staniforth Hext ..	P 9 Oct. 35	P 6 Oct. 37	4 Major Sadlier served in Sicily from July 1808 to June 1812, and was present at the capture of the Islands of Ischia and Procida. Served subsequently in the Peninsula, including the battle of Castalla and siege of Tarragona, action at Villa Franca, besides various minor affairs; served also in the American war, including the attack on Plattsburgh.
4	0	William Wilby	P 27 May 36	P 7 Oct. 37	
3	0	Joseph Palmer	P 23 June 37	P 8 June 38	
3	0	Jas. Alex. Madigan......	23 June 37	P 14 Dec. 38	
4	0	Wadham Wyndham Bond	P 4 Nov. 36	9 Mar. 39	
4	0	John Potter	22 April 36	10 Mar. 39	
3	0	John H. Glazbrook	P 6 Oct. 37	P 15 Mar. 39	
3	0	Edw. Jas. Baldwyn	P 20 Oct. 37	1 July 39	
1	0	James Keating	26 April 39	P 9 Aug. 39	
3	0	Wm. Mark Campbell....	P 10 Nov. 37	2 Oct. 39	
2	0	Thos. Charles Morgan ..	P 8 June 38	25 Oct. 39	

ENSIGNS.

2	0	John Lennox MacAndrew	P 14 Dec. 38	5 Capt. Otter served at Bhurtpore.
1	0	John Cowell Bartley	P 26 Apr. 39	6 Lieut. Curtayne served in the Burmese war in 1825 and 1826.
1	0	F. P. Haines	P 21 June 39	7 Capt. Burn served the campaign in the Eastern Islands, and was at the taking of Maccassar in 1814. Served the Mahratta campaign of 1817 and 18, and was severely wounded at Bhurtpore in 1826.
1	0	Arthur Byrne..........	25 Oct. 39	
1	0	Wm. Crawley	22 Nov. 39	
1	0	Henry Rice............	31 Dec. 39	
1	0	David Fra. Chambers ..	P 31 Jan. 40	
1	0	William Inglis	7 Feb. 40	
29	1/12	Paymaster.—James Burn,[7] 6 Feb. 35; *Ens.* 1 Oct. 11; *Lieut.* 16 June, 13; *Capt.* 19 Dec. 34.		
4	0	Adjutant.—John Potter, (*Lieut.*) 11 July, 37.		
3	0	Quarter-Master.—Samuel Sexton, 11 July, 37.		
		Surgeon.—William Parry, 17 April, 38; *Assist.-Surg.* 7 March, 22; *Hosp.-Assist.* 20 Dec. 13.		
5	0	Assistant-Surgeons.—Wm. Hutchinson Allman, M.D., 12 June, 35.		
2	0	James Mouat, 14 Dec. 38.		

Facings Blue—*Agent,* Messrs. Cox & Co.

[Emb. for Foreign Service, 1831.] **5th Regt. of Foot** (or *Northumberland Fusiliers*) [Serving in Cephalonia

'*Qua fata Vocant*," surmounting St. George and the Dragon. *On the corners of the 2nd colour the Rose and Crown; on the caps the* King's Crest; *also* St. George killing the Dragon. "WILHELMSTAHL"—"ROLEIA"—"VIMIERA"—"CORUNNA"—"BUSACO"—"CIUDAD RODRIGO"—"BADAJOZ"—"SALAMANCA"—"VITTORIA"—"NIVELLE"—"ORTHES"—"TOULOUSE"—"PENINSULA."

Years' Serv.			
		Colonel.	
59		ᛏ ᛭ Hon. Sir Charles Colville,[1] G.C.B. and G.C.H., *Ens.* 6 Dec. 1781; *Lieut.* 30 Sept. 87; *Capt.* 24 Jan. 91; *Major*, 2 Sept. 95; *Lieut.-Col.* 26 Aug. 96; *Col.* 1 Jan. 05; *Major-Gen.* 25 July, 10; *Lieut.-Gen.* 12 Aug. 19; *Gen.* 10 Jan. 37; *Col.* 5th Fusiliers, 25 March, 35.	
Full Pay.	Half Pay.		
36	0	*Lieut.-Colonel.*—William Sutherland,[2] *Ens.* 15 Dec. 04; *Lieut.* 1 July, 06; *Capt.* 18 Aug. 14; *Major*. p 25 Sept. 17; *Lieut.-Col.* p 16 May, 22.	
34	2 5/12	*Majors.*—ᛏ David England Johnson,[3] *Ens.* 9 Feb. 04; *Lieut.* 29 Dec. 04; *Capt.* 12 March, 12; *Brevet-Major*, 22 July, 30; *Regtl.-Major*, p 29 Dec. 37.	
14	5	Joshua Simmonds Smith, *Cornet*, 26 Dec. 21; *Lieut.* 25 May, 22; *Capt.* p 19 April, 27; *Major*, p 31 Dec. 33.	

		CAPTAINS.	2D LIEUT.	LIEUT.	CAPTAIN.	BREV.-MAJ.
24	1 6/12	Charles Deane	p 13 July 15	22 Oct. 22	p 15 May 27	
18	0	John Spence[4]	7 Nov. 22	25 June 24	p 5 Nov. 29	
31	0	ᛏ Thomas Canch[5]	28 Sept. 09	13 May 13	2 Nov. 30	
15	5/12	Charles May	10 May 25	p 25 Feb. 26	p 5 July 31	
20	0	Charles Wood	6 April 20	30 Dec. 24	p 2 Dec. 31	
14	1 8/12	John W. King	12 Aug. 24	13 Feb. 28	p 8 Feb. 31	
16	0	Philip M. N. Guy	p 23 Sept. 24	p 12 June 28	p 29 Dec. 37	
14	0	William Prime Jones	5 Oct. 26	p 5 Nov. 29	p 23 Apr. 39	
9	0	Augustus Blair	p 1 Nov. 31	p 24 April 35	p 1 Feb. 39	
24	4 1/12	William Clune	23 Sept. 12	1 Feb. 14	29 Nov. 39	
		LIEUTENANTS.				
23	0	Frederick A. Robinson	14 Aug. 17	p 12 Dec. 22		6 Paymaster Pennington served in the Peninsula from June 1809 to May, 1814, including Busaco, Redinha, Foz de Roz, Sabugal, Fuentes d'Onor, siege of Badajoz, May and June 1811, El Bodon, siege of Ciudad Rodrigo, Jan. 1812 (received two contusions on the 11th January, in the trenches, from the explosion of a 13-inch shell), siege of Badajoz, March and April, 1812, Salamanca, Vittoria, Nivelle, Orthes and Toulouse.
14	0	Theophilus Jenkins	2 Mar. 26	16 Dec. 31		
11	0	John Woodward	p 5 Nov. 29	p 10 May 33		
12	0	John Du Bourdieu	28 Feb. 28	8 July 34		
7	0	Fra. Rich. Pyner	22 Nov. 33	p 9 Feb. 38		
6	0	Cha. M. Dawson	p 26 Sept. 34	p 11 May 38		
6	0	Charles Durie	1 Aug. 34	p 6 July 38		
5	0	Thomas Place	p 16 Oct. 35	p 15 Mar. 39		
4	0	H. F. F. Johnson	22 Nov. 36	p 23 April 39		
3	0	Hugh P. Baker	p 29 Dec. 37	p 10 May 39		
5	0	Wm. Seymour Scroggs	p 12 June 35	p 21 June 39		
3	0	W. H. Kebbel	p 9 Feb. 38	p 23 Aug. 39		
2	0	Louis H. Hamilton	6 April 38	p 17 Jan. 40		
		2ND LIEUTENANTS.				
3	0	Chas. D. Osborn	p 12 Aug. 37			
2	0	Wm. Woodgate	p 6 July 38			
2	0	H.W. de la Poer Beresford	p 1 Feb. 39			
1	0	Wm. John Campbell	p 15 Mar. 39			
1	0	Wm. Chester Master	p 23 April 39			
1	0	Geo. Bryan Milman	p 10 May 39			
1	0	Francis Sutton	p 23 Aug. 39			
1	0	John Wallace Colquitt	p 17 Jan. 40			
33	6/12	*Paymaster.*—ᛏ Jas. M. Pennington[6], 25 Jan. 16; *Ens.* 5 Feb. 07; *Lieut.* 31 Mar. 08.				
4	0	*Adjutant.*—H. F. F. Johnson, (*Lieut.*) 13 Dec. 39.				
15	0	*Quarter-Master.*—Wm. Tiller, 5 May, 25.				
		Surgeon.—ᛏ Dun. Henderson, M.D., 23 March, 26; *Assist.-Surg.* 16 April, 12.				
21	3 10/12	*Assist.-Surgs.*—Thos. Hall, 30 June, 25; *Hosp.-Assist.* 19 May, 15.				
6	0	J. Arch. Duncan M'Bean, 12 Aug. 34.				

Facings Bright Green—*Agent*, Hopkinson, Barton & Knyvett.—*Irish Agent*, Borough & Co.

1 Sir Charles Colville served as Captain of the 13th regt. in St. Domingo in 1793, 4, and 5, and was wounded at the landing at Cape Tiberon; as Lieut.-Col. of the 13th regt. served the campaign of 1801 in Egypt. Sir Charles has received a cross and one clasp for Martinique, Fuentes d'Onor, Badajos, (severely wounded by a musquet-ball through the left thigh, and lost a finger off the right hand,) Vittoria (wounded) and Nivelle.

2 Colonel Sutherland served in the Ashantee War, on the Gold Coast, in 1824.

3 Major Johnson embarked with his regiment in 1806 for South America, and was present at the storming of Buenos Ayres. Present at Roleia, Vimiera, Corunna, Busaco, Sabugal (wounded), Fuentes d'Onor, Elbodon, Ciudad Rodrigo (severely wounded at the assault), and Salamanca.

4 Captain Spence served against the Ashantees from November 1822 to 1824.

5 Capt. Canch served in the Peninsula from Sept. 1809 to Dec. 1812, and from October 1813 to May 1814, including Busaco, Redinha, Sabugal (wounded), Siege of Badajoz, May 1811 (severely contused), Fuentes d'Onor, El Bodon, Ciudad Rodrigo (wounded at the assault), Siege and Capture of Badajoz (wounded), Salamanca, Nivelle, Orthes and Toulouse. Served in the American War, and was present at Plattsburgh.

Emb. for For. Service, 1821. 6th (or *Royal 1st Warwickshire*) *Regt. of Foot.* [Serving in the East Indies.

"*The Antelope.*"—On the three corners of the second colour, "*The Rose and Crown.*"—And on the Grenadier's caps, "*The King's Crest.*"—" ROLEIA "—" VIMIERA "—" CORUNNA "—" VITTORIA "—"PYRENEES"—" NIVELLE "—" ORTHES "—" PENINSULA "—" NIAGARA."

Years' Serv.		Colonel.
67		Sir George Nugent,[1] *Bart.* G.C.B. *Ensign*, 5 July, 1773 ; *Lieut.* 23 Nov. 75 ;
Full Pay	Half Pay	*Capt.* 28 April, 78 ; *Major,* 3 May, 82 ; *Lieut.-Col.* 8 Sept. 83 ; *Col.* 1 Mar. 94 ; *Major.-Gen.* 3 May, 96 ; *Lieut.-Gen.* 25 Sept. 1803 ; *Gen.* 4 June, 13 ; *Col.* 6th Regt. 26 May, 06. *Lieut.-Colonels.*
38	4 1/12	Henry Sullivan,[2] C.B. *Ensign*, p17 May, 98 ; *Lieut.* p20 Sept. 98 ; *Capt.* p10 July, 01 ; *Major,* p21 Jan. 08 ; *Lieut.-Col.* 1 July, 13 : *Col.* 22 July, 30.
28	6 7/12	p Wm. Henry Sewell, C.B. *Ens.* 27 March, 06 ; *Lieut.* p26 Feb. 07 ; *Capt.* p12 March, 12 ; *Brevet-Major*, 3 March, 14 ; *Brevet-Lieut.-Col.* 21 June, 17 ; *Regtl.-Major*, 11 Aug. 29 ; *Col.* 10 Jan. 37 ; *Regt. Lt.-Col.* 17 June, 39.
35	0	*Majors.*—John Algeo, *Ensign*, p18 June, 05 ; *Lieut.* 1 Jan. 06 ; *Capt.* p28 Feb. 12 ; *Major,* p26 June, 23 ; *Brevet-Lieut.-Col.* 28 June, 38.
36	0	p H. Bennet Everest,[3] *Ensign*, 22 Dec. 04 ; *Lieut.* 1 March, 07 ; *Capt.* p22 June, 20 ; *Major,* 23 Dec. 31.

		CAPTAINS.	ENSIGN.	LIEUT.	CAPTAIN.	BREV.-MAJ.
28	5/12	p John Crawfurd[4]	14 May 12	p17 Sept. 13	p17 May 21	10 Jan. 37
29	6	p George H. E. Murphy[5]	27 Nov. 05	2 July 07	25 Oct. 14	10 Jan. 37
26	2 5/12	p John Bonamy[6]	19 Dec. 11	10 Feb. 14	p24 Jan. 23	28 June 38
26	0	John Thomas Griffiths	6 Sept. 14	p17 May 21	1 Sept. 31	
23	0	William Pottinger	15 Dec. 17	9 April 25	p31 Oct. 34	
16	0	John Crofton	18 Dec. 24	p29 Aug. 26	p17 July 35	
15	0	John Lumley	p31 Dec. 25	p20 Mar. 29	p 8 April 37	
14	0	Maurice G. Dennis	9 May 26	5 July 27	p15 Dec. 37	
14	0	Robert Morris Beebee	p25 May 26	p20 Sept. 27	p21 June 39	
11	3 5/12	Tho. Sidney Powell	p13 May 26	p31 May 31	p13 Nov. 35	23 July 39
		LIEUTENANTS.				
20	0	George Alexander Gordon	6 April 20	20 Dec. 24		Echellar (wounded) ; Nivelle, Nive 9th, 10th, 11th, 12th, and 13th Dec., Orthes, and affair near Fort blaye.
17	11	Charles Davers Allen	17 Sept. 12	20 May 13		
12	0	John Belshes Home	p17 April 28	p 8 June 30		Served in the American war, and was present at the siege of Fort Erie, Oct. 1814.
15	0	Joseph Ralph	1 Jan. 26	11 June 30		
14	0	John Gray Wilson	p 1 Aug. 26	10 Dec. 29		4 Major Crawfurd served in the Peninsula from Jan. 1812 to July 1814, including operations of the covering army during the siege of Badajoz, 1812, as volunteer 79th regt. ; battle of Salamanca ; capture of Madrid ; battles of the Pyrenees, Nivelle, Nive, and Orthes (severe gun-shot wound).
12	0	William Frederic Jekyll	p28 Aug. 28	1 Sept. 31		
11	17 1/2	p 𝔚 F. Bree Muller[7]	3 Mar. 12	1 Apr. 14		
10	0	Frederick Bristow	p 8 June 30	9 May 33		
15	0	Francis Lucas	p 1 Oct. 25	24 Oct. 27		
10	0	John C. Mansergh	26 Nov. 30	11 July 34		
15	15 5/12	p Richard Henry Tighe	14 Dec. 09	12 Aug. 13		
9	0	Edward Staunton	17 May 31	4 Dec. 34		5 Major Murphy served in the Peninsula from Dec 1809 until the end of the war, including actions at Albeigana and Grijo ; passage of the Douro ; capture of Coimbra ; siege and capture of San Sebastian ; passage of the Bidassoa ; action at Bidort (wounded) ; Nivelle, Nive 9th 10th (wounded) 11th 12th and 13th Dec. ; blockade of Bayonne ; action at St Ellemo, and battle of Toulouse. Medal for Toulouse.
7	0	Robt. W. M'Leod Fraser	5 July 33	p17 July 35		
7	0	Morris Hall	p15 Mar. 33	7 Jan. 36		
6	0	Henry Augustus Sullivan	p21 Feb. 34	p 1 July 36		
7	0	Francis Dyke	p17 Jan. 34	9 Sept. 36		
5	0	William Reed	p 5 June 35	p15 Dec. 37		
5	0	Edward James Blanckley	22 May 35	17 Jan. 38		
10	0	George Hughes Messiter	15 June 30	29 Sept. 34		
4	0	Richard Sweet Cole	p12 Aug. 36	p25 Dec. 38		6 Major Bonamy served in the Peninsula from Sept. 1813 to June 1814, including battles of Nivelle, Nive 9th 10th and 11th Dec. and Orthes.
4	0	Chas. Napier North	20 May 36	28 Dec. 38		
3	0	Jas. Elphinst. Robertson	p 8 April 37	p21 June 39		
3	0	William T. Hall	28 April 37	p15 Nov. 39		
		ENSIGNS.				7 Lieut. Muller served at the taking of Genoa under Lord William Bentinck, and was engaged at Waterloo.
3	0	Henry Milnam Johnson	p15 Dec. 37			8 Paymaster Blakeman's services ; battles of Roleia, Vimiera, and Corunna ; expedition to Walcheren ; in the Peninsula from Nov. 1812 to May 1814 including battles of Vittoria, the Pyrenees, Heights of Echellar, Nivelle, Nive 9th to 13th Dec., Orthes and Toulouse.
3	0	George Finlay	p17 Nov. 37			
2	0	John Rees Croker	p25 Dec. 38			
2	0	David Ogilby	28 Dec. 38			
1	0	Fred. Lussan Loinsworth	p14 June 39			Served in the American War, and was at Fort Erie, Oct. 1814.
1	0	Edw. F. Crowder	15 June 39			
1	0	Thomas Rishton	p21 June 39			9 Quar.-Mast. Sheahan entered the army in 1793, and served from that period in every action in which the 6th regt. was engaged. He was wounded in the Pyrenees and Orthes.
1	0	Robert Edmund Stratton	15 Nov. 39			
36	0	*Paymaster.*—p John Blakeman,[8] 24 Jan. 05.				[at Orthes.
20	0	*Adjutant.*—George Alexander Gordon, (*Lieut.*) 10 March, 30.				
13	9/12	*Quarter-Master.*—p John Sheahan,[9] 30 April, 27.				
30	0	*Surgeon.*—p William Thompson, M.D. 19 Jan. 38 ; *Assist.-Surg.* 18 Oct. 10.				
14	0	*Assist.-Surgs.*—John Murtagh, M.D. 11 Feb. 30 ; *Hosp.-Assist.* 5 Dec. 26.				
13	0	Jas. Jackson, M.D. 29 July, 30 ; *Hosp.-Assist.* 27 Sept. 27.				

Facings Blue.—*Agent*, Messrs. Cox and Co.

1 Sir G. Nugent served in the first American war, and in Flanders, &c.
2 Col. Sullivan was employed during the Dutch and Caffre insurrection. Present at the action at Botus, and defeat of *La Preneuse* French frigate in Algoa Bay 1800. Present at the battle of Maida, and siege of Scilla Naval action off Cape St. Mary's on board H.M.S. *Halcyon*, with a Spanish squadron, 13th Dec. 1806. Served in the Pindarree war, and at the assault and capture of the Boria, Isle of Celebes. Suppressed three insurrections while commanding the Kandian provinces in Ceylon.
3 Major Everest's services :—battles of Roleia, Vimiera, and Corunna ; expedition to Walcheren ; in the Peninsula from Nov. 1812 to May 1814, including battles of Vittoria, the Pyrenees 25th, 26th, 27th, and 28th of July ; attack on the Heights of

Emb. for Foreign Serv. 11th Nov. 1839.] **7th Regiment of Foot, (or Royal Fusiliers.)** [Serving at Gibraltar.

In the centre of the colours, The "*Rose*" within the *Garter* and the *Crown* over it. And in the corners of the second Colour, The "*White Horse.*" "MARTINIQUE"— "TALAVERA"— "ALBUHERA"— "BADAJOZ"— "SALAMANCA"— "VITTORIA"— "PYRENEES"—"ORTHES"—"TOULOUSE"—"PENINSULA."

Years' Serv.				
		Colonel.		
46		℔ Rt. Hon. Sir Edw. Blakeney,[1] K.C.B. & G.C.H. *Cornet* 28 Feb. 1794; *Lieut.* 24 Sept. 94; *Capt.* 24 Dec. 94; *Major*, 17 Sept. 1801; *Lieut.-Col.* 25 April, 08: *Col.* 4 June, 14; *Major-Gen.* 27 May, 25; *Lieut.-Gen.* 28 June, 38; *Col.* 7th Fusiliers, 20 Sept. 32.		
Full Pay.	Half Pay.			
		Lieut.-Colonel.		
25	1¹⁰⁄₁₂	Frederic Farquharson, *Ens.* 17 Sept. 13; *Lieut.* 25 May, 14; *Capt.* ᴾ23 Sept. 19; *Major*, ᴾ29 June, 30; *Lieut.-Col.* ᴾ7 Sept. 32.		
		Majors.		
21	0	John Stuart, *Ens.* 22 Jan. 20; *Lieut.* 26 March, 23; *Capt.* ᴾ13 Aug. 25; *Major*, ᴾ6 May, 36.		
19	1⁶⁄₁₂	Thos. Rich. Baker, *Cornet*, ᴾ9 Dec. 19; *Lieut.* ᴾ1 April, 24; *Capt.* ᴾ18 Feb. 26; *Major*, ᴾ31 Aug. 38.		

		CAPTAINS.	ENSIGNS.	LIEUT.	CAPTAIN.	BREVET-MAJOR.
16	0	William Hope............	4 Nov. 24	ᴾ27 Oct. 25	ᴾ14 Feb. 28	
16	0	William Guard	ᴾ 6 Nov. 24	ᴾ31 Oct. 26	ᴾ10 Jan. 28	
15	³⁄₁₂	Lacy Walter Yea	ᴾ 6 Oct. 25	ᴾ19 Dec. 26	ᴾ30 Dec. 36	
13	0	M. R. S. Whitmore	26 June 27	ᴾ 5 Aug. 28	ᴾ16 Feb. 38	
13	0	W. B. Ponsonby........	13 Dec. 27	ᴾ31 May 31	ᴾ23 Feb. 38	
10	0	Ralph Bernal	ᴾ 8 June 30	ᴾ21 June 33	ᴾ27 July 38	
13	0	Catesby Paget	8 Nov. 27	ᴾ31 Aug. 30	ᴾ 9 Mar. 39	
10	2⁸⁄₁₂	Richard Wilbraham	ᴾ25 Mar. 28	25 May 33	ᴾ22 July 36	
8	0	Rich. Mordesley Best ..	ᴾ20 April 32	ᴾ16 Jan. 35	ᴾ 7 June 39	
8	0	*Sir* William O'Malley, *Bt.*	ᴾ28 Dec. 32	ᴾ 2 Oct. 35	ᴾ12 July 39	
		LIEUTENANTS.				
7	0	Ralph Tho. Brandling ..	ᴾ31 May 33	ᴾ 6 May 36		2 Quarter-Master Ledsam's services:—Expedition to Copenhagen in 1807; Peninsula from July 1810 to the end of the war, including the battles of Busaco, and Albuhera; siege and capture of Ciudad Rodrigo, and Badajoz; battles of Salamanca, Vittoria, Pampeluna, Orthes, and Toulouse. Present at the attack on New Orleans in 1815. 3 Dr. Shean served in the Peninsula from March 1813 to the end of the war, and was present at the battles of Vittoria, the Pyrenees, and the Nive.
7	0	T. St. V. H. C. Trouhridge	ᴾ24 Jan. 34	ᴾ30 Dec. 36		
7	0	*Hon.* Henry C. Boyle ..	ᴾ20 Sept. 33	ᴾ17 Feb. 37		
6	0	Thomas Butler	ᴾ 9 May 34	ᴾ 7 April 37		
6	0	*Hon.* W. P. M. Talbot ..	19 Dec. 34	ᴾ15 Sept. 37		
6	0	Geo. David Donkin	ᴾ15 Aug. 34	ᴾ 1 Dec. 37		
6	0	*Lord* James Butler	ᴾ 7 Nov. 34	ᴾ16 Feb. 38		
6	0	Robert Stuart..........	ᴾ23 May 34	11 June 37		
4	0	*Hon.* T. H. H. Thurlow .	ᴾ26 Feb. 36	ᴾ 9 June 38		
7	0	Murdoc Maclaine	ᴾ29 Nov. 33	ᴾ15 Dec. 37		
7	0	Arthur John Pack......	ᴾ 9 Aug. 33	ᴾ 5 May 37		
4	²⁄₁₂	Charles Stewart Cochrane	ᴾ 8 April 36	ᴾ17 Aug. 38		
5	0	Aubrey F. Beauclerk....	never	ᴾ 7 Aug. 35		
3	0	*Hon.* Wm. Packenham ..	ᴾ25 Aug. 37	ᴾ31 Aug. 38		
4	0	*Hon.* Cha. Luke Hare ..	ᴾ18 Mar. 36	ᴾ 7 Dec. 38		
2	0	David Dobbie..........	never	28 Dec. 38		
6	0	George Grogan	ᴾ16 Jan. 35	ᴾ 5 Oct. 38		
5	0	Richard Maunsell	ᴾ24 April 35	ᴾ 9 Mar. 39		
3	0	*Hon.* J. W. Fortescue ..	ᴾ14 July 37	ᴾ 5 June 39		
3	0	Alexander Fraser	ᴾ11 Aug. 37	ᴾ12 July 39		
5	0	John Keane............	ᴾ11 Sept. 35	17 Sept. 39		
10	0	*Paymaster.*—Thomas Gilley, 11 May, 38; *Lieut. & Adj.* 9 Nov. 30.				
2	0	*Adjutant.*—David Dobbie, (*Lieut.*) 28 Dec. 38.				
14	0	*Quarter-Master.*—℔ John Ledsam,[2] 20 April, 26.				
28	0	*Surgeon.*—℔ Robert Shean,[3] M.D. 26 Oct. 30; *Assist.-Surg.* 28 Jan. 13.				
14	0	*Assistant Surgeons.*—J. O'Brien, M.D. 18 Oct. 27; *Hosp.-Assist.* 1 Feb. 27.				
1	0	John Mure, M.D. 4 Oct. 39.				

Facings Blue.—*Agent*, Messrs. Cox & Co.—*Irish Agent*, Borough & Co.
[*Returned from the Mediterranean, April,* 1836.]

1 Sir Edward Blakeney has received a cross and one clasp for Martinique, Albuhera (severely wounded), Badajoz (severely wounded), Vittoria, and Pyrenees.

Emb. for Foreign Service, 1830.] **8th (or The King's) Regiment of Foot.** [Serving at Halifax Nova Scotia.

The "*White Horse*," "*Nec aspera terrent*," "*The Sphinx*," with the words "EGYPT"—"MARTINIQUE"—"NIAGARA."

Years' Serv.		Colonel.
57		ῗ Sir Henry Bayly,[1] G.C.H. *Ens.* 12 April, 1783; *Lieut. & Capt.* 28 Aug. 93; *Capt. & Lieut.-Col.* 5 Sept. 99; *Col.* 25 Oct. 09; *Major-Gen.* 1 Jan. 12; *Lieut.-Gen.* 27 May, 25; *Col.* 8th Regt. 13 Sept. 25.
Full Pay	Half Pay	
		Lieut.-Colonel.
32	6/12	ῗ Thos. Gerrard Ball,[2] *Ens.* 17 Sept. 07; *Lieut.* p 1 Dec. 08; *Capt.* p 7 April, 14; *Major,* p 24 June, 24; *Lieut.-Col.* p 2 Oct. 35.
		Majors.
26	2 1/12	Simcoe Baynes, *Ens.* 24 June, 12; *Lieut.* 28 Dec. 15; *Capt.* p 24 June, 24; *Major,* p 2 Oct. 35.
18	3 2/12	Charles St. Lo Malet, *Cornet,* p 6 Jan. 19; *Lieut.* p 26 May 25; *Capt.* p 25 Feb. 26; *Major,* p 10 Jan. 38.

		CAPTAINS.	ENSIGN.	LIEUT.	CAPTAIN.	BREVET-MAJOR.
19	2 10/12	H. Winch. Hartley	10 Sept. 18	1 Oct. 20	p 1 Oct. 25	28 June 38
15	0	Thomas Kenyon........	p 23 Feb. 25	p 24 Nov. 25	p 14 Apr. 29	
16	2 10/12	James Byron	p 13 Sept. 21	p 17 Dec. 25	p 10 May 33	
15	0	John Longfield	p 23 June 25	p 26 Sept. 26	p 30 Jan. 35	
15	0	William Chearnley.....	p 26 Nov. 25	p 15 Oct. 29	p 7 Aug. 35	
12	0	H. Welladvice Roper....	p 21 Nov. 28	p 21 Dec. 32	p 23 June 37	
20	9 1/12	ῗ David Gardiner[3]	27 June 11	24 Nov. 14	22 Nov. 37	
11	0	Walter Ogilvy..........	p 15 Oct. 29	p 8 Mar. 33	p 10 Jan. 38	
8	0	E. H. Greathed	p 22 June 32	p 10 May 33	p 27 Apr. 38	
8	0	John Terry Liston	p 27 July 32	p 7 Feb. 34	p 20 Nov. 38	
		LIEUTENANTS.				
15	0	Cyrus Plaistow Trapaud	p 9 June 25	p 18 Dec. 28		
8	0	Fra. Saunderson Holmes	p 8 Feb. 33	6 July 35		
7	0	Stephenson Browne	p 8 Mar. 33	p 4 Sept. 35		
7	0	John Eldridge West	p 7 Feb. 34	p 3 Feb. 37		
12	0	Henry Capadose........	26 Feb. 28	17 May 34		
6	0	Alfred A. Malet	p 30 Jan. 35	30 Apr. 37		
5	0	John Hinde	p 28 Feb. 35	p 30 June 37		
5	0	Mark P. Seward........	p 30 Oct. 35	p 1 Sept. 37		
7	0	F. Douglas Lumley	p 22 Oct. 33	8 Jan. 38		
5	0	Coulthurst Holder	p 22 Jan. 36	p 10 Jan. 38		
5	0	Hugh Hill	p 24 Nov. 35	p 27 Apr. 38		
4	0	Ernest Lavie	p 3 Feb. 37	p 20 Nov. 38		
3	0	John Long Marsden	p 17 Feb. 37	p 7 June 39		
		ENSIGNS.				
3	0	W. M. G. M'Murdo	1 July 37			
3	0	Thomas Clowes	p 1 Sept. 37			
3	0	C. F. B. G. Dickenson ..	p 10 Jan. 38			
2	0	P. A. Iremonger	p 27 Apr. 38			
2	0	Arthur Leslie	p 20 Nov. 38			
1	0	James Johnston........	p 7 June 39			
2	0	William Bayly	26 Jan. 39			
1	0	George Augustus Young	p 9 Dec. 39			
15	0	*Paymaster.*—Wm. Russell Lucas, 10 March, 37; *2nd Lieut.* 18 March, 25; *Lieut.*-3 Jan. 28.				
8	0	*Adjutant.*—Fras. Saunderson Holmes, (*Lieut.*) 10 March, 37.				
3	0	*Quarter-Master.*—Job Aldridge, 10 Feb. 37; *Ens.* 4 Feb. 37.				
16	12	*Surg.*—Peter Fraser,[4] 6 Dec. 36; *Asst.-Surg.* 10 Dec. 12; *Hosp.-Asst.* 16 July, 12.				
5	0	*Assistant-Surgeons.*—John Cha. Graham Tice, 15 Jan. 36.				
3	0	Isidore Anthony Blake, 15 Sept. 37.				

Facings Blue.—*Agent,* Messrs. Cox & Co.

1 Sir Henry Bayly served in Flanders: was present at the battle of Famars; the siege of Valenciennes, and was wounded at Lincelles. Sir Henry served also in Holland in 1799. Proceeded to the South of France in 1814, in command of the Brigade composed of the three provisional battalions of militia.

2 Col. Ball served in the Peninsula from June 1809 to Nov. 1813, including Busaco, Albuhera, Arroyo de Molino, Almaraz, Vittoria (wounded in the head), Maya (severely wounded in the left leg), in the Pyrenees, and siege of Badajoz in May 1811.

3 Captain Gardiner served the campaigns of 1812, 13, & 14, in the Peninsula.

4 Dr. Fraser served in the American war, and was at the capture of Oswego.

Emb. for Foreign Service, 1832.] **9th (or the East Norfolk) Regiment of Foot.** [Serving in Bengal.

The figure of "*Britannia*,"—" ROLEIA"—" VIMIERA"—" CORUNNA"—" BUSACO"—" SALAMANCA"—" VITTORIA"—" ST. SEBASTIAN"—" NIVE"—" PENINSULA."

Colonel.

Years' Serv.	Full Pay.	Half Pay.					
53			ወ Sir John Cameron,[1] K.C.B. *Ens.* 25 Sept. 1787; *Lieut.* 30 Sept. 90; *Capt.* 11 July, 94; *Major*, 9 Oct. 1800; *Lieut.-Col.* 28 May, 07; *Col.* 4 June, 14; *Major-Gen.* 19 July, 21; *Lieut.-Gen.* 10 Jan. 37; *Col.* 9th Regt. 31 May, 33.					
40	3½		*Lieut.-Colonels.*—John M'Caskill,[2] K.H. *Ens.* 10 March, 97; *Lieut.* 14 May, 1801; *Capt.* 6 March, 06; *Brevet-Major*, 12 Aug. 19; *Regtl.-Major*, ᵖ 11 March, 24; *Lieut.-Col.* ᵖ 17 Feb. 25; *Col.* 28 June, 38.					
34	7		ወ Sir Edm. Keynton Williams,[3] K.C.B. *Ens.* 30 Aug. 99; *Lieut.* ᵖ 18 April, 1800; *Capt.* 25th Sept. 07; *Brevet-Major*, 8 Oct. 12; *Brevet-Lieut-Col*, 21 June, 13; *Regtl.-Major*, 25 Oct. 14; *Regtl.-Lieut.-Col.* 1 June, 26; *Col.* 22 July, 30.					
27	2		*Majors.*—Abra. Beresford Taylor,[4] K.H. *Ens.* 14 Feb. 11; *Lieut.* 24 Dec. 12; *Capt.* 22 April, 25; *Major*, ᵖ 19 April, 33.					
32	0		ወ George Lenox Davis,[5] *Ens.* 15 Sept. 08; *Lieut.* 15 Oct. 11; *Capt.* 7 April, 25; *Major.* ᵖ 17 Oct. 37.					

		CAPTAINS.	ENSIGN.	LIEUT.	CAPTAIN.	BREV.-MAJ.
29	4 4/12	ወ Charles Barnwell[6]	30 July 07	30 Mar. 09	19 May 14	10 Jan. 37
16	0	Arthur Ogle	ᵖ 1 Apr. 24	ᵖ 8 Sept. 25	ᵖ 16 July 29	
26	0	Chas. Douglas	never	19 May 14	ᵖ 16 June 25	28 June 38
20	17	ወ Wm. Hen. Hartman ..	9 July 03	28 Mar. 05	30 Oct. 12	22 July 30
13	0	John Donnelly	ᵖ 17 May 27	ᵖ 16 July 29	ᵖ 30 Jan. 35	
30	0	Joseph Hammill	4 Jan. 10	13 May 12	28 Nov. 34	
23	1/12	Matthew Smith	16 Sept. 16	31 Dec. 23	8 Feb. 34	
12	0	Studholme Henry Metcalf	ᵖ 24 July 28	ᵖ 19 Apr. 31	ᵖ 28 Aug. 38	
11	0	Franklin Lushington ..	ᵖ 16 July 29	10 Oct. 33	ᵖ 30 Oct. 38	
12	0	John Charles Campbell..	ᵖ 15 May 28	ᵖ 7 Jan. 30	ᵖ 4 May 38	
		LIEUTENANTS.				
15	13 11/12	Walter Foster Kerr	ᵖ 23 Jan. 12	ᵖ 14 Oct. 13		
10	2/12	John Hosken	ᵖ 11 June 30	ᵖ 28 Feb. 34		
10	0	John W. Robinson	16 June 30	ᵖ 1 Aug. 34		
8	0	Arthur Borton	ᵖ 13 July 32	ᵖ 3 Apr. 35		
18	13 7/12	ወ Wm. Broom Farrant	ᵖ 1 Sept. 08	29 Jan. 12		
14	0	Robt. Joseph Edmonds..	ᵖ 30 Dec. 26	10 Jan. 31		
11	0	James Dunne	ᵖ 27 Apr. 29	ᵖ 17 Nov. 32		
13	0	John F. Field	ᵖ 28 June 27	21 Feb. 34		
8	0	Studholme Brownrigg ..	ᵖ 20 July 32	9 May 35		
8	0	Wm. W. Powell	ᵖ 16 Nov. 32	9 May 35		
7	0	Edmund F. A. Hartman	22 Nov. 33	ᵖ 29 Dec. 35		
6	0	Voland Vashon Ballard ..	ᵖ 7 Mar. 34	ᵖ 16 Sept. 36		
6	0	Charles Myers Creagh ..	ᵖ 14 Mar. 34	8 Nov. 36		
9	0	George Alex. Tytler	ᵖ 28 Oct. 31	ᵖ 13 Mar. 35		
5	0	Charles Elmhirst	ᵖ 14 Aug. 35	ᵖ 17 Oct. 37		
5	0	Duncan Munro Bethune	17 Apr. 35	21 Mar. 38		
5	0	Rich. Gibbons Morgan ..	ᵖ 29 Dec. 35	ᵖ 25 May 38		
5	0	William Shelton........	22 May 35	ᵖ 30 Oct. 38		
4	0	Fred. D. Lister	16 Sept. 36	ᵖ 22 Feb. 39		
4	0	James Slator Cumming..	ᵖ 22 July 36	21 Nov. 38		
4	0	George Cubitt	ᵖ 1 July 36	ᵖ 26 Apr. 39		
6	0	Lionel Hook	5 Sept. 34	4 Dec. 38		
2	0	Blayney Walshe	ᵖ 28 Aug. 38	31 Dec. 39		
		ENSIGNS.				
2	0	Chas. Spencer Gaynor ..	9 Nov. 38	Samuel Jordan Palmer .. ᵖ 26 April 39		
2	0	Archibald Bluntish......	7 Dec. 38	Alex. Taylor .... 21 June 39		
1	0	Donald B. Macleod	ᵖ 22 Feb. 39	Charles Henry M'Caskill 8 Nov. 39		
1	0	Arthur Layard	ᵖ 1 Mar. 39	Aug. Jardine Roberts.... 31 Dec. 39		
13	17 6/12	*Paymaster.*—Robert Bluntish, 14 Dec. 09.				
8	0	*Adjutant.*—Studholme Brownrigg,[7] (*Lieut.*) 25 May, 35.				
33	0	*Quarter-Master.*—ወ Joseph Scott,[7] 17 Dec. 07.				
20	7	*Surg.*—F. Sievwright, M.D. 25 Sept. 35; *Asst.-Surg.* 13 Mar. 17; *Hosp.-Asst.* [7 June, 13.				
6	0	*Assist.-Surgeons.*—William Harvey, 28 March, 34.				
3	0	Robert Harthill, 29 Dec. 39.				

Facings Yellow.—Agent, Messrs. Cox & Co.

Side notes:

4 Major Taylor served in the American war, including the battles of Chrystler's Farm, and Niagara (severely wounded through the right leg), siege of Fort Erie, Sept. 1814; present at the capture of Forts Loghur, Koarree, and Ryghur in the East Indies in 1818; also assault and capture of Roree in 1819. Served the campaigns in Ava, including the action at Dalla (wounded), attack on Panlang, Yangavehong, and Donebew.

5 Major Davis served in the Peninsula the latter part of 1808, until taken prisoner at Lugo, 9 Jan. 1809, where he was left dangerously ill; prisoner of war in France until April 1814.

6 Major Barnwell served in the Peninsula from July 1808 to the end of the war, including the battles of Roleia, Vimiera, Fuentes d'Onor, 1st siege of Badajoz, assault and capture of Ciudad Rodrigo, siege and storming of Badajoz, battles of Salamanca, Vittoria, Pyrenees, Nivelle, Nive, Orthes, and Toulouse.

7 Quarter-Master Scott was at the battle of Vimiera, capture of Oporto, battle of Vittoria, siege of San Sebastian, battles of the Nive 9th, 10th, and 11th Dec. 1813.

---

1 Sir John Cameron served in 1794, at the reduction of Martinique, (including the siege of Fort Bourbon and other minor affairs), St. Lucia, and Guadaloupe; and at the defence of the latter in the same year, including the sortie from, and assault of Fort Fleur d'Epee, the action of the 30th Sept. at Berville, and other combats to the 7th Oct, when he was severely wounded and taken prisoner. Served in the 9th Regt. in Portugal, Spain, and France, from 1808 to the end of the war, and has received honorary distinctions (a cross and three clasps) corresponding with those borne on the colours of the 9th Regt. with the exception of " Roleia," where his predecessor, in command of the 1st Battalion, fell mortally wounded. Besides the above, he was present in other general actions, and some of a partial nature, viz.; the assault of the fortified Convent of San Bartholomew, in front of San Sebastian, 17 July 1813, which was carried by the 9th Regt.; repulse of the sortie 27th Aug.; passage of the Bidassoa, and storming of the heights; investment of Bayonne, and sortie from the left bank of the Adour. Served in Canada in 1814 and 15. During the above service, Sir John was once severely and twice slightly wounded, and twice severely contused, he has also had two horses shot under him, one at Busaco, the other at the Nive.

2 For note 2 and 3 see next page.

10th (or the North Lincolnshire) Regiment of Foot.

The *Sphinx*, with the words, "EGYPT"—"PENINSULA."

Years' Serv.		
Full Pay	Half Pay	
50		**Colonel.**
		₿ ᏬᏁᏍ Sir John Lambert,[1] G.C.B. *Ens.* 27 Jan. 1791; *Lieut. & Capt.* 9 Oct. 93; *Capt. & Lieut.-Col.* 14 May, 01; *Col.* 25 July, 10; *Maj.-Gen.* 4 June, 13; *Lieut.-Gen.* 27 May, 25: *Col.* 10th Regt. 18 Jan. 24.
		Lieut.-Colonel.
28	3 7/12	₿ Holman Custance,[2] *Ens.* 20 Oct. 08; *Lieut.* 22 Feb. 10; *Capt.* P 26 May, 14; *Maj.* P 2 Sept. 24; *Lieut.-Col.* P 12 Dec. 26.
		Majors.
23	1 3/12	Gervas Power, 2nd *Lieut.* 12 Sept. 16; *Lieut.* 7 April, 25; *Capt.* P 8 April, 26; *Maj.* P 4 Sept. 35.
25	0	Saville Broom,[3] *Ens.* P 28 Dec. 15; *Lieut.* 15 Jan. 20; *Capt.* P 10 March, 25; *Maj.* 16 Sept. 36.

		CAPTAINS.	ENSIGN.	LIEUT.	CAPTAIN.	BREVET-MAJOR.
27	0	Thos. L. L. Galloway....	14 April 13	14 Nov. 22	P 26 May 25	28 June 38
20	0	Wm. Henry Adams	1 Feb. 21	P 11 Mar. 24	P 18 July 26	
15	1 1/12	Francis Dunne	P 29 May 23	P 23 June 25	P 30 Dec. 26	
15	0	John Wilmot	P 23 June 25	P 19 Sept. 26	P 15 Feb. 31	
14	1 2/12	Wm. M. Wetenhall	P 23 Sept. 24	P 16 Mar. 26	P 31 Aug. 30	2 Col. Custance served at Walcheren in 1809, and subsequently in the Peninsula, including the repulse of the French at Bejer, in front of Posta Banos pass, affairs in Roncesvalles pass, battle of Nivelle, attack on Cambo, crossing the Nive 9th Dec., action at St. Pierre d'Arrubé near Bayonne, 13th Dec. (twice wounded and severely), action at Sauveterre, passage of Gave d'Oleron, and Gave de Pau, battle of Orthes, affair at Tarbes, action at Aire (wounded), and battle of Toulouse.
15	0	Chris. L. Strickland	P 31 Mar. 25	P 8 April 26	P 24 May 33	
33	0	₿ John K. Jauncey[4]....	12 Mar. 07	10 Feb. 08	5 June 27	
14	3/12	Henry Onslow	P 24 Nov. 25	P 27 Mar. 27	P 4 Sept. 35	
15	0	Tho. Harte Franks.....	P 7 July 25	P 26 Sept. 26	P 1 Mar. 39	
14	0	George Staunton	P 5 Oct. 26	P 15 Feb. 31	P 7 June 39	
		LIEUTENANTS.				
22	0	Wm. Hen. Goode	21 May 18	P 31 July 23		
15	0	Henry C. Powell	9 April 25	P 17 July 26		
15	0	George Wright	P 10 Nov. 25	P 27 April 27		
14	0	Edward Shanly[5].......	1 June 26	10 Sept. 30		
13	0	W. G. D. Nesbitt	P 27 April 27	P 24 May 33		
13	0	John Green Paley	P 26 June 27	P 29 Nov. 33		
13	0	Fred. Wm. Hill	P 27 Dec. 27	P 13 Dec. 33		3 Major Broom was at the siege and capture of Malligaum in the East Indies in 1818. 4 Capt. Jauncey, expedition to Walcheren. Peninsula from July 1812 to June 1814, including battle of Castalla, siege of Tarragona, retreat from ditto, and second siege; retreat from Villa Franca after the battle of the Pass of Ordal; investment of Barcelona in 1814. Expedition to Naples in 1815. 5 Lieut. Shanly served the campaigns of 1813, 14, and 15, in Upper Canada, and was present at the battles of Chippewa and Lundy's Lane (wounded). 6 Quarter-Master Blenkinsop was present at the action before Alcoy in Spain. 7 Dr. Regan served in the expedition against New Orleans.
11	0	James Horsburgh	P 6 Aug. 29	26 Dec. 34		
10	0	Edw. Rich. White	P 8 June 30	P 6 Mar. 35		
9	0	Charles Harford	P 15 Feb. 31	P 4 Sept. 35		
8	0	Arthur B. Cane	11 Jan. 33	16 Sept. 36		
7	0	R. Lloyd Thomas	P 13 Dec. 33	P 1 Mar. 39		
6	0	William Fenwick	26 Dec. 34	P 7 June 39		
5	0	John Garvock.........	P 4 Sept. 35	31 Dec. 39		
		ENSIGNS.				
4	0	John Hen. Grant	2 April 36			
4	0	Hen. E. Longden	16 Sept. 36			
3	0	Sam. Goold Adams	P 8 Dec. 37			
2	0	J. W. E. Penrose	P 17 Aug. 38			
2	0	Geo. J. Thomas	P 25 May 38			
1	0	John James Bull	P 7 June 39			
1	0	Herb. Wat. Wms. Wynn	P 5 July 39			

25	3 3/12	*Paymaster.*—Robert Uniacke, 6 July, 26; *Ens.* 14 May, 12; *Lieut.* 9 Sept. 13	
5	0	*Adjutant.*—John Garvock, (*Lieut.*) 23 Aug. 39.	
11	0	*Quarter-Master.*—₿ Wm. Blenkinsop,[6] 13 Aug. 29.	
29	2	*Surgeon.*—J. Regan,[7] 2 Nov. 30; *Assist.-Surg.* 1 Sept. 14; *Hosp.-A.* 7 Oct. 09.	
		Assistant-Surgeon.—Stephenson Teevan, M.D. 23 Nov. 26: *Hosp.-Assist.* 16 June, 25.	

Facings Yellow.—*Agent,* Messrs. Cox & Co.
[*Returned from Corfu,* 28 Jan. 38.]

---

1 Sir John Lambert served in Flanders, and was at Lincelles and the sieges of Valenciennes, and Dunkirk; has received a Cross for Nivelle, Nive, Orthes, and Toulouse.

---

2 Col. M'Caskill was at the landing at Porto Rico, and siege of St. Juan, May, 1797. On passage to India when the fleet under convoy of Sir T. Trowbridge was attacked by the French Admiral Linois in the *Marengo* 84, a heavy frigate, and another ship, Aug. 1805; present at the sieges and captures of Forts Sattarah, Singhur, Woosootah, and a great many others. Also at the reduction of the stone fortress of Sholapore, and the attack and dispersion of 5,000 of the Peshwa's choicest troops strongly posted with their guns, 15 of which were captured under the walls of the fort, 11th May, 1818.

3 Sir Edm. Williams served the campaign of 1799 in Holland, including the actions of the 2nd and 6th Oct. (wounded); present at the battle of Maida in 1806, and the taking of Ischia in 1809. Served throughout the war in the Peninsula, including the following battles, sieges, &c., viz. Busaco (wounded), Badajoz, 1811, Salamanca (twice wounded, once severely), Burgos, Vittoria, Tolosa, St. Sebastian 1st, 2nd (wounded) and 3rd assaults, Bidassoa, Nivelle, Nive, Adour, and wounded at the investment of Bayonne.

Emb. for For. Service, 1827.] **11th (or North Devonshire) Regiment of Foot.** [Serving in Canada.

"SALAMANCA"—"PYRENEES"—"NIVELLE"—"NIVE"—"ORTHES"—"TOULOUSE"—"PENINSULA."

Years' Serv.		
Full Pay	Half Pay	
62		*Colonel.* ꘡ Sir Rufane Shawe Donkin,[1] K.C.B. & G.C.H. Ens. 21 Mar. 1778; Lieut. 9 Sept. 79; Capt. 31 May, 93; Major, 1 Sept. 95; Lieut.-Col. 24 May, 98; Col. 25 April, 08; Major-Gen. 4 June, 11; Lieut.-Gen. 19 July, 21; Gen. 28 June, 38; Col. 11th Regt. 15 March, 37.
36	1 1/12	*Lieut.-Colonel.*—꘡ George Leigh Goldie,[2] C.B. Cornet, 3 Sept. 03; Lieut. 14 Mar. 05; Capt. 4 Dec. 06; Brev.-Maj. 20 June, 11; Brev.-Lt.-Col. 12 Aug. 19; Regtl.-Major, 4 May, 26; Regtl.-Lieut.-Col. 13 Aug. 30; Col. 10 Jan. 37.
30	4 2/13	*Majors.*—꘡ B. Vigors Derinzy,[3] K.H. Ens. 26 May, 06; Lieut. 16 Mar. 08; Capt. 25 Oct. 14; Major, 4 Jan. 33.
41	0	꘡ Cecil Bisshopp,[4] C.B. Cornet, 10 Dec. 1790; Lieut. p14 Oct. 00; Capt. 23 June, 08; Brevet-Major, 27 May, 25; Brevet-Lieut.-Col. 19 Jan. 26; Regtl.-Major, 6 Sept. 34.

		CAPTAINS.	ENSIGN.	LIEUT.	CAPTAIN.	BREVET-MAJOR.
27	2 7/12	Wm. Chambre	9 July 11	27 May 12	p10 Jan. 22	10 Jan. 37
27	0	꘡ H. Keane Bloomfield	30 Sept. 13	p 7 Aug. 17	p 1 Apr. 24	28 June 38
33	0	꘡ Isaac Richardson[5]	5 Aug. 07	1 Oct. 08	7 Apr. 25	28 June 38
23	1	Edward Sterling Farmar	2 Jan. 17	p10 Jan. 22	p18 Oct. 33	
9	0	John Taylor Winnington	p 2 Dec. 31	p24 July 35	p 1 Sept. 37	
12	0	John Fordyce	p18 Dec. 28	p11 May 32	p 5 Aug. 36	
22	0	Edward Moore ········	21 May 18	7 Apr. 25	7 Feb. 39	
14	1/12	John Singleton	p17 June 26	p31 Dec. 27	p15 Feb. 39	
13	0	Hen. Blankley H. Rogers	p17 Jan. 28	p12 Apr. 33	p14 Oct. 36	
10	0	John Lee	31 Aug. 30	p19 June 35	p26 Apr. 39	
		LIEUTENANTS.				
15	0	John Tobin	p28 Dec. 25	p16 Aug. 27		
15	0	James Goold	p15 Sept. 25	21 May 29		
13	0	Bertram Charles Mitford	p27 April 27	p 3 May 31		
13	0	Arthur Kennedy	p24 May 27	p17 Feb. 32		
15	0	Edward Lionel Wolley ..	p29 Dec. 25	4 Jan. 33		
11	0	Gerald George Dunlevie	26 Mar. 29	p18 Oct. 33		
11	0	Lewis Alex. Boyd	21 May 29	p 9 Oct. 35		
9	0	Alexander Browne.....	p 3 May 31	p13 Nov. 35		
8	0	Alexander Cockburn	p 4 Dec. 32	p27 May 36		
7	0	James Forbes	p 1 Nov. 33	p10 July 37		
7	0	Edw. Lynch Blosse	p15 Nov. 33	p25 Jan. 39		
5	0	R. Brown T. Boyd.....	p20 Feb. 35	p15 Feb. 39		
5	0	Aug. Fred. Jenner	p 9 Oct. 35	p21 June 39		
		ENSIGNS.				
5	0	Sam. Symes Cox	p13 Nov. 35			
4	0	Valentine F. Story	p25 Nov. 36			
4	0	Geo. Edw. A. Tobin	p30 Dec. 36			
2	0	Walter F. Clark	p11 May 38			
2	0	Simon Fitzh. Jacson	p25 Jan. 39			
1	0	Alex. S. G. Jauncey	p15 Feb. 39			
2	0	Jas. Talbot Stanley	p 4 Jan. 39			
1	0	Jas. Hamilton Ross	p21 June 39			
32	3/12	*Paymaster.*—Alexander Boyd,[6] 8 Feb. 21; Ens. 14 Sept. 08; Lieut. 9 Aug. 09.				
5	0	*Adjutant.*—R. B. T. Boyd, (*Lieut.*) 15 Feb. 39.				
2	0	*Quarter-Master.*—J. J. Grant, 5 Oct. 38.				
24	5	*Surgeon.*—꘡ Daniel Leonard,[7] 2 Aug. 33; Assist-Surg. 11 May, 15; Hosp.-Assist. 12 Mar. 11.				
2	0	*Assistant-Surgeons.*—James Stewart, 17 April, 38.				

Patrick Brodie, 20 April, 26; *Hosp.-Assist.* 16 June, 25.

Facings, Green.—*Agent*, Messrs. Cox & Co.

[Right column notes:]
1 Sir Rufane Donkin was at the taking of Martinique, Guadaloupe, and St. Lucie; wounded at Ostend; accompanied the last expedition to Copenhagen, and has received a medal for Talavera.

2 Col. Goldie served in the Peninsula from March 1809 to Nov. 1813, including the passage of the Douro, battles of Talavera, Busaco, Albuhera, Vittoria, and the Pyrenees, besides many other minor actions, skirmishes, &c. Severely wounded in the Pyrenees, 30th July, 1813, by a musket-ball (long considered mortal) which is still lodged in the lungs. Medal for Albuhera. 3 (See bottom of page.)

4 Col. Bisshopp's services:—Campaign and battle of Corunna; expedition to Walcheren; campaign in the south of France; capture of Bhurtpore in 1826. 5 Major Richardson served in the Peninsula from Aug. 1809 to Oct. 1814, includ. bat. of Busaco; the subsequent retreat of the army to the lines before Lisbon; the adv. & purs. of the en. when they broke up from Santarem, Mar. 4, 1811; block. of Almeida; and bat. of Fuentes d'Onor. 6 Paymaster Boyd accompanied the expedition to Walcheren, and was present at the siege of Flushing. 7 Dr. Leonard served in the Peninsula from May 1811 to Sept 1814.

3 Major Derinzy's services :—Campaign and battle of Corunna (severely wounded in both knees); expedition to Walcheren; siege and capture of Flushing (wounded in left arm.) In the Peninsula, from Dec. 1810 until the end of the war, including affairs of Redinha and Pombal; re-capture of Campo Mayor; capture of Olivença; 1st siege of Badajoz; battle of Albuhera, siege and capture of Ciudad Rodrigo; siege and capture of Badajoz; battle of Salamanca; affair of Aldea de Ponte; retreat from Madrid; affairs of Osma and Jocauna; battle of Vittoria; blockade of Pampeluna; affairs of Roncesvalles, Zubisi, &c. battles of Pampeluna, 28th July, and of the Pyrenees, 30th July; affairs of Echallar, St. Estevan, &c; capture of San Sebastian; passage of the Bidassoa; battles of the Nivelle, (dangerously wounded (reported killed) through the body); and Nive; affairs of Bastide de la Clarence, and Gave d'Oleron. Twice wounded, musket ball in left arm, and by a splinter of a shell in the chest at the battle of Toulouse, but did not quit the field. Medal for Toulouse.

Emb. for Foreign Service, 1837.] **12th (or the East Suffolk) Regt. of Foot.** [Serving at the Mauritius.

"MINDEN"—"GIBRALTAR"—with the *Castle* and *Key*—"*Montis Insignia Calpe*"—"SERINGAPATAM"—"INDIA."

Years' Serv.		
53		**Colonel.** Hon. Robert Meade, *Ens.* 7 Nov. 1787; *Lieut.* 15 May, 93; *Capt.* 23 Sept. 93; *Major,* 30 Oct. 94; *Lieut.-Col.* 10 Mar. 95; *Col.* 29 April, 02; *Major-Gen.* 25 Oct. 09; *Lieut.-Gen.* 4 June, 14; *Gen.* 10 Jan. 37; *Col.* 12th Regt. 9 Oct. 23.
Full Pay	Half Pay	
28	1 6/12	**Lieut.-Colonel.** ‡ Joseph Jones,[1] *Ens.* 31 Jan. 11; *Lieut.* 5 Feb. 14; *Capt.* P 25 Sept. 23; *Major,* P 8 Oct. 30; *Lieut.-Col.* P 28 Aug. 35.
		Majors.
22	9/12	John Patton, *Ens.* 18 Sept. 17; *Lieut.* P 1 Mar. 21; *Capt.* P 10 Sept. 25; *Major,* P 31 Oct. 34.
18	1 2/12	H. Arthur O'Neill, *Cornet,* P 11 Oct. 21; *Lieut.* 10 Sept. 24; *Capt.* P 4 Feb. 26; *Major,* P 28 Aug. 35.

Full Pay	Half Pay	CAPTAINS.	ENSIGN.	LIEUT.	CAPTAIN.	BREVET-MAJOR.
15	3/12	Sir R. A. Douglas, Bt...	20 Dec. 24	P 17 Sept. 25	P 17 Jan. 28	
29	0	Sterling Freeman Glover	21 Feb. 11	25 Nov. 13	P 31 May 33	
14	0	Richard England	P 14 Sept. 26	18 Dec. 28	P 31 Oct. 34	
13	0	William Bell	P 3 April 27	P 8 Oct. 30	P 3 July 35	
12	0	Gerald Steph. Fitz Gerald	26 April 28	P 15 Feb. 31	P 24 Mar. 37	
25	1	Julius Henry Stirke	4 Aug. 14	P 25 Sept. 23	22 Nov. 36	
10	0	Edward Walhouse	P 8 Oct. 30	P 31 Oct. 34	P 11 Aug. 37	
28	0	Francis Marsh..........	5 Mar. 12	30 Dec. 19	4 Jan. 33	
7	0	J. M. Perceval..........	P 21 June 33	P 18 Mar. 36	P 18 May 38	
9	0	Charles Granet	P 19 July 31	P 23 Jan. 35	P 27 Apr. 38	
		LIEUTENANTS.				2 Lieut. Dunne served in the Peninsula from Sept. 1812 to Sept. 1814, including the battles of Vittoria, Pyrenees (wounded), Nivelle and Nive from 9th to 13th Dec.
21	7 4/12	‡ William Dunne[2]	16 July 12	21 Sept. 15		
6	0	Thomas Brooke	P 31 Oct. 34	P 29 July 36		
10	0	John Francis Kempt	P 16 June 30	19 May 37		
5	0	Francis Gilbert Hamley	P 7 Aug. 35	P 25 July 37		
5	0	James Boyd	P 28 Aug. 35	P 22 Aug. 37		3 Quarter-Master Swift served at Travancore in the East Indies in 1809, and at the attack and capture of the Isle of France in 1810.
4	0	Rich. John Allen Philipps	P 18 Mar. 36	P 1 Sept. 37		
10	0	Charles Robert Storey ..	P 16 June 30	29 Jan. 36		
6	0	Hew Dalrymple Fanshawe	4 July 34	P 25 May 38		
4	0	Rob. Geo. Duff	P 29 July 36	P 26 June 38		4 Dr. Cotton was at the siege and capture of Bhurtpore in 1825 and 26.
10	0	Samuel Reed	15 June 30	26 July 33		
4	0	Perrott Thornton	P 13 Jan. 37	P 22 Mar. 39		
6	0	William Robert Lewis ..	P 21 Feb. 34	26 June 38		
		ENSIGNS.				
4	0	John Arthur O'Toole....	P 30 July 36			
4	0	Henry D. Persse........	22 April 36			
3	0	Francis Grey Tidy	30 June 37			
3	0	Bennett W. Gillman....	P 23 Aug. 37			
2	0	John Marcon	P 18 May 38			
2	0	Augustus Fred. Braham..	P 26 June 38			
1	0	William Longfield	P 22 Mar. 39			
1	0	William Dickson Butcher	P 27 Sept. 39			
1	0	John Caldwell Bloomfield	P 24 Jan. 40			
29	3/12	*Paymaster.*—J. Wadeson, 9 Aug. 27; *Ens.* 27 June, 11; *Lieut.* 13 Oct. 12.				
4	0	*Adjutant.*—Henry D. Persse, (*Ens.*) 22 Nov. 36.				
11	0	*Quarter-Master.*—B. Swift,[3] 21 May, 29.				
27	0	*Surgeon.*—Thomas F. Cotton,[4] 13 Mar. 35; *Assist.-Surg.* 17 Aug. 15; *Hosp.-Assist.* 4 Oct. 13.				
5	0	*Assistant-Surgeons.*—John Booth, 17 July, 35.				
12	0	William Robertson, 29 July, 30; *Hosp.-Assist.* 8 May, 28.				

Facings Yellow—*Agent,* Messrs. Cox & Co.

1 Col. Jones served in the Peninsula from March 1812 to March 1814, including battle of Castalla; siege of Tarragona; battle of Villa Franca and retreat; taking of the forts in the Pass of Ballaguer, and blockade of Barcelona.

| Emb. for Foreign Service, 1823. | 13th (*or* 1st *Somersetshire*) *Foot.—Light Infantry.* | [Serving in Bengal. |

The *Sphinx*, with the words, "EGYPT"—"MARTINIQUE"—"AVA."

Colonel.

Years' Serv.	
64	Edw. Morrison, *Ens.* 20 Jan. 1777; *Lieut.* & *Capt.* 15 Sept. 80; *Capt.* & *Lieut.-Col.* 13 Jan. 90; *Col.* 26 Feb. 95; *Major-Gen.* 1 Jan. 98; *Lieut.-Gen.* 1 Jan. 05; *Gen.* 4 June, 14; *Col.* 13th Light Infantry, 15 Feb. 13.

Full Pay.	Half Pay.	
		Lieut.-Colonels.—Sir Robert Henry Sale,[1] K.C.B. *Ens.* 24 Sept. 95; *Lieut.* 12 April, 97; *Capt.* 23 March, 06; *Major*, 30 Dec. 13; *Lieut.-Col.* 2 June, 25; *Col.* 28 June, 38.
41	3 5/12	
41	0	William H. Dennie,[2] C.B. *Ens.* 1 Jan. 00; *Lieut.* P 4 Aug. 04; *Capt.* P 4 Oct 10; *Major*, P 19 April, 21; *Lieut.-Col.* P 6 July, 32.
34	0	*Majors.*—Edward T. Tronson,[3] *Ens.* 28 Nov. 06; *Lieut.* 26 Jan. 08; *Capt.* P 2 Sept. 19; *Major*, P 27 March, 35; *Brev.-Lieut.-Col.* 23 July 39.
31	3/12	ⓟ Tristram C. Squire,[4] *Ens.* 24 April, 09; *Lieut.* P 31 Jan. 10; *Capt.* P 18 Oct. 21; *Major*, 10 Jan. 37; *Regtal.-Major*, 21 April, 39.

		CAPTAINS.	ENSIGN.	LIEUT.	CAPTAIN.	BREV.-MAJ.
37	0	Robert Joseph Debnam[5]	25 June 03	10 June 04	P 1 April 10	22 July 30
24	2 11/12	Wm. Sutherland[6]	29 July 13	26 May 14	P 27 Oct. 28	
23	0	James Kershaw[7]	13 Feb. 17	2 Dec. 24	P 11 Aug. 29	23 July 39
32	0	Robert Pattisson[8]	31 Mar. 08	4 Jan. 10	30 Oct. 31	
15	0	J. G. Dalhousie Taylor	1 July 25	25 Oct. 27	P 6 July 32	
13	0	Horatio Nelson Vigors	P 12 April 27	P 11 Aug. 29	P 27 Mar. 35	
24	7/12	Henry Havelock[9]	20 July 15	P 24 Oct. 21	5 June 38	
22	5 1/12	ⓟ Rich. M. Meredith[10]	1 April 13	26 Jan. 15	2 Sept. 38	
21	6 7/12	Fra. Wm. Stehelin[11]	8 Oct. 12	8 Feb. 16	21 April 39	
18	0	A. P. Savage Wilkinson[12]	25 Dec. 22	16 Dec. 24	6 Sept. 39	
		LIEUTENANTS.				
13	0	Hamlet Wade		P 22 Feb. 27	9 Aug. 30	
13	0	James H. Fenwick		25 Oct. 27	30 Oct. 31	
12	0	Peter Raym. Jennings		P 5 Aug. 28	P 22 June 32	
10	0	Robert George Hughes		P 29 June 30	P 6 July 32	
10	0	Alex. Essex F. Holcombe		P 3 Dec. 30	12 Sept. 34	
9	0	George King		13 April 31	P 16 Jan. 35	
8	0	Rollo Gillespie Burslem		13 April 32	P 27 Mar. 35	
9	0	John Steward Wood		12 April 31	P 21 Aug. 35	
8	0	Frederick Holder		P 27 April 32	P 22 July 36	
8	0	Wm. Alex. Sinclair		P 23 June 32	2 Aug. 36	
8	0	Hon. E. J. W. Forester		P 28 Dec. 32	5 June 38	
6	0	Fred. Gordon Christie		8 April 34	20 July 38	
6	0	Thomas Oxley		18 July 34	P 3 Aug. 38	
6	0	J. Byron Hobhouse		P 27 June 34	P 4 Aug. 38	
5	0	David Rattray		P 27 May 35	2 Sept. 38	
5	0	Edward King		P 22 May 35	29 Jan. 39	
5	0	George Mein		19 June 35	21 April 39	
4	0	Richard Edward Frere		P 22 July 36	14 June 39	
3	0	Francis Levett Bennett		P 25 July 37	P 5 July 39	
4	0	George Wade		27 May 36	6 Sept. 39	
2	0	Henry Penny		P 9 Mar. 38	7 Feb. 40	
		ENSIGNS.				
2	0	John Wm. Cox			26 June 38	
2	0	William Williams			P 3 Aug. 38	
2	0	F. Van Straubenzee			P 17 Aug. 38	
1	0	Thos. Beckwith Speedy			15 Mar. 39	
1	0	T. F. P. C. Scott			P 26 Apr. 39	
1	0	G. G. C. Stapylton			14 June 39	
1	0	Edward B. Cureton			21 June 39	
1	0	Rob. S. Parker			P 5 July 39	
1	0	Arthur Oakes			31 Dec. 39	
1	0	George Talbot			7 Feb. 40	

Side notes (Lieutenants column):
4 Major Squire served the campaigns of 1810, 11, and 13, in the Peninsula; served in the Burmese war in 1824.
5 Maj. Debnam's services:—Campaign of 1804, including capture of Indore; siege of Bhurtpore 1805; campaigns of 1812, 15, 16, and 17, in India; capture of Rangoon and Burmese war.
6 Capt. Sutherland served throughout the Burmese war, including the capture of Cheduba; operations in front of Rangoon, Kokaign, Napadie, Melloon, and Pagam-Mew.
7 Major Kershaw served throughout the Burmese war, and was wounded at the capture of the island of Cheduba.
8 Capt. Pattisson was at cap. of Martinique 1809, and Guadaloupe 1810; served camps. of 1813 & 14 in Canada; served through, the Bur. war, includ. cap. of Rangoon, and storm, the following stockades:—Kemaroot, Kokaign (sev. wounded), Pagoda Hill, Napadee, Melloon, & Pagam-Mew.
9 Capt. Havelock served throughout the Burmese war.
10 Capt. Meredith served in the Peninsula from Nov. 1813 to June 1814, and was actively employed from the Pyrenees to the battle of Toulouse, at which he was present. Served in Canada in 1814 and 15; present at capture of Rangoon May 1824.
11 Lieut. Stehelin served the campaigns of 1813 and 14 in Canada. Served throughout the Burmese war, including capture of Cheduba and Kemaroot; operations before Rangoon, and attack of Pagoda Point.
12 Capt. Wilkinson served throughout the Burmese war.
13 Quart.-Master Sheridan served at the Ferrol, and throughout the campaign of 1801 in Egypt; present at the capture of Martinique 1809; served throughout the Burmese war.

22	7 9/12	*Paymaster.*—Harry Carew, 1 Feb. 31; *Ens.* 1 Jan. 11; *Lieut.* 19 March, 14.
13	0	*Adjutant.*—Hamlet Wade (*Lieut.*) 5 June, 38.
27	0	*Quarter-Master.*—Mark Sheridan,[13] 18 Feb. 13.
24	3 5/12	*Surgeon.*—ⓟ ⓒⓑ Denis Murray, M.D. 23 Nov. 32; *Assist.-Surgeon*, 22 June, 15; *Hosp.-Assist.* 9 Nov. 12.
15	0	*Assistant-Surgeons.*—J. Robertson, M.D. 13 Mar. 26; *Hosp.-Assist.* 29 Dec. 25.
4	0	George West Barnes, M.D. 8 April, 36.

Facings Yellow—*Agent*, Messrs. Cox & Co.

1 Sir R. H. Sale was at the battle of Mallavelly 27th March, 1799 siege and storming of Seringapatam (medal); campaign of 1804 in the Weynaud country; storming of the Travancore lines in 1809; capture of the Isle of France in 1810; present at the capture of Rangoon, and served throughout the Burmese war; wounded severely on the head 15th Dec. 24; and again at Mallown. Slightly wounded in the assault and capture of the Fortress and Citadel of Ghuznee, in Affghanistan, 23 July 1839.

2 Col. Dennie served the campaign of 1805 and 6 in India under Lord Lake; present at the capture of the Isle of France in 1810; also at the capture of Rangoon, and throughout the Burmese war; wounded in the head 15th Dec. 1824.

3 Col. Tronson was at the capture of Martinique 1809 and Guadaloupe 1810; served the campaigns of 1813 and 14 in Canada; served throughout the Burmese war, and was severely wounded at Pagaume 9th Feb. 1826.

Emb. for Foreign Service, 1836.] **14th (or Buckinghamshire) Regiment of Foot.** [Serving in the West Indies.

The *Royal Tiger*, superscribed "INDIA."—On the Bear-skin Caps of the Grenadiers and Drummers, the *White Horse*, "*Nec aspera terrent*."—"TOURNAY"—"CORUNNA"—"JAVA"—"WATERLOO"—"BHURTPORE."

Years' Serv.		
Full Pay.	Half Pay.	
57		**Colonel.** Sir James Watson,[1] K.C.B., *Ens.* 24 June, 1783; *Lieut.* 18 April, 92; *Capt.* 11 Mar. 95; *Major*, 3 Dec. 02; *Lieut.-Col.* 15 May, 06; *Col.* 4 June, 14; *Maj-Gen.* 19 July, 21; *Lieut.-Gen.* 10 Jan. 37; *Col.* 14th Regt. 24 May, 37.
34	2	**Lieut.-Colonel.**—₽ Mathias Everard,[2] C.B. & K.H. *Ens.* 28 Sept. 04; *Lieut.* 21 March, 05; *Capt.* 23 April, 07; *Brevet-Major*, 19 July, 21; *Regtl.-Major*, 11 Nov. 25; *Brevet-Lieut.-Col.* 19 Jan. 26; *Regtl.-Lieut.-Col.* 4 Aug. 29.
25	7/12	*Majors.*—Maurice Barlow, *Ens.* ᵖ21 July, 14; *Lieut.* 23 March, 15; *Capt.* ᵖ20 Dec. 21; *Major*, ᵖ12 June, 28.
19	0	James Watson, *Ens.* 22 Mar. 21; *Lieut.* ᵖ25 Dec. 22; *Capt.* ᵖ14 Dec. 32; *Major*, ᵖ10 Jan. 40.

		CAPTAINS.	ENSIGN.	LIEUT.	CAPTAIN.	BREV.-MAJ.
32	0	₽ Martin C. Lynch[4]	11 Feb. 08	31 May 09	22 June 26	
31	0	Cha. Rayner Newman[3]..	28 Sept. 09	15 Aug. 11	ᵖ 1 May 28	
31	0	Dickens M. Hazlewood[6]	10 May 09	ᵖ13 Dec. 10	10 July 31	
15	0	George Douglas	ᵖ 8 Oct. 25	ᵖ 5 April 27	ᵖ26 June 35	
15	0	Tho. Holmes Tidy[7]......	14 April 25	ᵖ28 Sept. 26	ᵖ 2 Oct. 35	
18	14	Joseph Smith	16 Feb. 08	14 Mar. 11	13 Mar. 27	
14	0	John Watson[7]..........	20 July 26	ᵖ17 May 27	ᵖ11 Aug. 37	
11	0	Geo. A. Wilson	ᵖ29 Sept. 29	ᵖ21 Dec. 32	ᵖ26 April 39	
17	16 2/12	George Beere	8 Feb. 07	29 Nov. 07	19 June 27	
9	0	Robert Spread Grady ..	ᵖ 3 Feb. 32	ᵖ 3 April 35	ᵖ10 Jan. 40	
		LIEUTENANTS.				
18	0	Robert Daly[8]	8 Aug. 22	6 Jan. 26		
15	0	Ralph Budd	10 Mar. 25	ᵖ16 Mar. 26		
12	0	Hen. M. F. Stirke	31 July 28	6 Sept. 34		
9	0	John Dwyer	ᵖ19 July 31	21 Nov. 34		
8	0	Collett Leventhorpe	ᵖ28 Sept. 32	ᵖ 2 Oct. 35		
7	0	Arth. W. Campbell	15 Mar. 33	25 Dec. 35		
6	0	Edward Archdall	6 Sept. 34	ᵖ25 Nov. 36		
11	2/12	Henry Pigott	ᵖ 9 July 29	14 June 33		
6	0	William Douglas	ᵖ23 May 34	1 Aug. 38		
5	0	Edward Prothero	ᵖ 2 Oct. 35	ᵖ26 April 39		
5	0	William Blundell	ᵖ30 Oct. 35	ᵖ10 Jan. 40		
4	0	John Spence	22 April 36	11 Jan. 40		
4	0	Rob. Wm. Romer	ᵖ30 Sept. 36	ᵖ24 Jan. 40		
		ENSIGNS.				
4	0	Arthur H. Elton	28 Oct. 36			
2	0	T. Edmonds Holmes	ᵖ28 Dec. 38			
1	0	John Peter Hall........	ᵖ26 April 39			
4	0	Manley Geo. Dwarris Hall	22 April 36			
1	0	Thomas Hamilton......	ᵖ31 Aug. 39			
1	0	David Tho. Armstrong ..	22 Nov. 39			
1	0	Loftus Hare	ᵖ31 Jan. 40			
30	2 10/12	*Paymaster.*—Peter Valentine Wood, 2 Aug. 31; *Ens.* 17 Sept. 07; *Lieut.* 3 Jan. 11; *Capt.* 13 Feb. 28.				
4	0	*Adjutant.*—John Spence, (*Lieut.*) 28 Oct. 36.				
17	0	*Quarter-Master.*—₽ Samuel Goddard,[9] 20 March, 23.				
		Surgeon.—Richard Dowse, 8 Jan. 36; *Assist.-Surg.* 25 Jan. 15.				
6	0	*Assist.-Surgs.*—Henry Drummond, M.D. 28 Nov. 34.				
5	0	John Thomson Telfer, 17 July, 35.				

4 Captain Lynch was at the siege of Flushing. Served at Malta and the Ionian Islands under Lord Wm. Bentinck. At Genoa and in the South of France in 1814. Present at the siege and capture of Bhurtpore, wounded at the assault 18th Jan. 1826.

5 Captain Newman was at the siege and storming of Bhurtpore.

6 Captain Hazlewood was at the siege and capture of Flushing, 1809. Present at the siege and capture of Bhurtpore, 1826.

7 Captains Tidy and Watson were at the siege and capture of Bhurtpore.

8 Lieut. Daly lost a leg at Bhurtpore.

9 Quarter-Master Goddard was at Waterloo, 18th June, and storming of Cambray, 24th June, 1815. Present at the Siege of Hattrass. Served the campaign of 1817 and 18, in the Deccan. Present at the siege and storming of Bhurtpore, 1826.

Facings Buff.—*Agent*, Mr. Charles Downes, 14, Warwick-street, Charing-cross.

1 Sir James Watson has received a medal for Java, and has performed distinguished service in the various wars in the East Indies.

2 Colonel Everard's services :—Expedition to South America, including taking of Maldonado ; actions previous to, and assault of Monte Video, where he commanded the Forlorn Hope. Campaign and battle of Corunna. Expedition to Walcheren, and siege of Flushing. Commanded 14th Regt. at the siege of Hatrass, 1816. Commanded Flank Battalion in the campaigns of 1817 and 18, under Lord Hastings. Commanded 14th Regt. at the siege and assault of Bhurtpore, 1826.

Emb. for For. Service, 1827.] **15th (or the Yorkshire E. R.) Regiment of Foot.** [Serving in Canada.

"MARTINIQUE"—"GUADALOUPE."

Years' Serv.						
57		**Colonel.**				
Full Pay.	Half Pay.	ᴾ Sir Moore Disney,¹ K.C.B., *Ens.* 17 April, 1783; *Lieut. & Capt.* 3 June, 91; *Capt. & Lieut.-Col.* 12 June, 95; *Col.* 29 April, 02; *Major-Gen.* 25 Oct. 09; *Lieut.-Gen.* 4 June, 14; *Gen.* 10 Jan. 37; *Col.* 15th Regt. 23 July, 14.				
		Lieut.-Colonel.				
13	3 6/12	Lord Charles Wellesley, *Ens.* ᴾ 16 Jan. 24; *Lieut.* ᴾ 21 Nov. 28; *Capt.* ᴾ 26 Feb. 30; *Brevet-Major,* 8 Sept. 31; *Regtl.-Major,* ᴾ 4 Oct. 33; *Lieut.-Col.* ᴾ 29 Dec. 37.				
		Majors.				
27	3/12	Thomas A. Drought, *Ens.* 11 Nov. 13; *Lieut.* ᴾ 16 Oct. 17; *Capt.* ᴾ 10 Oct. 22; *Major,* ᴾ 31 Dec. 30.				
15	8/12	Wm. Robert Brudenell Smith, *Ens.* 29 July, 24; *Lieut.* ᴾ 28 Jan. 26; *Capt.* ᴾ 20 Mar. 27; *Major,* ᴾ 21 June, 39.				

		CAPTAINS.	ENSIGN.	LIEUT.	CAPTAIN.	BREV.-MAJ.
32	3 8/12	Geo. Dennis Colman	29 Dec. 04	21 May 06	18 May 15	10 Jan. 37
17	1/12	Robert A. Cuthbert	ᴾ 25 Sept. 23	ᴾ 7 July 25	ᴾ 28 May 29	
15	0	James R. Brunker	9 April 25	9 Sept. 28	ᴾ 14 Sept. 32	
14	6/12	T. Halifax Western	2 Jan. 26	ᴾ 5 June 27	ᴾ 29 April 36	
14	0	George Pinder	ᴾ 24 Aug. 26	ᴾ 31 Dec. 30	ᴾ 21 Oct. 36	
16	0	R. H. J. B. McCumming	ᴾ 16 Dec. 24	ᴾ 6 Oct. 25	ᴾ 26 Nov. 30	
11	0	John A. Cole	14 Jan. 30	26 May 33	ᴾ 14 Dec. 38	
9	0	John Hope Wingfield ..	ᴾ 17 May 31	ᴾ 4 Oct. 33	ᴾ 18 Jan. 39	
10	0	Fitz William Walker....	ᴾ 31 Dec. 30	ᴾ 17 June 36	ᴾ 21 June 39	
8	0	Charles Horrocks	ᴾ 4 Jan. 33	ᴾ 21 Oct. 36	ᴾ 22 June 39	
		LIEUTENANTS.				
21	6 6/12	F. Lennox Ingall	8 April 13	14 Mar. 16		
15	0	Jas. Roy Norton	9 April 25	17 Dec. 30		
14	0	James Hay	16 Feb. 26	21 Dec. 32		
10	4 8/12	Robert Mac Gregor	6 Oct. 25	8 Aug. 27		
10	0	Hen. Scott Colman	ᴾ 19 Nov. 30	ᴾ 29 April 36		
7	0	H. B. F. Dickinson	5 July 33	ᴾ 23 Dec. 36		
7	0	Henry Grierson	ᴾ 9 Aug. 33	ᴾ 24 Feb. 37		
7	0	John Hen. Ashhurst	ᴾ 13 Dec. 33	ᴾ 16 Feb. 38	2 Captain Walker was at the siege of Flushing and taking of Tervere, in the island of Walcheren. Present at the crossing of the Bidassoa, and action before Bayonne.	
7	0	Hon. C. R. West	ᴾ 30 Aug. 33	ᴾ 5 June 35		
4	0	Daniel Capel	ᴾ 29 April 36	ᴾ 14 Dec. 38		
4	0	Hon. Francis Colborne..	ᴾ 1 Oct. 36	ᴾ 18 Jan. 39		
4	0	Henry Bond Head......	ᴾ 23 Dec. 36	ᴾ 21 June 39		
3	0	Chas. Edw. Astell	ᴾ 24 Feb. 37	ᴾ 22 June 39		
		ENSIGNS.				
3	0	J. Allix Wilkinson......	10 Mar. 37			
2	0	Alger R. Sewell	ᴾ 16 Feb. 38			
2	0	William Boyle	6 Dec. 38			
2	0	J. R. Barry............	ᴾ 14 Dec. 38			
2	0	Edward Pardoe	ᴾ 18 Jan. 39			
1	0	James Hutton.........	ᴾ 21 June 39			
1	0	John Smith...........	ᴾ 12 July 39			
1	0	C. Theodore de Montenach	ᴾ 13 July 39			

29	7 11/12	*Paymaster.*—ᴾ Charles Walker,² 1 July, 24; *Ens.* 24 Mar. 03; *Lieut.* 5 Dec. 04; *Capt.* 21 Oct. 13.	
14	0	*Adjutant.*—James Hay, (*Lieut.*) 16 Feb. 26.	
2	0	*Quarter-Master.*—J. Cartmail, 12 July, 39; *Ens.* 7 Dec. 38.	
		Surgeon.—Wm. Dobson, 29 Mar. 39; *Assist.-Surg.* 22 Sept. 25; *Hosp.-Assist.* 6 May, 15.	
		Assist.-Surgs.—Wm. Wallace, M.D. 8 Mar. 27; *Hosp.-Assist.* 17 Aug. 26.	
3	0	Henry Franklin, 29 Dec. 37.	

Facings Yellow—*Agent,* Messrs. Cox & Co.

---

1 Sir Moore Disney served under the Duke of York in Flanders; has received a Medal for Corunna; and commanded a brigade in the Expedition to Walcheren.

Emb. for For. Serv. 1819.] **16th (or the Bedfordshire) Regiment of Foot.** [Serving in Bengal.

Colonel.

Years' Serv.		
Full Pay	Half Pay	
55		🟉 Wm. Carr, *Visc.* Beresford,[1] G.C.B. & G.C.H. *Ens.* 27 Aug. 1785; *Lieut.* 25 June, 89; *Capt.* 24 Jan 91; *Major*, 1 March, 94; *Lieut.-Col.* 11 Aug. 94; *Col.* 1 Jan. 00; *Major-Gen.* 25 April, 08; *Lieut.-Gen.* 1 Jan. 12; *Gen.* 27 May, 25: *Col.* 16 Regt. 15 March, 23.
40	1 9/12	*Lieut.-Colonels.*—🟉 Adam Gordon Campbell,[2] *Ens.* 22 Nov. 98; *Lieut.* 14 Oct. 00; *Capt.* 29 Sept. 04; *Brevet-Major*, 4 June, 14; *Regtl.-Major*, 13 July, 26; *Lieut.-Col.* 8 Feb. 34.
35	5/12	🟉 George Macdonald,[3] *Ens.* 5 Sept. 05; *Lieut.* 25 July, 06; *Capt.* 17 Aug. 15; *Major*, P 13 Aug. 30; *Lieut.-Col.* 10 Jan. 37.
36	0	*Majors.*—S. G. Carter, *Ens.* 23 Mar. 04; *Lieut.* 27 March, 05; *Capt.* 25 Dec. 14; *Major*, 8 Feb. 34.
32	3 4/12	🟉 Henry Clements,[4] *Ens.* 7 April, 05; *Lieut.* 26 Aug. 07; *Capt.* 1 Sept. 13; *Major*, 10 Jan. 37.

			ENSIGN.	LIEUT.	CAPTAIN.	BREV.-MAJ.
		CAPTAINS.				
32	0	Robert Browne	12 May 08	8 June 09	7 Apr. 25	28 June 38
31	0	John Dalzell	1 Mar. 09	10 Sept. 12	1 Sept. 25	28 June 38
24	0	Henry M'Manus	18 July 16	16 Apr. 20	25 Oct. 27	
27	2/12	James Brand	11 Mar. 13	17 Aug. 20	25 Apr. 28	
20	0	Robt. Luxmoore	1 June 20	11 June 24	P 31 Aug. 30	
20	7	🟉 Charles Mudie[5]	4 Nov. 13	4 Oct. 15	P 26 Mar. 29	
25	0	Charles Murray	1 Sept. 15	13 Oct. 21	5 May 35	
14	1/12	Arthur Chas. Chichester	P 12 Dec. 26	P 10 Nov. 29	P 3 Apr. 35	
20	0	Chas. Fred. Thompson	17 Aug. 20	7 Apr. 25	10 Jan. 37	
14	0	Alex. Dick Colley	P 11 Feb. 26	P 22 Nov. 27	P 25 Dec. 35	
		LIEUTENANTS.				
20	0	Thomas Jones	24 Aug. 20	1 Sept. 25		
14	0	William Ashmore	P 18 Feb. 26	P 27 Apr. 27		
15	10 4/12	Alexander Munro	6 Oct. 15	26 Apr. 28		
16	8 7/12	William Bell	30 Nov. 15	26 Apr. 28		
14	0	John Willett P. Audain	14 Dec. 20	2 Oct. 28		
16	0	H. H. F. Clarke[6]	25 Nov. 24	1 May 26		
13	0	Francis Fairtlough	P 13 Mar. 27	21 Aug. 30		
13	1 10/12	Henry Copinger	28 Apr. 25	6 Mar. 28		
12	0	John Bruce	31 July 28	P 12 Apr. 31		
12	0	Francis Cassidy	P 25 Nov. 28	13 Dec. 31		
10	0	Chas. Jeffries Carter	18 June 30	28 Dec. 31		
9	0	Charles Hawker	22 Feb. 31	P 20 July 32		
12	0	John Macdonald	31 July 28	P 4 May 32		
9	0	Wm. Robt. Lyon Bennett	P 12 Apr. 31	P 24 Dec. 33		
9	0	Wm. Alphonso Kirk	30 Dec. 31	8 Feb. 34		
9	0	John Henderson	P 20 Jan. 32	28 Nov. 34		
8	0	Geo. Harris Wallace	P 20 July 32	5 May 35		
8	0	Crofton Ham. Fitzgerald	P 14 Dec. 32	27 July 35		
12	2/12	Hen. Durham Gibbs	P 30 Apr. 28	23 Mar. 33		
7	0	H. Anthony O'Molony	P 24 Dec. 33	10 Mar. 37		
4	0	George Stoney	P 13 May 36	P 11 Jan. 39		
6	0	Stephen Lawson	26 Dec. 34	22 Jan. 39		
5	0	Gilliam Maclaine Ross	8 May 35	9 Aug. 39		
		ENSIGNS.				
4	0	H. C. Miln Ximenes	P 11 Mar. 36			
3	0	Wm. Scott Carter	P 7 Apr. 37			
3	0	Felix Ashpitel	P 28 Apr. 37			
2	0	Thomas Garratt	9 Mar. 38			
1	0	Chas. Lorenzo de Winton	P 15 Feb. 39			
1	0	Lempster R. Elliot	9 Aug. 39			
1	0	John Octav. Chichester	P 26 Oct. 39			
1	0	Aylmer Strangford Craig	8 Nov. 39			

2 Colonel Campbell's services: Egyptian campaign of 1801, including the surrender of, and action to the westward of Alexandria, campaign and battle of Corunna, siege and capture of Flushing.

3 Colonel Macdonald accompanied the expedition to Hanover in 1805, joined the army in Sicily in 1806, and was employed with it in its various operations from 1806 to 1810; in 1810 went with the expedition to Naples, and was present at the capture of Ischia and Procida; returned to Sicily and employed against the French army in 1811; in 1812 was employed in Spain, including the battle of Castella, and siege of Tarragona; embarked for Canada in 1814, and was present at the operations before Plattsburgh; received three wounds at Waterloo, viz., in the leg, in the neck, and through the body, wounding the lungs.

4 Major Clements' services: Capture of the Cape of Good Hope in 1806; expedition to South America; campaign and battle of Corunna; expedition to Walcheren; Peninsula from 1810 to 1814, including Cavares and Merida, Salamanca, Begar, Vittoria, Valley of Bastian, and the Pyrenees.

5 Captain Mudie served in the Peninsula from Nov. 1813, to the end of the war, including the blockade of, and repulse of the sortie from Bayonne. Served the campaign of 1815, and was present at Quatre Bras and Waterloo.

6 Lieut. Clarke served in the Burmese war.

12	5/12	*Paymaster.*—Chas. H. Peirse, 23 Aug. 39; *Ens.* 6 Dec. 27; *Lieut.* 18 July, 30.
12	0	*Adjutant.*—John Bruce, (*Lieut.*) 3 March, 37.
11	13 5/12	*Quarter-Mast.*—Robert Douglas, 14 June, 33; *Ens.* 12 Oct. 15; *Lieut.* 10 Aug. 26.
		Surgeon.—William Steele, 29 May, 35; *Assist.-Surg.* 18 May, 12.
		Assistant-Surgeons.—Duncan Menzies, 29 July, 30; *Hosp.-Assist.* 1 Nov. 27.
14	0	Samuel Ingram, 25 March, 28; *Hosp.-Assist.* 15 June, 26.

Facings Yellow—*Agent*, Sir John Kirkland, No. 80, Pall Mall.

1 Lord Beresford has received a Cross and seven Clasps for Corunna, Busaco, Albuhera, Badajoz, Salamanca, (severely wounded) Vittoria, Pyrenees, Nivelle, Nive, Orthes, and Toulouse.

Embarked for Foreign Service, 1830 & 1831. **17th (or the Leicestershire) Regt. of Foot.** **Serving in the East Indies.**

The *Royal Tiger*, superscribed "HINDOOSTAN."

Colonel.

Years' Serv.		
Full Pay	Half Pay	
65		Sir Fred. Augustus Wetherall,¹ G.C.H. *Ens.* 23 Aug. 1775; *Lieut.* 27 Aug. 76; *Capt.* 17 May, 81; *Major*, 1 Mar. 94; *Lieut.-Col.* 20 May, 95; *Col.* 29 Apr. 1802; *Major-Gen.* 25 Oct. 09; *Lieut.-Gen.* 4 June, 14; *Gen.* 10 Jan. 37.

Lieut.-Colonels.—Wm. Croker,² C.B. *Ens.* ᴾ27 Mar. 03; *Lieut.* ᴾ2 June, 04; *Capt.* ᴾ20 Nov. 06; *Brevet-Major*, 12 Aug. 19; *Regtl.-Major*, ᴾ16 June, 25; *Lieut.-Col.* 1 April, 36.

37	0	
33	6/12	Thomas Hall,³ *Ens.* 26 Sept. 06; *Lieut.* 29 Aug. 07; *Capt.* ᴾ16 Sept. 13; *Brevet-Major*, 19 Jan. 26; *Regtl.-Major*, 24 July, 27; *Lieut.-Col.* ᴾ23 June, 38.
29	4 3/12	*Majors.*—John Pennycuick,⁴ K.H. *Ens.* 31 Aug. 07; *Lieut.* 15 Jan. 12; *Capt.* ᴾ14 June, 21; *Major*, ᴾ25 April, 34; *Brevet-Lieut.-Col.* 23 July, 39.
16	6 10/12	Chas. John Deshon, *Ens.* ᴾ18 Sept. 17; *Lieut.* ᴾ6 Oct. 25; *Capt.* ᴾ22 April, 26; *Major*, ᴾ16 June, 37.

		CAPTAINS.	ENSIGN.	LIEUT.	CAPTAIN.	BREV.-MAJ.
16	0	George Deedes	ᴾ 2 Sept. 24	ᴾ17 Sept. 25	ᴾ13 Aug. 29	
19	12	₱ Philip M'Pherson⁵	2 Nov. 09	13 June 11	13 Mar. 27	
15	0	Archibald Lockhart	ᴾ19 May 25	ᴾ 1 Aug. 26	ᴾ11 Oct. 33	
15	0	John Darley	ᴾ16 June 25	ᴾ 3 Oct. 26	ᴾ19 Dec. 34	5 Capt. M'Pherson served in the Peninsula, from Nov. 1809 to July, 1814, including the following battles, sieges, &c., viz., Coa, Mortiagoa, skirmish near and battle of Busaco, Coimbra, Alenguer, Pombal, Redinha, Miranda do Corvo, Sabugal, Fuentes d'Onor, Soiba, Ciudad Rodrigo, Jan. 1812, Badajoz, Mar. and Apr. 1812, Carvellejo, Petiegua, Salamanca, Nivelle, Bayonne, Nive, Tarbes, Tournefeuille and Toulouse.
14	0	Isaac Blackburne	ᴾ25 May 26	ᴾ19 July 27	ᴾ12 Feb. 36	
12	0	Croker Miller	ᴾ29 Jan. 29	ᴾ 5 Apr. 33	ᴾ19 Aug. 36	
10	0	John Erskine	ᴾ11 Feb. 30	ᴾ19 Dec. 34	ᴾ10 Feb. 37	
9	0	Wellington Hackett	ᴾ30 Dec. 31	ᴾ20 Nov. 35	ᴾ27 Oct. 37	
7	0	Legendre Ch. Bourchier¹⁰	ᴾ 5 Apr. 33	ᴾ12 Feb. 36	ᴾ20 July 38	
23	0	Lawrence Fyfe	ᴾ16 Oct. 17	10 Apr. 25	ᴾ14 Sept. 32	
		LIEUTENANTS.				
23	2/12	John Thomas Nagel	28 June 17	10 July 20		
15	0	₱ ⚔ David Cooper⁶	11 Aug. 25	1 May 28		6 Lieut. Cooper served in the Peninsula from Sept. 1810 to Aug. 1813, including battles of Fuentes d'Onor and Salamanca; sieges of Ciudad Rodrigo and Burgos. Present at Waterloo.
14	0	Wm. Fred. Harvey	ᴾ11 Apr. 26	ᴾ13 Aug. 29		
12	0	Edw. Barry Owen	26 Apr. 28	ᴾ21 Sept. 32		
7	0	Arth. Hyde Lucas	8 Mar. 33	ᴾ11 Dec. 35		
18	11 4/	₱ Rob. Gudgeon Johnston⁷	25 Oct. 10	20 Jan. 14		
12	0	Archibald Dickson	2 Apr. 28	8 Mar. 31		7 Lieut. Johnston served in the Peninsula, from Sept. 1811 to June 1814, including the battles of Vittoria, the Pyrenees from 25th July to 1st Aug., Nivelle, Nive, Orthes, Aire and Toulouse.
11	0	Fred. Augustus Wetherall	10 Dec. 29	ᴾ14 Dec. 32		
10	0	Eric Mackay Clarke	20 Oct. 30	6 June 35		
7	0	Js. Fitz Herbert de Tessier	ᴾ13 Sept. 33	1 Apr. 36		
10	0	Sep. Barty W. Wynyard	13 June 30	2 Apr. 36		
6	0	Savage Hall Corry	ᴾ19 Dec. 34	ᴾ29 Apr. 36		
7	0	Wm. Dunlop Baird	ᴾ29 Nov. 33	ᴾ29 July 36		8 Captain Moore was at the capture of various places in the West Indies, in 1801. Served in the Peninsula, including the battles of Nivelle, Nive, Orthes, and Toulouse. Wounded in Ireland, during the Rebellion in 1798, when a Militia Officer.
6	0	Henry Fane	ᴾ 1 Aug. 34	ᴾ30 July 36		
6	0	Jas. Thomas Mauleverer	ᴾ18 Apr. 34	ᴾ19 Aug. 36		
5	0	Oliver Paget Bourke	ᴾ11 Dec. 35	ᴾ27 Oct. 37		
12	0	Jas. Willington Kyffin	25 Sept. 28	23 Sept. 36		
4	0	Thos. Ormsby Ruttledge	ᴾ29 Apr. 36	ᴾ23 Apr. 38		
4	0	Harv. Well. Pole Welman	2 Apr. 36	28 Dec. 38		9 Quart.-Mast. Sarson served the Mahratta campaign of 1817 and 18.
4	0	Edw. Hen. Cormick	ᴾ29 July 36	ᴾ11 Jan. 39		
4	0	John Fra. Jones	ᴾ21 Oct. 36	ᴾ12 Apr. 39		
3	0	John Pennefather Perceval	17 Feb. 37	16 May 39		10 Captain Bourchier was severely wounded at the assault and capture of the Fort of Khelat, in Affghanistan, 13th Nov. 1839.
3	0	John L. Croker	18 Mar. 37	ᴾ18 Oct. 39		
		ENSIGNS.				
3	0	Edward Croker	ᴾ27 Oct. 37	Alex. M'Kinstry	ᴾ22 Feb. 39	
2	0	Edwin Colville Moore	1 June 38	Rich. J. Ross O'Conor	ᴾ12 Apr. 39	
2	0	Wm. Gordon	ᴾ20 July 38	Edw. Wm. John Knox	ᴾ18 Oct. 39	
2	0	T. P. G. Fitz-Mayer	28 Dec. 38	Robert Portal	ᴾ17 Jan. 40	

27	6/12	*Paymaster.*—₱ Joseph Moore,⁸ 5 April, 33; *Ens.* July, 1813; *Lieut.* 22 July, 13; *Capt.* 15 June, 32.
15	0	*Adjutant.*—₱ ⚔ David Cooper, (*Lieut.*) 21 May, 26.
17	0	*Quarter-Master.*—John Sarson,⁹ 14 Aug. 23.
20	7 4/12	*Surg.*—W. Milligan, M.D. 1 March, 39; *A.-S.* 10 Feb. 14; *H.-Assist.* 19 July 13.
2	0	*Assist.-Surgeons.*—Arthur S. Thomson, M.D. 19 Oct. 38.
		John Bathurst Thomson, M.D. 11 Jan. 39.

Facings White.—*Agents*, Messrs. Cox & Co.

1 Sir Frederick Augustus Wetherall commenced his military career in the 17th regiment,—served with it in the American war, and was present at the siege of Boston, the battles of Brooklyn, Whiteplains, Fort Washington, Prince Town, Brandwine, Germantown, Monmouth, &c. &c. Served in H. M.'s ship *Alfred*, in the battles off Cape Finisterre and St. Vincent's, previous to the relief of Gibraltar. He received two wounds at the taking of Martinique in 1794 as Aide-de-camp to the Duke of Kent; and was again wounded in action with a French frigate, and taken prisoner, on his passage from St. Domingo to Barbadoes with dispatches from Admiral Sir Wm. Parker and General Forbes, to Sir Ralph Abercrombie in 1795; he remained a close prisoner at Guadaloupe upwards of nine months, closely confined in a dungeon, in irons, without any other clothing than a shirt and a pair of trowsers, or any description of bedding; and on a daily allowance of three biscuits and a quart of water. Served in the East Indies, and was second in command on the expedition to Java, for which he received the thanks of both Houses of Parliament, and a Medal. His service abroad amounts to forty-one years.

2 Colonel Croker's services :—Siege of Gunnowri, 1807 ; campaign of 1808 and 9 against the Sieks ; campaign of 1814 and 15 against the Nepaul States ; Mahratta and Pindarree campaign of 1817 and 18.

3 Colonel Hall's services :—Capture of the Isle of France 1810 ; expedition to Java, 1811, including the actions at Batavia

Emb. for Foreign Service, 1837. — **18th (or Royal Irish) Regiment of Foot.** — [Serving in the East Indies.

On the three corners of the second Colour, the *Lion of Nassau,* "*Virtutis Namurcensis Præmium.*" The *Sphinx*, with the word, "EGYPT."

Colonel.

Years' Serv.			
53			
Full Pay	Half Pay		
44	0		
40	0		
17	4/12		
35	1 3/12		

Ⓟ Matthew Lord Aylmer,[1] G.C.B. *Ens.* 19 Oct. 87; *Lieut.* 26 Oct. 91; *Capt.* 8 Aug. 94; *Major,* 9 Oct. 00; *Lieut.-Col.* 25 March, 02; *Col.* 25 July, 10; *Major-Gen.* 4 June, 13; *Lieut.-Gen.* 27 May, 25; *Col. 18th Regt.* 23 July 32;

Lieut.-Colonel.—George Burrell,[2] *Ens.* 4 Feb. 97; *Lieut.* ᴘ 3 May, 97; *Capt.* 15 Aug. 05; *Major,* ᴘ 30 April, 07; *Brevet-Lieut.-Col.* 4 June, 13; *Regtl.-Lieut.-Col. & Col. in the Army,* 22 July, 30.

Henry Pratt,[3] *Ens.* 17 April, 00; *Lieut.* ᴘ 30 June, 01; *Capt.* 12 Oct. 09; *Major,* 22 July, 30; *Lieut.-Col.* 22 Oct. 39.

Majors.—Henry Williams Adams, *Ens.* 31 July, 23; *Lieut.* ᴘ 31 Dec. 25; *Capt.* ᴘ 10 June, 26; *Major,* ᴘ 18 Jan. 39.

Robert Hammill, *Ens.* 3 Dec. 03; *Lieut.* 22 Jan. 06; *Capt.* 29 July 11; *Brev.-Maj.* 22 July 30; *Regt.-Major,* 22 Oct. 39.

Years' Serv. Full	Half	CAPTAINS.	ENSIGN.	LIEUT.	CAPTAIN.	BREV.-MAJ.
35	0	Jeremiah Cowper	21 Nov. 05	25 Dec. 06	4 Sept. 23	28 June 38
35	0	Francis Wm. Dillon[4]	5 Dec. 05	6 Mar. 07	7 Apr. 25	28 June 38
29	4	Ⓟ Thomas Moore[5]	25 Oct. 07	8 Mar. 10	ᴘ 18 Feb. 26	
19	0	Nicholas R. Tomlinson ..	ᴘ 22 Mar. 21	ᴘ 21 July 25	ᴘ 8 Feb. 33	
25	1 10/12	John Grattan	ᴘ 8 July 13	4 Sept. 23	4 Mar. 36	
28	2 8/12	John J. Sargent	26 Oct. 09	13 Oct. 10	ᴘ 13 May 26	
14	0	Francis Wigston........	ᴘ 16 Mar. 26	ᴘ 1 June 32	ᴘ 18 Jan. 39	
14	0	Chas. J. Russell Collinson	ᴘ 25 May 26	ᴘ 4 Jan. 33	ᴘ 12 July 39	
11	0	Wm. Aug. Towns. Payne	ᴘ 23 May 29	ᴘ 7 June 33	ᴘ 20 Sept. 39	
18	9 3/12	Thomas Moyle	8 July 13	24 Nov. 14	22 Oct. 39	
		LIEUTENANTS.				
11	0	John Philip Mitford	ᴘ 4 June 29	ᴘ 16 May 34		
11	0	Clement Alex. Edwards	11 June 29	ᴘ 28 Nov. 34		
11	0	Charles Dunne	30 Apr. 29	ᴘ 20 Mar. 35		
8	0	Sir Harry Darell, *Bart.*	ᴘ 1 June 32	ᴘ 12 June 35		
8	0	Arthur Wilson	ᴘ 4 Jan. 33	26 June 35		
8	0	Hon. Chas. Hen. Stratford	ᴘ 8 Feb. 33	ᴘ 18 Mar. 36		
6	0	Geo. Wm. Davis........	ᴘ 16 May 34	20 July 38		
6	0	Standish Haly.........	ᴘ 28 Nov. 34	ᴘ 18 Jan. 39		
5	0	Sir Wm. Macgregor, *Bt.*	ᴘ 20 Mar. 35	ᴘ 29 Mar. 39		
5	0	Edward Jodrell	ᴘ 5 June 35	ᴘ 12 July 39		
6	0	James Wm. Graves ...	24 Oct. 34	31 May 39		
3	0	Geo. Fred. Call ...... :	ᴘ 7 Apr. 37	ᴘ 20 Sept. 39		
14	0	Charles Dunbar	ᴘ 3 Aug. 26	9 Nov. 32		
6	0	William Tyrrell Bruce ..	ᴘ 4 July 34	ᴘ 15 Apr. 36		
6	0	Charles Bentley	30 May 34	11 Mar. 37		
6	0	Christopher Vaughan Foss	29 Nov. 34	ᴘ 11 May 38		
6	0	Wm. Henry O'Toole	ᴘ 12 Dec. 34	31 May 39		
6	0	Wm. Augustus Gwynne..	ᴘ 11 July 34	23 Oct. 39		
6	0	John Joseph Wood......	19 Sept. 34	do.		
6	0	William Coates	ᴘ 6 Feb. 35	do.		
5	0	George Hilliard	ᴘ 13 Feb. 35	do.		
5	0	Alexander Murray	ᴘ 24 Apr. 35	do.		
2	0	Francis Swinburne......	20 July 38	24 Oct. 39		
		ENSIGNS.				
2	0	David Edwards	23 Nov. 38			
2	0	Hen. Felix Vavasour	ᴘ 7 Dec. 38			
2	0	Scroope Bernard	ᴘ 18 Jan. 39			
1	0	John Cochrane	ᴘ 21 Apr. 39			
1	0	Anth. W. S. F. Armstrong	ᴘ 21 June 39			
1	0	Isaac Henry Hewitt	ᴘ 12 July 39			
1	0	Wm. Peter Cockburn ..	ᴘ 21 June 39			
1	0	Henry Duncan Burrell ..	24 Oct. 39			
17	21 7/12	*Paymaster.*—George Isaac Call, 7 Dec. 36 ; *Cornet,* 4 March, 02 ; *Lieut.* 1 July, 04 ; *Capt.* 26 Dec. 11.				
8	0	*Adjutant.*—Arthur Wilson, (*Lieut.*) 16 May, 34.				
11	0	*Quarter-Master.*—James Carroll, 4 June, 29.				
20	7 3/12	*Surgeon.*—Ⓟ Don. M'Kinlay, M.D. 14 Oct. 26 ; *Assist.-Surg.* 5 Oct. 15 ; *Hosp.-Assistant,* 20 Sept. 13.				
5	0	*Assistant-Surgeons.*—Charles Cowen, 27 March, 35.				
1	0	John Baker, 15 Feb. 39.				

Facings Blue.—*Agent,* Messrs. Cox & Co.

Side notes:
1 Lord Aylmer has received a cross and one clasp for Talavera, Busaco, Fuentes d'Onor, Vittoria, and Nive.
2 Col. Burrell was at the capture of Guadaloupe in 1810. Served the campaign of 1814 in Upper Canada.
3 Col. Pratt served the campaign of 1801 in Egypt, and that of 1809 in St Domingo.
4 Major Dillon served in the expedition to St. Domingo in 1809.
5 Capt. Moore served in the Peninsula from 1808 to 1813, and was present at the siege of Ciudad Rodrigo, and both sieges of Badajoz. Severely wounded at the storming of Badajoz on the night of the 6th April, 1812.

and Weldevrieden ; storming the entrenched lines at Fort Cornelis ; storming the heights of Serandole, and capture of the Fort of Samarang ; present at the siege and storming of Bhurtpore, 1826
4 Colonel Pennicuick's services :—Expedition to Java, including the actions at Weldevrieden, Fort Cornelis, Djocjocarta, Probolings. Capture of Balli and Macassar in 1814. Served in the Burmese War in 1825 and 6. Wounded in the breast in an attack upon the enemy's field artillery, within the lines of Cornelis, 26th Aug 1811

19th (or the 1st Yorkshire North Riding) Regiment of Foot.

Colonel.
Sir Hilgrove Turner.[1] G.C.H. K.C. *Ens.* 20 Feb. 1782; *Lieut. & Capt.* 13 Oct. 89; *Capt. & Lieut.-Col.* 12 Nov. 94; *Col.* 1 Jan. 01; *Major-Gen.* 25 Apr. 08; *Lieut-Gen.* 4 June 13; *Gen.* 22 July, 30; *Col.* 19th Regt. 27 Apr. 11.

Years' Serv. — 58 Full Pay.

Lieut.-Colonel.
Thos. Hamilton, *Ens.* 15 July, 13; *Lieut.* 9 June, 14; *Capt.* 3 Nov. 25; *Major*, 23 Jan. 37; *Lieut.-Col.* P 28 Dec. 38.

Years' Serv.: 27 Full / 0 Half.

Majors.
Chas. Craufurd Hay, *Ens.* 27 June, 24; *Lieut.* P 24 Dec. 25; *Capt.* P 19 Sept. 26; *Major*, P 16 June, 37. — 16 / 0

Studholme John Hodgson,[2] *Ens.* 30 Dec. 19; *Lieut.* 3 Feb. 25; *Capt.* P 30 Dec. 26; *Major*, P 28 Dec. 38. — 20 / 10/12

Full	Half	CAPTAINS.	ENSIGN.	LIEUT.	CAPTAIN.	BREVET-MAJOR.
24	0	John Stirling	6 June 16	P 22 July 24	P 13 May 26	
21	3 1/12	Chas. Highmore Potts	8 Feb. 16	P 13 Nov. 17	P 31 Dec. 25	28 June 38
19	0	David Burns	17 Oct. 11	25 Jan. 16	20 July 30	
21	8 5/12	Thomas Beckham[3]	7 May 11	23 Feb. 13	P 8 June 30	
15	0	Francis Price	P 12 May 25	P 18 Feb. 26	P 7 Sept. 34	
13	11/12	John Semple	P 20 July 26	P 28 Sept. 30	P 5 Sept. 34	
25	0	Alexander Scott	17 Aug. 15	7 Apr. 25	23 Jan. 37	
15	0	Robert Lovelace	9 Apr. 25	12 Apr. 32	P 16 June 37	
8	0	Thomas Hilton	3 Mar. 32	29 July 36	P 30 Mar. 38	
7	0	John Duke Simpson	P 31 May 33	P 26 May 37	P 28 Dec. 38	
		LIEUTENANTS.				
15	0	William Bernard	17 Nov. 25	25 Jan. 28		
13	1 8/12	Frederick Deacon	P 8 Oct. 25	P 27 Jan. 32		
10	0	Mark Anthony H. Tuite	P 2 Nov. 30	P 21 Feb. 34		
10	0	Rich. A. M. Franklin	P 28 Sept. 30	17 Apr. 35		
8	0	Anthony Walshe	P 2 Nov. 32	23 Jan. 37		
6	0	Francis Seymour	P 2 May 34	P 16 June 37		
16	12 4/12	Geo. Rich. Langley	24 Nov. 12	7 Jan. 14		
18	8 5/12	Geo. Adamson Stanley	17 Feb. 14	25 May 15		
6	0	Jas. Temple Bowdoin	P 12 Sept. 34	P 30 Mar. 38		
5	0	James Cochrane	5 June 35	P 28 Dec. 38		
4	0	Henry Calley	29 July 36	P 2 Feb. 39		
7	0	George Tuite	P 7 Feb. 34	31 May 39		
5	0	William Dillon	P 13 Feb. 35	P 15 Feb. 39		
		ENSIGNS.				
3	0	Edw. J. Ellerman	P 10 Feb. 37			
3	0	H. Butler Stoney	P 5 May 37			
3	0	Robert Sanders	P 26 May 37			
3	0	Fred. Aug. Jeffreys	P 16 June 37			
2	0	James Ker	P 30 Mar. 38			
2	0	R. J. S. Mansergh	P 14 Sept. 38			
2	0	John Phillips	P 2 Feb. 39			
1	0	Hugh J. M. Campbell	31 May 39			

15	0	*Paymaster.*—Thos. R. Travers, 23 Nov. 38; *Ens.* 7 April, 25; *Lieut.* 10 June, 26.
4	0	*Adjutant.*—Henry Calley, (*Lieut.*) 2 Aug. 39.
5	0	*Quarter-Master.*—Richard Barrett, 30 Oct. 35.
16	0	*Surgeon.*—James Young,[4] M.D. 18 Oct. 39; *Assist.-Surg.* 14 Aug. 24; *Hosp.-Assist.* 18 May 24.
15	0	*Assistant-Surgeon.*—Thos Williams, M.D. 28 Sept. 26; *Hosp.-Assist.* 3 Nov. 25.

Facings Green.—*Agent*, Messrs. Cox & Co.—*Irish Agent*, Cane & Co.

[*Returned from Barbadoes*, 27 Aug. 1836.]

---

1 Sir Hilgrove Turner served in Flanders, and was present at the battles of St. Amand and Famars; siege of Valenciennes; action at Lincelles; investment of Dunkirk; actions at Lannoi and Vaux; Cateau, Basieu, Mouvais, and Templeuve, Tournay, and capture of Fort St. André. He served also in Egypt, and was at the battles of the 8th, 13th, and 21st March, 1801, &c.

2 Major Hodgson served in the Burmese war.

3 Capt. Beckham served the campaigns of 1812, 13, and 14 in the Peninsula.

4 Dr. Young served in Africa from 1824 to 1827 inclusive, and was present at the battle of Doodwa against the Ashantees, 7 Aug. 26.

20th (or the East Devonshire) Regiment of Foot.

"MINDEN"—"EGMONT-OP-ZEE"—The *Sphinx*, with the words "EGYPT"—"MAIDA"—"VITTORIA" "PYRENEES"—"ORTHES"—"TOULOUSE"—"PENINSULA."

Years' Serv.		
Full Pay.	Half Pay.	

Colonel.

| 59 | | ฿ Sir William Houstoun,[1] Bt. G.C.B. G.C.H. Ens. 18 July, 1781; Lieut. 2 April, 82; Capt. 13 Mar. 83; Major, 1 Mar. 94; Lieut.-Col. 18 Mar. 95; Col. 29 April, 1802; Major-Gen. 25 Oct. 09; Lieut.-Gen. 4 June, 14; Gen. 10 Jan. 37; Col. 20th Regt. 5 April, 15. |

Lieut.-Colonel.

| 42 | 3/12 | ฿ Henry Thomas,[2] C.B. Ens. 1 April, 98; Lieut. ᵖ 29 Dec. 98; Capt. 10 Sept. 05; Brevet-Major, 26 Aug. 13; Brevet-Lieut.-Col. 12 Aug. 19; Regtl.-Major, ᵖ 16 Dec. 24; Regtl.-Lieut.-Col. ᵖ 26 Nov. 25; Col. 10 Jan. 37. |

Majors.

| 20 | 0 | William Nelson Hutchinson, Ens. 24 Feb. 20; Lieut. 25 Oct. 23; Capt. ᵖ 17 June, 26; Major, ᵖ 4 Dec. 32. |
| 26 | 2 11/12 | ฿ John Maclean,[3] Ens. 2 May, 11; Lieut. 10 Dec. 12; Capt. 25 Dec. 30; Major, ᵖ 12 April, 39. |

		CAPTAINS.	ENSIGN.	LIEUT.	CAPTAIN.	BREVET-MAJOR.
25	3/12	Frederick Croad........	20 July 15	15 Dec. 18	ᵖ 27 Sept. 31	
15	1/12	Wm. Huntly Campbell..	ᵖ 27 Aug. 25	ᵖ 30 Dec. 26	ᵖ 19 July 31	
16	0	Fred. Contart Barlow ..	2 July 24	25 Oct. 27	ᵖ 18 Dec. 29	
15	0	Frederick Horn	ᵖ 26 Jan. 26	ᵖ 17 April 28	ᵖ 16 June 37	
13	0	Fra. Michael Fraser	12 April 27	ᵖ 17 Aug. 29	ᵖ 3 Nov. 37	
24	2 1/2	Charles Smith.........	ᵖ 20 Oct. 13	21 April 14	ᵖ 31 Dec. 25	28 June 38
13	7/12	R. Sherbourne Murray..	ᵖ 21 June 27	ᵖ 29 Mar. 33	ᵖ 19 June 35	
8	0	Benjamin Newman	ᵖ 23 Nov. 32	ᵖ 3 Nov. 37	ᵖ 12 April 39	
5	0	Hugh Dennis Crofton....	ᵖ 13 Mar. 35	29 Dec. 37	ᵖ 9 Aug. 39	
6	0	Lachlan Duff Gordon....	ᵖ 25 July 34	ᵖ 27 July 38	ᵖ 31 Dec. 39	
		LIEUTENANTS.				
20	5 4/12	Matthew Day.........	5 Oct. 15	2 Oct. 16		
20	0	Patrick Hennessey......	24 April 20	19 May 25		
16	0	Scrope Reynett Berdmore	25 Jan. 25	11 Oct. 27		
12	0	Eugene Brock..........	31 July 28	ᵖ 18 Aug. 29		
13	0	Henry Crawley	11 Oct. 27	11 June 30		
11	0	William Frith..........	ᵖ 12 Feb. 29	ᵖ 12 July 31		
4	0	John C. W. Vivian......	ᵖ 12 Feb. 36	ᵖ 15 Dec. 37		
5	0	Lord Mark Kerr........	19 June 35	14 Sept. 38		
4	0	Fred. Charles Evelegh ..	ᵖ 1 July 36	ᵖ 10 Nov. 37		
5	0	James B. Sharpe	27 Nov. 35	ᵖ 12 April 39		
5	0	Geo. B. C. Crespigny ..	ᵖ 29 Jan. 36	ᵖ 19 July 39		
3	0	Richard Leigh Lye......	ᵖ 3 Nov. 37	ᵖ 9 Aug. 39		
3	0	Philip Henry Crampton	ᵖ 24 Feb. 37	ᵖ 31 Dec. 39		
		ENSIGNS.				
2	0	George Steevens........	ᵖ 3 Aug. 38			
2	0	H. Wilkes Masterson....	ᵖ 6 July 38			
2	0	H. Otho de Crespigny ..	ᵖ 27 July 38			
1	0	William Baring	ᵖ 15 Feb. 39			
1	0	Robert Daly	ᵖ 12 April 39			
1	0	Sir Rich. Gethin, Bart.	ᵖ 19 July 39			
1	0	Maurice Cane	15 June 39			
1	0	Edm. Gilling Hallewell..	ᵖ 31 Dec. 39			

5 Dr. Griffith served in the Peninsula from Jan. 1810 to the end of the war, including the battles of Busaco, Fuentes d'Onor; siege and assault of Ciudad Rodrigo, Jan. 1812; siege and assault of Badajoz, Apr. 1812; battles of Salamanca, Vittoria, Pyrenees, Nivelle, Nive, Orthes, and Toulouse. Wounded at the affair of Vic Bigorre, 19th Jan. 1814. Served in India, Arabia, and the Burmese empire, from May, 1818, including the sieges of Asserghur, Ras-el-Kyma, and Zaia; siege and assault of Dwarka; affair of Beniaboo Ali; assault of a fortress on the banks of the Pegu river; assault of Syrian Pagoda; siege of Donabew, and battle near Prome.

27	0	*Paymaster.*—Charles South, 23 Aug. 27; Ens. 9 Dec. 13; Lieut. 17 Dec. 18.
13	0	*Adjutant.*—Henry Crawley, (Lieut.) 26 Jan. 38.
13	0	*Quarter-Master.*—Patrick Conolly, 19 April, 27.
31	0	*Surgeon.*—฿ M. Griffith,[5] 8 Feb. 17; Asst.-Sur. 24 Oct. 11; Hosp.-A. 4 Nov. 09.
		Assistant-Surgeon.—Andrew Foulis, 4 June, 29; 5 Dec. 26.

Facings Yellow.—*Agent*, Messrs. Cox & Co.

[*Returned from Bombay, May,* 1837.]

1 Sir W. Houstoun was at the taking of Minorca; served in the expeditions to Egypt and to Walcheren; and has received a medal for Fuentes d'Onor.

2 Col. Thomas has received a Medal and two Clasps for Nivelle, Orthes, and Toulouse.

3 Major Maclean served in the Peninsula, from 1812 to July, 1814, including the action of the 14th Nov. 1812, on the retreat from Salamanca, battles of Vittoria, Nivelle (wounded), Nive, and Toulouse. Present in the action before New Orleans, 8th Jan. 1815.

Emb. for Foreign Service, 1832—33.] **21st Foot, (or Royal North British Fusiliers.)** [Serving in the East Indies.

Colonel.

James, *Lord* Forbes,[1] *Ens.* 13 June, 1781; *Lieut. & Capt.* 21 April, 86; *Capt. & Lieut.-Col.* 23 Aug. 93; *Col.* 3 May, 96; *Major-Gen.* 29 April, 1802; *Lieut.-Gen.* 25 April, 08; *Gen.* 12 Aug. 19; *Col.* 21st Fusiliers, 1 June, 16.

Lieut.-Colonels—George Warren Walker,[2] *Cornet,* 17 May, 99; *Lieut.* P 18 June, 01; *Capt.* 5 April, 09; *Major,* 15 April, 17 : *Brevet-Lieut.-Col.* 5 Mar. 18 ; *Regtl.-Lieut.-Col.* 14 Feb. 22 ; *Col.* 10 Jan. 37.

George Deare, *Ens.* 30 Oct. 17; *Lieut.* 8 July, 22 ; *Capt.* P 30 Dec. 24 ; *Major,* P 26 Oct. 32 ; *Lieut.-Col.* 28 Dec. 38.

Majors.—John Picton Beete, *Second-Lieut.* 7 Sept. 20 ; *Lieut.* P 16 Sept. 24 ; *Capt.* P 6 Nov. 27 ; *Major,* P 26 June, 38.

₽ ₡₳ John Luard,[3] *Cornet,* P 25 May, 09 ; *Lieut.* P 3 June, 11 ; *Capt.* P 13 Dec. 21 ; *Major,* P 17 Oct. 34 ; *Brevet-Lieut.-Col.* 28 June, 38.

Years' Serv.		Rank / Name	2d LIEUT.	LIEUT.	CAPTAIN.	BREV.-MAJ.
Full Pay.	Half Pay.					
		CAPTAINS.				
25	1 5/12	William Jas. Sutherland	3 May 14	P 22 Sept. 14	P 29 June 20	10 Jan. 37
26	0	John Crofton Peddie....	4 May 14	P 29 June 20	P 26 Nov. 25	28 June 38
16	0	Wm. Henry Armstrong..	P 16 Sept. 24	P 26 Sept. 26	P 2 Mar. 32	
32	6	Angus Wm. Mackay[4]	P 24 July 02	P 30 June 08	27 July 32	
27	0	₽ Charles Lonsdale[5]	4 Feb. 14	27 April 20	11 Dec. 35	
12	0	Fred. Geo. Ainslie	P 24 April 28	P 5 Oct. 32	P 26 June 38	
16	0	Arthur L'Estrange......	30 Dec. 24	25 June 29	P 11 May 38	
27	0	₡₳ William Thain[6]	13 May 13	15 Aug. 15	17 Nov. 25	
9	0	Gustavus Wm. Nicolls ..	P 4 Oct. 31	P 26 Aug. 36	P 24 Aug. 39	28 June 38
9	0	John Ramsay Stuart....	P 20 Jan. 32	9 Aug. 35	P 10 Jan. 40	
		LIEUTENANTS.				
24	5 4/12	₽ Nicholas Wrixon[7]	P 4 April 11	13 May 13		
23	0	William John King[8] ...	1 Mar. 17	29 Jan. 20		
9	0	Malcolm Mac Gregor....	P 6 Sept. 31	P 12 Dec. 34		
12	0	Bonham Faunce......	P 15 May 28	11 Dec. 35		
8	0	Thos. Bythesea Mortimer	P 16 Nov. 32	2 July 37		
8	0	Alexander Seton........	P 23 Nov. 32	P 2 Mar. 38		
7	0	William Macknight	P 19 April 33	P 26 June 38		
6	0	Alfred Andrews	P 12 Dec. 34	P 17 Aug. 38		
5	0	William Domvile	P 24 April 35	P 18 Aug. 38		
13	7/12	Peter Craufurd	P 19 Sept. 26	P 31 Aug. 30		
12	0	Wm. Alexander Dely....	31 July 28	21 April 33		
9	0	And. Dav. A. Stewart ..	P 26 April 31	P 9 Aug. 33		
12	0	George Hutchinson	P 17 April 28	25 April 33		
9	0	Wm. Francis Ring......	28 Oct. 31	8 May 35		
8	0	Thomas Greene	P 23 Mar. 32	P 10 July 35		
7	0	Walter Murray	P 28 May 33	P 10 July 35		
8	0	Samuel Burges Lamb ..	P 14 Dec. 32	P 5 Feb. 36		
7	0	Henry Wm. Bace	15 Feb. 33	27 July 38		
4	0	B. Clichester Crookshank	25 Mar. 36	29 Dec. 38		
4	0	Arthur Lake Johnston ..	P 22 July 36	30 Dec. 38		
3	0	George Deare	P 15 Dec. 37	P 1 Feb. 39		
4	0	Arthur Geo. Shawe	1 April 36	23 Aug. 39		
3	0	John Lewis Mortimer....	9 Jan. 38	P 10 Jan. 40		
		SECOND LIEUTS.				
2	0	H. W. Martin..........	P 2 Mar. 38			
2	0	Frederic Holland	P 26 June 38			
2	0	John Watson	P 18 Aug. 38			
2	0	Robert Nicholson	P 7 Sept. 38			
2	0	J. R. Carnac	P 27 April 38			
2	0	Patrick Stuart	30 Dec. 38			
2	0	Cha. Geo. Brabazon	P 1 Feb. 39			
1	0	Oliver Tho. Graham	10 Jan. 40			
11	16 4/12	Paymaster.—Philip Jean, 1 Oct. 12.				
12	0	Adjutant.—Bonham Faunce, (Lieut.) 17 Sept. 39.				
1	0	Quarter-Master.—John Vale, 10 May, 39.				
29	1/12	Surgeon.—E. Pilkington, 30 Aug. 27 ; Assist.-Surgeon, 16 May, 11.				
6	0	Assistant-Surgeons.—J. Davidson, 30 June, 25 ; Hospital-Assist. 24 June, 15. Robert Smith, 26 Sept. 34.				

3 Colonel Luard served in the Peninsula, from Jan. 1811, until the end of the war, including battles of Pombal, Redinha, Condeira, Campo Mayor, Los Santos, Usagne, siege of Ciudad Rodrigo, siege of Burgos, siege of forts at, and battle of Salamanca, blockade of Pampelona, and battle of Toulouse. Present at Waterloo 18th June, 1815.

Siege of Bhurtpore 1825 and 6.

4 Capt. Mackay served in the campaign of 1807 in Egypt. Made prisoner of war in an engagement with the enemy in Calabria 16th June, 1809, and detained as such until 14th May, 1814. Present at New Orleans, 8 Jan. 1815.

5 Capt. Lonsdale's services:— campaigns in Germany in 1805 and 6; attack on Copenhagen and capture of the Danish fleet in 1807; campaign and battle of Corunna; expedition to Walcheren ; campaign of 1814 in Holland.

6 Major Thane served the campaign of 1813 & 14, in Germany and Holland, and was present at the bombardment of Antwerp, and storming of Bergen-op-Zoom. Shot through the left arm at Waterloo.

7 Lieut. Wrixon served in Spain from April 1812 to May, 1813, including the siege of Tarragona and battle of Castalla. Present at the siege and capture of Genoa.

7 Lieut. King served the campaigns of 1818 and 19 in Concan, in India. Served in the Burmese war in 1824 and 5, and received a severe contusion when leading the attack on the White Pagoda, an out work of the stockade of Donabew.

Facings Blue.—*Agent,* Messrs. Cox & Co.

1 Lord Forbes served in Flanders, and was present at the following battles and sieges : viz. Famars, Valenciennes, Dunkirk, Lincelles, Mouveaux, Tournay, Vaux, Cateau, Nimeguen, Fort St. André, &c. Lord Forbes afterwards accompanied the expedition to the Helder, and was present in every action but one which took place in that campaign.

2 Col. Walker's services:—siege of Agra and battle of Laswarree 1803 ; siege of Bhurtpore 1805, and campaigns of Lord Lake ; siege of Hattrass ; siege of Kaloonga under Major-Gen. Gillespie, who was killed.

22nd (or the Cheshire) Regt. of Foot.

Colonel.

Hon. Edw. Finch,[1] *Cornet*, 27 Dec. 1778; *Lieut.* 7 Oct. 79; *Capt.* 5 Feb. 83; *Lieut.-Col.* 3 Oct. 92; *Col.* 3 May, 96; *Major-Gen.* 1 Jan. 1801; *Lieut.-Gen.* 25 April, 08; *Gen.* 12 Aug. 19; *Col.* 22nd Regt. 18 Sept. 09.

Years' Serv.: 62

Lieut.-Colonel.

John Lysaght Pennefather, *Cornet*, P 14 Jan. 18; *Lieut.* P 20 Feb. 23; *Capt.* P 5 Nov. 25; *Major*, P 22 March. 31; *Lieut.-Col.* P 18 Oct. 39.

Full Pay 22 / Half Pay 5/12

Majors.

Samuel Brendram Boileau, *Ens.* P 4 Oct. 21; *Lieut.* P 1 Aug. 26; *Capt.* P 25 Nov. 28; *Major*, P 9 Dec. 36. (17 / 2)

John H. Poole, *Ens.* 24 Mar. 14; *Lieut.* 30 Sept. 19: *Capt.* 1 Nov. 30; *Major*, P 18 Oct. 39. (26 / 0)

Full	Half	CAPTAINS.	ENSIGN.	LIEUT.	CAPTAIN.	BREVET-MAJOR.
30	0	William Raban	3 Jan. 11	2 June 13	14 Feb. 28	
23	0	Arthur Myers	12 June 17	P 3 Feb. 20	P 24 June 24	28 June 38
15	0	David Rea Smith	P 3 Nov. 25	13 Feb. 28	P 26 April 31	
15	0	Fred. Darley George	P 24 Mar. 25	P 30 April 27	P 30 Aug. 33	
15	7/12	John M'Mahon Kidd	P 21 July 25	P 8 Nov. 27	P 28 Dec. 32	
12	0	Thos. Sydenham Conway	14 Feb. 28	P 26 April 31	P 9 Dec. 36	
20	9¾	B Archibald Campbell[2]	7 Mar. 11	5 Mar. 12	P 27 Oct. 37	
26	2/12	Joseph McLeod Tew [3]	10 Feb. 14	24 Mar. 26	6 April 38	
11	0	Wm. R. Preston	P 24 Sept. 29	P 22 Feb. 33	P 18 Oct. 39	
12	0	George Anderson	P 5 Sept. 28	P 19 Sept. 34	P 11 Aug. 37	
		LIEUTENANTS.				
23	3¾	George Munro	20 Jan. 14	29 Mar. 21		
22	6¾	Rob. Willington Kyffin	14 May 12	23 Dec. 13		
11	0	John Chalmers	P 3 Dec. 29	P 20 June 34		
13	2¼	Nathan Smith Gardiner	P 23 June 25	18 July 34		
13	0	And. Hamilton Russell	18 Jan. 28	23 July 34		
8	0	Thomas Chute	P 24 Feb. 32	P 9 Dec. 36		
6	0	Waldron Barrs Kelly	P 29 Aug. 34	P 1 April 36		
5	0	Chas. Thos. Powell	P 20 Nov. 35	P 10 Feb. 37		
5	0	Mark W. Goldie	P 29 Mar. 35	8 Sept. 38		
4	0	Hen. J. Coote	23 Sept. 36	P 17 Sept. 39		
4	0	Thomas Gaisford	P 23 Dec. 36	30 Sept. 39		
3	0	Thos. L. Parr Moore	P 11 Aug. 37	P 18 Oct. 39		
2	0	John Annah Ambrose	P 22 June 38	P 15 Nov. 39		
		ENSIGNS.				
3	0	Edward Dunbar	P 27 Oct. 37			
2	0	Fra. Pym. Harding	P 16 Mar. 38			
1	0	C. H. Montresor Smith	15 Mar. 39			
4	0	James Edw. Jerningham	P 25 Nov. 36			
1	0	William Somerville	P 9 Aug. 39			
1	0	Cha. Philip Jos. Stopford	P 17 Sept. 39			
1	0	John Brennan	17 Sept. 39			
1	0	Geo. Richard Coles	P 11 Nov. 39			

1 General Finch served in Flanders; and, in 1799, commanded the first battalion of his regt. (the Coldstream Guards) in the expedition to the Helder; and a brigade of Light Cavalry, and afterwards of Infantry in the campaign to Egypt. He also accompanied the expedition to Copenhagen in 1807.

2 Capt. Campbell served in the Peninsula from Aug. 1812 to the end of the war, and was present at the blockade of, and repulse of the sortie from Bayonne.

3 Captain Tew served in the American war in 1814 and 15.

4 Dr. M'Munn served the campaigns of 1813, 14, and 15, in Holland and Flanders, including the action at Merxem and bombardment of Antwerp.

26	0	*Paymaster.*—John M. Kennedy, 30 Oct. 28; *Ens.* 24 Feb. 14; *Lieut.* 6 Feb. 23.
6	0	*Adjutant.*—W. Barrs Kelly (*Lieut.*), 24 April, 38.
9	0	*Quarter-Master.*—Robert Harker, 6 Jan. 32.
23	3 11/12	*Surgeon.*—Robert Andrew M'Munn,[4] M.D. 1 Nov. 33; *Assist.-Surg.* 1 Sept. 14; *Hosp.-Assist.* 22 Nov. 13.
14	0	*Assist.-Surg.*—R. J. G. Grant, 14 Feb. 28; *Hosp.-Assist.* 7 Sept. 26.

Facings Buff.—*Agent*, Messrs. Cox & Co.—*Irish Agent*, Borough, Armit, & Cc.

[*Returned from Jamaica, 24 April, 1837.*]

Emb. for For. Service, 1838.] **23rd (*or* Royal Welsh Fusiliers) *Regt. of Foot.*** [Serving in Nova Scotia

In the centre of the Colour the *Prince of Wales's Feathers*, with the motto, "*Ich Dien.*"—In the second and third corners, the *Rising Sun* and the *Red Dragon*, and in the fourth corner, the *White Horse*, with the Motto, "*Nec aspera terrent.*"—"MINDEN"—the *Sphinx*, with the words "EGYPT"—"MARTINIQUE"—"CORUNNA"—"ALBUHERA"—"BADAJOZ"—"SALAMANCA"—"VITTORIA"—"PYRENEES"—"NIVELLE"—"ORTHES"—"TOULOUSE"—"PENINSULA"—"WATERLOO."

Years' Serv.						
57		| Colonel. Sir Jas. Willoughby Gordon, *Bt.* G.C.B. G.C.H. *Ens.* 17 Oct 1783; *Lieut.* 5 Mar. 89; *Capt.* 2 Sept. 95; *Major.* 9 Nov. 97; *Lieut.-Col.* 21 May, 1801; *Col.* 25 July, 10; *Major-Gen.* 4 June, 13; *Lieut.-Gen.* 27 May, 25; *Col.* 23rd Fusiliers, 23 April, 23.				
Full Pay.	Half Pay.					
		Lieut.-Colonel.				
34	2	William Ross,¹ *Ens.* 7 Sept. 04; *Lieut.* 5 June, 06; *Capt.* 16 Dec. 13; *Major,* P29 Aug. 26; *Lieut.-Col.* P24 Mar. 37.				
		Majors.				
29	0	Robt. Pattison Holmes,² *2nd Lieut.* 14 Feb. 11; *Lieut.* P12 Dec. 11; *Capt.* P4 Sept. 23; *Major,* 17 Dec. 30.				
25	0	Thomas Matheson, *2nd Lieut.* 17 Aug. 15; *Lieut.* P30 Oct. 23; *Capt.* P2 Aug. 26; *Major,* 20 Oct. 37.				

		CAPTAINS.	2ND LIEUT.	LIEUT.	CAPTAIN.	BREVET.-MAJOR.
18	0	William Cockell³	26 Dec. 22	P23 June 25	P29 Aug. 26	4 Capt. Enoch's services :— Expedition to Walcheren and siege of Flushing. Peninsula from 1810 to 1813, including sieges of Badajoz and Olivenza, 1811; battle of Albuhera, at Fuenta Grinalda, 25, 26th, & 27th Sept. 11; seg. of Ciudad Rodrigo, Jan. 1812; siege of Badajoz, March and April, 1812; battle of Salamanca, (severely wounded). Present on the 18th June, at Waterloo, storming of Cambray, and capture of Paris.
31	0	John Enoch⁴	30 Mar. 09	15 Aug. 11	22 July 30	
15	0	Henry Seymour	8 Apr. 25	P 1 Aug. 26	P15 Nov. 33	
14	0	Charles Crutchley	P 8 Apr. 26	22 July 30	P11 Dec. 35	
14	0	Scott Powell	P13 July 26	26 Oct. 30	P13 May 36	
12	2 8/12	William Alcock	P 8 Apr. 26	P11 Dec. 28	P24 Mar. 37	
11	0	Frederick Granville	P17 Sept. 29	P 1 Nov. 33	P28 Apr. 37	
11	0	John Lort Phillips	P 1 Oct. 29	P15 Nov. 33	P 4 Aug. 37	
12	0	Robt. Edgar Campbell	P21 Aug. 28	P19 Dec. 34	P30 Dec. 36	
10	0	Wm. Lemos Willoughby	P16 July 30	P10 Apr. 35	P 8 Dec. 37	
		LIEUTENANTS.				
15	0	Fred. J. Phillott	7 Apr. 25	P12 Dec. 26		
14	0	John Deakins	13 Apr. 26	P20 July 27		5 Paymaster Dunn served in the Peninsula in 1814. Present at Waterloo 18th June. Storming of Cambray (commanded ladder party 23d Fusiliers), and capture of Paris. 6 Quarter-Master Moore's services :—Campaign of 1799 in Holland, including the actions on the landing near the Helder, Zyp Dyke, Sand Hills, and Egmont-op-Zee, and taking of Hoorn by surprise. Egyptian campaign of 1801, including the action on landing, 8th March, and the actions of the 12th, 13th, and 21st March; siege and capture of Alexandria. Expedition to, and actions of the 17th and 24th Aug. 1807, in front of Copenhagen. Sieges of Forts Royal and Bourbon, and action in front of Fort Bourbon, Martinique. Peninsula from 1811 to the end of the war, including the following : viz. actions near Redulia, Condeiria, Aldea de Ponte; battles of Salamanca, Vittoria, Nivelle, Nive, Orthes, and Toulouse; sieges of Olivenza, Badajoz raised 13th May, 1811, Ciudad Rodrigo, Badajoz taken by storm, and forts near Salamanca. Present at Waterloo and the storming of Cambray.
10	0	W. Godfrey Clerke Monins	3 Aug. 30	P31 July 35		
10	0	Harry Geo. Chester	26 Oct. 30	7 Aug. 35		
10	0	Frederick Torrens	17 Dec. 30	P11 Dec. 35		
7	0	Hobart Grant Anderdon	P15 Nov. 33	P24 Mar. 37		
6	0	Geo. Watkins Rice	P 2 May 34	P17 June 36		
5	0	Charles Blackett	P27 Mar. 35	P28 Apr. 37		
5	0	George Ferguson	P17 Apr. 35	P28 Apr. 37		
5	0	Edward Battye	P31 July 35	P 4 Aug. 37		
5	0	J. Shuckburgh Capron	P21 Aug. 35	P 8 Dec. 37		
5	0	Wellington C. Cecil Baker	P11 Dec. 35	P 9 Jan. 38		
5	0	Arth. Beresford Brooke	9 May 35	P 6 Dec. 39		
		SECOND LIEUTS.				
4	0	F. A. D. Roebuck	P13 May 36			
3	0	A. W. W. Wynn	P24 Mar. 37			
3	0	A. J. Campbell	P28 Apr. 37			
3	0	Hon. F. J. R. Villiers	P 4 Aug. 37			
3	0	Thomas Ellis	20 Oct. 37			
3	0	Dudley Clarges Hill	9 Jan. 38			
1	0	Arch. Jas. Jones	P 5 Apr. 39			
1	0	Fra. Edward Evans	P 5 Apr. 39			

13	13½	*Paymaster.*— George Dunn,⁵ 15 Mar. 31; *2nd Lieut.* 15 Apr. 13; *Lieut.* 18 July, 15.
3	0	*Adjutant.*—Thomas Ellis, (*2nd Lieut.*) 8 Dec. 37.
13	0	*Quarter-Master.*— Garrett Moore,⁶ 8 Nov. 27.
19	3	*Surgeon.*—Saml. Wm. Chermside, M.D. 4 Jan. 39; *Assist.-Surg.* 2 Apr. 18.
4	0	*Assist.-Surgeons.*—James Connell, 10 Nov. 25; *Hosp.-Assist.* 16 June, 25. Andrew Furgusson, 23 Dec. 36.

Facings Blue.—*Agent*, Messrs. Cox & Co.—*Irish Agent*, Borough, Armit, & Co.

---

1 Colonel Ross served under Lord Lake in India in 1805 and 6. Present at the siege and storming of Fort Comona, in Bengal, 18th Nov. 07, on which occasion two-thirds of the officers were either killed or wounded. Siege and reduction of Fort Guinowric. Campaign of 1809 against the Seiks. Present at Waterloo, storming of Cambray, and capture of Paris.

2 Major Holmes served in the Peninsula, from 1812 to the end of the war, including the sieges of Ciudad Rodrigo and Badajoz, in 1812; battles of Nivelle, Nive, Orthes, and Toulouse. Present at Waterloo, storming of Cambray, and capture of Paris. Severely wounded at the storming of Badajoz by a musket ball in the right hand. Contused in the head, by a musket ball at Waterloo.

3 Captain Cockell was at the siege and capture of Bhurtpore, in 1826.

Emb. for Foreign Service, 1829.] **24th (or 2nd Warwickshire) Regiment of Foot.** [Serving in Canada.

The *Sphinx*, with the words, 'EGYPT"—"CAPE OF GOOD HOPE"—"TALAVERA"—"FUENTES D'ONOR"—"SALAMANCA"—"VITTORIA"—"PYRENEES"—"NIVELLE"—"ORTHES"—"PENINSULA."

Years' Serv.		Colonel.
49		ℙ 𝕮𝕭 Sir James Lyon,[1] K.C.B. and G.C.H. Ens. 4 Aug. 1791; Lieut. 26 April, 93; Capt. 5 April, 95; Major, 21 Feb. 99; Lieut.-Col. 13 May, 1802; Col. 4 June, 11; Major-Gen. 4 June, 14; Lieut.-Gen. 22 July, 30; Col. 24th Regt. 7 Sept. 29.
Full Pay.	Half Pay.	
		Lieut.-Colonel.
44	0	Charles Hughes,[2] Ens. 25 May, 96; Lieut. 11 May, 97; Capt. 28 Aug. 04; Brevet-Major, 4 June, 14; Regtl.-Major, 25 June, 24; Lieut.-Col. 10 Oct. 35.
24	4 1/12	Majors.—Hen. Dive Townshend,[3] Ens. ᴾ 16 July, 12; Lieut. ᴾ 14 Sept. 15; Capt. ᴾ 1 Nov. 21; Major, 10 Oct. 35; Brevet Lieut.-Col. 29 March, 39.
30	5 1/12	ℙ George Fitzgerald Stack,[4] K.H. Ens. 13 June, 05; Lieut. 4 Dec. 06; Capt. 25 May, 15; Major, 26 Oct. 35.

		CAPTAINS.	ENSIGN.	LIEUT.	CAPTAIN.	BREV.-MAJ.
20	7/12	ℙ 𝕮𝕭 John Stoyte[5]	21 Mar. 11	4 July 13	ᴾ 27 Jan. 25	28 June 38
20	1	Charles Hastings Doyle	23 Dec. 19	27 Sept. 22	ᴾ 16 June 25	28 June 38
29	0	ℙ Robert Marsh[6]	31 Oct. 11	ᴾ 13 Feb. 17	ᴾ 14 Apr. 29	
33	0	John Harris[7]	28 Aug. 07	21 July 09	11 May 30	8 Capt. H. W. Harris served in the Burmese war, and was present in the engagements at Paddeo, and Mahatee; severely wounded in the body and neck by musket shots at the attack of the Hills of Arracan.
18	0	Hen. Wm. Harris[8]	ᴾ 23 May 22	27 Sept. 24	ᴾ 30 Dec. 31	
15	0	Fred. Thomas Maitland..	9 Apr. 25	ᴾ 18 Feb. 26	ᴾ 12 Apr. 33	
31	3/12	ℙ John Adrian Lutman[9]	1 Feb. 09	13 May 13	13 Feb. 35	
16	0	Daniel Riley[10]	13 Jan. 25	15 Dec. 25	25 Oct. 35	
14	0	Robt. Griffith Williams..	ᴾ 3 Oct. 26	ᴾ 6 Sept. 31	ᴾ 24 Apr. 35	
15	0	Henry Young............	ᴾ 30 June 25	ᴾ 1 Aug. 26	ᴾ 3 Nov. 37	
		LIEUTENANTS.				9 Capt. Lutman's services :—Campaign and battle of Corunna (wounded in the left thigh ;) expedition to Walcheren, and siege of Flushing; Sicily from May 1810 to June 1812; Peninsula from June 1812 until the end of the war, including the battle of Castalla, siege of Tarragona, July and Aug. 1813, and blockade of Barcelona, Feb. to May 1814; served
15	0	Nicholas Leslie	8 Apr. 25	ᴾ 31 July 26		
15	0	Aug. Geo. Blachford....	ᴾ 12 Nov. 25	ᴾ 12 Dec. 26		
15	0	Hon. Charles Preston ..	ᴾ 19 Nov. 25	ᴾ 15 May 28		
15	0	Wm. Gustavus Brown ..	7 July 25	11 May 30		
14	0	John Massy Stack......	ᴾ 26 Sept. 26	ᴾ 30 Dec. 31		
14	0	William Spring	ᴾ 30 Dec. 26	ᴾ 4 June 32		
14	8/12	Edw. Sims James	ᴾ 22 Oct. 25	ᴾ 16 July 29		
12	0	Howell Paynter	26 Apr. 28	6 Jan. 33		
13	0	Fred. Chetwode	ᴾ 5 June 27	ᴾ 12 Apr. 33		10 Capt. Riley was in the engagement with a French squadron in the Mosambique channel 3rd July, 1810; served the Nepaul campaign of 1814 and 15.
12	0	John James Greig	ᴾ 15 May 28	ᴾ 21 Mar. 34		
11	13 7/12	John Monck Mason[11] ..	27 Sept. 15	25 Oct. 35		
22	8 3/12	ℙ Benjamin Beaufoy[12] ..	8 Mar. 10	8 Oct. 12		
7	0	Geo. Abercromby Ferrier	ᴾ 12 Apr. 33	ᴾ 1 June 38		11 Lieut. Mason served in Canada, Flanders, and France, in 1814 and 15; also in Canada in 1838, and commanded a company of volunteers at the taking of Grand Brule.
		ENSIGNS.				
5	0	Robt. Wm. Travers	23 Jan. 35			
3	0	Chas. R. Harris	ᴾ 17 Feb. 37			12 Lieut. Beaufoy was at the battle of Castalla, and at the siege of Tarragona in 1813; served also in American war.
4	0	Edm. Wodehouse	ᴾ 24 Mar. 37			
4	0	Thomas Spring	ᴾ 14 May 36			
3	0	E. J. Ing. Fleming	ᴾ 26 Jan. 38			13 Quarter-Master Murray's services :— Egyptian campaign of 1801; capture of the Cape of Good Hope in 1806; Nepaul campaigns of 1814, 15, and 16; Mahratta war in 1817 and 18.
2	0	Methuen Stedman	ᴾ 1 June 38			
2	0	Louis Bazalgette	26 June 38			
1	0	Jas. Gerald Fitz Gibbon..	25 Oct. 39			14 Dr. Lorimer served in the Peninsula from June 1810 to the end of the war.
27	0	Paymaster.—ℙ Alex. Tovey, 4 Feb. 19; Ens. 22 Oct. 13; Lieut. 11 June, 18.				
14	0	Adjutant.—Wm. Spring, (Lieut.) 4 Aug. 35.				
23	0	Quarter-Master.—James Murray,[13] 4 Dec. 17.				
17	12 1/12	Surgeon.—ℙ Wm. Lorimer,[14] 3 Nov. 37; Assist.-Surg. 22 June, 15; Hosp.-Assist. 10 June, 11.				
		Assist.-Surgeons.—Jas. Murray Drysdale, 10 Nov. 25; Hosp.-Assist. 19 Feb. 24. Geo. Ledingham, M.D. 8 Nov. 27; Hosp.-Assist. 31 Aug. 26.				

Facings Green.—*Agent*, Mr. Collyer.

1 Sir James Lyon commanded a detachment of the 24th regiment on board the *Marlborough*, in Lord Howe's actions of the 27th and 28th May, and 1st June, 1794. He was also present in the actions of the 13th and 21st March, 1801, in Egypt, and has received a medal and one clasp for Vimiera and Talavera.

2 Col. Hughes served the Egyptian campaign of 1801; engaged with a French squadron in the Mosambique channel 3rd July, 1810; served the Nepaul campaigns of 1814, 15, and 16, and was wounded at Harriapore; served during the Mahratta war of 1816 and 17; medal for services in Egypt.

3 Col. Townshend served in the American war, and was present at the taking of Fort Niagara, Blackrock, and Buffalo, and battle of Lundy's Lane; severely wounded through the left shoulder at the assault on Fort Erie, 14th Aug. 1814.

4 Major Stack was present at Talavera (wounded), Busaco, Espinelle, Fox d'Aronce; siege of Ciudad Rodrigo, and repulse of the sortie, 14th Jan. 1811; battle of Salamanca; surrender of Retiro; operations before, siege, and storming of the breaches (severely contused) at Burgos; battle of Orthes; besides a great many affairs and skirmishes. Severely wounded at Orthes; left arm amputated.

5 Major Stoyte was present at the storming of Badajoz 6th April, 1812, operations in front of, and battle of Salamanca; severely wounded at Salamanca; lost one finger, and wounded through the left hand and in the breast while carrying the colours, the standard of which was shot away; wounded through the right hand and taken prisoner at Bergen-op-Zoom; present on the 16th and 18th June at Waterloo.

6 Capt. Marsh served in the Peninsula from Aug. 1812 until the end of the war, including the battles of Vittoria, Echallar, Nivelle (wounded), and Orthes; served the Nepaul campaigns of 1815 and 16, and the Mahratta war of 1817 and 18.

7 Capt. John Harris was in the engagement with the *Belona* and *Minerva*, French frigates, and a corvette, in the Mosambique channel, 3rd July, 1810; served the Nepaul campaigns of 1814 and 15, including the taking of Harriapore; served in the Mahratta war in 1817. Served in Lower Canada in 1837, at the taking of Grande Brulée. In Upper Canada in 1838. Commanded the 24th regt. before Navy Island with the local rank of Major.

Emb. for For. Ser. Dec. 1839.] **25th (*or the King's own Borderers*) *Regt. of Foot.*** [Serving at the C. of Good Hope.

The *King's Crest* in two corners of the Colour, "*In Veritate Religionis confido.*" The *Arms of Edinburgh*, "*Nisi Dominus frustra;*" with the *White Horse* in the third corner of the Colour. "*Nec aspera terrent.*" "MINDEN"—"EGMONT-OP-ZEE." The *Sphinx*, with the word "EGYPT."—Flank Companies, "MARTINIQUE."

Years' Serv.		
Full Pay.	Half Pay.	
54		**Colonel.** 🅟 Sir Henry Fred. Campbell,[1] K.C.B. & G.C.H. *Ens.* 20 Sept. 86; *Lieut.* & *Capt.* 25 April, 93; *Capt.* & *Lieut.-Col.* 6 April, 96; *Col.* 25 Sept. 03; *Major-Gen.* 25 July, 10; *Lieut.-Gen.* 4 June, 14; *Gen.* 10 Jan. 37; *Col.* 25th Regt. 20th Oct. 31.
26	1	**Lieut.-Colonel.** Courtnay Chambers,[2] *Ens.* 10 June, 13; *Lieut.* & *Capt.* 6 July 15; *Major,* ᴾ 29 Oct. 25; *Lieut.-Col.* ᴾ 31 Aug. 30.
		Majors.
17	8 8/12	James Rob. Young, *Ens.* 27 July, 15; *Lieut.* 14 Dec. 18; *Capt.* ᴾ 13 May, 26; *Major,* ᴾ 31 Dec. 33.
18	3 3/12	Wm. James D'Urban, *Cornet,* 7 Oct. 19; *Lieut.* ᴾ 25 Sept. 23; *Capt.* ᴾ 8 April, 26; *Major,* ᴾ 16 Oct. 35.

		CAPTAINS.	ENSIGN.	LIEUT.	CAPTAIN.	BREVET-MAJOR.
37	8/12	John J. Hollis..........	9 July 03	1 Dec. 04	30 Mar. 09	22 July 30
15	0	Wm. O'Connor	9 Apr. 25	ᴾ 22 Dec. 25	ᴾ 14 Aug. 28	
15	0	A. Armstrong Barnes ..	21 July 25	28 May 29	ᴾ 1 July 36	
14	0	Richard Jenkins........	ᴾ 1 Feb. 27	ᴾ 4 June 28	ᴾ 16 June 37	
15	0	Samuel Wells	9 Apr. 25	ᴾ 8 Oct. 29	ᴾ 15 Sept. 37	
11	0	John Andros Guille	ᴾ 20 Apr. 29	31 Oct. 34	ᴾ 3 Nov. 37	
9	0	C. R. Knight	5 Apr. 31	ᴾ 16 Oct. 35	ᴾ 17 Nov. 37	
19	12 2/12	🅟 John Henry Cooke[3] ..	15 Mar. 09	19 Apr. 10	31 Dec. 23	28 June 38
7	0	Samuel B. Hamilton....	20 Sept. 33	ᴾ 14 July 37	ᴾ 12 Jan. 39	
7	0	Stephen Pons. Peacocke	ᴾ 25 Oct. 33	ᴾ 15 Sept. 37	ᴾ 23 Aug. 39	
		LIEUTENANTS.				
13	0	Wm. M'Donald	ᴾ 5 Apr. 27	ᴾ 31 Aug. 30		
13	0	Henry Pinder..........	ᴾ 6 Dec. 27	ᴾ 30 Oct. 34		
10	0	Skeffington Bristow	ᴾ 31 Aug. 30	ᴾ 22 May 35		
6	0	Edm. Bentley Frith	ᴾ 31 Oct. 34	ᴾ 3 Nov. 37		
5	0	W. C. E. Napier........	28 Aug. 35	ᴾ 17 Nov. 37		
5	0	Edw. R. Priestley	27 Nov. 35	ᴾ 13 Jan. 38		
4	0	Harry Gough	ᴾ 1 July 36	ᴾ 30 Mar. 38		
3	0	Stanhope M. Gildea	ᴾ 29 Apr. 37	ᴾ 11 May 38		
6	0	*Hon.* James Colborne ..	ᴾ 21 Mar. 34	26 June 38		
3	0	Thomas R. Conolly	ᴾ 15 Sept. 37	ᴾ 11 Jan. 39		
3	0	Neil Hulse Harenc......	ᴾ 17 Nov. 37	ᴾ 23 Aug. 39		
3	0	Rob. Henry Lindsell....	ᴾ 13 Jan. 38	ᴾ 15 Nov. 39		
2	0	Henry Francis Cust ...	ᴾ 30 Mar. 38	ᴾ 31 Dec. 39		
		ENSIGNS.				
3	0	C. G. Smith	ᴾ 1 Dec. 37			
2	0	James Ogilvy	ᴾ 31 Mar. 38			
2	0	F. J. B. Priestley	2 Mar. 38			
2	0	R. Mas. Taylor	ᴾ 11 Jan. 39			
2	0	Stewart Northey	ᴾ 18 Jan. 39			
1	0	Wm. Hodges T. Pattenson	ᴾ 23 Aug. 39			
1	0	Edward Wellesley	ᴾ 15 Nov. 39			
1	0	Henry Reynolds Werge	ᴾ 31 Dec. 39			
27	4 2/12	Paymaster.—🅟 ⚜️ Wm. Dean,[4] 10 Dec. 29; *Cornet,* 9 Feb. 09; *Lieut.* 14 Aug. 11.				
5	0	Adjutant.—Edward R. Priestley, (*Lieut.*) 13 Jan. 38.				
19	0	Quarter-Master.—John Potts, 10 Jan. 22.				
		Surgeon.—Jas. Findlayson Nivison, 20 Sept. 39; *Assist.-Surg.* 30 June, 25; *Hosp.-Assist.* 24 June, 15.				
15	0	Assistant-Surgeon.—James Sidey, M.D. 12 Jan. 26; *Hosp.-Assist.* 1 Dec. 25.				
1	0	Duncan Donald M'Cay M'Donald, 4 Oct. 39.				

1 Sir H. F. Campbell has received a medal and one clasp for Talavera and Salamanca. In the former battle he received a severe wound in the face.

2 Col. Chambers served the campaign of 1814 in Holland.

3 Major Cooke served four years in the 1st West York Militia prior to entering the 43rd Light Infantry, with which he served at Walcheren in 1809; in Portugal, 1811; siege and storming of Ciudad Rodrigo; siege and storming of Badajoz (wounded at the assault); battle of Salamanca; affair of San Munoz; battle of Vittoria (wounded); battles of the Pyrenees; San Sebastian; the attack on the heights of Vera, 7th Oct., when the left wing of the army crossed the Bidassoa; battles of the Nivelle and the Nive; affair at Tarbes; battle of Toulouse; battle in front of New Orleans, 8th Jan. 1815; served four years with the army of occupation in France. Employed on a special mission at Constantinople in 1836.

4 Paymaster Dean served in the Peninsula from April 1809 until the end of the war. Present at Waterloo.

Facings Blue.—*Agent*, Messrs. COX & CO.

[Emb. for Foreign Service, 1828.] **26th (*or the Cameronian*) Regiment of Foot.** [Serving in Bengal.

The *Sphinx*, with the words "EGYPT"—"CORUNNA."

Colonel.

Years' Serv.		
46		**P ᴋʜ John *Lord* Seaton,**[1] G.C.B. G.C.H., *Ens.* 10 July, 1794; *Lieut.* 4 Sept. 95; *Capt.* 12 Jan. 00; *Major*, 21 Jan. 08; *Lieut.-Col.* 2 Feb. 09; *Col.* 4 June, 14; *Major-Gen.* 27 May, 25; *Lieut.-Gen.* 28 June, 38; *Col.* of the Cameronians, 28 March, 38.
Full Pay.	Half Pay.	
32	2 4/12	*Lieut.-Colonels.*—**P** Hen. Oglander,[2] *C.B.*, *Ens.* P 20 Aug. 06; *Lieut.* 8 Sept. 08; *Capt.* P 2 April, 12; *Brevet-Major*, 14 Oct. 13; *Regtl.-Major*, 27 Oct. 14; *Lieut.-Col.* P 14 Dec. 15; *Col.* 10 Jan. 37.
35	1 6/12	Wm. James,[3] *Ens.* P 8 Dec. 03; *Lieut.* 23 Nov. 04; *Capt.* 5 Nov. 12; *Major*, 25 April, 28; *Lieut.-Col.* P 25 Dec. 35.
19	6 1/12	*Majors.*—Armine S. H. Mountain, *Ens.* 20 July, 15; *Lieut.* P 3 Dec. 18; *Capt.* P 26 May, 25; *Major*, P 30 Dec. 26.
26	1/12	Thos. Simson Pratt,[4] *Ens.* 2 Feb. 14; *Lieut.* P 20 April, 20; *Capt.* P 17 Sept. 25; *Major*, P 25 Dec. 35.

		CAPTAINS.	ENSIGN.	LIEUT.	CAPTAIN.	BREVET-MAJOR.
32	0	**P** William Johnstone[5] ..	25 Feb. 08	30 Mar. 09	P 20 April 20	10 Jan. 37
21	1 9/12	George Hogarth........	P 22 May 17	P 13 Sept. 21	P 12 Nov. 25	28 June 38
24	1	Hen. Fra. Strange	23 May 15	7 April 25	P 19 June 26	
30	0	Michael Pointon[6]	4 Oct. 10	2 July 12	13 Mar. 29	
26	0	William Cain[7]	6 July 14	12 June 19	9 Dec. 27	
19	0	James Paterson	P 17 May 21	P 4 Dec. 23	P 5 April 31	
22	3 5/12	James Piggott	6 April 15	9 April 25	14 Feb. 34	
33	0	Dobson Young[8]	3 Dec. 07	1 Aug. 10	30 May 34	
16	0	George Mylius	17 Oct. 24	P 28 Jan. 26	P 30 Aug. 31	
12	0	John Shum	P 19 Aug. 28	3 Oct. 32	P 22 Feb. 39	
		LIEUTENANTS.				
15	0	John Maule............	9 April 25	P 30 Aug. 26		
23	0	Thomas Ffrench........	4 Dec. 17	26 April 28		
22	0	Richard Thompson ...	P 1 Jan. 19	8 Nov. 27		
16	0	W. B. Staff............	4 Dec. 24	10 Mar. 27		
14	0	Edw. Regan Gregg	6 April 26	28 Sept. 27		
14	0	Thomas Seccombe......	P 6 July 26	31 Jan. 29		
16	0	E. W. Sibley[9].........	27 Nov. 24	16 Oct. 26		
11	0	Alex. M'Donald	13 Mar. 29	12 Oct. 32		
14	0	Edm. Pomeroy Gilbert..	P 28 Sept. 26	P 27 Sept. 31		
7	0	Henry Edgar	P 27 Sept. 33	P 24 Nov. 35		
7	18 3/12	Donald Robertson	24 Nov. 14	11 Dec. 35		
6	0	John M. Daniell.......	14 Feb. 34	P 25 Dec. 35		
7	0	John Wm. Johnstone ..	P 31 May 33	25 Feb. 37		
6	0	Charles Cameron	16 May 34	1 July 37		
6	0	James Willyams Grylls..	P 29 Aug. 34	P 29 April 37		
5	0	Hon. Wm. Godol. Osborn	P 11 Sept. 35	P 4 Aug. 37		
3	0	John Rodgers..........	P 31 Mar. 37	P 18 May 38		
4	0	George Sweeny	P 25 Nov. 36	P 26 June 38		
6	12 6/12	Alex. G. Moorhead	26 May 22	P 3 Dec. 25		
3	0	H. J. W. Postlethwaite..	P 11 Aug. 37	P 5 April 39		
6	0	Wm. Le Poer Trench ..	P 14 Nov. 34	P 14 June 39		
6	0	Walter Brisbane Park ..	26 Dec. 34	15 June 39		
5	0	Wm. Thomas Betts	24 Nov. 35	15 Nov. 39		
		ENSIGNS.				
3	0	John Cumming ..¨....	P 23 Sept. 37	Alex. Miller		15 Mar. 39
2	0	R. Palmer Sharp	P 18 May 38	Albany F. Wallace.....		P 5 April 39
2	0	Alf. R. Margary........	P 26 June 38	Rob. Colville Jones ...		P 9 Aug. 39
2	0	Hen. B. Phipps........	17 Aug. 38	Edw. G. Whitty.......		29 Nov. 39
13	0	*Paymaster.*—R. H. Strong, 1 June, 37; *Ens.* 7 Aug. 27; *Lieut.* 9 Dec. 31.				
11	0	*Adjutant.*—Alex. M'Donald, (*Lieut.*) 13 March, 29.				
12	0	*Quarter-Master.*—Joseph Goodfellow,[10] Feb. 28.				
28	0	*Surgeon.*—W. Bell, M.D. 15 March, 31; *Assist.-Surg.* 4 March, 13; *Hosp. Assist.* 24 Aug. 12.				
7	0	*Assist.-Surgeons.*—Chilley Pine, 2 Aug. 33.				
7	0	W. Godfrey Bace, M.D. 27 Dec. 33.				

Notes (right column):
4 Major Pratt served the campaign of 1814, in Holland, including the attack on Merxem, 2d Feb. and bombardment of Antwerp.
5 Major Johnstone was present at the battle of Corunna.
6 Captain Pointon served the Egyptian campaign of 1801, and was wounded in the right leg when engaging the French picquets in front of Alexandria.
7 Captain Cain served in the East Indies from Nov. 1813 to Dec. 1827, including the Nepaul and Deccan campaigns; also the siege and assault of Bhurtpore. Wounded in the left foot by a grape shot at the assault, 18th Jan. 1826.
8 Captain Young was at the storming and capture of Forts Comona (led the Forlorn Hope), Genowrie, and Ownona, in India, in 1807. Served the campaigns against Nepaul and the Mahrattas.
9 Lieut. Sibley served in the Burmese war.
10 Quarter-Master Goodfellow was at the capture of Hattras. Served the Mahratta campaigns of 1817-18. Present at the siege and capture of Bhurtpore.

Facings Yellow.—*Agent*, Messrs. Cox & Co.

1 Lord Seaton has received a cross and three clasps for Corunna, Albuhera, Ciudad Rodrigo, (where he was severely wounded), Nivelle, Nive, Orthes, and Toulouse.
2 Colonel Oglander's services:—Expedition to Copenhagen in 1807; Corunna campaign; expedition to Walcheren, Peninsula, from Aug. 1810, including the battles of the Coa, Almeida, Busaco, Redinha, Foz d'Aronce, Sabugal, Fuentes d'Onor; siege and capture of Ciudad Rodrigo; siege and capture of Badajoz; battle of Vittoria; Siege and capture of San Sebastian; and blockade of Bayonne. Lost left arm at the assault of Badajoz, and also wounded in the arm, thigh, and body, lost first finger of the right hand, and wounded in the body at the assault of San Sebastian.
3 Colonel James was at the capture of Martinique in 1809, and Guadaloupe in 1810.

Emb. for Foreign Service, 1835. **27th (or *Inniskilling*) *Regiment of Foot*.** **Serving at the Cape of Good Hope.**

A Castle with Three Turrets; St. George's colours flying in a blue Field. The White Horse. "*Nec aspera terrent.*" "ST. LUCIA." The *Sphinx*, with the words "EGYPT"—"MAIDA"—"BADAJOZ"—"SALAMANCA"—"VITTORIA"—"PYRENEES"—"NIVELLE"—"ORTHES"—"TOULOUSE"—"PENINSULA"—"WATERLOO."

Years' Serv.		
53		**Colonel.**
Full Pay.	Half Pay.	𝔓 Hon. Sir G. Lowry Cole,[1] G.C.B. *Cornet*, 31 March, 1787; *Lieut.* 31 May, 91; *Capt.* 30 Nov. 92; *Major*, 31 Oct. 93; *Lieut.-Col.* 26 Nov. 94; *Col.* 1 Jan. 1801; *Major-Gen.* 25 April, 08; *Lieut.-Gen.* 4 June, 13; *Gen.* 22 July, 30; *Col.* 27th Regt. 16 Dec. 26.
41	0	*Lieut.-Colonel.*—𝔓 𝔔𝔔 John Hare,[2] C.B. K.H., *Ens.* 29 Oct. 09; *Lieut.* 17 May, 00; *Capt.* 9 Sept. 05; *Brevet-Major*, 17 June, 13; *Brevet-Lieut.-Col.* 18 June, 15; *Regtl.-Major*, P 30 June, 18; *Lieut.-Col.* P 31 March, 25; *Col.* 10 Jan. 37.
		Majors.
35	0	𝔓 Duncan M'Pherson,[3] *Ens.* 19 Sept. 05; *Lieut.* 10 Nov. 06; *Capt.* 25 March, 24; *Major*, 27 Dec. 34.
17	0	Mont. Cholm. Johnstone, *Ens.* P 27 Feb. 23; *Lieut.* P 16 Dec. 24; *Capt.* P 19 Sept. 26; *Major*, P 27 July, 38.

		CAPTAINS.	ENSIGN.	LIEUT.	CAPTAIN.	BREVET-MAJOR.
15	4½	William Amsinck	1 Mar. 21	P 7 July 25	P 12 April 26	
24	2⁹⁄₁₂	William Sleator	20 April 14	7 April 25	P 11 Nov. 31	
15	0	John Maclean	8 April 25	P 30 Mar. 26	P 10 May 33	
15	0	Sam. E. Goodman	7 July 25	P 8 April 26	P 4 Oct. 33	
29	1⁄₁₂	𝔓 Arthur Byrne[4]	17 July 11	25 Aug. 13	5 Dec. 34	
13	7⁄₁₂	Richard Fawkes	P 1 Mar. 27	P 22 May 29	P 16 Jan. 35	
27	0	𝔓 𝔔𝔔 T. Charlton Smith[5]	24 June 13	5 Aug. 19	27 Mar. 35	
16	0	James Faunce Lonsdale	27 May 24	21 Dec. 26	P 27 July 38	
15	7⁄₁₂	Charles Vereker	9 April 25	P 27 Mar. 27	P 17 Aug. 38	
15	0	Geo. Anthony Durnford	3 Mar. 25	P 15 Dec. 25	6 Nov. 38	
		LIEUTENANTS.				
25	0	Walter Butler	P.15 Dec. 25	P 16 Sept. 26		
14	0	Usher Williamson	P 29 Aug. 26	P 11 Nov. 31		4 Captain Byrne's services:—Expedition to Copenhagen in 1807. Capture of Martinique in 1809. Peninsula from June 1810, to the end of the war, including the battles of Busaco and Albuhera; siege and storming of Badajoz, 1812; affair with the Advanced Guard of the French near Carazal; battles of Salamanca, Vittoria, the Pyrenees, Nivelle, Orthes, and Toulouse. Severely wounded in the Pyrenees, 26th July, 1813, and at Toulouse. Served also in the American war, including the battle at Plattsburgh.
13	0	Henry Butler	P 15 May 27	7 Sept. 32		
11	0	Rawdon S. E. Neynoe	10 June 29	P 10 May 33		
11	0	Thos. Percival Touzel	10 Sept. 29	P 4 Oct. 33		
9	0	Henry D. Cholmeley	P 13 July 31	P 13 Dec. 33		
14	0	Francis Smith	P 30 Dec. 26	P 19 May 33		
8	0	Hon. C. T. Skeff Foster	P 22 June 32	P 4 Aug. 37		
8	0	Andrew Vincent Watson	P 21 Dec. 32	P 18 May 38		
7	0	John Lewes	P 4 Oct. 33	P 27 July 38		
7	0	Frederick King	P 13 Dec. 33	P 17 Aug. 38		
5	0	Thomas Hare	27 Mar. 35	6 Nov. 38		
		ENSIGNS.				5 Captain Smith, previously to entering the army, served for a short period in the navy, and was three times wounded. Served in the Peninsula from June 1813 to the end of the war, and was present at the affair of Ordal. Severely wounded at Waterloo.
5	0	Lewis C. Irwin	P 10 April 35			
3	0	Herman Stapylton	P 4 Aug. 37			
3	0	E. N. Molesworth	P 1 Dec. 37			
3	0	Ben. Midgley	11 Dec. 37			6 Dr. Mostyn served in the Peninsula, from Jan. 1811 until the end of the war, including the siege of Badajoz, April 1812; battles of Salamanca, Vittoria, and the Pyrenees; storming of San Sebastian with the Volunteer party; battles of Orthes and Toulouse. Served in the American war, including the action at Plattsburgh. Present on the 18th June at Waterloo.
3	0	Barth. Tunnard	P 26 Dec. 37			
2	0	J. Thring Coxe	P 18 May 38			
2	0	G. L. Thomson	P 27 July 38			
2	0	James Somerville	P 17 Aug. 38			
1	0	John Sam. Manly	15 Feb. 39			
32	4⁄₁₂	*Paymaster.*—Victor Raymond, 9 March, 26; *Ens.* 11 Feb. 08; *Lieut.* 16 Nov. 09; *Capt.* 7 April, 25.				
3	0	*Adjutant.*—Benj. Midgley, (*Ens.*) 11 Dec. 37.				
9	0	*Quarter-Master.*—Geo. Thompson, 13 Sept. 31.				
30	0	*Surgeon.*—𝔓 𝔔𝔔 Thos. Mostyn,[6] 6 Oct. 25; *Assist.-Surg.* 19 Dec. 11; *Hosp. Assist.* 9 Nov. 10.				
5	0	*Assist.-Surgeons.*—Col. C. J. Delmege, M.D., 15 May, 35.				
1	0	George Barlow Fry, M.D. 5 July, 39.				

Facings Buff.—*Agent*, Messrs. Cox & Co.

1 Sir Lowry Cole commanded a brigade at the battle of Maida, and a division in the Peninsula and in France; he has received a Cross and four Clasps for Maida, Albuhera (wounded), Salamanca (severely wounded), Vittoria, Pyrenees, Nivelle, Orthes, and Toulouse.

2 Colonel Hare, previously to entering the 27th Regt. served in the Tarbert Fencibles, from which he volunteered to serve in the expedition to Holland in 1799, and was present at the landing at the Helder, and the landing and advance upon Ferrol. Served the Egyptian campaign of 1801, for which he has received a medal. Present at the capture of Ischia and Procida. Served in the Peninsula from August 1812 until the end of the war, including the taking of Alcoy; battles of Biar and Castalla; siege of, and operations before Tarragona, and blockade of Barcelona. Wounded at Waterloo.

3 Major M'Pherson served in Calabria in 1806. Present at the capture of Ischia in 1809. Served the campaigns of 1813 and 14, in the Peninsula, including the battles Biar and Castalla; siege of Tarragona; affair at Ordell (severely wounded through the body and left arm); and blockade of Barcelona. Served also in the American war, including the battle of Plattsburgh.

Emb. for Foreign Service, 1835.] **28th (or *North Gloucestershire*) Regt. of Foot.** [Serving in N. South Wales.

The *Sphinx*, with the words "EGYPT"—"CORUNNA"—"BARROSA"—"ALBUHERA"—"VITTORIA"—"PYRENEES"—"NIVELLE"—"NIVE"—"ORTHES"—"PENINSULA" "WATERLOO."

Years' Serv.		
Full Pay	Half Pay	
48		**Colonel.** Hon. Sir E. Paget,[1] G.C.B. *Cornet & Sub-Lieut.* 23 Mar. 1792; *Capt.* 7 Dec. 92; *Major*, 14 Nov. 93; *Lieut.-Col.* 30 April, 94; *Col.* 1 Jan. 98; *Major-Gen.* 1 Jan. 1805; *Lieut.-Gen.* 4 June, 11; *Gen.* 27 May, 25; *Col.* 28th Regt. 26 Dec. 15.
27	8/12	**Lieut.-Colonel.** Cudbert French,[2] K.H. *2nd Lieut.* p 3 Sept. 12; *Lieut.* p 1 April, 14; *Capt.* p 10 June, 24; *Major,* p 22 June, 32; *Lieut.-Col.* p 19 Dec. 34.
25	0	**Majors.** J. Messiter, *Ens.* 18 July, 15; *Lieut.* p 3 July, 23; *Capt.* p 19 Sept. 26; *Major,* p 27 Sept. 33.
29	1 8/12	Sydney John Cotton, *Cornet,* 19 April, 10; *Lieut.* 13 Feb. 12; *Capt.* p 1 Jan. 20; *Major* 18 Jan. 28.

		CAPTAINS.	ENSIGN.	LIEUT.	CAPTAIN.	BREVET-MAJOR.
33	0	Wm. Irwin[3]	p 10 Nov. 07	20 July 09	p 9 May 16	10 Jan. 37
26	6/12	Thomas Wheeler	24 May 14	p 18 Dec. 17	28 Sept. 32	
16	1 3/12	Wanley Elias Sawbridge	p 23 Oct. 23	28 Apr. 25	p 30 June 29	
14	0	F. Wimbleton P. Parker	p 10 June 26	p 3 Apr. 27	p 12 July 33	
14	0	Frank Adams	p 30 Dec. 26	23 Mar. 32	p 31 Dec. 33	
20	8 2/12	Wm. Hunter[4]	13 May 12	28 Apr. 13	p 27 Nov. 28	
11	0	Chas. Ferd. Ham Smith	18 June 29	p 27 Sept. 33	p 26 Dec. 37	
10	2 7/12	Maurice Chas. O'Connell	p 25 Mar. 28	25 Nov. 31	p 22 June 38	
27	1 5/12	George Minter	14 Nov. 11	15 Jan. 18	29 Apr. 32	
22	2 2/12	Wm. Lloyd Russell	17 Jan. 16	28 Feb. 22	20 Oct. 37	
		LIEUTENANTS.				
18	5 4/12	George Wardell	2 Jan. 17	9 Apr. 25	3 Major Irwin served in the Peninsula from the beginning of 1809, to the end of the war, including the passage of the Douro; battles of Talavera (wounded), Busaco, and Campo Mayor; first siege of Badajoz; battles of Albuhera, Aroyo de Molino, Almarez, Vittoria (severely wounded), Nivelle, Nive, Orthes, and Toulouse. Present on the 16th, (severely wounded) and 18th June. at Waterloo. 4 Capt. Hunter served in the Peninsula from Feb. 1813 to the end of the war, including the crossing of the Bidassoa (severely wounded by a musket shot through the body); battles of the Nive 10th, (wounded) 11th, and 12th December, Orthes, and Toulouse. 5 Paymaster Benson served in the Peninsula, from July, 1812, to the end of the war, including the battles of Vittoria, the Pyrenees, (wounded in the arm), Pampeluna, Nivelle, Nive, Orthes, and Toulouse. Served also in the American war, and was severely wounded in the right breast by a rifle ball at Plattsburgh.	
15	0	Mottram Andrews	9 April 25	p 24 July 28		
16	0	William Russell	3 Feb. 25	6 Nov. 26		
14	0	Fred. Browne Russell	2 Nov. 26	18 Feb. 30		
7	0	Robt. Julian Baumgartner	p 27 Sept. 33	p 30 June 37		
7	0	Henry Dalton Smart	p 31 Dec. 33	p 25 Aug. 37		
6	0	Chas. Henry Nicholetts	p 19 Dec. 34	p 6 Oct. 37		
12	19 4/12	Donald M'Phee	15 Dec. 08	29 Nov. 10		
7	0	Fra. Durell Vignoles	p 10 May 33	p 26 Dec. 37		
3	0	Edw. M. Love	p 23 June 37	p 17 Aug. 38		
3	0	John Edw. H. Pryce	p 30 June 37	p 1 Mar. 39		
3	0	W. G. Cormick	p 10 July 37	p 24 May 39		
3	0	G. Gravatt	p 25 Aug. 37	p 31 May 39		
		ENSIGNS.				
3	0	J. G. R. Aplin	p 7 Oct. 37			
3	0	H. Halsey Lake	p 15 Dec. 37			
2	0	Donald M'Gregor	4 May 38			
1	0	Percy Archer Butler	p 1 Mar. 39			
1	0	Henry Mostyn Owen	p 24 May 39			
1	0	Samuel Rawson	p 31 May 39			
1	0	Sidney Cotton	25 Oct. 39			
1	0	Eyre Coote Grant	26 Oct. 39			
20	8	*Paymaster.*—George Thos. Benson,[5] 20 May, 36; *Ens.* 13 Feb. 12; *Lieut.* 25 Aug. 13.				
2	0	*Adjutant.*—Donald M'Gregor, (*Ens.*) 17 Aug. 38.				
3	0	*Quarter-Master.*—William Kerr, 1 July, 38; *Ens.* 7 July, 37.				
		Surgeon.—James Campbell, 19 June, 35; *Assist.-Surg.* 25 Oct. 25; *Hosp. Assist.* 24 Feb. 20.				
		Assist.-Surgs.—A. S. Macdonell, 29 July 30; *Hosp.-Assist.* 15 Nov. 27.				
5	0	Archibald Alexander, 20 Feb. 35.				

Facings Yellow.—*Agent,* Messrs. Cox & Co.

1 Sir Edward Paget served in the campaign in Flanders and Holland in 94. He was present in the naval action off Cape St. Vincent, 14 Feb. 97; in the actions of the 8th, 13th, and 21st March, in Egypt (in the latter he was wounded), the investment of Cairo and Alexandria. Sir Edward lost his right arm in the action at Oporto, 12th May 09, and has received a Medal for Corunna.

2 Colonel French served the campaigns of 1813-14, in the Peninsula, including the battles of Nivelle, Orthes, and Toulouse.

29th (or the Worcestershire) Regiment of Foot.

"ROLEIA"—"VIMIERA"—"TALAVERA"—"ALBUHERA"—"PENINSULA."

Years' Serv.		
Full Pay	Half Pay	
47		*Colonel.* 🅟 🅒🅑 John *Lord* Strafford,[1] G.C.B. & G.C.H. *Ens.* 30 Sept. 1793; *Lieut.* 1 Dec. 93; *Capt.* 24 May, 94; *Lieut.-Col.* 14 March, 1800; *Col.* 25 July, 10; *Major-Gen.* 4 June, 13; *Lieut.-Gen.* 27 May, 25; *Col.* 29th Regt. 23 Jan. 28.
20	4 6/12	*Lieut.-Colonel.* Hon. C. A. Wrottesley,[2] *Cornet,* 21 Dec. 15; *Lieut.* ᴾ 5 July, 21; *Capt.* ᴾ 16 June, 25; *Major,* ᴾ 5 April, 31; *Lieut.-Col.* 3 July, 39.
34	1 1/12	*Majors.* 🅟 Thomas Bennett Hickin,[3] *Ens.* 2 May, 05; *Lieut.* ᴾ 31 Oct. 05; *Capt.* 9 May, 16; *Brev.-Major,* 10 Jan. 37; *Regtl.-Major,* ᴾ 31 May, 39.
34	6/12	Alex. Sharrock, *Ens.* 7 Aug. 06; *Lieut.* 30 June 08; *Capt.* 27 Apr. 27; *Major,* ᴾ 27 Sept. 39.

		CAPTAINS.	ENSIGN.	LIEUT.	CAPTAIN.	BREVET-MAJOR.
20	0	Rob. Percy Douglas	16 Mar. 20	ᴾ 19 Feb. 24	ᴾ 11 June 28	
15	0	George Congreve	8 Apr. 25	ᴾ 12 Jan. 26	ᴾ 12 June 28	
15	0	Christ. Edw. Eaton	ᴾ 28 Apr. 25	ᴾ 20 May 26	ᴾ 30 Dec. 31	
15	0	Henry Phillpotts	ᴾ 23 June 25	ᴾ 11 July 26	ᴾ 27 June 34	
14	0	W. Wickham Drake	ᴾ 25 Feb. 26	ᴾ 20 Aug. 29	ᴾ 14 July 37	
14	0	W. Gemmell Alves	ᴾ 20 May 26	ᴾ 10 Sept. 30	ᴾ 10 Nov. 37	
13	0	John George Weir	ᴾ 16 Aug. 27	ᴾ 30 Dec. 31	ᴾ 31 May 39	
15	0	Andrew T. Hemphill....	7 Apr. 25	16 Apr. 29	3 July 39	
10	0	*Hon.* W. F. Byng	never	ᴾ 31 Dec. 30	ᴾ 12 July 39	
11	0	Septimus Hen. Palairet..	ᴾ 28 Oct. 29	ᴾ 16 May 34	ᴾ 27 Sept. 39	
		LIEUTENANTS.				
10	0	John Owen Lucas	ᴾ 15 June 30	ᴾ 27 June 34		
8	0	Gregory Lewis Way	ᴾ 17 Feb. 32	30 July 36		
9	0	Edmund Geo. Nicolay ..	ᴾ 3 May 31	ᴾ 5 May 37		
7	0	George Brown	ᴾ 31 Dec. 31	ᴾ 14 July 37		
6	0	Arth. St. Geo. H. Stepney	ᴾ 16 May 34	ᴾ 10 Nov. 37		
7	0	H. Mont. Cuninghame ..	ᴾ 5 Apr. 33	ᴾ 21 Apr. 37		
5	0	Thomas A. Gerard......	ᴾ 15 May 35	ᴾ 11 Aug. 37		
5	0	Edmund Durbin	ᴾ 9 Oct. 35	ᴾ 8 Mar. 39		
4	0	George Molle	22 Nov. 36	ᴾ 31 May 39		
5	0	John M'Neale Walter....	ᴾ 31 July 35	3 July 39		
3	0	John Power	ᴾ 5 May 37	ᴾ 12 July 39		
3	0	Lewis Coker	11 Aug. 37	ᴾ 27 Sept. 39		
8	0	Cadwallader Edwards ..	ᴾ 21 Sept. 32	15 Dec. 37		
		ENSIGNS.				
2	0	H. P. L'Estrange	ᴾ 28 Dec. 38			
2	0	Kenneth Murchison	1 Feb. 39			
1	0	Thos. Edw. Wilbraham..	ᴾ 8 Mar. 39			
1	0	Frederick Coventry	ᴾ 31 May 39			
1	0	James Halkett	ᴾ 7 June 39			
1	0	George H. M. Jones	13 July 39			
1	0	Richard Francis Henry..	ᴾ 27 Sept. 39			
1	0	James Wm. Richardson	ᴾ 15 Nov. 39			

2 Col. Wrottesley was at the siege of Bhurtpore.

3 Major Bennett Hickin served in the Peninsula, from Aug. 1809, to the end of the war, including the capture of Oporto, battles of Talavera, Busaco, Albuhera, (wounded), Vittoria, Roncesvalles, Pyrenees (severely wounded at Pampeluna), Nivelle, Nive, Bayonne, Aire, Heights of Garris, Orthes, and Toulouse.

4 Dr. Ingham served in the American war, including the battles at Fort-George, Chippewa, and at the Falls of Niagara.

20	0	*Paymaster.*—James Espinasse, 8 Feb. 39; *Ens.* 8 Feb. 21; *Lieut.* 7 April, 25; *Capt.* 11 July, 37.
10	0	*Adjutant.*—John Owen Lucas, (*Lieut.*) 3 July, 39.
16	0	*Quarter-Master.*—🅟 Thomas Kneebone, 15 July, 24.
27	2 10/12	*Surgeon.*—Charles Thomas Ingham,[4] M.D. 25 June 26; *Assist.-Surg.* 16 Aug. 10; *Hosp.-Assist.* 24 May, 10.
2	0	*Assist.-Surgeon.*—Geo. Alex. Cowper, M.D., 30 March, 38.

Facings Yellow.—*Agent,* Messrs. Cox & Co.

[*Returned from the Mauritius, March,* 1838.]

1 Lord Strafford served in Flanders, Holland, and in the expeditions to Hanover, Copenhagen, and Walcheren, and has received a cross and one clasp for Vittoria, Pyrenees, Nivelle, Nive, and Orthes.

Emb. for For. Service, 1834.] **30th (or the Cambridgeshire) Regiment of Foot.** [Serving in Bermuda.

The *Sphinx*, with the words "EGYPT"—"BADAJOZ"—"SALAMANCA"—"PENINSULA"—"WATERLOO."

Years' Serv.						
47		Colonel.—🅑 Sir Thomas Bradford,[1] G.C.B. & G.C.H. *Ens.* 20 Oct. 1793; *Lieut.* 9 Dec. 93; *Capt.* 15 April, 94; *Major,* 9 Sept. 95; *Lieut.-Col.* 1 Jan, 1801; *Col.* 25 July, 10; *Major-Gen.* 4 June, 13; *Lieut.-Gen.* 27 May, 25; *Col.* 30th Regt. 18 April, 29.				
Full Pay.	Half Pay.					
34	0	*Lieut.-Colonel.*—🅑 Henry Edward Robinson,[2] *Ens.* 28 May, 06; *Lieut.* 9 Feb. 08; *Capt.* p 26 July, 22; *Major,* p 20 Sept. 27; *Lieut.-Col.* 1 Jan. 34.				
41	0	*Majors.*—Harry Smith Ormond,[3] *Ens.* 8 Nov. 99; *Lieut.* 28 Aug. 01; *Capt.* 24 Sept. 12; *Major,* 10 June, 29.				
37	0	John Tongue,[4] *Ens.* 9 July, 03; *Lieut.* p 24 May, 04; *Capt.* 7 March, 11; *Brevet-Major,* 22 July, 30; *Regtl.-Major,* 1 Jan. 34.				

		CAPTAINS.	ENSIGN.	LIEUT.	CAPTAIN.	BREV.-MAJ.
27	9 3/12	🅑 John Procter[5]	3 Dec. 03	8 June 04	4 May 09	22 July 30
25	2/12	John Gordon Geddes....	8 Nov. 15	27 Mar. 25	p 8 Apr. 26	
26	3/12	🅑 James Poyntz[6]	14 Apr. 14	19 July 15	28 Dec. 28	
25	9/12	Rob. Alex. Andrews	18 Aug. 14	27 Mar. 24	p 20 Aug. 29	
21	8	🅑 Wm. Baxter[7]	9 May 11	10 June 13	1 Jan. 34	
13	0	Hen. Jenkins Pogson....	p 15 Nov. 27	p 11 June 30	p 17 Oct. 34	
7	21	🅑 🅒🅑 Samuel Waymouth[8]	18 May 12	28 Mar. 13	13 Oct. 25	28 June 38
10	0	John Moore............	p 15 June 30	p 9 May 34	p 1 Mar. 39	
12	0	Charles Sillery	24 Nov. 28	20 July 30	p 15 Mar. 39	
9	0	Edward John Grant	p 9 Dec. 31	p 17 Oct. 34	p 22 Nov. 39	
		LIEUTENANTS.				
20	0	C. H. Marechaux		9 Dec. 20	6 Apr. 26	
13	0	Wm. Armstrong Steele..		16 May 27	8 Apr. 32	
13	0	Wm. Hodder Heard		16 Sept. 27	10 Dec. 33	
10	0	Edwin Godwin Pilsworth		p 31 Aug. 30	p 18 July 34	
7	0	Alex. John H. Lumsden		p 3 May 33	p 19 Dec. 34	
8	0	Sam. John Luke Nicoll..		p 27 Apr. 32	p 8 June 38	
6	0	*Hon.* J. Harlstonge Pery		p 9 May 34	p 30 Oct. 38	
6	0	Alex. Macdonald		18 July 34	31 Oct. 38	
6	0	P. C. Cavan		p 19 Dec. 34	p 1 Mar. 39	
5	0	Henry Shum		p 12 June 35	p 15 Mar. 39	
4	0	R. Dring O'Grady		p 30 July 36	p 26 Apr. 39	
4	0	John Tongue		p 2 Dec. 36	p 8 Nov. 39	
3	0	Henry Broome		p 8 Dec. 37	p 22 Nov. 39	
		ENSIGNS.				
2	0	D. J. B. Edwardes......		p 8 June 38		
2	0	Edward Edwards		p 30 Oct. 38		
1	0	Paget Bayly		p 8 Mar. 39		
1	0	Rob. Wm. Smith		p 15 Mar. 39		
1	0	Tho. Wm. Wilkinson....		p 1 Nov. 39		
1	0	Rich. Gervys Grylls		p 8 Nov. 39		
1	0	Louis G. F. Broome		p 22 Nov. 39		
1	0	Wm. Campbell Mollan..		p 10 Jan. 40		
15	0	*Paymaster.*—R. Ch. Macdonald, 8 May, 35; *Ens.* 10 April, 25; *Lieut.* 13 Dec. 27.				
6	0	*Adjutant.*—Alexander Macdonald, (*Lieut.*) 18 July, 34.				
16	0	*Quarter-Master.*—🅑 John Ward,[9] 21 Oct. 24.				
		Surgeon.—Joseph Trigance, 5 Dec. 34; *Assist.-Surg.* 9 Nov. 20; *Hosp.-Assist.* 7 March, 14.				
		Assist.-Surgeons.—Joseph Edmondson, 29 July, 30; *Hosp.-Assist.* 20 Dec. 26.				
4	0	James Cockburn, 15 April, 36.				

Notes to right of Lieutenants list:

7 Captain Baxter served in the Peninsula from July, 1811, to January, 1813, including the siege of the Forts at, and battle of Salamanca, where he was wounded; served also in the South of France in 1814.

8 Major Waymouth served in the Peninsula with the 2nd Life Guards; was severely wounded and taken prisoner (reported "supposed to be killed") at Waterloo, in charging the Cuirassiers. The effects of this wound were so severe that he was a year upon crutches in a state of excessive suffering, and it was six years before he could put on a boot. He was consequently compelled to make the sacrifice of his professional prospects by an exchange to half-pay when his name stood first for promotion by purchase.

9 Quarter-Master Ward served in the Peninsula from March, 1809, to June, 1813, including the siege of Cadiz, battle of Fuentes d'Onor, siege of Badajoz; and affair at Villa Murial; served also in the Netherlands.

Facings Yellow.—*Agent,* Messrs. Cox & Co.

1 Sir Thomas Bradford was present at the siege of Monte Video, and attack on Buenos Ayres. He has received a cross and one clasp for Corunna, Salamanca, Vittoria, St. Sebastian, and the passage of the Nive.
2 Colonel Robinson served in the Peninsula from June, 1809, to October, 1813, including the battles of Talavera, Busaco; lines at Torres Vedras; pursuit of Massena; siege of Ciudad Rodrigo; siege and storming of Badajoz (shot through the left arm at the assault 6th April, 1812); battle of Salamanca; retreat from Madrid; battles of Vittoria and the Pyrenees, (severely wounded, left leg fractured) 28th July, 1813.
3 Major Ormond's services:—Expedition to Copenhagen in 1801; Canadian campaigns of 1812, 13, and 14, including the battles of Fort George, Stoney Creek, and Chrystler's Farm.
4 Major Tongue commanded the left wing of the 30th Regiment at the siege of Asseerghur.
5 Major Procter's services:—Expedition to Copenhagen in 1807; Corunna campaign; Peninsula from 1812 until 1814; served also in the American War.
6 Captain Poyntz served in Portugal as a volunteer from February to November, 1811, including the sortie of the French from Almissa, and subsequent skirmish at Barber del Puesco, and battle at Fuentes d'Onor.

Emb. for For. Service, 1825.] **31st** (*or the Huntingdonshire*) *Regiment of Foot.* [Serving in Bengal.

"TALAVERA" — "ALBUHERA" — "VITTORIA" — "PYRENEES" — "NIVELLE" — "NIVE" — "PENINSULA."

Years' Serv.			
37		**Colonel.**	
Full Pay.	Half Pay.	◉ ☒ Sir Colin Halkett,¹ K.C.B. & G.C.H. *Lt.-Col.* 17 Nov. 1803; *Col.* 1 Jan. 12; *Major-Gen.* 4 June, 14; *Lt.-Gen.* 22 July, 30; *Col. 31st Regt.* 28 Mar. 38.	
		Lieut.-Colonels.— ◉ ☒ C. Horace Churchill, C.B. *Ens.* 19 June, 06; *Lieut. & Capt.* ᴾ 27 Aug. 12; *Brevet-Major,* 22 Nov. 13; *Brevet-Lieut.-Col.* 18 June, 15; *Regtl.-Major,* 27 July, 26; *Lieut.-Col.* 16 July, 30; *Col.* 10 Jan. 37.	
34	0		
34	0	◉ Samuel Bolton,² *Ens.* 5 Feb. 07; *Lieut.* 6 April, 09; *Capt.* ᴾ 24 Oct. 22; *Major,* 14 June, 33; *Lieut.-Col.* ᴾ 24 Nov. 35.	
24	4/12	**Majors.**—Thomas Skinner, *Ens.* 25 Jan. 16; *Lieut.* ᴾ 6 Aug. 19; *Capt.* ᴾ 9 Oct. 23; *Major,* ᴾ 24 Nov. 35.	
39	8/12	H. Clinton Van Cortlandt,³ *Cornet,* 8 May, 01; *Lieut.* 1 Nov. 03; *Capt.* 5 July, 14; *Brevet-Major,* 10 Jan. 37; *Regtl.-Major,* 17 Sept. 39.	

		CAPTAINS.	ENSIGN.	LIEUT.	CAPTAIN.	BREV.-MAJ.
35	1	Edward Wm. Bray⁴	12 Jan. 05	20 Apr. 08	6 Apr. 19	10 Jan. 37
30	2½	John Byrne	1 Oct. 08	21 Dec. 09	ᴾ 19 Apr. 21	26 Feb. 36
32	0	James Spence⁵	26 Nov. 08	ᴾ 20 Dec. 10	10 Feb. 25	28 June 38
29	0	◉ Charles Shaw⁶	13 May 11	13 Apr. 20	30 July 26	
22	5 10/12	◉ Lambert B. Urmston⁷	1 Apr. 13	11 May 15	ᴾ 12 Feb. 28	
15	0	Geo. Cuthbert Marshall	25 Aug. 25	11 June 29	ᴾ 24 Aug. 32	
30	2 8/12	☒ George Baldwin⁸	2 June 08	9 Nov. 14	14 June 33	
21	7 1/12	Holland Leckie M'Ghee	18 June 12	3 May 14	ᴾ 24 Nov. 35	
23	11	George Ogilvy	Jan. 07	5 Nov. 07	8 Apr. 25	28 June 33
19	7 1/12	Wm. Gibson Willes	9 Sept. 13	ᴾ 19 Dec. 16	26 Sept. 39	
		LIEUTENANTS.				
17	9 1/12	Thomas Bulkeley	never.	5 May 14		
21	0	Geo. Dobson Young	6 Apr. 19	25 Aug. 25		
16	0	Geo. Francis White	27 Jan. 25	3 Apr. 28		
14	0	John Cassidy Stock	23 Mar. 26	1 Feb. 29		
14	0	Robert Norman	ᴾ 7 Sept. 26	2 Sept. 29		
14	0	Thomas Pender	13 Sept. 26	1 Aug. 30		
12	0	Thos. Conyngham Kelly	3 Apr. 28	ᴾ 31 Aug. 30		
12	0	Edward Lugard	31 July 28	ᴾ 31 Oct. 31		
11	0	Frederick Spence	24 Dec. 29	ᴾ 1 Nov. 31		
10	0	Robt. John Eagar	11 June 30	ᴾ 25 Jan. 33		
9	0	James Croft Brooke	ᴾ 31 Oct. 31	2 Sept. 33		
9	0	John Snowden Scott	ᴾ 1 Nov. 31	ᴾ 6 Mar. 35		
8	0	Arthur Du Bourdieu	ᴾ 25 Jan. 33	27 Mar. 36		
10	4 8/12	Philip Le Couteur	ᴾ 8 Dec. 25	1 Apr. 36		
7	0	Hon. Geo. A. F. C. Graves	ᴾ 15 Mar. 33	ᴾ 30 Dec. 36		
5	0	George Frend	ᴾ 24 Nov. 35	ᴾ 14 July 37		
6	0	Hen. Knight Sayers	ᴾ 17 Oct. 34	7 July 37		
4	0	Dalway M'Ilveen	ᴾ 22 Jan. 36	ᴾ 12 July 39		
5	0	Theoph. John Bourke	10 May 35	26 Sept. 39		
5	0	John Æneas Duncan	ᴾ 7 Aug. 35	26 Oct. 39		
4	0	Joseph Greenwood	ᴾ 6 May 36	27 Oct. 39		
3	0	George Bainbridge Shaw	ᴾ 14 July 37	28 Oct. 39		
4	0	Thos. Henry Plasket	ᴾ 21 Oct. 36	29 Oct. 39		
		ENSIGNS.				
1	0	William Bray	21 June 39			
1	0	J. D. Carmichael Smyth	ᴾ 12 July 39			
1	0	Duncan Stew. Robertson	ᴾ 30 Aug. 39			
1	0	George Fred. Moore	25 Oct. 39			
1	0	Wm. Fred. Willes Atty.	ᴾ 15 Nov. 39			
1	0	John Lucas R. Pollard	17 Jan. 40			
1	0	Henry Wm. Hart	7 Feb. 40			
1	0	Robert Law	8 Feb. 40			
27	0	*Paymaster.*—John Henry Matthews,⁹ 21 Oct. 13.				
		Adjutant.—				
14	0	*Quarter-Master.*—Samuel Palmer, 8 May, 26.				
		Surgeon.—Henry Hart, M.D. 21 Sept. 30; *Assist.-Surg.* 31 Jan. 11.				
14	0	*Assist.-Surgeons.*—T. Eames Ayre, 2 Nov. 26; *Hosp.-Assist.* 17 July, 26.				
8	0	Charles Hugh James, 5 Oct. 32.				

Facings Buff.—*Agent*, Messrs. Price & Son.

*** Majors Bray and Spence, Captains Shaw and Baldwin, are the only officers now serving in the 31st regt. who suffered in that lamentable catastrophe, the burning of the *Kent*, East Indiaman, on the 1st March, 1825, in the Bay of Biscay.

4 Major Bray served the Mahratta campaigns of 1817, 18, and 19, and was present at the siege and capture of Ryghur, Amulnair, and Asseerghur.

5 Major Spence was present in the action of Stuola, near Genoa, 13th April, 1814, and subsequent attacks upon the city of Genoa until its surrender.

6 Captain Shaw was present at the battle of Albuhera. Also at the attack and surrender of Genoa in 1814, and, subsequently, at the surrender of Corsica.

7 Capt. Urmston served the campaigns of 1813 and 14 in the Peninsula, including the battles of the Nive, Orthes, and Toulouse. Served throughout the Burmese war, including the capture of Rangoon; storm and capture of the stockades of Kemwandirle and Kummerute; battles of Rangoon, Kokain, and Pagam-Mew; attack and capture of Donabew, Prome, and Maloom; actions of Simbike and Napadee.

8 Capt. Baldwin accompanied the expedition to Walcheren, and was at the siege of Flushing. Present on the 18th June at Waterloo, and the storming of Cambray.

9 Paymaster Matthews served in the Nepaul war in 1814 and 15; at the capture of Hattrass; in the Mahratta war in 1817 and 18; and at the capture of Bhurtpore.

1 Sir Colin Halkett has received a cross for Albuhera, Salamanca, Vittoria, and the passage of the Nive, and was severely wounded at Waterloo.

2 Col. Bolton served in the Peninsula, from 1808 to the end of the war, including the battles of Talavera, Busaco, Albuhera (wounded), Aroya de Molina, Vittoria, the Pyrenees, Nive, Orthes, Aire, and Toulouse.

3 Major Van Cortlandt was engaged at the following battles, sieges, &c. in the East Indies, viz. Lasna, Begaghur, Ruthowra, Agra, Deig, Bhurtpore, Allyghur, Coel, Delhi, Laswarrie, and Fallyghur, capture of Holkar. Also several skirmishes during the campaigns of 1803, 4, 5, and 6. Present at the sieges of Komona and Gunowrie in 1808, and at Kalunga in 1814. Served the campaigns against the Pindarrees in 1817 and 18.

Emb. for Foreign Service, 1830.] **32d (*or the Cornwall*) Regiment of Foot.** [Serving in Canada.

"ROLEIA"—"VIMIERA"—"SALAMANCA"—"PYRENEES"—"NIVELLE"— "NIVE"—"ORTHES"—"PENINSULA"—"WATERLOO."

Colonel.

Years' Serv.		
51		Sir Robert Macfarlane,[1] K.C.B. G.C.H. *Ens.* 26 May, 1789; *Lieut.* 22 May, 93; *Capt.* 25 Sept. 93; *Major*, 12 Nov. 94; *Lieut.-Col.* 19 Sept. 94; *Col.* 1 Jan. 1800; *Major-Gen.* 25 April, 08; *Lieut.-Gen.* 4 June, 13; *Gen.* 22 July, 30; *Col.* 32nd Regt. 26 Sept. 37.
Full Pay	Half Pay	

Lieut.Colonel.

| 26 | 4/12 | Thos. Henry Wingfield, *Lieut.* 7th Fusiliers, 11 Nov. 13; *Capt.* p 12 Sept. 22; *Major*, p 3 June 28; *Lieut.-Col.* 19 Jan. 39. |

Majors.

| 27 | 0 | ᛒ ☗ John Birtwhistle,[2] *Ens.* 14 April, 13; *Lieut.* p 14 Jan. 19; *Capt.* p 13 May, 24; *Brevet-Major*, 28 June, 38; *Regtl.-Major*, 19 Jan. 39. |
| 16 | 0 | Frederick Markham,[3] *Ens.* p 13 May, 24; *Lieut.* p 22 Oct. 25; *Capt.* p 16 April, 29; *Major*, p 28 Sept. 39. |

		CAPTAINS.	ENSIGN.	LIEUT.	CAPTAIN.	BREV.-MAJ.
28	7 8/12	ᛒ John Swinburn[4]	28 Aug. 04	16 May 05	15 Aug. 10	22 July 30
27	0	☗ George Browne[5]	10 June 13	30 Sept. 19	10 Feb. 32	15 June 38
21	0	Thomas Calder	15 July 19	7 April 25	16 Feb. 33	
13	0	John Thos. Hill	p 13 Mar. 27	p 16 April 29	p 13 Feb. 35	
13	0	Hen. Vaughan Brooke ..	p 12 July 27	p 11 June 30	p 22 May 35	
14	1 1/12	John Hen. Evelegh	8 April 25	p 28 Jan. 26	p 20 Jan. 32	
20	4 3/12	Thomas White	7 Dec. 15	25 Aug. 24	5 Oct. 38	
9	0	Osborne Markham......	p 27 Sept. 31	p 9 Mar. 34	p 3 Nov. 37	
19	7 10/12	Alexander Gardiner[6] ..	15 July 13	20 July 15	19 Jan. 39	
13	8/12	Edw. Osborne Broadley..	p 15 Aug. 26	p 29 Sept. 29	p 28 Sept. 39	
		LIEUTENANTS.				
15	0	Fra. John Griffin	13 Oct. 25	12 June 28		
15	0	☗ George Oke[7]	8 Dec. 25	26 June 28		
12	0	Cuthbert A. Baines	12 June 28	8 Oct. 30		
12	0	John Dillon............	p 26 June 28	10 Feb. 32		
11	0	Robert Campbell	p 2 Feb. 30	p 2 Aug. 33		
10	0	Thomas Forsyth........	p 15 June 30	p 22 May 35		
9	0	William Case	10 Feb. 32	9 Feb. 38		
7	0	Thos. Daniel Kelly......	12 April 33	10 Feb. 38		
7	0	John Erule Money......	p 18 April 33	5 Oct. 38		
7	0	J. E. W. Inglis	p 2 Aug. 33	19 Jan. 39		
17	2 9/12	Thomas Byrne	p 15 Mar. 21	18 Sept. 28		
5	0	Sam. Auchmuty Dickson	p 22 May 35	p 28 Sept. 39		
4	0	George Griffin	16 Dec. 36	22 Feb. 39		
		ENSIGNS.				
4	0	Rhys Jones	p 2 Sept. 36			
4	0	Thomas Robyns	p 7 Oct. 36			
3	0	E. W. D. Lowe	20 May 37			
3	0	Geo. Sam. Moore	9 Feb. 38			
1	0	John P. Pigott	p 15 Feb. 39			
1	0	Wm. Bellingham	8 Mar. 39			
1	0	Cha. Davers Rushbrooke.	p 24 May 39			
1	0	Henry Duberly	p 28 Sept. 39			
25	2 6/12	Paymaster.—☗ G. Moore,[8] 19 Oct. 26; *Ens.* 1 Oct. 12; *Lieut.* 6 Dec.13.				
7	0	Adjutant.—Thos. Daniel Kelly, (*Lieut.*) 12 April, 33.				
13	0	Quarter-Master.—ᛒ ☗ Thomas Healey,[9] 29 Nov. 27.				
35	8/12	Surgeon.—ᛒ Wm. Bampfield,[10] 21 Jan. 13; *Assist.-Surg.* 28 Jan. 08; *Hosp.-Assist.* 26 Dec. 04.				
8	0	Assist.-Surgeons.—Duncan M'Gregor, 4 Jan. 33.				
7	0	Alex. M'Grigor, 31 May, 33.				

Notes in right column:
5 Major Browne served at Waterloo on 16th and 18th June.
6 Capt. Gardiner served in the American war in 1815.
7 Lieut. Oke served at Waterloo on the 16th and 18th June.
8 Paymaster Moore served the campaign of 1814 in Holland, including the action at Merxem, and bombardment of Antwerp. Present at Waterloo.
9 Quarter-Master Healey's services:—siege of Copenhagen in 1807; battles of Roleia, Vimiera, and Corunna; expedition to Walcheren and siege of Flushing; Peninsula from June, 1811 to the end of the war, including the battles of Salamanca, the Pyrenees, Nivelle, Nive, and Orthes. Served at Waterloo 16th, and 18th June.
10 Dr. Bampfield was at the battles of Maida and Castalla; sieges of Tarragona and Barcelona.

Facings White—*Agent*, Messrs. Cox & Co.—*Irish Agent*, Borough, Armit & Co.

1 Sir Robert Macfarlane accompanied the expedition to Copenhagen in 1807. He served subsequently in Sicily as second in command under Lord William Bentinck.
2 Major Birtwhistle served the campaign of 1814 in the South of France. Present on the 16th (severely wounded) 17th, and 18th June, at Waterloo.
3 Major Markham was severely wounded in Canada, 23 Nov. 1837.
4 Major Swinburn's services:—siege of Copenhagen in 1807; campaign of 1808 in Portugal; (wounded in the head on the retreat to Vigo.) Present at the battles of the Coa, Fuentes d'Onor, Redinha (wounded in the hip), Sabugal, and Busaco. Joined the army at Toulouse in 1814. Present at New Orleans, Jan. 1815.

Emb. for Foreign Service, 1837.] **33d (or 1st Yorkshire, W. Riding) Regt. of Foot.** [Serving at Gibraltar.

"SERINGAPATAM"—"WATERLOO."

Years' Serv.		
61		*Colonel.*
Full Pay.	Half Pay.	Sir Charles Wale,[1] K.C.B. *Ens.* June, 1779; *Lieut.* 13 April, 80; *Capt.* 25 June, 83; *Major,* 1 Mar. 94; *Lieut.-Col.* 1 Jan. 98; *Col.* 25 April, 1808; *Major-Gen.* 4 June, 11; *Lieut.-Gen.* 19 July, 21; *Gen.* 28 June, 38; *Col.* 33d Regt. 25 Feb. 31.
34	0	*Lieut.-Colonel.* ⚜ Charles Knight,[2] *Ens.* August 06; *Lieut.* 25 Jan. 07; *Capt.* p 30 Aug. 10; *Brevet-Major,* 21 Jan. 19; *Regtl.-Major,* 25 Nov. 21; *Lieut.Col.* p 10 Sept. 30.
		Majors.
33	0	⚜ Joseph Mark Harty,[3] K.H. *Ens.* 23 April, 07; *Lieut.* p 1 May, 07; *Capt.* p 11 Mar. 13; *Major,* p 20 Dec. 27.
35	0	⚜ Thomas Reid,[4] *Ens.* 2 July, 05; *Lieut.* p 20 June, 06; *Capt.* 16 June, 15; *Brevet-Major,* 10 Jan. 37; *Regtl.-Major,* 10 Nov. 38.

		CAPTAINS.	ENSIGN.	LIEUT.	CAPTAIN.	BREV.-MAJ.
28	0	⚜ Richard Westmore[5]	28 May 12	p 1 April 13	23 June 25	28 June 38
29	0	George Whannell[6]	1 Mar. 11	16 Mar. 14	3 Nov. 25	28 June 38
18	11/12	Thos. Jas. Galloway	p 13 Sept. 21	2 June 25	p 27 Dec. 27	
15	0	Fred. Rudolph Blake	p 30 June 25	p 14 Aug. 27	p 23 Aug. 31	
17	0	Archibald Robertson	p 4 Dec. 23	p 31 Aug. 26	p 11 Dec. 28	
13	0	John Johnston	p 15 Aug. 27	16 Mar. 30	p 19 Oct. 38	
13	0	Thos. Bunbury Gough	p 27 Dec. 27	p 25 Jan. 31	p 23 Nov. 38	
11	0	George Aug. Vernon	2 July 29	p 12 April 31	p 28 Dec. 38	
20	8 7/12	⚜ Chas.Rob.Shuckburgh[7]	25 July 11	5 Aug. 13	21 June 39	
10	0	Henry Wm. Bunbury	p 29 June 30	p 30 Aug. 33	p 18 Aug. 38	
		LIEUTENANTS.				
14	0	John Williamson	p 30 Dec. 26	p 16 July 30		
13	0	Thos. Jacob Smith	p 13 Dec. 27	p 10 Sept. 30		
11	0	Warren Maude	p 20 Mar. 29	p 13 April 32		
10	0	Francis Todd	p 16 July 30	p 15 Mar. 33		
13	0	Thomas Plunkett	15 Nov. 27	p 5 April 33		
10	0	William T. Nixon	3 Aug. 30	p 22 Jan. 36		
9	0	Hen. Knight Erskine	6 Jan. 32	p 27 Feb. 36		
8	0	George Erskine	17 Aug. 32	p 3 June 36		
8	0	James Knight	p 28 Dec. 32	p 19 Oct. 38		
6	0	John Stuart	7 Mar. 34	p 23 Nov. 38		
5	0	E. Aug. Milman	p 27 Nov. 35	p 28 Dec. 38		
5	0	Edw. Winnington	p 22 Jan. 36	4 Jan. 39		
4	0	Chas. P. B. Walker	p 27 Feb. 36	21 June 39		
		ENSIGNS.				
4	0	Edmund Peel	p 18 Mar. 36			
4	0	Charles Mills	p 3 June 36			
2	0	Jas. Bruce Neil	p 19 Oct. 38			
2	0	Nich. Pelham Giveen	p 23 Nov. 38			
2	0	Rob. Gregory Wale	30 Oct. 38			
1	0	P. G. H. Somerset	p 29 Mar. 39			
1	0	John E. Collings	21 June 39			
1	0	Edw. Westby Donovan	10 Jan. 40			

4 Major Reid was at the capture of Bourbon and the Isle of France in 1810; served the campaigns of 1813 and 14 in Germany and Holland, including both attacks on Merxem, and the assault on Bergen-op-Zoom; served at Waterloo on the 16th, 17th and 18th June, and was severely wounded.

5 Major Westmore served the campaigns of 1813 and 14 in Germany and Holland, including both attacks on Merxem, and the assault on Bergen-op-Zoom; served at Waterloo on the 16th, 17th and 18th June, and was severely wounded.

6 Major Whannell served the campaigns of 1813 and 14 in Germany and Holland, including the attacks on Merxem, bombardment of the French fleet at Antwerp, and the attack on Bergen-up-Zoom.

7 Capt. Shuckburgh served in the Peninsula from 1811 to the end of the war, including the battle of Vittoria; blockade of Pampluna; battles of the Pyrenees, 25th, 26th, 28th, and 30th July; actions of Irun 31st Aug, Vera Heights; battles of Nivelle, Orthes, and Toulouse, besides various other minor actions and skirmishes.

15	14 7/12	*Paymaster.*—Patrick M'Grath, 4 Oct. 31; *Ens.* 7 Feb. 11; *Lieut.* 14 Jan. 13.
14	0	*Adjutant.*—John Williamson (*Lieut.*) 12 Mar. 31.
14	14 4/12	*Quarter-Master.*—⚜ Henry Oldershaw, 3 Aug. 32; *Ens.* 10 June, 12; *Lieut.* 3 Feb. 14.
24	1 6/12	*Surgeon.*—John Hall, 8 Nov.27; *Assist.-Surg.*12 Sept.22; *Hosp.-Assist.* 24 June 15.
13	0	*Assist.-Surgs.*—Denis Joseph Magrath, M.D. 29 June, 30; *Hosp.-Assist.* 1 Feb. 27.
8	0	J. M. C. M'Donald, 11 Jan. 33.

Facings Red—*Agent,* Messrs. Cox & Co.—*Irish Agent,* Borough, Armit & Co.

1 Sir Charles Wale served in the campaign of 1799 in Holland, and was present at the battles of the 10th and 19th Sept., and 2nd and 6th Oct. He has received a medal for Guadaloupe, where he was wounded in storming the heights of Matauba, 3 Feb. 10.

2 Col. Knight was at the capture of Bourbon and the Isle of France in 1810; served the campaign of 1814 in Holland, including the operations before Antwerp; served at Waterloo on the 16th, 17th and 18th June, and received a severe contusion; succeeded to the command of the 33d regiment during the action on the 18th June, and marched it out of the field.

3 Major Harty was at the capture of Bourbon and the Isle of France in 1810; served the campaigns of 1813 and 14 in Germany and Holland, including both attacks on Merxem, and the assault on Bergen-op-Zoom; served at Waterloo on the 16th, 17th and 18th June, and was slightly wounded.

Emb. for For. Service, 1829.] **34th (or the Cumberland) Regt. of Foot.** [Serving in Canada.

"ALBUHERA"—"VITTORIA"—"PYRENEES"—"NIVELLE"—"NIVE"—
"ORTHES"—"PENINSULA."

Years' Serv.		
Full Pay.	Half Pay.	
59		*Colonel.* ₽ Sir Thos. Makdougall Brisbane,¹ Bart. G.C.B. and G.C.H. *Ens.* 10 Jan. 1782; *Lieut.* 30 July, 91; *Capt.* 12 April, 93; *Major,* 5 Aug. 95; *Lieut.-Col.* 4 April, 1800; *Col.* 25 July, 10; *M ajor.-Gen.* 4 June, 13; *Lieut.-Gen.* 27 May, 25; *Col.* 34th Regt. 16 Dec. 26.
		Lieut-Colonel.
19	7/12	Rich. Airey, *Ens.* 15 March 21; *Lieut.* ᴾ4 Dec. 23; *Capt.* ᴾ22 Oct. 25; *Major,* ᴾ9 May, 34; *Lieut.-Col.* ᴾ10 Feb. 38.
		Majors.
17	5/12	George Ruxton, *Ens.* ᴾ7 Nov. 22; *Lieut.* 24 Jan. 25; *Capt.* ᴾ4 March, 26; *Major,* ᴾ4 Aug. 37.
21	0	Henry Deedes, *Ens.* ᴾ23 Dec. 19; *Lieut.* 2 Oct. 23; *Capt.* ᴾ19 Nov. 25; *Major,* ᴾ23 Feb. 38.

		CAPTAINS.	ENSIGN.	LIEUT.	CAPTAIN.	BREV.-MAJ.
23	1¾	Chas. Baillie Brisbane ..	21 Mar. 16	20 May 19	ᴾ 9 June 25	28 June 38
16	0	Edward Broderick	11 Mar. 24	ᴾ 7 Nov. 26	ᴾ 9 May 34	
11	3/12	James John Best........	6 Feb. 29	ᴾ29 June 30	ᴾ10 April 35	
11	0	R. Willoughby Byron ..	ᴾ27 Aug. 29	2 Aug. 33	ᴾ18 Sept. 35	
9	0	Philip Hamond	ᴾ 9 Dec. 31	ᴾ24 Dec. 33	ᴾ30 July 36	
19	0	Nicholas R. Brown	22 Mar. 21	2 June 25	2 May 37	
8	6 1/12	Joseph Hen. Mathews ..	ᴾ 4 Mar. 26	ᴾ21 Feb. 34	ᴾ 4 Aug. 37	
8	0	John Style Norris	ᴾ11 May 32	ᴾ28 Mar. 34	ᴾ22 Sept. 37	
7	0	Eustace Heathcote......	ᴾ,11 May 33	ᴾ13 Mar. 35	ᴾ23 Feb. 38	
30	1	Robert Bradfute........	9 Nov. 09	ᴾ20 Feb. 12	27 Mar. 28	
		LIEUTENANTS.				
12	0	Fred. Philip Glubb	2 Oct. 28	ᴾ10 May 33		
8	0	Charles F. Hervey	2 Nov. 32	ᴾ30 Dec. 34		
7	0	William E. James	2 Aug. 33	ᴾ10 April 35		
7	0	Hen. John Hutton	ᴾ24 Dec. 33	ᴾ18 Sept. 35		
6	0	Rich. D. Kelly	7 Mar. 34	ᴾ30 July 36		
6	0	Arth. Cyril Goodenough .	ᴾ 8 April 34	ᴾ25 Nov. 36		
6	0	Thomas Bourke	ᴾ 9 May 34	2 May 37		
6	0	Frederick H. Lang......	11 July 34	ᴾ 4 Aug. 37		
6	0	Folliott Duff	ᴾ30 Dec. 34	ᴾ29 Sept. 37		
5	0	John Simpson..........	ᴾ13 Mar. 35	ᴾ 3 Nov. 37		
5	0	Chas. Alfred Schreiber ..	ᴾ10 April 35	ᴾ23 Feb. 38		
4	0	Edw. P. A. Talbot......	ᴾ30 July 36	ᴾ 1 June 38		
4	0	John Gwilt	ᴾ25 Nov. 36	ᴾ10 Aug. 38		
		ENSIGNS.				
3	0	Bonfoy Rooper	ᴾ26 May 37			
3	0	Alex. C. Robertson......	ᴾ15 Sept. 37			
3	0	Fra. Chas. Harvey	ᴾ29 Sept. 37			
3	0	Wm. Bailey Money	ᴾ 3 Nov. 37			
2	0	H. Radford Norman	ᴾ23 Feb. 38			
2	0	J. Fryon Still	11 May 38			
2	0	Hen. Beckett Bertles....	ᴾ 1 June 38			
2	0	Joshua Hen. Kirby......	ᴾ10 Aug. 38			
13	0	*Paymaster.*—Chas. Boyse Roche, 30 Nov. 38; *Ens.* 18 Jan. 28; *Lieut.* 21 June, 32.				
4	0	*Adjutant.*—Edward Plantagenet Airey Talbot, (*Lieut.*) 20 Sept. 39.				
4	0	*Quarter-Master.*—Jones Duke, 10 Jan. 37.				
24	1	*Surgeon.*—William Bain, M.D. 29 Dec. 37 ; *Assist.-Surg.* 30 June, 25 ; *Hosp.-Assist.* 24 June, 15.				
7	0	*Assist.-Surg.*—Alexander Smith, 16 Nov. 33.				
4	0	James Gordon, 13 Jan. 37.				

Facings Yellow.—*Agent,* Messrs. Cox & Co.

1 Sir Thomas Brisbane joined the Duke of York's army in the beginning of the war, and was present in every action except that of the 22nd May 93, when he was confined from a wound received in the action of the 18th of the same month. He was subsequently present at the taking of various islands, forts, &c. in the West Indies. Sir Thomas has received a cross and one clasp for Vittoria, Pyrenees, Nivelle, Orthes, and Toulouse, where he was wounded.

Emb. for For. Service, 1837.] **35th (or Royal Sussex) Regiment of Foot.** [Serving at the Mauritius.

"MAIDA."

Years' Serv.		
Full Pay.	Half Pay.	
53		*Colonel.* Þ Sir John Oswald,¹ G.C.B. & G.C.M.G. *Second Lieut.* 1 Feb. 1788; *Lieut.* 29 Jan. 89; *Capt.* 24 Jan. 91; *Major*, 1 Sept. 95; *Lieut.-Col.* 30 Mar. 97; *Col.* 30 Oct. 1805; *Major-Gen.* 4 June, 11; *Lieut.-Gen.* 12 Aug. 19; *Gen.* 10 Jan. 37; *Col.* 35th Regt. 9 Oct. 19.
21	6/12	*Lieut.-Colonel.* Edward Kent S. Butler, *Ens.* 27 Aug. 18; *Lieut.* 7 April, 25; *Capt.* ᴾ 8 April, 26; *Major*, ᴾ 29 March, 33; *Lieut.-Col.* ᴾ 17 June, 36.
31	1	*Majors.* Aralander Tennant,² *Ens.* ᴾ 20 Oct. 08; *Lieut.* 10 June, 13; *Capt.* ᴾ 10 June, 26; *Major*, ᴾ 1 Aug. 34.
14	6/12	Benjamin F. Dalton Wilson, *Ens.* ᴾ 27 Aug. 25; *Lieut.* ᴾ 10 June, 26; *Capt.* ᴾ 20 April, 32; *Major*, ᴾ 17 June, 36.

		CAPTAINS.	ENSIGN.	LIEUT.	CAPTAIN.	BREV.-MAJ.
31	4 7/12	Edward Goate	9 May 05	8 Jan. 07	27 June 11	22 July 30
17	0	John Rowley Heyland ..	8 Jan. 24	ᴾ 7 Jan. 26	ᴾ 12 Apr. 31	
13	0	John Gordon	ᴾ 14 June 27	ᴾ 5 Apr. 31	ᴾ 5 Apr. 33	
13	0	J. H. Oakes Moore	25 Oct. 27	ᴾ 26 Apr. 31	ᴾ 31 Dec. 33	
15	0	John Oliver Munton	30 June 25	17 Aug. 32	ᴾ 20 Mar. 35	
9	0	James Fraser	ᴾ 5 April 31	ᴾ 1 Aug. 34	ᴾ 17 June 36	
12	1	Edward H. Hutchinson..	ᴾ 20 Mar. 27	ᴾ 10 Sept. 29	ᴾ 8 June 38	
14	10/12	James Tedlie	ᴾ 19 May 25	ᴾ 5 June 27	23 July 38	
28	6 10/12	Henry Cooper³.........	3 Oct. 05	18 June 07	25 Mar. 13	10 Jan. 37
9	0	Charles Beamish	ᴾ 26 Apr. 31	ᴾ 20 Mar. 35	ᴾ 31 Dec. 39	
		LIEUTENANTS.				
19	0	George Carnie	26 July 21	4 Oct. 27		
15	0	William Ward	18 Aug. 25	1 May 28		
14	0	Theophilus Faris	ᴾ 8 Apr. 26	ᴾ 25 Aug. 29		
15	0	George Bayly.........	10 Feb. 25	17 Apr. 30		
11	0	Thomas J. G. Chatterton	ᴾ 25 Aug. 29	ᴾ 31 Dec. 33		
7	0	Frederick English	ᴾ 22 Mar. 33	ᴾ 17 June 36		
7	0	Oliver Nicolls Chatterton	ᴾ 26 July 33	ᴾ 5 Aug. 36		
6	0	Thomas Goldie Harding .	ᴾ 31 July 34	ᴾ 26 Aug. 36		
6	0	Geo. Granville Baker....	ᴾ 1 Aug. 34	23 July 38		
5	0	Fred. Hugh Henry......	ᴾ 20 Mar. 35	7 Aug. 38		
5	0	Wm. Hutchinson Carrol	ᴾ 24 July 35	ᴾ 27 Sept. 39		
4	0	Henry Wheatstone	17 June 36	11 Oct. 39		
4	0	Jas. Farquhar Gordon ..	ᴾ 5 Aug. 36	ᴾ 31 Dec. 39		
		ENSIGNS.				
4	0	J. Talbot Crosbie	ᴾ 26 Aug. 36			
3	0	Rob. Otho Travers	ᴾ 15 Sept. 37			
3	0	Thomas Teulon	ᴾ 29 Dec. 37			
2	0	John A. Ewart	27 July 38			
2	0	James Moore	28 Aug. 38			
1	0	Wm. Thomas Harris	ᴾ 27 Sept. 39			
1	0	Geo. Cholmondeley Lees	ᴾ 9 Nov. 39			
1	0	Robert Henry Price	ᴾ 31 Dec. 39			
10	0	*Paymaster.*—Jas. Gust. Ham. Holmes, 24 Feb. 37; *Ens.* 11 June, 30; *Lieut.* 2 Aug. 33.				
4	0	*Adjutant.*—Hen. Wheatstone, (*Lieut.*) 5 Aug. 36.				
12	0	*Quarter-Master.*—Þ John Connon,⁴ 11 Sept. 28.				
		Surgeon.—Robert Sillery, M.D. 4 Jan. 39; *Assist.-Surg.* 18 April, 22; *Hosp.-Assist.* 24 May, 15.				
4	0	*Assistant-Surgeons.*—Arch. Gordon, M.D. 28 June, 36.				
1	0	Wm. Augustus Heise, M.D. 18 Oct. 39.				

Facings Blue.—*Agent*, Messrs. Cox & Co.

1 Sir John Oswald was at the capture of Martinique, St. Lucia, and Guadaloupe. He was severely wounded in Holland, 19 Sept. 1799, and has received a medal and two clasps for Maida, Vittoria, and St. Sebastian.

2 Major Tennant served at the siege of Flushing in 1809.

3 Major Cooper served at Walcheren in 1809, and subsequently in the American War

4 Quarter-Master Connon served in the Peninsula from Jan. 1810 to the end of the war, including the battles of Busaco and Fuentes D'Onor; sieges of Ciudad Rodrigo and Badajoz; battles of Salamanca, Vittoria, Pyrenees, and Orthes.

Emb. for Foreign Service, 1830.] **36th (*or Herefordshire*) Regt. of Foot.** [Serving in New Brunswick.

"Firm."—"HINDOOSTAN"—"ROLEIA"—"VIMIERA"—"CORUNNA"—"SALAMANCA"—"PYRENEES"—"NIVELLE"—"NIVE"—"ORTHES"—"TOULOUSE"—"PENINSULA."

Years' Serv.			
Full Pay	Half Pay		
62		*Colonel.* Sir Roger H. Sheaffe, *Bart. Ens.* 1 May, 1778; *Lieut.* 27 Dec. 80; *Capt.* 6 May, 95; *Major*, 13 Dec. 97; *Lieut.-Col.* 22 March, 98; *Col.* 25 April 1808; *Major-Gen.* 4 June, 11; *Lieut.Gen.* 19 July, 21; *Col.* 36 Regt. 21 Dec. 29.	
		Lieut.-Colonel.	
32	6 10/12	₱ Arch. M. Maxwell,[1] K.H. *2nd Lieut. Roy. Artil.* 1 July, 01; *Lieut.* 17 May, 03; *Capt.* 1 Feb. 08; *Brevet-Major*, 27 May, 25; *Regtl.-Major*, 12 Dec. 26; *Lieut.-Col.* ᴾ 25 Nov. 28.	
		Majors.	
32	0	₱ Geo. Cairnes,[2] *Ens.* 15 Dec. 08; *Lieut.* 2 Jan. 12; *Capt.* ᴾ 4 Nov. 24; *Major*, ᴾ 4 Dec. 32.	
34	0	₱ Thomas L'Estrange,[3] *Ens.* 9 Oct. 06; *Lieut.* 29 Feb. 08; *Capt.* 8 April, 25; *Brevet-Major*, 28 June, 38; *Regtl.-Major*, 14 Nov. 38.	

		CAPTAINS.	ENSIGN.	LIEUT.	CAPTAIN.	BREV.-MAJ.
28	3 6/12	₱ John De Lacy[4]	30 May 09	15 June 11	13 Feb. 27	
24	2 6/12	Charles Ashmore	25 Dec. 13	13 April 20	ᴾ 19 Aug. 28	
14	1/12	Charles Trollope........	ᴾ 19 Nov. 25	ᴾ 10 Oct. 26	ᴾ 23 Aug. 31	
14	0	Edward R. King	16 Feb. 26	31 July 28	ᴾ 4 Dec. 32	
14	0	Andrew Nugent........	ᴾ 7 Sept. 26	ᴾ 16 July 30	ᴾ 11 July 34	
13	0	John Henry Reeve......	ᴾ 18 Oct. 27	ᴾ 31 Aug. 30	ᴾ 6 May 36	
23	3 5/12	Jas. Murray Home[5]	24 Feb. 14	12 Dec. 16	11 Jan. 39	
15	0	John Hiern............	8 April 25	ᴾ 21 Feb. 28	31 May 39	
14	20 7/12	Henry Lecky	25 July 05	19 Oct. 08	ᴾ 23 May 16	10 Jan. 37
10	0	Robert Ross	13 June 30	ᴾ 11 July 34	ᴾ 14 Sept. 38	
		LIEUTENANTS.				
16	0	Alex. Connor	18 Dec. 24	ᴾ 7 Dec. 26	4 Captain De Lacy served in the Peninsula from Aug. 1809 to the end of the war, including sieges of Ciudad Rodrigo, Jan. and Feb. 1812; Badajoz, 6 April, 12; battles of Salamanca, Vittoria, Pyrenees, 28 July, to 2 Aug. 1813, Nivelle, Orthes, and Toulouse, 10 April, 14. Received a gun-shot wound in the right arm at Vittoria. Has served seven years in the West Indies since the peace. 5 Captain Home served the campaign of 1814 in Upper Canada.	
13	2 3/12	William Curteis	ᴾ 5 Nov. 25	ᴾ 20 Mar. 27		
10	0	John Pratt	ᴾ 8 June 30	8 June 35		
12	0	Lorenzo Rothe	ᴾ 6 Mar. 28	ᴾ 21 Aug. 35		
10	0	John Fleury	ᴾ 16 July 30	ᴾ 6 May 36		
10	0	Wm. Mauleverer	ᴾ 31 Aug. 30	ᴾ 13 Jan. 37		
8	0	Chas. A. Goodman......	2 Nov. 32	24 Feb. 37		
8	0	Alex. Thislethwayte	ᴾ 23 Nov. 32	ᴾ 24 Mar. 37		
5	0	Arthur Kinloch	24 July 35	ᴾ 28 Nov. 37		
5	0	N. Hynes	22 Oct. 35	29 Nov. 37		
4	0	James Nugent	ᴾ 15 April 36	11 Jan. 39		
4	0	Alfred Jas. Bourdillon ..	ᴾ 6 May 36	31 May 39		
4	0	Patrick L. M'Dougall ..	13 Feb. 36	ᴾ 11 May 39		
		ENSIGNS.				
4	0	E. W. Jennings........	ᴾ 13 May 36			
4	0	Edw. Chas. Butler	ᴾ 13 Jan. 37			
3	0	Wm. Ward Abbott	ᴾ 24 Mar. 37			
3	0	C. Wilson Carden	ᴾ 20 Oct. 37			
3	0	Robt. H. Carew........	ᴾ 28 Nov. 37			
2	0	R. Cairnes Bruce	ᴾ 30 Mar. 38			
2	0	Hen. W. Palmer	11 Jan. 39			
1	0	Edw. Warwick Harvey..	21 June 39			
20	16 8/12	*Paymaster.*—Humphrey Hen. Carmichael, 24 Feb. 14; *Ens.* 24 Sept. 03; *Lieut.* 27 Nov. 06; *Capt.* 31 Dec. 12.				
10	0	*Adjutant.*—John Pratt (*Lieut.*) 21 June, 39.				
5	0	*Quarter-Master.*—William Stuart, 10 July, 35.				
		Surgeon.—Wm. Lloyd, M.D. 18 Sept. 35; *Assist.-Surg.* 9 Nov. 14.				
14	0	*Assist.-Surg.*—Jas. Sheils, M.D. 29 July, 30; *Hosp.-Assist.* 25 Jan. 27.				
6	0	Charles Scott, M.D. 7 Nov. 34.				

Facings Grass Green.—*Agent*, Price & Son.—*Irish Agent*, Messrs. Borough, Armit & Co.

1 Colonel Maxwell served the campaign in Calabria, and commanded the artillery that besieged Scylla Castle. Served subsequently on the Eastern coast of Spain; embarked with Lord William Bentinck from Tarragona, after having assisted at two sieges of that fortress; took part in the Italian campaign, and was Brigade-Major to the artillery at the capture of Genoa.

2 Major Cairnes served at the siege of Flushing in 1809, and at different periods in the Peninsula.

3 Major L'Estrange served at Walcheren in 1809; and in the Peninsula from Oct. 1812 to the end of the war, including the battles of the Pyrenees, Nivelle, (wounded in the head), Nive, and Toulouse (severely wounded, lost a finger off the right hand.)

Emb. for Foreign Service, 1830.] **37th (or North Hampshire) Regt. of Foot.** [Serving in Nova Scotia.

"MINDEN"—"TOURNAY"—"PENINSULA."

Years' Serv.		
47		*Colonel.*
Full Pay	Half Pay	Hon. Sir Alexander Duff,[1] G.C.H. *Ens.* 23 May, 1793; *Lieut.* 15 Jan. 94; *Capt.* 16 Jan. 94; *Major,* 28 Mar. 94; *Lieut.-Col.* 14 April, 98; *Col.* 25 April, 1808; *Major-Gen.* 4 June, 11; *Lieut.-Gen.* 19 July, 21; *Col.* 37th Regt. 20 July, 31.
		Lieut.-Colonel.
42	7/12	Wm. Smelt,[2] C.B. *Cornet,* 16 March, 98; *Lieut.* p 11 Dec. 99; *Capt.* 21 March, 05; *Maj.* 28 Jan. 08; *Brev.-Lieut.-Col.* 4 June, 14; *Regtl.-Lieut.-Col.* 24 Nov. 14; *Col.* 22 July, 30.
		Majors.
31	2 9/12	p Henry Herbert Manners,[3] K.H. *2nd Lieut.* 23 April, 07; *Lieut.* 1 Feb. 09; *Capt.* 9 Sept. 19; *Major,* p 25 Dec. 25; *Brevet-Lieut.-Col.* 28 June, 38.
15	0	Joseph Bradshaw, *Ens.* p 12 May, 25; *Lieut.* p 12 Dec. 26; *Capt.* p 2 Dec. 31; *Major,* p 9 Dec. 36.

		CAPTAINS.	ENSIGN.	LIEUT.	CAPTAIN.	BREV.-MAJ.
36	0	p Henry Owen Wood[4] ..	6 July 04	25 Dec. 04	22 July 13	10 Jan. 37
31	5½	p ⟨⟩ John Thoreau[5] ..	26 Oct. 04	28 May 07	19 July 15	10 Jan. 37
14	0	Francis Skelly	p 6 July 26	18 Sept. 28	p 21 Sept. 32	
14	0	William Elliott	p 19 Sept. 26	p 31 Jan. 28	p 13 Dec. 33	
14	0	Geo. Briscoe Whalley ..	p 12 Dec. 26	p 12 Jan. 30	p 9 July 35	
13	0	Gilbert Wm. Franklyn ..	p 30 April 27	23 Nov. 30	p 9 Dec. 36	
26	0	John Harvey	14 April 14	10 April 25	9 Oct. 37	
9	0	J. R. Sheppard Wilson ..	p 19 April 31	p 10 Oct. 34	p 17 Nov. 37	
10	0	William Clay	8 June 30	p 21 Sept. 32	p 15 Feb. 39	
8	0	Patrick Fran. Durham ..	p 21 Sept. 32	p 10 July 35	p 1 Mar. 39	
		LIEUTENANTS.				
13	0	Thos. Edm. Le Blanc....	10 May 27	p 2 Dec. 31		
18	11¼	p Wm. Thorn. Servantes	27 June 11	29 Dec. 14		
10	0	Francis A. Cook........	31 Aug. 30	p 2 May 34		
8	0	Hen. Edw. Manners	p 29 June 32	9 July 35		
7	0	James Grignon	p 15 Mar. 33	p 9 Dec. 36		
6	0	Stanhope R. M. Byrne ..	p 10 Oct. 34	p 6 Oct. 37		
5	0	Wm. Glynne Griffith....	p 27 Feb. 35	p 17 Nov. 37		
5	0	Chas. Aug. Parkinson ..	p 10 July 35	p 6 April 38		
5	0	John Owen Lewis	p 11 July 35	9 July 38		
4	0	Eliott Tho. Seward......	p 9 Dec. 36	p 15 Feb. 39		
10	0	Sam. Baker Hayes......	p 11 June 30	p 13 Feb. 35		
3	0	Cha. Fra. Shum........	p 12 May 37	p 1 Mar. 39		
3	0	Wm. Hamilton	26 May 37	p 21 June 39		
		ENSIGNS.				
3	0	E. D. Atkinson........	p 6 Oct. 37			
3	0	W. G. M. Clibborn	17 Nov. 37			
3	0	A. M. Alex. Bowers	p 29 Dec. 37			
2	0	Hen. John Curteis	p 6 April 38			
2	0	H. Russell Manners	28 Aug. 38			
1	0	George Lawrence	p 15 Feb. 39			
1	0	Multon Lambard	p 1 Mar. 39			
1	0	Tho. Molyneux Keogh ..	p 21 June 39			

Remarks (for Captains column, Major Thoreau): 5 Major Thoreau served the campaign of 1805 in Hanover, 1808 to the end of the war, and in the Peninsula from Aug. including the battles of Roleia, Vimiera, Busaco; attack of Fort Christoval (wounded); siege of Badajoz; siege and capture of Ciudad Rodrigo; battle of Salamanca; capture of Madrid; battles of Vittoria, the Pyrenees, (wounded near Pampeluna), Orthes, and Toulouse. Served at New Orleans, and at Waterloo.

31	0	*Paymaster.*—p James Halfhide, 29 June, 09.
5	0	*Adjutant.*—J. O Lewis (*Lieut.*) 24 May, 39.
3	0	*Quarter-Master.*—Richard Hamilton, 2 Nov. 37.
15	0	*Surgeon.*—Alex. Browne, M.D. 22 Nov. 39; *Assist.-Surg.* 3 Aug. 26; *Hosp.-Assist.* 16 June, 25.
12	0	*Assist.-Surgs.*—John Wardrop Moore, 29 July, 30; *Hosp.-Assist.* 8 May, 28.
3	0	Charles Arnold Logie, 12 Jan. 38.

Facings Yellow.—*Agent,* Mr. Lawrie.—*Irish Agent,* Messrs. Cane & Co.

---

1 Sir Alex. Duff served in Flanders; accompanied the expedition from the East Indies to Egypt, where he served until the peace of 1802. Sir Alex. commanded the centre column in the attack upon Buenos Ayres.

2 Col. Smelt served in the American war, including the taking of Plattsburgh; storm and capture of Oswego; action at Lundy's Lane, and storming of Fort Erie 13th Aug. 14, where he was severely and dangerously wounded. Present at the capture of Rangoon, and other actions in Ava.

3 Col. Manners served at Obidos, Roleia, and Vimiera (wounded). Corunna campaign. Siege of Flushing (wounded). Campaigns of 1811 and 12 in the Peninsula, including the siege of Ciudad Rodrigo, action at Elbodon, siege of Badajoz, besides various skirmishes. Slightly wounded at the siege of Badajoz, and very severely on the night of the assault.

4 Major Wood served the campaign of 1814 in the Peninsula, including the investment of Bayonne.

38th (or the 1st Staffordshire) Regiment of Foot.

"Monte Video"—"Roleia"—"Vimiera"—"Corunna"—Busaco"—"Badajoz"—"Salamanca"—
Vittoria"—"St. Sebastian"—"Nive '—"Peninsula"—"Ava."

Years' Serv		
Full Pay	Half Pay	
72		**Colonel.** Sir Henry Pigot,[1] G.C.M.G. *Cornet*, 23 Jan. 1769; *Lieut.* 24 Sept. 72; *Capt.* 16 Mar. 75; *Major*, 4 April, 81; *Lieut.-Col.* 6 May, 83; *Col.* 20 Dec. 93; *Major-Gen.* 26 Feb. 95; *Lieut.-Gen.* 29 April, 1802; *Gen.* 1 Jan. 12; *Col.* 38th Regiment, 5 Dec. 36.
		Lieut.-Colonel.
40	1 10/12	Hugh Piper,[2] *Ens.* p 29 Mar. 99; *Lieut.* 13 Nov. 06; *Capt.* p 13 June,11; *Major*, 10 June, 28; *Lieut.-Col.* 28 May, 31.
		Majors.
30	0	p George Young,[3] *Ens.* 1 Nov. 10; *Lieut.* 24 Nov. 12; *Capt.* 10 Feb. 25; *Major*, 27 April, 34.
17	1 6/12	John Campbell,[4] *Ens.* 25 Nov. 21; *Lieut.* 1 July, 24; *Capt.* p 11 July, 26; *Major*, p 29 Dec. 37.

		CAPTAINS.	ENSIGN.	LIEUT.	CAPTAIN.	BREV.-MAJ.
25	0	James Pattoun Sparks ..	27 July 15	30 July 18	5 Sept. 26	
27	0	p Robert Matthew[5]	26 Sept. 13	25 Nov. 21	5 Jan. 27	
27	0	p Alexander Campbell[6]	17 Dec. 13	26 Nov. 21	25 Sept. 28	
16	0	J. Jackson Lowth[7]......	3 July 24	11 Sept. 25	p 23 Mar. 32	
22	0	Robert Carr	p 9 April 18	29 Dec. 23	11 Dec. 31	
13	0	Henry Knight Storks....	p 10 Jan. 28	p 2 Mar. 32	p 30 Oct. 35	
17	0	W. Littlejohn O'Halloran[8]	11 Jan. 24	20 July 26	p 29 Dec. 37	
24	7	p Robert Woodhouse[9] ..	17 Aug. 09	5 June 12	21 April 33	
9	0	Jos. Samuel Adamson ..	p 15 Mar. 31	p 27 Sept. 33	p 1 Dec. 37	
15	0	Charles Irvine..........	9 April 25	p 17 May 27	p 4 May 39	
		LIEUTENANTS.				
19	0	Frederick Tudor[10]	26 Nov. 21	18 Sept. 24		
15	0	Edward Evans	24 Mar. 25	5 Jan. 27	6 Capt. Campbell served the campaign of 1814, in the South of France, including the investment of Bayonne. Served throughout the Burmese war.	
14	0	John James Grant......	9 Mar. 26	p 12 Feb. 28		
15	0	Thomas Southall[11].....	2 Dec. 25	25 Sept. 28		
14	0	John Gage Lecky	p 22 April 26	p 26 Mar. 29		
12	0	Wm. Gamuel Edwards ..	14 Feb. 28	p 12 July 31	7 Captain Louth served throughout the Burmese war.	
9	0	John W. S. Smith	3 Feb. 32	4 Aug. 37		
8	0	Daniell O'Connell	p 4 May 32	p 22 Aug. 37	8 Capt. O'Halloran served at the siege and storming of Bhurtpore.	
8	0	John Robert Stawell....	p 25 May 32	p 10 Nov. 37		
6	0	Thomas Anderson	16 May 34	p 29 Dec. 37	9 Capt. Woodhouse served in the Peninsula from January, 1809, to Dec. 1811, including the battles of Talavera, Busaco, Fuentes d'Onor, and siege of Badajoz.	
3	0	Cockayne Frith	22 Aug. 37	p 4 May 39		
6	0	Wm. Donald Piper	21 Nov. 34	31 May 39		
3	0	Robert Charles Sinclair .	p 23 Aug. 37	p 20 Sept. 39		
		ENSIGNS.				
3	0	John Piper	p 10 Nov. 37		10 Lieut. Tudor served throughout the Burmese war.	
3	0	Charles J. Prichard	p 9 Jan. 38			
2	0	John R. Jackson........	11 May 38		11 Lieut. Southall served in the Burmese war from Nov. 1825.	
2	0	Charles R. Maxwell	p 19 Oct. 38			
2	0	Wm. James Loftus......	p 9 Nov. 38			
1	0	Henry Roe Evans	p 4 May 39			
1	0	R. Scott	31 May 39			
1	0	James Jarvis	p 20 Sept. 39			
14	3/12	*Paymaster.*—Wm. F. Vernon, 9 July, 30; *Ens.* 1 June, 26; *Lieut.* 5 July, 27.				
19	0	*Adjutant.*—Frederick Tudor (*Lieut.*) 17 Nov. 37.				
9	17 10/12	*Quarter-Master.*—George Green Watkins, 7 Oct. 36; *Ens.* 25 Dec. 13; *Lieut.* 23 July, 18.				
		Surgeon..—Hugh Lindsay Stuart, 17 Sept. 30; *Assist.-Surgeon*, 15 Dec. 25; *Hosp.-Assist.* 28 Dec. 20.				
14	0	*Assistant-Surgeon.*—Thos. Foss, 18 Jan. 27; *Hospital-Assist.* 15 June, 26.				

Facings Yellow.—*Agent*, Mr. Lawrie.—*Irish Agent*, Borough, Armit, & Co.
[*Returned from Bengal, May*, 1836.]

1 Sir Henry Pigot accompanied the brigade of Guards to Holland in 1793, and was present at the siege of Valenciennes, the action of Lincelles, and all the other engagements in which the brigade was engaged in the campaigns of 1793 and 94.
2 Colonel Piper served in the American war, including the capture of Moore island; also throughout the Burmese war.
3 Major Young served at the battle of Fuentes d'Onor; siege of Badajoz; attack of the Forts at, and battle of, Salamanca; capture of Madrid; siege of Burgos; twice engaged, and once wounded, on the retreat from Burgos; operations in front, investment of, and sortie from Bayonne. Served in the Burmese war.
4 Major Campbell served throughout the Burmese war.
5 Captain Matthew served at Badajoz, Salamanca, and Bayonne; at Graham's Town, when attacked by Caffres, in 1819; and throughout the Burmese war.

| Emb. for Foreign Service, 1826. | | 39th (or the Dorsetshire) Regiment of Foot. | | | Serving in the East Indies. |

"Primus in Indus."—"Plassey"—"Gibraltar"—with the *Castle and Key,* "*Montis Insignia Calpe*"—"Albuhera"—"Vittoria"—"Pyrenees"—"Nivelle"—"Nive"—"Orthes"—"Peninsula."

Years' Serv.		Colonel.
Full Pay. 46	Half Pay.	**Hon. *Sir* Robert Wm. O'Callagan,**[1] G.C.B. *Ens.* 29 Nov. 1794; *Lieut.* 6 Dec. 94; *Capt.* 31 Jan. 95; *Lieut.-Col.* 16 July, 1803; *Col.* 1 Jan. 12; *Major-Gen.* 4 June, 14; *Lieut.-Gen.* 22 July, 30; *Col.* 39th Regiment, 4 March, 33.
26	7/12	*Lieut.-Colonels.*—**[P]** Joseph Wakefield, *Cornet,* P 26 May, 14; *Lieut.* 29 Aug 15; *Capt.* P 29 July, 19; *Major,* 27 May, 34; *Lieut.-Col.* P 10 March, 37.
28	1/12	Thomas Wright,[7] *Ens.* 18 Dec. 12; *Lieut.* 22 April, 14; *Capt.* P 14 July, 25; *Major,* P 10 March, 37.; *Lieut.-Col.* 24 Apr. 39.
22	1 2/12	*Majors.*—Horatio Walpole, *Ens. & Lieut.* 8 May, 17; *Capt.* P 13 Jan. 25; *Major,* P 17 Nov. 37.
30	9 7/12	**P** Donald Urquhart,[2] *Ens.* 25 Mar. 01; *Lieut.* 17 Sept. 03; *Capt.* 21 May 08; *Brev.-Maj.* 27 May, 25; *Brev. Lieut.-Col.* 28 June, 38; *Regt.-Maj.* 24 Apr. 39.

		CAPTAINS.	ENSIGN.	LIEUT.	CAPTAIN.	BREV.-MAJ.
27	0	**P** John Fitz Gerald[3]	6 Oct. 13	7 April 25	27 May 34	
29	3 6/12	Wm. Boran Bernard[4]	12 April 08	12 Oct. 08	30 Dec. 28	
17	10 1/3	George Sleeman	12 May 13	5 Jan. 26	17 June 36	
15	0	Joseph Long Innes	8 April 25	14 Aug. 28	10 Jan. 37	
12	0	Chas. T. Van Straubenzee	P 28 Aug. 28	P 22 Feb. 33	P 10 Mar. 37	
14	0	William Wood	P 13 April 26	P 27 April 27	P 8 May 35	
27	9/12	John Blackall	14 Oct. 12	4 May 14	1 June 35	
9	0	Marmaduke Geo. Nixon ..	5 April 31	25 Mar. 33	P 28 Dec. 38	
17	0	Henry Francis Stokes[5] ..	24 July 23	1 Aug. 25	24 Apr. 39	
13	0	Frederick Dunbar	10 May 27	4 April 32	13 Oct. 39	
		LIEUTENANTS.				
13	0	Henry T. Griffiths	19 April 27	P 2 Nov. 32		1 Sir R. O'Callaghan has received a cross and two clasps for Maida, Vittoria, Pyrenees, Nivelle, Nive, and Orthes.
11	0	Bernard Gra. Layard	P 13 Aug. 29	12 Jan. 33		
8	0	Robert Newport Tinley ..	4 April 32	P 19 July 33		2 Col. Urquhart's services:—Expedition to Walcheren, and siege of Flushing; campaigns of 1813 and 14 in the Peninsula, including the crossing of the Bidassoa; battles of the Nivelle and Nive; severely wounded 9th Dec. 1813.
8	0	Robert Dean Werge	3 April 32	P 7 Aug. 33		
13	0	Charles Campbell	P 9 Aug. 27	3 May 33		
8	0	Henry A. Strachan	21 Sept. 32	2 June 35		
10	0	Arthur Herbert	P 18 Jan. 31	2 Sept. 34		
6	0	Æneas Wm. Fraser	P 6 June 34	P 4 Mar. 36		3 Capt. Fitz Gerald served in the Peninsula from May 1813 until the end of the war, including siege of San Sebastian (wounded at the assault, with the forlorn hope, 31 Aug. 1813); storming the heights of Vera, as a volunteer; battles of the Nivelle, Nive, Bayonne, Garrise, Orthes, and Toulouse.
6	0	William Munro	P 20 June 34	P 1 April 36		
5	0	H. Waget Davenport	P 30 May 35	P 2 Dec. 36		
10	0	James S. Atkinson	30 Sept. 30	3 Feb. 37		
5	0	Wm. Clarges Wolfe	P 30 Oct. 35	P 10 Mar. 37		
4	0	Edward Croker	P 4 Mar. 36	P 17 Nov. 37		
4	0	J. Fitz Roy Dalrymple ..	P 2 Dec. 36	P 8 Dec. 37		4 Captain Bernard served at the capture of the Isle of France in 1810; and at the surrender of Kurnool in the East Indies, in Jan. 1816.
4	0	Humphrey Gray	25 Mar. 36	1 July 38		
4	0	F. Hawtry Cox	P 26 Feb. 36	P 28 Dec. 37		
4	0	Wordsworth Smith	21 Oct. 36	23 Mar. 39		
3	0	Adam Hackett	P 10 Feb. 37	21 Apr. 39		
3	0	William Hardinge	P 10 Mar. 37	24 Apr. 39		
3	0	Charles J. Walker	7 April 37	13 Oct. 39		
3	0	Tho. Sargent Little	9 Dec. 37	19 Oct. 39		
2	0	Chas. Tho. Hamilton ...	P 17 Feb. 38	P 19 July 39		
		ENSIGNS.				
2	0	Owen Wynne Gray ...	9 Nov. 38			5 Capt. Stokes served throughout the Burmese war.
2	0	R. Hamilton Currie ...	P 28 Dec. 38			6 Captain Durnford served at the capture of the Isle of France in 1810; in the expedition to Java in 1811; capture of Kandy in 1815; and in the Kandyan rebellion in 1817 and 18.
2	0	James C. Harvey	25 Jan. 39			
1	0	Wm. Newport Tinley ..	P 15 Nov. 39			
1	0	Patrick Flynn	9 Jan. 40			7 Colonel Wright was severely wounded at the affair of Kittore in the East Indies, 18th Oct. 1839.
1	0	Hugh Geo. Colville	10 Jan. 40			
1	0	Edward Hardinge	P 11 Jan. 40			
34	0	*Paymaster.*—G. Augustus Durnford,[6] 13 Feb. 27; *Ens.* 28 June, 06; *Lieut.* 10 March, 10; *Capt.* 25 Dec. 26.				
6	0	*Adjutant.*—William Munro, (Lieut.) 24 May, 39.				
4	0	*Quarter-Master.*—John O'Brien, 19 Feb. 36.				[8 June 11.
24	5 3/12	*Surg.*—**P** Rob. Stark, M.D. 19 Nov. 30; *Assist.-Surg.* 21 Jan. 13; *Hosp.-Assist.*				
6	0	*Assist.-Surgs.*—James M'Gregor, 24 July, 34.				
5	0	John Sinclair, 24 April, 35				

Facings Green.—*Agent,* Messrs. Cox & Co.

Emb. for For. Service, 1823.] **40th (or the 2nd Somersetshire) Regiment of Foot.** [Serving in the East Indies.

The *Sphinx*, with the word "EGYPT" on the caps of the Flank Companies. "MONTE VIDEO"—"ROLEIA"—"VIMIERA"—"TALAVERA"—"BADAJOZ"—"SALAMANCA"—"VITTORIA"—·PYRENEES"—"NIVELLE"—"ORTHES"—"TOULOUSE"—"PENINSULA"—"WATERLOO.'

Years' Serv.		
45		**Colonel.** Sir Lionel Smith, Bart.¹* K.C.B. & G.C.H. *Ens.* March, 1795; *Lieut.* 28 Oct.
Full Pay.	Half Pay.	95; *Capt.* 22 May, 1801; *Major,* 22 April, 02; *Lieut.-Col.* 6 June, 05; *Col.* 4 June, 13; *Major-Gen.* 12 Aug. 19; *Lieut.-Gen.* 10 Jan. 37; *Col.* 40th Regt. 9 Feb. 37.
		Lieut.-Colonels.
36	9/12	Thomas Valiant, K.H, *Ens.* ᴾ31 March, 04; *Lieut.* 21 June, 05; *Capt.* ᴾ21 Aug. 17; *Major,* ᴾ24 Oct. 21; *Lieut.-Col.* ᴾ8 Oct. 25; *Col.* 28 June, 38.
45	0	Rob. Brice Fearon,¹ C.B. *Ens.* June, 95; *Lieut.* 4 Sept. 95; *Capt.* 21 April, 04; *Major,* ᴾ20 Dec. 10; *Brevet-Lieut.-Col.* 12 Aug. 19; *Regtl.-Lieut.-Col.* ᴾ8 May, 23; *Col.* 10 Jan. 37.
		Majors.
35	0	Richard Jebb,² *Cornet,* ᴾ12 Sept. 05; *Lieut.* ᴾ4 Aug. 08; *Capt.* ᴾ9 May, 11; *Brevet-Major,* 22 July, 30; *Regtl.-Major,* ᴾ1 May, 35.
26	1 5/12	George Hibbert, *Ens.* ᴾ25 Feb. 13; *Lieut.* 14 June, 15; *Capt.* ᴾ6 March, 23; *Major,* ᴾ13 Nov. 35.

		CAPTAINS.	ENSIGN.	LIEUT.	CAPTAIN.	BREV.-MAJ.
20	7/12	Evelyn Spen. Boscawen..	ᴾ26 Aug. 19	2 Sept. 24	ᴾ 1 Aug. 26	
15	0	James Stopford	ᴾ17 Sept. 25	ᴾ 2 Nov. 26	ᴾ10 Sept. 30	
15	0	Fitz Her. Coddington ...	ᴾ22 Sept. 25	ᴾ17 Jan. 28	ᴾ24 Dec. 32	
12	0	Thos. James Valiant	29 May 28	ᴾ17 Dec. 29	ᴾ 1 May 35	
23	1 10/12	Joseph Curtin..........	14 Sept. 15	8 April 25	18 July 35	
27	0	John Kelly	8 Nov. 13	20 Dec. 24	27 May 36	
16	0	John Gray	31 Aug. 24	4 May 26	ᴾ12 Sept. 34	
15	0	Joseph Boyer Oliver	ᴾ16 Dec. 25	ᴾ19 Sept. 26	7 Nov. 36	
17	9 6/12	John M'Duff	10 Feb. 14	26 June 27	ᴾ12 April 39	
17	0	Henry Caulfeild........	11 Dec. 23	ᴾ14 July 25	ᴾ 8 June 30	
		LIEUTENANTS.				
21	2 9/12	Thomas Miller	9 Jan. 17	19 April 27		1 Colonel Fearon's services: —Campaign of 1796 and 7, in the West Indies, including the storming of the Vigie (wounded in the knee by a bayonet); attack on Morn Fortunei, and surrender of St. Lucia. Campaign of 1799, in Holland, including the battles of the 19th Sept., 2nd and 6th Oct. Campaign of 1800 on the coast of France and Spain. Expedition to Quiberon Bay. Attack on Ferrol. Expedition to Vigo and Cadiz. Egyptian campaign of 1807, including the surrender of Alexandria; attack and storming of Rosetta. Campaign of 1814 and 15, in Italy, including the surrender of Naples and Genoa. Colonel Fearon commanded the troops on board the unfortunate ship *Kent,* when she was burned in the bay of Biscay, 1st March, 1825.
16	10 5/12	Boyce M'Kenzie........	31 Mar. 14	26 June 27		
18	8	John Perry Elliott......	28 Dec. 14	26 June 27		
17	8 10/12	James Adamson........	22 Feb. 15	11 June 17		
14	0	Ferdinand White	ᴾ 2 Nov. 26	10 Nov. 31		
11	0	Hen. Furey Wakefield ..	ᴾ17 Dec. 29	29 July 32		
10	0	Fred. Wm. Smith	ᴾ10 Sept. 30	ᴾ24 Dec. 32		
10	0	George Matthias White..	13 June 30	19 April 33		
9	0	James Todd	ᴾ22 Feb. 31	4 July 34		
7	0	John Martin B. Neill....	ᴾ22 Mar. 33	ᴾ 9 Jan. 35		
7	0	Hen. Crickitt Tyler	ᴾ 3 May 33	ᴾ 1 May 35		
6	0	Hen. Fancourt Valiant ..	ᴾ25 April 34	ᴾ13 Nov. 35		
9	0	Thomas L. K. Nelson....	25 Nov. 31	29 Jan. 36		
6	0	Wm. Augustus Fyers....	ᴾ17 Oct. 34	ᴾ20 May 36		
6	0	Henry Seymour	ᴾ 9 Jan. 35	7 Nov. 36		
5	0	Richard Armstrong	ᴾ 1 May 35	ᴾ 2 Mar. 38		2 Major Jebb served in Spain under Sir John Moore, including the actions at Sahagun and Benevente, and retreat to Corunna.
5	0	Henry Halkett	ᴾ29 May 35	ᴾ23 Mar. 38		
5	0	Alex. A. Nelson........	ᴾ 6 Mar. 35	ᴾ15 Mar. 39		
5	0	Edward Lee	ᴾ12 June 35	ᴾ12 April 39		
4	0	Rich. Olpherts	ᴾ 2 Dec. 36	ᴾ21 June 39		
10	0	John Dowman	ᴾ28 Sept. 30	ᴾ21 Dec. 32		
		ENSIGNS.				
4	0	F. T. L. G. Russell	ᴾ20 May 36			3 Capt. Naylor served at the capture of Loghur, Koaree, Ryghur, and several small Hill Forts in 1818. Served in the Serwent Warree State, and was severely wounded in both legs; (the right one badly fractured) at the assault of Rorce, 13th Feb 1819.
3	0	J. Young Vance	ᴾ21 April 37			
2	0	James Johnston.......	ᴾ23 Mar. 38			
1	0	Jas. Duncan Mac Andrew	ᴾ15 Mar. 39			
1	0	Edw. Hungerford Eagar	ᴾ12 April 39			
1	0	John W. Thomas	7 June 39			4 Dr. MacAndrew served at the siege of Flushing in 1809, and the campaigns of 1811, 12, and 13, in the Peninsula.
1	0	M. R. L. Meason	ᴾ21 June 39			
1	0	Robert Carey	15 Nov. 39			
28	0	*Paymaster.*—Charles Scarlin Naylor,³ 8 May, 35; *Ens.* 1 Sept. 12; *Lieut.* 25 Dec. 15; *Capt.* 9 May, 34.				
14	0	*Adjutant.*—Ferdinand White, *(Lieut.)* 1 Oct. 35.				
3	0	*Quarter-Master.*—Chas. Philips, 25 July, 37; *Ens.* 16 June, 37.				
23	7 10/12	*Surgeon.*—John MacAndrew,⁴ M.D. 30 April, 29; *Assist.-Surg.* 15 Feb. 10; *Hosp.-Assist.* 27 June, 09.				
14	0	*Assist.-Surgs.*—Arth. West, M.D. 15 June, 30; *Hosp.-Asst.* 25 Jan. 27.				
6	0	Henry Hadley, M.D. 28 Nov. 34.				

Facings Buff.—*Agent,* Messrs. Cox & Co.

1* Sir Lionel Smith has served chiefly in the East Indies. In 1809 and 10 he commanded an expedition to the Persian Gulf against the Pirates. Brought down by a sabre cut across the back of his head in the cavalry action at Ashta, 21st Feb. 1818.

Emb. for Foreign Service, 1822. — **41st (or Welsh) Regiment of Foot.** — Serving in the East Indies.

On the Colours and Appointments, the *Prince of Wales's Plume*, with the motto, "*Gwell Augau neu Chwilydd.*"—"DETROIT"—"QUEENSTOWN"—"MIAMI"—"NIAGARA"—"AVA."

Years' Serv.						
47		*Colonel.* ⁋ Sir R. Darling,¹ G.C.H. Ens. 15 May, 1793; Lieut. 2 Sept. 95; Capt. 6 Sept. 96; Major, 2 Feb. 1800; Lieut.-Col. 17 July, 01; Col. 25 July 10; Major-Gen. 4 June, 13; Lieut.-Gen. 27 May, 25; Col. 41st Regiment, 26 Sept. 37.				
Full Pay.	Half Pay.					
32	5/12	*Lieut.-Colonels.*—⁋ Richard England,² K.H., Ens. ᴘ 25 Feb. 08; Lieut. 1 June, 09; Capt. ᴘ 11 June, 11; Major, ᴘ 4 Sept. 23; Lieut.-Col. ᴘ 29 Oct. 25; Col. 28 June, 38.				
34	0	Wm. Booth,³ Ens. 8 May, 06; Lieut. 25 March, 09; Capt. 3 May, 21; Major, ᴘ 28 June, 27; Lieut.-Col. 11 July, 37.				
17	0	*Majors.*—Gore Browne, Ens. 14 Jan. 24; Lieut. ᴘ 11 July, 26; Capt. ᴘ 11 June, 29; Major, ᴘ 19 Dec. 34.				
26	2 5/12	⁋ Joseph Simmons,⁴ 2nd Lieut. 16 April, 12; Lieut. 23 Dec. 13; Capt. 18 Feb. 27; Major, 22 Aug. 37.				

		CAPTAINS.	ENSIGN.	LIEUT.	CAPTAIN.	BREV.-MAJ.
23	4 7/12	James Cochran⁵	ᴘ 17 Sept. 12	28 Dec. 15	26 Feb. 27	
18	3 9/12	George Carpenter	1 Oct. 18	1 Mar. 20	ᴘ 29 Oct. 25	28 June 38
30	1 9/12	William Dempster	9 Feb. 09	11 April 11	26 Feb. 28	
25	7/12	Perceval Browne⁶	25 Jan. 15	31 Mar. 23	18 Aug. 30	
17	2 1/12	John Wetherall	ᴘ 8 Nov. 21	ᴘ 27 Aug. 25	ᴘ 3 May 31	
21	5/12	Richard Price⁸	15 April 19	23 May 26	ᴘ 9 Mar. 32	
25	15 1/12	Archibald Hook	ᴘ Feb. 00	ᴘ 28 Mar. 00	12 Oct. 09	22 July 30
27	0	William Barnes⁷	ᴘ 4 Feb. 13	23 July 14	14 Sept. 35	
20	0	John Geo. Bedingfield⁸	2 Nov. 20	29 June 24	5 June 37	
19	0	Lawrance Tallan⁹	ᴘ 1 Nov. 21	27 Aug. 24	22 Aug. 37	
		LIEUTENANTS.				
20	0	⁋ Joseph Eyles Deere¹⁰	3 Aug. 20	3 Dec. 25		
15	0	Eugene Jas. Vaughan	4 Nov. 25	ᴘ 9 Nov. 26		
15	0	Samuel Geo. Stoddard¹¹	11 Feb. 25	17 Jan. 28		
13	0	William May	ᴘ 30 Jan. 28	18 Aug. 30		
12	2 3/12	Robert Donaldson	ᴘ 8 April 26	18 Sept. 32		
9	0	G. Sheaffe Montizambert	11 April 31	ᴘ 11 Jan. 33		
9	0	Robert Butler	12 April 31	ᴘ 25 Oct. 33		
9	0	Chas. Finch M'Kenzie	27 Sept. 31	28 May 34		
9	16 10/12	James Campbell	24 Feb. 15	24 Oct. 34		
8	0	Henry Downes	ᴘ 8 June 32	21 May 35		
6	0	Andrew Carden	ᴘ 14 Mar. 34	ᴘ 4 Dec. 35		
7	0	Wm. H. H. Anderson	20 Sept. 33	28 Aug. 36		
9	10 4/12	John Diddep	27 July 15	18 Oct. 36		
5	0	Thomas Burgh	ᴘ 8 May 35	5 June 37		
5	0	Walter Lawrence	ᴘ 18 Dec. 35	22 Aug. 37		
5	0	John Wallace	ᴘ 6 Mar. 35	ᴘ 10 Feb. 38		
4	0	James Eman	25 Mar. 36	16 Aug. 38		
4	0	J. De Blaquiere	ᴘ 30 Sept. 36	29 Jan. 39		
4	0	Thomas Owen Evans	30 Dec. 36	7 May 39		
3	0	Robert Pratt	ᴘ 16 June 37	ᴘ 27 June 39		
3	0	Cha. Anderson Morshead	11 July 37	ᴘ 28 June 39		
2	0	Anthony Sadlier	ᴘ 17 Aug. 38	ᴘ 30 Aug. 39		
3	0	John Mannin	22 Aug. 37	15 Nov. 39		
		ENSIGNS.				
2	0	Arth. W. Smith	25 Jan. 39			
1	0	Hen. F. Marston	8 Mar. 39			
1	0	Tho. M. L. Farmer	7 June 39			
1	0	Geo. Wm. Hessing	ᴘ 27 June 39			
1	0	Chas. Timothy Tuckey	ᴘ 28 June 39			
2	0	Alexander Stewart	ᴘ 11 May 39			
1	0	Geo. Davis Hutton	15 Nov. 39			
1	0	Warner West. Johnson	16 Nov. 39			
26	2	*Paymaster.*—F. Dickson,¹¹ 26 July, 27; Ens. 12 Mar. 12; Lieut. 27 Jan. 14.				
15	0	*Adjutant.*—Eugene Jas. Vaughan (*Lieut.*) 18 Sept. 32.				
2	0	*Quarter-Master.*—Wm. Burns, 16 Aug. 38; Ens. 16 Feb. 38.				
26	8/12	*Surgeon.*—⁋ Wm. Mortimer Wilkins,¹² 23 Dec. 36; Assist.-Surg. 22 June, 25; Hosp.-Assist. 10 Jan., 14.				
5	0	*Assist.-Surgs.*—Henry Fra. Minster, 29 May, 35.				
2	0	Arthur Charles Webster, 9 April, 38.				

Facings White.—*Agent*, Messrs. Cox & Co.

5 Capt. Cochran served the campaigns of 1813-14 in Canada, including the action at Moravian Town; the campaign of 1824-5 in Ava, including the capture of Rangoon and Martaban; siege and capture of Dameline; battles of Prome and Pagam-Mew.
6 Captain Browne served the campaigns of 1824-5 in Ava.
7 Captain Barnes served at the capture of Fort Anjui in Cutch, 25th Dec. 1815; the Mahratta campaigns of 1817-18; escalade of the Fort of Booge in Cutch, March 1819; siege of Ras-el-Kymah and Zou in Arabia, Dec 1819; escalade of Dwarka Ohamandel, Dec. 1820; action of Beni-Boo-Ally in Arabia, March 21.
8 Captains Price and Bedingfield served in the Burmese war.
9 Captain Tallan served throughout the Burmese war, including the capture of Rangoon; attack on Kimindine and Pagoda Point; capture of Fort Syriam; engagements in front of Rangoon, capture of Tantabain; siege and capture of Denobew; engagements near Prome; capture of Maloon and Pagam-Mew.
10 Lieut Deere served at Waterloo as a Volunteer, with the 91st Regt. Served also in the Burmese war.
11 Lieut Stoddard and Dickson (Paymaster), served in the Burmese war.
12 Dr. Wilkins served the campaign of 1814 in the Peninsula.

---

1 Sir Ralph Darling's services:—In 1793, the slaves in the island of Granada, assisted by the French from Guadaloupe, having revolted and murdered the Governor and upwards of forty of the principal inhabitants, he was employed with his Regt. (the 45th) in quelling the insurrection. In Jan., 1797, volunteered on the expedition against Trinidad, and was present at the destruction of the Spanish ships of war, and at the surrender of the island. In July 1799, proceeded with the expedition against

42d (or the Royal Highland) Regiment of Foot.

St. Andrew, "*Nemo me impunè lacessit.*"—The *Sphinx*, with the words "EGYPT"— "CORUNNA"—"FUENTES D'ONOR"—"PYRENEES"—"NIVELLE"—"NIVE" —"ORTHES"—"TOULOUSE"—"PENINSULA"—"WATERLOO."

Years' Serv.		
51	Full Pay.	Half Pay.

Colonel.

51		🄱 Rt. Hon. Sir George Murray,[1] G.C.B. & G.C.H. *Ens.* 12 March, 1789: *Lieut. & Capt.* 16 Jan. 94; *Capt. & Lt.-Col.* 5 Aug. 99; *Col.* 9 March, 1809; *Major-Gen.* 1 Jan. 12; *Lieut.-Gen.* 27 May, 25; *Col.* 42nd Highlanders 6 Sept. 23.
15	5 1/12	*Lieut.Colonel.*—George Johnstone, *Cornet,* ᴾ 5 Aug. 19; *Lieut.* ᴾ 9 Nov. 21; *Capt.* ᴾ 17 Nov. 25; *Major,* ᴾ 3 Oct. 26; *Lieut.-Col.* ᴾ 23 Aug. 39.
26	2 8/12	*Majors.*—🄱 James Macdougall,[2] *Second Lieut.* 11 June, 12; *Lieut.* 8 Sept. 13; *Capt.* ᴾ 10 Sept. 25; *Major,* 23 Oct. 35.
15	0	Duncan Alex. Cameron, *Ens.* 8 April, 25; *Lieut.* ᴾ 15 Aug. 26; *Capt.* ᴾ 21 June, 33; *Major,* ᴾ 23 Aug. 39.

		CAPTAINS.	ENSIGN.	LIEUT.	CAPTAIN.	BREV.-MAJ.
27	2 1/12	Daniel Frazer	31 Oct. 11	13 June 16	ᴾ 5 Nov. 25	28 June 38
15	0	Charles Dunsmure	9 Apr. 25	ᴾ 7 Nov. 26	ᴾ 30 Jan. 35	
14	0	William Guthrie	ᴾ 22 Apr. 26	ᴾ 20 Mar. 27	ᴾ 24 Feb. 37	
15	0	Archibald Campbell	ᴾ 26 Nov. 25	ᴾ 25 Dec. 28	ᴾ 10 Mar. 38	
15	0	Geo. Burrell Cumberland	11 Apr. 25	31 Dec. 28	ᴾ 30 Mar. 38	
25	1 8/12	Wm. Beales	24 June 13	13 Dec. 21	12 Aug. 36	
14	0	Thomas Tulloch	ᴾ 25 June 26	23 Oct. 28	ᴾ 12 July 33	
16	0	Lord Cecil Gordon	ᴾ 8 July 24	ᴾ 17 June 26	ᴾ 22 July 36	
18	7 4/12	George Montagu	8 Dec. 14	ᴾ 31 Oct. 22	ᴾ 22 Oct. 25	28 June 38
13	0	Rob. Williamson Ramsay	ᴾ 10 Jan. 28	12 June 30	ᴾ 23 Aug. 39	

		LIEUTENANTS.			
10	*0	J. Cameron Macpherson	ᴾ 10 Sept. 30	ᴾ 21 June 33	
8	0	Alexander Cameron	24 Feb. 32	ᴾ 30 Jan. 35	
8	0	Hon. Robert Rollo	ᴾ 10 Aug. 32	ᴾ 25 Sept. 35	
8	0	Thomas Kinlock	ᴾ 14 Sept. 32	ᴾ 24 Feb. 37	
9	0	Lord Chas. Lennox Kerr	ᴾ 5 Apr. 31	ᴾ 2 May 34	
8	0	H. Maurice Drummond	ᴾ 4 Dec. 32	ᴾ 15 Dec. 37	
7	0	Geo. Duncan Robertson	ᴾ 14 June 33	ᴾ 10 Mar. 38	
7	0	Charles Murray	ᴾ 21 June 33	ᴾ 30 Mar. 38	
7	0	Atholl W. Macdonald	ᴾ 9 Aug. 33	ᴾ 24 Apr. 38	
5	0	G. W. Macquarie	ᴾ 25 Sept. 35	ᴾ 31 May 39	
5	0	Duncan Cameron	23 Oct. 35	1 June 39	
3	0	Arch. Colin Campbell	ᴾ 24 Feb. 37	ᴾ 23 Aug. 39	
3	0	James Hunter	ᴾ 17 Nov. 37	ᴾ 27 Sept. 39	

		ENSIGNS.			
2	0	W. J. H. Johnstone	ᴾ 16 Mar. 38		
2	0	James Grant	ᴾ 30 Mar. 38		
2	0	Farquhar Campbell	ᴾ 30 Nov. 38		
1	0	Henry Sholto Douglas	ᴾ 31 May 39		
1	0	Thos. Rob. Drum. Hay	ᴾ 2 Aug. 39		
2	0	Thos. Francis Wade	2 Nov. 38		
1	0	Robert Bligh Sinclair	ᴾ 27 Sept. 39		
1	0	Augustus Paterson	ᴾ 10 Jan. 40		

1 Sir George Murray served the Campaign in Flanders in 1793 and 94; was wounded in Holland in 99; took part in the different battles, &c. in Egypt in 01, and accompanied the expedition to Copenhagen in 07. Sir George has received a cross and five clasps for Corunna, Talavera, Busaco, Fuentes d'Onor, Vittoria, Pyrenees, Nivelle, Orthes, and Toulouse.

2 Major Macdougall served the campaigns of 1813 and 14, in the Peninsula, including the affair of San Marcial; battles of Nivelle, Nive, 9th, 10th, 11th, 12th, and 13th Dec., Orthes, and Toulouse.

3 Quarter-Master King served in the Peninsula, from July, 1809, to August, 1812, including the battles of Busaco and Fuentes d'Onor. Present on 16th and 18th June, at Waterloo.

4 Dr. Paterson served in the Peninsula from Sept. 1810 to Dec. 1811. Served also in the Burmese war.

8	0	*Paymast.*—J. Wheatley, 12 Oct. 38; *Ens. & Adjt.* 20 July, 32; *Lieut.* 3 Apr. 35.	
5	0	*Adjutant.*—Duncan Cameron (*Lieut.*), 30 Oct. 38.	
22	0	*Quarter-Master.*—🄱 🄰 Finley King,[3] 31 Dec. 18.	
30	0	*Surgeon.*—🄱 James Paterson,[4] M.D., 25 May, 26; *Assist.-Surg.* 22 Aug. 11; *Hosp.-Assist.* 7 June, 10.	
15	0	*Assistant-Surgeon.*—James M'Gregor, 12 April, 26; *Hosp.-Assist.* 5 Jan. 26.	

Facings Blue.—*Agent,* Messrs. Cox & Co.—*Irish Agent,* Borough & Co.

[*Returned from Corfu, August,* 1836.]

the Dutch settlement of Surinam, and was employed in the arrangements for the capitulation, and present at the surrender of that colony. In April 1801 proceeded with the expedition against the Danish and Swedish islands, St. Croix, St. Thomas, St. Martin, and St. Bartholomew, and was present at their reduction. In September 1808, his Regt. (the 51st) being ordered on active service, he resigned his staff employment (Principal Assist. Adjt.-General) and took the command of it. Joined the army under Sir John Moore, in Spain, and was present during the advance and retreat, the action at Lugo, and battle of Corunna, for which last he received a Medal. In July 1809, was appointed Dep. Adjt.-General to the Force sent to the Scheldt under the Earl of Chatham, and was present at the siege and surrender of Flushing. On the return of the expedition he resumed his staff appointment at the Horse Guards.

2 Colonel England served at the siege of Flushing and campaign to Antwerp; subsequently at Tarrifa and in Sicily in 1810.

3 Colonel Booth's services:—Siege of Callinger (wounded at the assault). Nepaul war in 1814, including the sieges of Kolunga, Nahu, and Jetuck. Mahratta war in 1817-18, including the sieges of Singhur, Lattarak, Pourunder, and Wursetta. Burmese war in 1824-5, wounded at the storming of Martaban.

4 Major Simmons served in the Peninsula, from Sept. 1811 to the end of the war, including the storming of the Fort at Almarez; affair at San Munos; checking the French on the retreat from Madrid; cut off their Rear-Guard from Burgos; battle of Vittoria; skirmishing with the Rear-Guard, and driving the French into Pampeluna. 22d, 23d, and 24th June; storming the heights of Centra Barbera; storming of Eschelah; storming Vera Bridge and Heights; crossing the Bidassoa; storming Petets la Rhine; battles of Nivelle and Nive, 9th, 10th, 11th, and 12th Dec. Served throughout the Burmese war, including the storming of Rangoon and Syneham Pagoda; capture of Kimmadine; led the head of the left column in storming the trenches in front of the Dagon Pagoda; storming a strong stockade in front of the Dagon Pagoda. Commanded the left wing of the 41st Regt. in the field against the Kolampore Rajah.

[Emb. for Foreign Service, 1835.] **43rd (or Monmouthshire) Regiment of Foot** [Serving in Canada.]
(*Light Infantry.*)

"VIMIERA"—"CORUNNA"—"BUSACO"—"FUENTES D'ONOR"—"CIUDAD RODRIGO"—"BADAJOZ"—"SALAMANCA"—"VITTORIA"—"NIVELLE"—"NIVE"—"TOULOUSE"—"PENINSULA."

Years' Serv					
Full Pay.	Half Pay.	Colonel.			
47		John *Lord* Keane,[1] G.C.B. & G.C.H. *Ens.* 1793; *Lieut.* 29 April, 93; *Capt.* 12 Nov. 94; *Major*, 27 May, 1802; *Lieut.-Col.* 20 Aug, 03; *Col.* 1 Jan. 12; *Major-Gen.* 4 June, 14; *Lieut.-Gen.* 22 July, 30; *Col.* 43rd Light Infantry, 1 Aug. 39.			
		Lieut.-Colonel.			
34	0	H. Booth,[2] K.H. *Ens.* P 6 Mar. 06; *Lieut.* 11 June, 07; *Capt.* P 25 June, 12; *Major* P 29 Aug. 22; *Lieut.-Col.* 29 June, 30.			
		Majors.			
27	7/12	Jas. Forlong,[3] K.H. *Ens.* P 11 Mar. 13; *Lieut.* P 22 Dec. 14; *Capt.* P 20 Sept. 21; *Major*, P 1 July, 28.			
20	1/2	Jas. Bucknall B. Estcourt, *Ens.* P 13 July, 20; *Lieut.* P 9 Dec. 24; *Capt.* P 5 Nov. 25; *Major*, P 2 Oct. 36; *Brevet-Lieut.-Col.* 29 March, 39.			

		CAPTAINS.	ENSIGN.	LIEUT.	CAPTAIN.	BREV.-MAJ.
24	3 3/12	William Fraser[4]	8 Apr. 13	19 Jan. 14	P 9 Dec. 24	28 June 38
27	0	Chas. Ravenhill Wright[5]	25 Dec. 13	P 26 July 21	P 11 July 26	
18	0	Samuel Tryon	P 23 Jan. 23	P 10 Sept. 25	P 19 Feb. 28	
16	0	Wilbraham Egerton	P 4 Nov. 24	P 11 July 26	P 1 July 28	
15	0	*Hon.* A. Almoric Spencer	8 Apr. 25	P 5 July 27	P 6 Apr. 31	
15	0	William Bell	P 5 Nov. 25	P 1 July 28	P 23 Dec. 31	
15	0	Henry Bruere	P 1 Sept. 25	P 19 Feb. 28	P 8 Apr. 34	
15	0	George Talbot	2 Feb. 26	P 9 Sept. 28	P 3 Apr. 35	
14	0	Johnson Ford	P 7 Sept. 26	P 25 June 29	P 21 Oct. 36	
12	0	Fred. Paris Sanders	P 19 Feb. 28	16 July 30	P 31 Dec. 39	
		LIEUTENANTS.				
20	3 2/12	James Thomas	P 5 Dec. 16	9 Apr. 25		
17	0	Dan. Gardner Freer	20 Nov. 23	P 8 Apr. 26		
12	0	Thos. Aylmer Pearson ..	28 Feb. 28	P 23 Dec. 31		
12	0	Rich. Geo. Aug. Levinge	P 25 Nov. 28	P 8 Apr. 34		
11	0	John Meade	P 15 May 29	P 22 Aug. 34		
10	0	John Thos. Wm. Jones ..	16 July 30	P 6 Mar. 35		
8	0	Henry W. Paget	14 Dec. 32	P 1 May 35		
6	0	John Chidley Coote	P 4 July 34	P 15 Sept. 37		
6	0	Arth. Lowry Cole	P 22 Aug. 34	P 20 Nov. 38		
6	0	Henry Skipwith	P 24 Oct. 34	P 25 Jan. 39		
5	0	Wm. Rob. Herries	P 6 Mar. 35	P 12 April 39		
5	0	*Hon.* T. G. Cholmondeley	P 3 Apr. 35	P 31 Dec. 39		
		ENSIGNS.				
5	0	Robert Lambert	P 1 May 35			
5	0	*Hon.* C. H. Lindsay	P 5 June 35			
4	0	Albert S. Bruere	P 21 Oct. 36			
4	0	Jas. M. Primrose	6 Jan. 37			
3	0	*Lord* F. G. C. G. Lennox	P 15 Sept. 37			
2	0	O. A. O. Gore	P 20 Nov. 38			
2	0	*Hon.* John Kennedy	P 25 Jan. 39			
1	0	C. W. A. H. Wood	P 12 Apr. 39			
1	0	*Hon.* P. Egerton Herbert	17 Jan. 40			
29	2/12	*Paymaster.*—George Hood,[6] 25 Oct. 28; *Ens.* 21 Feb. 11; *Lieut.* 28 May, 12.				
17	0	*Adjutant.*—D. G. Freer (*Lieut.*), 8 March, 39.				
10	0	*Quarter-Master.*—Samuel Rand, 8 Oct. 30.				
26	1 7/12	*Surgeon.*—John Millar,[7] 5 Nov. 20; *A.-Surg.* 8 Feb. 21; *H.-Assist.* 24 May, 13.				
14	0	*Assistant-Surgeons.*—T. D. Hume, 11 Oct. 27; *Hosp.-Assist.* 26 Oct. 26.				
5	0	George N. Foaker, 1 May, 35.				

Notes right column:
3 Major Forlong served the campaigns of 1813 and 14, in Germany and Holland, including the actions at Merxem, bombardment of Antwerp, and storming of Bergen-op-Zoom. Severely wounded at Quatre-Bras, 16th June, 1815, right collar bone fractured and ball lodged in the right breast.

4 Major Fraser was severely wounded at the battle of the Nive.
5 Captain Wright served in the American war.
6 Paymaster Hood served the campaign of 1814, in the Peninsula. Present in the attack on New Orleans, 8th January, 1815.
7 Dr. Millar served the campaigns of 1813 and 14, in the Peninsula, and the expedition to New Orleans.

Facings White.—*Agent*, Messrs. Hopkinson, Barton, & Knyvett.—
Irish Agent, Borough & Co.

1 Lord Keane served the campaign in Egypt, in 1801, and has received a cross and two clasps for Martinique, Vittoria, Pyrenees, Nivelle, Orthes, and Toulouse. Sir John was severely wounded at New Orleans.
2 Colonel Booth served at the battle of Vimiera and Corunna; passage of the River Coa near Almeida; battles of Busaco, Salamanca, and Vittoria; attack on the heights of Vera.

Emb. for For. Service, 1822.] **44th** (*or the East Essex*) *Regiment of Foot.* [Serving in Bengal.

The *Sphinx*, with the words, "EGYPT"—"BADAJOZ"—"SALAMANCA"—"PENINSULA"—"BLADENSBURGH"—"WATERLOO"—"AVA."

Years' Serv.		
60		**Colonel.**
Full Pay	Half Pay	Gore Browne,[1] *Ens.* 5 July, 1780; *Lieut.* 3 March, 89; *Capt.* 8 June, 93; *Major*, 15 June, 94; *Lieut.-Col.* 30 Nov. 96; *Col.* 1 Jan. 1805; *Major-Gen.* 25 July, 10; *Lieut.-Gen.* 12 Aug. 19; *Gen.* 10 Jan. 37; *Col.* 44th Regt. 29 Jan. 20.
33	1 7/12	**Lieut.-Colonels.**—🅟 John Shelton,[2] *Ens.* 21 Nov. 05; *Lieut.* 26 Aug. 07; *Capt.* 17 June, 13; *Major,* 6 Feb. 25; *Lieut.-Col.* 6 Sept. 27.
36	0	🅟 Thomas Mackrell, *Ens.* 19 Sept. 04; *Lieut.* 25 May, 07; *Capt.* 11 June, 18; *Major*, 12 Nov. 25; *Lieut.-Col.* P25 June, 30.
24	2 10/12	**Majors.**—Day Hort Macdowall,[3] *Ens.* 15 April, 13; *Lieut.* P10 March, 14; *Capt.* 11 Sept. 17; *Major*, P18 July, 26.

Years' Serv.		CAPTAINS.	ENSIGN.	LIEUT.	CAPTAIN.	BREV.-MAJ.
24	1 0/12	Charles O'Neill	18 May 15	P27 June 16	P31 May 21	10 Jan. 37
34	0	John Kitson	25 Apr. 06	15 Jan. 07	3 Oct. 11	22 July 30
29	8	James Johnston[5]	3 Dec. 03	5 Aug. 04	7 Mar. 11	22 July 30
41	0	Benjamin Halfhide[6]	28 Oct. 99	7 Apr. 04	25 Aug. 09	22 July 30
26	2 8/13	Wm. Boxell Scott[7]	2 Apr. 12	15 Apr. 13	12 Apr. 31	
15	0	Arthur Horne..........	P19 Nov. 25	P27 Nov. 28	P21 Feb. 34	
23	4 3/13	Thomas Swayne[8]	24 Dec. 12	9 Aug. 14	30 Jan. 36	
17	0	Rob. Bradford M'Crea[9]..	16 Jan. 24	6 Dec. 25	P11 June 36	
16	0	Willoughby Cotton	P 2 Sept. 24	P 6 Nov. 24	P21 Nov. 28	
28	0	Alured Wm. Gray[10]	2 Feb. 13	23 Mar. 19	14 June 39	
		LIEUTENANTS.				
20	7/12	Thomas Robinson[11]	2 Mar. 20	10 Feb. 25		
16	0	James Douglas De Wend	29 Apr. 24	17 Dec. 25		
15	0	J. D. Young	16 Aug. 25	P 7 Jan. 27		
15	9 6/12	Edward Woolhouse	P 5 Oct. 15	P26 June 17		
18	0	Wm. Henry Dodgin	16 Jan. 23	29 May 28		
21	0	Thomas Collins	P 6 Jan. 20	P 7 July 25		
14	13 3/12	Cha. Ernest Turner[12] ..	17 May 13	12 Oct. 15		
12	0	Tho. Rich. Leighton ..	29 May 28	P 1 June 32		
13	0	Geo. Haddon Smith	21 Apr. 27	22 Oct. 33		
10	0	Wm. Evans............	29 June 30	23 Oct. 33		
9	0	Wm. George White	12 Apr. 31	29 Aug. 34		
12	4 7/12	Tho. Alex. Souter	30 June 24	8 May 35		
9	0	Fra. Montresor Wade ..	P20 Sept. 31	P26 June 35		
8	0	Arthur Hogg	P 1 June 32	30 Jan. 36		
7	0	Duncan Trevor Grant ..	P 5 July 33	1 Apr. 36		
16	0	C. K. Macan	19 Oct. 24	18 Apr. 27		
6	0	J. Chilton L. Carter	28 May 34	P23 Sept. 36		
6	0	Aug. Halifax Ferryman..	P27 June 34	30 June 37		
5	0	Edw. S. Cumberland....	P17 Apr. 35	P18 May 38		
5	0	Frederick Jenkins	P26 June 35	16 Aug. 39		
		ENSIGNS.				
5	0	Wm. MacMahon	P 6 Nov. 35			
4	0	Geo. H. Skipton	P11 June 36			
4	0	Wm. G. Raban	23 Sept. 36			
3	0	Robert Kipling	30 June 37			
3	0	Henry Cadett	28 Nov. 37			
2	0	F. J. Camp. Fortye	1 June 38			
2	0	Samuel Swinton........	P 9 Nov. 38			
1	0	Alured Wm. Gray	22 Nov. 39			
1	0	Frederick Shelton	P24 Jan. 40			
36	0	*Paymaster.*—Thos. Bourke, 12 Oct. 04.				
3	0	*Adjutant.*—Robert Kipling, (*Ens.*) 27 Dec. 37.				
23	4 3/12	*Quarter-Master.*—Robertus Rich. Halahan,[13] 14 Feb. 22; *Ens.* 23 July, 12; *Lieut.* 25 Aug. 15.				
27	0	*Surg.*—🅟 John Harcourt,[14] 7 May, 34; *Assist.-Surg.* 26 May, 14; *Hosp.-Assist.* 10 May, 13.				
4	0	*Assistant-Surgeons.*—Wm. Balfour, 4 March, 36.				
1	0	William Primrose, M.D. 9 Aug. 39.				

Facings Yellow.—*Agent,* Messrs Cox & Co.

3 Major Macdowall served the campaign of 1814 in Holland, including the action at Merxem 2d Jan., and Antwerp 2d Feb.

5 Major Johnston served at the taking of Madeira in 1807; capture of Guadaloupe and dependencies, St. Martins, and St. Eustatius in 1810; also 1 campaign against the Burmese.

6 Major Halfhide served the Nepaul campaigns of 1814, 15, and 16; also in Aracan in 1824.

7 Captain Scott served in the Burmese war.

8 Capt. Swayne served the campaigns of 1813 and 14 in Canada, including the action of Chippewa, and Fall of Niagara; siege and storm of Fort Erie, Aug. and Sept. 1814; served in the Burmese war, including the capture of several stockades in the neighbourhood of Rangoon, and on the advance of the army to Prome.

9 Capt. M'Crae served in the Burmese war, including the capture of Aracan, Ramree, and Chaudier.

10 Capt. Gray served in the actions of Jeetghur 3rd Jan. 1815, and Jubbulpore 19th Dec. 1817; and the campaign of 1825 in Aracan.

11 Lt Robinson served the campaign of 1825 in Aracan including the actions at Padona, Mahatee, and Aracan.

12 Lieut. Turner served the campaign of 1814 in Holland, including attack on Merxem & Bergen-op-Zoom.

13 Lieut. (Quarter-Master) Halahan served at the taking of Aracan in 1825.

14 Dr. Harcourt served in the Peninsula from June 1813 until the end of the war.

1 Gen. Browne served in Holland and was present in the battles of the 10th and 19th Sept., and 2nd Oct. 1799. He commanded the brigade that carried the town and fortress of Monte Video by assault, and was afterwards wounded at Walcheren.

2 Col. Shelton lost an arm at St. Sebastian.

45th (or the Nottinghamshire) Regiment of Foot.

"Roleia"—"Vimiera"—"Talavera"—"Busaco"—"Fuentes D'Onor"—"Ciudad Rodrigo"— "Badajoz"—"Salamanca"—"Vittoria"—"Pyrenees"—"Nivelle"—"Orthes"— "Toulouse"—"Peninsula"—"Ava."

Years' Serv.		
Full Pay	Half Pay	
48		**Colonel.** ℙ Sir Wm. Hen. Pringle,[1] G.C.B. *Cornet*, 6 July, 1792; *Lieut.* 24 Feb. 93; *Capt.* 15 Oct. 94; *Major*, 19 Sept. 94; *Lieut.-Col.* 5 Dec. 99; *Col.* 25 Oct. 1809; *Major-Gen.* 1 Jan. 12; *Lt.-Gen.* 22 July, 30; *Col.* 45th Regt. 29 Nov. 37.
31	9/12	**Lieut.-Colonel.**—ℙ Edw. French Boys,[2] *Ens.* ℙ 17 Nov. 08; *Lt.* 3 Apr. 10; *Capt.* ℙ 8 June 15; *Major*, 3 Feb. 29; *Lieut.-Col.* 21 June, 32.
16	1 5/12	**Majors.**—Elliott Armstrong, *Cornet*, ℙ 25 March, 23; *Lieut.* ℙ 23 June, 25; *Capt.* ℙ 10 June, 26; *Major*, ℙ 20 Feb. 35.
14	0	Francis Octavius Montgomery, *Ens.* ℙ 13 April, 26; *Lieut.* ℙ 28 April, 27; *Capt.* ℙ 15 Nov. 33; *Major*, ℙ 6 Sept. 39.

		CAPTAINS.	ENSIGN.	LIEUT.	CAPTAIN.	BREV.-MAJ.
32	0	ℙ Richard Stack[3]	24 Jan. 09	3 Mar. 11	12 Nov. 27	6 Dec. 39
25	2/12	Wm. Henry Butler[4]	10 Aug. 15	3 Nov. 18	5 Apr. 31	
25	0	John Macintire[5]	19 Aug. 15	25 Mar. 25	21 June 32	
16	0	Archibald Erskine	ℙ 24 June 24	16 Sept. 26	ℙ 16 Nov. 32	
11	0	Henry Cooper	ℙ 26 Feb. 29	ℙ 5 Apr. 31	ℙ 13 Nov. 35	
16	0	Edm. Wilson Lascelles[5]	23 Dec. 24	18 May 26	6 July 37	
12	0	Magens Mello	ℙ 22 May 28	ℙ 26 Apr. 31	ℙ 31 May 39	
11	0	Charles Hind	ℙ 8 Oct. 29	ℙ 7 Feb. 34	ℙ 22 Feb. 39	
7	0	Hallam D'Arcy Kyle	ℙ 12 July 33	ℙ 23 June 37	ℙ 24 May 39	
7	0	Jonas Stawell	ℙ 11 Oct. 33	1 Apr. 36	ℙ 6 Sept. 39	
		LIEUTENANTS.				
20	0	Thomas Prendergast[6]	17 Oct. 20	22 Apr. 25		
15	0	Fras. Percy Nott	23 June 25	10 May 26		
14	0	Charles Seagram	22 June 26	5 Mar. 31		
14	0	Hen. Wemyss Magee	15 Dec. 26	26 Nov. 30		
12	0	Donald Wm. Tench	31 July 28	ℙ 2 Dec. 31		
13	0	ℙ John Hine[7]	1 Aug. 27	30 Apr. 32		
9	0	Jocelyn Ing. Oakley	ℙ 26 Apr. 31	ℙ 20 Feb. 35		
6	0	Robert Bates	6 June 34	ℙ 25 Dec. 36		
5	0	G. A. L. Blenkinsopp	ℙ 4 Sept. 35	ℙ 31 May 39		
2	0	Hen. J. Shaw	ℙ 23 Mar. 38	ℙ 7 June 39		
2	0	Edw. Lawrence Tickell	ℙ 16 Feb. 38	ℙ 6 Sept. 39		
4	0	Charles Simeon	ℙ 13 May 36	ℙ 18 May 39		
4	0	Fran. Orl. H. Bridgeman	ℙ 28 Oct 36	ℙ 5 July 39		
		ENSIGNS.				
2	0	Wm. Smith[8]	26 June 38			
2	0	Hen. Thomas Vialls	ℙ 25 Dec. 38			
1	0	Henry W. Parish	ℙ 9 Mar. 39			
1	0	Jas. Butler Fellowes	ℙ 31 May 39			
1	0	Fred. Rich. Stack	1 June 39			
1	0	Stephen B. Gorgon	7 June 39			
1	0	R. J. Garden	21 June 39			
1	0	Wm. Cairnes Armstrong	ℙ 6 Sept. 39			
23	3 2/12	**Paymaster.**—Daniel O'Meara,[9] 20 Oct. 25; *Ens.* 25 Aug. 14; *Lieut.* 11 Jan. 16.				
13	0	**Adjutant.**—ℙ John Hine, (*Lieut.*) 1 Aug. 27.				
1	0	**Quarter-Master.**—Edwin Walters, 13 Dec. 39; *Ens.* 31 May, 39.				
19	8 4/12	**Surgeon.**—J. Ferguson,[10] 8 Mar. 39; *Ass.-Surg.* 3 Mar. 14.; *Hosp.-Ass.* 7 Mar. 13.				
13	0	**Assist.-Surgeon.**—Peter Baird, M.D. 29 July, 30; *Hosp.-Assist.* 13 June, 27.				

Notes on right column:

7 Lieut. Hine served in the Peninsula from April, 1809, to the end of the war, including the battles of Oporto, Talavera, Albuhera (twice wounded); assault and capture of Ciudad Rodrigo, and Badajoz; battles of Salamanca (wounded), Vittoria, Pyrenees, Nivelle, Nive, Orthes and Toulouse.

8 Ens. Smith served in the Burmese war.

9 Paymaster O'Meara served in Western Africa, under Governor M'Carthy, and in Caffraria in 1819 and 20.

10 Dr. Ferguson served the campaigns of 1813 and 14 in Canada; was engaged in an action on Lake Ontario and Lake Huron; also in the action of Michilimackinac.

Facings Green.—*Agent*, Messrs. Cox & Co.
[*Returned from Madras, March*, 1838.]

1 Sir Wm. Henry Pringle has received a Cross for Salamanca, Pyrenees, Nivelle, and Nive, and was severely wounded in France, Feb. 1814.

2 Col. Boys served in the Peninsula from 1809 to 1811, and again from 1813 to the end of the war, including the action at Sabugal, and battles of Fuentes d'Onor (wounded), Orthes, and Toulouse (wounded). Served also in the Burmese war.

3 Major Stack's services: Campaign and battle of Corunna. Actions in the Bay of Bengal in Nov. 1809, between the French frigates *La Venus, La Manche*, and *Creole* sloop-of-war, and the Hon. Company's ships *Wyndham, United Kingdom*, and *Charlton*, for his conduct on which occasion he received a gratuity from the Hon. Company. Capture of the Isle of France in 1810. Capture of Java in 1811, including the actions of the 10th, and 22nd; storming of Fort Cornelius, 26th Aug. (wounded); and storming of the Heights of Serondole, Sept. 1811. Relinquished the command of Amboyense corps at Samarang to go on service with his Regt. (the 14th), and was present at the capture of the piratical defences at Sambas, on the island of Borneo, July, 1813. Capture of the Fort of Hattrass. Mahratta campaigns of 1817 and 18. Wounded at the storming of Bhurtpore, 18th January, 1826. Served 28 years in the East Indies, without once returning to England during that long period.

4 Capt. Butler served in the Kandian campaigns of 1817 and 18, and was personally engaged, on various occasions, in affairs with the enemy.

5 Captains Macintire and Lascelles served in the Burmese war in 1825.

6 Lieut. Prendergast served throughout the Burmese war, including the taking of Prome, storming the enemy's works on the 1st, 2nd, and 5th Dec. 1825, and 19th Jan. 26, battle of Pagum-Mew, &c.

Emb. for For. Service, 1837.] **46th (or South Devonshire) Regt. of Foot.** [Serving at Gibraltar.

"DOMINICA."

Colonel.
ᵮ John Ross,¹ C.B. *Ens.* 2 June, 93; *Lieut.* 8 May, 96; *Capt.* 11 Jan. 00; *Major,* 15 Aug. 04; *Lieut.-Col.* 28 Jan. 08; *Col.* 4 June, 14; *Major-Gen.* 27 May, 25; *Lieut.-Gen.* 28 June, 38; *Col.* 46th. Regt. 1 Aug. 39.

Lieut.-Colonel.
Andrew Clarke,² K.H. *Ens.* 22 Aug. 06; *Lieut.* 29 July, 08; *Capt.* ᵖ 4 Feb. 13; *Major,* ᵖ 15 Dec. 25; *Brevet-Lieut.-Col.* 28 June, 38; *Regt.-Lieut.-Col.* ᵖ 11 Oct. 39.

*Majors.—*ᵮ Robert Garrett,³ K.H. *Ens.* 6 March, 11; 3 Sept. 12; *Capt.* 7 July, 14; *Major,* 19 Sept. 26.
Edward Hungerford Delaval Elers Napier, *Ens.* 11 Aug. 25; *Lieut.* 11 Oct. 26; *Capt.* ᵖ 21 June 31; *Major,* ᵖ 11 Oct. 39.

Years' Serv.						
Full Pay	Half Pay	CAPTAINS.	ENSIGN.	LIEUT.	CAPTAIN.	BREV.-MAJ.
47						
34	0					
15	14 10/12					
15	0					
32	3 1/12	Robert Martin⁴	15 Aug. 04	28 Mar. 05	21 Nov. 16	10 Jan. 37
24	0	Donald Stuart⁵	2 May 16	25 Feb. 20	1 Apr. 31	
22	0	Robert Campbell⁶	24 Dec. 18	13 June 22	15 June 32	
16	0	Charles W. Zuhlcke	24 June 24	4 May 26	ᵖ 29 May 35	
20	6 4/12	James Taylor	25 Aug. 14	4 Dec. 17	14 May 36	
31	3 10/12	ᵮ ᵒᵇ Richd. Handcock⁷	10 Sept. 05	5 Nov. 06	ᵖ 30 July 18	10 Jan. 37
9	0	Wm. Neville Custance	ᵖ 11 Oct. 31	ᵖ 26 June 35	ᵖ 16 Mar. 38	
11	0	Wm. Thomas Bremner	ᵖ 3 Dec. 29	ᵖ 21 June 31	ᵖ 5 April 39	
8	0	Geo. Heneage L. Wharton	ᵖ 1 June 32	ᵖ 19 June 35	ᵖ 11 Oct. 39	
6	0	Eustace A. T. d'Eyncourt	ᵖ 19 Sept. 34	ᵖ 29 Jan. 36	ᵖ 31 Dec. 39	
		LIEUTENANTS.				
18	0	William Child	13 Nov. 22	11 Aug. 26		
15	0	Joseph Davies	ᵖ 3 Dec. 25	ᵖ 14 Dec. 26		
14	0	Wm. James Yonge	ᵖ 27 July 26	ᵖ 17 May 27		
14	0	Wm. Lacy	20 Apr. 26	30 Aug. 27		
11	0	William Peacock	ᵖ 28 May 29	ᵖ 12 Dec. 34		
6	0	Wm. Clutton Marshall	ᵖ 28 Nov. 34	ᵖ 21 Oct. 36		
5	0	John Egerton Carrol	8 May 35	ᵖ 10 Feb. 37		
5	0	Geo. Martin Atkins	ᵖ 17 July 35	ᵖ 8 Apr. 37		
5	0	Arthur Geo. Vesey	ᵖ 29 May 35	ᵖ 25 Aug. 37		
5	0	Alex. Maxwell	ᵖ 19 June 35	ᵖ 28 Dec. 38		
5	0	Henry Mordaunt	ᵖ 29 Jan. 36	ᵖ 5 April 39		
3	0	Joseph Ischia Brome	ᵖ 10 Feb. 37	ᵖ 11 Oct. 39		
3	0	Eustace J. D. Moffatt	ᵖ 25 Aug. 37	ᵖ 31 Dec. 39		
		ENSIGNS.				
2	0	Hen. F. Sullivan	ᵖ 6 July 38			
4	0	David Fyffe	ᵖ 11 June 36			
2	0	William Fitz Gerald	ᵖ 28 Dec. 38			
1	0	Arthur Wombwell	ᵖ 5 Apr. 39			
1	0	H. B. Whittingham	31 May 39			
1	0	Philip Blundell Bicknell	ᵖ 11 Oct. 39			
1	0	Geo. Selsey Bigland	ᵖ 15 Nov. 39			
17	14 7/12	*Paymaster.—*William Iveson, 25 Aug. 08.				
14	0	*Adjutant.—*William Lacy, (*Lieut.*) 28 May, 37.				
10	0	*Quarter-Master.—*John Allan, 3 June, 30.				
28	0	*Surgeon.—*Michael Galeani,⁸ M.D. 7 Nov. 34; *Assist.-Surg.* 16 June, 25; *Hosp.-Assist.* 12 Nov. 12.				
6	0	*Assistant-Surgeons.—*Francis Burnett, M.D. 19 Dec. 34.				
14	0	Augustus H. Cowen, 29 July, 30; *Hosp.-Assist.* 2 Nov. 26.				

5 Capt. Stuart served at the siege and capture of Kittoor in the East Indies in Dec. 1824.

6 Capt. Campbell was employed on field service in India from Aug. 1820 to March 1825, including the siege of Kittoor.

7 Major Handcock accompanied the expedition to Hanover in 1805; joined the army in Sicily in 1806, and was employed with its various companies from 1806 to 1810; went with the expedition to Naples, and was present at the capture of Ischia and Procida; returned to Sicily and employed against the French army in 1811. Served in Spain during 1812 and 13, including the battle of Castalla, siege of Tarragona, and affair of Villa Franca.

8 Dr. Galeani landed at Leghorn, 14th March, 1814, and was present in the campaign of Italy with the advanced army, including the taking of the Castle of St. Maria, in Spezia; action at Seshi; siege and surrender of Genoa, and taking of the Castle of Savona and Novi.

Facings Yellow.—*Agent,* Messrs. Cox & Co.

1 General Ross has received a medal for Vimiera.
2 Colonel Clarke served at the capture of Guadaloupe in 1810.
3 Major Garrett received two wounds at the attack of the Forts at Salamanca, on which occasion the command of the Light Company of the Queen's and some Artillery devolved upon him, he being the only surviving officer of the column he attacked with. He was also severely wounded in the Pyrenees.
4 Major Martin served eight years in the field in Sicily; the campaign of 1807 in Egypt; taking of Genoa in 1814; two campaigns in the United States of North America, including the taking of Casteen and its dependencies on the River Ponobscot.

Emb. for For. Service, 1834.] **47th (or the Lancashire) Regt. of Foot.** [Serving at Malta.

"TARIFA"—"VITTORIA"—"ST. SEBASTIAN"—"PENINSULA"—"AVA."

Colonel.

Years' Serv.		
51		Sir Wm. Anson,[1] Bt. K.C.B. *Ens.* 13 June, 1789; *Lieut. & Capt.* 25 April, 93;
Full Pay	Half Pay	*Capt. & Lieut.-Col.* 28 Sept. 97; *Col.* 30 Oct. 05; *Major-Gen.* 4 June, 11; *Lieut.-Gen.* 12 Aug. 19; *Gen.* 10 Jan. 37; *Col. 47th Regt.* 25 March, 35.
47	2 6/12	*Lieut.-Colonel.*—Rich. Goodall Elrington,[2] C.B. *Ens.* 4 Dec. 90; *Lieut.* 19 Feb. 94; *Capt.* 1 June, 95; *Brevet-Major*, 25 April, 08; *Regtl.-Major*, p 3 May, 10; *Lieut.-Col.* 4 June, 13; *Col.* 22 July, 30.
35	0	*Majors.*—Philip Dundas,[3] *Ens.* 22 Aug. 05; *Lieut.* 25 Aug. 07; *Capt.* 16 Nov. 20; *Major*, p 28 June, 31.
15	4/12	John Gordon,[4] *Ens.* 12 April 25; *Lieut.* p 28 Jan. 26; *Capt.* p 25 Nov. 31; *Major*, p 24 March, 38.

		CAPTAINS.	ENSIGN.	LIEUT.	CAPTAIN.	BREV.-MAJ.
25	1 1/12	Edward Dundee[5]	never	Sept. 14	p 8 Oct. 29	
27	0	John Gordon	28 Sept. 13	13 Apr. 20	p 11 June 30	
14	3/12	H. W. Egerton Warburton	p 19 Jan. 26	p 25 Mar. 28	p 9 Mar. 32	
15	0	George Newcome	26 May 25	p 6 July 26	p 14 June 33	
12	0	Wm. O'Grady Haly	p 17 June 28	p 19 July 31	p 25 Apr. 34	
12	0	William Skipwith	p 19 June 28	p 18 Jan. 31	p 26 Feb. 36	
10	0	John Sutton	p 11 June 30	p 22 Oct. 33	p 17 Feb. 37	
10	0	John Brice Bidae	p 15 June 30	10 Dec. 33	p 24 Mar. 38	
10	0	Wm. Chs. Caldwell ...	p 8 Oct. 30	p 25 Apr. 34	p 9 Oct. 38	
9	0	Alexander Mitchell ...	p 5 July 31	p 27 June 34	p 14 June 39	

LIEUTENANTS.

18	0	John Lardner[6]		5 Sept. 22	12 July 25
16	0	Henry M'Nally[7]		12 Jan. 25	20 May 26
13	0	William Wise		p 21 Feb. 27	17 May 31
6	0	James Wm. Crowdy ...		p 28 Mar. 34	p 8 Apr. 36
7	0	Henry Bridges		19 July 33	p 17 Feb. 37
6	0	Desaguiliers West		p 25 Apr. 34	p 24 Mar. 38
6	0	Alan James Gulston ..		p 27 June 34	p 28 Sept. 38
6	0	William W. Rooke		5 Sept. 34	p 19 Oct. 38
5	0	Geo. Jas. Vernon		p 10 Dec. 35	p 2 Mar. 39
3	0	Tho. W. Elrington		p 17 Feb. 37	p 14 June 39
3	0	Wm. Armstrong		p 2 June 37	p 31 Dec. 39
6	0	Richard T. Farren		30 May 34	31 Jan. 40
3	0	John Sinnott		25 July 37	2 Feb. 40

8 Lieutenant (Quarter Master) Nagle served in the Peninsula from May 1811, to the end of the war, including the action at Aldea de Ponte; siege of Ciudad Rodrigo; siege of the forts at and battle of Salamanca; siege of Burgos (severely wounded); the whole of the skirmish in the Pyrenees, and near Pampeluna; engaged with the enemy 1st and 2d Aug. during their retreat; carrying their position 7th and 8th Aug.; action in front of San Sebastian; battles of Nivelle and Toulouse; besides a great many skirmishes. Served in the Burmese war.

ENSIGNS.

2	0	R. J. Elrington	p 24 Mar. 38
2	0	Cha. F. Fordyce	17 Feb. 38
2	0	W. D. P. Patton	p 28 Sept. 38
2	0	Rob. S. Torrens	p 19 Oct. 38
2	0	J. F. R. De Courcy ...	p 28 Dec. 38
1	0	John Wentworth Austen	p 14 June 39
1	0	James Villiers.........	p 31 Dec. 39
1	0	Rob. Nathaniel Clarke ..	31 Jan. 40

33	0	*Paymaster.*—James Clarke, 27 Sept. 30; *Ens.* 12 Aug. 07; *Lieut.* 5 Nov. 07; *Capt.* 19 Mar. 24.
3	0	*Adjutant.*—John Sinnott, (*Lieut.*) 25 July, 37.
24	4 1/12	*Quarter-Master.*—Mic. Nagle,[8] 4 Nov. 27; *Ens.* 9 April, 12; *Lieut.* 25 Dec. 14.
31	0	*Surg.*—H. T. Mostyn, M.D. 20 Oct. 25; *Assist.-S.* 4 Jan. 10; *Hosp.-A.* 8 July, 09.
15	0	*Assistant-Surgeons.*—Robert Battersby, 28 Sept. 26; *Hosp.-Assist.* 22 Dec. 25.
13	0	Thomas Fox, M.D. 29 July, 30; *Hosp.-Assist.* 15 Mar. 27.

Facings White.—*Agent*, Messrs. Cox & Co.

1 Sir. Wm. Anson has received a cross and three clasps for Corunna, Salamanca, Vittoria, Pyrenees, Nivelle, Orthes, and Toulouse.

2 Col. Elrington's services:—Campaigns in Holland from 1793 to Feb. 1795, including the attack on Famars, and siege of Valenciennes. Carribean war of 1795 and 6 in the West Indies; siege and storming of Monte Video and attack on Buenos Ayres. Attack and capture of Ras-el-Kimah in the Persian Gulf in 1809. Commanded a field force at the reduction of Palampore, Dresa, Kirjah, and Virampore in 1817; and a brigade during the Pindarree war. Commanded a brigade up the Persian Gulf in 1819, and from Dec. 1824, throughout the Burmese war. Shot through the body before Dunkirk, Sept. 1793, and through the thigh at the island of St. Vincent in July, 1796.

3 Major Dundas's services:—expedition to South America, including the taking of Maldonado, several skirmishes, and storming of Monte Video. Several skirmishes in the East Indies in 1811. Burmese war from Jan. 1826 until peace was proclaimed.

4 Capt. Gordon served the campaigns of 1816, 17, and 18, in Malwa; in the Persian Gulf in 1819 and 20; and in Ava in 1825 and 6. Wounded at Donabew 26th March, and on the Heights near Prome, 2d Dec. 1825.

5 Capt. Dundee served in the Peninsula in 1814; and in the Persian Gulf in 1819 and 20.

6 Lieut. Lardner served in the Burmese war from Dec. 1824 until peace was proclaimed.

7 Lieut. M'Nally served in the Peninsula, from May, 1808, until the end of the war, including Tarifa and Barrosa (wounded in the right leg); siege of Tarrifa; attack of Bohea; siege of Cadiz; attack of Arringuay bridge; retreat from Salamanca (wounded in the head 19th Nov. 1812); battle of Vittoria; siege of San Sebastian; capture of the island near St. Jean de Luz; battles of the Nive, 9th, 10th, 11th and Dec. and blockade of Bayonne. Served the campaigns of 1817 and 18 in Malwa; in the Persian Gulf in 1819 and 20, and in the Burmese war, including the siege of Donabew and Prome. Wounded through the body at Prome 2 Dec. 25.

Emb. for Foreign Service, 1838.] **48th (or Northamptonshire) Regt. of Foot.** [Serving at Gibraltar.

"DOURO"—"TALAVERA"—"ALBUHERA"—"BADAJOZ"—"SALAMANCA"—
"VITTORIA"—"PYRENEES"—"NIVELLE"—"ORTHES"—"TOULOUSE"—
"PENINSULA."

Years' Serv.		
62		*Colonel.* Sir Thos. Hislop,[1] *Bart.* G.C.B. *Ens.* 28 Dec. 1778 ; *Lieut.* 28 Jan. 83 ; *Capt.* 28 Jan. 85 ; *Major*, 16 Aug. 94 ; *Lieut.-Col.* 25 March, 95 ; *Col.* 29 Apr. 1802 ; *Major-Gen.* 25 Oct. 09 ; *Lieut.-Gen.* 4 June, 14 ; *Gen.* 10 Jan. 37 ; *Col.* 48th Regt. 25 Dec. 29.
Full Pay.	Half Pay.	
41	0	ᵽ T. Bell,[2] *C.B. Ens.* ᵖ 13 Nov. 99 ; *Lieut.* ᵖ 17 Jan. 01 ; *Capt.* 12 Sept. 05 ; *Brev.-Maj.* 26 Aug. 13 ; *Regtl.-Maj.* 25 Mar. 24 ; *Lieut.-Col.* ᵖ 20 Sept. 27.
		Majors.
30	2	Patrick MacDougall, *Ens.* 2 Mar. 08 ; *Lieut.* 16 Feb. 11 ; *Capt.* ᵖ 28 July, 14 ; *Major*, ᵖ 19 Dec. 26.
29	1 11/12	ᵽ Peter J. Willats,[3] *Ens.* 31 Aug. 09 ; *Lieut.* 2 June, 11 ; *Capt.* 22 Dec. 14 ; *Brevet-Major*, 10 Jan. 37 ; *Regtl.-Major*, 4 Nov. 38.

		CAPTAINS.	ENSIGN.	LIEUT.	CAPTAIN.	BREVET-MAJOR.
21	0	Hon. Arth. Alex. Dalzell	29 Apr. 19	ᵖ 5 Feb. 24	ᵖ 26 June 27	
16	0	William A. M'Cleverty ..	26 Mar. 24	26 Aug. 25	ᵖ 21 May 29	
20	0	William Codd..........	2 Mar. 20	25 Mar. 24	29 Mar. 33	
19	5	Robert Cole	21 Nov. 16	ᵖ 26 Dec. 22	ᵖ 14 Aug. 27	
18	3	Hunter Ward	ᵖ 9 Sept. 19	ᵖ 31 Dec. 22	ᵖ 10 Sept. 25	28 June 38
26	5 8/12	ᵽ ℞℞ Edward Duncan[4]	3 Sept. 08	28 Feb. 11	ᵖ 24 July 17	10 Jan. 37
21	6 7/12	Chas. Allen Young......	23 Mar. 19	ᵖ 20 Apr. 22	ᵖ 31 Dec. 27	
13	1 11/12	Jas. Webber Smith[5]	ᵖ 11 July 26	ᵖ 25 Dec. 35	ᵖ 7 Sept. 38	
10	0	Benjamin Riky	ᵖ 9 Nov. 30	30 May 34	ᵖ 8 Sept. 38	
21	7	Hender Mountsteven[6] ..	30 Dec. 12	6 Jan. 14	30 Nov. 38	
		LIEUTENANTS.				
15	0	Anthony Donelan	9 Apr. 25	7 Nov. 27		
12	0	Gordon Skelly Tidy	15 May 28	ᵖ 3 Dec. 29		
14	0	Rob. Chas. Hamilton....	ᵖ 3 Aug. 26	28 Apr. 31		
12	0	George Mowbray Lys ..	2 Mar. 28	20 Dec. 31		
11	0	John Massy............	ᵖ 3 Dec. 29	ᵖ 16 Sept. 36		
7	0	John Moore Ross	ᵖ 9 Aug. 33	ᵖ 13 Jan. 37		
6	0	Henry Wheeler	11 Feb. 34	27 Jan. 37		
7	0	Maurice Emmett	ᵖ 19 Apr. 33	ᵖ 1 Dec. 37		
5	0	John Edw. Hall........	ᵖ 21 Aug. 35	ᵖ 15 June 38		
5	0	Henry Bromley	ᵖ 4 Sept. 35	ᵖ 7 Sept. 38		
5	0	Cavendish S. Boyle	ᵖ 23 Oct. 35	ᵖ 8 Sept. 38		
5	0	Clifford Felix Henry....	ᵖ 25 Dec. 35	30 Nov. 38		
7	0	Henry W. Tobin.	ᵖ 12 Apr. 33	1 Feb. 39		
		ENSIGNS.				
3	0	Andrew Green	12 Jan. 38			
2	0	David Fullerton	ᵖ 15 June 38			
2	0	Robert Bateman	ᵖ 7 Sept. 38			
2	0	Robert Warburton......	ᵖ 8 Sept. 38			
2	0	John Minchin..........	ᵖ 14 Sept. 38			
2	0	Alexis Corcoran	30 Nov. 38			
2	0	Clement W. Strong	18 Jan. 39			
1	0	Geo. Dean Pitt	11 Oct. 39			

3 Major Willats served in the Peninsula from 1812 to the end of the war, including the siege and storming of Ciudad Rodrigo, siege and storming of Badajoz from 19th January to 6th April, 1812; operations near, and blockade of Bayonne.

4 Major Duncan served at the siege of Flushing in 1809, and in the Peninsula from Aug. 1812 to Oct. 1813, including the battle of Vittoria, and siege of San Sebastian, where he was severely wounded 31st August, 1813; present at Waterloo, the storming of Cambray, and capture of Paris.

5 Captain Smith was wounded in action at Coorg, Madras, April, 1834.

6 Captain Mountsteven served at the attack of various posts, &c. on the Frontiers of Canada, and within the United States in 1813, 14, and 15.

7 Paymaster Hartley served at the surrender of Martinique; and taking of Gaudaloupe in 1815.

23	4 4/12	*Paymaster.*—Bartholomew Hartley,[7] 30 Oct. 35 ; *Ens.* 15 Jan. 13 ; *Lieut.* 26 May, 14 ; *Capt.* 17 April, 35.
6	0	*Adjutant.*—Henry Wheeler, (*Lieut.*), 11 Feb. 34.
2	0	*Quarter-Master.*—James Earlsman Richardson, 9 Mar. 38.
		Surgeon.—Edward M'Iver, 18 Mar. 36 ; *Assist.-Surg.* 3 June, 13.
2	0	*Assist.-Surgs.*—Jas. T. O. Johnston, M.D. 3 Aug. 38.
2	0	Edward Wm. Stone, M.D. 5 Oct. 38.

Facings Buff.—*Agent,* Messrs. Cox & Co.—*Irish Agent,* Borough, Armit, & Co.

1 Sir Thomas Hislop served at Gibraltar during its bombardment and siege; was present at the surrender of various islands in the West Indies; and has received a medal for Guadaloupe. Sir Thomas performed distinguished service in the Pindarree and Mahratta war.

2 Colonel Bell served in the Peninsula from 1809 to the end of the war, including the passage of the Douro; battle of Albuhera (wounded); action at Aldea de Ponte; siege of Ciudad Rodrigo; siege and assault of Badajoz (severely wounded); battles of Salamanca, the Pyrenees, Nivelle, Orthes, and Toulouse. Col. B. has received a cross for the four last named battles.

Emb. for Foreign Service, 1821.] **49th** *(or Princess Charlotte's, or Herts.)* **Foot.** [Serving in Bengal.

"EGMONT-OP-ZEE"—"COPENHAGEN"—"QUEENSTOWN."

Colonel.

Years' Serv.		
51		Sir Gordon Drummond,[1] G.C.B. *Ens.* 21 Sept. 1789; *Lt.* 31 Mar. 91; *Capt.* 31 Jan. 92; *Maj.* 28 Feb. 94; *Lt.-Col.* 1 March, 94; *Col.* 1 Jan. 98; *Maj-Gen.* 1 Jan. 1805; *Lt.-Gen.* 4 June, 11; *Gen.* 27 May, 25; *Col.* 49th Regt. 21 Sept. 29.
Full Pay.	Half Pay.	

Lieut.-Colonels.

Full Pay	Half Pay	
34	0	R. Bartley,[2] *Ens.* 28 Feb. 06; *Lieut.* p12 Feb. 07; *Capt.* 10 Aug. 15; *Major,* p 5 Feb. 24; *Lieut.-Col.* 25 April, 28.
30	0	Edmund Morris,[3] *Ens.* 21 June, 10; *Lieut.* 21 April, 13; *Capt.* 1 Dec. 25; *Major,* p 13 Sept. 33; *Lieut.-Col.* p22 Nov. 36.

Majors.

32	1 4/12	p Thomas Stephens,[4] *Ens.* 28 Nov. 06; *Lieut.* 18 Aug. 08; *Capt.* 23 Dec. 13; *Major,* 4 June, 33.
29	0	Samuel Blyth, *Ens.* 21 Feb. 11; *Lieut.* 28 April, 13; *Capt.* 25 April, 28; *Major,* p 22 Nov. 36.

Captains.

			ENSIGN.	LIEUT.	CAPTAIN.	BREV.-MAJ.
28	0	Joseph Stean[5]	5 July 12	9 May 13	1 Apr. 29	
27	0	Gilbert Pasley[6]	26 Jan. 14	10 June 20	p 2 June 28	
15	0	Thos. Scott Reignolds	23 June 25	25 Apr. 28	p 26 Apr. 31	
26	14 6/12	p William Wilkinson[7]	12 Dec. 99	4 Mar. 01	1 Sept. 08	27 May 25
19	16 5/12	Charles Gregory	27 Feb. 05	2 Aug. 05	8 Dec. 13	10 Jan. 37
14	0	Wm. Raikes Faber	p 10 Apr. 26	p 28 Aug. 28	p 22 May 35	
20	9/12	Mitchell Geo. Sparks	4 Nov. 19	26 Dec. 23	28 June 36	
16	11 8/12	p David Mac Andrew[8]	15 Mar. 13	20 Apr. 15	18 Nov. 36	
15	0	William Johnston	p 7 Jan. 26	p 6 Nov. 27	p 22 Nov. 36	
16	9 1/12	Robert Campbell	21 Sept. 15	26 Apr. 28	22 Mar. 39	

Lieutenants.

14	0	Jas. Patrick Meik	p 26 June 26	p 10 Oct. 27	
12	0	John Leslie Dennis	25 Apr. 28	22 Sept. 30	
12	0	John Thornton Grant	28 Apr. 28	12 Nov. 30	
23	4 8/12	p Thomas Gibbons[9]	9 Sept. 12	7 Apr. 25	
11	0	Henry George Hart	1 Apr. 29	19 July 32	
11	0	J. Myers Montgomery	24 Dec. 29	2 Jan. 33	
11	0	Wm. Painter K. Browne	31 Dec. 29	4 Jan. 33	
9	0	Henry Garner Rainey	12 Apr. 31	8 June 33	
9	0	John Heatley	20 Sept. 31	28 Mar. 34	
8	0	James Ramsay	18 May 32	p 9 May 34	
7	0	Geo. Francis Bartley	p 12 July 33	p 19 Dec. 34	
7	0	Hugh Pearson	p 13 July 33	p 22 May 35	
11	0	Sam. Baxter D. Anderson	11 July 29	23 May 35	
6	0	John Hinton Daniell	p 14 Mar. 34	11 Nov. 36	
6	0	Arthur Robt. Shakespear	p 19 Dec. 34	p 17 Aug. 38	
6	0	Lachlan H. G. Maclean	26 Dec. 34	31 Aug. 38	
5	0	H. Seymour Michell	p 22 May 35	22 Mar. 39	
5	0	Sydney L. Horton	p 13 Feb. 35	22 Mar. 39	
4	0	Thos. P. Gibbons	p 8 July 36	15 June 39	
4	0	James Brockman	p 22 Nov. 36	23 July 39	
3	0	David M'Adam	28 Apr. 37	24 July 39	
4	0	Marcus A. Obert	p 12 Mar. 36	p 10 Jan. 40	

Ensigns.

3	0	Robert Blackall	p 19 Jan. 38	
2	0	Walter Tyler Bartley	20 July 38	
1	0	Joseph Hely	16 Feb. 39	
1	0	George Rand	8 Mar. 39	
1	0	Chas. Alex. Halfhide	21 June 39	
1	0	John M'Culloch O'Toole	22 June 39	
1	0	Clareveaulx Faunt	17 Sept. 39	
1	0	Wm. H. Clinton Baddeley	p 11 Oct. 39	

25	2 7/12	**Paymaster.**—R. Ware,[10] 23 June, 31; *Ens.* 25 Oct. 12; *Lieut.* 25 Sept. 13.
		Adjutant.—
3	0	**Quarter-Master.**—Henry Mayne, 23 June, 37.
30	7/12	**Surgeon.**—p James French,[11] M.D. 9 Dec. 24; *Assist.-Surg.* 8 Feb. 10.
5	0	**Assist.-Surgs.**—C. Flyter, 28 Aug. 35.
2	0	R. H. Garrett, M.D. 23 Nov. 38.

Facings Green.—**Agent,** Messrs. Cox & Co.

5 Capt. Stean's services:—campaign of 1799 in Holland, including the action at the landing, and battle of Egmont-op-Zee. Expedition to Copenhagen in 1801. Served during the war in North America in 1812, 13, and 14, and was wounded at Stoney Creek.

6 Capt. Pasley served at the siege of Hattras in 1817, and siege of Asseerghur in 1819.

7 Col. Wilkinson served at the capture of the Cape of Good Hope in 1806, and in the Peninsula from Aug. 1812 to Dec. 1813, including the battle of the Nive, where he was severely wounded, and for which battle he has received a medal. Brevet.-Lieut.-Col. 28 June 38.

8 Capt. Mac Andrew served in the Peninsula and France, in the 27th regt. including the battles of the Pyrenees, Nivelle, Orthes, and Toulouse, besides various affairs of outposts, &c.

9 Lieut. Gibbons served in the Peninsula from Sept. 1811, until the end of the war, including the battle of Salamanca; capture of the French rear-guard, 23rd July, 1812; capture of Madrid and Valadolid; siege of Burgos; battles of the Pyrenees, 28th, 29th, and 30th July; Maya Pass; battle of the Nive, 8th and 9th Dec.; blockade of Bayonne; battle of Orthes; affairs of Vic and Tarbes.

10 Paymaster Ware served in the Burmese war.

11 Dr. French served in the Peninsula from May, 1812, to the end of the war, including the battles of Salamanca and Vittoria; siege of San Sebastian, and battle of the Nive. Served in the American war at Bladensburgh, Washington, Baltimore, and New Orleans.

1 Sir Gordon Drummond served in Holland in 1794, and 95, and was present in Nimeguen during the siege, and at the sortie; embarked from Minorca in 1800, on the expedition to Egypt, and was present in the engagements of the 13th and 21st March; in the battle of Rhamania, and at the surrender of Grand Cairo and Alexandria. Sir Gordon commanded in the action near the Falls of Niagara, where he was severely wounded.

2 Col. Bartley served in the American war, including the action at Fort Erie; Fort George, 25th and 27th May; Stoney Creek; Fort George, 25th Aug. 13; and Crystler's Farm, where he was severely wounded.

3 Colonel Morris served in the American war, including the action at Stoney Creek.

4 Major Stephens accompanied the expedition to Walcheren, and was present at the siege of Flushing. Served in the Peninsula from March 1810 to the end of the war, including the battle of Busaco; siege of Almeida; battle of Fuentes d'Onor; storming the Forts at, and battle of Salamanca (severely wounded through the thigh); siege of Burgos; action of Cabecon; battle of Vittoria; blockade of Pampeluna; battles of the Pyrenees, Nivelle, Nive, Orthes and Toulouse, besides many other minor actions and skirmishes.

Emb. for For. Service, 1834.] **50th (or the Queen's own) Regt. of Foot.** [Serving in New South Wales.

The *Sphinx* with the words "EGYPT"—"VIMIERA"—"CORUNNA"—"ALMAREZ"—"VITTORIA"—"PYRENEES"—"NIVE"—"ORTHES"—"PENINSULA."

Years' Serv.					
58		*Colonel.*			
Full Pay	Half Pay	෴ Sir Geo. Townshend Walker,[1] Bt. G.C.B. *2nd Lieut.* 4 Mar. 1782 ; *Lieut.* 13 Mar. 83 ; *Capt.* 13 Mar. 89 ; *Major*, 28 Aug. 94 ; *Lieut-Col.* 6 Sept 98 ; *Col.* 25 Apr. 1808 ; *Major-Gen.* 4 June, 11 ; *Lieut.-Gen.* 19 July, 21 ; *Gen.* 10 Jan. 37 ; *Col.* 50th Foot, 23 Dec. 39.			
34	0	*Lieut.-Colonel.*—෴ Nicholas Wodehouse,[2] *Ens.* 3 Jan. 07 ; *Lieut.* 31 Aug. 07 ; *Capt.* ᴾ 26 Sept. 11 ; *Major*, ᴾ 18 Oct. 21 ; *Lieut.-Col.* ᴾ 2 Sept. 24 ; *Col.* 28 June, 38.			
33	2 4/12	*Majors.*—෴ Joseph Anderson,[3] K.H. *Ens.* 27 June, 05 ; *Lieut.* 6 Oct. 08 ; *Capt.* 20 Jan. 14 ; *Major*, ᴾ 16 Feb. 26.			
35	0	෴ Thomas Ryan,[4] K.H. *Ens.* 10 Oct. 05 ; *Lieut.* 28 April, 08 ; *Capt.* 30 Sept. 19 ; *Major*, 13 Aug. 30.			

		CAPTAINS.	ENSIGN.	LIEUT.	CAPTAIN.	BREV.-MAJ.
33	0	෴ William Turner[5]	9 Apr. 07	26 Aug. 08	4 Nov. 19	10 Jan. 37
24	0	James H. Serjeantson	ᴾ 16 May 16	2 Nov. 19	ᴾ 2 Sept. 24	28 June 38
33	0	෴ Fred. C. Montgomery[6]	18 Mar. 07	ᴾ 14 July 08	8 Apr. 25	28 June 38
16	2 4/12	William Fothergill	ᴾ 15 Nov. 21	25 Aug. 25	ᴾ 20 Sept. 27	
15	0	Peter John Petit	ᴾ 19 May 25	12 Feb. 28	ᴾ 28 May 33	
26	8/12	George M'Leod Tew	19 Aug. 13	30 Sept. 19	12 Jan. 34	
13	0	Hon. John Charles Best	ᴾ 21 June 27	ᴾ 29 Oct. 29	ᴾ 15 Aug. 34	
13	0	Henry Gunton	28 June 27	18 Jan. 33	ᴾ 27 Jan. 37	
11	0	J. Brathwaite Bonham	ᴾ 1 Oct. 29	ᴾ 28 May 33	ᴾ 20 July 38	
24	3 7/12	෴ James Weir[7]	13 May 13	30 Dec. 19	27 Nov. 38	
		LIEUTENANTS.				
21	0	William Sheaffe	4 Nov. 19	1 Aug. 22		
15	0	Wm. Langley Tudor	9 Apr. 25	ᴾ 26 Nov. 29		
15	0	Alex. C. D. Bentley	9 Apr. 25	17 Aug. 32		
9	0	Cha. Francis Gregg	ᴾ 16 Dec. 31	ᴾ 14 Feb. 34		
8	0	Richard Waddy	17 Aug. 32	4 May 36		
7	0	Henry Stapleton	ᴾ 2 Aug. 33	ᴾ 27 Jan. 37		
7	0	William Knowles	ᴾ 9 Aug. 33	ᴾ 20 July 38		
7	0	Geo. G. M. Cobban	ᴾ 16 Aug. 33	ᴾ 27 July 38		
8	0	Sam. Hood Murray	ᴾ 22 June 32	ᴾ 8 Dec. 37		
4	0	Henry Needham	16 Sept. 36	27 Nov. 38		
4	0	James John Enoch	16 Dec. 36	ᴾ 9 Feb. 39		
2	0	Cha. R. Grimes	ᴾ 16 Mar. 38	ᴾ 20 Dec. 39		
2	0	Harry Wainwright Hough	ᴾ 20 July 38	ᴾ 10 Jan. 40		
		ENSIGNS.				
4	0	Jas. G. Smyth	ᴾ 4 June 36			
3	0	Charles Green	ᴾ 23 June 37			
1	0	Arthur Bernard	ᴾ 8 Feb. 39			
1	0	Jos. John Grimes	ᴾ 9 Feb. 39			
1	0	James Russell	31 May 39			
1	0	John Fleming Parker	ᴾ 20 Dec. 39			
1	0	Simon Pepper Joyce	ᴾ 8 Mar. 39			

5 Major Turner's services :—Battles of Roleia, Vimiera, and Corunna; siege of Flushing; battle of Fuentes d'Onor, Arroyo de Molino, Almarez, Albadetarmos, Baighar, and Vittoria, where he was severely wounded; right arm amputated.

6 Major Montgomery's services :—Campaign and battle of Corunna; expedition to Walcheren and siege of Flushing; campaigns of 1811 and 12 in the Peninsula.

7 Captain Weir served in the Peninsula from November, 1812, to October, 1814, including the battles of Nivelle and Orthes.

8 Captain Bartley served the Corunna campaign, and subsequently in the Peninsula from March, 1811, to the end of the war, and was engaged at Almarez, Alba de Tormes, Baighar, Vittoria, Pyrenees 25th, 26th, and 27th July, Pampeluna 28th and 30th July.

32	7/12	*Paymaster.*—෴ George Bartley,[8] 23 June 25 ; *Ens.* 25 Oct. 07 ; *Lieut.* 13 April, 09 ; *Capt.* 9 Dec. 21.
15	0	*Adjutant.*—Wm. Langley Tudor, (*Lieut.*) 18 Jan. 33.
2	0	*Quarter-Master.*—Joseph Moore, 28 Aug. 38.
		Surgeon.—John Reid, 5 July 39 ; *Assist.-Surg.* 6 Oct. 14.
15	0	*Assist.-Surg.*—Robt. Ellson, 20 Oct. 25 ; *Hosp.-Assist.* 14 April 25.
5	0	Alexander Graydon, M.D., 15 May, 35.

Facings Blue.—*Agent*, Messrs. Cox & Co.

1 Sir George Walker served in Flanders in 1793, and was in the action of the 10th May, near Tournay; served in the expedition to Copenhagen in 1807, and subsequently in the expedition to the Scheldt. Sir George has received a cross and two clasps for Vimiera, Badajoz (severely wounded), and Orthes.

2 Colonel Wodehouse served in Portugal from May, 1808, to December, 1811, including the battle of Vimiera, campaign from Lisbon to Oporto, and battles of Busaco and Fuentes d'Onor; served the campaign of 1814 in the South of France, including the affair at Tarbes and battle of Toulouse.

3 Major Anderson's services :—Expedition to Calabria, including the battle of Maida and subsequent operations, and capture of the fortress of Catrone; expedition to Egypt in 1807; Peninsula from April, 1809, to January, 1812, including the battles of Talavera (wounded), and Busaco; retreat to the lines of Torres Vedras, and various affairs there ; with the advance at Espenilli; battle of Fuentes d'Onor; besides many other affairs and skirmishes; served at the capture of Guadaloupe in 1815.

4 Major Ryan accompanied the expedition to Walcheren in 1809; served in the Peninsula and received a severe sabre wound in the head, and several other wounds at Fuentes d'Onor.

| Emb. for For. Serv. 1838. | 51st (*or the 2nd Yorksh. W. Riding*) or The King's Own Light Inf. Regt. | Serving in Van Dieman's Land |

"MINDEN"—"CORUNNA"—"SALAMANCA"—"VITTORIA"—"PYRENEES"—
"NIVELLE"—"ORTHES"—"PENINSULA"—"WATERLOO."

Years' Serv.			
Full Pay.	Half Pay.		
46		*Colonel.* 𝔅 Sir Benj. D'Urban,[1] K.C.B. & K.C.H., *Cornet,* April, 1794; *Lieut.* 1 July, 94; *Capt.* 2 July, 94; *Major* 21 Nov. 99; *Lieut.-Col.* 1. Jan. 1805; *Col.* 4 June, 13; *Major-Gen.* 12 Aug. 19; *Lieut.-Gen.* 10 Jan. 37; *Col.* 51st Light Infantry, Dec. 29.	
31	0	*Lieut.-Colonel.*—𝔅 ☖ W. H. Elliott,[2] K.H. *Ens.* ᴾ 6 Dec. 09; *Lieut.* ᴾ 13 Aug. 12; *Capt.* ᴾ 9 Nov. 20; *Major* ᴾ 12 July, 31; *Lieut.-Col.* ᴾ 27 June 38.	
25	0	*Majors.*—Edw. St. Maur, *Ens.* ᴾ 22 June, 15; *Lieut.* ᴾ 16 Nov. 20; *Capt.* ᴾ 29 May, 23; *Major* ᴾ 1 July, 37.	
30	0	𝔅 ☖ Fred. Mainwaring,[3] *Ens.* 5 April, 10; *Lieut.* 15 April, 13; *Capt.* 4 Dec. 28; *Major* ᴾ 27 June, 38.	

		CAPTAINS.	ENSIGN.	LIEUT.	CAPTAIN.	BREV.-MAJ.
31	0	𝔅☖ Oliver D. Ainsworth[4]	11 April 09	26 July 10	14 Aug. 28	
24	5 9/12	𝔅 ☖ William Austin[5]...	5 Sept. 11	6 April 13	26 Sept. 34	
15	1	Seth Nuttall Fisher......	ᴾ 12 Feb. 24	ᴾ 13 May 26	ᴾ 3 April 35	
15	0	Edward Parker.........	ᴾ 14 April 25	4 Dec. 28	ᴾ 16 Dec. 36	
15	0	Arnold Chas. Errington..	ᴾ 4 Feb. 26	13 Sept. 31	ᴾ 14 July 37	
14	0	Harry Rolles	ᴾ 30 Dec. 26	ᴾ 11 Oct. 31	ᴾ 15 July 37	
12	0	Percy Rice............	14 Aug. 28	ᴾ 28 Nov. 34	ᴾ 2 Sept. 37	
11	2 11/12	Charles Holden.........	ᴾ 8 June 26	ᴾ 22 May 35	ᴾ 7 Oct. 37	
9	0	Wm. Henry Hare........	ᴾ 9 Aug. 31	ᴾ 25 Dec. 35	ᴾ 27 June 38	
23	1 6/12	Edward Forman........	31 Aug. 15	8 April 25	7 Sept. 38	
		LIEUTENANTS.				
9	0	Rich. D. Baker.........	13 Sept. 31	ᴾ 16 Dec. 36		
9	0	Augustus Thomas Rice...	ᴾ 11 Oct. 31	ᴾ 10 Mar. 37		
8	0	Edmund Isham.........	ᴾ 31 Aug. 32	ᴾ 1 July 37		
7	0	Hen. Chas. Capel Somerset	ᴾ 4 Oct. 33	ᴾ 14 July 37		
6	0	Henry M'Farlane.......	ᴾ 28 Nov. 34	ᴾ 15 July 37		
9	0	James Gates...........	11 July 31	27 Feb. 35		
5	0	Francis Carey.........	ᴾ 22 May 35	ᴾ 2 Sept. 37		
5	0	George Bagot	26 June 35	ᴾ 7 Oct. 37		
5	0	Hon. David Erskine....	ᴾ 31 July 35	ᴾ 27 June 38		
3	0	Edward Corbett.......	ᴾ 10 Mar. 37	ᴾ 21 June 39		
3	0	Car. A. H. Rumbold.....	ᴾ 1 July 37	ᴾ 26 July 39		
		ENSIGNS.				
3	0	Aug. J. W. Northey......	ᴾ 14 July 37			
3	0	Aug. Hen. Irby.........	ᴾ 15 July 37			
3	0	Fra. C. Doveton	ᴾ 2 Sept. 37			
3	0	Francis Chas. Skurray...	ᴾ 7 Oct. 37			
2	0	Walter Kirby	ᴾ 22 June 38			
2	0	W. Douglas Scott......	ᴾ 27 June 38			
2	0	Edw. Hen. Kelly.......	ᴾ 14 Sept. 38			
3	0	G. E. E. Warburton.....	6 Oct. 37			
1	0	Arthur S. Otway	21 June 39			
1	0	Arthur Miller Harris....	ᴾ 26 July 39			
30	0	*Paymaster.*—𝔅 ☖ John Gibbs,[6] 15 Feb. 10.				
5	0	*Adjutant.*—Francis Carey (*Lieut.*) 16 March, 38.				
27	0	*Quarter-Master.*—William Kenny,[7] 10 June, 13.				
25	0	*Surgeon.*—James Lowrie Tighe, 10 Jan. 40; *Assist.-Surg.* 20 Oct. 25; *Hosp.-Assist.* 24 June, 15.				
3	0	*Assist.-Surgeons.*—Wm. John Power, 14 July, 37.				
3	0	Thomas Bartlett, 4 Aug. 37.				

Notes column (right side):
4 Capt. Ainsworth served at the siege of Flushing, and subsequently in the Peninsula, including the battle of Fuentes d'Onor, and 2d siege of Badajoz. Present at Waterloo.

5 Capt. Austin served in the Peninsula, from Oct. 1811 to April, 1812, including the siege and storm of Ciudad Rodrigo. Served the campaign of 1814 in Holland, including the taking of the fortified village of Merxem. Present on the 18th June at Waterloo.

6 Paymaster Gibbs served in the Peninsula from Jan. 1811 until the end of the war, and was severely wounded in the advance on Llerena 26 March, 1812. Present at Waterloo.

7 Quarter-Master Kenny served at the taking of Castine in North America in 1814.

Facings Blue.—*Agent*, Sir John Kirkland, No. 80 Pall-Mall.

1 Sir Benjamin D'Urban has received a cross and five clasps for Busaco, Albuhera, Badajoz, Salamanca, Vittoria, Pyrenees, Nivelle, Nive, and Toulouse.

2 Col. Elliott served at the battle of Fuentes d'Onor; sieges of Badajoz, and Ciudad Rodrigo; affair near Moresco; battle of Salamanca; capture of Madrid and Retiro; siege and retreat from Burgos; battles of the Pyrenees, Nivelle, and Orthes. Present at Waterloo, and capture of Cambray.

3 Major Mainwaring served in the Peninsula, from March, 1811 to Jan. 1814, including the battle of Fuentes d'Onor; 2d siege of Badajoz; Val Moresco; Salamanca; retreat from Burgos; capture of Retiro, Madrid; battles of Vittoria, Pyrenees, and Nivelle. Present on the 18th June at Waterloo.

Emb. for Foreign Service, 1836.] **52d (or Oxfordshire) Regt. of Foot (Lt. Infantry).** [Serving at Barbadoes.

"HINDOOSTAN"—"VIMIERA"—"CORUNNA"—BUSACO"—"FUENTES D'ONOR"
"CIUDAD RODRIGO"—"BADAJOZ"—"SALAMANCA"—"VITTORIA"—
"NIVELLE"—"NIVE"—"ORTHES"—"TOULOUSE"—"PENINSULA"—
"WATERLOO."

Years' Serv.						
45		**Colonel.** ⓑ Sir Thomas Arbuthnot,[1] K.C.B. *Ens.* 23 Nov. 95: *Lieut.* 1 May, 96; *Capt.* 25 June, 98; *Major,* 7 April, 08; *Lieut.-Col.* 24 May, 10; *Col.* 4 June, 14; *Major-Gen.* 27 May, 25; *Lieut.-Gen.* 28 June, 38; *Col.* 52nd Light Infantry, 23 Dec. 39.				
Full Pay	Half Pay					
25	2/12	*Lieut.-Colonel.*—Wm. Blois, *Ens.* ᴾ 3 May, 15; *Lieut.* ᴾ 30 Aug. 21; *Capt.* ᴾ 14 July, 25; *Major,* ᴾ 12 Aug. 34; *Lieut.-Col.* ᴾ 11 May, 39.				
15	0	*Majors.*—Richard French, *Ens.* ᴾ 9 June, 25; *Lieut.* ᴾ 30 Dec. 26; *Capt.* ᴾ 2 Mar. 32; *Major,* ᴾ 11 May, 39.				
13		Henry Samuel Davis, *Ens.* 13 Apr. 27; *Lieut.* ᴾ 8 Oct. 30; *Capt.* ᴾ 17 July 35; *Major,* ᴾ 13 Dec. 39.				

		CAPTAINS.	ENSIGNS.	LIEUT.	CAPTAIN.	BREV.-MAJ.
14	0	Cecil Wm. Forester	ᴾ 1 Aug. 26	14 May 29	ᴾ 4 Dec. 35	
10	0	Hon. Harry Cav. Grey	ᴾ 9 Nov. 30	ᴾ 5 Apr. 33	ᴾ 25 Dec. 35	
14	1/12	Joshua Allen Vigors	ᴾ 19 Sept. 26	ᴾ 17 Sept. 29	ᴾ 19 Oct. 38	
14	0	Wm. Amherst Hale	ᴾ 30 Dec. 26	ᴾ 25 June 30	ᴾ 2 Nov. 38	
13	0	Fred. G. Bull	25 Oct. 27	ᴾ 8 Feb. 31	ᴾ 23 Nov. 38	
12	0	Hon. R. Le Poer Trench	ᴾ 15 Jan. 29	ᴾ 2 Mar. 32	ᴾ 11 May 39	
11	0	Evelyn H. F. Pocklington	ᴾ 10 Feb. 29	ᴾ 30 Aug. 33	ᴾ 24 May 39	
10	0	George Murray	ᴾ 25 June 30	ᴾ 12 Aug. 34	ᴾ 30 Aug. 39	
10	0	Bryan Palmes	ᴾ 8 Oct. 30	ᴾ 13 Mar. 35	ᴾ 20 Sept. 39	
10	0	Hon. Walter Arbuthnott	ᴾ 3 Aug. 30	ᴾ 4 Dec. 39	ᴾ 13 Dec. 39	
		LIEUTENANTS.				
11	0	George Hall		14 May 29	ᴾ 18 July 34	
7	0	John George Jarvis		ᴾ 30 Aug. 33	ᴾ 2 Nov. 38	
5	0	George Campbell		ᴾ 13 Mar. 35	21 Dec. 38	
6	0	Chas. Jas. Conway Mills		ᴾ 26 Dec. 34	ᴾ 28 Aug. 38	
3	3/12	C. Albert Denison		ᴾ 22 Sept. 37	ᴾ 11 May 39	
3	0	Hen. M. Brownrigg		ᴾ 1 Dec. 37	ᴾ 24 May 39	
2	0	J. H. Alleyne		ᴾ 25 May 38	ᴾ 31 May 39	
2	0	Frederick Carden		ᴾ 27 July 38	ᴾ 30 Aug. 39	
2	0	Chas. Geo. Fountaine		ᴾ 21 Sept. 38	ᴾ 20 Sept. 39	
2	0	Loftus W. Peacocke		ᴾ 19 Oct. 38	ᴾ 13 Dec. 39	
2	0	William Corbett		ᴾ 23 Nov. 38	ᴾ 31 Jan. 40	
		ENSIGNS.				
2	0	Rich. Davies de Winton		18 Jan. 39		
1	0	Rob. Octavius Cumming		22 Feb. 39		
1	0	Rob. B. Arthur Purvis		ᴾ 11 May 39		
1	0	Cha. Fra. Wedderburne		ᴾ 31 May 39		
1	0	Fred. J. Wilson		ᴾ 1 June 39		
1	0	John Archdall		ᴾ 30 Aug. 39		
1	0	Edgar Ratcliffe		ᴾ 20 Sept. 39		
1	0	Wm. Fred. Foxcroft Jones		ᴾ 21 Sept. 39		
1	0	John Mills Hawkins		31 Jan. 40		
1	0	M. Van Kerkwyk Bowie		ᴾ 1 Feb. 40		
15	1/12	*Paymaster.*—T. Miller Creagh, 21 June, 39; *Ens.* 23 Feb. 25; *Lieut.* 6 Mar. 26.				
5	0	*Adjutant.*—George Campbell, (*Lieut.*) 8 Nov. 39.				
3	0	*Quarter-Master.*—P. Clune, 29 Dec. 37.				
20	0	*Surgeon.*—John Wilson, 18 Oct. 39; *Assist.-Surg.* 1 July 24; *Hosp.-Assist.* 14 Dec. 20.				
2	0	*Assistant.-Surgeons.*—William Robinson, M.D. 11 Jan. 39.				
1	0	George William Macready, 23 Aug. 39.				

Facings Buff.—*Agent,* Sir John Kirkland

1 Sir Thomas Arbuthnot has received a cross and one clasp for Roleia and Vimiera, Corunna, Pyrenees, Nivelle, and Orthes.

Emb. for Foreign Service, 1829.] **53rd (or the Shropshire) Regt. of Foot.** [Serving in the Ionian Islands.

"NIEUPORT"—"TOURNAY"—"ST. LUCIA"—"TALAVERA"—"SALAMANCA"—"VITTORIA"—"PYRENEES"—"NIVELLE"—"TOULOUSE"—"PENINSULA."

Years' Serv		Colonel.				
36		P ☙ Lord Fitz Roy Jas. Hen Somerset,[1] K.C.B. *Cornet*, 9 June, 04; *Lieut.* 30 May, 05; *Capt.* 5 May, 08; *Major*, 9 June, 11; *Lieut.-Col.* 27 Apr. 12; *Col.* 28 Aug. 15; *Major-Gen.* 27 May, 25; *Lieut.-Gen.* 28 June, 38; *Col.* 53rd Regt. 19 Nov. 30.				
Full Pay.	Half Pay.					
21	3/12	*Lieut.-Colonel.*—Rich. Fred. Hill, *Ens.* P 24 June, 19; *Lieut.* P 12 June, 23; *Capt.* P 27 Aug. 25; *Major*, P 11 June, 30; *Lieut.-Col.* P 13 May, 36.				
16	1/12	*Majors.*—Philip Hill, *Ens.* P 11 Mar. 24; *Lieut.* P 17 Sept. 25; *Capt.* P 29 Aug. 26; *Major*, P 13 May, 36.				
16	10/12	Harry Shakespear Phillips, *Cornet*, P 8 Jan. 24; *Lieut.* P 12 May, 25; *Capt.* P 14 Feb. 28; *Major*, P 31 Aug. 38.				
		CAPTAINS.	ENSIGN.	LIEUT.	CAPTAIN.	BREV.-MAJ.
25	1 10/12	☙ John Lewis Black[2]	22 Apr. 13	10 Mar. 14	P 16 June 25	28 June 38
18	1 9/12	Rich. Fallowes Walond..	P 26 July 21	P 9 June 25	P 11 July 26	
15	0	Thomas Carnegy	P 17 Sept. 25	P 24 July 28	P 11 June 30	
15	0	Wm. George Gold	7 Apr. 25	26 June 28	P 29 June 32	
13	0	Edward Bond	P 8 Mar. 27	P 16 Sept. 29	P 26 Feb. 36	
15	0	William O'Brien	18 Jan. 26	P 8 June 30	P 13 May 36	
13	0	C. Edw. Dawson Warren	P 5 June 27	P 11 June 30	P 1 Dec. 37	
13	0	Richard Dyott	P 11 Oct. 27	P 14 June 31	P 31 Aug. 38	
12	0	Adolphus Fred. Bond ..	3 Apr. 28	P 29 June 32	P 12 Oct. 38	
12	0	Thomas Smart	P 24 July 28	P 14 Sept. 32	P 12 Apr. 39	
		LIEUTENANTS.				
19	0	J. Butler Wheatstone ..	1 May 21	31 Mar. 26		
14	0	John H. Allez	P 29 Aug. 26	P 26 Nov. 29		
11	0	Charles Inge	P 7 Jan. 30	P 26 Feb. 36		
10	0	Wellington Stewart	P 11 June 30	P 13 May 36		
8	0	Hon. St. G. Gerald Foley	P 29 June 32	P 27 May 36		
8	0	William Follows	13 Sept. 32	28 May 36		
8	0	Marley Hutchinson	P 14 Sept. 32	P 10 Mar. 37		
7	0	Rich. Butler Low	P 8 Nov. 33	P 1 Dec. 37		
6	0	Robert Spring	P 14 Feb. 34	P 4 Dec. 35		
5	0	Wm. R. Mansfield	27 Nov. 35	P 31 Aug. 38		
5	0	Charles Lempriere	P 4 Dec. 35	P 12 Oct. 38		
5	0	Wm. Rich. O. Gore	P 29 Dec. 35	P 12 Apr. 39		
6	0	Maximilian A. Nethercote	P 12 Aug. 34	P 30 July 36		
		ENSIGNS.				
4	0	G. P. Mansel	P 13 May 36			
4	0	R. Newton Phillips	P 27 May 36			
3	0	T. Harvey Bathurst	P 1 Dec. 37			
2	0	Wm. J. Verner	6 Apr. 38			
2	0	Hen. Martin Atkins	P 31 Aug. 38			
2	0	John Geo. Cooke	P 12 Oct. 38			
1	0	Cha. Hamilton Fenton ..	P 12 Apr. 39			
1	0	Edward Fellowes	P 22 Apr. 39			
29	6/12	*Paymaster.*—P John Quin Pardey,[4] 12 Feb. 36; *Ens.* 18 July, 11; *Lieut.* 17 Dec. 12; *Capt.* 31 Dec. 28.				
8	0	*Adjutant.*—William Follows (*Lieut.*) 13 Sept. 32.				
26	1	*Quarter-Master.*—P William Fair,[5] 15 Apr. 13; *Ens.* 14 Dec. 20.				
31	0	*Surgeon.*—P Charles Maclean,[3] M.D. 14 July, 25; *Assist.-Surg.* 27 Dec. 10; *Hosp.-Assist.* 8 July, 09.				
15	0	*Assistant.-Surgeons.*—Michael Bardin, 3 Aug. 26; *Hosp.-Assist.* 24 Nov. 25.				
12	0	Thos. Galbraith Logan, M.D. 29 July, 30; *Hosp.-Assist.* 8 May 28.				

Remarks column (right side):
4 Captain Pardey served in the Peninsula from Feb. 1813 to the end of the war.
5 Quarter-Master Fair served in the expedition to South America in 1807, including the storming and capture of Monte Video (wounded), attack and reduction of the enemy's camp at Colonia, advance and attack on Buenos Ayres, attack and reduction of the convent of St. Domingo, at which he was taken prisoner. In the Peninsula, under Sir John Moore, including the retreat to Corunna. Expedition to Walcheren, 1809.

Facings Red.—*Agent*, Messrs. Cox & Co.

1 Lord Fitz Roy Somerset performed the arduous and responsible duty of Aide-de-Camp and Military Secretary to His Grace the Duke of Wellington, throughout the campaigns in Spain, Portugal, France, and Flanders, and has received a cross and five clasps for Fuentes d'Onor, Badajoz, Salamanca, Vittoria, Pyrenees, Nivelle, Nive, Orthes, and Toulouse. His Lordship was wounded at Busaco, and lost his right arm at Waterloo.
2 Major Black served at Waterloo on the 16th and 18th June, and was slightly wounded on the 18th.
3 Dr. Maclean served at Walcheren in 1809; and in the Peninsula from Feb. 1810 to the end of the war, including the battles of Busaco, Salamanca, Vittoria, and the Pyrenees; crossing the Bidassoa; battles of Nivelle and Toulouse.

Emb. for Foreign Service, 1819.] **54th (or the *West Norfolk*) Regiment of Foot.** [Serving in the East Indies.

The *Sphinx*, with the words "EGYPT"—"AVA."

[This Regiment is in possession of a small brass piece of ordnance, taken by the Light Company, at Fort Marabout, in Egypt.]

Years' Serv. Full Pay.	Half Pay.					
62		**Colonel.** Isaac Gascoyne,[1] Ens. 8 Feb. 1779; Lieut. & Capt. 18 Aug. 84; Capt. & Lieut.-Col. 5 Dec. 92; Col. 3 May, 96; Major-Gen. 1 Jan. 1801; Lieut.-Gen. 25 April, 08; Gen. 12 Aug. 19; Col. 54th Regiment, 1 June, 16.				
27	1 5/12	**Lieut.-Cols.**—🄫 🄬 Mildmay Fane,[2] Ens. 11 June,12; Lt. 25 Sept. 13; Capt. P 28 July, 14; Maj. P 2 March, 20; Lt.-Col. P 12 June, 23; Col. 28 June, 38.				
41	0	🄫 John Reed,[3] Ens. P 26 March, 99; Lieut. 21 March, 00; Capt. 12 May, 08; Brevet-Major, 27 May, 25; Regtl.-Major, 2 June, 25; Lieut.-Col. P 20 July, 30.				
26	0	**Majors.**—🄬 John Clark,[4] K. H. Ens. 2 June, 14; Lieut. 27 Nov. 21; Capt. P 29 Aug. 26; Major, P 25 Dec. 26.				
24	11 7/12	W. Beetham,[5] En. 5 Oct. 04; Lt. 18 July, 05; Capt. 16 Ja. 12; Maj. P 8 Apr. 26.				
		CAPTAINS.	ENSIGN.	LIEUT.	CAPTAIN.	BREV.-MAJ
34	0	William Cox[6]	P 1 May 06	P 8 Aug. 07	21 Sept. 15	10 Jan. 37
26	0	🄬 Charles Hill[7]	12 May 14	26 Nov. 21	5 Jan. 26	
26	2 6/12	🄫 John Norman[8]	2 July 12	9 Nov. 15	9 July 32	
27	0	Aylmer Dowdall[9]	20 May 13	2 Mar. 17	2 May 29	
24	1	R. Tyrrell Rob. Pattoun[10]	11 Jan. 16	10 Aug. 23	2 Sept. 34	
15	0	Wm. Yorke Moore	P 15 Dec. 25	P 12 Dec. 26	P 19 July 33	10 Capt. Pattoun served at the storm and capture of Fort Bangalung; capture of the town of Lightburn in Rio Pongas in 1817, and Barsa Town, River Gambia, in 1818. 11 Capt. Wells served with the 13th Dragoons in the Peninsula, from Feb. 1810 to the end of the war, including the cavalry engagement between Campo Mayor and Badajoz (wounded): battles of Albuhera, Almarez, Vittoria, Pyrenees, Orthes, and Toulouse. Leg broken by a gun-shot wound on the 18th June at Waterloo. 12 Lieut. Dodd served in the Burmese war, including the actions of the 26th, 27th, and 29th March, 1825. 13 Lieut. Stoddard served in the Burmese war, including the actions at Mahattee and Aracan. 14 Paymaster Barlow served in the Peninsula from Aug. 1810 to April, 1812. Present at the battle of Jubblepore in the East Indies, 19th Dec. 1817. 15 Quarter-master Willox served the campaign of 1814 in Holland, including the action at Merxem 2d Feb. and bombardment of Antwerp. Present on the 17th and 18th June at Waterloo, and subsequent taking of Cambray. Served also in the Burmese war, including the actions at Mahattee and Aracan. 16 Dr. Stephenson served at the taking of Kandy in Ceylon in 1815; also in the Kandyan Rebellion in 1817 and 18, and was severely wounded in the left thigh 26th Oct. 1817.
14	0	Frederick Parr	P 20 April 26	P 12 April 27	P 7 Aug. 35	
22	2	🄫 🄬 Edward Wells[11]	26 June 16	25 Dec. 23	1 July 36	
12	0	Robert Parr	P 28 Feb. 28	P 21 May 29	P 22 Mar. 39	
14	1	Jasper Byng Creagh	9 Apr. 25	12 June 28	P 5 Oct. 32	
		LIEUTENANTS.				
17	0	George Holt		10 Aug. 23	12 Sept. 25	
16	0	John Beach Dodd[12]		24 May 24	31 Oct. 25	
24	0	John Stoddard[13]		3 Jan. 17	7 April 25	
26	0	Garnet Man		13 Jan. 25	15 Mar. 27	
15	0	J. Twisleton Bayley		16 Aug. 25	29 July 28	
12	0	John Ross Wheeler		30 July 28	P 25 Dec. 29	
12	0	Henry Brown		14 Aug. 28	P 31 Dec. 29	
14	0	Uriah Boyd		P 10 June 26	P 15 June 30	
13	0	J. Brett Chalk		P 12 July 27	23 Feb. 31	
11	0	Donald M'Donald		20 April 29	2 Jan. 32	
11	0	Launcelot Edward Wood		P 21 May 29	P 22 June 32	
11	0	Henry David Williams		P 25 Dec. 29	9 July 32	
8	0	Rowland Moffat		P 22 June 32	P 7 Aug. 35	
7	0	George Frederick Long		P 27 Sept. 33	P 17 June 37	
7	0	Charles Fade Heatley		19 April 33	7 July 37	
4	0	Seton Lionel Smith		12 Feb. 36	P 19 July 37	
		ENSIGNS.				
4	0	Thomas Mostyn		P 8 July 36		
4	0	Henry J. Warre		3 Feb. 37		
3	0	Pat. L. C. Paget		11 Aug. 37		
2	0	John Arthur Skurray		P 3 Aug. 38		
1	0	George Poulett		P 22 Mar. 39		
1	0	Geo. Cumming Miller		P 19 July 39		
1	0	Stephen Roland Woulfe		P 31 Jan. 40		
31	0	*Paymaster.*—🄫 Cuthbert Barlow,[14] 3 Jan. 28; Ens. 7 Jan. 10; Lieut. 13 Jan 14.				
17	0	*Adjutant.*—George Holt, (*Lieut.*) 2 Sept. 34.				
13	0	*Quarter-Master.*—🄬 James Willox,[15] 27 Sept. 27.				
26	0	*Surgeon.*—Thomas Gordon Stephenson,[16] M.D. 8 April, 36; *Assistant-Surg.* 2 July, 18; *Hosp.-Assist.* 21 Feb. 14.				
5	0	*Assistant-Surgeons.*—Richard Houstoun Everard, M.D. 19 June, 35.				
5	0	Edward Mockler, 25 Sept. 35.				

Facings Green.—*Agent,* Messrs. Cox & Co.

1 Gen. Gascoyne served the campaigns in Flanders, and was severely wounded at Lincelles, and again on the retreat from Mouvaix to Robaix.
2 Col. Fane served in the Peninsula from Dec. 1812 to March 1814, including the battle of Vittoria; assault and capture of San Sebastian, and battles of the Nive on 9 and 13 Dec. 13. Served at Waterloo on the 16th (severely wounded), & 18 June.
3 Col. Reed served at the siege of Flushing in 1809, and in the Peninsula from June, 1811, to March, 1814, including the action at and heights above Moresco; battle of Salamanca; capture of Madrid and Retiro; action at Olmas, and battle of Vittoria, where he was severely wounded in the right shoulder.
4 Major Clark was engaged at Waterloo on the 18th June, and storming of Cambray, 24th June, 1815. Served the campaigns of 1824 and 5 in India, including the taking of Rangoon, Kimendine, Kamaroot, and Mahattee. Led the attack upon the fortified heights at Aracan, and was severely wounded in the neck, arm, and left side.
5 Major Beetham served in the Egyptian expedition of 1807, also at the taking of Santa Maura.
6 Major Cox served at Travancore in 1809, and in Ava in 1825.
7 Capt. Hill was engaged at the 17th and 18th June, at Waterloo, and the subsequent taking of Cambray. Served in Caffraria in 1820 and 21. Also in the Burmese war, including the taking of Mahattee, and Aracan.
8 Capt. Norman was present at the battle of Vittoria, and severely wounded and taken prisoner in the Maya Pass, in the Pyrenees. He has since served 15 years in India.
9 Capt. Dowdall served the Mahratta campaign of 1818, including the taking of Loghur, Kooance, and Ryghur. Severely wounded at the storming of Ranjee in 1819, having sustained the total loss of sight of the right eye, a portion of the nose and jaw-bone. Served in the Burmese war, and was severely wounded at Dalla, near Rangoon, 9th Dec. 1824.

Emb. for For. Service, 1821.] **55th (or the Westmoreland) Regt. of Foot.** [Serving in th East Indies.

Colonel.

Years' Serv.		
56		₽ *Sir* William Henry Clinton,¹ G.C.B. *Cornet,* 22 Dec. 1784; *Lieut.* 7 Mar. 87; *Capt.* 9 June, 90; *Lieut.-Col.* 29 Dec. 94; *Col.* 1 Jan. 1801; *Major-Gen.* 25 April, 08; *Lieut.-Gen.* 4 June, 13; *Gen.* 22 July, 30: *Col.* 55th Regiment, 25 April, 14.
Full Pay.	Half Pay.	
39	1²⁄₁₂	*Lieut.-Cols.*—₽ James Holmes Schoedde,² *Ens.* May, 00; *Lieut.* 8 Oct. 01; *Capt.* P 19 Sept. 05; *Brev.-Maj.* 21 June, 13; *Rejtl.-Maj.* P 20 Jan. 25; *Lieut.Col.* P 20 Mar. 29.
25	2	Peter Edmonstone Craigie,³ *Ens.* P 3 June, 13; *Lieut.* P 29 Sept. 14; *Capt.* P 24 Oct. 21; *Major,* P 10 Aug. 26; *Lieut.-Col.* 21 Nov. 34.
26	0	*Majors.*—Charles Warren,⁴ *Ens.* 24 Nov. 14; *Lieut.* 13 Nov. 18; *Capt.* P 1 Aug. 22; *Major,* 21 Nov. 34.
14	0	David Lynar Fawcett, *Ens.* P 6 Apr. 26; *Lieut.* P 21 Nov. 28; *Capt.* 21 Nov. 34; *Major,* P 7 Feb. 40.

		CAPTAINS.	ENSIGN.	LIEUT.	CAPTAIN.	BREV.-MAJ.
32	1	Norman Maclean⁵	17 Sept. 07	23 Feb. 09	29 Mar. 27	
25	0	Colin Campbell	3 Oct. 15	23 June 21	P 20 Jan. 32	
28	5⁶⁄₁₂	Archdale Sharpin⁶	1 Jan. 07	23 Jan. 12	11 July 34	
12	0	John Horner	P 3 June 28	P 5 Apr. 31	P 7 Aug. 35	
24	5⁷⁄₁₂	₽ Arthur O'Leary⁷	18 Apr. 11	25 Jan. 14	27 Nov. 35	
14	0	Mackenzie Wilson	P 9 Aug. 26	P 5 Mar. 29	P 29 Jan. 36	
13	7¹⁰⁄₁₂	Fred. Wm. Edw. Barrell	17 Feb. 20	13 June 30	P 5 Feb. 36	
11	0	Hen. Chas. B. Daubeney	12 Mar. 29	9 Aug. 31	P 28 Oct. 36	
13	0	Aug. H. S. Young	6 Dec. 27	P 18 Nov. 31	P 7 June 39	
14	0	John Baillie Rose	P 8 Apr. 26	18 May 32	P 7 Feb. 40	

		LIEUTENANTS.			
14	0	Aug. Hen. Chaproniere	P 14 Dec. 26	12 June 30	
14	11³⁄₁₂	Wm. Thos. Colman	7 Sept. 15	13 June 30	
12	0	Thos. Ancrum Heriot⁸	P 21 Nov. 28	P 5 Apr. 31	
10	0	John Coats	P 2 Nov. 30	3 June 32	
13	0	Hector M'Caskill	29 Nov. 27	4 June 32	
9	0	Thomas De Havilland	P 5 Apr. 31	15 Feb. 33	
12	0	Edward Warren	P 26 Apr. 32	11 July 34	
8	0	Gus. Travers Brooke	P 22 June 32	20 Apr. 35	
8	0	Hume Edwards	P 26 July 33	P 7 Aug. 35	
7	0	W. Holland L. D. Cuddy	P 31 May 33	27 Nov. 35	
7	0	Henry Thomas Butler	P 1 Nov. 33	P 18 Mar. 36	
10	0	George Hamilton	P 16 June 30	22 July 36	
5	0	Joseph Rogers Magrath	P 7 Aug. 35	P 9 Dec. 36	
5	0	Wm. Peregrine Taylor	P 10 July 35	29 Mar. 38	
5	0	Edwin Gream Daniell	P 2 Oct. 35	P 7 Sept. 38	
6	0	Montague Barbauld	23 May 34	28 Dec. 38	
4	0	W. Haviland Fairtlough	P 12 Aug. 36	29 Dec. 38	
4	0	Henry H. Warren	P 9 Dec. 36	4 Feb. 39	
7	0	Wm. Charles Pinder	P 13 Dec. 33	P 3 June 36	
4	0	Edmund Pitman	P 27 Jan. 37	P 28 Sept. 39	
4	0	Henry Fred. Saunders	30 July 36	27 Dec. 37	
2	0	Daniel M'Coy	25 May 38	P 15 Nov. 39	
2	0	George King	P 19 Oct. 38	P 7 Feb. 40	

		ENSIGNS.		
2	0	John Frend	P 7 Sept. 38	
2	0	John Wilton	20 Dec. 38	
2	0	Chas. Augustus Daniell	P 18 Jan. 39	
1	0	Timothy Crowe	1 June 38	
2	0	George Schaw	P 14 June 39	
1	0	Tho. Oldham G. Rogers	P 28 Sept. 39	
1	0	Henry John White Egan	29 Nov. 39	
1	0	John Maguire	P 7 Feb. 40	

18	4⁄₁₂	*Paymaster.*—₽ Cyrus Daniell,⁹ 14 March, 22; *2nd Lieut.* 8 Nov. 21.
5	0	*Adjutant.*—Joseph Rogers Magrath, (*Lieut.*) 19 Sept. 37.
1	0	*Quarter-Master.*—James Wm. Grigg, 22 June, 39.
26	⁸⁄₁₂	*Surgeon.*—Archibald Shanks,¹⁰ M.D. 20 March, 35; *Assist.-Surg.* 17 March, 14; *Hosp.-Assist.* 9 Nov. 13.
		Assist.-Surgs.—J. Hartley Sinclair, M.D. 21 Dec. 26; *Hosp.-Assist.* 14 Apr. 26.
1	0	John Stewart Smith, M.D. 22 Nov. 39.

Facings Green.—*Agent,* Messrs. Cox & Co.

Notes on right side:

3 Col. Craigie served the campaign of 1814 in Holland, including the attacks on Merxem, and bombardment of Antwerp.

4 Major Warren and Lieut. Brook were wounded in action at Coorg, Madras, April, 1834.

5 Captain Maclean served in the Burmese war, including the capture of Zembyke and Melloon.

6 Capt. Sharpin served in the Mahratta war, and was present at the siege of Hattras.

7 Capt. O'Leary served the campaigns of 1811, 12, and 13, in the Peninsula, including the siege of Ciudad Rodrigo, battle of Salamanca, siege of Burgos, and retreat therefrom. Served in the Nepaul war, and was severely wounded in an attack on the heights of Harriapore, 1st March, 1816. Served also in the Mahratta war in 1817 and 18.

8 Lieut. Heriot was very severely wounded at Coorg.

9 Paymaster Daniell's services: Part of the campaign in Spain under Sir John Moore. Siege of Flushing. Peninsula, from July, 1813 to Feb. 1814, including the battle of the 31st Aug. in the Pyrenees; passage of the Bidassoa; battles of Nivelle, and operations in front of St. Jean de Luz; and battles on the Nive 9th, 10th, and 13th Dec. 1813.

10 Dr Shanks served the campaign of 1814 in Holland, including the attacks on Merxem, and bombardment of Antwerp.

1 Sir William Henry Clinton embarked with the Guards for Holland, and served the campaign of 1793 and 1794, and was present at the following battles, sieges, &c. viz.:—Famars, Valenciennes, Dunkirk, Lannoi, Premon, Cateau Cambresis, Fleurus, and the actions of the 10th, 17th, 18th, and 22d May, 1794.

2 Col. Shoedde served the Egyptian campaign of 1801. Served also in the Peninsula from 1808 to the end of the war, including the battles of Rolcia, Vimiera, Talavera, Fuentes d'Onor, sieges of Ciudad Rodrigo, and Badajoz, battles of Salamanca, Vittoria, Pyrenees, Nivelle, Nive, Orthes, and Toulouse, besides numerous minor actions and skirmishes. Medal for Nivelle.

Emb. for For. Service, 1831.] **56th (or the West Essex) Regiment of Foot.** [Serving in Jamaica.

"MORO"—"GIBRALTAR"—With the *Castle and Key*, "*Montis Insignia Calpe.*"

Years' Serv.		Colonel.			
53		*Sir* Hudson Lowe,[1] K. C. B. and G. C. M. G. *Ens.* 25 Sept. 1787; *Lieut.* 16 Nov. 91; *Capt.* 6 Sept. 95; *Major*, 5 July, 1800; *Lieut.-Col.* 25 June, 04; *Col.* 1 Jan. 12; *Major-Gen.* 4 June, 14; *Lieut.-Gen.* 22 July, 30; *Col.* 56th Regt. 23 July, 32.			
Full Pay.	Half Pay.				
		Lieut.-Colonel.			
24	2 10/12	William Hassall Eden, *Ens.* P31 March, 14; *Lieut.* P22 June, 20; *Capt.* P31 July, 23; *Major*, P29 Aug. 26; *Lieut.-Col.* P10 Aug. 39.			
25	1 8/12	*Majors.*—Forrester Owen Leighton, *Ens.* 30 Dec. 13; *Lieut.* 7 April, 25; *Capt.* P29 March, 27; *Major*, P20 May, 36.			
37	0	Peter Shadwell Norman, *Ens.* 9 July, 03; *Lieut.* 2 June, 04; *Capt.* 8 March, 10; *Brevet-Major.* 22 July, 30; *Regtl.-Major*, 15 July, 37.			
		CAPTAINS.	ENSIGN.	LIEUT.	CAPTAIN.	BREV.-MAJ.

33	0	Wm. Hen. Arthure......	19 Feb. 07	P21 Jan. 08	8 Apr. 25	28 June 38
27	0	Nicholas Palmer [2]	11 Nov. 13	3 May 21	P26 May 25	28 June 38
27	0	Rob. Shafto Vicars......	10 Dec. 13	P 9 Aug. 21	P22 Apr. 26	
33	7/12	Cha. O'Conor Higgins..	31 Dec. 06	14 July 08	6 Mar. 27	
12	0	John Wegg............	P18 Dec. 28	10 Mar. 33	P20 May 36	
15	0	Ed. Wm. Wilton Pawsey.	8 Apr. 25	P30 Dec. 26	P23 Sept. 36	
23	1 11/12	Ralph Piggott Ince.....	28 Sept. 15	8 Apr. 25	25 June 37	
24	0	Benjamin Walmsley.....	30 May 16	10 Apr. 25	15 July 37	
11	0	John Charlewood........	P23 Apr. 29	P 1 Aug. 34	P 6 Sept. 39	
18	0	Alex. Daniel Cuddy......	10 Oct. 22	18 May 26	13 Dec. 39	
		LIEUTENANTS.				
13	16	𝔅 William Telford [4]	5 Dec. 11	25 Aug. 13		
16	0	Ed. Elmore Nicolls......	7 Aug. 24	12 Apr. 27		
10	0	Hen. Bruce Barclay......	13 June 30	28 Oct. 34		
10	0	Thos. G. B. M'Neill.....	P25 Jan. 31	P25 Dec. 35		5 Lieut. Hollinsworth served the campaign of 1799 in Holland, including the actions of the 10th Sept. 2nd and 6th Oct. Egyptian campaign of 1801, including the actions of the 17th and 25th Aug. Present at the battle of Maida in 1806; also at the battles of Vimiera and Corunna. Expedition to Walcheren in 1809; and subsequently in the Peninsula, including the battle of Vittoria; action at Roncesvalles; the Pyrenees; affairs on entering France, and battle of Orthes, where he was severely wounded in the right thigh. 6 Dr. Neill served the campaign of 1814 in the Peninsula.
9	0	Wm. Adam Conran......	P11 Oct. 31	P20 May 36		
7	0	Edmund Fosbrooke......	P 6 Sept. 33	P28 June 36		
7	0	John Turner............	15 Mar. 37	3 Jan. 37		
6	0	Thos. Johnes Smith.....	P 1 Aug. 34	P24 Feb. 37		
8	0	Rich. Walter Lacy......	23 Mar. 32	15 Sept. 37		
15	0	𝔅 Henry Hollinsworth [5]	3 Dec. 25	29 May 28		
5	0	James Waddell.........	P 5 Feb. 36	2 May 38		
5	0	Soulden Oakeley........	P28 June 36	P 6 Sept. 39		
4	0	Eardley Norton........	P16 Sept. 36	13 Dec. 39		
		ENSIGNS.				
3	0	Lewis Cha. Conran......	P17 Mar. 37			
3	0	Arth. W. Byles	17 Nov. 37			
3	0	F. G. T. Deshon	29 Dec. 37			
5	0	Alex. Macpherson	9 Oct. 35			
2	0	R. H. Macdonnell	6 July 38			
1	0	Thomas Wallace Fraser..	30 Aug. 39			
1	0	George Wm. Patey	P 6 Sept. 39			
1	0	George Raban	31 Jan. 40			
26	0	*Paymaster.*—G. Burgoyne Sutherland, 19 Aug. 36; *Ens.* 8 Dec. 14; *Lieut.* 15 June, 20; *Capt.* 10 Oct. 26.				
8	0	*Adjutant.*—Rich. Walter Lacy, (*Lieut.*) 29 Dec. 37.				
5	0	*Quarter-Master.*—Thomas Debenham, 17 Feb. 35.				
27	0	*Surgeon.*—𝔅 Matthew Neill,[6] 29 Dec. 37; *Assist.-Surg.* 6 Nov. 23; *Hosp.-Assist.* 10 Jan. 14.				
14	0	*Assistant-Surgeons.*—Edw. Bradford, 20 March, 28; *Hosp.-Assist.* 5 Dec. 26				
5	0	Neil Stewart Campbell, M. D. 20 Feb. 35.				

Facings Purple.—*Agent*, Messrs. Cox & Co.—*Irish Agent*, Messrs. Borough, Armit & Co.

1 Sir Hudson Lowe was present at the attack of Martello Tower, storming of Convention Redoubt, and the sieges of Bastia and Calvi; served in the expedition to Egypt, and was present in the principal occurrences of that campaign; accompanied the expedition to the Bay of Naples, and commanded the first line of the advance. He was present at the attack and capitulation of Ischia; and subsequently at the attack and capitulation of Zante and Cephalonia.

2 Major Palmer served the campaigns of 1814 in Holland, including the actions at Merxem, and bombardment of the French fleet in the Scheldt.

4 Lieut. Telford served in the Peninsula from March 1812 to the end of the war, including the battle of Salamanca, retreat from Burgos, and action of Villa Murilla; affair at Osma, battle of Vittoria, carrying of the outworks of San Sebastian 17th July, and first assault on the body of the Fortress 25th July; also second assault and capture 31st Aug. 1813; battles of the Nivelle, 10th Nov., und Nive, 9th, 10th, and 11th Dec. 1813. Served subsequently in the American war.

| Emb. for For. Service, 1825. | **57th (or West Middlesex) Regiment of Foot.** | Serving in the East Indies. |

"ALBUHERA"—"VITTORIA"—"PYRENEES"—"NIVELLE"—"NIVE"—"PENINSULA."

Colonel.

Years' Serv.		
45		Right Hon. Sir Fred. Adam,[1] K. C. B. & G. C. M. G. Ens. 4 Nov. 1795; Lieut. 2 Feb. 96; Capt. 30 Aug. 99; Major, 9 July, 1803; Lieut.-Col. 28 Aug. 04; Col. 20 Feb. 12; Major-Gen. 4 June 14; Lieut.-Gen. 22 July, 30; Col. 54th Regt. 4 Dec. 35.
Full Pay.	Half Pay.	

Lieut.-Colonels.

39	6 8/12	James Allan,[2] C. B. Ens. P 1 Jan. 95; Lieut. P 18 Mar. 95; Capt. P 10 Sept. 99; Major, P 20 July 09; Brevet-Lieut.-Col. 4 June, 14; Regtl.-Lieut.-Col. 29 June, 26; Col. 10 Jan. 37.
34	0	George E. Jones,[3] K.H. Ens. 16 June, 06; Lieut. 16 April, 07; Capt. P 8 Oct. 12; Brev.-Maj. 22 July, 30; Regt.-Maj. P 4 Dec. 32; Lieut.-Col. P 8 Nov. 33.

Majors.—

42	5/12	Robert Hunt,[4] Ens. P 25, Jan. 98; Lieut. 6 Nov. 99; Capt. 11 May, 09; Brevet-Major, 22 July, 30; Regtl.-Major, 28 Sept. 30.
29	1/12	Philip Aubin,[5] Ens. P 14 Feb. 11; Lieut. 29 April, 13; Capt. 22 June, 26; Major, P 12 April, 31.

CAPTAINS.

Years	Half	Name	ENSIGN	LIEUT.	CAPTAIN	BREV.-MAJ.
35	7/12	Vance Y. Donaldson[6]	14 Sept. 04	25 Dec. 05	24 June 13	10 Jan. 37
31	0	James Jackson[7]	2 Mar. 09	19 June 11	7 Apr. 25	28 June 38
31	6 7/12	Harvey Welman[8]	P 5 Aug. 02	18 Feb. 04	2 Nov. 09	22 July 30
25	5/12	James Brown	P 15 June 15	5 Oct. 20	28 Sept. 30	
15	0	Thomas Shadforth	8 Apr. 25	P 10 Oct. 26	P 12 Apr. 31	
15	0	Clark Maries Caldwell	12 Jan. 26	P 27 Apr. 27	P 25 Jan. 31	
15	0	William John Saunders	9 Apr. 25	P 12 Feb. 30	P 12 Apr. 33	
23	2 4/12	Thomas Bainbrigge	24 May 15	P 3 Apr. 23	1 Aug. 35	
28	0	Mars Morphett[9]	1 Oct. 12	29 June 15	29 Jan. 36	
20	8	John Ovens[10]	2 July 12	5 July 14	9 Sept. 37	

LIEUTENANTS.

18	10	William Bate	2 Apr. 12	14 June 13	
17	0	Henry Hill	31 July 23	3 Aug. 26	
15	6	George Edwards	P 1 Apr. 19	25 Oct. 27	
14	0	Leonard Smith[11]	10 Aug. 26	22 Nov. 27	
14	0	Edmond Lockyer	3 Aug. 26	29 Sept. 30	
14	11 1/2	Wm. Justin Mac Carthy	15 June 15	30 Sept. 30	
12	0	William Tranter	P 11 Dec. 28	P 12 Apr. 31	
17	5 10/12	Thos. Fred. Richardson	25 Dec. 17	26 Apr. 28	
10	0	Henry Gahan	P 13 June 30	P 15 June 32	
10	0	A. T. Allan	29 Sept. 30	P 28 Dec. 32	
8	0	Fred. Hall Jackson	P 10 Feb. 32	P 13 June 34	
8	0	John Mockler	25 May 32	P 12 Sept. 34	
8	0	Wm. Bridger Goodrich	P 15 June 32	P 20 Feb. 35	
9	0	Henry Montagu Smyth	7 June 31	P 20 Mar. 35	
6	0	James Allan	P 13 June 34	P 20 Jan. 37	
10	0	William Jones	P 13 Aug. 30	27 Oct.	
6	0	Langford Frost	12 Aug. 34	9 Sept. 37	
5	0	Elphingston Junor	P 20 Feb. 35	P 9 Feb. 38	
5	0	Edward A. Thos. Lynch	P 20 Mar. 35	6 May 38	
5	0	Edward Stanley	8 May 35	10 June 38	
5	0	Geo. Henry Hunt	P 8 Jan. 36	P 29 Nov. 38	
4	0	John M'Namee	20 Jan. 37	25 Oct. 39	
9	2 1 10/12	Charles Jago	4 May 09	23 Jan. 12	

ENSIGNS.

3	0	F. C. W. Fitzpatrick	20 Oct. 37	
3	0	John Ahmuty	17 Nov. 37	
2	0	Warren Ahmuty	P 16 Feb. 38	
4	0	Fred. Thornton Raikes	1 Apr. 36	
2	0	Loftus Cassidy	P 9 Nov. 38	
2	0	David Edw. Armstrong	25 Dec. 38	
2	0	Hen. Braddel Croker	P 25 Jan. 39	
1	0	Lachlan Nicoll M'Lachlan	25 Oct. 39	

Paymaster.—

17	0	**Adjutant.—**Henry Hill, (Lieut.) 3 Aug. 26.
6	0	**Quarter-Master.—**James E. Langford, 21 Nov. 34.
25	0	**Surgeon.—**Alex. Braithwaite Morgan, 22 Nov. 39; Assist.-Surg. 27 Oct. 25; Hosp.-Assist. 21 Dec. 15.
6	0	**Assistant-Surgeons.—**Robert Henry Neville, 26 July 34.
2	0	George Robert Fraser, M. D., 27 July, 38.

Facings Yellow.—**Agent,** Mr. Lawrie, Charles-street, St. James's.

4 Maj. Hunt's services: Expedition to Hanover in 1805, and to Madeira in 1808. Campaign and battle of Corunna. Peninsula, from Feb. 1812 to the end of the war, and subsequently in the American war.

5 Major Aubin served in the Peninsula, from Nov. 1811 to the end of the war, including the battles of Vittoria, the Pyrenees, 25th, 28th, 30th, and 31st July; Nivelle, Nive, 9th, 11th and 13th Dec. 1813, besides many other minor actions and skirmishes. Severely wounded through the left side, in action at Couchez, 18th March, 1814.

6 Major Donaldson served in the Peninsula, from June 1809 to the end of the war, including the siege of Badajoz in April, 1811; battles of Albuhera, Vittoria, and the Pyrenees

7 Major Jackson served in the Peninsula, from Dec. 1809 to 1814, and was severely wounded through the left breast and in both arms at the battle of Albuhera, 16th May, 1811. Served subsequently in the American war.

8 Major Welman served at the battles of Roleia, Vimiera, and Corunna. With the expedition to Walcheren in 1809; & subsequently in the Peninsula, including the siege of Tarragona in 1811, and San Sebastian in Sept. 1813.

9 Capt. Morphett served the campaign of 1812 in the Peninsula, and received two slight and one severe wound at Salamanca. Present at the capture of Fort Jeytuch, East Indies, May, 1815

10 Capt. Ovens served in the Peninsula, from Nov. 1812 to the end of the war, including the battles of Vittoria, Pampeluna (wounded), Nivelle, Orthes & Toulouse. Served subsequently in the American war, including the action at Plattsburgh.

11 Lieut. L. Smith served in the Burmese war.

1 Sir Frederick Adam served in Holland, and was present in the actions of the 27th August, 19th September, and 2nd October, 1799; took part in the actions of the 8th, 13th, and 21st March, 1801, in Egypt. Sir Frederick was severely wounded near Alicant, 12th April, 1813; at the pass of Ordall he received two wounds, one which broke his left arm, and another which shattered his left hand; and he was also severely wounded at Waterloo.

2 Col. Allen was present at the capture of the Cape of Good Hope in 1795, and subsequently in 1806, including the battle of Blueberg. Served the whole of the Mysore campaign of 1799, including the battle of Mallavelly; siege and storm of Seringapatam, for which he has received a medal Engaged in the pursuit and dispersion of the Rebel Dundeah, and all his forces; the reduction and occupation of Tranquebar, and the whole of the southern Polygar war in 1800. Served in the Peninsula from 1810 to the end of the war. Medal for Toulouse. (Note 3 see foot of next page.)

58th (or the Rutlandshire) Regiment of Foot.

"GIBRALTAR"—with the *Castle and Key*, "*Montis Insignia Calpe.*"—The *Sphinx*, with the words "EGYPT"—"MAIDA"—"SALAMANCA"—"VITTORIA"—"PYRENEES"—"NIVELLE"—"ORTHES"—"PENINSULA."

Years' Serv.						
61		*Colonel.*				
Full Pay.	Half Pay.	₿ Frederick Maitland,[1] *Ens.* 1 Sept. 1779; *Lieut.* 19 Sept. 82; *Capt.* 2 Dec. 89; *Major*, 21 Aug. 93; *Lieut.-Col.* 2 July, 94; *Col.* 1 Jan. 1800; *Major-Gen.* 30 Oct. 05; *Lieut.-Gen.* 4 June, 11; *Gen.* 25 May, 25; *Col.* 58th Regiment, 11 Dec. 33.				
35	8/12	*Lieut.-Colonel.* John Wharton Frith,[2] *Ens.* P 17 July, 04; *Lieut.* 27 Feb. 05; *Capt.* 29 Jan. 12; *Major*, 22 July, 30; *Lieut.-Col.* P 16 Dec. 36.				
26	3/12	*Majors.*—William Firebrace,[3] *Ens.* 28 July, 14, *Lieut.* 20 June, 17; *Capt.* P 28 Mar. 22; *Major*, P 16 Dec. 36.				
26	1 1/12	Henry Houghton Irving, *Ens.* 1 Feb. 14; *Lieut.* 26 Dec. 16; *Capt.* P 3 June, 24; *Major*, 11 July, 37.				

Years' Serv. Full	Half	CAPTAINS.	ENSIGN.	LIEUT.	CAPTAIN.	BREV.-MAJ.
21	0	Rob. Henry Wynyard ..	25 Feb. 19	P 17 July 23	P 20 May 26	
16	0	Thomas John Grant	28 Mar. 24	P 21 July 25	P 18 Oct. 27	
27	0	Adam Beverhoudt[4]	21 Oct. 13	9 Apr. 16	29 Apr. 36	
15	0	Cyprian Bridge	8 Apr. 25	P 31 Jan. 28	P 16 Dec. 36	
14	10/12	Cha. Aug. Arney	P 5 Nov. 25	P 9 Aug. 31	P 1 July 37	
15	0	Alex. Boddam	P 5 Jan. 26	P 28 Sept. 30	P 11 Nov. 36	
9	0	Wm. Edward Grant	P 23 Dec. 31	P 13 May 36	P 23 Apr. 39	
13	0	F. J. Taggart Hutchinson	P 18 Dec. 27	P 17 May 31	P 17 Mar. 38	
21	1 5/12	William Henry Rogers ..	21 May 18	30 Sept. 19	P 21 Sept. 38	
7	0	Geo. Ponsonby Hume ..	P 28 June 33	P 16 Dec. 36	P 20 Sept. 39	
		LIEUTENANTS.				
14	5/12	Jonas Paisley Hardy....	29 Sept. 25	3 Nov. 26		
20	10 1/12	Robert Hutton[4]........	7 Mar. 10	30 July 12		
6	0	Joseph Hen. Laye	P 2 May 34	1 Dec. 37		
7	0	Dav. Elliott M'Kirdy ...	P 5 Apr. 33	P 30 Dec. 36		
5	0	Cha. Lavallin Nugent ..	P 21 Aug. 35	4 Feb. 38		
4	0	Charles Dresing	P 19 Feb. 36	2 June 38		
4	0	Moore Hill	P 26 Feb. 36	P 20 July 38		
4	0	Richard Denny	P 13 May 36	P 12 Oct. 38		
9	0	Wm. Dixwell Oxenden..	P 6 Apr. 31	P 3 Apr. 35		
4	0	John Perkins Mayers ..	29 July 36	P 23 Apr. 39		
4	0	Chas. Wm. Thompson ..	P 23 Dec. 36	P 3 May 39		
4	0	Alexander Macleod Hay	P 22 July 36	19 Oct. 38		
3	0	Michael King..........	15 Dec. 37	P 20 Sept. 39		
		ENSIGNS.				
2	0	Cha. C. Master	P 6 July 38			
2	0	Hen. C. Balneavis	7 July 38			
2	0	John S. Flack..........	26 June 38			
2	0	J. A. C. Petley	P 12 Oct. 38			
2	0	J. M'Lerie	28 Dec. 38			
1	0	Isaac Rhodes Cooper ..	P 23 Apr. 39			
1	0	John Wm. Saunders	P 3 May 39			
1	0	Michael Lionel Westropp	P 20 Sept. 39			
31	0	*Paymaster.*—₿ Edw. Fugion,[5] 23 Dec. 19; *Ens.* 4 May, 09; *Lieut.* 25 July, 11.				
2	0	*Adjutant.*—John M'Lerie, (*Ens.*) 28 Dec. 38.				
10	0	*Quarter-Master.*—Richard Timbrell, 19 Nov. 30.				
		Surgeon.—₿ John Munro, 8 Feb. 39; *Assist.-Surg.* 26 May, 14.				
8	0	*Assist.-Surgeon.*—Geo. Kincaird Pitcairn, M.D. 23 Nov. 32.				

Facings Black.—*Agent*, Messrs. Cox & Co.

[*Returned from Ceylon, June*, 1839.]

1 Gen. Maitland served at the relief of Gibraltar in 1787; and was continued for many years Military Secretary to Sir Ralph Abercrombie in the West Indies, and during about 30 years' service in that climate, he was at the reduction of every Island taken by the British arms; and commanded at the Saintes. In 1811, he was removed, by orders from home, from the Government of Granada to the Mediterranean, where he commanded the British army until the arrival of Lord W. Bentinck; and subsequently took a force of ten thousand men from Sicily to the eastern coast of Spain. Medal for Martinique.

2 Col. Frith was present in several affairs consequent upon the operations carried on by the division of the army under Col. Chambers in the Travancore war, particularly on the 15th January and 21st Feb. 1809. Served also at the capture of the Isle of Bourbon, and the Isle of France in 1810.

3 Major Firebrace served at the capture of Les Saintes, and Guadaloupe in 1815.

4 Capt. Beverhoudt and Lieut. Hutton served at the capture of Guadaloupe in 1815.

5 Paymaster Fugion served in the Peninsula from July, 1809 to the end of the war, including the battle of Salamanca; siege of Burgos; and battle of Orthes.

3 Col. Jones served with the expedition to South America in 1807; at the capture of the Isle of France in 1810. Served also in Ava, and commanded the 89th regiment in the general action and attack of the enemy's intrenched lines before Rangoon, 7th Dec. 1824.

Emb. for Foreign Service, 1834.] **59th (*or* 2nd *Nottinghamshire*) Regiment of Foot.** [**Serving at Corfu.**

"CAPE OF GOOD HOPE"—"CORUNNA"—"JAVA"—"VITTORIA"—"ST. SEBASTIAN"—"NIVE"—"PENINSULA"—"BHURTPORE."

Years' Serv.		Colonel.
62		ℙ Sir Fred. Philipse Robinson,¹ G.C.B. *Ens.* 11 Sept. 1778; *Lieut.* 1 Sept. 79; *Capt.* 3 July, 94; *Major*, 1 Sept. 94; *Lieut.-Col.* 1 Jan. 1800; *Col.* 25 July, 10; *Major-Gen.* 4 June, 13; *Lieut.-Gen.* 27 May, 25; *Col.* 59th Regiment, 1 Dec. 27.
Full Pay.	Half Pay.	*Lieut.-Colonel.*
35	0	Francis Fuller,² *Ens.* 16 Jan. 06; *Lieut.* 11 Oct. 07; *Capt.* ᴾ13 Feb.12; *Brevet-Major*, 22 July, 30; *Regtl.-Major*, 4 Aug. 30; *Lieut.-Col.* ᴾ22 Aug. 34.
		Majors.—Duncan Gordon,³ *Ens.* 30 July, 07; *Lieut.* 9 June, 08; *Capt.* 20 April, 15; *Major*, ᴾ4 July, 34.
33	0	
31	0	ℙ ℚℳ Nicholas Hovenden,⁴ *Ens.* 6 April, 09; *Lieut.* 12 Dec. 11; *Capt.* 19 Jan. 26; *Major*, ᴾ22 Aug. 34.

		CAPTAINS.	ENSIGN.	LIEUT.	CAPTAIN.	BREV.-MAJ.
31	0	ℙ Richard Manners⁵....	13 Apr. 09	ᴾ 8 Feb. 10	22 May 23	28 June 38
16	1/12	Wm. Fuller.............	25 May 24	6 Jan. 26	ᴾ 9 July 29	
19	0	Richard Floyer.........	ᴾ 1 May 21	ᴾ17 Sept. 25	ᴾ17 Jan. 28	
15	0	Geo. Netherton Harward	ᴾ 3 Nov. 25	ᴾ24 Aug. 26	ᴾ 2 Nov. 30	
11	0	Henry Hope Graham....	ᴾ15 Oct. 29	ᴾ 7 Sept. 32	ᴾ 7 Nov. 34	
21	7 4/12	John Levick	8 Oct. 12	24 Jan. 25	31 July 37	
10	0	Arnold E. Burmester....	31 Aug. 30	ᴾ 7 Mar. 34	ᴾ16 Mar. 38	
9	0	Geo. F. F. Boughey	ᴾ 1 Nov. 31	ᴾ11 July 34	ᴾ 1 June 38	
9	0	Rob. Spencer Boland....	15 Dec. 31	ᴾ 1 Feb. 33	ᴾ17 Nov. 37	
29	2	ℙ Wm. Graham⁶	13 July 09	12 May 12	7 Apr. 25	28 June 38
		LIEUTENANTS.				
14	0	James Mockler	22 Feb. 27	1 Nov. 31	6 Major Graham served at the siege of Flushing in 1809, and subsequently in the Peninsula, including the blockade of Bayonne. Served also in the American war, including the action at Bladensburgh and capture of Washington; action near Baltimore, and those in front of New Orleans on the 20th Dec 1814, and 8th Jan. 1815. Also at the taking of Fort Boyer.	
9	0	Adam J. Laing Peebles..	12 Apr. 31	ᴾ13 June 34		
9	0	Thomas Smith	ᴾ13 Sept. 31	ᴾ 4 July 34		
8	0	Edward Hen. Poyntz ..	ᴾ 7 Sept. 32	ᴾ22 Aug. 34		
7	0	Geo. Nares Heard	26 Apr. 33	ᴾ10 Apr. 35		
6	0	Wm. Wynne Lodder	ᴾ 7 Mar. 34	ᴾ 5 June 35		
6	0	William Foulis	ᴾ11 July 34	ᴾ17 Mar. 37		
6	0	Hon. Jas. Pierce Maxwell	ᴾ 6 June 34	ᴾ 5 May 37		
9	18 7/12	ℙ Edw. James Taylor⁷ ..	31 Dec. 12	28 Sept. 14	7 Lieut. Taylor served in the Peninsula, and was present at the battles of Nivelle and Orthes, besides several skirmishes.	
6	0	H. Wedderburn Cumming	ᴾ22 Aug. 34	ᴾ16 Mar. 38		
6	0	Henry Perrott	ᴾ 7 Nov. 34	ᴾ 1 June 38		
13	4/12	John Matcham Isaac....	4 Nov. 26	3 Sept. 29	8 Quarter-master Ellary served at the capture of the Cape of Good Hope in 1806; in the Travancore war in the East Indies in 1809; capture of the Isle of France in 1810; storming of Fort Cornelius and capture of Java in 1811, Balli and Macassar in 1814; Kandian campaign of 1818; and siege and assault of Bhurtpore in 1825 and 6. 9 Dr. Hibbert served in the Peninsula from 1812 to 1814, including the affair at Vigue; battle of Vittoria, and action of St. Jean de Luz.	
5	0	Wm. Fulton	ᴾ10 Apr. 35	ᴾ11 Oct. 39		
		ENSIGNS.				
5	0	Hen. W. Gordon	28 Aug. 35			
4	0	Eytre T. J. R. Nugent ..	12 Mar. 36			
4	0	John Tomline..........	ᴾ 4 June 36			
3	0	Thomas Peebles	ᴾ17 Mar. 37			
3	0	J. Herbert Clay	ᴾ 5 May 37			
2	0	Fra. Fuller	ᴾ16 Mar. 38			
2	0	Wm. Aug. Gaussen	ᴾ17 Aug. 38			
1	0	Cha. Townsend Wilson ..	ᴾ11 Oct. 39			
15	0	*Paymaster.*—Chas. Roberts, 23 June, 37; *Ens.* 10 April, 25; *Lieut.* 29 Sept. 29.				
9	0	*Adjutant.*—A. J. L. Peebles, (*Lieut.*) 1 Feb. 39.				
19	0	*Quarter-Master.*—William Ellary,⁸ 10 June, 21.				
29	6 4/12	*Surgeon.*—ℙ John Gray Hibbert,⁹ M.D. 26 May, 14; *Assist.-Surg.* 12 Oct. 09; *Hosp.-Assist.* 6 May, 05.				
19	0	*Assist.-Surgs.*—John Mair, M.D. 10 Nov. 25; *Hosp.-Assist.* 8 Nov. 21.				
3	0	Frederic Roberts, 11 Aug. 37.				

Facings White.—*Agent*, Messrs. Cox & Co.—*Irish Agent*, Messrs. Borough, Armit & Co.

1 Sir Fred. Robinson served in the first American war, and was subsequently at the taking of various Islands in the West Indies. Sir Frederick has received a medal and two clasps for Vittoria, St. Sebastian (severely wounded), and the passage of the Nive, where he was again severely wounded.

2 Col. Fuller was at the taking of Macassar in the island of Celebes, 9th June, 1814. Served also at the siege and capture of Bhurtpore in 1825 and 6.

3 Major Gordon served at the capture of the Isle of France in 1810, and of Java in 1811, and was wounded at the assault of Fort Cornelius. Served also at the siege and capture of Bhurtpore.

4 Major Hovenden served in the Peninsula, from Aug. 1812 to Nov. 1813, including the battle of Vittoria and storming of San Sebastian, 31 Aug. 1813, where he was severely wounded. Present at Waterloo, storming of Cambray, and capture of Paris. Served the Mahratta campaigns of 1817 and 18, and was engaged at the siege and storm of Bhurtpore.

5 Major Manners served in the Peninsula, from Aug. 1812 to May, 1814, including the battle of Vittoria, siege and storm of San Sebastian, Aug. 1813; battle of the Nive, 9th, 10th, and 11th Dec. 1813. Wounded at the storming of Bhurtpore, 18th January, 1826.

60th (or the King's Royal Rifle Corps.)

"*Celer et audax.*"

"Roleia"—"Vimiera"—"Martinique"—"Talavera"—"Fuentes d'Onor"—
"Albuhera"—"Ciudad Rodrigo"—"Badajoz"—"Salamanca"—"Vittoria"
"Pyrenees"—"Nivelle"—"Nive"—"Orthes"—"Toulouse"—"Peninsula."

Years' Serv.		
		Colonel-in-Chief.
		His Royal Highness A. F. Duke of Cambridge. (*See* Coldstream Guards.)
		Colonels Commandant.
46		1 ₿ Sir John Maclean,¹ K.C.B. *Ens.* 30 April, 1794; *Lieut.* 1 May, 94; *Capt.* 15 June, 97; *Major*, 2 Aug. 04; *Lieut.-Col.* 9 June 08; *Col.* 4 June, 14; *Major-Gen.* 27 May, 25; *Lieut.-Gen.* 28 June, 38; *Col.* 60th Rifles, 7 Jan. 35.
47		2 Hon. Patrick Stuart, *Cornet & Sub-Lieut.* 26 Sept. 93; *Lieut.* 6 June, 94; *Capt.* 12 April, 96; *Major*, 1 Feb. 03; *Lieut.-Col.*,25 Sept. 06; *Col.* 4 June, 14; *Major-Gen.* 19 July, 21; *Lieut.-Gen.* 10 Jan. 37; *Col.* 60th Rifles, 26 Sept. 37.

Full Pay.	Half Pay.		*Lieut.-Colonels.*
22	1	2	Hon. Aug. Fred. Ellis, *Cornet*, ᴾ 10 April, 17; *Lieut.* ᴾ 17 Dec. 18; *Capt.* ᴾ 24 Oct. 21; *Major*, ᴾ 12 Nov. 25; *Lieut.-Col.* ᴾ 18 Dec. 28.
22	1 2/12	1	Hon. Hen. Rich. Molyneux, *Ens.* ᴾ 22 May, 17; *Lieut.* ᴾ 24 Oct. 21; *Capt.* ᴾ 9 May, 23; *Major*, ᴾ 29 Aug. 26; *Lieut.-Col.* ᴾ 9 April, 29.
27	7/12		*Majors.*—2 ₿ J. Clavell Sladdon Slyfield,² K.H. *Ens.* 15 Oct. 12; *Lieut.* 30 Mar. 14; *Capt.* ᴾ 26 May, 25; *Major*, ᴾ 12 April, 31.
20	2 9/12	1	Walter Trevelyan, *2nd Lieut.* 18 Nov. 17; *Lieut.* 25 Sept. 25; *Capt.* ᴾ 19 Sept. 26; *Major*, ᴾ 28 Dec. 32.
18	9/12	2	Charles Markham, *Cornet*, ᴾ 28 June, 21; *Lieut.* ᴾ 23 June, 25; *Capt.* ᴾ 29 Aug. 26; *Major*, ᴾ 31 May, 33.
18	5	1	Wemyss Thos. Cockburn, *Cornet*, ᴾ 22 May, 17; *Lieut.* ᴾ 10 Dec. 18; *Capt.* ᴾ 26 Dec. 22; *Major*, ᴾ 25 Nov. 28.

			CAPTAINS.	2D LIEUT.	LIEUT.	CAPTAIN.	BREVET-MAJOR.
40	0	1	Melville Glenie³	23 Oct. 00	30 June 03	4 July 08	27 May 25
27	0	2	Ambrose Spong	15 Aug. 13	ᴾ 26 April 14	ᴾ 18 Nov. 24	28 June 38
16	0	2	Cosby Lewis Nesbitt ..	27 Mar. 24	ᴾ 2 June 25	ᴾ 18 Dec. 28	
16	0	1	Hon. G. Aug. Spencer..	ᴾ 12 Feb. 24	ᴾ 16 June 25	ᴾ 19 Dec. 26	
17	0	1	Edward Bagot	23 Oct. 23	ᴾ 10 Dec. 25	ᴾ 8 Nov. 27	
16	0	1	John Sutton Wilford ..	ᴾ 19 Nov. 24	ᴾ 25 Dec. 25	ᴾ 2 Nov. 30	
16	0	1	David Fitz Gerald	ᴾ 23 Dec. 24	ᴾ 28 Jan. 26	ᴾ 12 July 31	
14	1 3/12	1	Randal Rumley	ᴾ 30 Dec. 24	ᴾ 8 Oct. 25	ᴾ 14 Aug. 27	
16	0	1	Richard Gibbons......	ᴾ 18 Nov. 24	ᴾ 8 April 26	ᴾ 9 Aug. 32	
14	1 2/12	2	Fred. Wm. Hamilton..	10 June 25	ᴾ 8 April 26	ᴾ 4 Jan. 31	
16	0	1	Thomas Crombie......	ᴾ 12 Aug. 24	ᴾ 8 April 26	ᴾ 18 May 32	
15	0	2	Freeman Murray	ᴾ 24 Feb. 25	ᴾ 8 April 26	ᴾ 21 Dec. 32	
14	0	2	George Bulman	ᴾ 8 April 26	1 Nov. 30	ᴾ 29 May 35	
14	0	2	Chas. Orgell Leman ..	ᴾ 12 April 26	ᴾ 12 April 31	ᴾ 4 Sept. 35	
14	2/12	2	Edward Carter Giffard	23 Nov. 26	ᴾ 8 Feb. 31	ᴾ 9 Oct. 35	
14	0	2	Robert Atkins	ᴾ 24 Aug. 26	ᴾ 12 July 31	ᴾ 16 Sept. 36	
12	0	2	George Stewart	ᴾ 25 Nov. 28	ᴾ 11 Oct. 31	ᴾ 8 July 36	
11	0	1	Harrington Trevelyan	ᴾ 16 April 29	ᴾ 24 Aug. 32	ᴾ 7 April 37	
13	0	2	James St John Munro	ᴾ 29 Mar. 27	ᴾ 9 Aug. 32	ᴾ 17 Nov. 37	
9	12 10/12	1	John Temple	ᴾ 14 May 18	ᴾ 21 Oct. 24	ᴾ 28 Jan. 26	

1 Sir John Maclean accompanied his regiment (the 92nd) to Holland, in 1799, and was present at the battle of the 27th August, the taking of the Helder, and the actions of the 10th and 19th September, and 2nd October, near Alkmar, where he was severely wounded in two places. Accompanied the expedition to Egypt in 1801, and was present at the landing at Aboukir Bay, 8th March; at the battle of Alexandria, 21st March; and at every action which took place in Egypt during that campaign. Served in the expedition to Hanover, 1805 and 06; also in the expedition to Sweden, 1808. Embarked for the Peninsula in 1808; was present at the battle of Busaco; the action near Redinha; siege of Olivença; siege of Badajos, where he was severely wounded; the action near Canizal, where his battalion and the 40th regiment attacked a column of the enemy double their number, and put them to flight; the battles of Salamanca, Vittoria, the Pyrenees, near Pampeluna (wounded), Nivelle, Bayonne, Orthes, and Toulouse, where he was severely wounded, it being the fifth wound he received in the service of his country. Sir John has received a cross and two clasps.

2 Major Slyfield embarked with the 84th regiment, and joined the army near San Sebastian, 16th Sept. 1813. Present at the crossing of the Bidassoa; battles of Nivelle and Nive, (from 9th to 13th Dec.); and sortie from Bayonne.

3 Brevet-Lieut.-Col. 28 June, 1838.

60th (or the King's Royal Rifle Corps.)

Years' Serv. Full Pay.	Half Pay.		LIEUTENANTS.	2ND LIEUT.	LIEUT.	
15	0	1	Chas. Howe Spence ..	20 April 25	p 28 Sept. 26	4 Capt. Coxen served at the siege of Flushing in 1809, and subsequently in the Peninsula, including the lines of Torres Vedras; actions at Pombal, Redinha, Mirando de Corvo, Ponte de Rheux, Sabugal, Almeida; battle of Fuentes d' Onor; siege and storm of Ciudad Rodrigo; siege and storm of Badajoz, 16 March, 1812; battle of Salamanca; capture of Madrid; actions at Zamarnos and San Milan; battle of Vittoria; Lezacco, Vera bridge and heights; battles of Nivelle, Nive, (from 9th to 13th Dec.) Orthes, and affair at Tarbes. Severely wounded in the knee on the 18th June at Waterloo.
13	0	1	Henry Bingham	p 30 April 27	p 28 Sept. 32	
13	0	1	Thomas Bunbury	23 Jan. 28	p 28 Dec. 32	
12	0	2	John Jones..........	p 12 June 28	p 2 Dec. 31	
13	0	2	Thomas Townsend....	24 Jan. 28	20 June 33	
12	0	1	Hon. The. D. G. Dillon	31 July 28	p 21 June 33	
12	0	1	Wm. Fanshaw Bedford	p 18 Dec. 28	p 28 June 33	
11	0	1	Hon. H. Lyttle. Powys	p 2 April 29	p 19 Sept. 34	
11	0	1	Henry Wm. Ellis	p 14 May 29	p 17 April 35	
10	0	2	A. A. T. Cunynghame	p 2 Nov. 30	p 22 May 35	
10	0	1	Robert Aldridge	9 July 30	p 29 May 35	
8	0	2	Walling Everard	p 7 Sept. 32	p 15 May 35	
9	0	2	Rich. Byrd Levett....	p 12 April 31	p 4 Sept. 35	
10	0	2	Richard Maxwell	p 16 July 30	p 8 Feb. 33	
7	0	1	Fra. Roger Palmer ..	p 15 Mar. 33	p 24 April 35	
8	0	1	Geo. Hen. Courtenay	p 9 Mar. 32	p 8 April 36	
9	0	2	J. Kenneth Mackenzie	p 16 Dec. 31	p 16 Sept. 36	
8	0	2	Charles Wm. Jebb....	p 12 Oct. 32	p 17 Nov. 37	
8	0	2	Sir Ross Mahon, Bart.	p 14 Dec. 32	p 23 Nov. 38	
8	0	1	Wm. Stamer O'Grady	p 15 Jan. 33	p 31 Oct. 34	
6	0	2	John Stephen Robinson	p 11 April 34	p 19 Oct. 39	

2ND LIEUTS.

Years' Serv. Full Pay.	Half Pay.			2ND LIEUTS.	
6	0	1	Edw. J. Vesey Brown	p 12 Sept. 34	
6	0	1	Webbe Butler	p 19 Sept. 34	
5	0	1	Thomas Mitchell	27 Feb. 35	
5	0	2	Hen. R. Beresford....	p 22 May 35	
5	0	1	Henry Holbech......	p 29 May 35	
5	0	2	Hon. J. E. H. Thurlow	p 4 Sept. 35	
5	0	2	R. Ingram Dansey ..	p 5 Sept. 35	
4	0	2	Wm. Mark Wood	p 22 July 36	
4	0	2	Hon. Cornw. Maude..	p 16 Sept. 36	
4	0	2	John H. E. Ridley ..	p 23 Sept. 36	
4	0	1	Cha. Sedley Burdett..	p 21 Oct. 36	
3	0	2	Wm. Lewis Grant....	p 7 April 37	
3	0	1	Geo. Allan Hicks	p 27 Oct. 37	
3	0	2	Thomas Bateson	p 8 Dec. 37	
2	0	1	James Douglas	p 17 Aug. 38	
2	0	2	Hon. Adrian Hope ..	p 23 Nov. 38	
2	0	1	Cha. W. H. Sotheby..	p 25 Dec. 38	
1	0	1	Hon. A. C. L. Fitz Roy	p 17 May 39	
1	0	1	Hon. Elias R. Plunkett	p 20 July 39	
1	0	2	Rich. F. Waldo Sibthorp	p 20 Sept. 39	
1	0	1	John Breedon........	p 19 Oct. 39	

Paymasters.
| 31 | 1/12 | 1 | ⚐ Edward Coxen,⁴ 9 Feb. 26; 2nd Lieut. 5 April, 09; Lieut. 28 June, 10; Capt. 8 April, 25. |
| 13 | 0 | 2 | William Henry Fitzgerald, 20 Sept. 39; Ens. 17 Jan. 28; Lieut. 31 May, 33. |

Adjutants.
| 13 | 0 | 2 | Thomas Townsend (1st Lieut.) 24 Jan. 28. |
| 5 | 0 | 1 | Thomas Mitchell (2nd Lieut.) 27 Feb. 35. |

Quarter-Masters.
| 5 | 0 | 2 | ⚐ John Brannan, 18 Sept. 35; Ens. 5 Sept. 35. |
| 2 | 0 | 1 | Alan Waterhouse, 27 July, 38. |

Surgeons.
| | | 1 | Hugh Fraser, 30 Oct. 34; Assist.-Surg. 26 Jan. 15. |
| 24 | 1 6/12 | 2 | Peter Lamond, M.D. 7 June, 39; As.-Surg. 27 May, 24; Hosp.-Ass. 16 June, 15. |

Assistant-Surgeons.
5	0	2	David Morice, M.D. 29 May, 35.
		1	George Ferguson, 12 June, 28; Hosp.-Assist. 8 Nov. 26.
2	0	2	Johnstone Thomson Richardson, M.D. 1 Feb. 39.
2	0	1	Joshua Paynter, 11 Jan. 39.

[1st Battalion embarked for Foreign Service, 6 Oct. 30. Serving at Zante.]
[2nd Battalion embarked for Foreign Service, 15 Dec. 35. Serving at Corfu.]

Regimentals Green—Facings Scarlet—Agent, Messrs. Cox & Co.—Irish Agent, Borough, Armit & Co.

Emb. for Foreign Service, 1828.] **61st (or South Gloucestershire) Regt. of Foot.** [Serving at Ceylon.

The *Sphinx*, with the words, "EGYPT"—"TALAVERA"—"SALAMANCA"—"PYRENEES"—"NIVELLE"—"NIVE"—"ORTHES"—"TOULOUSE"—"PENINSULA"—Flank Companies, "MAIDA."

Years' Serv.						
78		\multicolumn{5}{l}{*Colonel.*}
Full Pay	Half Pay	\multicolumn{5}{l}{Rt. Hon. Sir George Hewett, Bt. G.C.B. *Ens.* 27 April, 1762; *Lieut.* 20 April, 64; *Capt.* 2 June, 75; *Major*, 31 Dec. 81; *Lieut.-Col.* 12 Oct. 87; *Col.* 1 March, 94; *Major-Gen.* 3 May 96; *Lieut.Gen.* 25 Sept. 1803; *Gen.* 4 June, 13; *Col.* 61st Regt. 4 April, 1800.}
26	8 5/12	\multicolumn{5}{l}{*Lieut.Colonel.*—Charles Forbes, *Ens.* 16 July, 06; *Lieut.* 11 March, 10; *Capt.* p 24 Oct. 21; *Major*, p 15 Aug. 26; *Lieut.-Col.* 28 June, 38.}
34	1 4/12	\multicolumn{5}{l}{*Majors.*—🅱 Henry Simmonds,¹ *Ens.* 21 March, 05; *Lieut.* 28 Nov. 05; *Capt.* p 31 March, 13; *Brevet-Major*, 10 Jan. 37; *Regtl.-Major*, 2 Dec. 37.}
33	3/12	\multicolumn{5}{l}{Henry Burnside,² *Ens.* 8 Oct. 07; *Lieut.* 18 Feb. 08; *Capt.* p 13 Nov. 17; *Brevet-Major*, 10 Jan. 37; *Regtl.-Major*, 28 June, 38.}

		CAPTAINS.	ENSIGN.	LIEUT.	CAPTAIN.	BREV.-MAJ.
31	0	🅱 Alex. M'Leod³	3 Aug. 09	p 12 Dec. 11	p 31 Dec. 25	28 June 38
27	0	Rob. Norris Verner	9 Dec. 13	30 Dec. 19	p 8 Oct. 30	
15	0	Frederick Barlow	8 Apr. 25	p 8 Apr. 26	p 12 Sept. 34	
15	0	William Jones	10 Apr. 25	p 12 Dec. 26	p 24 Nov. 35	
30	7/12	Peter Eason	5 Oct. 09	8 Oct. 10	21 June 33	
14	0	J. Barry Thomas	p 30 Dec. 26	p 9 Sept. 28	p 22 Nov. 36	
27	4 8/12	🅱 Charles Campbell⁴....	10 May 09	23 June 12	7 Nov. 27	
15	7 7/12	Fran. J. Swayne Hepburn	p 2 Apr. 18	p 12 May 25	28 June 38	
13	0	James Campbell........	22 Feb. 27	1 Apr. 31	p 25 Dec. 38	
14	0	Richard Gloster........	p 17 Aug. 26	18 Feb. 30	p 31 Dec. 39	
		LIEUTENANTS.				
14	0	John Geo. Philipps	p 19 Sept. 26	p 8 Oct. 30	5 Paymaster Toole served in the Peninsula from Feb. 1810 to March 1814, including the battles of Busaco, and Fuentes d'Onor; siege of Forts at, and battle of Salamanca (severely wounded in the left arm); battles of the Pyrenees (28th, 29th, 30th and 31st July) and Nivelle, where he was severely wounded in the right leg. 6 Quarter-Master Clarke served at the capture of Martinique in 1809, and Guadaloupe in 1810.	
14	0	Henry Vicars	p 26 Sept. 26	p 12 Apr. 31		
13	1 3/12	William Ward	p 18 July 26	p 4 Dec. 32		
9	0	Chas. Fred. H. Mayne ..	p 12 Apr. 31	p 13 Feb. 35		
9	0	Wm. Fra. Hoey	p 28 Oct. 31	5 Sept. 35		
10	0	John Tho. Bligh	p 28 Sept. 30	p 5 Feb. 36		
7	0	Wm. M. de Butts	24 Jan. 34	23 May 37		
6	0	Fra. John Stephens	p 12 Sept. 34	24 May 37		
5	0	Percival C. Fenwick	p 13 Feb. 35	p 10 Nov. 37		
5	0	Cha. Clement Deacon ..	p 28 Aug. 35	p 2 Dec. 37		
5	0	John Binney Gib	p 5 Feb. 36	28 June 38		
3	0	William J. Hamilton....	20 Apr. 37	5 July 39		
4	0	Wm. Jas. Tyrwhitt Walker	p 19 Aug. 36	p 31 Dec. 39		
		ENSIGNS.				
3	0	Tho. W. Hudson	p 16 June 37			
3	0	Tho. N. Dalton	22 June 37			
3	0	Wm. R. Browne........	29 June 37			
3	0	Edgar S. Smith	p 10 Nov. 37			
3	0	Geo. Edw. Coryton	p 2 Dec. 37			
2	0	Thomas Jones..........	9 Mar. 38			
2	0	George Howell	p 11 May 38			
1	0	Cha. Edward Prime	p 31 Dec. 39			
31	0	\multicolumn{5}{l}{*Paymaster.*—🅱 Archer Toole,⁵ 1 May, 28; *Ens.* 11 May, 09; *Lieut.* 30 Jan. 12.}
13	1 3/12	\multicolumn{5}{l}{*Adjutant.*—William Ward, (*Lieut.*) 26 Sept. 34.}
23	10/12	\multicolumn{5}{l}{*Quarter-Master.*—William Clarke,⁶ 16 Jan. 17.}
		\multicolumn{5}{l}{*Surgeon.*—James Smith, M.D. 15 Feb. 39; *Assist.-Surg.* 25 Sept. 12.}
1	0	\multicolumn{5}{l}{*Assist.-Surgeon.*—Francis Charles Annesley, 17 Sept. 39.}

Facings Buff.—*Agent*, Messrs. Cox & Co.—*Irish Agent*, Borough, Armit, & Co.

1 Major Simmonds served in the Peninsula from Feb. 1808 to Feb. 1813, including the battles of Talavera, Busaco, Albuhera; retreat from Madrid to Salamanca, and engaged every day during that retreat to Ciudad Rodrigo.

2 Major Burnside served at the capture of Martinique, and siege of Fort Deseix, March 1809; capture of Guadaloupe in 1810; and campaigns of 1813 and 14 in Canada.

3 Major M'Leod served the whole of the campaigns of 1810 and 11, first half of 1812, and the latter part of 1814, in the Peninsula, including the battles of Busaco, and Fuentes d'Onor, 3rd and 5th May 1811, and all the other operations.

4 Captain Charles Campbell served at the siege of Flushing in 1809; and subsequently in the Peninsula, including the battle of Castalla, and siege of Tarragona, under Sir J. Murray.

Emb. for Foreign Service, 1830.] **62nd (or Wiltshire) Regt. of Foot.** [Serving in the East Indies.

"PENINSULA."

Years' Serv.	Full Pay	Half Pay				
53	22	4 9/12	𝔓 Sir Archibald Campbell,[1] *Bart.* G.C.B. *Ens.* 28 Dec. 1787; *Lieut.* 26 April, 91; *Capt.* 17 May, 99; *Major*, 14 Sept. 04; *Lieut.-Col.* 16 Feb. 09; *Col.* 4 June, 14; *Major-Gen.* 27 May, 25; *Lieut.-Gen.* 28 June, 38; *Col.* 77th Regiment 23 Dec. 34. *Colonel*.			
30		1 9/12	*Lieut.-Colonels.*—𝔓𝔐 Thomas Reed, *Cornet*, 26 Aug. 13; *Lieut.* ᴾ 2 May, 15; *Capt.* ᴾ 19 Feb. 24; *Major*, ᴾ 15 June, 26; *Lieut.-Col.* ᴾ 11 Aug. 29.			
17		3/12	𝔓 𝔐 George Hillier, *Ens.* 23 March, 09; *Lieut.* 10 May, 10; *Capt.* 9 July, 12; *Brevet-Major*, 21 June, 17; *Regtl.-Major*, 17 Oct. 26; *Brevet-Lieut.-Col.* 24 July, 28; *Regtl.-Lieut.-Col.* 27 Sept. 35.			
13		0	*Majors.*—*Hon.* George Upton, *Ens.* ᴾ 24 April, 23; *Lieut.* ᴾ 29 Oct. 25; *Capt.* ᴾ 12 Dec. 26; *Major*, ᴾ 16 June, 37.			
			Francis J. Ellis, *Ens.* ᴾ 20 March, 27; *Lieut.* ᴾ 17 June, 29; *Capt.* ᴾ 10 May, 33; *Major*, ᴾ 16 March, 38.			

		CAPTAINS.	ENSIGN.	LIEUT.	CAPTAIN.	BREV.-MAJ.
15	0	Wm. T. Shortt.........	25 Mar. 25	ᴾ 30 Dec. 26	ᴾ 26 Feb. 29	
26	2 4/12	James Fraser Macdonell[2]	26 Dec. 11	23 Oct. 13	30 June 31	
27	0	George James Bower[3] ..	2 Nov. 13	3 Apr. 15	17 Aug. 32	
28	0	𝔓 Henry Astier[4]........	26 Nov. 12	24 Jan. 25	20 May 36	
14	0	George Herbert Clarke..	ᴾ 8 Apr. 26	ᴾ 7 June 27	ᴾ 4 Sept. 35	
11	0	William Ambrose Pender	ᴾ 25 June 29	3 Mar. 33	ᴾ 12 Jan. 38	
27	7/12	Colin Buchanan........	12 Nov. 12	7 Apr. 14	15 Jan. 38	
10	0	Wm. Mathias..........	ᴾ 8 Feb. 31	ᴾ 29 Mar. 33	ᴾ 16 Mar. 38	
22	10 4/12	Thos. Donaldson Price[5]..	ᴾ 8 Dec. 08	30 Apr. 12	28 Aug. 38	
10	17 6/12	𝔓 John Geo. Rawstorne[6].	22 July 13	18 Aug. 14	10 Oct. 38	

LIEUTENANTS.

11	0	Samuel Wood Graves....	ᴾ 5 Nov. 29	3 Aug. 33	
9	0	Henry Jackson.........	ᴾ 5 Apr. 31	ᴾ 20 Sept. 33	
9	0	George Evatt..........	30 Dec. 31	21 Sept. 33	
9	0	George Edward Olpherts.	ᴾ 20 Jan. 32	12 Oct. 33	
14	0	Henry Thos. Hutchins[7] .	8 Nov. 26	8 Apr. 34	
10	0	George Augustus Hatton.	ᴾ 2 Nov. 30	ᴾ 13 Nov. 32	
7	0	Henry Wells	ᴾ 8 Mar. 33	ᴾ 11 July 34	
7	0	Alexander Macleod......	ᴾ 10 Mar. 33	ᴾ 13 Mar. 35	
7	0	Robert Shearman.......	ᴾ 20 Sept. 33	29 Aug. 35	
6	0	Frederick Edw. Scobell...	ᴾ 20 June 34	ᴾ 11 Mar. 36	
6	0	Griffin Nicholas........	8 Apr. 34	26 May 36	
6	0	Charles Henry Gason....	ᴾ 10 Oct. 34	10 Mar. 37	
5	0	Thomas Knox Scott	ᴾ 13 Mar. 35	ᴾ 16 June 37	
5	0	John Grant............	ᴾ 30 Oct. 35	ᴾ 28 Nov. 37	
4	0	Augustus Harris........	ᴾ 4 Mar. 36	ᴾ 12 Jan. 38	
4	0	George Mackay.........	ᴾ 25 Mar. 36	ᴾ 23 Mar. 38	
5	0	George James Fulton....	13 Feb. 35	ᴾ 11 May 38	
3	0	John F. Egar..........	ᴾ 16 June 37	ᴾ 14 Sept. 38	
5	0	Arth. Maynard Herbert..	ᴾ 13 Nov. 35	14 Dec. 38	
4	0	William M'Nair	2 Dec. 36	15 Dec. 38	
3	0	George Sims...........	10 Mar. 37	16 Dec. 38	
7	0	John Tho. Jos. English..	ᴾ 7 Aug. 33	21 June 39	
3	0	Charles Young.........	ᴾ 28 Nov. 37	ᴾ 22 Nov. 39	

ENSIGNS.

3	0	James Elkington.......	ᴾ 12 Jan. 38	
2	0	Lennard Barrett Tyler..	ᴾ 23 Mar. 38	
2	0	John Dane............	ᴾ 11 May 38	
2	0	Robert Gubbins[8]	ᴾ 14 Sept. 38	
2	0	George E. Hillier.......	14 Dec. 38	
2	0	Wm. F. Dickson.......	25 Jan. 39	
1	0	Henry Meade Hamilton	ᴾ 9 Aug. 39	
1	0	John Burton Forster....	ᴾ 22 Nov. 39	

22	0	*Paymaster.*—C. H. J. Lane, 24 Jan. 29; *Ens.* 26 Mar. 18; *Lieut.* 27 May, 24.	
3	0	*Adjutant.*—George Sims, *(Lieut.)* 23 Apr. 39.	
6	0	*Quarter-Master.*—Wm. Guy, 16 Aug. 36; *Ens.* 2 May, 34; *Lieut.* 27 May, 36.	
26	5/12	*Surgeon.*—John Dempster,[9] M.D. 4 March, 36; *Assist.Surg.* 1 Sept. 14; *Hosp.*	
7	0	*Assistant-Surgeons.*—Kenneth M'Caskill, 2 Aug. 33. [*Assist.* 4 Oct. 13.	
1	0	Henry Mapleton, M.D. 12 July, 39.	

Facings Buff.—*Agent*, Messrs. Lawrie & M'Gregor, Charles-street, St James's.

Notes:
[2] Capt. Macdonell served at the taking of Genoa in 1814.
[3] Capt. Bower served at the siege of Hattrass, and throughout the Deccan campaigns in 1817 and 18. Also at the siege of Burtpore.
[4] Capt. Astier served in the Peninsula from 1812 to the end of the war, including the battles of Vittoria, the Pyrenees, Nivelle, Nive, Orthes, and Toulouse.
[5] Captain Price served in the American war, including the actions of Fort George, Stoney Creek, Lundy's Lane, Niagara, Chippewa; storming of Snake Hill, and action of Fort Erie. Slightly wounded in the shoulder in a sortie made by the enemy in front of Fort Erie.
[6] Captain Rawstorne served in the Peninsula, from Aug. 1813 to the end of the war, and was present at the battle of Orthes.
[7] Lieut. Hutchins served in the Burmese war as volunteer with the 87th regiment.
[8] Mr. Gubbins served with considerable distinction during two years in the Anglo-Spanish Legion, and was engaged in the actions of the 5th May, 6th June, 11th July, and 1st October, 1836; 10th, 15th, and 16th March, and 17th May, 1837. He has received two Medals.
[9] Dr. Demster served in the Burmese war.

1 Sir Archibald Campbell has performed great and distinguished service, both in the early and late wars in the East Indies, and Burmah. He has received a cross and one clasp for Albuhera, Vittoria, Pyrenees, Nivelle, and Nive.

Emb. for Foreign Service, 1828.

63rd (or West Suffolk) Regiment of Foot.

[Serving in the East Indies.

"EGMONT-OP-ZEE"—"MARTINIQUE"—"GUADALOUPE."

Colonel.

Years' Serv.		
59		Wm. Dyott,[1] *Ens.* 14 Mar. 1781; *Lieut.* 9 May, 82; *Capt.* 25 April, 93; *Major*,
Full Pay.	Half Pay.	19 May, 94; *Lieut.-Col.* 18 Sept. 94; *Col.* 1 Jan. 1800; *Major-Gen.* 25 April, 08; *Lieut.-Gen.* 4 June, 13; *Gen.* 22 July, 30; *Col.* 63rd, 7 April, 25.
40	1	*Lieut.-Colonels.*—᛫ ᛫᛫ Joseph Logan,[2] *Ens.* 20 Dec. 99; *Lieut.* 8 Aug. 01; *Capt.* 2 Feb. 09; *Brevet-Major*, 18 June, 15; *Regtl.-Major*, 27 July, 26; *Lieut.-Col.* P 17 Dec. 29.
38	0	James W. Fairtlough,[3] *Ens.* P 20 Aug. 02; *Lieut.* P 24 May, 04; *Capt.* P 14 Mar. 05; *Brev.-Maj.* 12 Aug. 19; *Regtl.-Major*, P 26 May, 25; *Lt.-Col.* 17 Sept. 33.
35	0	*Majors.*—Pery Baylee,[4] *Ens.* 25 April, 05; *Lieut.* P 8 Aug. 05; *Capt.* 5 Nov. 12; *Brevet-Major*, 22 July, 30; *Regtl.-Major*, 17 Sept. 33.
14	0	Arthur Cunliffe Pole, *Ens.* P 7 Nov. 26; *Lieut.* 5 June, 30; *Capt.* P 18 Oct. 33; *Major*, P 1 Dec. 37.

		CAPTAINS.	ENSIGN.	LIEUT.	CAPTAIN.	BREV.-MAJ.
30	2 9/13	᛫ Fred. Chid. Irwin,[5] K.H.	25 Mar. 08	17 Aug. 09	27 Mar. 27	28 June 36
30	0	Richard Fry	P 26 Apr. 10	P 18 June 12	5 June 30	
30	0	᛫ ᛫᛫ Park Per. Neville[6]	29 Mar. 10	17 July 11	27 Nov. 35	
20	9 1/12	᛫ ᛫᛫ Anth. G. Sidley[7]	1 Aug. 11	16 July 12	22 May 35	
16	9 1/12	Wm. Marcus Carew	4 Oct. 15	16 Nov. 26	22 Aug. 36	
23	8	᛫ Henry Croly[8]	27 Apr. 09	10 June 13	21 Apr. 37	
13	0	John Hodson Fearon....	10 Oct. 27	4 Feb. 32	P 3 Nov. 37	
15	0	George Green[9]	7 Apr. 25	29 June 27	P 10 Nov. 37	
11	0	Exham S. T. Swyny	P 1 Oct. 29	P 17 Oct. 33	P 8 Aug. 38	
20	13 5/12	John Foulston	1 Feb. 07	29 Sept. 08	31 Dec. 39	

3 Col. Fairtlough served at the bombardment of Ter Vere, and siege and capture of Flushing in 1809. Also at the capture of Guadaloupe in 1815.

4 Major Baylee served at the capture of Martinique in 1809, and Guadaloupe in 1810.

5 Major Irwin served in the Peninsula, from April, 1809, to Feb. 1814, including the capture of Oporto; battles of Talavera and Fuentes d'Onor; siege of Badajoz; siege and storm of Ciudad Rodrigo; siege of Badajoz, and capture of the castle by escalade, 7th April, 1812; battle of Salamanca; capture of Madrid and Retira; battles of Vittoria and the Pyrenees; besides various affairs and skirmishes on the advance and retreat of the army. Served also the Kandyan campaigns of 1817 and 18 in Ceylon.

6 Capt. Neville served in the Peninsula, from July 1810, to May, 1813, including the siege of Cadiz; battle of Fuentes d'Onor, 3rd and 5th May; sieges of Ciudad Rodrigo and Badajoz (severely wounded in the head and leg); battle of Salamanca, and siege of Burgos, where he was severely wounded through the left shoulder in the storm of the first line of the castle, 4th Oct. 1812. Served the campaign of 1814 in Holland, including the bombardment of Antwerp, and assault on Bergen-op-Zoom. Present at Waterloo. Served also in the Deccan war, including the capture of Asseerghur. Attached to the Nizam's troops at the capture of a predatory force in the Deccan, 11th Dec. 1820.

For 7, 8, 9, and 10, see next page.

		LIEUTENANTS.			
11	0	George Brookes Pratt ..	31 Dec. 29	P 19 July 33	
17	0	Chas. D. C. O'Brien	26 Mar. 23	24 Aug. 25	
8	19 2/12	John Spier	15 Nov. 12	10 Feb. 14	
12	0	Wm. Jas. Darling	5 Feb. 29	19 Sept. 33	
9	16	Cha. Higginbotham	P 29 June 15	20 Sept. 33	
12	12	Humphrey W. Coultman	1 Nov. 16	20 Sept. 33	
13	0	Hen. Tho. Crompton....	P 12 Apr. 27	P 16 Oct. 33	
9	0	Hen. Jos. Swyny	P 2 Dec. 31	P 18 Oct. 33	
8	0	Aug. Fred. Codd	P 21 Dec. 32	P 21 Feb. 34	
7	0	Thomas Harries	P 19 July 33	P 2 May 34	
7	0	Hen. R. Seymour	20 Sept. 33	P 20 Feb. 35	
7	0	John Thorp	P 27 Sept. 33	P 5 June 35	
7	0	Rob. Ladbroke Day	P 18 Oct. 33	P 7 Aug. 35	
7	0	Fra. Mostyn Owen......	P 1 Nov. 33	P 6 Nov. 35	
6	0	Patrick Lindesay	P 21 Feb. 34	P 5 Feb. 36	
6	0	Patrick Rob. Gordon....	P 2 May 34	20 June 36	
6	0	Vesey Berdmore........	9 Jan. 35	22 Aug. 36	
22	0	Giles Eyre	P 30 July 18	18 Jan. 23	
5	0	Gust. Nicolls Harrison ..	P 5 June 35	P 1 Dec. 37	
3	0	Jas. Rich. Lysaght......	3 Feb. 37	P 6 July 38	
17	17 2/12	᛫ John Fowle	19 Dec. 05	P 2 Apr. 07	
5	0	James B. Leatham......	P 5 Feb. 36	9 Jan. 39	
3	0	Charles Edward Fairtlough	P 12 May 37	P 31 Dec. 39	

		ENSIGNS.			
6	0	Theod. M. Haultain	27 June 34		
4	0	Wm. Jas. Hutchins	2 Dec. 36		
3	0	William Kenny	P 3 Nov. 37		
3	0	Wm. Fred. Carter	P 1 Dec. 37		
3	0	Henry Lees...........	P 27 Dec. 37		
2	0	S. F. C. Annesley	P 6 July 38		
1	0	John Hardie	P 29 Mar. 39		
1	0	Robert Fulton Cameron	31 Dec. 39		
15	0	*Paymaster.*—Richard Lane, 29 Sept. 37; *Ens.* 23 June, 25; *Lieut.* 25 Oct. 27; *Capt.* 16 March, 32.			
12	0	*Adjutant.*—W. J. Darling, (*Lieut.*) 8 Aug. 38.			
17	11	*Quarter-Master.*—᛫ Robt. Cart,[10] 11 Dec. 28; *Ens.* 24 Sept. 12; *Lieut.* 20 Jan. 14.			
24	3 5/12	*Surgeon.*—John W. Watson, M.D. 6 April, 26; *Assist.-Surg.* 4 March, 13; *Hosp.*			
5	0	*Assist.-Surgeons.*—Henry Pilleau, 22 Jan. 36. [*Assistant*, 10 Dec. 12.			

John Samuel Charlton, 1 March, 39.

Facings Green.—*Agent*, Mr. Collyer, Park-place, St. James's.

1 Gen. Dyott served in the West Indies in 1796; in Egypt 1801: and at Walcheren.
2 Col. Logan served with the expedition to Hanover in 1805; to Copenhagen in 1807; the Corunna campaign, and subsequently in the Peninsula, from 1812 to the end of the war. Wounded at Waterloo whilst in command of the 2d battalion Rifle Brigade.

Emb. for Foreign Service, 1834.] **64th (or 2nd Staffordshire) Regiment of Foot.** [Serving at Jamaica.

"ST. LUCIA"—"SURINAM."

Colonel.

Years' Serv.		
42		₽ Sir Rich. Bourke,¹ K.C.B. *Ens.* 22 Nov. 1798; *Lieut. & Capt.* 25 Nov. 99; *Major,* 27 Aug. 1805; *Lieut.-Col.* 16 Sept. 06; *Col.* 4 June, 14; *Major.-Gen.* 19 July, 21; *Lieut.-Gen.* 10 Jan. 37; *Col.* 64th Regt. 29 Nov. 37.
Full Pay.	Half Pay.	

Lieut.Colonel.

27	0	Jas. Edward Freeth,² *Ens.* 19 May, 13; *Lieut.* 23 April, 14; *Capt.* ᴾ 17 April, 17; *Major,* ᴾ 24 Dec. 29; *Lieut.-Col.* ᴾ 1 Dec. 37.

Majors.

28	8/12	₽ Severus Wm. Lynam Stretton,³ *Ens.* 11 June, 12; *Lieut.* 6 Jan. 14; *Capt.* ᴾ 13 Aug. 25; *Major,* ᴾ 2 Dec. 31.
19	11/12	Hon. Geo. Augustus Browne, *Ens.* ᴾ 27 April, 20; *Lieut.* ᴾ 28 Aug. 23; *Capt.* ᴾ 31 Dec. 25; *Major,* ᴾ 1 Dec. 37.

		CAPTAINS.	ENSIGN.	LIEUT.	CAPTAIN.	BREV.-MAJ.
17	0	James Draper	18 Dec. 23	ᴾ 19 Nov. 25	ᴾ 24 Dec. 29	
15	0	Digby Hen. Lawrell	ᴾ 28 Apr. 25	ᴾ 12 Dec. 26	ᴾ 4 Oct. 31	
15	0	Geo. Duberley	ᴾ 28 Jan. 26	ᴾ 24 Dec. 29	ᴾ 23 Aug. 33	
14	0	Maximilian J. Western	ᴾ 10 June 26	ᴾ 8 June 30	ᴾ 29 Dec. 35	
13	0	Edw. Curtis Fownes	ᴾ 15 Feb. 27	ᴾ 8 June 30	ᴾ 4 Nov. 36	
10	0	Wm. John James	ᴾ 20 July 30	ᴾ 20 Apr. 32	ᴾ 1 Dec. 37	
10	0	Francis Sealy	ᴾ 19 Nov. 30	ᴾ 21 Dec. 32	ᴾ 5 Oct. 38	
9	0	Charles Norris	ᴾ 25 Feb. 31	ᴾ 23 Aug. 33	ᴾ 23 Apr. 39	
13	19 1/12	₽ Lewis Moore Bennett	25 Feb. 08	30 May 09	ᴾ 3 Aug. 20	10 Jan. 37
9	0	G. C. Beresford Stirling	ᴾ 16 Aug. 31	ᴾ 11 July 34	ᴾ 20 Dec. 39	

LIEUTENANTS.

11	0	D'Oyly Wm. Battley		2 Apr. 29	22 Aug. 34
10	0	John Canavan		22 July 30	23 Aug. 34
6	0	Fred. Arthur Errington	ᴾ 21 Feb. 34	ᴾ 1 July 36	
6	0	Stephen Henry Smyth	ᴾ 11 July 34	ᴾ 4 Nov. 36	
5	0	Edw. Jones Coxe	ᴾ 16 June 35	22 Oct. 37	
5	0	Ambrose Barcroft Parker	ᴾ 13 Mar. 35	29 Nov. 37	
9	0	H. Altham Cumberlege	ᴾ 2 Dec. 31	22 Apr. 35	
5	0	James Dutton Smyth	ᴾ 29 Dec. 35	ᴾ 30 Dec. 37	
4	0	Ramsay H. Smith	ᴾ 1 July 36	ᴾ 6 July 38	
4	0	H. Redfearn Collinson	ᴾ 4 Nov. 36	ᴾ 5 Oct. 38	
3	0	W. W. Lyttleton	ᴾ 14 Apr. 37	ᴾ 23 Apr. 39	
5	0	Wm. Henry Lys	16 Oct. 35	13 May 39	
3	0	M. Edw. Smith	ᴾ 3 Nov. 37	ᴾ 20 Dec. 39	

ENSIGNS.

3	0	Hon. G. F. W. Yelverton	ᴾ 1 Dec. 37	
2	0	Wm. Baillie Jopp	ᴾ 6 July 38	
2	0	F. H. Kilvington	ᴾ 20 July 38	
2	0	N. T. Williams	ᴾ 5 Oct. 38	
2	0	Carey Handfield	14 Dec. 38	
1	0	Thomas Stirling	ᴾ 23 Apr. 39	
1	0	William Parker	11 Oct. 39	
1	0	George Amiel	ᴾ 20 Dec. 39	

30	6 1/12	*Paymaster.*—John Ralston,⁴ 29 Dec. 25; *Cornet,* 6 July, 04; *Lieut.* 10 July, 06, *Capt.* 26 May, 14.
5	0	*Adjutant.*—Edw. Jones Coxe, (*Lieut.*) 12 May, 39.
1	0	*Quarter-Master.*—James Howes, 6 Sept. 39.
		Surgeon.—Michael Fogarty, 27 Jan. 32; *Assist.-Surg.* 11 March, 11.
5	0	*Assistant-Surgeons.*—Rob. Keith Kynock, 4 Dec. 35.
1	0	Wm. Henry Brownson, M.D. 17 Sept. 39.

Facings Black.—*Agent,* Messrs. Cox & Co.—*Irish Agent,* Cane & Co.

3 Major Stretton served the campaigns of 1812 and 13 in the Peninsula, and was severely wounded by two gun-shots at the battle of Vittoria.

4 Capt. Ralston was embarked with a detachment of the 24th Light Dragoons in the outward bound Indian fleet, which maintained an action with a French squadron, under Admiral Linois, off the Mauritius, 6th Aug. 1805, and in which the enemy were beaten off. On the 6th Aug. 1809, he led the advanced squadron of his regiment in action with the rebels before Seringapatam, in which the latter were beaten and dispersed; and on the same date he commanded the outlying piquet in a night attack from the garrison of Seringapatam.

1 Sir Richard Bourke served in Holland in 1799, and was present in the actions of the 27th Aug. 10th and 19th Sept. 2nd and 6th Oct. where he received a severe wound through both jaws. Served as Quarter-Master-General in South America, and was present in the actions of the 19th and 20th Jan. 1807; at the siege and storming of Monte Video, and in the expedition against Buenos Ayres.

2 Col. Freeth served in the American war.

7 Captain Sidley served in the Peninsula from March, 1812, to Dec. 1813, including the battle of Salamanca; actions at Asma, Sabuganna de Morrilla (severely wounded), and Pyrenees, 31st Aug. Wounded on the 18th June at Waterloo. Served also in the Burmese war.

8 Captain Croly served at the siege of Flushing in 1809; battery firing in the Straits of Messina in 1811; in the Peninsula, from June, 1812, to the end of the war, including the battle of Castalla, siege of Tarragona; ditto, 2nd investment, retreat from Villa Franca, and investment of Barcelona. Served subsequently in the American war.

9 Captain Green served in the Burmese war.

10 Quarter-master Cart served in the Peninsula, from July, 1813, to the end of the war, including the battle of the Nive; blockade of and sortie from Bayonne.

Emb. for For. Service, 1829.] **65th (or 2d Yorksh. N. Riding) Regt. of Foot.** [Serving in Canada.

The *Royal Tiger*, superscribed "INDIA"—"ARABIA."

Years' Serv.		
61		*Colonel.*
Full Pay.	Half Pay.	Thomas Grosvenor,[1] *Ens.* 1 Oct. 1779 ; *Lieut. & Capt.* 20 Oct. 84; *Capt. & Lieut.-Col.* 25 April, 93; *Col.* 3 May, 96 ; *Major-Gen.* 29 April, 1802; *Lieut.-Gen.* 25 April, 08 ; *Gen.* 12 Aug. 19; *Col.* 65 Regt. 8 Feb. 14.
26	1 3/12	*Lieut.-Colonel.*—Henry Senior,[2] *Ens.* 6 May, 13 ; *Lieut.* 28 Dec. 15 ; *Capt.* p 24 April, 23 ; *Major,* p 12 March, 29 ; *Lieut.-Col.* p 19 Sept. 34.
33	0	*Majors.*—Peter Farquharson,[3] *Ens.* 1 Sept. 07; *Lieut.* p 1 May, 10 ; *Capt.* 2 June, 25 ; *Major,* p 24 Aug. 32.
17	5/12	Samuel Walker, *Ens.* p 10 Oct.22 ; *Lieut.* p 12 May, 25 ; *Capt.* p 1 Nov. 27 ; *Major,* p 19 Sept. 34.

		CAPTAINS.	ENSIGN.	LIEUT.	CAPTAIN.	BREV.-MAJ.
32	0	Sam. Robinson Warren[4]..	21 Apr. 08	23 Oct. 09	p 1 May 23	28 June 38
31	1 8/12	James Nokes[5].......	9 June 08	22 Feb. 10	20 Mar. 27	
24	10 6/12	John Thorne Weyland[6]..	31 July 06	1 Mar. 09	13 Mar. 27	
15	0	Charles Wise...........	p 7 July 25	p 22 Apr. 26	p 23 Apr. 29	
27	5 5/12	George Smyth	p 27 Aug. 08	4 July 11	3 Apr. 27	
23	7	James Patience	5 Apr. 10	24 Oct. 11	13 Nov. 27	
24	0	Alfred Fran. W. Wyatt ..	p 12 Dec. 26	p 23 Apr. 29	p 19 Sept. 34	
12	0	Cha. Emilius Gold	p 20 Mar. 28	p 28 Oct. 31	p 5 Feb. 36	
14	10 3/12	William Snow.........	19 Dec. 15	19 Mar. 24	p 15 Dec. 25	28 June 38
12	0	Geo. Freeman Murray ..	26 Apr. 28	p 29 June 32	p 5 Jan. 39	
		LIEUTENANTS.				
16	12 7/12	Rickard O'Connell[7] ..	12 May 12	15 July 13		
13	14 11/12	John Tho. Westropp	8 Oct. 12	23 Sept. 13		
12	0	Jas. Lewis Smith	p 21 Sept. 28	p 22 Oct. 33		
12	0	James Haining	27 Apr. 28	21 Feb. 34		
12	0	John Alex. Drought	p 25 Nov. 28	p 19 Sept. 34		
10	0	Wm. Pym Young	p 26 Oct. 30	p 27 Nov. 35		
9	0	Richard Newenham	14 June 31	p 5 Feb. 36		
9	0	John Sealy	p 1 Nov. 31	p 2 Sept. 36		
8	0	Francis Wise	p 29 June 32	p 12 Jan. 38		
7	0	Patrick Day Stokes ...	p 22 Oct. 33	p 13 Jan. 38		
6	0	Wm. Surtees Cook.....	p 27 June 34	p 5 Jan. 39		
5	0	St. Leger Barry	p 27 Nov. 35	10 Jan. 39		
5	0	Robert Haldane	p 5 Feb. 36	13 Dec. 39		
		ENSIGNS.				
4	0	Peter Wolfe	p 22 July 36			
4	0	J. Wms. Marshall	p 2 Sept. 36			
3	0	Cha. Guy Trafford	p 12 Jan. 38			
3	0	Oliver Nicolls.........	p 13 Jan. 38			
2	0	Cha. Wm. Sutton	p 6 July 38			
2	0	John Harvey	p 5 Jan. 39			
1	0	Christopher Rhatigan...	26 Apr. 39			
1	0	Duncan Bazalgette ...	p 31 Jan. 40			

5 Captain Nokes served in the Peninsula, from May, 1809, to Feb. 1814, including the battles of Talavera, Fuentes d'Onor, Salamanca, Vittoria, the Pyrenees and Nive, from 9th to 13th Dec.; sieges of Ciudad Rodrigo and Burgos. Present at the battle of Harriapore, in the Nepaul country, in 1816.
6 Captain Weyland served the campaigns of Upper Canada, from 1812 to 1815, including the actions of Fort George, &c. Severely wounded at Stoney Creek.
7 Lieut. O'Connell served in the Peninsula from April, 1812 to the end of the war, including the battles of Salamanca and Vittoria. Severely wounded at the capture of Badajoz on the night of the 6th April, 1812, where he served as a volunteer with the storming party.
8 Paymaster Blake served the campaigns of 1814 and 15 in Upper Canada.

24	2 9/12	*Paymaster.*—Stephen Blake,[8] 25 Feb. 22 ; *Ens.* 3 Feb. 14 ; *Lieut.* 3 Sept. 18.
12	0	*Adjutant.*—James Haining, (*Lieut.*) 21 Feb. 34.
2	0	*Quarter-Master.*—Thomas Paul, 26 Apr. 39 ; *Ens.* 25 Jan. 39.
23	6 10/12	*Surgeon.*—Copeland Grattan, M.D. 11 Sept. 28 ; *Assist.-Surg.* 14 June, 10.
5	0	*Assistant-Surgeons.*—John Edward Nicoll, 11 Aug. 35.
		Geo. Roche Smith, 13 Sept. 33.

Facings White.—*Agent,* Messrs. Cox & Co.—*Irish Agent,* Borough, Armit & Co.

1 General Grosvenor accompanied his regiment (the 3rd Foot Guards) to Holland in 1793, and afterwards into Flanders. In 1799 he went with the expedition to the Helder, and was present in the affair at the lines of Zuype (wounded), the battle of Alkmaer, and the actions of the 17th Sept. and 6th and 9th Oct. Commanded the picquets and out-posts at the siege of Copenhagen on the day of the sortie, when the Danes were repulsed. At the siege of Flushing, he was next in command to Sir Eyre Coote.
2 Col. Senior was severely wounded in the action between H. M. packet *Lapwing*, and the American privateer *Fox*, off Barbadoes, 30th Sept. 1813.
3 Major Farquharson served at the capture of the Isle of France in 1810. Capture of the fort of Now Nuggar in Kallywar, Feb. 1814. On the borders of Scindia's country in 1814 and 15. Capture of Forts of Joorin, Aug. 1815, Anjar and Khuncoote, Feb., Dhingee and Dwarka, March, 1816 Action and capture of Poona, 17th March, 1817. At Ashtee, 21st Feb. 1818, the Mahratta General Gokla killed, and Satteria Reya captured. Storm of Kutch Booje Fort, March, 1819. Capture of the Forts of Rass-el-Kyma and Zams, 8th and 22d Dec. 1819. Served also in Arabia in 1821, and was present in the action of Beni-Boo-Ali, 2nd March.
4 Col. Warren served in the expedition against pirates in the Persian Gulf in 1809, and was severely wounded in an attack on the fort of Luft. Capture of the Isle of France in 1810. Mahratta campaigns from 1815 to 1818, and again in an expedition up the Persian Gulf in 1819. Brevet Lieut.-Colonel 20 Dec. 39.

Emb. for For. Service, 1827.] **66th** (*or the Berkshire*) *Regiment of Foot.* [Serving in Canada.

"DOURO"—"TALAVERA"—"ALBUHERA"—"VITTORIA"—"PYRENEES"— "NIVELLE"—"NIVE"—"ORTHES"—"PENINSULA."

Years' Serv.			
54		*Colonel.*	
Full Pay.	Half Pay.	Richard Blunt,[1] *Ens.* 31 Jan. 1787; *Lieut.* 23 Feb. 91; *Capt.* 12 July, 93; *Major*, 17 May, 96; *Lieut.-Col.* 23 Aug. 99; *Col.* 25 Oct. 1809; *Major-Gen.* 1 Jan. 12; *Lieut.-Gen.* 27 May, 25; *Col.* 66th Regt. 25 March, 35.	
17	1 1/12	*Lieut.-Colonel.*—Tho. Henry Johnston, *Ens.* p 21 Feb. 22; *Lieut.* p 1 Oct. 25; *Capt.* p 24 Oct. 26; *Major*, p 20 May, 36; *Lieut.-Col.* p 28 Dec. 38.	
17	1 5/12	*Majors.*—Clopton Lewis Wingfield,[2] *Ens.* p 11 Oct. 21; *Lieut.* 27 Nov. 24; *Capt.* p 10 June, 26; *Major*, p 2 Feb. 38.	
15	0	Tho. Leigh Goldie, *Ens.* p 13 June, 25; *Lieut.* p 10 Dec. 25; *Capt.* p 24 Nov. 28; *Major*, p 28 Dec. 38.	

		CAPTAINS.	ENSIGN.	LIEUT.	CAPTAIN.	BREV.-MAJ.
32	0	John Clarke[3]	p 14 July 08	3 Oct. 09	p 13 Jan. 25	28 June 38
29	5 5/12	Thos. Hewit Baylie[4]	p 14 Aug. 06	25 June 07	6 Apr. 15	10 Jan. 37
15	3/4	Wm. Joshua Crompton	p 10 Sept. 25	p 12 Dec. 26	p 11 Apr. 34	
14	0	Wm. Longworth Dames	p 26 July 26	p 24 Nov. 28	p 27 June 34	
15	0	Tho. W. Nesham	p 14 Apr. 25	p 29 Aug. 26	p 4 May 33	
12	1/12	William Gordon	p 5 June 28	p 27 Apr. 32	p 12 May 37	
12	0	Cha. Edw. Michel	p 25 Nov. 28	23 Nov. 33	p 2 Feb. 38	
10	0	John Parker	p 26 Feb. 30	p 11 Apr. 34	p 28 Dec. 38	
9	0	Geo. Longworth Dames	p 5 Apr. 31	p 27 June 34	p 22 Feb. 39	
8	0	Geo. Grattan Biscoe	p 7 Apr. 32	p 12 Feb. 36	p 27 Sept. 39	
		LIEUTENANTS.				
21	0	Thomas Rainsford	17 Feb. 19	7 Apr. 25		
13	0	John Johnston	p 24 May 27	p 9 Mar. 32		
14	0	Robert Steele[5]	23 Mar. 26	26 Sept. 33		
14	0	George Maxwell	p 23 Feb. 26	29 May 28		
7	0	Le Marchant Carey	p 27 Sept. 33	10 Jan. 37		
7	0	T. Barnes *Lord* Cochrane	p 27 Sept. 33	p 12 May 37		
6	0	Ralph A. Chas. Daniell	p 11 Apr. 34	p 2 Feb. 38		
6	0	Hen. John Turner	p 9 May 34	p 22 Nov. 36		
5	0	E. M. Davenport	p 24 Apr. 35	6 Aug. 38		
4	0	*Hon.* E. A. F. H. Lambart	p 20 May 36	27 Dec. 38		
4	0	Fred. Chas. Trench	p 22 Nov. 36	p 28 Dec. 38		
4	0	Fred. John Trick	p 23 Dec. 36	p 15 Feb. 39		
4	0	Geo. A. Taylor	10 Jan. 37	p 22 Feb. 39		
3	0	Charles Henry Godby	p 12 May 37	p 27 Sept. 39		
		ENSIGNS.				
3	0	J. H. B. Birch	p 15 Dec. 37			
3	0	Hen. L. G. Scott	p 2 Feb. 38			
2	0	Edw. Berens Pratt	28 Aug. 38			
2	0	Bennett Langton	p 28 Dec. 38			
2	0	Henry Steele	1 Feb. 39			
1	0	Geo. Marshall Knipe	p 22 Feb. 39			
1	0	Fred. Joseph Belcher	p 27 Sept. 39			
25	6 5/12	*Paymaster.*—Kenneth Tolmie Ross, 11 Aug. 25; *Ens.* 22 June, 09; *Lieut.* 8 Oct. 12.				
4	0	*Adjutant.*—Hon. E. A. F. H. Lambart, (*Lieut.*) 27 June, 38.				
12	1	*Quarter-Master.*—William Hornby, 1 Feb. 27.				
		Surgeon.—J. Miller, M.D. 4 Jan. 39; *Assist.-Surg.* 8 Feb. 16.				
14	0	*Assist.-Surgeons.*—W. Linton, M.D. 18 Jan. 27; *Hosp.-Assist.* 9 Dec. 26.				
14	0	Philip Anglin, M.D. 13 Dec. 27; *Hosp.-Assist.* 31 Aug. 26.				

Facings Green.—*Agent*, Messrs. Cox & Co.—*Irish Agent*, Messrs. Cane & Co.

1 General Blunt served in Lord Moira's expedition, and in Flanders in 1794 and 95, and was actively employed in the West Indies, from 1795 until 1802. He has since served in Hanover, Madeira, and in the Peninsula.

2 Major Wingfield served two campaigns in the Burmese territories, and was in every action in which the 13th Light Infantry was engaged.

3 Major Clarke served in the Peninsula, from March, 1809, to the end of the war, including the battles of Oporto and Talavera; Lines of Torres Vedras; actions of Arroya de Molina, and Campo Mayor; battle of Albuhera; siege of Badajoz; battles of Vittoria, the Pyrenees, (from 25th to 31st July, and 2d Aug.), Nivelle, Nive, (9th and 13th Dec.); action of St. Palais; battles of Orthes, Aire and Toulouse, besides numerous skirmishes. At the battle of Albuhera, when in the command of a company of flankers, was struck down by a Polish lancer, and taken prisoner, but made his escape in a charge of cavalry.

4 Major Baylie served at the capture of the Isle of France in 1810; and of Java in 1811, including the actions of the 10th and 22d Aug., storming of the entrenched lines and forts of Cornelis, storming fortified heights of Serandole, storm and capture of Fort Onarang. Served in the campaigns of 1814 and 15, against the Nepaul States; also at the siege and capture of Hattras, and in the Mahratta campaign of 1817 and 18.

5 Lieut. Steele's services:—Campaign and battle of Corunna, where he was slightly wounded in the neck. Expedition to Walcheren. Peninsula, April, 1810 to 1814, including the siege of Cadiz and blockade of Bayonne.

Emb. for Foreign Service, 1832.] **67th (or South Hampshire) Regiment of Foot.** [Serving at Barbadoes.

The *Royal Tiger*, superscribed, "INDIA"—"BARROSA"—"PENINSULA."

Years' Serv. 45

Colonel.

Full Pay. / Half Pay.

Sir John Macdonald,[1] K.C.B. *Ens.* — April, 1795; *Lieut.* 2 Feb. 96; *Capt.* 22 Oct. 1802; *Major*, 28 Feb. 05; *Lieut-Col.* 17 Mar. 08; *Col.* 4 June, 14; *Major-Gen.* 27 May, 25; *Lieut-Gen.* 28 June, 38; *Col.* 67th Regt. 25 Aug. 28.

35 / 1 4/12 *Lieut.-Colonel.*—Thomas Bunbury,[2] K.H. *Ens.* 25 Mar. 04; *Lieut.* 24 Dec. 04; *Capt.* P 3 Nov. 08; *Major*, 14 April, 14; *Lieut.-Col.* P 5 July, 21; *Col.* 10 Jan. 37.

22 / 4/12 *Majors.*—Edward Basil Brooke, 2nd *Lieut.* 15 Dec. 17; *Lieut.* 9 April, 25; *Capt.* P 11 July 26; *Major*, P 5 July, 31.

18 / 8 9/12 William Nesbitt Orange,[3] *Ens.* 5 Feb. 14; *Lieut.* 19 Jan. 19; *Capt.* P 24 Oct. 21; *Major*, P 15 Aug. 34.

		CAPTAINS	ENSIGN.	LIEUT.	CAPTAIN.	BREV.-MAJ.
35	9	Geo. Cosby Harpour[4]..	20 April 96	29 Dec. 08	9 Dec. 19	10 Jan. 37
31	0	Thomas James Adair[5]..	25 May 09	20 Feb. 11	P 27 Mar. 23	28 June 38
31	0	Wm. White Warburton[6]..	17 Aug. 09	2 April 12	5 May 26	
15	0	Samuel Yorke Martin....	8 April 25	P 28 Jan. 26	P 24 Feb. 29	
17	2 1/12	Thomas Unett.........	P 27 Sept. 21	P 22 July 24	P 6 July 26	
18	0	Thos. Josephus Deverell..	7 Nov. 22	25 June 29	P 30 Aug. 31	
12	0	Chas. Christopher Davie..	P 11 Dec. 28	P 5 July 31	P 30 Dec. 37	
21	0	Thomas Byrne	4 Nov. 19	5 Mar. 23	22 Jan. 39	
11	0	Hon. Arch. G. Stuart....	P 30 April 29	P 30 Aug. 31	P 25 May 39	
25	2	Alexander Mackenzie ...	25 Oct. 13	5 Oct. 15	9 Aug. 35	
		LIEUTENANTS.				
16	0	Chas. Woodcock James..	27 Jan. 25	P 11 Dec. 28	8 Dr. Riach served the campaigns of 1813 and 14 in Germany and Holland, including the action at the Goerde in Hanover, 16th Sept. 1813; affair near Antwerp, Jan. 1814: attack on Merxem, and subsequent operations against the French fleet at Antwerp. Present at Waterloo on the 16th, 17th, and 18th June.	
15	0	George Alfred Currie....	1 Sept. 25	16 Mar. 32		
8	0	Henry James V. Kemble..	P 9 Mar. 32	P 5 Aug. 37		
8	0	John Elton M. Prower....	P 14 Dec. 32	28 Aug. 37		
8	0	Ferdinand Whittingham..	2 Nov. 32	P 19 Feb. 36		
6	0	John Porter	P 28 Mar. 34	P 29 Dec. 37		
5	0	Charles B. Hague.......	P 5 Sept. 35	P 30 Dec. 37		
7	0	William Pilsworth	P 24 May 33	18 Mar. 38		
5	0	Rodham C. D. Home....	P 16 Oct. 35	P 2 Nov. 38		
4	0	Henry Collette..........	P 26 Aug. 36	22 Jan. 39		
3	0	Thomas P. Onslow......	17 Nov. 37	P 25 May 39		
3	0	John Thomas Locke.....	26 Dec. 37	P 24 Aug. 39		
3	0	Capel Coape	P 29 Dec. 37	P 11 Oct. 39		
		ENSIGNS.				
3	0	Alexander Dury........	P 5 Aug. 37			
3	0	Wm. Robert Adair......	P 30 Dec. 37			
2	0	J. L. Campbell	30 Mar. 38			
2	0	Edw. H. Westropp......	P 2 Nov. 38			
1	0	Walter Caulfield Pratt...	P 25 May 39			
1	0	Henry Dawson	P 24 Aug. 39			
1	0	Rich. Morgan Humfrey..	P 11 Oct. 39			
1	0	Wm. Hayter Hussey	P 8 Nov. 39			

23 / 0 *Paymaster.*—James Robinson,[7] 26 Dec. 37; *Ens.* 20 Nov. 17; *Lieut.* 24 April, 20.

16 / 0 *Adjutant.*—Charles Woodcock James, (*Lieut.*) 26 Dec. 37.

1 / 0 *Quarter-Master.*—George Crispin, 25 Oct. 39; *Ens.* 22 Mar. 39.

24 / 4 5/12 *Surgeon.*—J. Riach,[8] M.D. 19 Nov. 30; *Assist.-Surg.* 2 July, 12; *Hosp.-Assist.* 18 May, 12.

6 / 0 *Assistant-Surgeons.*—Edward Hugh Blakeney, 17 Oct. 34.
2 / 0 Thomas Honor Wheeler, 28 Dec. 38.

Facings Yellow.—*Agent*, Messrs. Cox & Co.

1 Sir John Macdonald served the campaign of 1801 in Egypt, and has received a Medal and one Clasp for Barrossa and the passage of the Nive.
2 Col. Bunbury led the storming at Fort Zelaina, in Surinam, in 1804. Served the campaign of 1814 in Holland, including the attacks on Merxem, and the bombardment of the French fleet at Antwerp. Served also in the American war.
3 Major Orange served on the frontiers of Niagara in 1814 and 15. Served also at the siege and capture of Roahry, Rhyghur, and other places in the Southern Concan country in India in 1818.
4 Major Harpour served in Spain from Sept. 1810 to 1814, including the siege of Cadiz; battle of Barrosa; actions at Balaguere and Villa Franca; sieges of Terragona and Barcelona.
5 Major Adair served in Spain from Sept. 1810 to the end of the war, including the siege of Cadiz, battle of Barrosa, Fort San Philip, Balaguere, Villa Franca, Tarragona and Barcelona. Served also the Nepaul campaigns of 1817 and 18, and subsequently in the Deccan, including the siege and reduction of Rhyghur, Amulmer, and Asseerghur. Twice severely wounded by matchlock balls in the left arm, and right side at the siege of Asseerghur on the evening of the 19th March, 1819, in repulsing a sortie made by the garrison of the fort into the town.
6 Capt. Warburton served the Nepaul campaigns of 1817 and 18, and subsequently in the Deccan, including the capture of the forts at Rhyghur and Asseerghur.
7 Paymaster Robinson served at the siege of Asseerghur, March and April, 1819.

Emb. for Foreign Service, 1834.] **68th (or Durham) Regt. of Foot (Light Infantry).** [Serving at Jamaica.

"SALAMANCA"—"VITTORIA"—"PYRENEES"—"NIVELLE" "ORTHES"—"PENINSULA."

Years' Serv.					
49		*Colonel.* ℗ Sir William Johnston,[1] K.C.B. *Ens.* 3 June, 1791; *Lieut.* 7 Jan. 94; *Capt.* 4 April, 95; *Major*, 27 Feb. 1800; *Lieut.-Col.* 25 April, 08; *Col.* 4 June, 14; *Major-Gen.* 27 May, 25; *Lieut.-Gen.* 28 June, 38; *Col.* 68th Light Infantry, 6 April 38.				
Full Pay.	Half Pay.					
33	1 8/12	*Lieut.-Colonel.*—℗ ⓒⓑ John Cross,[2] K.H. *Ens.* 9 July, 05; *Lieut.* 29 May, 06; *Capt.* 31 Dec. 12; *Major*, 23 June, 25; *Lieut.-Col.* ℗8 Feb. 31.				
17	2 5/12	*Majors.—Lord* Wm. Paulet, *Ens.* ℗ 1 Feb. 21; *Lieut.* ℗ 23 Aug. 22; *Capt.* ℗ 12 Feb. 25; *Major*, ℗ 10 Sept. 30.				
15	0	Richardson Wm. Huey, *Ens.* 26 March, 25; *Lieut.* ℗ 19 Dec. 26; *Capt.* ℗ 11 June, 30; *Major*, ℗ 13 Oct. 38.				

		CAPTAINS.	ENSIGN.	LIEUT.	CAPTAIN.	BREV.-MAJ.
17	0	Harry Smyth........	℗ 10 July 23	℗ 13 Aug. 25	℗ 15 Oct. 29	
14	5/12	Donald H. A. Mackinnon	℗ 10 Nov. 25	℗ 5 June 27	℗ 4 Dec. 32	
15	0	Richard Leckonby Phipps	10 April 25	31 Dec. 28	℗ 3 May 33	
13	0	George Witham........	℗ 20 Mar. 27	℗ 26 Oct. 30	℗ 11 July 34	
12	0	Wm. Henry Gillman....	℗ 1 July 28	14 May 31	℗ 13 May 36	
11	0	Geo. M'Beath.........	℗ 15 Oct. 29	℗ 31 May 33	℗ 28 Oct. 36	
10	0	James Benners Parkinson	℗ 11 June 30	℗ 28 June 33	℗ 15 Sept. 37	
9	0	Alfred Edward Hill	℗ 9 Aug. 31	℗ 11 July 34	℗ 18 May 38	
8	0	Robert Hilaro Barlow ..	℗ 17 Aug. 32	℗ 26 June 35	℗ 5 Oct. 38	
7	0	Arthur Mainwaring	℗ 3 May 33	℗ 13 May 36	℗ 13 Oct. 38	

		LIEUTENANTS.			
17	0	℗ James Duff[3]........	15 May 23	20 July 25	
15	0	Evan Macpherson	8 April 25	℗ 20 Mar. 27	
7	0	John Moore Napier	℗ 31 May 33	℗ 20 May 36	
7	0	Mascie Domville Taylor..	℗ 10 May 33	18 Dec. 35	
7	0	Henry Smyth........	℗ 28 June 33	℗ 28 Oct. 36	
7	0	Herbert Blount	℗ 8 Nov. 33	℗ 15 Sept. 37	
7	0	Henry Aime Ouvry	℗ 17 Oct. 33	℗ 4 Sept. 35	
7	0	William Cross........	℗ 29 Nov. 33	℗ 19 Jan. 38	
6	0	John Johnston	℗ 11 July 34	℗ 18 May 38	
5	0	Percy Hill	℗ 24 April 35	℗ 5 Oct. 38	
5	0	Heneage G. Wynne	℗ 10 July 35	℗ 13 Oct. 38	

3 Lieut. Duff accompanied the expedition to Walcheren, and was twice wounded in the head in action with the enemy before Flushing, 5th Aug. 1809. Served in the Peninsula, from June, 1811, to the end of the war, including the action of Moresco, 20th June; heights above Moresco, 21st June, 1812; battle of Salamanca; capture of Madrid and Fort El-Retiro; action at Olmas, near Burgos, 20th Oct., and at San Munos, 17th Nov. 1812; battles of Vittoria, Pampeluna, Pyrenees, Eschelar, Lazacco, Nivelle, (severely wounded through the left foot), near Bayonne 12th and 13th Feb., and Orthes, besides minor actions and skirmishes.

		ENSIGNS.			
4	0	Lincoln C. Elwes	℗ 20 May 36		
4	0	William W. Horner	22 July 36		
3	0	Peter Chas. S. Grant....	℗ 15 Sept. 37		
2	0	William Rhodes	℗ 18 May 38		
2	0	Salway Browne	℗ 25 May 38		
2	0	Alfred Tipping	℗ 22 June 38		
2	0	Walter Y. Beale......	℗ 5 Oct. 38		
2	0	Robert G. Jephson....	℗ 19 Oct. 38		
1	0	Chas. Orlando Bridgeman	℗ 8 Mar. 39		
1	0	Graham Elmslie	℗ 23 Aug. 39		
12	3	*Paymaster.*—Lempster Bulkeley, 10 May, 39; *Ens.* 8 April, 25; *Lieut.* 29 May, 28; *Capt.* 9 Jan. 35.			
6	0	*Adjutant.*—John Johnston (*Lieut.*) 1 June, 38.			
5	0	*Quarter-Master.*—James Baxter, 15 July, 35.			
		Surgeon.—John Collis Carter, M.D. 19 Oct. 38; *Assist.-Surg.* 2 June, 25, *Hosp.-Assist.* 10 Jan. 14.			
6	0	*Assistant-Surgeons.*—Alexander Leslie, 18 July, 34.			
5	0	Charles Irving, 12 June, 35.			

Facings Green.—*Agent*, Messrs. Cox & Co.—*Irish Agent*, Borough & Co.

1 Sir Wm. Johnston embarked for Toulon in 1793, and was present at several affairs of out-posts, and at the action of the heights, when Gen. O'Hara was made prisoner. Served in Corsica, and was present at the capture of Bastia and Calvi (wounded). Accompanied the expedition to Tuscany in 1797. Served in the expedition against the Danish West India Islands in 1801, and the expedition to Walcheren. Commanded the 68th at the siege of Flushing. Sir Wm. has received a medal and two clasps for Salamanca, Vittoria, (severely wounded), and Orthes.

2 Col. Cross served in the Peninsula from 1808 to the end of the war, with the exception of a short period in 1809, including the campaign and battle of Corunna; action at Almeida on the Coa, 24 July, 1810; battle of Busaco. Actions at Pombal 11th March, Redinha 12th March (wounded), Miranda de Covo 14th March, Foz de Aronce 15th March, Sabugal 3d April, battle of Fuentes d'Onor 3rd and 5th May, 1811. Siege of Ciudad Rodrigo, from 8th to 19th Jan. Actions of San Munoz, 17th Nov. 1812, San Millan 18th June, 1813; battle of Vittoria: Lezacco bridge, Bidossoa, 30th Aug.; Vera 7th Oct. Nivelle, Nive (9th, 10th, and 11th Dec. 1813), Orthes, Tarbes, and Toulouse. Received a severe contusion on the 18th June at Waterloo. Col. Cross served in the Light Division as a volunteer, with the 1st battalion of the 52nd Light Infantry, when effective in the 2d battalion, from 31st Dec. 1812 to July, 1816.

Emb. for Foreign Service, 1831.] **69th (*or* South Lincolnshire) Regiment of Foot.** [Serving in Nova Scotia.

"JAVA"—"BOURBON"—"WATERLOO"—"INDIA."

Years' Serv.		
59		*Colonel.*

John Vincent,¹ *Ens.* 16 July, 1781; *Lieut.* 3 Aug. 82; *Capt.* 26 Oct. 86; *Major*, 6 May, 95; *Lieut.-Col.* 1 Jan. 1800; *Col.* 25 July, 10; *Major-Gen.* 4 June, 13; *Lieut.-Gen.* 27 May, 25, *Col.* 69th Regiment, 2 Jan. 36.

Full Pay.	Half Pay.	
		Lieut.-Colonel.
26	0	☷ Eaton Monins,² *Ens.* p 1 Dec. 14; *Lieut.* p 9 Sept. 19; *Capt.* p 23 June, 25; *Major*, p 19 Nov. 30; *Lieut.-Col.* p 2 Oct. 35.
		Majors.
27	1 8/12	ᛒ Robert Brookes,³ *Ens.* 16 May, 11; *Lieut.* 23 Aug. 13; *Capt.* p 27 Aug. 25; *Major*, p 3 May, 31.
19	3 7/12	Wm. Noel Hill,⁴ *Ens.* p 13 Nov. 17; *Lieut.* p 24 Oct. 21; *Capt.* p 14 Nov. 26; *Major*, p 4 Dec. 35.

		CAPTAINS.	ENSIGN.	LIEUT.	CAPTAIN.	BREV.-MAJ.
30	0	☷ Brooke Pigot⁵	19 July 10	p 9 May 11	p 29 Aug. 26	
23	10	ᛒ Rich. Wheeler Hooper⁶	28 Aug. 07	p 4 Jan. 10	p 8 Dec. 14	10 Jan. 37
13	0	Wm. Blackburne	p 27 Apr. 27	p 19 Nov. 30	p 6 Feb. 35	
12	0	Edm. Stephen Thomas ..	p 25 Nov. 28	p 28 Oct. 31	p 1 May 35	
30	0	George B. Rose⁷	25 Dec. 10	26 June 12	26 June 35	
10	0	Edmund Garland	p 19 Nov. 30	p 22 Aug. 34	p 9 Oct. 35	
25	1 8/12	Wm. Considine	23 Feb. 14	p 9 Sept. 19	p 25 June 29	
9	0	Charles James Coote	p 21 June 31	p 19 Dec. 34	p 14 Apr. 37	
22	0	Henry D. O'Halloran ..	1 Nov. 18	p 28 June 27	p 1 Sept. 38	
12	1 1/12	James Llewellyn Paxton	p 19 Apr. 27	p 12 Oct. 30	p 6 July 38	
		LIEUTENANTS.				
26	1 2/12	ᛒ Henry Bridger Tudor⁸	16 May 13	19 Oct. 20		
19	11 8/12	Charles Dutton	10 May 10	15 Oct. 12		
10	0	St. John Mundell	p 11 June 30	27 Mar. 33		
7	0	William Walker	2 Aug. 33	p 1 May 35		
7	0	Edward Hemphill	p 16 Aug. 33	p 24 July 35		
8	0	George Losack	p 11 May 32	p 9 Oct. 35		
9	0	W. J. B. M'Leod Moore	1 Nov. 31	4 Jan. 36		
6	0	Duval Knox O'Reilly....	p 18 July 34	p 7 Oct. 36		
6	0	Henry Wm. Knox Gore..	p 19 Dec. 34	12 May 37		
5	0	Alex. Magnay..........	p 1 May 35	p 1 Sept. 38		
5	0	Jas. Handasyde Edgar...	p 9 Oct. 35	p 28 June 39		
4	0	Charles Fred. Law......	p 7 Oct. 36	p 8 Nov. 39		
		ENSIGNS.				
5	0	Frederick Mundell......	p 24 July 35			
4	0	Thos. J. Kearney	27 Jan. 37			
3	0	Campbell Sawers	p 14 Apr. 37			
2	0	Percival Fenwick	p 28 Sept. 38			
2	0	Cha. W. Tuper	8 Feb. 39			
1	0	Tho. Cochrane Inglis....	p 14 June 39			
1	0	Tho. Geo. Lord Glamis..	p 28 June 39			
1	0	John Ballard Gardiner ..	25 Oct. 39			
1	0	Mar. Collingwood Hughes	p 8 Nov. 39			
19	0	*Paymaster.*—F. Henry Dalgety, 1 March, 39; *Ens.* 11 Jan. 21; *Lt.* 23 Mar. 26.				
3	0	*Adjutant.*—T. John Kearney, (*Ens.*) 30 March, 38.				
3	0	*Quarter-Master.*—James Hollis, 3 Nov. 37.				
25	0	*Surgeon.*—Francis O'Brien, 11 Jan. 39; *Assist.-Surg.* 27 Oct. 25; *Hosp.-Asst.* 12 July, 15.				
3	0	*Assist.-Surgeons.*—Edward Robertson, M.D. 11 Aug. 37.				
4	0	James Napper Irwin, 7 Oct. 36.				

Notes (right column):

6 Major Hooper served in the Peninsula from 1809 to 1811, and was severely wounded in the right shoulder at the battle of Albuhera. Served also in America in 1814 & 15.

7 Captain Rose commanded a section of the Forlorn Hope at the storming of the Arumbooly lines in Travancore, East Indies, 10th Feb. 09. Present in the engagement of Nagra Coil and Kotar, and at the Forts of Palanavarum and Woodaghery. Served also at the capture of Bourbon and the Isle of France, in 1810, and of Java in 1811.

8 Lieut. Tudor served in the Peninsula from 1813 to the end of the war.

Facings Green.—*Agent*, Messrs. Cox & Co.—*Irish Agent*, Mr. Atkinson.

1 General Vincent served in the West Indies, and was at the taking of St. Domingo. He served in the expedition to the Helder, and subsequently in the expedition to Copenhagen, under Sir Hyde Parker.

2 Colonel Monins served at Waterloo on the 18th June, with the 52nd Light Infantry, and with the army of occupation in France.

3 Major Brookes served in the Peninsula from July, 1811, to the end of the war, including the following battles, sieges, &c., viz.: Badajoz, Salamanca, Burgos, Palentia, Osma, Vittoria, San Sebastian, Aug. and Sept. 1813, Santa Clara (wounded), Bidassoa (wounded), Nivelle, Nive, 9th, 10th (wounded), and 11th Dec. and blockade of Bayonne. Proceeded to North America with the force that embarked from Bourdeaux, and served there until the termination of the American war.

4 Major Hill served in the Burmese War, including the actions of Prome and Tandwayn.

5 Captain Pigot served in Holland, Belgium, and France, from Dec. 1813 to Jan. 1816, including both actions at Merxem, and bombardment of the French fleet at Antwerp. Severely wounded in the head in the action of the 16th June at Quatre Bras.

Emb. for Foreign Service, 1834.] **70th (or the Surrey) Regiment of Foot.** [Serving in the West Indies.

Years' Serv.						
Full Pay	Half Pay	*Colonel.*				
57		Gage John Hall, *Ens.* 29 May, 1783; *Lieut.* 13 Dec. 83; *Capt.* 16 Dec. 94; *Major*, 23 Dec. 95; *Lieut.-Col.* 1 Jan. 01; *Col.* 25 July, 10; *Major-Gen.* 4 June, 13; *Lieut.-Gen.* 27 May, 25; *Col.* 70th Regiment, 30 Jan. 32.				
		Lieut.-Colonel.				
37	0	Joseph Kelsall, *Ens.* 17 Dec. 03; *Lieut.* p 21 Feb. 05; *Capt.* 11 Nov. 13; *Major*, 23 Nov. 32; *Lieut.-Col.* 28 June, 38.				
		Majors.				
31	0	p Edw. James White,[1] *Ens.* 30 Mar. 09; *Lieut.* 5 April, 10; *Capt.* 14 July, 25; *Major*, p 14 Dec. 32.				
37	$\frac{5}{12}$	Thomas Reed,[2] *Ens.* 9 July, 03; *Lieut.* 25 Sept. 04; *Capt.* 27 May, 13; *Brevet-Major*, 10 Jan. 37; *Regtl.-Major*, 28 June, 38.				
		CAPTAINS.	ENSIGN.	LIEUT.	CAPTAIN.	BREV.-MAJ.
30	0	William Taylor	p 7 Feb. 11	23 Apr. 12	1 Mar. 32	
27	0	Samuel Whyte	1 July 13	2 Mar. 20	16 Mar. 32	
26	0	John Brown	28 Apr. 14	7 Apr. 25	5 Sept. 33	
13	$2\frac{5}{12}$	Jas. John Graham	p 28 Oct. 24	p 8 Apr. 26	p 25 Feb. 30	
19	0	John Doyle O'Brien	15 Mar. 21	p 16 June 25	p 4 Dec. 35	
14	0	George Durnford	p 17 Oct. 26	p 8 Feb. 31	p 28 Nov. 37	
13	0	Edward Kelsall	p 10 Apr. 27	p 8 Mar. 31	23 Feb. 39	
9	0	Wm. Matthew Bigge	p 19 Apr. 31	p 26 Feb. 36	p 21 June 39	
11	16	John Johnston	1 Dec. 13	10 Apr. 16	28 Aug. 39	
8	0	Trevor Chute	p 10 Aug. 32	p 28 Oct. 36	p 2 Aug. 30	
		LIEUTENANTS.				
15	0	Cha. Fred. Gibson	9 Apr. 25	20 Sept. 33		
7	0	John Wm. Baird	p 5 Apr. 33	p 11 Nov. 36		
9	0	Hen. Cha. Whalley	p 14 June 31	13 Sept. 37		
8	0	Tho. Cha. Timins	16 Mar. 32	p 28 Nov. 37		
8	0	Jas. Palliser Costobadie	p 21 Sept. 32	28 June 38		
3	0	Wm. Rob. Brereton	p 1 Dec. 37	p 7 June 39		
4	0	Chas. Sheffield Dickson	p 16 Dec. 36	p 2 Nov. 38		
2	0	Edward F. Edwards	p 11 May 38	p 5 July 39		
6	0	George Reynolds	p 30 Dec. 34	27 Dec. 38		
3	0	John Hackett	17 Nov. 37	28 Aug. 39		
14	$10\frac{5}{12}$	Robert Carew	20 July 15	8 April 25		
1	0	Edw. Benj. Braddell	p 1 Mar. 39	p 31 Jan. 40		
		ENSIGNS.				
2	0	Geo. Evatt	13 July 38			
2	0	Oswald Pilling	30 Nov. 38			
1	0	Leopold S. C. Fraser	17 May 39			
1	0	Howell Hedd L. Clough	p 7 June 39			
1	0	Rob. Wilton Cooke	p 28 June 39			
1	0	Tho. Leonard Leader	p 5 July 39			
1	0	Fra. Vere Hopegood	p 15 Nov. 39			
1	0	Robert Kay	16 Nov. 39			
1	0	Joseph Edward Addison	p 31 Jan. 40			
31	0	*Paymaster.*—George Alfred Goldfrapp, 1 March, 32; *Ens.* 1 March, 09; *Lieut.* 3 Oct. 11; *Capt.* 3 Sept. 29.				
2	0	*Adjutant.*—George Evatt, *(Ens.)* 17 May, 39.				
6	0	*Quarter-Master.*—Robert Kaye, 12 Dec. 34.				
22	$3\frac{7}{12}$	*Surgeon.*—Wm. Kemlo,[5] M.D. 3 Nov. 37; *Assist.-Surg.* 20 Jan. 25; *Hosp.-Assist.* 12 May, 15.				
14	0	*Assist.-Surgs.*—John Maharg, M.D. 21 Feb. 28; *Hosp.-Assist.* 9 Dec. 26.				
3	0	Patrick Davidson, M.D. 12 Jan. 38.				

Facings Black.—*Agent*, Messrs. Cox & Co.—*Irish Agent*, Messrs. Cane & Co.

1 Major White's services:—Campaign and battle of Corunna, and expedition to Walcheren.
2 Major Reed served in the American War, including the actions at Baltimore, Bladensburgh, and capture of Washington.
5 Dr. Kemlo served at the siege of Bhurtpore.

Emb. for For. Service, 1838.] **71st (Highland) Regt. of Foot (Lt. Infantry.)** [Serving in Canada.

"HINDOOSTAN"—"CAPE OF GOOD HOPE"—"CORUNNA"—"ROLEIA"—
"VIMIERA"—"ALMAREZ"—"FUENTES D'ONOR"—"VITTORIA"—
"PYRENEES"—"NIVE"—"ORTHES"—"PENINSULA"—"WATERLOO."

Years' Serv.			
Full Pay	Half Pay.		
38		₽ Sir Sam. Ford Whittingham,¹ K.C.B. & K.C.H. *Ens.* 20 Jan. 03; *Lieut.* 25 Feb. 03; *Capt.* 14 Feb. 05; *Major*, 12 March, 10; *Lieut.-Col.* 30 May, 11; *Col.* 4 June, 14; *Major-Gen.* 27 May, 25; *Lieut.-Gen.* 28 June, 38; *Col.* 71st Light Infantry, 28 March, 38.	
		Lieut.-Colonel.	
16	3 5/12	Hon. Charles Grey, *2nd Lieut.* 16 Nov. 20; *Lieut.* ᴾ 10 April, 23; *Capt.* ᴾ 16 June, 25; *Major*, ᴾ 19 Feb. 28; *Lieut.-Col.* ᴾ 12 July, 31.	
		Majors.	
18	10/12	William Denny, *Ens.* ᴾ 10 Jan. 22; *Lieut.* ᴾ 23 June, 25; *Capt.* ᴾ 27 Sept. 33; *Major*, ᴾ 24 April, 38.	
12	5	Lord Arthur Lennox, *Ens.* ᴾ 24 June, 23; *Lieut.* ᴾ 22 Oct. 25; *Capt.* ᴾ 1 Aug. 26; *Major*, ᴾ 6 July, 38.	

		CAPTAINS.	ENSIGN.	LIEUT.	CAPTAIN.	BREV.-MAJ.
26	0	₩₽ A. Rob. L'Estrange²	7 Dec. 14	ᴾ 20 Dec. 21	ᴾ 7 Jan. 30	
26	0	₩₽ John Impett²	14 Apr. 14	ᴾ 5 Oct. 20	30 Jan. 35	
15	0	Wm. Jas. Myers	ᴾ 9 June 25	ᴾ 7 Jan. 30	ᴾ 29 Dec. 35	
13	0	Edward Foy	22 Nov. 27	ᴾ 15 June 30	ᴾ 18 Mar. 36	
15	0	Hen. Tristram Beresford	ᴾ 9 Feb. 26	ᴾ 26 Apr. 31	ᴾ 20 May 36	
14	0	Hen. Edmund Austen	ᴾ 10 June 26	ᴾ 27 Sept. 33	ᴾ 29 July 36	
14	0	Wilhelm Speer	ᴾ 26 Sept. 26	30 Jan. 35	ᴾ 24 Mar. 38	
9	0	Sir Hew Dalrymple, *Bt.*	ᴾ 15 Feb. 31	ᴾ 4 Sept. 35	ᴾ 24 Apr. 38	
12	0	Nath. Massey Stack	ᴾ 25 Nov. 28	ᴾ 29 Dec. 35	ᴾ 6 July 38	
23	0	George Cuming	27 Mar. 17	9 Apr. 25	31 Jan. 40	
		LIEUTENANTS.				
11	0	Jas. H. C. Robertson	2 July 29	30 Dec. 35		
9	0	R. T. W. L. Brickenden	ᴾ 26 Apr. 31	ᴾ 18 Mar. 36		
8	0	Charles Ready	ᴾ 13 July 32	ᴾ 19 Mar. 36		
7	0	William Wilkieson	ᴾ 21 June 33	ᴾ 20 May 36		
6	0	A. P. Gordon Cumming	ᴾ 6 Feb. 35	ᴾ 1 July 36		
5	0	Rob. Fran. Hunter	ᴾ 13 Mar. 35	ᴾ 29 July 36		
5	0	Thos. H. Colvill	22 May 35	ᴾ 8 Dec. 37		
5	0	William Hope	ᴾ 4 Sept. 35	ᴾ 24 Mar. 38		
5	0	Aug. T. Hamilton	ᴾ 29 Dec. 35	ᴾ 24 Apr. 38		
4	0	Barry Blennerhasset	ᴾ 18 Mar. 36	ᴾ 6 July 38		
		ENSIGNS.				
4	0	Wm. Fairholme	ᴾ 19 Mar. 36			
4	0	George Dance	ᴾ 8 Apr. 36			
4	0	G. A. Bayly	ᴾ 29 Apr. 36			
4	0	S. J. *Lord* Aberdour	ᴾ 20 May 36			
4	0	Lynedock Douglas	ᴾ 29 July 36			
3	0	Fra. G. Scott	4 Aug. 37			
3	0	G. A. C. Dashwood	ᴾ 8 Dec. 37			
2	0	J. E. Fleeming	ᴾ 24 Mar. 38			
2	0	R. R. Uniacke	ᴾ 24 Apr. 38			
2	0	Hon. H. H. H. Duncan	ᴾ 6 July 38			

22	9½	*Paymaster.*—₽ T. Dutton,³ 1 Apr. 36; *Ens.* 7 Sept. 09; *Lieut.* 14 Apr. 13.	
11	0	*Adjutant.*—James H. C. Robertson, (*Lieut.*) 13 Feb. 35.	
3	0	*Quarter-Master.*—Wm. Wakefield, 13 Dec. 39; *Ens.* 1 Feb. 38.	
		Surgeon.—₽ T. Bulkeley, M.D. 5 Nov. 12; *Assist.-Surg.* 25 March, 08.	
2	0	*Assistant-Surgeons.*—C. Campbell Hamilton Grant, 30 March 38.	
5	0	John Duncan Macdiarmid, 4 Dec. 35.	

Facings Buff.—*Agent,* Messrs. Cox & Co.

1 Sir Sam. Ford Whittingham was wounded at Talavera.
2 Captains L'Estrange and Impett served at Waterloo on the 18th June.
3 Paymaster Dutton served in the Peninsula, from Nov. 1812 to the end of the war, including the battles of Vittoria, the Pyrenees (wounded 25th July), Nivelle and Orthes. Served also in the American war, including the sieges of Fort Erie, and operations on the Niagara frontier.

Emb. for Foreign Service, 1828.] **72nd (or D. of Albany's own Highlanders.)** [Serving at the C. of G. Hope.

"HINDOOSTAN"—"CAPE OF GOOD HOPE."

Colonel.

P ĠĦ Sir Colin Campbell,[1] K.C.B. *Ens.* 3 Oct.1799; *Lieut.* 21 Aug. 1801; *Capt.* 9 Jan. 05; *Major*, 2 Sept. 08; *Lieut.-Col.* 3 May, 10; *Col.* 4 June, 14; *Major-Gen.* 27 May, 25; *Lieut.-Gen.* 28 June, 38; *Col.* 72nd Highlanders, 15 Aug. 36.

Lieut.-Colonel.

Charles George James Arbuthnot, *Ens. & Lieut.* 26 Dec. 16; *Capt.* P 16 March, 20; *Major*, P 3 July, 23; *Lieut.-Col.* P 1 Oct. 25; *Col.* 28 June, 38.

Majors.

Charles Maxwell Maclean, *Ens.* 29 Oct. 07; *Lieut.* 21 Dec. 09; *Capt.* P 24 July, 23; *Major*, P 1 Feb. 27.

Frederick Hope, *Ens.* P 11 July, 16; *Lieut.* P 24 Oct. 21; *Capt.* P 9 June, 25; *Major*, P 4 Oct. 33.

Years' Serv. Full Pay	Years' Serv. Half Pay	CAPTAINS.	ENSIGN.	LIEUT.	CAPTAIN.	BREV.-MAJ.
32	3 8/12	P John Doyle[2]	28 Sept. 04	13 Nov. 05	29 Sept. 13	10 Jan. 37
36	0	Peter Sutherland[3]	1 Sept. 04	15 Jan. 07	20 May 19	10 Jan 37
29	1/12	Henry Jervis	19 Dec. 11	29 Dec. 14	P 19 Sept. 26	
17	0	William Henry Robinson	8 Jan. 24	P 29 Aug. 26	P 21 June 30	
15	0	Thomas E. Lacy	8 Apr. 25	P 3 Oct. 26	P 11 July 34	
15	0	Robert Baillie	P 8 Oct. 25	P 3 Aug. 30	P 29 May 35	
14	0	Chas. Wm. M. Payne	P 1 Aug. 26	P 21 June 31	P 29 Dec. 35	
11	0	Edward John Fra. Kelso	14 May 29	P 2 Dec. 31	P 12 Aug. 36	
20	0	John Frith	6 Apr. 20	P 26 Aug. 24	7 Apr. 39	
11	0	Arthur Lowry Balfour	P 6 Aug. 29	P 29 Mar. 33	P 31 May 39	
		LIEUTENANTS.				
23	3 7/12	Lewis X. Leslie[4]	25 Dec. 13	P 1 July 24	3 Major Sutherland served at the capture of the Cape of Good Hope in 1806.	
17	9/12	Donough O'Brien	12 Sept. 22	2 July 29		
10	0	Andr. Sandilands Fisher	P 26 Feb. 30	P 21 Mar. 34	4 Lieut. Leslie served the campaign of 1814 in Canada.	
9	0	Charles Moylan	P 2 Dec. 31	P 29 May 35		
8	0	Hon. Charles Stuart	P 2 Mar. 32	P 29 Dec. 35	5 Captain Graham served at the capture of the Isle of France in 1810.	
8	0	William Rattray	3 Mar. 32	P 15 Apr. 36		
8	0	Thomas E. Pollard	11 Jan. 33	P 12 Aug. 36		
7	0	John Thomas Hope	P 29 Mar. 33	P 23 Dec. 36		
7	0	Thomas. Fred. Simmons	P 6 Dec. 33	P 28 Oct. 37		
6	0	A. Nowell Sherson	P 21 Mar. 34	P 8 Feb. 39		
6	0	George Pott Erskine	P 11 July 34	P 1 Mar. 39		
5	0	Jas. Aug. Harding	P 29 May 35	7 Apr. 39		
5	0	Hugh S. S. Burney	P 29 Dec. 35	P 14 June 39		
		ENSIGNS.				
4	0	J. Crighton Harris	P 12 Aug. 36			
4	0	William Adam	P 23 Dec. 36			
2	0	Wm. W. T. Cole	19 Oct. 38			
2	0	Geo. Ramsay Perceval	P 8 Feb. 39			
1	0	Wm. Hobart Seymour	P 1 Mar. 39			
1	0	John Wm. Garsford	P 31 May 39			
1	0	Hon. Cha. R. Pakenham	14 June 39			
1	0	Maurice Cane	15 June 39			

Paymaster.—William Graham,[5] 13 Oct. 25; *Ens.* 16 April, 05; *Lieut.* 21 April, 08; *Capt.* 7 April, 25. (35 / 0)

Adjutant.—Charles Moylan, (*Lieut.*) 14 April, 37. (9 / 0)

Quarter-Master.—William Hume, 24 April, 38. (2 / 0)

Surgeon.—Thomas Clarke, 15 Jan. 24; *Assist.-Surg.* 3 June, 13; *Hosp.-Assist.* 24 July, 1812. (28 / 0)

Assistant-Surgeons.—James Malcolm, 25 March, 28; *Hosp.-Assist.* 14 Dec. 26. (14 / 0)

William Michael Ford, 1 June, 26; *Hosp.-Assist.* 16 Feb. 26. (14 / 0)

Facings Yellow.—*Agent*, Messrs. Cox & Co.

---

1 Sir Colin Campbell has received a cross and six clasps for Talavera, Busaco, Fuentes d'Onor, Badajoz, Salamanca, Vittoria, Pyrenees, Nivelle, Nive, and Toulouse.

2 Major Doyle served with the expedition to South America, including the siege of and sortie from Monte Video, and storm by the enemy of Colonia. Served also in the South of France, from Dec. 1813 to the end of the war, including the blockade of and sortie from Bayonne, where he received a contusion on the left arm.

[Emb. for Foreign Service, 1827.] **73rd Regiment of Foot.** [Serving in North America.]

"MANGALORE"—"SERINGAPATAM"—"WATERLOO."

Years' Serv.		
Full Pay.	Half Pay.	
45		**Colonel.** 🎖 Wm. George, **Lord Harris**,¹ C.B. & K.C.H. *Ens.* 24 May, 1795; *Lieut.* 3 Jan. 96; *Capt.* 16 Oct. 1800; *Major*, 15 June, 04; *Lieut.-Col.* 29 Dec. 06; *Col.* 4 June, 14; *Major-Gen.* 19 July, 21; *Lieut.-Gen.* 10 Jan. 37; *Col.* 73d Regt. 4 Dec. 35.
36	0	*Lieut.-Col.*—🎖 Jas. Fred. Love,² C.B. K.H. *Ens.* 26 Oct. 04; *Lt.* 5 June,05; *Capt.* 11 July, 11; *Brev.-Major*, 16 March, 15; *Brev.-Lieut.-Col.* 5 May, 25; *Regtl.-Major*, 9 July,30; *Regtl.-Lieut.-Col.* 6 Sept. 34; *Col.* 28 June,38.
32	1 1/12	*Majors.*—🎖 Chas. Jowett Van der Meulen,³ *Ens.* 26 Nov. 07; *Lieut.* 10 Aug. 09; *Capt.* P 25 Nov. 23; *Major*, 7 April, 37.
15	2 2/12	William Eyre, *Ens.* P 17 Apr. 23; *Lieut.* P 5 Nov. 25; *Capt.* P 20 Mar. 27; *Major* P 19 July 39.

Years' Serv. Full	Half	CAPTAINS.	ENSIGN.	LIEUT.	CAPTAIN.	BREV.-MAJ.
22	0	Geo. Hankey Smith	P 7 May 18	P 7 Feb. 22	P 8 Apr. 26	
29	0	George Dawson⁴	7 May 11	7 Jan. 13	20 Mar. 28	
15	7/12	Adol. Lat. Widdrington	25 Jan. 25	P 26 Nov. 25	P 10 Nov. 29	
14	5/12	Anth. Coningham Sterling	P 29 Jan. 26	P 14 Apr. 29	P 11 Oct. 33	
13	2 2/12	John William Cross	21 Dec. 25	P 24 Jan. 28	P 28 Dec. 32	
15	0	Fred. Geo. Aug. Pinckney	8 Apr. 25	P 8 Apr. 26	P 23 Dec. 36	
15	0	Cha. Fred. Parkinson	10 Nov. 25	4 Sept. 28	P 22 Feb. 33	
14	0	Charles Wm. Combe	P 30 Aug. 26	P 12 June 30	P 12 July 39	
12	0	Thos. Fraser Sandeman	P 18 Dec. 28	P 27 July 32	P 19 July 39	
23	3 1/12	Charles Barry	23 Mar. 14	3 Feb. 15	P 21 July 25	28 June 38
		LIEUTENANTS.				
15	0	Benjamin Brown	P 7 July 25	15 May 28		
12	2 3/12	Oliver Barker D'Arcey	P 8 Apr. 26	P 9 Dec. 31		
12	0	Wm. Hen. Kenny	3 Apr. 28	15 Mar. 32		
15	0	David Cahill	10 Nov. 25	21 Dec. 32		
9	0	Maurice Chas. O'Connell	P 19 July 31	P 24 Jan. 34		
9	0	Wm. L. Y. Baker	25 Nov. 31	P 27 June 34		
10	0	Walter Beresford Faunce	P 18 Jan. 31	P 23 Dec. 36		
9	0	Edw. George Cubitt	P 9 Dec. 31	P 28 Apr. 37		
8	0	Wm. B. T. O'Connell	P 16 Mar. 32	P 16 June 37		
8	0	Aug. Wm. Murray	P 28 Dec. 32	P 28 Nov. 37		
6	0	Gerald Wardlaw	P 27 June 34	P 12 Apr. 39		
6	0	Rob. Carter Bamford	P 5 Sept. 34	P 12 July 39		
4	0	Melville G. B. Browne	P 23 Dec. 36	P 19 July 39		
		ENSIGNS.				
4	0	Douglas Jones	P 30 Dec. 36			
3	0	Wm. H. Fitz Gerald	P 5 May 37			
3	0	Rob. P. Campbell	P 16 June 37			
3	0	James F. Murray	P 28 Nov. 37			
2	0	Alfred A. Simmons	28 Dec. 38			
1	0	Geo. Edm. N. Nugent	P 12 Apr. 39			
1	0	Charles Littlehales	P 22 June 39			
1	0	John Davies	P 19 July 39			

3 Major Van der Meulen served in the Peninsula from May 1809 to Aug. 1811, and again from Sept. 1812 to the end of the war, including the battles of Talavera (severely wounded), Busaco, Albuhera (severely wounded), Vittoria, Pyrenees (severely wounded 28th July), Nivelle, Orthes and Toulouse, besides various minor engagements and skirmishes.

4 Captain Dawson served in the Kandian War in Ceylon.

5 Quarter-Master Hickson served the campaign of 1814 in Canada, and that of 1815 in the Netherlands and France.

6 Dr. Foster served the campaign of 1814 in Holland.

19	12 7/12	*Paymaster.*—John Court, 22 July, 36; *2nd Lieut.* 2 Nov. 08; *Lieut.* 7 Feb. 11.
15	0	*Adjutant.*—Benjamin Brown, (*Lieut.*) 17 Nov. 37.
22	5 1/12	*Quarter-Master.*—John A. Hickson,⁵ 11 Nov. 24; *Ens.* 25 Dec. 13.
25	1 1/12	*Surgeon.*—John Foster,⁶ M.D. 1 April, 36; *Assist.-Surg.* 9 Nov. 15; *Hosp.-Assist.* 22 Nov. 13.
6	0	*Assist.-Surgs.*—George Martin, M.D. 13 June, 34.
15	0	John James Russell, 25 April, 26; *Hosp.-Assist.* 16 June. 25.

Facings Green.—*Agent*, Messrs. Cox & Co.

---

1 Lord Harris joined the 76th regiment in India in 1797, and was present at the battle of Mallavelly; nearly all the affairs of out-posts, and in the storming party which carried Seringapatam. The battle of Blueberg, Cape of Good Hope; served in Holland in 1813 and 14, and commanded the brigade which carried the village of Merxem; severely wounded through the right shoulder at Waterloo. A superb sword was voted to Lord Harris by the officers of the 73d on his retiring from the command of that corps, in testimony of the high regard they entertained for his character and conduct.

2 Colonel Love served with the 52nd regiment in the expedition to Sweden under Sir John Moore, and afterwards in Portugal and Spain, including the advance into Spain, retreat to, and battle of Corunna, besides the different affairs on the retreat. Served afterwards in the Peninsula with the Light Division, including the storming of Ciudad Rodrigo, and all the affairs and battles in which the Light Division took a part up to 1812. During the campaign in Holland under Lord Lynedock, he was present at the attack on the fortified village of Merxem, and the bombardment of Antwerp. Present in the several affairs before New Orleans, and in the attack on that place, on which occasion he had two horses shot under him, and was slightly wounded in the arm by a rifle-ball. Served also the campaign of 1815, and received four severe wounds at the battle of Waterloo, when the 52nd regiment charged the French Imperial Guards. 225

Emb. for Foreign Service, 1834.] **74th Regiment of Foot.** [Serving at Trinidad.

The *Elephant*, superscribed "SERINGAPATAM"—"ASSAYE"—"BUSACO"—"FUENTES D'ONOR"—"CIUDAD RODRIGO"—"BADAJOZ"—"SALAMANCA"—"VITTORIA"—"PYRENEES"—"NIVELLE"—"ORTHES"—"TOULOUSE"—"PENINSULA."

Years' Serv.						
Full Pay.	Half Pay.	*Colonel.*				
49		Sir Phineas Riall,[1] K.C.H. *Ens.* 31 Jan. 1792; *Lieut.* 28 Feb. 94; *Capt.* 31 May, 94; *Major*, 8 Dec. 94; *Lieut.-Col.* 1 Jan. 1800; *Col.* 25 July, 10; *Major-Gen.* 4 June, 13; *Lieut.-Gen.* 27 May, 25; *Col.* 74th Regt. 20 May, 35.				
41	0	*Lieut.-Colonel.*—🅱 John Alex. Mein,[2] *Ens.* 14 Nov. 99; *Lieut.* 5 April, 01; *Capt.* 29 Feb. 04; *Major*, 11 Nov. 13; *Lieut.-Col.* 20 March, 23; *Col.* 28 June, 38.				
33	0	*Majors.*—🅱 Eyre John Crabbe,[3] K.H. *Ens.* 11 June, 07; *Lieut.* P 11 March, 08; *Capt.* 19 May, 14; *Major*, P 31 Jan. 28.				
28	1 5/12	Wm. White Crawley,[4] *Ens.* P 18 July 11; *Lieut.* P 19 Mar. 12; *Capt.* P 7 Nov. 22; *Brev.-Major*, 10 Jan. 37, *Regtl.-Major*, 13 Oct. 39.				
		CAPTAINS.	ENSIGN.	LIEUT.	CAPTAIN.	BREV.-MAJ.
30	4	🅱 John Casimir Harold[5]..	25 Sept. 06	28 May 07	16 Feb. 15	10 Jan. 37
26	1/12	Colin Alex. Campbell ..	P 25 Aug. 14	25 Jan. 25	P 25 Feb. 26	
31	2	🅱 John Alves[6]	5 Nov. 07	25 Dec. 10	13 Mar. 27	
21	0	Aug. Fran. Ansell	13 Jan. 20	P 19 Sept. 26	P 14 Dec. 32	
14	0	*Hon.* Tho. O'Grady	P 30 Dec. 26	P 24 Nov. 29	P 3 Oct. 34	
14	0	Edw. Clarges Ansell ...	10 Mar. 26	9 Nov. 30	P 23 Oct. 35	
25	2 5/12	John Campbell	P 16 Sept. 13	P 28 Sept. 20	15 Dec. 37	
13	0	Hen. Hewett Thompson..	P 12 Feb. 28	P 14 Dec. 32	P 17 May 39	
22	0	Annesley Eyre	14 May 18	20 Sept. 26	13 Oct. 39	
10	0	S. F. De Saumarez......	1 Oct. 30	P 11 July 34	P 22 Nov. 39	
		LIEUTENANTS.				
13	0	Duncan Fraser	P 13 Feb. 28	10 Dec. 33	5 Major Harold's services :— Campaign and battle of Corunna, Expedition to Walcheren and siege of Flushing.	
9	0	Geo. Tho. Evans........	P 17 May 31	P 29 Aug. 34		
9	0	Peter Wm. L. Hawker ..	P 9 Aug. 31	P 3 Oct. 34		
8	0	Walter Warde	P 29 June 32	P 7 Aug. 35	6 Capt. Alves served the whole of the campaigns of 1810, 11, 12, 13, and 14, with the 74th regiment, in the 3d division, without having ever been absent from it for a single day, including the battles of Busaco, Fuentes d'Onor, siege and storming of Ciudad Rodrigo, siege and storming of Badajoz, battle of Salamanca, capture of Madrid, battle of Vittoria, capture of Pampeluna, the battles in the Pyrenees, Nivelle, Orthes, and Toulouse, besides various affairs of out-posts.	
9	0	Edw. C. Munns........	13 Sept. 31	P 9 Jan. 35		
8	0	Geo. Wm. Fordyce	P 28 Dec. 32	P 5 Aug. 37		
7	0	Christ. B. Cardew......	27 Dec. 33	P 17 Mar. 38		
6	0	Geo. Monkland	P 11 July 34	25 May 38		
6	0	Acheson Eyre Obins	P 29 Aug. 34	P 10 Aug. 38		
5	0	Robert Walsh..........	P 7 Aug. 35	P 14 June 39		
3	0	John Inman	15 Dec. 37	13 Oct. 39		
10	0	William Hemphill......	13 June 30	P 9 Oct. 35		
2	0	Fitz H. W. L. Hancock..	P 17 Mar. 38	P 22 Nov. 39		
		ENSIGNS.			7 Paymaster Davies served in the Peninsula from Sept. 1811 to the end of the war, including the capture of Fort Picarina and Badajoz; battles of Salamanca, Vittoria, Pyrenees, Nivelle, Nivelle, Tarbes, Orthes & Toulouse. 8 Dr. Cumming served at New Orleans in 1814 and 15, and in the Burmese war in 1826.	
2	0	John Walker	9 Aug. 38			
2	0	Ormby Willington	P 10 Aug. 38			
2	0	J. Whitshed De Butts ..	P 18 Jan. 39			
1	0	Cha. Aylmer Coates	29 Mar. 39			
1	0	James Duff...........	P 17 May 39			
1	0	Tho. Williams Evans....	P 14 June 39			
1	0	Thomas Wallnutt	P 22 Nov. 39			
1	0	Denis Godley	23 Nov. 39			
29	0	*Paymaster.*—🅱 Richard Davies,[7] 1 Dec. 25; *Ens.* 6 June, 11; *Lieut.* 31 Dec. 12.				
13	0	*Adjutant.*—Duncan Fraser, (*Lieut.*) 21 April, 37.				
9	0	*Quarter-Master.*—Daniel M'Curdy, 26 Aug. 31.				
16	11/12	*Surgeon.*—Alex. Cumming,[8] 13 March, 35; *Assist.-Surg.* 23 Dec. 24; *Hosp.-Assist.* 7 March, 14.				
5	0	*Assist.-Surgs.*—John Kirby, 30 Oct. 35.				
1	0	Frederick Hillman Hornbrook, 1 March, 39.				

Facings White.—*Agent,* Sir John Kirkland.

1 Sir Phineas Riall has received a medal and one clasp for Martinique and Guadaloupe. Served in America in 1813, and was severely wounded at the battle of Chipawa.

2 Colonel Mein served in the East Indies from Nov. 1799 to Feb 1806, and was engaged at Amiednaghur, Assaye, Argaum, Gawelghur, Shandore, and Gulnah. Served also in the Peninsula at different periods from Jan. 1810 to Oct. 1812, including the battle of Busaco, and siege of Badajoz in March, 1812.

3 Major Crabbe served in the Peninsula from Jan. 1810 to the 31st Dec. 1812, and again from June 1813 to the end of the war, including the whole of the retreat to the lines of Torres Vedras; battle of Busaco; the advance from the lines to Guarda; first siege of Badajoz; siege and storm of Ciudad Rodrigo; siege and storm of Badajoz; battle of Salamanca, capture of Madrid, and subsequent retreat through Spain; battles of Nivelle, Nive, Vic, Tarbes, Orthes, and Toulouse, and the whole of the various minor affairs during that period. Wounded 15th March, 1811, at Foz d'Aronce, when commanding a party which drove a French piquet from the said village. Wounded again at Toulouse when attacking the Tete du Pont.

4 Major Crawley served the Nepaul campaigns of 1814 and 15, and in the Pindarree war in 1816 and 17

Emb. for Foreign Service, 1830.] **75th *Regiment of Foot.*** [Serving at the Cape of Good Hope.

The *Royal Tiger*, superscribed " INDIA"—" SERINGAPATAM."

Years' Serv.						
Full Pay	Half Pay	*Colonel.*				
50		❧ Sir Joseph Fuller,¹ G.C.H. Ens. 29 Sept. 1790; Lieut. & Capt. 22 Jan. 94; Capt. & Lieut.-Col. 18 June, 1801; Col. 25 July, 10; Major-Gen. 4 June, 13; Lieut.-Gen. 27 May, 25; Col. 75th Regt. 9 April, 32.				
37	0	Lieut.-Colonel.—❧ Pat. Grieve,² Ens. 9 July,03; Lieut. 1 Aug.04; Capt.16 May,09; Major, ᴾ 25 Nov. 19; Brev.-Lieut.-Col. 9 Nov. 30; Regtl.-Lieut.-Col. 7 July, 37.				
17	2/12	Majors.—Rob. Dampier Hallifax, Ens. ᴾ 31 July, 23; Lieut. ᴾ 23 June, 25; Capt. ᴾ 8 April, 26; Major, ᴾ 30 July, 36.				
21	1/12	Sam. Madden Fra. Hall, Ens. ᴾ 21 Jan. 19; Lieut. 7 April, 25; Capt. ᴾ 22 April, 26; Major, ᴾ 11 July, 37.				

		CAPTAINS.	ENSIGN.	LIEUT.	CAPTAIN.	BREV.-MAJ.
17	3/12	Jas. Hen. England......	ᴾ 12 Dec. 22	11 Aug. 25	ᴾ 29 Aug. 26	
16	0	John Hen. Hartley Boys.	27 June 24	ᴾ 28 Jan. 26	ᴾ 31 Dec. 30	
15	0	Peter Delancey	ᴾ 29 Jan. 26	ᴾ 30 April 29	ᴾ 8 Mar. 33	
15	0	Charles Herbert	ᴾ 19 Nov. 25	ᴾ 10 Oct. 26	ᴾ 27 Sept. 33	
14	0	Alexander Jardine	ᴾ 22 April 26	ᴾ 25 Feb. 30	ᴾ 11 Mar. 36	
13	0	William Sutton	ᴾ 5 June 27	ᴾ 16 Mar. 30	ᴾ 30 July 36	
13	0	Edward Knollys........	ᴾ 18 Oct. 27	ᴾ 2 Nov. 30	ᴾ 17 Feb. 37	
13	0	Geo. Bligh Moultrie	ᴾ 31 Dec. 27	ᴾ 31 Dec. 30	ᴾ 11 July 37	
24	2 7/12	John Bolton³	5 Nov. 13	26 Mar. 19	4 Sept. 35	
12	0	Basil Gray	30 July 28	31 Jan. 34	29 Nov. 39	
		LIEUTENANTS.				5 Quarter-master Berry served at Malta, Sicily, Spain, and North America, from Feb. 1805 to the 29th May,1815, including the capture of Ischia and Procida; siege and capture of Tarragona; siege of Barcelona in 1813 and 14; battle of Bladensburgh and capture of Washington; actions before Baltimore and New Orleans; siege and capture of Fort Bowyer. 6 Dr. Graham served in the Peninsula, from Jan. 1810, to the end of the war, including the battles of Busaco, Albuhera, Vittoria, Pyrenees, and Nivelle. Dr. Graham was on board the unfortunate ship *Kent*, which was burnt in the Bay of Biscay, 1st March, 1825.
15	0	Rob. Boyd Brown	ᴾ 16 June 25	ᴾ 10 Aug. 26		
10	0	William Brumell	ᴾ 11 June 30	ᴾ 10 Oct. 34		
9	0	William Lucas	ᴾ 4 Oct. 31	ᴾ 13 Mar. 35		
8	0	Rich. Price Puleston....	ᴾ 18 May 32	ᴾ 11 Mar. 36		
12	0	Edward Ricard	5 June 28	24 May 32		
8	0	William Brookes........	11 Jan. 33	16 Sept. 36		
7	0	Geo. Thorne George	ᴾ 6 Sept. 33	ᴾ 9 Dec. 36		
7	0	Chas. E. P. Gordon	13 Dec. 33	ᴾ 17 Feb. 37		
10	18 1/12	❧ William Carruthers⁴ ..	22 May 12	1 Dec. 13		
6	0	John Hamilton Cox	ᴾ 10 Oct. 34	ᴾ 11 July 37		
5	0	Geo. Wm. C. Stuart	ᴾ 27 Mar. 35	ᴾ 19 Jan. 38		
4	0	A. T. Hotham..........	ᴾ 11 Mar. 36	ᴾ 11 Jan. 39		
4	0	Thos. Geo. Walker......	ᴾ 28 June 36	ᴾ 27 Sept. 39		
		ENSIGNS.				
4	0	Hen. W. Goodwyn......	ᴾ 9 Dec. 36			
3	0	Geo. Lockwood	ᴾ 11 July 37			
3	0	St. John T. Gore........	ᴾ 19 Jan. 38			
2	0	Tho. Bar. Bicknell......	ᴾ 11 Jan. 39			
1	0	John Jas. Hamilton	28 Mar. 39			
1	0	John Fred. Galiffe	29 Mar. 39			
1	0	Edward John Dickson ..	ᴾ 27 Sept. 39			
1	0	Wm. Thomas Smith	ᴾ 31 Jan. 40			
14	0	*Paymaster.*—George Henry Eddy, 28 April, 37; Ens. 29 Aug. 26; Lieut. 20 Feb. 35.				
8	0	*Adjutant.*—William Brookes (*Lieut.*) 11 Jan. 33.				
14	12 2/3	*Quarter-Master.*—❧ Richard Berry,⁵ 10 March, 14.				
31	0	*Surgeon.*—❧ Edward Smith Graham,⁶ M.D. 22 Sept. 25; *Assist.-Surg.* 18 Oct. 10; *Hosp.-Assist.* 13 Dec. 1809.				
		Assistant-Surgeons.—George Anderson, 12 June, 35.				
5	0					
1	0	Alexander Gibb, M.D. 10 Jan. 40.				

Facings Yellow.—*Agent*, Messrs. Cox & Co.—*Irish Agent*, Borough, Armit & Co.

---

1 Sir Joseph Fuller served in Flanders in 1793 and 94, and was present at the sieges of Valenciennes and Dunkirk, and in all the actions of that campaign. In 1799, he served in the expedition to the Helder, and was present in the principal actions. Sir Joseph was at the passage of the Douro, 12th May, 1809, and and has received a medal for Talavera.
2 Colonel Grieve served at the siege of Tarragona.
3 Capt. Bolton served the Mahratta campaigns of 1817 and 18, and was present at the siege of Rhyghur.
4 Lieut. Carruthers served the campaigns of 1813 and 14 in the Peninsula with the 43rd Light Infantry in the light division.

Emb. for Foreign Service, 1834.] **76th Regiment of Foot.** [Serving at Barbadoes.

The *Elephant*, circumscribed "HINDOOSTAN"—"PENINSULA."

Years' Serv.		
48		**Colonel.**
Full Pay.	Half Pay.	❦ ☬ Sir Peregrine Maitland,¹ K.C.B. *Ens.* 25 June, 1792; *Lieut. & Capt.* 30 April, 94; *Capt. & Lieut.-Col.* 25 June, 1803; *Col.* 1 Jan. 12; *Major-Gen.* 4 June, 14; *Lieut.-Gen.* 22 July, 30; *Col.* 76th Regt. 19 July, 34.
		Lieut.-Colonel.
29	1¹⁰⁄₁₂	Joseph Clarke, *Ens.* 22 March, 10; *Lieut.* ᴾ 10 June, 13; *Capt.* ᴾ 24 Feb. 25; *Major*, 26 June, 33; *Lieut.-Col.* 17th Sept. 39.
		Majors.
22	⁴⁄₁₂	John Heneage Grubbe, *Ens.* ᴾ 20 Aug. 18; *Lieut.* ᴾ 24 Feb. 25; *Capt.* ᴾ 13 May, 26; *Major*, ᴾ 19 Jan. 39.
17	⁴⁄₁₂	Robert Fanshawe Martin, *Ens.* ᴾ 26 June 23; *Lieut.* ᴾ 20 Aug. 25; *Capt.* ᴾ 10 June 26; *Major* 17 Sept. 39.

		CAPTAINS.	ENSIGN.	LIEUT.	CAPTAIN.	BREV.-MAJ.
26	0	Rich. Gardiner	12 May 14	29 Sept. 25	ᴾ 5 April 33	
14	0	Robt. Clifford Lloyd	ᴾ 30 Dec. 26	ᴾ 8 June 30	ᴾ 3 June 36	
13	0	G. F. Cooper Scott	25 Oct. 27	ᴾ 3 May 31	ᴾ 1 July 36	
17	0	Robt. Shepherd	ᴾ 10 July 23	ᴾ 13 May 26	5 Jan. 37	
24	2	John Montgomerie	ᴾ 10 Mar. 14	11 Mar. 24	7 Feb. 38	
8	0	Charles Winter	ᴾ 24 Aug. 32	ᴾ 16 Oct. 35	ᴾ 1 Feb. 39	
15	0	Wm. Wild. J. Cockcraft	8 April 25	ᴾ 22 April 26	20 July 39	
16	0	Geo. Percy Pickard	29 April 24	11 Feb. 27	17 Sept. 39	
10	0	Francis Sadlier Prittie	ᴾ 13 Aug. 30	2 Aug. 33	ᴾ 8 Nov. 39	
7	0	Henry Brewster	ᴾ 18 Oct. 33	ᴾ 19 Aug. 36	ᴾ 9 Nov. 39	
		LIEUTENANTS.				
10	0	John B. Flanagan	8 Feb. 31	28 Aug. 35		
8	0	Cha. S. S. Evans	12 Oct. 32	ᴾ 3 June 36		
7	0	Charles Murray	ᴾ 29 Mar. 33	ᴾ 1 July 36		
5	0	Collingwood Fenwick	ᴾ 4 Sept. 35	ᴾ 7 April 37		
5	0	M. S. T. Dennis	ᴾ 18 Sept. 35	ᴾ 28 Nov. 37		
9	0	John Gore Ferns	3 May 31	23 Feb. 38		
4	0	Thomas Tydd	ᴾ 3 June 36	ᴾ 19 Oct. 38		
4	0	Arch. Rutherfoord	ᴾ 19 Aug. 36	ᴾ 1 Feb. 39		
3	0	Wm. H. More Simmons	10 Mar. 37	30 June 39		
3	0	Wm. Wood Senhouse	ᴾ 7 April 37	20 July 39		
2	0	Wm. Wood Whitter	ᴾ 23 Feb. 38	17 Sept. 39		
2	0	Jas. D. Beresford	2 Mar. 38	ᴾ 8 Nov. 39		
3	0	Henry A. Grant Evans	ᴾ 1 Dec. 37	ᴾ 9 Nov. 39		
		ENSIGNS.				
2	0	Henry Hearne Lacy	ᴾ 1 Feb. 39			
1	0	Geo. Robert Hopkins	28 Aug. 39			
1	0	Charles O'Donoghue	29 Aug. 39			
1	0	John Arch. Mac Queen	30 Aug. 39			
1	0	Henry Smith	17 Sept. 39			
1	0	Robt. Edw. Per. Brereton	18 Sept. 39			
1	0	Wm. Hugh Barton	ᴾ 8 Nov. 39			
1	0	John Wm. Frend	ᴾ 9 Nov. 39			
27	4¹⁰⁄₁₂	*Paymaster.*—Wm. Webster², 7 Sept. 26; *Ens.* 20 May, 08; *Lieut.* 1 Feb. 09.				
9	0	*Adjutant.*—John Gore Ferns (*Lieut.*) 30 June, 39.				
22	6³⁄₁₂	*QuarterMaster.*—John William Preston, 12 June, 28; *Ens.* 11 June, 12; *Lieut.* 19 Dec. 16.				
24	1⁶⁄₁₂	*Surgeon.*—William Birrell, M.D. 7 April, 37; *Assist.Surg.* 12 April, 21; *Hosp. Assist.* 3 June, 15.				
4	0	*Assistant-Surgeons.*—Robert Thomas Scott, 15 July, 36.				
2	0	J. D. Verd Leigh, M.D. 18 May, 38.				

Facings Red.—*Agent*, Messrs. Cox & Co.—*Irish Agent*, Borough, Armit & Co.

---

1 Sir Peregrine Maitland served in Flanders, and was present in several actions; served also at Ostend in 1798. He was present in the actions of Lugo and Corunna. Sir Peregrine has received a medal for the passage of the Nive.

2 Paymaster Webster served at the capture of Martinique in 1809; and in the American war in 1814.

Emb. for Foreign Service, 1837.] **77th (or East Middlesex) Regt. of Foot.** [Serving in Malta.

On the Colours and Appointments, the *Plume of the Prince of Wales*.
"SERINGAPATAM"—"CIUDAD RODRIGO"—"BADAJOZ"—
"PENINSULA."

Years' Serv.						
Full Pay.	Half Pay.	*Colonel.*				
47		Sir John Macleod, C.B. K.C.H. *Ens.* 9 Mar. 1793; *Lieut.* 2 May, 94; *Capt.* 24 June, 95; *Major,* 9 June, 99; *Lieut.-Col.* 1 Jan. 05; *Col.* 4 June, 13; *Major-General,* 12 Aug. 19; *Lieut.-Gen.* 10 Jan. 37; *Col.* of the 77th Regiment, 17 Feb. 40.				
31	2 11/12	*Lieut. Colonel.*—ᗷ George Paris Bradshaw,[2] K.H. *Ens.* p 2 Oct. 06; *Lieut.* p 16 June, 08; *Capt.* p 23 May, 16; *Major,* p 26 Dec. 22; *Lieut.-Col.* p 10 June, 26.				
29	1 9/12	*Majors.*—Nicholas Wilson, K.H. *Ens.* 31 Oct. 09; *Lieut.* 7 Oct. 13; *Capt.* p 24 Oct. 21; *Major,* p 30 Dec. 28.				
15	5/12	John Peter Nelley, *Ens.* p 13 Aug. 25; *Lieut.* p 10 June, 26; *Capt.* p 11 Oct. 31; *Major,* p 29 Nov. 39.				
		CAPTAINS.	ENSIGNS.	LIEUT.	CAPTAIN.	BREVET-MAJOR.
34	0	ᗷ James Algeo[3]	2 Sept. 06	4 Sept. 06	24 Feb. 25	28 June 38
31	0	ᗷ Richard Tatton[4]	28 July 09	7 June 11	7 Apr. 25	28 June 38
27	8	James Mason[5]	11 July 05	5 Mar. 07	18 Jan. 16	10 Jan. 37
16	4 4/12	Guy Clarke	17 Feb. 20	p 17 July 23	p 8 Apr. 26	
15	0	Wm. Jonathan Clerke	24 Feb. 25	p 10 June 26	p 18 Jan. 33	
22	15 7/12	George Stuart	1 Mar. 03	1 Sept. 04	21 Feb. 11	22 July 30
16	0	Alexander Tomkins	28 June 24	p 24 Dec. 25	p 8 Dec. 37	
11	0	Thos. Graham Egerton	24 Dec. 29	p 9 Mar. 32	p 23 Jan. 35	
13	0	Robt. Jocelyn Straton	10 Jan. 28	p 18 Jan. 33	p 26 Apr. 39	
12	0	George Dixon	p 30 Dec. 28	p 26 Dec. 34	p 29 Nov. 39	
		LIEUTENANTS.				
18	0	Paris W. Aug. Bradshaw	p 26 Dec. 22	24 Feb. 25		
21	6	William Galway	4 Nov. 13	27 July 20		
16	0	Dennis Herbert[6]	10 Feb. 25	5 Mar. 26		
15	0	Charles Lee	8 Apr. 25	p 30 Dec. 28		
11	0	John Edward Lewis	p 12 Jan. 30	23 Jan. 35	3 Major Algeo served in the Peninsula from Aug. 1813 until the end of the war.	
9	0	Henry Jervis White	p 23 Dec. 31	p 11 Sept. 35		
10	0	Henry Downe Griffith	13 June 30	6 Apr. 36		
9	0	William Forbes	p 2 Dec. 31	11 Aug. 35	4 Major Tatton served in the Peninsula from Aug. 1811 until the end of the war, and was present at the blockade of Bayonne.	
8	0	James A. Wheeler	21 Dec. 32	20 Mar. 37		
8	0	Molyn. Hyde Nepean	p 1 Feb. 33	25 Jan. 39		
6	0	R. Ambrose Morritt	p 27 Dec. 34	p 26 Apr. 39		
6	0	Montagu Denys	p 7 Nov. 34	6 Oct. 37		
4	0	Thos. Edmund Mulock	p 18 Mar. 36	p 29 Nov. 39		
		ENSIGNS.				
4	0	Jas. Dupre Brabazon	29 Apr. 36		5 Major Mason served with the expedition to the coast of America in 1813, and was engaged in several small actions; present at the capture of Moose Island in the Bay of Fundy in 1814.	
4	0	Robt. Baillie	3 Feb. 37			
2	0	Patrick Duff	p 7 Sept. 38			
2	0	Alex. B. Rooke	25 Jan. 39			
2	0	Alex. Aitken	1 Feb. 39			
1	0	Edw. Hen. L. Crofton	p 10 May 39		6 Lieut. Herbert served in the Burmese war.	
1	0	Osman F. Warrington	p 11 Oct. 39			
1	0	Luke Mahon	p 29 Nov. 39			
14	8 9/12	*Paymaster.*—Alexander John M'Pherson, 14 Dec. 38; *Ens.* 14 Aug. 17; *Lieut.* 18 Sept. 23.				
18	0	*Adjutant.*—Paris William Augustus Bradshaw (*Lieut.*) 28 Nov. 34.				
3	0	*Quarter-Master.*—Thomas Smedley, 7 April, 37.				
		Surgeon.—William Henry Burrell, M.D. 5 May, 37; *Assist.-Surg.* 12 April 21; Hosp.-Assist. 24 June, 15.				
4		*Assistant-Surgeons.*—Joseph Samuel Prendergast, M.D. 19 Feb. 36.				
5		John Drope M'Illree, 20 Feb. 35.				

Facings.—Yellow.—*Agent*, Messrs. Lawrie & M'Grigor.—*Irish Agent*, Messrs. Cane & Co.

---

2 Colonel Bradshaw's services :—Expedition to Madeira in 1807; expedition to Walcheren, 1809, including the landing at Ter-Vere, siege and bombardment of Flushing; Peninsula from June 1811 to the end of the war, including siege, assault, and capture of Ciudad Rodrigo and Badajoz; operations on the Bidassoa and Adour; blockade of and sortie from Bayonne.

78th (Highland) Regt. of Foot (or the Ross-shire Buffs.)
"Cuidich'n Rhi."—The Elephant, superscribed "ASSAYE"—"MAIDA"—"JAVA."

Year's Serv.		
Full Pay.	Half Pay.	*Colonel.*
52		ᴰ Paul Anderson,¹ C.B. *Ens.* 31 March, 1788; *Lieut.* 31 March, 91; *Capt.* 1 July, 95; *Major*, 25 June, 1801; *Lieut.-Col.* 17 Oct. 05; *Col.* 4 June, 13; *Major-Gen.* 12 Aug. 19; *Lieut.-Gen.* 10 Jan. 37; *Col.* 78th Highlanders 9 Feb. 37.
		Lieut.-Colonel.—Henry N. Douglas,² *Ens.* 23 Sept. 03; *Lieut.* 23 May, 05;
37	0	*Capt.* 14 Dec. 11; *Major,* ᴾ 22 Oct. 25; *Lieut.-Col.* ᴾ 28 April, 37.
26	2/12	*Majors.*—Martin Geo. Thos. Lindsay,³ *Ens.* ᴾ 16 Dec. 13; *Lieut.* ᴾ 5 Dec. 18; *Capt.* ᴾ 26 June, 23; *Major,* ᴾ 28 April, 37.
27	0	Jonathan Forbes,⁴ *Ens.* ᴾ 19 Jan. 14; *Lieut.* 13 April, 20; *Capt.* ᴾ 15 April, 24; *Major,* ᴾ 18 May, 38.

Full Pay	Half Pay	CAPTAINS.	ENSIGNS.	LIEUT.	CAPTAIN.	BREV.-MAJ.
27	0	Edw. Twopeny	27 Jan. 14	ᴾ 17 Aug. 20	ᴾ 22 Oct. 25	28 June 38
25	3 2/12	T. Hinton Hemmans	15 May 11	2 Dec. 13	ᴾ 8 Apr. 26	
18	0	R. J. Pop. Vassall	ᴾ 6 June 22	ᴾ 22 Oct. 25	ᴾ 13 May 26	
21	6 6/12	Ewan M'Pherson⁵	21 Jan. 13	5 Feb. 14	ᴾ 26 Apr. 27	
25	3 5/12	ᴰ Thos. John Taylor⁶	12 Mar. 12	7 Sept. 14	17 May 30	
22	0	Walter Hamilton	ᴾ 28 Jan. 19	ᴾ 15 Apr. 24	ᴾ 15 Mar. 33	
15	0	Colin Cam. M'Intyre	9 Apr. 25	ᴾ 17 July 28	ᴾ 28 Apr. 37	
22	8	ᴰ George Mitchell⁷	ᴾ 29 Nov. 10	29 July 13	5 Apr. 38	
13	0	John Burns	ᴾ 27 Apr. 27	ᴾ 15 Mar. 33	ᴾ 18 May 38	
15	0	John Edw. N. Bull	7 Apr. 25	ᴾ 15 June 26	19 Oct. 38	
		LIEUTENANTS.				
11	0	Abra. Wm. Browne	ᴾ 28 May 29	ᴾ 30 Aug. 33		
11	0	Henry Hamilton	ᴾ 13 Aug. 29	ᴾ 29 Nov. 33		
15	0	Jos. Rich. Lamert	10 Apr. 25	13 Dec. 32		
10	0	Dugald M'Neill	ᴾ 1 Feb. 31	ᴾ 7 Oct. 36		
8	0	Jas. Wood Collins	ᴾ 27 July 32	ᴾ 22 Nov. 36		
13	0	Fran. Rowland Nash	ᴾ 1 Mar. 27	26 Nov. 29		
7	0	J. Fowd. Haliburton	ᴾ 15 Feb. 33	ᴾ 28 Apr. 37		
7	0	Rich. Shields	ᴾ 5 July 33	ᴾ 25 Aug. 37		
7	0	D. St. Vin. Hamilton	ᴾ 30 Aug. 33	30 Nov. 37		
5	0	S. Montg. Eddington	ᴾ 11 Sept. 35	5 Apr. 38		
5	0	Fred. Edm. Caldwell	ᴾ 9 Oct. 35	ᴾ 18 May 38		
12	3	Alex. Grierson	ᴾ 9 June 25	ᴾ 15 Feb. 27		
4	0	Charles Pattison	ᴾ 7 Oct. 36	ᴾ 30 Aug. 39		
		ENSIGNS.				
5	0	Edward Hickey	ᴾ 22 May 35			
3	0	Grœme A. Lockhart	ᴾ 8 Dec. 37			
2	0	George Horrocks	ᴾ 18 May 38			
2	0	Dav. Doug. Wemyss	ᴾ 4 Aug. 38			
2	0	Th. Mayer Carvick	ᴾ 17 Aug. 38			
2	0	H. Douglas Gordon	ᴾ 18 Jan. 39			
1	0	Clare Skrine	ᴾ 30 Aug. 39			
1	0	Alex. Mackenzie	ᴾ 7 Feb. 40			

5 Captain M'Pherson served the Campaigns of 1814 and 1815 in Flanders, including the actions of the 13th Jan. and 2nd Feb. 1814, and the bombardment of Antwerp.

6 Capt. Taylor served the Campaigns of 1813 and 1814, including the investment of Pampeluna; the battles of the Pyrenees on the 28th, 29th, and 30th July, 1813; blockade of Bayonne; action of the lower Bidassoa 31st Aug. 1813; battle of Orthes; affair of Vic, and Tarbes, and battle of Toulouse where he was severely wounded.

7 Capt. Mitchell served the Campaigns of 1813 and 1814, including the battle of Vittoria, battles of the Pyrenees (wounded) 25th, 30th, and 31st July, 1813, of the Nive (wounded) 10th and 13th Dec. 1813, Orthes 27th Feb. Ayre 2nd March, and Toulouse 10th April, 1814.

8 Dr. Burt served the Campaigns of 1813 and 1814, including the Siege of St. Sebastian, and battle of Toulouse; present in the action at New Orleans 8th January, 1815.

21	6 4/12	*Paymaster.*—Monkhouse Graham Taylor, 26 Aug. 36; *Ens.* 10 June, 13; *Lieut.* 5 Sept. 22.
4	0	*Adjutant.*—Charles Pattison (*Lieut.*) 31 Aug. 39.
2	0	*Quarter-Master.*—Joseph Webster, 31 May, 39; *Ens.* 23 Nov. 38.
27	0	*Surgeon.*—ᴰ James Burt,⁸ 29 July, 36; *Assist.-Surg.* 4 Sept. 23; *Hosp.-Assist.* 7 June, 13.
		Assist.-Surgeon.—George Archer, M.D. 2 Nov. 30; *Hosp.-Assist.* 1 Nov. 27.

[*Returned from Ceylon*, 9 Feb. 38.]—*Facings* Buff.—*Agent*, Messrs. Cox & Co.

1 General Anderson was at the storming of Convention redoubts, Mozelle Fort, and the siege of Calvi, in Corsica; served subsequently in the West Indies, and received a severe contusion in the side in the storming of Morne Chapot, St. Lucia; served as Aide-de-Camp to Sir John Moore in the expedition to Holland; and afterwards in the expedition to Egypt, where he was severely wounded by a shot in the arm, in the action of 21st March; served in the expedition to Walcheren, and was present at the siege of Flushing. Gen. A. has received a medal for Corunna.

2 Colonel Douglas served the Campaign in Java, including the investment and storming of Fort Cornelis in August, and storming the Heights of Serondole in September, 1811; investment and storming of the Fortifications of Djocjocarta in June, 1812; commanded the detachment which took possession of the Island of Baviav; and on his return was appointed to the Staff, which he resigned to accompany his regiment in the expedition to the Island of Balli in May, and to Celebes July, 1814. Col. Douglas's services at the storming of Djocjocarta were noticed in the London Gazette, he having commanded the party which took the Sultan prisoner.

3 Major Lindsay served in Holland in 1814 and 15, and was present at the bombardment of Antwerp.

4 Major Forbes accompanied the 78th to Holland as a volunteer, and was present in action at Merxem 13th January, also on the 2nd February, 1814, and at the bombardment of Antwerp; served the Campaign of 1814 and 1815 in Flanders.

Record of the Service of the 78th Regiment.

Raised by letter of Service dated 7th March, 1793; inspected and passed July, 1793; proceeded to Holland September, 1794; returned to England May, 1795; proceeded to Quiberon August, 1795; returned January, 1796; proceeded to the Cape of Good Hope 1796; to Calcutta February, 1797, to Bombay, February 1803; to Goa February, 1807; to Java August, 1811; returned to England July 1817 proceeded to Ireland November, 1817, embarked for Ceylon April, 1826 returned to England February, 1838.

79th Regiment of Foot, (or Cameron Highlanders.)

"EGMONT-OP-ZEE,"—The *Sphinx*, with the words "EGYPT"—"FUENTES D'ONOR"—"SALAMANCA"—"PYRENEES"—"NIVELLE"—"NIVE"—"TOULOUSE"—"PENINSULA"—"WATERLOO."

Years' Serv						
50		*Colonel.*				
Full Pay	Half Pay	₽ Sir Ronald C. Ferguson,[1] G.C.B. *Ens.* 3 April, 1790; *Lieut.* 24 Jan. 91; *Capt.* 19 Feb. 93; *Major*, 31 May, 94; *Lieut.-Col.* 18 Sept. 94; *Col.* 1 Jan. 1800; *Major-Gen.* 25 April, 08; *Lieut.-Gen.* 4 June, 13; *Gen.* 22 July, 30; *Col.* 79th Highlanders, 24 March, 28.				
18	2	*Lieut.-Colonel.*—Robert Ferguson, *Ens.* 24 Feb. 20; *Lieut.* ᴾ2 Jan. 23; *Capt* ᴾ7 July, 25; *Major*, ᴾ31 Aug. 30; *Lieut.-Col.* ᴾ13 March, 35.				
20	0	*Majors.*—Andrew Brown, *Ens.* 26 Oct. 20; *Lieut.* 17 March, 25; *Capt.* ᴾ5 April, 31; *Major*, ᴾ26 May, 38.				
14	2/12	Hon. Lauderdale Maule, *Ens.* ᴾ24 Aug. 26; *Lieut.* 21 July 31; *Capt.* ᴾ22 May, 35; *Major*, ᴾ11 May, 39.				

		CAPTAINS.	ENSIGN.	LIEUT.	CAPTAIN.	BREV.-MAJ.
29	0	₽ ⚜ Wm. A. Riach[2]	17 Oct. 11	17 June 13	7 Apr. 25	28 June 38
20	7 8/12	Thos. Lewis Butler	13 Aug. 12	23 Sept.13	ᴾ 2 Feb. 30	
25	0	Duncan MacDougall	16 July 15	ᴾ 3 June 19	ᴾ18 July 34	
15	0	Wm. Henry Lance	ᴾ 7 July 25	ᴾ 2 Feb. 30	ᴾ 7 Aug. 35	
15	0	Robt. Manners	21 July 25	31 Dec. 30	ᴾ 8 July 37	
15	0	John Stewart Smyth	ᴾ10 Sept. 25	ᴾ 5 Apr. 31	ᴾ29 Dec. 37	
14	0	Thos. Isham	ᴾ 1 Aug. 26	ᴾ16 Mar. 32	ᴾ26 May 38	
13	0	James Cockburn	12 Apr. 27	ᴾ23 Aug. 33	ᴾ 8 June 38	
12	0	Ewen Cameron	31 July 28	ᴾ 6 Sept. 33	ᴾ29 Mar. 39	
18	0	Fra. Rawdon H. Lawrie[3]	18 Apr. 22	ᴾ13 Oct. 25	ᴾ 5 Jan. 39	
		LIEUTENANTS				
11	0	Geo. Jas. Gordon	ᴾ 2 Feb. 30	ᴾ18 July 34		
9	0	Edm. James Elliott	ᴾ 5 Apr. 31	ᴾ10 Oct. 34		
8	0	Wm. Craig Maxwell	ᴾ18 May 32	ᴾ13 Mar. 35		
8	0	James Ferguson	ᴾ27 July 32	ᴾ 7 Aug. 35		
7	0	Charles Skene	ᴾ12 Apr. 33	6 Nov. 35		
7	0	John Douglas	ᴾ 6 Sept. 33	ᴾ 8 July 36		
7	0	Robert Ferguson	ᴾ25 Oct. 33	ᴾ 8 July 37		
6	0	Wm. Monro	ᴾ10 Oct. 34	ᴾ29 Dec. 37		
5	0	John Douglas	ᴾ13 Mar. 35	ᴾ26 May 38		
5	0	Haskett Smith	ᴾ29 May 35	ᴾ 8 June 38		
5	0	Robt. J. M. Napier	ᴾ 7 Aug. 35	ᴾ14 Sept. 38		
5	0	Rich. C. H. Taylor	11 Dec. 35	ᴾ29 Mar. 39		
7	1	William Balfour	ᴾ20 Apr. 32	ᴾ 2 Sept. 36		
		ENSIGNS.				
3	0	Alex. C. Maitland	ᴾ 8 July 37			
3	0	Thomas Dundas	22 Sept. 37			
3	0	F. Acclom Milbank	ᴾ29 Dec. 37			
2	0	Alex. Buchanan	ᴾ26 May 38			
2	0	Rob. D. Clephane	ᴾ 8 June 38			
2	0	Hector MacNeal	ᴾ14 Sept. 38			
1	0	Thos. John Reeve	ᴾ11 May 39			
26	1 1/12	*Paymaster.*—⚜ Thos. Wm. Blewett Mountsteven,[4] 10 June, 36; *Ens.* 25 Nov. 13; *Lieut.* 25 Oct. 20; *Capt.* 8 May, 35.				
8	0	*Adjutant.*—James Ferguson (*Lieut.*) 11 May 39.				
2	0	*Quarter-Master.*—Alexander Cruickshanks, 12 Oct. 38.				
15	0	*Surgeon.*—James Alexander Ore, 6 Dec. 39; *Assist.-Surg.* 10 Nov. 25; *Hosp.-Assist.* 16 June, 25.				
13	0	*Assist.-Surgeon.*—Dan. Maclachlan, M.D. 21 Feb. 28; *Hosp.-Assist.* 14 Aug. 27.				

Facings Green.—*Agent*, Mr. Lawrie.

[*Returned from Canada, October*, 1836.]

1 Sir Ronald Ferguson served in Flanders in 1793, and received a wound in the knee. He was at the first and second taking of the Cape of Good Hope, and has received a medal for Roleia and Vimiera.
2 Major Riach served in the Peninsula from Oct 1811 until the end of the war, including the operations in covering the siege of Badajoz, March and April, 1812; battle of Salamanca, and siege of Burgos, Sept. and Oct. 1812; present on 16th June at Quatre Bras, and was severely wounded by a grape shot on the right side of the abdomen.
3 Captain Lawrie served at the siege and capture of Bhurtpore, in 1825 and 26.
4 Capt. Mountsteven was severely wounded at Waterloo.

Emb. for For. Service, 1837.] **80th Regt. of Foot** (*or Staffordshire Volunteers*). [Serving at New S. Wales.

The *Sphinx*, with the word "EGYPT."

Years' Serv.			
46		*Colonel.*	
		ⓓ Sir John Taylor,¹ K.C.B. *Ens.* Nov. 1794; *Lieut.* 6 Dec. 04; *Capt.* 9 Sept. 95; *Major,* 2 Sept. 1801; *Lieut.-Col.* 28 Feb. 05; *Col.* 4 June, 13; *Major-Gen.* 12 Aug. 19; *Lieut.-Gen.* 10 Jan. 37; *Col.* 80th Regiment, 15 March, 37.	
Full Pay.	Half Pay.		
		Lieut.-Colonel.	
34	0	Narborough Baker,² *Ens.* 17 April, 06; *Lieut.* ᴾ 10 March, 08; *Capt.* ᴾ 18 Nov. 19; *Major,* ᴾ 25 May, 32; *Lieut.-Col.* ᴾ 24 March, 37.	
		Majors.	
27	6	ⓓ Thomas Bunbury,³ *Ens.* 7 May, 07; *Lieut.* 17 Aug. 09; *Capt.* 25 Oct. 14; *Major,* ᴾ 21 Nov. 34.	
13	0	Sam. Lettsom, *Ens.* ᴾ 6 Mar. 27; *Lieut.* ᴾ 2 Apr. 29; *Capt.* ᴾ 4 Oct. 33; *Major,* ᴾ 17 Jan. 40.	

		CAPTAINS.	ENSIGN.	LIEUT.	CAPTAIN.	BREVET-MAJOR.
36	0	Jas. Winniett Nunn⁴....	7 Apr. 04	6 May 05	13 Dec. 10	22 July 30
18	0	Rich. Tasker Furlong ..	25 Jan. 23	ᴾ 5 Jan. 26	ᴾ 19 Dec. 34	
34	0	Wm. Kemp⁵	16 May 06	20 Nov. 07	14 Nov. 22	10 Jan. 37
10	0	Cha. Rob. Raitt........	13 June 30	ᴾ 4 Oct. 33	ᴾ 22 June 38	
8	0	Hor. Rob. M. Gulston ..	ᴾ 26 May 32	ᴾ 21 Nov. 34	ᴾ 23 June 38	
9	0	Geo. Brunswick Smyth..	ᴾ 18 Oct. 31	ᴾ 4 Mar. 36	ᴾ 26 June 38	
10	0	Rob. Alex. Lockhart....	ᴾ 11 June 30	ᴾ 5 Oct. 32	ᴾ 13 July 38	
15	0	Charles Steuart	ᴾ 10 Dec. 25	ᴾ 5 Feb. 29	ᴾ 9 Nov. 38	
6	0	*Hon.* Wm. A. S. Foster..	ᴾ 9 May 34	ᴾ 22 June 38	ᴾ 17 Jan. 40	
		LIEUTENANTS.			2 Col. Baker was at the capture of the Isle of France in 1810.	
21	0	Ronald Macdonald......	ᴾ 11 Feb. 19	23 Jan. 25		
15	0	George Black	9 Apr. 25	12 July 27	3 Major Bunbury served in the Peninsula from 1808 to the end of the war, including capture of Oporto, battles of Talavera and Barrosa, defence of Tarifa 1812, capture of Seville, defence of the Bridge of Puente Largo near Aranjues, battles of Nivelle and Nive (severely wounded), investment of Bayonne, and battle of Toulouse.	
13	0	Rich. Talbot Sayers	ᴾ 19 Apr. 27	ᴾ 25 May 32		
14	0	Rinaldo Scheberras	ᴾ 16 Mar. 26	16 Apr. 33		
11	15½	Jas. Deaves Morris	14 Apr. 14	25 June 18		
8	0	John Lightbody	ᴾ 25 May 32	ᴾ 9 May 34		
13	0	Owen Gorman⁶	26 Oct. 30	27 Feb. 36		
6	0	Wm. Hougham Tyssen ..	ᴾ 30 Jan. 35	ᴾ 23 June 38		
5	0	Hen. Theodore Torkington	ᴾ 14 Aug. 35	ᴾ 26 June 38		
7	0	Sam. Tolfrey Christie ..	ᴾ 22 Jan. 36	ᴾ 13 July 38		
10	20⁶⁄₁₂	Simon Fraser	7 Mar. 10	17 July 11	4 Major Nunn served the Egyptian campaign of 1807; present at the capture of Genoa in 1814.	
3	0	Abel Dottin Wm. Best...	ᴾ 21 Apr. 37	ᴾ 4 Oct. 39		
2	0	Lambert L. Montgomery	ᴾ 22 June 38	ᴾ 17 Jan. 40		
		ENSIGNS.			5 Major Kemp was at the taking of St. Domingo in 1809; served the campaign of 1814 in Holland, including the action at Merxem, and attack on Bergen-op-Zoom.	
2	0	Wm. Cookson..........	ᴾ 23 June 38			
2	0	Alex. Wm. Riley	ᴾ 26 June 38			
2	0	Anthony Ormsby	ᴾ 13 July 38		6 Quarter-Master, 15 Nov. 1827, from which date the period of service has been computed.	
2	0	Cha. Hen. Leslie	ᴾ 20 July 38			
3	0	H. A. Hollinsworth	8 July 37			
3	0	Wm. H. Hopper........	ᴾ 29 Dec. 37			
1	0	John Charles Hay	ᴾ 4 Oct. 39			
1	0	Hercules Atkin Welman	ᴾ 17 Jan. 40			
15	0	*Paymaster.*—Tho. Bloomfield Hunt, 1 Aug. 37; *Ens.* 19 Jan. 26; *Lieut.* 25 Oct. 33.				
8	0	*Adjutant.*—John Lightbody, (*Lieut.*) 24 March, 37.				
3	0	*Quarter-Master.*—Frederick Hayes, 10 Feb. 37.				
22	4⁹⁄₁₂	*Surgeon.*—Robt. Turnbull, 28 June, 36; *Assist.-Surg.* 14 May, 15; *Hosp.-Assist* 3 Oct. 13.				
4	0	*Assistant-Surgeons.*—Patrick Gammie, 17 June, 36.				
1	0	Arthur Colquhoun Macnish, 5 July, 39.				

Facings Yellow.—*Agent,* Mr. Lawrie.

1 Sir John Taylor served the campaign of 1799 in Holland, as Aid-de-Camp to Major-Gen. Hutchinson, with whom he went to Egypt, and was present in the different battles of that campaign. Sir John has received a medal and two clasps for Nivelle, Orthes, and Toulouse, and was severely wounded in France, Feb. 1814.

Emb. for For. Service, 1836.] **81st Regt. Foot. (or Loyal Lincoln Volunteers.)** [Serving at Barbadoes.

"MAIDA"—"CORUNNA"—"PENINSULA."

Years' Serv.			
Full Pay.	Half Pay.		
46		*Colonel.*	
		₧ Sir Richard Downes Jackson,¹ K.C.B. *Ens.* 9 July 1794; *Lieut. & Capt.* 24 May, 98; *Capt. & Lieut.-Col.* 4 Aug. 1808; *Col.* 4 June, 14; *Major-Gen.* 27 May, 25; *Lieut.-Gen.* 28 June, 38; *Col.* 81st Regt. 8 Jan. 29.	
21	8 6/12	*Lieut.-Colonel.*—Charles Chichester,¹* *Ens.* 5 Mar. 11; *Lieut.* 4 Nov. 12; *Capt.* ᴘ 23 Dec. 24; *Major,* ᴘ 29 Aug. 26; *Lieut.-Col.* ᴘ 12 July, 31.	
29	1/12	*Majors.*—₧ Rob. Henry Willcocks,² K.H. *Ens.* 12 Sept. 11; *Lieut.* 26 Aug. 13; *Capt.* 21 July, 25; *Major,* ᴘ 16 March, 32.	
18	2 3/12	Giles Vandeleur Creagh, 2nd *Lieut.* ᴘ 6 Jan. 20; *Lieut.* ᴘ 10 April, 25; *Capt.* ᴘ 1 Aug. 26; *Major,* ᴘ 27 Dec. 33.	

		CAPTAINS.	ENSIGNS.	LIEUT.	CAPTAIN.	BREV.-MAJ.
27	1 10/12	₧ Henry Dixon	ᴘ 5 Mar. 12	ᴘ 21 Dec. 15	ᴘ 21 Nov. 28	
20	1 5/12	Richard Hort	ᴘ 26 Jan. 19	ᴘ 4 May 22	ᴘ 27 Aug. 25	28 June 38
21	6 7/12	₧ Edw. Roley Hill³	23 Feb. 13	24 Feb. 14	ᴘ 26 Sept. 26	
16	0	Abraham Splaine	ᴘ 28 Oct. 24	ᴘ 22 Apr. 26	ᴘ 16 Mar. 32	
17	7 10/12	James Ward	25 May 15	ᴘ 23 June 25	ᴘ 6 July 32	
15	0	John Edw. Orange⁴	10 Apr. 25	15 Oct. 27	ᴘ 27 Dec. 33	
15	0	John Uniacke Jeffery	ᴘ 10 Apr. 25	ᴘ 21 Nov. 28	ᴘ 7 Nov. 34	
12	0	Cha. H. Edmonstone	ᴘ 23 Apr. 28	ᴘ 2 Mar. 32	ᴘ 13 Nov. 35	
16	9 6/12	Rich. Uniacke Howe⁵	18 Aug. 14	21 Sept. 15	20 Sept. 37	
10	0	Wm. Hen. C. Wellesley	ᴘ 29 June 30	ᴘ 5 Oct. 32	ᴘ 17 Jan. 40	

LIEUTENANTS.

13	0	Louis Guy⁶		8 Mar. 27	12 Apr. 27
9	0	Richard Hale		ᴘ 16 Feb. 31	ᴘ 1 Aug. 34
13	0	John Hamilton Stewart		23 July 27	2 Aug. 34
9	0	Tho. Sarsfield Perry		ᴘ 4 Oct. 31	ᴘ 7 Nov. 34
8	0	Edward Bowyer		ᴘ 16 Mar. 32	ᴘ 28 Nov. 34
10	0	Henry Farrant		9 July 30	13 Feb. 35
7	0	Henry Renny		ᴘ 27 Dec. 33	ᴘ 7 Aug. 35
6	0	Hon. R. A. G. Dalzell		ᴘ 21 Mar. 34	ᴘ 11 Sept. 35
6	0	Henry Edw. Sorell		ᴘ 16 May 34	ᴘ 6 Nov. 35
8	0	George W. Raikes		ᴘ 14 Dec. 32	ᴘ 23 Oct. 35
15	0	John Powell		29 Sept. 25	7 Oct. 32
5	0	Charles Hope Kerr		3 Oct. 35	ᴘ 22 Apr. 39
4	0	Chas. Wm. Thompson⁷		ᴘ 26 Feb. 36	ᴘ 17 Jan. 40

6 Lieut. Guy, as an officer in the Canadian Voltigeurs, was at the battle Chateauguay, 10th Oct. 1813, and Plattsburgh, 11th Sept. 1814.

7 Lieut. Thompson served as a Captain in the Anglo-Spanish Legion, and was engaged at Hernani, 30 Aug. 35; the operations on the heights of Arlaban, 16, 17, and 18 Jan. 36; and the action before San Sebastian, 5 May, 36, in which he was severely wounded in the hip and the hand.

8 Paymaster Thompson accompanied the 81st Regiment through all its services.

9 Quarter-Master Patterson's services:—battle of Maida, capture of Ischia, Peninsula from Sept. 1809 to the end of the war, including investment of Denia, battle of Castalla, and investment of Tarragona, June 1813.

ENSIGNS.

4	0	A. F. F. Boughey	ᴘ 30 July 36
3	0	Fred. Edw. Sorell	ᴘ 11 Aug. 37
2	0	John Oldright	21 Sept. 38
1	0	John Gilder	ᴘ 23 Aug. 39
1	0	John Bourchier	24 Aug. 39
1	0	Richard Crawley	ᴘ 19 July 39
1	0	James Woods	31 Dec. 39
1	0	Francis Lepper	ᴘ 7 Feb. 40
42	0	*Paymaster.*—₧ Arnold Thompson,⁸ 22 Aug. 05; *Ens.* 6 Sept. 98; *Lieut.* 9 July, 03.	
6	0	*Adjutant.*—Henry Edward Sorell, (*Lieut.*) 3 Nov. 37.	
11	0	*Quarter-Master.*—₧ James Patterson,⁹ 25 June, 29.	
		Surgeon.—David Rees, 7 June 33; *Assist.-Surg.* 12 May, 14.	
2	0	*Assist.-Surgeons.*—Edward Wm. Gray, 22 June, 38.	
1	0	Henry James Schooles, M.D. 28 June, 39.	

Facings Buff.—*Agent,* Messrs. Cox & Co.

1 Sir Rich. D. Jackson has received a cross and two clasps for Barrosa, Fuentes d'Onor, Salamanca, Nivelle, Nive, and Orthes.

1* Lieut.-Col. Chichester served as Brigadier-General with the Anglo-Spanish Legion during the years 1835, 6, and 7; was in the action before Ernani on the 30th August, 1835, in which he received two wounds; also at the relief of Bilbao in the same year. Commanded a brigade at Mendigur, and at Azua, on the 16th, 17th, and 18th Jan. 1836; in the battle before San Sebastian on the 5th of May, and at the passage of the Urmea and taking of passages on the 28th. Commanded at Alza when it was attacked on the 6th June by the Carlists with a chosen body of men, and had a horse wounded under him. Was engaged in the general action on the heights of Ametza on the 1st of October. In the operations on the 10th, 12th, 14th, and 15th of March, 1837, during which he had a horse wounded; and in the general action on the 16th of March, where he was wounded, and had two horses wounded. Commanded the British Legion, then formed into a division of two brigades, in the action of the 14th of May, and at the investment and storming of Irun on the 16th and 17th. For his services in Spain, Lieut.-Col. Chichester has received two medals.

2 Major Willcocks served in the Peninsula from May 1812 to the end of the war, including battle of Salamanca (wounded in the hand and leg), siege of Burgos, battle of Vittoria, siege and capture of San Sebastian, battles of the Nive (wounded in the right arm), and investment of Bayonne.

3 Capt. Hill served in the Peninsula from Sept. 1812 to the end of the war, including the affair of Munos, retreat from Burgos (as a volunteer), battle of Vittoria, Passage of the Bidassoa, battles of Nivelle and Toulouse.

4 Capt. Orange served in the Burmese war in 1825.

5 Capt. Howe was at the capture of *Castine*, United States, and *Adams*, United States frigate, 1st Sept. 1814.

Emb. for For. Service, 1837.] **82d Foot. (or the Pr. of Wales's Volunteers.)** [Serving at Jamaica.

On the Colours and Appointments, the *Prince of Wales's Plume.*—" ROLEIA"
—" VIMIERA"—" VITTORIA"—" PYRENEES"—" NIVELLE"—
" ORTHES"—" PENINSULA"—" NIAGARA."

Years' Serv.		Colonel.
Full Pay	Half Pay	
46		ꝓ Sir John Wilson,[1] K.C.B. *Ens.* 26 Mar. 1794; *Lieut.* 12 Aug. 95; *Capt.* 18 Jan. 99; *Major,* 27 May, 1802; *Lieut.-Col.* 22 Dec. 08; *Col.* 4 June, 14; *Maj.-Gen.* 27 May, 25; *Lieut.-Gen.* 28 June, 38; *Col.* 82nd Regt. 5 Dec. 36.
		Lieut.-Colonel.
41	0	ꝓ Geo. Marshall,[3] K.H. *Ens.* 6 Dec. 99; *Lieut.* 15 Aug. 04; *Capt.* 27 Oct. 08; *Brevet-Major,* 27 May, 25; *Regtl.-Major,* 23 Oct. 35; *Brevet-Lieut.-Col.* 28 June, 38; *Regtl.-Lieut.-Col.* ᴾ 21 June, 39.
		Majors.—ꝓ John F. Mackay,[2] *Ens.* 14 Dec. 04; *Lieut.* 19 Feb. 07; *Capt.* 16
36	0	Aug. 13; *Major,* ᴾ 5 July. 33.
26	3/12	ꝓ John Jas. Slater,[4] *Ens.* 20 May 14; *Lieut.* ᴾ 7 Jan. 19; *Capt.* ᴾ 17 Aug. 26; *Major,* ᴾ 21 June, 39

		CAPTAINS.	ENSIGN.	LIEUT.	CAPTAIN.	BREV.-MAJ.	
17	11 2/12	William Slater	9 Sept. 12	20 Jan. 14	ᴾ 25 Nov. 28		
15	0	Chas. Francis Maxwell ..	ᴾ 28 July 25	ᴾ 17 Aug. 26	ᴾ 16 Nov. 32		
12	0	Geo. Ogle Moore	18 Sept. 28	ᴾ 3 Dec. 30	ᴾ 12 July 33		
17	0	Jas. Alex. Robertson	ᴾ 6 Mar. 23	ᴾ 17 Sept. 25	ᴾ 8 June 32		
18	13 2/12	Benoit Bender[5]	ᴾ 29 Dec. 08	4 Apr. 10	26 Nov. 30		
29	9 1/12	ꝓ George Pinckney[6]	ᴾ 17 Sept. 01	22 Nov. 04	19 Nov. 12	22 July 30	
32	0	Richard Passley	8 Sept. 08	6 Nov. 09	16 Mar. 32		
10	0	Wm. Jas. Whittuck	ᴾ 3 Dec. 30	ᴾ 28 Aug. 35	ᴾ 21 June 39		
8	0	Thomys Wynn Hornby	1 Feb. 33	ᴾ 4 Sept. 35	ᴾ 2 Aug. 39		
15	0	John Du Vernet[7]	27 Mar. 25	ᴾ 8 Apr. 26	ᴾ 24 Apr. 35		
		LIEUTENANTS.					
19	9	Jas. Abbott[8]	ᴾ 9 Apr. 12	16 Feb. 15			
7	0	David Watson	ᴾ 12 July 33	ᴾ 24 Oct. 35			
7	0	Edw. Blagden Hale	ᴾ 2 Aug. 33	ᴾ 29 Jan. 36			
11	0	Henry Bates	9 July 29	28 Nov. 33			
6	0	Wm. Eccles	ᴾ 28 Feb. 34	ᴾ 28 Oct. 36			
5	0	Hen. L. Smith	21 Aug. 35	28 Sept. 38			
5	0	Jas. C. Maclachlan	ᴾ 4 Sept. 35	ᴾ 24 Nov. 38			
5	0	J. P. B. Puleston	ᴾ 24 Oct. 35	ᴾ 26 Apr. 39			
5	0	Fra. Geo. Sherlock	ᴾ 29 Jan. 36	ᴾ 31 May 39			
4	0	Fred. Wm. Diggle	ᴾ 14 Oct. 36	ᴾ 21 June 39			
3	0	E. R. W. Wingfield Yates	ᴾ 24 Mar. 37	ᴾ 2 Aug. 39			
2	0	Osborne West	ᴾ 11 May 38	ᴾ 13 Dec. 39			
6	0	James Bailie	ᴾ 28 Nov. 34	31 Dec. 39			
		ENSIGNS.					
2	0	C. T. Vesey Isaac	30 Oct. 38				
2	0	Thomas Lambert	ᴾ 24 Nov. 38				
1	0	Robert Crowe Fleming ..	ᴾ 26 Apr. 39				
1	0	Geo. Russell Nicholls	ᴾ 31 May 39				
1	0	Rob. Matthew Forster ..	ᴾ 12 July 39				
1	0	John Wildman Yates....	ᴾ 2 Aug. 39				
1	0	Geo. Edmund Halliday ..	ᴾ 23 Aug. 39				
1	0	James Pratt	ᴾ 13 Dec. 39				
33	0	*Paymaster.*—ꝓ Samuel Holdsworth,[9] 22 Sept. 25; *Ens. & Adjt.* 31 Dec. 07; *Lieut.* 1 Nov. 09.					
7	0	*Adjutant.*—David Watson, (*Lieut.*) 31 Oct. 39.					
8	0	*Quarter-Master.*—ꝗ Bernard Grant,[11] 28 Aug. 35; *Ens.* 28 Dec. 32.					
17	11 10/12	*Surgeon.*—ꝓ Pat. Pope,[10] M.D. 13 May, 36; *Assist.-Surg.* 24 Feb. 14; *Hosp.-Assist.* June, 1811.					
5	0	*Assistant-Surgeons.*—Arthur Anderson, M.D. 16 Oct. 35.					
14	3/12	Tho. Atkinson, M.D. 11 May, 26; *Hosp.-Assist.* 22 Dec. 25.					

Facings Yellow.—*Agent,* Mr. Lawrie.

5 Capt. Bender served in Canada from Dec. 1808 to Jan. 1815, and was present in the action of the 7th July, 1812, Monguago; taking of Detroit, taking several Block houses on the Miamie River; actions at River Aux Raisin, and Miamie, storming of Sanduskey, and Fort Niagara; engagement of 2nd Jan. 1814; Black Rocks, 2nd Feb., and at Buffalo.

6 Major Pinckney's services :—Expedition to South America, including the taking of Maldonado, and siege of Monte Video ; battles of Roleia and Vimiera; expedition to Walcheren ; received the flag of truce at the out-post, at the attack and capture of Ter Vere, Middleburgh, storming of Flushing.

7 Captain Du Vernet served in Ava in 1825, and 26.

8 Lieut. Abbott served in the American war.

9 Paymaster Holdsworth's services :—Expedition against Belle Isle June 1800; siege and capture of Flushing ; Peninsula from June 1812 to the end of the war, including battles of Vittoria, Mayo Pass, heights of Pampeluna 30th (wounded in the wrist by a musketball, & contused on the shoulder) and 31st July; heights of Lesacco 31st Aug.; battles of Nivelle and Orthes.

10 Dr. Pope was at the siege of Badajoz in 1812, and taken prisoner.

11 Qr.-Mast. Grant served the campaign of 1815, including the battle of Waterloo and capture of Paris.

1 Sir John Wilson has received a medal for San Sebastian.
2 Major Mackay's services :—Expedition to Copenhagen 1807 ; battles of Roleia, Vimiera, and Corunna ; expedition to Walcheren ; Peninsula from 1810 to Dec. 1813, including battles of Barrossa (severely wounded), Vittoria, Pass of Mayo 25th July, Pampeluna (severely wounded) 30th July, 1813.
3 Col. Marshall's services :—Expedition to Copenhagen in 1807 ; battles of Roleia, Vimiera, and Corunna ; Peninsula from Nov. 1812 to the end of the war, including battle of Vittoria, Pass of Mayo (wounded), Pampeluna 30th and 31st July, and 31st Aug. 1813 , Heights of St. Pee, severely wounded in the head. Present at Niagara, Sept. 1814, and slightly wounded.
4 Major Slater served in the Peninsula and also in America in 1814.

83rd *Regiment of Foot.*

"CAPE OF GOOD HOPE"—"TALAVERA"—"BUSACO"—"FUENTES D'ONOR"—"CIUDAD RODRIGO"—"BADAJOZ"—"SALAMANCA"—"VITTORIA"—"NIVELLE"—"ORTHES"—"TOULOUSE"—"PENINSULA."

Years' Serv. Full Pay.	Half Pay.	
		Colonel.
52		Hastings Fraser,[1] C.B. *Ens.* 9 April, 1788; *Lieut.* 3 Nov. 90; *Capt.* 7 Dec. 97; *Major* 28 July, 1802; *Lieut.-Col.* 7 Sept. 04; *Col.* 4 June, 13; *Major.-Gen.* 12 Aug. 19; *Lieut.-Gen.* 10 Jan. 37; *Col.* 83rd Regiment, 30 Sept. 35.
19	1 6/12	*Lieut.-Colonel.—Hon.* Henry Dundas, *Ens.* & *Lieut.* 18 Nov. 19; *Capt.* P 1 April, 24; *Major* P 11 July, 26; *Lieut.-Col.* P 3 Dec. 29.
34	1 9/12	*Majors.*—Botet Trydell,[2] *Ens.* 19 Oct. 04; *Lieut.* 30 Oct. 06; *Capt.* 17 Nov. 18; *Major* P 3 Dec. 29.
30	0	Peter Crofton,[3] *2nd Lieut.* 5 April, 10; *Lieut.* 9 Nov. 14; *Capt.* 15 Dec. 22; *Major* 2 March, 33.

Full Pay	Half Pay		Ensign.	Lieut.	Captain.	Brev.-Maj.
		Captains.				
22	5 8/12	𝔓 William Henry Law[4] ..	29 April 13	P 28 Nov. 16	P 14 July 25	28 June 38
31	0	𝔓 Joseph Swinburne[5] ..	16 Aug. 09	4 June 12	6 Oct. 25	28 June 38
22	2 3/12	Edward Townsend	23 May 16	P 28 Oct. 24	P 18 Feb. 26	
19	1 4/12	Robert Colquhoun	P 20 April 20	P 4 Dec. 23	P 16 Mar. 30	
27	5	𝔓 John Emslie[6]	26 Mar. 08	8 Nov. 09	22 May 29	
17	0	Henry Francis Ainslie....	29 Jan. 24	P 7 Nov. 26	P 5 April 31	
32	0	𝔓 𝔚 John Richardson[7]	1 Dec. 08	6 Sept. 10	17 Nov. 31	
13	0	Den. M'Carthy Stubbeman	P 22 Mar. 27	P 3 Aug. 30	P 5 June 35	
11	0	George Grey	14 Jan. 30	P 29 Mar. 33	P 22 Mar. 39	
10	0	Edward D'Alton.........	13 June 30	P 2 Aug. 33	P 20 Sept. 39	
		Lieutenants.				
20	0	John Rayson...........	1 Feb. 21	7 April 25		
15	0	John Kelsall...........	P 14 July 25	P 30 April 27		
16	0	William Garstin........	28 Oct. 24	29 May 28		
17	0	John Stubbs[8]...........	20 Apr. 26	25 June 30		
9	0	Henry Lloyd	P 5 Apr. 31	P 8 April 34		
8	0	Thos. John St. Aubyn....	P 24 Aug. 32	P 25 Sept. 35		
7	0	Benj. Handley Brown.....	P 12 Apr. 33	P 8 Dec. 37		
7	0	D. W. P. Labalmondiere ..	21 June 33	P 25 May 38		
7	0	Thos. Richard Derinzy...	P 2 Aug. 33	14 Nov. 38		
4	0	Walter Hamilton	P 10 June 36	P 1 Feb. 39		
6	0	Duncan Campbell........	P 8 April 34	P 15 Mar. 39		
6	0	Edward Steele...........	P 18 April 34	P 22 Mar. 39		
3	0	Wenman Wynniatt.......	P 8 Dec. 37	P 20 Sept. 39		
		Ensigns.				
5	0	Septimus A. F. Cary......	P 3 April 35			
2	0	Fra. John Hext.........	P 25 May 38			
2	0	Cha. Wilson Austin......	P 14 Dec. 38			
2	0	David Anderson........	28 Dec. 38			
2	0	John Thos. Downman ...	P 1 Feb. 39			
1	0	William Roger Puleston ..	P 15 Mar. 39			
1	0	*Hon.* Wm. Gage	P 22 Mar. 39			
1	0	John Williams Wallington	P 20 Sept. 39			

6 Capt. Emslie served in the Peninsula from June 1813 to the end of the war, including the battles of Nivelle, Orthes, and Toulouse. Served also in the Kandian rebellion in 1817 and 18.

7 Capt. Richardson served in the Peninsula from Dec. 1809 to the end of the war, including the general actions at Busaco, Salamanca, Vittoria, Pyrenees, 28th and 30th July, Nivelle (severely wounded in the left knee), Orthes, and Toulouse; partial actions at Rodiulia, Vale of Concales, Pyrenees, Heights of Vera; also engaged at the siege of Olavenza, first and last siege of Badajoz (wounded at the assault 7th April, 1812), siege of Ciudad Rodrigo, and storming the suburbs, and blockade of Pampeluna. Present at Waterloo.

8 Lieut. Stubbs served during the Kandian rebellion in 1817 and 18. Quarter-Master, 18th Sept. 23, from which date the period of service has been computed.

Full Pay	Half Pay	
17	10	*Paymaster.*—Richard Brough, 7 Oct. 24; * *Lieut.* 25 Dec. 13.
17	0	*Adjutant.*—John Stubbs, (Lieut.) 20 April, 26.
2	0	*Quarter-Master.*—Robert Imray, 8 June, 38.
		Surgeon.—William Gardiner, 5 May, 37; *Assist.-Surgeon,* 7 Feb. 11.
14	0	*Assist.-Surgeons.*—John Maitland, M.D. 12 June, 28; *Hosp.-Assist.* 16 Dec. 26.
6	0	Richard James O'Flaherty, 9 Jan. 35.

Facings Yellow.—*Agent,* Messrs. Cox & Co.

1 General Fraser served the three campaigns of 1790, 91, and 92, in the East Indies; was present at the siege and storming of Bangalore, the assault of Tippo's fortified camp, 6th Feb. 1792, and subsequent siege of Seringapatam. In 1803 he served at the siege and capture of Pondicherry. In 1797 he sailed on the projected Manilla expedition to Penang. In 1799 he took the field against Tippo Sultan, and was present at the battle of Mallavelly, and the siege and assault of Seringapatam. Gen. Fraser commanded the southern division of the army, during the whole of the Polygar war in 1801.

2 Major Trydell served at the capture of the Cape of Good Hope in 1806, and in the Kandian Insurrection of 1817 and 18 in Ceylon.

3 Major Crofton served in the Kandian Insurrection in 1817 and 18.

4 Major Law served in the Peninsula from Sept. 1813 to the end of the war, including the battles of Nivelle and Nive.

5 Major Swinburne served in the Peninsula from 1809 to the end of the war, including the battles of Oporto, Talavera (wounded in the right arm and foot), Busaco; actions at Pombal, Leria, Condeixa, Fleur-de-lis, Guarda, and Sabugal; battle of Fuentes d'Onor; first siege of Badajoz, action at Elbodon; siege of Ciudad Rodrigo; second siege of Badajoz, Salamanca, Vittoria, Pyrenees, Nivelle, Salvaterre, Orthes (wounded in the neck), Vigmagore, and Toulouse.

84th (*York and Lancaster*) Regt. of Foot.

The *Union Rose*, "NIVE"—"PENINSULA"—"INDIA."

Years' Serv.		
53		*Colonel.*
Full Pay.	Half Pay.	*Sir* Fitzroy J. Grafton Maclean,¹ *Bt. Ens.* 24 Sept. 1787; *Lieut.* 19 June, 88; *Capt.* 15 July, 93; *Lieut.-Col.* 18 Nov. 95; *Col.* 25 Sept. 1803; *Major-Gen.* 25 July, 10; *Lieut.-Gen.* 4 June, 14; *Gen.* 10 Jan. 37; *Col.* 84th Regiment, 28 July, 23.
31	5½	*Lieut.-Colonel.*—ᛔ Frederick Macbean,² K. H. *Ens.* 9 June, 03; *Lieut.* 6 May, 05; *Capt.* 24 Dec. 12; *Major,* p18 July, 26; *Lieut.-Col.* p2 Nov. 38.
25	2⁵⁄₁₂	*Majors.*—Richard Willington,³ *Cornet,* 1 Oct. 12; *Lieut.* 2 Oct. 14; *Capt.* p3 Dec. 25; *Brevet-Major,* 28 June, 38; *Regtl.-Major,* p2 Nov. 38.
17	0	Charles Franklyn, *Ens.* p17 July, 23; *Lieut.* p8 April, 26; *Capt.* p10 July, 28; *Major,* p28 Dec. 38.

		CAPTAINS.	ENSIGN.	LIEUT.	CAPTAIN.	BREV.-MAJ.
33	0	ᛔ Sam. Taylor Basden⁴..	21 May 07	9 Oct. 08	3 Oct. 27	
26	1	Alex M'Crae............	9 Sept. 13	p18 July 22	30 Aug. 31	
16	9	Hen. Bourke Clarke.....	23 Nov. 15	17 Aug. 26	18 July 33	
13	0	David Russell..........	p10 Jan. 28	p 1 Oct. 29	p 5 Apr. 33	
14	0	Tho. Geo. Veitch	17 Aug. 26	p10 July 28	p26 June 35	
18	4	Matthew B. G. Reed.....	p26 Feb. 18	p19 Nov. 25	p26 Feb. 36	
13	0	Charles James..........	p29 Nov. 27	p20 Jan. 32	p 9 Oct. 35	
15	0	Rich. Nassau Bolton....	p 7 July 25	15 Nov. 27	p 2 Nov. 38	
12	0	Samuel John Goslin.....	p10 July 28	p21 Sept. 30	p28 Dec. 38	
11	0	Wm. Hen. Kelly........	p 1 Oct. 29	18 July 33	p31 May 39	
		LIEUTENANTS.				
14	0	Jas. Alex. West.......	p 6 July 26	28 Feb. 28		
12	0	Thomas Bridge.........	p26 June 28	30 Aug. 31		
14	15⁷⁄₁₂	Roderick J. Hanley.....	7 July 11	25 May 12		
10	0	Arthur Coape..........	p19 Nov. 30	p22 Oct. 33		
10	0	Lawr. L. Esmonde White..	p18 Jan. 31	p26 June 35		
7	0	Rich. Lovelocke Coxe....	p21 Oct. 33	p10 June 36		
8	0	George M'Call..........	7 Sept. 32	p 1 Dec. 37		
7	0	Matthew Cassan........	p13 Dec. 33	10 May 38		
6	0	Thos. Davison.........	p23 May 34	p 2 Nov. 38		
5	0	Geo. Fra. Harrison.....	p26 June 35	p28 Dec. 38		
3	0	James Considine.......	26 July 37	p31 May 39		
4	0	Wm. Murray Mitchell ..	p5 Mar. 36	p1 Nov. 39		
		ENSIGNS.				
3	0	Cha. F. Campbell.......	15 Sept. 37			
3	0	Cha. F. Seymour	9 Jan. 38			
2	0	Thos. Lightfoot........	1 June 38			
2	0	Arth. Cav. Bentinck.....	p 2 Nov. 38			
2	0	John Willington Monck	p28 Dec. 38			
2	0	Geo. Fred. MacBean.....	4 Jan. 39			
2	0	Frederick Mills	p25 Jan. 39			
1	0	M. Mac Naughten Smith .	p31 May 39			
1	0	Speer Hughes..........	p31 Dec. 39			
31	0⁄₁₂	*Paymaster.*—ᛔ Joseph Nicholson,⁵ 7 Sept. 26; *Ens.* 11 Aug. 08; *Lieut.* 9 Aug. 10; *Capt.* 15 March, 21.				
3	0	*Adjutant.*—C. F. Seymour, (*Ens.*) 10 May, 39.				
3	0	*Quarter-Master.*—James Farrell, 12 May, 37.				
21	6²⁄₁₂	*Surgeon.*—Daniel Armstrong, 30 Oct. 38; *Assist.-Surgeon,* 22 Dec. 14; *Hosp.-Assist.* 6 Sept. 13.				
3	0	*Assistant-Surgeon,* Francis William Innes, M.D. 10 Feb. 37.				

4 Capt. Basden's services :—Expedition to Walcheren, and siege of Flushing; Peninsula from Aug. 1813 to the end of the war, including the battles of Nivelle and Nive, 9th, 10th, and 11th Dec. 1813.

5 Capt. Nicholson served in the Peninsula from April 1809 to the end of the war, including the battles of Talavera, Busaco, and Salamanca, where he was severely wounded.

[*Returned from the West Indies, May* 1838.]

Facings Yellow.—*Agent*, Messrs. Cox & Co.

1 Sir F. Maclean served many years in the West Indies, and was present at the reduction of various islands, &c. &c. He has received a medal for Guadaloupe.

2 Col. Macbean's services :—Battles of Roleia, Vimiera, and Corunna; expedition to Walcheren; Peninsula from Oct. 1812 to Nov. 1813, including the battle of Vittoria, Mayo Pass, Pyrenees 28th, 30th, and 31st July ; Pass of Echellar; served the campaign of 1815 in Upper Canada.

3 Major Willington served in the East Indies from May 1813 to May 1823, including the campaigns of 1815 and 16, in Kattywar and Kutch ; taking of Anjar ; Deccan campaigns of 1817 and 18 ; campaign of 1819 in Kandish, and in Kutch in 1820.

Emb. for Foreign Service, 1836.] **85th** (*Bucks Volunteers*) *or King's Light Inf. Regt.* [Serving in Canada.

"Aucto splendore resurgo."
" FUENTES D'ONOR"—"NIVE"—"PENINSULA"—"BLADENSBURG."

Years' Serv.			ENSIGN.	LIEUT.	CAPTAIN.	BREV.-MAJ.
Full Pay.	Half Pay.	*Colonel.*				
44		𝔹 Sir Wm. Thornton,[1] K.C.B. Ens. 31 March, 1796; Lieut. 1 March, 97; Capt. 25 June, 1803; Major, 13 Nov. 06; Lieut.-Col. 28 Jan. 08; Col. 4 June, 14; Major-Gen. 27 May, 25; Lieut.-Gen. 28 June, 38; Col. 85th Light Infantry, 9 April, 39.				
		Lieut.-Colonel.				
28	0	𝔹 Fred. Maunsell,[2] Ens. 16 March, 12; Lieut. P 28 Jan. 13; Capt. P 24 June, 19; Major, P 14 Aug. 27; Lieut.-Col. 23 May, 36.				
		Majors.				
28	0	𝔹 Henry John French,[3] Ens. 27 Aug. 12; Lieut. 21 July, 13; Capt. P 25 Sept. 23; Major, 23 May, 36.				
27	0	Wm. Thomas Hunt, Ens. 29 April 13; Lieut. 17 Nov. 14; Capt. P 9 April 25; Brev.-Maj. 28 June 38; Regt.-Maj. P 1 Nov. 39.				
		CAPTAINS.				
20	1 1/2	Manley Power..........	P 24 June 19	P 17 April 23	P 30 June 25	28 June 38
17	0	Herbert Edward Taylor..	22 Jan. 24	P 10 Sept. 25	P 11 June 30	
14	1 10/12	Francis John St. Quintin	8 April 25	P 28 Jan. 26	P 21 Nov. 28	
14	0	James Kennard Pipon ..	P 3 Aug. 26	P 9 Dec. 28	P 6 Mar. 35	
15	0	Henry Sabine Browne ..	P 23 June 25	P 11 July 30	P 30 Sept. 36	
12	0	Thos. M. M'N. Hamilton	P 24 April 28	P 1 Feb. 33	P 9 Nov. 38	
11	0	George Tennant	P 6 July 29	P 9 May 34	P 4 Oct. 39	
6	11	John Hamilton Dundas..	P 18 Dec. 23	P 16 June 25	P 8 Apr. 26	
9	0	George Cochrane Dickson	P 5 April 31	P 24 Nov. 35	P 1 Nov. 36	
13	0	Brook Taylor	P 15 May 27	P 15 June 30	P 28 Nov. 34	
		LIEUTENANTS.				
15	0	Henry Wynyard........		9 April 25	P 21 May 26	
13	0	William Todd..........	P 30 Aug. 27	P 2 Mar. 32		3 Major French served in the Peninsula, from Aug. 1813 to the end of the war, including siege of San Sebastian; passage of the Bidassoa; battles of the Nivelle and Nive, and investment of Bayonne. Served also in the American war, including the actions at Bladensburg, Baltimore, New Orleans, and Fort Boyer.
9	0	Henry Charles Curtis ..	P 30 Dec. 31	P 4 Mar. 36		
8	0	Oliver Jackson	P 2 Mar. 32	P 27 May 36		
8	0	John Blackburn	P 15 June 32	P 1 Sept. 37		
7	0	Alexander G. Grant	P 4 Oct. 33	P 18 Dec. 35		
6	0	Cholmeley Edw. Dering..	P 9 May 34	17 April 38		
6	0	John Wm. Grey........	P 16 May 34	P 1 June 38		
6	0	Compton Chas. Domville	P 16 May 34	P 9 Nov. 38		
5	0	Cecil Edward Bewes....	P 7 Aug. 35	P 4 Oct. 39		
4	0	John Horrocks	P 4 Mar. 36	P 1 Nov. 39		
		ENSIGNS.				
4	0	Chas. John Colville	P 27 May 36			
4	0	Alexander Patterson	23 Sept. 36			
3	0	Henry John Darell	P 5 May 37			
3	0	W. Wray Maunsell......	P 1 Sept. 37			
3	0	Thomas Edmund Knox..	26 Jan. 38			
2	0	T. C. M. Lethbridge	P 12 May 38			
2	0	Pat. W. Sydenham Ross	P 9 Nov. 38			
2	0	Charles K. K. Tynte....	P 10 Nov. 38			
1	0	Evelyn Latimer Parratt	P 4 Oct. 39			
1	0	*Lord* Spencer S. Compton	P 1 Nov. 39			
24	1	*Paymaster.*—George Ash Thompson, 27 Jan. 20; *Ens.* 16 Mar. 15; *Lieut.* 22 May, 17.				
4	0	*Adjutant.*—Alexander Patterson (*Ensign*) 16 Dec. 36.				
12	1 6/12	*Quarter-Master.*—George Edwards, 25 Oct. 27.				
29	7/12	*Surgeon.*—𝔹 George Griffin, 26 Sept. 84; *Assist.-Surg.* 28 April, 14; *Hosp.-Assist.* 11 June, 11.				
4	0	*Assistant-Surgeon.*—W. C. Humfrey, 18 Jan, 27; *Hospital-Assist.* 10 Jan. 26. William Carson, M.D. 7 Oct. 36.				

Facings Blue.—*Agent*, Messrs. Cox & Co.

1 Sir Wm. Thornton has received a medal for the passage of the Nive, and was twice wounded in the last American war.

2 Col. Maunsell served in the Peninsula, from August, 1813, to the end of the war, including siege of San Sebastian; passage of the Bidassoa; battles of Nivelle, 10th Nov., and Nive, 9th, 10th, and 11th Dec. Served also in the American war, and was slightly wounded at Bladensburgh, 24th Aug. and severely at New Orleans, 23d Dec. 1814.

86th (or the Royal County Down) Regiment of Foot.

On the Colours and Appointments, the *Harp* and *Crown*, with the Motto "*Quis Separabit.*" "INDIA"—The *Sphinx*, with the words "EGYPT"—"BOURBON"—On the Buttons, the *Irish Harp* and *Crown*.

Years' Serv.			ENSIGN.	LIEUT.	CAPTAIN.	BREV.-MAJ.
		Colonel.				
48		Sir Arthur Brooke,1 K.C.B. Ens. 31 Oct. 1792; Lieut. 26 Nov. 93; Capt. 19 Sept. 95; Major, 26 Dec. 1802; Lieut.-Col. 15 June, 04; Col. 4 June, 13; Major-Gen. 12 Aug. 19; Lieut.-Gen. 10 Jan. 37; Col. 86th Regiment, 24 May, 37.				
Full Pay.	Half Pay.	**Lieut.-Colonel.**				
37	1 1/12	Sir Michael Creagh,2 K.H. Ens. 9 May, 02; Lieut. 28 Feb. 04; Capt. 25 Nov. 09; Major, p 24 Oct. 21: Lieut.-Col. p 31 Dec. 30.				
		Majors.				
20	1/12	James Wm. Bouverie, Ens. p 29 June, 20; Lieut. p 3 July, 23; Capt. p 16 Aug. 25; Major, p 26 Nov. 29.				
31	0	James Creagh, Ens. 1 Jan. 10; Lieut. 4 March, 12; Capt. 7 April, 25; Brevet-Major, 28 June, 38; Regtl.-Major, p 18 Jan. 39.				
		CAPTAINS.				
36	0	Alexander Maclean3	6 Sept. 04	16 Sept. 05	30 June 17	10 Jan. 37
25	4/12	H. E. De Burgh Sidley..	4 May 15	21 Feb. 22	p 11 June 30	
18	3 5/12	Robert Henry Lowth ..	p 4 Feb. 19	p 1 April 24	p 15 May 27	
15	0	Lewis Halliday	7 April 25	p 4 May 26	p 31 Dec. 30	
23	3 8/12	John Holland	11 Mar. 14	21 Oct. 18	31 Oct. 34	
12	0	Archibald Hay	10 July 28	p 29 Mar. 33	p 8 April 36	
21	2	Richard Nugent Everard	p 27 Nov. 17	7 April 25	p 3 July 35	
18	7 5/12	J. Esten Dickinson	2 Aug. 15	13 Oct. 25	5 Sept. 36	
12	2 11/12	Owen Phibbs	p 31 Dec. 25	p 31 Dec. 30	p 18 Jan. 39	
9	16 2/12	Henry Sykes Stephens ..	14 June 15	8 Nov. 15	p 9 June 25	28 June 38
		LIEUTENANTS.				
21	0	James M'Intyre........	22 July 19	7 April 25	3 Major Maclean served at the capture of Bourbon in 1810. 4 Paymaster Ormond served at the capture of Martinique in 1809, and Guadaloupe in 1810.	
12	0	William Stuart	6 Mar. 28	p 28 Sept. 30		
16	0	Horatio Fenwick	19 Dec. 24	13 June 30		
13	0	Giles Keane	21 June 27	p 22 Feb. 31		
10	9 5/12	James Gilchrist	p 23 Nov. 20	31 Oct. 34		
9	0	Joseph Edwards........	p 11 Oct. 31	p 4 Dec. 35		
8	0	Charles Wm. Gore......	p 16 Nov. 32	p 3 Nov. 37		
6	0	Goring Rideout	p 23 Jan. 35	p 1 Dec. 37		
8	0	Hugh Thos. Bowen	18 May 32	p 6 June 34		
5	0	Henry Christmas Cash ..	p 4 Dec. 35	p 18 Jan. 39		
9	0	Charles Luxmore Bennett	p 3 Feb. 32	p 24 July 35		
6	0	Richard Baylis Bennett..	p 1 Aug. 34	p 12 Mar. 36		
3	22 6/12	John Lane	22 Dec. 14	12 Feb. 16		
		ENSIGNS.				
4	0	Hon. E. S. Plunkett	p 17 June 36			
4	0	Maurice Hartland Mahon	p 22 July 36			
4	0	John Harvey Thursby ..	p 26 Aug. 36			
3	0	Wm. F. Macbean	7 July 37			
3	0	William Edwards	p 1 Dec. 37			
2	0	Adolphus Fraser	p 4 Jan. 39			
2	0	W. W. R. Peacocke	p 18 Jan. 39			
1	0	Alexander Lecky	p 18 May 39			
21	5 5/12	Paymaster.—George Ormond,4 26 Feb. 29; Ens. 23 Sept. 13; Lieut. 6 Dec. 15.				
16	0	Adjutant.—Horatio Fenwick, (Lieut.) 26 Oct. 32.				
14	0	Quarter-Master.—Joseph Jerome, 23 March, 26.				
28	0	Surgeon.—John Coghlan, 5 Sept. 34; Assistant-Surgeon, 19 Sept. 22; Hosp.-Assist. 9 Nov. 12.				
14	0	Assistant-Surgeon.—J. Strath, 28 Sept. 26; Hosp.-Assist. 1 June, 26.				

Facings Blue.—*Agent*, Messrs. Cox & Co.

[*Returned from the West Indies, April*, 1837.]

1 Sir Arthur Brooke served on the Continent, from May, 1794, with the army under the Duke of York. In Dec. 1795, he went to the West Indies with the army under Sir Ralph Abercromby, and was present at the reduction of St. Lucia in 1796, and in the action of the 3rd May, in the same year. He next accompanied the army in the expedition to Egypt, and was in the actions of the 13th and 21st March, 1801. From 1804 to 1808, he served in Malta, and subsequently in Sicily and Spain. In 1813 he went to the Peninsula. The 1st June, 1814, embarked from Bordeaux for America, where he served with great distinction.

2 Sir Michael Creagh's services:—capture of the Cape of Good Hope in 1806, (slightly wounded); capture of the island of Bourbon (severely wounded by a cannot shot on the shoulder). Mahratta war in 1818, and Kandian war in 1819.

Emb. for For. Service, 1831.] **87th Regt. of Foot (or Royal Irish Fusiliers).** [Serving at the Mauritius.

"MONTE VIDEO"—"TALAVERA."—*An Eagle, with a Wreath of Laurel above the Harp, in addition to the Arms of the Prince of Wales, in commemoration of their distinguished Services on various occasions, and particularly at the Battle of* "BARROSA"—"TARIFA"—"VITTORIA"—"NIVELLE"—"ORTHES"—"TOULOUSE"—"PENINSULA" -"AVA."

Years' Serv.					
Full Pay	Half Pay	Colonel.			
47		₿ ᘮ Sir Thomas Reynell,[1] Bt. K.C.B. Ens. 30 Sept. 1793; Lieut. 3 Dec. 94; Capt. 29 July, 97; Major, 3 Aug. 1804; Lieut.-Col. 10 Mar. 05; Col. 4 June, 13; Major-Gen. 12 Aug. 19; Lieut.-Gen. 10 Jan. 37; Col. 87th Fusiliers, 15 Aug. 34.			
		Lieut.-Colonel.			
39	0	Henry C. Streatfeild,[2] Ens. Oct. 01; Lieut. ᴾ 13 Nov. 01; Capt. ᴾ 7 Nov. 05; Brevet-Major, 12 Aug. 19; Regtl.-Major, 18 May, 23; Lieut.-Col. ᴾ 4 Oct. 33.			
24	3 5/12	Majors.—₿ Henry Arthur Magenis,[3] Cornet, 1 Oct. 12; Lieut. 4 March, 13; Capt. ᴾ 9 Sept. 19; Major, ᴾ 20 Nov. 27.			
29	0	James Bowes,[4] Ens. 12 Sept. 11; Lieut. ᴾ April, 13; Capt. 23 Aug. 25; Major, ᴾ 18 Oct. 33.			

			2ND LIEUT.	LIEUT.	CAPTAIN.	BREV.MAJ.
		CAPTAINS.				
32	0	₿ James T. Moore[5]	13 Oct. 08	18 Feb. 12	18 Aug. 24	28 June 38
32	0	₿ James Kennelly[6]	11 Jan. 09	18 Nov. 13	12 Apr. 26	
26	1	Terence O'Brien	22 Apr. 13	19 Jan. 15	ᴾ 20 Mar. 28	
15	5/12	Lord Arthur Chichester	never	9 June 25	ᴾ 6 Dec. 27	
26	0	John Hassard[7]	22 Dec. 14	10 Aug. 18	ᴾ 16 July 30	
23	0	Fred. Holt Robe........	22 Oct. 17	8 Apr. 25	ᴾ 22 Oct. 33	
14	0	James Campbell........	ᴾ 6 July 26	ᴾ 31 July 28	ᴾ 10 Apr. 35	
14	0	Roger Keating	28 Mar. 26	ᴾ 11 Dec. 28	ᴾ 14 Mar. 34	
15	0	Henry B. Harvey	ᴾ 24 Dec. 25	ᴾ 24 Nov. 28	ᴾ 28 Dec. 32	
8	0	George Floyd Duckett ..	ᴾ 4 May 32	ᴾ 29 Aug. 34	ᴾ 5 July 39	
		LIEUTENANTS.				
24	10/12	George Mainwaring[8]	3 May 15	17 Sept. 17		
20	0	Robt. Russell Harris	19 Oct. 20	18 Aug. 24		
15	0	Patrick Francis Blake ..	26 Jan. 26	30 July 29		
12	0	Chas. Twistleton Graves	ᴾ 14 Feb. 28	ᴾ 25 Feb. 31		
11	0	Lord John Chichester ..	ᴾ 8 Sept. 29	ᴾ 10 Aug. 32		
9	0	Wm. Boyd	ᴾ 22 Feb. 31	ᴾ 17 Oct. 34		
9	0	Wm. Radcliff	ᴾ 27 Sept. 31	ᴾ 24 Apr. 35		
8	0	Henry Jephson	ᴾ 25 May 32	ᴾ 10 June 36		
9	0	C. H. Fitz Roy Vigors ..	ᴾ 28 Oct. 31	ᴾ 15 July 36		
9	0	Rich. Serrell O'Brien....	25 Nov. 31	19 Aug. 36		
7	0	Wm. Percy Lea	ᴾ 22 Feb. 33	ᴾ 21 Apr. 37		
6	0	Henry P. Faunt........	ᴾ 12 Sept. 34	ᴾ 9 July 38		
5	0	Charles Wm. D. Staveley	ᴾ 6 Mar. 35	ᴾ 4 Oct. 39		
		SECOND LIEUTS.				
4	0	Robt. Edwin Rich	ᴾ 10 June 36			
4	0	J. North Ouvry North ..	ᴾ 8 July 36			
4	0	Alfred Rush	ᴾ 15 July 36			
3	0	Wm. Shearman	ᴾ 21 Apr. 37			
3	0	J. Kent Egerton Holmes	8 Dec. 37			
2	0	Sam. Percy Lea	ᴾ 6 July 38			
1	0	Henry Moore	ᴾ 4 Oct. 39			
1	0	Richard Dores	25 Oct. 39			
31	3 2/12	Paymaster.—T. Drury,[9] 16 Apr. 29; 2nd Lieut. R. Marines, 7 Feb. 06; 1st. Lieut. 25 Oct. 11; 2nd Lieut. 95th Foot. (Rifle Brigade) 24 Dec. 13; Lieut. 20 Apr. 20.				
9	0	Adjutant.—R. S. O'Brien, (Lieut.) 26 June, 38.				
16	0	Quarter-Master.—₿ Stephen Carr,[10] 24 June, 24. [Hosp.-Assist. 30 Apr. 11.				
29	0	Surgeon.—ᘮ Rich. A. Pearson, M.D. 19 Nov. 30; Assist.-Surg. 13 May, 13;				
13	0	Assist.-Surgeons.—Stephen Lawson, 29 July, 30; Hosp.-Assist. 29 Nov. 27.				
1	0	James Gordon Inglis, M.D. 29 March, 39.				

Notes column (right side):
6 Captain Kennelly was present at the battle of Vittoria, the Pyrenees, Nivelle (wounded), and Toulouse, besides affairs of outposts. Served the Campaign in India of 1817 and 18, including the siege of Hatrass; and the Burmese war in 1825 and 26.
7 Capt. Hassard served the campaign of 1817 and 18, in India under the Marquis of Hastings; and in the Burmese war in 1825 and 6.
8 Lieut. Mainwaring served in Ava in 1825 and 26.
9 Captain Drury was present in several attacks upon the enemy on the coasts of the Mediterranean in 1806 and 7. Served the Campaign of 1809 and 10 in Arabia, including the siege and capture of Ras-ul-Kyhma, and the forts of Rums-Luft, an Sheenas. Present in the operations before New Orleans.
10 Quarter-master Carr served with peculiar distinction throughout all the actions of the 2nd battalion, and was wounded at Tarifa.

Facings Blue.—*Agent*, Messrs. Cox & Co.—*Irish Agent*, Messrs. Cane & Co.

1 Sir Thomas Reynell served in Flanders and Holland, in 1794 and 1795. At the Capture of Trinidad, in 1796. Served in Holland, in 1799. In 1800, served in Minorca, Malta, &c. Commanded the Light Company of the 40th at the landing in Egypt, and throughout the campaign. Sir Thomas was wounded at Waterloo.
2 Col. Streatfeild served the Mahratta Campaign of 1804, 5, and 6, including the assault of Bhurtpore with the Grenadiers of the 65th, when out of 17 officers and 300 men who marched to the assault, 14 officers and 190 men were either killed or wounded. At the capture of the Isle of France in 1810. Served the Mahratta Campaign of 1817 and 18, including the capture of Hatrass.
3 Major Magenis served with the 7th Fusiliers in the Peninsula and at New Orleans.
4 Major Bowes served in the Nepaul Campaign in 1816; present at the siege and capture of Hatrass in 1816 and 17; served the Mahratta Campaign of 1817 and 18; and in the Burmese war in 1825 and 26; wounded 25 Nov. 25.
5 Major Moore was present with the 2nd battalion in nearly every action in which it was engaged, the greater part of the time as adjutant, including the battle of Talavera (wounded in the right thigh, where the ball still remains), siege of Cadiz during the whole time, battle of Vittoria (two horses shot under him), the Pyrenees, Nivelle, Orthes (horse shot), Vic Bigorre (wounded), and Toulouse, besides various affairs of out posts &c. Served the Mahratta Campaign of 1817 and 18; and the Burmese war in 1825 and 26.

88th Regiment of Foot (or Connaught Rangers.)

On the Colours and appointments the *Harp and Crown*, with the motto, *"Quis Separabit."* The *Sphinx*, with the words "EGYPT"—"TALAVERA"—"BUSACO"—"FUENTES D'ONOR"—"CIUDAD RODRIGO"—"BADAJOZ"—"SALAMANCA"—"VITTORIA"—"NIVELLE"—"ORTHES"—"TOULOUSE"—"PENINSULA."

Years' Serv.					
Full Pay	Half Pay	*Colonel.*			
53		ⓟ Sir John Alex. Wallace,¹ Bt. K.C.B. *Ens.* 28 Dec. 1787; *Lieut.* 6 Apr. 90; *Capt.* 8 June, 96; *Major*, 9 July, 1803; *Lieut.-Col.* 28 Aug. 04; *Col.* 4 June, 13; *Major-Gen.* 12 Aug. 19; *Lieut.-Gen.* 10 Aug. 37; *Col.* 88th Regiment, 20 Oct. 31.			
		Lieut.-Colonel.			
33	1 7/12	ⓟ Robert O'Hara,² *Ens.* 29 Aug. 05; *Lieut.* ⓟ 3 Dec. 07; *Capt.* ⓟ 4 Apr. 11; *Major*, 14 May, 29; *Lieut.-Col.* 10 Nov. 37.			
16	1 11/12	*Majors.*—Ormsby Phibbs, *Cornet,* ⓟ 30 May, 22; *Lieut.* 7 Apr. 25; *Capt.* ⓟ 19 Sept. 26; *Major*, ⓟ 16 March, 38.			
16	0	Sir Wm. Payne Gallwey, *Bart.*, *Ens.* 29 July 24; *Lieut.* ⓟ 22 Sept. 25; *Capt.* ⓟ 21 Dec. 32; *Major*, ⓟ 1 Nov. 39.			

		CAPTAINS.	ENSIGN.	LIEUT.	CAPTAIN.	BREV.-MAJ.
20	7 10/12	Wm. Elliott	6 Aug. 12	2 Sept. 13	ⓟ 6 July 26	
15	0	Horatio Shirley	ⓟ 12 May 25	ⓟ 31 Oct. 26	ⓟ 5 July 33	
16	0	Rich. Warburton	8 Feb. 25	ⓟ 20 May 26	ⓟ 11 Nov. 36	
15	0	Edmund Rich. Jeffreys	16 June 25	ⓟ 11 Oct. 27	ⓟ 2 Feb. 38	
15	0	Edw. Adams	9 Apr. 25	31 Dec. 28	ⓟ 24 Feb. 38	
14	0	Peter Martyn	ⓟ 26 Dec. 26	2 Feb. 30	ⓟ 16 Mar. 38	
13	0	Wm. Irwin	ⓟ 15 Nov. 27	19 Nov. 30	ⓟ 26 Apr. 39	
11	0	Geo. Pat. O'Malley	ⓟ 10 Sept. 29	ⓟ 30 Apr. 33	ⓟ 10 Aug. 39	
10	0	Henry Townshend	ⓟ 28 Dec. 30	ⓟ 11 Nov. 36	ⓟ 11 Oct. 39	
8	0	Owen Lloyd Ormsby	ⓟ 21 Dec. 32	ⓟ 2 Feb. 38	ⓟ 1 Nov. 39	
		LIEUTENANTS.				
23	0	Gilbert Woollard	20 Nov. 17	27 May 22		
12	0	Wm. Mackie	5 Feb. 29	ⓟ 14 June 33		
10	0	Hen. Loftus Herbert	11 June 30	8 July 36		
7	0	Christ. Ellison	ⓟ 30 Apr. 33	ⓟ 24 Feb. 38		
6	0	Rob. Wm. Balfour	ⓟ 31 Oct. 34	ⓟ 16 Mar. 38		
5	0	Jas. Walker	ⓟ 5 June 35	ⓟ 7 Oct. 36		
4	0	Jas. M. Fowler	9 July 36	28 Aug. 38		
5	0	H. Beckw. Sawrey	ⓟ 6 Nov. 35	ⓟ 1 Mar. 39		
3	0	Geo. Fra. Stuart	ⓟ 23 June 37	ⓟ 5 Apr. 39		
3	0	Geo. Vaughan Maxwell	ⓟ 2 Feb. 38	ⓟ 26 Apr. 39		
2	0	Geo. Maxwell	ⓟ 16 Mar. 38	ⓟ 10 Aug. 39		
2	0	Joseph De Courcy Laffan	ⓟ 24 Feb. 38	ⓟ 11 Oct. 39		
2	0	Plomer J. Young	11 May 38	ⓟ 1 Nov. 39		
		ENSIGNS.				
2	0	F. R. MacGr. Dawson	ⓟ 4 Jan. 39			
2	0	Edward Norton	ⓟ 25 Jan. 39			
1	0	Septimus Adams	ⓟ 1 Mar. 39			
1	0	Edward Bayley	ⓟ 5 Apr. 39			
1	0	Edward Herbert Maxwell	ⓟ 26 Apr. 39			
1	0	George Rowan Hamilton	ⓟ 10 Aug. 39			
1	0	John Brooke Johnson	ⓟ 11 Oct. 39			
1	0	John Hardman Burke	ⓟ 1 Nov. 39			
25	7	*Paymaster.*—David Hay, 7 April, 08.				
4	0	*Adjutant.*—James M. Fowler, (*Lieut.*) 9 March, 38.				
9	0	*Quarter-Master.*—Thomas Mills, 19 Apr. 31.				
15	0	*Surgeon.*—Abraham James Nisbett Connel, M.D. 22 Nov. 39; *Assist.-Surg.* 16 June, 25; *Hosp.-Assist.* 10 Mar. 25.				
1	0	*Assist.-Surgeon.*—George Douglas Dods, M.D., 22 Nov. 39.				

Facings Yellow.—*Agent*, Messrs. Cox & Co.—*Irish Agent*, Messrs. Borough, Armit & Co.

[*Returned from the Ionian Islands, Sept.* 1836.]

1 Sir J. A. Wallace was at the battle of Seringapatam, the storming of Pagoda Hill, and of Tippoo's lines and camp, and the siege of Seringapatam, storming of Kistnagurrie, &c. &c. In 1798 served at the reduction of Minorca; from thence he joined the army under the command of Sir Ralph Abercromby, and was at the landing at Aboukir in Egypt, 8th March; the battles of the 13th and 21st, before Alexandria; at Rhamaine, Rosetta, and Grand Cairo. He has received a Medal and two Clasps for Busaco, Fuentes d'Onor, and Salamanca.

2 Colonel O'Hara served in Spain and Portugal from 1808 to 1811, including the battle of Vimiera, and retreat to Corunna; battle of Talavera; action of the Coa; battle of Busaco; action of Sabugal; affairs of Redinha, Miranda de Corvo, and Foz de Arroncé; battle of Fuentes d'Onor, and siege of Badajoz.

Emb. for Foreign Service, 1835.] **89th *Regiment of Foot*.** [Serving at Trinidad.

The *Sphinx*, with the words " EGYPT "—" JAVA "—" NIAGARA "—" AVA."

Years' Serv.		
Full Pay	Half Pay	**Colonel.**
49		₿ Sir Chas. B. Egerton,[1] G.C.M.G. & K.C.H. *Ens.* 16 Nov. 1791: *Lieut.* 21 Mar. 93; *Capt.* 22 April, 95; *Major*, 1 June, 98; *Lieut.-Col.* 14 Nov. 1802; *Col.* 4 June, 11; *Major-Gen.* 4 June, 14; *Lieut.-Gen.* 22 July, 30; *Col.* 89th Regt. 26 Sept. 37.
		Lieut.-Colonel.
41	0	J. L. Basden,[2] C.B. *Ens.* 12 Jan. 00; *Lieut.* P 17 March, 01; *Capt.* 4 Sept. 06; *Brev-Major*, 30 Dec. 13; *Regtl.-Major*, 25 Nov. 21; *Brev.-Lieut.-Col.* 22 July, 30; *Reg.-Lieut.-Col.* 6 July, 38.
35	0	*Majors.*—Walter Pearse,[3] *Ens.* 22 Aug. 05; *Lieut.* 9 Dec. 06; *Capt.* 27 March, 19; *Maj.* P 24 Dec. 33.
30	0	₿ A. S. H. Aplin,[4] *Ens.* 5 July, 10; *Lieut.* 24 Sept. 12; *Capt.* 9 March, 25; *Brev.-Major*, 28 June, 38; *Regtl.-Major*, P 7 July, 38.

Years' Serv. Full	Half	CAPTAINS.	ENSIGN.	LIEUT.	CAPTAIN.	BREV.-MAJ.
26	3	₿ Edw. Thorp[5]	7 Mar. 11	28 Jan. 13	P 13 Aug. 25	28 June 38
15	0	Robt. Lewis[6]	7 Apr. 25	P 2 Mar. 26	P 12 Feb. 28	6 Capt. Lewis served in the Burmese war.
27	0	₿ Edward Kenny[7]	17 June 13	1 Nov. 19	P 4 Dec. 32	
15	0	James Graham[8]	22 Apr. 25	19 Apr. 27	P 19 Apr. 33	7 Capt. Kenny served in the Peninsula, from June 1813, to the end of the war, including the action at Osma; battle of Vittoria; siege and capture of San Sebastian; passage of the Bidassoa (severely wounded above the left hip); St. Jean de Luz, and the series of actions between the 9th and 13th Dec 1813 in front of the intrenched camp near Bayonne. Served also in Ava, and was present in most of the operations throughout the war.
14	0	Mundy Pole	P 21 Sept. 26	P 21 June 27	P 24 Dec. 33	
27	1	John Milliquet Hewson[9]	2 Sept. 12	22 May 15	13 Mar. 35	
10	0	Wm. Alex. Poppleton	12 June 30	P 19 Apr. 33	P 7 July 38	
8	0	Caledon Rich. Egerton	15 June 32	P 28 Mar. 34	P 15 Mar. 39	
6	0	Geo. Calvert Clarke	P 30 May 34	P 7 Oct. 36	P 20 Sept. 39	
6	0	Charles Daly	P 25 July 34	P 17 Feb. 37	P 31 Dec. 39	
		LIEUTENANTS.				
8	0	Fred. Chas. Aylmer	P 4 Dec. 32	P 25 July 34		
10	0	John Spence	30 Sept. 30	P 12 Apr. 33		
9	0	Martin M. Dillon	16 Aug. 31	P 1 July 36		8 Captain Graham joined the 54th regt. in Burmah, as a volunteer, in Dec. 1824, and was present at the carrying the intrenched Fords of the Mahattee river, 27th March, and at the attack on the fortified heights of Arracan, 29th March, 1825; at the latter he was wounded in the side and face.
5	0	Chas. Montagu Walker	10 Apr. 35	P 10 Mar. 37		
8	0	John Duntze Macdonald	13 July 32	P 13 June 34		
5	0	Arthur Pigott	P 24 Apr. 35	2 July 38		
5	0	Wm. Hen. Thornton	3 Oct. 35	1 Nov. 38		
5	0	Henry Crawford	P 9 Oct. 35	8 Nov. 38		
4	0	Henry Edmunds	P 8 Apr. 36	P 15 Mar. 39		
4	0	Jas. R. Macdonald	P 7 Oct. 36	13 May 39		
3	0	Timothy Hutchinson	P 10 Mar. 37	P 28 June 39		
3	0	Charles Sandes	P 17 Feb. 37	P 20 Sept. 39		9 Capt. Hewson served in the American war, and was engaged at the battle of Niagara and siege of Fort Erie. Served also in the Burmese war. 11 Captain Bell served at the capture of the Isle of France in 1810, and in the Deccan in 1818. 12 Dr. M'Dermott served at New Orleans, 8th Jan. 1815.
2	0	Rob. B. Hawley	28 Aug. 38	P 31 Dec. 39		
		ENSIGNS.				
2	0	W. J. D. C. Aplin	P 7 July 38			
2	0	John Newbury	28 Dec. 38			
2	0	Oliver C. O'Brien	P 28 Dec. 38			
1	0	John Chas Romer	P 15 Mar. 39			
1	0	Chas. Doyle Patterson	21 June 39			
1	0	Fred. W. Oakley	P 28 June 39			
1	0	Geo. Aug. Fred. Ruxton	P 2 Aug. 39			
1	0	Tho. Dopping B. D'Arcy	P 10 Jan. 40			
32	0	*Paymaster.*—Wm. Bell,[11] 9 May, 34; *Ens.* 3 March, 08; *Lieut.* 9 May, 11; *Capt.* 25 Nov. 24.				
		Adjutant.—Henry Edmunds, (*Lieut.*) 12 May, 39.				
4	0	*Quarter-Master.*—James Dukes, 14 Dec. 20.				
16	3¾					
21	5 1/12	*Surgeon.*—Michael M'Dermott,[12] M.D. 5 April, 39; *Assist.-Surg.* 25 Dec. 23; *Hosp.-Assistant.* 7 Feb. 14.				
4	0	*Assistant-Surgeons.*—James Morison, 14 Oct. 36.				
1	0	George M'Clure, 29 March, 39.				

Facings Black.—*Agent*, Messrs. Cox & Co.

1 Sir C. B. Egerton commanded a detachment on board a line-of-battle ship, in Lord Howe's action of the 1st June, 1794. Served at the blockade of Malta, and surrender of Valetta, 5th Sept. 1800; from thence proceeded with Sir Ralph Abercromby's expedition to Egypt, and was present in the actions of the 13th and 21st March, 1801. Served with the army in Spain and Portugal in 1810 and 1811.

2 Col. Basden's services:—Mahratta war of 1803, 4, and 5, including the taking of Berhampore, Asseerghur, Argaum, Lasslgaum, Chawdore, Jaulnah and Gawilleghur. American war in 1813 and 14, and was engaged at Long Woods (severely wounded in the thigh); Fort Erie, Black Rock, Buffalo, and battle of the Falls (wounded). Served also through Burmese war.

3 Major Pearse served in the American war, and was engaged at Chrystler's Farm, and at Niagara, 25th July, 1814, where he was severely wounded through the arm. Served in the East Indies and the Burman empire, from Feb. 1816 to the end of the war, including the captures of forts Loghur, Issapore, Koarre, and Ryghur in 1818; assault on Rarree, 13th Feb, 1819; action near the Dagon Pagoda, 5th July, 24; assault of Mergui; Cockain; attacks on Pagham Mew, Zembeik, Mellown, and Donabew, besides many other affairs during the war.

4 Major Aplin served in the Peninsula, from Feb. 1811 to the end of the war, including the battle of Salamanca, siege of Burgos, and capture of Madrid. Served also throughout the Burmese war, and was present in numerous engagements with the enemy.

5 Major Thorp served in the Peninsula, from June, 1811, to the end of the war, including the affairs of Elbodon and Alfaytes, siege and storming of Ciudad Rodrigo; battles of the Pyrenees; crossing the Bidassoa; St. Jean de Luz, and different actions investing Bayonne, and sortie from Bayonne.

Emb. for For. Service, 1835.] **90th Regt. of Ft. (or Perthsh. Volun.) (Lt. Infan.)** [Serving at Ceylon.

"MANDORA."—The *Sphinx* with the word, "EGYPT"—"MARTINIQUE"—"GUADALOUPE."

Years' Serv.						
47		*Colonel.*				
Full Pay.	Half Pay.	Sir Hen. Sheehy Keating,[1] K.C.B. *Ens.* 31 Aug. 1793; *Lieut.* 31 Jan. 94; *Capt.* 8 Sept. 96; *Major,* 3 Sept. 1800; *Lieut.-Col.* 1 Aug. 04; *Col.* 4 June, 13; *Major-Gen.* 12 Aug. 19; *Lieut.-Gen.* 10 Jan. 37; *Col.* 90th Light Infantry, 26 Sept. 37.				
		Lieut.-Colonel.				
22	12 10/13	John Peddie, K.H.[2] *Ens.* 26 Sept. 05; *Lieut.* 26 Aug. 07; *Capt.* 23 Sept. 13; *Major,* p 16 June, 25; *Lieut.-Col.* p 28 Aug. 27.				
25	5 7/12	*Majors.*—John Singleton,[3] K.H. *Ens.* p 11 Jan. 10; *Lieut.* 25 July, 12; *Capt.* p 15 April, 24; *Major,* p 10 Jan. 28.				
20	9/12	Thomas Woodward Eyles, *Ens.* 30 Mar. 20; *Lieut.* p 6 Nov. 24; *Capt.* p 15 Aug. 26; *Major,* p 7 Feb. 40.				

		CAPTAINS.	ENSIGN.	LIEUT.	CAPTAIN.	BREV.-MAJ.
30	0	Horace Suckling [4]	22 Nov. 10	p 28 Feb. 12	p 21 Oct. 24	28 June 38
25	0	John Wilson	p 20 Apr. 15	8 Jan. 24	26 Mar. 29	
15	3/12	Geo. Darby Griffith	3 Mar. 25	p 24 Dec. 25	p 31 Dec. 28	
16	0	Fred. Eld	p 23 Dec. 24	p 26 Sept. 26	p 27 Sept. 31	
15	0	Hen. H. Cuming	7 Apr. 25	p 28 Sept. 26	p 2 Nov. 32	
15	0	Hen. Rob. Thurlow	p 11 Aug. 25	8 Jan. 29	p 27 Mar. 35	
14	0	Gervas S. Deverill.....	p 2 Nov. 26	p 13 Nov. 27	p 7 Mar. 34	
14	0	Geo. Douglas Bowyer ..	p 28 Dec. 26	p 7 Sept. 32	p 21 Sept. 38	
16	0	John Blaquiere Mann ..	10 Feb. 25	p 17 Nov. 25	2 June 38	
12	0	Vere Caldwell	p 5 Sept. 28	p 2 Nov. 32	p 7 Feb. 40	
		LIEUTENANTS.				
14	0	Marcus Geale	p 29 Sept. 26	3 Feb. 32		4 Major Suckling served in the Peninsula, from June, 1811, to Nov. 1813, including the siege of Badajoz, April, 1812, battle of Salamanca, retreat from Burgos, and siege of San Sebastian; wounded through the right hip and right hand at the assault 31st Aug. 1813. Served the campaigns of 1816, 17, and 18 in the Deccan.
11	0	Philip P. Gallwey	26 Mar. 29	19 Nov. 33		
10	0	Jas. D. G. Tulloch	18 July 30	14 Feb. 34		
9	0	Thos. Webb	p 31 May 31	p 27 Mar. 35		
9	0	John J. Doxat	3 Feb. 32	p 22 May 35		
8	0	John Hen. Bringhurst ..	p 7 Sept. 32	17 Mar. 38		
8	0	*Lord* S. A. Chichester ..	p 2 Nov. 32	p 22 June 38		
7	0	*Lord* James Beresford ..	p 1 Mar. 33	p 21 Sept. 38		
7	0	Cha. Montagu Chester ..	p 10 May 33	22 Sept. 38		
7	0	Frederick Woodgate	p 6 Dec. 33	p 25 Jan. 39		
6	0	Digby Fra. Mackworth..	p 2 May 34	p 7 Feb. 40		
		ENSIGNS.				
5	0	Cha. Vaughan Pugh	p 10 Apr. 35			
4	0	Robert Owen	22 Nov. 36			
3	0	K. W. S. Mackenzie	p 28 Apr. 37			
2	0	Thomas Ross	p 23 Mar. 38			
2	0	W. P. Purnell	24 Mar. 38			
2	0	Hen. Ashm. Evatt......	p 22 June 38			
2	0	Henry Lecky	p 25 Jan. 39			
1	0	Fra. B. Morley	p 5 Apr. 39			
1	0	James Wm. B. Peddie ..	25 Oct. 39			
1	0	Robert Grove	p 7 Feb. 40			
29	5	*Paymaster.*—Henry Yielding Eagar, 16 April, 18; *Ens.* 3 Dec. 06; *Lieut.* 17 March, 08.				
7	0	*Adjutant.*—Charles Montagu Chester. (*Lieut.*) 4 Aug. 36.				
3	0	*Quarter-Master.*—William Newland, 15 Sept. 37.				
		Surgeon.—John Kinnis, M.D. 22 June, 38; *Assist.-Surg.* 14 Dec. 24; *Hosp.-Assist.* 16 June, 15.				
5	0	*Assistant.-Surgeon.*—Richard Dane, M. D. 17 July, 35.				
4	0	Robert K. Prendergast, 7 Oct. 36.				

Facings Buff.—*Agent,* Messrs. Cox & Co.

1 Sir H. S. Keating served in the West Indies, and was severely wounded and detained as a prisoner at Guadaloupe. In conjunction with Commodore Rowley, he planned and conducted the operations of a gallant and successful attack upon the town and harbour of St. Paul's in the island of Bourbon.

2 Col. Peddie's services:—Battles of Roleia, Vimiera, and Corunna. Expedition to Walcheren. Campaign of 1812 in the Peninsula, including the battle of Salamanca, where he was severely wounded and lost his right arm.

3 Major Singleton served in the Peninsula, from 1811 to 1813, and was slightly wounded at the siege of the forts at Salamanca, and twice severely wounded at the battle of Salamanca.

Emb. for Foreign Service, 1835.] **91st (or the Argyllshire) Regiment of Foot.** [Serving at Cape and St. Helena.

"ROLEIA"—"VIMIERA"—"CORUNNA"—"PYRENEES"—"NIVELLE"—
"NIVE"—"ORTHES"—"TOULOUSE"—"PENINSULA."

Years' Serv.						
60		*Colonel.* Gabriel Gordon,¹ Ens. 6 Jan. 1781; Lieut. 26 Nov. 84; Capt. 10 July, 94; Major,				
Full Pay.	Half Pay.	16 May, 1800; Lieut.-Col. 9 March, 02; Col. 4 June, 11; Major-Gen. 4 June, 14; Lieut.-Gen. 22 July, 30; Col. 91st Regt. 19 April, 37.				
37	0	*Lieut.-Colonel.*—𝔓 𝕮𝕭 Robert Anderson,² K.H. Ens. 9 July, 03; Lieut. 12 Oct. 04; Capt. 30 April, 12; Major, ᴘ 23 Sept. 24; Lieut.-Col. ᴘ 2 Dec. 31.				
25	5	*Majors.*—Cornwall Burne, Ens. 4 Oct. 10; Lieut. 25 July, 15; Capt. ᴘ 3 Feb. 25; Major, ᴘ 8 Feb. 31.				
27	0	𝔓 𝕮𝕭 Norman Lamont,³ K.H. Ens. 26 Aug. 13; Lieut. 3 Sept. 18; Capt. 7 April, 25; Major, ᴘ 2 Dec. 31.				

		CAPTAINS.	ENSIGN.	LIEUT.	CAPTAIN.	BREV.-MAJ.
26	0	𝔓 𝕮𝕭 Dugald Ducat⁴ ..	24 Feb. 14	5 May 22	4 Aug. 28	
13	0	John Thornhill	ᴘ 5 Apr. 27	ᴘ 10 Sept. 28	ᴘ 8 Feb. 31	
31	0	𝔓 John Fraser⁵	29 May 09	12 Feb. 12	17 Aug. 32	
13	0	J. F. Glencairn Campbell	25 Oct. 27	ᴘ 27 Aug. 29	ᴘ 23 Nov. 32	
15	0	C. Cooke Yarborough ..	ᴘ 9 June 25	ᴘ 19 Sept. 26	ᴘ 4 Jan. 38	
13	6/12	Cha. Benj. Caldwell	ᴘ 10 Oct. 26	ᴘ 7 Oct. 29	ᴘ 4 Oct. 33	
14	4½	Thomas Eden Blackwell	26 Dec. 22	21 July 25	ᴘ 29 June 30	
11	0	David Forbes	ᴘ 8 Oct. 29	ᴘ 23 Nov. 32	ᴘ 24 July 35	
24	8 5/12	𝔓 John Marshall⁶	14 May 08	23 Nov. 09	20 Feb. 23	28 June 38
8	0	Wm. Glendowyn Scott ..	ᴘ 30 Mar. 32	ᴘ 12 June 35	ᴘ 22 Feb. 39	
		LIEUTENANTS.				
18	0	Geo. Adam Barnes......	12 Dec. 22	ᴘ 23 Sept. 24		
18	3/12	John Edward Barney ..	1 Aug. 22	ᴘ 9 June 25		
19	5	John Ward	8 Apr. 16	8 Sept. 28		
22	8	Wm. Wilson Hornsby ..	22 Mar. 10	22 Feb. 27		
12	0	John Campbell Cahill ..	28 Feb. 28	8 May 35		
8	0	Bertie E. M. Gordon....	ᴘ 26 Oct. 32	ᴘ 24 July 35		
8	0	Edw. W. C. Wright	21 Dec. 32	ᴘ 13 Nov. 35		
5	0	Colin Campbell	ᴘ 10 Apr. 35	ᴘ 2 Feb. 38		
5	0	Hen. J. Savage	5 June 35	ᴘ 11 May 38		
5	0	Rich. C. Onslow	ᴘ 12 June 35	ᴘ 25 Jan. 39		
5	0	James Christie	ᴘ 24 July 35	ᴘ 22 Feb. 39		
6	0	Rob. Fred. Middlemore..	19 Dec. 34	ᴘ 12 July 39		
5	0	John Brown	6 Nov. 35	31 Dec. 39		
		ENSIGNS.				
3	0	J. M. Pennington	ᴘ 26 Dec. 37			
2	0	F. Fraser Stokes	ᴘ 11 May 38			
2	0	Fred. J. Bayly	30 Oct. 38			
2	0	John George Hacket....	ᴘ 25 Jan. 39			
1	0	Wm. T. L. Patterson....	ᴘ 23 Feb. 39			
1	0	John Paton	ᴘ 23 Feb. 39			
1	0	Hen. Cha. Benyon Barton	ᴘ 12 July 39			
1	0	Peter L. Graham Cloete	17 Sept. 39			
15	0	*Paymaster.*—G. Had. Dalrymple, 31 Jan. 40; Ens. 5 Nov. 25; Lieut. 6 Dec. 27.				
5	0	*Adjutant.*—John Brown, (Lieut.) 14 Nov. 35.				
11	9 5/12	*Quarter-Master.*—William Barfoot, 13 July, 20.				
		Surgeon.—Nathaniel Morgan, 9 Aug. 39; Assist.-Surg. 28 Sept. 15.				
15	0	*Assist.-Surgs.*—Wm. C. Eddie, 12 Jan. 26; Hosp.-Assist. 1 May, 25.				
5	0	George M'Laren, M.D. 23 Oct. 35.				

5 Capt. Fraser served in the Peninsula from Aug. 1811 to the end of the war, including the siege and capture of the fortified convents at, and battle of Salamanca; siege of the castle of Burgos; battles of Vittoria, Pyrenees, Nivelle, and Toulouse. Severely wounded at Pampeluna 26th July, 1813.

6 Major Marshall's services:—Expedition to Portugal in 1808, including the battles of Roleia and Vimiera, advance into Spain and retreat through Gallicia under Sir John Moore, action at Lugo, and battle of Corunna. Expedition to Walcheren in 1809. Subsequently in the Peninsula, including the battles of Vittoria, the Pyrenees (26th, 27th, 28th, and 30th July), Nivelle, Nive, and investment of Bayonne, 9th, 10th, 11th, and 13th Dec. 1813, and battle of Orthes. Slightly wounded at Pampeluna, 28th July, 1813, and severely at Orthes.

Facings Yellow.—*Agent,* Messrs. Barron & Smith, Westminster.

1 General Gordon has received a medal and one clasp for Martinique and Guadaloupe.
2 Col. Anderson's services:—Expedition to Hanover in 1805 and 6. Battles of Roleia, Vimiera, and Corunna; expedition to Walcheren in 1809; to Swedish Pomerania in 1813, and campaign of 1814 in Holland, including the attack on Bergen-op-Zoom. Served at Waterloo 18th June, storming of Cambray, and capture of Paris.
3 Major Lamont served the campaigns of 1813 and 14 in the Peninsula, including the battles of the Pyrenees, Nivelle, Nive, Orthes, and Toulouse. Served at Waterloo, the storming of Cambray, and capture of Paris.
4 Capt. Ducat served in the Peninsula, from Aug. 1813 to the end of the war, including the battles of Nivelle, Nive, Orthes, and Toulouse. Served also at Waterloo, and at the storming of Cambray.

Emb. for Foreign Service, 1834.] **92nd (or Highland) Regt. of Foot.** [Serving at Malta.

"EGMONT-OP-ZEE"—"MANDORA"—The *Sphinx*, with the words "EGYPT"—"CORUNNA"—"FUENTES D'ONOR"—"ALMAREZ"—"VITTORIA"—"PYRENEES"—"NIVE"—"ORTHES"—"PENINSULA"—"WATERLOO."

Years' Serv.			
50		*Colonel.*	
Full Pay.	Half Pay.	Sir John Hamilton Dalrymple,¹ *Bart. Ens.* 28 Feb. 1790; *Lieut.* 30 April, 92; *Capt.* 26 April, 93; *Lieut.-Col.* 6 Dec. 98; *Col.* 25 April, 1808; *Major-Gen.* 4 June, 11; *Lieut.-Gen.* 19 July, 21; *Gen.* 28 June, 38; *Col.* 92nd Highlanders, 20 July, 31.	
		Lieut.-Colonel.	
29	7⅝	🅱 John M'Donald,² C.B. *Ens.* 17 Dec. 03; *Lieut.* 21 March, 05; *Capt.* 7 Sept. 09; *Brevet-Major*, 26 Aug. 13; *Regtl.-Major*, 25 Oct. 14; *Brevet-Lieut.-Col.* 4 Sept. 17; *Regtl.-Lieut.-Col.* ᴾ23 Sept. 24; *Col.* 10 Jan. 37.	
35	0	*Majors.*—🅱 🅲🅱🅱 Robert Winchester,³ K.H. *Ens.* 18 Sept. 05; *Lieut.* 6 Feb. 08; *Capt.* 19 July, 15; *Major*, 16 Aug. 25; *Brevet-Lieut.-Col.* 28 June, 38.	
22	1 4/12	John Alex. Forbes, *Ens.* ᴾ5 Dec. 16; *Lieut.* ᴾ22 May, 23; *Capt.* ᴾ24 Dec. 25; *Brev.-Major*, 28 June, 38; *Regtl.-Major*, ᴾ17 Sept. 39.	

		CAPTAINS.	ENSIGN.	LIEUT.	CAPTAIN.	BREV.-MAJ.
37	2 11/12	Stephen Noel⁴	8 Aug. 00	25 July 03	19 Mar. 12	22 July 30
16	1/12	Geo. Edw. Thorold	24 June 24	ᴾ 9 June 25	ᴾ19 Sept. 26	
23	2 3/12	Wm. Prittie Bayly	28 Sept. 15	ᴾ23 Oct. 23	ᴾ11 June 30	
16	7/12	Mark Kerr Atherley	ᴾ28 Aug. 23	ᴾ13 Aug. 25	ᴾ25 Nov. 28	
13	0	Thomas Ormsby	21 June 27	ᴾ12 Feb. 30	ᴾ15 Jan. 36	
12	0	Arch. Inglis Lockhart	ᴾ31 Dec. 28	ᴾ11 June 30	ᴾ19 Aug. 36	
22	3 8/12	Wm. Bletterman Caldwell	29 Sept. 14	ᴾ28 Oct. 24	ᴾ 9 Dec. 31	
11	0	Alex. Thos. W. Duff	ᴾ 4 June 29	ᴾ26 Nov. 30	ᴾ 8 Dec. 37	3 Col. Winchester's services:—Expedition to Copenhagen in 1807, and that to Walcheren in 1809. In the Peninsula, from October 1810, to the end of the war, including Lines of Torres Vedras, action of Arroya del Molino, taking of Almarez, defence of Alva de Tormes, battle of Vittoria, affairs of Puerto de Maya, 4th and 8th July, 1813, battles of the Pyrenees, 25th, 30th, and 31st July, 1813, affair of Roncesvalles, battle of Nivelle, affair of Cambo, battle of the Nive, 9th and 13th Dec. 1813, affair of Helette, action at Garris, affair of Ariverette, battle of Orthes, action at Aire, and affair at Tarbes. Present at Quatre Bras and Waterloo. Col. Winchester was slightly wounded in the Pyrenees, 25th July, severely at the Nive, 13th Dec. 1813, slightly at Quatre Bras, and severely at Waterloo. 4 Major Noel served in St. Domingo in 1796, 97, and 98, under Generals Boyer and Sir Brent Spencer, and was wounded in the right thigh, when the French attacked the Cordon of Posts. Served also at the capture of St. Lucia, Tobago, and the colonies of Demerara, Issequebo, and Berbice.
15	0	Robert Pitcairn	19 Jan. 26	ᴾ26 Oct. 30	ᴾ 6 Sept. 39	
10	0	Donald Stewart	30 Sept. 30	7 Feb. 34	ᴾ17 Sept. 39	
		LIEUTENANTS.				
17	0	Rob. M. Sutherland	25 Dec. 23	7 Aug. 24		
12	0	Arch. Neil Campbell	14 Aug. 28	8 April 31		
10	0	Arch. Hale Monro	ᴾ26 Nov. 30	ᴾ26 June 35		
8	0	James Cox	ᴾ16 Mar. 32	ᴾ19 July 34		
9	0	Patrick M'Leod Petley	ᴾ22 May 31	ᴾ21 Aug. 35		
9	0	Ken. Doug. Mackenzie	ᴾ25 Nov. 31	ᴾ19 Aug. 36		
8	17 1/2	Arch. Stewart	20 Mar. 15	12 July 33		
7	0	John T. C. Drake	7 Feb. 34	ᴾ10 Aug. 38		
11	0	Robert Petley	24 Dec. 29	ᴾ12 Aug. 34		
5	0	Edw. E. Haines	ᴾ26 June 35	ᴾ 1 Feb. 39		
5	0	Hon. H. B. W. Cochrane	ᴾ21 Aug. 35	ᴾ14 June 39		
5	0	Alex. Penrose Miller	ᴾ15 Jan. 36	ᴾ 6 Sept. 39		
4	0	James Caulfield Gordon	ᴾ18 Mar. 36	ᴾ17 Sept. 39		
		ENSIGNS.				
4	0	W. R. N. Campbell	ᴾ10 June 36			
4	0	Fra. W. Johnstone	ᴾ19 Aug. 36			
2	0	Arch. H. Tattnall	ᴾ10 Aug. 38			
2	0	P. H. Paterson	ᴾ17 Aug. 38			
2	0	William Dalzell	ᴾ 1 Feb. 39			
1	0	Geo. G. Hope Johnstone	ᴾ14 June 39			
1	0	Thomas Williams Davies	ᴾ 6 Sept. 39			
1	0	James Charles Gordon	ᴾ17 Sept. 39			
26	2 7/12	*Paymaster.*—J. Hope Johnstone Meiklejohn, 2 Mar. 20; *Ens.* 7 May, 12; *Lieut.* 10 Dec. 13.				
17	0	*Adjutant.*—Rob. Macleod Sutherland, (*Lieut.*) 7 Feb. 34.				
1	0	*Quarter-Master.*—John Forbes, 6 Sept. 39.				
		Surgeon.—C. Q. Palmer, 30 Dec. 34; *Assist.-Surg.* 17 April, 17.				
5	0	*Assist.-Surgeons.*—Melville Neale, 18 Sept. 35.				
1	0	John Crispigny Millingen, 20 Sept. 39.				

Facings Yellow.—*Agent,* Messrs. Cox & Co.—*Irish Agent,* Borough, Armit & Co.

1 Sir J. H. Dalrymple went to Flanders in 1794, and served on the Continent until the return of the British army, in 1795. In October, 1805, he accompanied the Expedition to Hanover. In July, 1807, he went to Zealand, and was present at the siege of Copenhagen.

2 Col. M'Donald's services:—Expedition to South America, and assault of Buenos Ayres; Peninsula, from Nov. 1808 to 1813; also in the South of France from March, 1814, including the battle of Busaco; Lines of Torres Vedras; affairs at Redinha, Pompal, and Campo Mayor; first siege of Badajoz; battle of Albuhera; second siege and assault of Badajoz; affairs at Alva de Tormes; battles of Vittoria, the Pyrenees, 25th, 30th, and 31st July, and Toulouse. Wounded in the head and right thigh at the assault of Buenos Ayres, 5th July, 1807; in the left leg and right groin in the Pyrenees, 30th July; and in the right shoulder and lungs at the assault of the fortified rock on the mountain Arolla, and surprising the enemy's posts in the valley of Banca, Pyrenees, 2d Oct. 1813.

Emb. for Foreign Service, 1838.] **93d (or Sutherland Highlanders) Regt. of Foot.** [Serving in Canada.

"CAPE OF GOOD HOPE."

Colonel.

Years' Serv.		
47	Full Pay	Half Pay

47 — 𝔅 Sir Jasper Nicolls,[1] K.C.B. *Ens.* 24 May, 1793; *Lieut.* 25 Nov. 94; *Capt.* 12 Sept. 99; *Major*, 6 July, 1804; *Lieut.-Col.* 29 Oct. 07; *Col.* 4 June, 14; *Major-Gen.* 19 July, 21; *Lieut.-Gen.* 10 Jan. 37; *Col.* 93rd Regt. 31 May, 33.

33 | 0 | *Lieutenant-Colonel.*—Robert Spark,[2] *Ens.* May, 07; *Lieut.* 3 Sept. 07; *Capt.* 17 Feb. 20; *Major*, p 25 Dec. 35; *Lieut-Col.* p 28 July, 38.

27 | 0 | *Majors.*—John Arthur, *Ens.* 25 Dec. 13; *Lieut.* 2 March, 20; *Capt.* p 8 Dec. 25; *Major*, p 30 Dec. 36.

21 | 0 | John Burgh, *Ens.* p 25 Nov. 19; *Lieut.* 7 April, 25; *Capt.* p 19 Sept. 26; *Major* p 28 July, 38.

		CAPTAINS.	ENSIGN.	LIEUT.	CAPTAIN.	BREV.-MAJ.
31	0	Charles Gordon[3]	22 June 09	15 Oct. 12	28 Feb. 28	
18	5 3/12	John Joseph Grier	11 Sept. 17	9 Apr. 25	p 31 July 28	
21	1 3/12	Robt. Carmichael Smyth	8 July 18	5 May 25	p 8 Apr. 26	
12	0	George Edward Aylmer	28 Feb. 28	p 13 Aug. 30	p 24 Nov. 35	
10	0	William Robt. Haliday	p 12 Feb. 30	p 3 Mar. 33	p 11 Nov. 36	
10	0	Wm. Bernard Ainslie	p 28 Sept. 30	p 24 Nov. 35	p 29 Sept. 37	
23	6 2/12	𝔅 Thos. Paul Williamson[4]	5 Dec. 11	24 Aug. 13	12 Jan. 38	
8	0	Neil S. Buchanan	p 21 Dec. 32	p 25 Dec. 35	p 28 July 38	
8	0	Wm. Pitt Trevelyan	p 4 Jan. 33	p 3 June 36	p 26 Apr. 39	
6	18	George Duff	p 6 Feb. 17	p 14 Oct. 19	p 9 Nov. 21	10 Jan. 37
		LIEUTENANTS.				
17	0	John Ambrose Russell	25 Dec. 23	28 Feb. 28		
14	0	James Neilson	p 19 Sept. 26	p 13 Aug. 29		
15	0	George Robert Pole	11 Aug. 25	24 Apr. 28		
14	0	William M'Donald[5]	23 Aug. 27	13 Jan. 34		
12	0	Jas. Montagu Brown	17 Apr. 28	14 Oct. 36		
6	0	John F. A. Hartle	21 Feb. 34	p 11 Nov. 36		
6	0	Robt. Murray Banner	p 19 Dec. 34	p 30 Dec. 36		
5	0	Andrew Agnew	p 17 Apr. 35	p 29 Sept. 37		
6	0	Lord. Cosmo Geo. Russell	p 12 Aug. 34	p 6 July 38		
5	0	Chas. Henry Gordon	p 24 Nov. 35	p 28 July 38		
5	0	Alex. S. L. Hay	p 25 Dec. 35	p 26 Apr. 39		
4	0	George Studdert	p 3 June 36	p 19 July 39		
4	0	George Douglas	20 May 36	p 30 Aug. 39		
		ENSIGNS.				
4	0	F. H. Crawford	14 Oct. 36			
4	0	Evan D. Macpherson	p 11 Nov. 36			
4	0	David Seton	p 30 Dec. 36			
3	0	E. Hunter Blair	p 29 Sept. 37			
2	0	Thos. M. Crawfurd	p 1 June 38			
2	0	George Seton	p 28 July 38			
1	0	Colin Maxwell	p 26 Apr. 39			
1	0	Geo. John White Melville	p 19 July 39			

4 Captain Williamson served the campaign of 1812, in the Peninsula, including the siege and assault of Badajoz 6th April, 1812; served the campaign of 1814 in Holland, including the attack on Bergen-op-Zoom.

5 Quarter-Master, 16 Nov. 1826, from which date the period of service has been computed.

6 Dr. Campbell served the campaigns of 1813 and 14 in the Peninsula, including the battle of Orthes; served also at New Orleans.

25 | 0 | *Paymaster.*—William Henry Wardell, 18 Dec. 28; *Ens.* 15 Aug. 15; *Lieut.* 21 Feb. 22.

14 | 0 | *Adjutant.*—William M'Donald (*Lieut.*) 23 Aug. 27.

— | — | *Quarter-Master.*—George Macdonald, 13 Dec. 39.

26 | 1 2/12 | *Surgeon.*—𝔅 John Campbell,[6] M.D. 27 Dec. 33; *Assist.-Surg.* 27 July, 15; *Hosp.-Assist.* 25 March, 13.

— | — | *Assistant-Surgeons.*—William Cruickshank, M.D. 5 Nov. 29; *Hosp-Assist.* 22 Nov. 27.

6 | 0 | George Taylor, 16 May, 34.

Facings Yellow.—*Agent*, Cox and Co.—*Irish Agent*, Borough, Armit & Co.

1 Sir Jasper Nicolls served in the Mahratta war, and was at the battle of Argaun, and at the siege and storm of Gawiel Ghur. In 1805 he embarked for Hanover, and in 1806 for Rio de la Plata. Commanded the 14th Regiment at Corunna, for which he has received a medal. In 1809, he served in Walcheren. In 1815 served in the Nepaul war; and, in 1816, commanded a brigade in the Pindarre and Mahratta war. Sir Jasper has been four times honourably mentioned for his conduct at Buenos Ayres, Corunna, Flushing, and Almorah.

2 Colonel Spark served in the American war in 1814 and 15, and was wounded at New Orleans 8th January, 1815.

3 Captain Gordon served in the American war in 1814 and 15, and was severely wounded in the left cheek at New Orleans 8th January, 1815.

Emb. for For. Service, 1838.] **94th *Regiment of Foot*.** [Serving in the East Indies.

Years' Serv.			
Full Pay.	Half Pay.		
44		*Colonel.* ₽ *Sir* Thomas M'Mahon, *Bt.* K.C.B. *Ens.* 2 Feb. 97; *Lieut.* 24 Oct. 99; *Capt.* 8 Oct. 03; *Major*, 6 Nov. 06; *Lieut.-Col.* 4 May 09; *Col.* 4 June, 14; *Major-Gen.* 27 May, 25; *Lieut.-Gen.* 28 June, 38; *Col.* 94th Regt. 28 March, 38.	
28	8 1/12	*Lieut.-Colonels.*—₽ George Wm. Paty,[1] C.B. & K.H. *Ens.* ₽ 28 April, 04; *Lieut.* 7 May, 05; *Capt.* ₽ 28 April, 08; *Major*, 2 June, 14; *Brevet-Lieut.-Col.* 4 Sept. 17; *Regtl.-Lieut.-Col.* ₽ 9 June, 25; *Col.* 10 Jan. 37.	
20	0	Charles Gascoyne, *Ens.* 7 Dec. 20; *Lieut.* ₽ 30 Jan. 23; *Capt.* ₽ 31 Dec. 25; *Major*, ₽ 23 Aug. 31; *Lieut.-Col.* 22 Oct. 39.	
15	3 3/12	*Majors.*—Henry Robert Milner, *Ens.* ₽ 7 Feb. 22; *Lieut.* ₽ 3 Dec. 25; *Capt.* ₽ 12 Dec. 26; *Major*, ₽ 5 July, 33.	
30	2 1/12	Geo. Topp Lindsay,[2] *Ens.* 21 Dec. 08; *Lieut.* 21 Sept. 09; *Capt.* ₽ 27 Dec. 20; *Brevet-Major*. 10 Jan. 37; *Regimental-Major*, 22 Oct. 39.	

		CAPTAINS.	ENSIGN.	LIEUT.	CAPTAIN.	BREV.-MAJ.
16	0	John W. Randolph......	25 Jan. 25	₽17 Nov. 25	₽ 9 Dec. 28	
17	6/12	Thomas Fred. Hart......	₽ 2 Jan. 23	₽ 8 Apr. 26	₽ 6 Sept. 31	
15	0	Corbett Cotton..........	9 Apr. 25	₽29 Mar. 27	₽ 4 May 32	
14	0	William Davenport......	₽17 Oct. 26	₽ 8 Oct. 29	₽22 July 36	
23	6 6/12	Henry Nicholls.........	25 July 11	₽15 Sept. 14	9 Feb. 38	
16	0	William Bell............	27 Mar. 24	23 Mar. 26	₽ 1 Dec. 37	
12	0	Robert Aldworth	₽15 Jan. 29	₽ 5 Apr. 33	₽ 8 June 38	
13	0	Robert M'Cleverty......	3 Jan. 28	₽23 Aug. 31	₽ 9 Nov. 38	
9	0	D. Fitz Gerald Longworth	₽ 3 May 31	₽27 Nov. 35	₽27 Sept. 39	
16	0	₽ William Spiller[3]	25 Nov. 24	6 Oct. 25	22 Oct. 39	
		LIEUTENANTS.				
14	1	Richard Lewis..........	₽28 July 25	30 Oct. 28		
8	0	William Carden Seton...	₽ 2 Mar. 32	₽22 July 36		
8	0	Francis Wm. Bowles....	₽14 Sept. 32	₽10 June 36		
6	0	George Maunsell........	₽11 July 34	₽ 8 Dec. 37		
10	0	Edw. Hen. Moore Kelly..	₽10 Sept. 30	₽31 July 35		
5	0	Tho. Fownes Seale......	₽ 8 May 35	₽27 Apr. 38		
5	0	Hen. Geo. Buller	₽26 June 35	₽ 8 June 38		
5	0	William Fisher.........	29 Jan. 36	₽ 9 June 38		
5	0	Thomas Jones..........	₽20 Feb. 35	23 May 37		
4	0	Edward Morris.........	₽22 July 36	₽ 9 Nov. 38		
4	0	Wm. H. Kirby..........	14 Oct. 36	₽28 Dec. 38		
3	0	G. A. Kooli D'Arcy.....	₽21 Apr. 37	26 Sept. 39		
3	0	Wm. Henry Dore	₽ 8 Dec. 37	₽27 Sept. 39		
18	0	Thomas Burke	8 Aug. 22	5 Oct. 26		
7	0	Alexander Crie Meik ...	₽10 May 33	14 Sept. 35		
5	0	Edward Smith Mercer ..	₽ 6 Mar. 35	₽11 June 36		
5	0	Virginius Murray	₽22 May 35	₽ 4 Nov. 36		
7	0	Albert Frend...........	31 Jan. 34	25 Aug. 37		
4	0	Adam Campbell........	19 April 36	19 Feb. 38		
4	0	Henry Clare Cardew....	₽ 8 July 36	₽14 Dec. 38		
6	0	Joseph Edwin Thackwell	₽ 6 June 34	23 Oct. 39		
3	0	James Stewart Menzies..	₽10 Feb. 38	24 Oct. 39		
2	0	Robert Dillon..........	₽ 8 June 38	₽29 Nov. 39		
		ENSIGNS.				
2	0	Robert Bruce..........	₽ 9 June 38			
2	0	Gilbert Mahon.........	₽ 9 Nov. 38			
2	0	Septimus Lyster........	₽28 Dec. 38			
1	0	Fred. Estwick	₽22 Feb. 39			
1	0	Thomas Henry Ashton ..	₽27 Sept. 39			
1	0	Alexander Maclean	15 Mar. 39			
1	0	Fred. Ximenes Groyune..	₽ 15 Nov. 39			
1	0	Cha. Campbell Hook....	₽29 Nov. 39			

1 Col. Paty served with the expedition to Copenhagen in 1807, and in the Peninsula from June, 1811, to the end of the war, including the siege and capture of Badajoz; battle of Salamanca; retreat from Madrid to Burgos; battles of Vittoria, the Pyrenees, Nivelle, and Nive 9th to 13th December, besides various minor affairs.

2 Major Lindsay served at the capture of the Isle of France in 1810.

3 Captain Spiller's services:— Battles of Vimiera (wounded in both thighs), and Corunna; expedition to Walcheren; Peninsula from July, 1811, to September, 1812; served also at New Orleans; received a wound by a musket shot in the right-hand (lost little finger), severe wound in the forehead, right temple, and under the chin, two wounds on the right thigh, and most severely burnt from head to foot by the explosion of a Mine at Ciudad Rodrigo.

26	5/12	*Paymaster*.—Wm. Bain M'Alpin, 22 Feb. 39; *Ens.* 6 Feb. 14; *Lieut.* 25 June, 24; *Capt.* 3 Aug. 38.
3	0	*Adjutant*.—George Abbas Kooli D'Arcy, *(Lieut.)* 3 Aug. 38.
2	0	*Quarter-Master*.—Thomas Waite, 17 Aug. 38.
		Surgeon.—Frederick Dix, 1 Nov. 27; *Assist.-Surg.* 19 Aug. 13.
3	0	*Assist.-Surgeons*.—Jas. Guy Piers Moore, 3 March, 37.
2	0	William Turnbull, M.D., 14 Sept. 38.

Facings Green.—*Agent*, Cox &c.

Emb. for Foreign Service, 1838.] **95th (or the Derbyshire) Regt. of Foot.** [Serving at Ceylon.

Years' Serv.			
45		*Colonel.*	
Full Pay	Half Pay	ʙ Sir John Buchan,¹ K.C.B *Ens.* 29 July, 95; *Lieut.* 21 Oct. 95; *Capt.* 15 March, 1802; *Major*, 30 June, 04; *Lieut.-Col.* 30 March, 09; *Col.* 12 Aug. 19; *Major.-Gen.* 22 July, 30; *Col.* 95th Regt. 5 Nov. 38.	
30	7$\frac{7}{12}$	*Lieut.-Colonel.*—ʙ James Campbell, K.H. *Ens.* 17 Sept. 03; *Lieut.* 25 Aug. 04; *Capt.* ᴾ 31 Mar. 08; *Major*, ᴾ 3 June, 19; *Lieut.-Col.* ᴾ 10 July, 24; *Col.* 28 June, 38.	
23	1$\frac{1}{12}$	*Majors.*—Hen Dundas Maclean, *Ens. & Lieut.* 5 Sept. 16; *Capt.* ᴾ 6 Nov. 24; *Major*, ᴾ 20 April, 32.	
34	0	ʙ John Walter,² *Ens.* ᴾ 15 July, 06; *Lieut.* 3 Sept. 07; *Capt.* ᴾ 24 Mar. 13; *Major*, 26 May, 31.	

		CAPTAINS.	ENSIGN.	LIEUT.	CAPTAIN.	BREV.-MAJ.
22	5$\frac{7}{12}$	Wm. Nonus Saunders⁵ ..	3 Sept. 12	23 May 15	ᴾ 18 Dec. 28	
14	4$\frac{8}{12}$	Hen. Churchill Tathwell	ᴾ 26 July 21	ᴾ 7 Oct. 24	ᴾ 19 Sept. 26	
17	1$\frac{5}{12}$	Thos. St. Leger Alcock..	ᴾ 28 Feb. 22	ᴾ 12 Dec. 26	ᴾ 20 Apr. 32	
32	2$\frac{6}{12}$	ʙ Joseph Robt. Raines³ .	19 Sept. 05	28 May 07	2 June 25	10 Jan. 37
12	3$\frac{8}{12}$	Chas. Augustus Brooke..	10 Apr. 25	17 Apr. 35	ᴾ 1 Dec. 37	
25	2	David Dickson	9 Sept. 13	9 Nov. 20	26 Jan. 38	
9	0	John G. Champion	2 Aug. 31	ᴾ 8 May 35	ᴾ 2 Feb. 38	
9	$\frac{2}{12}$	John Robt. Currie	ᴾ 28 Oct. 31	ᴾ 24 Apr. 35	ᴾ 8 June 38	
12	0	Wm. Fisher	8 Sept. 28	ᴾ 5 July 33	ᴾ 20 July 38	
17	0	James W. Dalgety......	26 June 23	5 Mar. 29	ᴾ 2 Dec. 37	
		LIEUTENANTS.				
17	9$\frac{2}{12}$	Wm. Armstrong Rogers	7 July 14	2 June 30		
10	0	Charles P. Hamilton....	29 June 30	ᴾ 13 Mar. 35		
14	1$\frac{9}{12}$	Edmund J. Cruice......	9 Apr. 25	13 June 30		
7	0	Alfred Thos. Heyland ..	ᴾ 4 Apr. 33	ᴾ 8 July 36		
5	0	John Randle Ford.....	ᴾ 13 Mar. 35	ᴾ 4 Aug. 37		
5	0	Henry Hume	ᴾ 9 May 35	ᴾ 1 Dec. 37		
14	0	Thos. James Dobson	ᴾ 14 Dec. 26	ᴾ 26 Nov. 30		
5	0	H. O. C. Master.......	ᴾ 18 Sept. 35	ᴾ 2 Feb. 38		
4	0	Geo. Cornwall	ᴾ 8 July 36	ᴾ 9 Mar. 38		
4	0	Edw. Thompson.......	ᴾ 30 Dec. 36	ᴾ 16 Mar. 38		
3	0	Rich. Pratt..........	ᴾ 5 May 37	ᴾ 8 June 38		
10	16$\frac{8}{12}$	John Wood...........	ᴾ 12 Jan. 14	ᴾ 15 June 32		
3	0	John Fitz Thos. Dennis..	ᴾ 4 Aug. 37	ᴾ 30 Oct. 38		
		ENSIGNS.				
3	0	Charles Rogers	ᴾ 17 Feb. 37			
3	0	F. Smythe	ᴾ 24 Feb. 37			
3	0	R. Collins Craigie	ᴾ 2 Feb. 38			
2	0	G. W. P. Bingham	ᴾ 16 Feb. 38			
2	0	Walter Venour	ᴾ 9 Mar. 38			
2	0	Fred W. Chapman......	ᴾ 16 Mar. 38			
2	0	Geo. Jas. Dowdall	ᴾ 8 June 38			
3	0	W. H. Underwood......	ᴾ 28 Apr. 37			

17	0	*Paymaster.*—ʙ F. Feneran,⁴ 15 Dec. 37; *Quart.-Mast.* 1 Dec. 23.	
17	9$\frac{2}{12}$	*Adjutant.*—William Armstrong Rogers (*Lieut.*) 3 July, 35.	
5	0	*Quarter-Master.*—Wm. Henry Rogers, 17 Feb. 38; *Ens.* 8 May, 35; *Lieut.* 16 Feb. 38.	
		Surgeon.—Joseph Ewing, 4 Dec. 35; *Assist.-Surg.* 7 Sept. 09.	
5	0	*Assistant-Surgeons.*—Duncan Affleck, 15 Jan. 36.	
3	0	Fred. Hobson Clark, 15 Sept. 37.	

Facings Yellow.—*Agent*, Mr. Lawrie.—*Irish Agent*, Messrs. Borough, Armit & Co.

1 Sir John Buchan has received a cross and one clasp for Guadaloupe, Vittoria, Pyrenees, Nivelle, and Nive.
2 Major Walter served in the Peninsula from October, 1813, to the end of the war, including the battles of Nivelle 10th Nov., and Nive 9th, 10th, 11th, and 12th December, 1813.
3 Major Raines served at the battles of Roleia, Vimiera, and Corunna, besides minor affairs during the retreat; served also at Walcheren.
4 Paymaster Feneran served the campaign of 1814 in Holland. Present at Waterloo.
5 Captain Saunders served in the American war, and was present at Chrystler's Farm and Niagara. Wounded in the right groin, left thigh, right cheek, and right arm.

96th Regiment of Foot.

Years' Serv.		
Full Pay	Half Pay	
46		**Colonel.** Sir Lewis Grant,[1] K.C.H. *Lieut.* 15 Feb. 1794; *Capt.* 11 June, 96; *Major,* 8 Sept. 02; *Lieut.-Col.* 18 Feb. 1804; *Col.* 4 June 13; *Major-Gen.* 12 Aug. 19; *Lieut.-Gen.* 10 Jan, 87; *Col.* 96th Regt. 9 April, 39.
36	1 2/3	**Lieut.-Colonel.**—₽ Alex. Cairncross,[2] K.H. *Ens.* ᴾ 25 June, 03; *Lieut.* 15 Sept. 04; *Capt.* 7 June, 10; *Major,* ᴾ 10 June, 26; *Lieut.-Col.* ᴾ 19 Sept. 34.
37	7/12	**Majors.**—William Hulme,[3] *Ens.* 25 Sept. 03; *Lieut.* 26 June, 05; *Capt.* 26 Aug. 13; *Brevet-Major,* 23 Dec. 17; *Regtl.-Major,* 9 March, 34; *Brevet-Lieut.-Col.* 10 Jan. 37.
20	0	C. Brownlow Cumberland, *Ens.* ᴾ 21 Dec. 20; *Lieut.* ᴾ 15 Oct. 25; *Capt.* ᴾ 10 June, 26; *Major,* ᴾ 19 Sept. 34.

		CAPTAINS.	ENSIGN.	LIEUT.	CAPTAIN.	BREV.-MAJ.
21	6	Peter Cheape	25 May 13	3 Aug. 15	ᴾ 24 Dec. 25	28 June 38
19	2	Bentinck H. Cumberland	ᴾ 19 Aug. 19	ᴾ 13 Oct. 25	ᴾ 14 Nov. 26	
16	0	Thos. Maitland Wilson ..	ᴾ 15 Apr. 24	ᴾ 13 May 26	ᴾ 23 Dec. 31	
14	1/12	Robt. Bush............	ᴾ 22 Apr. 26	ᴾ 5 June 27	ᴾ 23 Mar. 32	
25	4 1/12	₽ Loftus Fra. Jones[4]	7 Feb. 11	1 Oct. 12	9 Mar. 34	
13	0	Roderick Mackenzie	ᴾ 19 July 27	ᴾ 19 July 31	ᴾ 19 Sept. 34	
8	0	Edward Hill	ᴾ 29 Dec. 32	ᴾ 23 June 37	ᴾ 27 July 38	
20	0	Matthew Richmond	25 May 20	ᴾ 25 Sept. 23	ᴾ 16 Mar. 26	
22	0	Gerald Villiers Butler ..	ᴾ 22 Oct. 18	ᴾ 26 June 23	30 Sept. 39	
11	1 5/12	Wm. Cornwallis Symonds	ᴾ 12 Feb. 28	ᴾ 23 Mar. 32	3 Aug. 38	
		LIEUTENANTS.				
23	4/12	Alex. Mackenzie........	29 May 17	3 Nov. 19		
15	0	Philip Fred. de Meuron..	8 Apr. 25	ᴾ 10 June 26		
13	0	Jas. Clyde	ᴾ 5 June 27	ᴾ 23 Mar. 32		
13	0	Edward Barclay	ᴾ 12 July 27	ᴾ 14 Feb. 34		
11	0	Morris R. Campbell	2 July 29	19 Dec. 35		
8	0	Phillpotts Wright Taylor	ᴾ 16 Mar. 32	ᴾ 4 Mar. 36		
10	17 5/12	Nicholas Horsley[5]	18 Mar. 13	5 Oct. 15		
6	0	Wm. Arch. Eyton	ᴾ 14 Feb. 34	ᴾ 30 June 37		
5	0	Edw. W. Scovell........	29 Dec. 35	ᴾ 2 Nov. 38		
4	0	W. S. Nicholson	ᴾ 4 Mar. 36	19 Dec. 38		
14	0	James Chambre	ᴾ 27 July 26	ᴾ 12 Feb. 29		
4	0	Fra. J. Hugonin.......	ᴾ 12 Aug. 36	ᴾ 26 Apr. 39		
4	0	Richard R. Currer.....	16 Sept. 36	ᴾ 27 Sept. 39		
		ENSIGNS.				
3	0	Hon. John Stourton	ᴾ 30 June 37			
2	0	Fred. Pierce	ᴾ 18 Aug. 38			
2	0	Richard Roney	ᴾ 14 Sept. 38			
2	0	Livingston Mitchell	ᴾ 29 June 38			
2	0	James Pursloe	28 Dec. 38			
1	0	Selwyn Willson	ᴾ 12 July 39			
3	0	Clement Swetenham	31 Mar. 37			
1	0	Samuel Hobson	ᴾ 22 Nov. 39			

7 Dr. Shorland's services :—Campaign and battle of Corunna; campaign of 1810 and 1811 in Portugal, including the battle of Busaco. Served also during the whole of the war with the United States of America.

15	12 1/12	*Paymaster.*—₽ Edwin Griffiths,[6] 11 Jan. 33; *2nd Lieut.* 6 Jan. 13; *Lieut.* 12 Nov. 13.
11	0	*Adjutant.*—Morris R. Campbell, (*Lieut.*) 30 June, 37.
1	0	*Quarter-Master.*—Samuel Fox, 19 July, 39.
26	7 1/12	*Surgeon.*—₽ Jas. Shorland,[7] 14 July, 14; *Assist.-Surg.* 29 June, 09; *Hosp.-Assist.* 7 Oct. 07.
14	0	*Assistant-Surgeon.*—Adam Walker Murray, 8 Feb. 27; *Hosp.-Assist.* 6 July, 26.

Facings Yellow.—*Agent,* Messrs. Lawrie and M'Grigor.

[*Returned from North America,* Sept. 1835.]

1 Sir Lewis Grant was on board H. M. ship *Orion,* in the action with the French fleet 23d June, 95. Was subsequently at the capture of various places in the West Indies.

2 Col. Cairncross served in the Peninsula from Jan. 1810 to Oct. 1813, including the siege of Cadiz; lines at Torres Vedras; Massena's retreat from Portugal March and April 1811; affairs at Redinha, Pudents, Foz d'Aronce, and Sabugal; battle of Fuentes d'Onor, 3rd and 5th May; siege of Badajoz, June and July, 1811; action at El Bodon and Guinaldo; siege and storm of Ciudad Rodrigo; siege of Badajoz, and storm of the Castle by escalade on the night of the 6th April, 1812; battle of Salamanca; capture of Madrid, and Retiro, and Fort La China; Retreat to Portugal, Oct. and Nov. 1812, and battle of Vittoria. Wounded in the head at the storm of Ciudad Rodrigo, and severely through the right elbow joint at Vittoria.

3 Lieut.-Col. Hulme served in the Pindarree campaign, and commanded the flank companies in the general action of the 21st Dec. 17, for which he obtained the brevet rank of Major; he again commanded them when the fort of Fulnair was stormed 27th Feb. 1818.

4 Capt Jones served in the Peninsula from June, 1812, to the end of the war, including the battle of Salamanca; San Munos; San Milan; Vittoria, heights of Santa Barbara; Eschelar; Vera bridge and heights; crossing the Bidassoa, Nivelle (severely wounded); Orthes, Tarbes, Tournefeuille, and Toulouse. Served also during the whole of the operations against New Orleans.

5 Lieut. Horsley served the campaigns of 1813 and 14 in Germany and Holland, and was severely wounded (three wounds) at Bergen-op-Zoom.

6 Paymaster Griffiths served the campaigns of 1813 and 14 in the Peninsula. Served also in the American war, including the capture of Washington; battle before Baltimore, and the several operations on the coast. Present during the several attacks upon the enemy's lines before New Orleans. In the batteries upon the banks of the Mississippi at the blowing up of a man-of-war schooner. Taking of Fort Boyer.

97th (or *The Earl of Ulster's*) Regiment of Foot.

"*Quò fas et gloria ducunt.*"

Colonel.

Years' Serv		
42		
Full Pay	Half Pay	
		🄱 🄲🄰 Rt. Hon. Sir H. Hardinge,[1] K.C.B. *Ens.* 8 Oct. 1798; *Lieut.* 25 Mar. 1802; *Capt.* 7 Apr. 04; *Major,* 13 Apr. 09; *Lieut.-Col.* 30 May, 11; *Col.* 19 July, 21; *Maj.-Gen.* 22 July, 30.
32	4 9/12	*Lieut.-Col.*—🄱 John Campbell, *Ens.* ᴾ 9 July, 03; *Lieut.* ᴾ 17 Mar. 04; *Capt.* ᴾ 5 May, 08; *Brevet-Major,* 27 May, 25; *Regtl.-Major,* 27 Oct. 29; *Lieut.-Col.* 28 June, 38.
24	3 7/12	*Majors.*—🄱 Henry Fred. Lockyer,[2] K.H., *Ens.* ᴾ 25 Mar. 1813; *Lieut.* 19 Jan. 14; *Capt.* ᴾ 20 June 22; *Major,* ᴾ 12 June, 35.
31	5 3/12	Nicholas Lawson Darrah,[3] *2nd-Lieut.* 16 Aug. 04; *Lieut.* 2 April, 05; *Capt.* ᴾ 30 June, 08; *Brevet-Maj.* 27 May, 25; *Regtl.-Maj.* & *Brev.-Lt.-Col.* 28 June, 38.

		CAPTAINS.	ENSIGN.	LIEUT.	CAPTAIN.	BREV.-MAJ.
28	7 3/12	🄱 Thomas Smith[4].......	1 Dec. 04	25 Sept. 05	25 Oct. 14	10 Jan. 37
28	5 5/12	🄱 William Cannon[5].....	26 Aug. 07	7 June 10	7 April 25	28 June 38
26	0	Geo. Hutchison.........	never	14 July 14	ᴾ 26 June 27	
16	0	Wm. Trevor Stannus....	ᴾ 1 July 24	ᴾ 8 April 26	ᴾ 23 July 29	
15	0	Hon. Henry R. Handcock	8 April 25	ᴾ 20 Mar. 27	ᴾ 24 Feb. 32	
21	8	🄱 Donald Mackintosh[6]..	30 May 11	21 April 14	27 Sept. 34	
8	0	Aug. Fred. Welsford....	ᴾ 24 Feb. 32	ᴾ 25 July 34	ᴾ 19 Jan. 38	
20	5 6/12	Hector Harvest.........	20 April 15	7 April 25	28 June 38	
8	0	John Kinderley.........	ᴾ 14 Dec. 32	ᴾ 31 Dec. 36	ᴾ 22 Mar. 39	
12	0	Robert Lisle	ᴾ 11 Dec. 28	ᴾ 29 Aug. 34	ᴾ 6 Dec. 39	

		LIEUTENANTS.			
16	0	John M'Caskill........	25 Jan. 25	27 June 28	
7	0	Robt. Colvill	ᴾ 27 Dec. 33	ᴾ 10 Feb. 37	
6	0	Henshaw Russell.......	ᴾ 16 May 34	ᴾ 24 Mar. 37	
6	0	Rob. Hen. S. Jackson...	ᴾ 10 Oct. 34	ᴾ 2 Sept. 37	
4	0	Walter Boyd	12 Mar. 36	ᴾ 19 Jan. 38	
4	0	Tho. Onslow W. Ingram	ᴾ 13 May 36	ᴾ 9 Mar. 38	
6	0	David Craigie.........	ᴾ 7 Nov. 34	28 June 38	
5	0	Isaac Moore	20 Feb. 35	29 June 38	
8	0	John Hutton..........	27 April 32	28 Dec. 38	8 Captain O'Neill's services :— Expedition to Walcheren and siege of Flushing; capture of the Isle of France; Mahratta campaigns of 1817 and 18, including the capture of the Forts Singhur, Wossoola, Poorunder and Sholopore.
4	0	Wm. Garforth.........	ᴾ 31 Dec. 36	ᴾ 22 Mar. 39	
4	0	Geo. Mauleverer Gowan..	ᴾ 10 Feb. 37	ᴾ 17 May 39	
3	0	Rob. Beauchamp Giveen	ᴾ 2 Sept. 37	ᴾ 30 Aug. 39	
3	0	Frederick Wm. Lane....	ᴾ 19 Jan. 38	ᴾ 6 Dec. 39	

		ENSIGNS.		
2	0	William Murray.......	ᴾ 9 Mar. 38	9 Quarter-Master Sleator served in Sicily and the Peninsula, from 1805 until the end of the war in 1814.
2	0	George Dorehill	ᴾ 20 Nov. 38	
2	0	Alfred Padley	ᴾ 8 Feb. 39	
1	0	Richard Sutton........	ᴾ 17 May 39	
1	0	Edm. C. Leigh	5 July 39	
1	0	Fowler Burton	ᴾ 30 Aug. 39	
1	0	Thomas Lynch	ᴾ 6 Dec. 39	
1	0	Francis Wm. Sykes	ᴾ 31 Dec. 39	

28	4 1/12	*Paymaster.*—Charlton O'Neill,[8] 30 Dec. 36; *Ens.* 12 Oct. 08; *Lieut.* 2 May, 11; *Capt.* 27 June, 28.	
5	0	*Adjutant.*—Isaac Moore, *(Lieut.)* 20 Feb. 35.	
15	0	*Quarter-Master.*—🄱 Joseph Sleator,[9] 24 Feb. 25.	
24	4 9/12	*Surgeon.*—W. Austin, M.D. 21 Nov. 28; *Assist.-Surg.* 4 Mar. 13; *Hosp.-Assist.* 21 Nov. 11.	
4	0	*Assistant-Surgeon.*—Wm. Forbes Leith, 15 April, 36.	

Facings Sky Blue.—*Agent,* Cox & Co.—*Irish Agent,* Messrs. Cane & Co.

[*Returned from Ceylon, September,* 1836.]

1 Sir Henry Hardinge has received a cross and five clasps for Busaco, Albuhera, Badajoz, Salamanca, Vittoria, (severely wounded), Pyrenees, Nivelle, Nive, and Orthes. Sir Henry was severely wounded at Ligny, 16 June 1815, and lost his left hand.

2 Major Lockyer served in the Peninsula, from Aug. 1813 to the end of the war, including the battles of Nivelle, Nive, Orthes, Aire, (severely wounded on left wrist and elbow joint), and Toulouse.

3 Col. Darrah served in Scylla castle when besieged in 1807; and before the same place in 1809. At Mili, in Sicily, when a descent was made by the troops of Murat, king of Naples. Served also the campaign of 1814 in Holland, including the attack on Bergen-op-Zoom.

4 Major Smith served in the Peninsula from July, 1808 to the end of the war, including the battles of Roleia, Vimiera, Busaco, Fuentes d'Onor; siege of Ciudad Rodrigo; second siege and storm of Badajoz, 6th April, 1812; battles of Salamanca, Vittoria, (wounded in the left thigh), Sabugal, Villa Moreil; and passage of the Bidassoa.

5 Major Cannon served in the Peninsula, from Jan. 1810 to the end of the war, including the siege of Fort Matagorda in front of Cadiz in 1810, during its bombardment, which lasted two months; lines of Torres Vedras; battle of Fuentes d'Onor; first siege of Badajoz; action at Elbodon; storm of Ciudad Rodrigo (severely wounded in the chest); battles of Salamanca, Vittoria (slightly wounded in the right knee), Pyrenees, Nivelle, Orthes, and Toulouse.

6 Captain Mackintosh served at the siege of Copenhagen in 1807, and subsequently in the Peninsula, including the battles of Oporto and Talavera; siege of Cadiz in 1810; battle of Busaco; lines of Torres Vedras; battles of Fuentes d'Onor, Nivelle, Orthes, and Toulouse, besides several minor affairs and skirmishes. Wounded by the fragment of a shell at Orthes, while carrying the colours of the 88th regiment.

98th Regiment of Foot.

Years' Serv.						
42		*Colonel.*				
Full Pay.	Half Pay.	🅑 Sir Willoughby Cotton, G.C.B. & K.C.H. *Ens.* 31 Oct. 1798; *Lieut. & Capt.* 25 Nov. 99; *Capt. & Lieut-Col.* 12 June, 1811; *Col.* 25 July, 21; *Major-Gen.* 22 July, 30; *Col.* 98th Regt. 1 Aug. 39.				
30	2 6/12	*Lieut.-Colonel.*—🅑 Colin Campbell,[1] *Ens.* 26 May, 08; *Lieut.* 28 June, 09; *Capt* 9 Nov. 13; *Major,* ᴾ 26 Nov. 25; *Lieut.-Col.* ᴾ 26 Oct. 32.				
16	2 5/12	*Majors.*—Arthur Charles Gregory, *Ens.* ᴾ 24 Oct. 21; *Lieut.* ᴾ 1 Oct. 25; *Capt.* ᴾ 15 Aug. 26; *Major,* ᴾ 18 Oct. 31.				
16	7 3/12	Henry Eyre, *Ens.* ᴾ 28 Aug. 17; *Lieut.* ᴾ 20 April, 26; *Capt.* ᴾ 3 April 28; *Major,* ᴾ 17 Feb. 37.				
		CAPTAINS.	ENSIGN.	LIEUT.	CAPTAIN.	BREV.-MAJ.
20	6 6/12	William Roberts........	14 Apr. 14	7 Apr. 25	ᴾ 18 Oct. 31	
25	13	Peter Tripp[2]............	ᴾ 2 Sept. 02	ᴾ 3 Sept. 03	ᴾ 6 Nov. 05	12 Aug. 19
15	0	Thos. Maitland Edwards..	8 Apr. 25	ᴾ 3 Apr. 28	ᴾ 14 Dec. 32	
15	0	William Edie...........	ᴾ 14 Jan. 26	ᴾ 18 Oct. 31	ᴾ 29 Nov. 33	
10	0	Henry Douglas Cowper..	ᴾ 20 July 30	ᴾ 14 Dec. 32	ᴾ 4 Mar. 36	
25	9 6/12	🅑 John Macphail........	2 Jan. 06	29 Sept. 08	25 Oct. 14	
15	0	William Wallace.........	8 Apr. 25	25 Oct. 27	ᴾ 22 Sept 37	10 Jan. 37
11	0	Henry Darley.........	ᴾ 24 Sept. 29	26 Oct. 32	ᴾ 25 July 37	
8	0	Chas. Rich. Ilderton....	ᴾ 22 June 32	ᴾ 30 Jan. 35	ᴾ 4 Oct. 39	
9	0	Michael Gavin..........	ᴾ 2 Dec. 31	ᴾ 28 June 36	ᴾ 29 Nov. 39	
		LIEUTENANTS.				
21	5 10/12	Jas. Bell Kingsley......	10 Nov. 13	9 Nov. 14	4 Dr. Bourchier served in the Peninsula from 1809 to 1814, including the siege of Olivença; battles of Busaco and Albuhera (wounded in the right leg); siege of Badajoz in 1812. Present also in the attacks at Campo Mayor, and several others; and the retreat from Busaco and Burgos, and the various operations of the 2d division under the command of Lord Hill.	
22	9 9/12	Septimus Harrison[3]	24 Dec. 08	1 May 12		
8	0	Samuel Wm. Russell....	ᴾ 1 Feb. 33	9 Feb. 37		
7	0	Jas. C. Alex. Dunbar....	ᴾ 29 Nov. 33	ᴾ 22 Sept. 37		
7	0	Thos. Chas. Ormsby....	ᴾ 22 Mar. 33	20 Oct. 37		
6	0	Fred. Amelius Whimper..	ᴾ 23 Jan. 35	ᴾ 23 Mar. 38		
5	0	Thos. Heaton Lovett....	ᴾ 5 June 35	ᴾ 27 Apr. 38		
4	0	Daniel Rainier..........	ᴾ 4 Mar. 36	ᴾ 11 May 38		
4	0	John Morton Jeffery....	ᴾ 28 June 36	ᴾ 22 June 38		
3	0	E. J. Nixon.............	ᴾ 17 Feb. 37	ᴾ 26 Apr. 39		
5	0	Raleigh Henry Yea	ᴾ 13 Mar. 35	ᴾ 23 Feb. 38		
3	0	Edmund Haythorne	12 May 37	ᴾ 4 Oct. 39		
3	0	Chas. Edward Synge....	ᴾ 22 Sept. 37	ᴾ 29 Nov. 39		
		ENSIGNS.				
2	0	S. Erskine Rolland......	ᴾ 23 Feb. 38			
2	0	Steph. Edw. Colby......	ᴾ 22 June 38			
2	0	John Montresor	14 Dec. 38			
2	0	A. Hamilt. Harvest......	28 Dec. 38			
1	0	Francis Grantham	ᴾ 26 Apr. 39			
1	0	Charles Colby..........	ᴾ 30 Aug. 39			
1	0	Willoughby Har. Carter	ᴾ 4 Oct. 39			
1	0	John Alfred Street......	ᴾ 29 Nov. 39			
		Paymaster.—				
7	0	*Adjutant.*—T. C. Ormsby, *(Lieut.)* 22 March, 39.				
3	0	*Quarter-Master.*—James Fagan, 19 Jan. 38.				
33	3	*Surgeon.*—🅑 Thomas Bourchier,[4] 22 Aug. 11; *Assist.-Surg.* 24 May, 04.				
1	0	*Assistant-Surgeon.*—Edwin Adolphus, M.D. 20 Sept. 39.				

Facings White.—*Agent,* Messrs. Cox & Co.

[*Returned from the Cape of Good Hope, June,* 1837.]

1 Col. Campbell's services:—battle of Vimiera; advance and retreat of the army in Spain, and battle of Corunna. Expedition to Zealand. Peninsula, from Dec. 1809 to Jan. 1814, including the battle of Barrosa; defence of Tarrifa; expedition for the relief of Tarragona; affairs of Posts in the valley of Malaga; affair at Osma; battle of Vittoria; siege of San Sebastian, and assault of the outworks 17th July, and body of the fortress 25th July, 1813; on these assaults led the columns of attack. Passage of the Bidassoa and assault of the intrenched position on that river. Received two severe wounds at the assault of San Sebastian, one through the right hip, and one through the left thigh. Severely wounded at the assault of the intrenched position on the Bidassoa by a musket shot through the right thigh.

2 Col. Tripp served at the capture of Guadaloupe in 1815. Brevet Lieut.-Col. 28 June, 38.

3 Lieut. Harrison served the campaigns of 1814 and 15 in Nepaul, and commanded a company on the advanced guard in the action at Jeetghur, where he was wounded. Served also against the Mahrattas in 1816 and 17.

99th (or Lanarkshire) Regiment of Foot.

Years' Serv.			
Full Pay	Half Pay		
46		**Colonel.** ₱ Sir Hugh Gough,[1] K.C.B. *Ens.* 7 Aug. 94; *Lieut.* 11 Oct. 94; *Capt.* 25 June, 03; *Major*, 8 Aug. 05; *Lieut.-Col.* 29 July, 09; *Col.* 12 Aug. 19; *Major-Gen.* 22 July, 30; *Col.* 99th Regt. 23 Dec. 39.	
16	3 6/12	*Lieut.-Colonel.*—Sir John Gaspard Le Marchant,[2] *Ens.* 26 Oct. 20; *Lieut.* ᴾ 24 Oct. 21; *Capt.* ᴾ 30 June, 25; *Major*, ᴾ 14 Dec. 32; *Lieut.-Col.* ᴾ 18 Oct. 39.	
31	3 10/12	*Majors.*—₱ John Napper Jackson,[3] *Ens.* 1 July, 05; *Lieut.* 1 Jan. 06; *Capt.* 28 Feb. 12; *Major*, 11 June, 29.	
19	6 6/12	Edward Last, *Ens.* 13 Oct. 14; *Lieut.* ᴾ 20 Nov. 24; *Capt.* ᴾ 22 May 29; *Major*, ᴾ 18 Oct. 39.	

		CAPTAINS.	ENSIGN.	LIEUT.	CAPTAIN.	BREV.-MAJ.
32	5½	Gillies Macpherson[4]	9 July 03	22 May 04	7 May 12	22 July 30
14	2⅓	Geo. Marmaduke Reeves	1 July 24	ᴾ 8 Apr. 26	ᴾ 27 Apr. 27	
16	0	Jaffray Nicholson	ᴾ 20 Nov. 24	ᴾ 22 Apr. 26	ᴾ 5 July 33	
12	0	Philip Smyly	ᴾ 27 Mar. 28	ᴾ 18 June 30	ᴾ 18 July 34	
11	0	Edw. Maurice O'Connell	ᴾ 22 May 29	ᴾ 9 Dec. 31	ᴾ 28 Apr. 37	
25	2 11/12	John Armstrong	29 Oct. 12	19 Apr. 14	29 Sept. 37	
11	0	Geo. Robt. Cummin	ᴾ 7 Jan. 30	ᴾ 28 Sept. 32	ᴾ 21 Apr. 37	
17	1 1/12	John Parson Westropp	ᴾ 11 Jan. 22	ᴾ 23 June 25	ᴾ 27 Apr. 27	
14	0	Augustus Warren	ᴾ 19 Sept. 26	ᴾ 22 May 29	7 Oct. 39	
6	0	Henry Fred. Alston	ᴾ 21 Mar. 34	ᴾ 3 Mar. 37	ᴾ 18 Oct. 39	
		LIEUTENANTS.				
16	0	Henry Jas. Day	10 Feb. 25	11 June 29		
15	0	Robt. Webster	10 Apr. 25	26 June 30		
13	11 10/12	Lambert Cowell	ᴾ 24 Aug. 15	ᴾ 22 Jan. 18		
10	0	Wm. Mair	26 Nov. 30	22 Apr. 36		
5	0	Arch. W. Reed	ᴾ 4 Sept. 35	ᴾ 25 July 37		
9	0	Thos. Cassan	28 Oct. 31	26 July 37		
5	0	David Beatty	ᴾ 26 June 35	21 Jan. 38		
4	0	Henry Pardoe	ᴾ 8 July 36	ᴾ 2 Feb. 38		
5	0	Rich. Ramsbottom	ᴾ 7 Aug. 35	ᴾ 1 June 38		
4	0	Thos. Hussey Burgh	ᴾ 29 July 36	ᴾ 20 Nov. 38		
4	0	Isaac Hindley H. Gall	22 Nov. 36	7 Oct. 39		
3	0	Rupert Barber Deering	ᴾ 3 Mar. 37	17 Oct. 39		
3	0	Henry John Jauncey	ᴾ 28 Apr. 37	ᴾ 18 Oct. 39		
		ENSIGNS.				
3	0	S. Cosby Price	ᴾ 23 June 37			
3	0	Charles Blamire	ᴾ 25 July 37			
3	0	Edward Beatty	ᴾ 2 Feb. 38			
2	0	Pat. Johnston	ᴾ 20 Nov. 38			
1	0	Fred. Montgomerie	ᴾ 20 Sept. 39			
1	0	John Jas. Armstrong	17 Oct. 39			
1	0	Rob. Henry De Winton	ᴾ 18 Oct. 39			
1	0	William Roberts	ᴾ 1 Nov. 39			

5	23	*Paymaster.*—Edward Pratt, 18 Oct. 39; *Ens.* 3 Dec. 12; *Lieut.* 20 May, 14.	
3	0	*Adjutant.*—R. B. Deering, *(Lieut.)* 8 Feb. 39.	
6	0	*Quarter-Master.*—⟨⟩ Alexander Macdonald, 13 June, 34; *Ens.* 16 May, 34.	
24	7	*Surgeon.*—₱ William Williams,[5] 21 Sept. 30; *Assistant-Surgeon*, 19 Dec. 11; *Hosp.-Assist.* 9 July, 09.	
		Assistant-Surgeon.—Wm. Gibson Byrne, 19 Oct. 26; *Hosp.-Assist.* 8 Dec. 25.	

Facings Yellow.—*Agent*, Messrs. Lawrie & M'Grigor.—*Irish Agent*, Messrs. Cane & Co.

[*Returned from the Mauritius*, 5 *October*, 37.]

1 Sir Hugh Gough served at the capture of the Cape of Good Hope, and the Dutch Fleet in Saldanha Bay, 1795. Served afterwards in the West Indies, including the attack on Porto Rico, the brigand war in St. Lucia, and capture of Surinam. Proceeded to the Peninsula in 1809, and commanded the 87th regiment at the battles of Talavera, Barrosa, Vittoria, and Nivelle, for which he has received a cross. Sir Hugh had a horse shot under him on the 27th July, and on the 28th at Talavera, he was severely wounded in the side by a splinter of a shell; he also received a slight wound in the head at Tarifa.

2 Sir Gaspard Le Marchant served as Adjutant General to the Anglo-Spanish Legion, and Brigadier General in the Spanish service during the years 1835, 6, and 7. Was present at the relief of Bilboa and affair before that town in Sept. 1835. Engaged on the heights of Arlaban in Alava on the 16th, 17th, and 18th Jan.; in raising the siege of San Sebastian, and storming the Lines 5th May; passage of the Urmea, and taking of Passages 28th May; in the general action before Alza, Oct. 1836, besides several affairs in Guipuzcoa, as also in the general actions of the 10th, 13th, 15th, and 16th March before Hernani. For these services he received a medal.

3 Major Jackson served in the Peninsula from 1810 to the end of the war, including the battle of Fuentes d'Onor; siege of Ciudad Rodrigo; siege of Badajoz April 1812; battles of Salamanca, Vittoria, Pyrenees, 27th, 28th, 29th, and 30th July, Nivelle, Orthes, and Toulouse.

4 Major Macpherson served in the American war, including the taking of Castine and Hampden.
5 Dr. Williams served at Walcheren in 1809, and in the Peninsula from 1810 to 1812.

Rifle Brigade.

"Copenhagen"—"Monte Video"—"Roleia"—"Vimiera"—"Corunna"—"Busaco"—"Barrosa"—"Fuentes d'Onor"—"Ciudad Rodrigo"—"Badajoz"—"Salamanca"—"Vittoria"—"Nivelle"—"Nive"—"Orthes"—"Toulouse"—"Peninsula"—"Waterloo."

Colonel-in-Chief.

Years' Serv	
53	𝔓 𝔚𝔐 Arthur, *Duke of* Wellington, K.G. G.C.B. & G.C.H. 19 Feb. 20.

Colonels Commandant.

46	1 𝔓 𝔚𝔐 Sir A. F. Barnard,[1] K.C.B. & G.C.H. *Ens.* 26 Aug. 1794; *Lieut.* Sept. 94; *Capt.* 13 Nov. 94; *Major*, 1 Jan. 1805; *Lieut.-Col.* 28 Jan. 08; *Col.* 4 June, 13; *Major-Gen.* 12 Aug. 19; *Lieut.-Gen.* 10 Jan. 37.
48	2 𝔓 Sir Jas. Stevenson Barns,[2] K.C.B. *Ens.* 11 July, 92; *Lieut.* 2 Jan. 94; *Capt.* 27 Feb. 96; *Major*, 17 Sept. 02; *Lieut.-Col.* 6 Nov. 06; *Col.* 4 June, 14; *Major-Gen.* 19 July, 21; *Lieut.-Gen.* 10 Jan. 37.

Full Pay.	Half Pay.	
34	6/12	*Lieut.-Colonels.*—2 𝔓 George Brown,[3] C.B. & K.H. *Ens.* 23 Jan. 06; *Lieut.* 18 Sept. 06; *Capt.* 20 June, 11; *Major*, ᵖ 26 May, 14; *Brevet-Lieut.-Col.* 29 Sept. 14; *Regtl.-Lieut.-Col.* ᵖ 17 July, 23; *Col.* 6 May, 31.
34	0	1 𝔓 𝔚𝔐 John Charles Hope,[4] K.H. *Ens.* 8 Jan. 07; *Lieut.* 2 Feb. 09; *Capt.* 9 Nov. 20; *Major*, 22 July, 30; *Lieut.-Col.* ᵖ 4 Dec. 35.
24	3 6/12	*Majors.*—2 Geo. Milne Stevenson, *Ens.* 21 April, 13; *Lieut.* 11 Jan. 15; *Capt.* ᵖ 24 Oct. 21; *Major*, ᵖ 12 Aug. 34.
34	0	1 Thos. E. Kelly,[5] *Ens.* 1 April, 06; *Lieut.* 11 Feb. 08; *Capt.* 26 Dec. 22; *Brevet-Major*, 10 Jan. 37; *Regtl.-Major*, ᵖ 24 Feb. 37.
25	0	2 Richard Irton, *2nd Lieut.* ᵖ 11 May, 15; *Lieut.* ᵖ 20 May, 24; *Capt.* ᵖ 29 Aug. 26; *Major*, ᵖ 31 May, 39.
20	10/12	1 George Buller, *2nd Lieut.* 2 Mar. 20; *Lieut.* 28 Mar. 25; *Capt.* ᵖ 19 Aug. 28; *Major*, ᵖ 31 Dec. 39.

		CAPTAINS.	2ND LIEUT.	LIEUT.	CAPTAIN.	BREV.-MAJ.
22	0	1 Wm. Warren	ᵖ 26 Nov. 18	ᵖ 10 Jan. 22	ᵖ 31 Oct. 26	
31	0	2 𝔓 𝔚𝔐 Rob. Cochrane[6]	ᵖ 9 Nov. 09	8 May 12	22 May 28	
17	0	1 *Hon.* J. St. V. Saumarez	ᵖ 8 Jan. 24	ᵖ 28 Jan. 26	ᵖ 17 Dec. 29	
30	1	1 𝔓 𝔚𝔐 John Fry[7]	ᵖ 21 June 10	10 May 12	22 July 30	
16	0	1 Hen. Ferd. Beckwith	ᵖ 20 May 24	ᵖ 8 Apr. 26	ᵖ 31 Aug. 30	
16	0	1 Wm. Sullivan	ᵖ 14 Oct. 24	ᵖ 8 Apr. 26	ᵖ 21 June 31	
15	0	1 John Alex. Henderson	ᵖ 9 Dec. 24	ᵖ 31 Dec. 25	ᵖ 18 Jan. 31	
15	6/12	2 Wm. Crosbie	12 Apr. 25	ᵖ 29 Aug. 26	ᵖ 11 Oct. 33	
15	0	1 Robert Walpole	ᵖ 11 May 25	ᵖ 26 Sept. 26	ᵖ 24 Jan. 34	
15	0	2 Chas. Fred. Napier	9 Apr. 25	17 Apr. 29	ᵖ 12 Aug. 34	
15	0	2 Henry Capel	ᵖ 9 June 25	22 May 28	ᵖ 22 May 35	
15	0	2 Chas. Du Pre Egerton	ᵖ 13 July 25	ᵖ 25 Nov. 28	ᵖ 31 July 35	
15	0	2 James Dolphin	ᵖ 15 July 25	ᵖ 17 Dec. 29	ᵖ 4 Dec. 35	
13	1/12	2 Arth. J. Lawrence	ᵖ 4 Apr. 27	ᵖ 12 Feb. 30	ᵖ 24 Feb. 37	
14	0	1 John Rooper	ᵖ 7 Apr. 26	22 July 30	ᵖ 22 Aug. 37	
14	0	1 James Martin	ᵖ 9 Apr. 26	19 Aug. 30	ᵖ 3 Aug. 38	
14	0	2 Edw. Holt Glegg	ᵖ 3 Aug. 26	ᵖ 21 June 31	ᵖ 23 Apr. 39	
14	0	2 John Hamilton Esten	ᵖ 30 Aug. 26	ᵖ 30 May 32	ᵖ 31 May 39	
13	0	1 R. Henry Fitz Herbert	ᵖ 3 July 27	ᵖ 11 Jan. 33	ᵖ 25 Oct. 39	
12	0	2 Sidney Beckwith	17 Apr. 28	26 May 33	ᵖ 31 Dec. 39	

1 Sir Andrew Barnard served at St. Domingo from Apr. to Aug. 1795; served in the expedition under Sir Ralph Abercromby to the West Indies, and was at the reduction of Morne Fortunée. In 1799, served in the expedition to the Helder, and was present in the actions of the 27th Aug., 10th Sept. and 2d and 6th Oct. Sir Andrew has received a cross and four clasps for Barrosa (severely wounded), Ciudad Rodrigo, Badajoz, Salamanca, Vittoria, Nivelle (severely wounded), Orthes, and Toulouse. Slightly wounded at Waterloo.

2 Sir J. S. Barnes served under Gen. O'Hara, at Toulon, until its evacuation, and was present at the defence of Fort Mulgrave, and the sortie from Toulon. Served the whole of the campaign in Corsica, until the surrender of Calvi, including the storming of Convention Redoubts, capture of St. Fiorenzo, Bastia, and the siege of Calvi. In 1799, served the campaign in Holland, and was wounded at Alkinoor, 22 Oct. 99. Accompanied the expedition to the Ferrol, and served the whole of the campaign in Egypt in 1801, until the surrender of Alexandria. Served in the expedition to Walcheren, and in Spain and Portugal from March, 1810, until the conclusion of the war in 1814. He has received a cross for Busaco, St. Sebastian, Salamanca (severely wounded), and the Nive.

3 Col. Brown was at the siege and capture of Copenhagen in 1807; battle of Vimiera 21st Aug. 1808; passage of the Douro and capture of Oporto, with the previous and subsequent actions; battle of Talavera, 27th and 28th July, 1809 (severely wounded through both thighs); the action of the Light Division at the Bridge of Almeida, 24th July, 1810; battle of Busaco, and the different actions during the retreat of the French army from Portugal; actions at Sabugal, 3rd April, and battles of Fuentes d'Onor, 5th May, 1811; San Sebastian, Sept. 1813; Nivelle, 10th Nov.; Nive, 9th Dec. 1813, and investment of Bayonne. Served in the last American war, including the battle of Bladensburg and capture of Washington, 24th August 14. Slightly wounded in the head, and very severely in the left groin at Bladensburg.

Rifle Brigade.

Years' Serv. Full Pay.	Years' Serv. Half Pay.	LIEUTENANTS.	2ND LIEUT.	LIEUT.	
18	0	1 W. S. Ramsay Norcott	13 June 22	16 June 25	6 Capt. Cochrane was present
15	0	1 Thos. Wm. Smith	p 15 Sept. 25	24 Dec. 29	at Cadiz in Aug. 1811, and
12	0	1 Alexander Monro	p 19 Aug. 28	p 5 July 33	during the siege; at Orangues,
12	0	1 Keith W. Young	11 Sept. 28	p 11 Oct. 33	29th Oct.; San Munos, 17 Nov. 1812; San Milan, 18th June;
11	13 3/12	2 Frederick Belson	p 25 Jan. 16	p 24 Jan. 34	battle of Vittoria, 21st June;
10	0	1 Geo. Kerwan Carr....	p 29 June 30	p 31 July 35	bridge of Vera, 31 Aug. 13,
9	0	1 Wm. Henry Frankland	p 7 June 31	p 4 Dec. 35	(severely wounded in left arm;) Waterloo, 18th June, 1815,
9	0	2 Rob. Duncan Fergusson	p 5 July 31	p 6 May 36	wounded in left breast.
7	0	2 Wilmot Hen. Bradford	p 24 May 33	p 26 Aug. 36	7 Capt. Fry served in the
8	0	1 *Hon.* E. G. Monckton	18 May 32	20 Apr. 36	Peninsula from May, 1812, to the end of the war, including
9	0	2 Geo. Hughes Wilkins	16 Dec. 31	p 24 Feb. 37	the battles of Salamanca and
8	0	2 Rich. Luther Watson..	p 22 June 32	p 23 June 37	Vittoria. Severely wounded
8	0	2 Wm. Leigh Mellish ..	p 24 Jan. 33	p 2 Feb. 38	(left leg fractured) by a musket shot in the attack on the
8	0	2 Wm. Hen. Beresford..	p 25 Jan. 33	p 3 Aug. 38	heights of Vera, 7th Oct. 1813.
4	0	1 Arthur S. Murray	p 13 May 36	p 28 Dec. 38	Received four wounds on the
7	0	2 Alfred H. Horsford ..	12 July 33	p 23 Apr. 39	18th June, at Waterloo.
7	0	1 *Hon.* H. E. H. Gage ..	p 11 Oct. 33	p 31 May 39	8 Captain Holden served at
7	0	2 Edward Rooper	p 24 Jan. 34	p 5 July 39	the siege of Scylla Castle, in Calabria, in 1810; and at the
7	0	2 Geo. Sam. Jenkinson..	p 31 Jan. 34	p 12 July 39	attack and capture of the
5	0	2 Robert Reynard......	p 8 Jan. 36	p 8 Feb. 39	island of Pouza, on the coast of
6	0	1 Hen. S. Waddington..	p 15 May 34	p 25 Oct. 39	Naples, in 1813.
5	0	1 Rob. Vans Agnew	p 29 May 35	p 31 Dec. 39	9 Capt. Middleton served in the Peninsula and France from
		SECOND LIEUTENANTS.			13th March 1810, to 18th July,
5	0	1 Wm. Hale	p 31 July 35		1814, including the battle of Barrosa; siege
5	0	2 H. Oldfield Bowles ..	p 4 Dec. 35		of Ciudad Rodrigo, where he volunteered
5	0	1 Edw. A. Somerset ..	29 Jan. 36		with the storming party; Badajoz; battles of Salamanca, Vittoria, Nivelle, Nive, Orthes,
4	0	2 W. Shipley Warren ..	p 6 May 36		and Toulouse; besides various affairs of out-
4	0	2 Robert Craufurd	p 22 July 36		posts.
3	0	2 Geo. B. Dawson......	p 24 Feb. 37		10 Quarter - Master Trafford was present
3	0	2 Alex. Macdonell......	p 23 June 37		at the affair of Tarbes, 20th March; Tournefeuille, 27th March; battle of Toulouse, 10th
3	0	1 Rob. Moore Peel	p 2 Dec. 37		April, 1814; and battle of Waterloo, 18th June,
3	0	1 John Gibson	p 2 Feb. 38		1815.
2	0	1 *Sir* T. Munro, *Bart.*..	p 7 July 38		11 Dr. Ranken served in the Peninsula, from June 1811 to the end of the war, including the
2	0	2 W. Burnet Ramsay ..	p 27 July 38		battles of Vittoria, the Pyrenees, Nivelle, Nive,
2	0	1 Fred. F. J. Morrice ..	p 19 Oct. 38		Orthes and Toulouse; blockade of Pampeluna,
1	0	1 Cha. Edm. Law	p 23 Apr. 39		and sortie from thence; and the affairs of Vic Bigorre and Tarbes.
1	0	1 Fred. Rob. Elrington..	p 7 June 39		
1	0	1 *Lord* Alex. G. Russell	p 11 July 39		
1	0	2 Richard Lloyd	p 26 July 39		
1	0	2 George Dundas	p 25 Oct. 39		
1	0	2 Joseph Wilkinson	30 Dec. 39		
1	0	2 John Mitchell Eugene Shadwell	p 17 Jan. 40		
1	0	Chas. Hungerford Pollen	7 Feb. 40		

33 | 2 4/12 | *Paymasters.*—1 Wm. Holden,[8] 26 Feb. 24; *Ens.* 15 Dec. 04; *Lieut.* 31 Dec. 06; *Capt.* 12 July, 21.
32 | 0 | 2 p John Middleton,[9] 25 Nov. 26; *Ens.* 10 Mar. 08; *Lieut.* 4 Oct. 09; *Capt.* 7 [April, 25.
10 | 0 | *Adjutants.*—1 Geo. Kirwan Carr, (1st *Lieut.*) 30 Nov. 38.
1 | 0 | 2 Joseph Wilkinson, (2nd *Lieut.*) 31 Dec. 39.
3 | 0 | *Quarter-Masters.*—2 p ŒH Robert Trafford,[10] 2 June, 37.
1 | 0 | 1 Richard Taylor, 29 March, 39.
29 | 0 | *Surgeons.*—1 p Rob. Ranken,[11] 11 June, 30; *Assist.-Surg.* 16 April, 12; *Hosp. Assist.* 13 June, 11.
| | 2 Moses White, M.D. 29 July, 36; *Asst.-Surg.* 5 May, 25; *Hosp.-A.* 4 Apr. 14.
| | *Assist.-Surgs.*—1 Evans Garnons Lloyd, 18 Oct. 27; *Hosp.-Assist.* 25 Jan. 27.
1 | 0 | 2 Henry Downes, MD. 1 Nov. 39.

Regimentals Green.—*Facings* Black.—*Agent*, Messrs. Cox & Co.

[1st *Battalion returned from North America, Sept.* 1836.]
[2nd *Battalion returned from the Ionian Islands, June,* 1837.]

4 Colonel Hope's services :—Expedition to Copenhagen in 1807; to Sweden and subsequently to the Peninsula in 1808 and 9, including the retreat and battle of Corunna. Expedition to Walcheren. Campaigns of 1810 and 11 in the Peninsula, including the siege of Cadiz and battle of Barrosa, where he was severely wounded. Served also the campaign of 1814 in Holland. Present at Waterloo and the capture of Paris.

5 Major Kelly's services :—Expedition to Copenhagen in 1807. Capture of Martinique in 1809 and Guadaloupe in 1810. Campaigns of 1813, 14 and 15, in Lower Canada, including the action at Chateaugay and Plattsburgh.

1st West India Regiment of Foot.

"DOMINICA"—"MARTINIQUE"—"GUADALOUPE."

Years' Serv.						
Full Pay.	Half Pay.	Colonel.				
50		P ☖ *Sir* William Nicolay,¹ C.B. & K.C.H. 2nd *Lieut.* 28 May, 90; *Lieut.* 15 Aug. 93; *Capt.* 29 Aug. 98; *Major,* 26 June, 01; *Lieut.-Col.* 4 April, 05; *Col.* 4 June, 13; *Maj.-Gen.* 12 Aug. 19; *Lieut.-Gen.* 10 Jan. 37; *Col.* 1st West India Regt. 30 Nov. 39.				
21	12	*Lieutenant-Colonels.*—Wm. Bush, K.H. *Cornet,* P 7 Jan. 08; *Lieut.* P 29 June, 09; *Capt.* P 22 July, 13; *Major,* P 8 April, 26; *Lieut.-Col.* P 22 May, 29.				
39	5 8/12	Henry Capadose,² *Ens.* 24 Mar. 96; *Lieut.* 30 Oct. 99; *Capt.* 24 Mar. 04; *Brev.-Major,* 4 June, 14; *Regtl.-Major,* 17 Oct. 16; *Lieut.-Col.* 22 Apr. 36.				
36	1	*Majors.*—Wm. Maxwell Mills,³ *Ens.* 25 Oct. 03; *Lieut.* 24 Oct. 04; *Capt.* 18 April, 11; *Major,* 24 April, 28.				
31	0	John Cornell Chads,⁴ 2nd *Lieut.* Royal Marines, 4 May, 09; *Ens.* 83rd *Regt.* 3 March, 14; *Lieut.* P 1 Dec. 14; *Capt.* P 27 Jan. 20; *Major,* 22 April, 36.				

		CAPTAINS.	ENSIGN.	LIEUT.	CAPTAIN.	BREV.-MAJ.
17	12 1/12	P ☖ Robert Hughes⁵..	11 April 11	20 Oct. 12	13 Feb. 27	
19	12 10/12	Hector Downie⁶.......	14 Dec. 08	25 Feb. 10	26 Oct. 30	
13	0	Luke Smyth O'Connor...	P 27 April 27	22 Mar. 31	P 17 Jan. 34	
27	4 8/12	P Archibald Robertson⁷.	13 Apr. 09	6 Jan. 14	30 Dec. 34	
17	3	James Clarke.........	11 Jan. 21	P 19 July 27	21 April 36	
25	7/12	Wm. Devonish Deverell..	4 May 15	16 Nov. 20	7 April 37	
12	0	John David Blythe......	P 21 Nov. 28	P 3 Feb. 32	P 1 Dec. 37	
15	0	George Robeson........	21 July 25	17 April 28	1 June 39	
25	11 7/12	Rich. Straker Wickham...	2 Dec. 13	11 April 16	2 June 39	
24	2 11/12	P ☖ John Griffith ᵇ ..	29 July 13	4 May 15	29 July 36	
24	2 10/12	Thomas Moore	30 Mar. 14	25 Nov. 21	30 Sept. 36	
15	10 9/12	James Palmer..........	20 Apr. 15	6 June 16	25 Aug. 39	
17	11	William Burke.........	P 10 Dec. 12	27 Aug. 15	15 Sept. 39	
		LIEUTENANTS.				
13	0	John Fra. Grant.......	6 Dec. 27	9 Sept. 33		
8	0	Wm. Maxwell Mills....	P 20 July 32	P 17 Jan. 34		
12	0	Geo. Waller Meehan.....	17 April 28	14 April 36		
7	0	William Doran.........	15 Nov. 33	16 April 36		
7	0	Philip Phipps Trotman..	P 6 Dec. 33	P 17 April 36		
9	8 7/12	George Fahie Horsford..	30 Jan. 23	20 April 36		
11	4 1/12	Edward Lucas..........	9 April 25	21 April 36		
5	0	*Sir* J.R. Carm. Smyth,*Bt.*	P 29 May 35	P 26 Aug. 36		
4	0	Gustavus H. Reilly.....	P 21 April 36	P 1 Dec. 37		
4	0	Benjamin Mackenzie....	22 April 36	P 17 Feb. 38		
4	0	Wm. C. De Benyon Reade	20 April 36	26 April 38		
4	0	Fra. Milward W. Pogson	P 29 April 36	27 Oct. 38		
4	0	*Hon.* T. C. S. Foster....	P 10 June 36	1 June 39		
4	0	Alex. Wm. Mackenzie...	3 Feb. 37	1 June 39		
3	0	Edm. Hayter Bingham..	P 10 Mar. 37	1 June 39		
3	0	Edw. Alger. O'Donoghue	25 July 37	2 June 39		
2	0	S. W. Sutton Bush.....	18 Feb. 38	P 9 Aug. 39		
5	0	Edm. Phipps Mackie...	P 3 April 35	25 Oct. 39		
4	0	Ninian Craig	P 25 Mar. 36	26 Oct. 39		
4	0	Thomas Martin	27 May 36	27 Oct. 39		
2	0	R. J. H. Moffatt.......	26 June 38	15 Nov. 39		
2	0	H. Williams Wily......	27 June 38	15 Nov. 39		
14	1 6/12	James Mac Carthy.....	8 April 25	8 Oct. 27		
3	0	John Armstrong........	P 28 Oct. 37	7 Feb. 40		

1 Sir Wm. Nicolay's services:—sieges of Seringapatam and Pondicherry; capture of St. Lucia; campaign of 1808 in Spain, including the retreat to Corunna. Sir William was present at Waterloo.
2 Colonel Capadose served at the capture of Minorca in Nov. 1798.
3 Major Mills served at the capture of Martinique in 1809, and Guadaloupe in 1810.
4 Major Chads served with the expedition to Walcheren in 1809.
5 Capt. Hughes served in the Peninsula from 1809 to 1814, including the first siege of Badajoz, and the battles of Busaco, Vittoria (wounded), Salamanca, and the Pyrenees, besides various minor actions and skirmishes. Present at Waterloo on the 16th, 17th and 18th June, and was wounded on the 18th.

1st West India Regiment of Foot.

Years' Serv.			
Full Pay.	Half Pay.	ENSIGNS.	ENSIGN.
2	0	J. Hunter Mushet	p 19 Oct. 38
1	0	Mark Matthews	29 May 39
1	0	Stevenson Ballantine	30 May 39
1	0	Pierce Hackett	1 June 39
1	0	Robert Hughes	2 June 39
1	0	George Jeffrey[9]	4 June 39
1	0	John Andrew Wieburg	12 July 39
4	0	William Nepean Smith	20 Jan. 37
1	0	Joseph Alex. Hanna	17 Sept. 39
1	0	Henry St. John Clements	15 Nov. 39
		Paymaster.—	
2	0	*Adjutant.*—Seton Wm. Sutton Bush *(Lieut.)* 10 Jan. 40.	
1	0	*Quarter-Master.*—Richard Allard, 12 April, 39.	
		Surgeon.—J. Duncanson, M.D. 1 June, 38; *Assist.-Surg.* 27 Oct. 25; *Hosp.-Assistant*, 26 April, 15.	
4	0	*Assistant-Surgeons.*—Alexander Campbell, 12 Aug. 36.	
1	0	Robert Giles Montgomery, M.D. 5 July, 39.	

Facings White.—*Agents*, Messrs. Cox & Co.

6 Captain Downie served at the capture of Guadaloupe in 1810, including the attack on the Bridge of Noziere, 3rd February.

7 Captain Robertson served in the Peninsula from Jan. 1810 to the end of the war, including the siege of Cadiz, Feb. to Sept. 1810; lines at Torres Vedras; actions at Redinha, Cazal Nova, Foz d'Arronce, and Sabugal; battle of Fuentes d'Onor; first siege of Badajoz; actions at El Bodon, and Aldea de Ponte; siege and assault of Ciudad Rodrigo; siege and assault of Badajoz, April, 1812; battle of Salamanca; capture of Madrid; retreat to Portugal; battle of Nivelle; actions of La Bastide, Sauveterre, and Vic Bigorre; battles of Orthes (severely wounded in the left arm) and Toulouse.

8 Captain Griffith served the Egyptian campaign of 1801, and was wounded in the left thigh 21st March Served also in the Peninsula from July, 1812, to the end of the war, including the battle of Vittoria. Present at Waterloo on the 18th June.

9 Ensign Jeffrey served as a captain in the Anglo-Spanish Legion, and was engaged in the actions of the 5th May (severely wounded) and 1st Oct. (severely wounded), 1836; 10th, 12th (wounded), 14th, 15th and 16 March, 16th and 17th May, 1837. He has received two medals.

2nd West India Regiment of Foot.

Colonel.

Years' Serv.		
63	Francis Fuller,[1] *Ens.* 26 Jan. 1778; *Lieut.* 1 June, 78: *Capt.* 9 April, 81;	
Full Pay.	Half Pay.	*Major,* 21 Dec. 85; *Lieut.-Col.* 1 March, 94; *Col.* 1 Jan. 98; *Major-Gen.* 1 Jan. 1805; *Lieut.-Gen.* 4 June, 11; *Gen.* 27 May, 25.

Lieut.-Colonels.

Full	Half	
35	4 6/12	Francis Cockburn,[2] *Cornet,* 16 Oct. 00; *Lieut.* P 6 April, 03; *Capt.* 3 March, 04; *Major,* 27 June, 11; *Lieut.-Col.* 27 Oct. 14; *Col.* 10 Jan. 37.
45	0	Wm. Burke Nicolls,[3] *Ens.* 10 June, 95; *Lieut.* 4 April, 98; *Capt.* 3 Aug. 04; *Brevet-Major,* 4 June, 14; *Regtl.-Major,* 8 Jan. 24; *Lieut.-Col.* 12 Jan. 35.
31	0	Majors.—John Anderson,[4] *Ens.* 2 Nov. 09; *Lieut.* 24 Jan. 11; *Capt.* 16 Mar. 20; *Major,* 22 March, 27.
29	0	Thomas M'Pherson,[4] *Ens.* 8 Aug. 11; *Lieut.* 19 May, 13; *Capt.* 25 Dec. 23; *Major,* 12 Jan. 35.

Full	Half	CAPTAINS.	ENSIGN.	LIEUT.	CAPTAIN.	BREV.-MAJ.
37	0	Thomas Maling[5]	9 July 03	7 Sept. 04	11 July 05	12 Aug. 19
15	1 6/12	Herbert Mends	never	19 Feb. 24	19 Mar. 29	
20	7 8/12	John Jas. Peck[6]	27 May 13	24 May 21	P 8 June 30	
25	0	Edw. Cha. Soden	1 Feb. 16	27 June 24	10 Nov. 34	
15	0	James Allen	8 Dec. 25	28 May 28	24 July 35	
26	6/12	Rich. Percy Pack	16 Aug. 13	12 Apr. 20	12 Feb. 36	
9	0	Hen. C. Cobbe	15 Feb. 31	P 23 Jan. 35	P 3 Nov. 37	
17	0	E. S. Norman Campbell	P 2 Oct. 23	14 Jan. 20	P 7 Oct. 36	
18	8 1/12	Richard Elliott	28 July 14	30 Nov. 26	7 Aug. 39	
16	0	William Lardner[7]	27 June 24	22 Mar. 27	4 Oct. 39	

LIEUTENANTS.

Full	Half		ENSIGN.	LIEUT.	
15	0	Stephen John Hill	10 Nov. 25	13 Feb. 28	
12	0	Hen. Wase Whitfeild	13 Feb. 28	28 Oct. 31	2 Col. Cockburn served in South America in 1807; in the Peninsula in 1809 and 10; and in Canada from 1811 to 1814.
12	0	James Findlay	P 3 Apr. 28	18 Nov. 31	
12	0	Willoughby H. Nicolls	28 Aug. 28	22 Mar. 33	
13	14	Abraham P. Kenyon	24 June 13	24 June 13	3 Colonel Nicolls served at the capture of the Cape of Good Hope (both operations); also at the capture of the Isle of France.
7	0	James Edw. Boggis	P 12 July 33	P 17 Oct. 34	
9	0	Walter Craufurd Kennedy	27 Oct. 31	10 Nov. 34	
8	0	James Batchelor Davidson	25 May 32	13 Aug. 35	
5	0	Robt. Caldecott Morris	P 18 Dec. 35	P 25 Nov. 36	4 Majors Anderson and McPherson served in the American war.
8	18 1/2	Alexander Geddes	3 Feb. 14	27 Jan. 37	
6	0	L. C. W. H. Fitzgerald	P 17 Oct. 34	P 7 Apr. 37	5 Brev.-Lieut.-Col. 10 Jan. 37.
6	0	Anth. Hart Lapslie	11 July 34	5 Mar. 38	6 Capt. Peck served the campaigns of 1813 and 14 in the Peninsula.
4	0	Bartholomew O'Brien	P 15 Apr. 36	P 13 July 38	
5	0	John Miller	P 29 Dec. 35	25 Jan. 39	
6	0	B. Æ. S. Hutchinson	9 Dec. 24	10 Sept. 29	7 Capt. Lardner was severely wounded in retaking Fort Bullen, on the River Gambia, 11th Nov. 1831.
3	0	Robt. Murphy Nicolls	9 July 37	4 Oct. 39	
12	0	John Grogan	P 25 Nov. 28	P 20 Apr. 32	
3	0	William Anderson	10 July 37	25 Oct. 39	8 Quarter-master, 16 Aug. 33; from which date the period of service has been computed.
3	0	Jas. Delamain Mends	P 3 Nov. 37	26 Oct. 39	
7	0	John Potts[8]	5 Mar. 38	30 Dec. 39	
2	0	J. Gaggin Cox	1 June 38	31 Dec. 39	

ENSIGNS.

Full	Half		ENSIGN.	
2	0	J. Warren Glubb	16 Mar. 38	9 Dr. Richardson served at the capture of the Cape of Good Hope in 1806; reduction of Monte Video, and campaign of 1806 and 7 in South America; campaigns of 1808 and 9 in the Peninsula, including the battles of Roleia and Vimiera.
2	0	Geo. L. Woodd	30 Nov. 38	
1	0	Wm. M'Carthy Murray	22 Feb. 39	
1	0	Jas. Wm. Lovat Fraser	27 Sept. 39	
1	0	Joseph Hill	4 Oct. 39	
1	0	John Harger	25 Oct. 39	
1	0	Stephen Blaney Gordon	26 Oct. 39	
1	0	George Bennett	27 Oct. 39	
1	0	Geo. A. Crooks Kippen	P 6 Dec. 39	
1	0	—— Deckner	31 Dec. 39	
7	0	*Adjutant.*—John Potts, (*Lieut.*) 20 July, 38.		
2	0	*Quarter-Master.*—John Harpur, 5 March, 38.		
35	0	*Surgeon.*—John Richardson,[9] 5 Jan. 26; *Assist.-Surg.* 18 Feb. 08 *Hosp.-Assist.* 9 July, 05.		
4	0	*Assist.-Surgeons.*—Richard Tuthill, M.D., 8 Jan. 36.		
3	0	James Shirreff, 4 Aug. 37.		

Facings Yellow.—*Agent,* Messrs. Cox & Co.

1 Gen. Fuller served in the East Indies in 1782, 83, and 84, and commanded the 101st at the battle of Cuddalore in 1783. Served on the Continent in 1794 and 95. Embarked for the West Indies the latter end of 1795, where he continued to serve until 1802, and was present at the capture of various islands, &c. Embarked for the East Indies in 1806, where he was again actively employed.

Ceylon Rifle Regiment.

Years' Serv.			
Full Pay.	Half Pay.		

Lieut.-Colonels.

Full	Half	
37	0	࿋ Thomas Fletcher,¹ *Ens.* 28 July, 1803; *Lieut.* 13 March, 05; *Capt.* 12 Mar. 10; *Major,* ᴾ 6 Dec. 27; *Lieut.-Col.* ᴾ 27 Feb. 35.
32	0	࿋ James Macpherson,² *Ens.* 1 March, 08; *Lieut.* 28 Feb. 10; *Capt.* 25 April, 15; *Major,* ᴾ 6 July, 32; *Lieut.-Col.* ᴾ 27 March, 35.

Majors.

Full	Half	
29	4 4/12	࿋ James Anderson,³ *Lieut. 7th Fusiliers*, 28 Aug. 07; *Capt.* 1 Sept. 13; *Major,* 2 May, 34.
28	0	Samuel Braybrooke,⁴ *2nd Lieut.* 17 Dec. 12; *Lieut.* 29 April, 18; *Capt.* ᴾ 6 March, 23; *Major,* ᴾ 27 Feb. 35.

Full	Half	CAPTAINS.	ENSIGN.	LIEUT.	CAPTAIN.	BREV.-MAJ
19	3/12	Auchmuty Montresor ..	29 Mar. 21	25 Mar. 25	ᴾ 11 May 26	
32	7/12	Geo. Adol. Tranchell⁵ ..	2 Oct. 07	10 June 10	9 Oct. 26	
21	0	Peter Bennet Reyne ..	15 Apr. 19	15 Dec. 22	ᴾ 21 Dec. 26	
17	0	Thomas Wm. Rogers....	7 Jan. 24	ᴾ 4 May 26	ᴾ 7 June 27	
29	5	George Cochrane⁶	22 Jan. 07	7 Feb. 08	13 Feb. 27	
15	0	Henry Alex. Atchison ..	7 Apr. 25	7 Aug. 28	ᴾ 27 Feb. 35	
26	9 6/12	࿋ ⚜ Charles Wallett⁷	16 Aug. 04	9 Oct. 06	23 Mar. 15	10 Jan. 37
21	0	Thomas Skinner........	2 Dec. 19	8 Jan. 24	3 Apr. 36	
14	0	Brownlow Edw. Layard..	21 Dec. 26	ᴾ 28 Aug. 28	ᴾ 14 May 36	
23	6	Charles Kelson	26 Sept. 11	4 Mar. 13	10 June 32	
26	7/12	George Thomas Parke ..	3 Mar. 14	ᴾ 12 June 23	ᴾ 10 Aug. 26	
13	0	Charles Hamilton Roddy	ᴾ 15 Feb. 27	15 Apr. 29	ᴾ 27 Oct. 37	
15	9 7/12	Thomas Bonnor	ᴾ 5 Oct. 15	24 Dec. 18	ᴾ 30 June 25	28 June 38
11	0	William Dickson	ᴾ 3 Dec. 29	ᴾ 27 Feb. 35	ᴾ 5 July 39	
7	0	Wm. Twistleton Layard	ᴾ 22 Feb. 33	ᴾ 22 Nov. 36	ᴾ 16 Aug. 39	
20	7 6/12	࿋ ⚜ Thomas Lillie⁸ ..	1 Oct. 12	17 July 15	7 Dec. 38	

Full	Half	LIEUTENANTS.			
23	1 9/12	William Driberg	2 June 15	8 Aug. 22	
18	0	Rodney Mylius	16 May 22	30 May 24	
21	7 1/2	Thos. Eardley Hodges⁹	29 Jan. 12	4 Feb. 14	
26	0	James Stewart¹⁰........	10 May 14	11 Nov. 24	
26	0	Alexander Mackay......	1 Aug. 14	12 Nov. 24	
21	0	Cosby Warburton	22 July 19	18 June 25	
21	8 6/12	࿋ Richard Phelan¹¹	ᴾ 14 Feb. 11	26 Nov. 12	
19	0	David Meaden	8 Apr. 21	2 Feb. 26	
19	3 10/12	John Jas. Dwyer	20 Nov. 17	23 May 29	
16	5 11/12	John Burleigh	22 May 18	23 Mar. 21	
16	12 6/12	Mortimer Jones¹²	5 Mar. 12	4 Aug 13	
17	11 4/12	Louis Clare.............	10 Sept. 12	26 Jan. 14	
13	0	Simpson Nelson Burris..	ᴾ 17 Jan. 28	ᴾ 3 May 31	
9	17 6/12	William Caldwell	26 Aug. 13	2 Nov. 15	

3 Major Anderson served in the Peninsula, from 1809 to the end of the war, including the battles of Oporto, Talavera, and Busaco; first siege of Badajoz; battles of Albuhera and Salamanca; siege and capture of Ciudad Rodrigo and Badajoz; battles of Vittoria, Pampeluna, and Toulouse, besides other minor affairs.

4 Major Braybrooke served at the capture of the Kandyan territories in 1815, and in the Kandyan rebellion in 1817 and 18.

5 Captain Tranchell served in Travancore in 1809, and in the Kandyan country in 1815 and 18.

1 Col. Fletcher served the campaigns of 1808 and 9 in the Peninsula, including the battles of Roleia, Vimiera, and Corunna. Served also with the expedition to Walcheren.

2 Col. Macpherson's services:—Landed in Portugal, Sept. 1808; joined the 1st battalion 45th regiment in Almeida; proceeded with the brigade under Sir A. Cameron across the Douro to join the army under Sir John Moore; retreat to Lisbon. Campaign of 1809; affairs at Talavera 22d July, and Alberche 27th July; battle of Talavera 27th and 28th July; retreat to Portugal. Campaign of 1810; battle of Busaco, and retreat to lines of Lisbon. Campaigns of 1811; the affairs on Massena's retreat from the lines; action at Sabugal; battle of Fuentes d'Onor, 3d and 5th May; 2d siege of Badajoz, from 25th May to 15th June; action at Fuente Guinaldo, 26th June. Campaign of 1812; siege and storm of Ciudad Rodrigo, from 8th to 19th Jan.; (received a contusion at the assault); 3d siege and storm of Badajoz, from 10th March to 6th April, (severely wounded in the breast on mounting at the escalade); battle of Salamanca; capture of Madrid; affairs on the retreat from Madrid to Portugal. Campaign of 1813; battle of Vittoria; blockade of Pampeluna; battles of the Pyrenees; crossing the Bidassoa; storming the enemy's fortified entrenchments 7th and 9th Oct.; battle of Nivelle. Campaign of 1814; battle of Orthes, where he was severely and dangerously wounded, having received one shot in the right fore arm, and a second through the body. Received a severe bayonet wound in the leg at Ostend, June, 1815. Served in the Burmese war, and was severely wounded in the breast near Rangoon, 15th Dec. 1824. Col. Macpherson, although severely wounded at the time, climbed the flag-staff and pulled down the enemy's colours from the castle of Badajoz on the night of the storm.

Ceylon Rifle Regiment.

Years' Serv.			ENSIGN.	LIEUT.
Full Pay.	Half Pay.	LIEUTENANTS.		
13	0	Fran. Brownrigg Bayly............	2 Jan. 28	8 May 35
12	0	William Hardisty	p 29 May 28	8 Jan. 36
17	0	Albert Watson	17 July 23	14 Jan. 30
21	13	Frederick Ostheyden.............	27 Jan. 07	26 Jan. 11
10	0	Jas. Mitchell Macdonald	26 Oct. 30	p 29 July 36
6	0	Geo. Bulkeley Tattersall	p 16 May 34	p 28 Apr. 37
15	13	ᖴ Robert McBeath [13]	28 Oct. 12	30 Dec. 13
9	0	William John Kirk	27 Sept. 31	p 27 Oct. 37
6	0	William Price...................	p 13 June 34	8 May 38
6	0	Henry Charles Bird	p 13 June 34	22 May 38
6	0	Nicholas Fenwick	p 14 Nov. 34	p 17 Sept. 38
5	0	John Urban Vigors	p 27 Feb. 35	p 20 Nov. 38
5	0	Benjamin Bloomfield Keane.......	8 May 35	p 11 Jan. 39
4	0	Edward John Holworthy..........	p 12 Feb. 36	p 25 Jan. 39
4	0	Henry Gibbs Remmett...........	p 8 July 36	p 28 June 39
4	0	Henry Torrens Walker	28 Oct. 36	p 4 July 39
4	0	Henry Alexander Raitt...........	p 22 Nov. 36	p 5 July 39
4	0	Henry Du Vernet	25 Nov. 36	p 2 Aug. 39
3	0	Jones Butler Stevelly	p 27 Oct. 37	p 16 Aug. 39
		SECOND LIEUTENANTS.		
4	0	Christophilus Garstin	p 14 May 36	
3	0	Robert Watson	7 July 37	
3	0	Julius Brockman Travers.........	8 July 37	
3	0	Charles Thomas Smith...........	p 17 Nov. 37	
2	0	Charles A. Cobbe	p 6 July 38	
2	0	Francis Butler Templer...........	p 20 July 38	
2	0	Richard Brandram Gwilt.........	p 30 Oct. 38	
2	0	William Bagenall	2 Nov. 38	
2	0	J. R. Graham Pattison...........	p 28 June 38	
2	0	Johnson Bourne.................	p 11 Jan. 39	
1	0	John Brewse Kersteman	p 28 June 39	
1	0	Wm. Hopson Hopson	p 4 July 39	
1	0	Henry Lucas	p 5 July 39	
1	0	William Charles Vanderspar......	p 16 Aug. 39	
1	0	Frederick May	p 20 Sept. 39	
1	0	Robert Butler Stevelly	p 10 Jan. 40	

17	0	*Paymaster.*—Richard Jefferson, 6 May, 36; *2nd Lieut.* 23 Oct. 23; *1st Lieut.* 1 Sept. 26.	
		Adjutant.—	
14	0	*Quarter-Master.*—James Black,[14] 10 Aug. 26.	
		Surgeon.—David Ewing, 30 Sept. 36; *Assist.-Surg.* 3 June, 24; *Hosp.-Assist.* 7 Feb. 14.	
15	0	*Assist.Surgs.*—William Lucas, 25 May, 26; *Hosp.-Assist.* 3 Nov. 25.	
14	0	George Rumley, M.D. 19 April, 27; *Hosp.-Assist.* 12 Oct. 26.	
		Regimentals *Green*—Facings Black.—*Agent,* Sir John Kirkland, 80, Pall Mall.	

6 Capt. Cochrane served at the capture of Martinique, and Les Saintes in 1809, and Guadaloupe in 1810, and also in 1815.

7 Major Wallett's services:—Battles of Roleia and Vimiera; siege and capture of Flushing, 1809; in the Peninsula from June, 1811, to the end of the war, including the siege of Ciudad Rodrigo; battles in the Pyrenees on the 28th and 30th July; investment of Pampeluna; battles of Orthes and Nive; severely wounded in the thigh at Quatre Bras.

8 Capt. Lillie served in the Peninsula from Dec. 1812 to the end of the war, including the crossing of the Zadino; battle of Vittoria; blockade of Pampeluna from 5th to 18th July; pass of Roncesvalles, 28th July, battle of Pampeluna, 28th July, Nivelle, Nive (9th to 13th Dec.), Orthes (severely wounded) and Toulouse. Persent at Waterloo on the 18th June, and at the storming of Cambray.

9 Lieut. Hodges served at the capture of Genoa in 1814, and subsequently in the American war, including the capture of Washington and the engagements at Baltimore and New Orleans.

10 Lieut. Stewart served at the capture of Kandy in 1815, and in the Kandyan rebellion of 1817 and 18.

11 Lieut. Phelan served in the Peninsula, and was wounded on three different occasions. Served also in the American war.

12 Lieut. Jones served in the American war, and was engaged at Christler's Farm, Lundy's Lane (wounded), Fort Erie, and Chippewa.

13 Lieut. McBeath served in the Peninsula from March to 30 Dec. 1813, including the siege and capture of Balaguer; investment and taking of Tarragona.

14 Quarter-Master Black served the campaigns of 1813 and 14 in Germany and Holland, and was present at the attack upon Bergen-op-Zoom.

Royal African Colonial Corps.

Years' Serv.						
Full Pay.	Half Pay.					
35	2_{12}^{2}	Richard Doherty,[1] *Ens.* P10 Sept. 1803; *Lieut.* 22 Nov. 04; *Capt.* 21 May 12; Major, P 16 Sept. 24; *Lieut.-Col.* P 26 Sept. 26.				

Major.

28	0	₿ Francis Perry,[2] *Ens.* 8 Oct. 12; *Lieut.* 18 Feb. 13; *Capt.* 8 June, 26; *Major*, 8 Dec. 37.				

		CAPTAINS.	ENSIGN.	LIEUT.	CAPTAIN.	BREV.-MAJ.
18	0	James Jackson	1 Apr. 22	17 Feb. 24	3 Nov. 26	
27	0	Thompson Berwick	26 Jan. 14	26 June 24	24 May 32	
22	5$\frac{7}{12}$	Thomas Abbott[3]	13 Aug. 12	7 Apr. 14	18 Aug. 36	
10	3	William Shaw	15 Mar. 27	26 Apr. 31	19 Aug. 36	
9	0	Alexander Findlay	5 July 31	22 May 33	17 June 37	
8	17$\frac{3}{12}$	Richard Taylor	26 Oct. 15	28 July 36	P 15 Nov. 39	

		LIEUTENANTS.				
8	0	Edward O'Bryen	P 2 Mar. 32	10 Aug. 34		
7	0	Jas. Robt. Maxwell	23 May 33	6 Sept. 34		
7	0	Thomas Smales	P 31 May 33	20 May 36		
6	0	James Travers	28 Nov. 34	29 July 36		
6	0	Tho. Graham M'Intosh	29 Dec. 34	30 July 36		
6	19$\frac{2}{12}$	Edw. Southouse Glen	11 May 15	19 Aug. 36		
4	0	Wm. St. Leger Angelo	20 May 36	20 Oct. 37		
4	0	John Alex. Butcher	27 July 36	3 Nov. 37		
4	0	William Snowe	5 Aug. 36	27 Aug. 38		
4	0	Rich. Plunket Ireland	23 Dec. 36	28 Dec. 38		
4	0	Christopher Lynch	29 July 36	29 Dec. 38		
3	0	James Montgomery	20 Oct. 37	25 Oct. 39		
2	0	Tho. Vincent E. Reynolds	28 Dec. 38	P 15 Nov. 39		

		ENSIGNS.				
3	0	H. W. H. Graham	3 Nov. 37			
3	0	Henry Sall	8 Dec. 37			
2	0	C. S. H. Hingston	28 June 38			
2	0	Tho. Hislop J. Donaldson	25 Jan. 39			
1	0	Peter John Macdonald	25 Oct. 39			
1	0	G. Butler Triscott Colman	31 Dec. 39			

7	0	*Adjutant.*—Thomas Smales, (*Lieut.*) 20 Oct. 37.	
1	0	*Quarter-Master.*—Frederick Beckett Shaw, 24 Jan. 40.	
		Surgeon.—	
2	0	*Assist.-Surg.*—Edward John Burton, M.D. 11 May, 38.	

Facings Blue.—*Agent, Sir* John Kirkland, No. 80, Pall Mall.

---

[1] Col. Doherty served at the capture of Martinique in 1809, and Guadaloupe in 1810.
[2] Major Perry lost an arm at Salamanca, where he served as a volunteer.
[3] Captain Abbott served with the expedition to New Orleans. Mentioned in a public despatch to Lord Glenelg for gallant conduct whilst in command of an expedition in the interior of Africa.

Cape Mounted Riflemen.

Years' Serv.						
Full Pay.	Half Pay.					

Lieutenant-Colonel.

28	1	₽ ☿ Henry Somerset,[1] K.H. Cornet, 5 Dec. 1811; Lieut. 30 Dec. 12; Capt. 6 Oct. 15; Major, P 25 March, 23; Lieut.-Col. P 17 July, 24; Col. 28 June, 38.

Major.

27	4 10/13	₽ ☿ Wm. Burney,[2] K.H. Ens. 28 April, 08; Lieut. 1 May, 10; Capt. P 2 June, 14; Major, 6 Sept. 27.

		CAPTAINS.	ENSIGN.	LIEUT.	CAPTAIN.	BREV.-MAJ.
38	3 1/13	Pierce Lowen, K. H.[3]	19 May 99	25 July 05	13 June 11	22 July 30
28	1	Alex. B. Armstrong[4]	30 Jan. 12	5 Feb. 14	15 Sept. 25	28 June 38
25	5 5/12	₽ Charles Ross[5]	15 Mar. 10	4 Nov. 13	30 Apr. 37	
12	22 1/2	Henry Crause	14 Nov. 05	12 Oct. 07	16 Dec. 13	10 Jan. 37
20	0	Henry D. Warden	25 May 20	15 Sept. 25	1 Mar. 39	
16	0	Jas. Neil Rishton	10 Feb. 25	25 Dec. 27	2 Mar. 39	
		LIEUTENANTS.				
13	0	Thomas Donovan	15 Mar. 27	16 May 33		
10	0	Charles Peshall	9 Nov. 30	P 3 July 35		
8	0	Geo. T. C. Napier	23 Mar. 32	P 25 Aug. 37		
6	0	Geo. Edw. Cannon	P 1 Aug. 34	1 Mar. 39		
6	0	Fra. T. Le Touzel	P 23 Jan. 35	2 Mar. 39		
3	0	John Rob. O'Reilly	30 Apr. 37	3 Mar. 39		
4	0	Chas. Hen. Somerset	P 30 July 36	20 Sept. 39		
		ENSIGNS.				
2	0	William Harding	P 28 Dec. 38			
1	0	Wellington Lowen	1 Mar. 39			
1	0	Frederick Campbell	2 Mar. 39			
1	0	Honoratius Van Ryneweld	3 Mar. 39			
1	0	Charles B. Crause	27 Sept. 39			
1	0	John T. Bisset	7 Feb. 40			

28	0	Paymaster.—Wm. Gunn,[6] 31 May, 39; Quarter-Master, 6 Oct. 12.
13	0	Adjutant.—Thomas Donovan, (Lieut.) 20 Sept. 39.
13	0	Quarter-Master.—Detlif Sigfrid Schoufeldt, 25 Dec. 27.
34	3 3/12	Surgeon.—Wm. Parrott, 20 Oct. 25; Assist.-Surg. 10 March, 04; Hospital Assistant, 15 Oct. 03.
1	0	Veterinary Surgeon.—John Kingsley, 29 March, 1839.

Regimentals Green.—Agent, Sir John Kirkland.

1 Col. Somerset served the campaigns of 1813 and 14, including the battles of Vittoria, Orthes, and Toulouse.

2 Major Burney served at the capture of Ischia and Procida in 1809; siege of Cadiz in 1810; action of the Coa and Subugal; battle of Fuentes d'Onor; retreat from Burgos. Served the campaign of 1814 in Holland, including the action at Merxem, bombardment of Antwerp, and storming of Bergen-op-Zoom. Engaged in the Burmese war at the attack of Padowa Pass and the fortified position of Mahatee; storming the stockades and hills near, and taking the town and works of Aracan. Wounded on the 16th June, 1815, at Quatre Bras, by a musket shot in the left shin, and dangerously by a ball which entered the back part of the head.

3 Major Lowen served at the battle of Maida, and subsequently in Italy and the Mediterranean until the end of the war, including the capture of Ischia and Procida; reduction of the Ionian Islands, besides a variety of other desultory services.

4 Major Armstrong served at the capture of Genoa in 1814, and subsequently in the American war, including the capture of Washington, attack before Baltimore 13th Sept. 1814; and on New-Orleans, 8th Jan. 1815, where he was wounded and taken prisoner. Present when Graham's Town was attacked by about ten thousand Caffers, 22d April, 1819, and who were repulsed with great slaughter by three hundred men under the command of Col. Willshire.

5 Capt. Ross served in the Peninsula, from 1810 to 1813, including the siege of Cadiz; first siege of Badajoz; action at Fuentes de Guinalda; siege of Ciudad Rodrigo; second siege of Badajoz; battle of Salamanca, and capture of Madrid.

6 Paymaster Gunn served in Calabria in 1806; was present at the battle of Maida and taking of Catrone; served the campaign of 1807 in Egypt, including the attack on the forts and heights of Alexandria on the 19th, 20th, 21st March; siege of Rosetta, actions of El Hamet 20th and 21st April, and was there taken prisoner; served the campaigns of 1814 and 15 in Holland and the Netherlands, including the actions of the 13th January and 2d February, and the bombardment of Antwerp.

Royal Newfoundland Veteran Companies.

Years' Serv.						
Full Pay.	Half Pay.					

Major.

30	9/12	₿ ⚔ Robert Law,[1] K.H. *Ens.* 8 June, 1809; *Lieut.* 27 May, 11; *Capt.* P 18 Oct. 21; *Major,* P 29 Aug. 34.

Full Pay	Half Pay	CAPTAINS.	ENSIGN.	LIEUT.	CAPTAIN.	BREVET-MAJOR.
43	3	₿ William Sall, K.H.[2] ..	30 Oct. 94	26 Nov. 94	9 July 03	4 June 14
28	7 4/12	Har. Jeffares[3]	P 15 Feb. 10	4 Mar. 12	11 Aug. 25	28 June 38
24	16	William Bindon	21 Mar. 00	19 May 08	8 Apr. 25	28 June 38
		LIEUTENANTS.				
19	12 2/12	Richard Saunders	4 Nov. 09	25 Oct. 10		
16	17 5/12	Jas. Parsons Berry[4]	8 Jan. 07	26 Jan. 08		
14	14 7/12	Fred. Nepean Skinner ..	26 Mar. 12	25 Aug. 14		
12	15 5/12	J. Hunt (Acting Paymaster)	11 Dec. 12	9 Apr. 15		
11	20 1/12	₿ William Mason[5]	23 Feb. 09	19 Mar. 12		
7	21 9/12	Hector Munro[6]	5 Sept. 11	20 May 13		
8	14 6/12	John Nicholls..........	P 12 Feb. 18	7 Dec. 38		
		ENSIGNS.				
2	0	William Jenkins........	23 Feb. 38			
2	0	John Fletcher..........	4 Jan. 39			
1	0	John Gillespie	31 May 39			

Adjutant.

2	0	Wm. Jenkins, (*Ens.*) 5 July, 39.

Surgeon.

31	0	John Freeborn Pink, 10 Nov. 37; *Assist.-Surg.* 27 April, 20; *Hosp.-Assist.* 9 July 09.

Assistant-Surgeon.

1	0	William Sall, 10 May, 39.

Facings Blue.—Agent, Sir John Kirkland, No. 80, Pall Mall.

1 Major Law joined the army in Spain as a volunteer in 1808, and was attached to the 71st regiment; served with it in action at Lugo, on the retreat to, and at the battle of Corunna; served at the siege of Flushing, and the subsequent occupation of Walcheren; twice wounded by musket balls at Fuentes d'Onor, 3d and 5th May, 1811; severely wounded on the advance to Toulouse 21 March, 1814; continued uninterruptedly on service with his regiment (the 71st) in Portugal, Spain, and France, until the separation of the army at Bourdeaux in 1814; embarked in July, 1814, for New Orleans, but was recalled and sent to Belgium; was present with his regiment at Waterloo in Sir Frederick Adam's brigade, where he was very severely wounded by a cannon shot, which also killed his horse; served subsequently three years in France with the army of occupation. Major Law has served fifteen years in the Colonies since the Peace.
2 Col. Sall served at the taking of Maldonado and Monte Video in 1807; and in the Peninsula, from 1813 to the end of the war, and was present at the repulse of the sortie from Bayonne. Brevet Lieut.-Col. 22 July, 1830.
3 Major Jeffares was engaged at New Orleans, 8th Jan. 1815, and subsequently at the capture of Guadaloupe.
4 Lieut. Berry served nearly five years with the army in Sicily, and was present at the taking of the islands of Ischia and Procida. Served on board the *Weazle* Brig, cutting out gun-boats on the coast of Calabria in 1811.
5 Lieut. Mason served in the Peninsula, and was severely wounded in the right hip at the battle of the Nivelle. Served also in the American war, and was severely wounded at Niagara; in the right arm, where the ball still remains; in the neck, and seven buck shot wounds in the breast, and also one in the left arm.
6 Lieut. Munro served in the American war, was present in the action at Prescot, Chrystler's Farm, and Plattsburgh, besides various skirmishes.

Provisional Battalion at Chatham.

Years' Serv.		
Full Pay.	Half Pay.	

Lieutenant-Colonel.

26	10 4/12	₿ Thomas Weare,[1] K.H. *Ens.* 14 Sept. 04; *Lieut.* 25 June 05; *Captain,* 19 April 1810; *Brev.-Maj.* 21 June 13; *Regtl.-Major,* 1 June 26; *Brevet-Lieut.-Col.* 22 July 30; *Regtl.-Lieut.-Col.* 13 Apr. 38.

Surgeon.

34	0	Samuel Ayrault Piper, M.D. 20 Feb. 23; *Assist.-Surg.* 27 Dec. 06.

Agent, Sir John Kirkland.

1 Colonel Weare served with the British and Russian army in Italy in 1805; in Egypt, in 1807, against the Turks, including the second attack on Rosetta, the capture of guns and camels on the right bank of the Nile, and the retreat to Alexandria; at the reduction of the Islands of Ischia and Procida in 1809; at the taking of the Ionian Isles in 1809 and 10; and during the siege of Santa Maura as an acting Engineer Officer; in the Peninsula during the campaigns of 1812, 13, and 14, including the severe affair at Villa Moriel, the whole retreat from Burgos, the advance of 1813, affair of Osma, battle of Vittoria, both assaults and during the whole siege of San Sebastian, battle of the Nivelle, and some of the affairs at the Mayor's House in front of Bidart on the Bayonne road.

Royal Malta Fencible Regiment.

Colonel.

Count Francis Rivarola, K.C.H. *Ens.* 4 April, 1795; *Lieut.* 21 Feb. 98; *Capt.* 18 Mar. 04; *Major,* 6 Feb. 07; *Lieut.-Col.* 7 March, 11; *Col.* 19 July, 21; *Major-Gen.* 22 July 30.

Lieut.-Colonel.
* Marq. Guiseppe de Piro, C.M.G. 29 Dec. 37.

Captains.
* Francisco Bussiett, 11 Feb. 22.
* Giovanni Gouder, 24 Jan. 25.
* Paolo Ellul, 15 Jan. 27.
  James Galland, 29 Jan. 36.
* Carlo Cutajar, 17 Feb. 38.
* Paolo Camilleri, 9 Feb. 38.

Lieutenants.
* Vincenzo Bonavita, 25 Jan. 25.
* Salvatore Calleja, 25 April, 25.
* Mederico de Marchesi Alessi, 15 Jan. 27.
* Antonio Maltei, 15 Jan. 27.
* Guglielmo Petit, 17 Feb. 37.
* Salverio Gatt, 31 July, 37.
* Felice Rizzo, 27 Oct. 39.

Ensigns.
* Giuseppe Gouder, ditto.
* Georgio Virtu, 30 Dec. 34.
* Nicola Metrovich, 17 Feb. 37.
* William Gatt, 31 July, 37.
* Guiseppe Cavarra, 9 Feb. 38.
  Guiseppe Sesino, 27 Oct. 39.

Paymaster.
Vincenzo Rizzo, 25 Feb. 17.

Adjutant.
* Salverio Gatt. (*Lieut.*)

Quarter-Master.
* Paolo Salamone, 25 Jan. 39.

Surgeon.
J. Montanaro, 3 Aug. 38.

Assistant-Surgeon.
Michele F. Camilleri, M.D. 3 Aug. 38.

Facings Blue.—Agent, Sir John Kirkland.

---

5 Col. Hamilton served the campaign of 1799 in Holland, and was present in the different battles; with the expedition to South America, including the attack on Buenos Ayres, and all the skirmishes which took place before and after that event; in the Peninsula under Sir John Moore, including the battles of Roleia, Vimiera, and Corunna. Severely wounded (lost a leg) in action at Flushing, 7th Aug. 1809.

6 Col. Despard served at the siege and storm of Chumeer, (received a contusion on mounting the breach,) and three other forts in the East Indies, in 1807; siege of Gunourie; campaign against the Seiks in 1808 and 9; campaign of 1817 and 18 in the Deccan, including the battle of Jubbulpore.

7 Col. Falconar's services:—first Egyptian campaign; campaigns of 1805-6 in Italy, including battle of Maida, siege of Scylla, and capture of Catrone. Second Egyptian campaign, including the siege of Rosetta, and action at El Hamet. Campaign of 1814, in Holland, including action at Merxem and bombardment of Antwerp. Campaign of 1815, in Flanders. Besides the above, various other desultory services and skirmishes. Medal for services in Egypt.

8 Colonel Harvey served the Egyptian campaign of 1801, and has received the medal.

9 Paymaster Leech served in the Peninsula from Jan. 1813 to the end of the war, including the Passage of the Bidassoa, the battles of Nivelle 10th Nov., and Nive 9th, 10th, 11th, and 12th, Dec. 1813, and blockade of Bayonne; also at the escalade of Booj Booj in Cutch, March, 1819, and at the siege of Rhas-el-Khyma, and of Zoa in the Persian Gulf in 1819 and 20.

10 Lieut. Graham's services:—Expedition to South America in 1807, including the attack on Buenos Ayres; campaign and battle of Corunna; and subsequently in the Peninsula, including the actions at Barba del Puerco, of the Coa, near Almeida; battle of Busaco; actions at Redinha (wounded), Sabugal; battle of Fuentes d'Onor; sieges of Ciudad Rodrigo and Badajoz; battle of Salamanca, and numerous skirmishes. Wounded on the 18th June at Waterloo. Served also at Bhurtpore in 1826.

Recruiting Staff.

Years' Serv		
Full Pay.	Half Pay.	

Inspecting Field Officers.

Full Pay	Half Pay	Officer
45	0	₽ Alured Dodsworth Faunce,¹ C.B. *Ens.* 2 Dec. 1795; *Lieut.* 13 Oct. 96; *Capt.* 6 Aug. 1803; *Major*, 14 Feb. 11; *Brevet-Lieut.-Col.* 29 Sept. 14; *Lieut.-Col.* 24 Jan. 22; *Col.* 6 May, 31.
36	9⁄12	₽ John Fred. Ewart,² C.B. *Ens.* 1 Nov. 1803; *Lieut.* 10 Mar. 04; *Capt.* 17 April, 06; *Major*, 29 Oct. 12; *Lieut.-Col.* 15 Sept. 14; *Col.*, 10 Jan. 37.
37	10⁄12	₽ Edw. Fleming,³ C.B. *Ens.* ᴾ24 June, 02; *Lieut.* ᴾ6 July, 04; *Capt.* 30 May, 07; *Major*, 1 April, 13; *Lieut.-Col.* ᴾ18 July, 16; *Col.* 10 Jan. 37.
30	4 9⁄12	₽ George Dean Pitt,⁴ K.H., *Ens.*, 4 June, 1805; *Lieut.*, 5 Dec. 05; *Capt.*, 10 Aug. 09; *Major*, 13 Jan. 14; *Lieut.-Col.*, ᴾ18 Apr. 22; *Col.*, 10 Jan. 37.
44	0	₽ Nicholas Hamilton,⁵ K.H. *Ens.* 15 June, 1796; *Lieut.* 9 Dec. 96; *Capt.* 25 June, 03; *Major*, 18 June, 12; *Brev.-Lt.-Col.* 27 May, 25; *Col.* 28 June, 38.
33	2 9⁄12	₵₳ Charles King, K.H. *Cornet*, 9 May, 1805; *Lieut.* 30 Jan. 06; *Capt.* 18 Feb. 13; *Major*, 2 June, 25; *Lieut.-Col.* ᴾ18 Oct. 27.
41	0	Henry Despard,⁶ *Ens.* 25 Oct. 1799; *Lieut.* 25 June, 03; *Capt.* ᴾ19 Nov. 06; *Major*, ᴾ12 Aug. 19; *Lieut.-Col.* ᴾ13 Aug. 29.
41	3 7⁄12	Chesborough Grant Falconar,⁷ K.H. *Ens.* ᴾ1 Sept. 95; *Lieut.* 1 Nov. 99; *Capt.* 26 Dec. 05; *Brevet-Major*, 12 Aug. 19; *Regtl.-Major*, ᴾ26 June, 23; *Lieut.-Col.* ᴾ22 Oct. 25; *Col.* 28 June, 38.
42	1	Bissell Harvey,⁸ K.H. *Cornet*, ᴾ9 Nov. 97; *Lieut.* 24 Feb. 04; *Capt.* 11 April, 11; *Brevet-Major*, 16 May, 18; *Brevet-Lieut.-Col.* 10 Jan. 37.

Paymasters.

Full Pay	Half Pay	Officer
29	0	Francis Wemys, 25 May, 1811.
31	0	Nicholas Maunsell, 21 Aug. 1813; *Ens.* 27 Apr. 09; *Lieut.* 2 Nov. 09.
21	0	Hen. Benj. Brisco Adams, 16 Feb. 1819.
27	10	Edward Edmonds, 5 Sept. 1803.
33	0	₽ Richard Jellicoe, 24 Feb. 1814; *2nd Lieut.* 17 June 07.
24	10 8⁄13	₽ John Woodgate, 25 June, 1829; *Ens.* 17 Oct. 05; *Lieut.* 11 Feb. 08; *Capt.* 20 Feb. 12.
20	5 8⁄12	Henry Balthaser Adams, 30 Oct. 1828; *Ens.* 23 Feb. 15; *Lieut.* 12 June, 17; *Capt.* 17 Sept. 25.
32	6⁄12	₽ Francis Edward Leech,⁹ 19 Nov. 1807.
26	2 9⁄12	Hugh Percy Forster, 10 June, 1824; *Ens.* 24 July, 11; *Lieut.* 14 Dec. 15.

Full Pay	Half Pay	ADJUTANTS.	ENSIGN.	LIEUT.	ADJUTANT.
40	1	Thomas Shields	4 Feb. 00	3 Aug. 01	28 July 03
35	0	John Maguire	27 June 05	9 Oct. 06	4 Aug. 09
13	0	₽ ₵₳ William Graham ¹⁰	21 Sept. 27	28 Mar. 34	25 Dec. 35
16	14 10⁄12	₽ ₵₳ James Hope	1 Nov. 09	7 Jan. 13	29 Jan. 36
13	3 5⁄13	₽ James White	2 Jan. 24	7 Oct. 24	10 Feb. 37
15	0	Philip Henry Despard	17 Mar. 25	22 Nov. 27	24 Feb. 37
16	12 3⁄13	Robert M'Nair	22 Oct. 12	24 Mar. 14	14 July 37
1	0	Thomas Dagg	never	31 Dec. 39	31 Dec. 39
13	0	Denis Hanson	ᴾ30 May 27	24 Feb. 32	24 Jan. 40

1 Colonel Faunce served in Holland in 1799, and was present at the actions of the 2nd and 6th Oct. In 1805 accompanied the army to Hanover. In 1807 served in Zealand, and was at the siege and capture of Copenhagen. In 1808 served with the army under Sir John Moore, first at Gottenburgh, and afterwards throughout the operations in Portugal and Spain. In 1809 served with the army in the Scheldt. Served in the Peninsula from Nov. 1810 to Feb. 1813, including the storm and capture of Badajoz (wounded in the thigh), and battle of Salamanca. Served also in the American war, including the battle of Bladensburgh and capture of Washington, action near Baltimore, and operations before New Orleans in 1814 and 15; severely wounded 8th Jan. 1815. Medal for Salamanca.

2 Colonel Ewart accompanied the Expedition to Copenhagen in 1807. Served in the Peninsula in 1808 and 9 under Sir John Moore, and was wounded at Vimiera. Accompanied Expedition to the Scheldt. Served with the Light Division in the Peninsula from March 1811 to December 1812, including the battles of Fuentes d'Onor, and Salamanca; and the sieges of Ciudad Rodrigo, and Badajoz (wounded). Served in the West Indies from 1813 to 1816 inclusive, and was at the capture of Guadaloupe. Served in the East Indies from March 1819 to February 1823, and was employed as a Brigadier at the siege of Asseerghur.

3. Col. Fleming served in Calabria in 1806; at the capture of Alexandria, and attack on Rosetta in Egypt in 1807; in the Peninsula during the campaigns of 1808, 9, 10, and 11, and was present at the battles of Talavera (27th and 28th July 1809), and Albuhera, at which last he was severely wounded. Served in the West Indies, and with the expedition to the Southern States of America, in 1815.

4 Col. Pitt served at the capture of the Danish West India islands in 1807; and of Martinique in 1809. Served also in the Peninsula from Jan. 1811 to Jan. 1814, including the battle of Albuhera; actions at Usagre and Almaraz; siege of Badajoz; battles of Vittoria, Pampeluna, and the Pyrenees.

5 (For this and remaining notes, see bottom of preceding page.)

Royal Regiment of Artillery.

The Royal Arms and Supporters, with a Cannon, and the Motto "*Ubique*" over the Gun, and "*Quo fas et gloria ducunt*" below it.—"WATERLOO."—Rocket Troop: "LEIPSIC."

The figures in the first Column, prefixed to the Names, denote the Battalions to which the Officers belong.—H.B. Horse Brigade.—R.S. Rocket Service.—G.C. Gentleman Cadet.

₩ ℟ *Colonel-in-Chief.*—Lieutenant-General Right Hon. Sir Richard Hussey Vivian, *Bart.* G.C.B. and G.C.H., Master-General of the Ordnance.

Years Serv.		COLONELS-COMMANDANT.	SECOND LIEUT.	FIRST LIEUT.	CAPTAIN.	BREVET-MAJOR.	REG.-MAJOR.	LIEUT.-COLONEL.	BREVET-COLONEL.	REG.-COLONEL.	COLONEL COMM.	MAJOR-GENERAL.	LIEUT.-GENERAL.
59	H.B.	Benjamin Lord Bloomfield, G.C.B., G.C.H.	24 May 81	21 Nov. 87	9 Sept. 94	1 Jan. 05	1 June 06	3 Dec. 06	20 Feb. 12	never	4 Nov. 23	4 June 14	22 July 30
61	6	Henry Shrapnel 2	9 July 79	3 Dec. 81	15 Aug. 93	29 April 02	1 Nov. 03	20 July 04	4 June 13	20 Dec. '14	6 Mar. 27	12 Aug. 19	10 Jan. 37
61	5	George Wulff 3	ditto	14 Feb. 83	25 Sept. 93	ditto	20 July 04	28 Jan. 05	ditto	ditto	5 April 27	ditto	ditto
61	6	Sir Wiltshire Wilson, K.C.H. 4	ditto	28 Feb. 82	1 Nov. 93	ditto	ditto	10 Mar. 05	ditto	ditto	21 Jan. 28	ditto	ditto
60	7	Spencer Claudius Parry	3 Nov. 80	4 Mar. 86	14 Aug. 94	1 Jan. 05	1 June 06	1 June 06	4 June 14	ditto	27 Jan. 33	ditto	ditto
59	2	George Salmon	24 May 81	6 June 88	9 Sept. 94	ditto	1 June 06	18 June 07	ditto	3 July 15	7 Sept. 34	19 July 21	ditto
59	2	Richard Dickinson	29 June 81	17 May 90	6 Mar. 95	never	15 Sept. 06	ditto	ditto	29 July 20	28 April 36	ditto	ditto
58	3	Edward Pritchard 6	1 July 82	27 Oct. 90	ditto	never	18 June 07	30 April 09	12 Aug. 19	6 Aug. 21	3 July 37	22 July 30	ditto
52	3	℟ Robert Beevor 7	12 July 88	1 July 91	3 Oct. 95	never	1 Feb. 08	22 Mar. 11	ditto	17 Oct. 23	15 Mar. 38	ditto	ditto
48	8	℟ Sir J.H. Carncross, K.C.B.10	15 June 92	17 Jan. 93	28 Oct. 96	25 Feb. 08	1 May 09	14 Feb. 14	never	29 July 25	20 Sept. 39	10 Jan. 37	28 June 38

		Removed from the Corps, having the Rank of *Major-General.*	SECOND LIEUT.	FIRST LIEUT.	CAPTAIN.	BREVET-MAJOR.	REG.-MAJOR.	LIEUT.-COL.	BREVET-LIEUT.-COL.	REG.-LIEUT.-COL.	REG.-COLONEL.	MAJOR-GENERAL.	
58		₩ Sir J. Viney, C.B. and K.C.H. 8	1 July 82	24 Mar. 91	1 Oct. 95	never	1 Feb. 08	20 June 09	never	12 Aug. 19	4 Sept. 23	22 July 30	
46		₩ ℟ Sir A. Dickson, GCB,KCH.9	6 Nov. 94	8 Mar. 95	14 Oct. 01	6 Feb. 12	26 June 23	27 April 12	27 April 12	27 May 25	1 July 36	10 Jan. 37	
48		Alexander Watson 11.........	19 June 92	17 Jan. 08	9 Jan. 97	never	20 June 09	never	1 May 14	never	20 July 25	ditto	
48		E. V. Worsley	23 Jan. 93	15 Aug. 93	1 April 97	never	4 Sept. 09	20 Dec. 14	20 Dec. 14	never		ditto	
47		₩ Sir T. Downman, C.B., K.C.H. 12	24 April 93	11 Sept. 93	1 Nov. 97	never	22 Jan. 10	4 June 14	4 June 14	27 May 25		ditto	
47		Henry Eveleigh 13	ditto	1 Jan. 94	3 Nov. 97	25 July 10	8 May 11	17 Dec. 12	never			ditto	
47		Peter Fyers, C.B. 14.........	18 Sept. 93	ditto	16 July 99	4 June 11	14 Feb. 11	ditto	never			ditto	
47		Hon. W. H. Gardner 15......	ditto	ditto	ditto	ditto	20 Dec. 14	ditto	never			ditto	
47		Frederick Walker 16	18 Sept. 93	ditto	ditto	ditto	ditto	3 July 15	never			ditto	
47		₩ ℟ Alexander Macdonald, C.B. 17	1 Jan. 94	1 Aug. 94	2 Oct. 99	ditto	ditto	11 May 20	never			ditto	
47		₩ ℟ Percy Drummond, C.B. 18	ditto	ditto	7 Oct. 99	ditto	ditto	6 Nov. 20	never		13 Oct. 27	ditto	
47		Joseph Webbe Tobin	ditto	ditto	4 Feb. 00	1 Jan. 12	ditto	6 Aug. 21	never		31 Dec. 27	ditto	
45		₩ ℟ S. r J. May, K.C.B., K.C.H. 19	6 Mar. 95	7 Oct. 95	18 April 03	6 Feb. 12	2 May 25	27 April 12	22 July 30		10 Jan. 37	28 June 38	

Royal Artillery.

Years' Serv.		COLONELS.	SECOND LIEUT.	FIRST LIEUT.	CAPTAIN.	BREVET MAJOR.	REGIMTL. MAJOR.	BREVET LT.-COL.	REGIMTL. LT.-COL.	BREVET COLONEL.	REGIMTL. COLONEL.
Full Pay.	Half Pay.										
46	0	H.B. Robert Pynn, C.B. 20	30 May 94	14 Aug. 94	3 Dec. 1800	1 Jan. 12	28 Oct. 15	19 July 21	12 June 23	never	22 July 30
46	0	2 Rich. Secker Brough 21	..	2 Sept. 94	1 Jan. 98	25 July 10	31 Dec. 22	12 Aug. 19	4 Sept. 23	never	21 Nov. 33
46	0	ⓟ Andrew Bredin 22	..	9 Sept. 94	6 July 98	ditto	12 June 23	ditto	17 Oct. 23	never	28 July 33
46	0	5 James Power	..	30 Sept. 94	22 Feb. 99	4 June 11	ditto	ditto	26 Dec. 24	never	5 June 35
46	0	1 Charles Younghusband 23	9 Oct. 94	29 Oct. 94	18 April 01	4 June 13	26 June 23	never	5 Jan. 25	never	12 June 35
46	0	8 ⓟ George Crawford 24	ditto	31 Oct. 94	ditto	ditto	ditto	never	2 Mar. 25	never	27 April 36
45	0	4 Tho. John Forbes	6 Mar. 95	13 April 95	9 Sept. 02	ditto	17 Oct. 23	never	29 July 25	never	10 Jan. 37
45	0	7 ⓟ ⓒ Jas. Webber Smith, C. B. 25	ditto	3 Oct. 95	25 Nov. 02	ditto	26 Dec. 24	21 Sept. 13	ditto	22 July 30	ditto
45	0	5 Alexander Munro, K. H. 28	ditto	27 Jan. 96	2 May 03	ditto	9 July 25	never	ditto	never	ditto
45	0	4 Jas. Pattison Cockburn 29	ditto	ditto	17 May 03	ditto 14	ditto	never	ditto	never	ditto
45	0	H.B. ⓟ ⓒ Sir Hew Dalrymple Ross, K.C.B. 30	..	10 May 96	1 Sept. 03	31 Dec. 11	ditto	21 June 13	ditto	22 July 30	ditto
45	0	3 ⓟ Rob. Hen. Birch 31	9 Mar. 95	25 July 95	12 Sept. 03	4 June 14	ditto	never	12 Dec. 26	never	ditto
45	0	3 James Armstrong 32	ditto	31 July 95	ditto	ditto	ditto	never	13 Oct. 27	never	ditto
45	0	3 Thomas Paterson 33	1 Dec. 95	3 June 97	6 Dec. 03	ditto	5 Nov. 25	never	6 Nov. 27	never	ditto
44	0	4 Nath. Wilmot Oliver 34	2 June 96	13 Feb. 98	2 Mar. 04	ditto	14 Nov. 26	never	31 Dec. 27	never	23 June 37
44	0	6 Rich. John Jas. Lacy 35	8 Aug. 96	17 Mar. 98	20 July 04	ditto	The Regimental rank of Major was abolished 6th Nov. 1827.	never	23 Nov. 28	never	11 June 38
44	0	6 Frederic Campbell 36	12 Jan. 97	16 July 99	29 July 04	ditto		never	25 Nov. 28	never	28 June 38
44	0	1 George Turner, C. B. 37	14 Jan. 97	16 July 99	ditto	ditto		never	9 Dec. 28	never	10 Aug. 39
43	0	2 Rich. Fra. Cleaveland 38	24 Feb. 97	ditto	9 Oct. 04	ditto		never	30 Dec. 28	never	24 Nov. 39
43	0	8 ⓟ ⓒ Sir Rob. Gardiner, K.C.B.&K.C.H. 39	7 April 97	ditto	12 Oct. 04	27 April 12		3 Mar. 14		22 July 30	

LIEUT.-COLONELS.

43	0	9 P. Margetson Wallace 40	10 May 97	ditto	15 Nov. 04	4 June 14		never	ditto		
43	0	5 Richard Jones 41	12 May 97	ditto	5 Dec. 04	ditto		never	31 Dec. 28		
43	0	5 John Edw. Jones 42	14 July 97	ditto	20 Dec. 04	ditto		never	ditto		
43	0	7 ⓟ Thomas Alston Brandreth, C. B. 43	19 July 97	ditto	ditto	ditto		never	27 Oct. 29		
43	0	1 David Story 44	1 Sept. 97	18 July 99	1 Mar. 05	12 Aug. 19		never	10 Dec. 29		
43	0	1 ⓟ ⓒ Tho. Hutchesson 45	1 Dec. 97	2 Oct. 99	10 April 05	ditto		never	22 July 30		
42	0	H.B. ⓟ ⓒ Edw. Cha. Whinyates, C.B.& K.H. 46	1 Mar. 98	ditto	8 July 05	18 July 15		never	ditto		
42	0	9 ⓟ John Michell, C. B. 47	ditto	ditto	20 Sept. 05	29 Sept. 14		never	ditto		
42	0	3 ⓟ Hamelin Trelawny 48	28 April 98	ditto	28 Dec. 05	12 Aug. 19		never	27 May 31		

Royal Artillery.

Years' Service.		LIEUTENANT COLONELS.	SECOND LIEUT.	FIRST LIEUT.	CAPTAIN.	BREVET-MAJOR.	BREVET-LIEUT. COL.	REGIMENT. LIEUT. COL.	BREVET COLONEL.
Full Pay.	Half Pay.								
42	0	℗ Arthur Hunt 49	11 Nov. 98	18 April 01	1 June 06	12 Aug. 19	never	26 Oct. 31	
39	1 9/12	1 Stephen Kirby	1 Aug. 99	31 Dec. 00	ditto	ditto	never	20 July 34	
38	2 5/12	H.B. 6 George Cobbe 51	1 Oct. 99	1 Sept. 01	2 June 06	12 Aug. 19	never	7 Nov. 34	
36	4 5/12	℠ 4 Alex. Caralic Mercer 52	20 Dec. 99	1 Dec. 01	3 Dec. 06	ditto	never	5 June 35	
34	6 3/12	3 ℗ Wm. Greenshields Power, C. B. & K. H. 53	31 May 00	11 Feb. 02	13 June 07	21 Sept. 13	21 Jan. 17	12 June 35	10 Jan. 37
34	6 3/12	7 Jas. Stokes Bastard	15 Nov. 00	12 May 02	1 Feb. 08	27 May 25	never	27 April 36	
34	6 3/12	9 Thomas Cubitt 54	20 Dec. 00	11 June 02	ditto	ditto	never	25 May 36	
39	0	5 Cyprian Bridge 55	ditto	8 Aug. 02	ditto	ditto	never	4 June 36	
39	0	8 ℠ Tho. Gore Browne 56	23 Feb. 01	12 Nov. 02	ditto	ditto	never	1 July 36	
39	0	8 Duncan Grant 57	ditto	23 Nov. 02	ditto	ditto	never	12 July 36	
39	0	8 Henry Alex. Scott 58	28 Apr. 01	20 Apr. 03	ditto	ditto	never	10 Aug. 36	
39	0	0 John Cade Petley	1 Oct. 01	13 June 03	ditto	ditto	never	11 Nov. 36	
39	0	H.B. 4 ℠ Thomas Dyneley, C. B. 59	1 Dec. 01	1 July 03	28 May 08	18 June 15	never	10 Jan. 37	
38	0	R.S. 2 ℠ J. Boteler Parker, C. B. 60	1 Apr. 02	1 Sept. 03	5 June 08	21 Sept. 13	18 June 15	ditto	10 Jan. 37
38	0	1 Henry. Ch. Russell	ditto	12 Sept. 03	15 July 08	27 May 25	never	ditto	
38	0	6 ℗ Joseph Darby 61	1 July 02	ditto	22 Mar. 09	22 July 30	never	ditto	
38	0	H.N. 2 ℠ Edmund Yeamans Walcott 62	20 Dec. 02	ditto	23 Mar. 09	15 Aug. 22	never	ditto	
37	0	4 ℠ Samuel Rudyerd 63	15 Mar. 03	ditto	24 Mar. 09	22 July 30	never	ditto	
37	0	H.B. 2 ℗ William Cator 64	7 May 03	ditto	1 May 09	12 April 14	22 July 30	23 June 37	
37	0	8 ℠ Cha. Cornwallis Dansey, C. B. 65	19 July 03	ditto	1 Oct. 09	22 July 30	never	ditto	
37	0	3 Daniel Bisset	ditto	ditto	22 Jan. 10	ditto	never	ditto	
37	0	4 ℗ Adam Fife Crawford 66	17 Aug. 03	ditto	3 Aug. 10	ditto	never	ditto	
37	0	2 Hen. Wm. Gordon 67	ditto	ditto	ditto	1 June 13	never	ditto	
37	0	2 Sir Wm. Macb. G. Colebrooke, K. H. 68	ditto	ditto	27 Sept. 10	22 July 30	22 July 30	ditto	
37	0	1 Rich. Thomas King (3)	8 Sept. 03	ditto	8 May 11	ditto	never	ditto	
37	0	9 Wm. Daniel Jones 70	ditto	ditto	ditto	ditto	never	ditto	
37	0	2 ℗ Wm. Bolden Dundas, C. B. 71	ditto	ditto	11 July 11	21 Aug. 19	10 Jan. 37	23 June 37	
37	0	6 ℗ Frederic Arabin 72	ditto	ditto	ditto	22 July 30	never	18 Dec. 37	
37	0	5 ℗ Edward Tho. Michell, C. B. 73	ditto	13 Sept. 03	11 Aug. 11	17 Mar. 11	22 July 30	11 June 38	
37	0	4 Courtenay Cruttenden 74	ditto	24 Oct. 03	ditto	22 July 30	never	28 June 38	
37	0	7 ℗ Peter Faddy 75	ditto	1 Nov. 03	5 Sept. 11	22 July 30	never	10 Aug. 39	
37	0	3 Wm. Wylde 76	ditto	6 Dec. 03	16 Mar. 12	16 July 30	19 Aug. 36	20 Nov. 39	
37	0	8 Charles Edward Gordon 77	ditto	6 Dec. 03	17 Mar. 12	22 July 3)	never	24 Nov. 39	

266

Royal Regiment of Artillery.

Years' Serv. Full Pay.	Half Pay.		CAPTAINS.	2d LIEUT.	1st LIEUT.	CAPTAIN.	BREVET-MAJOR.
37	0	9	Philip Warren Walker 78..	3 Dec. 03	6 Dec. 03	1 June 12	22 July 30
37	0	2	P Alexander Maclachlan 79	ditto	ditto	17 June 12	ditto
37	0	H.B. P	Charles Blachley 80..	ditto	1 Mar. 04	21 June 12	ditto
37	0	4	P CB A. Macdonald C.B. 81	ditto	1 May 04	1 Oct. 12	18 June 15
37	0	3	P Hassel Richard Moor 82	22 Dec. 03	ditto	1 Dec. 12	22 July 30
37	0	1	Henry Geo. Jackson 83....	ditto	ditto	31 Dec. 12	ditto
37	0	6	Edward Sabine 84........	ditto	20 July 04	24 Jan. 13	10 Jan. 37
37	0	H.B. P	William Dunn 85	ditto	ditto	22 July 13	ditto
37	0	6	Zach. Clutterbuck Bayley 86	ditto	27 July 04	28 Aug. 13	ditto
37	0	8	Edwin Cruttenden 87	14 Jan. 04	29 July 04	25 Oct. 13	ditto
36	0	8	P CB James Sinclair 88..	9 June 04	15 Nov. 04	14 Feb. 14	ditto
36	0	5	James Gray 89	ditto	20 Dec. 04	1 May 14	ditto
36	0	1	James Fogo 90	18 June 04	21 Dec. 04	4 Oct. 14	ditto
36	0	H.B. P	Hon. Wm. Arbuthnot 91	16 July 04	ditto	20 Dec. 14	ditto
36	0	H B	P Henry Blachley 92 ...	10 Aug. 04	18 Feb. 05	ditto	ditto
36	0	8	Jas. Archibald Chalmer 93	ditto	1 Mar. 05	ditto	ditto
35	10/12	5	P CB Forbes Macbean 94..	15 Sept. 04	20 May 05	ditto	ditto
35	11/12	8	CB Wm. Henry Stopford 95	ditto	2 July 05	1 Apr. 15	ditto
35	1 3/4	4	Lloyd Dowse 96.........	29 Sept. 04	3 July 05	16 May 15	ditto
35	1 3/4	1	P George John Belson 97..	ditto	6 July 05	21 May 15	ditto
36	0	2	Peter Desbrisay Stewart 98	ditto	7 July 05	ditto	ditto
35	1 3/8	3	Robert Franck Romer	9 Nov. 04	16 July 05	23 May 15	ditto
34	2 3/4	6	Rich. Carr Molesworth 99..	ditto	17 July 05	20 June 15	ditto
33	2 1/3	4	Francis Rawdon Chesney 100	ditto	20 Sept. 05	ditto	2 Dec. 36
33	2 10/12	3	P CB William Bell 101 ..	23 Nov. 04	2 Dec. 05	3 July 15	10 Jan. 37
32	3 4/12	7	George Brodie Fraser	14 Dec. 04	3 Dec. 05	1 Aug. 15	ditto
32	3 4/12	H.B. P CB	Matthew Louis 102..	ditto	28 Dec. 05	26 Oct. 15	ditto
32	2 10/12	2	P Thomas Grantham 103 ..	ditto	29 Dec. 05	28 Oct. 15	ditto
32	3 6/12	7	Francis Haultain	ditto	23 Feb. 06	7 June 16	ditto
29	5 11/12	3	John Gordon 104	10 May 05	1 June 06	5 Aug. 16	ditto
29	6 2/12	3 P CB	W. Brereton C.B. K.H. 105	ditto	ditto	30 Sept. 16	21 Jan. 19
29	6 1/2	7 P	Poole Vallancey England 106	ditto	ditto	11 Mar. 17	10 Jan. 37
29	5 8/12	6	Irwine Whitty 107........	12 July 05	ditto	23 Oct. 18	ditto
29	5 1/2	6	Hen. Lewis Sweeting 108..	9 Aug. 05	ditto	1 May 19	ditto
30	5	5	P Frederick Wright 109 ..	13 Sept. 05	ditto	22 Apr. 20	ditto
30	4 11/12	8	P Jas. Humphreys Wood 110	ditto	ditto	11 May 20	ditto
30	4 8/12	3	William Ernst Jackson ..	ditto	ditto	29 July 20	ditto
30	4 8/12	9	P Basil Robinson Heron 111	ditto	ditto	6 Nov. 20	ditto
31	4	9	George Durnford	1 Nov. 05	ditto	6 Aug. 21	ditto
32	2 7/8	1	Charles Dalton 114	1 Mar. 06	ditto	30 Dec. 22	ditto
32	2 7/12	2	Jas. Robert Colebrooke 115	21 Mar. 06	3 June 06	31 Dec. 22	ditto
32	2 1/12	4	Rich. Burne Rawnsley	ditto	22 Oct. 06	12 June 23	28 June 38
32	2 1/2	2	P Wm. Augustus Raynes 116	25 Apr. 06	ditto	26 June 23	ditto
32	2	3 P CB	Rich. Hardinge, K.H. 117	23 May 06	19 Dec. 06	17 July 23	ditto
32	2	5	Joseph Hanwell	ditto	14 Jan. 07	ditto	ditto
33	9/12	7	Robert Andrews	1 July 06	15 Oct. 07	26 Nov. 24	ditto
33	7/12	5	Edmund Sheppard 118	ditto	1 Feb. 08	2 Mar. 25	ditto
33	9/12	3 P	Walter Elphinstone Lock 119	ditto	ditto	ditto	ditto
33	1	H.B. CB	Philip Sandilands 120	4 Oct. 06	ditto	ditto	ditto
33	1 1/12	5	Browne Willis	ditto	ditto	ditto	ditto
33	1 1/12	6	Benj. Hutcheson Vaughan	ditto	ditto	ditto	ditto
33	1 3/12	9	Thomas Gordon Higgins ..	ditto	ditto	ditto	ditto
32	1 5/12	9	CB Amherst Wright 121 ..	18 Dec. 06	ditto	ditto	ditto
34	0	R.S. CB	T. F. Strangways 122..	ditto	ditto	12 Dec. 26	
33	0	6	John Harbridge Freer	4 April 07	ditto	1 April 27	
33	0	7	Arch. White Hope	ditto	ditto	5 July 27	

Royal Regiment of Artillery.

Years' Serv. Full Pay.	Half Pay.		CAPTAINS.	2ND LIEUT.	1ST. LIEUT.	CAPTAIN.
33	1/12	5	John Lewis Smith.............	10 June 07	1 Feb. 08	6 Nov. 27
33	1/12	7	ɸ John Eyre 123	ditto	11 Feb. 08	ditto
33	1/12	3	Charles Otway	1 July 07	5 Mar. 08	ditto
33	2/12	4	ɸ William Elgee 124...........	ditto	20 May 08	ditto
33	2/12	4	John Morse Stephens	3 Oct. 07	5 June 08	ditto
33	3/12	2	⊞ William Lemoine	ditto	ditto	ditto
33	3/12	2	James Smith Law.............	3 Nov. 07	16 July 08	ditto
32	7/12	1	⊞ W. C. Anderson 125	ditto	1 Aug. 08	ditto
32	1/12	2	ɸ Charles Manners 126 .. .	ditto	24 Sept. 08	ditto
32	1	9	Reynolds Palmer	17 Dec. 07	1 Oct. 08	ditto
32	1	1	John Rom. Hornsby...........	ditto	15 Jan. 09	ditto
32	1	9	Andrew O. W. Schalch 127	ditto	10 Mar. 09	ditto
32	1	4	Richard Say Armstrong 128.....	ditto	22 Mar. 09	ditto
31	1 1/12	7	Mark Evans 130................	4 April 08	1 May 09	ditto
31	1 5/12	8	ɸ John Pascoe 131	ditto	29 July 09	ditto
32	0	9	George Temp. Rowland	ditto	10 Sept. 09	31 Dec. 28
31	1 4/12	8	ɸ George Spiller 132...........	2 May 08	7 Nov. 09	6 Nov. 27
30	2 7/12	4	ɸ J. N. Colquhoun 133......	1 June 08	8 Sept. 10	ditto
31	1 5/12	5	ɸ Anthony R. Harrison 134......	ditto	27 Oct. 10	ditto
31	1 7/12	1	George Charleton 135	6 July 08	29 Oct. 10	ditto
31	1 7/12	4	Richard Kendall 136...........	ditto	30 Oct. 10	ditto
32	0	7	ɸ Henry Richard Wright 137 ...	ditto	29 Dec. 10	11 July 29
30	1 9/12	8	ɸ Edward Jacob Bridges 138	1 Oct. 08	14 Mar. 11	6 Nov. 27
32	0	6	ɸ William Henry Bent 139......	26 Nov. 08	11 Aug. 11	27 Oct. 29
			SECOND CAPTAINS.			
30	2 2/12	9	Robert Clarke	ditto	12 Aug. 11	6 Nov. 27
30	2 1/12	1	ɸ Wm. Furneaux 140	ditto	18 Nov. 11	ditto
32	0	9	ɸ Hugh Morgan 141	21 Dec. 08	7 Feb. 12	30 June 30
31	0	H.B.	ɸ ⊞ Fr. Warde 142	4 Mar. 09	8 Mar. 12	3 July 30
31	0	H.B.	ɸ ⊞ W. B. Ingilby 143	1 April 09	9 April 12	22 July 30
31	0	2	ɸ ⊞ T. Or. Cater 144.........	ditto	16 April 12	ditto
31	0	H.B.	ɸ Henry Pester 145	1 May 09	16 June 12	ditto
31	0	5	ɸ Henry Stanway 146........	5 June 09	21 July 12	6 Nov. 30
31	0	2	ɸ Robert William Story 147......	6 Nov. 09	18 Mar. 13	27 May 31
31	0	8	ɸ Henry Slade 148.............	4 Dec. 09	23 July 13	20 June 31
31	0	5	George Gayton Palmer 149	20 Dec. 09	1 Oct. 13	26 Aug. 31
30	0	9	ɸ George James 150............	5 Mar. 10	25 Oct. 13	3 Sept. 31
30	0	2	Charles Henry Nevett	ditto	17 Dec. 13	26 Oct. 31
30	0	1	James Howell..................	2 April 10	ditto	27 Oct. 31
30	0	1	ɸ W. Hudson Lawrence 151.....	28 April 10	ditto	2 Feb. 32
30	0	R.S.	ɸ ⊞ J. Bloomfield 152	ditto	ditto	7 Feb. 32
30	0	H.B.	⊞ Edward Trevor 153......	4 June 10	17 Dec. 13	23 June 32
30	0	9	Richard Robinson Drew	ditto	10 Feb. 14	13 July 32
30	0	7	ɸ Henry Palliser 155...........	ditto	18 Feb. 14	27 Sept. 32
30	0	H.B.	ɸ Arch. Macbean 156	13 Dec. 10	23 July 14	28 Dec. 32
29	0	5	Harry Gough Ord..............	12 Dec. 11	20 Dec. 14	2 Feb. 33
29	0	9	Hugh R. Gillespie 157.........	ditto	ditto	7 May 33
28	3/12	5	Robert Long Garstin...........	ditto	ditto	1 Aug. 33
28	3/12	6	⊞ John Alexander Wilson......	11 Sept. 12	ditto	17 Oct. 33
27	6/12	8	Charles Robert Dickens 158......	ditto	29 Dec. 14	ditto
27	11/12	2	Richard Tomkyns 159	ditto	ditto	21 Nov. 33
27	1	7	Henry Williams 160	17 Dec. 12	20 May 15	17 Dec. 33
26	1 3/12	3	William Greenwood	ditto	22 May 15	22 Jan. 34
26	1 5/12	H.B.	ɸ Evan Morgan 161	ditto	23 May 15	10 Feb. 34
27	7/12	5	⊞ R. G. B. Wilson 162	ditto	20 June 15	8 July 34
26	1 7/12	5	⊞ Burke Cuppage 163	ditto	ditto	20 July 34
26	1 7/12	1	Robert Burn	ditto	ditto	14 Aug. 34
25	1 11/12	G.C.	⊞ R. B. Burnaby 164	ditto	28 June 15	9 Sept. 34
25	2 2/12	8	John H. Griffin 165	5 July 13	28 Oct. 15	21 Nov. 34
25	2 1/12	7	Thomas A. Lethbridge	ditto	17 Nov. 15	20 Dec. 34
25	2 6/12	4	John Somerville...............	ditto	9 Dec. 15	29 Dec. 34

Royal Regiment of Artillery.

Years' Serv. Full Pay.	Half Pay.		SECOND CAPTAINS.	2ND LIEUT.	1ST LIEUT.	CAPTAIN.
24	$2\frac{10}{12}$	4	R. Long. Cornelius	5 July 13	4 July 16	4 April 35
24	$2\frac{10}{12}$	1	Lewis Edward Walsh	ditto	13 July 16	6 May 35
24	$3\frac{1}{12}$	3	Wm. H. Hennis	13 Dec. 13	1 Aug. 16	5 June 35
23	$3\frac{5}{12}$	3	Fred. Aug. Griffiths	ditto	8 Oct. 16	19 Aug. 35
22	$3\frac{4}{12}$	2	Sir H. Chamberlain, Bart.	1 May 15	1 May 19	2 Sept. 35
22	$3\frac{4}{12}$	3	Daniel Thorndike	ditto	8 May 19	28 Dec. 35
22	3	9	Francis Holcombe	ditto	9 Nov. 19	6 Jan. 36
22	$2\frac{11}{12}$	8	Harry Stow	ditto	26 Dec. 19	4 Feb. 36
22	$2\frac{10}{12}$	6	William Fraser	ditto	5 Mar. 19	18 Mar. 36
23	$2\frac{5}{12}$	3	Charles Gostling	ditto	22 April 19	19 April 36
22	$2\frac{4}{12}$	4	Charles Henry Mee	ditto	11 May 19	27 April 36
22	3	7	Theophilus Desbrisay	ditto	12 May 19	25 May 36
23	$2\frac{9}{12}$	3	William John Stokes	10 July 15	2 April 21	29 June 36
23	$2\frac{6}{12}$	8	Chas. Bertie Symons	ditto	2 Dec. 21	1 July 36
22	$2\frac{6}{12}$	3	Wilkinson L. Kaye	11 Dec. 15	1 May 22	12 July 36
23	$1\frac{11}{12}$	1	Tho. Congreve Robe	ditto	30 Dec. 22	10 Aug. 36
23	$1\frac{4}{12}$	7	John Dyson	ditto	11 Aug. 23	10 Jan. 37
25	$\frac{1}{12}$	6	Geo. Mark Glasgow	ditto	15 Nov. 24	ditto
25	$\frac{1}{12}$	2	Richard Basset 166	ditto	26 Nov. 24	ditto
24	$\frac{1}{12}$	9	Wm. W. D'Arley	16 Dec. 16	10 Dec. 24	ditto
24	$\frac{1}{12}$	9	Edm. Neal Wilford	ditto	3 Jan. 25	ditto
24	$\frac{1}{12}$	4	John Tylden	ditto	13 Feb. 25	ditto
24	$\frac{1}{12}$	5	Wm. Hen. Pickering	ditto	9 April 25	ditto
24	0	4	William Dixon	ditto	29 July 25	ditto
24	0	6	William Stewart	ditto	ditto	ditto
24	0	4	J. Wheeler Collington	ditto	ditto	ditto
24	0	6	William Berners	ditto	ditto	ditto
24	0	3	Richard Shepherd	ditto	ditto	ditto
23	0	4	Geo. Hooton Hyde	7 July 17	ditto	19 Jan. 37
23	0	8	Thomas Peters Flude	ditto	ditto	29 Jan. 37
23	0	9	John Morris Savage	ditto	ditto	27 Mar. 37
23	0	3	James Smith Cremer	ditto	ditto	2 June 37
23	0	4	Wm. Young Fenwick	15 Dec. 17	ditto	23 June 37
23	0	5	Francis Weller	ditto	ditto	12 Sept. 37
23	0	7	Thomas Knatchbull	ditto	ditto	28 Nov. 37
23	0	7	J. Humphrey St. John	ditto	ditto	ditto
23	0	7	Rich. James Dacres	ditto	29 Aug. 25	18 Dec. 37
22	$\frac{3}{12}$	8	Chas. Wm. Wingfield	8 July 18	1 April 26	30 Dec. 37
22	$\frac{3}{12}$	7	Alexander Tulloh	ditto	10 July 26	20 April 38
21	$\frac{7}{12}$	4	J. Sidney Farrell	ditto	ditto	11 June 38
21	$1\frac{2}{12}$	2	John Knowles	5 Oct. 18	13 Dec. 26	6 Aug. 38
21	$1\frac{1}{12}$	8	Henry Poole	ditto	1 Feb. 27	13 Nov. 38
21	$1\frac{3}{12}$	1	Henry O'Brien	ditto	2 Feb. 27	11 Dec. 38
20	$1\frac{5}{12}$	6	Arthur Gossett	ditto	2 Mar. 27	1 May 39
20	$1\frac{10}{12}$	6	Samuel J. Skinner	23 Oct. 18	1 April 27	16 May 39
20	1	6	Robert Luard	8 Dec. 19	12 May 27	20 May 39
20	1	5	Henry Geo. Teesdale	ditto	26 May 27	23 May 39
20	$1\frac{1}{12}$	1	John Gore	8 Dec. 19	8 June 27	3 July 39
20	$\frac{6}{12}$	2	Noel Thomas Lake	5 July 20	5 July 27	10 Aug. 39
19	$\frac{1}{12}$	2	Piercy Benn	3 Feb. 21	13 Dec. 27	14 Aug. 39
19	$\frac{4}{12}$	8	John Deschamps	1 Aug. 21	6 Nov. 27	11 Sept. 39
19	0	1	George Burroughs	15 Dec. 21	ditto	19 Oct. 39
18	0	9	Wm. Mein Smith	1 June 22	ditto	20 Nov. 39
18	0	6	Tho. Ackers Shone	11 July 22	ditto	24 Nov. 39
			FIRST LIEUTENANTS.			
16	0	1	George Rogers	18 June 24	ditto	
16	0	9	James Turner	15 Nov. 24	ditto	
16	0	G.C.	Ashton Ashton Shuttleworth	10 Dec. 24	8 Nov. 27	
16	0	1	Geo. Wm. Bingham	26 Dec. 24	ditto	
15	0	H.B.	John Edward Dupuis	13 Feb. 25	ditto	
15	0	4	John Low	28 Feb. 25	ditto	

Royal Regiment of Artillery.

Years' Serv. Full Pay	Years' Serv. Half Pay		First Lieutenants.	2nd Lieut.	1st Lieut.
15	0	3	George Markland	9 April 25	12 Nov. 27
15	0	4	Robert Robertson	ditto	ditto
15	0	6	John Hill	10 April 25	ditto
15	0	2	Howe Curtis Bevan	5 May 25	ditto
15	0	G.C.	Charles Herrick Burnaby	9 June 25	14 Nov. 27
15	0	2	Wm. Fenwick Williams	14 July 25	16 Nov. 27
15	0	5	John Geddes Walker	29 July 25	ditto
15	0	7	Henry Geary	ditto	18 Nov. 27
15	0	4	John Herbert Caddy	ditto	ditto
15	0	7	Henry Joseph Morris	ditto	1 Jan. 28
15	0	H.B.	Richard Mathews Poulden	ditto	3 Jan. 28
15	0	9	John M'Coy	ditto	ditto
15	0	R.S.	Edw. Fitzherbert Grant	ditto	30 April 28
15	0	6	Wm. George Chart Caffin	16 Dec. 25	30 June 28
14	0	4	John Wray Mitchell	18 Oct. 26	9 Dec. 28
14	0	2	George John Beresford	ditto	31 Dec. 28
12	0	1	Rob. Fitzgerald Crawford	19 May 28	12 May 29
12	0	1	John St. George	ditto	11 July 29
12	0	H.B.	William Robert Nedham	ditto	12 July 29
12	0	9	Patrick Scott Campbell	ditto	19 Jan. 30
12	0	H.B.	Augustus Henry Frazer	ditto	1 Mar. 30
12	0	H.B.	Edward Charles Warde	ditto	30 June 30
12	0	9	Alexander Tytler	ditto	3 July 30
12	0	2	Henry Stephen Tireman	6 Aug. 28	4 July 30
12	0	6	Henry Coope Stace	ditto	5 July 30
12	0	7	Robert Roe Fisher	ditto	22 July 30
12	0	3	John William Ormsby	ditto	ditto
12	0	H.B.	Arthur Joseph Taylor	ditto	ditto
12	0	1	George Maclean	ditto	5 Aug. 30
12	0	3	William Baird Young	ditto	1 Oct. 30
11	0	8	William Harrison Askwith	18 Dec. 29	6 Nov. 30
11	0	5	Franklin Dunlop	ditto	25 Nov. 30
11	0	7	Francis Dick	ditto	26 Nov. 30
11	0	5	Alfred Tylee	ditto	1 April 31
11	0	5	Charles James Dalton	ditto	29 April 31
11	0	2	William Henry Forbes	ditto	27 May 31
11	0	H.B.	David Edward Wood	ditto	30 June 31
10	0	H.B.	Harcourt Popham	6 Nov. 30	20 July 31
10	0	6	Hugh Manley Tuite	ditto	26 Aug. 31
10	0	9	Wm. Emerton Heitland	ditto	3 Sept. 31
10	0	2	George Innes	ditto	4 Sept. 31
10	0	1	Fred. Eardley Wilmot	ditto	27 Sept. 31
10	0	2	James William Fitz Mayer	ditto	26 Oct. 31
10	0	5	Geo. Rob. Harry Kennedy	ditto	27 Oct. 31
10	0	H.B.	George Sandham	ditto	28 Oct. 31
10	0	H.B.	Chas. Vansittart Cockburn	ditto	2 Feb. 32
10	0	2	Frederick Wodehouse	17 Dec. 30	29 May 32
9	0	8	John Henry Francklyn	26 July 31	23 June 32
9	0	7	Hen. Thomas Fyers	ditto	13 July 32
9	0	R.S.	Gloucester Gambier	ditto	31 July 32
9	0	3	Francis Seymour Hamilton	ditto	17 Aug. 32
9	0	5	Edward Walter Crofton	ditto	29 Aug. 32
9	0	8	Samuel Philip Townsend	ditto	16 Oct. 32
9	0	H.B.	*Hon.* Robert French Handcock	ditto	23 Dec. 32
9	0	1	Powrie Ellis	ditto	28 Dec. 32
9	0	3	Robert Wynter	ditto	22 Jan. 33
9	0	4	Henry Hotham	16 Dec. 31	3 Feb. 33
9	0	6	Nathaniel Evanson Harrison	ditto	7 May 33
9	0	6	Charles Cheetham	ditto	16 July 33
9	0	4	Gilbert J. Lane Buchanan	ditto	1 Aug. 33
9	0	4	William Staines Paine	ditto	19 Aug. 33
9	0	H.B.	Walter Raleigh Gilbert	ditto	17 Oct. 33
9	0	8	Alex. Fred. William Papillon	ditto	23 Oct. 33
9	0	3	Henry Aylmer	ditto	21 Nov. 33
9	0	H.B.	George Chas. Rawdon Levinge	ditto	25 Nov. 33

Royal Artillery.

Years' Serv. Full Pay.	Half Pay.		FIRST LIEUTENANTS.	2ND LIEUT.			1ST LIEUT.		
9	0	1	Alex. Graham Wilkinson Hamilton..	16	Dec.	31	17	Dec.	33
9	0	2	William Fulford		ditto		22	Jan.	34
9	0	H.B.	Arthur Newcomen		ditto		10	Feb.	34
9	0	1	Alexander Irving		ditto		10	Mar.	34
9	0	6	Dionysius Airey		ditto		8	July	34
8	0	7	Stanley Bing Hornby..............	20	June	32	10	July	34
8	0	4	St. John Thomas Browne		ditto		11	July	34
8	0	6	Charles Bingham..................		ditto		20	July	34
8	0	9	Henry Sebastian Rowan............		ditto		14	Aug.	34
8	0	8	J. Noble Arbuthnot Freese........		ditto		9	Sept.	34
8	0	H.B.	Frederick Darby Cleaveland.......		ditto		25	Sept.	34
8	0	7	Henry Murray.....................		ditto		24	Oct.	34
8	0	8	Charles Smith....................		ditto		25	Oct.	34
8	0	8	Henry Austin Turner..............		ditto		20	Nov.	34
8	0	1	Thos. Beckett Fielding Marriott....	20	Dec.	32	21	Nov.	34
8	0	4	Thomas Elwyn....................		ditto		29	Dec.	34
8	0	5	Charles James Wright.............		ditto		30	Dec.	34
8	0	9	Geo. Augustus Fred. Derinzy.......		ditto		28	Jan.	35
8	0	6	William Hamilton Elliot...........		ditto		4	April	35
8	0	8	Peter Maclean....................		ditto		6	May	35
8	0	3	Charles Robert Wynne.............		ditto		5	June	35
8	0	5	Lowry Wm. Montgomery Wynne....		ditto		6	June	35
8	0	H.B.	Francis Ramsay		ditto		12	June	35
8	0	H.B.	William Wynn Jones...............		ditto		19	Aug.	35
8	0	5	Anthony Benn....................		ditto		2	Sept.	35
7	0	7	Robert Miller Mundy..............	21	June	33	28	Dec.	35
7	0	2	Charles Lionel Fitzgerald..........		ditto		6	Jan.	36
7	0	H.B.	George Drought Warburton........		ditto		17	May	36
7	0	3	Philip Reginald Cocks.............		ditto		18	Mar.	36
7	0	8	Robert Morse Fyers...............		ditto		19	Apr.	36
7	0	5	Richard Harvey...................		ditto		27	April	36
7	0	5	Walter Frederick Crofton..........		ditto		25	May	36
7	0	9	Henry Edward Morritt.............		ditto		4	June	36
7	0	5	Thomas De Winton		ditto		29	June	26
7	0	5	William Thomas Crawford.........		ditto		1	July	36
7	0	8	Pierrepont Henry Mundy..........	20	Dec.		2	July	36
7	0	8	George Edward Turner............		ditto		12	July	36
7	0	4	William Henderson................		ditto		13	July	36
7	0	H.B.	Alexander Stephen Dickson........		ditto		10	Aug.	36
7	0	9	Charles John Torrens..............		ditto		10	Jan.	37
7	0	8	George Carter Evelegh.............		ditto			ditto	
7	0	7	William James Smythe.............		ditto			ditto	
7	0	2	David William Paynter............		ditto			ditto	
6	0	2	George Robert Barker.............	21	June	34		ditto	
6	0	2	Peter Pickmore Faddy.............		ditto			ditto	
6	0	8	Arthur Thomas Phillpotts..........		ditto			ditto	
6	0	8	Hen. Rob. Eardly Wilmot..........		ditto			ditto	
6	0	8	John Olphert.....................		ditto			ditto	
6	0	1	William Bethell Gardner...........		ditto			ditto	
6	0	2	Percy William Hewgill............		ditto			ditto	
6	0	3	John Henry Lefroy	19	Dec.	34		ditto	
6	0	6	Chas. Jas. Buchanan Riddell........		ditto			ditto	
6	0	8	Arthur George Burrows...........		ditto			ditto	
6	0	3	Molyneux Chas. Marston..........		ditto		12	ditto	37
6	0	1	Edward Price.....................		ditto		28	ditto	37
6	0	6	Charles Colville Young		ditto		29	ditto	37
6	0	9	James William Domville...........		ditto		6	Feb.	37
6	0	7	Edwin Wodehouse................		ditto		22	ditto	37
6	0	7	George Ashley Maude		ditto		27	Mar.	37
5	0	2	John Farnaby Cator...............	18	June	35	5	Apr.	37
5	0	7	John Harvey		ditto		23	June	37
5	0	1	Evan Maberly....................		ditto		24	ditto	37

Royal Artillery.

Years' Serv					
Full Pay.	Half Pay.		FIRST LIEUTENANTS.	2ND LIEUT.	1ST LIEUT.
5	0	1	Hew Graham Ross...............	ditto	29 July 37
5	0	4	William Bland...................	ditto	12 Sept. 37
5	0	7	John Russell Domvile...........	ditto	26 ditto 37
5	0	4	Wm. Manley Hall Dixon.........	ditto	30 Oct. 37
5	0	2	*Hon.* Frederick Savile............	ditto	8 Nov. 37
5	0	9	Hen. Wm. Montresor............	ditto	28 ditto 37
5	0	6	Wm. Moffat Douglas Willan......	ditto	ditto
5	0	9	Collingwood Dickson	18 Dec. 35	29 ditto 37
5	0	3	Hyde Popham Parker	ditto	18 Dec. 37
5	0	7	*Hon.* Rob. Chas. Hen. Spencer......	ditto	30 Dec. 37
5	0	5	Henry J. Thomas................	ditto	1 Feb. 38
5	0	3	George Graydon.................	ditto	23 Mar. 38
5	0	9	Anth. Oldfield...................	ditto	20 April 38
5	0	5	H. Paget Christie................	ditto	11 June 38
4	0	6	Jas. B. Dennis...................	18 June 36	28 June 38
4	0	3	Dennis W. Pack.................	ditto	6 Aug. 38
4	0	3	John Travers....................	ditto	6 Oct. 38
4	0	3	*Hon.* G. Talb. Devereux............	ditto	13 Nov. 38
4	0	6	R. Blackwood...................	ditto	11 Dec. 38
4	0	3	Ralph S. Allen	ditto	1 May 39
4	0	6	William Swinton	ditto	16 May 39
4	0	8	Ed. William Rodwell............	ditto	20 May 39
4	0	1	Spencer Delves Broughton......	ditto	23 May 39
4	0	9	Allan H. Graham	ditto	3 July 39
4	0	4	John Miller Adye	13 Dec. 36	7 July 39
4	0	5	F. Alex. Campbell	ditto	10 Aug. 39
4	0	4	H. P. Goodenough	ditto	13 Aug. 39
4	0	4	Otto Bayer Mackie	ditto	14 Aug. 39
4	0	1	Chas. Anth. Balfour	ditto	31 Aug. 39
4	0	7	G. B. Shakespear	ditto	11 Sept. 39
4	0	4	Horace G. Alston	ditto	19 Oct. 39
3	0	6	Rich. H. Crofton	5 May 37	20 Nov. 39
3	0	9	Matthew Smith	ditto	24 Nov. 39

SECOND LIEUTENANTS.

3	0	8	W. J. Plunkett Wade. ditto	5 A. R. Wragge........	12 Mar. 39
3	0	8	Murray O. Nixon..... 14 Dec. 37	1 F. Wm. Haultain.....	ditto
3	0	5	H. Lynedoch Gardiner ditto	2 H. G. L. Cooper.....	ditto
3	0	9	Benj. Bathurst....... ditto	3 T. W. Lawrence......	ditto
3	0	2	H. B. O. Savile....... ditto	7 C. Wilson...........	ditto
3	0	3	R. Parker Radcliffe.. ditto	8 F. John Travers......	ditto
3	0	4	Thomas Knox....... ditto	3 M. C. Dixon........	ditto
3	0	5	Ch. Wright Younghusband............ ditto	7 C. F. Thorndike...... 1 H. Rogers...........	ditto ditto
3	0	6	Tho. Cromie Lyle.... ditto	4 J. Turner...........	ditto
2	0	2	Rob. Corcyra Romer.. 16 June 38	8 A. C. L. Fitz Roy....	ditto
2	0	6	George Wilder....... ditto	3 E. H. Fisher........	ditto
2	0	0	Charles Lawrence d'Aguilar .... ditto	4 G. Burrell .... 5 B. Willis	ditto ditto
2	0	0	Hugh Archibald B. Campbell.......... ditto	4 R. F. Mountain...... 9 G. J. Wyatt	ditto ditto
2	0	8	R. Bratton Adair.... ditto	9 S. Cleaveland........	ditto
2	0	3	Robert Talbot....... ditto	7 A. C. S. Somerset....	ditto
2	0	6	Henry Lempriere.... ditto	6 P. A. Morshead......	ditto
1	0	6	A. Thompson........ 12 Mar. 39	4 S. H. S. Inglefield....	ditto
1	0	4	H. Clerk .... ditto	6 Edw. Mourrier Boxer	20 Dec. 39
1	0	2	W. R. Gichard ...... ditto	3 C. Scudamore Longden	ditto
1	0	4	R. P. Jones .... ditto	2 Wm. Alex. Middleton	ditto
1	0	8	F. B. Ward .... ditto		
1	0	1	J. J. Brandling ...... ditto		
1	0	9	J. Inglis Macartney.. ditto		

FIELD TRAIN DEPARTMENT.

Director General of Artillery. . 🎖🎖 Maj.-Gen. *Sir* A. Dickson, GCB.KCH. 15 Mar. 38.
Commissary . . . . William Young, 28 Jan. 33.

Deputy Adjutant-General.
Major-Gen.—🎖🎖 *Sir* A. Dickson, G.C.B.
 & K.C.H. 10 April, 27.

Assistant Adjutant-General.
Lieut.-Col.—J. E. Jones, 19th Jan. 18.

Adjutants.
H. B. 2nd Capt.—🎖 Hen. Pester, 28 Dec. 32.
I. A. 2nd Lt.—🎖🎖 J. Wightman, 30 Aug. 34.
7 2nd Capt—T. A. Lethbridge, 22 Jan. 37.
4 2nd Capt.—J. Somerville, 22 Jan. 37.
3 2nd Capt.—F. A. Griffiths, 22 Jan. 37.
2 2nd Capt.—R. Basset, 22 Jan. 37.
9 2nd Capt.—J. M. Savage, 27 July, 37.
1 2nd Capt.—Wm. Furneaux, 14 Mar. 38.
8 2nd Capt.—C. W. Wingfield, 23 Sept. 38

Quarter-Masters.
7 Samuel Barnes, 1 Feb. 08.
4 William Gates, 15 Nov. 09.
1 George Landels, 1 July, 25.
5 Alexander Barker, 27 April, 26.
2 A. Fortune, 26 July, 27.
3 William Matthews, 25 July, 31.
6 James Fife, 10 Sept. 32.

8 William Porter, 25 Sept. 32.
9 Thomas Hendley, 23 Jan. 34.
H. B. J. Alexander, 26 Aug. 36.

Veterinary Surgeons.
Charles Percivall, 23 April, 18.
James Burt, 1 June, 07.
William Stockley, 24 April, 05.

Chaplains.
Matthew R. Scott, 10 April, 37.
George Baily Tuson, B.D. 1 April, 39.

Company of Gentlemen Cadets.
Captain.—The Master-Gen. of the Ordnance.
2nd Capt.—🎖🎖 Richard Beaumont Burnaby,
 9 Sept. 34.
1st Lieut.—Ashton Ashton Shuttleworth, 8
 Nov. 27.
1st Lt.—Cha. Herrick Burnaby, 14 Nov. 27.

Riding-House Establishment.
Lieut. Col.—Richard Jones, 31 Dec. 28.
1st Lieut.—Henry Philips, 31 July, 35. ;
Cornet 7th Hussars, 25 March 28.
1st Lieut.—Alexander M'Pherson, 1 Jan. 36.

COMMANDING OFFICERS OF ARTILLERY AND ENGINEERS AT HOME AND ON FOREIGN STATIONS.

GREAT BRITAIN.

	Artillery.		Engineers.	
			Lt.-Col. *Sir* J.M.F.Smith,*KH. London*	
			——— Moody . . . . *Waltham Abbey*	
Northern . . .	🎖🎖Col. *Sir* H. D. Ross, *KCB. Carlisle*		Captain Tait . . . . . *Newcastle*	
Eastern			Lieut.-Colonel Tylden . . *Harwich*	
Kent	Lt.-Gen. *Rt. Hon. Lord* ⎫ *Woolwich*		Captain Rutherford . . *Chatham*	
	Bloomfield, *GCB* & *GCH.* ⎭		🎖 Colonel Harding, *CB.*. *Woolwich*	
	Colonel Munro, *KH.* . . . *Dover*		🎖 Lieut.-Col. Thomson . *Dover*	
			Captain Smyth . . . . *Exeter*	
			🎖 Major Barry . . . . *Birmingham*	
			🎖 Major Rivers . . . . *Manchester*	
			🎖 Major Victor . . . . *Hull*	
Sussex				
South West . .	Colonel Forbes . . . . *Portsmouth* ⎫		Colonel Arnold, *KH.*	
Western	. . . . *Devonport* ⎭		🎖🎖 Col. *Sir* Geo. Cha. Hoste, *CB.*	
Jersey . . .	🎖🎖 Major Sinclair . . — —		Lieut.-Col. English	
Guernsey . . .	🎖 Captain Slade . . . — —		Lieut.-Colonel Calder	
North Britain .	Lieut.-Col. Gordon . . *Leith Fort*		🎖 ——— Blanshard, *CB.*	

IRELAND.

	🎖🎖Col. J. Webber Smith, *CB. Dublin*		🎖 Lt.-Col. Holloway, *CB. Dublin*	
Limerick . . .	🎖 Lieut.-Col. J. Michell, *CB.Limerick*			
Leinster	——— Cobbe . . *Island Bridge*		🎖 Major Marshall . . . *Leinster*	
Ulster	🎖 ——— Hunt . . *Charlemont*		Lieut.-Colonel Gordon . *Ulster Dist.*	
Munster . . .	Colonel Oliver . . . *Ballincollig*		🎖 ——— Slade . . *Munster*	
Connaught . .	🎖 ——— Birch . . . . *Athlone*		——— Walker . . *Connaught*	
Pigeon-house Fort	🎖 Lieut.-Colonel Arabin . *Dublin*			

FOREIGN STATIONS.

Gibraltar . . .	🎖🎖 Lieut.-Col. Browne .		🎖 Colonel *Sir* Cha. F. Smith, *CB.*	
Malta	——— Bastard . .	—	—	———Cardew
Ionian Islands .	🎖 🎖🎖 ——— Hutchesson .	—	—	Lieut.-Colonel Brown
West Indies . .	——— Grant . .	—	—	Major Fenwick
Jamaica . . .	🎖🎖 ——— Redyerd .	—	—	Major Gosset
Canada	Colonel F. Campbell . .			
Quebec . . .	Lieut.-Colonel Kirby. . .	—	—	⎱ 🎖🎖 Colonel Oldfield, *KH.*
Upper Canada .	——— Cubitt . .	—	—	
Nova Scotia . .	🎖🎖 ——— Mercer . .	—	—	🎖 Lieut.-Colonel Jones, *KH.*
Newfoundland .	Major Fraser	—	—	Lieut. Lloyd
Bermuda . . .	Lieut.-Colonel Bridge . .	—	—	🎖 Lieut.-Col. Emmett
St. Helena . .	🎖 ——— Trelawny . .	—	—	🎖 Capt. Alexander
Cape of Good Hope	🎖 ——— Brandreth, *CB.*.	—	—	🎖 Colonel Lewis, *CB.*
Ceylon . . .	🎖 Col. W. G. Power, *CB.KH.*	—	—	Lieut.-Colonel Dixon
Mauritius . . .	——— Jas. Power . . .	—	—	🎖 Colonel Fyers
Bahamas . . .	Lieut. Hornby	—	—	Capt. Budgen
Van Diemen's Land		—	—	Major Kelsall
New South Wales		—	—	🎖 ——— Barney

Paymasters to the Ordnance Department, Messrs. Cox & Co.

Notes to the Royal Artillery.

2 General Shrapnel served with the Duke of York's army in Flanders, and at the siege of Dunkirk.

3 General Wulff served at the siege of Fort St. Philip in Minorca in 1791 and 2; in the West Indies in 96, and proceeded from thence to Quebec, where he remained until 10th Sept. following, when he embarked to join his company in the West Indies. Volunteered his services with the expedition to the Helder in 1799, under Sir Ralph Abercromby, and served with that army until it returned to England.

4 Sir Wiltshire Wilson was present at the following sieges, actions, &c.—Valenciennes, Dunkirk, and Nieuport in 1793; Tournay and Nieuport in 1794; Quiberon Bay in 1795; Ostend in 1798; Capture of St. Lucie, and Tobago in 1803; and Surinam in 1804.

6 General Pritchard was present at the siege and surrender of Fort Bourbon, Martinique, in 1794, and was wounded by the bursting of a shell; was at Bass Terre, Guadaloupe, on the Republican troops regaining possession of the islands; at Morne, Mascot, when attacked.

7 General Beevor served in Flanders in 1793, 4 and 5; in Egypt in 1801 and 2; in Spain under Sir David Baird in 1808 and 9. Medal for services in Egypt.

8 Sir James Viney has received a medal and one clasp for Roleia and Vimiera, and Corunna.

9 Sir Alexander Dickson was at the capture of Minorca in 1798; blockade of Malta and surrender of La Valetta 1800; siege and capture of Monte Video, and attack on Buenos Ayres 1807; served throughout the campaigns of the Peninsula, France, and Flanders, including in 1809, the affair at Grigo, capture of Oporto, and expulsion of Marshal Soult from Portugal; in 1810, battle of Busaco and Lines of Lisbon; in 1811, affair at Campo Mayor, siege and capture of Olivença, first and second siege of Badajoz, and battle of Albuhera; in 1812, siege and capture of Ciudad Rodrigo, siege and capture of Badajoz, attack and capture of the forts at Almarez, siege and capture of the Forts, and battle of Salamanca, capture of the Retiro, Madrid, and siege of Burgos; in 1813, battle of Vittoria, siege and capture of St. Sebastian, Passage of the Bidassoa, battles of the Nivelle, and Nive; in 1814 passage of the Adour, and battle of Toulouse; served in the last American war, including the attack on New Orleans, and siege and capture of Fort Bowyer Mobile; present in the battles of Quatre Bras and Waterloo; commanded battering train in aid of the Prussian army in the sieges of Mauberg, Landrecies, Phillippeville, Marienberg, and Rocroy. Sir Alexander has received a cross and six clasps.

10 Sir J. H. Carncross served in the West Indies from 1797 to 1801; at Walcheren, 1809; and in the Peninsula and France, from 1811 to 14, including the battles of Salamanca, (siege of Burgos), Vittoria, Pyrenees, Nivelle, Nive, Orthes, and Toulouse; medal for Salamanca, and a cross and two clasps for the other actions.

11 General Watson served in Flanders in 1793, 4, and 5, including battles of St. Amand, Famars, siege of Valenciennes, battle of Lincelles, attack of Dunkirk, Lambric, Lannoy, Roubaix, Mouveaux, &c.; present in the actions of the 20th Sept. 2nd and 6th Oct. 1799 at the Helder; Battle of the Blue Bergh, and capture of Cape of Good Hope in 1806; attack and capture of Maldonado; capture of Monte Video, and attack on Buenos Ayres.

12 Sir Thomas Downman served in Flanders in 1793 and 4, including actions at Cateau, Lannoy, Roubaix, and was taken prisoner 18 May, 94; commanded a troop of horse artillery during the Corunna campaign; served in the Peninsula from Sept. 1810 to May 1813, including siege of Ciudad Rodrigo, and battle of Salamanca; medal for Salamanca.

13 General Evelegh served the Corunna Campaign.

14 General Fyers served the campaigns of 1794 and 5, in Holland; employed on the French coasts in mortar-ships, during 1796, 7, and 8; served two expeditions to the Baltic, and accompanied Lord Nelson to Revel, in Russia, and to attack the flotilla at Boulogne in 1801, (wounded); present at Copenhagen in 1807, and at the siege of Flushing; served the campaigns of 1813 and 14, in the Netherlands, including the attack on Bergen-op-Zoom.

Notes to the Royal Artillery.

15 General Hon. W. H. Gardner accompanied the expedition to Walcheren, and was present at the siege and capture of Flushing.

16 General Walker served on the Continent in 1794 and 5, and received three wounds in the retirement of the army across the Rhine near Arnheim, viz. one severely through the right arm below the elbow; the others above the elbow, and in the right hip.

17

18 General Drummond was present at the siege of Copenhagen in 1807; capture of the island of Walcheren, and siege of Flushing; battle of Waterloo.

19 Sir John May was employed afloat in bomb service from 1st Dec. 1797 to 16th April, 1801; present at Copenhagen in 1807. Served in the Peninsula and France from 18th Jan. 1809 to 26th June, 1814, including battles of Talavera, Busaco, Fuentes d'Onor, sieges of Ciudad Rodrigo, and Badajoz; siege of Forts at and battle of Salamanca; battle of Vittoria; siege of San Sebastian; passages of Bidassoa, Nivelle, and Nive; battle of Toulouse, and various skirmishes; present at Quatre Bras and Waterloo, and capture of Paris. Sir John received two musket-balls through the left thigh when charging the French rear guard on the morning after the battle of Salamanca, and a violent contusion at Vittoria; medal and three clasps.

20 Col. Pym served in Flanders in 1795 and 96; expedition to the Texel, 1797; expedition to Naples, 1805; battle of Maida, sieges of Scylla and Reggio in Calabria, and siege of Gaita, 1806; commanded Artillery in the expedition to Egypt in 1807; capture of Ischia and Procida, 1809; sieges and capture of Spezzia, Genoa, and Savona, 1814.

21 Col. Brough was at the captures of St. Lucia in 1796, and Guadaloupe in 1810.

22 Col. Bredin was at the capture of Grenada, St. Vincent, and St. Lucia, under Sir Ralph Abercrombie, and has served in the Peninsula.

23 Col. Younghusband served in St. Domingo in 1795, and at the siege of Flushing in 1809.

24 Col. Crawford was at the capture of Surinam in 1799, and Swedish and Danish islands in 1801, St. Lucia and Surinam in 1803. Served the whole of the Corunna campaign, and in the last American war.

25 Col. Smith was at the attack of Minorca in 1798; siege of Malta, 1800; defence of Porto Ferrajo, 1802; expedition to Walcheren, and siege of Flushing; served the campaigns of 1813, 14, and 15, including battle of Vittoria, passage of Bidassoa, Nive, siege of St. Sebastian, and battle of Waterloo. Medal and one clasp.

28 Col. Munro served the Egyptian campaign of 1801, including the action of 21st March, and siege of Aboukir; expedition to Walcheren, and siege of Flushing; in action at New Orleans, 23rd Dec. 1814, 1st and 8th Jan. 1815. Medal for services in Egypt.

29 Col. Cockburn was at the capture of the Cape of Good Hope in 1795; expedition to Manilla; capture of Copenhagen in 1807.

30 Sir H. D. Ross served in the Peninsula and France from 9th June, 1809 to Feb. 1814, including action at Coa, battle of Busaco, actions of Pombal and Redhina (wounded in the shoulder); Cayal Nova and Foz d'Oronces, (wounded in the leg); Sabugal, Fuentes d'Onor, Aldea Ponte, sieges of Ciudad Rodrigo and Badajoz, (dangerously wounded in the head); capture of forts at Salamanca, action at Castrajon, battle of Salamanca, capture of Madrid and Retiro, affair of San Munoz and St. Milan, battle of Vittoria and the Pyrenees, passage of the Bidassoa, Nivelle, and Nive, battle near Bayonne, 13 Dec. 1813; battle of Waterloo, 17th and 18th June, 1815. Cross and six clasps.

31 Col. Birch served in Ireland during the Rebellion of 1798; expedition to Walcheren; in the Peninsula, at Cadiz, and Seville, under Lord Lynedoch and Sir George Cook in 1810, 11, 12, and 13.

32 Col. Armstrong was at the capture of St. Lucia and Tobago in 1803; Surinam in 1804; and at St. Domingo in 1809.

33 Col. Paterson was at Copenhagen in 1807; and at Walcheren in 1809.

34 Col. Oliver served the Egyptian campaign of 1801, including the landing, 8th March, and battles of 13th and 21st March. Present at the siege of Flushing. Medal for services in Egypt.

35 Col. Lacy served in Holland in 1799, and in Spain and France, in 1812, 13, and 14, including the action at Castalla, the two sieges of Tarragona, and investment of Bayonne.

36 Col. Campbell served the Egyptian campaign of 1801, including the actions of the 8th, 13th, and 21st March; capture of Rosetta; several affairs on the march to, and capture of Cairo; capture of Alexandria. Medal for services in Egypt.

37 Col. Turner was at the capture of the Cape of Good Hope in 1806. Medal and one clasp for Orthes and Toulouse, and was also present at the affair of Tarbes.

38 Colonel Cleaveland served the Kandian campaign in which the king and his territory were captured.

Notes to the Royal Artillery.

39 Sir Robert Gardiner was at the capture of Minorca in 1798. Present at the battles of Roliea and Vimiera; battle of Corunna; expedition to Walcheren; battle of Barrosa; capture of Badajoz; battle of Salamanca; siege of Burgos; affair of Morales; battles of Vittoria, Orthes, Toulouse, and Waterloo. Cross and two clasps.

40 Colonel Wallace was on board the *Phœnix* Letter of Marque when she beat off a French Privateer near Barbadoes in Dec. 1800. Present at the siege of Flushing in 1809, and at the attack of Sucketts Harbour, United States, in 1813.

41 Colonel Richard Jones served in Holland in 1799, including the battles of Zuyp, Hoorn, Egmont, and Limmen. Present at the capture of Paris, and with the army of occupation until 2nd Dec. 1818.

42 Colonel John Edward Jones was employed afloat on board the bombs in 1801 and 02; commanded the artillery on board the *Volcano* bomb, and was present at the bombardment of Cronenburgh Castle, battle of Copenhagen, and bombardments of Boulogne under Lord Nelson.

43 Colonel Brandreth was at the siege of Malta in 1800; bombardment of Havre-de-Grace, 1803; Corunna campaign; expedition to Walcheren, and siege of Flushing; served the campaigns of 1812, 13, and 14, including the battles of the Pyrenees, Nivelle, and Toulouse. Medal and one clasp.

44 Colonel Story was at the blockade and capture of Malta in 1800; capture of the Danish Islands St. Croix and St. Thomas; bombardment and capture of Fort Dessaix, Martinique, Feb. 09; capture of Guadaloupe, Feb. 1810.

45 Colonel Hutchesson served in Holland in 1799; in the Peninsula and South of France from March 1813 to July 1814; Belgium and France from May 1815 to Nov. 1818, including the battle of Waterloo.

46 Colonel Whinyates served in the expedition to the Helder and campaign in North Holland in 1799; expedition to Madeira in 1801; Copenhagen 1807; Peninsula from Feb. 1810 to July 1813, including the battles of Busaco and Albuhera; affairs at Usagre, Aldea de Ponte, San Munos, attack and defeat of General Lalleman's cavalry at Ribera, and many other affairs. Severely wounded in the left arm at Waterloo.

47 Colonel John Michell served the campaign in Holland in 1799; in the Peninsula and South of France from Aug. 1813 to May 1814, including siege of San Sebastian, passage of the Bidassoa, Nivelle, and Nive, battles of Orthes, and Toulouse; in America from May 1814 to May 1815, including the attack of Washington and Baltimore, New Orleans, and other operations on the coast. Attached to the Prussian army in reducing the fortresses in the Netherlands. Medal and one clasp.

48 Colonel Trelawny served in Holland in 1799; in the Peninsula and South of France from Nov. 1813 to June 1814, including the passage of the Adour.

49 Colonel Hunt served in Ireland during the rebellion in 1798; at Cadiz from Feb. 1810 to Feb. 1812; in Belgium and France from 1814 to 1818, including the operations against the enemy in connection with the battle of Waterloo.

50 Colonel Nicolls served the Egyptian campaign of 1801, including the battles of the 8th, 13th, and 21st March: siege of Fort St. Julian, investment of Giza and Alexandria, received a contusion in the thigh from a cannon shot on the 13th March. Present at the storming of Buenos Ayres, July 1807; and at the siege of Flushing. Medal for services in Egypt.

51 Colonel Cobbe served the campaign in the West Indies in 1801, under Lieut.-Gen. Sir Thos. Trigge.

52 Colonel Mercer served in South America in 1807 and 8. Present at Quatre Bras and Waterloo.

53 Colonel W. G. Power served in Spain, Portugal, and France, from 14th Oct. 1808 to 4th June 1814, including battle of Talavera; sieges of Ciudad Rodrigo (wounded), and Badajoz, capture of French works at Almazaby: reduction of forts at, and battle of, Salamanca; siege of Burgos (wounded); siege of San Sebastian 11th July to 8th Sept. 1813; passage of the Bidassoa, Nive, and Adour.

54 Colonel Cubitt was at the battle of Maida, and siege of Scylla in 1806. Expedition to Walcheren 1809.

55 Colonel Bridge served the campaign on the Niagara Frontier, and on the North-West side of Lake Ontario, and Burlington Heights in Upper Canada, between Jan. 1813 and Aug. 1814. Wounded 7th May 1813. Permitted to wear the word "Niagara" on appointments.

56 Colonel Brown served at Walcheren in 1809. Present at Waterloo and Cambray.

57 Colonel Grant served in Hanover in 1805 under Lord Cathcart.

58 Colonel Scott served in the expedition to Walcheren, and was at the siege of Flushing.

Notes to the Royal Artillery.

59 Colonel Dyneley served the campaign of 1805 in Italy; present at the battle of Maida, and siege of Scylla, in 1806. Served in the Peninsula from July, 1811, to November, 1813, including siege of Ciudad Rodrigo (wounded in the head); siege of forts at Salamanca (wounded in the face); heights of St. Christovel; battles of Salamanca, Vittoria, and the Pyrenees, besides affairs of out-posts. Engaged at Waterloo.

60 Colonel Parker served at Walcheren, and was present at the siege of Flushing. Served in the Peninsula and South of France from February, 1812, to April, 1814; including the battle of Vittoria; both sieges of San Sebastian; battle of Orthes; affair at Tarbes and battle of Toulouse. Lost left leg at Waterloo. Medal for Vittoria.

61 Colonel Darby served in Hanover in 1805, and at the siege of Copenhagen in 1807, and the Corunna campaign.

62 Colonel Walcott served the Corunna campaign. Present at Waterloo.

63 Colonel Rudyerd served in bomb vessels on the coast of France in 1804. Present in two battles, and the capture of a fortress in the Travancore war, East Indies. Present at Quatre Bras and Waterloo.

64 Colonel Cator served campaign of Walcheren and siege of Flushing. In the Peninsula and South of France, from 1809 to 1814, including the siege of Cadiz; lines at Torres Vedras and at Santarem; battle of Barrosa (wounded); affair at Osma; battle of Vittoria; affair at Tolosa; passage of the Bidassoa, Nivelle, and Nive; at four days' engagements in front of Bayonne.

65 Colonel Dansey was at the sieges of Ischia, and Santa Maura. His services in the Peninsula, and France, and Flanders, include the following battles and sieges, viz :—Badajoz, Salamanca, Burgos (severely wounded), Vittoria, San Sebastian, Nivelle, Nive, besides various actions and skirmishes. Engaged 17th and 18th June at Waterloo, severely wounded on the 18th.

66 Colonel Crawford served in the lines in front of Sobral, Portugal, in 1809; was at the capture of Genoa in 1814; served in the last American War, including the taking of Washington, and engagements before New Orleans.

67 Colonel Gordon accompanied the expedition to Naples, December, 1805, and occupation of Sicily. Present at the battle of Maida, and attack and surrender of the Rock of Scylla in 1806.

68 Sir Wm. Colebrooke's services.—Campaigns of 1809 and 10, in India; expedition to Java in 1811, including the action of Weltyvreden; in batteries before Cornelis until wounded (in the groin) 22d August ; and the siege and capture of Jokjakarta. Expedition to Palemburg, in Sumatra, 1813; campaign of 1817 and 18, in India, against the Pindaries and Mahrattas: campaign of 1818 and 19 in Southern India. Present at sieges of Ras-el-Kyhman and Zaya, Arab fortresses.

69 Colonel King served in a Mortar-Boat in the Faro of Messina, for two months in 1810. Advanced into the United States with Sir George Prevost's army, and commanded a battery against Plattsburgh.

70 Colonel W. D. Jones served in the expedition to Naples in 1805; present at the attack and capture of Reggio Castle, in Calabria, in 1806; expedition to Egypt in 1807 ; in charge of the division of Mortar-Boats in the Faro of Messina in 1810.

71 Colonel Dundas was at the siege of Flushing in 1809; at Cadiz in 1810 and 11; detached from Cadiz to Tarragona in 1811; wounded in right ankle at Ciudad Rodrigo, and most severely and dangerously at Badajoz,—left arm amputated, left thigh dislocated, and hip bone shattered.

72 Colonel Arabin was present in the action after the troops effected a landing at Martinique, also at the siege of Fort Bourbon. Served in the Peninsula and France, from March, 1812, to Aug. 1814, including the battles of Biar and Castalla; siege and capture of Fort San Felipe; and battle of Ordal.

73 Colonel E. T. Michell was detached from Gibraltar in 1810, and commanded a Guerrilla division in the Serrania de Ronda ; present at the capture of Ronda, combats of El Brosque and of Bornos, night attack and capture of Arcos. Commanded the Artillery with the force occupying Tarifa in 1810, 1811, and 1812 ; engaged in all the affairs and operations at Tarifa, Vejer, Casas Viejas, Alcalà and Medina Sidonia; battle of Barrosa (shot through the shoulder) and final defence of Tarifa against Marshal Victor. In 1812 present at the assault and capture of forts at, and battle of Salamanca, combat of Castrejon, and many affairs of out-posts. Served in the Netherlands from December, 1813, to May, 1814, at the capture of Merxem, investment and bombardment of Antwerp, and in the night-attack on Bergen-op-Zoom, conducted one of the columns, and was severely wounded in several places.

74 Colonel Cruttenden was at the capture of Guadaloupe, in 1815; commanded the *Emma* troop ship when attacked by the *Nonsuch* American privateer, in the West Indies, which he beat off with great loss.

Notes to the Royal Artillery.

75 Colonel Faddy, prior to entering the Royal Artillery, was a midshipman on board the *Asia*, at the capture of the Dutch Fleet in Saldana Bay in 1795; present at the attack on Fort Jerome, St. Domingo, and at the siege and capture of the City of Santo Domingo in 1809; served in the Peninsula and France from July 1810 to June 1814, including the siege of San Sebastian; passage of the Adour, investment of, and sortie at, Bayonne, besides many affairs of out-posts.

76 Colonel Wylde served in Holland in 1813 and 14, and commanded a battery before Antwerp and at Bergen-op-Zoom.

77 Major Gordon served in the Peninsula and France from May 1813 to the end of the war, including sieges of Cadiz and San Sebastian, passage of Bidassoa, and Nivelle; actions in front of Bayonne (10th to 13th Dec.), battle of Orthes, occupation of Bourdeaux, and subsequent affairs on the Dordoyne and investment of the fortress of Blaye.

78 Major Walker was at the capture of Flushing in 1809; present in the campaigns on the Frontier of Niagara in 1813 and 14.

79 Colonel Maclachlan served in Spain in 1813 and 14; Brevet.-Lieut.-Col. 1 June, 32.

80 Major Blachley served in the Peninsula from July, 1809, to Dec. 1812, including battles of Busaco, Fuentes D'Onor, Salamanca, and siege of Burgos.

81 Colonel Macdonald was at the capture of the Cape of Good Hope in 1806, and proceeded from thence on the expedition to Buenos Ayres, where he was twice severely wounded and taken prisoner; served in the Peninsula and France, from June, 1809, to July, 1814, including the battles of Coa and Busaco; affairs of Redinha, Pombal, Condelia, and Fos de Roos; battles of Fuentes d'Onor, and Salamanca; affair of San Munos; battle of Vittoria; siege of San Sebastian; battles of the Pyrenees; affairs of the Gave Doltoron, and of Ayres; battle of Toulouse; severely wounded at Waterloo; Brevet-Lieut.-Col, 21 June, 17; Brevet-Colonel, 10 Jan. 37.

82 Major Moor served in the Peninsula from June, 1809, to June 1813, including battles of Busaco, Fuentes d'Onor, and Salamanca; sieges of Ciudad Rodrigo, and Badajoz; engaged at Castrajon, and twelve other affairs with the enemy.

83 Colonel Jackson served in Canada from April, 1813, to Aug. 1815, including Chrystler's Farm, and Plattsburgh; medal for the former. Brevet Lieut.-Col. 16 Aug. 39.

84 Major Sabine served the campaign on the Niagara Frontier in 1814, and commanded the batteries at the siege of Fort Eric.

85 Major Dunn served the campaign of 1805, in Italy; present at the battle of Maida, and capture of Scylla Castle in 1806; expedition to Egypt in 1807, including attack of Alexandria, Rosetta, &c.; battle of El Hamet, and taken prisoner; defence of Scylla Castle in 1808; served in the Peninsula in 1810 and 11, including siege of Ciudad Rodrigo; battles of the Coa, Busaco, Albuhera, and many other affairs; severely wounded in the groin by a musket-ball at Aldea de Ponte, 27 Dec. 1811; served in America in 1814, including the taking of Moos Island.

86 Major Bayley was at the battle of Maida, and siege of Scylla, in 1806; expedition to Egypt, and capture of Alexandria and Rosetta, in 1807; capture of Ischia in 1809; attack on an armed ship and gun-boats in the Bay of Scylla in 1810.

87 Major Cruttenden served the campaigns of 1813, 14, and 15, in Upper Canada, including attack and reduction of Oswego.

88 Major Sinclair served with the expedition to Zealand in 1807; expedition to Portugal, and battle of Corunna; expedition to the Scheldt; served in the Peninsula and France from Feb. 1811, to Aug. 1814, including the assault on Badajos in 1812; battles of Salamanca, Vittoria, and the Pyrenees; passage of the Bidassoa, Nivelle, and Nive; sortie from Bayonne, besides many other affairs; present at Waterloo.

89 Major Gray was at the capture of the Cape of Good Hope in 1806.

90 Major Fogo served in America during the whole war, including the battle of Platsburgh.

91 Major the Hon. W. Arbuthnot was present at the passage of the Douro, and the battles of Oporto, Talavera, and Busaco.

92 Major Blachley served in the Peninsula and France from Feb. 1812 to Aug. 1814, including the siege and capture of Badajoz; affair of Castrajon; battle of Salamanca; capture of Madrid, and Retiro; siege of Burgos; affair at Osma; battle of Vittoria; siege and capture of San Sebastian (both operations); passage of the Bidassoa, and the Nivelle; actions of the 9th, 10th, 11th, and 12th Dec. 1813, in front of Bayonne; passage of the Adour; investment of, and sortie from Bayonne; wounded in the head by a musket-ball at the sortie.

93 Major Chalmer served in the expedition to Walcheren, and was at the siege of Flushing.

94 Colonel Macbean was at the siege of Copenhagen in 1807; served the Corunna cam-

Notes to the Royal Artillery.

paign; the expedition to Walcheren, and siege of Flushing; present at Waterloo. Brevet Lieut.-Colonel, 16 Aug. 39.

95 Major Stopford served in South America in 1807 and 8; present at Quatre Bras and Waterloo, (received a contusion) and the capture of Paris.

96 Major Dowse served at Buenos Ayres in 1807.

97 Major Belson served in the Peninsula and France from July 1809 to July 1814, including the actions in front of Almeida; battle of Busaco; actions at Pombal; Redinha; in front of, and the heights of Caza Nova; Foz de Aronce; Sabugal; battle of Fuentes d'Onor; sieges of Ciudad Rodrigo, and Badajoz; battles of Vittoria, and the Pyrenees; passage of the Nivelle, and Nive; battle of Orthes, and many other actions and affairs of out-posts; severely wounded at Castrajon, 18 July, 1812.

98 Major Stewart served in Hanover in 1805, and at the siege of Copenhagen in 1807.

99 Major Molesworth served at the siege of Copenhagen in 1807.

100 Brevet-Lieut.-Colonel, 27 April, 1838.

101 Major Bell was at capture of the islands of St. Thomas and St. Croix in 1807; siege of fort Desaix, Martinique; capture of Les Saintes, near Guadaloupe; and bombardment and driving from the anchorage the French fleet in 1809; capture of Guadaloupe and adjacent islands in 1810. Served in the Peninsula and France from July 1813 to July 1814, including the passage of the Bidassoa, Nivelle, Nive, and four days' engagements near Bayonne; passage of the Adour, and investment of Bayonne; affairs at Vic Bigorre, and Tarbes; passage of the Garonne, and subsequent operations; battle of Toulouse (wounded); present at Quatre Bras and Waterloo, and capture of Paris.

102 Major Louis served in the Peninsula and France from Jan. 1813 to June 1814, including the battle of Vittoria, siege of San Sebastian; passage of the Nivelle, and Nive, and investment of Bayonne; present at Waterloo.

103 Major Grantham served at the siege of Cadiz.

104 Major Gordon was at the capture of the Danish Islands, St. Thomas and Santa Cruz in 1807; capture of Martinique and siege of Fort Bourbon; capture of Les Saintes in 1809; and capture of Guadaloupe in 1810.

105 Colonel Brereton served in the Peninsula, France, and Flanders, from December, 1809 to June, 1815, including the sieges of Cadiz, Matagorda (wounded), and San Sebastian; battles of Barrosa (wounded), Vittoria, the Pyrenees, Orthes, Toulouse, Quartre Bras, and Waterloo (severely wounded); besides the actions on retreat from Burgos, at San Munos, near Salamanca, Helette, St. Palais, Suaveterre, Aire, and Tarbes. Brevet-Lieut.-Col. 10th Jan. 37.

106 Major England served the expedition to the Weser in 1805 and 6; to the Cape of Good Hope and South America in 1806 and 7; campaign of 1813 in the Peninsula, including the battle of Vittoria and siege of San Sebastian.

107 Major Whitty was present at the reduction of the Danish Islands in the West Indies in 1807; capture of Guadaloupe in 1810, and of Paris in 1815.

108 Major Sweeting served the Candian campaign in Ceylon.

109 Major Wright was at the capture of Madeira, and served the Corunna campaign served with army of occupation in France.

110 Major Wood served in the Peninsula and France, from Feb. 1813 to the end of the war, including battle of Vittoria; blockade of Pampluna; battles of the Pyrenees; siege of San Sebastian; battle of the Nivelle; affairs of Vic Bigorre and Tarbes; battles of Orthes and Toulouse. Served the campaign in America, including attack on Plattsburgh.

111 Major Heron served at Scylla in Calabria, and expedition from Sicily in 1807; capture of Martinique, sieges of Pigeon Island and Fort Bourbon, 1810; served in the Peninsula and France from 30th May, 1812 to 8th Aug. 1814, including the affair at Osma; battle of Vittoria (wounded); both sieges of San Sebastian and storming of the town; passage of the Bidassoa, Nivelle, and Nive; actions on the 10th, 11th, and 12th Dec. 1813; in front of, and sortie from, Bayonne, April, 1814.

114 Major Dalton served at Walcheren, and was present at the siege of Flushing.

115 Major Colebrooke served the Walcheren campaign.

116 Major Raynes was at the siege of Copenhagen in 1807; served the Corunna campaign; expedition to Cadiz in 1810; battle of Barrosa; siege of Tariffa; action at Seville; battles of Vittoria, Pyrenees, and Nivelle; passage of the Adour, and operations before Bayonne.

117 Major Hardinge served in the Peninsula and France from 12th Aug. 1812, to 25 June 1814, including the battle of Vittoria; siege of San Sebastian; battles of Orthes and Toulouse. Present at Ligny, Quatre Bras, and Waterloo.

118 Major Sheppard served at Walcheren in 1809, and in Canada from March 1814 to Dec. 1816, including actions at Chippawa, and Lundy's Lane, before Fort Erie, and the attack on Snake Hill.

Notes to the Royal Artillery.

119 Major Lock was present at the battles of Roleia and Vimiera.

120 Major Sandilands served the Walcheren campaign. Present at Quatre Bras and Waterloo.

121 Major Wright was at the siege of Copenhagen in 1807. Served the campaign of 1813 and 14 in Germany under the orders of the Prince Royal of Sweden, and was present at the siege of Wittemberg, capture of Hanover and Lubeck, siege of Frederick Fort, and siege and surrender of Gluckstadt. Present on the 17th and 18th June at Waterloo. Medal for the siege of Gluckstadt.

122 Captain Strangways served the campaign of 1813 and 14 in Germany, including the battle of Gourd 16th Sept. and Leipsic 16th, 18th, and 19th Oct. 1813, for which the Swedish order of the sword was conferred on him, he having commanded the Rocket Troop after the death of Major Bogue killed in action. Present on the 16th and 18th June at Waterloo, where he was wounded.

123 Captain Eyre served the Corunna campaign.

124 Captain Elgee served in the Peninsula and France from Feb. 1809 to May 1814, including battles of Talavera and Fuentes d'Onor; siege of Burgos (contused wound in the leg); and investment of Bayonne.

125 Captain Anderson was at the siege and capture of Flushing and the subsequent operations in 1809. Bombardment of Antwerp, also previous and subsequent operations. Present at Waterloo and capture of Cambray and Paris.

126 Captain Manners served in the Peninsula from Feb. 1810 to Dec. 1813, including the battle of Barrosa (wounded); sieges of Tarifa and Cadiz.

127 Captain Schalch was at the capture of Guadaloupe in 1815.

128 Captain Armstrong served at Walcheren in 1809, and in Canada from May 1810 to July 1815, and was present in most of the engagements, &c. including the capture of Fort Niagara. Slightly wounded at Fort George, 27th May 1813.

130 Captain Evans served at Walcheren.

131 Captain Pascoe served in the Peninsula and France from Aug. 1809 to Feb. 1814, including the battles of Salamanca, Vittoria, Nivelle, Nive, passage of the Bidassoa, and other operations; sieges of Badajoz, Forts of Salamanca, Burgos, and San Sebastian. Army of occupation from 1815 to 1818.

132 Captain Spiller served at Walcheren, and was present at the siege of Flushing, and the attack and capture of Ter Vere.

133 Major Colquhoun served in Spain from 1812 until the close of the war. Brevet-Major 2nd Dec. 36.

134 Captain Harrison served in the Peninsula from Jan. 1810 to Sept. 1814, and was present at Cadiz, Isla, and Tariffa.

135 Captain Charlton served in the Canadas from 1811 to 1815, and was present in three general actions, one siege, several skirmishes, and at the storming of two forts. Received a contusion at the storming of Fort Erie.

136 Captain Kendall served at Walcheren in 1809. Present at the taking of Kandyan Provinces in 1815, and the subsequent operations there in 1817 and 18.

137 Captain Wright served at Cadiz during 1810, 11, and 12, and was at Fort Matagorda and Tariffa.

138 Captain Bridges served at Walcheren in 1809, and in the Peninsula and France from July 1811 to Aug. 1814, including the siege of Cadiz in 1811; battles of Vittoria and the Pyrenees; passage of the Bidassoa, Nivelle, Nive, and Adour; and the operations before Bayonne. Attached to the Prussian corps d'armée in 1815, under the command of Prince Augustus of Prussia, and employed in the reduction of Philippeville, Marienbourg and Rocroy. Adjutant to the Royal Artillery, serving with the force employed in Portugal in 1826; and Brigade Major to the Royal Artillery in the Canadas, in 1838.

139 Captain Bent served at Walcheren and at the bombardment of Flushing. Served in the Peninsula from Oct. 1810 to June 1813, including the sieges of Badajoz, battle of Albuhera, capture of General Gerard's corps at Arroga de Molinas, besides many other affairs. Severely wounded at San Munos.

140 Captain Furneaux served in the Peninsula from Oct. 1810 to April 1814, including the siege of Badajoz.

141 Captain Morgan served at Walcheren, and at the bombardment of Flushing. Served in the Peninsula and France from April 1812 to Aug. 1814, including the siege of Cadiz; battles of the Pyrenees; siege of San Sebastian (severely wounded); and battle of Toulouse.

142 Captain Warde was present at the siege of Cadiz and at Waterloo.

143 Captain Ingilby was present at the sieges of Ciudad Rodrigo, Fort of Salamanca

Notes to the Royal Artillery.

(wounded), and Burgos; battles of Busaco, Fuentes d'Onor, and 17th and 18th June at Waterloo.

144 Captain Cater served in the Peninsula from April 1810, including the siege of Cadiz. Present at Waterloo and at the taking of Cambray and Paris.

145 Captain Pester was present at the siege of Cadiz, and at the battle of Barrosa, where he was severely wounded.

146 Captain Stanway served in the Peninsula and France from Feb. 1812 to July 1814, including the siege of San Sebastian; passage of the Bidassoa, and the Adour.

147 Captain Story served in the Peninsula and France from Nov. 1812 to May 1814, including the siege of San Sebastian: passage of the Bidassoa, and the Adour.

148 Captain Slade served in the Peninsula and France from March 1812 to June, 1814, including the battles of Salamanca, the Pyrenees, and Orthes; siege of San Sebastian; passage of the Bidassoa, and Nivelle.

149 Brevet-Major, 11th July, 1837.

150 Captain James served in the Peninsula and France, from October, 1812, to April, 1814, including the battles of Vittoria, the Pyrenees, Nivelle, and Orthes. Served subsequently in the American War.

151 Captain Lawrence served in the Peninsula, from April, 1813, to April, 1814, including the siege of Tarragona.

152 Captain Bloomfield served in the Peninsula and France, from March, 1813, to June, 1814, including the battle of Vittoria, siege of San Sebastian, crossing the Bidassoa; battles of the Nivelle, Nive, Orthes, and Toulouse. Present at Waterloo.

153 Captain Trevor served the campaign of 1814 in Holland. Present at Waterloo and subsequent operations in France.

155 Captain Palliser served in the Peninsula and France, from November, 1812, to May, 1814, including the siege of San Sebastian, and battles of Vittoria, Orthes, and Toulouse. Served subsequently in the American War, including the battles of Bladensburgh, and Baltimore, and operations before New Orleans.

156 Captain Macbean served in the Peninsula and France, from July, 1812, to August, 1814, including the affair at Osma; battle of Vittoria; both sieges and capture of San Sebastian; passage of the Nivelle 10th November, and actions of the Nive, 9th, 10th, 11th, and 12th December, 1813.

157 Captain Gillespie served in the last American War, including the battle at Plattsburgh.

158 Captain Dickens served in Holland in 1813 and 14, including the attack on Merxem, and the cannonade against the enemy's ships of war in the basin.

159 Captain Tomkyns served the campaign of 1814 in Canada, including the actions near Fort George, and Lundy's Lane; blockade, attack, and final assault of Fort Erie. Present when the British lines on the Chippawa were attacked.

160 Captain Williams was engaged in the actions before New Orleans, and at the capture of Fort Boyer. Present at Waterloo and capture of Paris.

161 Captain Morgan served in the Peninsula and France from October, 1813, to June, 1814, including the passage of the Adour, and battle of Toulouse. Served the campaign of 1814 in Canada.

162 Captain R. G. B. Wilson served in Holland, Belgium, and France, from December, 1813, to January, 1816, including the 16th, 17th, and 18th June, at Waterloo.

163 Captain Cuppage served in the Peninsula and France, from February to August, 1814, including the sortie from Bayonne. Present 18th June, at Waterloo.

164 Captain Burnaby served the campaign of 1815, including the battle of Waterloo.

165 Captain Griffin served before Genoa in 1814.

166 Captain Basset was employed in raising the siege of Bilboa, 25th December, 1836. Present in the field actions on the 10th, 12th, 14th, 15th, and 16th March; attack and carrying by assault the town of Hernani, 12th May; and capitulation of the town of Fontarabia, 17th May, 1837.

Corps of Royal Engineers.

The Royal Arms and Supporters, with a Cannon, and the Motto, "*Unique*" over the gun, and "*Quo fas et Gloria ducunt*" below it.

Colonel-in-Chief.— Lieutenant General *Right Hon.* Sir Richard Hussey Vivian, *Bart.* G.C.B. & G.C.H. Master-General of the Ordnance.

Years' Serv. Full Pay.	Half Pay.	Colonels Commandant.	Second Lieut.	First Lieut.	Captain.	Brevet-Major.	Brevet Lt.-Col.	Reg.-Lt. Col.	Brevet-Col.	Regtl.-Colonel	Major-General	Lieut.-General
61	0	*Sir* Sam. Trevor Dickens,[1] K.C.H.	16 June 79	12 Mar. 89	29 Oct. 94	never	never	1 Mar. 05	4 June 13	30 Sept. 14	12 Aug. 19	10 Jan. 37
53	0	*Sir* Augustus De Butts, K.C.H.[1]*	22 Aug. 87	21 Nov. 92	3 Mar. 97	never	never	1 July 06	4 June 14	30 Dec. 14	19 July 21	ditto
52	0	Henry Evatt[2]	11 July 88	16 Jan. 93	29 Aug. 98	never	never	24 June 09	never	11 Nov. 16	27 May 25	28 June 38
42	6 8/12	*Sir* Fred. Wm. Mulcaster, K.C.H.[3]	14 June 92	27 Nov. 93	11 Sept. 98	25 July 10	never	1 May 11	never	7 Feb. 17	ditto	ditto
47	0	*Sir* How. Elphinstone, *Bt.* C.B.[4]	24 Apr. 93	5 Feb. 96	1 July 96	1 Jan. 12	never	21 July 13	never	2 Dec. 24	10 Jan. 37	
		Removed from the Corps, having the Rank of *Major-General*.										
47	0	Elias Walker Durnford[5]	24 Apr. 93	5 Feb. 96	11 Feb. 01	4 June 13	never	21 July 13	never	23 Mar. 25	10 Jan. 37	
47	0	*Sir* George Whitmore, K.C.H.	18 Sept. 93	ditto	28 Feb. 01	ditto	never	ditto	never	ditto	ditto	
42	0	*Sir* John Th. Jones, *Bt.* K.C.B.[6]	30 Aug. 98	14 Sept. 00	1 Mar. 05	6 Feb. 12	27 Apr. 12	11 Nov. 16	27 May 25	never	ditto	
47	0	Fred. Rennell Thackeray, C.B.[7]	18 Sept. 93	18 June 96	18 Apr. 01	19 May 10	never	21 July 13	never	2 June 25	ditto	
47	0	John Francis Birch, C.B.[8]	ditto	20 Nov. 96	ditto	6 May 11	never	ditto	never	29 July 25	ditto	
47	0	*Sir* Ste. R. Chapman, C.B. K.C.H.[8]*		ditto	ditto	30 Sept. 10	26 Apr. 12	ditto	never	ditto	ditto	
46	0	Gustavus Nicolls[9]	6 Nov. 94	3 Mar. 97	30 Mar. 02	4 June 13	never	1 Sept. 13	never	ditto	ditto	
45	0	Cornelius Mann	22 Apr. 95	29 Aug. 98	1 Dec. 02	ditto	never	30 Sept. 14	never	ditto	ditto	
44	0	George Wright[9]*	15 Aug. 96	ditto	3 Apr. 04	4 June 14	never	20 Dec. 14	never	ditto	ditto	
42	0	*Sir* John Fox Burgoyne, K.C.B.[10]	29 Aug. 98	1 July 00	1 Mar. 05	6 Feb. 12	27 Apr. 12	ditto	22 July 30	10 Jan. 37		
		Colonels.										
43	0	Charles Wm. Pasley, C.B.[11]	1 Dec. 97	28 Aug. 99	1 Mar. 05	5 Feb. 12	27 May 13	20 Dec. 14	22 July 30	12 Nov. 31		
42	0	Henry Goldfinch, C.B.[12]	1 Mar. 98	11 June 00	ditto	17 Dec. 12	21 Sept. 13	ditto	ditto	10 Jan. 37		
42	0	Jas. Robertson Arnold, K.H.[13]	ditto	ditto	ditto	never	never	ditto	never	ditto		
40	1 8/12	George Cardew	20 Dec. 98	18 Apr. 01	ditto	never	never	26 Nov. 16	never	ditto		
38	4	*Sir* Wm. Gosset, C.B. & K.C.H.[14]	ditto	ditto	2 Feb. 05	2 Feb. 14	3 Oct. 16	7 Feb. 17	never	ditto		
40	0	Thomas Fyers[14]*	2 May 00	ditto	21 Sept. 05	12 Aug. 19	never	23 Mar. 25	never	ditto		
40	0	Cha. Grene Ellicombe, C.B.[15]	never	1 July 01	1 July 06	27 Apr. 12	21 Sept. 13	ditto	22 July 30	ditto		
40	0	Edward Fanshawe, C.B.[16]	never	ditto	ditto	12 Aug. 19	never	ditto	never	ditto		
39	0	Thomas Cunninghame	2 July 01	30 Mar. 02	24 July 06	ditto	never	9 Apr. 25	never	ditto		
39	0	Thomas Colby	ditto	6 Aug. 02	1 July 07	19 July 21	never	29 July 25	never	ditto		
39	0	*Sir* Cha. Felix Smith, C.B.[17]	ditto	1 Oct. 02	18 Nov. 07	31 Dec. 11	21 Sept. 13	ditto	22 July 30	ditto		

282

Corps of Royal Engineers.

Years' Serv.		LIEUTENANT-COLONELS.	SECOND LIEUT.	FIRST LIEUT.	CAPTAIN.	BREVET-MAJOR.	BREVET-LIEUT. COL.	REGIMENT. LIEUT. COL.	BREVET-COLONEL.
Full Pay.	Half Pay.								
38	0	ⓟ George Judd Harding, C.B.[18]	1 Oct. 02	1 Dec. 02	18 Nov. 07	19 July 21	never	29 July 25	28 June 38
38	0	ⓟⓗ Sir George Chas. Hoste, C. B.[19]	20 Dec. 02	21 Dec. 02	ditto	17 March 14	ditto	ditto	ditto
37	0	John Ross Wright [20]	15 March 03	1 April 03	ditto	19 July 21	ditto	ditto	ditto
37	0	ⓟ Griffith George Lewis, C.B.[21]	1 Jan. 04	2 July 03	ditto	21 Sept. 13	ditto	ditto	
37	0	ⓟ Wm. Cuth. Elph. Holloway, C. B.[22]	1 Feb.	1 March 05	24 June 09	21 June 17	ditto	26 Feb. 28	
37	0	ⓟ Henry William Vavasour [22*]	1 June	ditto	ditto	never	ditto	28 Jan. 29	
36	0	George Graydon, K. H.[23]	1 Nov.	ditto	2 Dec. 09	ditto	ditto	22 May	
36	0	ⓟ Robert Thomson [24]	1 Dec.	ditto	10 July 10	ditto	ditto	26 Dec.	
34	7/12	Sir John Mark Fred. Smith, K. H.[25]	1 Fcb. 05	1 March 06	1 May 11	ditto	ditto	16 March 30	
32	2 9/12	ⓟ Rice Jones, K. H.[26]	1 April 06	1 July	ditto	ditto	ditto	8 June	
32	2 5/12	Thomas Moody [27]	2 ditto	ditto	ditto	23 May 16	ditto	2 Dec.	
29	5 5/12	ⓟⓗ John Oldfield, K. H.[28]	2 ditto	ditto	ditto	22 July 30	ditto	12 Nov. 31	
29	5 10/12	Matthew Charles Dixon [29]	1 Aug.	1 Dec.	ditto	ditto	ditto	25 June 35	
27	7 6/12	Patrick Doul Calder [30]	1 Nov.	1 May 07	13 May	ditto	ditto		
34	0	ⓟ William Henry Slade [31]	19 Nov.	ditto	4 March 12	23 June 14	ditto	10 Jan. 37	
34	0	William Burton Tylden [32]	6 Nov.	ditto	15 April	21 Jan. 19	ditto	ditto	
33	0	ⓟ John Neave Wells, C. B.[33]	4 May	14 July 07	20 May	never	ditto	ditto	
33	0	ⓟ Richard Zachary Mudge [33*]	21 July	1 March 08	21 July 13	ditto	ditto	ditto	
33	0	Archibald Walker	8 Sept.	1 April	ditto	ditto	ditto	ditto	
33	0	ⓟ Frederick English [34]	28 ditto	ditto	ditto	29 Sept. 14	ditto	ditto	
33	0	ⓟ Thomas Blanshard, C. B.[35]	1 Feb. 08	1 Aug.	ditto	never	ditto	ditto	
33	0	Alexander Brown [35*]	16 Feb.	ditto	ditto	5 July 21	ditto	ditto	
33	0	ⓟ Anthony Emmett [36]	10 May	24 June 09	1 Sept.	10 Jan. 37	ditto	9 Dec.	
32	0	ⓟ William Cuthbert Ward [37]	11 July	ditto		ditto	ditto	31 March 38	
32	0	James Gordon [38]							

CAPTAINS.

32	0	ⓟ George Barney [39]	11 July 08	24 June 09	1 Sept. 13	10 Jan. 37			
32	0	*Harry David Jones* [40]	17 Sept.	ditto	12 Nov. 14	ditto			
32	0	Richard Henry Bonnycastle [41]	28 Sept.	ditto	11 Feb.	ditto			
32	0	Anthony Marshall [42]	1 Oct.	1 Aug.	28 Feb.	ditto			
32	0	George Forbes Thompson	ditto	ditto	1 March	ditto			
32	0	Robert Sloper Piper [42*]	10 Jan. 09	1 Dec.	16 May	ditto			
32	0	*Sir George Gipps* [43]	11 Jan.	21 Dec.	30 Sept.	ditto			
32	0	ⓟ Philip Barry [44]	10 Feb.	1 March 10	1 Oct.	ditto			
26	5 7/12	ⓟ William Reid, C. B.[45]	ditto	23 April	20 Dec.	20 March 17	10 Jan. 37		
25	6 7/12	ⓟ William Redman Ord [46]	25 April	29 May	ditto	10 Jan. 37			

Corps of Royal Engineers.

Years' Serv. Full Pay.	Years' Serv. Half Pay.	CAPTAINS.	2ND LIEUT.	1ST LIEUT.	CAPTAIN.	BREV.-MAJ.
25	6	Roger Kelsall	12 July 09	1 May 11	16 June 15	10 Jan. 37
23	8	ᵬ Henry John Savage [47]	30 Sept. 09	ditto	1 Dec. 15	ditto
23	8	ᵬ Mar. A. Waters [48] ..	ditto	ditto	11 Nov. 16	ditto
23	7¹¹⁄₁₂	Pennel Cole	1 Feb. 10	ditto	7 Feb. 17	ditto
26	4	ᵬ Edward Matson [49] ..	7 May	ditto	9 Jan. 21	ditto
27	3⁵⁄₁₂	ᵬ James Conway Victor [50]	1 June	ditto	19 June	ditto
27	3	ᵬ Crighton Grierson [51] ..	ditto	ditto	1 July	ditto
28	1¹¹⁄₁₂	ᵬ Richard John Barou [52]	ditto	ditto	20 Dec. 22	ditto
30	³⁄₁₂	Thomas Howard Fenwick	21 July	ditto	2 Dec. 24	28 June 38
30	¹⁄₁₂	Lewis Alexander Hall ..	ditto	ditto	12 Jan. 25	ditto
29	0	Patrick Yule [53]	1 May 11	11 ditto	23 March	ditto
29	0	George Phillpotts [54]	ditto	7 June	ditto	ditto
29	0	Charles Jasper Selwyn [55]	ditto	18 July	ditto	ditto
29	0	W. Matthew Gosset [56] ..	14 Dec.	1 July 12	9 April	ditto
29	0	ᵬ Daniel Bolton [57]	ditto	ditto	7 June	ditto
29	0	F. William Whinyates [58]..	ditto	ditto	29 July	ditto
29	0	ᵬ Alex. Watt Robe [59] ..	ditto	ditto	ditto	ditto
29	0	Ralph Carr Alderson....	ditto	ditto	ditto	ditto
28	0	Charles Wright [60]	1 July 12	1 March 13	ditto	ditto
28	0	ᵬ Charles Rivers [61]	ditto	ditto	ditto	ditto
28	0	Fran. Ringler Thomson [62]	ditto	21 July	ditto	ditto
28	0	ᵬ H. Young Wortham [63]	ditto	ditto	24 Sept.	ditto
28	0	ᵬ Geo. Vaughan Tinling [64]	ditto	ditto	19 Oct. 26	
28	0	*Joshua Jebb* [65]	ditto	ditto	26 Feb. 28	
28	0	John Smyth [65]	ditto	ditto	29 Oct.	
27	0	Alexander Henderson ..	20 March 13	ditto	24 Feb. 29	
27	0	Thomas Battersbee......	ditto	ditto	22 May	
27	0	Arthur Walpole	ditto	ditto	27 Oct.	
27	0	George Tait............	ditto	ditto	16 Feb. 30	
27	0	*Hen. Rowl. Brandreth* [65]	ditto	ditto	16 Mar.	
27	0	Charles Ogle Streatfield..	ditto	ditto	21 June	
27	0	J. Ellison Portlock [65] ..	20 July	15 Dec. 13	22 June 30	
27	0	William Gregory	ditto	ditto	6 Oct. 31	
		SECOND CAPTAINS.				
27	0	Charles Carson Alexander	20 July	15 Dec. 13	7 Oct. 31	
27	0	Jas. Hunter Rutherford..	ditto	ditto	12 Nov.	
27	0	Arthur Kay [66]	ditto	ditto	10 Dec. 32	
27	0	George Curry Page	ditto	ditto	5 Jan. 33	
27	0	Henry Sandham........	ditto	ditto	1 May 34	
27	0	Colin Mackenzie........	ditto	ditto	26 Oct.	
27	0	T. Coryndon Luxmore ..	1 Jan. 14	1 Aug. 14	6 Nov.	
27	0	William Faris	ditto	ditto	1 March 35	
27	0	Edward Bullock Patten..	ditto	ditto	25 June	
26	⁶⁄₁₂	Fred. Henry Baddeley ..	ditto	ditto	ditto	
26	1¹⁄₁₂	George Dalton	ditto	ditto	19 Aug.	
25	1⁵⁄₁₂	Charles Burt	1 Aug.	1 July 15	15 Sept.	
24	2²⁄₃	George C. Degen Lewis..	ditto	ditto	5 Dec.	
23	2¹⁄₂	Gustavus C. Du Plat, K.H.	ditto	ditto	8 Feb. 36	29 March 39
21	4¹¹⁄₁₂	Thomas Budgen	ditto	ditto	13 May	
22	4	Vincent Joseph Biscoe ..	ditto	ditto	11 June	
20	5¹⁰⁄₁₂	Henry Powell Wulff	ditto	ditto	23 Sept.	
18	7⁵⁄₁₂	Montgomery Williams ..	24 March 15	1 May 16	10 Jan. 37	
18	7³⁄₁₂	John Hawkshaw........	ditto	ditto	ditto	
21	4⁷⁄₁₂	Thomas Hore	ditto	7 Feb. 17	ditto	
20	5	Thomas Foster	1 Sept.	7 Sept. 19	ditto	29 March 39
21	4	Geo. Fra. W. Bordes....	ditto	9 Jan. 21	ditto	
22	2¹¹⁄₁₂	John Isaac Hope	ditto	1 July	ditto	
23	1⁵⁄₁₂	Wm. Cameron Forbes ..	ditto	25 March 23	ditto	
24	⁷⁄₁₂	Richard John Stotherd..	ditto	13 March 24	ditto	
25	0	Alexander Gordon	ditto	2 Dec. 24	ditto	
25	0	Cowper Rose	ditto	12 Jan. 25	ditto	

Corps of Royal Engineers.

Years' Serv. Full Pay.	Years' Serv. Half Pay.	SECOND CAPTAINS.	2ND LIEUT.	1ST LIEUT.	CAPTAIN.
25	0	Wm. Biddlecomb Marlow............	1 Sept. 15	23 March 25	28 March 37
24	0	*Thomas Drummond*................	1 March 16	ditto	18 Aug.
24	0	Robert Kearsley Dawson............	ditto	ditto	ditto
24	0	Henry Pooley.....................	ditto	ditto	ditto
24	0	Francis Wm. Pettingal.............	ditto	ditto	20 Nov.
24	0	Samuel Hen. Wentworth............	ditto	ditto	9 Dec.
24	0	Henry Tucker.....................	ditto	9 April 25	25 Dec.
24	0	Benjamin Spicer Stehelin...........	1 Aug. 16	2 June	31 March 38
24	0	William Lancey...................	ditto	7 ditto	25 May
24	0	Charles Oldershaw.................	ditto	29 July 25	13 June
24	0	George St. Vincent Whitmore.......	ditto	ditto	24 Jan. 39
24	0	Henry Servante...................	ditto	ditto	27 May 39
24	0	Henry Owen Crawley	ditto	ditto	17 Aug. 39
24	0	John Twiss.......................	ditto	ditto	29 Sept. 39
23	8/12	Leicester Viney Smith	ditto	ditto	15 Oct. 39
22	2	John Walpole.....................	ditto	24 Sept.	28 Nov. 39
		FIRST LIEUTENANTS.			
19	1 1/12	Thomas Aiskew Larcom	1 June 20	9 Feb. 26	
17	11/12	Edward Vicars	28 March 22	8 April	
16	0	St. Aubyn Molesworth	28 Aug. 24	19 Oct.	
15	0	Robert Boteler...................	11 May 25	20 ditto	
15	0	*Edward Frome*...................	ditto	6 Dec.	
15	0	Richard Howorth.................	6 Aug. 25	11 April 27	
15	0	Charles C. Wilkinson	ditto	26 Feb. 28	
15	0	William Turnbull Renwick	ditto	7 Nov.	
15	0	Thomas Hosmer Rimington.........	ditto	28 Jan. 29	
15	0	William E. Delves Broughton	ditto	24 Feb.	
15	0	Richard J. Nelson.................	7 Jan. 26	22 May	
15	0	Robert Fenwick	ditto	23 ditto	
14	0	*George Burgmann*	15 March 26	27 Oct.	
14	0	Edward Aldrich...................	ditto	15 Feb. 30	
14	0	John Chaytor.....................	ditto	16 ditto	
14	0	Joshua Coddington	25 April 26	8 June	
14	0	Charles Bailey	ditto	21 ditto	
14	0	*William Thomas Denison*	ditto	22 ditto	
14	0	John Williams	22 Sept. 26	2 Dec.	
14	0	Edward William Durnford	ditto	5 Feb. 31	
14	0	Edward Thomas Lloyd	ditto	24 June	
14	0	Henry James	ditto	22 July	
14	0	William Robinson	ditto	6 Oct.	
14	0	Thomas R. Mould.................	ditto	7 ditto	
14	0	George Wynne	ditto	12 Nov.	
14	0	James Lynn	ditto	13 ditto	
13	0	William Stace....................	4 May 27	18 March 32	
13	0	Henry D. Harness.................	24 ditto 27	20 Sept.	
13	0	George A. Bennett.................	13 July 27	10 Dec.	
13	0	William Henry Ford...............	30 Aug. 27	5 Jan. 33	
13	0	St. George L. Lyster...............	ditto	4 Feb.	
13	0	Edmund T. Ford	ditto	5 ditto	
12	0	William Yolland..................	12 April 28	4 Sept.	
11	0	Charles Erskine Ford..............	29 April 29	1 May 34	
11	0	James Jenkin	23 Sept. 29	6 Nov.	
10	0	Richard Clement Moody	5 Nov. 30	25 June 35	
9	0	Frederick Augustus Yorke	5 Oct. 31	12 Aug.	
9	0	Charles Francis Skyring	ditto	19 Aug.	
8	0	George Rowan Hutchinson	29 May 32	15 Sept.	
8	0	Robert Gorges Hamilton	ditto	5 Dec.	
8	0	Henry Williamson Lugard	ditto	6 ditto	
8	0	William Charles Hadden	ditto	8 Feb. 36	
8	0	Roger Stuart Beatson	ditto	13 May	
8	0	Sampson Freeth	26 Sept.	ditto	
7	0	John Graham M'Kerlie............	27 Feb. 33	23 Sept.	
7	0	Julian Frederick Anthony Symonds ..	1 Aug.	24 ditto	

Corps of Royal Engineers.

Years' Serv. Full Pay	Years' Serv. Half Pay	FIRST LIEUTENANTS.	2ND LIEUT.	1ST LIEUT.
7	0	William George Hamley	5 Aug. 33	25 Sept. 36
7	0	Andrew Beatty	ditto	6 Nov. 36
7	0	John W. Gordon	1 Dec. 33	10 Jan. 37
7	0	Marcus Dill	ditto	ditto
7	0	James Fellowes	ditto	ditto
7	0	George B. G. Downes	ditto	ditto
7	0	Philip J. Bainbrigge	ditto	ditto
7	0	Archibald P. G. Ross	ditto	ditto
6	0	John Claridge Burmester	9 June 34	ditto
6	0	Edmund Ogle	ditto	ditto
6	0	Conolly M'Causland	ditto	ditto
6	0	John Cameron	12 Dec. 34	ditto
6	0	John S. Hawkins	ditto	ditto
6	0	James H. Freeth	ditto	ditto
6	0	Charles Duesberry Robertson	19 Dec. 34	31 Jan. 37
6	0	Charles Fanshawe	ditto	23 Feb.
5	0	Frederick E. Chapman	18 June 35	28 March
5	0	Thomas Fenwick	ditto	8 May
5	0	Theodosius Webb	ditto	18 Aug.
5	0	John Hodges Pipon	18 Dec. 35	20 Nov.
5	0	Thomas Rice Lyster	ditto	ditto
5	0	William Walter Fuller	ditto	9 Dec.
5	0	William Henry Roberts	ditto	25 Dec.
4	0	Gother Frederick Mann	18 June 36	31 March 38
4	0	Spencer Westmacott	ditto	25 May
4	0	Charles Acton Broke	ditto	13 June
4	0	Charles Edward Stanley	13 Dec. 36	14 June
3	0	William Collier Menzies	5 May 37	1 Aug.
3	0	Edward Reynolds	ditto	24 Jan. 39
3	0	Robert M. Laffan	ditto	1 April 39
3	0	Arthur Henry Freeling	14 Dec.	27 May 39
3	0	Harry St. George Ord	ditto	ditto
3	0	Frederick Le Mesurier	ditto	17 Aug. 39
3	0	David William Tylee	ditto	20 Sept. 39
3	0	Hampden C. B. Moody	ditto	22 Sept. 39
3	0	John Linton Arabin Simmons	ditto	15 Oct. 39
3	0	George Archibald Leach	ditto	28 Nov. 39

SECOND LIEUTENANTS.

Richard Tylden	14 Dec. 37	Henry Charles Cunliffe Owen		ditto
Philip John Stapleton Barry	ditto	G. F. D. Jervois		ditto
Henry Arthur White	ditto	T. L. J. Gallwey		ditto
Paul Bernard Whittingham	ditto	C. S. Miller		ditto
Phipps John Hornby	ditto	R. Burnaby		ditto
James William Gosset	ditto	A. D. Craigie		ditto
George Clement Baillie	16 June 38	Albert O'Donnel Grattan		ditto
Thomas Bernard Collinson	ditto	M. Vavasour		ditto
George Bent	ditto	James S. Baker		ditto
Edm. Yeamans W. Henderson	ditto	H. F. Keane		ditto
Archibald Randolph	ditto	*Hon.* W. Napier		ditto
George Sorell	16 June 38	William Cowper		20 Dec. 39
A. F. H. Dacosta	28 March 39	Charles John Gibb		ditto
J. Bayly		Charles Gordon Gray		ditto

Major of Brigade.—🅑 Colonel C. G. Ellicombe, C. B. 9 Jan. 21.
Scarlet.—*Facings*, Blue Velvet.
N. B. The officers in Italics are holding civil employment.

ROYAL SAPPERS AND MINERS.—(Officered by the Corps of Royal Engineers.)

Major of Brigade.—🅑 Brevet-Major Edw. Matson, 11 Feb. 31.
Adjutant.—Captain Henry Sandham, 1 Aug. 37.
Quarter-Master.—James Hilton, 9 Nov. 35.
Establishment at Chatham for instructing the Corps in Military Field Works.
Director.—🅑 Colonel C. W. Pasley, C.B., 27 May, 13.

Ordnance Medical Department.

Director-General.
Sir John Webb, K.C.H. 20 Nov. 09.

Assistant-Inspector.
Morgan Thomas, *Assist.-Surgeon*, 14 July, 14; *Surgeon*, 11 Nov. 11; *Assist.-Inspect.* 14 July, 36.

Years' Serv.		SURGEONS.	ASSISTANT-SURGEON.	SURGEON.
Full Pay.	Half Pay.			
35	$\frac{9}{12}$	Edward Simpson	25 April 05	5 Aug. 13
26	$8\frac{9}{12}$	Thomas Macmill Fogo, M.D.	22 Jan. 06	26 Sept. 14
33	0	James Stewart	1 Dec. 07	27 Jan. 27
32	0	J. Wallan Halahan, M.D.	5 Dec. 08	5 June 27
29	1	James Verling, M.D.	25 Jan. 10	3 July 27
28	$1\frac{5}{12}$	Alexander Ogilvie, M.D.	11 June 11	10 Aug. 29
28	0	Charles Tomlins Whitfield	12 May 12	1 June 30
28	0	Thomas Seaton	23 Oct. 12	25 Aug. 30
28	0	Thomas Haswell Quigley	3 Nov. 12	26 Aug. 30
27	$\frac{9}{12}$	James Parratt	9 Nov. 12	11 June 36
23	$4\frac{9}{12}$	Thomas Whitelaw	6 Jan. 13	14 June 36
21	$6\frac{5}{12}$	Wm. Frederic Nelson	12 Feb. 13	26 Oct. 36
19	$8\frac{5}{12}$	Stewart Chisholm	30 Nov. 13	11 Sept. 38
		APOTHECARY.		
41	0	William Harris, 1 Oct. 06; *Assist.-Surgeon*, 3 Sept. 99.		
		ASSISTANT SURGEONS.		
14	0	Thomas Colchester	27 Jan. 27	
13	0	William Richardson	17 April 27	
13	0	James E. Williams	11 May 27	
13	0	John Goldsworthy	12 June 27	
13	0	Wm. Kelly	31 Jan. 28	
12	0	Charles Dempsy	22 July	
9	0	John Atkins Davis	1 July 31	
9	0	Jas. Edw. Tho. Parratt	ditto	
9	0	George Farr	ditto	
9	0	Chas. Fred. Staunton, M.B.	ditto	
9	0	Johnson Savage, M.D.	ditto	
7	0	Benj. Geo. Calder, M.D.	1 May 33	
7	0	Robert Templeton, M.D.	6 May 33	
4	0	Joseph Ambrose Lawson, M.D.	11 June 36	
4	0	Wm. Alston Dassauville, M.D.	14 June 36	
4	0	Andrew Aylmer Staunton	20 Sept. 36	
4	0	James Somerville Litle	2 Nov. 36	
4	0	John Mackintosh, M.D.	23 Nov. 36	
3	0	George Thomas Ferris	20 Sept. 37	
2	0	Melbourne Broke Gallwey	18 June 38	
2	0	John Bent	25 April 38	
1	0	*Rich. Coffin Elliot	7 June 39	
1	0	*Ross Hassard	22 Aug. 39	
1	0	*Charles Young	ditto	

Paymasters to the Ordnance Department, Messrs. Cox & Co.

Notes to the Royal Engineers.

1 Sir Samuel Trevor Dickens was present at the landing at Ferrol, in August, 1800, and joined Sir Ralph Abercromby's army in the Mediterranean in September following.

1* Sir Aug. De Butts was at the sieges of Toulon, Bastia, and Calvi, and was favourably mentioned by Lord Hood in his despatches on the surrender of Bastia.

2 Gen. Evatt was present at the attack of Fort Fleur d'Epée, Guadaloupe, June, 1794, and at the defence of Fort Matilda, from 10th Oct. to 10th Dec. following. In 1795 at Dominica at the attack and capture of the French force landed for the reduction of the island. In 1797 served at the attack of the island of Porto Rico. Wounded at the Helder in 1799.

3 Sir Fred. Mulcaster served in Portugal, in 1797 and 98; acting as commanding engineer at the siege of Ciudadella in Minorca, in 1798, and remained in the Mediterranean until 1801.

4 Sir Howard Elphinstone was at the capture of the Cape of Good Hope in 1795; served in Egypt in 1801 as Commanding Engineer in the Indian Army under Sir David Baird. In 1806 was employed on a mission to Portugal. Embarked as Commanding Engineer under General Whitelock in the expedition to Monte Video. In 1808 embarked as Commanding Engineer with Sir Arthur Wellesley in the expedition to Portugal, and was severely wounded at Roleia. Served also in the Peninsula from 1812 to the end of the war, and was Commanding Engineer at the passage of the Adour, and blockade of and sortie from Bayonne. Sir Howard has received an Egyptian medal, and a medal and two clasps for Roleia, Nivelle, and Nive.

5 Gen. Durnford was present at the siege of Fort Bourbon, and capture of Martinique, St. Lucia, and Guadaloupe, in 1794.

6 Sir John Jones served the campaign in Calabria, &c.; was present at the battle of Maida; attack of Castle of Scylla; the retreat to Corunna; expedition to Walcheren, reduction of Flushing; served the campaigns of 1810, 11, and 12, in the Peninsula; has received a medal for Badajoz. Sir John was shot through the ancle joint at the siege of Burgos, Oct. 1812.

7 Gen. Thackeray was at the capture of Surinam in 1799, St. Martin's, St. Bartholomew's, &c. &c. in 1801; directed the siege of Scylla Castle, and that of the Fortress of Santa Maura in 1809; served with the army in Spain, in 1812; at the battle of Castalla, and siege of Tarragona in 1813, and remained with the army until 1814.

8 Gen. Birch served in Flanders, and Holland, in 1793, 94, and 95; the Egyptian campaign of 1801; taking of Copenhagen under Lòrd Cathcart; served in the north of Spain in 1808; taking of Flushing in 1809; blockade of Cadiz in 1810 and 11; has received a medal for Barrosa. Gen. B. was shot through the thigh near Valmesada, 7 Nov. 1808.

8* Sir Stephen R. Chapman served in Holland in 1799; at Copenhagen in 1807; and in the Peninsula from March 1809 to Feb. 1811.

9 Gen. Nicolls served in the American war during 1814 and 15, and was present at the capture of Moose Island, Castine, and Belfast, in the United States in 1814.

9* General Wright served in the West Indies during the war with France, from 1800 to 1805 inclusive, including the capture of the islands of St. Lucia and Tobago from the French. Commanded the batteries at the island of Trinidad under Sir Thomas Hislop, when that island was threatened with an attack by the combined squadrons of France and Spain. Served in North America, Canada, Nova Scotia, and New Brunswick during the whole of the late war with the United States, under Sir George Prevost and Sir John Sherbrooke; and with the latter officer served as Deputy Quarter Master General of the Forces in the provinces of Nova Scotia and New Brunswick. Served in the island of Ceylon, having volunteered his services in that island during the rebellion of the Kandyan provinces; and, on his return to England, visited the Court of Persia in an official capacity, and was the means of preventing the Shah of Persia from declaring war against the Hon. East India Company.

10 Sir John Burgoyne's services:—blockade of Malta, and surrender of Valetta, 5th Sept. 1800; landed in Egypt, 17th March, 1807; capture of Alexandria, 20th March; attack of Rosetta from 7th to 18th April, 1807; retreat to Corunna, 1809; passage of the Douro, 12th May; affair of Salamonde, 16th May; blew up Fort Conception in presence of the enemy, 21st July; battle of Busaco, 21st Sept.; retreat and lines of Lisbon; siege of Badajoz, 2nd to 13th June, 1811; action of Elbodon, 25th Sept. 1811; siege and storm of Ciudad Rodrigo, 8th to 19th January, 1812, siege and storm of Badajoz, 17th March to 6th April, 1812; siege and capture of Forts at Salamanca, 17th to 27th June, 1812; battle of Salamanca, 22nd July, 1812; advance to Madrid, and capture of Retiro Forts, 14th August, 1812; siege of Burgos, (wounded) 19th Sept. to 21st Oct. 1812; retreat from Burgos; advance of the army and cross the Ebro, May and June, 1813; battle of Vittoria, 21st June, 1813; siege and storming of St. Sebastian, (wounded) 15th July to 13th Aug. 13; siege of Castle of St. Sebastian, 31st Aug. to 9th Sept. 1813; passage of Bidassoa, 7th Oct. 1813; battles of the Nivelle and Nive; passage of Adour, 23rd February, and blockade of Bayonne; sortie from Bayonne, 14th April, 1814; attack of American lines before New Orleans; 8th Jan. 1815; capture of Fort Bowyer, from 8th to 11th Feb. 1815; Sir John has received a cross and one clasp.

11 Col. Pasley's services:—in 1806, in the defence of Gaeta; afterwards in the battle of Maida; siege of Copenhagen in 1807; in 1808 and 9, several skirmishes, and in the battle of Corunna; reconnoitered the enemy's coast under the fire of batteries, and afterwards at the siege of Flushing; Col. P. received a bayonet-wound through the thigh, and a musket-

Notes to the Royal Engineers.

wound, which injured the spine, in leading a storming party to attack an advanced work occupied by the French on the Dike in front of Flushing, 14th Aug. 1809.

12 Col. Goldfinch's services:—in 1807, expedition to Copenhagen; 1809, Oporto, Talavera; 1810, Busaco; 1813, Vittoria, Pyrenees, Nive; 1814, Orthes, Toulouse; has received a cross.

13 Col. Arnold's services:—blockade and surrender of Malta in 1800; the whole of the campaign in Egypt in 1801; including the attack and surrender of Aboukir Fort and castle, battle of Alexandria, and afterwards accompanied the division of the army which expelled the French from Grand Cairo, and took possession of that city; also present at the surrender of Alexandria to the British troops. Served several years in the West Indies, and at the last attack and surrender of the colonies of Demerara, Essequibo, Berbice, and Surinam, at which latter he was severely wounded in successfully leading the storming party against the Redoubt Frederick and Fort Leyden. Was several times handsomely mentioned in the public dispatches for his conduct at Surinam; and was on that occasion presented by the Committee of the Patriotic Fund with a sword of the value of one hundred pounds. He has since served several years in Bermuda and North America.

14 Sir Wm. Gosset served in Holland in 1799, and was major in command at the attack upon Algiers under Lord Exmouth in 1816.

14* Colonel Fyers served the Corunna campaign.

15 Col. Ellicombe served in the Peninsular from Nov. 1811 to the end of the war, including the siege and storm of Ciudad Rodrigo, 8th to 19th Jan. 1812; siege and storm of Badajoz, 17th March to 6th April, 1812; retreat from Burgos, 1812; advance of the army and cross the Ebro, May and June, 1813; battle of Vittoria, as Brigade-Major; siege and storm of St. Sebastian, 15th July to 9th Sept. 1813; passage of Bidassoa, 7th Oct. 1813; battle of Nivelle, 10th Nov. 1813; Nive, 10th, 11th and 12th Dec. 1813; passage of Adour, 23rd Feb. 1814, and blockade of Bayonne; sortie from Bayonne, 14th April, 1814. Medal for St. Sebastian.

16 Col. Fanshawe's services:—capture of Cape of Good Hope in 1806; expedition to South America, and siege and capture of Monte Video in 1807; with the army in Portugal in 1808; expedition to the Scheldt, and siege of Flushing in 1809.

17 Sir C. F. Smith's services:—capture of Santa Cruz, St. Thomas, and St. John in 1807; capture of Martinique (wounded) in 1809; senior engineer in charge of Cadiz and its environs in the operations connected with the battle of Barrosa in 1811; commanding engineer in the defence of Tariffa, and in the field operations which led to that event; chief engineer at Cadiz when the siege was raised in 1812; affairs of the 18th, and battle of Vittoria, 21st June, 1813; Villa Franca and Tolosa, 24th June; siege of St. Sebastian; capitulation of Paris, 7 July, 1815; army of occupation; has served 20 years in the West Indies.

18 Col. Harding's services:—1813, action of Castalla, May; attack of Denia, June; attack of Tarragona, June. 1815, sieges of Mauberg, Landrecy, Marienberg, Phillippeville, and Rocroy, with the Prussian army.

19 Sir Geo. Hoste's services:—battle of Maida, and siege of Scylla Castle in 1806; attack on Alexandria and Rosetta in Egypt, in 1807; taking of the islands of Ischia and Procida, and siege of Ischia Castle in 1810; action on board H. M.'s ship Spartin in the Bay of Naples, 3d May, 1810; two attacks on Antwerp, in 1812; led the Guards in the attack on Bergen-op-Zoom.

20 Col. Wright served in the expedition to the Helder in 1799.

21 Col. Lewis's services:—campaign in Naples and Calabria, in 1805 and 1806; battle of Maida and siege of the Castle of Scylla, in July and Aug. 1806; capture of Ischia and Procida, in the Bay of Naples, in Aug. 1809; and siege of the Castle of Ischia; siege of the Fort at Santa Maura; served the campaign of 1813 in the Peninsula; wounded at the assault of the breach of St. Sebastian, lost the left leg above the knee.

22 Col. Holloway served the campaigns of 1810, 11, and 12, in the Peninsula; wounded in the trenches before Badajoz, March, 1812; shot through the body 26th March, 1812, whilst storming the enemy's works.

22* Col. Vavasour served at the siege of Cadiz.

23 Col. Graydon was at the capture of Martinique, in 1809, and Guadaloupe, in 1810.

24 Col. Thomson was at the capture of Martinique, in 1809; served on the north coast of Spain, in 1812; and in the Netherlands, in 1813, 14, and 15.

25 Sir John Smith served in Sicily from 1807 to June 1812.

26 Col. Jones was at the passage of the Douro and capture of Oporto, May, 1809; battle of Talavera, July, 1809; battle of Busaco, Sept. 1810; siege of Badajoz, and battle of Albuhera, May, 1811; siege and capture of Ciudad Rodrigo, January, 1812.

27 Col. Moody has seen a great deal of active service in the West Indies, and has been twice wounded, for which he received the Brevet rank of Major, and the Cross of Knight of the Royal French Order of Military Merit.

28 Col. Oldfield served in Holland in 1814; from March to June 1815, second in command under Sir James Carmichael Smith in the Netherlands; as Brigade-Major with the Duke of Wellington's army at Waterloo, capitulation of Paris, and army of occupation.

29 Col. Dixon served in Canada during the war, from 1812 to 15, and was slightly wounded at the storming of Fort Sandusky; medal for Detroit.

30 Col. Calder served in the expedition to Walcheren, and siege of Flushing, in 1809.

31 Col. Slade was present at St. Sebastian in July and Aug. 1813; blockade and sortie at

Notes to the Royal Engineers.

Bayonne, March and April 1814; Col. Slade was one of the officers selected to accompany the boats from Socoa to the mouth of the river Adour, and to assist in laying the bridge across.

32 Col. Tylden served at the siege and capture of Fort Santa Maria, 29th March, 1814; Commanding Engineer in the action before Genoa under Lord Wm. Bentinck.

33 Col. Wells:—campaign of Portugal and Spain, in 1808 and 9, including action of Rolissa, and the battles of Vimiera and Corunna; campaign in Holland in 1809, including the siege of Flushing; blockade of Cadiz, from March, 1810, to the raising of the blockade in 1812, excepting about six months absence at Carthagena, and with the army in Estramadura, including the action of Barrosa, and the last siege of Badajoz, in March and April, 1812; served part of the campaign of 1813, until the army embarked at Bordeaux in 1814, including the passage of the Bidassoa, blockade of Bayonne, and the taking of a work at Laredo; campaign of Belgium and France, in 1815.

33 * Col. Mudge served in the Peninsula from March, 1809, to June, 1810.

34 Col. English's services:—campaign of 1808 and 9, from the period the British army landed in Portugal until the retreat to Corunna, including battles of Roleia, Vimiera, and Corunna; end of campaign of 1813, and campaign of 1814, including battles of Orthes and Toulouse; campaign of 1815, and with the army of occupation until August, 1817.

35 Col. Blanshard was at the blockade and sortie of Bayonne; served afterwards in the American war; and was present at the taking of Washington; the operations and engagement before Baltimore; field operations and engagement before New Orleans, taking by assault the lines on the right bank of the Mississippi, and capture of Fort Bowyer; joined Sir James Kemp's division in France, 22d June, 1815.

35 * Col. Alex. Brown served at Walcheren.

36 Col. Emmett's services, &c.:—sieges of Badajoz in 1811 and 12; passage of the Nive; Bayonne, Orthes, Toulouse; at New Orleans, at the attack on the American lines, and every affair on that expedition; at the siege of Fort Bowyer; slightly wounded at Badajoz in 1811; and on the advance towards Orthes; very severely wounded at the assault of Badajoz in 1812.

37 Col. Ward served with the army in Sicily in 1811 and 12; was present at the action of Castella, attack of Denia, and siege of Tarragona in 1813; served with the army in the Netherlands in 1814.

38 Col. Gordon's services:—attack on the Castle of Scylla, June, 1809; siege and capture of Santa Maura, March, 1810.

39 Major Barney served at the defence of Tariffa, in 1811 and 12; and at the captures of Guadaloupe and the Saintes in 1815.

40 Major Jones served in the expedition to Walcheren in 1809; served the campaigns of 1810, 11, 12, 13, and 14, including the actions and sieges of Cadiz, Tarragona, (1811), Badajoz (1812), Vittoria, St. Sebastian, passage of the Bidassoa, Nivelle, Nive, Bayonne; wounded leading the Forlorn Hope at the first assault of St. Sebastian. Appointed commanding engineer in charge of the fortifications on Montmâtre, after the entrance of the British troops into Paris in 1815.

41 Major Bonnycastle was at the siege and capture of Flushing, August 1809. Served in the war with the United States of America from 1812 to 1815, and was at the taking of Fort Castine, *John Adams* corvette, and fleet of merchantmen, and occupation of that part of the State of Maine east of the Ponobscot River; commanding engineer at the construction of the extensive works of the Castine Peninsula in the United States. With the army of occupation in France. Served the severe winter campaigns of 1837, 38 and 39, as commanding engineer in Upper Canada, and also held the command of the embodied militia, volunteers, &c. of the midland and other districts with the local and militia rank of Lieut.-Colonel.

42 Major Marshall served in the Peninsula from Jan. 1811 to Oct. 1813, including the first siege of Badajoz, siege and storm of Ciudad Rodrigo, siege and storm of San Sebastian. Slightly wounded at Ciudad Rodrigo, 16th January, 1812; severely wounded twice by musket-shots at San Sebastian, 31st August, 1813, when leading the advance of the column of attack up the great breach.

42 * Major Piper served six campaigns in the Peninsula, Flanders, and France, from March, 1810 to the 27th Jan. 16; viz. 5 campaigns in the Peninsula and South of France from 10 to 14, and one campaign in Flanders and France to the capitulation of Paris in 1815, and reduction of the army on the following year. From 1810 to 12 was employed in the Lines of Lisbon and Almaida; and from Jan. 12 to the conclusion of hostilities in 1815, held the command of a division of the Pontoon Train; (having been entrusted during that period with the organization and equipment of 4 several bridges;) threw the bridges of the Guadiana, Tagus, Bidassõa, Gave D'Oleron, Garronne and Seine, and served in the trenches at the last siege of Badajoz, from the morning of the 18th to the 23d of March, when, the bridges of communication below the town being destroyed and sunk, was dispatched (by order of the commander of the forces) to re-establish and remain with them— (passing shot, shell and ammunition during the nights, and provisions during the day time) —for the remainder of the operations; received the thanks of Sir Rowland Hill at the passage of the Tagus in August same year, on the advance of his column to Madrid; and subsequently, when on route to Salamanca (in consequence of the enemy's cavalry intercepting the communications through the Sierra-do-Gato) was commanded by written instructions from the commander of the Forces, to retire with the bridges on Alcantra de

Notes to the Royal Engineers.

la Reina and Badajoz, to Elvas, and finally to Abrantes; where, equipping a fresh train of boats for the operations of the ensuing year, advanced with the army from Sabugal and Freynada to the Ebro and Vittoria; passage of the Bidassôa in Oct. and latter part of the blockade of Pamplona; actions of the 9th and 11th Dec. 1813 at Bayonne; do. Toulouse in 1814; passed and repassed His Grace the Commander of the Forces and Staff during the operations of the day, from the right to the left bank of the river, on a fly-raft of three boats; and subsequently, advancing to Mongiscard on the Canal Royal du Midi, proceeded thence to Bordeaux; where, parking the whole of the bridges on the Glacis of the Chateau-Trompette, they were in July same year embarked for the use of the army in America. Proceeded to Ceylon, East Indies, 16th June, 16. Served as commanding engineer in the Kandyan Provinces, during the insurrections of 1817 and 18.

43 Sir George Gipps served in the Peninsula from March 1811 to the end of the war, including the siege of Badajoz, in March and April 1812, affair of the pass of Biar, battle of Castalla, and other smaller affairs in Catalonia in 1813 and 14; also at the capture of the Fort of Balaguer, siege of Tarragona, and blockade of Barcelona. Led one of the columns of assault at Fort Picurina, during the successful siege of Badajoz, on which occasion he was wounded in the left arm.

44 Major Barry served in the Peninsula from Aug. 1812, to Oct. 1813, and was severely wounded by a grape shot, 31st Aug. 1813, when leading a party to the breach at the storming of St. Sebastian.

45 Col. Reid served in the Peninsula from April 1810 to the end of the war, including the three several sieges of Badajoz, siege of Ciudad Rodrigo, siege of the Forts at and battle of Salamanca, siege of Burgos, battle of Vittoria, siege of San Sebastian, and battles of Nivelle, Nive, and Toulouse. Present at the attack on Algiers, under Lord Exmouth, in 1816. Severely wounded in the knee, repulsing a sortie at Badajoz, 10th May, 1811; in the leg during the assault of Ciudad Rodrigo, 19th January 1812; in the neck during the assault of St. Sebastian, 28th July 1813.

46 Major Ord served in Spain during 1810, 11, 12, 13, and one half of 1814, including the sieges of Cadiz and Tarragona.

47 Major Savage served in the Peninsula from Nov. 1813 to the end of the war, including the investment of, and repulse of the sortie from Bayonne.

48 Major Waters served in the Peninsula from April 1812 to September 1814. Was at Cadiz when the siege was raised in the former year. In 1815 he was present in the actions of Quatre Bras and Waterloo. He led one of the columns to the assault of Peronne on the 26th June 1815, and was at the capture of Paris.

49 Major Matson served in the Peninsula from Nov. 1812 to the end of the war, including the battle of Vittoria, siege of San Sebastian, and battles of Nivelle and Nive. Served also at New Orleans in 1814.

50 Major Victor served in the Peninsula from Dec. 1812 to the end of the war, including the battles of the Nive, Orthes, and Toulouse.

51 Major Grierson served at Cadiz during part of 1812 and 13, and afterwards on the eastern coast of Spain.

52 Major Baron served in the Peninsula from Jan. 1813 to the end of the war.

53 Major Yule served in the American war in 1814, and was at Chippewa, 5th July, 1814, and Niagara, 25th July, 1814.

54 Major Phillpotts was favourably noticed in Sir Gordon Drummond's despatch of the attack on Fort Erie, Sept. 1814.

55 Major Selwyn was at the attack of Guadaloupe, 10 Aug. 1815.

56 Major Gosset served in Canada in 1813 and 14.

57 Major Bolton served in the Peninsula from Oct. 1813 to the end of the war.

58 Major Whinyates was at the battle of Algiers, 27th Aug. 1816.

59 Major Robe joined the 4th division of the army in the Peninsula in 1813. In 1814 he was employed in the operations of the passage of the Adour; blockade of and sortie from Bayonne. Afterwards in the expedition to New Orleans. In 1815, 16, 17, and 18, with the Army in France.

60 Major Wright was wounded by a musket ball through the thigh, 12th Oct. 1821, at Zante, in an attack made by the Greeks upon a Turkish man-of-war.

61 Major Rivers landed at Passages, Dec. 1813, and joined the light division, Feb. 1814; took charge of a division of the boats fitted out at Socoa for the passage of the Adour; then joined the force for the siege of Bayonne; embarked for America in 1814.

62 Major Thomson was attached to the Prussian army in 1815, and served at Maubery, Landrecy, Phillipville, and Rocroi.

63 Major Wortham served the campaigns of 1813 and 14 in Spain and France, including the siege of St. Sebastian, from 20th August to 9th Sept. 1813; battle of Orthes, 27th Feb. 1814; battle of Toulouse, 10th April, 1814; served with the army in America, from 14th Sept. 1814, to 24th May, 1815, including the attack of the American Lines before New Orleans, 8th Jan. 1815, and the siege and capture of Fort Bowyer from 8th to 11th Feb. 1815.

64 Captain Tinling served in the Peninsula from Nov. 1813 to the end of the war.

65 Captains Jebb, Smyth, Brandreth, and Portlock, served in the last American war.

66 Captain Kay served in Holland and the Netherlands, in 1814 and 15.

Corps of Royal Marines.

"GIBRALTAR"—The *Globe*, with the motto "*Per Mare, per Terram.*" The *Crown*—The *Anchor* and *Laurel*—The Cypher of George the Fourth. (Post in the Line, between the 49th and 50th Regiments.)

Lieutenant-General.
Admiral *Sir* William Sidney Smith, G. C. B. 28 June, 1830.

Major-General.
Admiral Right Hon. Sir George Cockburn, G. C. B. 5 April, 1821.

Years' Service.				2ND LIEUT.	1ST LIEUT.	CAPTAIN.	BREV.-MAJOR.	LIEUT.-COL.	COLONEL.
Full Pay.	Half Pay.								
		COLONELS COMMANDANT.							
46	1	☙ Elias Lawrence, C. B. 1		8 May 93	14 Feb. 95	3 Dec. 01	4 June 13	15 Nov. 26	10 July 37
47	0	George Jones 2		19 June 93	24 April 95	16 July 03	4 June 14	22 July 30	ditto
47	0	☙ Thomas Adair, C. B. 3		1 Dec. 93	24 April 95	20 Sept. 03	ditto	22 July 30	ditto
45	0	William Conolly 4		8 May 95	7 April 96	15 Aug. 05	12 Aug. 19	16 April 32	ditto
		COLONELS AND 2ND COMMANDANTS.							
45	0	George Beatty 5		16 May 95	20 Nov. 96	15 Aug. 05	12 Aug. 19	16 April 32	27 Dec. 37
45	0	☙ Thomas Adams Parke, C. B. 6		19 May 95	23 Nov. 96	ditto	ditto	31 Dec. 32	26 April 38
44	0	☙ John Owen, C. B. & K. H. 7		1 Mar. 96	22 Oct. 98	4 May 07	19 July 21	10 Jan. 37	26 Aug. 39
44	4/12	John Wright, K. H. 10		21 April 96	10 June 99	27 July 08	16 Sept. 16	ditto	ditto
38	6	Thompson Aslett 11		1 June 96	2 May 00	ditto	27 May 25	10 July 37	ditto
		LIEUTENANT-COLONELS.							
33	11	☙ *Sir* Fra. Geary Gardner Lee 12		19 July 96	15 Jan. 01	2 Feb. 10	22 July 30	10 July 37	
36	7 4/12	Edward Smith Mercer 13		25 Mar. 97	17 July 03	22 Sept. 10	ditto	ditto	
34	8 7/12	William Walker 14		2 Sept. 97	3 Aug. 03	8 Jan. 12	ditto	ditto	
34	8 7/12	☙ John McCallum 15		29 Jan. 98	18 Oct. 03	12 May 12	ditto	ditto	
38	4 6/12	☙ Charles Menzies, K. H. 16 (*Comm. Artillery*)		17 Feb. 98	21 Dec. 03	13 April 13	10 Jan. 37	ditto	
34	8	☙ Henry John Murton 17		1 May 98	18 Feb. 04	20 Oct. 13	ditto	ditto	
33	8 7/12	William Fergusson 18		10 Sept. 98	29 April 04	23 Feb. 14	ditto	27 Dec. 37	
34	8	Richard Swale 19		24 Sept. 98	5 June 04	27 July 14	ditto	1 Jan. 38	
39	2 4/12	Joseph Walker 20		8 Dec. 98	18 Aug. 04	19 July 21	ditto	26 April 38	
40	1 1/12	Thomas Peebles 21		12 June 99	ditto	19 Dec. 22	ditto	7 Nov. 38	
40	1	Walter Powell		31 Jan. 00	21 Sept. 04	14 Nov. 23	18 Mar. 37	26 Aug. 39	
40	0	☙ W. Moulden Burton 22		4 Aug. 00	21 Dec. 04	8 April 24	28 June 38	ditto	
40	0	☙ Abraham H. Gordon 23		5 Jan. 01	18 July 05	18 Dec. 24	ditto		

Royal Marines.

Years' Service.		CAPTAINS.	2ND LIEUT.	1ST LIEUT.	CAPTAIN.
Full Pay.	Half Pay.				
40	0	ℭ David Marlay	11 Jan. 01	4 Aug. 05	5 Jan. 26
39	3/12	William Baker	14 ditto	15 ditto	21 Jan. 26
39	3/12	J. Montresor Pilcher 24..	15 ditto	ditto	11 Feb. 26
40	0	Thomas Stevens	15 ditto	ditto	11 Mar. 26
38	1	Richard Edwards	10 April	ditto	16 May 26
38	1	David Anderson Gibsone.	15 ditto	ditto	31 July 26
37	0	𝔓 David J. Ballingall 25..	1 July 03	ditto	ditto
37	0	Benjamin Bunce 25*	2 ditto	ditto	ditto
37	0	John Hewes 26	4 ditto	ditto	ditto
37	0	Donald Campbell 27	5 ditto	ditto	ditto
37	0	John Rawlings Coryton .	6 ditto	ditto	ditto
37	0	Hugh Mitchell	9 ditto	ditto	ditto
37	0	𝔓 Giles Meech 28	ditto	ditto	ditto
37	0	ℭ 𝔓 John Wilson 29	10 ditto	13 Sept. 05	ditto
37	0	Robert Mercer..........	11 ditto	18 Oct. 05	ditto
37	0	ℭ 𝔓 Willian Laurie 29*..	3 Nov.	1 Mar. 06	28 Sept. 26
37	0	Samuel Burdon Ellis	1 Jan. 04	29 Apr. 06	15 Nov. 26
36	4/12	ℭ Robert Gordon	ditto	13 May 06	31 Aug. 27
35	1	ℭ 𝔓 Alfred Burton 30...	1 Feb.	7 July 06	ditto
35	1	George Elliott Balchild ..	23 April	12 Mar. 07	20 Nov. 27
33	3	James Whylock	25 April	24 ditto	31 Aug. 27
33	2 10/12	ℭ Thomas Wearing 31 ..	5 May	24 Apr.	20 Dec. 27
31	4 7/12	𝔓 James Uniacke 32	28 Aug.	21 Aug.	31 Aug. 27
31	5	Stephen Giles	3 Oct.	13 Jan. 08	ditto
30	5 8/12	Charles Gray	10 ditto	24 Apr. 08	ditto
30	6	Herbert Bowen Mends 32*	23 ditto	27 May 08	ditto
31	5	Robert Ford 33	6 Nov.	27 July 08	20 Apr. 29
31	5	George Batt Bury	10 ditto	ditto	30 June 29
29	7	James Irwin Willes 33*..	12 ditto	ditto	15 Oct. 29
28	7 6/12	Thomas Waters	30 ditto	ditto	22 July 29
30	6	Frederic Layton	9 Jan. 05	ditto	ditto
30	6	Henry James Gillespie ..	11 Jan.	ditto	27 ditto
29	6 8/12	David M'Adam	19 April	ditto	7 Dec. 29
28	7	John Geo. Richardson 34.	18 Sept.	14 Feb. 09	17 Mar. 31
30	4 8/12	Samuel Garmston 35	27 Sept.	24 Aug. 09	16 Apr. 32
35	0	𝔓 John Harvey Stevens 36	28 ditto	2 Sept. 09	ditto
29	6	William Taylor	30 ditto	4 ditto	ditto
27	7 6/12	William Ford 37	3 Oct.	2 Nov. 09	ditto
35	0	Richard Charles Steele 38	5 ditto	11 Jan. 10	11 June 32
28	7	𝔓 Charles Compton Pratt	14 ditto	14 May 10	12 Oct. 32
25	10 3/12	Henry Ivatt Delacombe ..	21 ditto	30 June 10	ditto
26	9	George Hunt Coryton ..	9 Nov. 05	22 Sept. 10	ditto
26	9	John Ashmore	19 ditto	19 Dec. 10	ditto
25	9 6/12	Charles Fegan 39	30 ditto	26 Jan. 11	30 Sept 33
26	9	𝔓 G. Bruce Puddicombe	31 Dec.	20 April 11	12 Oct. 32
26	9	R. Lyde Hornebrook	8 Feb. 06	9 Jan. 12	ditto
24	10 6/12	Thomas Scott 40........	11 ditto	15 ditto	7 Jan. 34
23	11 3/12	Robert Leonarde 41	27 ditto	3 Mar. 12	28 Apr. 34
23	11	Thomas Rees Thomas ..	19 April	4 July 12	27 May
23	11	Arthur Morrison	8 May	3 Sept. 12	ditto
23	11	James Shute	21 June	30 Jan. 13	ditto
23	11	Charles Robinson 42	1 Aug.	11 May 13	ditto
23	11	William Lewis Dawes 43	22 Aug.	14 July 13	ditto
23	11	John Alex. Philips	26 ditto	17 ditto	ditto
25	8	Frederick Spry	1 April 07	5 Apr. 14	ditto
25	8	William Jolliffe	4 May	18 ditto	ditto
33	6/12	William Calamy 44......	18 June	14 June 20	24 Sept. 35
29	3 4/12	ℭ James Fynmore 45....	1 Sept. 08	4 May 22	15 Nov. 36
29	3	George Spurin	6 ditto	6 Dec. 22	6 Dec. 36
28	3 8/12	Richard William Pascoe .	12 ditto	10 May 23	23 May
29	3	Roger Sawry Tinklar ..	14 ditto	20 June 23	26 ditto
28	3 10/12	Thomas Sullock 46	16 ditto	22 Sept. 23	10 July
30	1 11/12	James Clarke	19 Sept. 08	14 Nov. 23	ditto
31	1	John Buckley Castieau ...	22 Sept. 08	13 April 24	ditto

Royal Marines.

Years' Service.		CAPTAINS.	2ND LIEUT.	1ST LIEUT.	CAPTAIN.
Full Pay.	Half Pay.				
29	3¼	Richard Searle 47	30 Sept. 08	13 April 24	10 July 37
31	1	John Tothill	8 Oct. 08	8 May 24	ditto
31	1½	Robert Henry 48	1 Nov. 08	22 June 24	ditto
31	1	ⓟ Fortescue Graham 49	17 Nov. 08	6 May 25	ditto
29	2²⁄₁₂	George Hugh Palliser	2 Jan. 09	20 June 25	ditto
30	1	Henry Smith	18 Feb. 09	13 Aug. 25	ditto
31	0	James Whitcomb	13 Mar. 09	11 Mar. 26	ditto
30	1¹⁄₁₂	Peter J. J. Dusautoy 50	14 Mar. 09	16 May 26	ditto
31	0	Edward Hearle	4 Apr. 09	25 Sept. 27	ditto
31	0	John M'Arthur	14 April 09	ditto	ditto
31	0	Joseph Childs	21 April 09	ditto	ditto
31	0	Hugh Evans	14 June 09	24 Nov. 27	16 Nov. 37
31	0	ⓟ Sam. Robt. Wesley 51	26 June 09	ditto	ditto
31	0	Thomas Park 52	30 Aug. 09	28 Feb. 28	7 Dec. 37
30	⁶⁄₁₂	George Griffin	18 Sept. 09	6 Mar. 28	9 Dec. 37
30	⁷⁄₁₂	Thomas Hicks Cater 53	12 Oct. 09	ditto	27 Dec. 37
22	8⁵⁄₁₂	ⓟ James Dowman 53*	28 Nov. 09	8 Mar. 28	1 Jan. 38
29	1⁷⁄₁₂	Charles Clarke	8 Feb. 10	24 Mar. 28	26 April 38
27	3	Richard Knowles Barnes	6 Mar. 10	4 June 28	ditto
28	2¹⁰⁄₁₂	John Law 54	14 Mar. 10	6 June 28	ditto
28	11³⁄₁₂	Chas. Robinson Miller 55	5 Oct. 00	10 May 05	4 May 38
28	2⁶⁄₁₂	Isaac Toby 56	3 April 10	9 Sept. 28	22 May 38
28	2	Edmund Nepean	27 Nov. 10	2 Oct. 28	1 June 38
25	4⁵⁄₁₂	Valentine Beadon 57	14 Feb. 11	6 Feb. 29	8 June 38
29	2¹⁄₁₂	William M'Kinnon	13 Mar. 09	18 April 26	ditto
24	5	Thomas Fynmore 58	6 April 11	23 April 29	3 Oct. 38
27	2	Francis Smith Hamilton	2 May 11	2 Oct. 29	7 Nov. 38
24	4½	John Tatton Brown 59	21 May 11	14 Nov. 29	28 Feb. 39
24	5⁶⁄₁₂	C. Cartwright Williamson	23 May 11	18 Dec. 29	26 Aug. 39
25	4	Edward Augustus Parker	23 Sept. 11	23 Feb. 30	ditto
		FIRST LIEUTENANTS.			
28	⁶⁄₁₂	Joshua Edleston	19 Nov. 11	22 July 30	
29	0	Henry Savage	2 Dec. 11	ditto	
22	6⁶⁄₁₂	Henry Bennett	26 Feb. 12	7 Dec. 30	
21	7⁵⁄₁₂	Charles William Pearce	26 Mar. 12	3 Feb. 31	
21	7⁵⁄₁₂	Ralph Carr 60	9 April 12	17 Feb. 31	
22	6⁹⁄₁₂	Thomas Hurdle 61	24 April 12	16 April 31	
21	7	ⓟ James Wood 62	25 April 12	14 May 31	
21	7	Edward Wm. Churchill	1 May 12	19 May 31	
21	7	Robert Wright	6 May 12	4 June 31	
21	7	William Gordon	13 July 12	10 Sept. 31	
21	7	Edward Appleton	26 Aug. 12	7 Oct. 31	
21	7	Thomas Peard Dwyer 63	19 Oct. 12	9 Nov. 31	
21	7	William Clendon	9 Nov. 12	19 Jan. 32	
21	7	Caleb Barnes	10 Nov. 12	22 Feb. 32	
19	8	John Colliss	26 Mar. 13	7 Mar. 32	
17	10³⁄₁₂	Peter Martin M'Kellar	17 April 13	4 April 32	
15	12	William Wood 64	10 May 13	16 April 32	
18	9³⁄₁₂	Thomas Stephens	18 Sept. 13	ditto	
17	10	Henry George Morrish	6 Dec. 13	11 June 32	
15	11⁵⁄₁₂	George Watson	20 Dec. 13	27 June 32	
17	9¹⁄₁₂	John Land	22 Dec. 13	11 July 32	
15	11	James Buchanan	22 Feb. 14	24 Aug. 32	
16	10	Henry George Mitford	23 Feb. 14	29 Aug. 32	
16	10	Samuel Hawkins	28 Feb. 14	12 Oct. 32	
15	9	James Kennett Wilson	15 Oct. 16	ditto	
19	0	William Lee	22 Aug. 21	ditto	
18	0	Robert Onslow Bridge	2 April 22	ditto	
18	0	Henry Wm. Parke 65	26 Nov. 22	ditto	
18	0	A. Blaxland Stransham 66	1 Jan. 23	ditto	
18	0	Edward Rea	3 Feb. 23	ditto	
17	0	Alexander Anderson 66	13 May 23	ditto	
17	0	George Logan 68	1 July 23	20 Feb. 33	
17	0	Robert Wright	7 Oct. 23	11 April 33	
16	0	John Fraser	8 May 24	23 Apr. 33	
16	0	Thomas Brown Gray	31 Jan. 25	1 Oct. 33	

Royal Marines.

Years' Service.		1ST LIEUTENANTS.	2ND LIEUT.	1ST LIEUT.
Full Pay.	Half Pay.			
15	0	Thomas Holloway	17 Mar. 25	9 Dec. 33
15	0	John Chas. Grey Courtis	30 May 25	28 Dec. 33
15	0	John Miller 66	18 July 25	7 Jan. 34
15	0	George James Hayes	26 Sept. 25	12 Feb. 34
15	0	Richard Johns	1 Oct. 25	4 Mar. 34
15	0	Peter Brames Nolloth	28 Jan. 26	19 Mar. 34
14	0	George Hollingworth	14 Feb. 26	28 Apr. 34
14	0	Fielding Alex. Campbell	23 Sept. 26	27 May 34
14	0	George Evans Hunt	16 Dec. 26	ditto
13	0	John Mitchell	5 Oct. 27	29 Nov. 34
13	0	Thomas Lemon	8 Oct. 27	5 Feb. 35
13	0	Peter Trant Payne	22 Oct. 27	30 Mar. 35
13	0	George Elliot	1 Nov. 27	6 Apr. 35
13	0	Alex. Humphrey Stevens	27 Nov. 27	24 Sept. 35
13	0	Thos. Chas. Cotton Moore	4 Dec. 27	26 Oct. 35
13	0	Augustus Flemyng	7 Jan. 28	28 Jan. 36
13	0	Wm. Bookey Langford	22 Jan. 28	22 Mar. 36
13	0	William Mackay Heriot	28 Jan. 28	24 Mar. 36
12	0	Hamilton Fleming	10 Mar. 28	15 Apr. 36
12	0	Charles Miller	19 Mar. 28	20 July 36
12	0	Henry Bremer	22 Mar. 28	7 Sept. 36
12	0	John Holland	26 Mar. 28	15 Nov. 36
12	0	A. Sandys Stawell Walsh	12 Apr. 28	6 Dec. 36
12	0	John George Aug. Ayles	13 May 28	10 Jan. 37
12	0	John Hawkins Gascoigne	4 June 28	23 May 37
12	0	John Urquhart	14 July 28	26 May 37
12	0	Wm. S. Langton Atcherly	29 Oct. 28	16 June 37
12	0	J. P. N. Forest Clapperton	30 Oct. 28	10 July 37
12	0	Thomas Fraser 70	26 Nov. 28	ditto
12	0	George Wm. Roper Yule	3 Jan. 29	ditto
12	0	John Hoskin Wright	5 Feb. 29	ditto
11	0	Robert John M'Killop	4 Mar. 29	ditto
11	0	Phineas Priest	8 Apr. 29	ditto
11	0	William Friend Hopkins	27 Apr. 29	ditto
11	0	Henry Pritchard Lewin	ditto	ditto
11	0	Henry Carr Tate	30 June 29	ditto
11	0	George Colt Langley	ditto	ditto
11	0	William King Schoveller	2 Oct. 29	ditto
11	0	Joseph Fran. Brittain 71	16 Nov. 29	ditto
11	0	George Walkup Congdon	4 Dec. 29	ditto
11	0	Rickard Williams Meheux	26 Dec. 29	ditto
11	0	Edward Hocker	30 Jan. 30	ditto
10	0	Francis Aug. Halliday	23 Feb. 30	ditto
10	0	Simon Frazer	ditto	ditto
10	0	Arthur John Molesworth	20 Mar. 30	ditto
10	0	John Wade	3 July 30	ditto
10	0	Hamnett Parke	27 July 30	ditto
10	0	Walter Cosser	10 Aug. 30	ditto
10	0	John Phillips	10 Nov. 30	ditto
10	0	William Henry March	20 Nov. 30	ditto
10	0	Chas. Allan Parker 72	4 Feb. 31	ditto
9	0	Edward Pownell Snowe	17 Mar. 31	ditto
9	0	Fra. Ed. Lascelles Craig	15 Apr. 31	ditto
9	0	Gallway Byng Payne	17 May 31	ditto
9	0	Frederick Maltby	19 May 31	ditto
9	0	Henry Crespin	3 June 31	ditto
9	0	Douglas Adam Dorratt	29 June 31	ditto
9	0	Joseph Oates Travers	10 Sept. 31	ditto
9	0	Geo. Aug. Fred. Danvers	9 Nov. 31	ditto
8	0	Robert Murray Curry	22 Feb. 32	ditto
8	0	Edward Stanley Browne	19 Mar. 32	28 Sept. 37
8	0	Joseph Reid Jackson	4 Apr. 32	7 Nov. 37
8	0	Charles Coleman Hewitt	ditto	13 Nov. 37
8	0	John James Winne	16 Apr. 32	16 Nov. 37
8	0	John Thompson Aslett	ditto	ditto

Royal Marines.

Years' Service					
Full Pay	Half Pay				

1ST LIEUTENANTS.

Full	Half	Name			
8	0	Berney Varlo		16 Apr. 32	24 Nov. 37
8	0	Henry Arnold		1 June	6 Dec.
8	0	Charles Fra. Hockin		11 ditto	9 ditto
8	0	Henry David Erskine		10 July	ditto
8	0	William Robert Maxwell		11 ditto	15 ditto
8	0	William Gun Mahon		19 Nov.	27 ditto
8	0	Thomas Dudley Fosbrooke		30 ditto	1 Jan. 38
8	0	Leo. Geo. Fred. March		5 Feb. 33	26 Apr.
7	0	Charles Joseph Hadfield............		15 ditto	ditto
7	0	William Sidney Budd		27 ditto	ditto
7	0	John Philips Stevens		7 May	ditto
7	0	Richard Carr Spalding		ditto	4 May
7	0	Edgar Walter		19 July	22 ditto
7	0	James Piers		16 Aug.	1 June
7	0	Hayes Marriott		11 ditto	16 ditto
7	0	Walter Welsford Lillicrap		1 Nov.	ditto
7	0	Chris. Dashwood Harrington........		ditto	16 Aug.
7	0	Thomas Baker Pleydell		ditto	3 Oct.
7	0	Samuel Netterville Lowder		ditto	7 Nov.
7	0	And. Roger Savage		11 Nov. 33	28 Feb. 39
7	0	Pitcairn Onslow		13 ditto	6 Apr. 39
7	0	Rich. Searle Bunce		10 Jan. 34	10 May 39
6	0	Gris. Fred. Phillips................		14 Feb.	26 Aug.39
6	0	Robt. Bruce Puddicombe		20 ditto	ditto

2ND LIEUTENANTS.

Full	Half	Name				
6	0	Edw. T. Parker Shewen	28 Feb.34	Geo. Brydge's Rodney..	19 Dec. 37
6	0	George Lambrick	14 Mar.	Jermyn Char. Symonds	ditto
6	0	Hugh Kennedy	21 ditto	John Maurice Wemyss..	ditto
6	0	Peter Fane Edge Daniel	4 Apr.	John Henry Mercer	1 Jan. 38
6	0	Robert Hockings	4 July	Walter Kirby..........	ditto
6	0	Wm. Lawrence Sayer ..	14 Nov.	George William Whiting	ditto
6	0	Richard George Conolly	26 Dec.	William Woollett Noble	16 ditto
5	0	Aug. D. Lyd. Farrant ..	31 July 35	Hen. Hotham M'Carthy	30 ditto
4	0	Henry Timpson........	5 Jan. 36	James Louttet Braimer	13 Mar.
4	0	Nicholas Moore	15 July	L. W. R. Denman	ditto
4	0	Hen. Chas. M. Hawkey	27 Sept.	Peregrine Hen. Fellowes	ditto
4	0	Frederick John White ..	19 Oct.	Wm. Chris. Per. Elliott	8 May
4	0	Ed. P. Hamett Ussher ..	27 Dec.	Charles William Adair..	ditto
3	0	Charles Ogilvy Hamley	21 Feb. 37	Richard Farmar	ditto
3	0	Henry Varlo	7 Apr.	William Jolliffe.......	12 June
3	0	William Statton Aslett ..	26 July	Robert Seps. Harrison ..	ditto
3	0	William Francis Foote..	1 Aug.	W. J. Pengelley	19 ditto
3	0	Charles Penrose Coode	ditto	Geo. Gardiner Alexander	14 Aug.
3	0	William Grigor Suther.	ditto	Henry Wm. Brooker....	15 ditto
3	0	Hen. Edward Delacombe	ditto	Charles Fred. Menzies	21 ditto
3	0	And. John B. Hambly ..	1 Aug.	Hugh Bowen Mends....	ditto
3	0	William Ramsay Searle	17 Oct.	John Huskisson........	4 Dec.
3	0	Henry Drury	19 ditto	J. H. Stewart	18 ditto
3	0	Geo. Sp. Percival Baker	24 ditto	David Blyth	ditto
3	0	Fred. Buckland Bluett..	ditto	J. E. Wilson Lawrence	27 ditto
3	0	Henry Atkins M'Callum	24 Oct. 37	Jas. Ainslie Stewart	11 May 39
3	0	Charles Louis	21 Nov.	James Pickard	ditto
3	0	Richard King Clavell ..	ditto	Hen. Chas. Penrose Dyer	ditto
3	0	John William Wearing..	ditto	Fra. Jas. Polkinghorne	ditto
3	0	Rich. Y. Stuart Moubray	5 Dec.	Wm. B. Thos. Rider....	10 Sept.
3	0	Alexander Ramsay	19 Dec.	Wm. Alfred G. Wright.	24 Sept.
3	0	Penrose Char. Penrose..	ditto	Wm. Jas. Burney	ditto

Royal Marine Artillery.

Lieut.-Colonel.
₽ Charles Menzies (16,) K.H., 10 July, 37.
Captains.
David A. Gibsone, 31 July, 26.
₽ J. Harvey Stevens, (36) 16 April, 32.
Richard C. Steele (38), 11 June, 32.
First Lieutenants.
Thomas Holloway, 9 Dec. 33.
John P. N. F. Clapperton, 10 July, 37.
Henry C. Tate, 10 July, 37.
Hamnet Parke, 10 July, 37.
Second Lieutenants.
John Maurice Wemyss, 19 Dec. 37.
Assistant-Surgeon.—James D. Simmie, 15 Sept. 27.
Deputy Adjutant-Gen.—☧ John Owen, C.B. K.H., (*Col.*) 1 Jan. 38.
Assistant Adjutant-General.—☧ ₽ J. Wilson (*Capt.*) 31 May, 34.
Paymasters.
George Varlo, 23 Aug. 05; *2nd Lieut.* 18 June, 93; *1st Lieut.* 24 April, 95; *Capt.* 15 July, 03.
And. Kinsman, 17 Jan. 21; *2nd Lieut.* 12 Nov. 93; *1st Lieut.* 24 April, 95; *Capt.* 24 July, 03; *Brevet-Major*, 4 June, 14.
John Lawrence, 20 July 30; *2nd Lieut.* 6 July, 03; *Lieut.* 15 Aug. 05; *Capt.* 31 July, 26.
George Hookey (73), 23 Mar. 36; *2nd Lieut.* 27 Jan. 06; *1st Lieut.* 8 Aug. 11; *Capt.* 12 Oct. 32.
Adjutants.
Peter M. M'Kellar, (*1st Lieut.*) 11 July, 34.
Thomas Hurdle, (*1st Lieut.*) 15 April, 34.
Thomas Stephens, (*1st Lieut.*) 10 July, 37.
William Wood, (*1st Lieut.*) 10 July, 37.
T. Browne Gray, (*1st Lieut.*) 26 April, 38.
William M. Heriot, (*1st Lieut.*) 16 June, 38.
Henry William Parke, (*1st Lieut.*) 14 Aug. 38.
Tho. P. Dwyer, (*1st Lieut.*) 25 Feb. 39.
Quarter-Masters.
Charles Miller, (*1st Lieut.*) 10 July, 37.
Henry Bennett, (*1st Lieut.*) 10 July, 37.
Henry Savage, (*1st Lieut.*) 9 Dec. 37.
George Watson, (*1st Lieut.*) 22 May, 38
Surgeons.
₽ Daniel Quarrier, (74) 10 Jan. 17.
Henry Parkin, 25 Sept. 22.
Isaac Ryall, 29 May, 28.
William Rae, (75) 5 Feb. 38.
Assistant-Surgeons.
William Cowling, 10 Oct. 22.
J. D. Simmie, 15 Sept. 27.
Alexander Blyth, 21 Nov. 29.
William J. Hunter, 1 Aug. 32.
Arthur Kift, 6 May, 34.
Isaac Dias, 22 Dec. 34.
John Baird, 23 Apr. 39.
Barrack-Masters.
Thomas Sheppard, 8 March, 26; *2nd Lieut.* 4 May, 93; *1st Lieut.* 18 Dec. 94; *Capt.* 1 Nov. 01; *Brevet-Major*, 4 June, 13.
Thomas Moore, 16 Aug. 27; *2nd Lieut.* 14 Jan. 01; *1st Lieut.* 15 Aug. 05; *Capt.* 21 Nov. 10.
Robert John Little, 12 Sept. 29; *2nd Lieut.* 4 July, 03; *1st Lieut.* 15 Aug. 05; *Capt.* 31 July, 26.
₽ Ambrose A. R. Wolrige, (76) 5 June, 32; *2nd Lieut.* 4 July, 03; *1st Lieut.* 15 Aug. 05; *Capt.* 31 July, 26.

Scarlet—Facings Blue.   Artillery—*Blue*—Facings Red, *Agent*, Messrs. Cox. & Co.

Notes to the Corps of Royal Marines.

1 Colonel Lawrence, prior to entering the Royal Marines, served four years and a half as Midshipman in the Royal Navy. In 1793 he served at Toulon; landed at Fort La Malgue and Fort Mulgrave during the siege. In 1798, at the capture of a French squadron of three frigates and two brigs off Toulon. In 1805 battle of Trafalgar; the ship in which he served, the Colossus, lost 200 in killed and wounded. In 1810, at Cadiz during the siege; was the senior captain of the expedition against Malaga. In 1814 and 15, served off New York on the American coast, until hostilities finally ceased.

2 Colonel Jones was at the defeat of the French Fleet by Lord Howe, 1 June 1794; and by Lord Bridport, 23 June, 1795. On board *La Revolutionare* when she captured the *Unite*, 12th April, 1798. Wrecked off Brest in 1804, and detained a prisoner of war until 1814.

3 Colonel Adair's services: Battle of the Nile; siege and capitulation of the Castle of St. Elmo, Naples, and town of Capua in 1798; blockade of Malta, and surrender of La Valetta; blockade of Cadiz, and present at an attack made by Spanish Gun Vessels when becalmed under the batteries of that town; on board H. M. S. *Genuix*, at the capture of *La Diane*, French frigate; served at New Orleans.

4 Col. Conolly served in Lord Bridport's action, 23rd June, 1795. In 1796, served in the Mediterranean, including the evacuation of Bastia, capture of Porto Ferrajo, and destruction of Martello Tower in St. Fiorenzo Bay. On board H. M. S. *Excellent* in the battle of Cape St. Vincent, 14th Feb. 1797. Capture of Admiral Perrie's squadron off Toulon in 1798, consisting of three frigates and two brigs. On board the *Hannibal*, in the battle of Algesiras, 6th July 1801, wounded and taken prisoner. On board H.M.S. *Penelope*, in the action off Flushing and Ostend, under Sir Sidney Smith, 16th May, 1804. Present at the siege of Copenhagen, and capture of Danish fleet in 1807, and at Nyebourg in 1808. In 1812, on board his Majesty's ship *Hamadryad*, when attacked by French privateers; debarked with detachments at Scheveling, and took possession of the Hague in 1814. During the above periods he has been very frequently engaged with the enemy in affairs of gun-boats and batteries, &c. &c. Has received a reward from the Patriotic Fund.

5 Col. Beatty's services: landed at the attack of Santa Cruz, Teneriffe, when Lord Nelson lost his arm; Battle of the Nile; siege of St. Jean d'Acre (wounded); was favourably mentioned in Sir Sidney Smith's despatch, and is the only officer now serving who participated in that celebrated defence. In 1803 he was at the capture of the *Harmonie* privateer, and the surprise and destruction of Fort Dunkirk, Martinique. The publication of the despatches connected with these events, in which he was most favourably mentioned, procured him a patriotic sword of the value of 50*l*. Captain of Marines in the *Courageux*, at the capture of the *Marengo* and *Belle Poule* in March 1805; and in the *Donegal*, Capt. P. Malcolm, when the small squadron under his command attacked two French frigates under the batteries of La Hogue, near Cape Barfleur, 10th November, 1810. He has been engaged in other affairs of minor importance, and was selected for the duty of accompanying Sir G. Cockburn with Napoleon in the *Northumberland* to St. Helena.

6 Colonel Parke was present in Duncan's victory near Camperdown, 11th Oct. 1797 commanded two companies of Marine Artillery in Spain in 1812, and three companies in America, from 1813 to 1816, including the attack and capture of the entrenched camp at Hampton; besides the above, he has been twelve times engaged with the enemy in boats and on shore.

7 Col. Owen's services:—Battle of Camperdown; defence of the island of St. Marcou; bombardment of La Hogue; boarding and capture of India ship *Chance* under the batteries at Mauritius; burning of French frigate *La Prenneuse*; boarding and capture of ship *Sea Nymph* in harbour of Port Louis; battle of Trafalgar; and, although wounded, was, nevertheless, the first person on board the Spanish 80 gun ship *Argonauta*; capture of Copenhagen; destruction of *Le Robuste* and *Lion*, French ships of the line, Cette; destruction of a French privateer brig in the port of Negaya; capture of a convoy at Languilla, the batteries being first carried by the Marines; destruction of the Forts of Alessis and Languilia by the Marines under his command, after having *charged with the bayonet and defeated a battalion of the French 52d of the line, of a very superior force.* Commanded a battalion on the North Coast of Spain, including the actions of Alza, 6th June; near Fontarabia, 11th July; and at Hernani, 16th March 1837, when the Royal Marines rendered such important services to the Queen of Spain and her Allies.

10 Colonel Wright's Services:— Engaged in most of Lord Nelson's attacks on Rota and Cadiz in 1797; battle of the Nile; campaign of Naples in 1799; surrender of Ovo and Novo, Fort St. Elmo, Capua, and Guata; cutting out of the *Guiep* at Vigo; Egypt in 1801; and battle of Algiers in 1816.

11 Colonel Aslett was present in the battle off Camperdown 11th Oct. 1797. Has been repeatedly in action with the Flotilla off Boulogne, Havre-de-Grace, but was employed principally blockading, Cadiz, Brest, Rochfort, Carthagena, and Toulon.

12 Sir Francis Lee was at Copenhagen; siege of Cadiz and various affairs of boats in the East Indies, and on the French coast.

13 Colonel Mercer was on board the *Topage* when she engaged two French frigates off

Notes to the Corps of Royal Marines.

Corfu, and in the boats of the *Topage* cutting out the enemy's armed vessels at Santa Maura in 1809; also in Albania in cutting out on various occasions.

14 Colonel Wm. Walker was employed from 1802 to 1805 at the taking of St. Lucia, Tobago, Demerara, and Berbice; wounded at the storming and taking of the battery called Petit Auce d'Allett; present in various attacks on the enemy's batteries, on a frigate and brig under fort Edward, Martinique.

15 Colonel M'Callum was at the capture of the *Victorin* French privateer in boats under his command in 1800; battle of Trafalgar; forcing the Dardanelles and destroying a Turkish squadron in 1807. Employed on various occasions in cutting out and destroying enemy's vessels.

16 Colonel Menzies commanded a detachment of Royal Marines landed at Port Jackson during an insurrection of convicts, in March, 1804; by his promptitude and exertions the town of Sydney and indeed the colony was in a great measure preserved and tranquillity restored. In 1806 he commanded one of the boats of His Majesty's Ship *Minerva*, cutting out five vessels from under Fort Finisterre. In the barge alone (50 miles from where the frigate lay at anchor) captured by boarding the *Buena Dicha* privateer, of three times the force of the boat, after a sharp conflict, in which several were killed and wounded. This attack was planned by Colonel Menzies. Commanded and headed the marines at the storming of Fort Finisterre, being the first who entered the Fort. In boats cutting out the Spanish vessel of war, *St. Joseph*, from the Bay of Arosa, where he landed and made prisoner the Spanish Commodore who delivered to him his sword. Commanded the Marines at the capture of Fort Guardia. Slightly wounded cutting out the French corvette, *La Moselle*, from under a battery in Basque Roads. Taking of Fort Camarinus and gun-boats from under its protection. Repeatedly engaged in severe boat-actions, and against batteries. Received a sword of honour from the Patriotic Fund.

17 Colonel Murton served in the North Sea, and the Helder expedition in 1799; served in the Egyptian expedition and the East Indies in 1801; the West Indies (slightly wounded) in 1804; coast of France, and engaged with the enemy's flotilla and batteries in 1805; the Mediterranean in 1806, engaged in cutting out the enemy's vessels from under batteries; and was voted a sword from the Patriotic Fund; in 1809, coast of Spain, and aiding the Guerillas; served in Holland in 1813.

18 Colonel Fergusson served at the capture of Rear Admiral Perrée's squadron from Egypt when in pursuit of the French and Spanish fleets in June, 1799. Blockade of Malta and capture of Admiral Perrée's squadron *Le Généreu* 74, *Ville de Marseilles*, &c. with a reinforcement and supplies for the relief of the garrison. Was wrecked and severely injured on board H.M.S. *Queen Charlotte* when burnt off Leghorn in 1800, only *four* saved out of a detachment of nearly 200 marines, including supernumeraries, in all upwards of 700 persons perished. Served at the siege of Genoa and Savona. Destruction of the fort of Port Espezie, and guns carried off by H.M.S. *Santa Dorothea* in 1800, to which ship he then belonged. Served in Egypt under the command of Sir Ralph Abercromby in 1801 (*medal*). In 1806 at Maida. Defence of Gaieta and surrender of Tropea; took possession of the latter town with his detachment. Served again in Egypt with the expedition under Major-General Fraser in 1807. He has been repeatedly engaged in severe boat actions, and against batteries, and debarked with detachments aiding in capturing and destroying ships and convoys on the enemy's coast.

19 Colonel Swale served in Holland in two general actions in 1799; in 1800 accompanied the expedition to Quiberon Bay, and was at the taking of a fort and two batteries at the Morbion and destroying a brig of war and other vessels. Present under Lord Keith at the fall of Genoa; also at the landing in Egypt, and the actions of the 13th and 21st March, 1801. In 1802 at the attack of Porto Ferrajo. Capture of the Cape of Good Hope, and a French frigate in 1806. Landed at Buenos Ayres, entered the city after a sharp contest in the field, and captured in his retreat with his detachment, two brass field-pieces, in the face of a superior force of the enemy. Served in the breaching battery before Monte Video, until the place was carried by assault. Assisted at the cutting out of two Danish schooners of war and the destruction of several of their gun-boats in 1810. Medal for services in Egypt.

20 Colonel Joseph Walker served at Copenhagen.

21 Colonel Thomas Peebles' services:—In action with Spanish gun-boats in the Gut of Gibraltar in 1799, and recapturing the *Lady Nelson* cutter by the boats of H.M.S. *Queen Charlotte*. Blockade of Malta in 1800, and capture of Admiral Perrée's squadron. On board H.M.S. *Queen Charlotte* when that ship was burnt off Leghorn, 17th March, 1800. Debarked in command of the marines of H.M.S. *Santa Theresa* and *Mutine* in a successful attack on the town of Finale, and relief of the Austrian garrison. Storming the Prima Galley (on the night of the 20th May) chained to the mole head batteries of Genoa by the boats of the fleet under Captain Beavor, R.N. Siege and bombardment of Genoa in conjunction with the Austrian army, and surrender of the city and French garrison under General Massena. On board H.M.S. *Minotaur* at the capture of *Le Pax* and *Esmeralda* Spanish ships from under the batteries of Barcelona, 1801. Wounded in H.M.S. *Caro-*

Notes to the Corps of Royal Marines.

line's boats off Ivica in action with a French zebeck and Spanish packet. Blockade of Leghorn and defence of Elba, and attack on vessels in the Mole of Leghorn by the boats of H. M. S. *Caroline* and *Salamine.* Served in the blockading fleets off Brest, Rochfort and Cadiz, frequently engaged in boat actions on those coasts. 1805. On board H. M. S. *Blanche* in the West Indies severely wounded and made prisoner in the action between that ship and a French squadron under Commodore Baudine. Served subsequently in the West Indies, and also in the Archipelago in 1830. Served several years on the staff as adjutant and deputy judge advocate. Has received a reward from the Patriotic Fund.

22 Colonel Burton served in the Baltic, coast of Spain, and West Indies, in 1801 and 2; North Sea and West Indies in 1803, 4, and 5; in the North Sea, and wrecked in the West Indies, in H.M.S. *Astrea*, in 1808; Adjutant 2nd battalion on the coast of Spain in 1812 and 13, and during the whole of the campaigns in America in 1813 and 14; has been frequently engaged with the enemy in boat affairs.

24 Captain Pilcher served with the boats of the British fleet, in 1801, in their occasional attack of the Spanish gun-boats and vessels off Cadiz. In 1803, served in His Majesty's Ship, *Raisonable*, in the North Sea; 1804, attack of the gun-boats and batteries at Boulogne; July 22, 1805, in the general action and defeat of the combined fleets of France and Spain. In August following, in action with *La Topaze*, French frigate. January 1806, landed with a battalion of Marines at the attack and capture of the Cape of Good Hope. In June following, with the same battalion, at the attack and defeat of the Spanish troops on the road to Buenos Ayres, and at the capture of that city: in August following, at the defence of that city against the Spanish forces, after three days' action, taken prisoner, with the rest of the British. 1811, served in the North Sea, in attacks with the Danish gun-boats. 1813 and 1814, off the coast of France and America. Appointed to the 2d batalion of Royal Marines, and was at the attack of the American army and its defeat on the road to Baltimore, when Maj.-Gen. Ross was killed. At the attack of the American troops at Farnham church: commanded upon this occasion the advance, consisting of small detachments of the 21st, 44th, and 85th regts. and marines. In 1815, was at the attack of the American Rifle force near Point à Petie, and the capture of that fort in West Florida. From 1819 to 1821, served in His Majesty's Ship, *Vigo*, at St. Helena, during the last nine months of Buonaparte's life, and assisted with the marines at his interment.

25 Capt. Ballingall prior to entering the Royal Marines, served as a Midshipman at Copenhagen in 1801; landed at Vimiera, 21 Aug., 1808; was a volunteer in the boats of the *Resistance* at the boarding and carrying *La Mouche*, French man-of-war schooner, under a constant fire of grape and musquetry; the commander fell by the hand of Capt. B. 26 Feb. 1809. Served as a volunteer at the cutting out of four French luggers laden with supplies for the French army, from the harbour of Santa Clara, north coast of Spain, on the night of the 27th Feb. 1809, under a galling fire of musquetry, and defended by two batteries which commanded the entrance; landed at the head of the Marines from the *Resistance*, carried a battery of four guns; and assisted in the capture and blowing up of a French man-of-war schooner, and destroyed her convoy, laden with supplies for the French army, 10th March, 1809; was subsequently at the siege of Cadiz; and in 1832 in the castles of Naupoli de Romania, with an allied garrison during an attack on that city.

25* Capt. Bunce served at the blockade of Brest, &c. during 1803, 4, 5, and 6. In 1810, served under Gen. Abercrombie and Admiral Birtie, at the capture of the Isle of France. In 1813, 14, and 15, served on board His Majesty's Ship *Rhine*, during which term, in the West Indies, when he was repeatedly employed in captures of American privateers and pirates in the boats of said ship.

26 Captain Hewes served on board the *Rainbow*, of 24 guns in the West Indies and was in a severe action with *La Nereide*, French frigate of 44 guns, off Cape Tiberon, and beat her off; employed on the coast of Catalonia and Corsica, and present at the cutting out *La Paix*, Genoese vessel armed with four guns, and moored to the batteries at Geraglio, near Cape Corse; he was at the attack on Leghorn in 1813, by Sir Josias Rowley, and present at the capture of Genoa by Lord Wm. Bentinck.

27 Captain Campbell served at Walcheren in 1809.

28 Captain Meech when embarked in the *Emerald* frigate, was engaged on the 13th March, 1808 in the attack on the Forts of Vivero Harbour (Coast of Spain), and in the destruction of the French Corvette *L'Apropos.* He was slightly wounded, and was presented with a sword from the Patriotic Fund. In 1811 and 12, he served in the 1st battalion (Royal Marines) in Portugal, and on the north coast of Spain: and in 1814 in the expedition against New Orleans.

29 Captain Wilson served in the battle of Trafalgar, and was sent with a guard on board the *Ildefonzo* (a Spanish ship of the line), and while he was thus situated the *Ildefonzo* was separated from the fleet and driven near to Cadiz; and, notwithstanding the circumstance of but thirty Englishmen being then on board, and Lieutenant Wilson the only commissioned

Notes to the Corps of Royal Marines.

English officer with five hundred Spaniards, the prize was nevertheless one of the four preserved for His Majesty's service. He served at the reduction of Les Saintes Islands in the West Indies; in the expedition to Walcheren; at the siege of Cadiz; in Portugal in 1810 and 11; in the action between the *Macedonian* and *United States*, and in the expedition against New Orleans; and he was one of the only two surviving officers from the wreck of the *Boreas* frigate. Served as adjutant of the Chatham Division.

29* Captain Lawrie served at Trafalgar on board the *Colossus*, which ship lost 200 men killed and wounded. In 1806 commanded the marines of the *Pompei* at the capture of the Island of Capri. Served in the same ship at the attack and capture of a Martello Tower on Cape Licora; forcing the passage of the Dardanelles, where he set fire to a Turkish ship of the line; assisted in the destruction of a battery of 31 guns, each carrying shot of 300 lbs. weight. Participated in the siege and capture of Copenhagen in 1807. In 1810 and 11 employed in the *Cambrian* in active service on the coast of Catalonia, and was presented with a gold medal by the Spanish Government for his conduct at the capture of Bagur and Palamos. Served at the siege of Tarragona in 1811; and in 1813 and 14 in the Peninsula, as a captain in the Spanish army.

30 Captain Alfred Burton previously to entering the Royal Marines served several years in the navy as Midshipman, in the North Sea, Baltic, and Mediterranean; and in the militia as Ensign. In 1804 Capt. B. served in the North Sea, and off Cadiz; in 1805, Trafalgar; 1807, siege of Copenhagen; 1809, Walcheren; from 1810 to 1813, Cadiz, coasts of Spain, Portugal, and France; at the attack on the forts and harbour of Courageux, north coasts of France, 19 July, 1815. Since the peace, he has served on the Coast Blockade, in the West Indies, and Mediterranean.

31 Captain Wearing was wounded at Trafalgar.

32 Captain Uniacke was in the general action with, and defeat of, the combined fleets of France and Spain, 22nd July, 1805; the Spanish line-of-battle ship *L'Firme* having struck, he was ordered to board and take possession of her, with forty marines, and had charge of several hundred prisoners until their arrival at Plymouth, from which period until May 1814 he was on active service, particularly on the coast of Spain, the West Indies, and during the whole of the expedition to America. At the capture of the New Orleans flotilla in 1814 he was wounded, and one of the few survivors in the Barge of the Sea Horse, with Capt. Lockyer, who led the boats of the squadron, boarded and carried the American Commodore, with the loss of the Lieutenant, both Midshipmen, and several of the crew killed and every individual wounded. Capt. Lockyer (who received three gun-shot wounds, and the Lieutenant fourteen alongside of him) bore testimony to his conduct in his public Dispatches in the following words:—" First Lieut. Uniacke, of the Royal Marines, (who is in general a volunteer on these occasions,) was most severely wounded, and gallantly supported me. For this event he was presented with 50*l*. from the Patriotic Fund. In the years 1823, 4, 5, and 6, he served on the South American station; and in 1834, 5, 6, and 7, on the East India station. Repeatedly engaged in battery and boat actions.

32* Captain Mends commanded the detachment of Marines on board H. M. Ship *Franchise*, and was one who boarded and assisted in cutting out the Spanish National Brig *Reposa* of 16 guns and 90 men, protected by a formidable battery and gun boats in the Bay of Campeachy, 6th Jan. 1806. For this action, where he was slightly wounded, he was presented with a valuable sword of honour by the Patriotic Fund. He served in the West Indies 1805, 6, and 7, and was frequently employed in boat and other service. He was in action with, and destruction of, the French squadron in the inner roads of Aix in 1809; then in the *Unicorn* frigate. He was at Corunna in the same ship during Sir John Moore's action, and assisted in getting the troops on board; likewise off Holland blockading the Texel fleet; and during the Counter revolution in 1813; then off Norway to the end of 1814.

33 Captain Robert Ford served in a battalion under the command of Col. Geo. Lewis in 1808; took possession of Fignara on the River Mandeigo for the landing of the army under the Duke of Wellington. Expedition to Walcheren. Commanded the Marines at the taking of Moos Island. Bombardment of Stoney Town, near New London; at the capture of Washington; succeeded to the command of a battalion of Marines in the action in front of Baltimore. In the action before New Orleans. Served with the Indians in the Floridas under the command of Lieut.-Colonel Edw. Nicolls, and various affairs of boats on the coast of America, and West Indies.

33* Captain Willes's services: Sir Richard Strachan's action, 4 Nov. 1805; West Indies, 1808 to 1812, including the capture of the city of St. Domingo in 1809; South Beveland, winter of 1813; Operations in the Chesapeake under Sir George Cockburn; Capture of Washington; Advance to Baltimore, in 1814; Capture of Cumberland Island on the coast of Georgia, and of the town of Saint Mary's, 1814; Coast of Africa, 1817; East Indies, 1832 to 1835. Various boat and other services.

34 Captain Richardson served in the Channel Fleet under Lords Gardiner and St

Notes to the Corps of Royal Marines.

Vincent; the Bellisle squadron under Sir Richard Keates, when endeavouring to intercept Jerome Bonaparte; and at the capture of *La Rhin* by *Mars* 74. With Admiral Murray and Brigadier General Crawford's expedition of 5000 men originally intended for Lima, but on arrival at Cape of Good Hope ordered to join General Whitelocke's army in Rio Plata; landed with Marines at Monte Video, and brigaded with detachments under command of the Hon. Lieut.-Colonel Deane, 38th Regt.; served in the Baltic, and, while passing the Sound, partially engaged the Castle of Cronenberg; joined the squadron under Sir Jas. Saumarez, in pursuit of Russian fleet, to Rogerswick Bay. Severely wounded on board *Africa* 64, in action with Danish Flotilla consisting of 26 heavy gun and mortar boats, in Keoge Bay, near Copenhagen, 20th October, 1808—*Africa* seven killed, fifty-six wounded. Blockade of Texel under Sir Samuel Hood, and Scheldt under Sir Richard Strachan and Sir Edw. Pellew; served with the Walcheren expedition in the *Theseus* 74, and dismantled and brought away its last gun-boat. Toulon fleet. Landed in company with other detachments of marines and seamen, and some Spanish troops on an island in the Bay of Rosas; dislodged French garrison and blew up the castle. Landed in company with other detachments of marines and seamen, 1812, at Sagona Bay, Island of Corsica,—destroyed and brought off great quantity of valuable ship timber. Affairs of coasts, &c. Served in Egypt and North America; and has received a reward from the Patriotic Fund.

35 Captain Garmston was at the taking of Fort Koupan, Isle of Temour, in 1811; capture of Java, in 1812; attack of Palembang, isle of Sumatra, and Sambass, isle of Borneo; Algiers in 1816. Present at the Sortie from Bilboa 15th May; the advance on the 28th May; and was wounded at the defence of the lines of San Sebastian 6th June, 1836.

36 Captain John Harvey Stevens served in the West Indies, &c. in 1806 and 1807, during the expedition to Walcheren in 1809, and was engaged in several flotilla affairs on the Scheldt. Served also at the successful defence of Cadiz and of Tarifa in 1810 and 1811; was engaged in several detached operations, particularly in one of a severe character on the river Guadalquiver. In 1813 was employed on the coast of America, where he was engaged in an attack on Craney Island, and at the taking of Hampton and Ocracoke under Sir George Cockburn. Served in Canada at the taking of Oswego, on which occasion he was mentioned in Sir Gordon Drummond's despatches. Engaged during a six weeks' siege of Fort Erie, and was intrusted with the construction of a field-work for the defence of the right of the position on Chippewa Creek, which was menaced by a very superior force. In 1816 he was on board the *Queen Charlotte* at the attack on Algiers under Lord Exmouth, by whom he was detached to fire carcasses at the enemy's vessels within the Mole. He was also present at the demonstrations before Algiers under Admiral Sir H. B. Neale. Capt. Stevens is now superintendent of the Marine Artillery Laboratory, which establishment originated in his proposition, and was organized by him.

37 Captain Wm. Ford served at the island of Anholt, in 1811, and at Nyburg; he was at the rupture of three Danish luggers from under the batteries.

38 Capt. Steele was the officer of Marine Artillery, in the *Ætna* bomb, in Basque Roads, at Lord Cochrane's action in 1809, also in the bombardment and siege of Flushing and other operations in the Scheldt in the same year; commanded the artillery in the defence of the island of Anholt, 27 March 1811; adjutant to the Brigade of Marine Artillery serving under Sir Sydney Beckwith, on the coast of America, and at the taking of Hampton, &c., afterwards to the end of the war in Canada; served in the north of Spain, from April 1836 to March 1838, took part in all the operations, including the battle of Hernani.

39 Captain Fegan was at the taking of the fort and town of Guadia; capture of the enemy's convoy under batteries near Marseilles; destruction of French forts near Port Vendre; the taking of Zante, Cephalonia, and Cerigo; capture of enemy's forts and convoy at Pezzero, in the Adriatic; action in the Bay of Naples, 3rd May, 1810, when Sir Jahleel Brenton, in the *Spartan*, defeated the whole of the enemy's squadron, and captured a brig of war; at the capturing an enemy's convoy from under the batteries of Terracino, in 1810; and at the destruction of several American privateers in the Bay of Fundy, by the *Spartan*.

40 Captain Scott was at the destruction of two ships of the line in the Bay of Cette, 26th Oct. 1809; in action with the French fleet off Toulon, 19th July, 1811; in the action at Navarino, 20th Oct. 1827.

41 Captain Leonard was at the storming of the enemy's works at the Island of Santa Maura, and at the siege of the fortress until its surrender in March, 1810. Served in three boat actions when belonging to the *Magnificent*. When in the Perlea he was in action with one line-of-battle ship and two frigates, off Toulon, from eight until three o'clock, Nov. 1811. In a boat action, and about the same time, engaged with the batteries and three armed schooners at the entrance of the Petit Pass, off Toulon.

42 Captain C. Robinson served at the siege of Copenhagen in 1807, and was engaged in the in-shore squadron with the Danish flotilla and crown batteries. In the action with and destruction of the French squadron in the inner roads of Aix, 12th April, 1809, in the

Notes to the Corps of Royal Marines.

Valiant, the senior officer's ship actually engaged. At the siege of Flushing, and the subsequent operations in the Scheldt in 1809. On the coast of France in 1810 and 1811 in boat affairs. In the 1st battalion of Royal Marines throughout the campaign of 1813 in the Chesapeake, commencing with the attack on Cranie Island. In the same battalion in the defence of Lower Canada in the winter of 1813 and in 1814 principally employed on the outposts of the army on the American frontier. In 1814 in command of a company of the 1st battalion Royal Marines in the capture of Cumberland Island, and the attack and capture of the fortified post and town of St. Mary's, Georgia.

43 Captain Dawes was at the siege of Copenhagen in 1807.

44 Captain Calamy has served in every quarter of the globe, and in the actions of Nyburg, Flushing, Isle of France, Java, and several minor affairs with gun-boats, &c.

45 Captain Fynmore, previously to entering the Royal Marines, served several years as midshipman in the navy; served in the expedition to Buenos Ayres; the battle of Trafalgar; and Algiers, in 1816.

46 Captain Sullock was at the capture of Les Saints, West Indies, and at the destruction of French frigates in 1809; capture of Guadaloupe in 1810; engaged in boats on the coast of France in 1811; served with battalion in Holland, in 1813 and 14, and in America in 1814 and 15, including Bladensburg, Washington, and Baltimore.

47 Captain Searle served at Walcheren in 1809.

48 Captain Henry was at the capture of Anholt, May, 1809; at Fort Mobile, 1815; the victory of Algiers, August, 1816; and was frequently engaged with boats in the Baltic, and with the American troops in the Floridas.

49 Captain Graham served in the expedition to Walcheren, and in coast operations in Spain and Portugal, and at the defence of Castro ; at the attack and capture of Hampton; attack and capture of the fortified town and position of St. Mary's, Georgia.

50 Capt. Dusautoy served at Walcheren; was at the capture of Genoa; and in two partial actions with French fleets off Toulon and Marseilles.

51 Captain Wesley served in a battalion formed from the Marines of the squadron under Sir Alex. Cochrane at the reduction of Guadaloupe and other French West India Islands in 1810; in several successful boat affairs under the batteries of Rochelle and Isle d'Aix in 1811 ; in coast operations (Spain,) and in the first battalion of Marines in Portugal 1812 ; at the attack and capture of Hampton, &c. in the Chesapeak, under Major-General Sir Sidney Beckwith, in 1813 in command of a division of gun-boats on Lake Champlain; employed in the blockade of the American flotilla at Platsburg ; at the defence of La Cole Mill (Canada): as adjutant to a battalion at the attack of the fortified town and position of St. Mary's (Georgia) in 1814 ; in repelling an attack of Algerine gun-boats in 1824 ; served as adjutant in Ireland and Mediterranean 1833, 4 and 5, and as adjutant to the battalion of Marines in the North of Spain, at the battle near Hernani, &c. in 1836 and 37.

52 Captain Park was actively employed in the Baltic during 1810, 11, and 12. From 1813 until the peace, served on the coast of America, and the West Indies, including the attack on Cranie Island, and landed at the taking of Hampton, in the Chesapeake.

53 Captain Cater was engaged in several affairs with gun-boats in the Baltic, in 1810. In 1813 he was at the destruction of a French frigate under the batteries near Cherbourg, and at the counter revolution in Holland, 21st Nov. 1813. From 1818 to 1821 the capture of a number of Slavers on the coast of Africa. Served in the north of Spain, including the sortie from Bilboa, 10th May; the advance of the 28th May; defence of the Lines of San Sebastian, 6th and 9th June ; and attack of Lines, 1st Oct. 1836.

53* Captain James Dowman served at the siege of Cadiz in 1810, 11, and 12, during which period he was repeatedly engaged in action against the enemy both on land and in boats, cutting out, &c. Served also at the blockading of the French fleet off Brest in 1813.

54 Captain Law was in the action with, and capture of the *Chesapeake* by the *Shannon*, 1st June, 1813 ; at the capture of Fort St. Elmo, and the batteries at Naples, 21st May, 1815.

55 Captain Miller was at the destruction of the Danish line at Copenhagen in 1801, under Lord Nelson; in 1809 at the taking of Ischia and Procida; destruction of French gun-boats, by boarding, in the Bay of Naples; capture of *La Lagire*, French privateer, of ten guns and 125 men, and her companion of one 24-pounder and twenty-five men by boarding. In 1810, at the capture of the enemy's convoy from under the batteries at Terracino. In command of the marines of the squadron at the island of Lissa, Nov. 1811, at the capture of the French frigate *La Pomone*. Was at the capture of a Portuguese pirate of 18 guns and 98 men, and several slave ships in 1816.

56 Captain Toby served from 1810 to 12 inclusive, on the Coast of France. From 1813 to 16, with the 1st battalion (Royal Marines) in America, and on the Lakes of Canada. Since the Peace, he has served in the Mediterranean, on the coasts of Africa, and South America. He has been frequently engaged in boat actions with batteries, &c. &c.

57 Captain Beadon served off the coast of France, from 1811 until 1814, including various boat actions; in 1815 at the capture of Naples and Gaieta. Severely engaged with pirates in the West Indies in 1824.

Notes to the Corps of Royal Marines.

58 Captain Thomas Fynmore was at the capture of a French privateer schooner of 16 guns and 96 men, besides other boat service in 1811. In the partial action with the French fleet off Toulon in 1814. Was landed at Mahon in command of a guard to protect the person of the Spanish governor from the threatened violence of the Walloon guards. Sent to the city of Florence in 1815, to place himself under the directions of General Count Nugent, commander-in-chief of the Austrian army, as extra aide-de-camp, and was at the taking of the city of Naples. In 1823 he was sent up to the city of Lima to protect English merchants' property against the attacks of the Negro slaves during the civil war. The 20th Oct. 1827, was at the battle of Navarino, for which service he was promoted by His Royal Highness the Duke of Clarence, but in consequence of belonging to a gradation corps the appointment was afterwards cancelled. Served with the French army at the reduction of the town and fortress of Patras and the Morea castle; served afterwards in the West Indies, North Sea, and off Oporto during the civil war between Don Pedro and Don Miguel. In 1833 joined the Royal Marine Battalion at Lisbon, commanded by Colonel Adair, C. B. In April, 1837, embarked on board H. M. S. *Castor* (36), on the 10th Oct. was landed in command of his detachment on the Albanian coast to attack Pirates. Served on the S. E. coast of Spain from 4th Jan. 38 to 30 Jan. 39.

59 Captain Brown's services:—attack on French forts at Ciota June 1812; attack and capture of the town of L'Escalia, in the Bay of Rosas, 1812; partial engagement with the French fleet, near Toulon, 1813; attack of Algiers; destruction of Greek pirates at Porto Bono, Isle of Candia, June, 1826.

60 Lieut. Carr served in the North Sea, coast of France, North and South America, Cape of Good Hope, &c. &c. from 1812 to 1815.

61 Lieut. Hurdle was at the attack on the forts and harbour of Courageaux in 1815; battle of Navarino in 1827.

62 Lieut. James Wood served from 1812 to 1815 at the Texel, Flushing, Cherbourgh, Basque Roads, north coast of Spain, and San Sebastian. During the war he served also in the West Indies, St. Helena, and Madeira.

63 Lieut. Dwyer served in the blockading squadrons off Flushing, the Texel, and off Brest. Since the peace he has served in the East and West Indies, and the Mediterranean.

64 Lieut. William Wood served in H. M. S. *Niger*, at the capture of the French frigate, *La Ceres*.

65 Lieut. Parke's services: — Co-operation with the Spanish forces and Legion near San Sebastian, and under Espartero in raising the siege of Bilboa.

66 Lieuts. Stransham, Anderson, and Miller, were at the battle of Navarino in 1827.

68 Lieut. Logan's services: — Co-operation with the French army in the Morea. Present at the siege of Patras. Co-operation with Spanish forces and legion near San Sebastian.

70 Lieut. Fraser landed for the protection of British property at Lima, during the revolution in Dec. 1835, when in possession of the rebels. For his conduct on that occasion, he was presented with a piece of plate by the merchants.

71 Lieut. Brittain was presented with a sword by the merchants of Bombay, for services performed against pirates in the Straits of Malacca.

72 Lieut. Parker was wounded through the arm at Prescott, in Upper Canada, 13th Nov. 1838.

73 Capt. Hookey served as Volunteer 1st class, in His Majesty's ship *Prince of Wales*, from Jan. to Dec. 1805, and was in the general action of the 22nd Dec. 1805. Served in the West Indies, from 1806 until 1809, including the capture of Les Saints, and Martinique, and several actions in boats cutting out French vessels, and destroying batteries, &c. From 1809 to 1811 served on board H. M. S. *Theban*, blockading the French flotilla at Boulogne; several times in action with them. Assisted in the boats cutting out a large French lugger at Dieppe. From 1812 to 1814, served on board His Majesty's ship *Daphne*, in the Baltic, and was several times in action with Danish gun-boats in the Belt.

74 Doctor Quarrier has served in every quarter of the globe. Present at the bombardment of Granville in 1803; St. Domingo in 1806. Served also in the Peninsula, including Corunna, siege of San Sebastian and passage of the Garrone. On board the *Leander* at the bombardment of Algiers in 1816; besides the above he has been engaged in several frigate actions.

75 Doctor Rae has served in every quarter of the globe; eight years in the East Indies at one period, and was at the destruction of the Dutch squadron in Surabaya in 1808. He has been in frequent engagements with batteries, and in the cutting out of numerous vessels, and in many boat-actions.

76 Captain Wolrige served in the year 1809 with Lord Cochrane in Basque Roads; and in the same year was engaged in action with gun-boats in the Baltic. From 1810 to 1812 defence of Cadiz and Tarrifa. Severely wounded at South Beveland in 1814, and received a reward from the Patriotic Fund. Present at the battle of Algiers in 1816.

COMMISSARIAT.

Years' Serv.			Treasury Clerk.	Deputy Asst. Commis. Gen.	Assistant Commis. Gen.	Deputy Commis. Gen.	Commissary General.
Full Pay.	Half Pay.						
		Commissary-General.					
		₿ R. Isham Routh	Never	Never	13 Nov. 05	9 Mar. 12	15 Aug. 26
		Dep.-Commiss.-General.					
		₿ Edw. Pine Coffin	Never	Never	1 Aug. 09	4 Aug. 14	
		₿ William Filder			10 Aug. 11	22 Oct. 16	
		₿ Tupper Carey			do.	19 July 21	
		William Hewetson		23 May 10	31 May 14	7 June 25	
		₿ Denzil Ibbettson	Never	5 Oct. 10	25 Dec. 14	10 Sep. 30	
		₿ Daniel Kearney		10 Aug. 11	19 July 21	13 Dec. 33	
		Charles Palmer [1]	Never	Never	4 May 15	20 Jan. 37	
		₿ William Miller		5 Aug. 11	22 Oct. 16	do.	
		Francis Edward Knowles		5 May 12	do.	do.	
		₿ John Banner Price ..		25 Dec. 14	9 Feb. 27	5 June 38	
		Asst.-Commiss.-General.					
		Charles Graham........		5 Sep. 14	7 June 25		1 Deputy Storekeeper General 4 May, 1815, transferred to the Commissariat with the Storekeeper General's Department in 1819, taking rank as Assistant Commissary General from date of Commission as Deputy Storekeeper General.
		₿ William Jennings		2 Mar. 12	do.		
		₿ F. W. A. C. Major ..		29 Apr. 12	do.		
		₿ Lovell Pennell		23 May 12	do.		
		John Tench............		25 May 12	do.		
		J. Kenneth Macbreedy ..		do.	do.		
		W. H. Robinson		2 Nov. 12	do.		
		₿ W. Randolph Eppes ..	24 Dec. 11	19 July 21	7 July 27		
		James Thompson		2 Nov. 12	23 Nov 27		
		Charles A. Clarke		15 Dec. 12	23 Nov. 27		
		Francis Robert Foote ..		30 Apr. 14	do.		
		Tannat H. Thomson		8 Dec. 12	10 Sep. 30		
		William Green		16 Mar. 13	10 Sep. 30		
		John Irvine		9 Sep. 14	2 Jan. 31		
		John Bland............		1 June 21	8 Mar. 31		
		₿ Henry Bowers	June 12	25 Dec. 14	13 Dec. 33		
		₿ George Maclean......	July 12	22 Oct. 16	24 May 34		
		₿ William Bishop		13 July 24	24 July 34		
		Thos. C. Weir		15 July 26	11 Apr. 36		
		₿ Edw. A. F. Cowan ..		5 Aug. 11	4 May 36		
		₿ Thomas Rayner......		22 Apr. 13	20 Jan. 37		
		John Davidson		25 Nov. 13	do.		
		John Leggatt		do.	do.		
		William Bailey		10 Jan. 14	do.		
		C. W. Beverley		15 Jan. 14	do.		
		John Lane		31 Jan. 14	do.		
		₿ William F. Bowman ..		4 May 14	do.		
		₿ James D. Watt......		do.	do.		
		Henry Laurie [2]	20 Dec. 19	19 July 21	19 Mar. 38		2 Transferred from Storekeeper General's Department, 20 Dec. 1819.
		Robert Lindsey		13 July 14	3 May 38		
		Joseph Verfenstein		25 Dec. 14	18 May 38		
		₿ Thomas Scobell		do.	5 June 38		
		Thomas Rae		do.	do.		

COMMISSARIAT.

Years' Serv.			Treasury Clerk.	Deputy Asst. Commis. Gen.	Assistant Commis. Gen.	Deputy Commis. Gen.	Commissary General.
Full Pay.	Half Pay						
		George C. Sanford		22 Oct. 16	5 June 38		
		Thomas Stickney		do.	do.		
		William Isaac Greig		13 May 14	28 June 38		
		William Ross		3 Nov. 14	do.		
		Oliver Goldsmith		17 Dec. 14	do.		
		William Low		do.	do.		
		Amos Lister[1]	Never	20 Dec. 19	22 Mar. 19		
		Dep. Asst. Commis.-Gen.					
		₱ Thomas Clarke		10 Aug. 11	[1] Transferred from Storekeeper General's Department (Assistant Storekeeper General, 20 December 1819).		
		Robert Lee		25 Dec. 14			
		Alexander Grant		do.			
		₱ Henry A. Bayley		do.			
		James Mason		do.			
		William Stevens........		do.			
		Robert Charters........		do.			
		₱ Peter Roberts	June 12	do.			
		Charles Williams		do.			
		John Jennings		do.			
		Colin Miller		do.			
		James Wilson..........		do.			
		₱ Charles Wemyss		25 Apr. 15	[2] Transferred from Storekeeper General's Department (Assistant Storekeeper General 25 April 1815).		
		Charles Morgan[2]	Never	do.			
		Kenneth Cameron[2]	do.	do.			
		Thomas Fraser		do.			
		₱ Henry Charles Darling		12 Sept. 16			
		₱ James William Reed..		22 Oct. 16			
		₱ Thos. R. Mitchison ..		do.			
		J. T. Goodsir		do.			
		₱ William Fletcher	June 12	do.			
		₱ William Milliken		do.			
		William Howe		do.			
		Charles Howard........		1 June 21			
		Samuel Carr		do.			
		Charles Bridgen........		do.			
		Jos. Steere Brown		do.			
		Thomas Davis Knight ..		do.			
		₱ John Rich. Comper ..		do.			
		Charles Swain		do.			
		Thomas Walker........		13 July 24			
		Fulford Bastard Feilde..		7 June 25			
		Langley Brackenbury ..		do.			
		Henry Francis Oriel		do.	[3] Transferred from Storekeeper General's Department, 20 Dec. 1819.		
		Thomas Eggar Trew[3] ..	20 Dec. 19	do.			
		Fergus Thos. Coxworthy[3]	do.	do.			
		Thos. Geo. S. Swan[3]	do.	do.			
		William Looker........		15 July 26			
		John M'Farlan		do.			
		Benjamin Stow	June 25	3 Apr. 27			
		R. Wharton Tweddell...		do.			
		Samuel Jos. Towesland..		18 Sep. 27			
		₱ Jos. Wm. Wybault ..		23 Sep. 27			
		James Tennent		do.			
		Richard Inglis		30 Oct. 27			
		James Skyrme		28 Nov. 27			

COMMISSARIAT.

Years' Serv. Full Pay	Half Pay	Name	Treasury Clerk.	Deputy Asst. Commis. Gen.	Assistant Commis. Gen.	Deputy Commis. Gen.	Commissary General.
		James Parr............		20 May 28			
		S. E. Hansord		do.			
		Slodden Castle		13 Jan. 29			
		Robert Ackroyd........		14 May 29			
		Frederick Thos. Mylrea..		10 Sept. 30			
		James Macpherson		do.			
		Thomas Wilson		do.			
		William Stanton		2 Jan. 31			
		B E. M. Archdeacon....		5 Oct. 32			
		William Baldy		do.			
		W. R. A. Lamont		do.			
		William Fred. Jones		do.			
		John Kent		do.			
		Stephen Owen		do.			
		John William Smith		1 Dec. 33			
		Fra. Bisset Archer......		2 Jan. 34			
		Thomas Graham		11 Dec. 34			
		William Henry Drake ..		16 Apr. 35			
		Johannes de Smidt		29 Aug. 36			
		Thos. Jas. Lempriere....		20 Jan. 37			
		George Shepheard		do.			
		Robert Neill		do.			
		Edward Thos. Grindley..		do.			
		William Hen. Maturin ..		do.			
		John William Bovell		do.			
		Wm. Hen. Dalrymple ..		do.			
		Randolph Routh		do.			
		Alexander Edwards		do.			
		William Fisher Mends ..	1 July 36	1 July 37			
		John Josiah Smith......		28 June 38			
		John Philip Camm		do.			
		Maximilian Malassez....		do.			
		Philip Turner..........		do.			
		John Trimmer		do.			
		Robert Low		do.			
		Edm. John M'Mahon ...		do.			
		Wm. Spearman Archer..		do.			
		John S. Davenport		do.			
		Willough. Clem. Wasey..		do.			
		James Aug. Erskine		do.			
		Henry Clarke..........	27 Aug. 37	27 Aug. 38			

Blue.—*Facings*—Black Velvet.

DUTIES AND ORGANIZATION.

The Commissariat are charged with the following duties:—In the Field they have hitherto had the custody of the Military Chest, and provided and paid for everything necessary for the subsistence and transport of an army. At the present time, on stations abroad, they have the charge of the Military Chests, negotiation of Bills for their supply, and receipt of all surplus monies arising from various sources in the hands of public departments, as also monies for remittance to England. They make advances to Regimental Paymasters on account of the Pay of the Troops, and to the Heads of the Ordnance and Naval Departments, on account of their respective services. They pay in detail the Staff, all money allowances and contingencies; also the Half Pay and re-

COMMISSARIAT.

tired allowances, Chelsea Pensions, Widows' Pensions, Compassionate allowances, and Naval Pensions, &c., to all persons resident at the several stations. They contract and pay for Provisions required on the spot for the supply of the Troops, and for land and water transport. In the West Indies they pay in detail the Assistant Commissioners and Stipendiary Magistrates under the Provisions of the Slave Compensation Act: at some stations they perform the duties of Naval Agents. In Canada, Nova Scotia, and Jamaica, they pay the Ecclesiastical Establishments, and at the former they have the custody and issue of Indian Presents, and charge of the Locks and Collection of the Tolls on the canals connected with the St. Lawrence. In New South Wales and Van Dieman's Land, they supply Provisions, Clothing, and Stores, of all descriptions for convict services. They enter into contracts for Ordnance Stores, Building Materials, &c., on the spot, and provide and pay for supplies for Army Hospitals, superintend the issue of provisions, forage, fuel, and light in kind made by Contractors, and issue such articles of Provision as are sent out for the use of the Troops from England. Their duties are blended with the Army, Ordnance, Navy, and many other branches of the public service. They are under the orders of and responsible for the execution of their duties to the General or Officers commanding at the various stations, and receive their instructions from the Board of Treasury, with whom they correspond through the Secretary on all points of service on which they are engaged.

See Report of Commissioners appointed to enquire into the expediency of Consolidating the Civil Departments of the Army, dated 21 July, 1837.

The following is the authority for its present organization :—

Commissary-in-Chief's Office, 19 March, 1810. His Majesty has been pleased to command that the following regulations should be established and acted upon in all future Promotions and Appointments in the Commissariat.

That the Gradation of Rank, be "Commissary-General," "Deputy Commissary-General," "Assistant Commissary-General," "Deputy Assistant Commissary-General," "Clerk." No person to enter but as Clerk,—to serve One year before eligible for Promotion.—Deputy Assistant to serve Four years, or Five from entrance as Clerk before eligible.—Assistant, Five years as Assistant, or Ten years from entrance as Clerk before eligible.—Deputy to be Three years in that rank before eligible.—Service to be counted as actual service on Full Pay. No person to be appointed Clerk previous to the age of 16.

The comparative ranks are Commissary-General as Brigadier-General.—Deputy as Major, after Three years, Lieutenant-Colonel.—Assistant as Captain.—Deputy Assistant as Lieutenant.—Clerk as Ensign. See Army Regulations.

MEDICAL DEPARTMENT.

Years' Serv. Full Pay	Half Pay		HOSPITAL ASSIST.	ASSIST. SURGEON.	REGTL. SURGEON.	STAFF SURGEON.	ASSIST. INSPECT.	BREVET DEP. INSP.	DEPUTY INSP.-GEN.	INSPEC. GENERAL.	WHERE STATIONED.
		Directors General.									
46	6/12	※ Sir James M'Grigor,[1] Bart. M.D. 13 June, 15	....	....	....	....	....	....	27 June 05	25 Aug. 09	London
		Geo. Renny, M.D. (*Ireland only*) 1 June, 95....	....	June 75	Jan. 80	....	....	....	....	....	Dublin
		Inspectors General of Hospitals.									
39	G	※ Thomas Draper,[3] (*West Indies only*)	25 Apr. 95	April 99	17 Apr. 04	1 Sept. 08	....	....	18 Jan. 16	24 Feb. 37	Barbadoes
35	5 10/12	※ Donald M'Leod,[4] M.D.	10 Sept. 99	30 Jan. 00	24 Nov. 03	9 Sept. 13	....	....	27 Nov. 28	1 June 37	Bengal
33	1 3/12	Joseph Skey, M.D.	....	....	....	....	18 July 05	11 Dec. 23	26 Oct. 20	15 Feb. 39	Québec
		Deputy Inspector-Generals of Hospitals.									
42	2 7/12	Robt. Moore Peile, M.D. (*Ireland only*)	19 June 98	....	....	1 July 95	....	....	25 Sept. 03		Dublin
36	1 3/12	Sir James Pitcairn,[5] M.D. (*Ireland only*) ...	....	....	....	Aug. 99	....	....	22 Oct. 03		Cork
37	3 4/12	※ Hugh Bone,[6] M.D.	8 Sept. 03	17 Sept. 03	13 July 09	26 Mar. 12	7 Sept. 15	27 May 25	1 Nov. 27		Corfu
33	7	※ James Gillkrest,[7] M.D.	10 Oct. 00	19 Aug. 01	15 Dec. 04	....	....	....	5 Nov. 29		Gibraltar
34	1 3/12	John Vaughan Thompson.............	....	3 July 00	25 June 03	25 Dec. 12	....	....	do.		Sidney, N. S. Wales
31	6 7/12	※ John Murray,[8] M.D.	Feb. 05	2 Mar. 09	28 May 12	9 Sept. 13	....	....	do.		Madras
37	0	※ Fred. Albert Loinsworth[9]	18 Feb. 03	22 July 04	8 June 09	7 July 14	....	....	do.		Bombay
33	2 2/12	※ Theodore Gordon,[10] M.D.	28 Nov. 03	23 Nov. 04	6 July 09	9 Sept. 13	7 Sept. 15	26 Nov. 18	29 Jan. 36		London
30	14 3/12	※ Arthur Stewart,[11] M.D.	5 Nov. 05	10 Apr. 06	3 Sept. 12	9 Nov. 26	27 Sept. 27	....	9 Dec. 36		Ceylon
25	5	※ Thomas Kidd,[12] M.D.	17 June 96	6 Apr. 97	25 July 99	27 Aug. 03	....	17 July 17	27 Jan. 37		Jamaica
24		※ John Frederick Clarke, M.D.	....	25 June 11	....	21 Dec. 26	4 Sept. 28	....	9 Aug. 39		Van Dieman's Land
		Assistant Inspectors of Hospitals.									
25	1 7/12	John Davy, M.D.	19 May 15	9 Nov. 15	1 Feb. 21	29 Mar. 21	8 Nov. 27	....	....		Chatham
29	7 6/12	John Shortt, M.D.[14]	June 04	19 Oct. 04	25 Mar. 24	....	1 June 38	....	....		Canada
25	2 6/12	※ * Brinsley Nicholson, M.D.	....	29 Apr. 13	5 Nov. 29	19 June 35	1 June 38	....	....		Cape of Good Hope
29	0	※ * Charles St. John,[16] M.D.	8 Aug. 11	3 Sept. 12	14 Feb. 22	9 Dec. 36	4 Jan. 39	....	....		Mauritius
32	7	※ Montagu Martin Mahony,[17] M.D.	....	29 Sept. 08	3 June 13	11 Aug. 35	30 Aug. 39	....	....		Malta
		Surgeons.									
26	3 3/12	※ James Elliot,[18]	23 May 01	12 Apr. 05	1 June 09	14 Oct. 13	....	....	....		Nova Scotia
30	0 7/12	William Hacket,[19] M.D.	....	12 June 01	25 Nov. 08	6 Jan. 14	....	....	....		
31	0	※ Alexander Stewart,[20] M.D.	14 June 09	27 Dec. 10	13 May 24	24 Nov. 25	....	....	....		Newry
27	4 11/12	William Munro............................	6 Sept. 08	16 Feb. 09	22 June 15	5 Jan. 26	....	....	....		Dublin
24	3	James Barry, M.D.	5 July 13	7 Dec. 15	....	22 Nov. 27	....	....	....		Barbadoes
25		John Robertson, M.D.	14 Mar. 14	22 June 20	....	10 Sept. 29	....	....	....		Edinburgh

Medical Department.

Years' Serv.		Full Pay.	Half Pay.		HOSPITAL-ASSISTANT.	ASSISTANT-SURGEON.	REGTL.-SURGEON.	STAFF-SURGEON.	WHERE STATIONED.
20	13.6/12			*Surgeons.* Francis Arthur M'Cann, M.D.		11 Sept. 06	13 Jan. 14	19 Nov. 30	St. Vincent.
31	1			⊕ Henry Franklin,[21]	13 Aug. 08	29 June 09	26 May 14	do.	Portsmouth.
31	5/12			⊕⊞ Abraham Armstrong,[22]	April 09	May 09	7 Mar. 16	do.	Corfu.
35	0			⊕ Colquhoun Grant,[23] M.D.	5 Feb. 05	6 Nov. 06	16 April 12	13 April 32	Royal Military College.
30	0			John Pickering, M.D.	24 April 10	29 April 13		29 June 32	St. Kitts.
27	0			Daniel Scott	8 Feb. 08	18 Mar. 24		17 Oct. 34	Barbadoes.
30	0			Alexander Melvin,[24]	26 July 10	26 Sept. 11	10 Dec. 23	3 Aug. 26	Coventry.
37	0			Michael William Kenny,[24]*		25 Sept. 03	13 Jan. 18	12 Feb. 36	Bristol.
24	11/12			Charles Whyte	19 Sept. 15	14 May 16	24 Aug. 26	30 Dec. 36	Glasgow.
32	4			⊕ John Lightbody,[25]	20 Aug. 04	20 June 05	15 Oct. 12	3 Mar. 37	Liverpool.
27	1 5/12			⊕ Peter Smith	25 June 12	11 Nov. 13	22 Mar. 31	7 April 37	Chatham.
24	0			Andrew Smith, M.D.	14 Mar. 16	27 Oct. 25		7 July 37	Leeds.
19	8 1/2			William Dawson, M.D.	18 Oct. 13	9 June 14	3 April 35	29 Dec. 37	Ceylon.
29	2 6/12			⊕⊞ Samuel Jeyes,[26] M.D.	14 Nov. 11	28 Nov. 11	2 May 22	7 Dec. 38	Canada.
28	0			⊕ George Barclay,[27] M.D.	17 Jan. 10	22 Aug. 11	23 Dec. 24	4 Jan. 39	do.
29	0			⊕ Walter Henry,[28]	11 April 11	19 Dec. 11	8 June 26	do.	do.
28	0			⊕⊞ Thomas Smith,[29] M.D.	29 Mar. 12	2 July 12	13 July 26	do.	do.
26	6/12			Joseph Farnden	24 Jan. 14	12 May 14	23 July 29	do.	Barbadoes.
27	0			Andrew Fergusson,[30] M.D.	21 June 13	20 July 15	28 Nov. 34	11 Jan. 39	do.
14	0			Thomas Spence	3 Aug. 26	8 Feb. 27		12 July 39	London.
30	1 7/12			⊕ Samuel Crozier Roe,[31] M.D.		4 Aug. 08	26 May 14	17 Sept. 39	Cork.
22	3 1/12			Alexander Sinclair, M.D.	20 July 15	9 May 16	28 Aug. 35	20 Sept. 39	Jamaica.
16	0			John Hawkey, M.D.	23 Dec. 24	16 June 25		do.	West Indies.
25	0			James Wilson, M.D.	3 June 15	30 June 25		do.	Sierra Leone.
20	6 8/12			William Fergusson	20 Dec. 13	13 May 24	24 Nov. 25	27 Sept. 39	
				Apothecaries.			Apothecary		
39	0			Henry O'Hara, M.D.			24 June 04		Dublin.
22	16 10/12			Edmund Starkie,[32]	13 May 01		8 Oct. 07		Chatham.
30	3/12			Jonathan Courtney	24 June 01		31 Aug. 09		Cape of Good Hope.
3	22 5/12			John Carter	11 Oct. 10		11 Mar. 13		Halifax, Nova Scotia.
31	2 1/12			⊕ George Hume Reade[33]			9 Sept. 13		Quebec.
28	1			⊕ Joseph Schembri	17 Jan. 07		14 Oct. 13		Corfu.
15	0			James Woolley Simpson	24 June 11		18 May 15		Malta.
14	0			Francis Matthias Bassano			18 Apr. 25		London.
				George Allman	8 Nov. 26	20 Sept. 27	28 Feb. 28		Jamaica.

Medical Department.

Years' Serv.			HOSPITAL ASSISTANT.	ASSISTANT SURGEON.	WHERE STATIONED.
Full Pay.	Half Pay.	Assistant-Surgeons.			
11	18	Henry Fisher, M.D.	never	28 Nov. 11	Dublin.
13	14	Thomas Rhys	25 Mar. 13	25 May 15	Honduras.
15	0	Michael Ryan, M.D.	10 Mar. 25	16 June 25	Canada.
24	1¾	Robert Dunkin Smyth	19 May 15	6 Oct. 25	Royal Mil. College.
44	0	John Cricklow Barker	24 Oct. 96	24 Nov. 25	Barbadoes.
12	3½	Wm. Scott M'Credie	6 Oct. 25	12 Jan. 26	Bermuda.
15	0	Peter Robertson............	24 Nov. 25	do.	Ceylon.
13	1⅚	John Forrest, M.D..........	10 Nov. 25	9 Feb. 26	Cape of Good Hope
15	0	John Gillice	18 Aug. 25	8 March 27	Chatham.
14	0	Alexander Thom	2 Nov. 26	do.	Mauritius.
14	0	William Hall	2 Nov. 26	8 May 28	Canada.
14	0	David Charles Pitcairn......	19 Dec. 26	29 July 30	Cork.
13	0	Alexander Campbell	27 Feb. 27	do.	Cape of Good Hope.
13	0	Michael Nugent............	do.	do.	Chatham.
13	0	James Clephane Minto	29 Mar. 27	do.	Cape of Good Hope.
13	0	Robert Allan	22 Nov. 27	do.	Mauritius.
13	0	Samuel Maitland Hadaway ..	29 Nov. 27	do.	Corfu.
13	0	Adam Thomson Jackson	do.	do.	Canada.
13	0	John Caw, M.D.............	3 Jan. 28	do.	Maidstone.
12	0	John Stewart	13 Mar. 28	do.	Chatham.
12	0	Peter Daly Murray	4 Aug. 28	do.	Ceylon.
10	2⅚	William Odell	14 Feb. 28	9 Nov. 30	Gibraltar.
11	1⅚	John Loftus Hartwell	13 Mar. 28	1 Feb. 31	Canada.
8	0	Robert Wood	never	31 Aug. 32	Cork.
8	0	John Mitchell, M.D.........	do.	13 Nov. 32	Gibraltar.
8	0	Edward Wm. Burton	do.	21 Dec. 32	Jamaica.
7	0	John Marshall	do.	29 March 33	
7	0	John Robert Taylor	do.	31 May 33	Canada.
7	0	James Stuart	do.	5 July 33	Cape of Good Hope.
7	0	Grigor Stewart	do.	12 July 33	
7	0	David Dyce	do.	15 Nov. 33	
7	0	Thomas Ross Jameson, M.D.	do.	10 Jan. 34	Jamaica.
6	0	Thomas Alexander	do.	10 Oct. 34	Do.
5	0	John Charles Cameron, M.D.	do.	27 March 35	Ceylon.
5	0	John Garnett Courtenay	do.	10 April 35	Cape of Good Hope.
5	0	Francis Robert Waring......	do.	8 May 35	Jamaica.
5	0	Robert Lawson	do.	15 May 35	Malta.
5	0	George Carr	do.	24 July 35	Chatham.
5	0	Peter Robertson............	do.	4 Dec. 35	Nova Scotia.
5	0	George Galland	do.	18 Dec. 35	Mauritius.
4	0	Archibald Stewart..........	do.	19 Feb. 36	Chatham.
4	0	Tho. Graham Balfour, M.D...	do.	29 April 36	London.
4	0	William Dick, M.D.	do.	13 May 36	Mauritius.
4	0	Robert Beresford Gahan	do.	17 June 36	Do.
4	0	Thos. Moore Fishbourne, M.D.	do.	22 July 36	Jamaica.
4	0	Lawrence Jameson..........	do.	12 Aug. 36	Cape of Good Hope.
4	0	Alexander Mackintosh, M.D.	do.	30 Sept. 36	Canada.
4	0	John Donald Grant	do.	30 Dec. 36	Nova Scotia.
4	0	William Denny	do.	13 Jan. 37	Jamaica.
3	0	Hugh Mackey	do.	17 Feb. 37	Corfu.
3	0	Luke Kelly, M.D............	do.	5 May 37	Ceylon.
3	0	John Grant................	do.	9 June 37	Ceylon.
3	0	Charles Stewart............	do.	7 July 37	Barbadoes.
3	0	Alex. Douglas Taylor........	do.	15 Sept. 37	Jamaica.
3	0	Thomas D'Arcy, M.D.	do.	29 Dec. 37	Canada.
3	0	William Home, M.D.........	do.	12 Jan. 38	Canada.
2	0	Charles Ross	do.	6 Apr.	Gambia.
2	0	Geo. Stewart Beatson, M.D...	do.	13 July	Ceylon.
2	0	Frederick Baillie	do.	19 Oct.	Corfu.

Medical Department.

Years' Serv. Full Pay.	Years' Serv. Half Pay.		ASSISTANT SURGEON.	WHERE STATIONED.
2	0	Frederick Foaker	19 Oct. 38	Corfu.
2	0	Simeon Henry Hardy, M.D.	2 Nov.	West Indies.
2	0	Wm. St. John Boyle, M.D.	30 Nov.	Sierra Leone.
2	0	Wm. Ord Mackenzie, M.D.	4 Jan. 39	Canada
2	0	Wm. Leslie Langley, M.D.	11 Jan.	West Indies.
2	0	John Gillespie Wood, M.D.	11 Jan.	Canada.
2	0	Charles Dawson	11 Jan.	Cork.
2	0	Charles Godwin, M.D.	18 Jan.	West Indies.
1	0	Benj. Usher Hamilton, M.D.	22 Feb.	Barbadoes.
1	0	Tho. John Coghlan, M.D.	29 Mar.	Cork.
1	0	Nicholas O'Connor, M.D.	5 Apr.	Barbadoes.
1	0	Geo. W. Powell, M.D.	7 June	Chatham.
1	0	Tho. Rose Dyce	7 June	Chatham.
1	0	Michael M'Bride	12 July	Malta.
1	0	James Johnston, M.D.	9 Aug.	Canada.
1	0	John Donald	23 Aug.	Canada.
1	0	Richard Bannatine	17 Sept.	Cork.
1	0	John Wordsworth	20 Sept.	Corfu.
1	0	John Newton	4 Oct. 39	Cork.
1	0	James Walker Chambers, M.D.	4 Oct.	West Indies.
1	0	Francis William Grant, M.D.	11 Oct.	Malta.
1	0	Alexander Greer, M.D.	11 Oct.	West Indies.
1	0	Charles Hart, M.D.	18 Oct.	West Indies.
1	0	William Duncan	8 Nov.	Sierra Leone.
1	0	Thomas Henry O'Flaherty	15 Nov.	Sierra Leone.
1	0	John Davies	22 Nov.	Mauritius.
1	0	James M'Gregor	5 Dec.	Gibraltar.
1	0	George Murray Webster	5 Dec.	Jamaica.
1	0	David Lucas	20 Dec.	Chatham.
1	0	James Alex. Fraser, M.D.	20 Dec.	C. of Good Hope
1	0	Joseph Burke	10 Jan. 40	Chatham.
1	0	Alex. B. Cleland, M.D.	21 Feb.	Chatham.

		DEPUTY PURVEYORS.	PURVEYOR'S CLERK.	DEPUTY PURVEYOR.	
		ꝓ Jonathan Croft		16 April 12	Sydney, N.S.W.
		ꝓ Francis Bishop		3 Sept. 12	Van Dieman's L.
		ꝓ Wm. Henry Clapp		15 Oct. 12	Cork.
29	1 6/12	ꝓ George Pratt [31]	25 Sept. 09	3 June 13	Chatham.
		ꝓ William Ivey		26 May 14	Dublin.
		Charles Warner		7 Sept. 15	Jamaica.
		Tho. Estwick Pierce		17 Jan. 22	Barbadoes.
		Matthew Wreford		3 Sept. 29	Plymouth.

Notes to Medical Department.

1 Sir James M'Grigor entered the service in Sept. 1793, as Surgeon of the 88th Regt.; he served in Holland and Flanders in 1794 and 5; in the West Indies in 1796; in the East Indies in 1798; in Egypt, as superintending Surgeon of the Anglo-Indian army in 1801; with the army at Walcheren in 1809; and in the Peninsula from 1811 to the end of the war.

3 Dr. Draper served in Sicily, 1806; in Egypt, 1807; the Corunna Campaign; Portugal in 1811; expedition to Holland in 1814.

4 Dr. M'Leod's services:—Campaign of 1799 in Holland; expedition to Belleisle, and Minorca; expedition to South America, including capture of Maldonado, Monte Video, and Buenos Ayres; campaign of 1808 and 9, including the battles of Roleia, Vimiera, and Corunna; expedition to Walcheren; in the Peninsula from June 1812 to the end of the war, including the battles of Salamanca, and Vittoria, and siege of San Sebastian; in America in 1814 and 15, including the action at Plattsburgh.

5 Dr. Pitcairn served in Holland in 1799, and in Egypt in 1801.

6 Dr. Bone's services:—Expedition to South America in 1807; campaign of 1808 and 9, including the battles of Roleia, Vimiera, and Corunna; expedition to Walcheren; Peninsula from May 1812 to the end of the war.

7 Dr. Gillkrest was present with the expedition in the West Indies in 1801 under Sir Thomas Trigge, including the capture of the islands of St. Martin, St. John, St. Bartholomew, St. Thomas, and Santa Cruz. Served as Surgeon of a regiment in the Light Division throughout the war in the Peninsula, including the battle of Vimiera; retreat to, and battle of Corunna, retreat from Burgos, actions of the Coa (near Almeida), Busaco, Sabugal, Fuentes d'Onor, Salamanca, Vittoria, the Pyrenees, Nivelle, Nive, and Toulouse; and the sieges of Ciudad Rodrigo and San Sebastian, at which latter he accompanied the storming party. Served also at New Orleans in 1815.

8 Dr. Murray went to the Mediterranean in 1805 in the expedition under Sir James Craig, and served in Malta, Naples, Calabria, Ischia and Procida, and in Sicily nearly five years. Served also in the Peninsula from 1810 to the end of the war.

9 Dr. Loinsworth served the campaign of 1808 and 9, and was present in the action at Lugo and battle of Corunna. Served also with the expedition against Guadaloupe in 1815.

10 Dr. Gordon's services:—Expedition to Hanover; campaign of 1808 and 9, including the battles of Roleia and Vimiera; and subsequently in the Peninsula, including the battles of Salamanca and Vittoria, siege of San Sebastian, retreat from Burgos, and passage of the Bidassoa, at which latter he was severely wounded in the head and neck.

11 Dr. Stewart's services:—Expedition to South America in 1807; in the Peninsula from March 1809 to Sept. 1812; present at Waterloo.

12 Dr. Kidd's services:—Expedition to Holland in 1799; expedition to South America in 1806 and 7; in the Peninsula from August 1808 to March 1813; campaign of 1813 and 14 in Germany and Holland.

14 Dr. Shortt served in the Peninsula from Sept. 1810 to the end of the war, and was at the defence of Cadiz from Oct. 1810 to the termination of the siege.

16 Dr. St. John served in the Peninsula from Sept. 1811 to the end of the war, and subsequently in the American war.

17 Dr. Mahony served in the Peninsula from April 1809 to the end of the war, including the passage of the Douro, battles of Talavera, and Busaco, siege of Olivença, battle of Albuhera, affair of Aldea de Ponte, sieges of Ciudad Rodrigo and Badajoz, affair of Fuenta de la Prima, battles of Salamanca and Vittoria, affair of Roncesvalles, battle near Pampeluna, affair of Eschalar, assault of San Sebastian, battles of Nivelle, Orthes, and Toulouse. Present also in the attack on New Orleans, 8th Jan. 1815.

18 Dr. Elliott's services:—Expedition to Naples in 1805; to Calabria in 1806, and was present at the battle of Maida; expedition to Walcheren and siege of Flushing; in the Peninsula from June 1812 to March 1813; expedition to Italy under Lord Wm. Bentinck.

19 Dr. Hacket served at Walcheren in 1809; in the American war, and was present at the different actions which took place there in 1813, and was wounded in the head. Served also the campaign of 1814 in Holland.

Notes to Medical Department.

20 Dr. Alex. Stewart served in the Peninsula from 1811 to the end of the war.

21 Dr. Franklin served in the Peninsula from Sept. 1808 to the end of the war, including the battles of Busaco, Vittoria, Pampeluna, Pyrenees, Nivelle, and Orthes; sieges of Olivença and Badajoz. Served also in the American War, including the action at Plattsburgh.

22 Dr. Armstrong served in the Peninsula from March 1810 to the end of the war, including the battles of Albuhera, Vittoria, Orthes, Pyrenees, and Toulouse. Present at Waterloo.

23 Dr. Grant served in the Peninsula from Jan. 1810 to the end of the war, including the battle of Busaco, first siege of Badajoz; siege of Ciudad Rodrigo; third siege of Badajoz; battles of Fuentes d'Onor, Salamanca, Vittoria, Pyrenees, Nivelle, Orthes, and Toulouse.

24 Dr. Melvin served at the capture of Guadaloupe in 1810.

24* Dr. M. W. Kenny served at the capture of the Cape of Good Hope in 1806; also at the capture of Bahadurpore and Asseerghur in the East Indies.

25 Dr. Lightbody served at Gibraltar during the epidemic in 1804; with the army in Sicily in 1807 and 8; in the Peninsula from March 1812 to April 1813; and again from April 1814 to the end of the war, including the defence of Alba de Tormes, and retreat from Salamanca.

26 Dr. Jeyes served in the Peninsula from Jan. 1813 to the end of the war, including the affair at Morales, battles of Vittoria, Pyrenees, Orthes, and Toulouse. Present at Waterloo.

27 Dr. Barclay served in the Peninsula in 1814, and subsequently in the American war.

28 Dr. Henry served in the Peninsula from May 1811, to the end of the war. Served also the campaign of 1816 against Nepaul.

29 Dr. Thomas Smith served the campaigns of 1813, 14, and 15, including the battles of Vittoria, the Pyrenees, Orthes, Toulouse, and Waterloo.

30 Dr. Andrew Ferguson served in the American war.

31 Dr. Roe's services:—Campaign and battle of Corunna; expedition to Walcheren; Peninsula from May, 1811, to the end of the war, including the battle of Albuhera; sieges of Ciudad Rodrigo and Badajoz; battles of Salamanca, Vittoria, Pyrenees, Nivelle, Orthes and Toulouse.

32 Dr. Starkie embarked with the Medical Staff for Egypt in 1801. Accompanied the expedition to Italy under Sir James Craig; served in Sicily and Calabria, and was at the capture of Regio.

33 Dr. Reade served in the Peninsula during the campaigns of 1812, 13 and 14.

34 Mr. Pratt joined the army in the Peninsula in Jan. 1810, and was present at the siege and capture of San Sebastian, and with the head-quarters during the operations in the Pyrenees.

OFFICERS

ON THE

RETIRED FULL PAY, AND HALF PAY,

INCLUDING

THE ROYAL REGIMENT OF ARTILLERY, CORPS OF ROYAL ENGINEERS, ROYAL MARINES, STAFF, AND MILITARY DEPARTMENTS.

N.B. *Officers whose names are in Italics are on retired full-pay.*

Officers above the rank of CAPTAIN *will be found in the list of Field Officers, at the beginning of the book, according to the dates of their Rank in the Army.*

CAPTAINS.

	CORNET, 2d LIEUT. or ENSIGN.	LIEUT.	CAPTAIN.	WHEN PLACED ON HALF PAY.	
Abbott, Christopher	11 Mar. 95	27 Jan. 96	18 July 05	26 Aug. 14	R. Marines.
ℬ Acton, George	9 Sept. 05	30 Oct. 06	9 Nov. 15	27 Mar. 16	27 Foot.
Adair, Johan Hein[1]	19 Sept. 05	28 Sept. 09	8 Jan. 24	15 May 35	Unattached.
Adair, William	2 Feb. 74	31 Oct. 76	1 June 80	25 Oct. 83	25 Foot.
Adams, Alexander	9 July 03	23 Nov. 04	15 Oct. 12	5 Dec. 14	1 Garr. Batt.
Adams, George	4 Dec. 99	26 July 04	15 Feb. 10	18 Jan. 21	21 Foot.
Adams, William	1 July 95	1 July 97	21 May 05		1 R. Vet. Bat.
Agnew, Charles	31 May 21	9 Dec. 24	8 April 26	8 April 26	Unattached.
ℬ *Agnew, Thos. Ramsden*[2]	19 Dec. 07	12 Oct. 09	22 June 15		2 R. Vet. Bat.
* Ainsworth, John	never	never	7 Dec. 99		128 Foot.
ℬ Alexander, Henry	13 June 11	26 Aug. 13	13 Aug. 25	15 Jan. 29	Staff Corp.
Alexander, *Sir* Jas. Edw.[3]	20 Jan. 25	26 Nov. 25	18 June 30	24 April 38	Unattached.
Allen, George	29 June 04	26 Feb. 05	19 Oct. 14		8 R. Vet. Bat.
* Allen, John Penn	never	never	25 Dec. 13		1814 1 Pr. B. of Mil.
* Allen, Robert	never	never	25 Dec. 13	25 Sept. 14	5 Foot.
ℬ Alpe, Hamond	11 Feb. 08	12 April 09	13 Jan. 20	15 Nov. 21	18 Dragoons.
* Amos, John Green	never	never	25 Dec. 13	25 Sept. 14	40 Foot.
Andrews, Charles	21 Mar. 11	23 June 14	27 Aug. 25	27 Aug. 25	Unattached.
ℬ Andrews, Francis	13 Aug. 07	1 June 09	28 Jan. 13	1814	45 Foot.
ℬ Andrews, Thomas	23 June 04	6 May 05	7 Apr. 08	1 Jan. 19	14 Foot.
Andros, William[4]	24 Sept. 12	13 May 14	16 June 25	10 Aug. 32	Unattached.
Antill, Hen. Colden	31 Aug. 96	24 May 99	11 Jan. 09	5 April 21	New.Bru.Fen.
Anton, Alexander	14 Sept. 04	25 Dec. 04	29 Feb. 16	25 Sept 17	8 W. Ind. Reg.
Appelius, Lewis Chas.	8 Oct. 12	7 Oct. 13	21 Dec. 15	25 Nov. 26	Unattached.
Appleton, William	30 June 01	12 Nov. 03	20 Sept. 10		1 R. Vet. Batt.
Arbuthnott, John, *Visc.*	27 Mar. 01	21 April 03	28 Aug. 04		Irish Brigade.
Arbuthnott, *Hon.* John	23 June 25	8 April 28	25 June 30	25 June 30	Unattached.
ℬ Archdall, Henry	25 Sept. 04	14 Nov. 05	26 Aug. 13	23 April 18	84 Foot.
Armstrong, John	25 Mar. 05	28 April 06	10 Mar. 14	25 May 17	37 Foot.
ℬ Armstrong, John	7 Aug. 03	26 Sept. 04	5 Jan. 15	25 Mar. 16	88 Foot.
ℬ Armstrong, John	28 Feb. 05	28 Aug. 06	4 Dec. 17	25 Nov. 18	99 Foot.
Armstrong, John	24 Mar. 95	1 June 97	15 Dec. 04		12 R.Vet.Batt.
ℬ Armstrong, Robert[5]	2 Apr. 07	20 April 09	13 Feb. 27	20 Nov. 35	23 Dragoons.
Armstrong, Thomas	28 Feb. 05	11 Sept. 05	8 May 17	25 Nov. 18	98 Foot.
Armstrong, Thomas	11 Jan. 16	20 Mar. 17	8 April 26	7 Sept. 38	Unattached.
ℬℳ Armstrong, William	18 May 09	14 June 10	4 Aug. 14	12 Aug. 19	African Co.
Arnold, Wm. Fitch	11 Oct. 10	7 Jan. 13	5 Feb. 18	20 May 19	Rifle Brigade.
Askew, Thomas	Feb. 93	26 June 93	26 Feb. 94		Waller's Co.
ℬ Atherton, John[6]	11 May 09	25 June 11	18 Dec. 29	10 July 35	52 Foot.
ℬ Atkin, William[7]	9 Mar. 10	2 July 11	31 Dec. 30	16 Dec. 36	81 Foot.

315

Captains.

	CORNET, ETC.	LIEUT.	CAPTAIN.	WHEN PLACED ON HALF PAY.	
Aubin, Thomas	3 Aug. 09	12 Apr. 10	1 Sept. 14	Dec. 14	8 Garr. Batt.
Aytoun, Mar. Chad. W.	3 Dec. 03	1 May 04	22 July 12	10 April 25	R. Artillery.
Baby, Anth. Duperon	Apr. 01	14 May 01	27 Jan. 12	21 Aug. 16	Bourbon Reg.
₱ ☖ Bacon, Cæsar	10 June 13	14 Oct. 13	10 July 17	25 Jan. 18	23 Dragoons.
Bagnold, Thomas M.	17 June 96	16 Sept. 00	27 July 08	2 Feb. 10	R. Marines.
Baker, Robert	31 Jan. 05	22 May 06	10 Aug. 15	4 May 20	57 Foot.
₱ Baker, William	3 Dec. 02	19 Nov. 03	11 Oct. 10	22 Dec. 25	60 Foot.
Balck, George Philip	29 Oct. 29	17 Apr. 35	1 June 38	26 June 38	Unattached.
₱ Baldwin, Anthony	never	27 Aug. 07	3 June 13	25 Feb. 16	7 Foot.
Baldwin, Connell Jas.	23 July 07	16 Mar. 08	10 Feb. 20	22 Feb. 27	Unattached.
Baldwin, John Hen.	20 Dec. 21	7 July 25	10 Feb. 29	12 Aug. 34	Unattached.
₱ Ball, Benj. Marcus	13 Aug. 07	25 May 09	21 April 14	17 Jan. 22	72 Foot.
Ball, Samuel	25 Dec. 76	31 Dec. 78	17 May 93	16 Feb. 95	R. Marines.
Bamford, Rich. Watkins	9 Apr. 25	20 Mar. 28	12 July 31	13 July 39	Unattached.
Barlow, B.	12 Dec. 16	13 May 19	23 Aug. 39	23 Aug. 39	Unattached.
Barnard, Hen. Gee	22 May 06	10 Dec. 07	15 July 13	2 Feb. 15	1 Drag. Gds.
Barnes, Joseph	1 June 95	1 April 97	13 Sept. 03		R. Artillery.
Barrett, Knox	10 Mar. 08	3 Jan. 10	25 May 26	5 April 27	Unattached.
Barron, John	14 Oct. 19	9 April 26	6 Jan. 32	6 Jan. 32	Unattached.
Barry, Bartholomew Edw.	27 Apr. 09	22 Mar. 10	17 Sept. 25	17 Sept. 25	Unattached.
Barton, Daniel	never	19 Dec. 27	12 July 33	8 Mar. 39	68 Foot.
Barton, Hugh	23 May 16	4 Aug. 25	22 April 26	30 Dec. 34	Unattached.
Barwell, Osborne	12 Sept. 11	2 April 12	1 Aug. 20	24 Jan. 28	Unattached.
Bateman, *Sir* John	never	18 Mar. 03	13 June 12	1 Nov. 14	R. Art. Drivs.
* Bates, Robt. Montelieu	never	never	25 Dec. 13	1814	1 P.Bn. of Mil.
₱ Baylee, Henry Gough	8 Oct. 12	9 June 14	13 Aug. 26	28 Aug. 38	Unattached.
Bayly, Paget	6 Aug. 03	9 May 05	23 Feb. 09	1814	2 Garr. Batt.
₱ ☖ Baynes, Geo. Macl.[8]	4 Apr. 07	1 Feb. 08	1 Aug. 27	25 Sept. 34	R. Artillery.
₱ ☖ Baynes, Thomas	27 Oct. 08	20 July 09	8 Jan. 24	20 Nov. 28	Unattached.
Bayntun, Charles		Mar. 93	15 Oct. 93	1 Feb. 98	Queen's Ran.
Beadon, Richard	11 May 96	never	25 Nov. 99	1811	92 Foot.
Bean, *Isaac*	9 July 03	1 Nov. 04	7 Nov. 05		28 Foot.
Beare, Wm. Gabbett	28 Jan. 26	26 Oct. 26	22 May 35	22 May 35	Unattached.
*Beattie, Vincent	never	never	25 Dec. 13	1814	1 Pr.Bn.of Mil.
Beatty, Samuel	7 Apr. 04	27 Oct. 08	25 Aug. 15	25 June 17	R.Waggon Tr.
₱ Beavan, John Griffiths [9]	2 June 12	3 Feb. 14	7 Aug. 28	15 Mar. 33	96 Foot.
Beaumont, John Percivall	6 Apr. 01	9 July 03	13 Oct. 08	25 Mar. 11	36 Foot.
*Beckham, Horatio	never	never	25 Dec. 13	25 Sept. 14	43 Foot.
Bell, George Rodney	9 July 03	23 Feb. 05	28 Dec. 09	1 May 28	Unattached.
Bell, Henry	28 Dec. 20	7 Apr. 25	17 Oct. 26	6 July 30	Unattached.
* Bell, James	never	never	25 Dec. 13	1814	3 Pr.Bn.of Mil.
Bellairs, John	10 Feb. 77	22 Mar. 80	28 Dec. 82	1783	90 Foot.
Belson, George	6 May 78	6 July 80	28 Apr. 95	28 April 95	R. Marines.
₱ Belton, Samuel	10 July 06	16 May 08	30 Dec. 24	29 Dec. 25	Unattached.
Bennett, James	9 Apr. 09	2 Dec. 13	20 Feb. 23	31 May 27	Unattached.
Bentham, John	3 Aug. 15	7 April 25	8 Feb. 31	17 May 39	6 Dr. Gds.
Bentinck, George	never	17 Jan. 22	8 April 26	31 Dec. 30	Unattached.
Beresford, Geo. de la Poer	8 Mar. 27	14 Feb. 28	19 Feb. 36	19 Feb. 36	Unattached.
Beretze, Francis	23 Dec. 02	10 Oct. 05	1 Aug. 13	25 June 26	1 R. Vet. Batt.
Berington, Thomas [10]	never	16 July 03	20 Feb. 13	1 Nov. 14	R. Art. Driv.
Berkeley, *Hon.* Cra. Fitzha.	29 Oct. 25	29 Jan. 27	22 Mar. 31	25 Aug. 37	Unattached.
Bernard, Peter	29 Jan. 24	11 Feb. 26	5 Nov. 29	17 May 31	Unattached.
Bernard, *Hon.* W. Smyth B.	9 Nov. 09	16 Aug. 10	10 Aug. 15	25 May 16	1 Drag. Gds.
Bertles, Henry	never	3 June 13	24 Jan. 40	24 Jan. 40	Unattached.
*Bettesworth, Henry	never	never	25 Dec. 13	25 Sept. 14	4 Foot.
☖ Biddulph, Theophilus	22 Dec. 04	22 May 06	14 Sept. 14	25 Mar. 16	6 Dragoons.
Bignell, Rich. Roe	3 Mar. 97	3 July 03	1 June 10	2 June 21	R. Marines.
Birch, George [11]	4 Apr. 08	1 Oct. 09	6 Nov. 27	31 July 32	R. Artillery.
₱ Birch, James [12]	12 July 09	1 May 12	20 Dec. 24	25 Sept. 25	R. Engineers.
Bird, Lewis Wm.	8 Dec. 03	5 Mar. 05	6 Oct. 08	2 May 16	18 Foot.
*Bischoffshausen,C.*Baron*	never	never	6 July 15	25 Sept. 16	For.Co.of Wag
₱ Bishop, James	25 May 04	23 Dec. 04	27 June 11	2 May 22	23 Foot.
Blachford, Oswald S.	6 Dec. 27	13 Sept. 31	1 Aug. 34	9 Feb. 38	59 Foot.
☖ Black, Samuel	5 Apr. 10	8 July 13	28 July 25	8 April 26	Unattached.

Captains.

	2D LIEUT, ETC.	LIEUT.	CAPTAIN.	WHEN PLACED ON HALF PAY.	
Blackall, John	6 July 09	8 July 13	14 Nov. 16	25 Nov. 18	98 Foot.
𝔅 Blackett, Christopher ..	19 Jan. 09	11 May 09	27 July 15	22 July 19	7 Dragoons.
Blackmore, Henry	6 July 96	2 Apr. 98	29 Apr. 03		2 R. Vet. Batt.
Blagrave, Joseph [13]	never	never	30 July 94	7 July 06	R. Art. Driv.
𝔅 Blakiston, John......	29 May 94	19 July 94	30 Sept. 13	25 Feb. 16	27 Foot.
Bland, James [14]	4 Sept. 04	25 Aug. 09	12 Feb. 26	23 Dec. 31	Unattached.
⦿𝔅 Blathwayt, Geo. Wm...	25 Nov. 13	4 May 15	9 June 25	9 June 25	Unattached.
Blathwayt, William	27 Apr. 15	25 Apr. 16	27 July 20	25 Oct. 21	3 Dragoons.
⦿𝔅 Blennerhasset, Aldw. [15]	23 Mar. 14	5 Oct. 15	26 Aug. 34	19 Jan. 38	Unattached.
Bloomfield, Edwin.......	13 Aug. 04	23 Apr. 05	15 Apr. 13	6 July 26	10 Foot.
Blunt, Richard	27 Mar. 23	31 Dec. 25	26 Sept. 26	27 Sept. 31	3 Foot.
Blyth, Augustus Fred.	19 Jan. 26	29 Aug. 26	5 Apr. 33	20 June 34	6 W. Ind. Reg.
Boardman, William [16]	5 Oct. 08	17 Sept. 09	25 Nov. 28	4 Nov. 36	Unattached.
Boates, William	15 June 15	9 Apr. 25	8 Apr. 26	15 Feb. 27	Unattached.
Boldero, Henry Geo.	1 Aug. 14	1 July 15	31 Dec. 27	17 Dec. 30	Unattached.
Bonner, John	4 May 01	5 Jan. 04	18 July 09		Ogle's Rec.Co.
Boulby, Thomas.........	23 May 06	3 Dec. 06	3 July 23	13 Oct. 26	R. Artillery.
Boulton, Richard	11 Apr. 94	never	13 July 97	25 Dec. 02	Coldstr. Gds.
Bourchier, Hugh Plunkett	12 May 14	20 Nov. 23	7 Aug. 35	6 Dec. 39	19 Dragoons.
Bowen, John Watts	19 Feb. 07	28 Jan. 08	12 May 14	1814	56 Foot.
Bower, John	24 Aug. 85	2 May 92	6 Aug. 93		45 Foot.
Bower, Thomas Bowyer ..	29 Nov. 21	4 Feb. 26	12 Dec. 26	16 Aug. 39	Unattached.
Bowie, James............	16 Dec. 95	3 May 96	14 Jan. 08	28 Dec. 17	103 Foot.
Bowness, John	26 Aug. 15	7 Apr. 25	11 June 30	8 July 36	Unattached.
Boyd, Edward	16 July 11	1 July 12	17 Aug. 26	25 Mar. 29	Staff Corps.
Boyes, Robt. Nairne [17]	26 May 14	8 June 15	9 Aug. 31	2 Aug. 33	3 W. Ind. Reg.
Brackenbury, John	19 Nov. 03	28 Nov. 05	15 Oct. 18	10 June 25	38 Foot.
Bradley, Wm. Brown	9 July 03	27 July 04	16 April 12	25 July 17	104 Foot.
Brannan, Peter	1 Sept. 19	13 Nov. 22	18 Mar. 38	23 Aug. 39	Unattached.
Bray, Edm. Moore	9 July 03	14 Feb. 05	18 Aug. 08	25 Sept. 15	York Lt. Inf.
Brereton, Robert [18]........	24 Jan. 05	25 June 06	17 Aug. 15	9 Mar. 32	Unattached.
Brett, William	11 Apr. 94	23 Jan. 12	26 May 25	16 June 25	Unattached.
Breynton, John	6 June 75	27 Dec. 78	16 Mar. 91		Indep. Co.
Brice, Vaughan	29 Dec. 04	23 Feb. 06	16 Sept. 13	25 Nov. 17	66 Foot.
*Bridge, Samuel.........	never	never	2 Dec. 99	1800	82 Foot.
Briggs, Abraham	26 Feb. 07	29 Dec. 08	8 Apr. 25	26 May 25	5 Foot.
Broadhead, Bingley	22 Oct. 25	20 Sept. 26	5 July 33	23 Aug. 39	Unattached.
Broadhead, John Richard..	8 July 19	24 Oct. 21	23 July 25	25 Oct. 27	Unattached.
Brodie, Hugh............	11 Jan. 05	2 July 06	8 Sept. 14		2 R. Vet. Batt.
Brooke, *Sir* A.B.deCapell,*Bt*	19 Aug. 13	27 July 15	26 Feb. 18	26 Feb. 18	17 Dragoons.
Brooke, Robert	15 Oct. 88	6 Feb. 93	4 June 94		Indep. Co.
Brown, David...........	1 Dec. 04	12 Sept. 05	24 May 10	7 Dec. 14	1 Garr. Batt.
Brown, Edward [19]	22 Dec. 08	18 Jan. 10	25 Oct. 27	21 Mar. 34	Unattached.
Brown, Francis	26 Sept. 27	12 June 30	22 May 35	Nov. 39	60 Foot.
Brown, George	2 Oct. 96	1 Oct. 01	15 Feb. 09		R. Marines.
Brown, Hugh............	12 Feb. 06	16 Jan. 12	10 Feb. 34		R. Marines.
Brown, James............	7 Nov. 87	2 Nov. 90	12 Sept. 95		82 Foot.
𝔅 Brown, John Bernie	25 June 02	20 Mar. 04	25 Aug. 13	25 Sept. 18	60 Foot.
Brown, Nathaniel	30 June 04	27 Mar. 05	2 Jan. 17	25 June 17	62 Foot.
𝔅 ⦿𝔅 Brown, Thomas [20]..	23 Oct. 06	15 Dec. 07	20 July 15	25 Feb. 16	79 Foot.
Browne, Arth. Arundel	30 June 25	13 April 26	27 April 29	22 Nov. 36	Unattached.
Browne, Brotherton	1 Sept. 11	1 Sept. 13	8 April 26	8 April 26	Unattached.
Browne, David	May 99	11 Aug. 99	24 Nov. 07		8 R.Vett.Batt.
Browne, John............	12 Sept. 05	7 Nov. 06	15 July 13	25 May 18	100 Foot.
Browne, Lawrence........	5 Oct. 04	1 Aug. 05	13 Mar. 10	18 Sept. 16	4 Ceylon Reg.
Browne, Peter	14 May 07	1 Feb. 09	30 Nov. 15	12 June 28	Unattached.
Browne, P. Rutledge Montg.	31 Oct. 11	24 Dec. 12	29 Aug. 26	28 June 31	Unattached.
𝔅 Browne, *Hon.* Thomas ..	6 Aug. 07	14 July 08	12 Aug. 12	25 Mar. 16	16 Dragoons.
Browne, William	16 Aug. 99	28 April 04	30 May 09	9 Dec. 19	24 Dragoons.
Brutton, John	15 Mar. 08	19 July 21	11 April 36		R. Marines.
Bryan, George	22 May 97	never	25 Nov. 99	26 May 03	Gren. Gds.
Buchan, George	16 Aug. 04	8 May 05	11 Feb. 13	20 Dec. 18	83 Foot
Buchanan, John Graham ..	15 Feb. 16	9 April 25	2 Aug. 39	2 Aug. 39	Unattached.
Buckworth, Peter Everard	2 July 94	never	4 June 98	25 Dec. 02	Gren. Gds.

Captains.

	CORNET, ETC.	LIEUT.	CAPTAIN.	WHEN PLACED ON HALF PAY.	
Bulkeley, Charles	14 April 19	19 April 22	31 May 25	24 Feb. 32	Unattached.
Buller, Edmund Rich.	24 April 24	20 Nov. 25	9 April 29	9 April 29	Unattached.
Buller, George William	27 July 20	13 Jan. 25	20 May 26	19 Oct. 32	Unattached.
₽ ₡₥ Burges, Som. Wald.[21]	1 Oct. 12	never	20 Oct. 14	8 May 17	5 W. Ind. Reg.
Burke, Alexander[22]	8 Mar. 10	5 Nov. 12	20 Feb. 35	1 April 36	Unattached.
₽ Burke, Edmund	20 Oct. 12	21 Oct. 13	10 Nov. 15	3 Aug. 20	York Chass.
₡₥ Burke, James[23]	21 May 12	30 Mar. 14	7 July 25	7 July 25	Unattached.
Burnaby, Edwin	4 Nov. 19	12 June 23	8 April 26	12 Oct. 26	Unattached.
Burnett, Rich. Parry	10 July 99	5 May 00	13 June 05	1 Nov. 16	Veteran Co.
₽ Burton, John Curzon[24]	4 April 07	1 Feb. 08	6 Nov. 27	25 Nov. 33	R. Artillery.
Burton, Joseph	5 Oct. 04	4 Nov. 05	21 April 14	19 Oct. 20	37 Foot.
Bussche, George	never	never	13 Sept. 98	25 June 02	20 Dragoons.
Butler, Edward	9 Nov. 15	24 Feb. 20	1 Oct. 25	1 Oct. 25	Unattached.
Burler, Rich. Alexander	20 July 19	25 Sept. 23	10 Sept. 25	5 Nov. 29	Unattached.
₽ ₡₥ Butler, Theobald	8 Oct. 06	28 April 08	28 Nov. 34	28 Nov. 34	Unattached.
Butler, Theophilus	16 July 07	27 Dec. 10	19 May 14	25 July 14	4 Drag. Gds.
Butler, Walter	22 May 04	27 Jan. 07	26 Oct. 30	6 April 38	65 Foot.
₽ Butler, William	16 Aug. 04	27 June 05	25 June 12	25 July 17	27 Foot.
Bygrave, Joseph	never	never	25 Dec. 13	8 May 28	Unattached.
₽ Calcott, Geo. Berkeley	10 Sept. 07	6 April 09	26 Oct. 15	4 Dec. 23	7 Foot.
₽ Caldecot, Henry	20 July 09	10 June 13	12 Aug. 24	17 Mar. 25	2 Drag. Gds.
Calder, William	14 July 14	24 June 24	6 July 35	27 Jan. 37	Unattaehed.
Caldwell, Arthur James	22 May 14	18 Nov. 19	20 Jan. 25	30 July 29	Unattached.
Cameron, Angus	21 Sept. 85	3 Sept. 88	24 Jan. 91		Indep. Co.
₽ Cameron, John[25]	3 April 06	11 May 07	26 May 14	21 Aug. 35	Unattached.
Cameron, William	6 Aug. 03	14 Dec. 04	6 Nov. 11	6 Nov. 17	13 Dragoons.
₽ ₡₥ Campbell, Alexand.[26]	14 Dec. 09	20 July 13	28 Nov. 33	3 Nov. 37	35 Foot.
Campbell, Alexander	4 July 03	15 Aug. 05	31 July 26		R. Marines.
₽ Campbell, Archibald[27]	26 April 10	29 July 13	11 June 29	11 Aug. 29	2 Ceylon Reg.
₡₥ *Campbell, Donald*[28]	9 July 03	7 April 04	22 June 09		2 R. Vet. Batt.
Campbell, Donald	12 Aug. 03	21 Mar. 05	5 Mar. 12	20 Aug. 18	94 Foot.
Campbell, Duncan	21 May 96	4 Mar. 00	27 July 08	22 Oct. 19	R. Marines.
Campbell, George	9 July 03	1 April 05	9 Dec. 13	20 April 15	26 Foot.
Campbell, John	1 July 03	15 Aug. 05	31 July 26		R. Marines.
Campbell, John	16 Dec. 95	15 June 96	25 June 03		4 R. Vet. Batt.
Campbell, John[29]	2 April 12	1 April 13	26 Dec. 25	10 Sept. 30	26 Foot.
₽ Campbell, John	6 June 05	23 Aug. 07	19 May 14	25 Feb. 16	91 Foot.
Campbell, John	25 Dec. 04	24 June 05	11 July 11	10 Oct. 16	8 W. Ind. Reg.
Campbell, Moses	14 Jan. 08	13 Feb. 11	26 Feb. 28	26 Feb. 28	Unattached.
₽ Campbell, Patrick	July 98	22 Nov. 98	25 Nov. 06	25 Dec. 18	48 Foot.
Campbell, Walter	23 June 25	25 June 29	20 Sept. 33	5 April 39	Unattached.
₽ Campbell, William (1st)[30]	28 Feb. 11	25 June 12	12 April 27	28 June 31	Unattached.
₽ Campbell, William (2nd)[31]	25 Mar. 13	21 July 25	12 July 39	12 July 39	Unattached.
Cardew, Henry[32]	1 Oct. 08	1 Aug. 09	24 Feb. 14		R. Engineers.
Carloss, John Baxter	11 Sept. 06	29 Sept. 09	7 April 25	15 Mar. 33	96 Foot.
₽ Carnegie, W. F. Lindsay[33]	22 Dec. 03	20 July 04	1 July 13	1 Dec. 19	R. Artillery.
Carpenter, Digby Thos.	23 Mar. 96	22 July 97	18 Aug. 08	6 July 15	61 Foot.
Cartan, William	17 July 15	12 Dec. 22	31 Aug. 38	31 Aug. 38	Unattached.
Carteret, John Daniel de	9 July 03	21 Jan. 04	5 May 14	1814	96 Foot.
Cary, Wm. Lucius	never	*25 Dec. 13	26 May 25	20 Jan. 32	Unattached.
Castieau, Thos. James	3 Mar. 14	7 April 25	23 Oct. 35	25 Aug. 37	Unattached.
Cates, James	16 Mar. 15	19 May 22	17 Feb. 25	2 Jan. 28	Unattached.
Cathcart, *Hon.* Adolphus F.	7 Nov. 22	9 June 25	13 July 32	27 July 32	Unattached.
₽ Cattanach, John	25 Oct. 03	16 Sept. 05	10 Feb. 14	1814	92 Foot.
Caulfeild, William	5 May 08	7 Dec. 09	9 Nov. 20	25 Oct. 21	6 Drag. Gds.
₽ Caulfield, Daniel[34]	4 April 05	18 June 07	26 May 23	14 Sept. 32	7 Foot.
₽ Chadwick, William	9 July 03	2 Feb. 05	20 Feb. 12	25 Aug. 14	34 Foot.
₽ Chaloner, John	14 June 00	12 Nov. 03	11 Feb. 08	21 Jan. 13	Indep. Co.
*Chambers, John	never	never	25 Dec. 13	1814	2 Pr.Bn.of Mil.
Chancellor, John	30 Jan. 06	19 May 07	14 Sept. 09	10 July 23	61 Foot.
Chapman, John James[35]	13 Sept. 05	1 June 06	21 April 20	2 June 29	R. Artillery.
₽ *Chapman, Joseph*	23 Jan. 00	6 June 04	9 Mar. 09		1 R. Vet. Batt
Charlton, Saint John	10 Feb. 14	10 Nov. 14	12 Oct. 20	25 Oct. 21	14 Dragoons.

Captains.

	ENSIGN, ETC.	LIEUT.	CAPTAIN.	WHEN PLLCED ON HALF PAY.	
Chawner, Edw. Hoare	9 June 25	10 June 26	7 Sept. 32	7 Sept. 32	Unattached.
Cheape, John	17 June 77	28 Dec. 78	14 April 80	1783	95 Foot.
* Cheape, John	never	never	9 July 03	1805	5 Garr. Batt.
Cheney, Edward..........	28 Dec. 20	19 Jan. 26	20 Mar. 27	20 Mar. 27	Unattached.
Cheney, Ralph	31 Dec. 27	22 June 32	8 Dec. 37	14 Feb. 40	Unattached.
Chepmell, Charles	May 04	23 Nov. 04	1 Oct. 12	25 April 26	Unattached.
Chesshire, Edward........	20 Oct. 96	11 May 97	15 Dec. 04	24 Sept. 12	49 Foot.
Chichester, Arthur.......	27 Sept. 01	14 Jan. 02	12 Dec. 05	19 Mar. 07	Liverpool Reg.
Chichester, George[36]	18 Sept. 17	7 Mar. 22	12 Nov. 25	24 Aug. 32	Unattached.
Chichester, *Lord* Ham. Fra.	never	7 Dec. 26	28 Dec. 32	13 April 38	9 Foot.
Chichester, Hen. T. *Earl of*	10 June 24	28 April 27	3 Jan. 28	3 Jan. 28	Unattached.
Chisholm, Andrew........	18 June 07	3 Aug. 09	14 May 29	20 June 34	Unattached.
𝔓 𝕮𝕭 *Chisholm, Donald*[37]		10 Oct. 05	20 July 15		4 R. Vet. Bn.
Christie, Napier Turner....	5 April 21	10 Sept. 25	1 Aug. 26	23 Oct. 35	Unattached.
Christie, Thomas		14 Aug. 00	3 April 01		99 Foot.
Clark John	3 Sept. 01	5 Aug. 04	7 May 12	25 Dec. 14	38 Foot.
Clarke, Charles	never	16 Nov. 15	26 July 31	2 Aug. 31	York Ran.
𝕮𝕭 Clark, Pryce[38]	2 Mar. 15	27 June 22	16 July 33	20 Sept. 39	Unattached.
Clayfield, Edw. Ireland....	19 July 15	28 Mar. 22	17 Sept. 25	17 Sept. 25	Unattached.
Cleather, Edw. John......	15 Oct. 12	22 Oct. 17	24 Aug. 32	24 Aug. 32	Staff Corps.
Clements, Frederick Wm.	16 Feb. 14	23 Feb. 15	8 April 25	12 July 26	African Corps.
Clements,*Hon.*Wm. Sydney	9 Dec. 24	31 Oct. 26	5 April 31	20 Mar. 35	Unattached.
𝔓 𝕮𝕭 Clerke, *Sir* W. H. *Bt.*	10 Jan. 11	25 July 11	25 April 22	2 May 23	42 Foot.
Clive, Edward	27 April 15	21 Jan. 19	23 June 25	22 May 28	Unattached.
𝔓 Close, Charles[39]........	28 April 04	13 Oct. 04	17 Dec. 13	23 April 24	R. Artillery
𝔓 Close, Henry Jackson....	13 July 06	5 Dec. 06	16 Jan. 12	25 Sept. 20	22 Dragoons.
Cochrane, Robt. Mortmier[40]	17 Nov. 08	25 Dec. 10	6 Feb. 12	1 Nov. 36	GlengarryFen.
Cock, Wm. Beddeck	30 Jan. 06	27 Aug. 11	12 Oct. 32		R. Marines.
Cockburne, Wm. Horace ..	10 April 09	25 June 12	2 June 25	27 Dec. 27	Unattached.
Cocker, Barnard William ..	23 May 16	27 April 20	8 April 26	24 May 28	Unattached.
Coghlan, Robt. Elisha	28 Sept. 20	10 Mar. 25	8 April 26	14 Feb. 28	Unattached.
Colby, Hen. *Augustus*,[41] ..	12 July 08	24 June 09	2 Sept. 13		R. Engineers.
Collard, Thomas..........	7 Sept. 04	31 Oct. 05	3 Feb. 14	25 Feb. 16	81 Foot.
𝕮𝕭 Colleton, Thomas Wm.	21 Nov. 11	25 Nov. 13	19 April 31	25 Oct. 31	Staff Corps.
Collins, Graves Chamney ..	20 May 99	8 Oct. 01	24 July 12	1814	61 Foot.
Collis, Peter	11 Mar. 12	14 June 15	8 Feb. 32	28 Aug. 38	Unattached.
Colman, Thomas	28 May 07	26 July 08	26 Oct. 30	27 May 36	Unattached.
Colt, William	13 Dec. 26	27 Aug. 29	13 Mar. 35	21 Oct. 36	Unattached.
𝔓 Colthurst, Fitzmau. W.[42]	12 Jan. 09	12 Oct. 09	26 Oct. 30	28 May 33	75 Foot.
𝔓 𝕮𝕭 Colthurst, Jas. R.[43]	12 Nov. 07	13 Oct. 09	29 Sept. 25	25 June 30	Sub. In.of Mil.
𝔓 Colthurst, Nicholas	27 Nov. 06	29 Mar. 08	25 Oct. 14	11 June 30	Unattached.
Colton, William..........	1 Dec. 99	10 Sept. 03	30 Nov. 07		2 R. Vet. Batt.
Colville, Frederick........	22 Sept. 08	never	9 Dec. 13	25 Feb. 19	Sc. Fus. Gds.
Coney, Bicknell	1 Dec. 13	31 July 17	20 Dec. 23	20 Dec. 23	17 Dragoons.
Connop, Henry	2 Sept. 19	10 Feb. 25	22 April 26	26 April 27	Cape Reg.
𝔓 Connor, Charles[14]	23 Feb. 09	27 June 11	7 Aug. 27	15 Dec. 37	Unattached.
Conrady, Martinus[45]	30 April 13	28 Sept. 18	26 Nov. 29	20 Nov. 38	Unattached.
Conroy, *Sir* John *Bt.* KCH.	8 Sept. 03	12 Sept. 03	13 Mar. 11	17 June 22	R. Artillery.
Cook, Jervis	26 May 06	28 Oct. 12	27 May 34		R. Marines.
* Cooke, John............	never	never	25 Dec. 13	1814	56 Foot.
Cooper, *Hon.* A. H. Ashley	8 April 25	20 May 26	21 June 31	5 Sept. 34	Staff Corps.
* Cooper, Robert Henry ..	never	never		1814	2 Pr.Bn.of Mil.
Cooper, Robt. Hen.Spencer[46]	20 Mar. 13	21 July 13	23 May 29	15 Feb. 30	R. Engineers.
Coote, Chidley	never	9 June 14	14 July 25	20 June 26	Unattached.
Corsy, Charles Juste de....	3 Mar. 03		6 Sept. 06	1811	96 Foot.
𝔓 Costley, Theoph. Byers..	9 May 05	1 Jan. 07	7 Oct. 13	1814	45 Foot.
ℭ Cottell, James[47]........	17 Sept. 98	5 May 04	18 April 14	20 Mar. 35	R. Marines.
𝔓 Cottingham, Edward ..	20 April 09	19 July 10	28 Jan. 13		Yk.Chasseurs.
Cotton, Edw. Antonius[48]	1 July 06	1 Feb. 08	29 July 25	29 July 25	R. Artillery.
Couche, Thomas..........	9 Oct. 00	29 Nov. 01	17 Oct. 05	28 Dec. 17	103 Foot.
Courtney, Henry Fred. ..	2 Dec. 95	15 June 96	18 July 05		10R.Vet.Batt
Cowper, *Hon.* Wm. Francis	31 Dec. 27	24 Feb. 32	25 Dec. 35	25 Dec. 35	Unattached.
𝔓 Cox, Charles	17 Sept. 03	16 May 05	14 April 08	9 Nov. 15	41 Foot.
Cox, Charles	14 Feb. 05	9 Oct. 06	1 April 13	2 July 18	87 Foot.

Captains.

	CORNET, ETC.	LIEUT.	CAPTAIN.	WHEN PLACED ON HALF PAY.	
Cox, Edmund [49]	7 July 14	11 Nov. 17	10 Aug. 32	17 April 35	Unattached.
* Cox, John	never	never	25 Dec. 13	1814	77 Foot.
Cox, John George	6 Aug. 03	25 Jan. 04	20 Feb. 11	8 July 19	40 Foot.
Cox, Joseph Lucas	4 July 05	19 Mar. 07	20 Sept. 24	13 Jan. 25	Unattached.
Coxwell, Edward [50]	20 Dec. 05	1 June 06	11 July 22	10 Feb. 34	R. Artillery.
* Coyney, Walter Hill	never	never	26 Nov. 99	1800	Indep. Co.
Cracknell, James, Thos.	17 Aug. 07	19 June 21	26 Oct. 35		R. Marines.
Cradock, Adam Williamson	9 July 03	21 Mar. 05	7 Oct. 12	25 Nov. 14	15 Foot.
ℬ ℭℳ Cradock, Thomas [51]	20 Feb. 06	7 May 07	30 Jan. 23	3 Aug. 26	Unattached.
Craick, Douglas Hamilton			24 June 83	25 Oct. 83	29 Foot.
Craig, William Henry	25 June 97	27 July 03	26 Aug. 11	16 April 12	R. Marines.
ℬ Craigie, John	3 Oct. 05	15 April 06	2 Dec. 13	1814	47 Foot.
Cranfield, Geo. Darley	16 June 06	12 May 07	7 April 25	14 Sept. 26	Unattached.
Crawfurd, *Sir Robt. Bart.*	21 April 79	22 Mar. 80	14 Aug. 83	31 Dec. 89	9 Foot.
ℬ Creswell, George [52]	3 Sept. 07	1 Dec. 08	13 Nov. 32	17 July 35	Unattached.
Creswell, William	18 Aug. 99	22 Mar. 00	5 Feb. 06		8 R. Vet. Batt.
Crichton, John	2 April 88	25 Jan. 92	26 April 98		Hanger's Co.
ℬ Croasdaile, George	15 April 13	23 Feb. 15	8 April 26	21 May 29	Coldst. Gds.
Croker, Edward	8 Jan. 07	14 April 08	24 June 16	18 Oct. 20	84 Foot.
Crosbie, *Sir William, Bart.*	4 Mar. 13	13 July 15	24 Feb. 17	1 June 26	Unattached.
Cross, Wm. Jennings	1 April 19	1 Dec. 25	29 Aug. 26	29 Aug. 26	Unattached.
Crowther, Rich. J. F.	2 Dec. 98	18 Aug. 04	19 July 21		R. Marines.
Cruikshank, Patrick	3 Mar. 04	23 July 04	24 Oct. 11	27 June 16	11 Foot.
ℬ Cubitt, Henry Finley [53]	21 Mar. 06	15 Sept. 06	12 June 23	15 Mar. 27	R. Artillery.
Cudbertson, John	5 Oct. 04	8 Oct. 06	17 Mar. 14	21 Sept. 15	45 Foot.
Cumming, John Johnstone	26 Mar. 05	19 Aug. 06	28 Feb. 16	25 Nov. 15	8 W. Ind. Reg.
Cuppage, Adam [54]	11 Mar. 13	3 Aug. 15	13 Nov. 35	13 Nov. 35	Unattached.
Cuppage, Alexander	25 Aug. 09	29 Dec. 12	28 Mar. 16	11 June 30	Unattached.
Curtis, Henry [55]	22 Dec. 03	20 July 04	25 Jan. 13	21 April 21	R. Artillery.
Cust, *Hon.* Peregrine Fra...	31 Mar. 08	3 May 10	17 Oct. 11	25 Mar. 16	3 Drag. Gds.
Custance, Neville	2 July 12	9 Sept. 13	15 June 26	12 Oct. 26	1 R. Vet. Batt.
Daintry, Michael	22 June 20	9 June 25	10 Feb. 29	10 Feb. 29	Unattached.
ℬ Dallas, Robert Wm.	1 Sept. 08	13 Oct. 11	15 Mar. 15	21 May 18	14 Foot.
Dalton, Wm. Serjeantson	12 Sept. 22	9 Feb. 26	26 April 31	17 April 35	Unattached.
Daniel, Hen. Nixon [56]	13 Dec. 10	20 Feb. 14	23 Dec. 32	20 Dec. 34	R. Artillery.
ℬ D'Arcey, Edward	13 April 09	22 Aug. 10	3 Aug. 15		6 R. Vet. Batt.
D'Arcy, John	3 Mar. 08	29 April 08	8 April 25	8 Oct. 31	Veteran Co.
D'Arcy, Judge Thos.	31 Dec. 94	26 Sept. 95	11 May 08		4 R. Vet. Co.
Darling, Chas. Henry	7 Dec. 20	29 Sept. 30	30 Oct. 30	30 Oct. 38	Unattached.
Darrock, Duncan	25 Mar. 19	25 Jan. 23	19 Nov. 25	1 Nov. 27	Unattached.
ℬ Davern, John	27 Mar. 06	11 Nov. 07	31 Aug. 15	8 June 30	27 Foot.
Davies, Arthur	22 Nov. 21	17 Feb. 25	3 Oct. 26	3 Oct. 26	Unattached.
ℳ Davies, David [57]	16 April 07	18 June 07	19 July 15	24 July 28	Unattached.
* Davies, John	never	never	27 Nov. 99	25 Dec. 99	4 Foot.
Davies, John	4 April 08	20 June 09	6 Nov. 27	9 Sept. 34	R. Artillery
Davis, Alfred [58]	21 Sept. 15	27 May 19	19 Jan. 26	13 Aug. 30	Unattached.
ℬ Davis, James [59]	2 April 07	19 June 08	1 Mar. 33	1 Aug. 37	Unattached.
Davis, William	26 Feb. 07	23 Feb. 14	27 May 34		R. Marines.
Dawe, Charles	28 Jan. 08	15 Feb. 10	1 Mar. 21	9 Jan. 29	Unattached.
ℬ ℳ Day, James [60]	10 June 07	1 Feb. 08	6 Nov. 27	3 Feb. 28	R. Artillery.
Day, John	15 Oct. 03	21 Feb. 05	10 May 13	11 Nov. 19	96 Foot.
Dayrell, Francis	11 July 16	22 July 24	17 Sept. 25	17 Sept. 25	Unattached.
ℬ Deacon, Chas. Parke [61]	1 April 02	12 Sept. 03	16 Dec. 08	1 Aug. 22	R. Artillery.
ℳ Deacon, Thomas [62]	5 April 13	3 Aug. 15	29 April 36	29 April 36	Unattached.
ℬ De Burgh, Anth. Philip	7 Mar. 10	18 April 11	6 June 15	25 Dec. 16	Portuguese S.
De la Condamine, Thos.	16 June 14	18 Mar. 25	15 June 32	15 June 32	Unattached.
Delancey, John	27 Aug. 15	8 June 20	14 July 25	30 July 29	Unattached.
De Lisle, Hirzel Fred.	23 Sept. 13	12 Feb. 24	22 April 26	14 Feb. 28	Unattached.
Delmont, Frederick	8 June 96	11 Aug. 00	27 July 08	1 Jan. 16	R. Marines.
Dennis, James	11 June 07	15 June 09	7 April 25	6 Oct. 25	Unattached.
ℬ Dennis, John Cripps	11 June 95	17 Feb. 99	15 April 13	25 Dec. 14	32 Foot.
Denny, Robert		2 Oct. 05	30 Nov. 09		2 R. Vet. Batt.
ℬ Derenzy, Geo. Webb	27 Nov. 06	25 Dec. 07	20 April 15	25 Feb. 16	82 Foot.

Captains.

	2D LIEUT, ETC.	LIEUT.	CAPTAIN.	WHEN PLACED ON HALF PAY.	
D'Erp, Balthazar, *Baron* ..	never	never	30 Dec. 97		60 Foot.
Des Vœux, *Sir Charles Bt.*	5 Sept. 95	26 April 96	25 Dec. 02	21 April 04	63 Foot.
Des Vœux, Henry	8 April 25	9 Feb. 26	26 Nov. 29	22 Aug. 34	Unattached.
₧ Devey, Henry Fryer	never	30 Aug. 07	8 Sept. 13	25 Aug. 14	7 Foot.
Devon, Wm. Henry	11 Feb. 06	15 Jan. 12	23 Dec. 33		R. Marines.
Dewell, Thomas	14 Feb. 04	29 July 04	17 Dec. 14	1 Mar. 27	R. Artillery.
Dick, John	26 Sept. 95	24 June 96	19 Sept. 04	27 Oct. 08	112 Foot.
Dickson, Lothian Sheffield	27 Jan. 25	27 Nov. 28	4 Oct. 33	9 Dec. 37	Unattached.
Dillon, Timothy	25 Dec. 98	15 Dec. 00	12 May 13		2 R. Vet. Batt.
Dillon, William	6 Aug. 12	18 April 16	19 April 31	24 July 31	Staff Corps.
Disney, Algernon	2 May 01	28 April 03	28 Feb. 05	28 Feb. 05	York Hussars.
Dixon, Henry, M.	25 April 22	19 Jan. 26	24 Sept. 29	8 Feb. 39	88 Foot.
Dixon, John	10 Mar. 14	12 Feb. 18	5 Nov. 25	5 Nov. 25	Unattached.
* Dobbs, Francis	never	never	25 Dec. 13	25 Sept. 14	12 Foot.
Dodd, Thomas	1 July 82	16 Mar. 91	6 Mar. 95		R. Artillery.
* Dodsworth, Benjamin ..	never	never	25 Dec. 13	1814	3 Pr.Bn.of Mil.
Dodsworth, *Sir Edwd., Bt.*	28 Mar. 87	20 April 91	27 Feb. 93	1795	105 Foot.
Donoughmore, J. *E. of*, K.P.	25 Sept. 07	never	19 Nov. 12	27 May 19	Gren. Gds.
* Doran, James Goddard ..	never	never	25 Dec. 13	25 Sept. 14	14 Foot.
₧ Douglas, Arch. Murray ..	20 Jan. 08	13 Feb. 09	28 April 14	25 Feb. 17	52 Foot.
Douglas, Hen. Hamilton ..	12 Mar. 14	14 April 18	30 June 24	16 July 25	78 Foot.
₧ Douglas, Joseph........	14 July 08	20 Dec. 10	8 April 26	14 Aug. 28	Unattached.
Douglass, Robert	20 Mar. 17	3 Dec. 18	6 July 30	24 Oct. 34	Unattached.
Dowland, John	1 Nov. 04	28 Mar. 05	1 June 15	16 Nov. 18	67 Foot.
₵₧ Down, Richard	7 Mar. 11	31 Mar. 14	29 Sept. 25	7 April 26	Unattached.
Downes, Wm. James......	10 Aug. 26	7 Sept. 32	22 Nov. 36	25 June 38	11 Dragoons.
₧ Doyle, Michael Taylor ..	3 July 05	10 July 06	1 Feb. 10	25 July 16	5 Foot.
Doyne, Richard	12 Mar. 12	9 Nov. 14	19 Nov. 25	19 Nov. 25	Unattached.
₧ Drewry, Frederick Geo.	19 May 08	12 Oct. 09	10 Aug. 26	30 Sept. 36	12 Foot.
₵₧ Dromgoole, N. Fleming	1 Nov. 04	4 July 05	29 July 13	25 June 17	35 Foot.
Drought, Barth. Elliott....	4 Sept. 02	6 July 04	21 June 10	1814	48 Foot.
₧₵₧ Drought, John Head	3 Mar. 08	8 Sept. 08	10 Oct. 16	25 Mar. 17	93 Foot.
Druitt, Edward	18 Oct. 04	6 Mar. 06	3 Feb. 14	25 May 17	37 Foot.
Drummond, George	14 Oct. 24	8 Dec. 25	30 Dec. 26	30 Dec. 26	Unattached.
₧ Drummond, J. M'Gregor	15 Dec. 08	23 May 11	4 Dec. 23	4 Dec. 23	82 Foot.
Drury, John	12 Oct. 05	9 April 10	11 July 32	28 April 34	R. Marines.
₧ Drysdale, Alexander....	1 July 04	10 Oct. 05	10 Feb. 14	27 Mar. 16	27 Foot.
Duff, Benjamin	16 Feb. 26	30 June 29	22 June 32	24 April 35	27 Foot.
Duncan, William[63]........	10 May 05	1 June 06	11 Mar. 17	15 Mar. 25	R. Artillery.
Dundas, Rich. Leslie......	17 June 19	17 Sept. 25	28 Jan. 26	13 Nov. 32	87 Foot.
Dungan, William	4 Aug. 14	17 Oct. 16	19 Sept. 26	19 Sept. 26	Unattached.
Dunmore, Alex. *Earl of* ..	1 Aug. 26	14 Aug. 27	10 Aug. 32	27 June 34	Unattached.
Dunn, Thomas	20 Jan. 03	11 Aug. 04	22 Sept. 08	18 Feb. 19	14 Foot.
Dunne, Richard..........	8 April 25	2 Mar. 26	16 May 34	23 Nov. 38	Unattached.
₧ Durie, John Adam	12 Nov. 03	18 Sept. 05	28 April 14	1814	92 Foot.
₧ Duval, David[64]	26 Mar. 11	14 Nov. 11	28 Oct. 24	20 July 32	Unattached.
Duval, John	9 July 03	24 Jan 05	18 Oct. 10	16 April 29	Unattached.
₧ ₵₧ Eason, R. Prescott[65]	8 Jan. 07	17 May 09	7 April 25	6 April 38	2 Ceylon Reg.
₧ ₵₧ Eaton Charles	4 Dec. 06	7 June 08	21 April 14	14 Aug. 23	10 Foot.
Eckford, Alexander	8 June 97	24 July 03	30 May 11	1 Sept. 14	R. Marines.
₧ Edmonds, Hamilton[66] ..	6 Feb. 08	23 Feb. 09	13 Feb. 27	18 Nov. 31	60 Foot.
Edwards, John	20 Feb. 12	30 Dec. 13	8 Mar. 39	8 Mar. 39	Unattached.
₵₧ Edwardes, David John	1 Nov. 05	1 June 06	1 June 22	29 July 26	R. Artillery.
Edwardes, *Hon.*Geo.Warren	6 May 24	15 June 26	3 July 27	12 Feb. 36	14 Foot.
Elliott, Edw. Francis......	1 Aug. 14	1 July 15	10 June 26	10 June 26	Unattached.
₧ ₵₧ Elliott, Rich. Chas.	5 June 09	23 June 11	28 Aug. 27	28 Aug. 27	Unattached.
₵₧ Elliott, William	4 Jan. 10	27 Nov. 12	14 April 18	22 Jan. 24	11 Foot.
Ellis, Dixie..............	10 Sept. 03	1 June 09	10 Aug. 20	2 Nov. 20	Yk.Chasseurs.
Ellis, Geo. Moore	28 Nov. 05	10 Sept. 07	25 May 20	16 Nov. 28	34 Foot.
₧ Ellis, Hercules[67]	5 Aug. 07	20 April 09	11 Aug. 25	4 Nov. 36	Unattached.
Ellis, Joseph	29 Aug. 05	22 Sept. 08	29 Sept. 25	7 June 27	Unattached.
Ellis, Richard	July 07	25 Sept. 07	24 Sept. 12	25 May 16	18 Dragoons.
* Ellis, Thos. David	never	never	25 Dec. 13	1814	81 Foot.

321

Captains.

	CORNET, ETC.	LIEUT.	CAPTAIN.	WHEN PLACED ON HALF PAY.	
᙭᙭ Elmsall, J. Edw. Greaves	22 April 13	16 Feb. 15	2 Mar. 20	25 Oct. 21	1 Drag. Gds.
Elphinstone, J. *Lord*, GCH.	4 Aug. 23	4 June 28	4 Dec. 32	12 Nov. 36	Staff Corps.
Elrington, John Henry	5 Nov. 94	10 Mar. 95	12 June 00	1 Dec. 08	28 Dragoons.
Elton, Isaac	2 Sept. 25	7 Nov. 26	5 July 31	29 Dec. 37	Unattached.
Elton, Robert James	20 Dec. 23	8 April 26	31 Dec. 27	22 Jan. 29	Unattached.
Emerson, John[68]	30 July 07	12 April 09	13 Feb. 27	23 Sept. 36	Unattached.
Emery, Thomas	30 Jan. 06	7 Jan. 08	20 Jan. 20	1 Dec. 20	53 Foot.
Eminson, Thomas	18 June 94	20 May 95	3 May 00	9 May 03	23 Dragoons.
᙭ Enderby, Samuel[69]	31 Oct. 11	16 April 12	27 May 19	17 Feb. 32	Yk.Chasseurs.
ᖴ Evans, Aug. Fitz Gerald	10 Mar. 08	9 Nov. 09	20 Mar. 27	11 Jan. 31	37 Foot.
* Evans, Edward	never	never	25 Dec. 13	1814	3 Pr.Bn.of Mil.
* Evans, Henry	never	never	25 Dec. 13	1814	2 Pr.Bn.of Mil.
Evans, James[70]	16 July 04	28 Jan. 05	20 Dec. 14	20 June 31	R. Artillery.
Evans, John	31 Aug. 95	13 Sept. 98	21 Nov. 05	25 June 16	Newf. Fen.
Evatt, F. (Adj. 23 May, 00)	25 June 02	28 Feb. 05	25 Mar. 13		VeteranComp.
Fairtlough, Fran. Graham	never	3 Oct. 94	24 July 00		4 R. Vet. Batt.
Fairtlough, William	28 Feb. 00	21 Mar. 04	7 Feb. 07	25 June 16	Sicilian Reg.
ᖴ Falkiner, Samuel	25 Sept. 06	11 June 07	5 Feb. 18	22 Feb. 27	Unattached.
Farmar, Jasper	21 July 96	15 Jan. 01	10 Nov. 08	1 Jan. 16	R. Marines.
Farmar, Richard	1 July 03	15 Aug. 05	31 July 26		R. Marines.
Fauquier, Henry T.	13 Jan. 97	16 July 99	20 July 04		R. Artillery.
Faverman, Zaccheus[71]	20 Feb. 96	1 June 98	24 Mar. 07	2 Feb. 10	R. Marines.
* Fellowes, John	never	never	25 Dec. 13	1814	1 Pr.Bn.of Mil.
Fenton, John Spread	19 Sept. 05	13 June 06	8 April 25	10 July 28	Unattached.
ᖴ Ferguson, Adam	1 Dec. 05	23 Oct. 06	4 Feb. 08	8 Oct. 16	101 Foot.
* Ferguson, Geo. Richard	never	never	19 Sept. 05	11 Oct. 16	Canadian Fen.
Ficklin, Robert	20 July 15	7 April 25	10 Aug. 26	26 Feb. 30	Unattached.
Fife, Adam	28 April 06	15 Nov. 07	15 Oct. 12	25 Nov. 16	69 Foot.
Findlater, Alex. Napier	6 Mar. 06	15 Feb. 08	25 Aug. 23	25 Aug. 23	24 Foot.
Finey, Alen George	26 July 08	19 April 10	5 June 27	5 June 27	Unattached,
Finucane, Geo. Thurles	22 Sept. 08	15 Mar. 10	17 July 28	May 39	36 Foot.
Fischer, John Nich. (*Lieut.*)	6 July 03	15 Aug. 05	12 April 11	10 Sept. 14	R. Marines.
Fisk. Wm. Hawley	27 April 15	25 Oct. 15	8 April 26	17 Feb. 37	Unattached.
Fitzgerald, John George			31 Aug. 15		7 R. Vet. Batt.
Fitz Gerald, Massy	30 Jan. 23	25 June 29	13 Mar. 35	7 July 37	Unattached.
* Fitzherbert, John	never	never	25 Dec. 13	1814	80 Foot.
Fitz Roy, George	12 Feb. 18	11 Jan. 21	26 May 25	15 June 30	W. Ind. Rang.
Fitz Roy, W. Sim. Haughton	23 Nov. 20	7 April 25	8 Mar. 27	27 Aug. 29	86 Foot.
Fleming, Arthur	17 Aug. 99	27 May 01	1 June 06		R. Artillery.
Fletcher, James Vernon	8 April 13	14 April 14	6 April 20	11 June 30	Unattached.
Folkes, Richard	20 May 95	10 Aug. 96	28 Nov. 01		Indep. Co.
᙭᙭ Foot, George[72]	4 Oct. 06	1 Feb. 08	29 July 25	29 July 25	R. Artillery.
Forbes, Charles	23 June 25	15 Aug. 26	21 Dec. 32	7 Aug. 35	Unattached.
ᖴ Forbes, Hugh[73]	12 April 09	20 Nov. 10	25 Mar. 25	28 Aug. 35	8 Foot.
Forbes, John	21 Nov. 11	21 Oct. 13	13 Oct. 36	7 June 39	Unattached.
Ford, Charles[74]	1 July 06	1 Feb. 08	29 July 25	7 May 33	R. Artillery.
Forde, William	4 July 05	12 June 07	27 July 20	7 July 25	Unattached.
Forman, George	6 Aug. 07	22 Sept. 08	13 Mar. 27	24 Sept. 36	Unattached.
ᖴ᙭᙭ Forster, Henry[75]	1 July 06	16 Oct. 07	26 Dec. 24	7 Feb. 32	R. Artillery.
Fortescue, *Hon.* Geo. Matt.	12 Jan. 09	22 Mar. 10	24 Dec. 12	25 Oct. 16	25 Dragoons.
Foskett, Joseph	24 Apr. 23	22 Oct. 25	7 Nov. 26	31 Aug. 30	Unattached.
Foss, Christopher	26 June 01		28 July 07	4 Feb. 15	6 Garr. Batt.
Foster, Isaac	25 May 11	14 Sept. 18	15 April 29	10 May 39	Unattached.
Fothergill, Henry	21 Aug. 17	25 Jan. 25	12 Dec. 26	24 May 39	28 Foot.
Fothergill, Thomas	28 Mar. 05	10 Oct. 05	2 Nov. 09	26 Mar. 18	Greek Lt. Inf.
ᖴ Fowden, Wm.	10 Oct. 05	6 April 07	4 Jan. 10	2 May 22	22 Dragoons.
Fox, Barry	1 Jan. 07	10 Jan. 08	7 Dec. 15	25 Mar. 17	97 Foot.
Fraser, Andrew	10 Feb. 96	4 Aug. 99	10 April 07		7 R. Vet. Batt.
Fraser, Evan Baillie	9 Jan. 23	15 Dec. 25	12 Dec. 26	14 June 33	Unattached.
Fraser, Thomas	16 Jan. 08	19 Feb. 10	2 July 12	25 June 17	83 Foot.
Fraser, William	12 Jan. 96	1 May 97	9 July 03		6 R. Vet. Batt.
ᖴ᙭᙭ Frederick, Edward	21 Aug. 06	7 May 07	28 April 14	7 April 26	Unattached.
* Frederick, *Sir* Richard, *Bt.*	never	never	27 Nov. 09	25 May 02	9 Foot.

322

Captains.

	ENSIGN, ETC.	LIEUT.	CAPTAIN.	WHEN PLACED ON HALF PAY.	
Frederick, Roger	4 Oct. 08	18 Oct. 09	2 July 12		7 R. Vet. Batt.
Freeman, John[76]	27 June 05	30 July 07	9 April 25	26 April 33	42 Foot.
Freeman, T. Inigo Wickham	19 Dec. 16	9 Nov. 21	12 Nov. 25	12 Nov. 25	Unattached.
French, Acheson	17 June 07	2 Feb. 07	7 April 25	9 Nov. 30	Gren. Gds.
⅋ French, Edward Francis	3 May 10	10 Sept. 12	7 Jan. 19	8 April 26	Unattached.
French, Lucius Henry[77] ..	16 Nov. 26	20 Aug. 29	28 June 39	28 June 39	Unattached.
⅋ French, Thomas Wm.	9 May 05	16 July 07	5 Dec. 19	13 Aug. 29	71 Foot.
Fresson, Meatchelle, Fra. A.	19 Nov. 96	29 Nov. 07	29 Aug. 15	28 Sept. 19	60 Foot.
Frome, Francis	26 Sept. 95	1 May 97	18 Oct. 13	1 May 19	66 Foot.
Fry, John	24 Oct. 99	25 June 03	2 May 11	25 May 16	11 Foot.
*Fry, Oliver	never	17 Oct. 94	14 Oct. 01		R. Artillery.
⅋ Fullarton, Archibald ..	19 Mar. 01	15 Oct. 03	2 April 12		6 R. Vet. Batt.
⅋ Fuller, Fred. Hervey[78] ..	21 Jan. 04	4 April 05	2 Aug. 15	22 May 28	Unattached.
Fuller, John Thomas[79]	1 July 06	1 Feb. 08	13 Feb. 25	13 Feb. 25	R. Artillery.
Fullerton, Alexander Geo.	18 Feb. 28	19 Nov. 30	24 Dec. 33	7 Mar. 34	Unattached.
⅋ Furnace, Norbury......	25 Dec. 06	16 Mar. 08	30 Dec. 19	3 April 23	60 Foot.
⅋ Fyers, Edward[80]	23 April 08	24 July 09	21 July 13		R. Engineers.
⅋ Fyfe, William..........	2 June 04	29 Aug. 05	16 Sept. 13	1814	92 Foot.
* Fyler, Thomas..........	never	never	25 Dec. 13	25 Sept. 14	5 Foot.
* Gabbett, John..........	never	never	25 Dec. 13	25 Sept. 14	88 Foot.
Galbraith, George	28 June 05	30 Oct. 06	9 Dec. 19		4 R. Vet. Batt.
Gale, Alex. Robinson	15 July 05	14 Jan. 07	6 April 19	20 July 20	26 Foot.
Galloway, David	4 Mar. 06	10 April 12	21 May 34		R. Marines.
Gammell, Andrew........	17 Aug. 20	12 May 25	19 Sept. 26	19 Sept. 26	Unattached.
⅋ Gapper, Edmund	1 Aug. 04	5 May 05	3 June 12	25 June 17	83 Foot.
⅋ ⅏ Gardiner, John[81] ..	9 April 09	30 Aug. 10	16 June 25	11 Mar. 36	2 Drag. Gds.
Gardner, James	27 July 15	8 May 19	15 June 26	5 Oct. 26	Unattached.
* Gardner, Richard	never	never	29 Nov. 99	25 May 02	4 Foot.
Gardner, Hon. Sam. Martin	2 Mar. 05	1 May 05	17 Aug. 08	28 Dec. 17	103 Foot.
Garner, John Hutchinson ..	25 June 12	21 April 14	1 Mar. 21	25 Oct. 21	40 Foot.
Garth, Thomas	23 Nov. 15	6 June 16	24 Aug. 20	25 Oct. 21	15 Dragoons.
⅋ Gascoyne, Thos. Bamber[82]	5 Nov. 07	25 Mar. 09	7 Feb. 22	13 May 36	3 Ceylon Reg.
Gauntlett, James	9 July 03	24 April 04	18 Dec. 06	1814	90 Foot.
George, John	28 Feb. 10	7 Nov. 11	8 April 25	6 Dec. 27	Unattached.
Gerard, Robt. Tolver	3 July 28	16 Dec. 30	17 Mar. 37	22 Feb. 39	Unattached.
Gifford, Geo. St. John ..	20 Feb. 96	25 April 97	3 Sept. 04		11 R.Vet.Batt.
⅋ Gilbert, Francis Yarde[83]	1 May 11	10 June 11	23 Mar. 25	6 June 25	R. Engineers.
Gilbert, James Anthony ..	16 Dec. 16	28 Feb. 25	10 Jan. 37	28 Nov. 37	R. Artillery.
Gilbert, Thomas..........	24 May 75	3 Dec. 76	1 June 81	26 Nov. 82	R. Marines.
Gilbert, Walter Raleigh ..	26 Dec. 70	7 July 75	25 Aug. 94		123 Foot.
* Giles, Joseph	never	never	25 Dec. 13	25 Sept. 14	9 Foot.
Gilpin, Richard Thos.	29 Nov. 21	30 Dec. 24	24 Dec. 25	24 Dec. 25	Unattached.
Ginger, Joseph	25 Sept. 03	6 Mar. 05	1 May 11	21 Dec. 20	6 Foot.
⅋ Girdlestone, James	20 Nov. 06	25 Dec. 07	20 Dec. 10	29 Dec. 25	Unattached.
⅋ Girling, Thos. Andrews	28 Aug. 04	21 Sept. 05	13 Oct. 14	24 May 29	5 Foot.
⅋ Glasse, Francis	14 Aug. 01	9 Jan. 08	13 Sept. 08	8 Jan. 18	25 Foot.
Glenie, Isaac	19 Sept. 05	17 July 06	14 Dec. 15	25 Sept. 16	Nova Sco.Fen.
Glumer, Weddo de	never	never	30 Dec. 97	16 Mar. 02	4 Foot.
Gold, Henry Yarburgh	11 April 25	18 Sept. 28	5 April 31	6 Dec. 39	Unattached.
Goode, John[84]..........	5 Sept. 11	12 Nov. 12	26 Feb. 35	20 Feb. 39	Unattached.
Goodwin, S. Osnaburgh ..	25 Dec. 13	31 Oct. 22	22 Dec. 35	Feb. 39	Unattached.
Gordon, David	4 Aug. 00	30 May 03	10 Dec. 10	25 Nov. 18	5 W. Ind. Reg.
Gordon, James	27 Nov. 23	26 May 25	12 Nov. 29	15 Mar. 31	3 W. Ind. Reg.
Gordon, Thomas	1 June 20	9 June 21	1 May 28	10 May 33	R. Wagg. Tr.
⅋ ⅏ Gordon, Thomas[85]..	7 Mar. 11	2 July 12	26 Mar. 31	7 Mar. 32	Unattached.
Gorse, William[86]	11 Nov. 12	28 July 14	14 Aug. 35	14 Aug. 35	Unattached.
* Gould, Charles	never	never	25 Dec. 13	25 Sept. 14	1 Foot.
Gould, Fran. Augustus	4 May 15	13 Mar. 17	23 10 Dec. 25	7 Sept. 32	Unattached.
⅋ Gould, John[87]	31 Aug. 07	22 Mar. 09	13 Feb. 27	26 July 31	Unattached.
* Gould, Thomas	never	never	25 Dec. 13	25 Sept. 14	14 Foot.
Gouttebernard, J. M. de la		25 May 98	3 Mar. 06	1816	8 W. Ind. Reg.
Grace, Robert............	23 June 96	20 Oct. 00	27 July 08	25 Mar. 15	R. Marines.
Graham, Alexander	27 June 05	25 Dec. 06	21 Feb. 11	25 April 16	25 Foot.

323

Captains.

	CORNET, ETC.	LIEUT.	CAPTAIN.	WHEN PLACED ON HALF PAY.	
☉☩ Graham, Jas. Reg. Tovin	30 Jan. 14	8 June 15	16 Mar. 20	25 Oct. 21	2 Dragoons.
ℙ Grant, Charles	July 04	17 Sept. 04	8 June 09	6 July 15	45 Foot.
Grant, James	20 Dec. 21	30 June 25	6 Mar. 27	6 Mar. 27	Unattached.
Grant, James	4 Nov. 12	6 Nov. 14	3 May 33	17 July 35	Unattached.
Grant, John	15 Feb. 10	5 Mar. 12	13 Aug. 30	14 Dec. 32	24 Foot.
Grant, John	25 Oct. 98	12 April 99	21 Mar. 05	4 April 11	Indep. Co.
Grant, Lachlan	1 Aug. 04	3 Feb. 06	9 Sept. 14	25 Feb. 16	78 Foot.
Grant, Robert............	8 May 17	18 July 26	11 Dec. 28	11 June 30	Unattached.
Grantham, Valentine......	26 July 04	6 Nov. 05	2 Mar. 09	30 Nov. 15	48 Foot.
Grantt, John	16 Dec. 95	23 June 96	27 Dec. 14	25 Dec. 17	72 Foot.
Graves, William H.	6 Jan. 08	26 Oct. 08	8 April 25	23 Nov. 36	Unattached.
ℙ *Gray, Robert*..........	2 May 00	9 July 03	10 Aug. 09		6 R. Vet. Batt.
Green, John Cranston	13 Jan. 14	23 June 14	24 Dec. 21	24 Oct. 21	1 Dragoons.
ℙ Gregor, Gordon Wm. Fra.	23 May 06	14 May 07	17 June 13	25 Dec. 14	23 Foot.
Gregory, Hen. Jas. Mitchell	21 July 08	29 Dec. 09	5 Aug. 19	5 Octr 22	2 Ceylon Reg.
* Gregory, John Barnes ..	never	never	25 Dec. 13	1814	56 Foot.
ℙ ☩ Grenfell, William ..	11 April 11	11 Mar. 13	24 Dec. 18	26 Oct. 20	21 Dragoons.
Grey, Chas. Bacon........	21 Nov. 11	20 May 13	9 Aug. 21	25 Oct. 21	9 Dragoons.
Grey, *Hon.* Hen. Booth ..	12 May 25	13 April 26	17 Dec. 30	9 Aug. 33	Unattached.
Grey, Matthew Robt.	7 Aug. 17	24 Oct. 21	12 Aug. 24	10 Sept. 30	6 W. Ind. Reg.
Grimes, Henry[88]........	19 Oct. 20	23 Oct. 23	27 April 34	14 June 38	Unattached.
ℙ Grimes, John	6 Oct. 08	1 Nov. 10	25 May 22	30 May 22	76 Foot.
Groeme, George..........		27 Dec. 77	17 Sept. 80		72 Foot.
Groombridge, John Wm. ..	11 Jan. 00	1 Jan. 01	19 April 10	4 May 20	91 Foot.
Grover, John	20 Aug. 12	31 Mar. 14	12 Dec. 26	12 Dec. 26	Unattached.
ℙ Grubbe, Thos. Hunt[89] ..	28 Mar. 11	15 Oct. 12	8 April 26	18 Nov. 31	Unattached.
Gunning, Matthew	8 Aug. 99	4 Sept. 01	11 April 11	19 April 21	25 Dragoons.
Gwynne, Hen. Lewis Edw.	25 April 05	26 June 06	23 Aug. 10	25 Feb. 17	62 Foot.
ℙ Hacket, Richard	never	26 Oct. 07	17 Dec. 13	6 Aug. 18	14 Foot.
Hadley, William	21 April 04	6 May 05	2 Dec. 13		5 R. Vet. Batt.
Haig, William	9 May 06	9 Oct. 12	27 May 34	17 Nov. 34	R. Marines.
Haigh, William Preston ..	11 July 08	24 June 09	1 Sept. 13		R. Engineers.
Halcott, Matthew Chas. ..	2 Feb. 15	10 April 23	7 Jan. 26	7 Jan. 26	Unattached.
Hamilton, Geo. James	8 Sept. 74	17 July 76	7 Feb. 80		Indep. Co.
ℙ Hamilton, John	10 June 04	5 June 05	17 Feb. 14	25 Dec. 14	42 Foot.
ℙ Hamilton, Thomas......	29 Aug. 04	7 Sept. 05	24 Sept. 12	25 July 17	27 Foot.
Hammill, Thomas Cochrane	8 Oct. 07	5 April 10	26 June 27	26 June 27	Unattached.
Hance, William James....	11 June 07	4 April 08	29 June 15		1 R. Vet. Batt.
ℙ ☩ Harding, Robert[90]..	6 June 06	6 April 07	17 Oct. 23	17 Oct. 23	R. Artillery.
ℙ Hardwick, William	27 Aug. 04	12 Feb. 05	1 Mar. 10	26 Nov. 18	2 Foot.
Hare, *Hon.* Richard	10 Jan. 22	23 June 25	11 July 26	17 Mar. 37	Unattached.
Hare, Robert	28 May 18	30 Oct. 23	27 April 27	15 June 32	Unattached.
ℙ ☩ Hare, William Henry	17 Dec. 07	20 July 09	18 Nov. 19	25 July 22	51 Foot.
Harison, William Thomas..	7 Sept. 20	14 April 25	17 Oct. 26	14 Nov. 34	Unattached.
ℙ ☩ Harris, Isaac Watkins	8 Dec. 08	20 June 11	7 April 25	9 April 26	Unattached.
☩ Harris, William	16 April 12	21 Jan. 13	2 June 25	8 June 30	Unattached.
☩ Harrison, Hugh[91]	21 Nov. 05	18 June 07	11 June 12	16 May 22	5 Foot.
Harrison, John	20 July 15	28 Oct. 24	3 Dec. 29	15 Mar. 39	Unattached.
ℙ Hart, Francis Hen.	5 Jan. 05	15 Jan. 07	8 April 25	26 May 25	84 Foot.
Hart, Richard	27 Mar. 05	25 April 06	25 Mar. 25	19 May 25	66 Foot.
* Haselfoot, Charles	never	never	25 Dec. 13	25 Aug. 14	3 Foot.
* Haselfoot, Wm. Henry ..	never	never	25 Dec. 13	25 Aug. 14	3 Foot.
Hastings, *Sir* C. Abney, *Bt.*	17 Jan. 08	15 Sept. 08	7 Mar. 11	17 Nov. 14	105 Foot.
Haviland, Hen. Hone	8 May 95	11 April 96	15 Aug. 05	7 Mar. 10	R. Marines.
Haviland, Richard........	never	16 Aug. 99	28 Nov. 05	1807	R. Waggon Tr.
Hawke, *Hon.* Stanhope....	17 July 23	12 May 25	26 Sept. 26	2 Dec. 31	Unattached.
Hawker, Hen. Frederick ..	24 Oct. 11	22 Feb. 16	12 April 32	10 Jan. 34	12 Foot.
Hawkins, Geo. Palmer....	30 Nov. 09	6 Jan. 11	15 May 27	15 May 27	Unattached.
Hawkins, John	25 Aug. 06	3 Nov. 08	1 July 20	7 Sept. 26	Unattached.
Hay, David Balfour	25 Nov. 95	7 Dec. 96	7 Dec. 97	9 July 02	26 Dragoons.
Hay, Francis	24 Mar. 04	1 Aug. 04	21 Sept. 09	21 Aug. 17	34 Foot.
Hay, John	8 July 03	15 Aug. 05	31 July 26		R. Marines.
Hay, John	2 April 94	15 April 94	5 Aug. 99	1802	12 W. Ind. Reg.

Captains.

	ENSIGN, ETC.	LIEUT.	CAPTAIN.	WHEN PLACED ON HALF PAY.	
Hay, William............	15 Mar. 10	7 Nov. 13	22 April 36	10 Nov. 37	Unattached.
ῼ Hayes, Hen. Browne....	6 May 04	4 Dec. 04	19 Dec. 11	15 Mar. 18	84 Foot.
Hayes, Robert	20 Mar. 96	1 April 99	13 Jan. 07	22 Nov. 14	R. Marines.
Hayne, Richard	7 July 17	9 April 25	24 Aug. 32	24 Aug. 32	Staff Corps.
ῼ Healey, John	4 June 08	8 Sept. 08	26 June 23	25 Jan. 24	39 Foot.
Healey, Robert Thomas ..	24 Oct. 26	8 June 30	24 April 35	7 April 37	Unattached.
Heath, Macclesfield Wm...	1 Aug. 14	1 July 15	13 May 36	25 May 38	R. Engineers.
* Heathcote, Cockshutt ..	never	never	25 Dec. 13	1814	53 Foot.
ῼ ꨳ Heaviside, Richard..	26 May 08	20 Sept. 09	15 June 15	14 Dec. 26	Unattached.
Hebden, Henry	25 May 15	7 April 25	13 May 26	26 April 27	Unattached.
Helden, Robt. Ongley	7 Mar. 00	3 Sept. 01	6 Mar. 06	25 Jan. 17	89 Foot.
ῼ Hemsworth, Thos. Rich.	9 July 03	27 Aug. 04	15 Sept. 08	25 Dec. 14	31 Foot.
Henderson, David	28 Nov. 06	23 Jan. 15	5 Jan. 15	25 Feb. 16	10 Foot.
Hendry, Andrew	8 July 09	9 Jan. 28	24 Nov. 37		R. Marines.
Heneage, Thomas	28 Mar. 92	21 Feb. 93	18 Mar. 94		Indep. Co.
ῼ Henry, Graham........	6 Nov. 06	2 Mar. 08	25 Oct. 14	29 Nov. 27	Unattached.
Henryson, John.........	1 April 06	1 July 06	1 May 11		R. Engineers.
Herriot, Andrew	4 Mar. 98	14 Feb. 04	6 Oct. 13		R. Marines.
Hewett, John............	12 Nov. 05	24 Sept. 10	12 Oct. 32		R. Marines.
ꨳ Hibbert, J. Nembhard	13 Jan. 14	30 Mar. 15	7 Sept. 20	25 Oct. 21	1 Drag. Gds.
ῼ *Hickie, Bartholomew* ..	2 June 04	18 April 05	31 Dec. 12		7 R. Vet. Bat.
Hill, Geo. Stavely	9 Sept. 19	6 June 22	25 Mar. 29	27 Dec. 33	Unattached.
ῼ ꨳ Hill, Henry[92]	19 Jan. 15	5 May 15	28 June 36	28 June 36	Unattached.
Hill, Nicholas Thomas	20 Oct. 08	13 Sept. 10	25 Oct. 17	25 July 19	Staff Corps.
Hill, Rich. Kirwan	2 Feb. 15	25 April 22	14 May 29	19 Oct. 38	Unattached.
Hill, St. Leger	27 Aug. 04	22 Aug. 05	29 Jan. 18	14 Nov. 22	12 Dragoons.
ꨳ Hincks, John[93]	8 Nov. 06	1 Feb. 08	29 July 25	29 July 25	R. Artillery.
Hinde, Hen. Reynolds ...	29 Jan. 00	13 Jan. 02	29 Nov. 05	25 Mar. 11	36 Foot.
ῼ ꨳ Hobbs, Thomas[94] ..	19 Sept. 05	7 Feb. 08	20 July 15	25 May 20	25 Foot.
ῼ Hobkirk, Samuel	25 April 06	7 April 08	3 Dec. 12	25 Mar. 17	43 Foot.
ῼ ꨳ Hodges, Geo. Lloyd[95]	28 Aug. 06	7 Jan. 08	31 Dec. 30	31 Dec. 30	Unattached.
Hogg, George	26 May 25	22 April 26	23 April 29	6 July 32	90 Foot.
ꨳ Holbech, Edward	5 Oct. 04	18 Dec. 05	25 May 09	11 April 22	91 Foot.
Holland, William	26 Mar. 07	28 Sept. 08	21 July 14	25 June 17	83 Foot.
Holmes, Christ. Francis ..	25 June 12	14 Oct. 14	12 Feb. 29	9 June 37	Unattached.
Holt, Wm. Foden[96]	21 Aug. 06	13 Aug. 07	28 Dec. 30	28 April 37	Unattached.
Home, Francis	4 June 07	10 Aug. 08	24 Mar. 17	22 May 17	81 Foot.
Hookey, George..........	27 Jan. 06	8 Aug. 11	12 Oct. 32	23 Mar. 36	R. Marines.
Hopkins, Henry..........	7 Oct. 02	24 June 03	21 Aug. 06	2 Nov. 09	11 Garr. Bat.
Hopkins, Henry..........	15 July 12	2 Mar. 20	25 Sept. 35	25 Sept. 35	Unattached.
Hopkins, Rich. Thompson..	12 April 27	11 June 30	21 Nov. 34	8 June 38	Unattached.
Hore, Walter	5 Mar. 77	1 June 78	15 Feb. 82	1 Mar. 84	103 Foot.
Hornbrook, Thos. Beckford	25 Aug. 99	1 Sept. 04	8 May 24	5 Jan. 26	R. Marines.
* Horndon, John Doidge ..	never	never	25 Dec. 13	25 Sept. 14	4 Foot.
Horsell, Bartholomew	10 Sept. 03	12 Jan. 04	26 Nov. 12	1814	R. Wag. Train
ῼ *Hort, Josiah Geo.*[97]	19 Sept. 05	26 Feb. 07	23 Aug. 10		12 R. Vet. B.
Horton, James	11 July 11	2 July 12	31 Dec. 28	25 June 29	Staff Corps.
Horton, William	6 Aug. 99	8 May 00	21 Nov. 11	25 Sept. 14	6 Foot.
Hotham, Augustus	20 Dec. 21	19 May 25	19 Dec. 26	28 Dec. 32	Unattached.
Hotham, George[98]	24 Mar. 15	1 May 16	10 Jan. 37	17 Aug. 39	R. Engineers.
ῼ Houlton, George	20 Nov. 06	6 Oct. 08	2 Nov. 15	25 Mar. 17	49 Foot.
Howard de Wal. C. A. *Lord*	never	24 April 17	3 Oct. 22	3 Oct. 22	8 Foot.
Howard, *Hon.* Henry	21 July 25	14 May 26	9 Nov. 30	29 Nov. 33	Unattached.
Hugo, Thomas	1 July 05	2 July 05	22 July 13	25 Feb. 16	91 Foot.
ῼ *Hulme, John Lyon*[99] ..	24 June 09	10 July 10	20 Dec. 14		R. Engineers.
Hulme, Wm. Browne......	never	11 Dec. 96	31 May 09	1814	Staff Corps.
Hulse, Charles	never	3 Oct. 26	10 Dec. 30	10 May 31	Rifle Brigade.
ῼ ꨳ Humbley, William[100]	15 April 07	13 Oct. 08	20 July 15	25 Dec. 18	Rifle Brigade.
Humby, John	30 July 04	10 June 07	31 Aug. 27		R. Marines.
ꨳ Hume, Gustavus Thos.	13 Dec. 13	21 Nov. 16	10 June 24	6 July 29	Unattached.
ῼ Humfrey, Benj. Geale...	16 June 08	20 Oct. 08	31 Mar. 14	19 May 25	56 Foot.
Humphreys, John Goullin[101]	14 May 07	14 July 08	8 April 25	18 Nov. 31	Coldst. Gds.
Hunt, Edward Hugh	2 Jan. 17	18 July 22	26 May 25	3 May 31	Unattached.
Hunter, Edward..........	13 July 09	11 Aug. 13	18 May 38	18 May 38	Unattached.

F F

Captains.

	2D LIEUT. ETC.	LIEUT.	CAPTAIN.	WHEN PLACED ON HALF PAY	
Hunter, Geo. James[102]	1 Oct. 08	13 Mar. 11	6 Nov. 27	23 Oct. 33	R. Artillery.
Hunter, James	23 April 12	22 Aug. 15	14 Aug. 23	14 Aug. 23	70 Foot.
Hunter, John	27 Nov. 17	24 Oct. 21	4 Feb. 26	4 Feb. 26	Unattached.
Hurdle, Thomas	15 Jan. 98	1 Dec. 03	18 Mar. 13		R. Marines.
Hussey, Thomas..........	28 April 97	18 July 03	24 Sept. 10	1 Sept. 14	R. Marines.
Hutchinson, James[103]	8 Dec. 04	26 Sept. 06	25 May 19	18 Oct. 33	1 Garr. Batt.
Jacks, Walter............	26 May 03	7 Mar. 05	21 Oct. 13	25 Dec. 18	20 Dragoons.
Jackson, George..........	30 April 07	13 Jan. 08	12 Oct. 15	25 June 16	GlengarryFen.
Jacques, John	30 Mar. 78	12 Oct. 93	27 Aug. 03		1 R. Vet. Batt.
𝔍 Jago, Darell[104]	5 July 13	26 Oct. 15	20 Nov. 34	6 Jan. 36	R. Artillery.
James, Demetrius Grevis ..	19 April 96	8 June 99	29 June 08	25 Feb. 12	R. Marines.
𝔍 *James, Henry*[105]	7 Dec. 07	19 July 21	18 Mar. 36		R. Marines.
𝔍 James, William	never	4 Mar. 13	8 May 17	25 Feb. 19	Sc. Fusil. Gds.
Jameson, James	16 Aug. 01	17 Dec. 03	31 Oct. 10	25 Feb. 16	4 Foot.
Jarvis, Sam. Raymond	7 April 06	19 June 06	7 Sept. 15	25 Jan. 23	7 Dragoons.
* Jeffrey, George	never	never	25 Dec. 13	25 Sept. 14	26 Foot.
* Jeffreys, Richard	never	never	25 Dec. 13	1814	53 Foot.
Jeffries, James	12 May 08	28 Mar. 11	7 April 25	7 July 25	Unattached.
Jeffries, Sam. Barton.....	28 Oct. 05	4 Feb. 08	16 Dec. 19	16 Dec. 19	25 Dragoons.
Jenkins, Morgan James...	31 Oct. 11	14 Oct. 12	18 Sept. 28	19 July 33	Unattached.
Jenour, Matthew	25 Mar. 04	2 Jan. 06	13 Jan. 14	23 July 29	Unattached.
Jerningham, *Hon.* C. W. S.	10 June 26	24 April 28	2 Dec. 31	2 Dec. 31	Unattached.
Jesse, William	9 April 25	23 Feb. 26	25 Aug. 37	6 April 38	Unattached.
Inge, William...........	14 May 18	11 April 22	16 Sept. 24	12 July 27	Unattached.
𝔍 𝔍 Ingram, Jno. Nelson[106]	25 Nov. 06	18 Oct. 08	7 April 25	2 Sept. 36	Unattached.
𝔍 𝔍 Johnson, H. Caven.[107]	6 Feb. 05	26 May 06	14 May 12	4 May 20	7 Dragoons.
Johnson, Yarrall	12 Aug. 03	22 Dec. 04	9 June 13	3 July 23	63 Foot.
Johnson, Frederick Wm...	31 Dec. 25	7 Dec. 26	15 June 30	25 Sept. 35	78 Foot.
Johnston, George	26 Jan. 19	24 June 24	30 Dec. 26	28 May 28	60 Foot.
Johnston, James Wm.	22 Dec. 03	29 July 04	20 Oct. 13	1 Jan. 25	R. Artillery.
Johnston, William........	4 Mar. 01	27 July 02	1 Feb. 10	12 Dec. 25	Unattached.
𝔍 Johnstone, James	29 Dec. 08	30 Aug. 10	10 June 13	25 Feb. 16	7 Foot.
Jolliffe, *Sir* Wm. G. H. *Bt.*	10 April 17	26 Aug. 19	22 April 24	24 June 24	Bourbon Reg.
𝔍 𝔍 Jones, Charles.......	23 July 07	10 Mar. 08	7 Oct. 13	29 Mar. 21	Yk.Chasseurs.
Jones, Chas. Fred. Burrell	12 Nov. 25	12 Dec. 26	21 Mar. 34	1 May 35	Sub.Ins.of Mil
Jones, Ebenezer	15 Dec. 07	10 April 25	9 Sept. 28	9 Sept. 28	Unattached.
* Jones, Edward	never	never	25 Dec. 13	25 Aug. 14	29 Foot.
Jones, Fielding Shawe	22 April 99	19 Aug. 01	23 June 14	25 Mar. 16	6 Dragoons.
Jones, John Evans	21 Sept. 05	5 April 09	19 May 31		R. Marines.
Jones, Nicholas Burnell ..		22 May 84	9 May 89	1802	8 W. Ind.Reg.
Jones, Thomas	18 Nov. 99	20 May 00	31 Dec. 03	2 July 07	Irish Brigade.
𝔍 Jones, William	25 Feb. 08	5 Jan. 09	30 Sept. 19	5 June 23	52 Foot.
* Jones, William	never	never	25 Dec. 13	1814	1 Pr.Bn.of Mil
Jordan, Jacob............	4 July 16	17 Jan. 22	7 Nov. 26	29 Mar. 27	Unattached.
Irwin, Thomas	26 Aug. 09	29 Oct. 12	3 Dec. 18	25 Oct. 21	6 Dragoons.
𝔍 Judge, Arthur[108]	8 June 05	12 Sept. 05	28 Sept. 13	4 Dec. 17	11 Foot.
Kean, Henry[109]	8 Oct. 06	8 July 08	13 Mar. 27	20 July 30	60 Foot.
Keane, Geo. Michael......	27 Mar. 23	27 Aug. 25	19 Dec. 26	17 Mar. 37	Unattached.
Keating, James Singer	5 Feb. 18	24 Oct. 21	8 April 26	8 April 26	Unattached.
Keats, John Smith	16 Dec. 16	2 Mar. 25	5 July 29	31 May 33	R. Wagg. Tr.
Keens, John	2 Nov. 09	14 Nov. 11	5 June 27	5 June 27	Unattached.
𝔍 𝔍 Keily, Townsend R.[110]	8 June 09	25 Oct. 10	26 May 25	19 Jan. 26	Unattached.
Kellenbach, Frederick	never	30 Dec. 97	5 Dec. 05		2 R. Vet. Batt.
Kellet, John	28 April 93	9 Oct. 94	3 Oct. 01	1 Feb. 04	R. Marines.
Kellow, Robert	6 July 03	15 Aug. 05	31 July 26		R. Marines.
Kelly, John..............	9 July 03	7 Sept. 04	4 June 13	25 April 16	25 Foot.
Kelly, William	26 Oct. 99	23 July 04	15 Feb. 11		2 R. Vet. Batt.
Kernmis, Thos. Arthur....	never	22 April 26	9 Dec. 30	4 July 34	Unattached.
Kendall, George	9 Dec. 98	18 Aug. 04	19 July 21	19 July 21	R. Marines.
Kennedy, Hugh Fergusson	31 July 23	16 June 25	27 Nov. 28	31 Dec. 31	Unattached.
𝔍 Kent, John.............	27 April 03	28 Aug. 04	10 May 09	12 Dec. 17	53 Foot.
𝔍 Ker, Richard Hall[111]	31 May 10	10 June 13	6 Feb. 35	6 Feb. 35	Unattached.

Captains.

	CORNET, ETC.	LIEUT.	CAPTAIN.	WHEN PLACED ON HALF PAY.	
Kerr, Robert	5 Mar. 06	23 Dec. 06	14 Aug. 15	12 Aug. 24	40 Foot.
Kerr, Samuel	29 Oct. 09	14 Oct. 10	25 Nov. 28	25 Nov. 28	Unattached.
* Ketti'oy, James	never	never	25 Dec. 13	25 Aug. 15	51 Foot.
ⓟ Killikelly, Michael	22 May 04	5 June 06	8 July 13	25 Dec. 14	32 Foot.
ⓟ King, Charles [112]	16 June 08	27 Dec. 10	27 April 27	27 April 27	Unattached.
King, George	5 Feb. 07	15 April 07	17 Nov. 14	5 Mar. 29	Unattached.
King, James	25 Sept. 06	10 Dec. 06	28 Feb. 11	1 Jan. 18	73 Foot.
ⓟ King, John Duncan [113] ..	28 Aug. 06	18 Feb. 08	16 Mar. 30	28 Dec. 30	Unattached.
King, John Lewis	3 Jan. 22	24 Jan. 25	15 Aug. 26	25 Dec. 28	2 Foot.
King, Sir R.Duckworth,Bt.	28 Feb. 22	29 May 25	22 April 26	5 Feb. 36	Unattached.
ⓟ King, Thos. Newton [114]..	4 Oct. 06	1 Feb. 08	29 July 25	30 June 30	R. Artillery.
Kingsley, Charles	13 Nov. 04	17 July 06	13 June 11		9 R. Vet. Batt.
Kingsley, Edward	27 June 05	25 Feb. 07	5 Nov. 12	25 Feb. 16	58 Foot.
* Kinneir, Joseph Hall	never	never	25 Dec. 13	1814	2 Pr.Bn.of Mil
ⓟ Kirby, Michael	25 June 12	29 Feb. 16	31 May 21	19 April 23	65 Foot.
Kirk, William.	22 Mar. 00	27 April 04	28 Dec. 09	1 Dec. 17	47 Foot.
ⓟ Kirkley, Tho. Harrison [115]	1 May 11	25 Feb. 13	1 June 34	4 May 38	Unattached.
Kirwan, Andrew Hyacinth	never	5 Aug. 13	29 Oct. 25	25 Nov. 28	Unattached.
Kirwan, Henry	18 April 00	28 Nov. 00	22 May 04	25 July 12	15 Foot.
ⓟ Kirwan, Richard	never	27 Oct. 07	16 Mar. 15	24 July 28	Unattached.
Knapman, Wm. Stephens..	1 Nov. 03	17 Jan. 06	31 July 26		R. Marines.
ⓟ Knipe, Geo. Frederick ..	29 May 96	16 July 00	2 July 13	18 May 15	23 Foot.
Knipe, John	4 April 00	28 Sept. 01	30 Jan. 12	25 Aug. 14	60 Foot.
Knox, Charles............	8 April 26	9 Aug. 27	4 Mar. 36	10 Feb. 38	Unattached.
ⓟ Kyle, Alexander........	13 May 05	7 April 07	11 Oct. 10	25 Dec. 18	94 Foot.
Lambert, Sir Hen. John,Bt.	6 April 09	never	27 May 13	12 Aug. 15	86 Foot.
Lamotte, Chas. Wyndham	6 Nov. 27	28 Oct. 31	22 July 36	10 Nov. 37	Unattached.
Lancey, Thos. Furbor	14 Dec. 11	1 July 12	10 April 25		R. Engineers.
Lane, Charles [116]...........	15 May 12	23 Oct. 13	9 July 33	7 Mar. 34	Unattached.
ⓟ Lane, Henry [117]	never	1 Sept. 01	1 Jan. 06	1 July 16	R.Art.Drivers
Langrishe, Hugh Henry ..	never	5 July 15	27 April 25	27 Oct. 25	Unattached.
Langdon, Gilbert	3 May 95	27 Jan. 96	14 June 20		R. Marines.
Langford, Buller Rolle ..	28 April 95	27 Jan. 96	15 Aug. 05	22 Nov. 09	R. Marines.
ⓟ ⓦ Langton, Edward ..	23 May 05	25 July 05	12 May 12	8 April 17	52 Foot.
Lanphier, J. Phillips Cosby	27 Mar. 06	7 Sept. 09	19 April 18	6 Oct. 25	25 Foot.
Latham, Matthew	15 Nov. 05	8 April 07	11 Feb. 13	20 April 13	Portuguese S.
La Touche, Robert	28 Sept. 20	15 July 24	14 Jan. 26	12 Oct. 26	Unattached.
* Laurence, Frederick	never	never	25 Dec. 13	25 Sept. 14	43 Foot.
* Law, Edward Bedwell ..	never	never	25 Dec. 13	25 June 16	R. Wagg. Tr.
Law, James Horton	22 July 13	7 May 18	9 Sept. 25	11 Jan. 28	Unattached.
Lawlor, Provo William [118]..	1 July 06	1 Feb. 08	8 April 25	20 April 38	R. Artillery.
Lawrence, John	6 July 03	15 Aug. 05	31 July 26	20 July 30	R. Marines.
* Laxon, John	never	never	25 Dec. 13	25 Sept. 14	7 Foot.
Layard, Brownlow Villiers	24 July 23	20 Jan. 26	21 Nov. 34	26 Feb. 36	Unattached.
Leahy, Henry............	25 April 06	28 Aug. 07	18 Oct. 10	7 Aug. 17	95 Foot.
ⓦ Leatham, James	26 Sept. 05	12 June 06	19 July 15	28 April 25	Yk. Chasseurs
* Lechmere, Capel........	never	never	25 Dec. 13	1814	3 Pr.Bn.of Mil
Le Couteur, John	15 Nov. 10	21 Nov. 11	15 May 17	25 Aug. 17	104 Foot.
Lee, David...............	never	never	14 Mar. 11		9 R. Vet. Batt.
ⓟ Leech, John	3 Sept. 03	7 Mar. 05	10 June 13		5 R. Vet. Batt.
ⓟ L'Estrange, Edward [118]*	10 Nov. 08	19 April 10	9 Nov. 30	14 June 39	Unattached.
Lefroy, Anthony			22 May 94	17 Sept. 02	4 Foot.
Le Hunt, Charles	6 May 07	15 May 09	25 June 18	25 Oct. 21	90 Foot.
ⓟ Le Mesurier, Peter	15 Dec. 04	19 June 06	22 Mar. 10	16 Dec. 19	103 Foot.
ⓟ Le Mesurier, W. Abraham	6 July 04	7 May 05	15 Mar. 10	19 Nov. 29	Unattached.
ⓟ Lempriere, Wm. Chas.[119]	8 June 04	23 Oct. 04	17 Dec. 13	26 Nov. 27	R. Artillery.
Leslie, John..............	20 July 15	12 Dec. 22	23 Oct. 35	9 Mar. 38	Unattached.
Levett, Theophilus........	26 May 25	14 Aug. 28	23 Aug. 33	25 June 38	11 Dragoons.
Lewis, Alexander	15 June 97	27 May 01	13 June 11	22 Mar. 27	Unattached.
ⓟ Lewis, Charles [120]	9 June 30	30 Dec. 09	19 Mar. 32	26 Jan. 38	Unattached.
Lewis, Philip George......	3 May 00	26 Aug. 01	29 Oct. 12	25 April 17	5 W. Ind.Reg.
ⓟ Lewis, Roger Lambert ..	Feb. 08	16 June 08	11 June 18	27 Nov. 18	38 Foot.
Lewis, Thomas Locke	20 Mar. 13	21 July 13	8 June 30	5 Jan. 33	R. Engineers.

Captains.

	CORNET, ETC.	LIEUT.	CAPTAIN.	WHEN PLACED ON HALF PAY.	
Lewis, Westenra Warner ..	4 Jan. 05	26 Oct. 06	7 Dec. 20	16 Sept. 24	74 Foot.
Lindsay, Wm. Chacon	11 Sept. 12	1 April 15	23 Oct. 33	3 July 39	R. Artillery.
ᛃ Lister, Thomas St. George	24 April 05	11 May 07	26 Aug. 13	8 Mar. 21	Portuguese S.
ᛃ Litchfield, Richard[121] ..	26 Nov. 08	5 Sept. 11	6 Nov. 27	6 Nov. 27	R. Artillery.
Little, Robert John	4 July 03	15 Aug. 05	31 July 26	12 Sept. 29	R. Marines.
Lloyd, Kingston Dodd	27 Nov. 11	21 April 14	31 May 27	31 May 27	Unattached.
Lloyd, Mark	20 July 15	24 June 19	10 May 39	10 May 39	Unattached.
* Lloyd, John Vaughan ..	never	never	23 Mar. 01	1802	46 Foot.
Loftus, Frederick	7 Oct. 19	9 June 25	8 April 26	8 April 26	Unattached.
ᛃ Logan, Abraham	20 Oct. 00	17 July 01	25 April 09		9 R. Vet. Batt.
*Long, John	never	never	25 Dec. 13	25 Aug. 14	70 Foot.
*Long, John Amhurst	never	never	25 Dec. 13	1814	52 Foot.
Louis, Marcus	Jan. 95	8 Sept. 95	23 May 00		5 R. Vet. Batt.
Lowe, Sherbrooke	18 Aug. 15	17 May 21	12 Dec. 26	28 June 39	Unattached.
ᛃ Lynch, Martin	30 Aug. 04	8 Sept. 05	24 Dec. 12	25 July 17	27 Foot.
Lyon, George	8 Nov. 21	31 May 25	30 Dec. 26	30 Dec. 26	Unattached.
Lyon, William	17 July 23	21 July 25	30 Dec. 26	2 Aug. 33	6 W. Ind. Reg.
M'Arthur, Malcolm G.....	5 May 95	15 Mar. 96	15 Aug. 05	1 Sept. 14	R. Marines.
M'Barnet, Donald	5 April 01	8 July 03	30 Mar. 09	1814	92 Foot.
M'Carthy, Chas. Callaghan	18 Aug. 08	4 Oct. 09	13 Mar. 27	20 June 34	Unattached.
ᛃ *M'Carthy, J. E. Connor*	9 July 03	2 April 05	4 Feb. 13		2 R. Vet. Batt.
ᛃ ᛃ M'Conchy, James[122]	7 Jan. 13	20 July 15	11 Dec. 35	11 Dec. 35	Unattached.
M'Dermid, John	2 Sept. 95	21 Oct. 95	28 Aug. 04		3 R. Vet. Batt.
M'Donald, Alexander	25 Nov. 99	3 Sept. 02	15 April 07	1814	56 Foot.
ᛃ M'Donald, Donald[123]..	12 Sept. 08	24 June 09	20 Oct. 13	28 Sept. 24	R. Engineers.
M'Donald, Henry Thomas	9 July 03	27 Mar. 05	31 Mar. 14	22 Dec. 17	53 Foot.
M'Donald, James	21 Sept. 15	27 Dec. 19	6 Oct. 25	23 Nov. 32	Unattached.
M'Donald, William	14 Jan. 05	10 April 06	8 Sept. 14	20 May 17	York Lt. Inf.
M'Donell, Alexander	28 Sept. 04	7 Nov. 05	16 Mar. 15		6 R. Vet. Batt.
M'Donell, Forbes James ..	29 April 95	26 Jan. 97	17 April 05		2 R. Vet. Batt.
M'Dougall, Duncan	30 June 01	3 Dec. 03	13 June 11	Mar. 17	21 Foot.
M'Gie, George	24 April 96	13 June 99	27 July 08	1 Jan. 16	R. Marines.
M'Innes, Matthew........	9 July 00	5 Mar. 12	11 Oct. 32	15 Feb. 39	8 Dragoons.
M'Inroy, William	10 Sept. 28	8 Oct. 29	29 Nov. 33	17 Aug. 38	Unattached.
M'Intyre, Angus	26 Aug. 07	2 April 10	27 Aug. 24	9 July 29	Unattached.
M'Iver, George	31 Mar. 14	2 Mar. 20	14 Feb. 32	5 April 39	Unattached.
M'Kenzie, Alexander	28 Mar. 81	18 April 93	1 May 98		R. Marines.
M'Kenzie, William	2 Feb. 01	26 Jan. 03	24 Oct. 10	12 Aug. 19	6 Foot.
M'Kenzie, William	25 Feb. 08	15 Feb. 11	13 Mar. 27	13 Mar. 27	Unattached.
M'Laine, Alexander	1 Mar. 06	19 Aug. 07	7 April 25	15 Sept. 25	Unattached.
M'Lean, Hector Hugh	7 April 04	10 Sept. 06	17 Mar. 15	25 Feb. 16	93 Foot.
M'Lean, Malcolm	28 Feb. 00	25 June 03	7 Nov. 05		4 R. Vet. Batt.
M'Leod, John............	17 July 96	15 Jan. 01	5 Oct. 08	26 Sept. 14	R. Marines.
M'Leod, Robert..........	22 May 93	24 April 95	2 July 03		R. Marines.
M'Leod, William	4 June 07	27 April 09	13 Mar. 27	13 Mar. 27	Unattached.
M'Mahon, Alex. St. Leger	15 Jan. 07	1 Sept. 10	7 July 25	7 July 25	Unattached.
M'Mahon, Mortimer	23 Nov. 04	16 Oct. 06	29 Sept. 14	25 Feb. 16	8 Foot.
ᛃᛃ M'Millan, Henry	1 Oct. 02	10 April 05	18 July 15	19 Sept. 16	21 Dragoons.
M'Murdo, Alured Charles[124]	1 Jan. 14	29 June 26	22 Mar. 31	22 Mar. 31	Unattached.
M'Nab, John	12 May 05	14 July 06	12 Aug. 13	25 Sept. 16	Nova Sco. Fen.
ᛃ M'Nab, Robert[125]......	15 Oct. 12	9 April 25	27 Mar. 36	5 April 38	Unattached.
M'Namara, John Michael	25 Mar. 79	12 Oct. 82	15 June 96		R. Marines.
M'Neill, Alexander	18 May 08	13 July 09	13 April 15	30 April 18	10 Foot.
M'Pherson, Daniel	26 June 06	18 Jan. 08	6 Feb. 12		2 R. Vet. Batt.
M'Pherson, William	23 April 05	9 May 05	19 Aug. 13	25 June 17	83 Foot.
M'Queen, Simon[126]	14 Aug. 13	23 Oct. 16	1 June 32	1 June 32	Unattached.
M'Vicar, John	27 Aug. 04	28 Oct. 08	20 July 15	25 Dec. 18	R. Waggon Tr.
ᛃ Macdermid, John	2 Feb. 04	28 Mar. 05	21 Aug. 10	23 April 18	100 Foot.
Macdonald, Alexander	13 Nov. 23	7 July 25	11 June 30	18 June 30	62 Foot.
Macdonald, Charles Kerr ..	15 May 23	26 Nov. 25	7 Nov. 26	7 Nov. 26	Unattached.
Macdonald, John[127]	7 June 10	21 May 12	8 June 20	9 Aug. 31	Unattached.
Macdonald, Ranald	18 July 15	3 Dec. 18	19 Nov. 30	22 Mar. 33	Unattached.
Macdonald, Ronald	5 Feb. 01	26 July 04	2 Jan. 12	20 April 20	12 Foot.

Captains.

	2D LIEUT. ETC.	LIEUT.	CAPTAIN.	WHEN PLACED ON HALF PAY.	
*Macdonald, R. G. Livings.	never	never	25 Dec. 13	1814	52 Foot.
Macdonell, John	5 Oct. 95	3 July 96	9 July 03		3 R.Vet. Batt.
ℬ MacDonnell, Ewen [128]	20 Jan. 14	27 Mar. 23	6 May 35	28 Nov. 37	Unattached.
Macfarlane, Andrew	20 Oct. 04	26 Oct. 04	10 Sept. 12	25 Feb. 16	91 Foot.
Mac Gregor, John [129]	19 Oct. 09	28 Nov. 11	29 Sept. 27	28 Mar. 34	Unattached.
ℬ Mackay, James	21 May 04	17 Sept. 04	22 Mar. 10	25 Feb. 16	72 Foot.
Mackay, Robert	24 July 00	24 Nov. 03	10 July 07		7 R. Vet. Batt.
Mackay, William	8 Oct. 99	6 April 01	22 May 06		9 R. Vet. Batt.
Mackenzie, Alexander	30 Nov. 15	8 April 25	1 Aug. 26	7 Mar. 34	Unattached.
Mackenzie, Alex. Wedder..	14 Jan. 07	11 Jan. 08	23 Jan. 12	6 Nov. 17	3 Garr. Batt.
Mackenzie, Donald	11 July 00	17 Dec. 03	21 Mar. 11		8 R. Vet. Batt.
Mackenzie, John Taylor	6 Sept. 04	7 Oct. 05	7 Feb. 11		7 R. Vet. Batt.
Mackey, John Alexander	9 April 25	20 Nov. 27	3 Dec. 29	8 Oct. 30	59 Foot.
ℬ Maclean, Alexander	31 Dec. 03	23 April 05	15 Oct. 12	21 Nov. 16	79 Foot.
Maclean, James [130]	22 July 13	8 Nov. 14	22 Nov. 21	18 Sept. 23	103 Foot.
Macleane, William	1 Dec. 04	27 May 07	25 May 22	3 Jan. 28	Unattached.
Macleod, Arthur Lyttelton	12 Dec. 22	9 June 25	15 Feb. 33	1 Feb. 39	Unattached.
Macneil, Archibald	10 Feb. 96	26 July 97	13 Aug. 05		3 R. Vet. Batt.
Macpherson, Charles [131]	16 Nov. 15	14 Jan. 20	9 June 37	9 June 37	Unattached.
Macpherson, Donald	15 Aug. 05	14 Jan. 08	23 Nov. 18	16 April 29	Unattached.
ℬ Macpherson, Lachlan [132]	31 Mar. 14	7 April 25	19 May 37	19 May 37	Unattached.
Macpherson, Duncan	12 Oct. 04	1 Feb. 07	11 Aug. 15	5 July 21	97 Foot.
Macpherson, Ewen	13 Nov. 23	5 Nov. 25	10 Oct. 26	14 June 38	Unattached.
Macquarie, Hector	26 Sept. 11	12 Feb. 14	25 Dec. 38	25 Dec. 38	Unattached.
ℬ 🅆🅂 Maddock, William	6 Aug. 99	25 July 01	12 Oct. 15	25 Feb. 16	79 Foot.
Majendie, John Routledge	1 June 20	15 May 23	30 June 25	17 May 37	Unattached.
Mairis, Valentine Hale	11 May 13	28 Jan. 19	10 June 26	10 June 26	Unattached.
Maitland, John Madan [133]	15 July 13	14 April 14	11 Sept. 17	26 Feb. 24	52 Foot.
Maitland, Patrick	20 Feb. 23	7 July 25	8 April 26	8 April 26	Unattached.
Mallard, John Hicks	8 Dec. 07	19 July 21	24 Mar. 36		R. Marines.
Mallock, Samuel	9 Jan. 01	4 Aug. 05	1 July 25		R. Marines.
ℬ Mancor, Andrew	26 Oct. 04	16 June 07	3 Sept. 12	1 Aug. 16	59 Foot.
Mandeville, Edward	10 April 25	12 Dec. 26	22 Oct. 37	11 Oct. 39	90 Foot.
Mansfield, John	15 Sept. 96	11 Jan. 00	26 Jan. 04		2 R. Vet. Batt.
🅆🅂 Marcon, Edward	11 May 11	20 May 13	3 Jan. 22	6 Feb. 23	79 Foot.
Marlow, John	1 July 01	18 May 03	1 Feb. 08	24 Feb. 23	R. Artillery.
Marryat, George	19 Feb. 24	23 June 25	18 Dec. 27	31 Dec. 29	Unattached.
Martin, Henry Clinton [134]	20 Dec. 99	25 Dec. 01	13 Jan. 07		R. Artillery.
Masboug, Ladislasde Villiers	never	never	30 Dec. 97	1799	60 Foot.
Mascall, John Richard	7 Sept. 08	19 Dec. 22	10 Jan. 37		R. Marines.
Massey, George [135]	never	never	1 Sept. 01		R. Art. Drivers
🅆🅂 Master, Richard Thos. [136]	21 Jan. 13	never	1 July 15	25 Feb. 19	Gren. Gds.
Matheson, David	28 July 14	12 Mar. 18	28 June 36	28 June 36	Unattached.
Matheson, John	5 Aug. 03	17 April 04	6 Dec. 10	25 April 16	78 Foot.
Mathew, Geo. Benvenuto	7 July 25	19 Sept. 26	19 April 31	23 Sept. 36	Unattached.
Mathias, Gabriel [137]	18 Dec. 06	11 Feb. 08	29 Aug. 25	17 Mar. 36	R. Artillery.
Matson, Henry	16 Sept. 13	2 June 14	30 Nov. 38	30 Nov. 38	Unattached.
Maule, John	24 Sept. 05	19 May 09	15 Sept. 31	30 Nov. 32	R. Marines.
🅆🅂 Maunsell, John Edm. [138]	14 June 05	1 June 06	24 Mar. 17	14 Nov. 26	R. Artillery.
Maxwell, Henry	4 Mar. 13	13 Jan. 14	10 April 23	18 May 26	Unattached.
Maxwell, William	1 April 24	18 Feb. 26	11 June 30	11 June 30	Unattached.
* May, Joseph	never	never	25 Dec. 13	1814	53 Foot.
Mayer, Philip	30 Dec. 97	5 Aug. 00	23 Nov. 09	25 Jan. 18	60 Foot.
Mayne, Simon William	1 April 24	7 July 25	1 Feb. 27	12 April 39	19 Dragoons.
Mayne, William	16 Dec. 16	26 Dec. 24	25 Oct. 27	25 Oct. 27	Unattached.
Meech, Thomas Crosby	5 Sept. 05	26 Dec. 05	1 Oct. 12	3 May 21	62 Foot.
Meek, Jacob [139]	21 Mar. 10	22 Oct. 12	23 June 25	26 April 34	Unattached.
ℬ *Melhuish, S. Camplin [140]*	25 April 09	28 May 10	20 Dec. 14		R. Engineers.
Mellis, John	10 June 26	3 April 28	24 Jan. 40	24 Jan. 40	Unattached.
ℬ Mends, Hugh Bowen	13 Nov. 06	27 Nov. 06	12 Feb. 14	26 Feb. 29	Staff Corps.
Metcalfe, Thos. Levet	5 Aug. 99	23 May 00	25 April 05		6 R. Vet. Batt.
🅆🅂 Methold, Edward	17 Sept. 12	28 Mar. 15	11 Oct. 21	11 Oct. 21	3 Drag. Gds.
Meynell, Edw. Francis	8 July 13	26 Aug. 13	19 June 17	30 May 22	79 Foot.
Michell, Walter Taylor	10 June 94	24 April 95	21 Dec. 03	5 Oct. 13	R. Marines.

Captains.

	ENSIGN, ETC.	LIEUT.	CAPTAIN.	WHEN PLACED ON HALF PAY.	
Micklethwait, John	1 Oct. 12	19 Aug. 13	7 July 25	7 July 25	Unattached.
Miller, Thomas	5 May 04	26 Sept. 04	17 Feb. 14	8 April 26	Unattached.
Millerd, Thomas	29 Mar. 22	27 Feb. 24	8 April 26	8 April 26	Unattached.
𝕻 Milles, Wm. Hickes	25 Nov. 07	29 June 09	22 April 13	11 April 23	55 Foot.
Milligan, William	17 Dec. 18	1 Jan. 24	18 July 26	15 Mar. 31	Unattached.
Mills, Samuel	4 Feb. 26	3 Jan. 28	28 Dec. 38	28 Dec. 38	Unattached.
𝕻 Minchin, John Paul	14 Aug. 04	8 Oct. 06	26 Nov. 12	6 April 20	100 Foot.
Mitchell, Andrew	25 Feb. 04	3 April 05	27 June 11		7 R. Vet. Batt.
𝕻 Mitchell, Parry	26 Aug. 07	20 Sept. 10	8 Sept. 25	10 Aug. 26	66 Foot.
Mitchell, Thomas Peter....	1 June 00	5 April 01	11 April 11	3 June 13	69 Foot.
𝕮𝕭 Molesworth, A. Oliv.[141]	17 Dec. 12	20 June 15	10 July 34	28 Dec. 35	R. Artillery.
Molesworth, Arthur	6 Feb. 05	27 July 08	12 Oct. 30	9 Dec. 34	R. Marines.
𝕻 𝕮𝕭 Molloy, John [142]	17 Dec. 07	5 June 09	5 Aug. 24	28 May 29	Unattached.
Molyneux, John	20 July 15	16 Sept. 19	21 July 25	18 Nov. 31	52 Foot.
Montagu, *Lord*, Wm. Fran.	23 July 18	8 Mar. 21	8 April 26	2 Feb. 30	Unattached.
𝕮𝕭 Montogu, Willoughby[143]	26 Nov. 08	11 Aug. 11	6 Nov. 27	6 Nov. 27	R. Artillery.
Montgomery, Alex. Rich...	16 May 05	28 May 06	17 Sept. 12	16 Dec. 13	23 Foot.
𝕻 Montgomery, Richard[144]	7 Sept. 12	20 Mar. 23	12 June 35	12 June 35	Unattached.
Moore, Charles	3 May 00	25 Sept. 01	25 April 11	1815	67 Foot.
Moore, Frederick	3 April 17	12 Sept. 22	23 June 25	16 Aug. 33	22 Dragoons.
Moore, Henry............	6 July 15	17 Feb. 23	23 April 26	23 April 26	Unattached.
Moore, Humphrey	7 Nov. 04	27 July 08	23 April 29		R. Marines.
𝕮𝕭 Moore, James Stewart	1 Aug. 11	7 April 13	15 April 19	25 Dec. 19	24 Dragoons.
Moore, Thomas	20 Jan. 98	23 Sept. 03	21 Nov. 10	16 Aug. 27	R. Marines.
Moray, Francis, *Earl of* ..			22 Nov. 90	Jan. 91	Indep. Co.
𝕻 Mordaunt, Lewis	1 Sept. 04	20 Feb. 06	26 July 12	25 Dec. 14	61 Foot.
Morgan, Charles	11 Sept. 05	11 Nov. 08	17 Mar. 31		R. Marines.
𝕻 Morgan, Edward	never	4 Feb. 08	5 Mar. 12	22 Aug. 22	75 Foot.
𝕻 Morgan, George Gould..	4 July 11	never	26 Oct. 15	25 Feb. 19	Coldstr. Gds.
Morgan, John	1 Jan. 04	11 May 06	31 Aug. 27		R. Marines.
𝕻 Morle, John	18 Aug. 08	14 Sept. 10	2 Sept. 13	29 April 19	3 W. Ind. Reg.
Morrice, William	17 Aug. 97	1 Aug. 03	24 Oct. 11	3 Mar. 12	R. Marines.
* Morris, Griffith Jeffrey ..	never	never	25 Dec. 13	25 Sept. 14	22 Foot.
Morris, John Boden	14 July 25	9 Feb. 26	18 Jan. 31	8 April 36	Unattached.
𝕻 Morris, Samuel	31 Jan. 05	2 April 06	25 Nov. 13	25 Dec. 14	28 Foot.
Morrison, Hans	7 May 07	15 Feb. 08	13 Feb. 27	6 Dec. 27	60 Foot.
𝕻 Mortimer, Charles......	20 Nov. 06	9 Feb. 08	9 Mar. 24	12 April 31	Unattached.
Mortimer, Edmund	20 May 26	31 Dec. 27	18 July 34	18 July 34	Unattached.
𝕻 Morton, Harcourt	25 April 08	10 Nov. 08	12 Jan. 14	25 Mar. 16	14 Foot.
Mottley, Thos. Martin	11 Dec. 15	15 Nov. 24	10 Jan. 37	30 Dec. 37	R. Artillery.
Mulkern, Martin	23 April 12	1 Mar. 16	14 July 25	14 July 25	Unattached.
Mundy, Chas. Godfrey	13 April 96	never	23 Oct. 99	25 Dec. 02	Gren. Gds.
Munro, Hugh	14 April 90	14 Mar. 92	15 May 94		Invalids.
Murray, Chas. Robert	1 Aug. 22	19 May 25	8 April 26	25 Nov. 28	Unattached.
Murray, John Digby......	never	5 Jan. 14	2 April 18	18 Aug. 25	Unattached.
Musters, Henry	never	9 Dec. 30	5 June 35	26 Jan. 38	4 Foot.
𝕻 Muter, Robert	5 Mar. 07	3 Mar. 08	27 May 19	25 Oct. 21	7 Foot.
Muttlebury, James Eyre ..	19 Feb. 18	28 Jan. 24	19 Dec. 26	9 July 29	57 Foot.
Nash, Chas. Widenham[145]..	9 July 12	15 June 15	7 Aug. 27	7 Aug. 27	Unattached.
Neale, Wm. Payne	2 Oct. 23	27 Aug. 25	15 June 30	15 June 30	Unattached.
𝕻 Ness, James Burdett....	27 Aug. 04	26 Aug. 06	10 June 13	3 Sept. 18	71 Foot.
Nestor, James............	16 Sept. 04	15 Nov. 05	24 Oct. 11	14 Mar. 22	19 Foot.
Newbery, George	31 Jan. 11	1 Oct. 12	24 Feb. 16	24 May 16	44 Foot.
Newburgh, Ar. R. Camac..	25 April 17	16 July 21	17 June 23	21 May 25	Unattached.
Newell, George	never	7 Oct. 94	15 Aug. 00		4 R. Vet. Batt.
Newhouse, William [146] ..	14 Sept. 15	17 Sept. 18	13 Jan. 37	14 Dec. 38	Unattached.
𝕻 Newman, John	17 July 06	25 Nov. 07	25 Oct. 14	25 Dec. 16	Portuguese S.
Newton, Wm. Henry	20 June 00	25 Dec. 00	4 Dec. 06	3 Dec. 14	6 Garr. Batt.
Neynoe, Charles Fitz Roy..	25 May 20	9 Dec. 24	29 Sept. 29	21 May 36	Unattached.
Nicholas, James..........	21 Sept. 05	6 April 09	4 Jan. 31	30 Sep. 33	R. Marines.
𝕻 Nicolls, Augustus[147] ..	5 Oct. 09	1 Sept. 13	17 Mar. 37	17 Mar. 37	Unattached.
𝕻 *Nichols, William*	4 Aug. 04	11 July 05	27 Jan. 14		2 R. Vet. Batt.
𝕻 Nicholson, Huntley [148] ..	10 Oct. 11	5 Aug. 13	24 Mar. 38	17 Sept. 39	Gren. Gds.

Captains.

	CORNET, ETC.	LIEUT.	CAPTAIN.	WHEN PLACED ON HALF PAY.	
₽ ₩ Nisbet, Robert	30 Nov. 09	26 Dec. 11	19 Nov. 18	19 Nov. 18	20 Dragoons.
₽ ₩ Nixon, James Lock..	27 Aug. 12	never	12 May 14	6 July 20	60 Foot.
Nooth, Henry Stephen	never	14 May 12	29 Jan. 24	13 May 24	6 Drag. Gds.
Norris, John	12 Sept. 05	20 Dec. 08	17 Mar. 31	20 July 36	R. Marines.
North, Philip [149]	5 Aug. 13	21 Sept. 20	15 Feb. 31	13 Nov. 32	Unattached.
Northey, Wm. Brook	never	1 Aug. 22	20 April 26	25 May 28	Coldstr. Gds.
Nunn, John	4 June 12	7 Sept. 15	15 Nov. 39	15 Nov. 39	Unattached.
₽ Nunn, John Loftus [150] ..	9 Mar. 10	17 Jan. 11	27 April 32	27 April 32	Unattached.
Nunn, John Oliver Howe ..	26 Aug. 13	9 Sept. 15	22 April 26	15 May 28	80 Foot.
Oates, William Coape	22 Aug. 11	7 Oct. 13	27 July 15	25 Aug. 16	Glengarry Fen
O'Brien, Donatus	26 July 21	25 Mar. 24	20 July 38	20 July 38	Staff Corps.
O'Brien, Lucius [151]	1 July 82	28 Oct. 90	6 Mar. 95		R. Artillery.
O'Bryen, Charles	10 Nov. 93	24 April 95	22 July 03	8 June 10	R. Marines.
₽ O'Dell, Henry Edward [152]	8 July 06	25 Feb. 08	9 Jan. 22	20 Sept. 39	67 Foot.
Odlum, Henry	24 Mar. 03	16 Dec. 03	15 Oct. 07		5 R. Vet. Batt.
O'Donell, Neal	23 Nov. 96	1 Sept. 98	21 Aug. 06		4 R. Vet. Batt.
Ogilvie, John Gilbert......	5 June 23	18 Feb. 26	3 May 31	24 Feb. 37	Unattached.
O'Grady, John	20 Sept. 10	22 Sept. 13	26 May 31	29 July 36	96 Foot.
₽ O'Hegerty, Charles	21 Mar. 05	22 Feb. 09	16 Sept. 13	25 Mar. 16	60 Foot.
O'Meara, John	7 Oct. 13	2 Mar. 26	19 Nov. 30	21 June 31	3 Drag. Gds.
₽ O'Neill, Charles........	16 June 08	4 Jan. 10	5 June 27	30 Jan. 35	2 Foot.
* O'Neill, Daniel	never	never	25 Dec. 13	25 Sept. 14	70 Foot.
Onslow, *Sir* Henry *Bt*.....	20 Dec. 98	3 Dec. 00	1 June 06	9 June 19	R. Artillery.
₩ Ormsby, Arthur [153]....	2 June 14	27 Jan. 23	15 Jan. 36	25 Aug. 37	Unattached.
₽ Orr, Martin [154]	never	28 June 10	28 Oct. 31	23 Feb. 38	Unattached.
Osborne, William	30 Jan. 23	13 Aug. 25	31 Oct. 26	7 Mar. 34	Unattached.
Ouseley, William	20 May 18	31 Jan. 22	9 June 25	9 Aug. 31	Unattached.
Owen, Robert............	4 April 98	3 July 00	29 May 07	2 July 18	12 Foot.
₩ Packe, Geo. Hussey [155]	24 June 13	6 Jan. 14	27 June 16	25 Mar. 17	21 Dragoons.
* Page, Robert	never	never	25 Dec. 13	25 Sept. 14	9 Foot.
₩ Pakenham, William ..	30 Aug. 04	10 April 05	20 Dec. 14	1 July 22	R. Artillery.
Palliser, Rich. Bury	2 Nov. 13	9 April 18	12 Aug. 24	6 April 26	Unattached.
Palmer, Edw. Despard	Dec. 99	22 May 00	7 Sept. 09	13 Nov. 17	67 Foot.
Palmer, John............	5 July 13	27 Oct. 15	5 April 31	5 April 31	Unattached.
Parker, John	29 Nov. 21	12 May 25	19 Sept. 26	19 Sept. 26	Unattached.
₩ Parker, Stephen [156] ..	9 Feb. 09	11 April 11	20 Mar. 27	9 Oct. 35	Rifle Brigade.
Parlby, George	1 Aug. 16	3 Oct. 19	30 Sept. 25	7 Dec. 26	Unattached.
₽ ₩ Paschall, G. Fred. [157]	17 Mar. 12	19 Oct. 12	23 Mar. 26	19 Dec. 34	Unattached.
₽ Passley, John Panton [158]	31 Oct. 05	5 Dec. 07	8 Jan. 18	25 Sept. 18	60 Foot.
Patriarche, Philip	13 May 95	6 Oct. 96	15 Aug. 05	29 Nov. 14	R. Marines.
* Patrick, James	never	never	25 Dec. 13	25 Sept. 14	70 Foot.
₽ Patten, Wm. Brown [159]..	14 June 05	1 June 06	11 Mar. 17	1 Feb. 26	R. Artillery.
₽ Pattenson, Cooke Tylden	19 Feb. 07	9 Mar. 09	18 Aug. 14	25 Dec. 18	Rifle Brigade.
Petterson, Theophilus	2 Dec. 96	4 Oct. 01	20 Feb. 09	5 May 23	R. Marines.
Pattoun, George..........	28 Feb. 06	13 Mar. 12	15 May 34	28 Feb. 39	R. Marines.
Paul, Gregory............	7 Aug. 00	2 Jan. 06	20 June 11	25 Feb. 16	57 Foot.
Payne, *Sir* Charles, *Bt.* ..	25 July 11	6 Feb. 12	10 April 17	15 June 20	25 Dragoons.
Payne, William			1 April 95	22 June 99	8 Foot.
Peard, William Love	19 Oct. 04	1 Aug. 05	15 Jan. 18	10 Dec. 23	62 Foot.
Pearson, Charles	15 Dec. 17	18 May 25	22 April 26	6 Feb. 35	Unattached.
Peevor, George	1 Dec. 07	1 Jan. 10	2 Sept. 24	9 June 25	3 Foot.
₽ Pemberton, G. Keating [160]	5 Mar. 10	17 Dec. 13	3 Oct. 31	8 July 34	R. Artillery.
Penny, William	1 Feb. 06	15 June 08	19 June 27	30 Mar. 32	Unattached.
Penruddocke, Thomas	15 Nov. 97	never	25 Nov. 99	25 Dec. 02	Scots Fus. Gds.
Pepyat, Geo. Bownell ...	31 Jan. 06	3 Sept. 11	12 Oct. 32		R. Marines.
Perry, Joseph	2 June 04	18 April 05	7 Dec. 13	24 Mar. 25	34 Foot.
Petre, John..............			3 May 00	3 Dec. 02	22 Dragoons.
Pettat, Thomas John	4 May 26	14 April 29	13 Sept. 31	8 June 32	Unattached.
* Pettingal, Francis	never	never	25 Dec. 13	1814	1 Pr. Bn. Mil.
* Phelp, Edward Tufton ..	never	never	25 Dec. 13	1814	2 Pr. Bn. Mil.
₽ Phibbs, Wm. Harloe [161]..	30 Oct. 10	24 June 13	3 June 36	11 May 38	Unattached.
₽ ₩ Phillimore, Wm. R.	13 Dec. 10	never	13 Dec. 13	22 July 24	81 Foot.
Phillipps, James Winsloe ..	8 April 19	17 July 23	11 Feb. 26	19 Nov. 29	Unattached.

Captains.

	2D LIEUT. ETC.	LIEUT.	CAPTAIN.	WHEN PLACED ON HALF PAY.	
Phillipps, Henry	30 May 22	22 Oct. 25	25 Nov. 28	18 Dec. 35	Unattached.
P Phillips, Robt. Fryer[162]	4 Oct. 06	1 Feb. 08	29 July 25		R. Artillery.
Pickwick, Wm. Eleazer ..	13 Nov. 17	7 April 25	11 July 26	30 April 29	Unattached.
Pigott, Robert	16 June 04	13 Nov. 04	9 July 07	25 June 16	1 Gar. Batt.
P Pigott, William	19 Mar. 03	28 Aug. 04	5 Nov. 07	9 July 18	11 Foot.
Pinkerton, Robert........	9 Mar. 96	15 Dec. 98	19 June 07	16 Oct. 15	R. Marines.
P ℞ Pitman, William[163]..	6 Aug. 12	27 Sept. 13	12 April 31	10 Jan. 34	Unattached.
Pitts, Francis	25 Nov. 21	17 Feb. 25	15 April 36	15 April 36	Unattached.
Place, James	Dec. 07	15 Dec. 08	14 Sept. 20	12 June 23	2 Gar. Batt.
* Pococke, John Blagrave	never	never	6 Dec. 99	25 June 02	15 Foot.
Pode, William	8 June 09	12 Jan. 11	17 May 21	25 Oct. 21	33 Foot.
Pole, Samuel	5 June 23	27 Aug. 24	15 Aug. 26	15 Aug. 26	Unattached.
P Pollock, Samuel	30 May 05	21 May 06	18 Feb. 13	25 Mar. 17	43 Foot.
℞ Poole, Wm. Halstead[164]	11 Sept. 12	10 May 15	25 Nov. 33	22 Jan. 34	R. Artillery.
P Pope, Edward[165]	1 Sept. 04	26 Sept. 05	29 Sept. 13	14 Aug. 16	27 Foot.
P℞ Portarlington, J. E. of	24 Oct. 21	10 Sept. 25	9 Aug. 31	9 Aug. 31	Unattached.
P Porteous, Alexander....	17 July 06	23 July 07	20 April 15	25 July 15	60 Foot.
Porter, William	28 Oct. 94	13 Jan. 95	9 July 03		3 R. Vet. Batt.
Portman, H. W. Berkeley	13 April 20	16 Sept. 24	10 Dec. 25	25 Nov. 28	Unattached.
P Potter, Thomas	13 Nov. 06	2 Mar. 09	25 Oct. 14	25 Dec. 16	Portuguese S.
P Powell, Francis	8 May 05	26 Feb. 06	14 May 12	1814	45 Foot.
Powell, Peter	26 Oct. 04	2 Mar. 06	4 Feb. 13	26 Feb. 30	2 W.Ind. Reg.
Power, Thomas	19 June 06	25 Mar. 08	6 Nov. 13	2 Dec. 19	60 Foot.
Powys, Thomas	never	30 April 12	2 Jan. 18	30 April 29	Unattached.
Poyntz, James	24 July 84	8 Nov. 88	28 Aug. 94		Kelso's Reg.
Pratt, Henry	13 Oct. 04	25 Oct. 05	22 Nov. 10	25 Feb. 16	58 Foot.
*Pratt, James............	26 May 81	22 Jan. 83	12 Feb. 07		1 R. Vet. Batt.
P Prendergast, James	28 Aug. 06	26 Nov. 07	7 April 25	1 Nov. 27	Unattached.
Prendergast, Stephen	6 Aug. 06	13 Nov. 06	11 Feb. 13	25 Mar. 26	84 Foot.
* Price, Charles..........	never	never	25 Dec. 13	25 Sept. 14	35 Foot.
P Price, David	25 Dec. 05	23 April 07	8 Oct. 12	25 Dec. 14	36 Foot.
P Price, Rice	Mar. 08	21 July 08	27 April 20	25 Dec. 21	57 Foot.
* Prickett, William	never	never	25 Dec. 13	25 June 16	R. Wag. Tr.
P ℞ Pringle, J. Watson[166]	23 Aug. 09	1 May 11	21 July 15		R. Engineers.
P.℞ Prior, Tho. Murray[167]	6 Aug. 03	22 Feb. 06	28 Nov. 34	28 Nov. 34	Unattached.
Prosser, Frederick........	22 Dec. 14	18 Oct. 16	1 Aug. 22	2 April 29	Unattached.
Prosser, Walter	24 April 81	11 July 82	24 June 95		Indep. Co.
Protheroe, W. Gar. Bridges	11 Mar. 01	12 Nov. 03	8 Oct. 07	18 Nov. 19	56 Foot.
Purcell, Tobias	28 Sept. 09	17 Sept. 12	30 Aug. 27	14 May 29	Unattached.
P Purefoy, Brinsley	27 Feb. 00	31 Dec. 03	20 July 09		10R.Vet.Batt.
Pyne, Arthur............	31 Jan. 71	12 May 76	5 June 81		Invalids.
P Pyner, Francis	25 Feb. 07	25 Mar. 08	4 April 13	25 Feb. 16	58 Foot.
P Quentin, Geo. Edward ..	28 July 08	17 May 09	25 Oct. 14	25 Dec. 16	Portuguese S.
Quested, Thomas	7 Oct. 05	11 Jan. 10	27 June 32		R. Marines.
Quill, John Thomas[168]	22 June 09	3 Sept. 12	5 Oct. 38	5 Oct. 38	Unattached.
℞ Rainforth, William ..	2 Dec. 12	23 Dec. 13	6 Feb. 35	9 June 38	Unattached.
℞ Ramsay, Thomas	19 June 06	16 Feb. 08	17 May 10	25 Mar. 16	14 Foot.
Randall, Charles	11 Oct. 97	23 Aug. 99	14 Feb. 11	27 Sept. 31	Unattached.
Rannie, William..........	21 May 07	29 Jan. 08	5 Oct. 32	22 Feb. 39	Unattached.
* Ravenscroft, Charles	never	never	3 Dec. 03	1814	R.Waggon Tr.
Rawlison, George[158*]......	4 May 05	7 Aug. 06	11 Aug. 14	25 Feb. 16	8 Foot.
℞ Rawson, William	16 Aug. 99	29 Mar. 04	4 May 09	2 July 18	27 Foot.
Read, Constantine........	7 Nov. 16	7 April 25	24 Aug. 32	24 Aug. 32	Staff Corps.
Read, William	25 Sept. 03	6 Feb. 05	13 Jan. 14	1816	90 Foot.
P Reardon, Rodol. Hobbs[169]	26 Aug. 08	1 Feb. 10	26 Oct. 30	26 Oct. 30	Unattached.
P Rees, Charles..........	21 April 03	2 June 04	3 Feb. 12	25 Dec. 14	53 Foot.
Reeves, Thomas	18 Sept. 04	3 Mar. 06	3 Mar. 14	9 Sept. 16	15 Foot.
Reeves, Thomas	7 Sept. 04	9 Oct. 05	25 June 07	8 April 19	24 Foot.
P Reid, Frederick[170]......	never	18 May 03	1 Nov. 12	1 Nov. 14	R. A. Drivers.
P Reynett, James Henry ..	19 Sept. 04	4 June 06	23 July 12	1814	45 Foot.
Reynolds, James	1 July 95	4 Nov. 95	6 Sept. 04		1 R. Vet. Bat.
P ℞ Rice, Stephen[171]....	7 Oct. 13	17 April 15	25 Dec. 38	25 Dec. 38	Unattached.

332

Captains.

	ENSIGN, ETC.	LIEUT.	CAPTAIN.	WHEN PLACED ON HALF PAY.	
Rich, John Sampson [172]	1 Mar. 08	30 April 09	9 Dec. 28	6 Nov. 30	R. Artillery.
Rich, Rob. James Evelyn	12 Aug. 24	29 June 26	1 Feb. 31	14 Feb. 31	66 Foot.
Richards, George	25 Jan. 98	18 Oct. 03	19 April 12	18 Mar. 13	R. Marines.
Richards, Hood	5 Aug. 19	29 Jan. 24	14 Nov. 26	14 Nov. 26	Unattached.
Richardson, Charles	13 Nov. 99	24 April 04	10 Feb. 14	25 May 16	59 Foot.
Richardson, Frederick	19 April 15	18 Dec. 24	17 Sept. 29	28 Dec. 32	5 Foot.
Richardson, Mervyn	19 July 15	2 May 24	4 Feb. 26	4 Feb. 26	Unattached.
Richardson, Thomas	3 Sept. 07	10 Mar. 08	22 May 16	4 Sept. 17	7 Dragoons.
¶☼ Richardson, Wm. S. [173]	23 Feb. 13	5 June 15	24 Dec. 25	24 Dec. 25	Unattached.
Rickards, Henry	29 Aug. 07	23 Sept. 08	3 Mar. 25	18 May 26	Unattached.
* Rickards, William	never	never	25 Dec. 13	25 Aug. 16	64 Foot.
Ridding, William	21 Oct. 95	9 Oct. 97	3 Aug. 12	5 Mar. 18	59 Foot.
Riddle, William	17 Nov. 03	20 July 04	10 Mar. 10	25 Sept. 16	4 Ceylon Reg.
* Riddlesden, Richard	never	never	25 Dec. 13	25 Sept. 14	4 Foot.
Ridge, Geo. Cooper		1795	17 June 06	4 Dec. 06	16 June 08	4 Foot.
Ridge, Rob. Stuart [174]	8 Sept. 14	28 Dec. 21	29 Sept. 37	29 Sept. 37	Unattached.
¶☼ Ridgway, John A. [175]	25 Jan. 10	9 May 12	24 Dec. 29	19 July 31	Unattached.
* Ridgway, Samuel	never	never	25 Dec. 13		1814	85 Foot.
Rivers, Jas. John Campbell	18 Mar. 06	17 April 12	27 May 34		R. Marines.
¶☼ Roberts, John [176]	21 April 08	12 Oct. 09	7 April 25	21 June 27	Unattached.
Roberts, John Cramer	18 Jan. 15	13 June 16	14 July 25	14 July 25	Unattached.
Robertson, Alexander	16 Nov. 09	28 Nov. 10	6 Mar. 27	6 Mar. 27	Unattached.
Robertson, Charles	21 Aug. 05	10 Jan. 07	6 May 13	18 Mar. 19	Meuron's Reg.
Robertson, Frederick	22 Dec. 03	20 July 04	23 July 13	10 Oct. 21	R. Artillery.
* Robertson, John	never	never	25 Dec. 13	25 Sept. 14	14 Foot.
Robertson, Patrick	10 Jan. 01	4 Aug. 05	13 Aug. 25	4 Feb. 35	R. Marines.
Robinson, Beverley	10 May 05	1 June 06	20 Jan. 17	1 April 17	R. Artillery.
Robinson, Joseph	21 April 14	18 Nov. 24	7 June 39	7 June 39	Unattached.
Robinson, Wm. Henry	1 April 01	15 Aug. 05	18 April 26	22 May 30	R. Marines.
Roche, Joseph	15 Dec. 04	10 Feb. 07	16 May 11		3 R. Vet. Bat.
Rollo, Robert A. [177]	17 Aug. 03	12 Sept. 03	29 Dec. 10	12 April 20	R. Artillery.
Rollo, *Hon.* Roger	13 Aug. 94	9 Sept. 94	18 April 01	24 Nov. 02	R. Artillery.
Rose, George Pitt	11 July 22	22 April 24	29 Aug. 26	15 Sept. 37	9 Dragoons.
¶ Rose, Hugh Hay	14 July 04	3 Oct. 05	25 Oct. 14	25 Dec. 16	Portu. Serv.
Rose, H. M. St. Vincent	8 Jan. 18	28 Nov. 21	9 June 25	20 April 26	Unattached.
Rose, James Pratt	11 Feb. 08	1 June 09	31 Aug. 15	25 Nov. 17	66 Foot.
¶ Rose, Thomas	6 July 04	8 Oct. 06	15 Sept. 14	25 Dec. 14	32 Foot.
Rose, William	8 Feb. 94	3 Sept. 94	15 Nov. 94		97 Foot.
¶Ross, J.(*Q.M.*6 July 96) [178]	never	9 Sept. 00	30 Dec. 36	30 Dec. 36	Unattached.
Rous, *Hon.* Wm. Rufus	never	17 Dec. 12	18 Nov. 19	24 April 23	Portuguese.
Rowan, William	27 May 02	6 April 09	9 June 20	1 Nov. 21	84 Foot.
¶ *Royal, John*	4 May 09	3 Oct. 11	10 Nov. 13		2 R. Vet. Bat.
¶ Royds, William	16 Feb. 08	15 Feb. 09	9 June 14	25 Feb. 17	52 Foot.
¶ Rudkin, Mark	12 July 05	29 Jan. 07	21 May 13	25 May 28	47 Foot.
Runnacles, Anthony	11 Dec. 15	22 Sept. 23	10 Jan. 37	27 Mar. 38	R. Artillery.
¶ Ryves, John	12 Oct. 99	19 May 00	25 Mar. 08	25 Feb. 16	58 Foot.
Salmond, James	31 Dec. 27	11 Jan. 31	30 Oct. 35	27 Jan. 38	Unattached.
Sampson, W. H.	14 Oct. 13	15 April 19	3 Nov. 35	1 Feb. 39	Unattached.
Sanderson, Edward	18 Mar. 95	6 Sept. 95	25 June 03	2 Feb. 08	Scotch Brig.
¶ Sandes, John [179]	18 Mar. 13	4 May 15	17 May 31	28 June 33	Unattached.
¶ Sandwith, Fred. Browne	8 Oct. 06	29 Aug. 07	31 Mar. 14	25 Dec. 14	38 Foot.
Sandys, Miles	23 Oct. 79		6 Mar. 83		1783	104 Foot.
¶ Saunderson, Wm. Basset	6 Mar. 07	28 April 08	4 Mar. 13	9 May 22	50 Foot.
Sayer, Joshua Saffrey	10 Aug. 99	1 Sept. 04	20 June 23		R. Marines.
¶ Scargill, James [180]	12 April 10	21 Oct. 12	17 Jan. 28	6 July 32	Unattached.
¶☼ Schreiber, George	23 Dec. 13	11 July 16	9 Nov. 21	9 Nov. 21	18 Dragoons.
Schultz, John Frederick	11 Dec. 07	23 June 08	16 Nov. 14	19 Sept. 22	Portu. Serv.
Scott, Charles	13 Feb. 06	16 Jan. 12	19 Mar. 34	11 April 36	R. Marines.
Scott, Chas. Rochfort	2 Jan. 12	20 July 15	25 June 30	25 June 30	Staff Corps.
Scott, Rich. Andrew	28 Feb. 14	19 Mar. 25	24 Aug. 32	24 Aug. 32	Staff Corps.
Scriven, John	28 Feb. 96	21 Oct. 98	4 May 07	9 Aug. 14	R. Marines.
¶ Seward, Elliot [181]	29 Sept. 04	3 July 05	10 May 15	16 Jan. 18	R. Artillery.
Shand, John Muller	9 Feb. 01	28 Aug. 04	15 Jan. 12	25 Jan. 17	89 Foot.

Captains.

	2D LIEUT. ETC.	LIEUT.	CAPTAIN.	WHEN PLACED ON HALF PAY.	
Sharp, Henry Jelf	21 May 18	14 July 25	17 Oct. 26	22 Feb. 31	Unattached.
Sharp, William	24 April 93	5 Oct. 94	23 Feb. 97		Indep. Comp.
Shaw, George	30 April 07	20 April 08	20 July 15	25 Dec. 18	96 Foot.
Shawe, Rich. Fleetwood ..	5 June 23	14 July 25	27 April 27	6 Jan. 32	Unattached.
Shawe, Francis Manby	never	6 May 13	5 Oct. 20	13 April 26	Unattached.
Shearman, John	19 Feb. 00	27 Nov. 06	15 Feb. 10	20 Dec. 21	7 Foot.
Sheppard, Walter Cope....	8 May 23	10 Nov. 25	9 April 29	25 June 31	Unattached.
𝔓 Sherran, William	22 Aug. 99	10 July 01	8 Sept. 08	25 Sept. 16	43 Foot.
𝔓 Shinkwin, Rich. Walter	10 Sept. 12	9 Feb. 20	16 Sept. 36	7 June 39	Unattached.
Short, William Henry	24 Dec. 79	30 Oct. 80	30 July 89	1 Mar. 98	25 Foot.
𝔓 Shum, William	10 Dec. 07	21 Feb. 10	27 May 13	25 Mar. 16	3 Dr. Gds.
Siborn, William	9 Sept. 13	8 Nov. 15	31 Jan. 40	31 Jan. 40	Unattached.
Silver, Jacob	11 Sept. 13	15 Oct. 18	11 Mar. 24	8 April 26	Unattached.
Sime, Robert	3 Mar. 99	22 April 01	15 Mar. 10	30 May 16	78 Foot.
Simmons, Thos. Frederick[184]	23 May 06	1 Feb. 07	22 Sept. 23	12 Mar. 29	R. Artillery.
Simpson, Alexander	28 Sept. 96	24 Oct. 99	5 Nov. 07	15 May 17	5 W. I. Regt.
Sisson, Joseph	18 Sept. 06	26 Aug. 08	7 April 25	14 Sept. 26	Unattached.
Sitwell, William Hurt	20 April 20	17 Sept. 25	30 Aug. 26	23 Mar. 32	Unattached.
𝔓 Skene, Alexander	28 May 07	25 July 09	11 Nov. 13		4 R. Vet. Bat.
Skinner, Henry Bryant[183]	10 Mar. 09	20 Jan. 26	10 July 37		R. Marines.
Skirrow, James	3 Dec. 03	28 Jan. 05	2 Sept. 13	25 Dec. 28	48 Foot.
Skynner, Aug. Chas.......	3 Oct. 16	3 Mar. 25	12 April 27	20 Dec. 39	15 Dragoons.
Slater, Henry Francis	1 May 15	6 Nov. 20	4 June 36	19 Aug. 39	R. Artillery.
Sleigh, William	3 May 00	25 Feb. 04	19 Mar. 12	25 April 17	99 Foot.
Small, Robert............	4 Oct. 11	20 Sept. 14	20 Oct. 25	29 Oct. 25	Unattached.
Smart, George John	5 Sept. 22	27 July 25	30 Dec. 26	31 Dec. 30	Unattached.
Smith, Edm. Carrington ..	28 Dec. 19	10 Feb. 25	8 April 26	8 April 26	Unattached.
Smith, Henry Nelson	1 Mar. 10	1 May 11	26 Aug. 19	1 Feb. 20	R. Engineers.
Smith, John	17 Aug. 99	27 May 01	1 June 06		R. Artillery.
Smith, John	25 Oct. 07	9 Nov. 09	11 May 23	24 May 27	Unattached.
Smith, John	2 April 20	24 May 33	26 Aug. 36	31 Mar. 37	Unattached.
Smith, Robt. Geo. Suckling	17 Dec. 12	28 June 15	25 Sept. 34	28 Nov. 37	R. Artillery.
Smyth, William Thomas ..	29 Sept. 25	25 Nov. 28	24 July 35	31 Aug. 38	35 Foot.
Somerville, Mark, *Lord*[184]	8 Sept. 03	6 Dec. 03	16 April 12	2 Dec. 19	R. Artillery.
ℚℜ Souter, David.........	16 May 11	24 Sept. 12	2 Feb. 30	26 Jan. 38	66 Foot.
Southwell, Hon. Chas. KH.	never	3 July 95	17 Sept. 03		12 R. V. Bat.
𝔓 ℚℜ Spalding, John[185] ..	20 Jan. 14	30 Mar. 26	26 June 38	26 June 38	Unattached.
Spearman, James Morton..	10 July 15	23 Jan. 21	25 Oct. 27	25 Oct. 27	Unattached.
𝔓 Spearman, John	22 Mar. 98	9 Aug. 99	28 April 08	26 Nov. 18	5 Foot.
Spedding, John	never	12 Aug. 95	25 May 98	23 Nov. 04	Irish Brigade.
Spry, Henry	6 Jan. 01	25 July 05	20 June 25	13 Aug. 25	R. Marines.
Spurin, John	7 Feb. 97	19 Nov. 01	22 July 09	15 Sept. 26	R. Marines.
𝔓 Stainforth, John	Mar. 03	23 July 03	19 Feb. 07	11 July 16	2 Gar. Bat.
Stampa, Anthony	30 Dec. 97	25 July 00	10 Oct. 09	2 Feb. 26	Unattached.
𝔓 Stanford, Francis[186]	21 Oct. 13	1 Sept. 20	1 Mar. 39	1 Mar. 39	Unattached.
* Stanier, George	never	never	3 Dec. 99	1800	82 Foot.
𝔓 Stanley, Mark Anth.[187]..	15 June 09	16 Aug. 10	29 Dec. 24	10 Feb. 32	Unattached.
* Stapleton, Wm. Philip ..	never		25 Dec. 13	25 Aug. 15	51 Foot.
Stapley, Thomas	30 April 05	5 Aug. 06	26 July 21	17 Aug. 32	Unattached.
Staunton, William........	10 Jan. 95	8 June 96	20 Nov. 01	1806	118 Foot.
Steele, John	never	never	28 Sept. 99	4 Feb. 08	105 Foot.
𝔓 Stephens, Henry Wm...	31 Aug. 04	13 June 05	26 Feb. 07	25 Feb. 16	6 Foot.
Stephenson, Edward	27 Oct. 08	12 Sept. 11	27 April 27	27 April 27	Unattached.
Stephenson, Wm. Walter ..	30 Jan. 12	19 Aug. 13	24 Oct. 21	24 Oct. 21	Rifle Brigade.
𝔓 Sterne, William	7 Sept. 04	26 Sept. 06	24 June 13	12 Nov. 18	83 Foot.
Steuart, James	20 April 15	15 Dec. 25	13 Nov. 35	14 Feb. 39	Unattached.
ℚℜ Steuart, John[188]	17 June 13	10 Nov. 14	12 Nov. 25	2 April 29	Unattached.
ℚℜ Steuart, Robert	12 Aug. 12	11 Aug. 14	3 Mar. 25	19 Jan. 26	Unattached.
Steward, John Chas. Tucker	15 Dec. 92	25 Sept. 94	11 Nov. 95	25 Dec. 02	Scots F. Gds.
Steward, Thomas Carr ..	5 July 03	15 Aug. 05	31 July 26		R. Marines.
𝔓 ℚℜ Stewart, Allan[189] ..	10 Dec. 12	19 July 15	3 June 28	27 May 36	Unattached.
𝔓 Stewart, Daniel	13 April 09	21 Nov. 10	19 Dec. 16	23 July 18	3 Foot.
Stewart, David Ogilvy	30 April 99	3 July 01	7 Mar. 05	7 Dec. 14	2 Gar. Bat.
𝔓 ℚℜ Stewart, Duncan[190]	13 June 05	1 Jan. 07	3 Aug. 15	25 Dec. 26	Unattached.

Captains.

	CORNET, ETC.	LIEUT.	CAPTAIN.	WHEN PLACED ON HALF PAY.	
Stewart, Hen. Wm. Seymour	22 Oct. 18	24 Oct. 21	25 May 26	12 June 30	Unattached.
Stewart, James	16 May 05	15 Jan. 06	9 June 14	14 Mar. 21	87 Foot.
Stewart, James			28 Aug. 94		Cheshire Reg.
₧ Stewart, James	18 Oct. 10	1 April 12	2 June 25	22 Nov. 27	Unattached.
Stewart, Joseph King	11 Dec. 17	16 Dec. 19	8 April 26	8 April 26	Unattached.
₧ ☾ Stewart, Robert	31 Oct. 05	13 May 08	27 April 20	1 May 28	Unattached.
Stewart, Walter James	7 July 03	15 Aug. 05	31 July 26	27 Sept. 27	R. Marines.
₧ St. George, Stepney	28 May 07	6 Aug. 07	16 June 25	25 May 26	Unattached.
* Still, Nathaniel Tyron	never		25 Dec. 13	25 Sept. 14	5 Foot.
St. Leger, John	26 Oct. 15	2 Dec. 19	25 Sept. 23	25 Aug. 25	Port. Serv.
Stockenstrom, Andrew	12 Sept. 11	7 June 14	25 May 20	20 July 20	Corsican Ran.
Stocker, Ives	14 Dec. 11	1 July 12	29 July 25		R. Engineers.
Stopford, Thomas	22 April 26	20 Nov. 27	12 April 33	17 April 35	Unattached.
Story, George Walter	7 Feb. 22	26 May 25	6 July 30	6 July 30	Unattached.
Straith, Hector	6 July 09	29 Aug. 11	26 Aug. 24	12 Jan. 26	Unattached.
Straker, James	26 May 04	25 Oct. 04	29 Sept. 14	27 May 24	York Chas.
Strange, Charles	6 May 19	25 Dec. 23	21 Nov. 28	21 Nov. 28	Unattached.
Strangwayes, Thomas	17 Feb. 03	9 June 04	4 June 11	13 Jan. 20	12 Foot.
Strangways, George Fox	5 Oct. 20	8 April 25	25 June 29	8 June 38	Unattached.
Strangways, Wm. Henry	6 July 03	15 Aug. 05	31 July 26		R. Marines.
Straubenzee, Charles	28 Oct. 95	5 Sept. 96	14 Dec. 04	15 Oct. 07	6 W. I. Reg.
Stuart, Charles Augustus	26 Nov. 06	18 Feb. 08	14 Oct. 24	16 April 29	Unattached.
Stuart, Hon. James	11 Jan. 21	7 April 25	6 Nov. 27	18 Oct. 39	Unattached.
Stuart, Hon. John	12 July 15	14 Nov. 16	27 Aug. 25	27 Aug. 25	Unattached.
Stuart, John Morton	11 June 12	6 Jan. 14	16 May 22	22 Sept. 25	Unattached.
☾ Stupart, Francis [191]	5 May 08	14 Dec. 09	20 July 15	25 Mar. 16	2 Dragoons.
Sturgeon, Philip	14 July 80	18 April 93	27 April 97	30 Nov. 04	R. Marines.
Suckling, Nelson Fleming	16 Jan. 23	23 June 25	13 Mar. 27	13 Mar. 27	Unattached.
₧ *Sutherland, Andrew*	7 April 04	27 June 05	13 May 13		5 R. Vet. Bat.
Sutherland, Edward	27 Nov. 16	14 April 25	25 Dec. 38	25 Dec. 38	Unattached.
Sutherland, Geo. M'Kay	2 Aug. 15	14 Oct. 24	5 June 28	21 Nov. 28	23 Dragoons.
Sutherland, Hugh Alex.	2 July 94	11 Oct. 94	10 July 01	15 April 13	10 Foot.
Sutton, Samuel Ives	22 Sept. 25	16 Nov. 26	11 June 30	20 Oct. 37	Portu. Serv.
Sweeny, Charles Fred.	12 April 10	7 May 12	29 Dec. 37	29 Dec. 37	Unattached.
Sweeny, James	9 Sept. 13	9 April 25	15 Feb. 39	15 Feb. 39	Unattached.
Sweny, Welbore Ellis	1 May 13	6 Feb. 17	19 Nov. 25	21 Sept. 30	9 Foot.
Synnot, Walter	7 June 93	3 Sept. 95	7 Dec. 97	1803	89 Foot.
₧ Templeton, Edward	25 July 05	29 May 06	4 May 15	4 Nov. 19	47 Foot.
₧ Tench, Henry	9 July 03	15 Dec. 04	24 July 12	25 Feb. 16	10 Foot.
Tenison, Barton [192]	7 Mar. 11	22 Oct. 12	14 Dec. 15	4 Jan. 33	Unattached.
* Terry, John	never	never	25 Dec. 13	1814	74 Foot.
Terry, John	6 May 05	6 Aug. 07	31 Jan. 11	24 Aug. 20	101 Foot.
* Terry, Stephen	never	never	5 Dec. 99	3 Sept. 01	8 Foot.
₧ Thatcher, Sackville Z. [193]	1 Nov. 10	26 Aug. 13	8 Feb. 39	6 Dec. 39	Unattached.
Thompson, Edward	9 Nov. 07	1 Mar. 10	13 June 16	10 Aug. 19	Staff Corps.
₧ Thompson, E. Colley [194]	31 Mar. 08	31 May 10	14 Sept. 32	14 Sept. 32	Unattached.
₧ Thompson, James	19 June 06	15 Oct. 07	23 May 16	25 Jan. 17	89 Foot.
Thomson, James	18 Aug. 07	19 July 21	26 Dec. 35		R. Marines.
Thorne, William	17 Mar. 99	26 Jan. 01	14 May 07	25 June 16	1 Gar. Bat.
Thursby, Charles	3 Oct. 26	10 Nov. 29	28 June 31	1 June 32	29 Foot.
Tinling, Chas. Hugh Lyle	20 Nov. 17	3 May 21	30 Dec. 34	3 Aug. 38	7 Foot.
☾ Tompkins, New. Rich.	21 Nov. 11	10 Dec. 13	19 Sept. 26	15 June 30	Unattached.
Toole, William	5 Dec. 05	25 Aug. 07	9 Nov. 14	19 April 17	40 Foot.
Toomer, Edward Alexander	28 Feb. 97	6 Mar. 02	15 Jan. 10	2 June 21	R. Marines.
Torriano, C. Strangways [195]	25 April 06	22 Oct. 06	26 June 23	15 April 29	R. Artillery.
Townsend, Sam. Irwin	14 July 83	never	28 Aug. 99	16 July 03	Gren. Gds.
☾ Trafford, Sigismund [196]	7 June 10	25 July 11	9 Nov. 15	25 Mar. 16	1 Dragoons.
Trevillian, Maurice Ceely	4 Mar. 13	30 Sept. 13	13 Sept. 21	13 Sept. 21	14 Dragoons.
Triscott, Joseph	2 June 97	21 July 03	26 Oct. 10	1 Sept. 14	R. Marines.
Trollope, Arthur	21 Feb. 28	23 Aug. 31	24 Mar. 37	16 Aug. 39	20 Dragoons.
₧ Trotter, John [197]	26 Nov. 08	1 Nov. 11	19 Jan. 30	26 Aug. 31	R. Artillery.
Trotter, Robert Knox	12 May 25	6 July 26	9 Aug. 27	2 Dec. 36	Sub.In.of Mil.
Trower, Anthony	1 Mar. 03	2 Dec. 04	15 July 13	25 June 15	4 Ceylon Reg.

Captains.

	ENSIGN, ETC.	LIEUT.	CAPTAIN.	WHEN PLACED ON HALF PAY.	
Tucker, John Tudor [196]....	7 July 06	14 April 13	27 May 34		R. Marines.
Tupman, John	31 Oct. 99	24 Mar. 00	19 July 10	29 April 19	4 W. I. Regt.
Turner, Edw. Geo. T. Page	4 May 09	4 Jan. 10	25 Dec. 12	4 May 15	3 Dragoons.
Turner, Richard	12 Feb. 98	1 Dec. 03	9 Feb. 13	16 Feb. 14	R. Marines.
☗☗ Turner, William	23 May 11	6 Feb. 12	3 Nov. 19	27 June 22	78 Foot.
Tweed, Augustus	3 May 10	12 Sept. 11	5 June 27	5 June 27	Unattached.
ᛈ Tweedie, Michael [199]	1 May 09	17 June 12	22 July 30	17 Dec. 33	R. Artillery.
ᛈ ☗☗ Tyndale, Chas. W. [200]	9 May 11	3 June 13	5 Aug. 24	1 Sept. 37	Unattached.
Ussher, John [291]	30 May 09	31 July 11	28 Dec. 32	13 Jan. 37	Unattached.
Vandeleur, Thos. Pakenham	27 April 15	5 Dec. 22	16 Dec. 24	15 Jan. 29	Unattached.
Vanderpant, Dirk	21 Aug. 99	11 June 01	22 May 02	25 June 02	9 Foot.
Vane, Charles Birch	30 Dec. 26	17 Dec. 30	19 July 39	19 July 39	Unattached.
Varlo, George.............	18 June 93	24 April 95	15 July 03	23 Aug. 05	R. Marines.
ᛈ Vaughan, Herb. Henry [202]	29 June 09	16 Jan. 12	4 Sept. 23	25 Jan. 31	Unattached.
ᛈ Ventry, T. T. Arem. *Lord*	never	5 Feb. 07	8 Aug. 11	11 Dec. 17	43 Foot.
Vernon, Bowater Henry ..	17 Oct. 16	8 July 24	28 Jan. 26	28 Jan. 26	Unattached.
ᛈ Vetch, James [202]*	1 July 07	1 Mar. 08	21 July 13	11 Mar. 24	R. Engineers.
ᛈ Vincent, George.........	1 Sept. 04	7 June 05	5 Oct. 15	25 Feb. 16	4 Foot.
ᛈ Vincent, John Read	14 Sept. 04	18 April 05	29 July 13	25 Feb. 16	4 Foot.
Vincent, Thomas	20 Oct. 13	10 Aug. 15	28 June 27	12 Dec. 34	York Rangers
ᛈ Visme, Francis de	22 Mar. 10	31 Dec. 12	19 Mar. 18	21 Feb. 22	60 Foot.
Vyvyan, Thomas	15 Aug. 04	28 Feb. 05	25 Dec. 07	13 July 15	41 Foot.
ᛈ Wainman, William	25 Sept. 06	10 Nov. 08	13 Feb. 12	25 Mar. 16	14 Dragoons.
ᛈ Wainwright, Henry M. [203]	14 Jan. 08	3 Sept. 09	3 Jan. 26	26 Nov. 30	Unattached.
Wake, Richard William ..	10 April 25	22 April 26	16 July 30	25 May 32	African Corps
ᛈ Wakefield. Gilbert......	27 June 11	8 Sept. 12	25 July 22	24 Oct. 27	Unattached.
ᛈ Walker, *Harry*.........	16 Jan. 04	28 Aug. 04	22 July 13		1 R. Vet. Batt
ᛈ Walker, Isaac...........	27 Feb. 06	10 Nov. 07	26 Mar. 12	27 April 15	45 Foot.
Walker, Thomas..........	29 June 15	29 Feb. 16	9 Nov. 21	9 Nov. 21	19 Dragoons.
ᛈ Walker, William	6 July 09	13 June 11	22 Mar. 15	15 June 15	24 Foot.
ᛈ Walker, William	Dec. 08	14 Sept. 08	30 Dec. 19	9 Aug. 20	7 W. I. Regt.
Waller, Aldcroft..........	25 Feb. 08	1 Jan. 10	12 Nov. 12	17 Dec. 18	96 Foot.
* Waller, John	never	never	25 Dec. 13	25 Dec. 19	88 Foot.
Wallis, William Ogle......	9 April 76	28 April 78	26 Feb. 90		Indep. Co.
Walsh, John	23 Nov. 04	1 Dec. 05	20 June 15	24 Feb. 23	R. Artillery
Ward, John...............	17 Sept. 03	20 Mar. 05	22 Oct. 12	26 Oct. 16	24 Foot.
* Warner, Richard.......	never	never	25 Dec. 13	25 Sept. 14	5 Foot.
Warren, George	31 Dec. 03	8 Dec. 04	6 Dec. 10	25 Dec. 18	3 W. I. Regt.
Warrington, Thornhill	13 Nov. 98	22 Nov. 98	23 Jan. 12	2 July 23	76 Foot.
Waterman, Henry	6 Aug. 07	23 June 08	3 May 21	18 Dec. 28	Unattached.
ᛈ Watkins, Wm. Nowell ..	16 June 03	2 June 04	8 Mar. 10	25 Oct. 21	48 Foot.
Watson, *Hon*. Richard	26 June 17	23 Nov. 20	19 May 25	10 Sept. 30	Unattached.
Watson, William	11 April 09	26 April 10	26 Nov. 18	7 Mar. 22	21 Dragoons.
Webb, Chas. Campbell	5 Nov. 00	2 July 01	1 July 13	1816	72 Foot.
Webb, Daniel Peploe......	5 Oct. 15	11 July 22	12 Dec. 26	18 Dec. 28	Unattached.
Webb, John	20 Dec. 04	18 July 05	3 July 29	3 July 29	Unattached.
ᛈ Webbe, *John Wynne*....	15 Mar. 08	20 July 10	23 Sept. 13		7 R. Vet. Batt
Webb, Robert [204]	24 Sept. 05	19 May 09	7 Mar. 32		R. Marines.
Webb, Samuel	4 Jan. 00	14 Mar. 05	31 Mar. 14	23 Oct. 23	42 Foot.
☗☗ Webb, Vere [205]........	12 May 12	9 Dec. 13	19 Aug. 30	6 Sept. 31	Unattached.
☗☗ Webster, James C. [206]..	21 April 14	13 July 20	12 Nov. 25	1 Dec. 27	Unattached.
Webster, Thomas	28 May 94	20 July 95	25 June 03	1805	York Rangers
Weeks, Forster Israel	25 May 05	31 July 06	6 Feb. 12	25 Aug. 16	Glengarry Fe.
Welch, Stephen J. W. F. ..	27 Aug. 25	19 Sept. 26	6 Sept. 27	6 Sept. 27	Cape Reg.
Welchman, Geo. Thomas ..	31 Aug. 05	27 July 08	17 Mar. 31		R. Marines.
ᛈ Wellings, George	14 Feb. 11	14 Nov. 11	23 Mar. 15	25 June 23	Unattached.
☗☗ Wells, Fortescue [207] ..	4 Oct. 06	1 Feb. 08	29 July 25	29 July 25	R. Artillery
* Welsh, Conway	never	never	25 Dec. 13	25 Sept. 14	40 Foot.
Wemyss, James	10 April 17	31 Jan. 21	22 Oct. 25	22 Oct. 25	Unattached.
Westropp, Lionel John	9 July 03	28 April 04	5 Mar. 07	28 Oct. 19	95 Foot.
Wetherall, Charles [208]......	15 Aug. 13	8 Aug. 16	29 June 24	27 June 34	Unattached.

Captains.

	CORNET, ETC.	LIEUT.	CAPTAIN.	WHEN PLACED ON HALF PAY.	
₽ ⚜ Wharton, William [209]	4 Dec. 06	11 Dec. 06	13 Aug. 12	1 June 20	43 Foot.
White, Frederick	21 Sept. 20	11 Aug. 25	26 Sept. 26	5 June 35	Unattached.
₽ White, John	5 April 01	12 Jan. 05	24 July 12	1814	61 Foot.
₽ Whitle, Robert	25 Aug. 08	22 Feb. 10	22 Dec. 24	6 Dec. 27	Unattached.
₽ Whitley, James	22 Aug. 05	17 Dec. 06	17 June 13	25 Feb. 16	9 Foot.
Wieburg, John Andrew [210]..	10 Dec. 12	21 April 14	13 Jan. 37	13 Jan. 37	Unattached.
Wightman, George	5 July 00	30 May 09	17 Mar. 14	1814	48 Foot.
Wilford, Ernest Christian..	2 Sept. 14	14 Mar. 23	19 April 31	19 April 31	Staff Corps.
₽ *Wilkinson, William*	never	29 Aug. 07	2 Sept. 13		3 R. Vet. Batt.
Willard, Leonard Kilham	23 Aug. 99	3 April 01	1 Dec. 04		11 R.Vet.Batt.
₽ Williams, James........	9 April 07	10 Aug. 08	14 Sept. 13	25 Feb. 16	11 Foot.
Williams, Joseph	2 July 97	28 July 03	8 Oct. 11	1 Sept. 14	R. Marines.
Williams, Robert	25 Nov. 15	24 Oct. 21	8 April 26	8 April 26	Unattached.
Williams, Rowland Edward	12 Jan. 05	25 July 05	13 Oct. 08	25 June 16	7 W. Ind. Reg.
Williams, William	23 June 94	7 April 95	23 Sept. 99	25 Dec. 01	40 Foot.
Wills, Thomas Lake	12 Feb. 97	3 Dec. 01	9 Aug. 09	27 Nov. 15	R. Marines.
Willson, Thomas..........	12 Sept. 05	4 Feb. 08	7 Mar. 16	25 Mar. 16	20 Dragoons.
Wilson, Edward..........	5 June 06	9 Feb. 08	28 June 10	25 Feb. 16	57 Foot.
Wilson, James	19 May 14	20 Dec. 24	7 April 37	5 May 37	Coldstr. Gds.
Wilson, John	22 June 04	10 June 07	31 Aug. 27		R. Marines.
Wilson, Joseph Fraser	5 April 10	10 June 11	13 Feb. 27	13 Feb. 27	Unattached.
Wilson, Peter Theodore ..	29 Mar. 95	27 Jan. 96	15 Aug. 05	24 Dec. 05	R. Marines.
Wily, Daniel	14 Sept. 04	13 Mar. 06	11 Aug. 14	25 June 17	83 Foot.
Winckley, Thomas	20 Feb. 88	14 Dec. 91	5 Sept. 95	17 Feb. 03	4 Foot.
Windham, Joseph Smyth ..	22 Dec. 08	14 Dec. 09	5 Nov. 12	25 Dec. 14	17 Dragoons.
* Winnington, Hen. Jeffreys	never	never	25 Dec. 13	25 Sept. 14	39 Foot.
Wishart, Alexander	14 Nov. 05	26 May 08	6 Sept. 21	6 Sept. 21	15 Foot.
Witts, John..............	12 May 96	1 Nov. 99	27 July 08	30 Sept. 13	R. Marines.
₽ Wolfe, Edward	29 Dec. 04	9 Jan. 06	9 Sept. 13	25 Dec. 14	28 Foot.
Wolfe, Richard [211]	7 Feb. 11	3 Dec. 12	10 Dec. 33	19 Mar. 37	Sub.Ins.of Mil
Wolrige, Ambrose A. R. ..	4 July 03	15 Aug. 05	31 July 26	5 June 32	R. Marines.
Wolseley, Rob. Benj.[212]....	5 Oct. 04	27 May 07	8 April 25	13 April 32	22 Dragoons.
⚜ Wood, John Manley ..	19 May 14	6 Sept. 21	10 Sept. 25	10 Sept. 25	67 Foot.
Woodford, John..........	30 Dec. 13	17 July 23	29 Oct. 25	12 July 33	Unattached.
Woods, Richard..........	2 Dec. 06	28 Dec. 09	13 Aug. 12		8 R. Vet. Batt.
₽ Woolcombe, Robert [213] ..	1 July 06	18 June 07	18 June 24	18 June 24	R. Artillery.
Workman, Thomas	3 Jan. 11	2 April 12	3 Aug. 30	8 Mar. 31	Unattached.
Worsley, James White	1 July 12	21 July 13	8 April 26	1 Jan. 33	Sub.Ins.of Mil
Wortley, *Hon.* Chas. Stuart	25 Nov. 19	21 Nov. 22	26 May 25	29 Oct. 29	88 Foot.
₽ Wrench, E. Ommanney	Mar. 02	6 Feb. 06	7 July 08	25 July 14	9 Dragoons.
₽ Wrench, Wm. Handfield	1 April 07	22 Oct. 07	7 May 18	29 Nov. 21	AfricanCorps.
Wright, George	11 July 03	25 Oct. 05	31 July 26	30 Sept. 33	R. Marines.
* Wright, Samuel	never	never	25 Nov. 99	24 Feb. 00	35 Foot.
Wright, Thomas..........	6 Feb. 06	19 Feb. 07	3 Nov. 18	30 Dec. 19	95 Foot.
Wulff, Kenelm Chandler ..	29 Oct. 08	12 July 11	6 Nov. 27	6 Nov. 27	R. Artillery.
Wyatt, Alex. H. L.	17 Sept. 25	24 Feb. 29	29 June 32	31 Dec. 39	Unattached.
Wyatt, Samuel	28 Feb. 07	1 Feb. 08	1 Mar. 27	19 April 36	R. Artillery.
Wyke, George		16 Nov. 94	9 Aug. 99		Indep. Co.
Wyndham, Alex. Wadham	16 Mar. 20	25 Nov. 24	12 Dec. 26	26 July 27	Unattached.
Wynn, *Sir* William	3 April 94	27 May 95	11 Jan. 00		Invalids.
₽ Wynne, Abraham Wm.[214]	16 April 07	3 Oct. 09	24 July 17	29 Mar. 27	Unattached.
Wynne, John	16 Dec. 20	1 Aug. 27	13 Aug. 39	28 Sept. 39	R. Artillery.
Yarmouth, R. S. C. *Earl of*	24 Feb. 20	24 Oct. 21	25 Mar. 23	17 April 23	22 Dragoons.
Yeoman, Constantine	5 Mar. 10	21 Oct. 13	31 Aug. 26	13 Dec. 32	Staff Corps.
Young, James............	11 Oct. 21	28 Jan. 26	31 July 28	19 Mar. 29	88 Foot.
Young, William..........	10 July 03	12 Sept. 05	31 July 26		R. Marines.
₽ Younghusband, Robert..	Nov. 01	22 April 02	1 Jan. 11	25 Dec. 17	53 Foot.

Notes to the Captains.

1 Captain J. H. Adair served at the capture of Martinique and Les Saintes in 1809; of Guadaloupe in 1810, and again in 1815.
2 Captain T. R. Agnew served the campaigns of 1808, 9, 12, and 13 in the Peninsula, and was present at the capture of Oporto, battle of Talavera, and subsequent affairs; also at the battle of Vittoria, where his leg was so severely fractured as to require three separate amputations of the thigh.
3 Sir James Alexander served with the armies in the field during the late Burman, Persian, Turkish, Portuguese, and Kaffir wars.
4 Captain Andros served the campaigns of 1814 and 15 in Ghuzerat and Kutch, and was present at the capture of the forts of Joosin, Anjar, Khuncoote, Dhingee, and Dwarka. Served also throughout the Mahratta campaigns of 1816, 17, and 18, including the battle before, and subsequent capture of Poona, and the affair of Ashtee.
5 Captain Robert Armstrong served in the Peninsula, from July, 1809 to Jan. 1810, and again from Oct. 1811 to Feb. 1814, including the battle of Talavera; storming the forts, and battle of Salamanca; siege of Burgos, and blockade of Pampeluna.
6 Captain Atherton's services :—Peninsula from 1810 to the end of the war, and was present at the sieges of Cadiz and Tarifa. Deccan campaign of 1817 and 18. Expedition to the Persian Gulf in 1819 and 20, including the siege of Ras-el-Khyma, &c. Burmese war in 1825 and 6.
7 Captain Atkin served at Walcheren in 1809, and in the Peninsula from Dec. 1810 to the end of the war, including the battle of Albuhera; sieges of Ciudad Rodrigo and Badajoz; battle of Salamanca; forts at Burgos and Madrid; covering the retreat from Burgos; battle of Vittoria; siege of San Sebastian; action in the Pyrenees, and investment of Bayonne, besides various affairs of minor importance. Wounded in crossing the Bidassoa, 7 Oct. 1813, and again before Bayonne, 28 Feb. 1814.
8 Captain G. Macleod Baynes served in the Peninsula, from Sept. 1812 to the end of the war, including the battles of the Pyrenees (30th July), Nivelle, and Toulouse. Served also at Quatre Bras and Waterloo.
9 Captain Beavan served in the Peninsula, from March 1813, to the end of the war, and was present at the investment of Bayonne.
10 Captain Berington served at Walcheren in 1809.
11 Captain George Birch served at the siege of Flushing in 1809.
12 Captain James Birch served at the siege of Cadiz.
13 Captain Blagrave served with expeditions to Quiberon Bay, 1795, and to the Helder in 1799.
14 Captain Bland served in the Mahratta war, including the captures of Nagpore and Asseerghur. Commanded two companies of the Royals at the taking of the Hill Forts in Candeish. Received a contusion on the head from a matchlock ball in Nullyghaum, and was severely wounded in the leg at Asseerghur.
15 Captain Blennerhasset served at Quatre Bras and Waterloo 16th, 17th, and 18th June. Also in Ava in 1825.
16 Captain Boardman served at the capture of the French West India Islands in 1809, and in 1815.
17 Captain Boyes served in the American war, and was present in the actions at Bladensburg, Baltimore, and New Orleans.
18 Captain Brereton (as a volunteer with the 63d regiment), was present in every action and service with the corps throughout the campaign of 1799 in North Holland. Present at the sieges and capture of Ter Vere, and Flushing, in Walcheren in 1809. Also at the capture of Guadaloupe in 1815, including the assault of the heights of Baliffe (wounded) and Boulogne, and the fortified position of Morne Honnell. Severely wounded at Egmont-op-Zee, 6th Oct. 1799, and slightly at Ferrol, 1800.

Notes to the Captains.

19 Captain Edward Brown served at the capture of Guadaloupe in 1815.
20 Captain Thomas Brown was severely wounded at Quatre Bras.
21 Captain Burges was severely wounded at Waterloo.
22 Captain Alexander Burke served in the American war, including the action at Plattsburgh.
23 Captain James Burke was slightly wounded at Quatre Bras, and severely at Waterloo.
24 Captain J. C. Burton served on the eastern coast of Spain from March 1813, to the end of the war.
25 Captain John Cameron's services:—Campaign of 1808 and 9, including the battle of Corunna. Expedition to Walcheren. Peninsula, from Jan. 1810 to the end of the war, including the battles of Busaco, Fuentes d'Onor, Salamanca, Nivelle, Nive, and Toulouse.
26 Captain Alexander Campbell (h. p. 35 regiment). Served in the Peninsula from Sept. 1812 to the end of the war, and subsequently in the Netherlands and France, including the battles of the Pyrenees, Nivelle, Nive, Orthes, Toulouse, and Waterloo. Served also in the Burmese war in 1824, 5, and 6.
27 Captain Archibald Campbell served in the Peninsula from April, 1810, to the end of the war, including the battle of Busaco ; Lines at Torres Vedras, affair at Campo Mayor, battle of Albuhera, 1st and 2nd sieges of Badajoz, affair at Arroya de Molinos, battles of Vittoria, Pyrenees, Pampeluna, (severely wounded in the side), Nive 9th Dec., and Bayonne 13th Dec., taking Isle de Role, battles of Orthes, Aire, and Toulouse. Head severely injured 24th June, 1813, when pursuing the enemy to Pampeluna.
28 Captain Donald Campbell was slightly wounded at Waterloo.
29 Captain John Campbell (h. p. 26th regiment), served at New Orleans.
30 Captain Wm. Campbell (1st), served in the Peninsula, from August, 1811, to June, 1813, including the storming of Badajoz, battle of Salamanca, advance to Madrid, siege of Burgos, affair of Villa Muriel on the retreat from Burgos.
31 Captain Wm. Campbell (2d) served in the Peninsula with the Rifle Brigade.
32 Captain Cardew served at Walcheren in 1809.
33 Captain Carnegie served in Portugal, from Nov. 1809 to 1811.
34 Captain Daniel Caulfield served in the Mediterranean and the Peninsula, from April, 1806, to the end of the war, including the captures of Santa Maura, and the islands of Ischia and Procida, and siege of Tarragona. Served also in the American war, including the actions of Bladensburg, Baltimore, and New Orleans, at which last he was slightly wounded.
35 Captain John J. Chapman served with the expedition to Walcheren, and was present at the siege of Flushing.
36 Captain George Chichester served during the rebellion in Ceylon in 1818. Served also at the siege of Bhurtpore, and was wounded at the assault.
37 Captain Donald Chisholm was slightly wounded at Quatre Bras.
38 Captain Pryce Clark was engaged on the 17th and 18th June, at Waterloo, and subsequent taking of Cambray. Served in Caffraria in 1820 and 21.
39 Captain Charles Close joined the army under the Duke of Wellington at the close of the Peninsular war.
40 Captain Cochrane served on the frontiers of the United States throughout the last war with America, including the actions at Fort George, Niagara, and Fort Erie.
41 Captain Colby served at Walcheren in 1809.
42 Captain F. M. Colthurst served in the Peninsula from August, 1810, to the end of the war.
43 Captain James R. Colthurst was slightly wounded at Waterloo.
44 Captain Charles Connor's services:—Expedition to Walcheren in 1809. Campaigns of 1813 and 14 in the Peninsula, including the following, viz. Vittoria, Pass of Roncesvalles, Pyrenees, Echelar, Nivelle, and Orthes. Besides the above, he served during Sir John Moore's campaign in Spain, as a volunteer with the 15th Hussars, and was in the actions at Rueda, and Benevente.
45 Captain Conrady served at the taking of Kandy and the Kandyan Provinces in Ceylon in 1815. Also at the suppression of the rebellion in 1817 and 18.
46 Captain R. H. Spencer Cooper served the campaign of 1814 in Holland.
47 Captain Cottell served at the battle of Trafalgar.
48 Captain Cotton served at the capture of the islands of Ischia and Procida in 1809, and at the siege of Genoa in 1814.
49 Captain Edmund Cox served at the siege and capture of Hattras, and the Mahratta campaigns of 1817 and 18. Also in the Burmese war in 1825 and 6.
50 Captain Coxwell served at Copenhagen in 1807, and at Flushing, 1809.
51 Captain Thomas Cradock was severely wounded at Waterloo.
52 Captain George Cresswell's services:—Rebellion in Ireland. Campaign of 1799 in

Notes to the Captains.

Holland, including the actions of the 27th Aug., 10th and 19th Sept., 2d and 6th October. Expedition to Hanover, 1805. Siege and capture of Copenhagen, 1807. Peninsula, from March, 1810, to the close of the war, including the operations in Alemtejo and investment of Badajoz, 1811 ; heights of Christoval; first siege of Badajoz, and sortie from thence; siege and capture of Badajoz ; battle of the Nivelle ; passage of the Adour, and battle of Orthes (dangerously wounded), besides other desultory services.

53 Captain Cubitt's services :—Copenhagen, 1807. Walcheren, 1809. Peninsula, from Feb. 1813 to the end of the war, including the battles of Vittoria, Pyrenees, Orthes, and Toulouse.

54 Captain Adam Cuppage's services :—Campaigns in Guzerat, Kuttywar, and Kutch, from Nov. 1814 to May, 1816, including the taking of Juria Bunder, Dwarka, Kuncott, and Dinghee. Throughout the Mahratta war. Expedition to the Persian Gulf in 1819 and 20, including the capture of Ras-el-Kymah. Expedition to the coast of Arabia in 1821 ; wounded in the action of Beni-Boo-Alli, 2d March, 1821.

55 Captain Curtis served at Walcheren in 1809, and was present at the capture of Flushing.

56 Captain Daniel served in the American war.

57 Captain David Davies was slightly wounded at Quatre Bras, and severely at Waterloo.

58 Captain Alfred Davis was present at the affair of Maheidpore, 21st Dec. 1817, and the taking of Talnair, 1818.

59 Captain James Davis served at the siege of Cadiz.

60 Captain James Day served the campaigns of 1813, 14, and 15, including the battles of Vittoria, Nivelle, Nive, Orthes, and Waterloo. Severely wounded in the face at the battle of Nivelle, and slightly in the leg at Waterloo.

61 Captain C. P. Deacon served at Naples in 1804 ; in Sicily and Calabria in 1805 and 6, including the battle of Maida. Peninsula, including the siege of San Sebastian ; and, subsequently, in the American war, including the actions at Bladensburg, Baltimore, and New Orleans. On board the *Volcano* in the engagement with the *Saucy Jack*, American Privateer.

62 Captain Thomas Deacon served on the Continent, from June 1813 to Jan. 1816, including the battle of Goerde, actions at Merxem, and battle of Waterloo, where he was severely wounded. Served also in the Kandyan rebellion in 1817 and 18.

63 Captain Duncan served with the expedition to Bremen in Germany in 1805. Served also in the American war, including the capture of Moose Island.

64 Captain David Duval served at the siege of Cadiz. Served also in the American war.

65 Captain Eason served throughout the Peninsular war, including the passage of the Vouga, combat of Grijon, passage of the Douro, battle of Busaco, action of Campo Mayor, 1st siege of Badajoz, and battle of Albuhera. Present at Quatre Bras and Waterloo, at which last he was severely wounded.

66 Captain Edmonds served in the Peninsula, from March, 1809, to the end of the war, and was slightly wounded at the battle of Talavera, 28th July, 1809.

67 Captain Hercules Ellis served in the Peninsula, from March, 1809, to the end of the war, including the 1st siege of Badajoz, and battles of Busaco, Fuentes d'Onor, Vittoria, and the Pyrenees.

68 Captain Emerson served at the taking of Santa Maura, storming the enemy's outposts in 1809, and at the taking of the Ionian Islands.

69 Captain Enderby served at Belgaum and Sholapore in 1818, and at Bhurtpore in 1825 and 6. In addition to the above he served three years in the royal navy as midshipman, and was on board the *Defence* at the battle of Trafalgar.

70 Captain James Evans served at Walcheren, and was present at the siege of Flushing.

71 Captain Fayerman served in Egypt under Sir Ralph Abercromby, and has received a medal.

72 Captain Foot served the campaign of 1814 and 15 in Holland, Belgium, and France, including the attack on Merxem, bombardment of the shipping at Antwerp, attack on Bergen-op-Zoom, and battle of Waterloo.

73 Captain Hugh Forbes served in the Peninsula, from June, 1811, to the end of the war, including the siege and capture of Ciudad Rodrigo and Badajoz ; and battles of Salamanca, Vittoria, Pyrenees, Nivelle, Orthes, and Toulouse.

74 Captain Charles Ford served at the siege of Flushing in 1809, and at New Orleans in 1814.

75 Captain Forster's services :—Expedition to Copenhagen, 1807. Campaign under Sir John Moore, including the cavalry action at Sahugun, and battle of Corunna. Severely wounded at Waterloo, by a grape-shot in the foot.

76 Captain John Freeman served in Egypt in 1807.

Notes to the Captains.

77 Captain Lucius H. French served at the bombardment of Algiers under Lord Exmouth, 27th Aug. 1816, as a Midshipman in the Royal Navy.

78 Captain F. H. Fuller proceeded to the Peninsula in 1808, and was present at the capture of Oporto, battles of Talavera, Busaco, and Fuentes d'Onor, besides various skirmishes.

79 Captain J. T. Fuller served at the siege of Copenhagen in 1807, and at the bombardment of Algiers, 27 Aug. 1816.

80 Captain Fyers served in the Peninsula during the campaign of 1809.

81 Captain John Gardiner's services:—Expedition to Walcheren, and siege of Flushing, 1809. Peninsula, from May, 1812, to the end of the war, including the battles of Vittoria and the Pyrenees; passage of the Bidassoa; battles of Nivelle, Nive (9th to 13th Dec.), Orthes, Tarbes, and Toulouse. Present at Quatre Bras and Waterloo, 16th, 17th, and 18th June. Wounded in the face in the Pyrenees (not returned), and severely in the thigh at Waterloo.

82 Captain Gascoyne served in the Peninsula from 1809 to 1813, and was severely wounded in the leg at the battle of Salamanca. Served also in Ceylon during the Kandyan rebellion in 1818.

83 Captain F. Y. Gilbert served in the Peninsula, from December, 1812, to the end of the war.

84 Captain Goode served in the American war, including the operations in the Chesapeake, battle of Bladensburg and capture of Washington; destruction of the American flotilla. Served also at the attack and capture of Guadaloupe in 1815.

85 Captain Thomas Gordon served the campaigns of 1814 and 15, and was present at the repulse of the sortie from Bayonne, and battle of Waterloo. Served afterwards in the East Indies, and was engaged at the battle of Maheidpore.

86 Captain Gorse served at the capture of Guadaloupe in 1815.

87 Captain John Gould's services:—Expedition to Walcheren and siege of Flushing, 1809. Peninsula, from June, 1813, to the end of the war, including the siege of San Sebastian; battles of the Bidassoa, Nivelle, and Nive, and all the operations round Bayonne. American war, including the action at Plattsburg.

88 Captain Grimes served throughout the Burmese war.

89 Captain Grubbe served in the Peninsula the latter part of 1812, and was present in action with the enemy, 16th Nov. 1812, on the retreat from Burgos. Served also at New Orleans.

90 Captain Harding served in the Peninsula from Aug. 1811 to the end of the war, including the battles of Salamanca, and Vittoria; siege of San Sebastian; and battles of Orthes and Toulouse. Present at Waterloo.

91 Captain Hugh Harrison was severely wounded at Waterloo.

92 Captain Henry Hill served in the Peninsula, from May, 1811, to June, 1813, and was present at the action near Elbodon, battle of Salamanca, and with the advance and rearguard to and on the retreat from Burgos. Served the campaign of 1815, and was present at Waterloo.

93 Captain Hincks served at the siege of Copenhagen in 1807. Present at Waterloo on the 17th and 18th June.

94 Captain Hobbs was severely wounded at Quatre Bras.

95 Captain Hodges served in the Peninsula, from 1812 to 1814, including the battles of Vittoria and the Pyrenees, besides various minor actions and skirmishes. Present at Waterloo.

96 Captain Holt served in the American war, including the taking of Castine; operations on the American coast, and upon the Ponobscot.

97 Captain Hort served in Lower Calabria, and Sicily, and accompanied the expedition under Major-General Ackland to the Bay of Naples in 1806. Served the campaign under Sir John Moore, and lost his right leg at the battle of Corunna.

98 Captain George Hotham served at the bombardment of Algiers under Lord Exmouth.

99 Captain J. L. Hulme served in the Peninsula, from March, 1810, to the end of the war, including the 2d siege of Badajoz, battles of Nivelle, and Nive (10th to 13th Dec.), passage of the Adour, investment of and repulse of the sortie from Bayonne.

100 Captain Humbley was severely wounded at Waterloo.

101 Captain Humphreys served at the capture of Martinique and the Saintes in 1809, and of Guadaloupe in 1815.

102 Captain George J. Hunter served during the campaign of 1814 on the Niagara frontier, including the action at Chippewa, and attack on Fort Erie.

103 Captain Hutchinson's services:—Campaign of 1795 in Holland. Attack on Porto Rico, and capture of Surinam, 1799. Expedition to South America in 1807, including the attack and capture of Monte Video and Buenos Ayres. Capture of the Isle of France, 1810. Siege and capture of Hattras, 1817. Mahratta war, 1818. Burmese war in 1825 and 6.

Notes to the Captains.

104 Captain Jago served the campaign of 1815, and was present at Quatre Bras and Waterloo, 16th, 17th, and 18th June.

105 Captain Henry James was present at the capture of Fort San Philippe (Balaguer), and siege of Tarragona in 1813; and at the bombardment of Algiers in 1816.

106 Captain Ingram served with the 3d battalion of the Royals during the whole of the Peninsular war. Present at Quatre Bras and Waterloo, 16th, 17th, and 18th June, and the subsequent operations.

107 Captain H. C. Johnson was slightly wounded at Waterloo.

108 Captain Judge accompanied the 27th regiment on the expedition to Hanover in 1805. Joined the army in Sicily in 1806, and was employed with it (in a Grenadier battalion) during its various operations to 1810. Sailed with the force for Naples, and was present at the capture of Ischia and Procida in 1809. Returned to Sicily, and appointed Deputy Assistant Quarter-Master General; employed against the French army in 1811. Served with that department during 1812 and 13 at the battle of Castalla, twice in active siege before Tarragona, in affair at Villa Franca, and the pass of Balaguer. Rejoined 27th regiment, and sailed from Bourdeaux for Canada; present at the battle of Plattsburg, and severely contested passage of the Saranac.

109 Captain Henry Kean served at the capture of Guadaloupe in 1809, and Martinique in 1810, and again in 1815.

110 Captain Keily was severely wounded at Waterloo.

111 Captain R. H. Ker served in Spain and France from March, 1814, to the end of the war, and was present at the investment of Bayonne.

112 Captain Charles King served the campaigns of 1810, 11, 12, and part of 1813 and 14, including the siege and capture of Badajoz, and battle of Orthes. Severely wounded at the storming of the castle of Badajoz, 6th April, 1812.

113 Captain J. D. King served in Holland and the Peninsula, from July, 1809, to the end of the war, including the capture of Walcheren, and siege of Flushing; battle of Busaco, action at Fuente Grinaldo, affair at Alasa del Ponte, battles of Vittoria, and the Pyrenees, 25th, 26th, 27th, and 28th July, 1813. Severely wounded in the right shoulder in the Pyrenees, 28th July, 1813.

114 Captain King served the Corunna campaign.

115 Captain Kirkley served in the Peninsula, from May, 1812, to the end of the war, including the action at San Milan, battles of Vittoria, and the Pyrenees (25th to 28th July), bridge of Vera, crossing the Bidassoa, battles of Nivelle, Nive (9th to 13th Dec.), Orthes, Tarbes, and Toulouse. Served afterwards in the American war, and was present in the actions before New Orleans, 18th Dec. 1814, and 8th Jan. 1815, and was slightly wounded.

116 Captain Charles Lane served in the American war; also at the taking of several islands in the Persian Gulf in 1819 and 20.

117 Captain Henry Lane's services:—Expedition to Quiberon Bay, 1795; the Helder, 1799; to Egypt, 1801; Peninsula, 1809 to 1813.

118 Captain Lawlor served in the American war, under Sir Gordon Drummond.

118* Captain L'Estrange's services:—Campaign in Spain, and battle of Corunna. Capture of the Isle of France, 1810. Capture of Java, 1811; engaged with a Dutch Brigade at St. Nicholas; storming of a strong Dutch Fort on the coast of Bantum. On board H.M.S. *Roscius*, at the boarding and capture of eleven French gun-boats. Present at the siege and storm of Cornelius, and storm and capture of the heights of Serandole. Capture of the town and fortress of Sambus, Isle of Borneo, March, 1813. Nepaul war, 1815. Siege and capture of Hattras, March, 1817. Mahratta campaign, 1817 and 18. Siege and storm of Bhurtpore.

119 Captain Lempriere's services:—Campaign in Spain under Sir John Moore, 1808 and 9. American war in 1814 and 15, including the capture of Washington, and all the operations in the Chesapeake, and before New Orleans. Attached to the Prussian army at the sieges of Mauberg, Phillipville, Rocroy, &c. &c.

120 Captain Charles Lewis served in the Peninsula from Aug. 1813, to the end of the war. Also in the Burmese war in 1825 and 6.

121 Captain Litchfield served the campaigns of 1812, 13, and 14, including the action at Puerta del Almarez, and battles of Vittoria, Orthes, and Toulouse. Served afterwards in the American war, including the action at Plattsburg.

122 Captain M'Conchy served in the south of France, from 1st March, 1814, to the end of the war. Also the campaign of 1815, and was present at Quatre Bras and Waterloo, at which last he was severely wounded in the left shoulder.

123 Captain Donald M'Donald served at Walcheren in 1809, and at the siege of Cadiz in 1813.

124 Captain M'Murdo served at the siege of Hattras in 1817, and afterwards in the Pindarree war.

Notes to the Captains.

125 Captain Robert M'Nab served in the Peninsula, from Jan. 1813, to the end of the war, including the battles of Vittoria, Pyrenees, Nivelle, Nive, Orthes, Vic Bigorre, and Toulouse.

126 Captain M'Queen served in the American war, and was present at the taking of Castine and Hampden, and the *John Adam.*

127 Captain John Macdonald served in the American war, and was severely wounded in the head and leg at New Orleans.

128 Captain Mac Donnell served in the Peninsula from Jan. 1814, to the end of the war, including the affair at Tarbes, and battle of Toulouse.

129 Captain Mac Gregor served in East Indies, and was severely wounded at the battle of Maheidpore, 22d Dec. 1817, and at the assault on Fort Talnair, 27th Feb. 1818.

130 Captain James Maclean embarked in Nov. 1813, for the western coast of Africa, where he served on several expeditions, and was present in almost every affair and skirmish which took place on the various parts of the coast at which he was stationed, including the attack and capture of the town of Barra, River Gambia, July, 1817.

131 Captain Charles Macpherson served in the East Indies, and was present at the siege of Asseerghur, March, 1819.

132 Captain Lachlan M'Pherson served in the Peninsula from Jan. 1810, to the end of the war, including the battles of Busaco, and Fuentes d'Onor, first siege of Badajoz, sieges and captures of Ciudad Rodrigo and Badajoz, battles of Vittoria, Pyrenees, Nivelle, Orthes, and Toulouse. Severely wounded in the head at Vittoria, and in the left knee at Toulouse.

133 Captain J. M. Maitland landed at Leghorn with Lord Wm. Bentinck. Served with the advance, and was frequently engaged with the enemy. Present also at the attack upon Genoa.

134 Captain Martin served on the expedition under Sir Tho. Trigge against the Danish and Swedish West India Islands in 1801, and on the expedition under Lieut. General Greenfield, against the French Islands in 1803.

135 Captain Massey served on the Continent in 1793, 4, and 5, and at the Helder in 1799.

136 Captain Master went with the expedition to the Hague, and served the campaign of 1813 and 14 in Holland, and was present at the taking of Merxem, the bombardment of Antwerp, and storming of Bergen-op-Zoom. Served the campaign of 1815; carried the King's Colour of the 3d battalion Grenadier Guards at Quatre Bras and Waterloo, 16th, 17th, and 18th June; present with the storming party at Peronne, and at the capture of Paris.

137 Captain Mathias served at the capture of Guadaloupe in 1809, and Martinique in 1810.

138 Captain Maunsell served the campaign of 1815, and was present at Waterloo.

139 Captain Meek served with the expedition under Lord Wm. Bentinck, in the Genoese territory in 1814.

140 Captain Melhuish served in the Peninsula from May, 1811, to the end of the war, including the siege and storming of Badajoz, and repulse of the sortie in 1812; passage of the Adour, and investment of and repulse of the sortie from Bayonne. Led the attack at Badajoz by escalade at the bastion of St. Vincent. Twice slightly wounded at the siege of Badajoz; also slightly wounded at the investment of Bayonne, and again at the sortie.

141 Captain A. O. Molesworth served the campaign of 1815, and was engaged at Cambray 23d and 24th June, and was present at the capture of Paris.

142 Captain Molloy served in the Peninsula with the Rifle Brigade. Severely wounded at Waterloo.

143 Captain Montogu was present at the siege of Dantzick in 1813. Served the campaign of 1815, and was present at Waterloo.

144 Captain Richard Montgomery served in the Peninsula from March, 1812, to the end of the war, including the battles of Salamanca (slightly wounded), Pyrenees, Nivelle, and Nive.

145 Captain Nash served in the American war, and was present at the action of Lundy's Lane, storming of Fort Erie, 15th Aug. 1814 (severely wounded in the leg by a musket ball, and afterwards blown up by the explosion of a powder magazine), and action at Chippewa.

146 Captain Newhouse served the Mahratta campaign of 1817 and 18, and was wounded 31st Jan. 1818. Served also with the expeditions to the Persian Gulf, in 1819 and 1821.

147 Captain Augustus Nicolls served in the Peninsula from Feb. 1810, to the end of the war, including the battles of Busaco, Albuhera, Vittoria, Orthes and Toulouse, and affairs at Aroya del Molino, Garice, and Aire.

148 Captain Nicholson was present at the battles of Nivelle, Nive, Orthes, and Toulouse. Served also in the Burmese war, including the engagements of the 20th, 25th, and 26th Nov. 1825.

Notes to the Captains.

149 Captain North served in Holland and France, from Nov. 1813 to Feb. 1816.

150 Captain J. Loftus Nunn served in the Peninsula from Feb. to July, 1811, and again from Sept. 1812, to the end of the war, including the battles of Vittoria and the Pyrenees (wounded through the left arm); taking the heights of Vera; battles of the Nivelle, Nive (9th to 13th Dec.), Orthes, and Toulouse.

151 Captain Lucius O'Brien served in the West Indies, from April, 1787 to Nov. 1794, and was present at the siege of Fort Bourbon, Martinique; capture of St. Lucia and Guadaloupe; 2d attack of Guadaloupe, and storming of Point-a-Petre.

152 Captain O'Dell served with the expedition to South America in 1807, and subsequently in the Peninsula, including the battles of Busaco and Fuentes d'Onor; actions at Sabugal and Elbodon; first siege of Badajoz, siege of Ciudad Rodrigo, siege and capture of Badajoz; battles of Salamanca (wounded), Vittoria, Nivelle, Orthes, and Toulouse.

153 Captain Ormsby served the campaign of 1815, and was present at the battle of Waterloo, and storming of Cambray, at which last he was slightly wounded. Served afterwards in the East Indies, including the siege and capture of Hattras; the Deccan campaign of 1817 and 18; and the siege and capture of Bhurtpore.

154 Captain Orr served in the Peninsula from Feb. to Aug. 1811, and again from April, 1812, to the end of the war, including the siege of Badajoz (April and May, 1811), battle of Albuhera (wounded in the left knee and elbow), affair of Osma, battle of Vittoria, affair of Roncesvalles, battles of Pampeluna, Nivelle, Orthes, and Toulouse.

155 Captain Packe was slightly wounded at Waterloo.

156 Captain Stephen Parker served in Holland, Flanders, and France, from Dec. 1813 to Dec. 1815, including the action at Merxem, bombardment of Antwerp, attack on Bergen-op-Zoom, and battles of Quatre Bras and Waterloo.

157 Captain Paschall served in the Peninsula from Oct. 1813 to the end of the war, including the battle of Nivelle, and Orthes. Present at Waterloo 18th June.

158 Captain Passley served the Peninsula campaigns of 1811, 12, and 13, including the battles of Vittoria, the Pyrenees, and Nivelle, besides various minor actions and skirmishes. Severely wounded at the battle of the Nivelle.

159 Captain Patten served in Portugal and Spain under Sir Arthur Wellesley and Sir John Moore, and was present at the battles of Roleia and Vimiera. Served also on the eastern coast of Spain, and in the south of France in 1813 and 14, including the battle of Castalla, siege of Tarragona, affair of Molinos del Rey, and blockade of Barcelona.

160 Captain Pemberton served in the Peninsula from Feb. 1814 to the end of the war.

161 Captain Phibbs served in the Peninsula from Nov. 1813, to the end of the war, including the battles of Nivelle, Orthes, and Toulouse. Served afterwards in the American war, and was present at the taking of Plattsburg. Lost left arm, and shot through both legs at the battle of Nivelle.

162 Captain R. F. Phillip's services:—Expedition to Walcheren. Campaigns of 1812 and 13 in the Peninsula, including the battles of Salamanca, Vittoria, Pyrenees, and Nivelle; and the sieges of the forts of Salamanca and San Sebastian.

163 Captain Pitman's services:—In the Peninsula from August, 1812, to the end of the war, including the battle of Vittoria, and capture of San Sebastian. Campaign of 1815, including the battle of Waterloo. Siege and capture of Bhurtpore.

164 Captain Poole served the campaigns of 1814 and 15, including the bombardment of the French fleet at Antwerp, and the battle of Waterloo.

165 Captain Pope's services:—Expedition to Naples under Sir James Craig, 1805, battle of Maida, 4th July, 1806. Capture of the islands of Ischia and Procida, 1809. Peninsular campaigns of 1813 and 14, including the battles of Biar and Castalla, siege of Tarragona, blockade of Barcelona, affairs of Ordal and Col de Balaguer.

166 Captain Pringle served in the Peninsula, from Jan. 1810 to the end of the war, including the battles of Nivelle and Nive (wounded), and investment of Bayonne. Served also the campaign of 1815, and was severely wounded at Waterloo.

167 Captain Prior served in the Peninsula with the 11th Light Dragoons, and was present at the battle of Salamanca, and various out-post affairs. Served also the campaign of 1815; commanded the skirmishers of the 18th Hussars on the 17th June, and received the first fire of the French army on that day; present at the battle of Waterloo and capture of Paris.

168 Captain Quill served at the capture of Guadaloupe in 1815.

168* Captain Rawlison's services:—Expedition to Egypt in 1807. Taking of the island of Zante, 1809. Siege of Santa Maura, 1810.

169 Captain Reardon served in Portugal and Spain in 1808 and 9, including the battle of Roleia and Vimiera, action at Lugo, and battle of Corunna.

170 Captain Reid served in the Peninsula, and was present at the battles of Corunna, Talavera, Busaco, Fuentes d'Onor and Vittoria.

171 Captain Rice served the campaigns of 1814 and 15 under the Duke of Wellington, and was present at the battle of Waterloo.

Notes to the Captains.

172 Captain J. S. Rich served at Walcheren in 1809, and in Holland from Dec. 1813 to May, 1814.
173 Captain Wm. S. Richardson was severely wounded at Waterloo.
174 Captain R. S. Ridge served the Mahratta and Pindarree campaigns of 1817 and 18, and afterwards with the expedition to the Persian Gulf, including the siege of Ras-el-Kyma.
175 Captain J. A. Ridgway served in the Peninsula from May, 1812, to the end of the war, including the battle of Vittoria. Served also the campaign of 1815, and was present at the battle of Waterloo. Severely wounded by a musket-shot in the right shoulder, at the taking of Vera heights, and lost the fore-finger of the left hand by a musket-shot at Waterloo.
176 Captain John Roberts was slightly wounded at Waterloo.
177 Captain Robert A. Rollo served in Egypt in 1807.
178 Captain Ross was present with the 5th regiment at the sieges of Calvia and Bastia, in Corsica, under Sir C. Stewart in 1795 and 6. Served nine years in India, and was at the taking of Kandy, in the island of Ceylon, in 1803. Served at the affair at Lugo, and battle of Corunna, under Sir John Moore in 1808 and 9 ; and afterwards at the taking of Flushing.
179 Captain Sandes served in the Peninsula from March, 1813, to Feb. 1814, including the battle of Vittoria, and siege of San Sebastian in July and Aug. 1813. Served also in the Mahratta war in 1817 and 18; and with the expedition to the Persian Gulf in 1819 and 20.
180 Captain Scargill served at Tarifa under Colonel Skerrit.
181 Captain Seward served in the Peninsula from Oct. 1810 to Feb. 1813, including the siege of the forts at and battle of Salamanca, and siege of Burgos, from 19th Sept. to 21st Oct. 1812.
182 Captain Simmons served at the bombardment of Fort Desaix, and the attack and capture of Martinique in 1809.
183 Captain Skinner served at the attack on New Orleans.
184 Lord Somerville served at Copenhagen in 1807, and at Walcheren in 1809.
185 Captain Spalding's services :—Capture of the Cape of Good Hope, 1806 ; wounded 8th Jan. Expedition to South America, 1807. Peninsula from 1808 to the end of the war, including the battles of Roleia, Vimiera, Corunna, Almarez (wounded), Vittoria, Pyrenees, Pampeluna, Nive, Orthes, and Toulouse ; besides various minor actions and skirmishes. Campaign of 1815, including the battle of Waterloo.
186 Captain Stanford served in the south of France, from 1814 to the end of the war, and was present at the battle of Toulouse.
187 Captain Stanley served in the Peninsula from Oct. 1812, to the end of the war, and was present at Vittoria, Roncesvalles, Pampeluna, and Orthes.
188 Captain John Steuart was severely wounded at Quatre Bras.
189 Captain Allan Stewart served in the Peninsula from 1812 to the end of the war, and was present at Vittoria, Nivelle, Vera, Nive, Orthes, Tarbes, and Toulouse. Served the campaign of 1815, including the battles of Quatre Bras and Waterloo, at which last he was very severely wounded by a musket-ball through the left shoulder, and a sabre thrust through the left arm.
190 Captain Duncan Stewart was severely wounded at Quatre Bras.
191 Captain Stupart was severely wounded at Waterloo.
192 Captain Tenison served in the Burmese war.
193 Captain Thatcher served in the Peninsula from Aug. 1811, to the end of the war, including the action at Fuenta Grinaldo, sieges of Ciudad Rodrigo and Badajoz (wounded), battles of Salamanca (wounded), Vittoria, Pampeluna, Pyrenees, Nivelle, Nive, Orthes, and Toulouse. Wounded at Vera.
194 Captain E. Colley Thompson served in the Peninsula from Oct. 1808 to Feb. 1813, including the battles of Talavera and Busaco, action at Campo Mayor, first siege of Badajoz and Olivenza, and battle of Albuhera.
195 Captain Torriano served at Walcheren, and was present at the siege of Flushing.
196 Captain Trafford was slightly wounded at Waterloo.
197 Captain John Trotter served at Walcheren ; also at Cadiz during the latter part of the siege.
198 Captain Tucker served in the American war.
199 Captain Tweedie was present in the batteries of the Faro under Sir James Stewart. Served also the campaign of 1814 in the South of France, including the battle of Toulouse.
200 Captain Tyndale served in the Peninsula from March 1812 to the end of the war, and was engaged at Moresco, Salamanca, the Retiro Madrid, Vittoria, the Pyrenees, Lezacca, Nivelle, and Orthes. Served also the campaign of 1815, including the battle of Waterloo (slightly wounded), taking of Cambray, and capitulation of Paris.
201 Captain Ussher served the Nepaul campaigns of 1816 and 17.

Notes to the Captains.

202 Capain Vaughan served in the Peninsula from July 1810 to Jan. 1812, including the battle of Barrosa and siege of Cadiz. Served afterwards in the East Indies, including the Mahratta campaigns of 1817 and 18, and sieges of Ryghur, Amulneer and Asseerghur.

202* Captain Vetch served at the siege of Cadiz.

203 Captain Wainwright served in the Peninsula from June 1810 to the early part of 1813, including the siege of Cadiz, battle of Barrosa, and storming of Tarifa by the French. Served afterwards in the East Indies, including the expedition to the Persian Gulf under Sir Keir Grant, and the Burmese war.

204 Captain Robert Webb served in H. M. S. *Superb* at the battle off St. Domingo, 6th Feb. 1806. Copenhagen, 1807. Walcheren, 1809. Wounded in an attack on an armed convoy in the Adriatic, 22d May, 1812.

205 Captain Vere Webb served the campaigns of 1814 and 15 in Holland, the Netherlands, and France, including the actions at Merxem, bombardment of Antwerp, and battle of Waterloo, at which last he was slightly wounded.

206 Captain Webster was severely wounded at Quatre Bras.

207 Captain Wells served at Madeira in 1807 and 8; at Walcheren, 1809; and the campaign of 1815, including the battles of Quatre Bras and Waterloo.

208 Captain Wetherall served in the Mahratta war in 1817, 18, and 19, and was engaged at Bodamy, Belgaum, Sholapore, and Capauldroog.

209 Captain Wharton's services:—Expedition to Walcheren, siege and capture of Flushing, 1809. Campaign of 1811 in Spain and Portugal, including the battle of Fuentes d'Onor and siege of Badajoz. Campaigns of 1813, 14, and 15, in Swedish Pomerania, Hanover, and the Netherlands, including the battles of Goerde 16th Sept. 1814, and Quatre Bras and Waterloo (16th, 17th, and 18th June), at which last he was severely wounded through both thighs by a musket ball.

210 Captain Wieburg served the campaigns in the Netherlands, and was wounded in the righ hand and below the right ancle before Nimeguen in May, 1795. Served also at the taking of the Danish West India Islands in 1807, and Martinique and the Saintes in 1809, and Guadaloupe in 1810. Wounded above the ankle in both legs at Martinique.

211 Captain Richard Wolfe's services:—Taking of Palembang in Sumatra, 1813. Taking of Bali, and also the fortified Kittore at Macassar, 1814. Deccan campaign, 1817 and 18. Kandyan war, 1818.

212 Captain Wolseley served at the captures of St. Martin and Guadaloupe in 1810, and again at the latter in 1815.

213 Captain Woolcombe served in the Peninsula from the commencement of 1809 to the end of the war, including the battles of Fuentes d'Onor (slightly wounded) and Castalla, and the siege of Tarragona.

214 Captain A. Wm. Wynne served in the Peninsula from the 1st Aug. 1808, to Nov. 1813, including the battles of Roleia, Vimiera, Talavera, Fuentes d'Onor, Salamanca, Vittoria; sieges of Ciudad Rodrigo, Badajoz and San Sebastian; passage of the Bidassoa, besides various minor affairs and skirmishes. Twice slightly wounded, viz., at Redinha, and at Fuentes d'Onor.

LIEUTENANTS.

	CORNET, 2d LIEUT. or ENSIGN.	LIEUT.	WHEN PLACED ON HALF PAY.	
Ackland, Graves	18 Nov. 13	23 April 18	7 June 19	61 Foot.
Acklom, George................	20 May 26	8 Jan. 29	3 Nov. 37	38 Foot.
Ackroyd, William	26 Dec. 76	1 Jan. 79	15 May 87	R. Marines.
Acome, Thomas................	24 May 15	3 July 17	19 July 19	York Rangers.
Adams, Samuel	3 May 84	27 May 07	3 June 07	50 Foot.
Addison, John	1 Sept. 14	17 Oct. 16	6 June 22	2 Dragoon Guards.
Adey, William Gyde	20 Oct. 80	15 July 81		72 Foot.
Agar, Thos. (Qr. Master, 5 Oct. 09)	never	25 Mar. 13		4 R. Veteran Bat.
Alcock, Henry	10 Mar. 08	22 Feb. 10	22 July 19	63 Foot.
Alder, Walter K.	1 Nov. 03	1 Feb. 06	7 Oct. 14	R. Marines.
🞖 Alderson, John[1]	21 April 13	13 Aug. 15	25 Mar. 17	33 Foot.
Alexander, John...............	27 April 11	18 Sept. 29	23 Feb. 30	R. Marines.
Alexander, William	14 Feb. 16	22 Mar. 18	25 July 19	24 Dragoons.
Allan, William	24 Feb. 13	3 Mar. 14	26 Nov. 18	7 Foot.
Allen, Francis	never	25 Feb. 14		3 Prov. Batt.
* Allen, George	never	25 Dec. 13	25 Mar. 16	88 Foot.
🞖 *Allen, John* [2]	10 Aug. 04	1 Dec. 05	1 Feb. 19	R. Art. Drivers.
Allen, John....................	10 Sept. 12	26 Sept. 13	25 Dec. 14	38 Foot.
Allen, John....................	8 Mar. 10	28 May 12	6 May 16	84 Foot.
Allen, Joseph	Dec. 02	24 Dec. 02	11 May 16	52 Foot.
Alley, Tottenham	23 Aug. 10	5 June 11	25 July 16	Corsican Rangers.
🞖 Allingham, John Delancey ..	7 Oct. 13	25 Sept. 17	15 Oct. 20	24 Dragoons.
🞖 🞖 Alston, James[3]	14 May 12	21 Oct. 13	9 May 17	1 Foot.
Alt, Daniel	31 Mar. 14	26 July 15	6 Dec. 33	Staff Corps.
Altenstein, Henry, *Baron*	16 Jan. 09	10 Nov. 09	9 Dec. 24	6 W. I. Regiment.
* Ames, John..................	never	25 Mar. 14		1814 1 Prov. Batt.
Amyatt, Augustus	24 June 12	22 Dec. 13	27 Feb. 23	26 Foot.
Amyott, Richard Garrett	2 Aug. 99	21 Aug. 04	5 Dec. 14	R. Marines.
Anderson, Thomas.............	23 Nov. 09	25 June 12		3 R. Veteran Bat.
Anderson, William	4 Oct. 04	3 Nov. 08		5 R. Veteran Bat.
Anderson, William	14 Dec. 25	15 Nov. 27	4 Jan. 33	27 Foot.
Andrew, Charles...............	28 April 10	17 Dec. 13	19 Dec. 20	Royal Artillery.
Arbuthnott, *Hon.* Mariott	6 Mar. 18	14 Sept. 20	5 June 28	8 Foot.
Archer, John..................	Aug. 07	26 Feb. 08		6 R. Veteran Bat.
Archer, Thomas................	4 Feb. 08	11 Feb. 08	18 Feb. 08	112 Foot.
* Arden, William	never	25 Dec. 13	25 Sept. 14	4 Foot.
Armstrong, Andrew	3 June 12	4 Feb. 14	14 Mar. 16	4 Foot.
Armstrong, Francis Wheeler	1 Sept. 08	21 June 10	24 Oct. 22	Coldstream Gds.
Armstrong, John		10 Mar. 95		R. Irish Art.
Armstrong, John	19 Oct. 09	23 April 12	25 Feb. 16	40 Foot.
🞖 Armstrong, John Cooper [4]	1 Jan. 07	17 Dec. 08	1 July 16	R. Art. Drivers.
Armstrong, Montgomery	10 June 13	25 May 15	25 Dec. 18	York Rangers.
Armstrong, Richard	16 May 07	7 Mar. 10	12 Mar. 18	70 Foot.
Armstrong, Thomas	17 June 13	10 Oct. 16	20 Nov. 23	8 Dragoons.
Armstrong, William	28 Dec. 15	25 Feb. 22	30 June 25	Unattached.
Armstrong, Wm. Blosse	12 Mar. 12	29 April 13	25 July 14	9 Dragoons.
Armstrong, Wm. Henry	27 Aug. 07	22 Sept. 08		2 R. Veteran Bat.
Arnott, Alexander.............	27 April 09	28 Feb. 12	25 Mar. 17	26 Foot.
Athol, John *Duke of*...........	25 Oct. 97	1 Feb. 98	9 May 00	3 Foot.
Atkin, Christopher	1 Mar. 98	21 Aug. 00	7 May 03	15 Foot.
Atkin, James	24 Nov. 12	13 July 15	30 Mar. 20	58 Foot.
Atkin, John	30 Jan. 12	19 Oct. 15	25 Feb. 16	88 Foot.
Atkin, William	12 May 14	11 Jan. 21	25 Aug. 21	88 Foot.
*Atkinson, Charles	never	25 Dec. 13	25 Sept. 14	14 Foot.
Atkinson, John	28 Feb. 05	12 Sept. 05	25 Nov. 18	98 Foot.
🞖 Austin, Edward Frederick	11 July 11	30 Sept. 13	9 Jan. 14	47 Foot.

347

Lieutenants.

	CORNET, ETC.	LIEUT.	WHEN PLACED ON HALF PAY.	
Austin, Joseph	6 April 09	22 Aug. 10	25 Dec. 15	42 Foot.
Austin, Thomas	17 May 10	6 Dec. 13		5 R. Veteran Bat.
Avarne, Thomas Jeffrey Jonah	12 Aug. 13	6 Feb. 17	25 July 17	67 Foot.
Avery, Thomas	18 Nov. 95	1 Sept. 97	9 July 98	R. Marines.
Aynge, George	6 Oct. 12	6 Jan. 13	1 Aug. 16	R. Art. Drivers.
Ayshford, Aaron Moore	17 Aug. 09	15 April 12	31 Mar. 14	12 Foot.
Babington, Murray	6 June 80	14 Nov. 82	30 Nov. 91	10 Foot.
₧ Bace, William	9 Feb. 09	2 Oct. 11	19 Dec. 16	3 Foot.
Bagshaw, Stephen Granby	25 Jan. 16	6 July 20	12 Jan. 26	23 Dragoons.
Bailey, Charles Courant	1 Oct. 07	25 Aug. 09		5 R. Veteran Bat.
Bailey, Edward	1 May 04	24 Mar. 07	1 Sept. 14	R. Marines.
Bailey, James Alderson	5 May 14	21 Dec. 15	3 Jan. 22	60 Foot.
₧ Baillie, Andrew	29 June 09	27 June 11	3 July 17	30 Foot.
Baily, John	7 Feb. 06	24 Oct. 11	1 Sept. 14	R. Marines.
Bain, John	20 April 09	11 April 11	2 Dec. 14	61 Foot.
Bainbrigge, Thos. Parker	1 Oct. 07	3 May 10	20 Nov. 23	48 Foot.
Baird, John	26 Mar. 06	9 July 09	25 April 18	Cape Reg.
Baker, George	16 Dec. 11	27 July 30	3 Feb. 31	R. Marines.
Baker, Thomas	2 Dec. 99	19 July 00	25 July 02	15 Foot.
Balderson, John Robert	21 Jan. 13	27 Jan. 14		7 R. Veteran Batt.
Baldock, Charles Robert	2 April 10	17 Dec. 13	8 Nov. 19	Royal Artillery.
Bale, William	3 July 06	28 Oct. 07	23 Oct. 16	3 Foot.
Ballietchet, John	5 Oct. 05	29 Dec. 09	1 Sept. 14	R. Marines.
Ball, Howell	20 May 13	18 Mar. 15		Garrison Co.
Ball, Robert	27 Oct. 07	14 Nov. 09	22 Oct. 16	59 Foot.
Ball, William	25 Jan. 10	11 Mar. 13	9 Nov. 20	22 Foot.
Bamford, John	1 July 98	17 May 03		Scotch Brigade.
*Banko, Christopher	never	25 Dec. 13	25 Mar. 16	88 Foot.
Baring, Frederick	15 Nov. 11	8 Feb. 13	4 Aug. 37	51 Foot.
Barlow, John Thomas	8 Aug. 05	19 Mar. 07	20 Dec. 19	93 Foot.
Barnes, James	28 Nov. 11	7 Oct. 18	23 July 20	73 Foot.
Barnetson, Alexander	1 Mar. 06	29 Sept. 07	28 Mar. 22	92 Foot.
Barnewall, Bartholomew	never	10 Oct. 95		79 Foot.
Baron, Jonathan	8 Oct. 04	13 Feb. 08	27 Aug. 24	R. Marines.
Barret, Thomas	15 April 13	8 June 15	25 Feb. 16	3 Foot.
₧ Barrington, Edward	28 Mar. 11	13 Feb. 12	12 Dec. 25	Unattached.
Barry, St. George Ryder	23 June 14	25 Oct. 15	14 Nov. 16	13 Dragoons.
Bartlet, Frederick George	20 Aug. 13	18 May 20	7 Oct. 24	7 Foot.
₧₳ Bartlet, William	3 Feb. 14	11 Aug. 15	25 Nov. 16	69 Foot.
*Bass, John	never	25 Dec. 13		1814 2 Prov. Bn. of Mil.
Bassett, Joseph Davie	12 Mar. 89	18 Aug. 90	1792	75 Foot.
Bate, Frederick	1 Dec. 12	15 July 13	1 Nov. 14	R. Art. Drivers.
Bate, Henry Cotsford	6 Mar. 95	3 Oct. 95	17 Feb. 03	R. Artillery.
Battersby, James	13 May 13	30 May 14	25 June 17	30 Foot.
Battley, William	14 Nov. 11	7 Feb. 13	25 Dec. 16	60 Foot.
Batwell, Andrew	31 July 00	9 Feb. 01	20 Feb. 05	40 Foot.
₧ Bayly, Frederick [5]	5 June 09	21 June 12	20 June 29	R. Artillery.
Bayly, Thomas	25 Aug. 13	19 Oct. 14	25 Mar. 16	1 Foot.
Bayntun, Edward	31 Mar. 04	28 Mar. 05	24 Oct. 16	2 Garr. Batt.
₧ Beamish, Bernard	5 Feb. 08	11 Oct. 08	25 Dec. 21	84 Foot.
Beauchamp, Chas. Eustace	5 Oct. 18	15 Mar. 27	6 Feb. 37	R. Artillery.
Beauchant, Theophilus, Sam.	9 Nov. 05	22 Sept. 10	3 May 17	R. Marines.
₧ Bedell, Walter Death	19 Mar. 07	11 Aug. 08	23 Nov. 15	24 Foot.
Belford, William	18 Mar. 13	25 Jan. 25	25 Nov. 33	48 Foot.
Bell, James	28 Mar. 06	25 Jan. 09	19 July 23	2 Ceylon Reg.
Bell, John Allan	20 June 05	18 June 07		104 Foot.
Bell, Robert	never	12 Nov. 08	1810	R. Waggon Train.
Bell, Samuel	15 Sept. 08	3 Jan. 11	25 Dec. 18	90 Foot.
Bellock, Charles	18 Dec. 01	16 Aug. 02	24 Aug. 02	York Hussars.
Bellot, Charles Joseph de	never	30 Dec. 97		60 Foot.
₧ Belstead, Henry	29 Aug. 11	9 June 13	7 July 29	89 Foot.
Bennett, Bryan O'Donnell	26 May 14	24 April 16	30 Mar. 26	77 Foot.
₧ Bennett, James	19 Nov. 12	21 Oct. 13	25 Mar. 16	14 Dragoons.

Lieutenants.

	2D LIEUT. ETC.	LIEUT.	WHEN PLACED ON HALF PAY.	
Bennett, John..................	22 Aug. 06	6 July 13	17 July 13	R. Marines.
Bennett, John (*Qr. Mast.* 3 Mar. 04)	never	8 Mar. 10		5 R. Veteran Batt.
Benson, Wm. W. H.............	7 July 25	11 Dec. 28	7 Feb. 40	30 Foot.
Benwell, Thomas	21 Sept. 13	17 Mar. 15	25 Feb. 16	4 Foot.
Berford, Richard	25 Oct. 07	12 Sept. 09	30 Sept. 19	2 Foot.
Berkeley, Aug. Fitzhardinge	4 June 12	28 Jan. 13	15 May 16	R. Waggon Train.
Berry, Marlborough Parsons	8 Dec. 96	26 Mar. 99	18 Mar. 13	3 Foot.
Berry, Warton, Pennyman	2 Feb. 80	30 Sept. 87		97 Foot.
Bersma, Henry	20 April 09	22 Feb. 10	25 April 17	5 West India Reg.
ℬ ℭℳ Best, Charles Lewis	18 Jan. 08	12 May 12	24 Feb. 16	1st Line Ger. Leg.
Bezant, John..................	3 Feb. 06	5 Sept. 11	6 Mar. 15	R. Marines.
Birch, George..................	15 Aug. 11	20 Aug. 12	15 Mar. 17	64 Foot.
ℬ ℭℳ Black, James	16 May 11	22 July 13	19 April 17	91 Foot.
ℬ *Black, John*[6]..............	15 June 09	30 Dec. 10		3 R. Veteran Batt.
Blackiston, Thomas Henry	1 Aug. 14	1 July 15		R. Engineers.
Blackwell, Daniel	28 Jan. 13	2 Mar. 20	2 Nov. 20	2 Garr. Batt.
Blagg, James	25 Aug. 09	14 Mar. 11	25 Feb. 15	25 Foot.
Blagrave, James...............	18 Dec. 06	8 May 11	24 Oct. 19	89 Foot.
Blair, Thos. Newenham.........	23 Sept. 12	15 June 15	25 April 16	7 West India Reg.
Blake, James Bunbury..........	25 Jan. 25	5 Sept. 26	12 Mar. 29	43 Foot.
Blake, John	5 July 13	4 July 15	22 Jan. 25	R. Artillery.
Blake, Isidore.................	10 May 10	31 Aug. 13	30 Aug. 23	8 Dragoons.
Blake, Robert	30 April 12	23 Sept. 13		9 R. Veteran Bat.
Blakeney, Richard.............	2 July 03	15 Aug. 05	4 Aug. 19	R. Marines.
Blakeway, John...............	21 Dec. 20	8 Sept. 25	25 Jan. 28	Cape Reg.
Blanchard, William	24 June 12	13 Oct. 14	25 Sept. 16	Nova Scotia Fen.
Bland, Robert John	29 Aug. 11	12 June 15	8 Nov. 17	70 Foot.
Blankeney, John Edward		18 April 93	22 Aug. 96	R. Marines.
Blaydes, Chas. Benjamin........	11 Aug. 29	19 April 33	23 April 39	Unattached.
ℬ *Blood, Thomas*[7].............	18 Nov. 13	8 Sept. 14		8 R. Veteran Batt.
ℬ ℭℳ Blood, Thomas[8]	25 Oct. 22	18 July 26	28 Mar. 34	Unattached.
Bloomfield, *Hon.* J. A. D.		9 April 18	25 Dec. 18	Coldstream Gds.
Blucke, Rob. Stewart...........	8 Feb. 06	16 Dec. 11	1 Sept. 14	R. Marines.
Blucke, William................	17 Sept. 05	21 Jan. 09	1 Sept. 14	R. Marines.
ℬ *Blyth, John Willis*[9].........	never	24 Oct. 03	1 Aug. 16	R. Art. Drivers.
ℬ ℭℳ Boase, John[10]............	Aug. 07	9 June 08	19 June 27	94 Foot.
Boghurst, Edward.............	4 June 10	17 Feb. 14	1 Aug. 27	R. Artillery.
Boileau, John Peter	18 Mar. 13	11 July 16	14 Aug. 17	90 Foot.
ℭℳ Boldero, Henry	25 Jan. 13	16 Aug. 13	25 June 18	27 Foot.
Bolton, Philip	17 Jan. 10	25 July 11	17 Jan. 22	63 Foot.
Bolton, Samuel	4 May 09	20 Mar. 10	27 April 15	23 Foot.
Bond, Andrew	7 Mar. 11	8 Oct. 12	10 July 20	21 Dragoons.
Bond, William Spittle	16 Mar. 01	15 Aug. 05	2 Feb. 15	R. Marines.
Bonnor, Thomas...............	Nov. 96	16 Mar. 97		Corsican Reg.
*Booth, William	never	25 Dec. 13	25 Sept. 14	14 Foot.
Bordes, Breon Charles	10 June 26	3 April 27	2 Dec. 36	13 Foot.
ℭℳ Bott, Charles	19 Dec. 11	22 April 13	25 Oct. 16	R. Waggon Train.
Bottomley, James	never	4 Dec. 99	25 June 02	15 Foot.
Boucher, Francis de	never	30 Dec. 97	1809	60 Foot.
*Bourillion, Julius.............	never	25 Dec. 13	25 Sept. 14	4 Foot.
Bourke, John..................	12 Jan. 81	9 May 82	1783	Fish's Corps.
Bourke, Miles.................	30 Oct. 06	6 Mar. 11	25 April 17	98 Foot.
Bourne, William	20 Nov. 78	11 Sept. 81	26 Mar. 90	R. Marines.
Bovill, Edward	3 Sept. 12	16 Sept. 13	2 May 17	29 Foot.
Bowdler, George Andrew	18 May 08	22 Sept. 08	30 Oct. 17	99 Foot.
Bowles, Humphrey	May 02	20 July 02	20 July 02	2 Dragoons.
Bowsar, Charles William	30 Mar. 08	21 May 08	10 Feb. 20	84 Foot.
Boyd, Arthur..................	20 May 13	16 Feb. 14	24 Oct. 16	2 Garr. Bat.
Boyd, *Sir* John, *Bt.*...........	8 July 08	2 May 11	25 June 16	1 Garr. Bat.
Boyd, Robert.................	13 Oct. 08	15 Aug. 11		7 R. Veteran Bat.
Boys, Richard	31 Aug. 30	22 Mar. 33	23 Dec. 36	Canadian Fen.
Brackenbury, William	15 Mar. 08	16 Aug. 09	3 Oct. 16	101 Foot.
Bradburne, Francis	8 June 15	3 Sept. 16	3 Sept. 16	16 Dragoons.
Braddell, John Armstead	15 Oct. 07	25 May 09	25 Mar. 11	36 Foot.

Lieutenants.

Name	2D LIEUT. ETC.	LIEUT.	WHEN PLACED ON HALF PAY.	
Bradford, William	7 Mar. 10	29 Oct. 12	29 May 17	8 Foot.
Bradshaw, Francis Green	5 Jan. 05	5 Dec. 05	12 Mar. 18	52 Foot.
Brady, Bernard	13 April 09	18 May 13	25 Dec. 18	97 Foot.
Brady, William	4 Oct. 11	24 Dec. 12	25 Oct. 19	60 Foot.
⚔︎ Bramwell, John [11]	29 July 13	18 July 15	25 Feb. 17	92 Foot.
Brandling, Charles John	20 April 20	25 Mar. 23	25 Mar. 25	3 Foot.
Brannan, James	6 June 16	25 Dec. 23	1 June 32	Unattached.
T. Brattle, Thomas [12]	8 July 03	15 Aug. 05	11 Aug. 14	R. Marines.
⚔︎ Brauns, Aug. Chris. Gottlieb.	15 Nov. 11	17 Feb. 14	22 April 19	Staff Corps.
⚔︎ Brearey, Christ. Spencer	21 July 08	2 Nov. 09	5 May 25	27 Foot.
Brenner, Edward	29 June 02	27 Oct. 03		2 R. Veteran Bat.
Brereton, Thomas	25 Nov. 99	25 Mar. 02		Rifle Brigade.
⚔︎ Breton, John Frederick [13]	1 Oct. 08	15 Mar. 11	1 Oct. 23	R. Artillery.
Brett, James Joseph	26 April 15	24 April 24	24 Dec. 29	30 Foot.
Bretthauer, Christian William	12 June 10	6 Oct. 11	25 April 16	60 Foot.
P ⚔︎ Brice, Alexander Adair	8 Aug. 11	21 May 12	5 Oct. 20	66 Foot.
⚔︎ Bridge, George Dandridge [14]	7 April 13	3 Oct. 15	25 June 17	73 Foot.
Bridger, James	25 Feb. 08	2 Jan. 09	25 Mar. 16	16 Dragoons.
*Bridger, John	never	30 Mar. 14	1814	1 Prov. Bn. of Mil
Bridgewater, Thomas	never	29 Nov. 99	25 Oct. 00	36 Foot.
Brierly, William	9 May 11	2 Sept. 13	25 Mar. 17	77 Foot.
Brock, James Loftus	28 May 07	20 Sept. 08	2 Oct. 17	6 Foot.
Brohier, Cyrus	25 Mar. 08	5 July 10	16 Jan. 23	York Chasseurs.
Brohier, John Boyle	21 Jan. 08	3 June 09	25 Dec. 18	61 Foot.
P ⚔︎ Brook, Thomas	29 Aug. 07	9 May 09	16 June 25	51 Foot.
Broomfield, Alex. Scott	25 July 10	10 April 17	20 Nov. 22	68 Foot.
⚔︎ Brown, Alexander	25 Dec. 13	3 Aug. 15	25 Mar. 17	42 Foot.
Brown, Charles	8 Mar. 10	7 Oct. 13	25 Dec. 14	50 Foot.
⚔︎ Brown, Eugene	14 Sept. 09	9 July 12	25 April 17	91 Foot.
Brown, Francis Carnac	27 July 07	1 April 10	8 July 18	80 Foot.
Brown, John	16 April 07	26 Aug. 08	10 Dec. 12	82 Foot.
Brown, Lewis Joseph	8 Oct. 12	24 Feb. 14	25 June 17	97 Foot.
Brown, Richard	14 Aug. 79	27 April 83	1 Sept. 83	R. Marines.
Browne, Andrew	8 Sept. 25	6 July 26	14 May 29	52 Foot.
Browne, Andrew	3 Feb. 12	3 Nov. 14	17 Sept. 23	53 Foot.
Browne, Courtney	27 April 09	3 Jan. 11	6 Dec. 14	1 Garr. Bat.
Browne, Daniel	16 June 08	5 Mar. 12	30 Aug. 20	43 Foot.
Browne, Valentine	16 April 12	10 Aug. 15	25 Mar. 17	13 Foot.
⚔︎ Browne, *Hon.* William	19 Sept. 11	26 Nov. 12	3 Jan. 22	52 Foot.
Browning, Thomas	26 Aug. 13	17 Oct. 16	18 Oct. 19	68 Foot.
Bruce, John	6 June 04	12 April 05	1 Aug. 16	R. Art. Drivers.
Brumby, Charles	29 Oct. 12	25 Feb. 14	25 Oct. 16	Meuron's Reg.
P Brydges, John Wm. Egerton	15 Dec. 08	15 Feb. 10	25 Dec. 15	14 Dragoons.
Bryson, Patrick	6 Feb. 06	8 Oct. 11	17 Jan. 26	R. Marines.
Bryson, William	27 June 05	21 Jan. 13		3 R. Veteran Bat.
Bubb, Anthony	20 Feb. 12	16 Dec. 13	1814	61 Foot.
Buchanan, Drummond	10 Aug. 09	28 Nov. 11	25 Dec. 18	90 Foot.
P Buchanan, William Theo.	10 Dec. 12	2 Sept. 13	25 July 16	13 Dragoons.
Buckeridge, Fran. Hotchkin	6 April 20	7 April 25	13 April 26	30 Foot.
Buckley, William Henry	4 Oct. 28	28 July 25	2 Nov. 32	Unattached.
Budd, Samuel Hayward	23 Jan. 12	29 Oct. 12	1815	Dillon's Reg.
Bulger, Andrew	26 Oct. 04	30 July 06	25 June 16	Newf. Fen. Corps.
Bullen, Richard	30 Jan. 12	1 Sept. 15	25 Nov. 17	66 Foot.
Buller, John	22 Aug. 05	19 Mar. 07	7 Oct. 19	85 Foot.
Bunyon, Charles Spencer	1 Aug. 26	16 July 29	16 Sept. 30	Unattached.
*Burchell, Frederick	never	25 Dec. 13	1814	2 Prov. Bn. of Mil.
Burdon, Charles	17 Mar. 96	1 April 99	11 Nov. 01	R. Marines.
Burge, Benjamin	April 94	31 May 94		71 Foot.
Burges, Samuel	10 April 08	9 Feb. 09		10 R. Veteran Bat.
⚔︎ Burgess, Francis	4 June 12	16 Dec. 13	25 Mar. 17	54 Foot.
Burgh, John Henry De	17 Dec. 07	1 Mar. 10	13 Sept. 21	21 Dragoons.
Burke, Richard	6 Sept. 04	14 Nov. 05	25 April 16	101 Foot.
Burn, Henry Wilson	25 Nov. 13	2 Mar. 16	21 Nov. 28	1 Foot.
Burn, James	13 Oct. 08	19 Feb. 11	1814	72 Foot.

Lieutenants.

	ENSIGN, ETC.	LIEUT.	WHEN PLACED ON HALF PAY.	
Burne, Lawford	6 Nov. 06	11 Aug. 08	16 Nov. 20	22 Dragoons.
Burne, William Brampton	29 Dec. 14	25 May 15	25 Oct. 21	15 Dragoons.
⚜ Burnet, John	27 May 13	8 May 15	25 Feb. 16	52 Foot.
Burroughes, Tho. D'Eye	4 May 20	24 Oct. 21	24 Oct. 21	14 Dragoons.
Burslem, James Godolphin	24 Sept. 96	1 June 98	1 Mar. 19	R. Artillery.
₱ Burton, Richard	13 Nov. 09	5 Nov. 12	25 Nov. 19	94 Foot.
Busteed, Charles	Dec. 07	22 Sept. 08	25 Sept. 17	1 Garr. Bat.
Busteed, John	2 April 12	29 Sept. 14	25 Mar. 17	16 Foot.
Busteed, Michael	30 Nov. 09	8 Aug. 11	1813	57 Foot.
Bustin, Wm. Ridsdale	3 Sept. 12	1 June 15	16 May 16	10 Foot.
Butler, Richard	16 July 12	9 June 14	25 Feb. 16	91 Foot.
Butler, Thomas Lapp	5 Aug. 13	20 July 15	13 June 34	Unattached.
⚜ Butler, Whitwell	never	12 Jan. 14	25 Feb. 19	Scots Fusilier Gds.
₱ Butterworth, Henry	25 Aug. 07	27 April 09	11 May 20	35 Foot.
Byng, *Hon.* Gerald Frederick F...	Nov. 99	26 Jan. 01		53 Foot.
Byrne, Redmond	5 Mar. 12	3 Mar. 14	25 Mar. 16	15 Foot.
₱ Cahill, Nicholas	10 Mar. 08	30 Aug. 10	11 May 15	36 Foot.
Cameron, Alexander	20 April 09	3 Oct. 11	9 Dec. 19	42 Foot.
Cameron, Donald	13 Dec. 04	7 Aug. 05	5 June 06	42 Foot.
₱ Cameron, Donald	never	7 May 11	23 Sept. 19	60 Foot.
₱ ⚜ Cameron, Dugald	19 April 09	1 May 11	13 Nov. 17	89 Foot.
Cameron, Duncan	22 April 13	21 April 14	27 June 16	1 Foot.
Cameron, James	14 Dec. 09	9 Dec. 19	7 Oct. 36	27 Foot.
Cameron, James	25 Aug. 08	21 Mar. 11	10 July 17	77 Foot.
Cameron, John	17 Aug. 06	13 Aug. 07	25 Dec. 15	2 Garr. Bat.
₱ Cameron, Lachlan M'Lean	13 Oct. 12	20 May 14	26 Feb. 29	Unattached.
Cameron, Peter Robert	10 Dec. 12	1 Aug. 15	5 Feb. 24	53 Foot.
Cameron, Thos. Cochrane	26 Aug. 13	8 Feb. 21	1 Nov. 33	Unattached.
Campbell, Alexander	10 Sept. 05	10 Oct. 08	1 Sept. 14	R. Marines.
* Campbell, Alexander	never	25 Dec. 13	1814	93 Foot.
Campbell, Alexander	13 Dec. 10	5 Nov. 11	25 July 17	104 Foot.
₱ *Campbell, Andrew*	27 Aug. 07	31 May 09		4 R. Veteran Bat.
Campbell, Archibald				O'Conner's Rec.Co.
Campbell, Charles	24 June 13	29 Sept. 14	25 Sept. 18	99 Foot.
Campbell, Charles Moore	2 Jan. 06	27 Aug. 07	25 April 16	10 Foot.
₱ Campbell, Charles William	21 May 09	2 May 11	17 April 17	39 Foot.
Campbell, Donald	16 Sept. 13	8 Dec. 14	25 Feb. 16	57 Foot.
Campbell, Dugald	18 Feb. 11	8 July 13	31 Jan. 19	72 Foot.
Campbell, Duncan	1 May 95	27 Jan. 96	9 Dec. 01	R. Marines.
Campbell, Duncan	29 Oct. 05	25 July 10	1 Sept. 14	R. Marines.
Campbell, George Andrew	5 Nov. 08	18 Dec. 24	28 Feb. 28	R. Marines.
Campbell, James	7 Feb. 05	27 July 08	30 Jan. 24	R. Marines.
₱ Campbell, James	14 Feb. 11	22 Oct. 13	25 Mar. 17	50 Foot.
Campbell, James	19 July 15	28 April 24	23 April 26	Unattached.
Campbell, John	21 Oct. 95	19 Mar. 01		8 R. Veteran Bat.
Campbell, Rupert	26 Sept. 31	7 July 37	27 July 38	38 Foot.
₱ *Campbell, Thomas*	3 May 00	2 Mar. 04		11 R. Veteran Bat.
⚜ Campbell, Thomas	24 Jan. 11	3 Sept. 12	25 Sept. 17	40 Foot.
Campbell, William	15 April 13	18 May 14	25 May 16	49 Foot.
* Candler, Stephen Campbell	never	4 Dec. 99	1800	52 Foot.
Canning, Edward	8 April 13	12 Aug. 15	25 Mar. 17	33 Foot.
Cannon, James	4 Jan. 15	22 June 15	25 Nov. 16	3 Garr. Bat.
Cardew, John Trevanion	21 June 05	27 July 08	10 Sept. 24	R. Marines.
Carey, James	7 Sept. 04	26 Mar. 05	19 Mar. 17	101 Foot.
₱ Carey, Michael [15]	27 Oct. 08	7 Mar. 11	7 Sept. 32	40 Foot.
₱ ⚜ Carey, Thomas, K.H. [16]	1 July 11	25 Mar. 12	27 April 16	Ger. Leg.
Carlisle, Robert Needham	11 June 30	16 Nov. 32	20 Oct. 37	20 Foot.
Carnaby, Alexander	2 Nov. 09	24 Nov. 14	25 Mar. 17	76 Foot.
Carr, Dawson	12 July 10	1 Nov. 10	25 Dec. 22	60 Foot.
Carr, John	25 Dec. 13	29 Mar. 26	28 Sept. 30	14 Foot.
Carr, Ralph	2 July 11	27 Jan. 14	16 April 17	21 Foot.
* Carrington, Walter Welland	never	25 Feb. 14	1814	1 Prov. Bn. of Mil.
Carrington, William	22 Jan. 07	12 July 08		2 R. Veteran Bat.

Lieutenants.

	CORNET, ETC.	LIEUT.	WHEN PLACED ON HALF PAY.	
Carrington, William Henry	19 May 93	1 April 95	12 Sept. 99	R. Marines.
Carroll, John	3 Dec. 14	28 Mar. 16	25 Jan. 17	89 Foot.
Carroll, John	6 Mar. 06	26 Nov. 06	15 April 19	Scots Fusilier Gds.
P Carson, James	6 Nov. 09	4 June 12	1 Oct. 29	Unattached.
Carter, George	7 May 07	28 Sept. 07	25 Feb. 16	6 Foot.
Carteret, Hugh de	24 Oct. 13	27 June 16	25 Mar. 17	12 Foot.
Cary, Dering	27 Feb. 10	14 May 12	25 Mar. 17	44 Foot.
Cary, George Marcus	2 Oct. 12	17 July 15	25 Dec. 18	Rifle Brigade.
Cary, William	14 May 12	30 Sept. 12	14 July 25	Unattached.
Cassan, Edward Sheffield	18 July 10	25 June 12	19 Dec. 22	West Ind. Rangers.
Cassel, James	5 July 03	15 Aug. 05	12 Nov. 14	R. Marines.
Caulfield, John	3 June 13	26 June 16	19 May 18	22 Foot.
Cauty, George	15 Dec. 08	20 Mar. 10	19 July 19	York Rangers.
Cauty, Thomas Henry Horatio	26 Jan. 12	23 Dec. 13	19 Aug. 16	Bourbon Reg.
Chads, William Catherwood	15 Oct. 05	5 June 10	1 Sept. 14	R. Marines.
Chadwick, Richard	22 June 09	16 May 11	15 May 17	7 Foot.
Chadwick, William	18 Jan. 10	18 Jan. 12		5 R. Veteran Bat.
Challis, John Henry	26 Feb. 08	1 Sept. 08		1 R. Veteran Bat.
Chamberlayne, Jos. Chamberlayne	5 July 09	24 Oct. 12	1 April 20	R. Artillery.
Chambers, John	17 Sept. 27	27 May 34	16 June 37	R. Marines.
Chambers, Samuel	6 Mar. 10	10 Sept. 11	9 Dec. 19	54 Foot.
Chambers, Samuel	16 Nov. 80	26 June 83		68 Foot.
Chambres, William Chambers	3 Oct. 05	18 Nov. 09	1 Sept. 14	R. Marines.
Champion, Edward Kendall	7 July 14	12 Feb. 24	29 Dec. 25	Unattached.
Chapman, George [17]	29 April 13	29 June 15		8 R. Veteran Bat
P ⚜ Chapman, William	4 April 09	26 April 10	18 Mar. 19	Rifle Brigade.
Charsley, Charles	2 May 11	7 Nov. 13	6 Sept. 17	56 Foot.
Charteris, Charles	16 June 95	12 April 96	25 June 02	28 Dragoons.
Chatfield, Frederick	24 Nov. 18	19 Nov. 21	19 Nov. 21	20 Foot.
P Chetham, Isaac	6 Aug. 11	10 Dec. 12	25 Mar. 17	40 Foot.
Chisholm, Alexander	1 Feb. 10	9 June 11	25 Mar. 17	African Corps.
Choiseul, Xavier	20 Mar. 07	2 May 11	25 Feb. 15	27 Foot.
Christian, John	23 Feb. 09	11 May 12	19 April 17	88 Foot.
Cinnamond, Joseph	2 Nov. 03	22 Feb. 06	25 April 15	R. Marines.
Clare, Benjamin	21 Dec. 12	11 Dec. 14	25 Dec. 18	60 Foot.
Clark, Edward Stevens	30 Jan. 12	10 June 13	25 Mar. 17	44 Foot.
Clark, Frederick	11 June 12	16 Feb. 14	20 Sept. 31	14 Foot.
Clark, George	7 Aug. 00	19 Jan. 05	25 April 12	R. Marines.
Clark, John	20 May 13	25 Aug. 14	25 Nov. 18	99 Foot.
P Clark, Robert	12 April 09	26 Dec. 11	25 Mar. 19	68 Foot.
Clark, Thomas	8 June 93	24 April 95	8 Jan. 01	R. Marines.
P Clark, Thomas Noble	25 Feb. 08	11 April 11	19 Feb. 25	24 Dragoons.
Clark, William	7 May 12	9 Dec. 13	25 Nov. 16	3 Garr. Batt.
Clarke, John Thorp	5 Nov. 12	7 June 15	25 Feb. 16	3 Foot.
Clarke, Marshal	3 Feb. 14	12 Oct. 20	25 Aug. 21	88 Foot.
Clarke, Thomas	31 May 10	25 Jan. 13		2 R. Veteran Batt.
Clarke, Walter	18 July 16	9 Nov. 18	1 Feb. 20	24 Dragoons.
Clarke, William	3 July 03	15 Aug. 05	1 Jan. 10	R. Marines.
Clason, Patrick	13 April 09	3 Jan. 11	9 April 18	79 Foot.
Clay, William Waldegrave Pelh.	1 July 13	19 April 21	10 Oct. 22	43 Foot.
Cleary, Richard Stanton	2 June 08	23 Mar. 09	30 Sept. 19	76 Foot.
P Cleghorn, George	5 Oct. 09	11 July 11	23 July 18	52 Foot.
Clements, George Edward	28 Mar. 10	30 April 12	16 Mar. 20	71 Foot.
Clendining, Andrew	26 April 27	9 April 29	26 Dec. 37	45 Foot.
Cliffe, Wastel	31 Aug. 81	3 Aug. 85	31 Jan. 88	42 Foot.
⚜ Clues, Josiah	12 April 15	15 Oct. 16	25 Jan. 17	83 Foot.
Coates, Richard Aylmer	22 Oct. 12	27 Jan. 14	29 Oct. 29	47 Foot.
Cobbold, Frederick	23 Aug. 10	15 Aug. 11	2 Feb. 30	Unattached.
* Cochrane, William	never	25 Dec. 13	25 Sept. 14	32 Foot.
Cockburn, Phineas C.	30 Dec. 13	23 Feb. 15	18 Sept. 23	70 Foot.
Colclough, M'Carty	25 April 11	23 Sept. 13	25 May 17	62 Foot.
Colcroft, John	28 Feb. 12	27 May 13	9 Nov. 20	74 Foot.
Cole, Charles	21 Nov. 99	7 April 02	25 June 02	16 Dragoons.
Cole, John William	16 July 07	16 Nov. 09	13 Nov. 17	21 Foot.

Lieutenants.

Name	2D LIEUT. ETC.	LIEUT.	WHEN PLACED ON HALF PAY.	
₽ Collingwood, William Dixon ..	13 July 09	8 Oct. 12		5 R. Veteran Batt.
₡₠ Collins, Benjamin Marshall ..	27 April 09	1 Nov. 10	30 Dec. 18	6 West India Reg.
₽ Collins, Charles	24 May 10	8 Oct. 13		8 R. Veteran Batt.
Collins, Joseph Ambrose	19 Sept. 13	14 Dec. 14	25 Dec. 18	3 West India Reg.
₽ Collis, John	1 Dec. 06	16 June 08		61 Foot.
Collis, William	22 April 06	1 July 12	1 Sept. 14	R. Marines.
Colls, William	1 Feb. 16	25 Sept. 17	26 Feb. 18	York Lt. Infantry.
Comerford, George	13 Jan. 14	16 Nov. 15	25 June 17	57 Foot.
Compson, George	29 June 09	24 Dec. 11	25 Mar. 17	25 Foot.
* Condonne, Robert Patrick	never	25 Dec. 13	25 Sept. 14	14 Foot.
Condy, Nicholas	9 May 11	24 Feb. 13	25 Dec. 18	43 Foot.
Coningham, William	24 Nov. 13	4 April 16	13 Mar. 17	63 Foot.
Conway, Samuel	1 May 14	24 Feb. 20		10 R. Veteran Batt.
Cook, Benjamin	1 June 09	24 Oct. 10	24 April 17	1 Dragoons.
₽ Cooke, Adolphus	30 Mar. 09	16 July 12	9 Aug. 21	76 Foot.
Coombe, Joseph¹⁸	1 Jan. 00	7 Sept. 04	25 Oct. 05	R. Marines.
* Cooper, Charles Kelly	never	25 Dec. 13	25 Oct. 14	52 Foot.
Cooper, Samuel	12 July 21	10 Sept. 25	25 Dec. 28	2 Foot.
Coote, Charles	7 June 21	29 April 24	24 Feb. 32	Unattached.
₡₠ Coote, John¹⁹	9 Nov. 09	27 May 12		10 R. Veteran Batt.
Coote, Richard Gethin Creagh²⁰ ..	25 Sept. 13	10 May 15	1 Feb. 31	35 Foot.
Coppinger, John Murray	14 April 26	19 May 34	30 Mar. 35	R. Marines.
Corham, William	4 Mar. 96	13 Nov. 98	5 Dec. 01	R. Marines.
* Corrigan, James	never	25 Dec. 13		1814	74 Foot.
Corry, Somerset	28 Sept. 09	16 April 12	16 Sept. 13	18 Foot.
Cosby, William	18 Sept. 04	8 May 06	2 April 18	5 West India Reg.
Cotter, Charles	9 Aug. 14	30 Sept. 24	14 Aug. 28	Unattached.
₽ Cottingham, Thomas	11 May 12	5 Aug. 13	25 Dec. 18	52 Foot.
Couche, John	1 Jan. 04	26 April 06	13 Jan. 16	R. Marines.
Coulthard, Robert	27 July 09	23 Nov. 09	7 May 18	1 Dragoon Gds.
₽ Courtenay, William Allan	14 June 09	23 Aug. 13	4 April 16	39 Foot.
Coveney, James	never	20 Feb. 16	23 Oct. 17	60 Foot.
Coventry, Richard²¹	11 Jan. 10	20 Aug. 12		4 R. Vet. Batt.
Cowan, William	1 June 78	12 Aug. 79	1 Jan. 91	67 Foot.
₽ Cowcher, John	14 Jan. 07	23 May 09	25 Aug. 14	3 Foot.
Cowderoy, Thomas Frederick	9 Feb. 15	1 July 19	16 Mar. 20	21 Dragoons.
₽ Cowley, Charles	24 May 09	10 Sept. 12	18 July 16	39 Foot.
₽ ₡₠ Cox, Charles Thomas	29 June 09	29 May 11	25 Oct. 20	71 Foot.
Cox, Douglas Leith	30 Nov. 09	29 Oct. 12	16 Mar. 32	Unattached.
Cox, Samuel	22 Dec. 09	19 Mar. 28	6 Feb. 29	R. Marines.
Cozens, George	27 July 09	5 Dec. 11	27 Mar. 17	101 Foot.
₽ Crabtree, George Longbottom..	11 Mar. 12	29 Oct. 12	10 April 23	5 Dragoon Gds.
Crampton, Josiah	6 Sept. 04	22 May 04	25 Dec. 18	97 Foot.
Crauford, William	22 May 12	24 Aug. 15	25 Mar. 17	70 Foot.
Crause, Charles	3 Aug. 00	12 Dec. 04	31 Oct. 14	R. Marines.
₡₠ Crawford, Alexander Spiers²²	18 May 14	27 July 15	3 Feb. 25	67 Foot.
Crawford, John Charles	11 July 11	27 Dec. 15	29 Sept. 19	52 Foot.
Crawford, Joseph	4 July 11	23 July 12	24 Oct. 16	2 Garr. Bat.
₽ Crawley, William	7 Nov. 11	31 Dec. 12	25 Mar. 17	27 Foot.
Creagh, Arthur Gethin	6 June 05	10 April 06	3 Dec. 07	17 Foot.
Cree, John		24 July 02	1805	York Rangers.
₽ Crewe, Kinder	never	4 June 12		2 R. Veteran Bat.
Crisp, Robert	4 June 12	5 Feb. 14	25 Mar. 29	1 Foot.
Crispo, Sidney Smith	11 Mar. 28	18 July 36	7 Nov. 37	R. Marines.
Cromp, Thomas²³	18 Aug. 79	1 May 83	5 June 04	R. Marines.
Crookshank, Richard...........	23 July 12	4 Feb. 13	25 Sept. 14	4 Dragoon Gds.
Cross, Richard	16 Mar. 30	22 June 32	21 April 37	20 Foot.
Cross, Richard	28 Oct. 13	7 April 25	17 July 28	24 Foot.
Croudace, William.............	19 April 10	4 Feb. 14	25 Aug. 22	2 Ceylon Reg.
Crow, William	Sept. 99	18 Nov. 99	25 Nov. 02	9 Foot.
₽ Crowe, Charles	14 Aug. 11	24 Dec. 12	25 Mar. 17	27 Foot.
Crowe, James................	16 Dec. 13	13 June 16	6 Feb. 17	2 Garr. Bat.
Crowe, Joseph	26 Oct. 10	29 Mar. 12	28 June 19	60 Foot.
Crowther, Jeremiah	15 Jan. 04	27 Aug. 04	1806	R. Waggon Train.

Lieutenants.

Name	2D LIEUT. ETC.	LIEUT.	WHEN PLACED ON HALF PAY.	
Crozier, Acheson	2 July 03	15 Aug. 05	1 May 17	R. Marines.
₽ Cubitt, Edward George	31 Oct. 11	23 Jan. 12	8 Jan. 24	4 Dragoons.
Cull, George [21]	5 Aug. 99	1 Sept. 04	10 Jan. 16	R. Marines.
Cumberlege, Cleland	31 Dec. 25	25 Aug. 29	28 Sept. 30	1 Foot.
Cumming, Alexander	27 Jan. 14	6 Oct. 14	25 Dec. 14	26 Foot.
Curling, Henry	22 Oct. 25	20 Aug. 29	30 Dec. 34	52 Foot.
Curtayne, Francis	16 Feb. 09	11 Oct. 10	29 Aug. 23	8 Dragoons.
Curzon, Hon. John H. Roper	14 Oct. 24	15 Nov. 27	30 Dec. 31	37 Foot.
Cusine, John	22 Mar. 10	4 Mar. 13	13 Dec. 26	Unattached.
₽ Cuthbert, Kingston	2 Dec. 06	13 Oct. 08	25 Jan. 16	82 Foot.
Cutting, Thomas	9 Jan. 13	13 Sept. 14	24 Feb. 16	Ger. Leg.
₽ Dalgairns, William [25]	7 Sept. 09	5 July 10	24 July 17	55 Foot.
Dalgety, Alexander	19 June 06	28 July 08	25 Sept. 16	89 Foot.
Dalgleish, Robert	1 April 12	1 July 13	25 June 17	73 Foot.
Dalrymple, Alexander	May 95	1 Sept. 95		46 Foot.
D'Alton, Edward Richard	3 June 12	7 Sept. 13	1814	Chass. Brit.
₽ Dalton, John [26]	15 April 09	13 June 12	1 Nov. 14	R. Art. Drivers.
Dalton, Matthew Aylmer	15 Oct. 12	18 May 14	25 Mar. 16	Sicilian Reg.
Dalton, Philip Tuite	3 Oct. 11	1 April 13	25 July 14	9 Dragoons.
Daly, George	17 Mar. 14	4 Oct. 15	30 Oct. 17	99 Foot.
Dalzell, William John	1 May 15	29 July 20	17 Jan. 24	R. Artillery.
Damerum, George	5 Oct. 20	23 Sept. 24	23 April 29	104 Foot.
Daines, Mansell	6 Feb. 12	25 May 15	25 Mar. 16	6 Dragoons.
₽ Daniel, Robert	never	11 April 09	19 Mar. 18	7 Foot.
₠ Daniell, Robert [27]	21 Sept. 09	15 July 11	9 Dec. 19	59 Foot.
₽ D'Arcy, William	29 Feb. 96	25 July 04		1 R. Veteran Bat.
Darcy, Isaac Roboteau	15 April 07	2 Oct. 09		8 R. Veteran Bat.
* Dardis, George	never	25 Feb. 14	1814	1 Prov. Bn. of Mil
Darke, John	Nov. 00	28 Aug. 01	11 Jan. 21	Coldstream Gds.
Daubuz, James Barill	3 Aug. 20	24 Oct. 21	22 Mar. 27	Unattached.
Davidson, Duncan	5 July 21	11 April 22	10 Mar. 25	Coldstream Gds
Davies, Charles Nice	25 June 06	8 April 07	1815	53 Foot.
Davies, Christopher	13 Oct. 27	28 Dec. 78	20 Dec. 87	42 Foot.
Davies, David	21 Nov. 06	1 Oct. 13	8 May 27	R. Marines.
Davies, Edward John	1 Aug. 05	27 Aug. 07	28 Jan. 19	30 Foot.
Davis, Charles Winter	3 Sept. 12	24 Feb. 14	17 Sept. 29	30 Foot.
Davis, John	7 Aug. 06	19 Nov. 07		2 R. Veteran Bat
Davis, William	9 Sept. 99	5 Feb. 01	25 July 02	16 Foot.
Davis, William Henry	21 Jan. 13	25 May 15	18 April 17	8 West India Reg.
Davison, James	18 Aug. 14	5 Oct. 15	7 Nov. 17	99 Foot.
₽ Davison, John	19 Sept. 05	3 Sept. 06	2 Jan. 22	11 Foot.
Davys, Edmund Soden	11 Nov. 08	16 May 11	25 Dec. 18	90 Foot.
Dawson, William	6 May 12	6 May 13	25 April 16	Ger. Legion.
Day, Alexander	14 May 99	18 Aug. 04	1 Oct. 14	R. Marines.
₽ Day, John	2 Nov. 08	21 Mar. 11	25 Feb. 16	11 Foot.
Dean, Robert	1 Jan. 13	5 June 15	20 Oct. 16	16 Dragoons.
Delamain, Edward Smith	20 Feb. 11	28 July 14	2 July 20	60 Foot.
De Lancey, Oliver	3 June 13	16 Nov. 16	22 June 20	10 Dragoons.
₽ Delmé, Henry Peter	7 Mar. 11	3 Sept. 12	25 Feb. 16	88 Foot.
* Denford, Charles	never	25 Dec. 13	1814	95 Foot.
Denison, George	18 June 12	29 Jan. 18	20 July 20	19 Foot.
Dennis, Harloe	25 May 14	30 Nov. 15	25 Aug. 16	101 Foot.
Dent, Robert	21 Dec. 20	16 Dec. 24	29 Sept. 25	Unattached.
Desbarres, Henry Windham	26 May 14	8 Dec. 14	2 Feb. 26	Unattached.
Dick, George	25 Oct. 07	5 April 10	19 Aug. 19	4 West India Reg
₠ Dickson, Charles Lennox	11 June 12	21 April 14	7 Sept. 26	Unattached.
Dickson, David	8 Dec. 15	23 Dec. 24	3 July 28	42 Foot.
Digges, Charles	4 Mar. 13	11 May 15	3 Oct. 18	W. Ind. Rangers
₽ Dighton, Robert [28]	27 April 09	7 Sept. 12	7 Nov. 34	Unattached.
Dillon, Anthony	9 April 16	17 Nov. 25	2 Oct. 35	Unattached.
Dillon, Edward Walter Percy	21 April 08	5 Oct. 09	23 Dec. 19	63 Foot.
Dillon, Thomas	3 July 06	2 Feb. 09		8 R. Veteran Bat.
*Disney, Henry	never	25 Dec. 13	25 May 17	37 Foot.

354

Lieutenants.

	ENSIGN, ETC.	LIEUT.	WHEN PLACED ON HALF PAY.	
Disney, James Robert	10 Nov. 14	20 July 15	25 Aug. 19	York Chasseurs.
Dixon, John William	2 Nov. 09	14 Aug. 11	1814	48 Foot.
d&d Dobbs, William [29]	22 Aug. 13	29 Sept. 14	17 April 17	1 Foot.
Dobree, Augustus Fred.	23 Sept. 08	28 Sept. 09	28 Dec. 20	36 Foot.
Dobyns, Robert William	19 July 09	27 Mar. 11	2 Sept. 16	7 West India Reg.
Dodd, Edward Henry	15 Mar. 21	10 Aug. 26	15 Mar. 27	87 Foot.
p d&d Dodwell, George	6 July 04	25 April 05	30 May 16	23 Dragoons.
Dolmage, Julius	14 Aug. 00	28 Aug. 01	12 Sept. 05	4 Foot.
Donaldson, John	4 Mar. 06	21 Aug. 00		8 R. Veteran Bat.
Donnelly, John	21 Nov. 13	18 July 15		2 R. Veteran Bat.
Dormer, Charles	28 Nov. 16	2 Dec. 19	16 May 34	Unattached.
Doswell, Henry	18 Sept. 05	1 Feb. 09	1 April 17	R. Marines.
Douglas, Cunningham	9 April 09	18 July 11	5 May 15	18 Foot.
Douglas, William Henry	3 Dec. 12	9 Nov. 13	25 Aug. 24	5 Foot.
Douglass, Edmond Alexander	9 April 12	20 July 15	25 Nov. 16	3 Garr. Bat.
d&d Dowbiggin, William Henry [30]	22 Mar. 10	8 Aug. 11	25 Aug. 21	16 Foot.
p Dowker, Thomas	20 April 09	15 Mar. 10	24 Nov. 14	38 Foot.
d&d Dowling, Joseph	18 Jan. 10	13 Aug. 12	26 July 27	Unattached.
Downer, George P. Maxwell	3 Feb. 14	19 Jan. 15	25 Mar. 17	York Lt. Inf. Vol.
Downie, Alexander	10 June 13	18 May 21	25 Nov. 22	6 Foot.
Dover, Joseph	13 May 11	9 Dec. 13	13 July 15	48 Foot.
Doyne, Robert Stephen	22 Sept. 25	28 Sept. 26	17 Sept. 29	7 Dragoons.
d&d Drake, Edward	25 Nov. 13	15 June 15	25 April 16	28 Foot.
Drawbridge, Charles [31]	21 Dec. 08	3 Dec. 11	24 Aug. 20	R. Artillery.
Dreghorn, Allan Hamilton	26 Mar. 12	6 May 13		7 R. Veteran Bat.
Drew, Matthew	28 Jan. 07	25 May 08	25 Dec. 18	R. Waggon Train.
Drew, Tank. Chamberlain	7 Nov. 11	20 Aug. 12	25 Mar. 17	45 Foot.
p d&d Drummond, Geo. Duncan	30 May 11	28 Jan. 13	25 June 26	3 R. Veteran Bat.
Du Chastelet, Maximilian	12 Sept. 05	3 Dec. 07	25 May 16	60 Foot.
Dudley, Samuel	25 Aug. 14	17 Nov. 14	17 Nov. 14	11 Dragoons.
Duggan, Arthur	10 June 13	23 Mar. 15	25 Dec. 18	96 Foot.
Dunbar, James	28 Feb. 05	26 Dec. 05	16 Mar. 20	21 Dragoons.
Dunlop, Archibald	18 Nov. 03	1 April 06	17 Aug. 18	R. Marines.
Dunn, Thomas	5 Oct. 05	1 Sept. 08	25 Jan. 18	12 Foot.
d&d Dunnicliffe, Henry [32]	12 Dec. 11	20 Dec. 14	1 April 19	R. Artillery.
p d&d Duperier, Henry [33]	7 Oct. 13	23 Feb. 14	10 Nov. 21	18 Dragoons.
Durell, Thos. Vavasour	15 Nov. 15	13 Dec. 18	14 Oct. 19	1 W. Ind. Reg.
Dusautoy, James	5 Feb. 77	21 Jan. 79		R. Marines.
Dyer, Robert Turtliff	16 Feb. 05	27 July 08	14 Dec. 14	R. Marines.
Eagar, Alexander	31 Mar. 14	14 Dec. 15	25 Feb. 16	57 Foot.
Eagar, James	10 Nov. 08	21 June 11		7 R. Vet. Batt.
Eagar, Jeffrey	26 May 14	19 June 17	14 Nov. 19	York Rangers.
Eagles, Edward Bampfield	29 Sept. 04	28 Mar. 07	1 Sept. 14	R. Marines.
Earle, Alexander Hamilton	4 Dec. 09	28 Aug. 13	10 Aug. 21	R. Artillery.
Easter, Jeremiah	31 Mar. 08	26 July 09	25 July 14	23 Dragoons.
p Eaton, John	22 June 09	17 Jan. 11	25 Mar. 16	20 Dragoons.
Eberstein, Franz. B. von	28 Nov. 05	10 Dec. 07		7 R. Vet. Batt.
Eccles, Cuthbert	19 Nov. 12	20 May 14	25 Mar. 17	83 Foot.
Ede, Denzil	7 June 99	18 Aug. 04	1 Jan. 16	R. Marines.
Ede, John	14 Mar. 96	1 Jan. 99		R. Marines.
Edgworth, Thos. Bridgman	17 Feb. 95	30 Dec. 95	19 Mar. 96	R. Marines.
p Edington, John	7 Feb. 11	23 Jan. 12	3 April 16	81 Foot.
Edmonds, Robert	6 July 09	4 Jan. 10	25 Mar. 17	27 Foot.
Edridge, Frederick Leeds	5 July 20	5 July 27		R. Artillery.
p Edwards, Benj. Hutchins [34]	14 May 12	21 Oct. 13	1 July 36	Unattached.
Edwards, Charles	27 Sept. 13	24 Dec. 18	3 Mar. 25	71 Foot.
Edwards, John	2 Sept. 07	16 Dec. 07	28 Jan. 13	27 Foot.
Edwards, John	15 Aug. 78	24 April 82	1783	97 Foot.
Edwards, Richard	24 May 06	20 Oct. 12	1 Sept. 14	R. Marines.
Edwards, Stephen	27 Sept. 04	3 April 06	15 Mar. 10	7 Garr. Batt.
Edwards, Thomas	11 April 09	8 Oct. 12	8 July 19	66 Foot.
d&d Edwards, William	3 June 24	5 Jan. 26	22 Mar. 29	89 Foot.
Edwards, Wright	2 Sept. 12	10 Nov. 13	11 July 22	58 Foot.

Lieutenants.

	CORNET, ETC.	LIEUT.	WHEN PLACED ON HALF PAY.	
Edyvean, Robert Bradlick	31 May 10	4 Mar. 13	28 Dec. 17	103 Foot.
Egan, James	3 July 11	2 Feb. 14	25 April 17	21 Foot.
Eliot, Charles	14 Oct. 13	11 Jan. 21	15 Jan. 24	43 Foot.
Elley, John	20 Mar. 11	8 June 13	25 Dec. 18	West Ind. Rangers.
Elliot, Henry	11 July 03	5 Nov. 05	11 Dec. 16	R. Marines.
Elliott, George Henry	15 June 09	8 Feb. 10	2 April 12	44 Foot.
Ellis, William	1 Feb. 10	9 June 12	25 Jan. 17	89 Foot.
Elrington, Thos. Gerard	5 Mar. 12	12 Feb. 14	25 May 17	62 Foot.
Elton, William	31 Dec. 18	10 Feb. 20	21 Mar. 22	19 Dragoons.
*Emery, John	never	25 Mar. 14	1814	3 Prov. Bn. of Mil.
Enzinger, John	21 Sept. 09	20 Oct. 14		8 R. Vet. Batt.
Erroll, Wm. Geo. *Earl of*, KT. GCH.	24 April 17	3 May 21	23 Jan. 23	45 Foot.
Erskine, Robert	2 April 22	25 June 24	5 July 31	African Corps.
Eustace, James	24 Dec. 83	23 May 86	30 April 92	Irish Brigade.
Evans, George	30 Aug. 07	19 Nov. 07	25 Sept. 17	1 Garr. Batt.
Evans, John	1 Mar. 10	13 April 13	25 Dec. 14	28 Foot.
Evans, John	26 Dec. 08	21 June 10	23 July 20	83 Foot.
ℳ *Evans, Matthew*[45]	1 Dec. 05	1 Jan. 07		R. Art. Drivers.
Evans, Ralph	24 Sept. 12	16 Feb. 14	25 May 17	62 Foot.
ℬ Evans, Thomas	26 Nov. 12	19 Jan. 14	25 Feb. 17	38 Foot.
Every, John	15 June 01	17 Mar. 02	25 June 02	15 Dragoons.
Eyma, John Adrian	11 Sept. 11	15 Oct. 12	1814	R. Waggon Tr.
Fairtlough, Hen. Blacker	26 Dec. 04	27 July 08	1 April 17	R. Marines.
Fallon, Charles	7 Sept. 15	16 July 17	11 Mar. 19	23 Dragoons.
Farie, James		16 Jan. 78	1783	82 Foot.
Farmer, Richard	28 Nov. 99	11 Aug. 01	25 Sept. 02	36 Foot.
ℬ Farmer, Wm. John George	31 Oct. 11	6 Dec. 13	10 April 17	9 Foot.
ℬ Fensham, Daniel	28 Mar. 11	22 Oct. 12	25 Dec. 18	Rifle Brigade.
Fenton, William	15 Aug. 05	31 July 06	8 Mar. 21	69 Foot.
Ferguson, Arch. (Q.-M. 24 May 10)	never	2 May 16		1 R. Vet. Batt.
ℬ Ferguson, Donald	14 May 12	10 Dec. 13	25 Dec. 18	Rifle Brigade.
Ferguson, George	18 May 13	3 Dec. 14	25 Mar. 17	97 Foot.
Fergusson, James	23 June 13	21 April 14	25 Feb. 16	57 Foot.
Fergusson, Thomas	13 April 09	5 Aug. 13	14 May 29	8 Foot.
Ferrier, Walter	30 April 95	23 Mar. 96		Indep. Co.
Ffennell, Richard	25 April 06	26 Oct. 06	10 Dec. 18	98 Foot.
Ffinney, Edw. Hamilton	27 Dec. 23	13 June 39	1 April 36	46 Foot.
Finch, Edward[sc]	18 June 07	20 July 09	4 Sept. 17	13 Dragoons.
Finch, Hugh Frederick	3 Aug. 15	6 May 19	19 Dec. 22	9 Dragoons.
Finn, James Glover	7 June 09	13 Aug. 12	25 Aug. 17	56 Foot.
Fitchett, John	23 Dec. 00	8 Oct. 02		7 Garr. Batt.
Fitz Gerald, James	21 Nov. 11	21 April 14	25 Mar. 17	77 Foot.
Fitz Gerald, Rich. Henry	1 Oct. 12	23 Mar. 15	26 May 25	Unattached.
ℳ *Fitz Gibbon, Gerald*	26 Aug. 13	20 July 15	26 April 17	23 Foot.
Fitz Gibbon, William	29 May 11	16 Sept. 13	25 Sept. 17	83 Foot.
Fitzherbert, George	25 Oct. 09	31 July 11	25 Jan. 18	14 Foot.
ℬ Fleetwood, James	4 Oct.	10 30 April 12	9 Oct. 23	25 Dragoons.
ℬ *Fleming, Hugh*	11 Jan. 10	26 Mar. 13		7 Royal Vet. Batt.
Fleming, Jn. (Q.-Mas. 25 Dec. 04)	25 Nov. 06	5 June 07		3 Royal Vet. Batt.
ℬ Flood, Ross	26 Mar. 12	31 Mar. 14	22 April 24	4 Foot.
Follett, Frederick	2 Feb. 15	16 May 16	27 Nov. 23	71 Foot.
Fonblanque, John Samuel Mar de Grenier	3 Jan. 10	18 June 12	25 Mar. 17	21 Foot.
Foot, Randal	11 July 26	6 Aug. 29	3 Feb. 32	14 Foot.
Foote, John Hollis Rolle	18 April 11	29 April 13	25 Feb. 16	9 Foot.
Foote, Robert	Sept. 01	30 Oct. 01	9 Mar. 03	11 Dragoons.
Forbes, Alexander	10 July 82	7 Dec. 85		100 Foot.
Forbes, Nathaniel	31 Jan. 82	15 May 84		102 Foot.
Forbes, Peter	18 Mar. 13	21 Aug. 17	25 Jan. 19	95 Foot.
Ford, Arthur White	27 April 09	3 Oct. 11		2 R. Vet. Batt.
ℬ Ford, John[37]	25 May 09	30 May 11	15 Nov. 21	3 West Ind. Reg.
" Forster, John Augustus	never	25 Dec. 13	1814	2 Prov. Bn. of Mil.
*Fortescue, George	never	25 Mar. 14	1814	3 Prov. Bn. of Mil.

Lieutenants.

	CORNET, ETC.	LIEUT.	WHEN PLACED ON HALF PAY.	
Fortescue, John Mill............	19 Aug. 13	7 Mar. 16	1 Oct. 17	103 Foot.
Fortune, John	23 Oct. 13	23 May 15	24 Oct. 15	2 Garr. Batt.
Forward, Samuel	7 June 15	8 June 20	8 June 20	21 Dragoons.
Fothergill, *Joshua*	19 April 10	10 June 13		1 R. Vet. Batt.
₽ Fowke, John	20 Feb. 12	19 Aug. 13	25 Dec. 18	68 Foot.
Fowler, William................	11 May 96	1 Nov. 99	1 July 02	R. Marines.
Francklin, Michael George	7 June 33	11 Nov. 36	20 Dec. 39	73 Foot.
₽ Franklin, Rob. Deane	3 Aug. 09	25 Aug. 13	8 June 15	36 Foot.
₡ Fraser, Andrew Simon [38]	16 Sept. 13	20 July 15	18 Jan. 27	Unattached.
Fraser, Archibald	26 Aug. 07	3 Jan. 12	12 Dec. 16	101 Foot.
Fraser, Arthur John	14 Sept. 04	12 Jan. 05	6 Dec. 14	2 Garr. Batt.
₽ Fraser, David................	9 May 11	2 Dec. 13	25 Mar. 17	82 Foot.
Fraser, Donald	11 Mar. 11	3 July 13	25 Mar. 16	1 Foot.
Fraser, Hugh..................	6 Sept. 10	6 June 14		4 R. Veteran Batt.
Fraser, John Nugent............	12 Jan. 26	20 Jan. 32	16 Feb. 39	Unattached.
Fraser, Simon	4 May 92	1 July 95	1 July 02	42 Foot.
Freame, Wm. Horwood..........	8 Dec. 13	14 Dec. 25	2 Feb. 26	58 Foot.
₡ Freear, Arthur William	6 June 09	24 June 11	20 Nov. 17	30 Foot.
Freeman, Alfred P. I. Walsh	1 Oct. 96	14 May 12	22 Feb. 16	15 Foot.
Freeman, Richard Francis	5 April 99	11 Nov. 99	2 July 03	30 Foot.
French, Hyacinth	27 July 09	17 May 13	25 Dec. 18	97 Foot.
French, Lucius	3 Sept. 12	4 May 16	25 July 17	67 Foot
French, William................	8 May 06	11 Nov. 07	3 Aug. 20	36 Foot.
French, William Lasinby	8 June 95	19 Jan. 97	10 Aug. 02	R. Marines.
Froger, Leopold de	15 Jan. 08	30 Aug. 09	24 July 22	63 Foot.
Fullarton, John	22 July 13	7 Dec. 14	7 April 16	71 Foot.
Fuller, William	25 July 95	20 Feb. 99	16 Feb. 09	4 Foot.
₽ Gaggin, Pierce	15 Aug. 11	9 Feb. 14	18 April 17	6 Foot.
₡ Gairdner, Patrick	27 July 12	30 Jan. 14	25 April 16	German Legion.
Gale, William................	12 April 15	26 June 17	22 Sept. 20	1 Dragoons.
Gallagher, John................	10 June 04	22 May 04	25 Sept. 18	98 Foot.
Galwey, John	4 April 81	6 Feb. 83	1783	75 Foot.
*Gamlen, Charles Arthur.......	never	16 Mar. 14	1814	3 Prov. Bn. of Mil.
Gapper, Abraham Arthur........	30 May 11	14 July 14	25 Mar. 17	13 Foot.
Garden, John Campbell	16 Dec. 07	4 Oct. 10	25 June 16	NewfoundlandFen.
Gardiner, Arthur	25 Mar. 08	11 July 11	7 Dec. 14	2 Garr. Batt.
Gardiner, Wm. Gregory	21 Mar. 11	12 Aug. 12	24 May 21	Rifle Brigade.
₽ ₡ Gardner, Andrew	14 Nov. 11	30 Sept. 13	25 Mar. 17	27 Foot.
Garstin, James	26 Oct. 07	12 Nov. 09	10 Nov. 17	15 Foot.
*Gatlive, John	never	30 Nov. 99	25 June 01	36 Foot.
Gatty, Joseph..................	10 Dec. 11	26 Oct. 12	13 Nov. 17	60 Foot.
Gay, John	24 Sept. 12	2 Feb. 14	9 Aug. 19	Garrison Com.
Geddes, Alexander.............	16 May 11	14 Jan. 13	29 Dec. 15	5 W. Ind. Reg.
Geddes, James	17 Mar. 13	9 June 14	25 Dec. 14	42 Foot.
₡ Gerard, Arthur	29 April 13	16 Mar. 15	25 Feb. 16	4 Foot.
Gibb, Harry Will. Scott	11 July 14	27 Sept. 18	1 Dec. 22	R. Artillery.
Gibbings, Thomas	20 Dec. 10	4 Feb. 14	25 Mar. 17	81 Foot.
Gibbon, Stephen	20 May 12	10 Nov. 14	1 May 17	29 Foot.
Gibbons, Thomas	8 June 04	1 Dec. 05	1 Jan. 36	R. Artillery.
₽ Gibbs, William	6 Aug. 07	8 Feb. 10	14 June 21	8 Dragoons.
Gibson, William	11 Feb. 08	13 Sept. 10		1 R. Vet. Batt.
₽ *Gibson, Wm. Joseph*..........	27 Sept. 04	11 Mar. 06		8 R. Vet. Batt.
₽ *Gichard, Edward*	21 Aug. 06	28 July 08	25 April 16	4 Foot.
Giffard, Thos. Frederick	9 July 12	5 May 14	20 May 24	18 Foot.
₽ ₡ Gilborne, Edward [39]	4 Oct. 08	18 Oct. 09	25 Dec. 18	71 Foot.
₽ Gilder, Matthew William	19 July 10	26 Aug. 13	16 April 17	6 Foot.
Gilfillan, Wm. Fred. Anderson....	4 Mar. 12	6 May 13	28 June 19	60 Foot.
Gill, George	29 Jan. 06	26 Aug. 11	1 Sept. 14	R. Marines.
Gillespie, Joshua	10 Nov. 08	7 Mar. 11	6 Feb. 15	5 Garr. Batt.
Gillies, John	12 May 25	8 Oct. 30	10 May 39	Unattached.
Gillman, Wm. Howard..........	18 Dec. 12	16 July 13	1 July 16	R. Artillery Driv.
Gillmore, Joseph Albert	12 Nov. 12	1 Sept. 14	7 Aug. 17	27 Foot.
Gilse, Frederick de	6 Feb. 06	26 Sept. 09	7 Mar. 15	R. Waggon Tr.

Lieutenants.

	2D LIEUT, ETC.	LIEUT.	WHEN PLACED ON HALF PAY.	
Glanville, William	15 June 15	7 May 18	21 Nov. 28	71 Foot.
Glassen, Caldwell	4 May 10	11 Sept. 28	29 Aug. 29	R. Marines.
Glendinning, Adam	16 Dec. 05	26 June 06		9 R. Veteran Batt.
⚜ Glendinning, Thomas	9 Dec. 13	20 July 15	27 Sept. 17	60 Foot.
⚜ Glynn, Henry	25 Nov. 13	20 Sept. 15	25 Feb. 16	40 Foot.
Glover, Edward	13 Nov. 32	7 Nov. 34	10 Feb. 37	60 Foot.
Goddard, Geo. Anthony	14 Dec. 09	21 Jan. 13	7 Sept. 15	50 Foot.
Godfrey, Whiteside	16 July 06	3 July 08		5 R. Veteran Batt.
Goodacre, Richard	25 Aug. 07	1 Oct. 09	25 May 17	Depôt.
*Goodair, William	18 Aug. 78	5 Mar. 82		Indep. Co.
⚐ Goodall, William	30 Mar. 09	21 Dec. 09	6 June 16	52 Foot.
Gordon, Alexander	22 May 06	3 Mar. 08	25 Oct. 10	92 Foot.
⚐ Gordon, George	20 Feb. 12	6 Jan. 14	30 Dec. 19	85 Foot.
Gordon, *Sir* John, *Bt.*	23 May 97	24 April 98	26 May 03	4 Foot.
Gordon, John	23 Dec. 77	29 June 80	1783	81 Foot.
Gordon, John Ponsonby	17 Jan. 22	15 Aug. 26	15 Aug. 26	Unattached.
Gordon, Lewis	Feb. 02	27 May 02	25 Oct. 02	35 Foot.
Gordon, *Sir* Orford Gordon, *Bt.*	10 Mar. 14	27 July 15	25 Nov. 16	3 Garr. Batt.
Gordon, William	27 May 12	16 Sept. 13	20 May 17	York Lt. Inf. Vol.
⚐ *Goslett, Jos.* (*Q.-Mas.* 13 July 09)	never	30 Nov. 15		2 R. Vet. Batt.
Goudie, John	23 May 11	1 Dec. 14	28 May 19	72 Foot.
⚐ Gould, Thomas	20 June 05	16 April 06	13 Oct. 14	11 Dragoons.
Goulden, George	8 Nov. 10	22 Sept. 13	25 Mar. 17	82 Foot.
⚐ ⚜ Græme, Geo. Drummond [40]	14 May 12	30 Aug. 12	25 April 16	German Legion.
Graham, Alexander		5 Dec. 79	1783	90 Foot.
Graham, Hector	26 Oct. 09	8 June 11	18 Nov. 19	60 Foot.
⚐ Graham, James	25 Feb. 08	11 April 11	25 July 17	27 Foot.
Graham, Mitchell	15 Dec. 81	12 June 94	2 April 96	R. Marines.
Graham, Walter	24 May 10	4 June 12		6 R. Veteran Batt.
Grant, Alexander	10 Dec. 79	3 Dec. 81		Invalids.
Grant, Alexander	20 Oct. 08	24 Dec. 10	11 Oct. 16	Canadian Fen. Co.
Grant, Charles		5 Jan. 78	13 May 83	81 Foot.
Grant, Geo. Colquhoun	15 June 09	2 Jan. 11	19 Dec. 22	2 Ceylon Reg.
*Grant, James		never	25 Dec. 13	25 June 16	R. Waggon Train.
*Grant, James		never	25 Dec. 13	1814	R. Waggon Train.
⚐ Grant, John [41]	1 Oct. 06	8 May 11	21 Oct. 25	R. Artillery.
⚐ Grant, John [42]	28 Mar. 10	24 July 11		2 R. Veteran Batt.
⚐ Grant, John [43]	5 Oct. 09	15 April 13	31 Aug. 38	Unattached.
Grant, Robert	28 Sept. 15	31 May 21	13 Sept. 21	10 Dragoons.
Grant, William	12 Sept. 94	22 Nov. 94	5 Mar. 95	34 Foot.
Grant, William	16 Aug. 04	17 Apr. 05	15 Mar. 10	7 Garr. Batt.
Grant, William	21 Oct. 08	19 Apr. 10	17 Sept. 12	7 Garr. Batt.
Grape, Henry	3 Oct. 00	9 Apr. 05	22 Oct. 14	R. Marines.
⚐ Grattan, James	9 Aug. 10	4 July 11	18 Aug. 14	9 Dragoons.
Graves, William	23 Sept. 05	12 May 09	2 Sept. 09	R. Marines.
Gray, Arthur Maynard	28 Jan. 19	11 Aug. 25	23 April 29	7 West Ind. Reg.
Gray, John	3 Apr. 79	9 Dec. 80	1784	4 Foot.
Greatrex, Charles Butler	15 Oct. 05	1 June 10	1 Sept. 14	R. Marines.
Greaves, Charles	25 Oct. 27	8 June 30	9 May 34	Unattached.
Greaves, Spencer	7 Nov. 26	3 June 28	1 Aug. 31	14 Foot.
Green, Samuel	31 Oct. 10	10 Sept. 12	23 Dec. 24	78 Foot.
Greene, Edward [44]	13 Dec. 13	1 Aug. 16	1 Feb. 19	R. Artillery.
Greene, George	31 Aug. 95	1 Oct. 96	5 Jan. 04	10 Foot.
Greene, John	12 Mar. 12	10 June 13	24 May 21	22 Dragoons.
Greene, John	8 Nov. 09	29 Dec. 12	25 June 17	83 Foot.
Greene, William	18 Dec. 24	7 Aug. 27	21 June 30	54 Foot.
Greer, Alexander		8 Jan. 01	17 Sept. 02	6 Foot.
Greer, William	6 July 09	9 July 12	25 May 17	11 Foot.
Greetham, John Henry	2 April 22	25 June 24	28 Mar. 32	Unattached.
Gregg, Wm. Osburne	21 Sept. 09	23 Oct. 13	25 June 16	84 Foot.
Grenier, Lewis	13 Jan. 13	9 Dec. 19	1 Aug. 22	61 Foot.
⚜ Grier, Robert [45]	26 Feb. 10	13 May 12	27 Mar. 17	44 Foot.
Grierson, Charles	25 May 15	2 Mar. 20	25 Oct. 21	1 Drag. Gds.
Grieve, George	9 July 03	15 Aug. 05	28 Mar. 15	R. Marines.

Lieutenants.

	CORNET, ETC.	LIEUT.	WHEN PLACED ON HALF PAY.	
Griffin, John	8 May 11	23 Sept. 13	25 May 17	37 Foot.
Griffith, Charles	2 July 03	15 Aug. 05		R. Marines.
ℬ Griffith, David	3 Sept. 12	28 July 14	11 Apr. 22	36 Foot.
ℬ Griffiths, Edwin [46]	6 Jan. 13	12 Nov. 13	1 July 16	R. Artillery Driv.
ꟼ Griffiths, Henry	4 Aug. 14	24 May 15	12 Mar. 29	Staff Corps.
ℬ Griffiths, John George [47]	10 Feb. 11	1 Nov. 12	1 Nov. 14	R. Artillery Driv.
Griffiths, Thomas	23 Nov. 09	28 Feb. 12		8 R. Vet. Batt.
Griffiths, Valentine	20 Sept. 04	9 Dec. 07	1 Sept. 14	R. Marines.
Griffiths, William Stuart	8 Oct. 12	21 Jan. 14	5 Oct. 15	23 Foot.
ℬ Grimes, Robert [47]*	4 Mar. 09	16 Mar. 12		R. Artillery.
Grove, Charles Thomas.........	4 June 12	13 Oct. 14	24 Feb. 16	14 Foot.
* Grove, James	never	25 Feb. 14	1814	1 Prov. Bn. of Mil.
Grovestins, August de	12 April 98	4 July 01	29 Oct. 09	Hompesch's M. Rifl.
ℬ Grueber, Daniel.............	24 Dec. 12	21 April 14	25 Mar. 17	39 Foot.
Guest, Edward	25 Aug. 07	10 Sept. 12		2 R. Veteran Batt.
Guitton, Nathaniel R.	22 Aug. 08	5 June 11	16 Jan. 17	Corsican Rangers.
Gümoëns, Nich. Theo. de	22 Nov. 09	27 April 11	1815	Dillon's Reg.
Gun, John	11 Jan. 10	15 Oct. 12	13 Nov. 17	15 Foot.
Gunn, George.................	4 Mar. 06	1 April 12	1 Sept. 14	R. Marines.
Gunn, William	26 Aug. 04	20 June 05	20 May 13	72 Foot.
Gunning, Alexander	29 Oct. 07	2 Jan. 10	1815	61 Foot.
ℬ ꟼ Gunning, George [48]	19 July 04	2 Sept. 07	10 Jan. 22	1 Dragoon Gds.
ꟼ *Hackett, William*	never	19 Dec. 11		1 R. Veteran Batt.
Hadwen, Thomas	21 May 18	18 Mar. 24	13 Feb. 35	89 Foot.
ℬ ꟼ Haggup, William	30 Aug. 10	13 May 12	14 Feb. 28	Unattached.
Haire, John	12 Nov. 06	18 Feb. 08	1815	1 Garrison Batt.
Halahan, R. Newton Chr.........	12 Mar. 12	24 May 15	25 April 16	25 Foot.
* Hall, Chambers	never	25 Dec. 13	25 Sept. 14	14 Foot.
Hall, Robert	2 April 12	3 Aug. 13	25 Feb. 16	71 Foot.
Hall, William Sanford	19 Dec. 11	22 April 13	11 July 17	18 Foot.
Halls, Thomas	5 July 93	24 April 95		R. Marines.
ℬ Hamer, Mich. Greatheed	6 April 02	23 April 12	2 April 18	5 Foot.
ℬ Hamilton, George	3 Oct. 05	23 April 07	25 Oct. 27	Unattached.
ℬ Hamilton, George .... :	29 April 13	4 Aug. 15	22 Sept. 37	Unattached.
ℬ Hamilton, James Banbury	25 Sept. 09	23 July 12	18 Dec. 28	10 Dragoons.
ꟼ Hamilton, John	26 July 12	17 Aug. 15	25 Mar. 16	German Legion.
Hamilton, Robert Campbell		13 Feb. 94	25 June 03	35 Foot.
ℬ Hamilton, Thomas	2 Aug. 10	31 Oct. 11	26 Mar. 18	29 Foot.
Hamilton, William Henry.......	27 Oct. 08	18 Jan. 10	1 Jan. 18	14 Foot.
Hammersley, William	4 July 15	28 Feb. 16	12 Aug. 17	3 Garrison Batt.
Hann, Robert................	1 Mar. 09	20 Mar. 11		5 R. Veteran Batt.
Hardcastle, William Augustus	7 Mar. 11	29 April 19	14 Mar. 22	75 Foot.
Harden, William	22 Feb. 10	22 Oct. 13	25 Feb. 16	2 Garrison Batt.
Hardman, Hen. Anthony........	16 June 06	15 Jan. 07	25 April 16	7 West India Reg.
ꟼ Hardman, Samuel	19 May 13	9 Dec. 13	6 June 16	10 Dragoons.
Hargrove, John Langford	18 Oct. 10	28 Mar. 12		10 R. Vet. Batt.
*Harland, John	never	25 Feb. 14	1814	1 Pr. Bn. of Mil.
Harman, Joshua...............	5 Oct. 13	3 Aug. 14	25 Oct. 16	Watteville's Reg.
Harrington, Henry	20 May 06	12 Oct. 12	1 Sept. 14	R. Marines.
Harris, Charles	11 Aug. 13	12 June 16	25 Oct. 17	60 Foot.
Harris, William	31 July 12	25 Jan. 13		8 R. Veteran Batt.
Hart, John	13 June 11	12 Aug. 13	25 Dec. 18	2 Foot.
ꟼ Hartley, Jas. Campbell	24 Jan. 14	24 May 15	25 Mar. 16	14 Foot.
Hartman, Rawlins.............	6 Aug. 07	17 Dec. 08	1814	96 Foot.
Hasleham, Wm. Gale	11 Feb. 08	25 Aug. 09		6 R. Veteran Batt.
Hassard, Richard		20 Dec. 94		R. Irish Artillery.
Haswell, John Stepney	10 Dec. 98	18 Aug. 04	30 Aug. 14	R. Marines.
Hatheway, Charles	25 Mar. 13	25 Aug. 14	25 April 16	New Brunsw. Fen.
Havelock, Thomas.............	3 Sept. 95	28 Jan. 96	9 May 16	7 Foot.
Hawkins, George	23 Dec. 13	3 Feb. 20	25 Aug. 21	86 Foot.
Hawkins, George Drew.........	17 Oct. 04	24 Mar. 08	1 Sept. 14	R. Marines.
Hawkins, John	5 Nov. 12	1 Dec. 14	25 Mar. 17	32 Foot.
Hay, Alexander Murray	10 Nov. 14	22 July 24	12 April 32	Unattached.

Lieutenants.

	ENSIGN, ETC.	LIEUT.	WHEN PLACED ON HALF PAY.	
Hazen, John	24 April 13	23 June 14	25 Mar. 17	49 Foot.
Hearn, John Heming	5 May 08	18 Feb. 10	25 Oct. 22	60 Foot.
𝖀𝖁 Hearn, William Marcus⁴⁹	10 June 12	7 July 14	25 Mar. 16	44 Foot.
𝖀𝖁 Hearne, George Henry	16 Mar. 09	29 Oct. 10	29 Aug. 16	4 Foot.
Heath, Philip	16 Dec. 16	29 July 25	3 Dec. 30	R. Artillery.
*Heath, Thomas	never	25 Dec. 13	25 Sept. 14	38 Foot.
𝕻 Heathcote, Jos. Chappell	13 Sept. 10	10 Dec. 12	27 Mar. 28	Cape Corps.
Hedding, Wm. Levitt	7 Jan. 13	21 Sept. 15	25 Mar. 31	35 Foot.
Heddle, Alexander	4 May 09	20 Mar. 10	25 Dec. 21	African Corps.
Hegarty, Luke	19 Sept. 95	31 July 96	1803	81 Foot.
Hely, Jas. Joseph Fred.	25 Aug. 07	1 Sept. 09	13 July 15	31 Foot.
𝖀𝖁 Hemsley, Henry	25 April 13	18 July 15	5 Dec. 22	28 Foot.
Hemsworth, Wm. John	25 Nov. 06	28 Dec. 07	30 Mar. 15	50 Foot.
Henderson, Jas. Allen	28 Mar. 10	26 Feb. 12	25 Sept. 18	10 Foot.
Henderson, Walter	31 Dec. 07	18 Oct. 10	11 June 18	72 Foot.
𝕻 Henderson, William	4 July 11	17 Oct. 14	25 May 17	5 Foot.
Hendley, Hen. Earbery	4 Jan. 10	20 Mar. 12	29 Dec. 17	3 Ceylon Reg.
Henry, Charles	28 Nov. 10	16 Mar. 15	25 June 16	Sicilian Reg.
*Herbert, John James	never	25 Dec. 13	25 Sept. 14	41 Foot.
Herbert, Issac	8 Dec. 99	31 Mar. 08		8 R. Veteran Batt.
Herrick, Edward Henry	8 Oct. 12	22 June 15	25 Mar. 16	15 Foot.
𝕻 Herron, Samuel	7 Sept. 09	30 May 11	6 Nov. 23	24 Foot.
Hewat, William	19 Sept. 11	22 Oct. 13	25 May 17	62 Foot.
Hewetson, Henry	30 Nov. 09	10 Dec. 12	25 Mar. 26	101 Foot.
𝖀𝖁 Hewetson, John	13 May 13	28 Sept. 15	25 Mar. 31	35 Foot.
Hewett, James Waller	9 May 11	7 July 13	24 Jan. 18	1 Foot.
Hewett, William	14 June 10	23 Jan. 12		7 R. Veteran Batt.
𝖀𝖁 Hewitt, Robert⁵⁰	21 Oct. 13	3 Nov. 19	16 Dec. 19	61 Foot.
Heyland, Langford	8 April 26	15 May 27	22 Mar. 32	101 Foot.
Hickman, Richard	7 Jan. 08	19 July 21	1 Mar. 27	R. Marines.
Hicks, Raymond	16 Oct. 06	21 June 10		5 R. Veteran Batt.
Higgin, Robert	11 Aug. 13	4 May 15	25 Mar. 17	12 Foot.
Higgins, Alexander Boyd	2 Nov. 09	21 June 10	4 Dec. 17	1 Foot.
Higginbotham, Henry	13 May 13	2 April 18	25 Sept. 20	22 Dragoons.
*Hilder, Jesse	never	25 Dec. 13	25 Sept. 14	15 Foot.
Hilditch, Charles	2 July 07	15 Sept. 08	11 Oct. 10	3 Foot.
𝕻 Hill, Richard	28 Dec. 09	2 Mar. 12	12 Feb. 18	45 Foot.
Hillas, Thomas	16 Aug. 04	13 June 05	8 April 13	96 Foot.
𝕻 Hilliard, Christopher	7 July 08	22 Feb. 10	25 Nov. 18	5 Foot.
Hilton, William Legh	21 May 12	1 Dec. 14	22 Feb. 22	98 Foot.
*Hinde, Edward	never	25 Dec. 13	1814	Rifle Brigade.
Hingston, Francis Bernard	13 Oct. 08	5 Dec. 11	17 Feb. 20	84 Foot.
Hockings, Richard		7 Sept. 94	6 July 04	92 Foot.
𝖀𝖁 Hodder, Edward⁵¹	29 July 13	10 Aug. 15	25 Nov. 16	69 Foot.
Hodgetts, Thomas	4 Sept. 30	13 Mar. 35	20 Jan. 37	Unattached.
Hodson, Alderson	25 Jan. 10	22 Aug. 11	22 June 20	2 Foot.
Hoey, Richard Hudson O'Reilly	11 Nov. 13	17 Aug. 26	30 Oct. 35	85 Foot.
Hojel, James				Caithness Fen. Inf.
𝕻 Holborn, Charles	9 June 07	6 Feb. 12	2 Oct. 17	10 Dragoons.
Hole, William	10 Dec. 12	7 Feb. 14	25 Mar. 17	43 Foot.
Holgate, Edward Milton	8 May 11	23 Sept. 13	25 Jan. 16	82 Foot.
Holland, Rupert Charles	27 Sept. 05	11 Aug. 09	1 April 17	R. Marines.
𝕻 Hollis, William Henry	26 Aug. 07	5 May 08	24 July 17	57 Foot.
𝖀𝖁 Holman, Charles	10 Sept. 12	11 Nov. 13	25 Dec. 18	52 Foot.
𝕻 Holmes, Benjamin Hayes	2 Nov. 09	13 Aug. 12	25 Mar. 17	36 Foot.
Holmes, Chas. Wm. Scott D.	21 April 14	7 Sept. 15	13 April 17	3 Dragoons.
𝕻 Holmes, David	21 Oct. 12	20 Jan. 14	14 April 17	9 Foot.
Holmes, James	23 Feb. 96	17 Sept. 98	12 Dec. 04	R. Marines.
*Holt, George Francis	never	25 Dec. 13	1814	2 Pr. Bn. of Mil.
Holyoake, Henry	22 Oct. 13	24 Feb. 15	1818	84 Foot.
𝕻 Home, John	11 Oct. 10	26 Nov. 12	3 July 17	3 Foot.
Home, William	24 Nov. 04	7 Jan. 06	15 Jan. 24	York Light Inf.
𝕻 𝖀𝖁 *Hood, James*⁵¹*	28 Aug. 07	3 Aug. 09		9 R. Veteran Batt.
Hopkins, Charles	22 Jan. 12	9 Dec. 12	25 Mar. 17	74 Foot.

Lieutenants.

	2D LIEUT. ETC.	LIEUT.	WHEN PLACED ON HALF PAY.	
₽ Hopkins, Wm. Randolph......	14 Sept. 08	5 Oct. 13	25 July 16	5 Foot.
₡₳ Horan, Thomas James⁵²	12 Oct. 09	11 June 12	25 Mar. 17	32 Foot.
Houghton, William	6 Feb. 12	4 May 15	25 Mar. 16	15 Foot.
How, Johnson..................	26 July 09	14 Jan. 28	9 Sept. 28	R. Marines.
How, Thomas...................	16 Oct. 05	8 June 10	1 Sept. 14	R. Marines.
Howard, Henry	25 Mar. 06	25 April 12	1 Sept. 14	R. Marines.
Howard, Thomas	25 Oct. 07	31 Oct. 09	4 Feb. 15	6 Garrison Batt.
₽ Howells, Jonathan...........	1 June 08	1 Dec. 00	27 Dec. 21	77 Foot.
Howsham, William	2 Sept. 08	5 Jan. 09	13 June 16	20 Dragoons.
Hubbard, Armiger Watts	9 May 04	4 May 07	28 Aug. 21	R. Marines.
Hubbard, James................	1 Nov. 05	20 Aug. 10	1 Sept. 14	R. Marines.
Hudson, Henry	16 Oct. 10	27 Mar. 12	25 Oct. 19	60 Foot.
Hudson, John..................	14 April 12	30 Sept. 13	8 Sept. 19	4 West India Reg.
Hughes, Edward	12 Nov. 12	9 Sept. 13	25 Dec. 18	19 Foot.
₡₳ Hughes, George	29 April 13	4 Oct. 15	3 Aug. 22	73 Foot.
Hughes, Henry Francis.........	8 June 09	6 Feb. 12	25 Aug. 16	Glengarry Fen.
Hull, Arthur Hill	24 Aug. 25	6 Nov. 27	28 June 31	50 Foot.
₽ Humphreys, Chas. Gardiner ..	9 May 11	11 Mar. 13	4 Sept. 17	14 Dragoons.
Humphreys, John	3 Aug. 09	12 Mar. 12	1816	72 Foot.
₽ Hunt, Michael	13 April 09	8 Aug. 11	2 Mar. 15	61 Foot.
Hunt, William	14 Jan. 14	29 June 15	5 Feb. 29	Staff Corps.
Hunter, Thomas................	25 Feb. 16	27 Nov. 18	10 Nov. 21	18 Dragoons.
Hunter, William Dodsworth.....	23 April 05	17 April 06	25 Nov. 16	64 Foot.
Hurring, Thomas	14 May 12	12 Aug. 16	28 Aug. 23	17 Dragoons.
Hurt, Francis	Nov. 00	16 June 01	25 June 02	15 Dragoons.
Hutchinson, John	12 Nov. 12	6 Nov. 15	24 April 23	60 Foot.
Hutton, William	26 May 24	14 May 33	28 Sept. 37	R. Marines.
Huyghue, Samuel	30 Aug. 10	26 Jan. 15	25 Oct. 17	60 Foot.
₽ Hyde, Frederick	29 Oct. 10	16 Sept. 13	6 May 17	4 Foot.
₽ Jackson, Charles	27 Aug. 07	29 June 09	21 Aug. 17	3 Foot.
Jackson, Frederick............	24 Aug. 26	8 Sept. 32	29 Aug. 34	27 Foot.
Jackson, James	2 May 04	15 April 07	26 June 12	R. Marines.
Jackson, John.................	19 May 14	24 May 20	25 Oct. 21	4 Foot.
Jackson, William	3 Oct. 11	29 June 15	15 Mar. 17	64 Foot.
Jacob, John Villiers	28 Aug. 89	17 Mar. 93	27 Nov. 93	77 Foot.
₡₳ Jagoe, Jonathan⁵³	3 April 11	10 June 13	25 Mar. 17	32 Foot.
James, David William	10 May 13	16 April 32	15 Dec. 37	R. Marines.
James, Joseph Gillam	11 Feb. 08	19 April 10	25 Nov. 16	69 Foot.
James, Robert	18 May 11	5 Dec. 13	13 April 15	56 Foot.
James, Robert U. D.	28 May 07	27 July 14	1 Sept. 14	R. Marines.
Jameson, Thomas	15 Dec. 08	15 Oct. 10	25 Dec. 18	3 West India Reg.
Jameson, William	21 May 12	2 Feb. 14	7 Aug. 17	37 Foot.
Jappie, William	14 May 11	29 April 13	25 Mar. 17	14 Foot.
₽ Jarvey, James	13 Nov. 07	26 April 10	15 May 17	7 Foot.
Ibbotson, Henry	1 April 12	12 June 15	5 Oct. 17	103 Foot.
Jeffreyson, George..........	28 July 95	12 Jan. 96		2 R. Veteran Batt.
₽ Jeffries, Joseph	8 May 11	5 July 13	14 May 18	1 Foot.
Jennings, George	18 July 05	19 Mar. 07	25 Aug. 16	1 Garrison Batt.
Jennings, Richard Bennet......	9 Mar. 32	29 Jan. 36	22 July 36	38 Foot.
Jenoway, Richard Oldham	24 Aug. 07	14 Jan. 08	25 Mar. 17	1 Foot.
Jervis, Thomas	30 July 18	25 Sept. 23	6 May 24	24 Foot.
₽ Illius, William	30 April 12	29 June 13	25 Dec. 18	Rifle Brigade.
Ince, Charles..............	22 May 06	17 Jan. 08		1 R. Veteran Batt.
Inglis, Edward	1 Oct. 12	17 June 13	25 Mar. 16	3 Dragoon Gds.
Inman, Thomas Withy	4 Jan. 10	7 Oct. 13	16 Mar. 15	45 Foot.
₡₳ Innes, Alexander	19 July 10	15 Oct. 12	24 Nov. 26	Unattached.
Innes, Robert	2 Dec. 13	4 Apr. 15	25 Dec. 28	48 Foot.
Johns, James	6 Dec. 05	29 Jan. 11	1 Sept. 14	R. Marines.
₡₳ Johnson, J. (*Q. Mas.* 14 Sep. 26.)	8 May 34	11 Mar. 37	26 July 39	40 Foot.
Johnson, William Proude	21 May 10	4 Nov. 13	22 Sept. 17	103 Foot.
Johnson, William Stephen	19 Aug. 12	15 June 15	18 April 17	29 Foot.
* Johnston, Galbraith	never	25 Dec. 13	1814	2 Prov. Bn. of Mil.
Johnston, George	25 Dec. 78	27 Sept. 81	1783	56 Foot.

Lieutenants.

	ENSIGN, ETC.	LIEUT.	WHEN PLACED ON HALF PAY.	
Johnston, John	6 Aug. 07	8 Aug. 10	11 Oct. 16	Canadian Fen. Co.
Johnston, John Rollo	22 Sept. 25	19 Sept. 26	7 July 38	Unattached.
Johnston, William Bacon	1 June 26	11 April 27	9 Oct. 35	89 Foot.
Johnstone, William	28 Oct. 78	25 Mar. 83	1783	86 Foot.
Jones, David Richard	16 Sept. 29	29 Dec. 35	1 June 38	45 Foot.
Jones, Edward	31 Mar. 08	2 Dec. 13		10 R. Veteran Batt.
Jones, Jeremy	9 May 11	10 Feb. 13	9 April 19	60 Foot.
Jones, John	23 Apr. 07	28 Feb. 11	6 July 21	22 Dragoons.
Jones, John Parslow	22 Mar. 09	25 Sept. 27	3 Mar. 34	R. Marines.
⚔ ⛨ Jones, Richard	28 Mar. 11	8 Oct. 12	21 Apr. 17	40 Foot.
Jones, Vaughan	12 Nov. 07	12 Jan. 09	25 May 10	8 Garrison Batt.
Jones, William	25 Mar. 12	21 May 13	25 Mar. 17	44 Foot.
Jones, William	25 Nov. 13	25 Oct. 15	25 Feb. 16	German Legion.
Jones, William John Williams	14 Mar. 15	27 Nov. 16	22 May 17	101 Foot.
Jordan, Edward	25 Aug. 07	10 Aug. 08	16 Oct. 17	26 Foot.
Joynour, Reuben		8 Feb. 83	1783	89 Foot.
⚔ *Ireland, James Stanley*	22 Feb. 10	17 Sept. 12		6 R. Veteran Batt.
Irvine, Robert	22 July 13	4 May 15	11 July 16	7 West India Reg.
⛨ Irving, Jacob Œmilius⁵⁴	24 Mar. 14	18 May 15	5 Nov. 18	13 Dragoons.
Irving, Robert	16 May 11	7 July 14	26 Oct. 15	32 Foot.
Irwin, Alexander⁵⁵	4 Mar. 13	24 Nov. 14	13 Jan. 37	3 Foot.
Irwin, Charles	22 Apr. 13	9 Oct. 18	5 Aug. 29	Unattached.
Irwin, John Robert	25 Feb. 08	28 Dec. 09	1814	54 Foot.
⚔ ⛨ Isaacson, Egerton Cha. Har.	30 Dec. 12	14 July 14	25 Sept. 23	Garrison Com.
Juxon, John	30 Jan. 06	30 Dec. 07		6 R. Veteran Batt.
Kane, John Daniel	23 Dec. 13	25 Dec. 14	25 April 16	60 Foot.
Kane, John Joseph	21 Oct. 13	4 May 15	25 Mar. 17	4 Foot.
Kayes, William	14 May 12	10 Aug. 14	1815	73 Foot.
Kearnes, John	5 Jan. 14	26 Feb. 18	25 July 19	68 Foot.
⚔ Keatinge, George	10 Nov. 08	30 May 11	25 Dec. 25	4 Foot.
Keene, James	10 Dec. 10	25 Feb. 04	9 May 05	35 Foot.
⚔ Keep, William Thornton	29 Aug. 11	8 Sept. 13	25 Dec. 14	28 Foot.
Keir, John	28 April 06	21 Aug. 06	29 Sept. 08	5 Foot.
⚔ Kelly, John	17 Dec. 07	10 April 11	1815	87 Foot.
Kelly, William	never	17 Dec. 94		R. Irish Artillery.
Kelsall, Joseph	never	21 Sept. 15		8 R. Veteran Batt.
Kemple, John	6 June 11	26 Mar. 12	10 Jan. 26	99 Foot.
* Kendall, Richard	never	25 Dec. 13	25 June 16	R. Waggon Train.
⚔ Kennear, David⁵⁶	1 Dec. 12	19 May 13	1 July 16	R. Artillery Driv.
⚔ ⛨ Kennedy, Francis⁵⁷	13 April 09	21 Feb. 11	26 Feb. 24	51 Foot.
Kennedy, John	19 Dec. 05	5 Feb. 08	2 Jan. 17	4 Ceylon Reg.
* Kennedy, Patrick Henry	never	25 Dec. 13	1814	2 Prov. Bn. of Mil.
Kent, James	14 Sept. 15	24 Dec. 18	4 Oct. 19	W. India Rangers.
Kentish, Edward	30 Mar. 79	16 Oct. 82	1 Sept. 83	R. Marines.
Kenworthy, William	17 June 13	1 Oct. 18	25 Sept. 22	48 Foot.
Kepple, Henry	23 Nov. 28	11 July 34	26 July 39	Unattached.
Ker, John	31 Dec. 12	25 June 18	25 Dec. 18	90 Foot.
Kerr, Charles	23 Feb. 09	7 Mar. 11	11 April 16	72 Foot.
Kerr, James	9 July 03	18 Feb. 04		4 R. Veteran Batt.
Kerr, John Henry	21 Jan. 13	23 Nov. 20	15 Mar. 21	104 Foot.
⛨ Kerr, Robert	11 Feb. 11	25 May 15	25 Mar. 17	60 Foot.
Kersteman, Harry Gobins	12 Dec. 11	20 Sept. 14	2 Sept. 22	R. Artillery.
⛨ *Kett, Charles George*⁵⁸	13 Dec. 13	30 Sept. 16		R. Artillery.
Kettlewell, Evans	3 June 07	21 April 08	25 Dec. 18	96 Foot.
Kierulf, William Duntzfelt	1 Jan. 19	2 Jan. 20	11 April 20	22 Dragoons.
Kingsborough, Robert, *Visc.*	6 July 14	24 Dec. 18	12 June 26	Unattached.
Kingscote, Thomas Henry	never	15 May 17	8 Aug. 22	14 Dragoons.
Kingsley, Daniel	17 Oct. 11	10 Sept. 12	17 Aug. 32	Unattached.
Kingsley, Jeffries	24 June 13	25 Nov. 13	19 Feb. 18	3 Dragoons.
⚔ Kingsmill, Parr	14 Sept. 08	8 May 11	19 April 17	88 Foot.
Kingsmill, William	15 Sept. 08	30 May 11		10 R. Veteran Batt.
Kirke, William Fetcham	15 Aug. 05	12 Feb. 07		11 R. Veteran Batt.
Knight, Alfred⁴⁹	18 June 12	14 Feb. 14	13 Nov. 33	90 Foot.

Lieutenants.

	CORNET, ETC.	LIEUT.	WHEN PLACED ON HALF PAY.	
Knight, Richard Lott	16 May 11	15 July 19	25 Dec. 23	22 Foot.
Knight, William	14 Feb. 05	28 May 07	3 Dec. 18	28 Foot.
Knox, Francis	23 Mar. 08	23 May 10	14 Aug. 17	31 Foot.
La Berthodierre, P. Marie	15 Aug. 10	12 Nov. 12	20 June 16	8 West India Reg.
₽ Lacy, Samuel Walter	4 Oct. 10	16 Sept. 13	24 June 24	10 Foot.
La Grange, Jas. Warrington	10 Mar. 14	5 Oct. 15	25 Mar. 16	3 Dragoon Gds.
* Lambert, John	never	25 Mar. 14	1814	3 Prov. Bn. of Mil.
₽ Lane, Ambrose	28 May 11	28 July 13	25 June 17	83 Foot.
Lane, Ambrose	13 Aug. 07	7 Mar. 11	25 Sept. 18	98 Foot.
Lane, Francis	30 Sept. 11	7 Dec. 13	25 May 17	37 Foot.
₽ Lane, John	13 Oct. 12	28 April 14	3 Jan. 19	Rifle Brigade.
Lane, John	22 June 15	30 Dec. 20	24 April 28	Unattached.
₽ Lane, John Barnet	1 Oct. 12	30 Aug. 15	25 Mar. 16	3 Dragoon Gds.
Lang, John	23 Aug. 10	10 Dec. 12	1 June 20	23 Foot.
₽ Langdon, Colwell	6 April 09	21 Dec. 09	20 Sept. 19	60 Foot.
* Langdon, John	never	25 Dec. 13	1814	2 Prov. Bn. of Mil.
Langford, Richard Coplen	12 Sept. 08	13 Oct. 81	19 Mar. 85	66 Foot.
Lapasture, Henry de	21 Dec. 15	19 Mar. 18	29 Mar. 21	67 Foot.
Laplain, John	10 Oct. 11	6 Dec. 13	6 Sept. 17	56 Foot.
Latham, John	1 July 13	14 July 14	1814	92 Foot.
Laurie, James	15 Mar. 04	24 Sept. 06	7 April 17	R. Marines.
Lawson, John	10 Oct. 22	17 Aug. 26	5 Sept. 35	Unattached.
Lawson, William	20 June 99	14 Nov. 06		Garrison Co.
Laye, George	14 July 14	29 April 19	24 Mar. 25	24 Foot.
Lea, William	16 Jan. 04	24 July 05	25 Dec. 18	20 Dragoons.
Leach, Henry	never	5 July 15	25 Dec. 18	Scots Fus. Gds.
₽ Leaf, John Walton	31 Dec. 12	7 Dec. 13	25 July 16	52 Foot.
Leathes, Edward	14 Nov. 16	25 Sept. 23	6 May 24	8 Dragoons.
Leavach, John	17 Aug. 09	3 July 11	17 Feb. 20	3 West India Reg
Lee, Edward	26 Aug. 07	2 Feb. 09	24 Feb. 20	85 Foot.
Lee, George	30 April 12	5 Aug. 13	19 Mar. 18	21 Foot.
Leevis, Coakley	18 April 05	28 Oct. 07	6 Feb. 15	5 Garr. Batt.
₽ Legget, John	23 Feb. 08	15 Sept. 08	16 Oct. 16	3 Dragoon Gds.
Leigh, Geo. Henry John	4 Dec. 28	3 April 35	4 Aug. 37	20 Foot.
Leonard, Thomas	15 Mar. 10	1 Nov. 11	5 Aug. 16	Meuron's Reg.
Lerche, Gotlieb	14 May 12	19 Aug. 13	20 Feb. 16	R. Waggon Tr.
Leslie, Angus	12 Mar. 12	10 Feb. 14	25 Mar. 17	93 Foot.
Leslie, Anthony	2 Mar. 09	6 Feb. 12	25 Aug. 16	Glengarry Fen.
Leslie, John	25 April 16	9 Nov. 21	9 Nov. 21	18 Dragoons.
₽ L'Estrange, George	16 Jan. 12	17 June 13	11 July 22	Scots Fusil. Gds.
L'Estrange, Torriano Francis	20 Oct. 14	16 Oct. 17	16 Nov. 20	Coldstream Gds.
⚀⚀ Lewin, Carrigue [60]	3 Aug. 09	27 June 11	4 April 22	19 Dragoons.
₽ ⚀⚀ Lewin, Thomas Ross	27 Nov. 06	15 Dec. 08	26 Sept. 22	32 Foot.
Lewis, Henry	1 Sept. 06	4 Aug. 13	1 Sept. 14	R. Marines.
Lewis, James Cossley	6 June 05	28 Jan. 07	1814	56 Foot.
Lewis, Robert	23 Oct. 06	7 April 08	4 Feb. 19	15 Foot.
Lewis, Thomas	12 May 14	10 Oct. 15	25 Nov. 16	3 Garrison Batt.
Lewis, William	12 Mar. 10	10 May 14	20 July 20	19 Foot.
Liardet, Frederick	25 May 15	10 April 25	20 Sept. 26	Unattached.
Lidderdale, John	4 June 96	21 Feb. 99	6 Aug. 03	9 Foot.
Lind, Robert	11 Feb. 08	10 Oct. 09		1 R. Veteran Batt.
Lindsay, Alexander		25 Feb. 95		104 Foot.
₽ Lindsey, Henry John	5 Dec. 11	11 Jan. 16	31 Jan. 28	Unattached.
Lisle, Benjamin de	6 Dec. 10	2 Sept. 12	11 Oct. 16	Canadian Fen.
ℭ Lister, John [61]	23 Feb. 05	27 July 08	26 Nov. 25	R. Marines.
Little, John	27 April 09	9 Sept. 12	25 July 17	27 Foot.
Little, John William	1 Jan. 19	11 Mar. 24	11 July 29	Unattached.
* Little, Tenison	never	25 Dec. 13	25 Sept. 14	1 Foot.
Lloyd, Charles	5 June 06	28 Oct. 12	14 Nov. 26	R. Marines.
⚀⚀ Lloyd, Edward Bell	30 May 11	12 Mar. 12	5 Aug. 19	16 Dragoons.
Lloyd, John Ormsby	25 Nov. 13	14 May 18	15 Oct. 19	74 Foot.
Locke, William	9 June 14	3 July 17	20 Mar. 23	5 Dragoon Gds.
₽ ⚀⚀ Lockwood, Purefoy [62]	18 April 11	22 April 13	25 Aug. 16	30 Foot.

Lieutenants.

	CORNET, ETC.	LIEUT.	WHEN PLACED ON HALF PAY.	
Logan, David	1 Mar. 79	16 Sept. 82	1 Oct. 92	R. Marines.
Logie, John	27 Dec. 05	30 Mar. 11	6 Mar. 28	R. Marines.
Long, Edmund Slingsby	3 Aug. 04	8 Aug. 05	5 Aug. 13	23 Foot.
Long, William	17 Mar. 14	7 April 25	21 Nov. 28	Unattached.
Lonsdale, Alured	20 May 26	3 Aug. 30	8 April 36	84 Foot.
₽ ᴍ Lonsdale, William	1 Feb. 10	15 May 12	25 Mar. 17	4 Foot.
Lorimer, Charles Hunt	12 Jan. 05	28 April 06		8 R. Veteran Batt.
₽ Lorimer, William	25 July 05	18 June 07	25 Nov. 14	42 Foot.
₽ Love, James [63]	6 Nov. 09	19 Mar. 13	1 April 19	R. Artillery.
Lovelace, Henry Philip	25 Aug. 09	24 May 11	23 Aug. 27	Unattached.
Lovelock, John Birmingham	3 Aug. 09	4 July 11	25 Oct. 21	29 Foot.
Lovett, G. W. Molyneux	27 April 20	30 Nov. 24	6 Jan. 32	30 Foot.
Lovett, Henry William	2 June 04	18 June 07	19 Nov. 07	9 Foot.
* Lovett, Joseph Venables	never	25 Feb. 14	1814	3 Prov. Bn. of Mil.
Lovett, Thomas	1 April 09	17 April 12	1 Mar. 22	R. Artillery.
Lowe, Addison	18 Aug. 08	6 April 10		1 R. Veteran Batt.
Lowe, John	21 Sept. 12	16 June 14	25 Dec. 15	Nova Scotia Fen.
₽ Lowry, Armar	31 Dec. 12	28 July 14	1814	45 Foot.
Lowry, John	7 June 10	24 Dec. 12	13 July 20	95 Foot.
Lozon, Victor	Sept. 07	26 Feb. 08	14 April 08	62 Foot.
ᴍ Lucas, Jasper	6 Jan. 13	19 July 15	25 Mar. 17	32 Foot.
Luckett, James	31 Dec. 99	19 June 01	14 April 03	10 Dragoons.
* Luckhurst, Thomas	never	25 Jan. 14	1814	3 Prov. Bn. of Mil.
Lugard, John	20 May 95	11 Nov. 95	16 July 03	62 Foot.
Lupton, William	28 Nov. 11	9 Feb. 13	25 June 17	60 Foot.
₽ ᴍ Lye, Benjamin Leigh	4 Aug. 08	30 June 11	5 June 17	11 Dragoons.
Lynam, Charles	25 June 12	16 Nov. 15	25 Mar. 16	15 Foot.
Lynch, Anthony Francis William	2 Jan. 12	7 Dec. 13	28 Dec. 17	56 Foot.
Lynch, Edward Crean	11 Dec. 23	21 Jan. 26	8 April 34	22 Foot.
Lynch, Samuel Smith	7 April 14	16 Nov. 15	21 June 33	77 Foot.
Lynd, Robert	14 Feb. 16	31 Oct. 18	4 April 23	65 Foot.
Lyon, George	4 Sept. 06	10 Feb. 08	25 Nov. 18	99 Foot.
Lyster, Arthur O'Neil	2 Sept. 24	13 June 30	7 Sept. 33	46 Foot.
Lyster, Henry	29 May 17	7 Sept. 20	25 Oct. 21	7 Dragoons.
Lyster, William John		12 Mar. 83	25 June 10	8 Garr. Batt.
M'Anally, Charles	26 Nov. 06	31 Dec. 07	5 Oct. 20	84 Foot.
₽ ᴍ *M'Arthur, Charles* [64]	9 Nov. 09	17 Oct. 11		2 R. Veteran Batt.
M'Arthur, James Earle	17 May 11	4 Dec. 13	12 Oct. 19	14 Foot.
M'Arthur, John Doyne	9 July 03	18 Feb. 04		3 R. Veteran Batt.
M'Bean, Alexander	25 April 13	27 Nov. 13	25 Mar. 16	German Legion.
M'Carthy, Justin Thadeus Cour.	17 Jan. 33	13 Jan. 38	10 May 39	R. Marines.
M'Carthy, William	7 Oct. 13	18 July 16	25 Mar. 17	16 Foot.
M'Clintock, James	12 May 12	23 Nov. 15	25 Feb. 16	88 Foot.
M'Clure, Arthur	15 Jan. 07	26 April 09	5 Feb. 18	1 Foot.
₽ M'Cormick, James	25 May 09	17 Mar. 14	25 Dec. 18	94 Foot.
₽ *M'Crohan, Denis Eugene*	16 May 12	21 Oct. 13		3 R. Veteran Batt.
M'Cullock, James Murray	2 Nov. 98	17 July 04	11 June 16	R. Marines.
M'Dermott, James	15 Oct. 12	31 Mar. 14	25 Mar. 16	20 Dragoons.
M'Dermott, Thomas	1 Nov. 94	25 Feb. 05		7 R. Veteran Batt.
M'Dermott, William H. E.	28 Jan. 19	21 July 25	25 May 29	20 Foot.
M'Donald, Charles Alexander	2 July 12	3 Oct. 16	25 June 18	32 Foot.
M'Donald, Colin	25 Nov. 08	21 Feb. 11	25 Feb. 16	72 Foot.
₽ ᴍ M'Donald, Donald	22 Oct. 12	7 June 15	25 Feb. 16	40 Foot.
M'Donald, Duncan	9 July 03	19 Oct. 04		9 R. Veteran Batt.
M'Donell, Angus	6 Feb. 12	24 Feb. 14	25 Aug. 16	Glengarry Fen.
ᴍ M'Donough, Thomas	31 Aug. 07	30 Oct. 09	21 June 27	34 Foot.
M'Dougall, Hugh	4 June 12	14 April 14	25 Feb. 16	91 Foot.
M'Dougall, John Robert	6 May 77	12 Dec. 81	1783	8 Foot.
₽ M'Dougall, Patrick	28 Dec. 09	13 May 12	1814	48 Foot.
M'Dougall, Thomas William John	10 Mar. 28	5 July 30	6 Dec. 37	R. Marines.
M'Duff, Alexander	23 Feb. 09	9 July 12	15 May 18	100 Foot.
ᴍ M'Duffie, Donald	4 Feb. 13	10 Mar. 14	27 April 17	40 Foot.
M'Farlane, William	11 July 11	1 April 14	28 Aug. 23	17 Dragoons.

Lieutenants.

	CORNET, ETC.	LIEUT.	WHEN PLACED ON HALF PAY.	
M'Farlane, William	1 April 95	2 June 96	April 98	Campbell's Rec. Co.
M'Goldrick, Æneas	11 Nov. 13	15 Jan. 18	25 Feb. 22	62 Foot.
M'Gregor, John	12 May 20	22 Dec. 24	25 Dec. 28	46 Foot.
M'Gregor, John	11 Dec. 06	6 Feb. 08	23 June 25	3 West India Reg.
M'Illree, Robert William	25 Oct. 07	28 Feb. 11	25 Dec. 18	96 Foot.
ℬ M'Intosh, A. (Q. Mas. 12 Apr. 10.)	never	25 Dec. 14		4 R. Veteran Batt.
M'Intyre, Peter	21 Sept. 05	16 Mar. 09	1 Sept. 14	R. Marines.
M'Iver, Donald	22 Feb. 10	9 April 12	17 May 21	77 Foot.
M'Kay, John	6 Feb. 12	13 July 15	25 Aug. 16	Glengarry Fen.
M'Kellar, John	7 April 08	11 Oct. 09	25 Dec. 16	2 Garrison Batt.
M'Kenzie, John	31 Dec. 12	8 Sept. 14	11 Oct. 16	Canadian Fen.
M'Kenzie, William Fleming	18 April 11	10 Feb. 14	5 Feb. 29	Staff Corps.
M'Kinnon, John	18 Dec. 06	15 Mar. 10	25 July 17	104 Foot.
M'Lachlan, Lachlan	21 Sept. 96	11 Dec. 97	24 July 00	3 West India Reg.
ℬ M'Laren, Alexander Donald	3 June 12	31 Mar. 14	25 Feb. 16	91 Foot.
M'Lean, Archibald	24 Sept. 12	9 Mar. 15	25 Mar. 17	56 Foot.
M'Lelland, Robert	28 Dec. 06	27 Aug. 07		1 R. Veteran Batt.
M'Leod, James	21 Jan. 08	11 June 08		2 R. Veteran Batt.
M'Leod, William	26 June 10	20 Oct. 13	16 Sept. 23	34 Foot.
M'Leroth, Thomas	17 June 13	16 April 32	22 April 33	R. Marines.
M'Manus, Henry		23 June 04	25 Mar. 17	62 Foot.
M'Millan, John	17 Sept. 13	31 Aug. 15	10 Mar. 16	82 Foot
M'Mullen, Isaac	29 Nov. 10	19 Nov. 12	25 Mar. 17	11 Foot.
M'Nabb, John	28 Sept. 15	25 Mar. 24	18 May 26	Unattached.
M'Namara, Henry	1 Jan. 01	27 Nov. 01	25 June 02	62 Foot.
M'Namara, Michael	2 Nov. 09	28 Oct. 10	28 June 19	60 Foot.
M'Nicol, Duncan	16 Oct. 04	29 Feb. 08	15 Oct. 22	R. Marines.
ℬ M'Nicol, Nicol	14 May 12	10 Feb. 14	16 April 17	27 Foot.
M'Neil, Donald	23 Aug. 10	4 June 14	17 July 18	Cape Reg.
M'Phee, John	25 Feb. 13	17 July 15	25 Mar. 17	79 Foot.
ℬ M'Pherson, Æneas	25 June 12	26 Sept. 13	25 April 16	59 Foot.
ℳ M'Pherson, Alexander[65]	15 Dec. 08	22 Oct. 12	25 Mar. 17	92 Foot.
M'Queen, Robert	14 Sept. 13	1 Oct. 14	25 Dec. 18	25 Dragoons.
M'Rae, Farquhar	24 June 05	21 Jan. 08	7 Feb. 22	66 Foot.
M'Rae, Theodore	26 July 15	14 May 18	25 Dec. 18	African Corps.
Mac Alester, Charles Somerville	3 Nov. 80	27 Aug. 85		81 Foot.
Macalpine, James	5 Mar. 12	15 Aug. 13	25 July 20	8 Dragoons.
Macartney, Charles	11 Dec. 28	13 Nov. 34	1 Nov. 38	11 Dragoons.
Macdonald, Angus	3 May 10	13 Jan. 14	25 June 16	90 Foot.
Macdonald, James	29 Dec. 77	9 Sept. 80	1783	76 Foot.
ℬ Macdonald, John	22 April 13	20 May 14	25 Mar. 17	74 Foot.
ℳ Macdonald, John	18 May 09	30 April 12	9 May 17	91 Foot.
Macdonald, John	6 Feb. 14	26 June 19	12 June 23	4 West India Reg.
Macdonald, Stephen	22 Dec. 12	5 April 14	25 April 16	German Legion.
ℬ Mac Donell, Alexander	5 June 09	5 April 10		7 R. Veteran Batt.
Macdonell, Donald Æneas	7 Aug. 13	29 Nov. 15	25 Sept. 17	98 Foot.
Macdonell, Duncan	26 Sept. 94	15 July 95		Elford's Co.
Mac Donogh, Montagu	13 Feb. 12	8 July 13	25 Feb. 16	4 Foot.
ℬ Macdougall, Colin	12 Oct. 09	19 July 13	1815	91 Foot.
Mac Gachen, John	5 Dec. 11	28 Dec. 14	20 Feb. 19	72 Foot.
Mac Gibbon, Robert	22 Nov. 10	14 May 12	25 Mar. 17	45 Foot.
Mac Gregor, John[66]	9 May 11	26 Jan. 14		4 R. Veteran Batt.
ℳ Machell, John Thomas	12 Aug. 13	24 Feb. 14	10 Nov. 21	18 Dragoons.
Macintire, Andrew	27 Feb. 12	9 Oct. 27	28 Sept. 30	York Rangers.
Mackay, Hugh	30 Dec. 81	25 Dec. 82		Queen's Amer. Ran.
ℬ Mac Kay, Lachlan[67]	31 Oct. 11	23 Sept. 13	18 Jan. 31	42 Foot.
Mackay, Hugh Donald	1 April 13	31 Mar. 14	1 Oct. 17	5 West India Reg.
Mackay, Niel	9 May 05	27 Feb. 06	25 Oct. 19	76 Foot.
Mackay, Robert	7 Sept. 09	26 July 10	27 Jan. 19	22 Foot.
Mackenzie, Alastair	8 Jan. 24	19 Sept. 26	4 Oct. 31	30 Foot.
Mackenzie, William	20 July 15	7 Sept. 20	25 Oct. 21	3 Dragoons.
ℬ *Mackie, John*	1 June 09	23 Jan. 13		7 R. Veteran Batt.
ℳ Mackinlay, John[68]	12 May 08	2 Nov. 09	25 Feb. 17	92 Foot.
Mackintosh, John	5 July 03	15 Aug. 05	12 Mar. 23	R. Marines.

Lieutenants.

	ENSIGN, ETC.	LIEUT.	WHEN PLACED ON HALF PAY.	
Mackintosh, Phineas.............		27 Nov. 94	1800	91 Foot.
Maclauchlan, James Augustus....	5 Mar. 12	24 Feb. 14	25 July 17	104 Foot.
Maclean, George.................	18 Jan. 15	15 Aug. 26	25 Jan. 30	African Corps.
ᛈ Maclean, John	11 Dec. 06	17 Dec. 07	25 Dec. 17	53 Foot.
ᛘ Macnab, Duncan	16 Dec. 13	17 July 17	25 Dec. 18	52 Foot.
Macnab, John...................	4 July 11	16 Feb. 15	25 Dec. 18	94 Foot.
* Macnamara, Michael	never	25 Feb. 14	1814	1 Prov. Bn. of Mil.
Macpherson, Duncan.............	26 Mar. 08	2 Jan. 12	13 Dec. 16	52 Foot.
Macpherson, Lachlan	21 Aug. 09	20 Mar. 00		52 Foot.
Madden, Henry.................	25 July 95	22 Feb. 99		R. Irish Art.
ᛈ Magee, James Fitz Maurice....	22 Aug. 11	12 Aug. 13	25 Mar. 17	38 Foot.
Magin, William	2 July 03	15 Aug. 05	25 Sept. 09	R. Marines.
Maher, Martin.................	6 April 09	17 Jan. 11		7 R. Veteran Batt.
Mahon, Edmond	12 Mar. 12	15 June 15	4 Nov. 17	70 Foot.
Mahon, James...................	2 Jan. 12	2 Feb. 14	25 Dec. 14	26 Foot.
Major, Stephen	3 Oct. 09	26 July 10	25 Mar. 17	13 Foot.
ᛈ ᛘ Mann, James[69]............	5 Aug. 13	18 Aug. 14	18 July 16	1 Foot.
Manners, George	15 Dec. 08	12 Sept. 11	25 Mar. 17	25 Foot.
Manners, John	24 Feb. 96	26 Sept. 98	29 Nov. 08	R. Marines.
Marcer, Richard Harvey	1 Aug. 09	18 Aug. 04	9 Jan. 16	R. Marines.
Marchington, Joseph.............	12 April 07	7 May 12	15 Oct. 16	13 Dragoons.
Marder, Henry	22 Nov. 98	1 June 99	24 Jan. 03	71 Foot.
Markham, Thomas...............	24 Aug. 81	30 Sept. 82	1783	83 Foot.
Marklove, John	8 April 13	20 June 16	28 Dec. 17	56 Foot.
Marrie, James[70]	8 Mar. 96	8 Dec. 98	18 Feb. 04	R. Marines.
Marsh, Henry...................		8 July 95		Indep. Co.
Marsh, John	27 June 05	9 Nov. 07		9 R. Veteran Batt.
Marshall, Ralph	3 Feb. 08	12 April 10	12 June 23	89 Foot.
Marshall, Thomas	2 Sept. 98	1 April 04	14 Aug. 07	R. Marines.
ᛈ ᛘ Martin, Benjamin	26 Dec. 98	3 June 02	11 Nov. 18	85 Foot.
Martin, Edward		3 Dec. 00		R. Artillery.
ᛘ Martin, Henry	28 May 12	31 Mar. 14	25 Mar. 16	44 Foot.
ᛈ ᛘ Martin, Henry	3 June 12	21 Oct. 13	25 Dec. 18	51 Foot.
Martin, Johnston	25 Jan. 12	29 Oct. 12	24 April 16	Bourbon Reg.
Martin, Robert	18 Nov. 78	24 Aug. 81	1 Sept. 83	R. Marines.
Martin, Richard Bartholomew....	12 April 21	9 April 26	15 June 30	Unattached.
Martin, Thomas.................	25 Sept. 87	16 Jan. 93	7 April 03	35 Foot.
Martin, William Neufville	15 April 12	3 Mar. 14	15 Mar. 17	64 Foot.
Martyn, Charles	25 June 02	25 Dec. 02		7 R. Veteran Batt.
Mason, Francis	25 June 05	9 Oct. 06	22 Mar. 10	8 Garr. Batt.
Mason, James...................	5 Jan. 09	9 May 11	25 Mar. 17	11 Foot.
Mason, Robert	7 Mar. 94	24 April 95	18 Oct. 03	R. Marines.
* Mason, Robert James..........	never	25 April 14	1814	1 Prov. Bn. of Mil.
Masters, John...................	9 Mar. 15	7 July 37	26 Jan. 39	
Masters, Stephen	13 Nov. 05	15 Jan. 07	2 July 17	30 Foot.
Matheson, Roderick	6 Feb. 12	5 Aug. 13	4 Dec. 16	Glengarry Fen.
ᛈ Mathews, Joseph	6 April 09	13 June 11	25 June 17	83 Foot.
ᛈ Mathison, John Augustus......	8 May 11	12 Aug. 13	25 Mar. 17	77 Foot.
ᛘ Matthews, John Powell......	3 Nov. 14	7 April 25	31 Dec. 30	10 Foot.
ᛘ Matthews, William M'Donald[71]	25 Dec. 13	7 Jan. 19	26 Jan. 26	62 Foot.
Maunsell, George	18 Oct. 10	28 Jan. 12	25 June 16	87 Foot.
* Mawby, Joseph	never	9 Mar. 14	1814	3 Prov. Bn. of Mil.
Mawhood, William John	7 Oct. 77	21 Nov. 78	1783	80 Foot.
Maxwell, John	18 July 11	24 Dec. 12	1816	8 West India Reg.
Maxwell, Joseph................	7 Mar. 11	19 May 13	25 Sept. 18	99 Foot.
Mayhew, Henry	7 Mar. 00	23 May 04	7 Dec. 14	1 Garr. Batt.
Meade, Thomas Harold..........	4 Oct. 10	27 July 12	10 July 17	13 Foot.
Meares, John	20 Mar. 09	18 Sept. 27	2 Oct. 28	R. Marines.
Meech, Robert	17 Jan. 10	19 June 11	10 Aug. 20	43 Foot.
Mellish, William................	29 Nov. 05	17 Nov. 08	16 Mar. 15	R. Waggon Tr.
Mence, Haffez..................	13 Aug. 12	27 April 15	25 Mar. 17	32 Foot.
Menzies, Alexander ......: ...	25 Aug. 08	11 May 09		5 R. Veteran Batt.
Menzies, George................	15 Oct. 12	16 Mar. 15	25 Mar. 17	93 Foot.
Mercer, Alexander..............	15 April 13	1 June 15	25 Mar. 17	42 Foot.

Lieutenants.

	2D LIEUT. ETC.	LIEUT.	WHEN PLACED ON HALF PAY.	
Meredith, Boyle	29 Mar. 10	1 July 13	24 Oct. 22	16 Foot.
Meredith, George	9 Aug. 96	1 Oct. 01		R. Marines.
ⓦ Meuron, John Frederick de ..	15 April 12	19 Aug. 12	24 Feb. 16	German Legion.
ⓦ Middleton, Thos. Falkner	28 Oct. 13	4 May 15	25 July 16	1 Dragoon Gds.
ℙ Miles, George................	25 May 09	16 May 11	14 Mar. 22	7 Foot.
Miles, John....................	15 Dec. 99	5 Feb. 01		8 R. Veteran Batt.
ℙ Miles, John Marshall	10 Dec. 12	23 Feb. 14	25 Mar. 17	43 Foot.
ℙ ⓦ Mill, James [72]	12 April 09	18 Sept. 11	4 April 22	2 West India Reg.
Miller, David	19 April 05	27 July 08	4 Jan. 25	R. Marines.
Miller, Donald	30 May 11	6 April 14	25 Oct. 21	33 Foot.
* Miller, Gavin	never	25 Dec. 13	26 Sept. 14	19 Foot.
Miller, Henry	14 Mar. 04	15 Sept. 06	1 Sept. 14	R. Marines.
ⓦ Miller, John................	13 Jan. 25	22 April 26	30 June 37	66 Foot.
Miller, William	10 July 15	7 April 21	25 Jan. 25	R. Artillery.
Miller, Zaccheus [73]	20 May 97	19 July 03		R. Marines.
Mills, James	3 Dec. 25	12 Dec. 26	3 Sept. 29	30 Foot.
Mills, Thomas..................	28 Jan. 13	25 Aug. 14	25 May 18	100 Foot.
ℙ *Milne, James Miles*	2 Mar. 08	31 Mar. 10		5 R. Veteran Batt.
Milnes, Alfred Shore...........	5 July 13	15 Jan. 16	5 Sept. 22	R. Artillery.
Milnes, Thomas Milnes Smith	28 Nov. 11	9 Feb. 15	25 Mar. 17	28 Foot.
Minchin, Charles Humphrey	1 Jan. 14	1 Aug. 14	24 June 19	R. Engineers.
Minchin, George................	25 Mar. 13	25 Dec. 14	25 May 16	New Brunsw. Fen.
Minty, John	21 Feb. 11	27 Oct. 14	26 Feb. 15	2 Garr. Batt.
Mitchell, John	7 Mar. 11	4 Mar. 13	25 Jan. 17	78 Foot.
Mitchell, Robert...............	15 Feb. 10	11 Feb. 13	25 Mar. 17	28 Foot.
ℙ ⓦ Moffat, Abraham	5 Aug. 13	22 June 15	25 Feb. 16	71 Foot.
ℙ Mogridge, James Edward......	11 April 09	28 June 10	2 Oct. 17	34 Foot.
ⓦ Moller, Charles Champion ..	16 June 14	19 April 15	23 April 17	18 Dragoons.
Monck, Charles Stanley	10 Oct. 11	31 Dec. 12	25 Mar. 17	44 Foot.
Money, George	1 Jan. 12	15 July 13	25 Mar. 17	12 Foot.
Money, Richard	23 Mar. 94	1 Mar. 00	25 Sept. 02	24 Dragoons.
Monro, Frederick	20 Dec. 09	3 Sept. 13	23 June 24	R. Artillery.
Monro, Hector William Bower....	9 Dec. 13	3 May 14	29 May 23	65 Foot.
ℙ Moody, Thomas	30 June 08	1 June 09	10 Aug. 20	Meuron's Reg.
Moore, James Adolphus [74]......	14 Oct. 05	14 May 10	8 Sept. 20	R. Marines.
* Moore, Joshua John	never	25 Dec. 13	25 Sept. 14	14 Foot.
Moore, Richard	26 June 99	16 May 00	29 Nov. 02	27 Foot.
Moore, Samuel	27 May 13	7 Mar. 16	4 June 18	7 Foot.
* Moore, Samuel	never	25 Dec. 13	25 Sept. 14	38 Foot.
ℙ ⓦ Moorhead, Charles	23 Aug. 10	3 Sept. 12	25 Dec. 18	71 Foot.
Moreton, Moses	26 Nov. 07	28 Apr. 08	4 Sept. 17	54 Foot.
Morgan, Edward	9 July 03	15 Aug. 05	25 Jan. 16	R. Marines.
Morgan, John	2 Jan. 12	11 Aug. 13	25 Jan. 18	12 Foot.
Morgan, Thomas................	2 Oct. 00	30 Mar. 05	17 Oct. 14	R. Marines.
Moriaty, James Robert	11 Sept. 05	10 Nov. 08	1 Sept. 14	R. Marines.
Moley, Edward Lacy	16 Aug. 10	13 Jan. 13	25 Mar. 17	York Rangers.
ℙ Morphy, Richard	2 April 12	26 Aug. 13	25 Mar. 17	3 Foot.
Morris, Francis Anthony	18 Jan. 16	19 Feb. 24	10 June 25	88 Foot.
Morrish, James	30 May 05	27 July 08	1 Sept. 14	R. Marines.
ℙ *Morrison, J. Whiteford*	26 Aug. 07	17 Aug. 09		9 R. Veteran Batt.
Morton, William	10 Nov. 13	1 Sept. 16	25 Nov. 17	66 Foot.
Morton, William	9 Aug. 99	21 Feb. 00		French's Rec. Co.
Moss, George	23 Dec. 13	16 Nov. 15	18 Aug. 16	8 West India Reg.
Mosse, Henry Alexander	31 Dec. 07	4 Jan. 10	25 Mar. 19	94 Foot.
Mosse, Peter Benjamin..........	20 May 10	3 May 12	25 Sept. 17	80 Foot.
Mostyn, Robert	28 Aug. 08	26 Sept. 11	18 April 17	81 Foot.
Moulin, Andrew du	10 Aug. 96	16 Mar. 97	23 July 02	9 Foot.
* Mount, Edward	never	25 Dec. 13		1814 R. Waggon Train.
ⓦ Mount Edgcumbe, E. A. *Earl of*	never	12 Jan. 14	25 Feb. 19	Grenadier Gds.
Mountford, Joseph..............	12 April 06	2 June 12	1 Sept. 14	R. Marines,
Muckleston, Edward	14 Dec. 08	27 June 11	13 Oct. 17	25 Foot.
Mulhallen, Robert	8 Oct. 12	31 Aug. 15	25 Mar. 16	3 Dragoon Gds.
Munro, Donald	14 June 10	6 Mar. 12		7 R. Veteran Batt.
ℙ Munro, Frederick [75]	20 Dec. 09	3 Sept. 13	23 June 24	R. Artillery.

Lieutenants.

	ENSIGN, ETC.	LIEUT.	WHEN PLACED ON HALF PAY.	
Munro, John	22 Nov. 98	17 Sept. 01		3 R. Veteran Batt.
Murchison, Kenneth	23 July 07	21 June 10		3 R. Veteran Batt.
ℳ Mure, George	never	14 April 14	15 June 20	Grenadier Gds.
Murray, Alexander............	18 Mar. 97	12 July 03	15 Nov. 03	R. Marines.
Murray, Edward..............	28 Feb. 05	25 Sept. 07	25 Nov. 18	99 Foot.
Murray, Edward	28 April 13	11 Aug. 14	9 June 25	Unattached.
ℙ Murray, Francis	29 June 09	7 July 14	25 Dec. 18	94 Foot.
ℙ Muskett, Thomas Willis[76]	17 May 07	11 Mar. 09	1 July 16	R. Art. Drivers.
* Myers, William	never	25 Dec. 13	1814	2 Prov. Bn. of Mil.
Nangle, George	29 Jan. 06	30 June 08	4 Sept. 17	76 Foot.
Nankivell, James	16 Dec. 99	16 Nov. 00		98 Foot.
ℙ Nantes, Richard.............	never	19 Oct. 09	1814	55 Foot.
Napier, Duncan Campbell	24 Feb. 14	4 May 15	5 Aug. 16	Meuron's Reg.
Napper, Alexander	26 Oct. 07	16 Mar. 09	11 July 16	81 Foot.
ℙ Nash, Henry	29 Oct. 12	28 April 14	13 April 17	9 Foot.
Nash, James	24 Jan. 99	11 Dec. 99	6 April 03	4 Foot.
ℳ Nash, John[77]	18 Nov. 13	19 July 15	11 May 17	79 Foot.
* Nash, William...............	never	25 Jan. 14	1814	3 Prov. Bn. of Mil.
Nason, Henry................	19 Sept. 11	29 Feb. 16	25 Dec. 16	8 West India Reg.
Nayler, Charles	24 June 13	2 June 14	25 May 15	63 Foot.
Naylor, Edward[78]	6 May 99	18 Aug. 04	16 Dec. 15	R. Marines.
Neligan, Thomas	28 Nov. 10	11 Nov. 13	25 Sept. 17	83 Foot.
ℙ Nelson, John Clarke..........	16 May 11	25 Aug. 13	18 May 15	28 Foot.
Nembhard, Thomas Hay	16 Aug. 27	5 April 33	2 Nov. 38	38 Foot.
Nesfield, William Andrews	26 June 12	30 Mar. 14	25 Dec. 18	48 Foot.
* Newbolt, Francis	never	25 Dec. 13	1814	R. Waggon Train.
Newman, Joseph	21 July 08	19 Oct. 10	25 Dec. 14	31 Foot.
Newton, Beauchamp Bartholomew	28 Mar. 16	28 June 21	4 Dec. 23	34 Foot.
Newton, Hibbert	27 July 09	13 April 13	25 Mar. 17	32 Foot.
Newton, John................	16 Sept. 95	2 Dec. 95	23 Aug. 02	15 Dragoons.
Newton, Thomas Charles	23 April 13	7 Sept. 15	25 June 16	R. Waggon Train.
Newton, Walter	6 Apr. 09	2 Nov. 10	2 Aug. 20	21 Dragoons.
Neynoe, Joseph	17 July 00	25 June 03		5 R. Veteran Bat.
ℳ Nicholson, John	25 Dec. 13	5 April 15	25 Mar. 16	14 Foot.
Nicholson, Ralph	29 May 10	31 Dec. 12	27 July 20	101 Foot.
ℙ Nicholson, Richard	27 Dec. 10	7 Oct. 13	25 July 16	5 Foot.
Nicholson, Robert Dring	29 Nov. 10	21 April 14	25 Feb. 16	58 Foot.
𝒯 Nicolas, Paule Harris[79].......	6 July 05	27 July 08	1 Sept. 14	R. Marines.
Nicoll, Benjamin David.........	1 Jan. 06	1 Sept. 08	1 Aug. 16	R. Art. Drivers.
Niess, John.................	5 Nov. 12	8 Feb. 16		3 R. Veteran Bat.
Nisbett, Henry	20 Mar. 06	16 Feb. 09	25 Dec. 18	24 Dragoons.
ℙ ℳ Nixon, William Richmond..	26 July 10	11 May 12	25 Nov. 19	52 Foot.
Norman, William	7 Mar. 10	14 May 12	25 April 26	69 Foot.
Norris, Robert	9 May 16	18 Mar. 18	31 Dec. 18	20 Dragoons.
Nowlan, Thomas.............	12 Aug. 13	18 May 15	26 Oct. 30	West India Rang.
ℙ Nowlan, William	3 Jan. 06	12 Jan. 09	22 June 20	91 Foot.
ℳ Nugent, Edward............	23 Dec. 13	7 Dec. 20	14 Dec. 26	Unattached.
Nugent, Walter	8 June 09	9 Nov. 09	25 Mar. 11	26 Foot.
ℳ Oakes, *Sir* Henry Thomas, *Bt.*	22 Oct. 12	11 Feb. 14	25 Mar. 17	95 Foot.
O'Brien, Cunningham Por.	4 Mar. 13	14 Sept. 15	25 Mar. 17	95 Foot.
O'Brien, James..............	6 Dec. 10	28 July 12		6 R. Veteran Batt.
* O'Brien, John	never	25 Dec. 13	25 Sept. 14	16 Foot.
O'Connell, Maurice	22 Sept. 13	4 Oct. 15	21 Aug. 23	York Rangers.
O'Connor, Bernard Richard	18 May 09	22 Nov. 10	18 July 16	44 Foot.
ℙ O'Connor, James	22 Oct. 12	19 Jan. 15	2 April 16	27 Foot.
ℙ O'Connor, Maurice	10 Aug. 08	25 Oct. 10	20 Jan. 20	97 Foot.
ℙ O'Connor, Patrick	23 Oct. 07	6 Oct. 08	22 Jan. 18	11 Foot.
O'Dell, Edm. Westropp	12 Sept. 05	13 Aug. 07	25 Sept. 18	98 Foot.
O'Dogherty, Francis Blake	17 June 95	26 Jan. 97	16 June 00	R. Marines.
O'Flyn, Andrew	3 Feb. 08	27 Oct. 08	19 Aug. 19	87 Foot.
ℙ Ogilvy, David...............	18 May 09	17 Feb. 14	25 Dec. 18	94 Foot.
O'Halloran, Maurice	25 July 11	10 June 13	25 May 17	62 Foot.

Lieutenants.

	CORNET, ETC.	LIEUT.	WHEN PLACED ON HALF PAY.	
ぱ ㎜ O'Hara, Patterson........	8 Nov. 10	2 Sept. 12	25 Mar. 16	59 Foot.
O'Kelly, James	8 Mar. 10	16 Nov. 12	20 Mar. 23	4 Foot.
Olding, Nicholas Purdue		25 June 81		Donkin's Corp.
* Oliver, John.................	never	25 Dec. 13	25 Sept. 14	33 Foot.
Olpherts, Robert	18 June 18	13 April 20	20 Sept. 26	Unattached.
O'Neill, Henry	30 June 25	29 Aug. 26	11 July 37	Unattached.
O'Neill, John Augustus...........	8 June 15	31 Aug. 15	25 May 16	13 Dragoons.
O'Neill, John	9 April 12	29 Feb. 16	15 Feb. 33	Unattached.
㎜ Onslow, Phipps Vansittart⁶⁰..	17 Dec. 07	16 Dec. 08	9 Dec. 24	R. Artillery.
O'Regan, Thomas	21 Feb. 05	2 Oct. 06		4 R. Veteran Batt.
ぱ O'Reilly, John	25 April 11	16 Sept. 13	25 May 16	11 Foot.
Ormsby, Henry Michael	2 Jan. 12	1 Oct. 12	25 Mar. 17	36 Foot.
ぱ Ormsby, James	10 Oct. 06	14 Mar. 08	10 Feb. 20	25 Dragoons.
ぱ Ormsby, Sewell	7 Mar. 05	8 Jan. 07	11 Dec. 17	6 Foot.
Orr, James	26 Nov. 04	27 July 08	1 April 17	R. Marines.
ぱ ㎜ *Orr, John* ⁶¹	3 Oct. 11	29 April 13		8 R. Veteran Batt.
Orr, John	14 July 08	13 Oct. 08	25 Dec. 17	89 Foot.
ぱ Orrell, Andrew	30 May 11	21 April 14	25 June 17	34 Foot.
ぱ Osborne, Darragh	18 June 07	11 May 09	9 May 22	100 Foot.
O'Sullivan, Eugene	3 June 08	20 Feb. 12	18 Sept. 17	98 Foot.
Ottey, John..................	14 May 12	9 Dec. 13	25 May 17	37 Foot.
Ottley, Benjamin Robert	14 Mar. 11	16 July 12	25 April 22	61 Foot.
Oughton, James	20 Feb. 12	20 Oct. 16	25 Mar. 19	61 Foot.
ぱ Owens, John Walker	29 Sept. 08	7 Feb. 11	25 Sept. 17	31 Foot.
㎜ Pagan, Samuel Alexander ⁶²...	31 Oct. 11	7 April 14	14 Feb. 22	55 Foot.
Paget, Robert	4 June 12	17 Feb. 14		7 R. Veteran Batt.
Palling, John Graveley	21 Dec. 13	21 Nov. 17	25 July 19	24 Dragoons.
Palmer, Humphrey	3 Aug. 09	11 Oct. 10	27 April 15	47 Foot.
Pannell, Robert	30 Mar. 12	2 Aug. 13	25 June 19	60 Foot.
Parke, Samuel	9 Feb. 09	4 Mar. 11	7 Sept. 15	2 Garrison Batt.
Parker, Frederick	4 Mar. 09	7 Jan. 26	6 Mar. 28	R. Marines.
Parker, Henry	18 Nov. 11	22 July 30	29 June 31	R. Marines.
Parker, John Frederick	21 Mar. 82	29 May 83	31 Jan. 84	105 Foot.
Parker, Kenyon S...............	26 Nov. 05	15 Jan. 11	1 Sept. 14	R. Marines.
*Parker, Michael	never	25 Jan. 14	1814	3 Prov. Bn. of Mil.
Parker, Thomas Robert	6 Aug. 07	23 Sept. 08		6 R. Veteran Batt.
㎜ Parkinson, Robert............	22 April 13	4 May 15	30 Oct. 17	R. Waggon Train.
ぱ Parratt, Killebrant Mered. ⁶³	29 Oct. 08	11 July 11	12 Sept. 22	R. Artillery.
ぱ ㎜ Parry, James	10 Sept. 12	27 Jan. 14	25 Mar. 17	28 Foot.
*Parry, Thomas	never	25 Feb. 14	1814	3 Prov. Bn. of Mil.
Parsons, Rich. Tapper	18 May 99	18 Aug. 04	5 May 08	R. Marines.
Paterson, Alexander	25 July 12	4 June 13	25 April 16	German Legion.
Paton, George	12 July 10	1 July 12	25 Sept. 16	22 Dragoons.
Patten, William	14 July 25	16 Nov. 27	28 Sept. 39	R. Artillery.
Patterson, Edward	1 Sept. 08	20 Sept. 10	25 Sept. 17	31 Foot.
Patterson, John Williams........	18 April 11	3 Sept. 12	11 Oct. 19	60 Foot.
ぱ Pattison, Joseph	21 Feb. 11	2 Jan. 12	3 Nov. 14	5 Dragoon Guards.
Pawley, George	21 Mar. 05	9 Oct. 06	14 April 08	Murray's Rec. Cos.
ぱ Paxton, Archibald Frederick ..	26 June 11	19 Dec. 11	23 July 17	11 Dragoons.
Peach, John Carroll	3 Sept. 12	25 Aug. 14	25 Feb. 19	African Corps.
Peacock, Robert................	9 Dec. 13	14 July 14	25 Mar. 16	44 Foot.
Pearson, Matthew	April 94	19 July 94		95 Foot.
Pearson, William Rex	11 Mar. 09	11 Feb. 26	3 Mar. 29	R. Marines.
Peddie, William	2 Jan. 10	30 Jan. 12	20 April 17	21 Foot.
Peel, Edmund.................	15 Mar. 15	13 Mar. 17	2 May 22	25 Foot.
Peel, Robert Haworth	7 Mar. 16	17 Oct. 16	16 June 30	Unattached.
Peers, Henry de Linné	29 Jan. 12	22 July 13	17 Aug. 20	53 Foot.
ぱ Pell, Edwin	27 July 09	25 Mar. 13	25 Sept. 17	36 Foot.
ぱ Penfold, Edward	29 Aug. 11	25 Mar. 12	25 Mar. 17	14 Dragoons.
Pengelly, Edward	5 July 03	15 Aug. 05	21 Jan. 23	R. Marines.
ぱ Pennefather, Richard	14 June 10	26 Sept. 11	31 July 17	87 Foot.
ぱ *Pennington, Rowland*	8 Sept. 08	23 May 11		5 R. Veteran Batt.
Pepper, Theobald	14 Sept. 08	27 June 11	25 Mar. 16	3 Dragoon Guards.

Lieutenants.

	2D LIEUT. ETC.	LIEUT.	WHEN PLACED ON HALF PAY.	
Perceval, Charles	13 June 11	4 Mar. 13	19 Oct. 20	68 Foot.
Percy, Francis	22 July 13	16 Oct. 17	25 Dec. 18	51 Foot.
Perham, John	26 June 06	9 Feb. 13	9 Sept. 26	R. Marines.
Perham, William	20 Sept. 05	20 Feb. 09	1 Sept. 14	R. Marines.
Perkins, Thomas Steele	4 Dec. 98	18 Aug. 04	16 Jan. 16	R. Marines.
Perring, *Sir John, Bt.*	2 May 11	13 Feb. 12	25 Dec. 18	25 Dragoons.
* Perrott, Robert	never	2 Dec. 99	25 May 02	4 Foot.
Perry, Henry	5 Jan. 05	18 Aug. 14	31 Jan. 15	R. Waggon Train.
Perry, Richard Lavite	20 Dec. 10	3 Sept. 12	25 Mar. 17	44 Foot.
Peterson, Charles	15 Mar. 31	26 June 35	1 Nov. 38	11 Dragoons.
⑱ Petre, Henry William	14 May 07	26 Jan. 00	18 Feb. 19	18 Dragoons.
Phair, William Barry	9 July 07	7 Dec. 09	25 July 17	104 Foot.
Phibbs, Rutledge	18 Oct. 10	13 Aug. 12	18 July 16	10 Foot.
⑫ ⑱ Philipps, Grismond	3 Aug. 09	5 Sept. 11	26 Aug. 19	97 Foot.
Phillips, John (*Cornet*)	17 Nov. 96		25 Nov. 02	R. Waggon Train.
* Phillips, John	never	25 Nov. 99		Independ. Cos.
⑫ Phillips, Robert Jocelyn	20 July 09	6 Oct. 12	25 Mar. 15	27 Foot.
Phillipson, John Burton	25 April 02	14 Mar. 05	18 Feb. 19	1 Dragoon Guards.
⑱ Philpot, Edward [64]	16 Aug. 06	1 Sept. 08	1 Aug. 16	R. Art. Drivers.
Pickard, Henry William [85]	17 Dec. 12	21 May 15	29 April 31	R. Artillery.
Pickring, Joseph	8 Oct. 12	16 Nov. 13	25 Feb. 16	4 Foot.
Pictet, Armand Jaques [86]	9 Feb. 15	6 April 20	21 Feb. 28	Unattached.
Pictet, Frederick	25 June 12	22 Jan. 14	24 Sept. 19	60 Foot.
Pigou, Laurence	17 Nov. 14	8 Aug. 16	25 Mar. 17	2 Dragoon Guards.
Pigou, William George	3 Oct. 16	8 Feb. 21	1 May 23	83 Foot.
Pike, John	20 Oct. 08	25 June 12		6 R. Veteran Batt.
Pinhey, William Towley	1 Oct. 05	25 Sept. 09	1 April 17	R. Marines.
Pinniger, Broome	2 April 12	1 Dec. 13	28 Dec. 17	6 West India Regt.
Piper, Thomas	14 Jan. 01	15 Aug. 05	11 Nov. 08	R. Marines.
Playfair, Andrew William	26 April 10	7 Nov. 11	25 July 17	104 Foot.
* Plowman, Thomas	never	25 Dec. 13	1814	R. Waggon Train.
⑫ Plunkett, Edmund Henry [87]	2 Mar. 07	13 July 09	22 June 32	14 Foot.
Plunkett, Thomas Richard	6 Mar. 11	1 July 13	6 Oct. 25	18 Dragoons.
⑫ Poe, Purefoy	13 June 09	1 July 13	17 April 17	30 Foot.
⑱ Polhill, William	1 July 13	13 Dec. 15	10 Jan. 19	23 Dragoons.
Pontcarré, E. L. E. C. De	12 Mar. 06	26 July 10	17 Jan. 15	R. For. Artillery.
Pook, George Anthony	9 May 11	25 Nov. 13	7 June 33	61 Foot.
⑫ Poole, Walter Croker	21 Dec. 09	26 Mar. 12	1815	88 Foot.
Porter, Henry	7 July 03	15 Aug. 05	9 Sept. 14	R. Marines.
Porter, Robert	7 Dec. 00	3 Mar. 12	11 April 16	7 Foot.
⑫ Pountney, Henry James	31 May 09	16 June 11	13 Feb. 17	71 Foot.
Powell, James Bruce	22 June 09	26 Feb. 12	16 April 18	12 Foot.
Powell, John Harcourt	10 Dec. 12	30 Mar. 13	25 Jan. 15	7 Dragoons.
⑫ Pratt, George	4 Dec. 06	9 Mar. 09	25 July 17	27 Foot.
Pratt, Richard	1 Dec. 04	10 Sept. 07	25 June 18	50 Foot.
Price, Stephen	10 Oct. 09	10 Oct. 10	25 Dec. 18	60 Foot.
* Prichard, Thomas	never	28 Nov. 99	25 June 01	36 Foot.
Pridham, William [88]	13 June 99	18 Aug. 04	23 Oct. 16	R. Marines.
⑫ Priest, *John* [89]	13 July 05	1 Jan. 06		R. Art. Drivers.
Pringle, James	3 Aug. 09	5 Aug. 13	18 April 17	81 Foot.
Pritchard, John		19 Oct. 94		3 R. Veteran Batt.
Probyn, John	4 June 01	14 April 04	16 June 08	20 Foot.
Purcell, Ignatius	never	21 Dec. 94		R. Irish Artillery.
Purdon, Philip	10 Sept. 12	27 Dec. 13	25 Mar. 17	41 Foot.
Purefoy, Arnold Nesbitt	12 June 09	1 April 13	14 Dec. 32	21 Foot.
* Pycroft, Charles	never	25 Dec. 13	25 Sept. 14	14 Foot.
⑱ Quill, Henry [90]	16 Mar. 09	17 Dec. 12		9 R. Veteran Batt.
Ragg, Samuel	1 Feb. 10	5 Mar. 12		1 R. Veteran Batt.
Rainsforth, Charles	2 Sept. 12	5 Feb. 16	28 Feb. 20	67 Foot.
Rainsforth, Charles	2 Feb. 15	8 April 25	19 May 25	Unattached.
Ramsden, George	10 July 15	7 Nov. 21	30 Mar. 25	R. Artillery.
Rancland, John	22 Sept. 12	6 July 14	28 Dec. 17	56 Foot.
⑫ Ranie, Frederic James	31 Dec. 12	6 Aug. 18	1 Oct. 37	95 Foot.

Lieutenants.

Name	CORNET, ETC.	LIEUT.	WHEN PLACED ON HALF PAY.	
Rankin, Coun Douly	21 June 10	2 Nov. 11	4 April 16	8 Foot.
Rankine, David	25 Feb. 13	17 Nov. 14	25 Dec. 18	Rifle Brigade.
Ratcliffe, William	25 Aug. 07	13 April 09	6 Dec. 14	1 Garrison Batt.
Rawlins, John Hart	18 Feb. 13	20 Nov. 17	3 Dec. 18	13 Foot.
Rawstorne, Fleetwood	3 July 06	7 July 08	8 April 26	Unattached.
ℬ Raymond, William	12 Jan. 09	1 Aug. 11	9 Nov. 15	31 Foot.
Rea, Andrew Charles	27 Sept. 04	21 Nov. 07	1 April 17	R. Marines.
Rea, Charles	22 June 96	4 Oct. 00		R. Marines.
ℬ Read, Robert	21 Mar. 11	23 April 13	26 May 25	Unattached.
Reade, John	30 June 04	28 April 06	31 May 10	103 Foot.
Reed, Thomas Borrett	24 April 12	17 Mar. 31	7 Oct. 31	R. Marines.
Rees, Edward	9 July 03	15 Aug. 05	8 June 15	R. Marines.
Reeves, Lewis Buckle	23 April 04	12 Mar. 07	1 April 17	R. Marines.
Reeves, Thomas	2 Nov. 04	27 July 08	1 April 17	R. Marines.
Reeves, Samuel (Qr. Mas. 27 Oct. 14)	never	21 Dec. 15		2 R. Veteran Batt.
ℬ ℳ Reid, Thomas[91]	8 Feb. 08	1 May 09	1 July 16	R. Art. Drivers.
Renny, Henry Laws	20 July 13	15 Dec. 13		R. Engineers.
ℬ Renwick, George	18 July 09	12 July 10	14 Mar. 10	6 Foot.
Reveley, George Williamson	15 May 11	6 July 14	20 June 19	30 Foot.
ℬ Reynett, William France	20 July 09	28 Feb. 11	24 Dec. 18	73 Foot.
ℬ Reynolds, John	21 July 08	14 Dec. 09	24 Feb. 25	99 Foot.
ℳ Reynolds, Thomas Matthew[92]	20 Feb. 12	10 Mar. 14	8 April 24	12 Foot.
Rhodes, John	9 May 11	26 Oct. 15	25 Dec. 18	19 Foot.
ℬ Ribton, *Sir* John, *Bt.*	6 Feb. 11	25 June 12	5 Feb. 18	23 Foot.
Rich, Henry	21 Jan. 12	4 Feb. 13	30 Nov. 20	4 West India Regt.
Richardes, William Eardley[93]	11 July 14	25 Jan. 19	12 May 24	R. Artillery.
* Richardson, Francis	never	13 Nov. 08	1810	R. Waggon Train.
ℬ Richardson, George Henry	27 Aug. 07	23 Nov. 09	15 May 17	38 Foot.
* Richardson, James	never	25 Dec. 13	1814	3 Prov. Bn. of Mil.
Richardson, John[94]	4 Aug. 13	27 July 15	1 Oct. 18	92 Foot.
Richardson, John	8 June 09	11 Sept. 11	11 Oct. 16	Canadian Fen.
ℬ *Richardson, Thomas Lothian*	never	10 Sept. 03		R. Art. Drivers.
ℬ ℳ *Richardson, William[95]*	15 Aug. 11	20 Oct. 13		10 R. Veteran Batt.
Richmond, James	26 Nov. 07	1 May 12	25 July 19	24 Dragoons.
Richmond, Sylvester	9 Aug. 11	24 April 13	3 Oct. 22	48 Foot.
Ricketts, Alfred	8 July 13	22 Dec. 14	25 Feb. 16	9 Foot.
Ricketts, Philip	19 Feb. 07	25 Mar. 08	20 April 20	44 Foot.
ℳ Riddoch, Alexander	11 June 12	2 Feb. 15	25 Mar. 16	4 Foot.
ℬ Riddock, William	8 April 13	15 Mar. 15	25 Feb. 16	4 Foot.
Rideout, Henry Wood	21 Sept. 15	19 April 18	20 July 20	19 Foot.
Riet, William Vander	6 June 14	13 April 15	25 Dec. 16	Cape Regiment.
Rigby, Samuel	28 June 10	3 Nov. 11	27 June 16	New Bruns. Fen.
ℬ ℳ Ripley, William	15 Mar. 10	2 May 11	1 Aug. 16	52 Foot.
Ritchie, James	20 Feb. 17	21 Feb. 27	25 Sept. 27	1 Foot.
Robb, David	14 July 08	16 Oct. 09	6 Jan. 20	25 Dragoons.
ℳ Roberts, Harry Harvey	10 Dec. 12	7 Jan. 14	25 Dec. 16	51 Foot.
Roberts, James	15 Jan. 07	24 May 09	4 July 22	7 Foot.
ℬ ℳ Roberts, John[96]	1 Sept. 08	1 Dec. 09	1 July 16	R. Art. Drivers.
Roberts, John	28 Dec. 15	8 April 25	22 April 26	Unattached.
ℬ Robertson, Alexander	15 June 09	4 July 11	18 April 16	27 Foot.
Robertson, Allan	5 April 10	24 Dec. 12	25 Mar. 17	1 Foot.
Robertson, Donald	8 June 09	7 Jan. 13	25 Mar. 17	82 Foot.
ℳ Robertson, James[97]	6 Jan. 14	20 July 15	25 Feb. 16	79 Foot.
ℬ Robinson, Andrew Delepere	18 Jan. 10	10 Oct. 11	4 April 16	57 Foot.
Robinson, Anthony	24 Nov. 02	17 Dec. 06		3 R. Veteran Batt.
Robinson, Daniel	18 May 07	27 July 14	1 Sept. 14	R. Marines.
Robinson, Fenton	13 Dec. 13	1 Aug. 16	20 June 22	R. Artillery.
Robinson, George	15 Sept. 08	7 Nov. 09	25 April 19	60 Foot.
ℬ ℳ Robinson, James[98]	10 Dec. 07	17 May 10	20 Mar. 23	50 Foot.
Robinson, John	14 Mar. 05	8 Jan. 07	30 Sept. 19	85 Foot.
Robinson, Issac Byrne	17 Dec. 18	3 Nov. 25	8 Feb. 34	92 Foot.
ℬ Robinson, William Henry	28 Nov. 11	27 Aug. 13	11 Feb. 15	45 Foot.
Roch, George	11 May 14	9 July 18	25 Dec. 18	98 Foot.
ℳ Rochford, Charles	26 Feb. 13	15 June 15	25 Aug. 21	Rifle Brigade.

Lieutenants.

	ENSIGN, ETC.	LIEUT.	WHEN PLACED ON HALF PAY.	
* Rochfort, John	never	25 Dec. 13	1814	100 Foot.
Rogers, Adam	25 Oct. 07	15 Mar. 09	4 Feb. 15	6 Garrison Batt.
Rogers, Jacob Glynn	6 Oct. 14	5 Mar. 18	28 Dec. 38	Unattached.
Rogers, John	10 April 11	30 June 29	14 May 31	R. Marines.
ⓂⒶ Rogers, Robert Naylor[99]	29 July 13	14 June 15	12 Nov. 36	Unattached.
Rolfe, Joseph	3 July 01	14 Sept. 04	25 Mar. 17	53 Foot.
Rollo, James	27 Mar. 12	5 Aug. 13	25 May 16	59 Foot.
Rooke, Lewis	6 Oct. 04	16 Jan. 08	1 Sept. 14	R. Marines.
Rooney, Bernard	4 Nov. 13	24 May 15	24 Oct. 15	2 Garrison Batt.
Rose, Hugh	31 Dec. 12	25 May 19	19 Aug. 24	24 Foot.
Rose, John	12 Feb. 94	13 Feb. 94	11 Oct. 98	Irish Brigade.
Roseingrave, Matthew	2 April 07	11 Feb. 08	25 Sept. 17	10 Foot.
Ross, Emilius	10 Aug. 15	26 June 27	July 39	Unattached.
ⓂⒶ Ross, Ewen[100]	13 April 09	26 Nov. 12	25 Mar. 17	92 Foot.
Ross, Hamilton	30 July 94	15 July 95	1803	81 Foot.
Ross, James Fraser	26 Feb. 08	4 May 09	5 Mar. 18	42 Foot.
Ross, John	25 May 15	11 Sept. 17	17 Feb. 22	African Corps.
Ross, John		21 Sept. 05	8 Mar. 10	7 Garrison Batt.
Ross, Robert	6 Mar. 11	29 July 13	25 May 16	11 Foot.
Rotely, Lewis	27 July 05	27 July 08		R. Marines.
Rothwell, William	10 July 11	25 Nov. 13	12 Oct. 26	Unattached.
Rouse, Richard	3 Nov. 98	18 Aug. 04	13 Dec. 05	R. Marines.
Rousseau, Peter	10 Sept. 12	8 June 14	25 Dec. 16	Cape Regiment.
Rowan, John Hill	15 Nov. 27	8 July 32	31 Aug. 39	Unattached.
Ⓟ Royse, Abraham Foord	20 May 13	15 June 15	2 April 17	87 Foot.
Rudland, Jones	9 May 11	20 May 13	25 May 18	10 Foot.
Ruel, John Godfrey	2 Sept. 05	29 July 08	1 Sept. 14	R. Marines.
Russell, Henry James	4 Aug. 08	10 Aug. 13	25 Aug. 19	60 Foot.
Russell, James	never	27 July 15		3 R. Veteran Batt.
Russell, William	10 Sept. 07	10 Dec. 12		5 R. Veteran Batt.
Russwurm, Alexander	12 Jan. 13	3 Feb. 14	12 June 28	50 Foot.
Ⓟ Rutherford, James[101]	15 Feb. 10	27 Oct. 14	15 June 15	23 Foot.
Ruvynes, Charles Aug. de	11 Nov. 07	6 Feb. 12	25 Dec. 18	20 Dragoons.
Ryan, John Dennis	29 Aug. 15	10 Oct. 16	25 Sept. 20	2 Dragoons.
Ⓟ Ryan, Richard	1 July 13	7 Sept. 15	25 Dec. 18	96 Foot.
Ryan, William	10 July 10	21 April 14	25 Dec. 18	63 Foot.
Ryneweld, William Van	29 Nov. 06	14 July 08	23 May 16	93 Foot.
Sabine, John	6 June 05	14 April 08	25 Dec. 18	African Corps.
St. John, John	15 July 13	9 Aug. 15	25 Mar. 17	12 Foot.
St. John, Richard Fleming	16 Dec. 16	8 April 25	1 Oct. 30	R. Artillery.
Sampson, William	27 Oct. 04	29 June 08	18 June 16	R. Marines.
Sampson, William	23 Mar. 09	8 Sept. 12	25 Jan. 16	27 Foot.
Sanders, David Morison	12 May 13	9 Mar. 20	25 May 26	Unattached.
Sandilands, William Nimmo	14 Dec. 09	11 Nov. 12	25 April 16	7 West India Regt.
Sandon, John Kidgell	1 June 79	1 Dec. 82	9 May 83	R. Marines.
Sandwith, Geo. Aug. Elliot	14 Oct. 05	25 April 10	1 Sept. 14	R. Marines.
Sandys, Myles	1 Dec. 08	5 April 10	2 April 18	40 Foot.
Sargent, Samuel	1 Nov. 09	17 Oct. 10	20 Feb. 23	1 R. Veteran Batt.
Sarsfield, Bingham	1 Aug. 11	30 Dec. 14	27 July 26	Unattached.
Ⓟ Sarsfield, Thomas	25 July 11	21 Oct. 13	6 April 15	47 Foot.
Saunders, Andrew Childers	19 Aug. 13	31 Mar. 14	25 Mar. 16	1 Dragoons.
Saunders, Joseph	12 Oct. 09	28 Dec. 12	25 Sept. 17	1 Garrison Batt.
Saunders, Robert Francis	16 Mar. 09	7 Dec. 09	8 Jan. 20	68 Foot.
ⓂⒶ Saunders, Robert John[102]	26 Nov. 08	11 Aug. 11	1 April 21	R. Artillery.
Ⓟ Sawkins, William	26 Dec. 11	6 Jan. 14	25 July 17	3 Garrison Batt.
Sawyers, John	24 Dec. 04	27 July 08	14 June 18	R. Marines.
Saxby, Robert	25 Sept. 05	15 June 09	1 Sept. 14	R. Marines.
Ⓟ Sayer, George	11 July 11	27 Aug. 13	25 Mar. 17	55 Foot.
Sayers, Arthur	6 Sept. 05	9 Oct. 06	26 Aug. 13	27 Foot.
Sayers, William	22 Aug. 11	15 July 13	7 Sept. 26	Unattached.
Scanlan, John Fitzgibbon	7 April 06	12 May 12	1 Sept. 14	R. Marines.
Schaffalizky, Frederick	30 Oct. 06	15 June 09	1814	104 Foot.
Schaw, John Sauchie	11 Dec. 15	1 June 22	1 June 22	R. Artillery.

Lieutenants.

	CORNET, ETC.	LIEUT.	WHEN PLACED ON HALF PAY.	
Schneider, Robert Wilmot	10 April 25	8 April 26	29 Nov. 27	Unattached.
Scobell, John	27 Jan. 96	20 Oct. 97	27 Nov. 02	R. Marines.
Scott, David	28 Nov. 11	25 Jan. 13		7 R. Veteran Batt.
Scott, Edward	never	10 Dec. 99	25 June 02	7 Foot.
ℬ Scott, Henry	22 Aug. 10	11 May 12	15 Jan. 18	5 Foot.
Scott, John	20 April 96	3 Mar. 00	25 Nov. 16	3 Garrison Batt.
ℬ Scott, Percy	22 June 12	28 Nov. 15	20 Aug. 17	98 Foot.
Scott, Thomas	25 Aug. 08	28 Feb. 12	25 Dec. 18	94 Foot.
Scott, William Fitz Gerald	30 Dec. 12	14 Dec. 14	20 Sept. 33	6 West India Regt.
Searanke, John	27 Aug. 12	18 Feb. 13	11 May 15	4 Dragoon Guards.
* Sebborne, Thomas Hall	never	25 Dec. 13	25 Sept. 14	3 Foot.
ℳ Sedley, John Somner	6 May 13	23 Oct. 17	25 Dec. 18	Staff Corps.
Segrave, O'Neil	23 June 25	13 May 26	26 Mar. 30	Unattached.
Semple, John	never	20 Oct. 94		R. Irish Artillery.
Serjeant, John	10 Oct. 05	22 Jan. 10	1 Sept. 14	R. Marines.
ℳ Seward, Charles	24 Feb. 14	13 Aug. 15	25 Nov. 16	69 Foot.
Sewell, Ballantine	7 Aug. 99	18 June 01		1802 49 Foot.
Seymour, C. Marlborough	11 Aug. 08	29 June 09	11 May 15	32 Foot.
Shadforth, Henry	14 Oct. 19	4 Dec. 23	21 Mar. 29	Unattached.
Shadwell, Henry Eugene	24 June 05	22 Jan. 07	17 Dec. 18	35 Foot.
Shafto, William Henry	5 Aug. 13	28 Sept. 15	25 Mar. 17	16 Foot.
Sharman, Charles	never	12 Dec. 94		R. Irish Artillery.
Sharpe, John	14 April 08	19 April 09	10 Sept. 12	54 Foot.
Sharpin, Henry	4 Feb. 13	7 Nov. 15	10 Feb. 32	53 Foot.
ℳ Sharpin, William [103]	12 Dec. 12	20 Dec. 14	1 July 23	R. Artillery.
ℳ Shaw, Sir Charles [103*]	21 Jan. 13	9 Dec. 13	25 Dec. 18	90 Foot.
Shaw, George	17 May 14	4 Sept. 23	13 July 26	Unattached.
Shaw, Hugh	31 Oct. 11	21 Oct. 13	25 Mar. 17	74 Foot.
Shaw, James Peter	29 Feb. 04	8 Jan. 07	29 June 15	33 Foot.
Shaw, Samuel	17 Oct. 05	29 Sept. 08	30 Sept. 19	4 Foot.
Shawe, John Wingfield	10 Oct. 16	16 Mar. 20	27 July 20	18 Dragoons.
Shawe, Meyrick	never	23 June 14	25 Mar. 17	30 Foot.
Shelley, Sir Timothy, Bt.	15 Dec. 79	20 June 81	11 June 83	22 Dragoons.
ℬ ℳ Shelton, John Willington [104]	21 July 08	22 Mar. 10	27 Nov. 17	28 Foot.
Shepard, Henry Richardson	15 Aug. 09	28 Feb. 12	25 Oct. 21	12 Foot.
ℬ Sheppard, Thomas	Aug. 07	28 Mar. 08	17 Oct. 16	59 Foot.
Shewbridge, Henry	23 Dec. 12	12 Dec. 14	25 Dec. 18	60 Foot.
Shiel, Theobald	never	1 April 26	13 July 26	60 Foot.
Short, Charles	15 Oct. 18	26 Sept. 23	22 Feb. 31	21 Foot.
ℬ Shotton, Benjamin	1 Sept. 04	20 Mar. 06	20 Nov. 17	16 Dragoons.
ℬ ℳ Sicker, George	25 June 02	20 Feb. 05	30 July 18	23 Dragoons.
Simmons, James F.	5 July 13	23 Dec. 15	1 April 19	R. Artillery.
ℬ Simoneau, Louis	20 Feb. 11	1 June 12	25 Nov. 16	Meuron's Regt.
Simpson, James	23 May 11	23 Sept. 13	28 Nov. 16	89 Foot.
Simpson, John	1 Nov. 03	1 Jan. 06	6 Oct. 14	R. Marines.
Sinclair, George	17 Feb. 14	14 June 21	24 Nov. 25	92 Foot.
Sinclair, John	30 May 05	10 Dec. 07		8 R. Veteran Batt.
* Singleton, Jonathan Felix	never	25 Dec. 13		1814 2 Prov. Bn. of Mil.
Skelton, William	1 Sept. 07	16 Mar. 08	7 Sept. 15	84 Foot.
Skene, William	25 July 94	21 Feb. 95		Independ. Co.
Slaney, Moreton	21 Nov. 05	24 Aug. 07	1 Dec. 20	25 Dragoons.
ℬ Slattery, Bartholomew	14 April 13	23 Mar. 15	26 Mar. 16	27 Foot.
Sleator, John	25 June 10	20 April 14		5 R. Veteran Batt.
Sloan, James	5 Oct. 04	1 July 06		4 R. Veteran Batt.
ℬ Sloan, James	23 April 05	29 Jan. 07	3 Feb. 20	68 Foot.
Small, Francis Walsh	23 Aug. 10	14 Nov. 11	11 June 30	Unattached.
Smith, Alexander	12 Sept. 99	1 Sept. 04	15 Dec. 06	R. Marines.
ℳ Smith, Alexander	4 Aug. 08	22 Feb. 10	30 Sept. 19	42 Foot.
Smith, Boys Jenkin	13 Oct. 08	13 Sept. 10		8 R. Veteran Batt.
Smith, Edward	22 Feb. 10	20 Jan. 14	25 Feb. 16	58 Foot.
Smith, Edward Atkins	25 July 09	2 May 11	11 April 22	31 Foot.
Smith, George Charles	23 June 04	4 Aug. 05	24 Jan. 22	63 Foot.
Smith, Henry	12 Nov. 12	16 Nov. 15	28 Dec. 27	6 West India Regt.
* Smith, Henry Pasco	never	25 Dec. 13	25 Sept. 14	12 Foot.

Lieutenants.

	2D LIEUT. ETC.	LIEUT.	WHEN PLACED ON HALF PAY.	
Smith, Henry Porter	16 June 14	24 June 19	24 May 21	Rifle Brigade.
Smith, Hugh William	28 Mar. 10	29 Oct. 11	13 Aug. 12	67 Foot.
Smith, James	30 May 11	21 Oct. 13	25 Dec. 18	20 Dragoons.
Smith, James Berridge	1 Oct. 12	26 Aug. 13	30 Oct. 23	21 Dragoons.
⚜ Smith, James Ramsay	13 Oct. 14	20 Mar. 24	6 July 26	38 Foot.
Smith, John	10 April 09	7 Oct. 12	9 Mar. 20	14 Foot.
ℙ Smith, John	12 May 12	8 Feb. 14	19 April 17	27 Foot.
⚜ Smith, John	26 Oct. 15	12 July 22	30 July 29	Staff Corps.
* Smith, John	never	25 Feb. 14	1814	2 Prov. Bn. of Mil.
Smith Joseph,(*Qr. Mas.* 28 Apr. 08)	never	7 Sept. 15		3 R. Veteran Batt.
Smith, Leonard Fleming	5 June 12	19 May 14	14 May 15	26 Foot.
ℙ Smith, Michael	29 Aug. 11	23 Aug. 13	20 April 17	40 Foot.
Smith, Peter	never	30 April 04		R. Art. Drivers.
Smith, Peter	1 Dec. 12	15 July 13	1 Nov. 14	R. Art. Drivers.
ℙ Smith, Ralph	22 Sept. 08	22 Mar. 10	8 May 23	53 Foot.
Smith, Robert	4 April 05	20 Feb. 06	11 July 16	1 Foot.
Smith, Thomas Flynn	26 Feb. 06	26 Mar. 07		7 Foot.
Smith, Thomas Francis	4 June 12	25 June 18	20 Oct. 23	24 Foot.
Smith, William[105]	14 Jan. 07	3 Mar. 09	1 July 16	R. Art. Drivers.
ℙ Smith, William	11 Oct. 10	26 Oct. 15	25 Sept. 17	31 Foot.
ℙ⚜ Smith, William	1 Sept. 13	19 July 15	25 Feb. 16	71 Foot.
Smith, William	6 Aug. 12	4 Feb. 14	25 Oct. 17	78 Foot.
ℙ⚜ Smith, William	28 June 10	21 July 13	27 April 17	91 Foot.
Smyth, James Ryan	3 Sept. 12	21 June 15	25 Mar. 16	15 Foot.
Smyth, Thomas	29 June 09	28 Aug. 11	25 Jan. 17	34 Foot.
Smyth, William	16 May 11	3 June 19	30 Dec. 19	Scots Fusilier Gds.
Sneyd, William	17 Feb. 83	14 April 83	1783	88 Foot.
Spaight, Henry	3 Mar. 14	11 Oct. 21	23 June 25	2 Dragoon Guards.
Spalding, Warner Reeve	26 Mar. 07	13 Nov. 10		8 R. Veteran Batt.
Spencer, Thomas[106]	never	2 Aug. 03	1 June 04	R. Art. Drivers.
Sperling, John[107]	14 Dec. 11	1 July 12	24 Jan. 24	R. Engineers.
Spinks, William	25 Dec. 02	25 April 11		3 R. Veteran Batt.
Spong, Francis Mallett[108]	1 Dec. 09	5 June 11	1 Nov. 14	R. Art. Drivers.
Spooner, Henry	21 Nov. 99	12 June 01	25 June 02	15 Dragoons.
Spotiswood, Andrew	4 July 11	3 Feb. 14	25 Mar. 17	21 Foot.
Sproule, Edward	26 Jan. 08	1 Feb. 10	5 Nov. 18	69 Foot.
ℙ Stacey, Edwin	30 May 11	26 Mar. 12	25 Aug. 14	12 Dragoons.
⚜ Stainforth, George	29 July 13	19 July 15	25 Mar. 17	23 Foot.
Stanley, Edward	2 Sept. 04	1 Jan. 06		R. Art. Drivers.
Stannus, Thomas	3 Aug. 05	1 Oct. 05	3 July 17	7 Dragoons.
Stansfield, Robert	19 Sept. 26	2 Nov. 32	4 Aug. 37	20 Foot.
Stapleton, David	25 Aug. 08	3 May 10	19 June 17	41 Foot.
Stapleton, Richard	19 April 14	7 April 25	24 May 27	Unattached.
Stapleton, William Bull	26 Nov. 12	25 Feb. 13	9 Nov. 15	Staff Co. of Caval.
ℙ Stavely, John	25 Dec. 06	9 Mar. 09	12 Nov. 18	4 Foot.
ℙ Stawell, William	19 Sept. 11	9 Nov. 15	25 Dec. 17	98 Foot.
Steade, Charles	never	22 Feb. 16	23 Oct. 17	60 Foot.
Steed, Edward Henry	29 Sept. 14	26 April 17	25 Dec. 18	25 Dragoons.
ℙ Steel, William Robert	7 May 06	16 June 08	2 Mar. 15	48 Foot.
Steele, Matthew Frederick[109]	9 April 25	16 Feb. 31	30 Dec. 34	91 Foot.
Steele, *Sir* Robert, *Knt.*	10 July 03	15 Aug. 05	4 Aug. 17	R. Marines.
* Steggall, William Charles	never	25 Dec. 13	25 Sept. 14	43 Foot.
Stevenson, John	18 Sept. 80	29 April 82		Strathaven's Co.
Stewart, Alexander	20 Mar. 15	26 Oct. 26	5 July 27	84 Foot.
Stewart, Charles	25 July 09	17 Oct. 11	24 Jan. 21	4 Foot.
ℙ Stewart, Duncan	9 Mar. 09	22 Feb. 10	30 Oct. 17	104 Foot.
Stewart, Edward Hobbs	3 Dec. 96	4 Oct. 01	1 Feb. 17	R. Marines.
Stewart, James	9 June 14	16 Oct. 18	9 Sept. 24	53 Foot.
Stewart, Mervyn	12 Jan. 15	25 Jan. 16	10 July 20	21 Dragoons.
Stewart, Thomas	21 Mar. 11	3 Mar. 13	1 Dec. 25	23 Foot.
Stobart, Henry[110]	12 Dec. 11	29 Aug. 14	10 July 26	R. Artillery.
Stobie, John	April 08	14 June 08		4 R. Veteran Batt.
Stock, Frederick	23 June 04	16 May 05	5 Nov. 07	R. Irish Artillery.
Stokes, Joseph Southwell	29 Oct. 12	26 Aug. 15	28 Oct. 17	80 Foot.

Lieutenants.

	ENSIGN, ETC.	LIEUT.	WHEN PLACED ON HALF PAY.	
Stokes, John	3 July 97	2 Jan. 98	8 Aug. 98	67 Foot.
Stowards, Robert	7 Mar. 11	2 July 13		10 R. Veteran Batt.
Street, John	21 Oct. 13	26 July 15	2 Oct. 17	49 Foot.
Stretch, Bolton Edward	21 Oct. 13	4 May 15	9 Aug. 33	7 Foot.
Stritch, William Luke	24 Dec. 12	4 Aug. 14	25 Mar. 17	95 Foot.
ℙ Strode, George	30 Mar. 09	5 April 10	25 Feb. 17	20 Foot.
Stronach, William	24 Mar. 15	11 Nov. 16	31 Dec. 24	R. Engineers.
⚅ Strong, William Burrough [111]	14 May 12	16 Dec. 13	25 Mar. 17	44 Foot.
⚅ Stuart, Charles	19 May 08	16 Jan. 12	19 April 17	91 Foot.
Stuart, Charles George	9 May 11	20 April 14	25 Mar. 16	88 Foot.
Stuart, George	10 Nov. 13	2 Jan. 17	11 Jan. 20	86 Foot.
ℙ Stuart, George Evans	28 Feb. 12	20 Jan. 14	25 Dec. 14	61 Foot.
Stuart, James	9 July 03	14 April 04		3 R. Veteran Batt.
ℙ Stuart, James Thomas Simon	12 Jan. 09	23 Nov. 09	20 May 19	73 Foot.
Stuart, Peter	never	14 Oct. 06		1 R. Veteran Batt.
⚅ Stuart, Robert Thomson	5 Aug. 13	18 July 15	25 Mar. 17	28 Foot.
Stuart, William	24 April 04	24 Mar. 07	25 June 16	R. Marines.
* Suberkrub, John Jacob	never		1814	3 Prov. Bn. of Mil.
Sullivan, Bartholomew	26 Nov. 06	6 Oct. 13	2 Sept. 26	R. Marines.
ℙ Sullivan, James	18 May 09	20 June 11	24 June 24	19 Foot.
* Sullivan, John	never	25 Dec. 13	15 Aug. 14	49 Foot.
Sunbolf, George	18 Feb. 08	28 Feb. 11	18 June 18	33 Foot.
Supple, Edward	28 Sept. 09	11 July 11	20 Sept. 18	10 Foot.
Supple, Kerry	4 Aug. 13	14 Feb. 16	28 May 17	60 Foot.
Sutherland, Alexander	2 Nov. 96	4 Nov. 99	25 April 02	9 Foot.
Sutherland, Edward	9 Sept. 12	26 Aug. 13	12 July 33	Unattached.
Sutherland, Kenneth	21 June 97	25 Mar. 01		2 R. Veteran Batt.
Sutherland, Sutherland Hall	22 June 15	15 Feb. 16	4 April 23	65 Foot.
Suttie, George Grant	never	17 April 17	25 Dec. 18	Scots Fusilier Gds.
Sutton, John	14 May 12	25 Aug. 14	17 Oct. 16	4 West India Regt.
Swanson, Thomas	25 May 08	25 Oct. 10	17 Mar. 13	42 Foot.
Sweeting, George	never	4 Aug. 14	16 Dec. 19	7 Foot.
Swiny, Shapland William	16 May 11	29 April 13	11 July 16	39 Foot.
Swyer, William [112]	20 Feb. 98	21 Dec. 03	13 May 06	R. Marines.
ℙ Sydserff, John Buchan	24 Oct. 11	6 Jan. 14	25 Mar. 17	82 Foot.
Symonds, William	27 Jan. 07	2 July 07	25 Mar. 17	60 Foot.
ℙ Syret, James	23 Jan. 12	26 Aug. 13	25 Mar. 17	9 Foot.
Taaffe, William	14 Feb. 11	14 May 12	2 Dec. 19	60 Foot.
Tane, Thomas Jas. Waldegrave	2 July 03	15 Aug. 05	17 Aug. 14	R. Marines.
Tapp, John William	14 July 98	9 Feb. 00		R. Artillery.
Tapp, William	12 Mar. 12	13 Jan. 14	4 April 16	18 Foot.
ℙ Tasker, James	30 Nov. 04	16 Oct. 06	24 April 17	57 Foot.
ℙ Tatlock, Thomas	8 Mar. 09	15 Aug. 11	2 Oct. 17	62 Foot.
Tayloe, John	12 Mar. 12	27 April 15	25 Mar. 17	77 Foot.
ℙ Taylor, Edward	10 Sept. 12	27 Jan. 14	30 Nov. 20	87 Foot.
⚅ Taylor, Francis	8 Nov. 10	10 Sept. 12	22 Nov. 33	46 Foot.
ℙ Taylor, Francis William	22 Aug. 11	25 Mar. 13	25 Mar. 17	14 Dragoons.
* Taylor, George	never	23 Mar. 14	1814	3 Prov. Bn. of Mil.
Taylor, Ingram Pank	14 Jan. 06	14 June 11	1 Sept. 14	R. Marines.
Taylor, John	25 Dec. 13	1 June 20	25 Nov. 21	74 Foot.
Taylor, John	30 July 12	14 July 14	25 Dec. 18	90 Foot.
Taylor, Joseph Henry	16 Dec. 19	26 July 26	2 Feb. 30	Unattached.
Taylor, Nathaniel	21 May 12	13 July 15	25 Dec. 18	90 Foot.
Taylor, Thomas	12 Oct. 09	5 May 12	30 May 17	26 Foot.
Taylor, Thomas	10 April 09	13 Dec. 10	1 May 17	41 Foot.
Taylor, William	25 Dec. 78	2 Dec. 81	22 Jan. 83	R. Marines.
* Thackeray, Joseph	never	25 Dec. 13	25 Sept. 14	51 Foot.
ℙ Thackwray, Matthew	21 June 10	25 Feb. 13	25 Mar. 17	29 Foot.
Thiballier, Hubert	3 July 06	26 Dec. 06	11 June 18	3 Foot.
⚅ Thoburn, Robert	11 Feb. 08	12 Jan. 09	25 Feb. 16	35 Foot.
Thom, John	31 Oct. 05	15 April 07		12 R. Veteran Batt.
ℙ Thomas, James	7 April 08	4 May 09	2 Feb. 15	50 Foot.
ℙ *Thompson, Benjamin*	11 July 11	29 Aug. 16		1 R. Veteran Batt.

Lieutenants.

	CORNET, ETC.	LIEUT.	WHEN PLACED ON HALF PAY.	
🅦 Thompson, Henry Walker....	16 Sept. 13	20 July 15	25 Mar. 17	74 Foot.
Thompson, John	15 May 28	15 Aug. 34	26 May 38	Unattached.
🅟 Thompson, Ralph Keddey	26 Mar. 12	21 Oct. 13	2 April 18	26 Foot.
🅟 Thompson, Tho. Jones	10 Nov. 08	24 May 10	28 Dec. 26	Unattached.
Thomson, Stackhouse	25 Feb. 05	21 Nov. 05	20 Sept. 10	8 Garrison Batt.
Thomson, Colin	21 Nov. 05	31 Mar. 08	29 Aug. 16	23 Dragoons.
* Thomson, Andrew	never	1 Mar. 14		3 Prov. Bn. of Mil.
Thomson, David.............	Dec. 07	3 Mar. 08		3 R. Veteran Batt.
🅟 *Thomson, James*	17 Aug. 08	19 April 10		10 R. Veteran Batt.
Thomson, Jeremiah	7 Aug. 99	25 Oct. 00	25 Sept. 02	17 Foot.
Thomson, Joseph	29 April 13	7 Sept. 15	25 Mar. 16	15 Foot.
Thornley, Thomas	21 Oct. 13	28 Sept. 15	3 April 17	43 Foot.
🅟 Thornton, John	27 Aug. 07	2 Aug. 10	17 July 17	42 Foot.
Thorold, Frederick	3 Oct. 26	16 Jan. 29	18 May 32	Unattached.
🅟 *Thweng, George A.*[113] ...	never	1 May 04		R. Art. Drivers.
🅦 Tighe, Daniel	never	26 Nov. 14	15 Feb. 21	Grenadier Guards.
Tinling, Charles Stubbs......	5 April 15	3 July 23	24 Nov. 25	Unattached.
Tipping, John Whitmere	17 June 13	7 Mar. 16	25 Feb. 19	Staff Corps of Cav.
Tisdall, James...............	3 Jan. 11	14 April 13	25 Jan. 16	10 Foot.
🅟 Tittle, John Moore.........	7 July 08	1 Nov. 10	12 April 21	African Corps.
Tolcher, Christopher	20 July 15	9 July 18	25 Dec. 18	2 Foot.
Toole, Francis Norris........	11 Nov. 24	17 Aug. 26	12 June 30	43 Foot.
Torrance, David	14 Sept. 09	8 Oct. 12	4 Jan. 17	15 Foot.
Tottenham, John William......	3 Mar. 17	12 Sept. 22	26 Dec. 22	86 Foot.
Tour, Augustus de la.........	26 July 10	1 Mar. 15	1 Feb. 17	R. Foreign Art.
🅟 Towell, George	9 Aug. 10	13 May 12	6 Nov. 23	8 Dragoons.
Towers, William Riley	10 Feb. 00	5 April 01		6 Garrison Batt.
🅟 Town, Edward	26 Nov. 12	17 Mar. 14	9 Nov. 15	Dillon's Regiment.
Townly, James	11 April 06	20 May 12	6 July 27	R. Marines.
🅟 Townsend, John	21 Dec. 08	1 Dec. 11	6 Feb. 26	R. Artillery.
Townsend, Joseph	1 Sept. 15	20 Dec. 22	21 April 23	R. Engineers.
Townsend, Richard	29 Oct. 94	22 Feb. 96		54 Foot.
Townsend, Robert Lawrence ...	2 Dec. 13	13 Jan. 20	30 Aug. 21	18 Dragoons.
Townshend, William	18 Oct. 04	29 Oct. 06	15 Jan. 18	83 Foot.
Trant, William	23 April 07	25 May 08	11 Dec. 17	80 Foot.
Travers, Joseph		29 Aug. 22	7 Sept. 22	60 Foot.
Trebeck, Thomas	11 Dec. 15	18 June 24	18 June 24	R. Artillery.
Trench, Thomas[114]	21 Dec. 08	2 Dec. 11	25 Aug. 20	R. Artillery.
Trevenen, James..............	28 Nov. 11	1 July 13	30 Nov. 20	2 West India Regt.
Tristram, Barrington.........	11 Sept. 12	11 May 15	1 Feb. 19	R. Artillery.
Trollope, *Sir John, Bt.*....	10 July 17	24 Oct. 22	25 Sept. 23	10 Dragoons.
🅟 *Trotter, Robert*	15 Feb. 11	16 April 12		9 R. Veteran Batt.
Tuckett, Harvey Garnett Phipps ..	7 Sept. 15	10 Oct. 22	2 Nov. 38	11 Dragoons.
Tucker, J. Owen Edwards......	16 July 29	18 Oct. 33	14 April 37	20 Foot.
Tucker, Thomas Elliott.......	23 June 08	13 Dec. 10	25 Oct. 21	84 Foot.
🅟 🅦 Tudor, Charles...........	6 April 04	26 Oct. 08	25 Jan. 18	23 Dragoons.
Tudor, Henry.................	1 June 14	5 May 16	5 April 21	37 Foot.
Tunstall, Gabriel	13 Jan. 14	25 July 16	8 Nov. 27	Unattached.
🅟 Tunstall, William	11 May 09	21 Jan. 12	22 April 19	36 Foot.
Turnbull, John	never	8 July 93		Scotch Brigade.
Turner, Francis Mark	19 Dec. 99	7 Aug. 01	17 Oct. 16	7 Foot.
🅟 Turner, Thomas	25 Aug. 07	16 Mar. 09	25 Dec. 14	23 Foot.
Turner, Young	19 April 10	1 May 11	25 June 16	Sicilian Regiment.
Tuton, Charles	25 May 15	8 June 15	25 Nov. 16	3 Garrison Batt.
🅟 Tweedie, James	18 May 08	27 Feb. 12	28 Nov. 16	7 Foot.
Twyford, John................	10 Oct. 05	15 Mar. 10	1 Sept. 14	R. Marines.
Tytler, Patrick	never	5 May 04		{ 4 R. Veteran Batt. *Fort-Major of Stirling Castle.*
Valentine, John	12 Nov. 12	22 Oct. 13	25 Nov. 18	99 Foot.
🅟 Vallancey, Richard.........	1 Sept. 07	20 July 09	23 July 18	1 Foot.
Vanderbrouck, Francis	never	30 Dec. 97		60 Foot.
🅟 Vaughan, George	16 May 11	15 July 13	25 June 17	57 Foot.

376

Lieutenants.

Name	CORNET, ETC.	LIEUT.	WHEN PLACED ON HALF PAY.	
Vaughan, Travers Hartley	5 Mar. 12	25 Mar. 14	25 Aug. 16	New Brunsw. Fen.
Vavasour, Thomas Hippon	3 Mar. 14	15 Feb. 16	25 June 17	73 Foot.
Veitch, Charles	Jan. 08	22 July 08	4 Feb. 15	6 Garrison Batt.
Vereker, Henry	25 Sept. 11	11 Feb. 13	11 Feb. 17	18 Foot.
⚜ Vereker, Henry Thomas	23 April 07	29 Sept. 08	7 Mar. 22	62 Foot.
Vernon, John Russell	30 June 25	7 Aug. 27	28 Sept. 30	1 Foot.
⚜ Vesey, John	21 Sept. 09	2 Aug. 10	21 Oct. 17	76 Foot.
Victor, George	18 April 09	25 Sept. 27	6 June 28	R. Marines.
Vieth, Frederick William	14 Mar. 11	3 Aug. 13	29 Dec. 25	Unattached.
Villiers, Alex. Hen. Charles	12 Feb. 07	16 June 08		2 R. Veteran Batt.
Vowell, John	25 Mar. 08	2 Nov. 09	25 Mar. 17	25 Foot.
Uniacke, Thomas Fane	15 Dec. 08	11 June 11	28 Mar. 22	Rifle Brigade.
Upton, William	3 Oct. 08	20 Oct. 08	25 May 14	15 Foot.
Urquhart, Donald	27 Oct. 10	30 Mar. 12	25 Dec. 17	60 Foot.
Wade, George	9 May 11	14 Jan. 13	25 Mar. 17	18 Foot.
Waite, Richard Godsell	28 Oct. 07	15 Nov. 09	27 July 20	83 Foot.
Walbridge, Henry William	3 Nov. 08	2 Jan. 12	30 Dec. 19	York Chasseurs.
Walby, Samuel	19 Mar. 13	4 May 15	25 Dec. 18	R. Waggon Train.
⚜ Waldie, James Henry	17 Oct. 11	13 Feb. 12	7 Sept. 20	29 Foot.
Walford, John Thomas	5 May 08	22 June 09	21 Aug. 23	72 Foot.
Walker, Alexander	27 Oct. 07	26 Feb. 11	25 Dec. 18	96 Foot.
Walker, Allen	21 Sept. 99	8 Jan. 04		7 R. Veteran Batt.
Walker, James	11 May 05	27 July 08	15 Oct. 22	R. Marines.
Walker, James	14 Oct. 13	23 May 16	25 Dec. 18	96 Foot.
Walker, James	12 Nov. 12	16 Feb. 14	25 Dec. 18	African Corps.
Walker, John Allen	5 Oct. 20	7 April 25	15 Feb. 27	34 Foot.
Walker, Roger Boyce	15 Nov. 10	10 June 13	9 July 18	43 Foot.
Wall, Henry	17 Feb. 06	25 Feb. 12	24 April 13	R. Marines.
Wall, Richard	7 Nov. 05	1 May 09		7 R. Veteran Batt.
⚜ Wallace, Hugh Ritchie	14 July 09	16 Nov. 09	9 July 18	7 Foot.
Wallace, Robert Grenville	17 Dec. 13	4 May 16	7 Dec. 20	York Chasseurs.
⚜ Waller, Kilner	20 Sept. 10	25 Feb. 13	3 April 16	57 Foot.
Walsh, Arthur Blaney	8 April 13	1 Feb. 16	25 Aug. 19	West India Ran.
⚜ Walsh, Lawrence De Courcy	14 May 07	8 June 09	25 Aug. 23	34 Foot.
Walsh, Patrick	31 July 10	2 Nov. 09	25 June 16	Newfoundld. Fen.
Walsh, William	9 June 08	24 Jan. 10	26 Nov. 18	51 Foot.
Ward, Alexander	June 95	11 Nov. 95	1 Aug. 98	Irish Brigade.
Ward, Henry	30 Jan. 07	11 Dec. 13	23 Feb. 30	R. Marines.
* Ward, John	never	25 Dec. 13	25 Sept. 14	15 Foot.
Ward, John	18 Nov. 19	8 April 26	8 May 28	103 Foot.
Wardell, John	17 Mar. 11	1 Aug. 18	20 July 20	19 Foot.
Waring, Edward	8 Dec. 25	15 Mar. 27	25 Feb. 29	African Corps.
Warren, Edward Townsend	8 Aug. 11	13 Oct. 14	25 Dec. 16	90 Foot.
Warren, Robert	25 April 06	15 Oct. 07		7 R. Veteran Batt.
⚜ Warren, William Ouseley[115]	25 Mar. 13	24 Nov. 14	25 May 32	Unattached.
⚜ Watson, Andrew	10 June 13	16 Aug. 15	25 Sept. 23	24 Foot.
Watson, Edward		7 Aug. 94	1795	79 Foot.
⚜ Watson, Feltham	25 April 06	8 Feb. 08	23 June 13	57 Foot.
⚜ Watson, George[116]	28 Feb. 12	22 Oct. 12	14 Sept. 32	Unattached.
* Watson, James	never	25 Dec. 13	1814	89 Foot.
Watson, John	18 Aug. 08	20 May 13	25 Dec. 33	48 Foot.
Watson, Thomas Brereton	23 Nov. 09	21 Nov. 11	18 April 16	8 Foot.
Watson, William Henry	11 Nov. 11	7 May 12	25 Mar. 16	6 Dragoons.
Watt, Thomas	8 Jan. 78	2 Aug. 80	1783	71 Foot.
Watton, Edward John	27 Aug. 99	9 June 04	15 May 05	20 Foot.
Watton, John Budder	3 Oct. 11	3 Dec. 12	25 Dec. 18	R. Waggon Train.
Watts, Henry	24 Jan. 15	25 Feb. 18	11 Nov. 29	Unattached.
Wauch, David	8 Nov. 10	19 May 14	25 July 14	6 Dragoon Guards.
Weaver, William Henry	12 Dec. 11	1 Oct. 14	1 Jan. 8	R. Artillery.
* Webster, James	never	25 Dec. 13	1814	3 Prov. Bn. of Mil.
Webster, William Francis	6 Feb. 23	12 July 33	18 Oct. 39	2 Ceylon Regt.
Weight, Edward	10 Aug. 15	28 Feb. 22	10 Mar. 25	8 Dragoons.

Lieutenants.

	2D LIEUT. ETC.	LIEUT.	WHEN PLACED ON HALF PAY.	
* Weir, Richard	never	25 Dec. 13	1814	2 Prov. Bn. of Mil.
𐌐 Weir, Robert Lewis	6 Oct. 12	15 Dec. 14	25 Mar. 16	27 Foot.
𐌐 Weir, Thomas	19 Sept. 11	22 Aug. 13	25 June 17	1 Foot.
𐌐 Weir, William	31 Mar. 08	17 Oct. 11	25 July 17	27 Foot.
Welch, John West	3 Oct. 08	19 Oct. 09	25 Sept. 14	11 Foot.
Welstead, William	12 Sept. 11	12 Aug. 13	10 Oct. 16	8 West India Regt.
West, Henry	10 July 77	1 July 79	29 Oct. 92	R. Marines.
West, John Wade	16 Dec. 95	4 Jan. 97	25 Mar. 16	14 Foot.
Westcott, John Hancock	20 July 09	12 Aug. 12	23 April 17	7 Foot.
Whaley, Robert	8 Oct. 12	22 April 13	2 Jan. 17	14 Dragoons.
⛨ Wheatley, Edmund	23 Oct. 12	26 April 14	25 April 16	German Legion.
𐌐 Wheatley, William	19 Feb. 06	19 May 09	18 Mar. 19	39 Foot.
Wheeler, James	3 July 96	11 Dec. 00	1 July 02	R. Marines.
Whimster, James	27 Nov. 10	5 Aug. 13	25 June 16	Sicilian Reg.
*Whitby, James	never	25 Feb. 14	1814	1 Prov. Bn. of Mil.
White, George	28 Feb. 12	13 May 13	25 Mar. 17	36 Foot.
𐌐 White, Henry	5 April 10	29 April 12		7 R. Veteran Batt.
White, William	13 Sept. 08	10 May 23	27 Jan. 36	R. Marines.
Whiteford, John	12 Sept. 11	8 Aug. 15	25 Mar. 17	13 Foot.
Whitehead, William	1 Mar. 10	15 April 13	25 Mar. 17	13 Foot.
Whitfield, William	23 April 12	13 April 14	25 Mar. 17	62 Foot.
Wigley, George James	13 July 08	25 Mar. 10	20 May 19	63 Foot.
𐌐 Wigton, James	25 Mar. 08	2 Sept. 08	25 Mar. 15	9 Foot.
𐌐 *Wilford, John* [117]	1 Dec. 05	1 Sept. 06		R. Artillery Drivers.
Wilkins, William	6 Aug. 07	30 Dec. 12	25 Aug. 16	1 Garr. Batt.
⛨ Wilkinson, Henry	8 May 10	12 May 12	14 May 16	40 Foot.
Wilkinson, John Alexander	6 Oct. 08	3 Oct. 11	11 Sept. 23	24 Foot.
⛨ Willett, Augustus Saltren	5 June 06	27 Aug. 07	7 Feb. 22	22 Dragoons.
Willey, Edward	22 Oct. 18	23 May 22	19 June 23	19 Dragoons.
𐌐 Williams, Charles	24 June 13	29 May 17	24 Dec. 19	53 Foot.
Williams, George Blennerhasset	28 Feb. 05	17 Sept. 07		3 R. Veteran Batt.
Williams, Henry Micajah	22 Nov. 04	26 Sept. 05	25 Jan. 16	90 Foot.
Williams, Robert	26 Sept. 06	28 Jan. 08	25 Sept. 26	53 Foot.
𐌐 Willis, George Brander [118]	2 May 08	17 Nov. 09	3 April 23	R. Artillery.
𐌐 Wills, James [119]	1 Dec. 12	17 April 13	1 Nov. 14	R. Artillery Drivers.
Wilson, Alexander Lockhart	11 Feb. 13	6 April 20	28 June 21	83 Foot.
Wilson, Charles	28 April 09	7 May 12	25 Aug. 17	56 Foot.
Wilson, Henry	22 June 09	29 April 12	2 Sept. 19	37 Foot.
Wilson, Henry	21 July 25	29 Nov. 27	11 Oct. 31	89 Foot.
Wilson, P. (Qr. Mast. 20 June 05)	never	10 Nov. 14		4 R. Veteran Batt.
Wilson, Robert	14 April 06	20 June 12	1 Sept. 14	R. Marines.
Wilson, Wm. Henry Bowen Jordan	10 Sept. 25	12 Oct. 26	1 Feb. 31	Garrison Co.
Wilton, John Lucas	13 Mar. 27	16 Mar. 32	28 Dec. 38	54 Foot.
Winckworth, John	14 Nov. 10	22 Feb. 16	16 July 17	75 Foot.
Windle, John Shepard	11 Dec. 06	25 Jan. 08	16 May 22	53 Foot.
Winton, James	10 Aug. 99	27 Oct. 99	25 Sept. 02	17 Foot.
Wisdom, John	25 Dec. 06	10 Dec. 07	20 July 09	17 Foot.
𐌐 ⛨ Wood, Frederick [120]	28 April 04	14 June 05	25 Mar. 17	11 Dragoons.
Wood, George	28 Feb. 12	2 Dec. 13	20 Mar. 19	95 Foot.
* Wood, George	never			Independent Co.
Wood, Geo. Horsley	25 Nov. 13	12 April 21	29 Jan. 27	67 Foot.
𐌐 Wood, Henry	25 Mar. 13	13 Aug. 18	11 Nov. 24	23 Foot.
Wood, William Sumpter	22 July 19	26 Dec. 21	24 July 28	30 Foot.
Woodcock, Thomas	29 Aug. 11	2 April 12	25 May 15	4 Dragoon Guards.
Woodgate, William Harding	13 Dec. 27	11 Oct. 31	13 April 38	45 Foot.
Woods, William	7 April 08	28 Dec. 09	15 Feb. 16	6 Dragoons.
Worsley, George	8 Dec. 03	21 Mar. 05	10 Sept. 12	39 Foot.
𐌐 ⛨ Worsley, Thos. Taylor [121]	14 Feb. 11	2 Oct. 12	11 Feb. 16	45 Foot.
Wraxall, Charles Edward	11 Sept. 12	1 April 15	1 Aug. 19	R. Artillery.
⛨ Wray, Hugh Boyd	23 Jan. 11	10 Sept. 12	19 April 17	40 Foot.
Wrey, William Long	27 Jan. 13	25 Aug. 14	28 Jan. 17	19 Dragoons.
Wright, Alexander	1 Oct. 95	27 Mar. 96		11 R. Veteran Batt.
Wright, Edward	Dec. 01	13 Aug. 02	25 Oct. 02	35 Foot.
Wright, John	8 June 09	10 Sept. 12	25 July 17	27 Foot.

Lieutenants.

	ENSIGN, ETC.	LIEUT.	WHEN PLACED ON HALF PAY.	
₧ Wright, John	14 June 11	5 Feb. 12	22 Mar. 27	Unattached.
Wright, William	2 Aug. 80	3 Aug. 85		81 Foot.
₧₡₨ Wright, William [122]	11 Mar. 13	20 July 15	25 Dec. 18	Rifle Brigade.
Wrighte, William	20 May 12	26 May 14	19 April 17	3 Foot.
* Wynter, John Jonathan	never	25 Dec. 13	25 Feb. 16	63 Foot.
Wynter, William Rose	27 Aug. 05	12 Dec. 05	9 July 07	22 Dragoons.
Yarnold, Benjamin	23 July 12	17 Sept. 31	29 Nov. 34	R. Marines.
Yelverton, *Hon.* Barry Charles....	5 Oct. 32	13 Sept. 33	11 Aug. 37	79 Foot.
Yonge, Weston	24 Oct. 13	19 Oct. 15	1817	84 Foot.
₧ ₡₨ Yonge, William Crawley ..	14 May 12	29 April 13	13 Feb. 23	17 Foot.
Young, Alexander (*Adj.* 2 July 96)	1 June 97	8 Oct. 02	25 May 03	30 Foot.
Young, Edward Wynyard	9 April 25	2 July 29	5 Sept. 34	60 Foot.
Young, Hen. Harman	3 April 06	25 Nov. 08	22 Jan. 18	31 Foot.
Young, Henry	31 May 09	1 Aug. 11		6 R. Veteran Batt.
Young, John George	20 Jan. 14	12 Aug. 24	14 May 29	90 Foot.
Young, Robert	3 Oct. 11	6 Sept. 14		1 R. Veteran Batt.

Notes to the Lieutenants.

1 Lieutenant Alderson was severely wounded at Quatre Bras (right arm amputated.)
2 Lieut. John Allen (R. Artillery Drivers), served in the Peninsula from 1809 to 1814, and was present at the battle of Talavera.
3 Lieut. Alston was slightly wounded at Quatre Bras.
4 Lieut. J. Cooper Armstrong served at Copenhagen in 1807, and in the Peninsula from 1812 to 1814.
4* Lieut. Bace commanded the 61st regiment at the battle of Toulouse, for which he has received a medal.
5 Lieut. Frederick Bayly's services :—Peninsula from June, 1810, to the end of the war, including the battles of Busaco and Castella. American war in 1814 and 15, including the attacks on Baltimore and New Orleans, at which last he was slightly wounded. At the taking of the following fortresses when serving with the Prussian army in 1815, viz.: Mauberg, Landrecies, Philippeville, and Rocroy.
6 Lieut. John Black served in the Peninsula with the 74th regiment, including the action at El Bodon, capture of Madrid, retreat from Madrid into Portugal, battles of Vittoria and the Pyrenees, (27th to 31st July, and 1st and 2d Aug.), passage of the Bidassoa, blockade of Pampeluna, battles of Nivelle, and Nive (9th to 13th Dec.), affairs of Vic Bigorre and Tarbes, battle of Orthes, action at Aire, and battle of Toulouse.
7 Lieut. Blood (8th R. Veteran Batt.) served in the Peninsula from June, 1811, to the close of the war, including the sieges and stormings of Ciudad Rodrigo and Badajoz, battle of Salamanca, retreat from Madrid to Portugal, battle of Vittoria, the successful storming of San Sebastian (with the stormers of the Light Division), battles of Nivelle, Nive (9th to 13th Dec.) and Orthes, at which last he was severely wounded by a ball which entered his right knee: he was also severely wounded on the top of the breach at San Sebastian, a musket-ball having struck him in the face and passed through his nose.
8 Lieut. Blood's (unattached) services :—Campaign of 1794 in Flanders, including the actions of the 17th and 26th April, 10th, 17th, and 18th May. Peninsula from 1809 to the end of the war, including the battles of Talavera, Fuentes d'Onor, Salamanca, Vittoria, and Nive. Campaign of 1815, including the battle of Waterloo. Siege of Bhurtpore, 1826. Wounded in Flanders in 1794.
9 Lieut. Blyth served in the Peninsula, and was present at the first siege of Badajoz and battle of Albuhera, at which latter he was wounded.
10 Lieut. Boase was severely wounded at Quatre Bras.
11 Lieut. Bramwell was severely wounded at Quatre Bras (right leg amputated.)
12 Lieut. Brattle's services :—Battle of Trafalgar, on board H. M. S. *Africa* 64. Joined the force under General Whitelock at Monte Video, 1807. Action with Danish gun-boats, near Copenhagen, 20th Oct. 1808 (severely wounded). Served afterwards with the Channel Fleet, off Brest, Basque Roads, and Belle Isle.
13 Lieut. Breton served the campaign of 1815, and was present at the battle of Waterloo.
14 Lieut. Bridge was severely wounded at Waterloo.
14* Lieut. Burslem served at the siege of Houat, and commanded a detachment of Artillery in a night attack on the batteries at Morbihan. Landed at Ferrol with the army under the command of Sir James Pulteney, and attached to the reserve on the heights. Served the campaign of 1801 in Egypt, including the siege of Aboukir and battle of Alexandria, at which latter he lost his right leg by a cannon-shot. Medal for services in Egypt.
15 Lieut. Michael Carey served in the Peninsula from March, 1809, to the end of the war, including the passage of the Douro, battles of Talavera (severely wounded in the head), and Busaco, first siege of Badajoz, battle of Fuentes d'Onor, siege of Ciudad Rodrigo, 2nd siege and storming of Badajoz, battles of Salamanca, Orthes, and Toulouse.
16 Lieut. Thomas Carey was slightly wounded at Waterloo.
17 Lieut. George Chapman served the campaign of 1814 in Holland, including the attack of Bergen-op-Zoom, action at Merxem, and bombardment of Antwerp, at which last he was severely wounded on trench duty, and lost his right leg.
18 Lieut. Coombe served in Egypt in 1801, and has received the Egyptian medal.
19 Lieut. John Coote was slightly wounded at Waterloo.
20 Lieut. R. G. C. Coote served in the Burmese war.
21 Lieut. Coventry served in the East Indies from March, 1783 to Aug. 1798, including the siege of Cannanore, relief of Mangalore, siege of Paulautcherry, affair of Kisnaporam, siege and assault of Bangalore, battle near Seringapatam, siege of Savandroog (severely wounded in the right hip when with the forlorn hope), actions of the 6th and 7th Feb. 1792, siege of Pondicherry, siege of Trincomalee and capture of Ceylon. Served also at the capture of the Cape of Good Hope in 1802, and of the Isle of France in 1810.
22 Lieut. A. S. Crawford was slightly wounded at Waterloo.
23 Lieut. Cromp served in Egypt in 1801, and has received the Egyptian medal.
24 Lieut. Cull served in Egypt in 1801, and has received the Egyptian medal.

Notes to the Lieutenants.

25 Lieut. Dalgairns was wounded at the storming of Bergen-op-Zoom.

26 Lieut. John Dalton served in the Peninsula, and was present at the siege of Ciudad Rodrigo, and the battles of Vittoria, Orthes and Toulouse.

27 Lieut. Daniell (h. p. 59th regiment), was slightly wounded at Waterloo.

28 Lieut. Dighton served in Spain and Portugal from April, 1810, to July, 1812, including Massena's retreat. Served also in the south of France in 1814, and was present at the investment of Bayonne, and repulse of the sortie from thence (slightly wounded.)

29 Lieut. Dobbs was severely wounded at Waterloo.

30 Lieut. Dowbiggin was slightly wounded at Waterloo.

31 Lieut. Drawbridge served at Walcheren, and was present at the siege of Flushing.

32 Lieut. Dunnicliffe served the campaign of 1815, and was present at Quatre Bras and Waterloo.

33 Lieut. Duperier was severely wounded at Waterloo.

34 Lieut. Benj. Edwards served in the Peninsula from 1811 to the end of the war, including the third siege of Badajoz (wounded), and the battles of Salamanca, Nivelle (wounded), Nive, and Toulouse.

35 Lieut. M. Evans served at Copenhagen in 1807; at Flushing in 1809, and subsequently in the Peninsula, including the sieges of Ciudad Rodrigo and Badajoz, and battle of Salamanca. Present also at the battle of Waterloo.

36 Lieut. Edward Finch served at the capture of Martinique in 1809, and subsequently in the American war, and was present at York, Sackett's Harbour, Stoney Creek, and Fort George.

37 Lieut. John Ford served the campaigns of 1809, 10, 11, 13, and 14, and was present at the siege of Flushing, defence of Cadiz, and battles of Fuentes d'Onor, Nivelle, Nive, and Toulouse, besides other actions of less importance.

38 Lieut. A. S. Fraser was slightly wounded at Quatre Bras.

39 Lieut. Gilborne served at the siege of Flushing, and subsequently in the Peninsula, including the battles of the Pyrenees and the Nive, actions at Aire and at Bayonne, and battles of Orthes and Toulouse. Served also the campaign of 1815, including the battle of Waterloo and capture of Paris.

40 Lieut. Græme was severely wounded at Waterloo.

41 Lieut. John Grant (R. Artillery) served with the expedition to Walcheren, and was present at the siege of Flushing. Served afterwards in the Peninsula from Oct. 1813 to Feb. 1814.

42 Lieut. John Grant (2nd R. Vet. Batt.) served in the Peninsula from September, 1808, to the end of the war, including the action at Alcantares, and battles of Talavera and Busaco. Wounded in the thigh by a rifle ball at Alcantares, and received a sabre cut in the face near Salamanca.

43 Lieut. John Grant (unattached) served in the Peninsula from Aug. 1811, to Dec. 1813, including the action at Alba de Tormes, retreat from Madrid, and battles of Vittoria and the Pyrenees. Wounded in the side at the Maya Pass.

44 Lieut. Edward Greene served with the battering train attached to the Prussian besieging army, and was employed in taking several fortresses on the French frontier, July and Aug. 1815.

45 Lieut. Grier was severely wounded at Quatre Bras.

46 Lieut. Edwin Griffiths served in the Peninsula from June, 1813, to May, 1814, and afterwards in the American war, and was present at Washington, Baltimore, and New Orleans, and taking of Fort Bowyer.

47 Lieut. J. G. Griffiths served in the Peninsula, and was present at the battle of Vittoria, siege of San Sebastian, and battles of the Pyrenees, Orthes and Toulouse.

47* Lieut. Grimes served in the Peninsula from March 1811 to Sept. 1812, and was present at the siege of Ciudad Rodrigo, and the successful siege of Badajoz, at which latter he was severely wounded in the right thigh by a cannon-shot.

48 Lieut. George Gunning was slightly wounded at Waterloo.

49 Lieut. Wm. M. Hearn was severely wounded at Quatre Bras.

50 Lieut. Robert Hewitt was severely wounded at Quatre Bras.

51 Lieut. Hodder was severely wounded at Waterloo.

51* Lieut. Hood served in South and North Beveland, and at Walcheren, in 1809. Joined the army in the Peninsula on its retreat from Burgos in 1812, and served with it until the end of the war, including the battles of Vittoria, the Pyrenees, Nivelle, Nive, Orthes, and Toulouse, besides a great many minor actions and skirmishes. Served also the campaign of 1815, and was engaged with the enemy on the 16th, 17th, 18th, and 19th June, at and near Waterloo; the storming of Cambray, and capture of Paris. Severely wounded at the battle of Toulouse.

52 Lieut. Horan was slightly wounded at Quatre Bras, and severely at Waterloo.

53 Lieut. Jagoe was severely wounded at Waterloo.

54 Lieut. J. Æ. Irving was slightly wounded at Waterloo.

55 Lieut. Alex. Irwin's services :—Siege and capture of Hattras, 1816 and 17. Mahratta campaign, 1817 and 18. Burmese war, 1825 and 6.

Notes to the Lieutenants.

56 Lieut. Kennear served in the Peninsula from Nov. 1813 to May, 1814, and afterwards in the American war, and was present at Bladensburg, Washington, Baltimore, and New Orleans.

57 Lieut. Francis Kennedy's services:—Siege and capture of Flushing, 1809. Campaigns of 1811, 12, 13, 14, and 15, including the siege of Badajoz, covering the second siege of Ciudad Rodrigo, crossing the Esla, retreat from Burgos, battles of Fuentes d'Onor, Salamanca, Vittoria, Pampeluna, Pyrenees, Nivelle, Orthes and Waterloo, and taking of Cambray.

58 Lieut. Kett served the campaign of 1815, including the battle of Waterloo and taking of Cambray.

59 Lieut. Alfred Knight served at the capture of Genoa in 1814, and afterwards at the taking of Castine and Hamiltown in the United States of North America.

60 Lieut. C. Lewin was slightly wounded at Waterloo.

61 Lieut. Lister served at the battle of Trafalgar.

62 Lieut. Lockwood's services:—Peninsula campaigns of 1811, 12, and 13, including the assault and capture of Badajoz, battle of Salamanca, and action at Villa Murial on the retreat from Burgos. Campaign of 1814 in Holland, including Fort Frederick Henry. Campaign of 1815. Severely wounded at Quatre Bras by a musket ball which passed through the frontal bone and lodged on the brain, to extract which the operation of the trepan was resorted to.

63 Lieut. Love served in the Peninsula from July 1810 to Dec. 1812, including the sieges of Ciudad Rodrigo and Badajoz (wounded), storming the Forts at Almarez, siege of the Forts at (wounded) and battle of Salamanca, and siege of Burgos. Served afterwards in the American war, and was present in the action at Plattsburg.

64 Lieut. Charles M'Arthur was slightly wounded at Waterloo.

65 Lieut. Alex. M'Pherson was severely wounded at Quatre Bras.

66 Lieut. Mac Gregor served the Nepaul campaigns of 1814, 15, and 16, and was present at the taking of Harriapore.

67 Lieut. Lachlan Mac Kay served in the Peninsula from 1812 to the end of the war, including the battles of the Pyrenees, Nivelle, Nive, Orthes, and Toulouse.

68 Lieut. Mackinlay was severely wounded at Quatre Bras.

69 Lieut. Mann was severely wounded at Quatre Bras.

70 Lieut. Marrie was present at the battle of Copenhagen in 1801.

71 Lieut. Wm. M'Donald Matthews was slightly wounded at Waterloo.

72 Lieut. Mill was severely wounded at Waterloo.

73 Lieut. Zac. Miller served in Egypt in 1801, and has received the Egyptian medal.

74 Lieut. J. A. Moore served in the American war.

75 Lieut. Fred. Munro served in the Peninsula from March 1812 to the end of the war, including the sieges of the Forts at Salamanca, Burgos, and San Sebastian, and the battles of Salamanca, Vittoria, the Bidassoa, and St. Jean de Luz.

76 Lieut. Muskett served at Walcheren in 1801, and afterwards in the Peninsula, including the sieges of Ciudad Rodrigo and Badajoz. Served also in Holland in 1814, including the action at Merxem and attack on Bergen-op-Zoom.

77 Lieut. John Nash was slightly wounded at Waterloo.

78 Lieut. Naylor served in Egypt in 1801, and has received the Egyptian medal.

79 Lieut. Nicolas served at the battle of Trafalgar.

80 Lieut. Onslow's services:—Siege of Flushing, 1809. Campaign of 1814, in Holland, including the bombardment of the French Fleet at Antwerp.

81 Lieut. John Orr (8th R. Vet. Bn.) was severely wounded at Waterloo.

82 Lieut. Pagan was severely wounded at Waterloo.

83 Lieut. Parratt served at Walcheren in 1809, and in the Peninsula from 1811 to the end of the war, including the sieges of Cadiz and San Sebastian, battle of Nivelle, actions at Vic Bigorre and Tarbes, and battles of Orthes and Toulouse.

84 Lieut. Philpot served the campaign of 1815, and was present at the battle of Waterloo.

85 Lieut. Pickard served the campaign of 1814 in Lower Canada, under Sir George Prevost, and was present at the attack on Plattsburg. Served also the campaign of 1815 in Upper Canada under Sir Gordon Drummond.

86 Lieut. A. J. Pictet served in the Burmese war, and was present at the taking of Donabew.

87 Lieut. Edmund H. Plunkett's services:—Campaign of 1808 and 9 in Portugal and Spain, including the battles of Roleia, and Vimiera, retreat to and battle of Corunna. Expedition to Walcheren, 1809, and subsequently in the Peninsula, including the battle of Orthes. Served afterwards in the American war, and was present at the siege of Fort Erie.

88 Lieut. Pridham served in Egypt in 1801, and has received the Egyptian medal.

89 Lieut. Priest served in Portugal and Spain in 1808 and 9, and was present at the battle of Corunna.

90 Lieut. Quill was severely wounded at Quatre Bras.

91 Lieut. Reid served at Corunna and at Walcheren in 1809, in the Peninsula in 1813 and 14: also the campaign of 1815, including the battle of Waterloo, where he was wounded.

Notes to the Lieutenants.

92 Lieut. Thos. M. Reynolds was severely wounded at Waterloo.
93 Lieut. Richardes served the campaign of 1815, and was present at the sieges of Mauberge, Philippeville, and Landrecies.
94 Lieut.John Richardson (h. p. 92d Regt.) served in the American war, and was present in the actions of Brownstown, River Raison, Miami, Sandusky, and Moraviantown, at which last he was taken prisoner. Served as a Major in the Anglo-Spanish Legion, and received three wounds at the storming of the Carlists' lines in front of SanSebastian. Obtained a medal.
95 Lieut. Wm. Richardson was severely wounded at Waterloo,
96 Lieut. John Roberts (R. Art. Drivers) served at Corunna in 1809 ; and in Holland in 1814, including the action at Merxem and bombardment of Antwerp. Served also the campaign of 1815, and was present at the battles of Quatre Bras and Waterloo.
97 Lieut. James Robertson was severely wounded at Quatre Bras.
98 Lieut. James Robinson was severely wounded at Quatre Bras.
99 Lieut. R. N. Rogers served the campaign of 1815, and was present at the battles of Quatre Bras and Waterloo.
100 Lieut. Ewen Ross was severely wounded at Quatre Bras.
101 Lieut. Rutherford served in the Peninsula with the late 94th Regt., and was present at the siege of Cadiz, actions at Pombal and Redinha, lines at Lisbon, Massena's retreat, action at Sabugal, battle of Fuentes d'Onor, first siege of Badajoz, battles of Vittoria, Pyrenees, Nivelle, Orthes, and Toulouse.
102 Lieut. R. J. Saunders served the campaign of 1815, and was present at the battle of Waterloo.
103 Lieut. Wm. Sharpin served the campaigns of 1814 and 1815 in Holland, the Netherlands, and France, and was present at the battle of Waterloo.
103* Sir Charles Shaw served the campaigns of 1814 and 15 in Holland, Flanders, and France, including the reconnoisance of Bergen-op-Zoom, attack on Merxem, and attempt to burn the French Fleet at Antwerp, and battle of Waterloo. In 1831, joined the army of the Queen of Portugal, and served throughout the civil war in that country, including all the general actions, sorties, and skirmishes during the defence of Oporto, affair of Torres Vedras, and battle of Almoster: in the above service he was seven times wounded. In 1835, he was appointed a Brigadier-General in the British Auxiliary Legion in Spain, and till Aug. 1836, he took a leading part in all the contests in which the Legion was engaged, including the successful assault on the Carlists' lines before San Sebastian (severely wounded), and for which a medal was given.
104 Lieut. Shelton served in the Peninsula with the 28th Regt., and was present at the battle of Busaco, lines at Torres Vedras, affair of Campo Mayor, siege of Olivença, battles of Albuhera (severely wounded), Pyrenees, Nivelle, Nive, in front of Bayonne (11th to 13th Dec.), and Toulouse. Served also the campaign of 1815, and was present at the battle of Waterloo, where he was severely wounded by a shell which shattered his right arm, and broke his ribs.
105 Lieut. Wm. Smith (R. Artillery Drivers), served at Walcheren in 1809, and the campaigns of 1813, 14, and 15 in Holland, Belgium, and France, and was wounded at Merxem.
106 Lieut. Spencer served with the expedition to the Helder in 1799.
107 Lieut. Sperling served in Holland in 1814.
108 Lieut. Spong served in the Peninsula in 1811 and 12.
109 Lieut. M. F. Steele served at the capture of Java in 1811, as an officer of Royal Marines.
110 Lieut. Stobart served in the American war under Sir Gordon Drummond.
111 Lieut. Strong was severely wounded at Quatre Bras.
112 Lieut. Swyer served in Egypt in 1801, and has received the Egyptian medal.
113 Lieut. Thweng served in the Peninsula, and was present at the battles of Talavera and Busaco, and siege of Badajoz.
114 Lieut. Trench served at Walcheren, 1809.
115 Lieut. Wm. O. Warren served the campaign of 1815, and was present at the battles of Quatre Bras and Waterloo.
116 Lieut. George Watson served in the Peninsula from June, 1813, to the end of the war, and was present at the battle of Toulouse.
117 Lieut. Wilford served in the Peninsula, and was present at the siege of Burgos, and battles of Vittoria and Toulouse.
118 Lieut. Willis served at Walcheren, and was present at the siege of Flushing. Served also the Peninsular campaigns of 1811, 12, and 14, including the 2nd and 3rd sieges of Burgos, investment of Bayonne and repulse of the sortie from thence.
119 Lieut. Wills served in the Peninsula, and was present at the siege of San Sebastian and battle of Toulouse.
120 Lieut. Fred. Wood was severely wounded at Waterloo.
121 Lieut. T. T. Worsley was severely wounded at Waterloo.
122 Lieut. Wm. Wright (h. p. Rifle Brigade) was severely wounded at Waterloo.

SECOND AND SUB-LIEUTENANTS, CORNETS, AND ENSIGNS.

	CORNET, 2d LIEUT. or ENSIGN.	WHEN PLACED ON HALF PAY.	
Adam, James	21 Mar. 14	1 April 17	R. Sappers and Miners.
Agassis, Lewis	21 Aug. 09	14 May 17	R. Marines.
Aickin, Francis	25 May 15	5 Dec. 19	14 Dragoons.
Ainslie, Robert	14 Mar. 88		77 Foot.
Allen, William	10 Mar. 09	31 May 23	R. Marines.
Anderson, William	12 July 09	1 Jan. 16	R. Marines.
Andrews, Richard	7 Mar. 16	7 Mar. 16	81 Foot.
Arney, William Sheve	28 July 14	25 Dec. 16	25 Dragoons.
Ashe, William	27 Nov. 97		Kingston's Rec. Co.
Atkinson, Charles	13 Nov. 11	11 Aug. 14	R. Marines.
Atkinson, Francis	7 April 08	25 Mar. 10	7 Garrison Battalion.
Atkinson, Joseph	5 Dec. 11		3 R. Veteran Battalion.
Austin, William	26 Nov. 12		11 R. Veteran Battalion.
Babington, Humphry	15 Mar. 10	25 Mar. 15	1 Garrison Battalion.
Bache, Thomas Ogle	17 Aug. 15	25 Jan. 18	23 Dragoons.
Backhouse, John Iggulden	17 Mar. 31	26 Feb. 30	R. Marines.
Backhouse, Peter	5 Aug. 15	2 Oct. 23	8 Dragoons.
Bakewell, Robert	17 Jan. 15	25 July 17	27 Foot.
Barker, Anthony	1 Mar. 15	25 April 16	New Brunswick Fen.
Barrett, William Newman	6 May 13	30 Sept. 19	60 Foot.
Barry, James	21 Feb. 11	1 Jan. 16	R. Marines.
Barry, James	30 July 11		R. Marines.
Baugh, James	7 Dec. 12	1 Sept. 14	R. Marines.
Bayley, John	3 Mar. 13	30 July 18	13 Dragoons.
Bell, John		1814	3 Prov. Batt. of Militia.
Bellon, Achilles	24 Dec. 94		130 Foot.
Berkeley, G. C. Grantley Fitzhardinge	7 Nov. 16	28 Aug. 23	82 Foot.
Bernard, Walter	20 Oct. 14	27 Nov. 17	60 Foot.
Bevan, Michael	19 Nov. 04	8 Oct. 24	R. Marines.
Bevan, Robert	24 July 12		6 R. Veteran Battalion.
Biddulph, Walter	7 Sept. 08	24 April 15	R. Marines.
Biggs, Lionel	9 Nov. 15		3 R. Veteran Battalion.
Bignell, Charles Phillips	18 Oct. 26	7 Sept. 29	R. Artillery.
Bishop, Vesey	11 July 80		R. Marines.
Black, James	8 July 15	25 June 16	R. Waggon Train.
Black, Thomas	24 Feb. 14	22 May 23	19 Foot.
Blackiston, William	4 April 09	7 Mar. 11	36 Foot.
Blake, Edward John	26 Mar. 12	1 Jan. 16	R. Marines.
Blake, Frederick	5 Nov. 12		1 R. Veteran Battalion.
Bliss, Nathaniel		1814	3 Prov. Batt. of Militia.
Blois, Sir Charles, Bart.	14 July 90		Horse Grenadier Guards.
Blythe, Samuel	25 Dec. 13	10 Jan. 21	94 Foot.
Bolomey, Louis William James	26 Sept. 13	24 Feb. 16	German Legion.
Bonavia, Calcedonio	25 Oct. 15		Maltese Mil. Artif.
Bond, Thomas	25 May 10	1 Jan. 16	R. Marines.
Booth, James	17 May 10		4 R. Veteran Battalion.
Boulton, William	11 June 12		4 R. Veteran Battalion.
Bourke, James	22 April 13		10 R. Veteran Battalion.
Bowden, George	30 July 10	1 Jan. 16	R. Marines.
Boyce, Thomas	16 July 13	1 Aug. 16	R. Artillery Drivers.
Boyd, John	5 Dec. 82	1783	80 Foot.
Brackenbury, Richard	24 June 83		70 Foot.
Bradburne, Fred. Angelo	16 Jan. 17	7 Mar. 22	9 Dragoons.
Bradley, Edward Sands	13 Oct. 14	25 Sept. 18	99 Foot.

Second and Sub-Lieutenants, Cornets, and Ensigns.

	2D LIEUT. ETC.	WHEN PLACED ON HALF PAY.	
Branch, George Fergusson	16 April 32	14 July 37	R. Marines.
Brandon, Joseph	24 Dec. 02	24 Dec. 02	64 Foot.
Bremner, Peter	23 June 13		6 R. Veteran Battalion.
Brew, Charles		1814	2 Prov. Batt. of Militia.
Brew, William			2 Prov. Batt. of Militia.
Brisac, Douglass Pettiward	12 June 12	1 Jan. 16	R. Marines.
Brohenshire, Joseph	7 May 07		11 R. Veteran Battalion.
Brooks, John Thomas	2 Feb. 15	25 Mar. 16	14 Dragoons.
Bruyeres, Henry Pringle	1 Sept. 15	21 Feb. 23	R. Engineers.
Burke, James	20 May 13		8 R. Veteran Battalion.
Burrows, James	21 June 10		4 R. Veteran Battalion.
Burton, Emanuel	17 Aug. 15	14 Sept. 26	Unattached.
Bury, Phineas	23 Jan. 17	23 Jan. 17	57 Foot.
Bush, Thomas	26 May 14		5 R. Veteran Battalion.
Butcher, John Lewis	18 Oct. 09	1816	8 West India Regiment.
Cameron, Donald	8 July 00	9 Aug. 02	40 Foot.
Cameron, Ewen	7 June 15		3 R. Veteran Battalion.
Cameron, James		1814	3 Prov. Batt. of Militia.
Campbell, Alexander Brodie	24 June 02	24 June 02	49 Foot.
Campbell, Archibald	27 Aug. 07	1811	Barrack Artillery.
Campbell, Colin	28 Oct. 09	26 Oct. 14	R. Marines.
Campbell, George	20 Mar. 17	7 Feb. 22	58 Foot.
Campbell, James	2 Sept. 08	17 June 13	R. Marines.
Campbell, James	11 Nov. 13	1814	92 Foot.
Carden, Paul Kyffin	22 Jan. 11	3 Aug. 20	R. Marines.
Carey, John Westropp	23 June 14	30 Dec. 19	30 Foot.
Carige, John Herbert	21 Sept. 15	24 Aug. 20	3 Garrison Battalion.
Carroll, Thomas	20 Nov. 17	26 Oct. 20	53 Foot.
Cassan, Edward Sheffield	8 April 25	25 Nov. 36	German Legion.
Chambers, Montagu	9 Nov. 15	1 Oct. 18	71 Foot.
Charles, Deskford	1 July 11		R. Sappers and Miners.
Child, George Richard	24 July 09	14 Nov. 17	R. Marines.
Chittem, John	14 Nov. 11		4 R. Veteran Battalion.
Church, Boneval	20 Jan. 14	25 Oct. 19	R. Waggon Train.
Clark, William Richard	3 Sept. 08	18 Aug. 14	R. Marines.
Clarke, George Dacres	5 July 80	21 April 89	R. Marines.
Clarke, James R.[1]	1 Nov. 05		R. Artillery.
Codrington, Sir C. B. Bart.	14 Aug. 82	24 June 83	21 Dragoons.
Coffin, Nathaniel	21 Mar. 83	11 Jan. 86	15 Foot.
Coleman, Charles	13 Feb. 98	1 Jan. 03	R. Marines.
Colley, William	15 April 96	3 Mar. 06	R. Marines.
Collier, James	26 July 08	24 Oct. 11	R. Marines.
Collings, William Moore	3 Mar. 14	23 Oct. 23	85 Foot.
Collins, William	25 Nov. 80		R. Marines.
Collins, Stephen Edward	14 Dec. 12	1 Sept. 14	R. Marines.
Collyer, George Samuel	24 Jan. 83	24 Jan. 83	87 Foot.
Cooke, Charles	27 May 82	1783	89 Foot.
Cordeaux, Charles	23 Jan. 14	1 Nov. 14	R. Artillery Drivers.
Corstorphin, Andrew	18 Aug. 13	1 Sept. 14	R. Marines.
Cosnard, John	11 May 91		88 Foot.
Couche, Richard	28 April 08	15 Sept. 17	R. Marines.
Coventry, Frederic	22 Dec. 14	25 Dec. 18	20 Dragoons.
Cowper, William	28 May 15	25 April 16	Foreign Corps of Wagg.
Cranage, John	26 Aug. 94		Independent Co.
Crespin, George Henry Legassick	11 Jan. 00	25 May 02	R. Marines.
Crombie, James[2]	31 Aug. 20		2 R. Veteran Batt.
Crossgrove, James	29 July 13	4 Feb. 19	104 Foot.
Crown, George Frederick	17 Feb. 14	1 Sept. 14	R. Marines.
Crozier, Henderson	12 May 14	25 Dec. 14	22 Foot.
Cruse, Thomas	1 Sept. 14	21 Oct. 14	R. Marines.
Cullen, Edward	20 Feb. 99		R. Artillery.
Cumming, Alexander	17 Feb. 14	26 Aug. 19	42 Foot.
Currie, James	25 May 15		4 R. Veteran Batt.

Second and Sub-Lieutenants, Cornets, and Ensigns.

	2D LIEUT. ETC.	WHEN PLACED ON HALF PAY.	
Currie, Robert William (*Cornet*)	19 Sept. 16	2 Oct. 23	60 Foot.
Curzon, Geo. Henry Roper	16 Dec. 16	2 Jan. 21	R. Artillery.
Daly, Lawrence	3 Jan. 11		75 Foot.
Dalyell, John	21 Dec. 15	30 Jan. 23	1 Dragoon Guards.
D'Anfossy, *Le Chevalier*	29 June 15	1 Aug. 15	R. Artillery.
Dardis, John	29 Oct. 12	26 Dec. 16	14 Foot.
Davenport, George	27 Jan. 14	25 Dec. 14	36 Foot.
Davis, John Henry	21 May 08		R. Marines.
Davis, Robert	7 Mar. 10	1 Jan. 16	R. Marines.
Davis, William	12 Aug. 09		R. Marines.
Dawson, Geo. Edward	5 Dec. 16	4 July 22	91 Foot.
Day, John	10 Dec. 14	25 Aug. 23	60 Foot.
Deaman, Thomas	28 April 14		Bradshaw's Rec. C.
Deane, Thomas	26 Mar. 83	1783	96 Foot.
Deans, Robert	25 April 11		6 R. Veteran Battt
De Beauvoir, *Sir* John Edmund	3 Mar. 14	14 May 18	104 Foot.
De Fauche, Charles	15 June 15	25 Mar. 17	60 Foot.
Dennis, William	25 June 13	25 Jan. 15	Dillon's Regt.
Devereux, George Alfred	2 Oct. 09	12 Aug. 14	R. Marines.
Dewell, Arthur	13 May 99	23 June 04	R. Marines.
D'Heillimer, George	5 Aug. 13	25 Mar. 16	Sicilian Reg.
Dillon, John	5 Mar. 18	1 April 24	3 Dragoon Guards.
Dillon, Theobald Augustus	21 April 14	25 Feb. 16	58 Foot.
Dixon, John Smart	20 July 15	4 Jan. 21	94 Foot.
Dixon, Richard	27 June 00	24 Aug. 02	York Hussars.
Dobree, Harry Hankey	24 June 02	24 June 02	7 Dragoons.
Dobree, Richard John	24 July 02	24 July 02	22 Dragoons.
Dodd, Charles W. Macarmick	6 Aug. 13	25 June 16	Newfoundland Fen.
Donovan, Henry Douglas	25 Aug. 13	13 Feb. 17	9 Foot.
Douglas, John	27 July 15		4 R. Veteran Batt.
Downing, John Flynn	4 Jan. 21		5 R. Veteran Batt.
Drinkwater, Thomas	4 April 09	1 Jan. 16	R. Marines.
Duckers, Charles	24 Dec. 12	21 Mar. 16	82 Foot.
Dudley, Benjamin	17 April 07	19 April 10	81 Foot.
Dufresne, Louis Flavien	13 Nov. 13	11 Oct. 16	Canadian Fen.
Durell, Philip	14 July 84		Independent Company.
Durnford, Andrew Mont. Isaacson	18 May 20		2 R. Veteran Batt.
Eaves, John	2 Dec. 06		R. Sappers and Miners.
Edgar, Charles Frederick	12 Jan. 05	1 Sept. 08	2 West India Regt.
Edgelow, George	14 July 14		8 R. Veteran Batt.
Egan, Timothy	25 Dec. 13	25 Sept. 19	R. Waggon Train.
Elliot, John Furzer	4 June 09	23 April 19	R. Marines.
Ensor, James	19 Mar. 97	31 May 02	R. Marines.
Evans, Daniel	16 Dec. 12	1 Sept. 14	R. Marines.
Evans, John	31 Aug. 95	25 Dec. 97	Irish Brigade.
Evans, John	9 May 11	6 Dec. 14	1 Garrison Batt.
Evans, William	11 Oct. 81	1 Sept. 83	R. Marines.
✠ Ewart, Charles	22 Feb. 16		5 R. Veteran Batt.
✠ Eyre, Richard Cocks .... (*2nd Lieut.*)	22 April 14	7 Aug. 17	81 Foot.
Eyre, Thomas Dowling	11 Nov. 11	28 Dec. 14	R. Marines.
Fagg, John William Thomas	3 May 21	25 Oct. 21	4 Dragoon Guards.
Fanning, Frederick	3 Aug. 13	29 June 25	R. Marines.
Farrell, Thomas	19 Oct. 15	8 Sept. 25	62 Foot.
✠ Fenn, John	10 Feb. 14	25 Dec. 18	R. Waggon Train.
Fenyhough, Thomas	25 Nov. 99	27 Aug. 03	40 Foot.
Field, John Stroud	7 April 09	6 June 15	R. Marines.
Fitzgerald, John	19 Aug. 13	25 Oct. 21	29 Foot.
Fitz Gerald, Nicholas	9 Dec. 99	2 Feb. 03	22 Dragoons.
Fletcher, James	11 Feb. 85		100 Foot.
Fletcher, *Sir* William Alexander, *Bart.*	15 May 17	15 May 17	3 Dragoon Guards.
Flexman, James	27 Jan. 08	11 Jan. 16	R. Marines.

Second and Sub-Lieutenants, Cornets, and Ensigns.

	ENSIGN, ETC.	WHEN PLACED ON HALF PAY.	
Flint, William Richard	3 Sept. 10	1 Jan. 16	R. Marines.
Foote, Samuel Townsend	1 Aug. 05		47 Foot.
Forbes, John	1 June 96		107 Foot.
Ford, James Bouverie	25 May 15		6 R. Veteran Batt.
Ford, William	29 April 09	6 Jan. 19	R. Marines.
Forsey, John	29 April 13	25 Oct. 14	Staff Corps of Cavalry.
Forster, George	25 July 01	1802	8 West India Regiment.
Forsyth, Robert	23 July 12		7 R. Veteran Battalion.
Fosbery, Henry William	17 Feb. 14	25 Oct. 21	12 Foot.
Fosbrooke, Robert	25 Dec. 13	1814	2 Prov. Batt. of Militia.
Francis, Henry, *Ens.*	6 Aug. 13	13 Jan. 20	Rifle Brigade.
Fraser, William (*Lieut.* 27 Jan. 37)	1 April 13	27 July 38	60 Foot.
Fraser, John	29 Dec. 14		72 Foot.
French, Peter	12 Mar. 83		Strathaven's Co.
Frett, John	21 Feb. 14	1 Sept. 14	R. Marines.
Fullom, John	24 Aug. 15		2 R. Veteran Battalion.
Gage, John Ogle	25 Dec. 13	8 May 23	9 Dragoons.
Garden, Alexander	3 Mar. 14	25 July 17	104 Foot.
Gardiner, James	8 Feb. 16	29 May 17	10 Dragoons.
Gardner, Charles	15 Dec. 14	31 Dec. 18	4 Ceylon Regt.
Gardner, John	28 Sept. 15		7 R. Veteran Battalion.
Geffrard, John	24 Jan. 91		Indep. Co.
Gibbs, William	1 Aug. 11		8 R. Veteran Battalion.
Gillbee, James	13 April 13	25 Mar. 16	Sicilian Regiment.
Glanville, Francis (*Lieut.*)	20 April 15	11 April 22	19 Dragoons.
Gleadowe, William	12 Feb. 18	25 Dec. 18	25 Dragoons.
Goldrisk, John Thomas	26 July 21	26 July 21	8 Dragoons.
Gordon, Alexander	25 Oct. 80	6 Feb. 90	R. Marines.
Gordon, Anthony	26 Dec. 11		5 R. Veteran Battalion.
Gordon, Francis	6 Oct. 84	23 Mar. 85	16 Foot.
Gordon, John	3 Mar. 04		7 R. Veteran Battalion.
Gould, Matthew	25 Dec. 06		4 R. Veteran Battalion.
Graham, Henry	13 June 15	25 Feb. 18	103 Foot.
Graham, Humphrey	19 July 98		Hanger's Rec. Co.
Grant, Alexander	12 Oct. 15	25 Mar. 16	1 Foot.
Grant, John	4 July 98		Bradshaw's Rec. Co.
Grattan, Charles	1 Dec. 12		R. Sappers and Miners
Grattan, Richard	1 Dec. 79		103 Foot.
Gray, John		1814	3 Prov. Bn. of Mil.
Graydon, James	15 Dec. 14	25 July 17	27 Foot.
Griffith, Hugh Davies	11 July 16	21 Oct. 19	22 Dragoons.
Griffith, Richard	15 Aug. 00		R. Irish Artillery.
Gritton, Henry	8 Sept. 08	20 Feb. 17	R. Marines.
Gunn, William	23 Aug. 15	24 April 16	Bourbon Regiment.
Gunthorpe, Joshua Rowley	4 June 95	16 Oct. 95	R. Marines.
Hagerty, William	5 June 09	30 May 17	R. Marines.
Hailes, Augustus	28 June 11	1 Jan. 16	R. Marines.
Hallum, James	31 Mar. 08	30 Mar. 20	R. Marines.
Hamilton, James	2 May 16	25 Feb. 19	4 West India Regiment.
Hamilton, John	24 Mar. 00	25 Mar. 02	1 Foot.
Hammond, William	17 Oct. 14	1 Jan. 16	R. Marines.
Hamond, William	26 Sept. 87		71 Foot.
Handcock, Tobias	4 May 15	26 Mar. 16	27 Foot.
Hannay, James	26 Aug. 82	21 Feb. 91	R. Marines.
Harby, William	27 Oct. 14		2 Garrison Battalion.
Harding, John	5 Mar. 12	25 Mar. 17	34 Foot.
Harper, Joseph James	29 May 83	25 June 15	Bruce's Co.
Harrison, Samuel Wyment	16 July 00	25 June 02	4 Dragoon Gds.
Harrison, William	26 Dec. 16	26 Dec. 16	38 Foot.
Hart, William[3]	25 May 15	25 Sept. 17	R. Waggon Train.
Harvey, John	29 Dec. 13	8 Nov. 28	R. Marines.
Harvey, John	24 Dec. 12	25 April 16	Corsican Rangers.

Second and Sub-Lieutenants, Cornets, and Ensigns.

	CORNET, ETC.	WHEN PLACED ON HALF PAY.	
Harwood, Edward	12 Oct. 13	25 Dec. 14	32 Foot.
Haslewood, Joseph	24 April 83	1783	89 Foot.
Hay, Archibald James	12 Nov. 12	25 April 16	2 Hussars German Leg.
Haydon, Joseph	27 Mar. 07	27 May 00	R. Marines.
Haydon, Robert Luckcombe	24 Feb. 14	1 April 19	20 Foot.
Haydon, William	25 Dec. 13	6 Mar. 17	6 West India Regiment.
Hays, Henry Horace	5 Jan. 15	25 June 18	81 Foot.
Haymard, Joseph Peter	29 Sept. 14	25 April 17	5 West India Regiment.
Hayter, George	10 June 13	1814	R. Waggon Train.
Hearne, Thomas William	15 Feb. 81	1 Sept. 83	R. Marines.
Heaviside, John	6 Nov. 06	18 Dec. 06	18 Dragoons.
Hemmings, John Exham	1 June 97		Invalids.
Henderson, James	20 Oct. 15		1 Garrison Battalion.
Heslop, John	18 Feb. 83		Invalids.
Hewett, Frederick	9 Sept. 12	1 Jan. 16	R. Marines.
Hewson, George	2 April 12	25 Dec. 14	24 Foot.
Hill, John	12 Jan. 82	12 May 91	R. Marines.
Hinton, John Thomas	25 May 12	1 Jan. 16	R. Marines.
Hoare, Charles Vyvyan	12 Mar. 11	3 Aug. 15	R. Marines.
Hobro, Edward		1814	1 Prov. Bn. of Militia.
Hodges, Edward Boucher	11 Aug. 13	14 Dec. 20	R. Marines.
Hodgins, Alexander	24 Sept. 12		12 R. Veteran Battalion.
Hodgson, Frederick Æmilius	10 Feb. 14	1814	R. Waggon Train.
⚔ Holland, Thomas Edward	25 Dec. 13	14 Jan. 19	83 Foot.
Holmes, Richard	20 Nov. 80	6 April 90	R. Marines.
Home, David	9 Dec. 13	9 July 18	69 Foot.
Hopkins, George	16 Feb. 15	11 Feb. 19	60 Foot.
Horne, John	14 Mar. 01	13 Aug. 02	15 Foot.
Horton, James	19 Mar. 07		2 Garrison Battalion.
Houlditch, John	20 Aug. 98		Horse Grenadier Gds.
Hoyland, John	1 April 15	1 Mar. 17	R. Sappers and Miners.
Hughes, Edward Hughes Ball	28 Aug. 17	11 Feb. 19	7 Dragoons.
Hugoe, Samuel	1 Oct. 11	1 Jan. 23	R. Marines.
Huntley, Joseph Martin	28 Mar. 11	2 Feb. 15	47 Foot.
Huthnance, John	12 Nov. 13	1 Nov. 14	R. Artillery Drivers.
Jack, Thomas[4]	23 Feb. 13		R. Artillery Drivers.
Jackson, John	22 Feb. 09	1 Jan. 16	R. Marines.
⚔ Jagger, Joseph[5]	16 July 13	1 Aug. 16	R. Artillery Drivers.
Jeffreys, Humphrey	2 Aug. 83		69 Foot.
Jenkins, John	19 Jan. 10	1 Jan. 16	R. Marines.
Innes, John	20 April 64		73 Foot.
Innes, Robert	14 May 13	8 Mar. 21	94 Foot.
John, David	25 Dec. 06		10 R. Veteran Battalion.
Johnston, Hamilton Trail	25 Aug. 10	1 Jan. 16	R. Marines.
Jones, John Henry Whitmore	22 May 17	9 Nov. 20	21 Dragoons.
Jones, Stopford Thomas	15 Nov. 10	25 Mar. 16	61 Foot.
Jop, Robert	11 May 15	25 April 16	25 Foot.
Karr, Peter	29 July 13		4 R. Veteran Battalion.
Katzman, Christian	23 Jan. 14	24 April 22	60 Foot.
Kennett, Charles Leighton	21 Sept. 15	20 April 20	4 West India Regiment.
King, George	16 Mar. 08	30 Aug. 14	R. Marines.
King, Robert Daubeny	20 April 15	14 June 15	14 Foot.
Knight, Christmas	25 Jan. 13		7 R. Veteran Battalion.
Kruger, Carl Wevel von	22 Jan. 14	23 Sept. 24	2 Ceylon Regiment.
Kyles, James	19 Oct. 15		2 R. Veteran Battalion.
Laing, James	15 June 15	25 June 17	83 Foot.
Lamb, John	9 Nov. 15		2 R. Veteran Battalion.
Lamborn, John Sherard	24 Aug. 32	24 July 35	R. Marines.
Lane, George Dawkins	15 Feb. 12	1 Jan. 16	R. Marines.
Lane, James Reece	15 April 07	7 Nov. 12	R. Marines.
Lanfranchi, Ruggero	3 Sept. 01		Queen's Germans.

Second and Sub-Lieutenants, Cornets, and Ensigns.

	ENSIGN, ETC.	WHEN PLACED ON HALF PAY.	
Langdale, Marmaduke Robert	17 June 02	25 July 02	9 Foot.
Langford, Edward	24 June 02	24 June 02	49 Foot.
Lawrence, George	24 Oct. 21	3 Nov. 25	55 Foot.
Layfield, George	8 June 20		3 R. Veteran Battalion.
Leatham, Francis	4 Nov. 13	25 April 17	62 Foot.
Lee, Frederick Richard	6 Dec. 13	21 Dec. 15	96 Foot.
Lee, John	8 Sept. 14	25 April 16	78 Foot.
Lee, Robert Newton	29 June 15	13 Nov. 23	2 Ceylon Regiment.
Leissring, Charles	24 Sept. 12	2 Sept. 17	7 West India Regiment.
Lennan, Edward	3 Aug. 15	16 April 18	7 West India Regiment.
Lepine, John	7 Oct. 93	27 Nov. 93	73 Foot.
Levick, Jonathan	8 Dec. 14	25 Dec. 17	1 Garrison Battalion.
Lewis, James	29 Feb. 16	25 Nov. 16	3 Garrison Battalion.
Lewis, Stephen	19 May 14	6 July 20	73 Foot.
Lidderdale, Thomas Robertson	14 Aug. 00		6 West India Regiment.
Lloyd, Henry Vereker	31 Jan. 16	25 Oct. 21	86 Foot.
Lloyd, Samuel	24 Feb. 09	10 April 16	R. Marines.
Loft, John Henry	30 Dec. 13	12 Mar. 18	15 Dragoons.
Loftin, George	19 Jan. 07	22 Dec. 09	R. Marines.
Lomas, Ralph	8 Aug. 99	1 Sept. 02	R. Marines.
Losack, Augustus	18 May 15	5 Aug. 19	84 Foot.
Lum, William Purefoy	25 Dec. 13	27 July 20	35 Foot.
Lyons, Anthony Munton	3 Nov. 12	1 Sept. 14	R. Marines.
Lyte, Thomas	22 July 80	19 Sept. 88	R. Marines.
M'Alister, Angus	20 April 15	25 Dec. 18	94 Foot.
M'Aulay, Aulay	27 Feb. 79	7 June 80	R. Marines.
M'Conechy, James	10 Mar. 12	1 Jan. 16	R. Marines.
M'Culloch, George	14 Nov. 11		7 R. Veteran Battalion.
M'Dermott, Geo. Augustus	2 Dec. 13	10 Aug. 20	Rifle Brigade.
M'Donald, Ronald	19 Dec. 11		2 R. Veteran Battalion.
M'Donell, Alexander	6 Feb. 12	25 Aug. 16	Glengarry Fencibles.
M'Intosh, Robert	15 July 13	25 Dec. 18	94 Foot.
⌘ M'Kay, Joseph [6]	6 Oct. 14	1 Aug. 16	1 Foot.
M'Kinnon, John	24 June 83	1783	64 Foot.
M'Lachlan, Neil	7 Sept. 04		64 Foot.
M'Lauchlan, James	28 April 14	1814	92 Foot.
M'Leod, Norman	11 Aug. 14	8 Mar. 21	6 Foot.
M'Taggart, Angus	25 Nov. 12		1 R. Veteran Battalion.
Macdonnell, Charles	8 June 15	24 May 21	32 Foot.
Mackay, George	1 July 13	1815	1 Garrison Battalion.
Mackay, John	24 Feb. 20		3 R. Veteran Battalion.
Mackay, William	16 June 14		2 R. Veteran Battalion.
Mackreth, Henry Williams	21 Oct. 13	15 June 15	26 Foot.
Maclachlan, Colin	9 July 00	25 June 15	72 Foot.
Maclean, Alexander	24 June 13	25 June 16	Newf. Fencibles.
Maclean, Samuel	22 April 15	1 Mar. 17	R. Sappers and Miners.
Mac William, John	14 Sept. 15	15 May 18	100 Foot.
Madden, Robert	16 July 13		R. Artillery Drivers.
Maloney, James	28 Feb. 11		7 R. Veteran Battalion.
Manico, Edward	2 Feb. 11	1 Jan. 16	R. Marines.
Mansell, William	20 April 15	20 April 20	79 Foot.
Manson, William	5 Dec. 82	1783	87 Foot.
Margitson, Joseph	6 Sept. 15	25 Feb. 16	27 Foot.
Marsack, Geo. Hartwell	13 June 11	25 Nov. 14	31 Foot.
Marshall, Lawrence Jopson	27 Feb. 17	27 Feb. 17	7 Dragoon Guards.
Marshall, Thomas	25 Feb. 09	6 Mar. 15	R. Marines.
Mason, Richardson	14 April 13	25 Dec. 18	94 Foot.
Mason, Robert James	26 April 09	17 May 11	R. Marines.
Maule, William	3 May 00	25 June 02	28 Dragoons.
⌘ Maxwell, Wm. Aug. Riddell (*Cornet*)	25 Oct. 15	13 Dec. 27	Unattached.
₿ *Mead, Charles*[7]	1 May 13		R. Artillery Drivers.
Meredith, James Henry	2 May 11	1 Jan. 16	R. Marines.
Merritt, Thomas	25 Dec. 82		Queen's Am. Ran. *Cav.*

Second and Sub-Lieutenants, Cornets, and Ensigns.

	ENSIGN, ETC.	WHEN PLACED ON HALF PAY.	
Middleton, Robert	11 May 20		10 R. Veteran Battalion.
Millar, Robert[8]	7 Oct. 13	24 Jan. 34	92 Foot.
Milliken, John	1 June 01		63 Foot.
Monk, John	30 May 12	14 Sept. 14	R. Marines.
Montgomery, Robert	2 Dec. 13	25 Jan. 19	95 Foot.
Moon, John	31 May 10		11 R. Veteran Battalion.
Mooney, John	25 April 98	26 April 98	R. Marines.
Moore, Charles William	31 May 09	22 Sept. 17	R. Marines.
Moore, James	7 Sep. 09		97 Foot.
Moore, John		1814	1 Prov. Bn. of Militia.
Morehouse, George	25 Oct. 13	25 April 16	New Brunswick Fen.
Morgan, James Hungerford	8 Sept. 08	2 Jan. 21	R. Marines.
Morris, John	27 July 15	15 May 17	4 Foot.
Mortashed, John	27 Jan. 14	25 Oct. 21	35 Foot.
Moss, Henry	31 Aug. 13	1 Sept. 14	R. Marines.
Murphy, John Good	23 Oct. 00		54 Foot.
Murray, Adam	18 Jan. 16	13 Feb. 18	84 Foot.
Nason, George	9 Oct. 15	25 June 22	68 Foot.
Nelson, Richard	27 Jan. 14	18 July 16	3 Foot.
Newson, George	26 Feb. 13	25 May 16	Greek Lt. Infantry
Nicholls, John	26 Aug. 99	16 May 00	4 Foot.
Nicholson, William	2 July 18	2 July 18	28 Foot.
Nixon, John Isaac	7 Dec. 15	1 Jan. 18	4 Foot.
North, Roger	9 Mar. 13	11 Nov. 24	R. Marines.
Nugent, Christopher Edm. John	25 June 02	24 June 02	17 Dragoons.
O'Connell, Daniel	7 Sept. 31	17 April 33	R. Marines.
O'Shea, Thomas	5 July 15	25 Nov. 16	3 Garrison Batt.
Owen, Robert Hassall	22 Feb. 11	1 Jan. 16	R. Marines.
Palling, Henry	8 July 13	Jan. 19	95 Foot.
Parsons, Guy	16 May 09		R. Marines.
Partington, James	1 Dec. 14	25 Oct. 17	8 West India Regiment.
Pasheller, Charles	16 Nov. 80	1 Sept. 83	R. Marines.
Patterson, Thomas	6 April 13	1 Sept. 14	R. Marines.
Pawsey, George	20 Nov. 81	8 Mar. 91	R. Marines.
Payler, Thomas	7 Nov. 11		Bradshaw's Rec. Co.
Pearce, Edmund Wentworth	11 June 94	20 June 95	18 Foot.
Pegg, William	17 June 02	31 Mar. 03	28 Dragoons.
Pellet, James	28 Jan. 13	17 Nov. 14	38 Foot.
Pepperell, John Down	22 Nov. 10		1 R. Veteran Battalion.
Philipps, George	15 April 12	1 Jan. 16	R. Marines.
Pitt, Henry	2 Sept. 12	1 Jan. 16	R. Marines.
Plenderleath, David	6 May 02	25 May 02	4 Foot.
Pogson, Bedingfield	21 Feb. 98	1 Feb. 03	R. Marines.
Porter, John Hall	4 Feb. 11	1 Jan. 16	R. Marines.
Porter, Samuel	3 Jan. 98	25 June 03	38 Foot.
Potts, Robert Clowes	15 Feb. 83	1783	88 Foot.
Poussin, Balthazard	23 Dec. 13	25 Mar. 16	Corsican Rangers.
Powell, William Edward (*Ensign*)	21 Mar. 11	12 Sept. 22	18 Dragoons.
Prendergast, Maurice	22 Feb. 13	25 April 16	2 Hussars German Leg.
Prosser, Edmund Bond	28 Nov. 82	1 Sept. 83	R. Marines.
Pulliblank, Edward Cooper	18 July 09	16 Jan. 16	R. Marines.
Radcliffe, *Sir* Joseph, *Bart.*	19 July 15	22 April 19	23 Dragoons.
Radcliffe, Thomas	1 Sept. 09	1 Sept. 14	R. Marines.
Raye, Henry Robert	14 Dec. 12	1 Sept. 14	R. Marines.
Read, James	21 Jan. 11	1 Jan. 16	R. Marines.
Read, Thomas	1 Feb. 06	7 May 10	R. Marines.
Reid, Thomas	3 May 00	9 Feb. 03	22 Dragoons.
Rendlesham, Frederick, *Lord*	31 Oct. 16	21 Dec. 20	21 Dragoons.
Resius, Frederick	1 June 15	4 Oct. 19	60 Foot.
Rickard, Martin	25 Dec. 13	25 Dec. 18	R. Waggon Train.

Second and Sub-Lieutenants, Cornets, and Ensigns.

Name	CORNET, ETC.	WHEN PLACED ON HALF PAY.	
Ridge, James Stuart	22 Feb. 14	29 June 20	6 West India Regiment.
Ridsdale, Griffith Twistleton	3 June 13	1814	47 Foot.
Robertson, William	1 July 12		R. Sappers and Miners.
Robson, John Charles	27 July 30	17 Oct. 33	R. Marines.
Roch, James	31 Dec. 82		103 Foot.
Rogers, Thomas	17 Oct. 99	25 Aug. 02	40 Foot.
Rose, Colin	23 Feb. 15	25 June 16	90 Foot.
Rose, Philip	17 Nov. 13	1814	56 Foot.
Ross, David Robert	2 May 16	13 April 20	23 Dragoons.
Ross, Henry Paget Bayly	16 Dec. 12	1 Sept. 14	R. Marines.
Ross, Horatio (*Cornet*)	19 Oct. 20	20 Nov. 23	59 Foot.
Ross, John	20 Oct. 10	4 Feb. 15	6 Garrison Battalion.
Ross, William	20 June 83	1783	10 Foot.
St. John, Oliver	9 Sept. 13	4 Feb. 15	6 Garrison Battalion.
Sallery, William Ogle	19 Feb. 07	23 Aug. 10	7 Garrison Battalion.
Saunders, Edward	14 Jan. 14	1 April 17	R. Sappers and Miners.
Sargent, Richard	15 Dec. 13	1 Sept. 14	R. Marines.
Savage, Rowland	2 Dec. 14	12 Mar. 18	1 Foot.
Sayer, Benjamin	14 Oct. 82	1 Sept. 83	R. Marines.
Schalch, Philip	11 Dec. 15	14 Dec. 21	R. Artillery.
Scott, William	16 June 14	1814	61 Foot.
Scully, William	24 June 02	24 June 02	13 Dragoons.
Senior, John	30 June 16	8 Sept. 19	4 West India Regiment.
Serjeant, George	11 April 12	1 Jan. 16	R. Marines.
Shackel, William	21 Sept. 15	25 June 16	R. Waggon Train.
Shaw, Leander	25 May 15		1 R. Veteran Battalion.
Shaw, Richardson	18 April 83	1783	89 Foot.
Shepherd, William	18 Nov. 13	14 Nov. 16	R. Waggon Train.
▣ Shore, John [9]	19 May 13	15 Nov. 14	R. Artillery Drivers.
Simpson, John B. (*Cornet*)	17 Oct. 16	5 Aug. 24	48 Foot.
Simpson, John W.	2 Aug. 10	1 Jan. 16	R. Marines.
Sired, William	24 Aug. 20		2 R. Veteran Battalion.
Skinner, William Dunstan	25 July 12	23 Sept. 24	R. Marines.
Skues, George	25 Oct. 13	1 Sept. 14	R. Marines.
Smith, John	22 Oct. 03	25 June 15	72 Foot.
Smith, John	1 June 11		R. Sappers and Miners.
Smith, Michael Cusac	19 Aug. 13	10 June 19	11 Dragoons.
Smith, Peter	25 Oct. 14	25 April 16	New Brunswick Fen.
▣ Smith, Wm. Staytor (*Lieut.* 17 Oct. 08)	25 Dec. 06	8 Nov. 19	72 Foot.
Smithwick, Robert	3 Oct. 10	1 Jan. 16	R. Marines.
Spark, John	8 April 12		R. Sappers and Miners.
Sparkes, Thomas	7 April 13	1814	56 Foot.
Spearman, Ralph William	30 Jan. 21	25 Aug. 21	21 Foot.
Standish, Richard	28 June 11	1 Jan. 16	R. Marines.
Staples, Edmund Robert	28 Nov. 16	25 Feb. 19	Staff Co. of Cavalry.
Stevens, Samuel	23 Feb. 81	1783	Elford's Co.
Stevens, William	1 Nov. 15	1 April 17	R. Sappers and Miners.
Stevenson, George	29 Dec. 14	22 July 19	6 Dragoons.
Stewart, Robert	25 May 15		7 R. Veteran Battalion.
Stratton, William	1 April 13		R. Sappers and Miners.
Strudwick, George Lucas	25 April 81		Wall's Corps.
Stuart, Alexander	4 Sept. 17	4 Sept. 17	3 Dragoon Guards.
Sunderland, Henry	26 July 21	7 Mar. 22	52 Foot.
Sutherland, Alexander	12 Nov. 12		1 R. Veteran Battalion.
Swallow, Samuel	23 Nov. 81	1 Sept. 83	R. Marines.
Sweeney, Francis Bernard	20 Jan. 14	25 April 17	62 Foot.
Swinhoe, Robert	1 Mar. 16	25 April 19	25 Dragoons.
Symmers, George	17 May 81		Indep. Co.
Sympson, Robert	25 Feb. 83		60 Foot.
▣ Talbot, James (*Lieut.*)	16 Feb. 15	23 May 22	2 Dragoon Guards.
Talmash, Arthur Cæsar (*Lieut.*)	24 Aug. 15	13 Oct. 20	6 Dragoons.
Taylor, Robert [10]	22 Jan. 08		R. Artillery.

Second and Sub-Lieutenants, Cornets, and Ensigns.

	CORNET, ETC.	WHEN PLACED ON HALF PAY	
Taylor, William	16 May 16	5 Sept. 16	7 West India Regiment.
Temple, Gustavus Hancock	15 May 09	18 Mar. 13	R. Marines.
Thacke, Robert	6 Feb. 12	20 Dec. 25	R. Marines.
Thierry, Lewis de	8 Feb. 14	1 Sept. 14	R. Marines.
Thomas, Mark	9 Nov. 15	25 Nov. 18	98 Foot.
Thompson, Augustus	5 Aug. 13	5 Aug. 24	42 Foot.
Thompson, Thomas	9 Dec. 13	1814	96 Foot.
Thomson, George	5 May 14	25 Jan. 18	12 Foot.
Thomson, Thomas	29 Feb. 12	24 Sept. 23	R. Marines.
Thornton, Robert Innes	1 Aug. 16	1 Aug. 16	78 Foot.
Tickell, John Arscott	8 Sept. 08	7 Oct. 19	R. Marines.
Todd, William	2 Feb. 10	1 Jan. 16	R. Marines.
Toy, John	13 Nov. 10		5 R. Veteran Battalion.
Tracy, Henry	23 May 13		R. Artillery Drivers.
Traill, Thomas	28 Oct. 14	25 Mar. 16	21 Foot.
Trewhitt, Henry	30 Dec. 13	8 Jan. 18	34 Foot.
Talk, John Augustus	7 July 84		86 Foot.
Turnbull, William George	12 Aug. 13	25 June 18	73 Foot.
Turner, William	6 Feb. 12	25 June 16	Sicilian Regiment.
Tweedie, David	28 Aug. 12	1 Jan. 16	R. Marines.
Tyndale, Joseph	19 Aug. 99	27 Aug. 03	4 Dragoons.
Vaux, John Gustavus	23 Sept. 13	1 July 16	R. Artillery Drivers.
Veitch, William	30 Jan. 12	30 May 16	58 Foot.
Vincent, John Tunnadine	18 Nov. 80	1 Sept. 83	R. Marines.
Wade, Thomas	5 Dec. 08	1 Jan. 16	R. Marines.
Walker, Samuel	30 July 12	11 Feb. 24	R. Marines.
Walker, Thomas	2 Dec. 08	29 Nov. 14	R. Marines.
Walker, William Hislop	16 Nov. 15	25 Feb. 25	3 West India Regiment.
Wallace, Alexander	1 July 11		R. Sappers and Miners.
Wallace, James (*Ensign*)	14 April 14	22 June 23	22 Dragoons.
Walrond, Bethell	17 Dec. 18	18 May 22	15 Dragoons.
Walsh, George	14 April 14	25 June 20	45 Foot.
Walter, George	17 Jan. 11	1 Jan. 16	R. Marines.
Walter, Rawlins George	1 April 09	1 Jan. 16	R. Marines.
Walters, Henry	13 Dec. 13	1 Sept. 14	R. Marines.
Ward, John	14 Dec. 07	20 Aug. 14	R. Marines.
Watkins, Westropp Peard	18 Feb. 13	30 May 22	22 Foot.
Watson, Atherton	31 May 91	12 April 93	91 Foot.
Watson, James	21 Sept. 12	8 April 26	R. Marines.
Watts, David John	20 May 08	1 Jan. 16	R. Marines.
Watts, William	8 Oct. 03	24 May 04	2 Dragoon Guards.
Way, Hollis Bull	28 Nov. 80	1 Sept. 83	R. Marines.
Way, John	5 July 80	1 Mar. 84	103 Foot.
Webster, James	24 Nov. 02	24 Nov. 02	27 Foot.
Weir, Hector John	10 Dec. 82	1 Sept. 83	R. Marines.
Weir, Henry	18 Feb. 14	1 Sept. 14	R. Marines.
Weiss, Frederick	24 Jan. 14	25 July 18	60 Foot.
Whaley, George	24 Sept. 02	25 Sept. 02	17 Foot.
Wheadon, John	11 April 12	1 Jan. 16	R. Marines.
Wheler, Edward	17 July 17	25 Dec. 18	20 Dragoons.
White, *Sir* T. Wollaston, *Bart.*	19 Oct. 20	9 July 23	10 Dragoons.
Wilcocks, John Lodge	3 May 00	25 June 02	1 Dragoon Guards.
Wilde, Joshua John	18 Nov. 81	1 Sept. 83	R. Marines.
Wildey, Thomas	3 Oct. 16	25 Dec. 17	7 Dragoons.
Wilkins, Samuel Martin	7 Jan. 06		86 Foot.
Wilkinson, John Byng	13 July 15	4 June 18	23 Dragoons.
Williams, John	9 Mar. 81	1 Sept. 83	R. Marines.
Williams, William	12 Oct. 15		Garr. and Vet. Co.
Williamson, William Hamilton	27 May 19	9 Jan. 23	6 Dragoons.
Wills, John	23 May 00		Kingston's Rec. Co.
Wilson, Edward Lumley	24 Oct. 02	24 Oct. 02	Homp. M. Rif.
Wolff, Alexander Joseph	25 Dec. 21	11 Nov. 24	11 Foot.
Wolseley, Arthur	30 June 83		Queens' Amer. Ran(*Inf.*)

Second and Sub-Lieutenants, Cornets, and Ensigns.

	2D LIEUT. ETC.	WHEN PLACED ON HALF PAY.	
Woodcock, Frederick	3 Aug. 12	20 Feb. 15	R. Marines.
Woolhouse, Andrew Mackason	13 Aug. 25	17 July 28	Unattached.
Yate, John	18 July 07		R. Marines.

Services of the Second Lieutenants, Cornets, and Ensigns.

1 Second Lieut. James R. Clarke served on the Continent in 1794 and 95, and was present in several skirmishes, and at the siege of Nimeguen, where he was wounded.

2 Ensign Crombie was at the capture of the Cape of Good Hope in 1806. Served also the campaign before New Orleans in 1814 and 15, and was severely wounded.

3 Cornet Hart served at the taking of the Cape of Good Hope and capture of the Dutch Fleet in Saldanah Bay in 1796.

4 Second Lieut. Jack served in Holland in 1799, and was three times wounded. Served also in the American war, including the actions at Le Bleuf, Chippewa (wounded), and Lundy's Lane.

5 Second Lieut. Jagger served in the Peninsula, including the battle of Talavera. Served also the campaign of 1815, and was present at the battle of Waterloo.

6 Ensign M'Kay was slightly wounded at Waterloo.

7 Second Lieut. Mead served the Peninsular campaign of 1814.

8 Ensign Millar served in the Peninsula, and was present at the battles of Nivelle, Nive, and Toulouse.

9 Second Lieut. Shore served in the Peninsula, from Sept. 1813, to the end of the war.

10 Second Lieut. Robert Taylor's services:—Siege of Fort Bourbon and captures of Martinique, St. Lucia and Guadaloupe, 1794. In 1795, when the Caribs rose to take the Island of St. Vincent, he commanded the Artillery in the field for ten months, during which period he was in eleven different engagements.

PAYMASTERS.

	CORNET, 2d LIEUT. or ENSIGN.	LIEUT.	PAY-MASTER.	WHEN PLACED ON HALF PAY.	
Acton, Edward	never	never	9 Mar. 12	6 Dec. 14	2 Garr. Batt.
Aitkin, Alexander	do	do	26 Aug. 13	17 Feb. 21	42 Foot.
Albert, Hugh Lewis	do	do	5 Feb. 98	23 Oct. 17	39 Foot.
Amey, Henry James	do	do	1 Mar. 06	30 Sept. 16	German Legion
Armstrong, James	do	do	6 Jan. 14	25 Aug. 17	67 Foot.
Bannerman, Alexander ..	do	do	23 Feb. 04	1811	78 Foot.
Bell, William	do	do	12 Dec. 11	19 Aug. 19	56 Foot.
Bews, John............	do	do	28 Nov. 11	1 July 36	73 Foot.
Biggs, Edward	do	do	30 Nov. 15	25 Nov. 26	22 Foot.
Boustead, John	do	do	21 June 10	1 May 36	Ceylon Rif. Regt.
P Bowden, Wm. Carey..	do	do	12 May 08	4 Nov. 24	21 Dragoons.
P Boyle, William[1]......	21 July 08	6 Feb. 12	3 Nov. 25	1 May 32	21 Foot.
P Brenan, Justin	never	never	11 Mar. 13	5 Nov. 18	88 Foot.
Brenan, Patrick........	do	do	11 Nov. 13	23 May 22	97 Foot.
Bromley, William	do	do	19 Nov. 07	25 Dec. 16	2 Garr. Batt.
Burnet, John	do	do	25 June 02	11 April 11	16 Dragoons.
Cameron, Allan	19 April 05	30 Jan. 06	16 July 21	25 April 24	5 Foot.
Campbell, Duncan......	never	never	15 Mar. 98		88 Foot.
Carmichael, Robert	do	do	8 Aug. 06	25 Dec. 14	42 Foot.
Chapman, Benjamin	do	do	27 Aug. 03	23 Dec. 19	German Legion.
Chase, John Woodford ..	do	do	24 Oct. 05	1811	Malta Regiment.
Christie, George........	do	do	25 Dec. 06	25 July 17	8 W. India Regt.
Collins, Michael	8 Aug. 16	do	21 Mar. 27	June 39	76 Foot.
Cox, Charles	never	do	29 Jan. 06	7 May 29	75 Foot.
Creser, Richard	10 Jan. 11	3 June 13	14 Jan. 19	17 Nov. 25	27 Foot.
Cross, Anthony	never	never	6 Nov. 01	11 Sept. 06	24 Dragoons.
Cross, Henry	do	do	15 Oct. 08	25 June 17	83 Foot.
Crowe, George William..	do	do	7 Mar. 11	25 Dec. 24	27 Foot.
Cuyler, Henry	do	do	24 July 16	1 Jan. 36	Rec. District.
Dana, William Pulteney	do	do	25 April 07	25 Dec. 16	6 Garr. Batt.
Dawe, Andrew Moore ..	do	do	8 Oct. 07	5 April 33	53 Foot.
P CB Deane, William ..	do	do	13 Aug. 02	1822	18 Dragoons.
De Carteret, George....	do	do	15 Feb. 98		5 R. Vet. Batt.
Dive, Hugh............	do	do	31 Mar. 08	21 Aug. 23	10 Foot.
Doughty, Edward	do	do	2 April 12	8 Sept. 19	4 W. India Regt.
Drayton, Samuel Box ..	do	do	25 Nov. 13	25 Mar. 16	15 Foot.
Este, William..........	do	do	28 Oct. 13	13 Nov. 17	57 Foot.
Finch, Charles	do	do	13 Feb. 12	25 Jan. 18	12 Foot.
Fisher, James	do	do	23 July 03	25 Mar. 17	Rec. District.
P Fraser, William[2]	20 July 94	21 Oct. 95	7 Feb. 04	1 Dec. 33	36 Foot.
Furlong, Charles John[3]..	29 Sept. 08	3 Jan. 10	22 April 24	26 July 33	Unattached.
Gapper, Peter..........	20 June 05	25 Dec. 06	14 Nov. 16	11 Nov. 19	104 Foot.
Geddes, Adam Gordon ..	never	never	31 Mar. 14	25 June 21	10 R. Vet. Batt.
Goddard, John	do	do	29 Aug. 11	27 Feb. 21	15 Foot.
P CB Gordon, James ..	do	do	4 April 05	2 Mar. 20	92 Foot.
Grant, Peter	do	do	29 Aug. 98	15 May 06	55 Foot.
P Grosser, John........	do	do	1 Aug. 11	14 Feb. 22	69 Foot.
Haldane, William	do	do	8 July 13	27 June 22	3 West Ind. Reg.

Paymasters.

	ENSIGN, ETC.	LIEUT.	PAY-MASTER.	WHEN PLACED ON HALF PAY.	
ℙ Hall, Henry William..	never	never	4 April 05	29 July 19	39 Foot.
Hall, John	do	do	2 Oct. 12	25 Sept. 28	Rec. District.
Halpin, William........	do	do	6 Jan. 7	25 June 16	German Leg.
Hanbury, Capel S.......	26 May 14	23 Nov. 15	26 Dec. 21	27 Mar. 28	1 Dragoons.
ℙ Hancorne, Christopher	never	never	13 June 05	25 Feb. 16	4 Foot.
Harman, Robert........	do	do	26 May 08	19 Oct. 26	17 Dragoons.
Harvey, Geo. Frederick..	do	do	3 Nov. 13	1814	Rec. District.
Heath, Edwin..........		do	*1814	28 June 27	30 Aug. 39	88 Foot.
ℙ ℚ Hilliard, Henry⁴..	25 Feb. 08	16 Nov. 09	22 Mar. 21	10 May 39	68 Foot.
Home, David	never	never	20 June 98	2 April 18	35 Foot.
Hounsom, George	do	do	29 Oct. 07	24 April 26	2 R. Vet. Batt.
Hunter, Thomas........	12 May 14	1 Oct. 25	3 Nov. 25	1 Oct. 36	7 Dragoon Gds.
Johnson, Ralph Boetler..	never	never	27 Oct. 10	25 June 15	45 Foot.
ℙ Johnstone, Jas. (Capt. 15 July 13)⁵	19 June 06	11 Feb. 08	17 July 23	1 Mar. 32	70 Foot.
ℙ Jolliffe, Cornwall	never	never	27 June 05	1817	34 Foot.
ℙ Jones, Michael	do	do	21 April 98	25 Aug. 19	80 Foot.
Irvine, J. Christ. Caulfield	do	do	27 Sept. 10	13 Oct. 25	80 Foot.
Irvin, Martin	5 May 04	16 Jan. 06	17 May 04	25 Dec. 14	61 Foot.
Ker, Thomas	27 April 09	12 July 10	14 May 17	30 June 20	103 Foot.
King, Thomas.........	never	never	5 Sept. 11	25 Dec. 18	98 Foot.
ℚ Knight, John	do	do	20 Jan. 14	25 May 16	German Leg.
Knyvett, Henry	do	do	25 Oct. 02	1 Nov. 26	Chief Pay. Dep.
ℙ Lediard, Thomas......	do	do	4 April 11	25 Dec. 17	66 Foot.
Ledingham, George	1 Aug. 05	17 July 06	16 Sept. 19	30 Nov. 38	34 Foot.
Leech, James	never	never	1 Feb. 98	23 June 08	3 Dragoon Gds.
ℙ ℚ Lutyens, Daniel..	do	do	19 Oct. 04	19 Oct. 38	3 Dragoon Gds.
M'Dougall, Wm. Adair..	do	do	1 July 13	12 Oct. 38	42 Foot.
ℙ M'Leod, Martin......	8 Oct. 12	18 Jan. 15	15 Jan. 24	15 Jan. 30	25 Foot.
Mackay, James	13 Mar. 15	14 Sept. 15	15 July 21	3 Nov. 25	60 Foot.
Mackay, James Duff	never	never	26 Nov. 12	1814	50 Foot.
ℚ Mackenzie, Hugh ..			8 Nov. 98	16 Aug. 24	71 Foot.
Mackenzie, Hugh Bailey	1 Feb. 13	do	24 May 29	14 Dec. 38	77 Foot.
Mackie, William	never	do	24 Jan. 05	25 July 17	27 Foot.
Malassez, Nicholas	do	do	30 Dec. 97	29 Oct. 02	Hompesch. M.R.
Mitchell, Daniel........	do	do	25 Dec. 13	1814	Rec. District.
Moir, William..........	do	do	16 Aug. 10	25 Feb. 23	Ceylon Regt.
ℙ ℚ Moore, Rob.(Capt. 20 July, 15)⁶	9 Oct. 06	14 April 08	10 June 24	1 Oct. 34	40 Foot.
ℙ Moss, William	never	never	3 Mar. 04	25 Aug. 16	York Lt. Inf.
O'Keefe, James	do	do	16 Jan. 12	1 April 37	48 Foot.
Phillips, W. Hollingworth	do	do	26 April 03	1 Nov. 33	Rec. District.
Pillon, John	do	do	26 Nov. 18	29 July 25	54 Foot.
Raymond, William	do	do	5 Dec. 99	25 Dec. 08	17 Foot.
Read, George	do	do	6 May 13	11 Nov. 24	5 Foot.
Reilly, Bernard	do	do	28 June 10	1 Nov. 36	18 Foot.
ℚ Robinson, P. Vyvyan	do	do	28 Jan. 13	28 June 27	88 Foot.
ℙ Rodgers, James⁷	17 May 27	do	7 Oct. 36	1 June 37	26 Foot.
Roddy, Chas. Pakenham	never	do	18 April 05	25 May 17	89 Foot.
Rose, Hickman Leland ..	do	do	26 Jan. 15	16 Aug. 21	30 Foot.
Sarjeant, William	do	do	31 Mar. 03	25 May 14	34 Foot.
Sherwood, Henry	do	do	1 May 04	23 July 18	Brunsw. Caval.
Smyth, Francis Robert..	do	do	12 Sept. 04		Rec. District.
Sprakeling, William	do	do	14 Dec. 15	25 Sept. 20	Rec. Dist.
ℙ ℚ Strange, Alex⁸ ..	do	do	11 April 11	16 Aug. 31	62 Foot.

Paymasters.

	2D LIEUT. ETC.	LIEUT.	PAY-MASTER.	WHEN PLACED ON HALF PAY.	
ℬ Teighe, Thomas	never	never	8 Sept. 04	25 June 16	German Legion.
Terry, Henry	13 Sept. 10	19 May 14	27 Dec. 27	1 June 35	99 Foot.
ℬ ℭℳ Thomson, J. Crooke	never	never	31 Jan. 11	22 Oct. 16	1 Foot.
Tiddeman, Henry	do	do	28 May 07	26 Mar. 18	75 Foot.
ℬ Tierney, Thomas	do	do	23 July 12	6 Sept. 27	43 Foot.
Tod, Alexander	do	do	28 June 10	25 April 16	38 Foot.
Trattle, John Kerr	do	do	26 July 10	11 Aug. 25	88 Foot.
Trick, Thomas	do	do	14 Sept. 09	12 July 14	1 R. Vet. Batt.
Wainwright, David	do	do	7 Sept. 08		11 R. Vet. Batt.
Wardell, Charles	1 Sept. 10	20 Dec. 13	7 Feb. 21	25 Jan. 28	42 Foot.
Wardell, John	never	never	1 May 05	25 June 26	24 Dragoons.
Wetherall, William	do	do	17 Aug. 99		87 Foot.
ℬ White, John Lewis	do	do	25 Feb. 13	8 Oct. 18	81 Foot.
ℬ White, Warren Hastings	do	do	17 Sept. 12	21 Sept. 15	German Legion.
ℬ ℭℳ Williams, James	do	do	4 Oct. 10	25 April 16	44 Foot.
Worsley, Cha. Corn. Sey.	do	do	25 Nov. 13	19 Jan. 18	60 Foot.
ℬ Wright, James	do	do	25 Mar. 10	25 Dec. 18	94 Foot.

Notes to the Paymasters.

1 Paymaster Boyle served in the Peninsula from May 1809 to the end of the war, including the battle of Busaco, affairs of Foz d'Aronce and Campo Mayor, siege and capture of Olive**n**a, assault and capture of Badajoz, capture of the Retiro. Slightly wounded in the ear at Fort St. Christoval 10th May, 1813, and again in the face in the Pyrenees 28th July, 1813.

2 Paymaster Fraser served in South America and was present at the attack on Buenos Ayres; in Portugal and Spain under Sir John Moore, including the battles of Vimiera and Corunna; at Walcheren, 1809; and in the Peninsula from Jan. 1811 to the end of the war, including the battles of Salamanca, Pyrenees, Nivelle, and Toulouse.

3 Paymaster Furlong was in the action before Genoa, and the taking of that city 17th April, 1814. Served afterwards in the American war, including the operations in the Chesapeak, battle of Bladensburg and capture of Washington; action before Baltimore and the subsequent service in the Chesapeak; operations of the army before New Orleans, the actions of the 23d Dec. 1814, and 1st Jan. 1815, and storm of the American lines before New Orleans; taking of Fort Bowyer. On board the *Golden Fleece* Transport, when attacked by an American Privateer off the island of St. Domingo, 28th Nov. 1814.

4 Paymaster Hilliard served in the Peninsula from June 1809 to the end of the war, including the battle of Busaco, affair of Campo Mayor, first siege of Badajoz, battle of Albuhera, affairs at Aroya de Molinos and Almarez. Served also the campaign of 1815, including the actions at Quatre Bras and Waterloo, at which latter he was severely wounded.

5 Captain Johnstone served at the siege of Copenhagen in 1807; and in the Peninsula from March 1809 to Oct. 1811, and again from Feb. 1812 to Feb. 1813, including the capture of Oporto, battles of Talavera (wounded), Busaco, and Albuhera (severely wounded); and first siege of Badajoz, besides minor actions and skirmishes.

6 Captain Moore served in the Peninsula from Feb. 1810 to the end of the war, including the battle of Busaco, first siege of Badajoz, siege of Ciudad Rodrigo (wounded in the trenches, 15 Jan. 1812), and third siege of Badajoz (severely wounded at the assault 6th April, 1812). Accompanied the expedition to New Orleans. Served also the campaign of 1815, including battle of Waterloo, where he was again severely wounded.

7 Paymaster Rodgers served in the Peninsula from May 1813 to the end of the war, including the siege of Tarragona. Served afterwards in the East Indies, and was present at Amulmir, Malligaum, and Asseerghur.

8 Paymaster Strange served at the siege of Fort St. Philip in the Island of Minorca in 1782, and was slightly wounded in the right knee. In action with the Irish rebels near Clonakilty in 1798. Served the campaigns in the Peninsula, Flanders, and France from 1811 to 1815 inclusive.

ADJUTANTS.

	CORNET, 2d LIEUT. or ENSIGN.	LIEUT.	ADJUTANT.	WHEN PLACED ON HALF PAY.	
Austin, George	30 Nov. 15	never	30 Nov. 15	25 Aug. 17	73 Foot.
Badham, Thomas	6 Dec. 10	7 Dec. 13	6 Dec. 10	14 Aug. 17	35 Foot.
Bangs, Wm. Rickett	3 Feb. 12	10 June 14	3 Aug. 13	25 Mar. 16	47 Foot.
Brew, William [1]	3 May 00	29 Jan. 01	20 Mar. 99	1814	2 Pr. Bn. of Mil.
Brown, James	never		10 Feb. 94		Northern Fen. In.
Brown, John Thomas ..		26 Oct. 99		25 June 14	1 Pr. Bn. of Mil.
Bruce, Thomas	never	never	18 July 99		Winds. Foresters
Bury, Wm. Aug.	10 Mar. 14	never	10 Mar. 14	25 Dec. 14	22 Foot.
Campbell, David	never	never	7 Mar. 94		Roth.&Caith.F.I
Cook, Robert	2 Dec. 03	19 Nov. 05	2 Dec. 03	10 Nov. 16	Newfound. Fen.
Crause, John	29 Dec. 08	25 April 11	6 April 15	25 May 17	Recru. District.
Crawford, James	17 April 06	5 May 07	17 April 06		8 R. Vet. Batt.
Doyle, Thomas Henry ..	25 July 16	never	18 April 22		1 R. Vet. Batt.
Ellis, Richard..........	29 Jan. 07	17 July 12	2 Feb. 09	25 Dec. 18	97 Foot.
Fahey, John	14 Sept. 15	never	14 Sept. 15	25 Mar. 16	81 Foot.
Farnan, John	7 April 13	10 Aug. 14	7 April 13	25 Feb. 16	8 Foot.
Fisher, Samuel S.	5 Sept. 11	18 Oct. 15	21 Nov. 11	25 Mar. 16	88 Foot.
Fitz Gerald, Dennis	15 July 13	never	15 July 13	25 June 16	41 Foot.
Fletcher, Richard	28 Oct. 08	7 Mar. 11	4 Mar. 13	25 May 17	Rec. District.
Fraser, Alexander	25 Mar. 13	24 June 15	25 Mar. 13	25 Feb. 16	New Bruns. Fen.
Halden, John	18 July 16	never	18 July 16	25 Sept. 17	7 Foot.
Haven, Henry	never	never	4 Sept. 00		Nug. Rec. Corps.
Henry, John	9 June 14	never	9 June 14	25 Feb. 16	91 Foot.
Holmes, John..........	never	never	11 May 97		Durham Fen.Inf.
Hopper, Jacob	1 Jan. 07	19 Jan. 08	1 Jan. 07	25 Mar. 14	Recruiting Dist.
Ingram, James	10 Mar. 97	never	10 Mar. 97		Breadal.Fen.Inf.
Kirkwood, James	27 Oct. 14	never	1 Nov. 19		6 R. Vet. Batt.
Leith, John Kenneth....	12 June 17	never	12 June 17	17 Sept. 18	12 Foot.
Leslie, James	15 Feb. 10	21 Nov. 11	20 May 13	5 Feb. 18	57 Foot.
Livingstone, Jeremiah ..	5 Oct. 15	never	5 Oct. 15	30 Nov. 16	Glengarry Fen.
Lowrie, James	24 Feb. 20	never	26 Sept. 22		2 R. Vet. Batt.
Mackenzie, Thomas	never	never	19 Feb. 83		77 Foot.
Morison, Daniel					W. Lowland F. I.
Muller, William	never	never	30 Mar. 83	1783	85 Foot.
Neale Abel	31 Dec. 07	1 Jan. 10	31 Dec. 07	25 Dec. 18	25 Dragoons.
Osborne, Francis	9 Dec. 19	never	9 Dec. 19	15 Mar. 21	62 Foot.
Packett, John	23 May 14	never	23 May 14	1815	Greek Lt. Inf.
Parlour, William	5 Aug. 13	5 Mar. 16	5 Aug. 13	28 Dec. 17	6 W. Ind. Regt.
Peacocke, George	never	never	31 Mar. 83	1783	88 Foot.
Peckett, Sampson	25 Feb. 13	20 Nov. 16	14 Oct. 13	25 June 17	34 Foot.
Reed, Lancelot	never	never	24 Jan. 83	1783	75 Foot.
Sinclair, John	14 Aug. 06	never	19 April 10		1 R. Vet. Batt.
Stewart, James	1 July 95	22 Aug. 96	16 Oct. 06		2 R. Vet. Batt.
Tassie, George	13 Dec. 10	never	13 Dec. 10		7 R. Vet. Batt.
Taylor, Thomas	never	never	18 Dec. 99		York Fen. Inf.
Thompson, Thomas	never	never	6 June 99		Ross & Cro. F. I.
Trotter, Thomas......	27 Oct. 14	never	27 Oct. 14	25 Oct. 16	27 Foot.
Turner, Alexander	29 Dec. 14	2 April 18	1 Oct. 18	23 June 25	3 W. Ind. Regt.
Walford, Edw. Lorkin ..	25 June 02	never	16 Jan. 00	2 Sept. 02	R. Wagg. Train.
Whitaker, Thomas......	24 June 13	never	24 June 13	25 Sept. 16	72 Foot.
Young, Robert	30 Mar. 20	never	30 Mar. 20		1 R. Vet. Batt.

1 Lieut. and Adjutant Brew served with the 2d Dragoon Guards in the campaigns of 1793, 4, and 5, in Flanders and Holland, under the Duke of York; and also proceeded with that regiment on the Walcheren expedition in 1809. Volunteered for Foreign service as Adjutant from the Royal West Middlesex Militia to the 2d Provisional Battalion, and accompanied it to France in 1813.

QUARTER-MASTERS.

	QUARTER-MASTER.	WHEN PLACED ON HALF PAY.	
Adey, Thomas	29 June 15		5 Royal Veteran Battalion.
Allen, Thomas	21 Oct. 13	6 Dec. 14	1 Garrison Battalion.
Amaron, Charles		25 Sept. 07	23 Dragoons.
Anderson, John	11 Oct. 05	25 June 16	6 West India Regiment.
Anderton, William		1 Jan. 31	1 Life Guards.
Armstrong, John	25 April 05	16 Dec. 19	58 Foot.
Atkins, William		25 Dec. 09	7 Dragoons.
Austin, John Radford	2 Mar. 14	1814	2 Provisional Batt. of Militia.
Austin, Nathaniel	1 May 14	25 June 17	3 Ceylon Regiment.
₧ ℗℗ Bagshaw, Isaac	13 Oct. 14	19 Sept. 22	84 Foot.
Banks, William		25 Feb. 20	1 Life Guards.
Barrow, Joseph		25 Mar. 12	10 Dragoons.
Bathurst, William		1 Jan. 31	1 Life Guards.
Beer, William		25 Mar. 26	2 Life Guards.
Bell, Robert	25 Sept. 12	29 Dec. 17	5 West India Regiment.
Benton, William	1 Nov. 04		72 Foot.
Bett, Thomas	1 Aug. 04		Royal Artillery.
Bishop, William			1 Life Guards.
₧ ℗℗ Blackier, Thomas[1]	16 Sept. 19	22 Feb. 39	7 Dragoons.
Blay, Samuel Sutton	5 Mar. 12	25 June 16	72 Foot.
Blythman, William	28 Sept. 15	25 Nov. 16	69 Foot.
₧ Booth, Jonathan[2]	4 May 26	27 July 38	60 Foot.
Brew, Francis[3]	17 May 21	23 June 37	49 Foot.
Brookman, James		25 Mar. 11	11 Dragoons.
℗℗ Brown, John	15 June 15	30 Mar. 38	1 Dragoon Guards.
Browning, Henry			Cambridge Fencible Cavalry.
Bryon, Daniel		25 June 18	19 Dragoons.
Buchanan, Wm. (Ens. 24 Feb. 20.)	6 Feb. 12		1 Royal Veteran Battalion.
Buchanan, William	12 Dec. 11		3 Royal Veteran Battalion.
Bulcock, Henry		25 Sept. 05	24 Dragoons.
Burns, Cormick	11 Mar. 13	1814	96 Foot.
Burrough, Thomas	26 Aug. 13	10 July 17	60 Foot.
Burt, James Elias		25 Dec. 02	23 Dragoons.
Calder, James	8 Feb. 35	6 Sept. 30	92 Foot.
Calueve, Pierre de			Royal Waggon Train.
Cambidge, Robert		25 Aug. 02	21 Dragoons.
₧ ℗℗ Cameron, Angus[4]	13 Feb. 12	12 Oct. 38	79 Foot.
Campbell, Jeremiah	28 July 14	11 Nov. 24	12 Foot.
Campbell, William	31 Jan. 22	10 Feb. 37	80 Foot.
Campbell, John	1 Mar. 93		Argyll Fencible Infantry.
Carden, James		1 Mar. 98	30 Dragoons.
Carey, Peter Martin	10 Aug. 96		Corsican Regiment.
Carkeek, Stephen			Cornwall Fencible Cavalry.
Carpenter, William			Cambridge Fencible Cavalry.
₧ Carr, James[5]	2 Nov. 26	6 Sept. 39	64 Foot.
Cart, Richard	7 Aug. 23	1 Jan. 31	R. Horse Guards.
Carter, John Henry		do	1 Life Guards.
Carter, William			Rutland Fen. Cav.
₧ Castray, Luke[6]	25 Mar. 24	19 Jan. 38	98 Foot.
Chalmers, William	27 July 05		94 Foot.
Cherriman, John	4 Jan. 10	25 Sept. 18	11 Dragoons.
Clark, Alexander	16 Jan. 07		R. Artillery.
Clark, Joseph			1 Life Guards.

Quarter-Masters.

Name	QUARTER-MASTER.	WHEN PLACED ON HALF PAY.	
Clarke, William	24 April 28	25 Aug. 29	Staff Corps.
Clayton, Thomas			Hants Fen. Cav.
Clifford, Richard	29 May 94	1795	119 Foot.
Cockburn, James	13 July 15	24 June 24	8 Dragoons.
☖ Collins, John	12 June 17	10 Nov. 21	18 Dragoons.
☖ *Colquhoun, Robert*	21 Aug. 06		Grenadier Guards.
Cooke, James		25 April 11	15 Dragoons.
Cooper, Henry		25 May 22	1 Life Guards.
Costello, Pierce		1 Mar. 98	32 Dragoons.
Crabtree, George	25 Oct. 09	21 May 18	87 Foot.
Crooks, Wm. Smedley		1 Jan. 31	2 Life Guards.
Cross, George	10 Mar. 14	1814	86 Foot.
Crymble, William	27 May 13		64 Foot.
Dallas, Alexander	3 Aug. 20	18 Nov. 24	Bourbon Reg.
Dandy, John	7 Mar. 22	7 Sept. 26	90 Foot.
Daum, Joseph	7 Feb. 08	25 Dec. 09	2 Dragoon Guards.
☖ Davidson, James [7]	14 Feb. 28	22 July 36	41 Foot.
Davies, Thomas	10 Dec. 12		1 Roy. Vet. Batt.
Davis, James		25 Jan. 10	8 Dragoons.
Delhanty, Henry		18 Sept. 04	22 Dragoons.
Dewson, Jeremiah Wilkes,[8] (*Ens.* 7 Oct. 13, *Lieut.* 25 Feb. 19)	3 Aug. 26	12 July 39	15 Foot.
Dixon, James (*Cor.* 13 Oct. 19)	25 June 24	8 Jan. 29	104 Foot.
Dobson, William			1 Life Guards.
Dowling, Robert		25 Dec. 22	4 Dragoon Guards.
Duncan, James			Perth. Fen. Cav.
Duncan, John	10 Mar. 14	25 Feb. 16	93 Foot.
Dunn, Thomas			Pembroke Fen. Cav.
Duxbury, Thomas	18 Mar. 13	9 May 16	14 Foot.
Dwelly, Thomas	15 Oct. 12	25 July 37	Coldstream Guards.
Ebdon, Richard		25 Mar. 10	3 Dragoons.
Eccles, Elkanah	25 Feb. 11	25 May 16	Greek Lt. Inf.
Edwards, Peter		8 Jan. 03	10 Dragoons.
Edwards, Thomas Willock [9]	3 Dec. 12	17 Feb. 32	84 Foot.
Ellington, John		11 Mar. 22	2 Life Guards.
Elliott, James	23 Nov. 04	26 April 39	65 Foot.
Ellis, John		25 June 02	22 Dragoons.
Emmott, William	25 Sept. 28	1 Jan. 31	R. Horse Guards.
Everitt, Joseph		25 Feb. 11	8 Dragoons.
Eyres, Benjamin		25 Sept. 14	10 Dragoons.
Fairbrother, Carter	7 Nov. 29	1 Jan. 31	R. Horse Guards.
Farrants, James	9 May 11	29 Mar. 18	103 Foot.
Finlay, William	28 Aug. 94		Glasgow Corps.
Frith, Joseph	25 Dec. 28	1 Jan. 31	Royal Horse Guards.
Flaherty, Hugh	1 Dec. 14	25 May 18	100 Foot.
Fox, Peter	25 Dec. 19	20 Nov. 23	Garrison Companies.
Fraser, Alexander	28 Sept. 09	11 Oct. 16	Canadian Fencibles.
Fraser, Donald	25 Nov. 05		74 Foot.
Frost, John	31 May 28	1 Jan. 31	Royal Horse Guards.
Gallie, Hugh	25 Feb. 10		9 Royal Veteran Battalion.
Gaze, James			Norfolk Fen. Cav.
Gillie, John		25 Dec. 22	12 Dragoons.
Glover, James			Lancashire Fen. Cav.
Godwin, John			Hants. Fen. Cav.
Grady, William	1 Oct. 07		12 Foot.
Green, Thomas		25 Oct. 26	1 Life Guards.
Greig, George		1 Jan. 31	2 Life Guards.
Grimwood, Thomas	25 Nov. 11	25 July 14	56 Foot.
Grove, Joseph		25 June 16	3 Dragoon Guards.
Guest, Charles			Pembroke Fen. Cav.

Quarter-Musters.

	QUARTER-MASTER.	WHEN PLACED ON HALF PAY.	
Haddon, Richard		25 Mar. 10	10 Dragoons.
Hagan, John		25 Oct. 83	Tarleton's Dragoons.
⚜ Hall, John	29 Sept. 14	14 Jan. 19	6 West India Regiment.
Hamilton, William		17 Nov. 00	Lanark & Dumbarton Fen. Cav.
⚜⚜ Hanna, William[10]	8 Jan. 20	27 May 36	4 Foot.
Harding, John	31 Oct. 03	8 May 17	3 Foot.
⚜ Hardy, Luke	13 Jan. 25	3 Aug. 26	New Brunswick Fencibles.
⚜ Hardy, Thomas	13 Feb. 12	25 Aug. 22	Royal Horse Guards.
Harris, William	25 Jan. 10		14 Foot.
Harrison, Alexander	22 Jan. 13	25 Sept. 17	1 Garrison Battalion.
Harrison, Dan. Chas. Rogers	8 Sept. 08	15 July 16	11 Foot.
Harwood, Sacheverel	9 July 03	25 July 16	Malta Regiment.
Haslam, Richard	25 Aug. 09	17 June 13	5 Dragoon Guards.
Haydon, Francis			Essex Fen. Cavalry.
Heartley, Andrew	12 Dec. 22	1 Jan. 31	Royal Horse Guards.
Henstock, Henry	1 Feb. 16	25 July 16	5 Foot.
Hewetson, Hamilton		25 June 02	4 Dragoon Guards.
Hill, James			Lothian Fen. Cav.
⚜ Hill, William	25 Dec. 26	29 Mar. 39	Rifle Brigade.
Hilliard, John			Cornwall Fen. Cav.
Hoath, Charles	5 Nov. 07	8 Aug. 16	60 Foot.
Hodder, John			1 Fencible Cav.
Holmes, Benjamin		25 June 02	1 Dragoon Guards.
Hope, William			Roxburgh Fen. Cav.
Horne, Robert	5 April 08	25 Aug. 18	2 Dragoon Guards.
Horner, Isaac	21 Oct. 95	1 Mar. 98	33 Dragoons.
Horton, Edward	26 Feb. 29	9 Nov. 30	1 Dragoons.
Houghton, John[11]	14 Dec. 09	15 Sept. 37	14 Dragoons.
Hudson, Edward	28 Sept. 09	25 Dec. 14	23 Foot.
Hurst, William		1 Mar. 98	32 Dragoons.
Jackson, Henry	28 April 27	1 Jan. 31	Royal Horse Guards.
Jackson, John		25 Jan. 13	3 Dragoons.
Jackson, John			Dumfries Fen. Cav.
Jennings, John			Essex Fen. Cav.
Innes, William	22 Dec. 00		Nugent's Rec. Co.
⚜ Johnson, Samuel[12]	14 Dec. 15	9 Mar. 38	48 Foot.
Johnston, Alexander	24 Sept. 12	28 Sept. 20	60 Foot.
Jolley, John			2 Life Guards.
Joseph, James		1 Jan. 31	1 Life Guards.
Julyan, Thomas			Cornwall Fen. Cav.
Kelly, Rich. Seymour	26 Jan. 26	July 38	Staff Corps.
Kenyon, Henry (*Ens.* 29 Oct. 12)	15 June 20		2 R. Veteran Battalion.
Kewin, Miles	2 July 12		5 R. Veteran Battalion.
⚜⚜ Kinkee, Frederick[13]	1 July 24	18 Aug. 25	19 Dragoons.
⚜ Kyle, Archibald[14]	13 Aug. 22	28 Aug. 35	82 Foot.
Lambster, Daniel		25 Aug. 14	15 Dragoons.
Landless, John			Lothian Fen. Cav.
Ledger, Thomas		25 April 11	15 Dragoons.
⚜ Lewis, J. H. (*Ens.* 12 Mar. 14)[15]	19 Oct. 15	3 Aug. 32	33 Foot.
Loggan, Edward	20 July 13	6 Feb. 15	2 Garrison Battalion.
Lord, Robert	16 Oct. 12		Royal Horse Guards.
Lowrey, William			Berwick Fen. Cav.
M'Clenahan, Thomas	4 Nov. 13	25 Dec. 16	2 Garrison Battalion.
M'Cord, Charles		1 Mar. 98	33 Dragoons.
M'Guire, Bernard		25 Aug. 10	9 Dragoons,
M'Intyre, Joseph	7 April 01		Ross and Cromarty Fen. Inf.
M'Laine, Lauchlan	6 April 15	2 Sept. 16	7 West India Regiment.
M'Naughtan, William		25 Mar. 14	2 Dragoons.
M'Pherson, John[16]	9 Sept. 13	2 Mar. 38	72 Foot.
Macdonald, William	14 April 14	25 July 17	104 Foot.

Quarter-Masters.

	QUARTER-MASTER.	WHEN PLACED ON HALF PAY.	
Mackay, Donald	12 Oct. 04	18 Mar. 13	42 Foot.
Machay, George	3 Sept. 01		93 Foot.
Mackenzie, John	16 Mar. 20	2 Jan. 23	7 Foot.
Mackenzie, John	1 Jan. 24	17 Aug. 38	94 Foot.
Maitland, John	22 July 13	25 May 17	37 Foot.
Maitland, Peter	9 Feb. 09	15 Sept. 37	90 Foot.
Manley, John	22 Oct. 12	25 Dec. 14	36 Foot.
Mann, Robert	19 May 94		90 Foot.
Mansfield, William [17]	21 April 11		22 Foot.
Marsh, Thomas	11 Nov. 95		Loft's Rec. Co.
Masterman, John		25 June 02	10 Dragoons.
Masters, James		1814	1 Provisional Batt. of Militia.
Merrie, William		25 Aug. 10	2 Dragoons.
Midwinter, Thomas			1 Life Guards.
Miller, George		1 Jan. 31	2 Life Guards.
Mingay, John	12 May 83		92 Foot.
Minikin, John	30 June 04		73 Foot.
Mitchell, Henry		25 Oct. 14	8 Dragoons.
Moore, George	18 Dec. 06		57 Foot.
Moore, John	26 Oct. 15	25 Nov. 16	3 Garrison Battalion.
⌐ Morgan, John [18]	1 Jan. 24	29 Dec. 37	52 Foot.
Morris, William	15 Oct. 14		19 Foot.
Mulholland, Andrew	28 May 12	25 Dec. 14	18 Foot.
Mulligan, Richard	30 Jan. 03		56 Foot.
Newell, John		25 Nov. 11	1 Dragoon Guards.
Nickson, John		25 Mar. 16	1 Dragoon Guards.
North, William			2 Life Guards.
⌐ O'Brien, Bartholomew [19]	1 Feb. 27	17 July 35	5 Dragoon Guards.
Ottey, John [20]	30 July 00	18 Sept. 35	60 Foot.
Page, William	13 Feb. 12	25 Jan. 18	12 Foot.
Palmer, Samuel			Cinque Ports Fencible Cavalry.
Paterson, Charles			Princess Royal's Own Fen. Cav.
Pattle, Daniel Moss			Norfolk Fencible Cavalry.
Pegley, Robert	24 Feb. 20		4 Royal Veteran Battalion.
⌐ Perrie, William	7 Dec. 26	25 Dec. 35	2 Dragoons.
Peters, John James (*Lt.* 12 Dec. 18)	12 Feb. 24	1 June 38	28 Foot.
Petto, Samuel	13 April 09	25 May 17	1 Foot.
Pilton, William	1 Jan. 13	1 July 25	Royal Artillery Drivers.
Pittard, Thomas			Oxford Fencible Cavalry.
⌐ Powell, John [21]	21 June 10	7 April 37	77 Foot.
⌐ Pratt, David (*Cornet*, 5 Sept. 11; *Lieut.* 26 Oct. 12) [22]	25 Jan. 16	23 Sept. 36	16 Dragoons.
Price, Samuel			Pembroke Fencible Cavalry.
Proudfoot, William			Perth Fencible Cavalry.
Quaile, Robert Orr		25 Feb. 27	17 Dragoons.
Reid, Archibald		28 Nov. 05	30 Dragoons.
Rendell, John Gill	14 Mar. 11	25 Feb. 16	40 Foot.
⌐ Reynolds, Richard	9 Mar. 09	12 Feb. 24	1 West India Regiment.
Rice, Thomas			Cinque Ports Fencible Cavalry.
Roberts, James		25 Feb. 14	16 Dragoons.
Roberts, John	28 April 08		81 Foot.
Rodgers, William	26 May 25	1 May 28	66 Foot.
Rogers, Thomas		25 Dec. 18	25 Dragoons.
Rusher, John	20 April 26	8 June 38	83 Foot.
Russell, Richard		25 Jan. 20	25 Dragoons.
Ruttledge, John		25 Dec. 09	9 Dragoons.
Ryall, John			Dumfries Fen. Cav.
Salter, Robert	20 Nov. 94		Fife Fen. Inf.

Quarter-Masters.

	QUARTER-MASTER.	WHEN PLACED ON HALF PAY.	
Sanderson, Jos. Prossor	28 May 07	28 May 18	47 Foot.
Satchell, Carrol (*Ens.* 6 July, 15)	7 Mar. 22		3 Royal Veteran Battalion.
Sawyers, Edward	30 April 12		6 Royal Veteran Battalion.
Sewell, William	20 Jan. 14	25 Feb. 19	Staff Corps of Cavalry.
Shaw George	12 Feb. 07	1 May 17	8 Foot.
Shirley, John	14 Sept. 26	1 Jan. 31	Royal Horse Guards.
❡ Sidley, George	14 April 08		23 Foot.
Simpson, Edward		1 Jan. 31	2 Life Guards.
Smart, Robert	2 April 07		6 Foot.
Smith, James		25 Jan. 13	16 Dragoons.
Smith, John		25 May 17	9 Dragoons.
Smith, Samuel		25 June 03	23 Dragoons.
Smith, Thomas		23 Sept. 04	28 Dragoons.
Staples, John	21 Jan. 03	29 Oct. 22	2 Ceylon Regiment
Steel, Joseph		1 Jan. 31	1 Life Guards.
Stephens, John [23]	14 Sept. 15	9 Dec. 31	African Corps.
Stevens, George	13 Aug. 18	28 July 25	5 West India Regiment.
❡ Stewart, James	16 April 07	25 Oct. 21	36 Foot.
Stott, Christopher		1 June 18	1 Life Guards.
ᛘ Stubbs, Joshua [24]	5 May 08	26 June 35	48 Foot.
Sutherland, George	7 Mar. 94		Rothsay and Caithness Fen. Inf.
❡ Thompson, William	6 May 19	7 Apr. 37	Scots Fusilier Guards.
Thomson, Joseph	11 May 15		4 Royal Veteran Battalion.
Thomson, William	17 Mar. 14	25 Dec. 14	22 Foot.
Trower, George	13 Aug. 12	25 Oct. 21	41 Foot.
❡ *Troy, Thomas*	5 Aug. 13		Royal Horse Guards.
❡ Varley, Thomas	20 Mar. 06	12 Dec. 22	Royal Horse Guards.
❡ *Waddell, William*	8 July 13		1 Dragoons.
Wagstaff, William	24 Oct. 05	25 Mar. 16	1 Dragoon Guards.
Wales, John		25 April 15	6 Dragoons.
Wallis, Samuel [25]	1 Feb. 23	3 Nov. 37	60 Foot.
Walsh, William	16 June 08		21 Foot.
❡ Watmough, Peter	22 Feb. 09		Royal Horse Guards.
Watson, John Thomas	10 Oct. 11	26 Mar. 18	5 Foot.
Webster, William		1 Jan. 31	2 Life Guards.
ᛘ Weston, Charles [26]	28 Dec. 15	9 Aug. 33	Scots Fusilier Guards.
Wilkinson, William		1 Jan. 31	2 Life Guards.
Williamson, David	25 April 96		Breadalbane Fen. Inf.
Wilton, Samuel		25 June 02	2 Dragoon Guards.
Winkworth, William			Cambridge Fen. Cav.
Witham Robert	10 Mar. 13	17 Feb. 20	84 Foot.
Wood, Thomas			Cambridge Fen. Cav.
Worsley, Jas. (*Ens.* 25 Oct. 15)[27]	29 Mar. 21	5 Oct. 38	11 Foot.
Wright, Thomas [28]	11 Aug. 25	17 Aug. 38	9 Dragoons.
Wynne, Rich. Miles	25 Dec. 13	1814	3 Prov. Bn. of Mil.
Yates, Joseph	9 April 12	25 June 17	83 Foot.

Notes to the Quarter-Masters.

1 Quarter-Master Blackier served the campaign in Spain under Sir John Moore, from Nov. 1808 to Jan. 1809. Served also the campaign of 1815, including the battle of Waterloo.
2 Quarter-Master Booth served the campaign in Spain from Oct. 1808 to Jan. 1809.
3 Quarter-Master Brew served the campaigns of 1812, 13, and 14 in North America, including the actions of Stoney Creek and Chrystler's Farm, at which latter he was wounded.
4 Quarter-Master Cameron served in the Peninsula, France, and Flanders from May 1813 to Oct. 1818, including the battles of the Pyrenees (28th, 29th, and 30th July), Nivelle, Nive, Toulouse, Quatre Bras, and Waterloo. Engaged in quelling the late insurrection in Upper Canada.
5 Quarter-Master Carr's services :—Campaign in Holland in 1799; wounded in the right leg by a musket-shot and taken prisoner at the battle of Egmont-op-Zee. Egyptian campaign of 1801. Battle of Maida, 1806. Peninsular campaigns from July 1808 to Jan. 1809, and from Oct. 1812 to the end of the war, including the battles of Vimiera, Corunna, Vittoria, Pyrenees, Orthes, and Toulouse.
6 Quarter-Master Castray served in the Peninsula from Jan. 1808 to Jan. 1809, and from May 1810 to the end of the war, including the following battles, sieges, &c. viz. Roleia, Vimiera, Lugo (wounded in the head), Corunna, Fuentes d'Onor, bridge of Almeida, Ciudad Rodrigo, Badajoz (3rd operation, and wounded in the head and the leg at the assault), Vittoria, Pyrenees, San Sebastian, Nivelle, Nive, Bridge of Vera (wounded through the knee), Orthes, and Toulouse.
7 Quarter-Master Davidson served the campaigns of 1814 and 15 in Holland, Flanders, and France, including the action at Merxem, bombardment of Antwerp (wounded), storming of Bergen-op-Zoom, battles of Quatre Bras and Waterloo (twice wounded), and Capture of Paris.
8 Lieut. and Quarter-Master Dewson served the campaign of 1814 in Holland under Lord Lynedoch.
9 Quarter-Master T. W. Edwards served in the East Indies from Nov. 1796 to 1830, during which long period he was actively employed in nearly all the campaigns and engagements which took place, commencing with the battle of Malavelly, and terminating with the Burmese war. Medal for the capture of Seringapatam.
10 Quarter-Master Hanna was present at the assault and capture of Badajoz, battles of Salamanca and Vittoria, and siege of San Sebastian. Served in the American war in 1814 and 15, and was present at Washington, Baltimore, and New Orleans. Served also the campaign of 1815 including the battle of Waterloo.
11 Quarter-Master Houghton has seen a great deal of active service in the East Indies, where he served from April 1810 to Oct. 1819.
12 Quarter-Master Samuel Johnson served in the Peninsula from June 1809 to the end of the war, including the battle of Albuhera. Served afterwards in the American war.
13 Quarter-Master Kinkee served in the Peninsula, France, and Flanders from Jan. 1813 to the end of the war, including the action at Morales de Toro, and battles of Vittoria, Pyrenees, Orthes, and Waterloo.
14 Quarter-Master Kyle's services :—Siege and capture of Copenhagen in 1807. Campaign in Portugal and Spain in 1808 and 9, including the battles of Roleia and Vimiera. Expedition to Walcheren in 1809, including the siege and capture of Flushing. Campaigns in the Peninsula from June 1812 to the end of the war, including the siege of San Sebastian, and battles of the Pyrenees, Nivelle, and Orthes. Latter part of the American war, including the siege of Fort Erie.
15 Quarter-Master Lewis's services.—Campaign in Spain and battle of Corunna. Expedition to Walcheren, 1809. Peninsular Campaigns from 1811 to the end of the war.
16 Quarter-Master M'Pherson served in Ireland during the rebellion in 1798, including the battle of Ballynamuck. Served also at the capture of the Cape of Good Hope in 1806, and was present at the battle of Blueberg.
17 Quarter-Master Mansfield served during twenty years in the East Indies, including the storming of Fort Barrabatty in 1803, where he was wounded, and the Mahratta cam-

Notes to the Quarter-Masters.

paigns of 1804, 5, & 6 under Lord Lake. Served also at the capture of the Isle of France in 1810.

18 Quarter-Master Morgan, with the exception of a few months, served throughout the whole of the Peninsular war, including the following battles, sieges, &c. viz. Corunna, Almeida, Busaco, Pombal, Redinha, Miranda de Corvo, Condeixa, Foz d'Aronce Sabugal, Fuentes d'Onor, Ciudad Rodrigo, (a volunteer on the storming party, and wounded in the left leg), and Badajoz, again a volunteer on the storming party, and severely contused on the head.

19 Quarter-Master O'Brien served in the Peninsula from August 1811 to the end of the war, including the action at Llerena (wounded), and battles of Vittoria, Orthes, and Toulouse.

20 Quarter-Master Ottey served at the Helder in 1799, including the actions of the 27th August, 10th and 19th Sept. 2nd and 6th October. Served afterwards in the East Indies from Jan. 1803 to Aug. 1815, including the siege of Bhurtpore, expedition to the Persian Gulf in 1809, and capture of the Isle of France.

21 Quarter-Master Powell served in the East Indies from May 1788 to Sept. 1807, including the reduction of Cannanore, campaign against Tippoo terminating at Seringapatam 14th Feb. 1792; capture of Cochin 20th Oct. 1795; capitulation of Columbo and its dependencies, 16th Feb. 1796; campaign against Tippoo in 1799, including the affair of Seedasseer, and the reduction of Seringapatam; assault and capture of Jamalabad, Sept. 1799; campaign against Doondia Waugh; campaign in Wynaad (severely wounded through the left wrist by a musket-shot on a reconnoitring party 22nd Jan. 1801); assault of Pangalamcourchy; assault and capture of Anakenny. Served also in the Peninsula from June 1811 to the end of the war.

22 Lieut. and Quarter-Master Pratt served in the Peninsula from April 1809 to the end of the war, including the passage of the Douro, and battles of Talavera, Busaco, Fuentes d'Onor, Salamanca, Vittoria, and investment of Bayonne. Served also at Bhurtpore under Lord Combermere.

23 Quarter-Master John Stephens served in the Nepaul war in the East Indies.

24 Quarter-Master Stubbs served at the blockade of Malta in 1800; and in the Peninsula from June 1809 to the end of the war, including the battles of Talavera and Busaco, siege and capture of Badajoz, and battles of Vittoria, Pampeluna, Orthes, and Toulouse.

25 Quarter-Master Wallis served in the Burmese war.

26 Quarter-Master Weston served with the expedition to Hanover in 1805, and with that to Copenhagen in 1807. Served also in the Peninsula from 30th Dec. 1808 to the end of the war, including the passage of the Douro and capture of Oporto, battles of Busaco and Fuentes d'Onor, siege of Ciudad Rodrigo, covering the siege of Badajoz, battle of Salamanca, capture of Madrid, siege of Burgos, battle of Vittoria, siege of San Sebastian, passage of the Bidassoa, actions at Bidart (9th to 13th Dec.), passage of the Adour, investment of Bayonne, and repulse of the sortie from thence.

27 Quarter-Master Worsley proceeded to Naples under Sir James Craig in 1805, and served in the Light Brigade under General Kempt in the following years; landed at Messina, and was at the destruction of the enemy's gun-boats in the Bay of Bagno; also in the Bay of St. Euphemia, with the division of gun-boats under Lieut. Colonel O'Toole. Served also at the capture of the Islands of Ischia and Procida; and has been upwards of twenty times engaged with the enemy's gun-boats.

28 Quarter-Master Thomas Wright served in South America in 1807 under General Whitelock; also at Walcheren, including the siege of Flushing in 1809 under Lord Chatham.

COMMISSARIAT DEPARTMENT.

COMMISSARIES-GENERAL.		
ⓟ Adams, Joseph Hollingworth.	20 Jan.	37
Bethune, John D. (*Lieut.-Col.*)..	18 July	99
ⓟ Bisset, *Sir* John, KCH.	31 July	11
Cocksedge, Henry............	20 Jan.	37
ⓟ Dalrymple, *Sir* Charles	29 Jan.	12
ⓟ Dickens, James............	19 July	21
ⓟ Drake, John	30 Aug.	33
Drummond, James	25 Aug.	08
ⓟ Dunmore, Thomas	25 Dec.	14
Granet, Augustus	25 Dec.	14
ⓟ Haines, Gregory	30 Aug.	33
ⓟ Kennedy, *Sir* R. H. KCH. KC.	3 Nov.	08
Luscombe, Tho. Popham	15 Aug.	26
Petrie, William	20 Jan.	37
Turquand, Peter	19 July	21
Wood, *Sir* Gabriel............	8 July	06
ⓟ Wright, Charles	19 July	21

DEPUTY-COMMISSARIES-GENERAL.		
Allan, David	13 June	13
Anderson, Richard John	16 Aug.	11
ⓟ Auther, William	20 Jan.	37
ⓟ Barney, Richard	19 July	21
Bent, Thomas Hamlyn........	19 Mar.	07
ⓟ Booth, William	18 Dec.	18
ⓟ Boyes, Robert	7 Nov.	09
Brown, Richard..............	29 May	90
Brown, William..............	19 July	21
Couche, Edward	12 Aug.	06
ⓟ Cumming, William	10 Sept.	30
Daniell, Francis..............	2 Feb.	07
ⓟ Dobree, John Saumarez	7 June	25
Fernandes, Alexander	21 Mar.	05
Forbes, Charles John..........	25 July	15
Forbes, John	19 July	21
ⓟ Gauntlett, William	18 Mar.	12
ⓟ Greive, William	3 Feb.	13
Hagenau, John Frederick......	25 Dec.	14
Hayward, William............	20 Jan.	37
Hill, Hugh	20 Jan.	37
Hopkins, Samuel	25 Dec.	14
Humphreys, John Thomas	2 April	10
Hunter, Henry Lannoy........	31 May	98
ⓟ Laidley, John..............	20 Jan.	37
ⓟ Laidley, William	20 Jan.	37
Low, Isaac	25 May	97
ⓟ Lukin, William	2 Sept.	14
ⓟ Lutyens, Charles	26 June	09
Mackay, William	7 June	25
Malassez, Nicholas............	20 Jan.	37
Maturin, William	10 Sept.	36
Miles, George................	8 Sept.	10
ⓟ Moore, George	10 Sept.	30
ⓟ Nugent, Geo. Steph. N. Hodges	22 Oct.	16
ⓟ Ogilvie, James	22 Mar.	12
Osborn, Thomas..............	28 June	38
Ramsay, Thomas Wharton	28 June	38
ⓟ Robinson, Edward Cooke....	22 Oct.	16
ⓟ St. Remy, P. C. Lelievre de..	19 July	21
Schmidchen, Augustus	27 July	12
Singer, Paulus Æmilius,(*Ireland.*)	1 April	00
Somerville, Alexander	19 July	21
ⓟ Spurrier, John	10 Sept.	30
ⓟ Strachan, Alexander	10 Sept.	30
Sweetland, John..............	16 Nov.	02
Teckell, John, (Musters)	19 Nov.	05
Telfer, Buchan Fraser	25 Dec.	14
Webb, William	15 Jan.	22
ⓟ Wemyss, William	25 Dec.	14
Wethered, Thomas............	21 Mar.	07
ⓟ White, George	20 Nov.	15
Wild, Henry James	20 Jan.	37
Williams, Richard	28 June	38
Woodhouse, James, CMG.	7 June	25

ASSISTANT-COMMISSARIES-GENERAL.		
Allsopp, Robert	10 Sept.	30
Arnold, Thomas..............	28 June	38
Bailey, Michael	20 Jan.	37
Beech, William	24 Feb.	10
Birney, George, (*Ireland.*)	25 June	08
ⓟ Carruthers, David..........	24 Feb.	10
ⓟ Chalmers, Andrew	20 Jan.	37
Chiaranda, Francis Leonard....	10 Sept.	30
Child, George................	4 May	15
Colvill, Robert, (*Ireland.*)......	23 Feb.	09
Courtenay, George Townsend ..	26 Sept.	06
Cramer, Henry John	4 May	15
Crookshank, George	3 Aug.	14
Daniel, John Edgecumbe	23 Nov.	27
Davidson, Peter Fraser	19 July	21
Dillon, William (*Ireland.*)	25 June	03
Dinwiddie, Gilbert Hamilton ..	28 June	38
Engelbach, Thomas Lewis	1 May	01
Ely, Ernest..................	20 Jan.	37
Francklin, James Bontineau....	31 Mar.	14
Furmidge, William	7 June	25
Gelston, Thomas (*Ireland.*)....	25 June	03
Gilbert, Henry	9 May	17
Gilmor, Robert	10 Jan.	14
Goldrisk, James (*Ireland.*)	1 Jan.	99
ⓟ Gomm, Richard Stonier	1 Nov.	14
Grant, John (*Ireland.*)........	1 April	00
Grellier, George	3 Feb.	07
Grindlay, Robert	30 July	25
Hanagan, William (*Ireland.*) ..	24 May	98
ⓟ Head, *Sir* George	25 Dec.	14
Heydinger, William Charles ..	25 May	12
Hughes, William (*Ireland.*)....	25 Sept.	06
ⓟ Kearney, Thomas	10 Aug.	11
Kuper, Augustus	28 Nov.	12
Lane, John	25 Dec.	14
Ledwith, William (*Ireland.*) ..	25 Mar.	14
Lithgow, William	22 Oct.	16
ⓟ M'Leod, Donald	25 Dec.	14

Commissariat Department.

Name	Date	Name	Date
₽ M'Nab, Duncan	10 Sept. 30	Eyl, John Geo.	25 Dec. 11
Macdonell, Hugh	1 Aug. 09	Faxardo, Augus. Maria Guax	25 Dec. 14
Matthey, Alphonso	9 Nov. 13	Finlay, John	23 May 10
Nightingale, Allen Jackson	23 Nov. 27	Fitzgerald, James David	22 Oct. 16
Palmer, Constantine John	4 Feb. 06	Freeborn, John	25 Dec. 14
₽ Priestley, William Henry	19 July 21	Gilbert, Thomas Morley	4 May 15
Pryce, Josiah	25 Oct. 27	₽ Gillespie, Joshua	24 Jan. 12
Ragland, William	20 Jan. 37	Graham, Frederick	22 Oct. 16
Ragueneau, Charles	10 Sept. 30	Greig, William	25 April 15
₽ Riddell, Archibald	do	Grist, James Bond	19 July 21
Rogerson, Ralph	31 Mar. 14	Gunning, Charles	24 May 13
Ross, William	28 June 38	Harper, Charles	22 Oct. 16
Skelton, Thomas Lourey	22 Oct. 16	Harris, Anthony Charles	25 Dec. 14
Swainson, William	29 Mar. 13	Hazard, Joseph	19 July 21
Swinney, George	20 Jan. 37	Hodson, James	25 Dec. 14
₽ Trotter, Alexander	do	Hoffay, Ernest Albert	do
White, Thomas	19 July 21	Horne, James	do
₽ Wilkinson, John Walter	10 Aug. 11	Le Mesurier, Henry	4 May 14
₽ Wood, John	25 April 15	Llufriu, Bartholomew	22 Oct. 16
Woolrabe, John	20 Jan. 37	Malassez, Cha. Thomas	20 May 28
₽ Wybault, Patrick Robert	25 Dec. 14	Marter, Thomas Peter	4 May 15
Yeoland, George	10 Sept. 30	Montgomerie, Frederick	22 Oct. 16
		₽ O'Meara, William	9 Mar. 12
DEPUTY ASSISTANT COMMISSARIES GENERAL.		Paty, John	20 May 28
		Petrie, Samuel	25 Dec. 14
Alder Benjamin	22 Oct. 16	Richardson, Fran. Moseley	do
Anderson, John David	11 Oct. 14	Robinson, Augustus Facey	25 April 15
Bain, George	20 May 28	Robinson, William	3 April 27
Bayley, Thomas	10 Aug. 11	Rodney, *Hon.* Mortimer	27 Aug. 12
Baynes, Sir E. Stuart, KCMG.	16 Dec. 13	₽ Schaumann, Augustus	26 Dec. 12
Beltz, Samuel	31 Mar. 14	₽ Schnitter, John Solomon	3 Feb. 13
Billings, Francis Thomas	9 Sept. 14	Sclater, Wm. Salusbury	3 April 27
₽ Birch, Augustus	22 Oct. 16	Sedgwick, Thomas	12 July 14
₽ Boyes, Geo. Thos. Wm. Blaney	3 Feb. 13	Sisson, Marcus Jacob	22 Oct. 16
Brock, John Savery	25 Dec. 14	Smith, Tho. Tringham	9 Nov. 13
Browne, Joseph Steere	19 July 21	Stanton, William	19 July 21
Byndloss, Edward	31 Dec. 13	Stayner, Thos. Allen	11 May 13
Calder, Patrick	2 Jan. 13	Streatfield, Wm. Sandeforth	4 May 15
Campbell, James	15 Jan. 22	Thornton, Charles	13 July 14
₽ Charlier, Joseph	25 Dec. 14	Thynne, Henry	25 Dec. 14
Coates, William	1 Oct. 13	Tidmarsh, Charles	29 Dec. 14
Curran, Boaventura Rom.	25 Dec. 14	Turner, Thomas	22 Oct. 16
David, John	11 Oct. 14	Wathen, Augustus	25 Dec. 14
Davies, Peter	15 Jan. 14	Whitehead, Hen. Lowe	do
Davis, Lionel	4 Jan. 14	Wickens, James	5 Feb. 14
Dilke, William	22 Oct. 16	Withers, George	11 Mar. 14

MEDICAL DEPARTMENT.

	HOSPITAL ASSISTANT/ASSISTANT SURGEON.	REGIMENTAL SURGEON.	STAFF SURGEON.	ASSIST-INSPEC. or PHYSICIAN	BREVET DEP.-INSP.	DEPUTY INSP.-GEN.	BREVET INSP.-GEN.	INSPECTOR GENERAL.	PRINCIPAL INSP.-GEN.
PRINCIPAL INSPECTORS-GENERAL.									
Gordon, Theodore, *M.D.*[1]	24 June 88	16 Oct. 93	April 96	Nov. 96	never	30 May 00	27 May 25	15 Nov. 27	Feb. 10
Somerville, William, *M.D.*	25 Mar. 95	Mar. 05				25 Mar. 05		never	28 Dec. 15
INSPECTORS-GENERAL.									
Adolphus, Jacob, *M.D.*[2]	2 Oct. 95	10 Oct. 02	5 Oct. 04	29 June 09	never	17 25 Nov. 19	27 May 25	15 Nov. 27	
Baxter, Alexander, *M.D.*[3]	31 Aug. 98	30 Aug. 99	12 April 05	3 Sept. 12	never	3 Aug. 15	10 Dec. 23	3 July 28	
Blackwell, Adair[4]	19 Mar. 92	never	29 July 95	July 01	never	27 Oct. 08	never	18 Jan. 16	
Borland, James, *M.D.*	20 Dec. 90	never	2 April 94	Sept. 95	never	5 Dec. 99	never	22 Jan. 07	
Erly, John, *M.D.* (*Local*)[5]	4 Dec. 95	25 June 97	18 April 00	never	never	14 Sept. 15	27 May 25	23 July 33	
Farrell, Charles, *M.D.*	never	16 Nov. 99	1 Jan. 96	3 Sept. 12	never	9 Oct. 17	27 May 25	22 July 30	
Fellowes, Sir James, *M.D.*	June 94	never	never	1 Aug. 11	never	11 Mar. 13	never	29 April 13	
Fergusson, William, *M.D.*[6]	8 April 94	never	19 May 94	28 Oct. 95	never	Dec. 00		18 April 13	
Franck, James, *M.D.*	never	never	never	Sept. 05	never		never	4 April 00	
Grant, Sir James Robert, *M.D.*[7]	22 Jan. 92	24 Feb. 94	April 00	10 June 94	never	16 April 07	never	14 July 14	
Gunning, John	never	never	never	never	never	17 Sept. 12	never	1 Feb. 16	
Gunning, Thomas[8]	never	23 Mar. 97	11 April 00	never	never	11 July 11	17 July 17	1 Jan. 28	
Higgins, Summers, *M.D.*[9]	never	1 Sept. 97	15 Oct. 03	Jan. 09	never	12 Nov. 12	27 May 25	22 July 30	
Hogg, William	30 Nov. 89	never	1 Jan. 95	29 Sept. 95	never	17 Sept. 07	27 May 25		
Hume, John Robert, *M.D.*[10]	28 Oct. 98	9 May 00	9 July 08	17 Aug. 09	never	26 May 14	never	3 Dec. 18	
Keate, Robert	Aug. 94	never	never	10 May 98	5 Sept. 99	never	never	21 Jan. 07	
Nixon, Thos. (*Surg.-Maj.* 9 June, 14)	never	26 Dec. 96	20 Mar. 99	never	never	never	never	10 Nov. 24	
Phillips, John	16 May 94	never	17 Sept. 94	never	never	27 Aug. 08	19 July 21		

407

Medical Department.

	HOSPITAL ASSISTANT	ASSISTANT SURGEON.	REGIMENTAL SURGEON.	STAFF SURGEON.	ASSISTANT INSPEC. OF PHYSICIAN	BREVET DEP.-INSP.	DEPUTY INSP.-GEN.	BREVET INSP.-GEN.	INSPECTOR GENERAL.
Pyun, *Sir* William, *MD. KCH.*	never	Mar. 96	24 Aug. 00	never	never	never	20 Dec. 10	never	25 Sept. 16
⫽ Robb, John, *MD.*[11]	28 May 97	20 Sept. 97	1 Jan. 04	never	16 Feb. 14	never	12 May 28	25 Nov. 18	22 July 30
Roberts, Rich. Worthington, (*Ordnance*)	23 Apr. 96	1 May 97	1 Oct. 97	20 July 09	never	never	22 July 15	never	17 Nov. 24
Strachan, James, *MD.*[12]	20 May 93	never	10 Dec. 94	4 April 00	never	never	18 Jan. 16	27 May 25	22 Aug. 37
Tegart, Edward[13]	June 96	never	4 April 00	1794	1799	10 Mar. 10	25 May 09	17 July 25	25 Mar. 24
⫽ Thomson, Thomas, *MD.*[14]	never	never	May 91	Nov. 95	never	never	21 Jan. 13	27 May 25	22 July 30
Tudor, William[15]	Mar. 92	never					13 Nov. 03	19 July 21	
⫽ Warren, John[16]	never	never	9 April 94	8 Oct. 94	never	22 Aug. 05			18 Jan. 16
Whitelock, James[17]	25 Oct. 89	never	30 May 94	18 June 07	never	never	3 Sept. 03	19 July 21	
⫽ ⫽ Woolriche, Stephen[18]	never	never					26 May 14	9 Dec. 23	22 July 30

DEPUTY-INSPECTORS-GENERAL.

Albert, George Frederick, *MD.*[19]	never	never	never	30 Aug. 99	never	never	4 Nov. 13		
⫽ Arthur, James, *MD.*[20]	never	1 June 01	18 Aug. 08	15 Oct. 12	29 Mar. 21	never	22 July 30		
⫽ Arthur, John, *MD.*	never	14 Sept. 04	5 Sept. 11	never	3 Aug. 15	27 May 25	22 July 30		
Bancroft, Edward Nathaniel, *MD.*	never	never	never	never	5 Oct. 95	17 July 17			
⫽ Barry, William, *MD.*[21]	15 April 08	4 Jan. 10	never	19 Nov. 21	never	never	10 Nov. 25		
⫽ Browne, Andrew[22]	27 Aug. 95	25 June 97	28 Mar. 01	30 July 94	never	never	22 July 30		
Buckle, Dickens[23]	never	never	never	never	never	never	18 Jan. 30		
Calvert, Robert, *MD.*	never	never	never	25 Sept. 14	22 Oct. 07	25 Nov. 18	29 Jan. 36		
⫽ Clark, John, *MD. KH.*[24]	never	12 July 09	never	4 June 12	3 July 23	1 Oct. 20	22 July 30		
⫽ Collier, Charles[25]	Sept. 06	4 Oct. 06	Aug. 09	never	1798	19 July 21			
Crawford, Stuart, *MD.*[26]	never	never	never	never	never	never	20 Jan. 32		
⫽ Daun, Robert, *MD.*[27]	22 Oct. 03	17 Dec. 03	4 Aug. 14	19 Jan. 32	never	17 July 17	18 Feb. 13		
Duncan, Thomas[28]	4 Feb. 94	1 Feb. 97	9 July 03	8 Aug. 11	31 Jan. 11	never			
⫽ Forbes, Charles Fergusson, *MD. KH.*[29]	May 98	9 Jan. 99	22 Dec. 04	1808	never	27 May 25	16 Sept. 13		
Grasett, Henry[30]	27 Dec. 94	never	1 Mar. 97	31 Jan. 11	never	27 May 25			
Griffin, Goldsmith Edmund[31]	5 Jan. 99	19 Dec. 99	12 Nov. 03	23 June 08	never	never	22 July 30		
⫽ Guthrie, George James	23 June 00	5 Mar. 01	20 Mar. 06	4 Jan. 10	never	never	23 Mar. 30		
Hartle, Robert[32]	1 Dec. 96	22 Nov. 01	25 Feb. 05	28 Jan. 13	never	6 Mar. 30			
⫽ Howell, John, *MD.*[33]	11 June 01	28 Aug. 04	17 Mar. 08	16 April 12	never	never	11 Nov. 11		
Kaersley, Joseph, *MD.* (*Ordnance*.)	5 Nov. 93	never	8 Dec. 93	never	never	never			

Medical Department.

	HOSPITAL ASSISTANT.	ASSISTANT SURGEON.	REGIMENTAL SURGEON.	STAFF SURGEON.	ASSIST.- INSPEC. or PHYSICIAN	BREVET DEP.- INSP.	DEPUTY INSP.-GEN.
Knipe, John Augustus [34]	1 April 97	1 May 97	3 Oct. 05	28 May 12	never	17 July 17	26 Oct. 26
Lamert, Matthew [35]	22 Oct. 95	31 Dec. 99	25 June 01	never	never	never	22 July 30
Lindsey, Owen, MD. [36]	never	31 Dec. 03	2 Nov. 09	5 Nov. 12	never	never	22 July 30
MacDougle, James, MD. [37]	never	never	never	never	25 Aug. 09	never	17 Sept. 13
McMillan, Quinten	12 Sept. 95	4 Mar. 97	25 Mar. 01	20 July 09	never	14 May 18	
McMullin, John, MD.	never	never	never	never	19 Oct. 09	25 Nov. 18	22 July 30
Macleod, Swinton [38]	25 Mar. 00	25 June 01	9 July 03	never	never	never	5 Nov. 29
Marshall, Henry [39]	24 Feb. 06	17 April 06	15 April 13	21 Dec. 13	never	never	22 July 30
Meade, Sir John, MD. KH. [10]	25 Aug. 95	25 Dec. 96	19 Feb. 01	8 June 09	never	never	29 April 13
Porteus, Edward [41]	21 Dec. 97	23 Aug. 99	18 Sept. 99	17 Dec. 03	never	never	13 May 13
Robinson, Isaac [42]	20 Oct. 94	never	16 Sept. 95	never	never	never	22 July 30
Thomas, Joseph	Apr. 00			2 June 04	never	never	26 May 25
West, Sir Augustus, MD. [13]	26 May 04	7 Nov. 05	never	25 Mar. 13	never	29 April 18	18 Nov. 24
White, Andrew [44]	9 Nov. 99	10 Sept. 03	30 May 05	23 May 11	never	never	25 Sept. 17

ASSISTANT INSPECTORS AND PHYSICIANS.

Durie, William, KH. (Ordnance)	never	20 Nov. 97	18 Nov. 05	never	26 Sept. 14		
Evans, Lewis, MD. [45]	7 April 06	26 Nov. 07	never	never	26 May 14		
Faulkner, Sir Arthur Brooke, MD. [46]	never	never	never	never	28 July 08		
Greaves, William [47]		never	9 April 94	April 95	30 Aug. 99		
Hume, Thomas, MD.	never	never	never	never	16 June 08		
Jones, Griffith [48]		15 Oct. 00	28 Mar. 11	19 Nov. 30	9 Dec. 36		
Kenning, Samuel, MD.	never	26 April 99	1 Aug. 06	never	22 July 15		
Knight, Edward, MD. [49]	never	never	never	never	1809		
L'Affan, Sir J. de Courcy, Bt. MD.	never	never	never	never	13 June 11		
Maclagan, David, MD. [50]	never	10 Sept. 07	never	never	26 May 14		
Morewood, Geo. Alexander, MD. [51]	never	never	never	never	7 Sept. 07		
Morison, Charles, MD.		10 Sept. 03	20 June 11	never	29 June 15		
Robson, William, MD. [52]	never	7 Mar. 05	never	never	30 Sept. 13		
Sibbald, William, MD. [53]	Aug. 10	13 Dec. 10	never	7 Sept. 15	22 Nov. 27		
Walker, Thomas, MD. [54]		20 June 05	3 Sept. 12	never	18 Feb. 13		
Wright, James, MD.	20 May	23 June 04	8 Sept. 08	never	26 May 14		

Medical Department.

SURGEONS.	HOSPITAL-ASSIST. &c.	ASSISTANT SURGEON.	SURGEON.	
₽ Abell, Joseph	4 Nov. 05	10 April 06	15 July 13	60 Foot.
Abercrombie, John	9 June 98	6 Mar. 99	19 July 00	60 Foot.
Adams, James	9 Mar. 04	3 Oct. 04	15 April 13	4 Ceylon Reg.
Allan, Colin, *MD*		8 May 06	25 Mar. 26	Staff.
₽ Allardyce, James	never	4 Aug. 01	30 May 09	5 Garr. Batt.
₽ Amiel, Romaine⁵⁵	1 Nov. 94	1796	24 Feb. 25	1 R. Vet. Batt.
₽ Anderson, Andrew, *MD*.⁵⁶	1 Mar. 05	4 Feb. 08	25 June 12	Staff.
Anderson, Charles			5 July 89	Scotch Brigade.
₽ Anderson, Thomas	25 June 95	27 June 98	4 April 00	3 Foot
Annesley, Charles, *MD*.⁵⁷	22 Jan. 05	5 May 08	21 Jan. 13	2 Dragoons.
₽ Armstrong, Arch. Nicholls	never	14 May 04	21 July 14	5 R. Vet. Batt.
Arnott, Archibald, *MD*.	never	25 Dec. 96	23 Aug. 99	20 Foot.
Ayton, Robinson	23 Sept. 05	1 May 06	10 Sept. 12	34 Foot.
Bacot, John	never	2 July 03	9 June 14	21 Dragoons.
Baird, John, *MD*.	8 July 11	21 Jan. 13	12 Dec. 26	Staff.
Banks, James			20 June 98	Staff.
₽ Batt, Thomas⁵⁸	9 Dec. 05	25 April 06	15 July 13	7 Foot.
Beck, Edward	19 Dec. 04	1 Aug. 06	11 Nov. 11	Ordnance.
Beckett, Thomas (*Savoy*)			8 July 95	Staff.
₽ Berry, Titus	never	never	24 June 03	Staff.
Black, Ebenezer	19 May 06	2 Mar. 09	21 Jan. 13	18 Dragoons.
Blake, Andrew, *MD*.	never	14 Mar. 05	28 July 14	16 Foot.
₽ Boggie, John, *MD*.	17 Oct. 99	8 Jan. 01	15 Oct. 07	Staff.
₽₩ Bolton, John	never	never	14 Sept. 91	7 West Ind. Reg.
₽ Bolton, Robert Henry, *MD*	26 Nov. 07	9 Feb. 09	7 Oct. 13	78 Foot.
₽ Boutflower, Charles	never	4 April 00	3 Sept. 12	Staff.
₽ Boyle, Alexander, *MD*.	21 Sept. 99	11 Dec. 99	12 Nov. 03	Staff.
Bradley, Nicholas Phineas	22 Sept. 04	1 Aug. 06	11 Nov. 11	Ordnance.
Brady, Jas. Patricius, *MD*.(Dist.)	Jan. 01	25 Dec. 02	3 Mar. 08	Staff.
Brandes, Christian Louis			2 July 07	Staff.
₽ Brown, Frederick, *MD*.	19 May 08	4 Jan. 10	8 Sept. 25	73 Foot.
₽ Brown, Joseph	19 Jan. 08	25 Feb. 08	28 Oct. 13	Staff Corps of Cav.
Brown, Robert	8 July 99	11 Jan. 00	11 Dec. 06	Staff.
Burton, Edward	9 May 11	21 Jan. 13	1 June 26	Staff.
₽ Byrtt, William⁵⁹	18 Aug. 06	7 July 08	9 Sept. 13	24 Foot.
Cahill, Alexander	20 Aug. 03	15 Oct. 07	25 Aug. 00	25 Foot.
₽ ₩ Callander, John	1805	7 May 07	25 Mar. 13	R. Wagg. Tr.
Campbell, Dougal, *MD*.	never	1 Aug. 06	8 July 15	Ordnance.
Carnegie, John, *MD*.	Feb. 04	25 Feb. 04	5 Sept. 11	62 Foot.
Carter, John	never	25 Sept. 03	2 Mar. 09	60 Foot.
Carver, Walter		25 June 01	6 April 09	4 R. Vet. Battalion.
Cavenagh, James Gordon	28 Sept. 93	31 Jan. 99	21 Feb. 00	62 Foot.
₩ Chenevix, Geo. (Surg.-Maj. 4 Sept. 36)	never	17 Dec. 12	24 Feb. 25	Coldstream Guards.
Clark, Thomas			16 Sept. 95	19 Foot
Cloak, Nicholas	10 Aug. 03	25 Feb. 05	28 July 14	86 Foot.
₽ Coates, Edw. Fred. (Local)	never	20 Aug. 07	10 Oct. 11	Staff.
Coates, William Henry	8 April 94	never	16 June 95	Staff.
₽ Coldstream, John	3 April 94	29 Oct. 02	25 Sept. 09	26 Foot.
₽ ₩ Collins, John, *MD*.	17 July 08	1 Dec. 08	28 Mar. 16	60 Foot.
Coombe, Charles	never		April 01	14 Nov. 05	Coldstream Guards.
Cooper, Samuel	7 Jan. 13		26 May 14	Staff.
Corfield, Charles	13 Sept. 90	25 Dec. 96	25 Feb. 99	38 Foot.
Cotgrave, Jonathan	7 Feb. 92	never	6 May 95	Staff.
₽ Coulson, Alexander	April 00	11 Sept. 02	31 Jan. 11	48 Foot.
₽ Cross, James	7 Jan. 11	11 Mar. 13	19 Nov. 30	83 Foot.
Cuddy, Stephen	never	1 Aug. 06	1 Nov. 14	Ordnance.
Cunningham, Alexander⁶⁰	13 July 04	26 Oct. 04	6 Feb. 12	86 Foot.
₽ Davies, Daniel Owen⁶¹	20 April 10	25 Mar. 13	26 Oct. 30	18 Foot.
Davies, Henry, *MD*.	3 Aug. 03	20 Oct. 08	5 Sept. 11	100 Foot.
₽ Dealey, Charles⁶²	Feb. 11	4 Mar. 13	19 Oct. 32	77 Foot.
Desailly, Joseph	July 99	8 May 01	3 Sept. 12	4 Foot.
Dick, John	never	17 May 98	26 Sept. 12	5 Foot.
Dickinson, Nodes	17 Oct. 95	never	25 June 98	Staff.

Medical Department.

Name	HOSPITAL-ASSISTANT ASSIST. &c.	ASSISTANT SURGEON.	SURGEON.	
Docker, Thomas	never	never	3 Aug. 15	Staff.
ᛘ ᛘᛘ Douglas, Robert	May 01	June 02	6 June 05	West India Rangers.
Easton, John	never	12 May 98	23 Apr. 09	15 Dragoons.
Egan, Myles			3 Dec. 93	131 Foot.
ᛘ Este, Michael Lambton[63]	never	4 Sept. 00	3 Oct. 12	1 Life Guards.
Ferris, Henry	28 May 97	June 97	1 Jan. 04	Ordnance.
Fitzpatrick, Nicholas	25 April 03	1 Jan. 04	11 Nov. 11	Ordnance.
Fletcher, Joseph	7 July 99	4 April 00	2 May 07	Ordnance.
ᛘ Forster, Thomas	never	8 Dec. 03	26 July 10	3 Foot.
Foster, Francis		22 May 97	26 Sept. 05	56 Foot.
ᛘ Fraser, Arch. Campbell	never	Dec. 08	20 July 15	Staff.
ᛘ Freer, John, MD.	21 Jan. 09	16 Nov. 09	24 Feb. 25	97 Foot.
ᛘ ᛘᛘ Galliers, William	2 May 03	25 Mar. 04	10 Sept. 07	Staff.
Garrett, George, MD.	1 May 97	4 Sept. 06	18 June 12	70 Foot.
ᛘ ᛘᛘ Gibson, J. Bushby (Reg.)	8 Aug. 03	17 Sept. 03	7 Dec. 09	Staff.
Gibson, Robert	never	8 Dec. 04	23 Nov. 20	Grenadier Guards.
Gill, William	28 Nov. 03	1 May 05	3 Mar. 08	90 Foot.
Gillham, John Allen		15 Mar. 99	19 May 01	Coldstream Guards.
ᛘ Glasco, John (Reg.)	never	21 April 08	8 Feb. 16	Staff.
Goodrich, Robert[64]	12 May 12	11 Mar. 13	8 Feb. 27	6 Foot.
Grant, John	never	11 April 00	15 Oct. 03	Staff.
ᛘ ᛘᛘ Grant, Robert	never	15 June 97	27 Aug. 03	Staff.
Grieve, William			1 May 97	77 Foot.
ᛘ Griffith, John	6 April 06	7 May 07	17 Sept. 12	Staff.
ᛘ Hamilton, Arthur[65]	15 Feb. 09	17 May 10	20 Oct. 25	45 Foot.
Hamilton, Charles	never	20 April 09	27 Jan. 20	54 Foot.
Hamilton, Gavin			30 Aug. 99	46 Foot.
Hamilton, Henry	never	26 Oct. 04	10 Aug. 09	13 Foot.
ᛘ Harper, William	29 Oct. 95	23 June 04	15 Oct. 12	Staff.
Hay, Wm. Alexander	never	never	12 Jan. 96	Scots Fusilier Gds.
ᛘ Heine, Henry	never	never	21 April 01	Staff.
Heir, Matthew	1797	27 Nov. 02	2 Nov. 04	60 Foot.
Henley, John	never	4 Aug. 08	13 June 16	Staff.
Hichens, Richard	never	1 Sept. 06	22 July 15	Ordnance.
Hodson, John, MD. (Reg.)[66]	23 May 01	Sept. 12	29 Oct. 12	Staff.
ᛘ Hogg, Thomas	8 Sept. 94	30 Nov. 97	22 Jan. 07	76 Foot.
Home, George	12 May 15	18 Aug. 25	23 Sept. 36	85 Foot.
Horsman, William			3 Jan. 82	71 Foot.
ᛘ Hosack, James	never	22 Oct. 07	25 May 09	Staff.
Hughes, James	never	never	18 Nov. 95	3 Prov. Bn. of Mil.
ᛘ Humfrey, Richard	8 April 94	never	18 Nov. 95	Staff.
Hutchesson, Francis Pery	1 Aug. 05	1 Aug. 06	20 Nov. 13	Ordnance.
Jackson, Thomas[79]	25 Oct. 95	11 Sept. 97	25 Jan. 00	14 Foot.
Jameson, David, MD.	10 June 06	15 Oct. 07	6 Mar. 17	1 Dragoons.
ᛘ Jebb, Frederick	never	6 July 04	25 Mar. 13	Staff.
ᛘ Johnson, Edward, MD.	April 07	19 Nov. 07	15 July 13	39 Foot.
ᛘ Jones, William, MD.[67]	never	12 May 03	9 Mar. 09	1 Dragoon Guards.
ᛘ ᛘᛘ Jones, William, MD. (Reg.)	12 Nov. 05	21 Nov. 05	3 Sept. 12	Staff.
Keby, William	16 June 01	8 Oct. 03	11 Nov. 11	Ordnance.
Kell, James Butler		25 Feb. 04	10 Feb. 14	1 Foot.
Kellock, Alexander			25 Dec. 82	Queen's Amer. Ran.
ᛘ Kettle, William	Aug. 05	10 April 06	26 Aug. 13	49 Foot.
ᛘ Kindell, Alexander	15 Oct. 03	3 Dec. 03	25 Sept. 14	Staff.
Leath, John, MD.		1 Jan. 05	12 April 10	Staff.
Ledbrooke, Tobias	never	never		1 Prov. Bn. of Mil.
ᛘ Lewis, John	25 Sept. 99	24 Mar. 03	28 Mar. 16	York Chasseurs.
M'Arthur, James, MD. (Reg.)[68]	24 Jan. 14	27 April 15	4 April 25	Staff.
ᛘᛘ M'Donald, Alexander, MD.	never	2 Sept. 07	30 Sept. 26	Ordnance.
M'Grigor, John, MD.	never	1 Aug. 06	8 July 15	Ordnance.
Mackechnie, Andrew	never	9 July 04	30 July 12	Staff Corps.
ᛘ M'Lean, Daniel	8 Sept. 03	8 Oct. 03	20 July 09	Staff.
M'Mullen, Stephen, MD.		25 June 99	18 Nov. 13	Staff.
Macarthur, Peter[60]	24 May 95	8 Dec. 04	5 Sept. 05	1 R. Vet. Bat.
Mac Donnell, James, MD.	29 Nov. 13	14 Dec. 15	21 Sept. 30	57 Foot.

Medical Department.

	HOSPITAL-ASSIST. &c.	ASSISTANT SURGEON.	SURGEON.	
P Macnish, William, *MD.*	10 Aug. 03	4 Aug. 04	6 June 09	23 Foot.
Macredie, Thomas		3 Mar. 08	24 Jan. 11	71 Foot.
Mann, George (Reg.)	30 Aug. 99	17 Mar. 03	3 July 06	Staff.
Markham, Henry Wm.[69]	11 June 07	3 Dec. 07	2 Dec. 13	56 Foot.
P Marsdin, William (Reg.)	never	25 Mar. 97	24 Aug. 97	Staff.
P ФА Matthews, James, *MD*...	8 July 99	19 Dec. 99	9 July 03	Staff.
Mein, Pulteney, ...	never	25 Dec. 96	3 May 00	73 Foot.
Melville, Alexander, *MD*.....	24 Mar. 04	10 Sept. 07	26 Sept. 11	Staff.
Millar, Archibald (Reg.)	7 Nov. 04	15 Dec. 04	12 April 21	Staff.
Moffat, David	never	1 June 02	1 June 05	3 Ceylon Reg.
Morgan, John	11 Dec. 05	2 Oct. 06	16 Feb. 14	Ordnance.
Morle, Wm. Burgess	19 Mar. 02	22 Sept. 02	2 Nov. 09	59 Foot.
Murray, John	28 Oct. 94	25 Dec. 96	17 July 05	19 Dragoons.
O'Brien, John Terence			28 May 94	94 Foot.
O'Connor, James, *MD*........	1 June 91	never	16 Sept. 95	22 Dragoons.
P Paddock, John	25 Nov. 95	4 April 05	2 Oct. 06	Staff.
Parker, Wm. John Brown......	19 Oct. 01	8 Nov. 04	3 Aug. 15	10 Foot.
Paton, William, (*Dist.*)	26 Dec. 94		4 June 07	Staff.
Peach, George, (*Reg.*)	11 Mar. 00	4 April 00	15 Aug. 05	Staff.
Pollok, William, *MD*.	8 Sept. 03	24 Oct. 03	8 Oct. 18	53 Foot.
Poole, Matthew, *MD*.	never	never	30 June 96	Staff.
P Pooler, John	10 Oct. 94	16 June 98	9 July 03	Staff.
ФА Powell, James............	11 Dec. 05	4 June 07	28 May 14	Ordnance.
Preston, John			30 July 96	Staff.
P Prichard, Octavius.........	21 Jan. 07	25 Feb. 08	13 May 13	New Brunsw. Fen.
P Purdon, George	never	7 May 07	30 Sept. 13	32 Foot.
Purdon, Henry, *MD*.	1 April 93	never	20 June 98	Staff.
Pyper, Robert, *MD*.	2 Dec. 95	25 June 97	30 Jan. 00	4 Dragoon Guards.
Radford, John Hopkins, (*Dist.*)..	Sept. 94	25 May 02	9 April 07	Staff.
Reynolds, Michael (*Reg.*)	1 May 94	26 July 97	1 Dec. 02	Staff.
P Ridgway, T. H. *MD.* (*Reg.*)[70]	9 Mar. 07	30 July 07	5 Nov. 12	Staff.
Roberts, William	never	7 Nov. 05	29 Oct. 12	1 Foot.
P Robertson, Henry, *MD*.	Sept. 09		25 Feb. 13	Staff.
Robertson, William	9 July 05	13 Oct. 06	29 July 13	41 Foot.
P ФА Robinson, Benjamin	22 Oct. 94	never	2 Feb. 95	12 Dragoons.
Rowe, George	never	25 Aug. 00	18 June 07	Malta Reg.
P Salmon, Edw. (*Surg.-Major,* 4 Dec. 23.)[71]	never	16 Aug. 97	25 May 08	Scots Fusilier Guards.
P Sandford, R. Walthall (*Reg.*)[72]	26 June 07	26 Nov 07	9 Sept. 13	Staff.
Sandieman, John	17 Mar. 06	16 Mar. 08	12 Oct. 14	Ordnance.
Savery, John Robert	17 Feb. 09	1 June 09	28 Dec. 20	1 West India Reg.
P ФА Scott, Francis, *MD.*[73] ..	never	14 May 03	25 Jan. 10	Rifle Brigade.
P ФА Scott, Robert, *MD*.	24 June 10	5 Nov. 12	8 Nov. 27	Staff.
Scratchley, James	30 June 04	1 Aug. 06	11 Nov. 11	Ordnance.
P Shekleton, Robert	never	5 Nov. 07	9 Sept. 13	51 Foot.
Shelley, John Nichols	13 July 05	22 Aug. 05	25 Feb. 11	1 Greek Light Inf.
Sillcock, Isaac	11 May 01	10 Mar. 04	16 Feb. 09	12 Foot.
Smet, John Francis	3 Oct. 94	25 Dec. 96	9 Aug. 08	52 Foot.
P Smyth, William	never	7 April 04	22 Aug. 11	45 Foot.
P Spence, William	3 Oct. 04	20 Nov. 04	4 Feb. 13	Staff.
Spencer, Richard	7 April 00	5 June 00	9 July 03	York Rangers.
P Stanford, Jos. Arthur, *MD*...	22 Oct. 03	25 Oct. 03	4 Jan. 10	Cape Reg.
P ФА Steed, George, *MD*.	4 Mar. 05	15 Aug. 05	17 Jan. 11	1 Dragoons
Stewart, Charles	never	12 Sept. 03	26 Nov. 07	25 Foot.
P Stewart, John Edmonstoune	10 Dec. 10	25 June 12	2 Nov. 30	84 Foot.
P Stratton, Robert	25 Sept. 99	21 Mar. 00	3 Oct. 05	Staff.
P Taberger, John, *MD*.		3 Nov. 04	22 July 09	Staff.
P Taylor, John	4 Sept. 94	never	30 April 90	Staff.
Tedlie, Edward, *MD*.[74]	never	14 Nov. 04	9 Dec. 24	25 Foot.
Thom, Alexander	never	9 Mar. 97	30 Aug. 99	Staff.
Thomas, Thomas			7 Feb. 80	93 Foot.
Thomson, John, *MD*.	never	never	21 Sept. 15	Staff.
Thornton, William	9 Sept. 00	23 July 03	6 Oct. 08	09 Foot.
Trevor, Andrew[75]	Sept. 93	never	9 May 94	33 Foot.

Medical Department.

	HOSPITAL-ASSIST. &c.	ASSISTANT SURGEON.	SURGEON.	
Tucker, John	Sept. 94	never	18 Mar. 95	Staff.
Turner, William	9 June 98	15 May 02	9 Aug. 10	7 R. Vet. Batt.
฿ Vallange, William, *MD*.	8 July 06	7 Dec. 09	19 Jan. 15	69 Foot.
฿ ใช้ Van Millingen, J. G.,*MD*.	16 May 01	26 Jan. 02	16 Nov. 09	Staff.
฿ Vassall, William, *MD*.		12 Nov. 03	15 June 09	24 Foot.
Vermeulen, George		12 April 10	2 Dec. 13	60 Foot.
Volmar, G. Ber.(Apoth.14 Oct.05)	never	never	15 June 09	Staff.
Wake, Baldwin	April 94	never	6 May 95	111 Foot.
Walker, J. Harding, *MD*.[76] ...	25 Oct. 08	2 Nov. 09	22 Nov. 15	92 Foot.
฿ Walker, Roger Chambers	21 Feb. 97	24 June 99	3 Dec. 03	3 Dragoons.
฿ Wallace, William	1 Feb. 88	never	11 May 91	Staff.
Ward, John Richard		21 Aug. 06	4 Dec. 23	Scots Fus. Gds.
Waring, Charles	25 Feb. 08	6 July 09	6 Jan. 14	5 Foot.
ใช้ Watson, Sam.Wm.(Surg.-Maj. 11 Nov. 24)		20 Mar. 99	14 July 09	Grenadier Guards.
West, Henry	4 Oct. 99	25 June 01	27 Nov. 06	10 Dragoons.
White, John	25 May 81	never	25 Dec. 01	Staff.
White, Peter	21 Dec. 07	15 Nov. 10	7 Oct. 13	72 Foot.
ใช้ Whymper, William, *MD*. ..		14 Nov. 05	25 Dec. 13	Coldstream Guards.
฿ Widmer, Christopher	June 04	15 Aug. 05	24 Oct. 11	Staff.
Williams, James		1 Nov. 99	12 June 04	84 Foot.
฿ Williams, John, *MD*.[77]	5 May 05	20 June 05	3 Sept. 12	Staff.
Williams, Richard, *MD*.	9 Aug. 13	24 Feb. 14	29 June 32	68 Foot.
฿ Wood, David, *MD*.	20 Mar. 00	2 Oct. 00	3 Nov. 08	Staff.
Woods, Thomas	19 Aug. 99	30 Aug. 99	19 Sept. 05	Staff.
Wright, Robert	never	never		2 Prov. Bn. of Mil.
Wybrow, William	never	26 Dec. 96	3 July 99	17 Dragoons.
฿ Wylde, John Fewtrell	10 April 98	14 Mar. 05	12 Feb. 07	7 R. Vet. Batt.
Young, Thomas	4 Dec. 03	1 Jan. 04	11 Nov. 11	Ordnance.
฿ Young, Thomas[78]	10 Dec. 10	9 Sept. 13	4 May 26	71 Foot.
Young, Colin, *MD*.	never	1 Mar. 98	15 Oct. 07	6 R. Vet. Batt.

APOTHECARIES.

			APOTHECARY.	
Cowen, John			14 Nov. 97	
฿ Graham, John...............	19 April 08	never	31 Aug. 09	
Hoffe, Philip	11 Aug. 95	never	21 April 04	
Huggan, Andrew	21 June 13	never	25 Nov. 13	
฿ Jones, Samuel...............	Aug. 09		31 Aug. 09	
฿ Matthews, Richard..........	20 Dec. 03		6 April 09	
Maxwell, John	19 April 99	25 Dec. 02	11 July 05	
Middleton, George	never	never	7 Sept. 15	
Newton, John Hayne..........	18 Oct. 95	never	28 May 07	
O'Brien, Edward			20 June 98	
฿ Wheadon, William..........			18 Oct. 10	
White, Henry			14 April 04	
Wightman, George...........			25 July 03	

ASSISTANT-SURGEONS.

Apreece, Thomas	never	21 June 10		Ordnance.
Attree, William	never	1 Aug. 06		Ordnance.
Backhouse, Thomas	1 Dec. 12	24 Feb. 14		5 Royal Vet. Batt.
ใช้ Bartlett, James, *MD*.......	May 12	16 July 12		9 Royal Vet. Batt.
Beard, Thomas	12 Nov. 12			Ordnance.
Benza, Pasquale Maria	8 Aug. 15	26 Jan. 26		Staff.
฿ Bremner, Alexander	6 July 10	3 Sept. 12		3 Foot.
฿ ใช้ Brisbane, Thomas, *MD*.....	19 June 12	3 June 13		58 Foot.
Browne, Francis	12 Oct. 26	24 July 28		26 Foot.
Burke, Thomas	never	4 Aug. 08		27 Foot.
฿ Campbell, Alexander........	24 Feb. 14	13 July 15		3 Dragoon Guards.
Cannon, Æneas, *MD*.	11 June 11	23 July 11		Ordnance.

Medical Department.

Name	HOSPITAL- ASSIST. &c.	ASSISTANT SURGEON.	
Chislette, Henry		15 Dec. 04	81 Foot.
Clarke, Charles Edward		4 June 01	Grenadier Guards.
Coleman, John	never	31 Aug. 97	7 Dragoon Guards.
Cooper, Bransby	20 May 12	2 Dec. 12	Ordnance.
Cunin, William	never	21 Mar. 16	3 Royal Veteran Battalion.
Cupples, Charles	18 July 12	4 Dec. 12	Ordnance.
Curtis, Thomas Venden	10 Nov. 13	29 Aug. 14	Ordnance.
⅓ Develin, Henry William	20 July 09	20 May 13	49 Foot.
Devitt, Mitchell, *MD.*	26 May 15	8 Feb. 16	47 Foot.
Dolmage, Gideon	never	10 Dec. 33	18 Foot.
Douglas, John	Aug. 10	26 Sept. 11	8 Foot.
Dumbreck, David, *MD.*	3 Nov. 25	12 Jan. 26	Staff.
Dyason, William			4 Garrison Battalion.
Dyce, Robert, *MD.*	8 Feb. 21	22 Sept. 25	Staff.
Eddowes, James	never	25 Aug. 10	Ordnance.
Emerson, Thomas	25 April 93	8 Nov. 03	104 Foot.
⅓ Evers, George	3 June 15	23 Dec. 24	14 Foot.
Fitzmaurice, George Lionel	6 July 29	1 July 31	Ordnance.
Fryer, William Henry	15 Dec. 26	8 May 28	Staff.
Furnivall, John James, *MD.*	never	1 Dec. 09	Ordnance.
⅓ Gatty, Henry	26 April 13	20 Nov. 13	Ordnance.
⅓ Gibb, Wm. Richardson, *MD.*	6 July 11	25 July 12	88 Foot.
Hendrick, John, *MD.*		3 July 17	34 Foot.
⅓ Hewat, Richard	4 Jan. 11	15 June 15	65 Foot.
Holden, Horatio Nelson	1 Feb. 27	2 Aug. 31	21 Foot.
Hollier, Edward		7 Oct. 13	37 Foot.
Hollmann, Joseph		30 Dec. 97	60 Foot.
Huggins, John	10 Jan. 14	28 Dec. 15	58 Foot.
⅓ Hurst, James	10 June 12	28 Oct. 13	37 Foot.
Jarvis, James		3 Oct. 00	65 Foot.
Ince, Henry Robert		26 June 00	10 Royal Veteran Battalion.
Inglis, Charles	never	4 April 10	Ordnance.
Johnston, Arthur, *MD.*	July 11	28 May 12	60 Foot.
Jones, John		6 July 04	1 Royal Veteran Battalion.
Joseph, Lawrence Alfred	5 Dec. 26	24 Jan. 28	4 Dragoon Guards.
Irwin, Walter Devereux		21 Dec. 97	11 Foot.
Kehoe, Patrick		June 10	25 June 19	52 Foot.
⅓ Kenny, Matthias, *MD.*	never	1 Dec. 10	Ordnance.
Knott, William	16 June 15	5 May 25	6 Dragoons.
La Cloche, Thomas	7 Nov. 97	24 Dec. 02	7 Royal Veteran Battalion.
⅓ Lawder, James	never	12 Nov. 12	66 Foot.
Ligertwood, Andrew	8 April 05	11 July 05	3 Royal Veteran Battalion.
Locke, Wm. Oliver	never	29 Mar. 07	Ordnance.
Lukis, Thomas	never	9 April 12	50 Foot.
⅓ ⅓ M'Clintock, Hugh	29 Mar. 12	5 Nov. 12	Staff.
M'Crae, Farquhar, *MD.*	never	28 Sept. 32	6 Dragoons.
M'Culloch, Samuel	18 Aug. 12	1 Jan. 13	Ordnance.
M'Gregor, Alexander, *MD.*	never	6 Dec. 33	Staff.
M'Laine, John	never	6 Dec. 06	60 Foot.
M'Lean, George Gordon	7 Feb. 14	1 Sept. 14	35 Foot.
M'Swyny, Eugene, *MD.*	never	3 Dec. 12	25 Dragoons.
MacBain, Giles	15 Feb. 10	19 Mar. 12	62 Foot.
Martin, George	Feb. 09	28 Feb. 11	67 Foot.
Martin, James	29 Dec. 14	10 Oct. 16	9 Foot.
Millar, James, *MD.*	never	7 June 32	Staff.
Miller, John, *MD.*	never	7 Mar. 07	Ordnance.
Millet, Edward, *MD.*	June 05	25 June 19	4 Foot.
Morgan, Evan		1 Nov. 99	35 Foot.
Mullarky, Daniel	22 Nov. 13	6 Oct. 25	27 Foot.
Nixon, James	29 June 15	8 Jan. 16	Ordnance.
Nugent, Morgan	8 Dec. 12	20 Nov. 13	Ordnance.
O'Beirne, James, *MD.*	never	11 Oct. 10	Ordnance.
O'Connor, J. Lynch, *MD.*	10 Nov. 13	28 May 14	Ordnance.
O'Toole, John	12 Mar. 12	11 Nov. 13	51 Foot.

Medical Department.

	HOSPITAL-ASSIST. &c.	ASSISTANT SURGEON.	
O'Donnell, John	7 Mar. 14	25 Jan. 25	77 Foot.
Poett, Joseph		Dec. 09	14 Dec. 09	4 Royal Veteran Battalion.
Price, Thomas	19 Feb. 05	13 Nov. 06	96 Foot.
𝕮 Raleigh, Walter, *MD*.	30 Nov. 13	12 Oct. 14	Ordnance.
Ranclaud, Mark Alexander	never	26 June 09	Ordnance.
Rankin, Wm. Thomas, *MD*.	25 Jan. 26	28 Sept. 26	84 Foot.
Reilly, William			Staff.
Robins, Jacob William		27 June 02	Corsican Rangers.
Rolland, Jas. Henderson...........	29 May 28	29 July 30	Staff.
Ross, William Baillie, *MD*.	7 April 25	16 June 25	5 Royal Veteran Battalion.
𝕮 Rudge, Edward	20 May 12	3 Dec. 12	Ordnance.
St. Croix, Benjamin de	14 May 01	1 Dec. 25	Staff.
Sprague, John Hanmer	5 May 10	14 June 10	8 Royal Veteran Battalion.
Sproule, James Alex.		17 Mar. 14	2 Royal Veteran Battalion.
Swift, Richard	never	19 Aug. 13	60 Foot.
Thompson, John	never	1 Dec. 09	Ordnance.
ℙ Tobin, John	7 Dec. 09	19 Dec. 11	9 Dragoons.
Topham, James Anthony	5 May 25	11 May 26	10 Foot.
Tuthil, Michael H.	1 April 14	19 Dec. 14	Ordnance.
Venables, Robert, *MD*.	28 Aug. 11	11 Nov. 11	Ordnance.
𝕮 Verner, Edw. Donovan	9 June 13	29 Nov. 13	Ordnance.
Vowell, Christ. Maxwell...........	29 Mar. 27	18 Dec. 28	73 Foot.
ℙ Walbran, Francis George [81]	7 Oct. 12	24 Feb. 14	45 Foot.
Webb, Boloyne Gordon	28 Dec. 26	29 July 30	Staff.
Wilkinson, John William		28 Sept. 91	Royal Marines.
Williams, David	20 Dec. 13	12 Aug. 19	67 Foot.
Woodroff, John, *MD*.		Dec. 03	25 June 19	Staff.

PURVEYORS.	DEPUTY PURVEYOR	PURVEYOR
ℙ Hodges, Edward	29 June 09	9 Sept. 13
ℙ James, William	19 Mar. 00	29 June 09
Usher, William	13 Nov. 00	2 June 14

DEPUTY PURVEYORS.

ℙ Bacon, Harry	21 Dec. 09
Bonnin, Henry Gousse	28 Sept. 09
Cleave, Richard	29 June 09
ℙ Copeland, Alexander	31 Aug. 09
Cornish, Thomas	7 Sept. 15
ℙ Dunn, John.....................	9 Sept. 13
Edghill, James	6 Oct. 14
Everitt, Hen. Yarburgh	26 May 14
ℙ Findley, Thomas	10 Mar. 14
Gibbons, Samuel	14 Mar. 00
ℙ Harrington, Joseph..............	9 Sept. 13
ℙ M'Pherson, Lachlan	19 Aug. 13
Moore, John	25 Sept. 14
Newcomb, Joseph	26 May 15
ℙ O'Reilley, Henry William........	5 Jan. 09
Power, Hugh	12 June 06
𝕮 Robinson, George................	7 Sept. 15
Sheppard, David Parker............	28 Sept. 09
ℙ Smyth, Thomas	3 Sept. 12
ℙ Soare, Charles	15 Oct. 12
Tucker, Richard	5 Nov. 29
ℙ Wallington, James	9 Sept. 13
ℙ Winnicki, Christopher	24 June 02
ℙ Winter, George	15 Oct. 12
ℙ Winter, John	21 Dec. 09

Medical Department.

HOSPITAL ASSISTANTS.	HOSPITAL-ASSISTANT
Blackwood, John	25 April 14
Bocca, Pasquale	7 Mar. 14
Brereton, Charles	9 Nov. 13
Bruce, Alexander	4 July 15
Carter, Henry Collis	11 Jan. 10
Ker, James	9 Nov. 15
M'Cabe, Patrick	7 Oct. 12
Randazzo, Francis	12 Oct. 15
Robertson, Patrick, *MD*	24 June 15

VETERINARY SURGEONS.	VETERINARY SURGEON.	
Berington, James	16 Dec. 13	Depot.
Cumming, Robert Stewart	24 April 05	Royal Artillery.
Darvill, Richard	13 Dec. 10	7 Dragoons.
Field, Jeremiah	24 April 13	2 Life Guards.
Goodwin, Joseph	24 April 05	R. Artillery.
Grellier, James	21 Feb. 00	R. Waggon Train.
Gross, George	29 July 13	25 Dragoons.
Hogreve, Henry*	12 July 06	15 Dragoons.
Lythe, John	1 June 09	Royal Artillery.
O'Connor, Charles	7 Mar. 08	Royal Artillery.
Peers, James	21 Feb. 05	16 Dragoons.
Percivall, William	30 Nov. 12	Royal Artillery.
Price, Edmund	13 June 16	17 Dragoons.
Ryding, William	2 May 00	1 Dragoons.
Steed, Edward Henry	15 Mar. 98	Depot.
Thompson, Robert	17 April 01	14 Dragoons.

CHAPLAIN'S DEPARTMENT.

CHAPLAINS.			
Barrington, Gilbert	31 Aug. 95	Hughes, John	25 Dec. 09
Carey, Nicholas	19 Feb. 95	James, Maurice	25 Nov. 13
Cautley, William Grainger	25 Dec. 09	Jepson, George	8 April 83
Cracroft, John	23 May 12	Irwin, Henry	
Crigan, Claudius	15 July 95	Kirkbank, William	9 June 84
Dayman, Charles	18 Oct. 11	Lyon, Charles Jobson, *BA*	9 April 16
Denius, Nathaniel Robert	29 June 16	Mackereth, Mark Anthony	25 Dec. 10
Dobbs, John	24 Sept. 94	Morgan, James	21 Mar. 82
Forsyth, Morris	18 Mar. 95	Neve, Frederick	13 Nov. 99
Frith, Edward Cockayne	4 May 11	Preston, Joseph	19 July 94
Frith, William Cockayne	25 June 12	Rose, John	11 July 83
Goff, Thomas	28 July 98	Stonestreet, George Griffin	4 April 14
Guinness, Hosea	3 Dec. 94	Symonds, Henry John	12 April 13
Hill, Samuel	20 Sept. 10	Timbrill, John	30 June 95
Hudson, Joseph, *MA*	25 Nov. 25	Trail, Archibald Hamilton	31 May 95

* Mr. Hogreve served in the Peninsula, France, and Flanders, from Dec. 1811 to the end of the war, including the third siege of Badajoz, and battles of Vittoria, Toulouse, and Waterloo.

Notes to the Medical Officers.

1 Doctor Gordon served with the South African expedition under General Whitelock in 1807.
2 Doctor Adolphus served in Ireland during the Rebellion in 1798; and with the Walcheren expedition in 1809.
3 Doctor Baxter served in Holland in 1799. Joined the 48th Regt. in the Peninsula in 1810, where he served until the end of the war. Served also in the American war in 1814.
4 Doctor Blackwell served at the capture of St. Fiorenza, Calvi and Bastia, in Corsica : also the Egyptian campaign of 1801.
5 Doctor Erly served in the Egyptian campaign of 1801. In Portugal from the latter part of 1808 to April 1809. Expedition to Walcheren. Served afterwards in the Peninsula from Feb. 1812 to the end of the war, and subsequently in the American war.
6 Doctor W. Fergusson served in Holland in 1794 ; in St. Domingo in 1796, 7, and 8 ; again in Holland in 1799 ; with the Expedition to Sweden, and subsequently to the Peninsula under Sir John Moore, and afterwards under the Duke of Wellington.
7 Sir James Robert Grant served at Walcheren in 1809 ; and the campaign of 1815, including the battle of Waterloo.
8 Doctor Thomas Gunning served in Holland in 1799. Embarked for the Mediterranean with Sir James Craig's expedition in April 1805, and was employed on active service at Naples, Sicily, Maida, the taking of the Islands in the Bay of Naples, and the Ionian Islands. Wounded at the taking of Santa Maura.
9 Doctor Higgins served the Egyptian campaign in 1801. Served in the Peninsula during the greater part of the war, including the battles of Talavera, Fuentes d'Onor, Vittoria, and the subsequent affairs until after the capture of San Sebastian.
10 Doctor Hume served in Egypt in 1801. Also in the Peninsular war.
11 Doctor Robb served in Holland in 1799; expedition to Hanover in 1805; to South America in 1807. Served throughout the whole of the Peninsular war, and afterwards in the American war.
12 Doctor Strachan served at Walcheren in 1809.
13 Doctor Tegart served in Ireland during the Rebellion in 1798. Blockade and reduction of Malta, 1800. Expedition to Hanover, 1805 ; Copenhagen and Madeira, 1807, and subsequently to Portugal under Sir John Moore, where he served that memorable campaign terminating with the battle of Corunna. Served afterwards in the Peninsula from 1809 to 1813.
14 Doctor Thomson served in Egypt; also at the capture of Martinique, the Saintes, and Guadaloupe. Served also in the Peninsula from 1813 to the end of the war ; and afterwards with the expedition against New Orleans.
15 Doctor Tudor served on the Continent in 1793, 94, and 95 ; and with the expedition to the Helder in 1799.
16 Doctor Warren served the Corunna campaign.
17 Doctor Whitelock served in Holland under the Duke of York in 1794.
18 Doctor Woolriche served in Holland under the Duke of York. Expedition to Copenhagen 1807. Served also in the Peninsula, France, and Flanders under the Duke of Wellington.
19 Doctor Albert served at the Helder in 1799. Also the campaign of 1814 in Holland under Lord Lynedoch.
20 Doctor James Arthur served in the Peninsula from 1809 to the end of the war.
21 Doctor Barry served in the Peninsula from Aug. 1808 to Aug. 1811, and again from Aug. 1813 to the end of the war. Also the campaign of 1815, including the battle of Waterloo.
22 Doctor Browne served in the Peninsula, with the 9th Regt. including the actions at Roleia, Vimiera, and Oporto. Slightly wounded in the right thigh 11th April 1802, during the mutiny of the 8th West India Regt. at St. Rupert's.
23 Doctor Buckle served with the expedition to Ostend under Sir Eyre Coote, in 1798.
24 Doctor Clark served in the Peninsula from Nov. 1809 to the end of the war.
25 Doctor Collier served at the capture of Martinique in 1809 ; and in the Peninsula from the latter part of 1812 to the end of the war.
26 Doctor Crawford served at the Helder in 1799.
27 Doctor Daun served at the capture of the Cape of Good Hope in 1806. Also the campaign of 1815, including the battle of Waterloo.

Notes to the Medical Officers.

28 Doctor Duncan has seen a great deal of active service in the East Indies.

29 Doctor Forbes served with the expedition to the Ferrol in 1800. Egyptian campaign of 1801. Capture of St. Lucia and Tobago, 1803. Served also throughout the whole of the Peninsular war.

30 Doctor Grasett served at the capture of Trinidad in Jan. 1797; and of Malta in 1800. Served also in the Peninsula from May 1809 to Feb. 1813.

31 Doctor Griffin served at the Helder in 1799.

32 Doctor Hartle served on the expedition to St. Lucia in 1803, and accompanied the storming party to Morne Fortune. Present at Dominica when the French attacked the island in 1805. Served also at the capture of the Islands of St. Thomas and St. Croix in 1807, and Martinique, in 1809, including the actions of the 1st and 2nd Feb. Also at the capture of Guadaloupe in 1815.

33 Doctor Howell served in Calabria in 1806, and was at the battle of Maida. Served the Egyptian campaign of 1807; and subsequently in the Peninsula from April 1810 to Oct. 1812. Slightly wounded on the left shoulder by the Bedouin Arabs in Egypt, while employed on a mission to the Mamelukes, and severely wounded in the loins in Portugal, the ball still remaining unextracted.

34 Doctor Knife served in Ireland during the Rebellion in 1798, siege of Copenhagen, and battle of Kiog, 1807. Campaign in Portugal and Spain in 1808 and 9.

35 Doctor Lamert served in St. Domingo in 1796 and 97; in Egypt in 1801 (wounded in the action of the 13th March); Copenhagen in 1807; campaign in Portugal and Spain under Sir John Moore, including the battles of Roleia and Vimiera, retreat to, and battle of Corunna; expedition to Walcheren 1809; and subsequently in the Peninsula until 1811.

36 Doctor Lindsey served in the Peninsula from Jan. 1810 to the end of the war.

37 Doctor MacDougle served at Walcheren in 1809; and in the Peninsula from Dec. 1810 to Aug. 1813; and in Holland and the Netherlands from Dec. 1813 until after the battle of Waterloo.

38 Doctor Macleod served the Egyptian campaign of 1801. Campaigns in the Peninsula from June 1809 to July 1812, and from early in 1813 to the end of the war.

39 Doctor Marshall served in South America in 1807.

40 Sir John Meade served at the capture of Trinidad, after which he accompanied the expedition to Porto Rico. Egyptian campaign of 1801. Campaign in South America in 1807. Campaigns in the Peninsula from July 1808 to July 1810.

41 Doctor Porteus served the Egyptian campaign of 1807; and in Dec. 1812 he joined the army in Alicante and served with that division of the army until the British troops finally evacuated the eastern coast of Spain; he then proceeded to Genoa.

42 Doctor Robinson served in Holland in 1794 and 95; subsequently in the West Indies under General Forbes; and in the Peninsula, France and Flanders from April 1809 to the end of the war, including the capture of Oporto, and battles of Talavera, Salamanca, Busaco, Fuentes d'Onor, Vittoria, and Waterloo. Served also at Bhurtpore under Lord Combermere.

43 Sir Augustus West served in Hanover in 1805; at Copenhagen and Sweden in 1807; Portugal and Spain 1808; Walcheren 1809; and in the Peninsula from 1809 to the end of the war.

44 Doctor White served in Egypt in 1801; and subsequently in the Peninsula.

45 Doctor Evans served in the Peninsula with the 29th Regt. and on the staff.

46 Sir Arthur Brooke Faulkner served in Spain in 1808; and at Walcheren in 1809.

47 Doctor Greaves served on the Continent in 1794 and 95; and at the Helder in 1799.

48 Doctor Jones served at the capture of the Islands of Ischia and Procida in 1809. Employed in the gun-boats in the Faro of Messina under Sir John Stewart. Present at the capture of the Ionian Islands and siege of Santa Maura, under Sir John Oswald. Served the campaign in Catalonia under Lord William Bentinck. Served afterwards in the American war, including the actions at Bladensburg and Baltimore, capture of Washington, and operations against New Orleans.

49 Doctor Knight served at Walcheren in 1809.

50 Doctor Maclagan served at Walcheren in 1809. Served also in the Peninsula from Dec. 1811 to the end of the war.

51 Doctor Morewood served at Walcheren in 1809; in the Peninsula in 1812; and in the American war in 1813.

52 Doctor Robson served in the Peninsula from Dec. 1811 to the end of the war.

53 Doctor Sibbald served in the Peninsula during the campaigns of 1813 and 14, including the battles of Orthes and Toulouse. Served subsequently in America at New Orleans.

54 Doctor Walker served at Walcheren in 1809. Served with the exception of a few months, throughout the whole of the Peninsular war.

55 Doctor Amiel served with the expedition to Quiberon Bay, Isle Dieu, Portugal, &c. Served also several campaigns in the Peninsula.

Notes to the Medical Officers.

56 Doctor Andrew Anderson served in Naples and Calabria, and was present at the battle of Maida, and siege of Scylla Castle. Expedition to Walcheren and siege of Flushing 1809. Peninsula from Jan. 1809 to Nov. 1813, including the siege of Cadiz, battles of Busaco, Fuentes d'Onor and Salamanca, siege of Burgos Castle, and actions in the Pyrenees.

57 Doctor Annesley was at the siege and capture of Santa Maura in March 1810; siege and capture of Trieste, Oct. 1813. Served against the Vice Roy of Italy under General Nugent and Colonel Robertson in 1813, and was at the taking of Comachio, Ferrara, Ravenna, Bologna, and Genoa.

58 Doctor Batt served with the expedition to Hanover in 1805; campaign in the Peninsula in 1808 and 9, including the battle of Vimiera, retreat to Corunna, passage of the Douro, and battle of Talavera. Expedition to Walcheren, 1809. Peninsular campaigns of 1811 and 12, including the advance in pursuit of Massena, and battles of Fuentes d'Onor and Salamanca.

59 Doctor Byrtt's services:—Expedition to South America under General Whitelock. Campaign in the Peninsula from July 1808 to Jan. 1809, including the battle of Vimiera. Expedition to Walcheren. Peninsula from Dec. 1812 to the end of the war, including the battles of Orthes and Toulouse.

60 Doctor Cunningham served the campaigns in Upper Canada in 1813 and 14 under Sir Gordon Drummond.

61 Doctor D. O. Davies served in the Peninsula from June 1810 to the end of the war, including the sieges of Cadiz and Tarifa, and battles and affairs of Barrosa, Vittoria, Pyrenees, Nivelle, Nive, St. Palais, Aire, Tarbes, Orthes, and Toulouse. Served also at the attack on New Orleans.

62 Doctor Dealey served in the Peninsula in 1811 and 12, including the battle of Albuhera, and first siege of Badajoz.

63 Doctor Este served the Egyptian campaign of 1801, including the actions of the 8th (slightly wounded), 13th, and 21st March, and siege of Alexandria. Served also in the Peninsula from Oct. 1812 to the end of the war, including the battles of Vittoria, Pampeluna, Orthes, and Toulouse. Medal for services in Egypt.

64 Doctor Goodrich served in the Peninsula from May 1812 to May 1814.

65 Doctor Arthur Hamilton served in the Peninsula from 1809 to the end of the war, including the capture of Oporto, battle of Busaco, first siege of Badajoz, battle of Albuhera, action at Arroya de Molinos, battle of Vittoria, action before Bayonne 13th Dec., and battle of Toulouse.

66 Doctor Hodson served in Egypt in 1801.

67 Doctor Jones (h. p. 1st Dr. Gds.) served at Copenhagen in 1807; in the Peninsula under Sir John Moore; and at Walcheren, 1809.

68 Doctor M'Arthur served at the capture of Guadaloupe in 1815.

69 Doctor Markham served at the siege of Copenhagen in 1807, and at the occupation of Martinique in 1815.

70 Doctor Ridgway's services:—Siege of Copenhagen, 1807. Campaign in the Peninsula from May 1808 to Jan. 1809, including the actions of Obidos, Roleia, and Vimiera, advance into Spain, and retreat to Corunna. Expedition to Walcheren, and siege of Flushing, 1809. Peninsular campaigns from May 1810 to May 1811, and from May 1812 to the end of the war, including the retreat to the Lines of Lisbon and subsequent advance to Santarem, defence of Cadiz, battles of Barrosa and Salamanca, advance to and retreat from Madrid.

71 Doctor Salmon served in Holland in 1799, including the actions of the 27th Aug., 10th and 19th Sept., 2d and 6th October. Served also in the Peninsula from Jan. 1809 to June 1810, from March 1811 to March 1813, and from March 1814 to the end of the war, including the passage of the Douro and capture of Oporto, affair at Salamanca, battle of Fuentes d'Onor, sieges of Ciudad Rodrigo and Badajoz, battle of Salamanca, capture of Madrid, siege of Burgos, investment of Bayonne, and repulse of the sortie.

72 Doctor Sandford served at Copenhagen in 1807; and in the Peninsula from 1812 to the end of the war, including the siege of Burgos, and battles of Salamanca, Pyrenees, Orthes, and Toulouse. Served also in the Burmese war.

73 Doctor Francis Scott's services:—Capture of the Cape of Good Hope in 1806. Expedition to Walcheren, 1809. Peninsular campaigns from April 1813 to the end of the war, including the following battles and affairs, viz. Vera and Vera heights, Nivelle, Orthes, Tarbes, and Toulouse. Also the campaign of 1815, including the battle of Waterloo.

74 Doctor Tedlie served the campaign and capture of Travancore in 1809. Capture of Bourbon and the Isle of France, 1810. Capture of Java, 1811.

75 Doctor Trevor served the campaign in Flanders in 1794, and was present with his regt. (the 33rd) in all the operations in that country, and in the retreat of the army through Holland. Served subsequently in the East Indies from 1796 to 1808, and was present at the battle of Mallavelly, and at the storming and capture of Seringapatam.

Notes to the Medical Officers.

76 Doctor J. H. Walker served at New Orleans in 1814 and 15 under Sir Edward Pakenham.

77 Doctor John Williams served throughout the whole of the Peninsular war, and was present with the troops when engaged with the enemy in ten general actions and successful sieges, viz. the Douro, Busaco, Fuentes d'Onor, Ciudad Rodrigo, Badajoz, Salamanca, Vittoria, San Sebastian, Orthes, and Toulouse, besides many others of less importance. Served subsequently in North America during the latter part of the war with the United States.

78 Doctor Young (h. p. 71st Reg.) served in the Peninsula from May 1811 to the end of the war, including the capture of Badajoz, and battles of Vittoria, the Pyrenees, Nivelle, Nive, Orthes (taken prisoner), and Toulouse.

79 Doctor Jackson served at the reduction of Grenada in 1796 (from the revolted Negroes); at Martinique, and on the expedition to Porto Rico, and in Demerara in 1797; with the army under Lord Cathcart in Germany in 1805 and 6; at the capture of the Isle of France in 1810; and of Java in 1811, including the whole of the operations. In 1812 at the siege and capture of Djocjocarta in the interior of Java; in June 1813 at the assault and destruction of the piratical forts of Sambas in the Island of Borneo; in 1815, Nepaul campaign; in 1817, assault and capture of Hattras; in 1817 & 18, the whole of the Pindarree campaign in the centre of India.

80 Doctor Macarthur was severely wounded at the storming of Seringapatam.

81 Doctor Walbran served in the Peninsula, and was present at the siege of Ciudad Rodrigo, and battles of Vittoria and Toulouse.

OFFICERS

ON THE

FOREIGN HALF-PAY.

GERMAN LEGION.

		RANK IN THE ARMY.		WHEN PLACED ON HALF-PAY.	
LIGHT DRAGOONS.					
1st.					
Lieut.-Col.	𝔓 𝕶𝕳 John, *Baron* Bülow, CB. KH.	1 Aug.	1810	24 Feb.	1816
Captains	𝕶𝕳 Hans von Hattorf	8 June	07	do	
	𝔓 𝕶𝕳 Frederick von Uslar Gleichen¹	3 Jan.	09	do	
	𝕶𝕳 Bernard von Bothmer	28 Aug.	10	do	
	𝕶𝕳 Henry George von Hattorf	25 Feb.	12	do	
	𝕶𝕳 George de Ramdohr	8 Mar.		do	
	𝕶𝕳 Charles Elderhorst	10 Mar.	13	do	
	Hartwig von Witzendorff	13 June		do	
	𝕶𝕳 Morris de Cloudt	17 Sept.		do	
	𝕶𝕳 Benedix, *Baron* Decken	18 Sept.		do	
Lieutenants	𝕶𝕳 Augustus Fischer	13 Mar.	12	do	
	Frederick Natermann	do		do	
	Charles Fred. Tappe	24 Dec.		25 Apr.	15
	𝕶𝕳 Otto von Hammerstein	13 May	15	24 Feb.	16
	𝕶𝕳 Conrad Poten	6 July		do	
	𝕶𝕳 Henry Nanne	7 July		do	
	𝕶𝕳 Lewis Kirchner	8 July		do	
Cornets	𝕶𝕳 Frederick Breymaun	15 Mar.	14	25 Feb.	16
	Charles von der Decken	18 Apr.		do	
	𝕶𝕳 Ludewig von Müller	22 Apr.		do	
	𝕶𝕳 Hannach Boguslaw Leschen	27 May		do	
	George von Uslar Gleichen	13 May	15	do	
	𝕶𝕳 Edward Trittau	14 May		24 Feb.	
	Hen. Anth. Fred. Cleve	7 July		do	
	Christian von Bülow	25 Oct.		do	
Vet.-Surgeon	𝕶𝕳 Ludolph Heuer	25 May	05	do	
2d.					
Captains	𝕶𝕳 Charles, *Baron* Marschalck	24 Nov.	1809	24 Feb.	1816
	𝕶𝕳 William Seeger	27 Aug.	12	do	
	𝕶𝕳 George Braun	3 July	15	do	
	𝕶𝕳 Augustus Poten	15 Oct.		do	
Lieutenants	𝕶𝕳 Ludolph de Hugo	24 Mar.	12	do	
	𝕶𝕳 Joannes Justinus von Fumetti	do		do	
	Augustus Kuhls	28 May		do	
	𝕶𝕳 Carl Schaeffer	2 Oct.		do	
	𝕶𝕳 Herman Hen. Con. Ritter	18 Sept.	13	do	
	𝕶𝕳 Ern. Theo. Chr. Meier	15 Mar.	14	do	
	𝕶𝕳 Ferdinand Küster	21 Nov.	15	do	
Cornets	𝕶𝕳 O. W. F. J. C. von Bulow	8 Oct.	13	do	
	Ferd. Carl Edmund Kuhls	10 Apr.	15	do	
	Ernest von Voss	4 July		do	
	Ferdinand von Stolzenberg	21 Nov.		do	
	Christian Schaumann	23 Nov.		do	
Surgeon	𝕶𝕳 Frederick Detmer	13 July	13	do	
Vet.-Surgeon	Conrad Dallwig	29 Apr.	13	21 Aug.	

1 Captain Von Uslar Gleichen has received a **medal** for the battle of Vittoria.

Foreign Half-pay.

HUSSARS.
1st.

		RANK IN THE ARMY.		WHEN PLACED ON HALF-PAY.	
Captains	....George de Muller ....Major	4 June	1814	25 June	1814
	※ George, *Count* von der Decken	11 July	11	24 Feb.	16
	※ Frederick von der Decken	18 Nov.		do	
	※ Louis Krauchenberg................	13 Jan.	13	do	
	※ Gustavus Schaumann	10 Oct.		do	
	※ Frederick Baertling ············	27 Jan.	14	do	
	※ Hieronimus von der Wisch	6 April		do	
Lieutenants	..※ Conrad Poten	14 July	11	do	
	※ Leopold Sigismond Schultze	19 Nov.		do	
	Frederick Holtzermann	20 June	13	do	
	※ Henry Cristoph. Behrens	19 Nov.		do	
Cornets	......※ Franz. Geo. von Oldershausen	27 Jan.	14	do	
	※ William Theodore Gebser	14 Feb.		do	
	※ Frederick Jacob Rahlwes	26 April		do	
	※ William de Hassell	13 Sept.		do	
Adjutant	....※ Siegesmund Freudenthal ...... *Lieut.*	27 Mar.	13	do	
Assist.-Surgs.	※ Frederick Deppee	6 Dec.	05	do	
	※ Henry Gehse	3 Mar.	12	do	

2d

Captains	....George Chr. von Donop	19 Nov.	07	do	
	Urban Cleve	19 July	11	do	
	Theodor von Stolzenberg..............	14 Nov.	12	do	
Lieutenants	..Johann Daniel Borchers	23 Aug.	11	do	
	Frederick Grahn	28 Mar.	12	do	
	Dav. Cha. Corn. Wieboldt	29 Aug.		do	
	Michael Löning	16 Nov.		do	
Cornets	......Frederick Herman Meyer	16 Dec.	12	do	
	Ernest Soest	27 Nov.	13	do	
	Herman Westfeld	23 Mar.	14	do	
	Victor Von Aiten	27 April		do	
	Theodore von Marschalck	28 July	15	do	
Adjutant	....Henry Gotze ....*Lieut.*	28 Mar.	12	do	
Assist.-Surg.	Achatz William Holscher	19 April	06	do	
Vet.-Surg.	Frederick Eicke	2 Jan.	07	do	

3rd.

Major	....※ G. *Baron* von Krauchenberg, CB. KCH. *Lt.-Col.*	18 June	15	do	
Captains	....Fred. *Baron* von Poten	16 Mar.	10	do	
	※ Quintus, *Baron* Goeben	2 May	11	do	
	※ William von Schnehen...............	20 Sept.		do	
	※ Johann Christian Ulrich Heise	13 Nov.	12	do	
	Ivan Gott. F. *Baron* Hodenburg	16 Sept.	13	do	
	※ August. de Harling	8 Oct.		do	
	※ George Meyer	27 Dec.		do	
	※ Diede. Wm. von der Hellen	17 Feb.	14	do	
	Gustavus Meyer	5 July	15	do	
Lieutenants	..※ John Christ. Fred. Nanne	13 Nov.	12	do	
	※ John Henry D'Homboldt	14 Nov.		do	
	※ Charles Augustus Reinecke..........	15 Nov.		do	
	※ Christian Oehlkers	9 Oct.	13	do	
	※ Lewis Krause	10 Oct.		do	
	※ Fred. Adol. Zimmermann	27 Dec.		do	
	※ Eberhard Gerstlacher	17 Feb.	14	do	
	※ Anthony Frederick Hoyer	5 July	15	do	
	※ Frederick de Fresnoy	29 July		do	
	Philip Volborth	30 Oct.		do	
Cornets	......※ Alex. *Baron* Hammerstein............	9 Oct.	13	do	
	※ Rudolph. Fredrichs	10 Oct.		do	
	※ Conrad von Dassel	22 Oct.		do	
	※ Hans, *Baron* Hodenberg	1 Dec.		do	
	George Julius Meyer	5 May	14	do	
	Carl. Died. U. O. F. Cleve	9 July	15	do	
	Carl. Fred. Deichmann	23 Oct.		do	
Paymaster	..※ John William Wieler	20 Aug.	11	do	
Assist.-Surg.	..※ Geo. Lewis Bauermeister...........	7 Sept.	13	do	
Vet.-Surg.	....Frederick Eidmann...................	12 July	06	do	

Foreign Half-pay.

LIGHT INFANTRY. 1st.		RANK IN THE ARMY.		WHEN PLACED ON HALF-PAY.	
Col.-Com.	🎖🎖 Charles, *Count* Alten, GCB. GCH. Major-Gen.	25 July	1810	24 Feb.	1816
Major	Henry William Dammers	4 June	14	do	
Captains	🎖 Frederick de Gilsa	16 April	11	do	
	🎖 Gustavus, *Baron* Marschalck	26 Jan.	14	do	
	🎖 Augustus Wahrendorff	4 July	15	do	
	🎖 Christopher Heise	23 Aug.		do	
Lieutenants	🎖 George Breymann	20 Mar.	12	do	
	🎖 William de Heugel	do		do	
	🎖 Charles Kessler	20 July	13	do	
	🎖 Adolphus Koester	22 Oct.		do	
	🎖 Nicholas de Miniussir	29 Jan.	14	do	
	🎖 Harry Leonhart	25 Mar.		do	
	🎖 John Frederick Kuntze	28 April		do	
Ensigns	🎖 William Rubenz	7 Aug.	13	do	
	🎖 Gustavus George Best	26 Nov.		do	
	🎖 Adol. von Gentzkow	27 Nov.		do	
	🎖 Otto de Marschalck	16 May	14	do	
	🎖 Adolphus Heise	28 May		do	
	Cha. Martin A. Heckscher	20 Aug.	15	do	
Adjutant	🎖 John Fred. Wm. Buhse ....*Ens.*	29 May	15	do	
2nd.					
Major	🎖 Geo. *Baron* von Baring, CB. KCH. *Lt.-Col.*	18 June	15	do	
Captains	William Stolte	24 April	11	do	
	🎖 Charles Meyer	1 July	15	do	
Lieutenants	🎖 James Oliver Lindham	8 July	11	do	
	🎖 William Doring	10 April	14	do	
	Henry Fred. Schaumann	2 May		25 Oct.	1815
Ensigns	🎖 George Frank	5 Jan.	14	24 Feb.	1816
	🎖 Henry Augustus Knop	14 Jan.		do	
	🎖 Lewis Charles Baring	11 April		do	
	George de Bachellé	13 April	15	do	
	Chr. Aug. Jacob Behne	26 June		do	
Assist.-Surg.	Joseph Tholon	6 Oct.	15	do	

BATTALIONS OF THE LINE. 1st.				
Majors	🎖 Wm. von Robertson, CB. KCH. *Lt.-Col.*	18 June	15	do
	Cha. von Kronenfeldt, KH	17 Aug.		do
Captains	🎖 Frederick, *Baron* Goeben	17 Mar.	12	do
	🎖 George, *Baron* Goeben	18 Mar.		do
	🎖 Leopold von Rettberg	18 Aug.	13	do
	Ernest, *Baron* Hodenberg	22 Sept.		do
	🎖 Lewis von Holle	26 June	15	do
	🎖 Frederick von Rössing	2 Sept.		do
Lieutenants	🎖 Christian Hen. von Düring	17 Aug.	09	do
	🎖 Ludolph Kumme	18 Aug.		do
	Ernest Wilding, KH.	22 May	11	do
	William Schröder	18 Mar.	12	do
	🎖 Diederich de Einem	do		do
	🎖 George Wichmann	30 Oct.		do
	🎖 Charles von Weyhe	24 Nov.		do
	🎖 William Wolff	21 May	13	do
	🎖 Adolph. von Arentsschildt	18 Aug.		do
	🎖 Fred. Augustus Muller	22 Sept.		do
	🎖 William Best	26 Nov.		do
Ensigns	🎖 Augustus, *Baron* Le Fort	9 Sept.		do
	🎖 Augustus von Brandis	6 Jan.	14	do
	🎖 Arnold William Heise	7 Jan.		do
	🎖 Frederick Kersting	19 Feb.		do
	Adolphus de Beaulieu	21 Mar.		do
	🎖 Cha. Aug. von der Hellen	7 May		do
Adjutant	🎖 Frederick Schnath............*Lieut.*	18 Mar.	12	do
Assist.-Surgs.	Frederick Harzig	7 Dec.	05	do
	🎖 Philip Langeheineken	31 Jan.	11	do

Foreign Half-pay.

BATTALIONS OF THE LINE.		RANK IN THE ARMY.		WHEN PLACED ON HALF-PAY.	
2nd.					
Captains	Wm. *Baron* Decken, KH. ... *Major*	18 June	1815	24 Feb. 1816	
	Aug. Chas. Fred. Hartmann	3 Jan.	09	do	
	Ferd. Adolphus, *Baron* Holle	28 May	15	do	
Lieutenants	William Kulemann	7 Sept.	09	do	
	Godfrey Tiensch	17 Mar.	12	do	
	Augustus Frederick Schmidt	do		do	
	Chas. Augustus Lewis Billeb	do		do	
	George Mejer	1 Oct.		do	
	Francis La Roche	27 Mar.	14	do	
	George Fabricius	29 April		do	
	Augustus Ferdinand Ziel	17 June		do	
	Lewis Henry de Sichart	28 May	15	do	
Ensigns	Charles Lewis de Sichart	16 Feb.	14	do	
	Frederick Diestelhorst	14 April		do	
	Gust. Fred. Wm. Hartmann	8 May		do	
	Henry Garvens	24 May		do	
	Thilo von Uslar Gleichen	29 May		do	
	Augustus Luning	17 June		do	
Adjutant	Adolphus Hesse ... *Lieut.*	17 Mar.	12	do	
3rd.					
Captains	Lewis de Dreves ... *Major*	18 June	15	do	
	George, *Baron* Holmhorst	30 Oct.	07	do	
	Lewis Bacmeister	23 Aug.	09	1 Oct.	14
	Albert Cordemann	8 Sept.	14	24 Feb.	16
	Frederick Erdmann	19 June	15	do	
	Hans von Uslar Gleichen	20 June		do	
	George Appuhn	25 July		do	
Lieutenants	George W. F. von Weyhe	30 Oct.	07	do	
	Charles Brauns	14 Sept.	10	do	
	Christian de Soden	18 Mar.	12	do	
	Lawrence Heise	do		do	
	Augustus Kuckuck	do		do	
	Julius Brinkmann	11 May		do	
	Henry Delmel	20 Mar.	13	do	
	Lewis de Bachellé, *Baron* von dem Brinck	20 Sept.		do	
	Henry Edward Kuckuck	8 Dec.		do	
Ensigns	Frederick de Storren	18 Feb.		do	
	Frederick von Schlutter	6 May		do	
	Augustus William Kuckuck	8 Jan.	14	do	
	Richard Hupeden	9 Jan.		do	
Adjutant	Fred. Bern. Schneider ... *Lieut.*	18 Mar.	12	do	
Surgeon	Lewis Stuntz	14 Aug.	05	do	
4th.					
Co Com.	Sig. Christophe Gustave, *Baron* Low, KCB. KCH ... *Maj.-Gen.*	25 July	10	do	
Captains	William Heydenreich	31 Mar.	07	do	
	George Ludewig	13 Dec.	08	do	
	Frederick Ludewig	20 Oct.	12	25 May	15
	Frederick Otto	25 May	15	24 Feb.	16
	Justus Formin	9 June		do	
	Frederick Keszler	21 June		do	
	Christian Bacmeister	7 July		do	
	William Pape	19 Aug.		do	
Lieutenants	Caspar von Both	13 Dec.	08	do	
	Adolphus Ludewig	19 Mar.	12	do	
	Hen. Fred. Theo. de Witte	31 Oct.		do	
	Ernest Brinckmann	4 Mar.	13	do	
	Frederick von Lasperg	8 Oct.		do	
Ensign	William Luning	7 May		do	
	Augustus Schulze	15 June		do	
	Frederick von Brandis	26 July		do	
	James Mannsbach	21 Sept.		do	
	Ferd. von Uslar Gleichen	30 May	14	do	

Foreign Half-pay.

BATTALIONS OF THE LINE.		RANK IN THE ARMY.		WHEN PLACED ON HALF-PAY.	
4th.					
Ensigns	🎖 Arnold Appuhn	6 June	1813	24 Feb.	1816
	🎖 Lewis von Soden	25 May	15	do	
Adjutant	🎖 Adol. von Langwerth .... Lieut.	19 Mar.	12	do	
Qr.-Master	Augustus Becker	25 Sept.	04	do	
Assist.-Surg.	John Henry Wicke	28 Feb.	12	do	
5th.					
Majors	Augustus Kuckuck	4 June	14	do	
	🎖 Philip Henry Fred. Mejer	do		do	
Captains	Julius Bacmeister	26 Sept.	11	25 July	15
	🎖 William Mejer	19 Mar.	12	24 Feb.	16
	John George Hagemann	16 Dec.		25 July	15
	Charles, *Baron* Linsingen	16 April	13	24 Feb.	16
	Henry, *Baron* Dachenhausen	8 Dec.		do	
	🎖 Eberhard de Brandis	27 July	15	do	
	🎖 Charles Berger	21 Aug.		do	
Lieutenants	Theodore Gallenbreg	26 Sept.	11	do	
	🎖 Geo. Aug. Hen. Buhse	27 Sept.		do	
	🎖 Geo. Fred. Cha. von Schauroth	20 Mar.	12	do	
	🎖 John Fred. Charles de Witte	do		do	
	🎖 Augustus Winckler	do		do	
	🎖 Charles Schlaeger	do		do	
	Adolphus Rothard	do		do	
	Joseph Korschann	25 Sept.	12	25 July	15
	🎖 George Klingsöhr	16 Dec.		do	
	🎖 Lewis de Geissmann	16 April	13	24 Feb.	16
	Lewis Jaenicke	16 Mar.	14	do	
	🎖 George Wischmann	10 April	15	do	
	🎖 Bernard Croon	12 April		do	
Ensigns	🎖 Ferdinand Scharnhorst	27 Mar.	13	do	
	🎖 Charles Winckler	10 Jan.	14	do	
	🎖 Lewis Klingsohr	22 Mar.		do	
	Ernest Baring	25 May		do	
	🎖 Adolphus Scharnhorst	7 June		do	
	Geo. Cha. Aug. von Loesecke	15 April	15	do	
	Carl Peter Arnold Meier	16 April		do	
	🎖 Rudolph Carstens	15 May		do	
Adjutant	🎖 William Walther .... Ensign	22 Nov.	13	do	
Assist.-Surg.	🎖 George Hartog Gerson	9 Aug.	10		
6th.					
Lieut.-Colonel	John Wm. de Ulmenstein	23 Oct.	10	24 May	16
Captains	Charles Von Brandis	14 Mar.	12	do	
	John And. Christ. Anthony	11 May		do	
	Ernest, *Baron* Magius	25 Jan.	14	do	
	Eberhard Kuntze	9 Sept.		do	
	Barth. Geo. von Honstedt	20 Aug.	15	do	
Lieutenants.	Joseph Kersting	16 Jan.	08	do	
	J. Philip Anth. Schaedtler	18 Feb.	09	do	
	Ernest, *Baron* Heimburg	16 Mar.		do	
	Otto Schaumann	20 Sept.	10	do	
	Christ. Arnold Volger	25 Jan.	11	do	
	Frederick Hurtzig	21 Mar.	12	do	
	William Kirch	do		do	
	Ernest Mensing	do		do	
	Francis, *Baron* Acton	4 April	14	do	
	🎖 Christ. Lewis Von Ompteda	26 May		do	
Ensigns	Christian George Seelhorst	16 Oct.	12	do	
	🎖 Adolphus W— Steiglitz	22 Mar.	14	do	
	Alexander Autran	2 April		do	
	🎖 Lew. Albrecht von Ompteda	15 April		do	
	Herman Schwencke	8 June		do	
	Edward von Brandis	9 June		do	
Adjutant	Fra. Matthias Debs .... Lieut.	25 Feb.	12	do	
Qua.-Master.	John Charles Kruger	4 Jan.	13	do	
Assist.-Surg.	Solomon Jurdan Einthoven	29 Feb.	12		

Foreign Half-pay.

BATTALIONS OF THE LINE. 7th.		RANK IN THE ARMY.		WHEN PLACED ON HALF PAY.	
Major	William Chuden	28 Aug.	1813	24 May	1816
Captains	Ernest de Becker	16 Jan.	08	13 Nov.	13
	Frederick Munter	21 Sept.	10	24 May	16
	Henry William Volger	12 Mar.	11	do	
	Arnold Backmeister	21 Mar.	12	do	
	Gottlieb de Hartwig	26 Oct.	15	do	
Lieutenants	John George Leop. de Mutio	4 Jan.	09	do	
	Augustus de Offen	12 Mar.	11	do	
	Frederick von Diebitsch	23 July		do	
	ᛗ Charles Poten	23 Mar.	12	do	
	Theodore von Sebisch	do		do	
	George Munderloh	do		4 Sept.	13
	Charles von Blottnitz	2 April	14	24 May	16
	Christian Frederick Eichhorn	3 April		do	
	Augustus Steffen	27 May		do	
Ensigns	ᛗ Arnold Erich Backhaus	18 July		do	
	ᛗ Gottlieb von Suckow	23 Mar.		do	
	ᛗ Charles Ernest F. Neuschaffer	19 April		do	
	ᛗ Franz Frederick Backhaus	29 April		do	
	Augustus von Hodenberg	2 June		do	
Adjutant	John Ernest Stutzer ...... Lieut.	28 Oct.	09	do	
Assist.-Surg.	ᛗ Henry Schuchardt	16 Jan.	14	do	
8th.					
Captains	ᛗ Frederick Marburg	27 Mar.	12	24 Feb.	16
	ᛗ George Delius	11 Sept.	14	do	
	ᛗ George Lewis Otto Hotzen	23 June	15	do	
	ᛗ Frederick Luderitz	24 June		do	
	ᛗ Charles Poten	8 Sept.		do	
Lieutenants	ᛗ Ferdinand von Weyhe	16 Aug.	09	do	
	ᛗ Frederick Ziermann	27 Mar.	12	do	
	ᛗ Augustus Helmich	12 Sept.	14	do	
Ensigns	Frederick Dorndorf	12 July	12	do	
	ᛗ Godlove Kunoth	13 July		do	
	ᛗ William de Moreau	11 Oct.		do	
	ᛗ Augustus Spiel	23 Mar.	14	do	
	ᛗ Frederick Henry Muller	13 April		do	
	ᛗ Henry Seffers	3 June		do	
	ᛗ Geo. Fred. Godfrey Lunde	12 Sept.		do	
Adjutant	ᛗ Frederick Brinckmann ... Lieut.	10 April	11	do	
Qua.-Master.	Christian Tobing	14 Dec.	07	do	
Assist.-Surg.	ᛗ Ernest Sander	4 July	06	do	

ARTILLERY.

Colonel	Fred. Count von der Decken, GCH. Lt. Gen.	4 June	1814	do	
Major	ᛈ ᛗ Sir Julius Hartmann, KCB.KCH. Lt. Col.	17 Aug.	12	do	
Captains	ᛈ Sir Victor von Arentsschildt, CB. KCH. Major	25 Nov.	13	do	
	Charles Baron Witzleben	23 Dec.	05	do	
	ᛈ ᛗ Charles de Rettberg[1]	12 April	06	do	
	ᛈ Lewis Daniel[2]	26 Nov.	08	do	
2nd Captains	ᛗ George Wiering	23 Nov.	09	do	
	ᛗ William Braun	11 Dec.	12	do	
	Lewis Jasper	25 Nov.	13	do	
	William de Schade	26 Nov.		do	
	ᛗ Frederick Erythropel	16 May	15	do	
1st Lieuts.	Victor Preussner	5 June	07	do	
	Ferdinand de Brandis	28 Sept.		do	
	ᛗ Henry Mielman	26 Nov.	08	do	

[1] Captain de Rettberg has received a medal and two clasps for Talavera, Busaco, and Badajoz.
[2] Captain Daniel has received a medal and a clasp for Orthes and Toulouse.

Foreign Half-pay.

ARTILLERY.		RANK IN THE ARMY.		WHEN PLACED ON HALF-PAY.	
	Henry Stöckmann	13 Dec.	1812	24 Feb.	1816
	William Rummel	14 Dec.		do	
	🎖 William de Goeben	25 Nov.	13	do	
	🎖 William de Scharnhorst	26 Nov.		do	
	Frederick Drechsler	27 Nov.		do	
	Augustus Pfannkuche	28 Nov.		do	
	🎖 Henry Hartmann	26 Mar.	14	do	
	Henry Bostlemann	16 May	15	do	
2nd Lieuts.	Frederick Seinecke	12 Dec.	12	do	
	Henry Wohler	13 Dec.		do	
	🎖 Lewis Haardt	14 Dec.		do	
	🎖 Lewis Heise	15 Dec.		do	
	Lewis Scharnhorst	15 Nov.	13	do	
	🎖 Lewis de Wissell	30 Nov.		do	
	🎖 Chas. Herman Ludowieg	16 Feb.	14	do	
	Augustus Capelle	19 May		do	
	John Fred. Schlichthorst	20 May		do	
	Franz Röttiger	26 Nov.		do	
	Adolphus Rechtern	24 July	15	do	
	Lewis Hagemann	25 July		do	
Paymaster	John Blundstone	9 April	05	do	
Surgeon	Henry Kels	18 Dec.	05	do	
Assist.-Surg.	🎖 George Crone	10 Feb.	10	do	
Vet.-Surgeon.	John Frederick Hilmer	22 Aug.	06	do	

ENGINEERS.					
Captains	Victor Prott, *KCH.*	29 Mar.	05	do	
	Charles Ernest Appuhn	25 Nov.	08	do	
	Charles Wedekind	12 Oct.	09	do	
2nd Captains.	George Fred. Meinecke	24 Nov.	10	do	
	Augustus Schweitzer	15 July	12	do	
	William Müller	13 Dec.			
1st Lieuts.	William Unger	14 Aug.	11	do	
	John Luttermann	21 Nov.	12	do	

STAFF.					
Brig. Majors.	Ern. de Kronenfeldt	*Capt.* 20 Feb.	13		
	🎖 J. Godf. de Einem	*Capt.* 28 April	14	do	
	Fr. Chr. *Baron* Heimburg	*Capt.* 26 July	15	do	
	Lewis Benne, *KH.*	*Capt.* 8 Aug.		do	
	🎖 George Baring	*Capt.* 20 Nov.		do	
Chaplain	Frederick Bambke	17 Mar.	04	do	

MISCELLANEOUS CORPS.

BRUNSWICK CAVALRY.					
Lieut.-Col.	*Ernest von Schrader	26 Sept.	1809	24 June	1816
Major	* Wilh. von Weissen *Lt.-Col.*	4 June	14	do	
Captains	*William de Wulffen	28 Sept.	09	14 June	
	*Alexander von Erichsen	7 Mar.	11	do	
	*Gustavus Conrad Alex. von Girsewald	4 Nov.	13	do	
Lieutenant	William von Lubeck	1 Nov.	13	24 Feb.	16
Cornets	Chas. Fred. Edw. Michelet	22 July	13	24 June	
	Frederick Moeller	10 Mar.	14	do	
Adjutant	William Butze *Lieut.*	26 Sept.	09	do	
Qua.-Master.	Ferdinand de Bothmer	21 June	10	do	
Vet. Surgeon.	Frederick von Ohlen	7 Feb.	11	do	

Foreign Half-pay.

BRUNSWICK INFANTRY.		RANK IN THE ARMY.		WHEN PLACED ON HALF-PAY.
Major	*Friedrich Dornberg	28 May	1812	1814
Captains	*Heinrich von Doebell	27 Sept.	09	do
	* Fred. Lewis de Wachholtz	do		do
	* Frederick von Wolffradt	16 Aug.	10	do
	*Henry von Brandenstein	20 Feb.	11	do
	*Fred. F. Fer. von Steinwehr	21 do		do
Lieutenants	Ernest von Patzinsky	27 Sept.	09	do
	*Fred. John Adrian von der Heyde	do		do
	*Carl. Ernest Berner	do		do
	J. D. W. L. von Schwarzenberg	21 Feb.	11	do
	Frederick Hausler	27 June		do
	Albert von Greisheim	27 Aug.		24 June 1815
	Augustus Grutteman	10 Dec.	12	14
	Adolph. Otto von Broembsen	5 May	13	do
	Charles Haberland	1 April	14	do
Ensigns	Johannes Cornelius Schot	1 April	13	do
	Michael Charles Edwards	28 Oct.		do
	E. A. William de Bernewitz	1 Dec.		do
Paymaster	Griffin Jones	21 Oct.	13	do
Qua.-Master	John Reind'l	23 May	11	do
Surgeon	Charles Wehsarg	12 Aug.	13	do
Assist.-Surg.	Lewis Aug. T. Heimburgh	28 Oct.	13	do

CHASSEURS BRITANNIQUES.

Major	*A. Le Theur de Combremont	7 Mar.	11	do
Captains	Nich. Philibert de Brem ...... Major	4 June	14	do
	Felix le Page	1 May	01	1808
	Fridolin de Freuller	2 Sept.	06	1814
	Francois Jos. Spitz	22 Aug.	08	do
Lieutenants	Etienne de Planta	3 Dec.	07	2 Nov. 15
	J— N— de Ponchalon	24 May	10	1814
	Jean Nepomucene Stoeber	28 June		do
	Armand Casimir G. Duflef	18 Oct.		do
	Etienne Epiphane Julien	18 Feb.	11	do
	Pietro Santa Columba	8 Aug.		do
	Antoine Servais	3 June	12	do
	Silvain de Precorbin	4 June		do
	Jos. Ignace Goussencourt	22 July	13	do
	Frederick Wolf	21 April	14	do
Ensign	Francis Kander	14 July	14	do
Chaplain	Francois Nicolle	4 May	09	do
Adjutant	Pierre F. Louis Boussingault ...... Lieut.	3 April	10	do
Assist.-Surg.	Ignation Stumpa	12 April	10	do

CORSICAN RANGERS.

Captains	Joseph Panattieri	6 Jan.	07	1817
	Jean de Susini	8 Jan.		do
	Jacques Guanter	27 May	13	do
	Adrian Manfredi	19 May	14	do
	Paul Zerbi	10 Aug.	15	do
Lieutenants	Philip de Furer	6 Nov.	06	25 July 1816
	Peter Francis Ciavaldini	6 Jan.	07	1817
	Antonio Astuto	2 June	08	do
	Jean Baptiste Zerbi	13 Sept.	10	do
	Louis de Kamptz	31 May	11	do
	Antonio D'Odiardi	10 Feb.	12	do
	Jean Baptiste Carabelli	11 Feb.		1816
	Raphael Pagano	12 Feb.		1817
	Dominico Antonio Peretti	25 June		do
	Francois Salvatelli	21 Jan.	13	do
	Giovanni Ant. Vincenti	19 May	14	do
Ensigns	Louis Crocicchia	25 June		do
	Joseph Susini	19 May	14	do

Foreign Half-pay.

		RANK IN THE ARMY.		WHEN PLACED ON HALF-PAY.	
DILLON'S.					
Captains	Charles de Boylesve	3 Sept.	1806	1814	
	Pierre du Sage	8 Feb.	10	do	
	Jean de Chesse	20 Mar.	11	do	
GREEK LIGHT INFANTRY.					
Captain	Joseph Coppon	7 Jan.	13	do	
Lieutenants	Pietro Antonio Salvatori	2 July	13	do	
	Pierre Astuto	25 June	14	do	
MALTA.					
Lieutenant	Ern. Fer. Cha. Bern. Richter	20 Mar.	1805	1811	
MEURON'S					
Major	Cha. Emanuel May	17 June	13	25 Sept.	1816
Captains	Nich. Julien de Bergeon	23 May	00		10
	Elias Merckhel	28 Dec.	03	do	
	George Alexander Dardel	24 Sept.	04		08
	Frederick Matthey	25 Apr.	08	25 Sept.	16
	Rudolphe Amedée de May (d'Uzistort)	28 Feb.	10	do	
Lieutenants	Laurent Boyer	25 Sept.	1798		
	Frederick, *Baron* Bibra	1 Sept.	1806	25 July	1816
	Johan Theo. de Misani	10 Sept.		25 Sept.	
	Charles Jos. Zehupfenning	9 Mar.	09	25 July	
	Francois de Graffenried	1 Mar.	10	do	
	Charles de Gumoens	28 April	11	25 Sept.	
	Antoine Fred. de Graffenried	30 April	11	do	
	August. de Loriol	28 Sept.	14	do	
	Charles Cæsar de Meuron	do		do	
	Jules Cæsar Saum	15 Jan.	16	do	
Assist.-Surg.	Ludwig Aug. Winter	1 Sept.	03	25 July	1816
ROLL'S					
Major	Cha. de Vogelsang .... *Lieut.-Col.*	25 July	1810	25 July	1816
Captains	Nicholas Muller .... *Maj.*	4 June	1814		1816
	Ferd. *Compte* de la Ville	21 Oct.	04	25 Dec.	17
	Benoit Ryhiner	3 Sept.	07		1816
	Lewis Muller	25 Jan.	10	do	
	Antoine Courant	5 Apr.		do	
	Frederick Rusillion	21 Apr.	14	do	
Lieutenants	Joseph Tugginer	30 Oct.	1806	do	
	Jost Muller	5 Nov.	07	do	
	Amanz Glutz	23 May	08	do	
	Pierre P. Auguste de Courten	15 Dec.		do	
	John Peter Sorgenfrey	21 Dec.		do	
	Hector de Salis	22 Dec.		do	
	Charles Pannach	25 Jan.	10	do	
	Jean Juliani	18 Feb.	11	do	
	Edmund de Tugginer	26 Feb.		do	
	Otto Henry Salinger	28 Feb.		do	
	Henry d'Holbreuse	15 Oct.	12	do	
	Joseph Gurtler	9 Dec.		do	
	Edward de Tugginer	29 Sept.	13	do	
	Nicholas Stutzer	30 Sept		do	
	Charles Crato Trott	28 April	14	do	
	Jean Baptiste Phil. Stutzer	27 Oct.		do	
Ensigns	Patricio Schmid	11 Dec.	1812	do	
	Charles de Bronner	22 June	15	do	
Chaplains	John Becker	9 Dec.	1794	1810	
	William Peter Macdonald	1 July	1812	1816	
Surgeon	John Aug. Romhild	22 Dec.	1804	do	
Assist.-Surg.	William Heyn	do		do	
	Charles Gemmellaro	25 Nov.	13	do	

Foreign Half-pay.

		RANK IN THE ARMY.		WHEN PLACED ON HALF-PAY.	
SICILIAN					
Captains	Francesco Stuart	19 Oct.	1815	20 Mar.	1816
	Charles Felix Cavallace	27 Dec.		do	
Lieutenants	Henry Stuart	12 June	1808	25 Mar.	
	Thomas de Fossi	6 April	09	do	
	Joseph Bartoli	8 Nov.		do	
	Baldassare Ossorio	9 Nov.		do	
	Marino Zugiani	8 Feb.	10	do	
	Gustave de Roquefeuil	23 Aug.		do	
	Andrieu Vieusseux	11 April	11	do	
	Francis Rivarola	6 Feb.	12	do	
Ensigns	Charles Hegler	28 Feb.	12	do	
	Gaetano D'Angelo	6 Oct.	14	do	
Qua.-Master	John Nurg	3 Nov.	08	do	

WATTEVILLE'S					
Lieut.-Colonel	Rudolphe May	21 May	12	24 Oct.	16
Captains	Amand de Courten......*Maj.*	4 June	18		15
	Pancrace Ledergerw	9 July	06	26 Oct.	16
	Cha. Zehender De Thiel	25 Mar.	11	do	
	Jean Christian Weyssen	25 Aug.	13	25 Mar.	
Lieutenants	Albert Steiger	6 May	07	24 Oct.	16
	Cæsar Augus. Champeaux	7 May		do	
	Albert Manuel	5 Sept.	10	do	
	Charles Louis Sturler	6 Sept.		25 July	
	Charles Thormann	25 Mar.	11	24 Oct.	
	Frederick Fischer	26 Mar.		25 July	
	Francis Dicenta	28 Aug.		24 Oct.	
	Amedée Rodolph de Bersy	29 Aug.		do	
	Rodolph de Watteville	22 Feb.	14	do	
	Charles May	23 Feb.		do	
Ensigns	Fra. Louis Con. Fischer	25 Jan.	14	do	
	Jean Albert Fischer	27 Jan.		do	
Chaplain	Peter James de la Mothe	23 April	12	do	
Adjutant	Joseph Mermet......*Lieut.*	27 Jan.	08	do	
Assist.-Surg	Jean Baptiste Boidin	1 May	1801	25 July	16

YORK LIGHT INFANTRY					
Captains	Abraham Louis Hebert	25 Aug.	14	25 Mar.	17
	Arthur Leon de Tinseau	15 June	15	25 July	16
Lieutenants	Antoine Louis de Mendibus	8 July	11	19 Mar.	17
	John Ordon	10 July		do	
	Alexander Schmitt	13 Sept.	13	24 May	16
	John Ernest Symkath	14 Sept.		19 Mar.	17
	Jean Julian, *Chevalier* de Gannes	13 July	15	do	
Ensign	Louis Tholon	do		25 July	16
Qua.-Master	Nicholas Crouwell	28 Nov.	16	19 Mar.	17

VETERAN BATTALION					
Captains	Frederick Bothe	4 April	09	24 Feb.	16
	Frederick Wyneken	8 July	11	do	
	George Fred. And. Rautenberg	17 Mar.	12	do	
	Charles Ebell	23 Mar.		do	
	Christian, *Baron* Goeben	27 Feb.	15	do	
Lieutenants	John William Tatter	19 Aug.	09	do	
	George de Witte	20 Aug.	11	do	
	William Fahle	14 Mar.	12	do	
	☙ Frederick von Fincke	20 Mar.		do	

441

Foreign Half-pay.

		RANK IN THE ARMY.		WHEN PLACED ON HALF-PAY.	
VETERAN BATTALION.					
Ensigns	George Augustus Rumann	25 June		24 Feb.	16
	William Riddle	30 Jan.	14	do	
Ensigns	Henry Brackmeyer	31 Jan.	14	do	
	Henry William Müller	17 Aug.	15	do	
	John Henry Wegener	18 Aug.		do	
	Frederick Schultze	20 Aug.		do	
Adjutant	August. Henry Schaefer ......Lieut.	15 Feb.	13	do	
Assist.-Surg.	John Christ. Fred. Fischer	17 Feb.	14	do	

WAGGONERS.

Lieutenants	Andrew Philip Cramer	21 June	10	25 Sept.	16
	*David Crusius	14 May	15	25 April	
	Philip Aug. von Harlessem	18 May		25 June	
	Augustus Barckhausen	7 July		25 April	
Cornets	John Albert Kropp	1 June	15	25 July	16
	Henry von Jeinsen	25 July		do	
	Henry Van Sande	do		do	

MEDICAL DEPARTMENT.

Surgeons	Joseph Tholon	4 June	1807
	Charles Groskopff	4 Feb.	13

GARRISONS

AND

MILITARY ESTABLISHMENTS.

ALDERNEY.

		PER ANN. £ s. d.	DATE OF APPOINTMENT.
Town-Major	..*Major* O'Hara Baynes....................	69 19 2	25 Dec. 1827

BELFAST.

Town-Major	..*Lieut*. Peter Stuart.......................	63 13 8	24 Dec. 1818

BERWICK.

Governor	......*Lieut.-Gen Sir* James Bathurst, *KCB*. 568 15 10		1 Feb. 1833
Town-Adjutant.	*Ensign* William Mansell..................	69 19 2	25 Nov. 1819

CAPE BRETON.

Town-Adjutant.	*Lieut*. Edw. Sutherland	86 13 9	12 July 1833

CARLISLE.

Town-Major	..*Lieut*. Duncan Macdonald................	69 19 2	30 Sept. 1813

CARRICKFERGUS.

Governor	......*Lieut.-Gen. Sir* W. Hutchinson, *KCH*.....159 4 0		12 Feb. 1830

CHARLESFORT AND KINSALE.

Governor	......*Gen. Sir* Warren Marmaduke Peacocke, *KCH. KC.* 318 8 0		3 Aug. 1830
Fort-Major	....*Lieut*. John Black	63 13 8	5 Dec. 1822

CHESTER.

Governor	......*Gen*. Edward Morrison 173 7 6		2 Nov. 1796
Lieut.-Governor	*Gen. Sir* John Fraser, *GCH*. 173 7 6		13 Nov. 1828

DARTMOUTH.

Governor	......Arthur Howe Holdsworth................		10 Sept. 1807
Fort-Major	....*Major* Robert Kelly	69 19 2	11 Dec. 1828

DUBLIN.

Town-Major	..*Major* Walter White 173 7 6		25 July 1825

DUMBARTON CASTLE.

Governor	......*Gen.*Thomas *Lord* Lynedoch,*GCB.GCMG.* 284 7 11		22 May 1829

DUNCANNON FORT.

Fort-Major	....*Lieut*. Thomas Austin....................	63 13 8	27 July 1820

Garrisons.

EDINBURGH CASTLE.

	PER ANN. £ s. d.	DATE OF APPOINTMENT
Governor ...... 🏅 *Maj.-Gen.* Cha. M. *Lord* Greenock, *KCB*.		17 Feb. 1837
Lieut.-Gov. .... *Gen.* F. Tho. Hammond, *GCH.*	173 7 6	20 July 1831
Fort-Major .... *Lieut.-Col.* Bissell Harvey, *KH*	86 13 9	16 Nov. 1822
Chaplain ...... *Rev.* William Beattie Smith		24 April 1838

GALWAY.

Town-Major .. *Ensign* James Hamilton	62 13 8	1 April 1819

GIBRALTAR.

Town-Major .. *Col.* Daniel Falla	182 10 0	4 July 1822
Town-Adjutant. *Lieut.* Archibald Campbell	91 5 0	26 Feb. 1816

GRAVESEND AND TILBURY FORT.

Governor ...... *Gen. Hon. Sir* G. L. Cole, *GCB*	284 7 11	15 Jan. 1818
Lieut.-Gov. .... *Col.* Peter Dumas	173 7 6	23 July 1832
Fort-Major .... *Major* Thomas Kelly	69 19 2	13 Jan. 1814

GUERNSEY.

Fort-Maj.& Adj. *Major* John Hankey Bainbrigge	82 2 6	22 Nov. 1839

HULL.

Governor ...... *Gen.* William *Earl* Cathcart, *KT.*	568 15 10	18 June 1830
Lieut.-Gov. .... *Major-Gen. Sir* Cha. Wade Thornton, *KCH.*	173 7 6	25 Sept. 1816
Town-Major .. *Lieut.-Col.* Robert Simson, *KH.*	69 19 2	2 Oct. 1823

JERSEY.

Governor ...... *Gen.* W. C. *Visc.* Beresford, *GCB. GCH.* ..		29 Jan. 1829
Fort-Maj.& Adj. *Lieut.-Col.* Robert Fraser, *KH.*	82 2 6	25 Mar. 1823

INVERNESS, OR FORT GEORGE.

Governor ...... *Lieut.-Gen. Right Hon. Sir* George Murray, *GCB. GCH...*	474 10 0	7 Sept. 1829
Fort-Major .... *Captain* Andrew Fraser	86 13 9	20 Sept. 1813

LAND-GUARD FORT.

Lieut.-Gov. .... *Lieut.-Col.* Charles Augustus West	173 7 6	20 June 1811

LONDONDERRY AND CULMORE.

Governor ...... 🏅 *Lieut.-Gen.* John *Lord* Strafford, *GCB. GCH.*		15 June 1822
Town-Major .. John Nicholson	63 13 8	26 May 1830

MALTA.

Town-Adjutant. *Lieut.-Col.* Robert Terry	91 5 0	18 Aug. 1825
Quarter-Master. *Lieut.* John Colcroft	136 17 6	26 Oct. 1826

MILFORD-HAVEN.

Governor ...... *Sir* John Owen, *Bart.*		14 June 1821

MONTREAL.

Town-Major .. 🏅 *Ensign* Colin Macdonald	86 13 9	30 Jan. 1835

Garrisons.

NEW BRUNSWICK.

		PER ANN. £ s. d.	DATE OF APPOINTMENT.
Town-Major	..*Lieut.* John Gallagher	86 13 9	25 Feb. 1819

NEW GENEVA.

Fort-Major	....Anthony Wharton	159 4 0	26 Dec. 1816

PLACENTIA.

Lieut.-Gov.	.....*Major-Gen.* George James Reeves, *CB. KH.*	173 7 6	14 June 1819

PLYMOUTH.

Governor	......🎖 *Gen.* Rowland *Lord* Hill, *GCB. GCH. KC.*	1221 4 7	18 June 1830

PORTSMOUTH.

Town-Major	..*Lieut.* Henry White	69 19 2	2 Oct. 1823
Town-Adjutant.	*Lieut.* Thomas Vavasour Durell	86 13 9	18 Aug. 1825
Physician	....*Sir* James M'Grigor, *Bart. MD.*	173 7 6	13 June 1811
Surgeon	......Isaac Chaldecott	44 2 1	3 Nov. 1790

QUEBEC.

Governor	......*Major-Gen.* William Goodday Strutt	346 15 0	4 April 1800
Lieut.-Gov.	....*Gen.* William Thomas Dilkes	173 7 6	2 Oct. 1829

ST. HELENA.

Town-Major	..*Lieut.* George Adam Barnes	173 7 6	6 Nov. 1835

ST. JOHN'S, NEWFOUNDLAND.

Fort-Major	....*Capt.* John And. Nicolas Wieburg	86 13 9	4 May 1838

ST. JOHN'S, OR PRINCE EDWARD'S ISLAND.

Town-Major	..*Capt.* Ambrose Lane	86 13 9	1 Jan. 1819

ST. MAWES.

Capt. or Keeper.	*Gen. Sir* Geo. Nugent, *Bt. GCB.*	104 18 9	2 Nov. 1796
Deputy-Gov.	..🎖 *Major-Gen. Sir* Alexander Cameron, *KCB.*	44 2 1	23 Oct. 1828

SCARBOROUGH CASTLE.

Governor	......🎖 *Col.* James Grant, *CB.*	15 4 2	30 Jan. 1832

SHEERNESS.

Governor	......*Gen.* S. *Visc.* Combermere, *GCB. GCH.*	284 7 11	25 Jan. 1821
Lieut.-Gov.	.....*Lieut.-Col.* Robert Walker	173 7 6	20 May 1813
Fort-Major	....*Major* Oswald Pilling	69 10 0	17 Jan. 1834

STIRLING CASTLE.

Governor	......*Gen. Sir* Martin Hunter, *GCMG. GCH.*	284 7 11	23 July 1832
Deputy-Gov.	..*Col. Sir* Archibald Christie, *KCH.*	173 7 6	15 Feb. 1831
Major	........Patrick Tytler	86 13 9	5 Aug. 1795
Chaplain	......*Rev.* Robert Watson	76 0 10	26 April 1838

Garrisons.—Military Establishments.

TOWER OF LONDON.

		PER ANN. £ s. d	DATE OF APPOINTMENT.
Constable	....❦ *Field-Mar.* Arthur, *Duke of* Wellington, KG. GCB. GCH.	947 9 7	29 Dec. 1826
Lieutenant	....*Gen.* John Sulivan Wood		26 Feb. 1833
Deputy-Lieut.	....❦ *Lieut.-Col.* John Gurwood, *CB.*	346 15 0	15 Nov. 1839
Major	........*Capt.* John Henry Elrington	173 7 6	4 July 1816
Chaplain	......*Rev.* Robinson Rishton Baily	115 11 8	25 Mar. 1830

TYNEMOUTH CASTLE AND CLIFF FORT.

Lieut.-Gov.	.....*Lieut.-Gen.* William Thomas	173 7 6	6 Sept. 1826

WIGHT ISLAND.

Governor	......James Edw. *Earl of* Malmesbury	474 10 0	22 Aug. 1807
Capt. of Sandown Fort	....*Capt. Sir* Wm. Wynn	173 7 6	29 Mar. 1810
——— Yarmouth Castle	..❦ *Major-Gen. Sir* J. Waters, *KCB.*	173 7 6	22 April 1831
——— Carisbrooke Castle.	*Lieut.-Gen. Sir* W. Paterson, *KCH.*	173 7 6	20 Feb. 1817
——— Cowes Castle	....❦ *Gen.* H. W. *Marq. of* Anglesey, *KG. GCB. GCH.*	173 7 6	25 Mar. 1826

FORT WILLIAM.

Lieut.-Gov.	.....❦ *Lieut.-Gen. Rt. Hon. Sir* James Kempt, *GCB. GCH.*	173 7 6	10 Oct. 1812

MILITARY ESTABLISHMENTS.

CHELSEA HOSPITAL.

Governor	......*Gen. Hon. Sir* Edward Paget, *GCB.*	500 0 0	10 Jan. 1837
Lieut.-Gov.	.....*Gen. Sir* George Townshend Walker, *Bt. GCB.*	400 0 0	24 May 1837
Major	........*Lieut.-Col.* Henry Le Blanc	300 0 0	22 Sept. 1814
Adjutant	......*Col.* John Morillyon Wilson, *CB. KH.*	100 0 0	16 Nov. 1822
Chaplain	......*Rev.* George Robert Gleig		19 Feb. 1834
Phys. and Surg.	..William Somerville, *MD.*	365 0 0	8 Oct. 1819

ROYAL MILITARY COLLEGE.

Governor	......❦ *Major-Gen. Sir* Geo. Scovell, *KCB.*	1000 0 0	3 Feb. 1837
Lieut.-Gov.	.....❦ *Col.* Thomas William Taylor, *CB.*	383 5 0	3 Feb. 1837
Captains of Companies of Gentlemen Cadets.	{ *Lieut.-Col.* Charles Wright, *KH.*	129 5 5	12 Sept. 1805
	❦ *Lieut.-Col.* Charles Diggle, *KH.*	129 5 5	10 Aug. 1820
Chaplain, &c.	...*Rev.* William Wheeler, *DD.*	300 0 0	25 Mar. 1804
Adjutant	......*Major* George Procter	163 2 6	24 Feb. 1818
Quarter-Master.	*Lieut.* John Whitacre Tipping	97 6 8	10 Sept. 1830
Surgeon	......John Pickering, *MD.*	255 10 0	29 June 1832
Assist.-Surg.	...Robert Dunkin Smyth	136 17 6	1 Mar. 1833

ROYAL MILITARY ASYLUM.

Chelsea.

	PER ANN. £ s. d.	DATE OF APPOINTMENT.
Commandant ..Lieut.-Col. James Williamson	400 0 0	17 Sept. 1812
Sec. and Adjt.. *Capt. John Lugard	182 10 0	13 Sept. 1804
Quarter-Master.William Henry Brownson	180 0 0	8 Mar. 1839
Surgeon ......Samuel George Lawrance	273 15 0	24 July 1828
Assist.-Surg. ..William Smith	136 17 6	26 Dec. 1834

Southampton.

Commandant ..⚜ Col. George Evatt	273 15 0	25 June 1816
Assist.-Surg. ..John Hennen, *MD*	36 17 6	11 Sept. 1828

ROYAL HIBERNIAN SCHOOL.

Surgeon ......⚜ William Finnie		25 Mar. 1836

GENERAL OFFICERS RECEIVING REWARDS FOR DISTINGUISHED SERVICES.

GENERAL.
Thomas Scott
John M'Kenzie
Sir William Wilkinson, *GCMG*.
James Robertson
Pinson Bonham
William Eden

LIEUTENANT-GENERAL.
Benjamin Gordon
Sir Alexander Halkett, *KCH*.
John Granby Clay
Sir Thomas Browne, *KCH*.
John M'Nair, *CB*.

John Montagu Mainwaring
Henry Elliot
Samuel Huskisson
Dennis Herbert

MAJOR-GENERAL.
Sir Andrew Pilkington, *KCB*.
Sir William Gabriel Davy, *KCH*.
Mark Napier
Sir Alexander Leith, *KCB*.
Sir Thomas Pearson, *CB*. *KCH*.
Sir Dugald Little Gilmour, *KCB*.
Sir William Macbean, *KCB*.

OFFICERS

TO WHOM

HONORARY DISTINCTIONS

HAVE BEEN GRANTED,

IN COMMEMORATION OF THEIR SERVICES IN THE
FOLLOWING BATTLES OR ACTIONS.

Maida........	4 July	1806
Roleia	17 Aug.	08
Vimiera	21 do.	
Sahagun, Benevente, &c... (actions of Cavalry)........	Dec. 1808 & Jan.	09
Corunna......	16 Jan.	
Martinique............ (attack and capture)	Feb.	
Talavera	27 & 28 July.	
Guadaloupe .... (attack and capture)	Jan. & Feb.	10
Busaco	27 Sept.	
Barrosa	5 Mar.	11
Fuentes d'Onor............	5 May.	
Albuhera	16 do.	
Java .... (attack and capture)	Aug. & Sept.	
Ciudad Rodrigo.......... (assault and capture)	Jan.	12
Badajoz .... (do. do.)	17 Mar. & 6 Apr.	
Salamanca	22 July.	
Fort Detroit, America .... (capture of)	Aug.	
Vittoria	21 June	13
Pyrenees	28 July to 2 Aug.	
St. Sebastian .... (assault and capture)	Aug. & Sept.	
Chateauguay, America......	26 Oct.	
Nivelle	10 Nov.	
Chrystler's Farm, America	11 do.	
Nive......	9 to 13 Dec.	
Orthes	27 Feb.	14
Toulouse	10 Apr.	

On the 7th October, 1813, a General Order, of which the following is an abstract, was issued by the Commander-in-Chief:—

Whereas considerable inconvenience has arisen from the number of Medals which have been issued in commemoration of the brilliant and distinguished events in which the success of His Majesty's arms has received the Royal approbation, the Prince Regent has been pleased to command that the following Regulations shall be adopted in the grant and circulation of such marks of distinction: viz.—

1st. That one Medal only shall be borne by each Officer recommended for such distinction.

2nd. That for the second and third events, which may be subsequently commemorated in like manner, each individual recommended to bear the distinction shall carry a gold Clasp attached to the ribbon to which the Medal is suspended, and inscribed with the name of the Battle or Siege to which it relates.

3rd. That upon a claim being admitted to a fourth mark of distinction a Cross shall be borne by each Officer, with the names of the four Battles or Sieges respectively inscribed thereupon; and to be worn in substitution of the distinctions previously granted to such individuals.

Officers who have received Honorary Distinctions.

4th. Upon each occasion of a similar nature that may occur subsequently to the grant of a Cross, the Clasp shall again be issued to those who have a claim to the additional distinction, to be borne on the ribbon to which the Cross is suspended, in the same manner as described in No. 2 of these Regulations.

His Royal Highness was further pleased to command that the distribution of Medals or Badges for Military services of distinguished merit shall be regulated as follows: viz.—

1st. That no General or other Officer shall be considered entitled to receive them, unless he has been personally and particularly engaged upon those occasions of great importance and peculiar brilliancy, in commemoration of which such marks of distinction are to be bestowed.

2nd. That no Officer shall be considered a candidate for the Medal, or Badge, except upon the special selection and report of the Commander of the Forces upon the spot, as having merited the distinction by conspicuous services.

3rd. That the Commander of the Forces shall transmit to the Commander-in-Chief, Returns, signed by himself, specifying the names and ranks of those Officers whom he shall have selected as particularly deserving.

4th. The Commander of the Forces in making the selection will restrict his choice to the undermentioned ranks: viz.—

> General Officers.
> Commanding Officers of Brigades.
> Commanding Officers of Artillery, or Engineers.
> Adjutant-General, and Quarter-Master-General.
> Deputies of ditto, and ditto, having the rank of Field-Officers.
> Assistants, Adjutant and Quarter-Master-Generals, having the rank of Field-Officers, and being at the head of the Staff, with a detached Corps, or distinct division of the Army.
> Military Secretary, having the rank of Field-Officer.
> Commanding Officers of Battalions, or Corps equivalent thereto; and Officers who may have succeeded to the actual command during the engagement, in consequence of the death or removal of the original Commanding Officer.

The Crosses, Medals, and Clasps, are to be worn by the General Officers, suspended by a Ribbon of the colour of the sash, with a blue edge, round the neck; and by the Commanding Officers of Battalions, or Corps equivalent thereto; and Officers who may have succeeded to the actual command during the engagement; the Chiefs of Military Departments, and their Deputies and Assistants (having the rank of Field Officers); and such other Officers as may be specially recommended, attached by a Ribbon of the same description, to the button-hole of their uniform.

Those Badges which would have been conferred upon the Officers who have fallen at or died since the Battles and Sieges, shall, as a token of respect for their memories, be transmitted to their respective families.—*Vide the London Gazette, 9th October,* 1813.

Officers who have received Honorary Distinctions.

NAMES AND PRESENT RANK.	DISTINCTIONS.	SIEGES, BATTLES, ETC.	RANK OR COMMAND AT THE TIME.
🟊 ⚔ Abercromby, Col. Hon. Alex. CB. late of Coldst. Gds.	Cross	Albuhera, Vittoria, Pyrenees, Orthes	Lieut.-Col. 28 F. commanding a Brigade Assistant Quar.-Mas.-Gen.
Agnew, Lieut.-Col. Patrick Vans, CB. ..E. I. Comp. Serv.	Medal	Java	Deputy-Adjutant-General
Alex, Lieut.-Col. Luke, CB. ....late of 55 F.	do.	Martinique, Guadaloupe	3 W. I. R.
🟊 Allan, Col. James, CB. ....57 F.	Medal	Toulouse	Major 94 F.
🟊 ⚔ Alten, Major-Gen. Charles, Count, GCB. GCH. late Ger. Leg.	Cross and 3 Clasps	Albuhera, Salamanca, Vittoria, Nivelle, Nive, Orthes, Toulouse	A Brigade / A Division
🟊 Anderson, Lieut.-Gen. Paul, CB. ....78 F.	Medal	Corunna	Acting Dep.-Adj.-Gen.
🟊 Anderson, Col. Sir Alexander, CB. ....Unatt.	Cross and 3 Clasps	Badajoz, Salamanca, Vittoria, Pyrenees, Nivelle, Orthes, Toulouse	Lieut.-Col. 11 Portuguese
🟊 ⚔ Anglesey, Gen. the Mar. of, KG. GCB. GCH. 7 Dr.	Medal	Sahagun, &c.	Commanding the Cavalry
Annesley, Major Marcus ....Unatt.	do.	Salamanca	Captain 61 Regiment
🟊 Anson, Gen. Sir George, GCB. ....4 Dr. Gds.	Medal and 2 Clasps	Talavera, Salamanca, Vittoria	A Brigade of Cavalry
🟊 Anson, Gen. Sir William, Bt. KB. ....47 F.	Cross and 3 Clasps	Corunna, Salamanca, Vittoria, Pyrenees, Nivelle, Orthes, Toulouse	Col. commanding 1 Ft. Gds.
🟊 Arbuthnot, Lieut.-Gen. Sir Thomas, KCB. ......52 F.	Cross and 1 Clasp	Roleia and Vimiera, Corunna, Pyrenees, Nivelle, Orthes	A Brigade
🟊 Arbuthnot, Major-Gen. Sir Robert, KCB.	Cross and 3 Clasps	Busaco, Albuhera, Badajoz, Nivelle, Nive, Orthes, Toulouse	Assistant Adjutant-Gen.
🟊 Arbuthnott, Major-Gen. Hon. Hugh, CB.	Medal	Busaco	Assistant-Quar.-Mas.-Gen.
🟊 Arentschildt, Major Sir V. von, CB. KCH. late Ger. L.	Medal and 2 Clasps	Busaco, Fuentes d'Onor, Toulouse	Military Secretary to Lord Beresford
🟊 Armstrong, Col. Sir Richard, CB. ....Unatt.	do	Busaco, Vittoria, Pyrenees	Major 52 F
🟊 Askew, Lieut.-Gen. Sir Henry ....h. p. 8 Garr. Bn.	Medal	Nive	Portuguese Artillery / 16 Portuguese / 10 Caçadores
🟊 Auchmuty, Col. Samuel Benj. CB.	Medal and 1 Clasp	Orthes, Toulouse	Light Companies
🟊 Aylmer, Lieut.-Gen. Lord, GCB. ....18 F.	Cross and 1 Clasp	Talavera, Busaco, Fuentes d'Onor, Vittoria, Nive	Assistant-Adjutant-Gen. Deputy-Adjutant-Gen. A Brigade
🟊 Bace, Lieut. William ....h. p. 3 F.	Medal	Toulouse	1 Battalion 61 F.
🟊 Balvaird, Col. William, CB. ....Unatt.	Medal and 1 Clasp.	Nivelle, Nive	Capt. 3 Battalion 95 F.
🟊 ⚔ Barnard, Lieut. Gen. Sir Andrew F. KCB. KCH. Rifle Brig.	Cross and 4 Clasps	Barrosa, Ciudad Rodrigo, *Badajoz, Salamanca, Vittoria, Nivelle, Orthes, Toulouse	A Battalion 95 F. / * A Division

450

Officers who have received *Honorary Distinctions*.

NAMES AND PRESENT RANK.	DISTINCTIONS.	SIEGES, BATTLES, ETC.	RANK OR COMMAND AT THE TIME.
Barns, Lieut.-Gen. *Sir* J. Stevenson, *KCB*. Rifle Brig.	Cross	Busaco, St. Sebastian, Salamanca, Nive	Lieut.-Col. 3 Battalion 1 F.
Bathurst, Lieut.-Gen. *Sir* James, *KCB*.	do	Roleia and Vimiera, Corunna, Talavera, Busaco	Military Secretary
Baynes, Lieut.-Col. Henry, *KH*. ...... h. p. R. Art.	Medal	Talavera	
Beckwith, Col. Charles, *CB*. .... h. p. Rifle Brig.	do	Toulouse	Assistant-Quar.-Mas.-Gen.
Bell, Col. John, *CB*	Cross	Pyrenees, Nivelle, Orthes, Toulouse	Assistant-Quar.-Mas.-Gen.
Bell, Lieut. Col. Thomas, *CB*. .... 48 F.	do	Pyrenees, Nivelle, Salamanca, Orthes	Major 48 F.
		Corunna	Major-General
Beresford, Gen. *Viscount*, *GCB. GCH*. .... 16 F.	Cross and 7 Clasps	Busaco, Albuhera, Badajoz, Salamanca, Vittoria, Pyrenees, Nivelle, Nive, Orthes, Toulouse	Lieut.-Gen. and Marshal commanding Portuguese
Berkeley, Major-Gen. *Sir* Geo. H. F. *KCB*.	Cross and 3 Clasps	Busaco, Fuentes d'Onor, Badajoz, Salamanca, Vittoria, St. Sebastian, Nive	Assistant-Adjutant-Gen.
Blake, Col. *W. W. CB*. .... late 11 Dr.	Medal	Roleia and Vimiera	
Blakeney, Lieut.-Gen. *Rt. Hon. Sir* Edward, *KCB. GCH*. .... 7 F.	Cross and 1 Clasp	Martinique, Albuhera, Badajoz, Vittoria, Pyrenees	Lieut.-Col. 7 F.
Bouverie, Lieut.-Gen. *Sir* Henry Frederick, *KCB*.	do	Salamanca, Vittoria, St. Sebastian, Nive, Orthes	Assistant-Adjutant-General
Bradford, Lieut.-Gen. *Sir* Thomas, *GCB. GCH*.	do	Corunna, Salamanca, Vittoria, St. Sebastian, Nive	Portuguese Brigade
Brandreth, Lieut.-Col. Thomas Alston, *CB*. ... R. Art.	Medal and 1 Clasp	Pyrenees, Toulouse	
Braun, Capt. William .... late Ger. Leg.	Medal	Albuhera	A Brigade
Brisbane, Lt.-Gen. *Sir* Thos. M. Bt. *GCB. GCH*. 34 F.	Cross and 1 Clasp	Vittoria, Pyrenees, Nivelle, Orthes, Toulouse	9 Portuguese Caçadores
Broome, Lt.-Col. *Gustavus*, *CB*. .... late of 95 F.	Cross	Salamanca, Pyrenees, Nivelle, Nive	Capt. 40 F.
Browne, Lieut.-Col. Fielding, *CB*. ... h. p Rifle Brig.	Medal	Badajoz	28 F.
Browne, Col. *J. Frederick*, *CB*. .... late of 28 F.	do	Barrosa	Col. 7 Portuguese
Buchan, Major-Gen. *Sir* John, *KCB*. .... 95 F.	Cross and 1 Clasp	Guadaloupe, Vittoria, Pyrenees, Nivelle, Nive	§ 1 Dragoon Ger. Leg.
Bulow, Lieut.-Col. John, *Baron*, *CB*. late Ger. Leg.	Medal and 2 Clasps	Salamanca, Vittoria, Toulouse	A Brigade
Bunbury, Lieut.-Gen. *Sir* Henry Edward, *Bt. KCB*.	Medal	Maida	Deputy-Quar.-Mas.-Gen.
Bunce, Lieut.-Col. Richard, ... late of R. Marines.	do	Java	Capt. R. Marines
Burgoyne, Maj.-Gen. *Sir* John F. *KCB*. from R. Eng.	Cross and 1 Clasp	Badajoz, Salamanca, Vittoria, *St. Sebastian, *Nive	*Comm. R. Engineers
Burslem, Col. *Nathaniel*, *KH*. .... late of 67 F.	Medal	Java	Deputy-Quar.-Mas.-Gen.
Caldwell, Lieut.-Col. Alexander .... E. I. Co. Serv.	do	do.	
Cameron, Lieut.-Gen. *Sir* John. *KCB*. .... 9 F.	Cross and 3 Clasps	Vimiera, Corunna, Busaco, Salamanca, Vittoria, St. Sebastian, Nive	9 F.
Cameron, Maj.-Gen. *Sir* Alexander, *KCB*.	Medal and 2 Clasps	Ciudad Rodrigo, Badajoz, Salamanca	Rifle Brigade

Officers who have received Honorary Distinctions.

NAMES AND PRESENT RANK.	DISTINCTIONS.	SIEGES, BATTLES, ETC.	RANK OR COMMAND AT THE TIME.
Campbell, Gen. *Sir* Henry Frederick, *KCB. GCH.* 25 F.	Medal and 1 Clasp	Talavera, Salamanca	{ Brig.-Gen. and Major-Gen. comm. a Brigade of Gds.
Campbell, Lieut.-Gen. *Sir* Colin, *KCB.* ...72 F.	Cross and 6 Clasps	{ Talavera, Busaco, Fuentes d'Onor, Badajoz, Salamanca, Vittoria, Pyrenees, Nivelle, Nive, Toulouse	{ Assistant-Adjutant-Gen. Assistant-Quar.-Mas.-Gen.
Campbell, Lieut.-Gen. *Sir* Archibald, *Bt. GCB.* ...62 F.	Cross and 1 Clasp	Albuhera, Vittoria, Pyrenees, Nivelle, Nive	Brig.-Gen. Portuguese
Campbell, Col. *Sir* Guy, *Bt. CB.* ......Unatt.	Medal	Pyrenees	Major 6 F.
Campbell Col. *Archibald, CB.* ....late of 46 F.	do	Nive	16 Portuguese
Campbell, Col. *John, CB.* ....late of 22 F.	Medal and 1 Clasp	Orthes, Toulouse	Suc. to comm. of L. Comps. 52 F.
Campbell, Lieut.-Col. Patrick, *CB.* ....h. p. 52 F.	do	Nivelle, Nive	A Light Battalion
Campbell, Major William ....Unatt.	do	Pyrenees, Nivelle	3 Portuguese
Carncross, Maj.-Gen. *Sir* Joseph Hugh, *KCB.* ....h. p. 1 F.	Cross and 2 Clasps	Vittoria, St. Sebastian	
Carroll, Maj.-Gen. *Sir* W. Parker, *CB.* R. Art.	Medal	Salamanca, Vittoria, Pyrenees, Nivelle, Nive, Orthes	Brig.-Gen. Spanish Army
Chapman, Maj.-Gen. *Sir* S. R. *CB. KCH.* R. Eng.	do	Albuhera	1 Dragoons
Charleton, Lieut.-Col. Edward, *KH.* ....Unatt.	do	Busaco	A Brigade
Clifton, Maj.-Gen. *Sir* Arthur B. *KCB. KCH.* 17 Dr.	Medal and 1 Clasp	Toulouse	
Cole, Geo. *Hon. Sir* Galb. Lowry, *GCB.* ....27 F.	Cross and 4 Clasps	Fuentes d'Onor, Vittoria	A Division
		Maida	A Brigade
		Albuhera, Salamanca, Vittoria, Pyrenees, Nivelle, Orthes, Toulouse	A Division
Colville, Gen. *Hon. Sir* Charles, *GCB. GCH.* 5 F.	Cross and 1 Clasp	Martinique	A Brigade
		Fuentes d'Onor, Badajoz, Vittoria, Nivelle	A Division
Combermere, General Stapleton, *Lord Viscount, KCB.* *GCH.* ....h. p. Insp. F. O. 1 Life Gds.	do	Talavera, Fuentes d'Onor, Salamanca, Orthes, Toulouse	{ Maj.-Gen.com.Brig. Cavalry Lieut.-Gen. com. Cavalry.
Conyers, Colonel Charles E. *CB.* ....late of Gren. Gds.	Medal	Orthes	82 F.
Cooke, Lieut.-Col. *R. H. CB.* ....late of 83 F.	do	St. Sebastian	Detachment of Guards
Cother, Lieut.-Col. *Charles, CB.* ....late of 42 F.	do	Vittoria	71 F.
Cowell, Lieut.-Col. *William, CB.*	Medal and 1 Clasp	Nivelle, Orthes	A Light Battalion
Creagh, Colonel *Andrew, CB.* ....late of 81 F.	Medal	Roleia and Vimiera	{ A Light Comp. of a Brigade as Brevet-Major of 29 F.
Crosse, Colonel William, *CB.* ....Unatt.	Cross	Nivelle, Nive, Orthes, Toulouse	Major 36 F.
Cumming, Lt.-Gen. *Sir* Henry John, *KCH.* ....12 Dr.	Medal	Salamanca	Colonel comm. 11 Light Dr.

Officers who have received Honorary Distinctions.

NAMES AND PRESENT RANK.	DISTINCTIONS.	SIEGES, BATTLES, ETC.	RANK OR COMMAND AT THE TIME.
⚔ Dalmer, Maj.-Gen. Thomas, *CB*.	Medal and 1 Clasp	Salamanca, Vittoria	A Light Battalion
Dalton, Major D. H. ... *E. I. Comp. Serv.*	Medal	Java	Bengal Light Infantry Battalion
Daniel, Captain Lewis ... late Ger. Leg.	Medal and 1 Clasp	Orthes, Toulouse	Artillery Ger. Leg.
⚔ Darling, Lieut.-Gen. *Sir* Ralph, *GCH*. ... 41 F.	Medal	Corunna	Lieut.-Col. 51 F.
⚔ Davy, Maj.-Gen. *Sir* William Gabriel, *CB. KCH*.	Medal and 1 Clasp	Roleia and Vimiera, Talavera	Major 5 Batt. 60 F.
⚔ Derinzy, Major B. V. ... 11 F.	Medal	Toulouse	7 Caçadores
Dewar, Lieut.-Col. James ... *E. I. Comp. Serv.*	do.	Java	Major 3 Bengal Vol. Bat.
⚔ Dick, Maj. Gen. *Sir* R. H. *KCB*.	Medal and 2 Clasps	Busaco, Fuentes d'Onor, Salamanca	42 F.
⚔ Dickson, Maj.-Gen. *Sir* Jer. *KCB*.	Cross and 1 Clasp	Vittoria, Pyrenees, Nivelle, Orthes, Toulouse	Assist. Quarter-Master-Gen.
⚔ Dickson, Maj.-Gen. *Sir* Alex, *GCB. KCH*. .. R. Art.	Cross and 6 Clasps	Albuhera, Busaco, Ciudad Rodrigo, Badajoz, Salamanca, *Vittoria, *St. Sebastian, *Nivelle, *Nive, *Toulouse	Comm. Portuguese Artillery *Comm. Art.
Dilkes, General William Thomas	Medal	Barrosa	Brigadier General
⚔ Disney, General *Sir* Moore, *KCB*. ... 15 F.	do	Corunna	do
Dixon, Lieut.-Col. Matthew Charles ... R. Eng.	do	Detroit	Commanding Royal Engineers
⚔ Donkin, Gen. *Sir* Rufane Shawe, *KCB. GCH*. ... 11 F.	do	Talavera	Col. commanding a Brigade
⚔ Douglas, Maj.-Gen. *Sir* James, *KCB*.	Cross and 3 Clasps	Busaco, Salamanca, Pyrenees, Nivelle, Nive, Orthes, Toulouse	Colonel 8 Portuguese A Brigade
⚔ Douglas, Maj.-Gen. *Sir* Neil, *KCB. KCH*.	Cross	Pyrenees, Nivelle, Nive, Toulouse	
Douglas, Lieut.-Col. Robert, *CB*. ... late of R. Art.	do	Salamanca, Vittoria, Pyrenees, Nivelle	
⚔ Downes, Maj.-Gen. *Sir* Ulysses, *Lord*, *KCB*.	Cross and 1 Clasp	Vittoria, Pyrenees, Nivelle, Nive, Toulouse	A.D.C. to the D. of Wellington
Downmann, Maj.-Gen. *Sir* Thos. *CB. KCH*. .. R. Art.	Medal	Salamanca	
Doyle, Colonel *Sir John Milley, KCB*.	Cross and 1 Clasp	Fuentes d'Onor, Ciudad Rodrigo, Vittoria, Pyrenees, Orthes	Colonel 19 Portuguese
⚔ Duffy, Colonel John, *CB*. ... late of 12 Garr. Batt.	Medal	Badajoz	Brevet-Major 43 F.
⚔ Dundas, Maj.-Gen. *Hon. Sir* R. L. *KCB*.' ... Unatt.	Cross and 3 Clasps	Talavera, Salamanca, Vittoria, Pyrenees, Nivelle, Nive, Toulouse	R. Staff Corps
⚔ D'Urban, Lieut.-Gen. *Sir* B. *KCB. KCH*. ... 51 F.	Cross and 5 Clasps	Busaco, Albuhera, Badajoz, Salamanca, Vittoria, Pyrenees, Nivelle, Nive, Toulouse	Brigadier-General Portuguese
Eden, General William	Medal	Java	Quarter-Master-General
⚔ Effingham, General Kenneth Alex. Earl of, *GCB*. ..3 F.	Medal and 1 Clasp	Vittoria, Nive	A Division
⚔ Ellicombe, Colonel C. Grene, *CB*. ... R. Eng.	Medal	St. Sebastian	
⚔ Elphinstone, Maj.-Gen. *Sir* Howard, *CB. Bt.* .. R. Eng.	Medal and 1 Clasp	Nivelle, Nive	

Officers who have received Honorary Distinctions.

NAMES AND PRESENT RANK.	DISTINCTIONS.	SIEGES, BATTLES, ETC.	RANK OR COMMAND AT THE TIME.
⚜ Erskine, Colonel W. H. Knight, *CB*. ....h. p.	Medal	Badajoz	Major 27 F.
⚜ Eustace, Maj.-Gen. W. C. *CB. KCH*.	Medal and 1 Clasp	Fuentes d'Onor, Salamanca	Chass. Britt.
⚜ Fane, General *Sir* Henry, *GCB*. ....1 Dr. Gds.	Cross and 1 Clasp	Roleia & Vimiera, Corunna, Talavera, Vittoria, Orthes	A Brigade of Cavalry
⚜ Faunce, Col. Alured Dodsworth, *CB*....Insp. Fd. Off.	Medal	Salamanca	4 F.
⚜ Ferguson, Gen. *Sir* Ronald Craufurd, *GCB* ....79 F.	do	Roleia and Vimiera	A Brigade as Major-Gen.
⚜ Fergusson, Col. James, *CB*. ....h. p.	do	Badajoz	Captain 43 F.
⚜ Fitz Gerald, Maj.-Gen. *Sir* John F. *KCB*.	Cross	Badajoz, Salamanca, Vittoria, Pyrenees	{ A Light Battalion / A Brigade
Forbes, Col. David, *CB*. ....h. p. 78 F.	Medal	Java	Flank Battalion
⚜ ⚜ Freemantle, Col. John, *CB*. ....Unatt.	do	Orthes	A.D.C. to the D. of Wellington
⚜ ⚜ Friedrichs, Lieut.-Col. Augustus C....late Ger.Leg.	do	Toulouse	Major 2 Dr. Ger Leg.
⚜ Fuller, Lieut.-Gen. *Sir* Joseph, *GCH*. ....75 F.	do	Talavera	Lieut.-Col. comm. Coldst. Gds.
⚜ *Fuller*, Lieut.-Col. *Francis*, *CB*. ....late of 59 F.	Medal	St. Sebastian	
⚜ *Galiffe*, Lt.-Col. *John*, *CB*. ....late of 60 F.	Cross	Vittoria, Nivelle, Orthes, Toulouse	A Light Battalion
⚜ Gardiner, Major, Gen. *Sir* John, *KCB*. ..Dep. Adj. Gen.	Medal and 1 Clasp	Nivelle, Orthes	A Brigade
⚜ ⚜ Gardiner, Col. *Sir* Robert, *KCB. KCH*....R. Art.	Cross and 2 Clasps	Barrosa, Badajoz, Salamanca, Vittoria, Orthes, Toulouse	
⚜ Gibbs, Maj.-Gen. *Sir* Edward, *KCB*.	Medal and 2 Clasps	Ciudad Rodrigo, Badajoz, Vittoria	52 F.
⚜ ⚜ Gilmour, Maj.-Gen. *Sir* Dugald Little, *KCB*.	Cross	Busaco, Fuentes d'Onor, Nive, Toulouse	95 F.
⚜ ⚜ Gleichen, Captain F. von Uslar ...late Ger. Leg.	Medal	Vittoria	
⚜ Goldfinch, Col. Henry, *CB*. ....R. Eng.	Cross	Vittoria, Nive, Orthes, Toulouse	
⚜ Goldie, Col. George Leigh, *CB*. ....11 F.	Medal	Albuhera	Maj. 66 F.
⚜ ⚜ Gomm, Maj.-Gen.*Sir*W.M.*KCB*.from Coldst. Gds.	Cross and 1 Clasp	Badajoz, Salamanca, Vittoria, St. Sebastian, Nive	Assist.-Qua.-Mast.-Gen.
⚜ Gordon, Lt.-Gen. Gabriel ....91 F.	Medal and 1 Clasp	Martinique, Guadaloupe	Dep.-Quar.-Mast.-Gen.
⚜ Gordon, Col. William A., *CB*. ....h. p. 95 F.	Medal	Nive	A Light Battalion
⚜ Gough, Maj.-Gen. *Sir* Hugh, *KCB*. ....99 F.	Cross	Talavera, Barrosa, Vittoria, Nivelle	87 F.
⚜ ⚜ Greenock, Maj.-Gen. *Lord*, *KCB*. from R. Staff C.	Medal and 2 Clasps	Barrosa, Salamanca, Vittoria	Assist.-Qua.-Mast.-Gen.
⚜ Greenwell, Maj.-Gen. *Sir* Leonard, *KCB. KCH*.	do	Badajoz, Fuentes d'Onor, Orthes	45 F.
Griffiths, Lt.-Col. Hugh ............E.I.Comp.Serv.	Medal	Java	Capt. 5 Bengal Vol. Bn.
⚜ Guise, Lt.-Gen. *Sir* John Wright, *Bt. KCB*.	Cross	Fuentes d'Onor, Salamanca, Vittoria, Nive	Col. Com. 3 F. Gds.
⚜ ⚜ Halkett, Lt.-Gen. *Sir* Colin, *KCB. GCH.* ..31 F.	do	Albuhera, Salamanca, Vittoria, Nive	Col. Com. a Brig. Ger. Leg.

454

Officers who have received Honorary Distinctions.

NAMES AND PRESENT RANK.	DISTINCTIONS.	SIEGES, BATTLES, ETC.	RANK OR COMMAND AT THE TIME.
💰 💰 *Halkett*, Lt.-Col. *Hugh*, CB. KCH. late Ger. Leg.	Medal and 1 Clasp	Albuhera, Salamanca	2 Light Inf. Ger. Leg.
💰 💰 Hardinge, Maj.-Gen. Rt. Hon. Sir Hen., KCB. 97 F.	Cross and 5 Clasps	Busaco, Albuhera, Badajoz, Salamanca, Vittoria, Pyrenees, Nivelle, Nive, Orthes	Dep.-Quarter-Master-Gen. Portuguese
💰 Hare, Col. Richard Goddard, CB. Unatt.	Medal and 1 Clasp	Nivelle, Nive	Assist.-Adjut.-General
💰 *Harrison*, Lt.-Col. *John Bacon*, CB. late of 50 F.	Medal and 2 Clasps	Pyrenees, Nive, Orthes	50 F.
💰 💰 Hartmann, Lt.-Col. Sir *Julius*, KCB. KCH. late Ger. Leg.	Cross and 2 Clasps	Talavera, Albuhera, Salamanca, Vittoria, St. Sebastian, Nive	Art. Ger. Leg.
Harvey, Maj.-Gen. Sir *John*, KCB. KCH.	Medal	Chrystler's Farm	Dep.-Adjutant-General
Harvey, Col. Sir *Robert John*, CB. h. p.	do.	Orthes	Assist.-Quar.-Mast.-Gen. Port.
Hawker, Gen. *Samuel*, GCH. 3 Dr. Gds.	do.	Talavera	Col. Comm. 14 Lt. Dr.
Hawkins, Lt.-Col. *John P.*, CB. late of 68 F.	Medal and 2 Clasps	Vittoria, Pyrenees, Nivelle	68 F.
💰 *Hay*, Col. *James*, CB. Unatt.	Medal and 1 Clasp	Vittoria, Nive	16 Lieut. Dr.
Heriot, Lt.-Col. *Frederick*, CB. h. p. Canad. Volt.	Medal	Chrystler's Farm	Canadian Voltiguers
Herford, Lt.-Col. *Wm. I.* late of 23 F.	Medal and 1 Clasp	Orthes, Toulouse	Major 23 F.
Herzberg, Lt.-Col. F. A. de late Bruns. Inf.	Cross	Salamanca, Vittoria, Pyrenees, Nivelle, Orthes	Brunswick Infantry
💰 💰 Hill, General *Rowland*, *Lord*, GCB. GCH. KC. R. H. Gds.	Cross and 3 Clasps	Roleia and Vimiera, Corunna, Talavera, Vittoria, Pyrenees, Nivelle, Nive, Orthes	A Brigade A Division A Corps
💰 💰 *Hill*, Col. Sir *Robert C.*, CB. late of R.H. Gds.	Medal	Vittoria	A Brigade of Cavalry
💰 Hill, Col. Sir *Dudley St. Leger*, CB. Unatt.	Cross and 1 Clasp	Fuentes d'Onor, Badajoz, Salamanca, Vittoria, St. Sebastian	8 Caçadores
Hislop, General, Sir *Thomas*, Bt. GCB. 48 F.	Medal	Guadaloupe	Maj.-Gen comm. a Division
Holcombe, Lt.-Col. *Harcourt Fort*, CB. late of R. Art.	do.	Badajoz	Assist.-Adjutant-General
💰 Hope, Col. Sir *James Arch.*, KCB. Unatt.	Cross and 1 Clasp	Vittoria, Nivelle, Nive, Orthes, Toulouse	Maj.-Gen. comm. a Division
Houstoun, General Sir *William*, Bart. GCB. GCH. 20 F.	Medal	Fuentes d'Onor	Major 18 Hussars
Hughes, Col. *James*, CB. h. p. 18 Dr.	Medal and 2 Clasps	Vittoria, Orthes, Toulouse	1 Batt. 52 F.
💰 *Hunt*, Lieut.-Col. *John Philip*, CB. late of 11 F.	do.	Badajoz, Salamanca St. Sebastian	Colonel of Light Division
💰 Jackson, Maj.-Gen. Sir *Rich. Downes*, KCB. 81 F.	Cross and 2 Clasps	*Barrosa, Fuentes d'Onor, Salamanca, Nivelle, Nive, Orthes	*Lt.-Col. comm. a Detach. Coldst. Gds.
Jackson, Lieut.-Col. *Henry George* R. Art.	Medal	Chrystler's Farm	Assist.-Qua.-Mast.-Gen.
💰 Johnston, Lieut.-Gen. Sir *William*, KCB. 68 F.	Medal and 2 Clasps	Salamanca, Vittoria, Orthes	Lieut.-Col. 68 Regt.

Officers who have received Honorary Distinctions.

NAMES AND PRESENT RANK.	DISTINCTIONS.	SIEGES, BATTLES, ETC.	RANK OR COMMAND AT THE TIME.
⚜ Jones, Maj.-Gen. *Sir* John Thos. *Bt. KCB.*from R.Eng.	Medal	Badajoz	Lieut.-Col. 13 F.
⚜ Keane, Lieut.-Gen. John, *Lord, GCB. GCH.* ....43 F.	Cross and 2 Clasps	Martinique .... Vittoria, Pyrenees, Nivelle, Orthes, Toulouse	Colonel comm. a Brigade
⚜ ᴹ Kempt, Lieut.-Gen. *Sir* James, *GCB. GCH.* ..2 F.	Cross and 3 Clasps	Maida .... Badajoz, Vittoria, Nivelle, Nive, Orthes, Toulouse.	Lieut.-Col. Light Infantry A Brigade
⚜ ᴹ Kerrison, Lt.-Gen. *Sir* Edw. *Bt. CB. GCH.* 14 Dr.	Medal	Orthes	Lieut.-Col. 7 Hussars
⚜ King, Maj.-Gen. *Sir* Henry, *CB.* .....h. p. Port. Serv.	Medal	Vittoria	82 F.
⚜ Knight, Lieut.-Col. Edward ....h. p. Port. Serv.	do	do	Major 11 Portuguese
⚜ Kyle, Captain Alexander ....h. p. 94 F.	do	do	Captain 94 F.
⚜ ᴹ Lambert, Lieut.-Gen. *Sir* John, *GCB.* ....10 F.	Cross	Nivelle, Nive, Orthes, Toulouse	A Brigade
⚜ Langlands, Major George..........late 13 R. Vet. Batt.	Medal and 1 Clasp	Ciudad Rodrigo, Badajoz	Capt. 74 F.
⚜ Leith, Major-Gen. *Sir* Alexander, *KCB.*	Cross and 1 Clasp	Vittoria, Pyrenees, Nivelle, Nive, Orthes	31 F.
L'Estrange, Major-Gen. Geo. Guy Carleton, *CB.* ...	Medal	Albuhera	Major comm. 2 Batt. 31 F.
Lightfoot, Col. Thomas, *CB.* ....h. p. 45 F.	Medal and 2 Clasps	Vittoria, Pyrenees, Toulouse	Major 45 F.
Lillie, Lieut.-Col. *Sir* John Scott, *CB.* ....h. p. 31 F.	Cross	Pyrenees, Nivelle, Orthes, Toulouse	Lieut.-Col. 7 Caçadores
Lindsay, Col. *Martin, CB.* ....late of 78 F.	Medal	Java	
⚜ Londonderry, Gen. Charles Wm. *Marq. of, GCB.* *GCH.* ....10 Dr.	Cross and 1 Clasp	Sahagun and Benevente.......... Talavera, Busaco, Fuentes d'Onor, Badajoz	A Brigade of Cavalry Adjutant-General
⚜ Low, Major-Gen. S. C. G. *Baron, KCB. KCH.*late Ger.L.	Medal and 1 Clasp	Talavera, Salamanca	
⚜ Lumley, Gen. *Hon.* *Sir* Wm. *GCB.* ......6 Dr.	Medal	Albuhera	Major-Gen. comm. Cavalry
⚜ Lynedoch, Gen. T. *Lord, GCB. GCMG.* ....1 F.	Cross	Barrosa .... Ciudad Rodrigo, Vittoria, St. Sebastian	Commanding the Forces A Division
⚜ ᴹ Lyon, Lieut.-Gen. *Sir* James, *KCB. GCH.* ..24 F.	Medal and 1 Clasp	Vimiera, Talavera	Lieut.-Col. 97 F.
⚜ M'Donald, Col. John, *CB.*..........92 F.	do	Vittoria, Pyrenees	A Portuguese Brigade
M'Nair, Lieut.-Gen. John, *CB.*	Medal	Martinique	Lieut.-Col. comm. a Brigade
Macbean, Major-Gen. *Sir* William, *KCB.*	Cross	Busaco, Salamanca, St. Sebastian, Nive	⎰ 19 Portuguese ⎱ 24 do
⚜ Macdonald, Lieut.-Gen. *Sir* John, *KCB.* ......67 F.	Medal and 1 Clasp	Barrosa .... Nive	Deputy-Adjutant-General Assistant-Adjutant-General
⚜ *Macdonald*, Lieut.-Col. *Robert, CB.* ....late of R. Art.	Medal	Salamanca	
Macdonell, Lieut.-Col. *George, CB.* ......late of 79 F.	do	Chateauguay	Glengarry Lt. Infantry

Officers who have received Honorary Distinctions.

NAMES AND PRESENT RANK.	DISTINCTIONS.	SIEGES, BATTLES, ETC.	RANK OR COMMAND AT THE TIME.
Macdonell, Major-Gen. *Sir* James, *KCB. KCH.*..Unatt.	Medal	Maida	Major Batt. 78 Regiment
Maclaine, Col. Hector ....84 F.	do	Nivelle	Major comm.
Maclean, Gen. *Sir* Fitzroy Grafton, *Bt.*............	do	Guadaloupe	Brigadier-General
Maclean, Lieut.-Gen. *Sir* John, *KCB.*............60 F.	Cross and 2 Clasps	Salamanca, Vittoria, Pyrenees, Nivelle, Orthes, Toulouse	Lieut.-Col. 3 Batt. 27 F.
Macpherson, Col. Robt. Barclay, *CB. KH.* h. p. 71 F.	Medal and 1 Clasp	Vittoria, Orthes	Major 88 F.
Maitland, Gen. Frederick ....58 F.	Medal	Martinique	Major-Gen. comm. a Division
Maitland, Lieut.-Gen. *Sir* Peregrine, *KCB.*...76 F.	do	Nive	Col. comm. 1st. Brig. of Gds.
Manners, Major-Gen. *Lord*, Charles S. *KCB.*	Medal and 2 Clasps	Salamanca, Vittoria, Toulouse	3 Dragoons
Manners, Lieut.-Col *Russell*, *CB.*....late of 74 F.	Cross	Fuentes d'Onor, Ciudad Rodrigo, Badajoz, Orthes	74 F.
Mansel, Lieut.-Col. *John*..........late of 53 F.	Medal and 1 Clasp.	Salamanca, Toulouse	A Provisional Battalion
May, Major-General *Sir* John, *KCB. KCH.* from R. Art.	Cross and 3 Clasps	Badajoz, Salamanca, Vittoria, St. Sebastian, Nivelle, Nive, Toulouse	Assistant-Adj.-Gen. R. Art.
Meade, Lieut.-Gen. *Hon.* John, *CB.*................	Medal	Busaco	Lieut.-Col. 45 F.
Michell, Lieut.-Col. John, *CB.*...............R. Art.	Medal and 1 Clasp.	Orthes, Toulouse	Capt. Portuguese Artillery
Michell, Major Chas. D. *KH.*......h. p. Port. Serv.	do	Vittoria, Toulouse	Major, succeeded to command of 48 F.
Middlemore, Major-Gen. George, *CB.*................	Medal	Talavera	Lieut.-Col. 38 F.
Miles, Col. *Sir Edward, CB.*............late of 89 F.	Medal and 1 Clasp.	Salamanca, St. Sebastian	Capt. comm. 2 Batt. 95 Regt.
Miller, Col. *Sir George, CB.*..................Unatt.	Medal	Nivelle	Light Companies
Mitchell, Lieut.-Col. *James, CB.*........late of 92 F.	do	Orthes	Major 23 Portuguese
Murphy, Major George H. E. .... 6 F.	do	Toulouse	
Murray, Lieut.-General *Sir* George, *GCB. GCH.* 42 F.	Cross and 6 Clasps	Corunna, Talavera, Busaco, Fuentes d'Onor Vittoria, Pyrenees, Nivelle, Orthes, Toulouse	Quarter-Master-General
Napier, Major-Gen. Mark	Medal	Guadaloupe	90 F.
Napier, Major-Gen. *Sir* Charles James, *KCB.*........	do	Corunna	Major commanding 50 F.
Napier, Major-Gen. *Sir* George Thomas, *KCB.*	Medal and 1 Clasp	Ciudad Rodrigo	Major 52 F. commanding the Advance
Napier, Col. William F. P. *CB.*........h. p. 43 F.	Medal and 2 Clasps	Salamanca, Nivelle, Nive	Major 43 F.
Nickle, Col. Robert, *KH.*..............................Unatt.	Medal	Nivelle	Capt. 88 F.
Nicol, Major-Gen. Charles, *CB.*..........from 66 F.	do	Nive	
Nicolls, Lieut.-Gen. *Sir* Jasper, *KCB.*.........93 F.	do	Corunna	Lieut.-Col. 2 Batt. 14 F.

Officers who have received Honorary Distinctions.

NAMES AND PRESENT RANK.	DISTINCTIONS.	SIEGES, BATTLES, ETC.	RANK OR COMMAND AT THE TIME.
O'Callaghan, Lieut.-Gen. *Hon. Sir* Robt. *GCB*. 39 F.	Cross and 2 Clasps	Maida, Vittoria, Pyrenees, Nivelle, Nive, Orthes	Lieut.-Col. Grenadiers Col. commanding 39 F. and a Brigade
Oglander, Col. Henry, *CB*. 26 F.	Medal	St. Sebastian	Capt. 47 F.
Oke, Lieut.-Col. John ......h. p. 61 F.	do	Toulouse	61 F.
Orange, General, *the Hereditary Prince of*, *GCB*.	Cross and 2 Clasps	Ciudad Rodrigo, Badajoz, Salamanca, Vittoria, Pyrenees, Nivelle	A. D. C. to the Duke of Wellington
Oswald, Gen. *Sir* John, *GCB. GCMG*. 35 F.	Medal and 2 Clasps	Maida, Vittoria, St. Sebastian	Col. comm. a Brigade Major-General commanding a Division
Paget, Gen. *Hon. Sir* Edward, *GCB*. 28 F.	Medal	Corunna	Major-General
Pakenham, Maj.-Gen. *Hon. Sir* Herc. Rob., *KCB*.	Cross	Busaco, Fuentes d'Onor	Assistant-Adjut.-General
Parker, Col. John Boteler, *CB*. R. Art.	Medal	Ciudad Rodrigo, Badajoz	
Patrickson, Col. *C. C., CB*. late of 43 F.	do	Vittoria, Toulouse	43 F.
Pearson, Major-Gen. *Sir* Thomas, *CB. KCH*.	Medal and 1 Clasp	Albuhera	Major 23 F.
Plenderleath, Lieut.-Col. *Charles, CB*. late of 49 F.	Medal	Chrystler's Farm	Inspect. Field Officer
Power, Captain Thomas ....h. p. 60 F.	do	do.	49 F.
Prevot, Captain Joseph F. de........late Chass. Britt.	do	St. Sebastian	Succeed. to com. of 47 F.
Pringle, Lieut.-Gen. *Sir* William Henry, *GCB*. 45 F.	Cross	Nivelle	
Purvis, Lieut.-Col. Charles ....h. p. Canad. F.	Medal	Salamanca, Pyrenees, Nivelle, Nive	A Brigade
Pynn, Lieut.-Col. *Sir* Henry, *CB*. late of Port. Serv.	Medal and 2 Clasps	Vittoria, Fuentes d'Onor, Pyrenees, Orthes	Major 1 Dr.
			18 Portuguese
Quentin, Lieut.-Gen. *Sir* George Aug. *KCH*.	Medal and 1 Clasp	Orthes, Toulouse	10 Hussars
Rainey, Major John ....late of 82 F.	Medal	Roleia and Vimiera	Assist.-Qua.-Mast.-Gen.
Rettberg, Captain Charles de .....late Ger. Leg.	Medal and 2 Clasps	Talavera, Busaco, Badajoz	
Riall, Lieut.-General *Sir* Phineas, *KCH*.	Medal and 1 Clasp	Martinique, Guadaloupe	Lt.-Col. comm. a Brigade
Rice, Col. Samuel, *CB. KH*. Unatt.	Medal	Nivelle	51 F.
Roberts, Lieut.-Col. William ......late of R. Art.	do	Barrosa	
Robertson, Maj.-Gen. *George D*.	do	Maida	Major 35 F.
Robinson, Lieut.-Gen. *Sir* Fred. P. *GCB*. 59 F.	Medal and 2 Clasps	Vittoria, St. Sebastian, Nive	A Brigade
Rolt, Colonel John, *CB*. Unatt.	Cross and 1 Clasp	Vittoria, Nivelle, Nive, Orthes, Toulouse	Lt.-Col. 17 Portuguese

Officers who have received Honorary Distinctions.

NAMES AND PRESENT RANK.	DISTINCTIONS.	SIEGES, BATTLES, ETC.	RANK OR COMMAND AT THE TIME.
Ross, Lieut.-Gen. John, *CB*..........46 F.	Medal	Vimiera	Lt.-Col. 2 Bn. 52 F.
Ross, Colonel *Sir* Hew Dalrymple, *KCB*...R. Art.	Cross and 2 Clasps	Busaco, Badajoz, Salamanca, Vittoria, Nivelle, Nive	Assist.-Adjut.-General
Rowan, Lieut.-Col. *Charles*, *CB*....late of 52 F.	Medal and 2 Clasps	Ciudad Rodrigo, Badajoz, Salamanca	A. D. C. to the Duke of Wellington
Russell, Col. *Lord* Geo. William, *GCB*........Unatt.	Medal	Toulouse	
St. Clair, Colonel Thomas S., *CB, KH*.........do	do	Nive	Lieut.-Col. 5 Cacadores
Salaberry, Lieut.-Col. *Cha. de, CB*. late h. p. Canad.Voltig.	do	Chateauguay	Comm. advanced Detach.
Saunders, Gen. John Stratford	do	Talavera	Colonel comm. 61 F.
Schoedde, Lieut.-Col. James Holmes ....55 F.	do	Nivelle	
Scovell, Maj.-Gen. *Sir* Geo. *KCB*.	Cross and 1 Clasp	Vittoria, Pyrenees, Nivelle, Nive, Toulouse	Cav. Staff Corps
Seaton, Lieut.-Gen. John *Lord*, *GCB. GCH*........26 F.	Cross and 3 Clasps	Corunna, Albuhera, Ciudad Rodrigo, *Nivelle, *Nive, Orthes, Toulouse	Military Secretary; 66 F. comm. a Brigade; 52 F. *a Brigade
Seton, Col. William Carden, *CB*..........h. p. 88 F.	Medal and 1 Clasp	Badajoz, Salamanca	88 F.
Slade, General *Sir* John, *Bt. GCH*........5 Dr. Gds.	Medal and 1 Clasp	Corunna, Fuentes d'Onor	Brigadier-General
Smith, Colonel James Webber, *CB*......R. Art.	do	Vittoria, St. Sebastian	Major-General
Smith, Colonel, *Sir* Charles Felix ......R. Eng.	do		
Snodgrass, Colonel Kenneth, *CB*............Unatt.	Cross	St. Sebastian	13 Portuguese
Somerset, Lieut.-Gen. *Lord* Robert Edw. Henry, *GCB*...........4 Dr.	Cross and 1 Clasp	Nivelle, Nive, Orthes	1 Cacadores
Somerset, Lieut.-Gen. *Lord* Fitzroy James Hen. *KCB*........53 F.	Cross and 5 Clasps	Talavera, Salamanca, Vittoria, Orthes, Toulouse; Fuentes d'Onor, Badajoz, Salamanca, Vittoria, Pyrenees, Nivelle, Nive, Orthes, Toulouse	Lieut.-Col. 4 Dr.; A Brigade of Cavalry; A. D. C. and Military Secretary to the D. of Wellington
Stanhope, Maj.-Gen. *Hon*. Lincoln, *CB*.	Medal	Talavera	Major 16 Light Dr.
Stewart, Maj.-Gen. William	do	Albuhera	
Stone, Lieut.-Col. Bayntun ....h. p. 58 F.	do	Nivelle	A Provisional Battalion
Stovin, Col. *Sir* Frederick, *KCB. KCMG*......Unatt.	Cross and 2 Clasps	Salamanca, Vittoria, Pyrenees, Nivelle, Orthes, Toulouse	Assist.-Adjut.-Gen.
Strafford, Lt.-Gen. John, *Lord*, *GCB. GCH*....29 F.	Cross and 1 Clasp	Vittoria, Pyrenees, Nivelle, Nive, Orthes	A Brigade
Stretton, Colonel Sempronius, *CB*....h. p. 84 F.	Medal	Pyrenees	Captain comm. 40 F.
Taylor, Lieut.-Gen. *Sir* John, *KCB*..........80 F.	Medal and 2 Clasps	Nivelle, Orthes, Toulouse	88 F.

Officers who have received Honorary Distinctions.

NAMES AND PRESENT RANK.	DISTINCTIONS.	SIEGES, BATTLES, ETC.	RANK OR COMMAND AT THE TIME.
⊕ Thomas, Colonel Henery, *CB.* .... 20 F	Medal and 2 Clasps	Nivelle, Orthes, Toulouse..........	A Light Battalion
⊕ Thomson, Colonel Alexander, *CB.* ...... h. p. 98 F.	Medal	St. Sebastian	Assistant Engineer
⊕ Thornton, Lieut.-Gen. *Sir William, KCB* ...... 96 F.	do	Nive...............................	Lieut.-Col. 85 F.
⊕ *Thornton*, Colonel *Henry, CB.* .... late of 82 F.	Cross	Talavera, Nivelle, Orthes, Toulouse	Lieut.-Col. 40 F.
⊕ Tonson, Colonel Jacob, *CB.* .... h. p. 37 F.	Medal	Nive...............................	Major 84 F.
⊕ Trevor, Lieut.-Gen. *Hon.* Henry Otway, *CB.*..	do	Salamanca	Comm. Coldst. Gds.
⊕ Turner, Colonel George, *CB.* .... R. Art.	Medal and 1 Clasp	Orthes, Toulouse	
⊕ Tweeddale, Maj.-Gen. George, *Marq. of, CB. KT.*	Medal	Vittoria............................	Assist.-Qua.-Mast.-Gen.
⊕ Upton, Lieut.-Gen. *Hon.* Arthur Percy, *CB.* ...	Medal and 1 Clasp	Vittoria, Nive	do
⊕ ⚔ Vandeleur, Gen. *Sir* John, *GCB* .... 16 Dr.	Cross	Ciudad Rodrigo, Salamanca, Vittoria, Nive	A Brigade
⊕ ⚔ Vere, Maj.-Gen. *Sir* Charles Broke, *KCB*......	Cross and 5 Clasps	Albuhera, Badajoz, Salamanca, Vittoria, Pyrenees, Nivelle, Nive, Orthes, Toulouse	Assist.-Qua.-Mast.-Gen.
⊕ Vernon, Col. Henry Chas. Edw. *CB.* ...... Unatt.	Medal	Salamanca	Staff
⊕ ⚔ Vigoureux, Col. C. A. *CB.* .... h. p. 45 F.	Medal and 1 Clasp	Fuentes d'Onor, Vittoria	A Light Battalion
⊕ Viney, Maj.-Gen. *Sir* James, *CB. KCH.* .. R. Art.	do	Corunna, Roleia, and Vimiera	Comm. R. Art. at Corunna
⊕ ⚔ Vivian, Lieut.-Gen. *Right Hon. Sir* Richard.	do	Sahagun and Benavente	Lieut.-Col. 7 Dr.
Hussey, *Bt. GCB. GCH.* .... 1 Dr.		Orthes	Col. comm. a Brigade of Cav.
Wale, Gen. *Sir* Charles, *KCB.* .... 33 F.	Medal	Guadaloupe	Brigadier-General
⊕ Walker, Gen. *Sir* George, T. *Bt. GCB.* ...... 50 F.	Medal and 2 Clasps	Vimiera	Col. comm. 50 F.
⊕ Wallace, Lieut.-Gen. *Sir* John Alexander, *Bt. KCB.* 88 F.	do	Badajoz, Orthes	Major-General
⊕ *Ward*, Col. *John Richard, CB.* .... late of 2 Dr.	do	Busaco, Fuentes, d'Onor, *Salamanca	*Comm. a Brigade 2 Batt. 27 F. Lt. Inf. 4 Div.
⊕ Wardlaw, Maj.-Gen. John	Medal	Nive...............................	1 Battalion 36 F. 76 F.
⊕ ⚔ *Waters*, Maj.-Gen. *Sir* John, *KCB.*	Cross and 4 Clasps	Badajoz, Salamanca, Vittoria, Pyrenees, Nivelle, Nive, Orthes, Toulouse	Assistant-Adjutant-General
Watson, Lieut.-Gen. *Sir* James, *KCB.* .... 14 F.	Medal	Java...............................	Lieut.-Col. 14 F.
⊕ Watson, Maj.-Gen. *Sir* Henry, *CB.*	do	Salamanca	1 Portuguese Cavalry
⊕ Way, Maj.-Gen. *Sir* Gregory H. B. *CB.*	do	Albuhera	Major 29 F. succeeded to the command

Officers who have received Honorary Distinctions.

NAMES AND PRESENT RANK.	DISTINCTIONS.	SIEGES, BATTLES, ETC.	RANK OR COMMAND AT THE TIME.
₿ ✠ Wellington, Field Marshal Arthur, *Duke of*, *KG. GCB. GCH.*, Constable of the Tower of London, and Lord Warden of the Cinque Ports	Cross and 9 Clasps	Roleia, and Vimiera, Talavera, Busaco, Fuentes d'Onor, Ciudad Rodrigo, Badajoz, Salamanca, Vittoria, Pyrenees, Nivelle, Nive, Orthes, Toulouse	COMMANDER OF THE FORCES.
Wetherall, Gen. *Sir* Fred. Aug. *GCH.* .... 17 F.	Medal	Java	Major-General
₿ ✠ White, Lieut.-Col. *Wm. Grove*, *CB.*......late of 94 F.	Medal and 1 Clasp	Vittoria, Pyrenees	Commanding 48 F.
₿ ✠ Wilkins, Lieut.-Col. *Geo. CB. KH.* late of Rifle Brig.	Medal	Salamanca	Major 95 F.
₿ Wilkinson, Lieut.-Col. *William* .... 49 F.	do	Nive	
₿ Williams, Col. *Sir* Edm. Keynton, *KCB.* .... 9 F.	Cross and 1 Clasp	Busaco, Salamanca, Vittoria, St. Sebastian, Nive	4 Caçadores
₿ ✠ Wilson, Lieut.-Col *Geo. Davis*, *CB.* late Port. Serv.	Medal	Badajoz	Brigad.-Gen. Portuguese
₿ Wilson, Lieut.-Gen. *Sir* John, *KCB.* .... 82 F.	do	St. Sebastian	{ Detachment 48 F. { A Light Battalion
₿ Wilson, Maj.-Gen. *Sir* James, *KCB.*..............	Cross and 1 Clasp	Albuhera, Badajoz, Salamanca, Vittoria, Toulouse	
₿ Woodford, Lieut.-Gen. *Sir* Alex. *KCB. GCMG.* ..	Medal and 2 Casps	Salamanca, Vittoria, Nive	Assistant-Qua.-Mast.-Gen.
₿ ✠ Woodford, Maj.-Gen. *Sir* John Geo. *KCB. KCH.* from Gren. Gds. ... late of 60 F.	Cross	Nivelle, Nive, Orthes, Toulouse	
₿ *Woodgate*, Col. *William*, *CB.*	Medal	Fuentes d'Onor	
₿ Yale, Lieut.-Col. William Parry .... Unatt.	do	Albuhera	
₿ Zuhlcke, Col. Geo. Henry, *CB.* ..... h. p. Port. Serv.	Medal and 2 Clasps	Vittoria, Pyrenees, Orthes	2 Caçadores

OFFICERS

NOW HOLDING RANK IN THE ARMY

OF THE

MOST NOBLE ORDER OF

ST. GEORGE, OR THE GARTER.

(According to the Dates of Appointment.)

KNIGHTS. (KG.)

Field Marshal *His Majesty the King of Hanover, KP. GCB.*
Field Marshal *His Royal Highness A. F. Duke of Cambridge, GCB. GCMG. GCH.*............Colds. Gds.
Field Marshal *His Majesty the King of the* Belgians, *GCB. GCH.*
Field Marshal 👑 Arthur, *Duke of Wellington, GCB. GCH.*.....Gren. Gds.

General 👑 H. *Marq. of* Anglesey, *GCB. GCH.*..............7 Hussars.
👑 Charles, *Duke of* Richmond, Aide-de-Camp to the Queen.
Colonel *His Royal Highness Prince* George W. F. C. of Cambridge.
His Royal Highness Francis Albert Augustus Charles Emanuel, *Duke of* Saxe, *Prince of* Saxe Cobourg and Gotha.

OFFICERS

NOW HOLDING RANK IN THE ARMY

OF THE

MOST ANCIENT AND NOBLE ORDER OF THE THISTLE.

KNIGHTS. (KT.)

General, William, *Earl* Cathcart 2 Life Gds.
Major-General, George, *Marquess of* Tweeddale, *CB.*

George, *Marquess of* Huntly
Aide-de-Camp to the Queen.
Lieutenant, William George, *Earl of* Errol, *GCH.*...........................h. p.

OFFICERS

NOW HOLDING RANK IN THE ARMY

OF THE

MOST ILLUSTRIOUS ORDER OF ST. PATRICK.

KNIGHTS. (KP.)

Field Marshal, *His Majesty the King of* Hanover, *KG. GCB.*
General, Edmund, *Earl of* Cork

James, *Marquess of* Thomond, Aide-de-Camp to the Queen.
Major Fra. N., *Marquess of* Conyngham, *GCH.*.......................Unatt.
Captain, John, *Earl of* Donoughmore..h.p.

OFFICERS

NOW HOLDING RANK IN THE ARMY

OF THE

MOST HONOURABLE ORDER OF THE BATH

KNIGHTS GRAND CROSSES. (GCB.)

Field Marshal *His Majesty the King of* Hanover, *KG. KP.*
Field Marshal *His Royal Highness the Duke of* Cambridge, *KG. GCMG. GCH.* Coldstream Gds. 60 F.
His Majesty the King of the Belgians, *KG.* and *GCH.*

⚔ Alten, Maj.-Gen. C. *Count, GCH.* (*Honorary*) ....late Ger. Leg.
⚔ Anglesey, Gen. H. *Mar. of, KG. GCH.* 7 Dr.
Anson, Gen. *Sir* George ....4 Dr. Gds.
Aylmer, Lt.-Gen. M. *Lord* ....18 F.
Beresford, Gen. W. Carr, *Visc. GCH.* 16 F.
Bloomfield, Lt. Gen. B. *Lord, GCH. (Civil)* R. Art.
Bradford, Lt.-Gen. *Sir* T. *GCH.* ....30 F.
Brisbane, Lt.-Gen. *Sir* T. M. *Bt. GCH.* 34 F.
Campbell, Lt.-Gen. *Sir* Arch. *Bt.* ....77 F.
Clinton, Gen. *Sir* William H. ....55 F.
Cockburn, *Rt. Hon. Sir* G. M.-Gen. R. Mar.
Cole, Gen. *Hon. Sir* Galb. Lowry ....27 F.
⚔ Colville, Gen. *Hon. Sir* Chas. *GCH.* 5 F.
Combermere, Gen. Staple. *Visc. GCH.* 1 L.G.
Cotton, M.-Gen. *Sir* Willoughby, *KCH.* 98 F.
⚔ Dickson, Maj.-Gen. *Sir* A. *KCH.* R. Art.
Doveton, Lt.-Gen. *Sir* J. ......E. I. C. Ser.
Drummond, Gen. *Sir* Gordon ....49 F.
Effingham, Gen. K. A. *Earl of* ....3 F.
Fane, Gen. *Sir* Henry ....1 Dr. Gds.
Ferguson, Gen. *Sir* Ronald Craufurd...79 F.
Gordon, Lt.-Gen. *Sir* James Willoughby, *Bt. GCH.* ....23 F.
Grey, Gen. *Hon. Sir* Hen. Geo. *GCH.* 13 Dr.
Hewett, Gen. *Rt. Hon. Sir* George, *Bt.* 61 F.

⚔ Hill, Gen. Rowland, *Lord, GCH.* and *KC...* R. Horse Gds. Gen. Comm.-in-Chief.
Hislop, Gen. *Sir* Thomas, *Bt.* ....48 F.
Houstoun, Gen. *Sir* Wm. *Bt. GCH...* 20 F.
Keane, Lt.-Gen. John, *Lord, GCH.* ..43 F.
⚔ Kempt, Lt.-Gen. *Rt. Hon. Sir* James, *GCH.* ....2 F.
⚔ Lambert, Lt.-Gen. *Sir* John ....10 F.
Londonderry, Gen. C. W. *Marq. of, GCH.* 10 Dr.
Ludlow, Gen. G. J. *Earl* ....Sco. Fus. Gds.
Lumley, Gen. *Hon. Sir* William ......6 Dr.
Lushington, Maj.-Gen. *Sir* J. L. E. I. C. Ser.
Lynedoch, Gen. Thomas, *Lord, GCMG.* 1 F.
Murray, Lt.-Gen. *Rt. Hon. Sir* G. *GCH.* 42 F.
Nugent, Gen. *Rt. Hon. Sir* Geo. *Bt.* ....6 F.
O'Callaghan, Lt.-Gen. *Hon. Sir* R. W. 39 F.
⚔ Orange, Gen. *H. R. H. W. F. H. the Hereditary Prince of*
Oswald, Gen. *Sir* John, *GCMG.* .....35 F.
Paget, Gen. *Hon. Sir* Edward........28 F.
Pringle, Lt.-Gen. *Sir* Wm. Henry ....45 F.
Robinson, Lt.-Gen. *Sir* F. P. ....59 F.
Russell, Col. *Lord* Geo. Wm. (*Civil*) Unatt.
⚔ Seaton, Lt.-Gen. John, *Lord, GCH.* 26 F.
Smith, *Sir* Wm. Sidney, Lt.-Gen. of R. Mar.
⚔ Somerset, Lt.-Gen. *Lord,* R. E. H. 4 Dr.
⚔ Strafford, Lt.-Gen. Jn. *Lord, GCH.* 29 F.
⚔ Vandeleur, Gen. *Sir* John O ......16 Dr.
⚔ Vivian, Lt.-Gen. *Rt. Hon. Sir* R. H. *Bt. GCH.* ....1 Dr.
Walker, Gen. *Sir* Geo. Townsend, *Bt.* 50 F.
⚔ Wellington, Field Marshal Arthur, *Duke of, KG. GCH.* Gren. Gds., Rifle Brig., Constable of the Tower of London, and Lord Warden of the Cinque Ports.
Worsley, M.-Gen. *Sir* Hen. .....E. I. C. Ser.

KNIGHTS COMMANDERS. (KCB.)

⚔ Adam, Lt.-Gen. *Rt. Hon. Sir* Frederick, *GCMG* ....57 F.
Anburey, Maj.-Gen. *Sir* Thos...E. I. C. Ser.
Anson, Gen. *Sir* William, *Bt.* ....47 F.
Arbuthnot, Lt.-Gen. *Sir* Thomas ....52 F.
Arbuthnot, Maj.-Gen. *Sir* Robert
Barnard, Lt.-Gen. *Sir* Andr. *GCH.* Rifle Br.
Barns, Lt.-Gen. *Sir* Jas. Stevenson, ...do.
Bathurst, Lt.-Gen. *Sir* Jas. Gov. of Berwick
⚔ Berkeley, Maj.-Gen. *Sir* G.H.F.

Blakeney, Lt.-Gen. *Rt. Hon. Sir* Edw. *GCH.* ....7 F.
Bourke, Lt.-Gen. *Sir* Richard ....64 F.
Bouverie, Lt.-Gen. *Sir* Henry F. *GCMG.*
Brooke, Lt.-Gen. *Sir* Arthur ....86 F.
Buchan, Maj.-Gen. *Sir* John ....95 F.
Bunbury, Lt.-Gen. *Sir* Henry Edward, *Bt.*
Burghersh, Lt.-Gen. J. *Lord, GCH.*
Burgoyne, Maj.-Gen. *Sir* J. F.
Caldwell, M. Gen. *Sir* J. L.....E. I. C. Ser.

Most Honourable Order of the Bath.

KNIGHTS COMMANDERS.—*Continued.*

Ⓚ Cameron, Maj.-Gen. *Sir* Alex.
Cameron, Lt.-Gen. *Sir* John .... 9 F.
Campbell, Gen. *Sir* Henry F. *GCH.* 25 F.
Ⓚ Campbell, Lt.-Gen. *Sir* Colin .... 72 F.
Carncross, Maj.-Gen. *Sir* Jos. Hugh, R. Art.
Casement, Maj.-Gen. *Sir* W..... E. I. C. Ser.
Ⓚ Clifton, Maj.-Gen. *Sir* Ar. B. *KCH.* 17 Dr.
Corsellis, Maj.-Gen. *Sir* Thos... E. I. C. Ser.
Deacon, Maj -Gen. *Sir* Chas. .. E. I. C. Ser.
Ⓚ Dick, Maj.-Gen. *Sir* R. H. *KCH.*
Dickson, Maj. Gen. *Sir* Jeremiah
Disney, Gen. *Sir* Moore ....15 F.
Donkin, Gen. *Sir* Rufane S. *GCH.* .. 11 F.
Douglas, Maj.-Gen. *Sir* James
Douglas, Maj.-Gen. *Sir* Neil, *KCH.*
Doveton, Maj.-Gen. *Sir* John .. E. I. C. Ser.
Downes, Maj.-Gen. *Sir* Ulysses, *Lord*
Doyle, Col. *Sir* J. M.
Dundas, Maj.-Gen. *Hon. Sir* R. L.
D'Urban, Lt.-Gen. *Sir* Benj. *KCH.* .. 51 F.
Ⓚ Evans, Col. *Sir* De Lacy
Fitz Gerald, Maj.-Gen. *Sir* J. F.
Foulis, M.-Gen. *Sir* David ...... E I. C. Ser.
Fraser, Maj.-Gen. *Sir* Hugh........ do.
Gardiner, M.-Gen. *Sir* John, Dep. Ad. Gen.
Gardiner, Col. *Sir* Robert, *KCH.* .. R. Art.
Gibbs, Maj.-Gen. *Sir* Edward
Gilmour, Maj.-Gen. *Sir* D. L.
Ⓚ Gomm, Maj.-Gen. *Sir* Wm. M.
Gough, Maj.-Gen *Sir* Hugh .... 99 F.
Grant, Lt.-Gen. *Sir* Wm. Keir, *GCH.* 2 Dr.
Ⓚ Greenock, Maj.-Gen. *Lord*
Greenwell, M.-Gen. *Sir* Leonard, *KCH.*
Guise, Lt.-Gen. *Sir* John Wright, *Bt.*
Ⓚ Halkett, Lt.-Gen. *Sir* Colin, *GCH.* 31 F.
Ⓚ Hardinge, Maj.-Gen. *Rt. Hon. Sir* Henry 97 F.
Harvey, Maj.-Gen. *Sir* John, *KCH.*
Hope, Col. *Sir* James A............Unatt.
Houstoun, Maj.-Gen. *Sir* Rob... E. I. C. Ser.
Jackson, Lt.-Gen. *Sir* Rich. Downes .. 81 F.
Johnston, Lt.-Gen. *Sir* William ...... 68 F.
Jones, Maj.-Gen. *Sir* J. T. *Bt.*
Keating, Lt.-Gen. *Sir* Henry Sheehy .. 90 F.
Leighton, Maj.-Gen. *Sir* David .. E. I. C. Ser.
Leigh, Maj.-Gen. *Sir* Alexander
Lowe, Lt.-Gen. *Sir* Hudson, *GCMG.* 56 F.
Ⓚ Lyon, Lt.-Gen. *Sir* James, *GCH.* 24 F.

Macbean, Maj.-Gen. *Sir* Wm.
M'Mahon, Lt.-Gen. *Sir* Thomas, *Bt.* ... 94 F.
Macdonald, Lt.-Gen. *Sir* John ...... 67 F.
Ⓚ Macdonell, Maj.-Gen. *Sir* Jas. *KCH.*
Macfarlane, Gen. *Sir* Robert, *GCH.* ... 32 F.
MacGregor, M.-Gen. *Sir* E. J. M. *Bt. KCH.*
M'Lean, Lt.-Gen. *Sir* Hec. ..... E. I. C. Ser.
Maclean, Lt.-Gen. *Sir* John..........60 F.
Macleod, Maj.-Gen *Sir* Don. .. E. I. C. Ser.
Maitland, Lt.-Gen. *Sir* Peregrine .... 76 F.
Malcolm, Lt.-Col. *Sir* James, late R. Mar.
Manners, Lt.-Gen. *Lord* Cha. S....... 3 Dr.
Ⓚ May, M.-Gen. *Sir* John, *KCH.* from R. Ar.
Napier, M.-Gen. *Sir* Cha. Jas.
—— M.-Gen. *Sir* Geo. Tho.
Nicolls, Lt.-Gen. *Sir* Jasper .... 93 F.
O'Halloran, Maj.-Gen. *Sir* J. .. E. I. C. Ser.
Pakenham, Maj.-Gen. *Hon. Sir* H. R.
Pilkington, Maj.-Gen. *Sir* Andrew
Reynell, Lt.-Gen. *Sir* Thomas, *Bt.* .. 87 F.
Richards, M.-Gen. *Sir* Wm. .. E. I. C. Ser.
Rose, M.-Gen. *Sir* John .... do.
Ⓚ Ross, Col. *Sir* Hew D..........R. Art.
Russell, M.-Gen. *Sir* Jas. ...... E. I. C. Ser.
Sale, Col. *Sir* Robert H. .... 13 F.
Savage, M.-Gen. *Sir* John Boscawen, *KCH.*
Scott, M.-Gen. *Sir* Hopt. S. ..... E. I. C. Ser.
Ⓚ Scovell, Maj.-Gen. *Sir* George, Gov. of the R. Mil. College.
Smith, Lt.-Gen. *Sir* Lionel, *Bt. GCH.* 40 F.
Ⓚ Somerset. Lt.-Gen. *Lord* Fitz Roy 53 F.
Stovin, Col. *Sir* Frederick, *KCMG*...Unatt.
Taylor, Lt.-Gen. *Sir* John .... 80 F.
Ⓚ Thackwell, Col. *Sir* Joseph, *KH.*..3 Dr.
Thornton, Lt.-Gen. *Sir* Wm. .... 85 F.
Ⓚ Vere, Maj.-Gen. *Sir* Cha. Broke
Wale, Gen. *Sir* Charles............... 33 F.
Wallace, Lt.-Gen. *Sir* J. A............88 F.
Waters, Maj.-Gen. *Sir* John.Capt. Yarm.Cast.
Watson, Lt.-Gen. *Sir* Jas..............14 F.
Whitehead, M.-Gen. *Sir* Tho. .. E. I. C. Ser.
Whittingham, Lt.-Gen. *Sir* S. F. *KCH.* 71 F.
Williams, Col. *Sir* E. K................9 F.
Willshire, Col. *Sir* Thomas............2 F.
Ⓚ Wilson, Lt.-Gen. *Sir* J............82 F.
Wilson, M.-Gen. *Sir* James
Woodford, Lt.-Gen. *Sir* Alex. *GCMG.*
Ⓚ Woodford, M.-Gen. *Sir* J. G. *KCH.*

COMPANIONS. (CB.)

Ⓚ Abercromby, Col. *Hon.* Alex.
A'Court, Col. C. Ashe, *KH.*
Adair, Col. Thomas .... R. Mar.
Agnew, Lt -Col. Pat. Vans, late of E.I.C. Ser.
Auchmuty, Col. Sam. B.
Alen, Lt.-Col. Luke
Allan, Col. Jas. .... 57 F.
Anderson, Lt.-Gen. Paul ....78 F.
Anderson, Col. *Sir* Alex. ....Unatt.
Andrews, M.-Gen. Aug........E. I. C. Ser.
Arbuthnott, Maj.-Gen. *Hon.* Hugh
Arentsschildt, Maj. *Sir* V. von, *KCH.*

Ⓚ Arguimbau, Col. Lawrence
Armstrong, Col. *Sir* Richard ....Unatt.
Ⓚ Askew, Lt.-Gen. *Sir* Hen.
Baddeley, M.-Gen. W. C. ...... E. I. C. Ser.
Ⓚ Bailey, Lt.-Col. M. W.
Bainbrigge, Col. Philip, Assist. Qua. Mast.Gen.
Balvaird, Col. William .... Unatt.
Ⓚ Baring, Lt.-Col. G. *Baron* von, *KCH.*
Basden, Lt.-Col. James Lewis ....89 F.
Battersby, Lt.-Col. Fra. ....late Unatt.
Battine, Col. William..........E. I. C. Ser.
Ⓚ Beckwith, Col. Charles

Most Honourable Order of the Bath.

COMPANIONS—(C.B.)—*Continued.*

Bell, Col. John
Bell, Lt. Col. Thomas............... 48 F.
Birch, Maj.-Gen. John Francis
Bisshopp, Lt.-Col. Cecil .... 11 F.
Blair, Col. Thomas Hunter .... Unatt.
Blake, Col. Wm. Williams
Blanshard, Lt.-Col. Tho. .... R. Eng.
Bosset, Col. C. P. de, *KH.*
Bowen, M.-Gen. Herbert ...... E. I. C. Ser.
Bowyer, Lt.-Col. C............. late of do.
Brandreth, Lt.-Col. Thomas A. ... R. Art.
🎖 Brereton, Lt.-Col. Wm. *KH.* .. R. Art.
🎖 Bridger, Lt.-Col. J. P.
Brotherton, Col. T. W. .... 16 Dr.
Brown, Col. George, *K.H.* .... Rif. Br.
Brown, Lt.-Col. Gust.
Browne, Col. John F.
🎖 Browne, Col. Fielding
🎖 Bulow, Lt.-Col. J., *Baron*
Bryant, Col. *Sir* Jer. .... E. I. C. Ser.
Butterworth, Major W. J............do.
🎖 Calvert, Col Felix.............. Unatt.
🎖 Cameron, Lt.-Col. Duncan.. late of 79 F.
Cameron, Major John .... E. I. C. Ser.
Campbell, Major *Sir* Edw. A. ...... do.
🎖 Campbell, Col. *Sir* Guy, *Bt.* .... Unatt.
Campbell, Col. Archibald .... late of 46 F.
🎖 Campbell, Col. John.... late of 22 F.
🎖 Campbell, Col. William...... h. p. 23 F.
🎖 Campbell, Lt.-Col. Patrick.. h. p. 52 F.
Campbell, Lt.-Col. Charles Stewart h. p. 1 F.
Carey, Maj.-Gen. *Sir* Octavius, *KCH.*
Carrol, Maj.-Gen. *Sir* W. P. *KCH.*
Caulfield, Col. James .. late of E, I. C. Serv.
🎖 Chalmers, Col. Wm. *KH.*
Chapman, M.-Gen. *Sir* S. R. *KCH.* R.Eng.
Cheape, Lt.-Col. John........... E. I. C. Ser.
🎖 Cheney, Col. E.
🎖 Childers, Col. Michael ...... late Unatt.
Church, Lt.-Col. *Sir* R. *GCH.*
🎖 Churchill, Col. C. H. 31 F. Qua.-Mast.-Gen. E. Ind.
🎖 Clarke, Lt.-Col. Isaac B. .. late of 2 Dr.
Cock, Lt.-Col. Henry .... E. I. C. Ser.
Colvin, Lt.-Col. John.............. do.
Conyers, Col. Cha. Edw.
🎖 Cooke, Lt.-Col. R.H.
Cother, Lt.-Col. Charles
Couper, Col. Geo. *KH.*.............. Unat.
Cowell, Lt.-Col. William
Creagh, Col. Andrew
Croker, Lt.-Col. William .... 17 F.
Crosdill, Lt.-Col. J. .... late of E. I. C. Ser.
Cross, Col. William .... Unatt.
Cunliffe, M. Gen. *Sir* R. H. *Bt.* E. I. C. Ser.
D'Aguilar, Col. Geo. C. Unatt. Dep. Adj.-Gen. in Irel.
🎖 Dalmer, M. Gen. Thomas
🎖 Damer, Lt.-Col. *Hon.* Geo. Lionel D.
🎖 Dansey, Lt.-Col. Cha. Cornw. .. R. Art.
Davy, Maj.-Gen. *Sir* W. Gabriel, *KCH.*
Dawes, Col. Thomas H.
De la Motte, M. Gen. Peter.... E. I. C. Ser.
Dennie, Lt.-Col. William H. .... 13 F.

Dickson, M. Gen. William .... E. I. C. Ser.
🎖 Dorville, Lt.-Col. Philip........ Unatt.
Douglas, Lt.-Gen. *Sir* Howard, *Bt. GCMG.*
🎖 Douglas, Lt.-Col. Robert.. late of R.Art.
Downman, Maj.-Gen. *Sir* Thomas, *KCH.*
Doyle, Lt.-Gen. *Sir* C. W. *GCH.*
🎖 Drummond, Maj.-Gen. Percy
Duffy, Col. John .... Unatt.
Dundas, Lt.-Col. *Hon.* Henry........ 83 F.
Dundas, Lt.-Col. Wm. Bolden ...... R. Art.
🎖 Dyncley, Lt.-Col. Tho........... do.
Eden, Lt.-Col. John, Unatt. Dep. Adj.-Gen. in Canada
🎖 Egerton, Col. Rich............ Unatt.
Ellicombe, Col. Charles Grene...... R. Eng.
Elphinstone, Maj.-Gen. *Sir* Howard, *Bt.*
🎖 Elphinstone, Maj.-Gen. Wm. Keith
Elrington, Col. Richard Goodall ...... 47 F.
Erskine, Col. William Howe Knight
Eustace, Maj.-Gen. William C. *KCH.*
Evans, M. Gen. Thomas
Evans, Col. R. L. .... late of E. I. C. Ser.
Everard, Lt.-Col. Mathias, *KH.*...... 14 F.
Ewart, Col. John Fred.
Fagan, Col. C. S. .... E. I. C. Ser.
Fair, Maj.-Gen. A............... do.
Fanshawe, Col. Edward .... R. Eng.
Faunce, Col. A. D.
🎖 Fead, Lt.-Col. George
Fearon, Col. Robert Bryce .... 6 F.
Fergusson, Col. Jas. .... h. p.
Finch, Col. *Hon.* John .... Unatt.
Fitzgerald, Lt.-Col. Cha. late of E. I. C. Ser.
Fleming, Col. Edw. .. Insp. Fd. Off. Rec. Dist.
Forbes, Col. David
Fraser, Lt.-Gen. Hastings............ 83 F.
Frederick, M. Gen. Edward.... E. I. C. Ser.
Freke, Col. Henry
🎖 Fremantle, Col. J. .... Unatt.
🎖 Fuller, Lt.-Col. Francis.... late of 59 F.
Fyers, Maj.-Gen. Peter
Gabriel, Colonel Robert Burd, *KH.*
Galiffe, Lt.-Col. John
Galloway, Col. Arch........... E. I. C. Ser.
Godwin, Col. Henry
🎖 Gold, Col. Charles
Goldfinch, Col. Henry .... R. Eng.
Goldie, Col. Geo. Leigh .... 11 F.
🎖 Goodman, Col. Stephen Arth. *KH.*
Gordon, Col. William Alex.
🎖 Gore, Col. *Hon.* Cha. *KH.* Unatt. Dep. Quart.-Mast.-Gen. in Canada
Gore, Maj. Henry Ross
Gosset, Col. *Sir* Wm. *KCH.* .... R. Eng.
Graham, Lt.-Col. Charles .... E. I. C. Serv.
🎖 Grant, Col. Jas. Gov. of Scarboro' Castle
Greenhill, Maj.-Gen. James D... E. I. C. Ser.
Grey, M. Gen. John
🎖 Gurwood, Lt.-Col. John .... Unatt.
🎖 Halkett, Lt.-Col. Hugh, *KCH.*
Hall, Lt.-Col. Henry .... E. I. C. Ser.
🎖 Hamerton, Maj.-Gen. J. M.
Hamilton, M.-Gen. Christopher
Harding, Col. Geo. Judd .... R. Eng.

Most Honourable Order of the Bath.

COMPANIONS—(CB.)—Continued.

Hare, Col. Richard Goddard ....Unat.
🎖 Hare, Col. John, *KH.* ....27 F.
🎖 Harris, Lt.-Gen. W. G. *Lord, KCH.* 73 F.
Harrison, Lt.-Col. John Bacon
Harvey, Col. *Sir* Rob. John
Hawkins, Lt.-Col. John P.
🎖 Hay, Col. James ....Unatt.
Herbert, Lt.-Col. Charles......E. I. C. Ser.
Herford, Lt.-Col. Wm. L.
Heriot, Col. F. G.
Herries, Col. *Sir* Wm. L. *KCH.*.....Unatt.
🎖 Hill, Col. *Sir* R. C.
Hill, Col. *Sir* D. St. Leger ....Unatt.
Holcombe, Lt.-Col. Har. Fort.
Holloway, Lt.-Col. W. C. E. ......R. Eng.
Home, Col. Robert ....E. I. C. Ser.
Hopkinson, Lt.-Col. *Sir* C...late of do.
🎖 Hoste, Col. *Sir* Geo. Cha. ....R. Eng.
Hughes, Col. James
Hughes, Lt.-Col. Samuel......E. I. C. Ser.
Hull, M.-Gen. William ....do.
Hunt, Lt.-Col. J. P.
Hunter, Col. George....late of E. I. C. Ser.
Innes, Col. William ....E. I. C. Ser.
Irvine, Maj. Arch......late of E. I. C. Ser.
🎖 Jessopp, Major John......late of 22 F.
Johnson, Lt.-Col. John..late of E. I. C. Ser.
Johnstone, M.-Gen. F. J. T. ..E. I. C. Ser.
Kenah, Col. Thomas
🎖 Kennedy, Lt.-Col. Alex. Kennedy Clark, *KH.* 7 Dr. Gds.
Kennedy, Col. James ....E. I. C. Ser.
🎖 Kennedy, Col. Jas. Shaw ......Unatt.
🎖 Kerrison, Lt.-Gen. *Sir* Edw. *Bt. GCH.* 14 Dr.
King, Maj.-Gen. *Sir* Henry, *KCH.*
🎖 Krauchenberg, Lt.-Col. G. *Baron* von, *KCH.*
🎖 Lautour, Col. P. A. *KH.*
Lawrence, Col. Elias..............R. Mar.
🎖 Leach, Lt.-Col. Jonathan
L'Estrange, Maj.-Gen. G. G. C.
Lewis, Col. George ....late of R. Mar.
Lewis, Col. Geo. Griffith ....R. Eng.
Lightfoot, Col. T.
Lillie, Lt.-Col. *Sir* John Scott
Limond, M.-Gen. *Sir* James ..E. I. C. Ser.
Lindsay, M.-Gen, Alex. ....do.
Lindsay, Col. Martin
Lisle, Lt.-Col. Robert
🎖 Lluellyn, Col. Richard
🎖 Love, Col. Jas. Fred. *KH.* ......73 F.
Low, Lt.-Col. John ....E. I. C. Ser.
Lumsden, Maj. Tho...............do.
🎖 Lygon, Maj.-Gen. *Hon.* E. P.
M'Donald, Col. John................92 F.
M'Douall, Col. Robert
M'Nair, Lt.-Gen. John
🎖 Macdonald, Maj.-Gen. Alex.
🎖 Macdonald, Col. Alex. ....R. Art.
🎖 Macdonald, Lt.-Col. Ranald, *KH.* 4 F. Dep. Adj.-Gen. Bombay
🎖 Macdonald, Lt.-Col. Robt. late of 35 F.

Macdonald, Lt.-Col. Robt. ....late of R. Art.
Macdonell, Lt.-Col. George
Maclaine, Col. *Sir* Arch. ....Unatt.
Macleod, Lt.-Gen. *Sir* John, *KCH.* .. 77 F.
Macleod, M.-Gen. Cha. ......E. I. C. Ser.
Macleod, Lt.-Col. George Francis
Macpherson, Col. R. Barclay, *KH.*
Manners, Lt.-Col. Russell
Mansel, Lt.-Col. John
Manson, Lt.-Col. Alex.........E. I. C. Ser.
Maxwell, Maj.-Gen. *Sir* Cha. Wm. *KCH.*
Mayne, Maj.-Gen. John ......E. I. C. Ser.
Meade, Lt.-Gen. *Hon.* John
🎖 Mercer, Col. Douglas ....Unatt.
Michell, Lt.-Col. Edw. T............R. Art
Michell, Lt.-Col. John .... do.
Middlemore, M.-Gen. Geo.
Miles, Col. *Sir* Edward
🎖 Miller, Lt.-Col. F. S.
🎖 Miller, Col. George............Unatt.
Milnes, Lt.-Col. Colin J.
🎖 Mitchell, Lt.-Col. Jas. ....late of 92 F.
🎖 Money, Col. Arch.
Monteath, Lt.-Col. Thomas ....E.I.C.Serv.
Montgomerie, Maj. P. .... E.I.C.Serv.
Morgan, Lt.-Col. John .... do.
Morison, Col. William .... late of do.
🎖 Murray, M. Gen. *Hon.* Henry
🎖 Muttlebury, Lt.-Col. George
Napier, Col. Thos. E.
Napier, Col. W. F. P.
Nicol, M. Gen. Charles
🎖 Nicolay, Lt.-Gen. *Sir* W. *KCH.* 1W.I.Reg.
O'Donnell, Lt.-Col. H. A. late of E.I.C.Serv.
O'Donoghue, Lt.-Col. J. W.
Ogilvie, Col. James ....Unatt.
Oglander, Col. Henry ....26 F.
🎖 O'Malley, Col. George..........Unatt.
Orchard, Lt.-Col. Joseph ......E.I.C.Serv.
O'Reilly, Lt.-Col. Walter F.
Oswald, Lt.-Col. Robert
Otway, Lt.-Gen. *Sir* Loftus Wm.
Owen, Col. John, *KH.* Dep. Adj. Gen. R. Mar.
Parke, Col. Thos. Adams.......... do.
🎖 Parker, Col. John Boteler ......R. Art.
🎖 Parkinson, Col. Edward
Parlby, M. Gen. B. B. ........E.I.C.Serv.
Pasley, Col. Charles William ......R. Eng.
Patrickson, Col. C. C.
Paty, Col. Geo. Wm. *KH.* ....94 F.
Pearson, Maj.-Gen. *Sir* T. *KCH.*
Pelly, Lt.-Col. Raym.
Persse, Lt.-Col. William.............16 Dr.
Pitman, M.-Gen. Robert........E.I.C.Serv.
Plenderleath, Lt.-Col. Charles
Pollock, Maj.-Gen. Geo..........E.I.C.Serv.
Pollok, Maj.-Gen. Thos......... do.
Pottinger, Lieut. Eldred........ do.
Power, Col. William G..............R. Art.
Proctor, Col. Hen. Adolphus
Purton, Major John ..........E.I.C.Serv.
Pym, Col. Robert ....R.Art.
Pynn, Lt.-Col. *Sir* Henry
🎖 Quentin, Lt.-Gen. *Sir* Geo. Aug. *KCH.*

Most Honourable Order of the Bath.

COMPANIONS—(C.B.)—Continued.

Rainey, Col. Hen. *KH*. . . . . .Unatt.
Reade, Col. *Sir* Thomas
Reeves, Maj.-Gen. Geo. J. *KH*.
Reid, Lt.-Col. Wm. . . . . R. Eng.
🎖 Rice, Col. Samuel, *KH*. . . . . Unatt.
Richards, Maj.-Gen. Alfred . . . . E.I.C.Serv.
Roberts, Lt.-Col. Abraham. . . . . . .   do.
Roberts, Col. H. T. . . . . late of do.
Robertson, Maj.-Gen. Geo. Duncan
Robertson, Lt.-Col. W. von, *KCH*.
Rolt, Col. John . . . . .Unatt.
🎖 Rooke, M.-Gen. *Sir* Hen. W. *KCH*.
Ross, Lt.-Gen. John . . . . 46 F.
🎖 Rowan, Lt.-Col. Charles
🎖 Rowan, Col. William . . . . Unatt.
Russel, Col. Lechmere . . . . E.I.C.Serv.
St. Clair, Col. Thos. Staunton, *KH*. . . Unatt.
Salter, Maj.-Gen. Jas. F. . . . . E.I.C.Serv.
🎖 Saltoun, Maj.-Gen. Alex. *Lord*, *GCH*.
Saluberry, Lt.-Col. C. de, late h.p.Can. Voltig.
Sandwith, Maj.-Gen. Wm. . . . . . . E.I.C.Serv.
Sandwith, Lt.-Col. Bentham . . . . . . do.
Scott, Lt.-Col. John . . . . .4 Dr.
Seton, Col. William Carden
Sewell, Col. Wm. Hen. . . 6 F.Dep.Qua.Mast.
 Gen. E. Indies
Skinner, Col. James . . . . E.I.C.Serv.
🎖 Sleigh, Maj.-Gen. J. W. . . . . 9 Dr.
Smelt, Col. William . . . . 37 F.
🎖 Smith, Col. Henry Geo. . . . . .Unatt.
Smith, Col. *Sir* C. F. . . . . .R. Eng.
🎖 Smith, Col. J. W. . . . . .R. Art.
Smith, Lt.-Col. Robert . . late of E. I. C.Serv.
Smyth, Lt.-Col. C. M. Carmichael, E.I.C.Serv.
Snodgrass, Col. Kenneth . . . . Unatt.
Stalker, Lt.-Col. Foster . . . . E.I.C.Serv.
Stanhope, Maj.-Gen. *Hon.* Lincoln
Stanhope, Col. *Hon.* Leicester . . . . . .Unatt.
Stannus, M.-Gen.*Sir* Ephraim G., E.I.C.Serv.
🎖 Staveley, Col. William . . . . .Unatt.
Steel, Lt.-Col. S. W. . . . . .E.I C.Serv.
Stevenson, Lt.-Col. Thomas. . . .   do.
🎖 Straton, Lt.-Gen. *Sir* Jos., *KCH*. 8 Dr.
🎖 Stretton, Col. Sempronius
Sullivan, Col. Henry . . . . .6 F.
Taylor, M.-Gen. H. G. A. . . . . . . E.I.C.Serv.
Taylor, Lt.-Col. Cha. Cyril . . . . . . Part.Serv.

🎖 Taylor, Col. T. W. Lt. Gov. R. Mil. Coll.
Thackeray, M.-Gen. Fred. Rennell
Thomas, Col. Henry . . . . .20 F.
Thomson, Col. Alexander
Thomson, Capt. Geo. . . . . E.I.C.Serv.
Thorn, Col. Nathaniel, *KH*.Ass.Qua.Ma,Gen.
Thornhill, Lt.-Col. George
Thornton, Col. Henry
Tickell, Col. Richard . . . . E.I.C.Serv.
Timbrell, Major Thos. . . . .   do.
Tonson, Col. Jacob
🎖 Torrens, Col. Robert. .A. G. in East Ind.
Trevor, Lt.-Gen. *Hon.* Henry Otway
Tulloch, Lt.-Col. Alex. . . . . E.I.C.Serv.
Turner, Col. George . . . . R. Art.
Tweeddale, M.-Gen. Geo. *Marq. of*, *KT*.
Upton, Lt.-Gen. *Hon.* A. P.
Vernon, Col. Hen. C. E. . . . . .Unatt.
🎖 Vigoureux, Col. C. A. . . . . h. p.
Viney, Maj.-Gen. *Sir* James, *KCH*.
Wade, Lt.-Col. *Sir* C.M. . . . . . . E.I.C.Serv.
Wade, Col. Tho. Fra. . . . . .Unatt.
Wahab, Col. James . . . . . late of E.I.C.Serv.
🎖 Walker, Lt.-Col. Leslie, *KH*.
Ward, Col. John Rich.
Warre, Col. *Sir* William . . . . .Unatt.
Waters, Col. Edmund E. . . . . . . E.I.C.Serv.
Watson, M.-Gen. *Sir* Henry
Watson, Lt.-Col. W. L. . . . . late of E.I.C.Serv.
Way, Maj.-Gen. *Sir* G. H. B.
Wells, Lt.-Col. John Neave . . . . R. Eng.
Wemyss, Col. Thos. Jas.
Wetherall, Col. Geo. Aug. *KH*. . . . . .1 F.
Wheeler, Lt.-Col. Hugh M. . . . . E.I.C.Serv.
Whinyates, Lt. Col. Edward C. *KH*. . R.Art.
Whish, Col. William S. . . . . E.I.C.Serv.
White, Lt.-Col. Wm. Grove
🎖 Wilkins, Lt.-Col. George, *KH*.
Williamson, Lt.-Col. William . .E.I.C.Serv.
Wilson, Col. *Sir* J.M. *KH*.Adj. to Chel. Hosp.
Wilson, M.-Gen. Thomas . . . . . .E.I.C.Serv.
Wilson, M.-Gen Francis W. . . . .   do.
Wilson, Lt.-Col. G. D.
Wood, Col. William, *KH*.
Woodgate, Col. William
Wynyard, Col. Edward . . . . .Unatt.
Zuhlcke, Col. Geo. Hen.

OFFICERS OF THE ORDER.

Dean—John Ireland, Dean of Westminster.
Genealogist—Walter Aston Blount, Esq. *Chester Herald*.
Bath King of Arms—Algernon Greville, Esq.
Registrar and Secretary—Captain Michael Seymour, R. N.
Deputy—Sir William Woods, *KH. Garter King of Arms*.
Gentleman Usher—George Frederick Beltz, Esq. *KH. Lancaster Herald*.
Messenger—James Pulman, Esq. *Richmond Herald*.
Officer of Arms Attendant on the } *Sir* William Woods, *KH. Garter King*
  Second and Third Classes.   }   *of Arms*.
Secretary to Second and Third Classes.—*Sir* Harris Nicolas, *KCMG. KH.*

OFFICERS
NOW HOLDING RANK IN THE ARMY
OF
THE MOST DISTINGUISHED ORDER
OF
SAINT MICHAEL AND SAINT GEORGE.

GRAND MASTER.

Field Marshal *His Royal Highness* Aug. F. *Duke of Cambridge, KG. GCB. GCH.*

KNIGHTS GRAND CROSSES. (GCMG.)
Field Marshal *H.R.H.* Aug. F. *Duke of Cambridge, KG. GCB. GCH.* Coldst. Guards, and 60th Foot.
Lt.-Gen. *Sir* Howard Douglas, *Bt. CB.*
❦ Lt..Gen. *Rt. Hon. Sir* Frederick Adam, *KCB.* 57 F.
❦ Lt.-Gen. *Sir* Alexander Woodford, *KCB.*
Colonel *Sir* Frederick Hankey.
Lt.-Gen. *Sir* Hen. Frederick Bouverie, *KCB.*
Gen. *Sir* Henry Pigot, 38 F.
Gen. Thomas *Lord* Lynedoch, *GCB.* 1 F.
Lt.-Gen. *Sir* C. Bulkeley Egerton, *KCH.* 89 F.
Lt.-Gen. *Sir* Hudson Lowe, *KCB.* 56 F.
Maj.-Gen. *Sir* Patrick Ross, *KCH.*
Gen. *Sir* John Oswald, *GCB.* 35 F.
Gen. *Sir* Martin Hunter, *GCH.*

Gen. *Sir* William Wilkinson.

KNIGHTS COMMANDERS. (KCMG.)
Colonel *Sir* Fredrick Stovin, *KCB.*
Dep. Assistant Com. Gen. Sir Edward Stuart Baynes, h. p.
Maj.-Gen. *Count* F. Rivarola, *KCH.* R.Malta Fen. Reg.

COMPANIONS. (CMG.)
Lt.-Col. Thomas Drake, Unatt.
Major Charles Andrews Bayley, Unatt.
Lt.-Col. *Marq.* Guiseppe de Piro, R. Malta Fen. Reg.
Colonel Henry Balneavis, *KH.* Unatt.
Dep. Com. Gen. James Woodhouse, h. p.
❦ Major John W. Parsons, Unatt.

OFFICERS OF THE ORDER.
Chancellor .... *Sir* Harris Nicolas, *KCMG. KH.*
King of Arms .... *Sir* Charles Douglas, *CMG.*
Registrar at Corfu ....
Chancery of the Order ...∴... The Colonial Department, Downing Street.

OFFICERS
NOW HOLDING RANK IN THE ARMY,
WHO ARE PERMITTED TO WEAR
FOREIGN ORDERS.

The Orders mentioned in this List belong to the following Countries, and the Dates are those of the Institution of the Order:—

Austria—Maria Theresa (3 Classes) 18 June, 1757.
    Leopold (3 Classes) 14 July, 1806.
Bavaria—Maximilian Joseph (3 Clas.) 1 Jan. 1806.
Belgium—Leopold (3 Classes.)
France—Military Merit (3 Classes) Mar.1759.
    Legion of Honour (5 Classes) 13 May 1802.
Greece—Saviour (4 Classes.)
Hanover—Guelphs (3 Classes) 18 June, 1815.
Naples—St. Januarius (1 Class) July, 1738.
    St. Ferdinand and Merit, (3 Clas.) 1 April 1800
    St. George and Reunion (3 Clas.) 1 Jan. 1819.
Netherlands—Wilhelm (4 Clas.) 30 Apr. 1815.
Persia—Lion and Sun (3 Classes) 1801.
Portugal—Tower and Sword (3 Clas.) 17 Apr. 1748.
    St. Bento d'Avis (2 Classes) 1789.

Prussia—Black Eagle—18 Jan. 1701.
    Military Merit—1740.
    Red Eagle (3 Classes) 12 June, 1792.
Russia—St. Andrew—30 Nov. 1698.
    St. Alexander Newski—1722.
    St. Ann (2 Classes) 3 Feb. 1735.
    St. George (4 Classes) 26 Nov. 1769.
    St. Wladimir (5 Classes) 4 Oct. 1782.
Sardinia—St. Maurice and St. Lazarus (2 Classes) 13 Nov. 1572.
Saxony—St. Henry (3 Classes) 7 Oct. 1736.
Spain—Charles the Third (3 Clas.) 19 Sept. 1771.
    San Fernando (5 Clas.) 31 Aug. 1811.
    St.Hermenigilde(2Clas.)10July,1815.
    St.Isabella the Catholic (3 Clas.) 1815.
Sweden—Sword (3 Classes) 17 Apr. 1748.
Turkey—Crescent (2 Classes) 6 July, 1804.
Tuscany—St. Joseph, (3 Classes) 1807.
Wirtemburg—Military Merit (3 Clas.) 1759.

ROYAL HANOVERIAN GUELPHIC ORDER.

KNIGHTS GRAND CROSSES. (GCH.)

Field Mar. His R. H. Aug. Frederick, *Duke of* Cambridge, *KG. GCB. GCMG.*
Field Mar. His Majesty *The King of the* Belgians, *KG. GCB.*

🕮 Alten, M.-Gen. C. *Count GCB.* late Ger. Leg.
🕮 Anglesey, Gen. H. W. *Marq. of, KG. GCB.* 7 Dr.
🕮 Barnard, Lt.-Gen. *Sir* A. F. *KCB.* Rif.Br.
Bayly, Lt.-Gen. *Sir* Henry............8 F.
Beresford, Gen. Wm. Carr. *Visc. GCB.* 16 F.
Blakeney, Lt.-Gen. *Rt. Hon. Sir* Edw. *KCB.* 7 F.
Bloomfield, Lt.-Gen. Benj. *Lord, GCB.* R.Art.
Bradford, Lt.-Gen. *Sir* Tho. *GCB.*.....30 F.
Brisbane, Lt.-Gen. *Sir* T.M. *Bt. KCB.* 34 F.
Burghersh, Lt.-Gen. J. *Lord, KCB.*
Campbell, Gen. *Sir* Hen. Fred. *KCB.* 25 F.
Champagne, Gen. *Sir* Josiah ....17 F.
Church, Lt.-Col. *Sir* R. *CB.* late Greek Lt.In.
Cockburn, General George
Cockburn, Maj.-Gen. *Sir* Jas. *Bt.*
🕮 Colville, Gen. *Hon. Sir* Cha. *GCB.* 5 F.
Combermere, Gen. S. *Visc. GCB.* 1 Life Gds.
Conyngham, Maj. F. N. *Marq. KP.* Unatt.
Crosbie, Gen. *Sir* J. Gustavus
Darling, Lt.-Gen. *Sir* Ralph ....41 F.
Decken, Lt.-Gen. F. *Count* von der, late Ger. Leg.
Donkin, Gen. *Sir* R. S. *KCB.*........11 F.
Doyle, Lt.-Gen. *Sir* Chas. Wm. *CB.*
Duff, Gen. *Hon Sir* Alex............37 F.
Elphinstone, Capt. J. *Lord (Civil)* ..Unatt.
Erroll, Lieut. W. G. *Earl of, KT.* ....h. p.
Fitz Clarence, Col. *Lord* Frederick ..Unatt.
Fraser, Gen. *Sir* John .. Lt. Gov.of Chester.

Fuller, Lt.-Gen. *Sir* Joseph..........75 F.
Gordon, Lt.-Gen. *Sir* J. Willoughby, *Bt. GCB.* Quar.-Mast.-Gen..........23 F.
Grant, Lt.-Gen. *Sir* Wm. Keir, *KCB.* 2 Dr.
Grey, Gen. *Hon. Sir* H. G. *GCB.* ... 13 Dr.
🕮 Halkett, Lt.-Gen. *Sir* Colin, *KCB.* 31 F.
Hammond, Gen. Fra. Tho.
🕮 Hill, Gen. R. *Lord, GCB. KC.* R.Horse Gds. and Gen. Comm. in Chief
Houstoun, Gen. *Sir* Wm. *Bt. GCB.* ...20 F
Hunter, Gen. *Sir* Martin, *GCMG.* Gov. of Stirling Castle
Keane, Lt.-Gen. John, *Lord, GCB.* ..43 F.
🕮 Kempt, Lt.-Gen. *Rt. Hon. Sir* Jas. *GCB.* 2 F.
🕮 Kerrison, Lt.-Gen. *Sir* Edw. *Bt. CB.* 14 Dr.
Londonderry, Gen. C. W. *Marq. of, GCB.* 10 Dr.
🕮 Lyon, Lt.-Gen. *Sir* Jas. *KCB.* ..24 F.
Mackenzie, Gen. *Sir* Alexander, *Bt.*
Macfarlane, Gen. *Sir* R. *KCB.* ......32 F.
Murray, Lt.-Gen. *Rt. Hon. Sir* G. *GCB.* 42 F.
🕮 Saltoun, Maj.-Gen. A. *Lord, C.B.*
🕮 Seaton, Lt.-Gen. John, *Lord, GCB.* 26 F.
Slade, Gen. *Sir* John, *Bt.* ......5 Dr. Gds.
Smith, Lt.-Gen. *Sir* Lionel, *Bt. KCB.* 40 F.
Stephenson, Maj.-Gen. *Sir* Benj. Charles
🕮 Strafford, Lt.-Gen. J. *Lord, GCB.* 29 F.
Turner, Gen. *Sir* Hilgrove ....19 F.
🕮 Vivian, Lt.-Gen. *Rt. Hon. Sir* R. H. *Bt. GCB.*......................1 Dr.
🕮 Wellington, Fd. Mar. A. *Duke of, KG. GCB.* Gren. Gds. and Rifle Bag.
Wetherall, Gen. *Sir* Fred. Aug. ......17 F.
Wheatley, Maj.-Gen. *Sir* Henry

KNIGHTS COMMANDERS. (KCH.)

Adams, Lt.-Gen. *Sir* G. P.
Arentsschildt, Maj. *Sir* V. von, *CB.*l.Ger.Leg.
Arthur, Col. *Sir* Geo............. h. p.
🕮 Baring, Lt.-Col.G. *Baron* von, *CB.*l.G.L.
Barton, Lt.-Gen. *Sir* Robert
Bisset, Comm. Gen. *Sir* John..........h. p.
🕮 Bowater, Maj.-Gen. *Sir* Edw.
Browne, Maj.-Gen. *Sir* John
Browne, Lt.-Gen. *Sir* Thomas
Browne, Col. *Sir* Thos. H. ....h. p.
Campbell, Maj.-Gen. *Sir* Jas. late of R. Mar.
Carey, Maj.-Gen. *Sir* Octavius, *CB.*
Carrol, Maj.-Gen. *Sir* Wm. Parker, *CB.*
Chabot, Maj.-Gen. Louis W. *Visc.* late of 50 F.
Chapman, M.-Gen. *Sir* S. R. *CB.* from R. E.
Christie, Col. *Sir* Arch. Dep. Gov. Stirl. Cas.
🕮 Clifton, M.-Gen. *Sir* Ar. B. *KCB.* 17 Dr.
Conroy, Capt. *Sir* John, *Bt.* ..h. p. R. Art.
Cotton, M.-Gen. *Sir* Willoughby, *GCB.* 98 F.
Cumming, Lt.-Gen. *Sir* H. J. ......12 Dr.
Cust, Lt.-Col. *Hon. Sir* Edward ....Unatt.
Dalbiac, Lt.-Gen. *Sir* Jas. Chas. 3 Dr.Gds.
Davy, Maj.-Gen. *Sir* Wm. Gabriel, *CB.*

De Butts, Lt.-Gen. *Sir* Augustus ..R. Eng.
D'Este, Col. *Sir* Aug. Fred. ....Unatt.
🕮 Dick, Maj.-Gen. *Sir* Robt. Hen. *KCB.*
Dickens, Lt.-Gen. *Sir* S. Trevor....R. Eng.
🕮 Dickson, Maj.-Gen. *Sir* Alex. *GCB.* from R. Art.
🕮 Douglas, Maj.-Gen. *Sir* Neil, *KCB.*
Downman, M.-Gen. *Sir* T. *CB.* from R. Art.
D'Urban, Lt.-Gen. *Sir* Benj. *KCB.* ..51 F.
Egerton, Lt.-Gen. *Sir* Charles Bulkeley, *GCMG.*......................89 F.
Eustace, Maj.-Gen. Wm. Cornwallis, *CB.*
Gardiner, Col. *Sir* Robert, *KCB.* ..R. Art.
Gosset, Col. *Sir* William, *C.B.* ....R. Eng.
Grant, Lt.-Gen. *Sir* Lewis ....16 F.
Greenwell, Maj.-Gen. *Sir* Leonard, *KCB.*
Halkett, Lt.-Gen. *Sir* Alex.
🕮 Halkett, Lt.-Col. Hugh. *CB.* late G. Leg.
Hanbury, Maj.-Gen. *Sir* John
🕮 Harris, Lt.-Gen. W. G. *Lord, CB.* 73 F.
Harvey, Maj.-Gen. *Sir* John, *KCB,*
🕮 Hartmann, Lt.-Col. *Sir* J. *KCB.* late Ger. Leg.

Royal Hanoverian Guelphic Order.

KNIGHTS COMMANDERS—Continued.

Hawker, Lt.-Gen. *Sir* Thomas ..6 Dr. Gds.
Herries, Col. *Sir* Wm. Lewis, *CB*. ..Unatt.
Higgins, Col. *Sir* Sam. G. late of Scots Fusil. Guards.
Hutchinson, Lt.-Gen. *Sir* W. G. Gov. of Carrickfergus
Kearney, Maj.-Gen. *Sir* James
Kennedy, Comm.-Gen. *Sir* R. H....... h. p.
King, Maj.-Gen, *Sir* Henry, *CB*.
☗ Krauchenberg, Lt.-Col. G. *Bar.* von, *CB*. late Ger. Leg.
Linsingen, Maj. E. *Baron* .. late Ger. Leg.
Lloyd, Lt.-Gen. *Sir* Evan .... 7 Drag. Gds.
Low, Maj.-Gen. S. C. G. *Baron*, *KCB*. late Ger. Leg.
☗ Macdonell, Maj.-Gen. *Sir* Jas. *KCB*. from Coldstream Gds.
Macgregor, Maj.-Gen. *Sir* Evan J. M. *Bt. KCB*.
Macleod, Lieut-Gen. *Sir* John, *CB*.
Macra, Col. *Sir* John............. Unatt.
Martin, Lt.-Col. David ..... late Ger. Leg.
Maxwell, Maj.-Gen. *Sir* Cha. Wm. *CB*.
☗ May, Maj.-Gen. *Sir* John, *KCB*. from R. Art.
Montresor, Lt.-Gen. *Sir* T. Gage, 2 Dr. Gds.
Mulcaster, Lt.-Gen. *Sir* Fred. Wm. R.Eng.
☗ Nicolay, Lt.-Gen. *Sir* Wm., *CB*. 1 W. I. Reg.
O'Connell, Maj.-Gen. *Sir* M. Cha.
Paterson, Lt.-Gen. *Sir* Wm. Capt. of Carisbrook Castle.
Peacocke, Gen. *Sir* W. M. *KC*. Gov. of Kinsale.
Pearson, Maj.-Gen. *Sir* Thomas, *CB*.
Prott, Capt. Victor.........late Ger. Leg.
Pym, Insp. Gen. *Sir* Wm............h. p.
☗ Quentin, Lt.-Gen. *Sir* Geo. Aug. *CB*.
Reynett, Col. *Sir* J. H...............h. p.
Riall, Lt.-Gen. *Sir* Phineas........ 74 Ft.
Rivarola, Maj.-Gen. *Count* Fra. *KC.MG*. R. Malta Fenc.
☗ Robertson, Lt.-Col. W. von, *CB*. late Ger. Leg.
☗ Rooke, Maj.-Gen. *Sir* H. W. *CB*. late of Scots Fus. Gds.
Ross, Maj.-Gen. *Sir* Patrick *GC.MG*. late of 75 Ft.
Savage, Maj.-Gen. *Sir* John B. *KCB*. from R. Marines.
☗ Straton, Lt.-Gen. *Sir* Joseph, *CB*. 8 Dr.
Thornton, Maj.-Gen. *Sir* C. Wade, late of R. Art.
☗ Townsend, Col. *Hon.* Horatio G. P. Unatt.
Trench, Maj.-Gen. *Sir* Fred. Wm.
Tuyll, Maj.-Gen. *Sir* William
Viney, Maj.-Gen. *Sir* James, *CB*. from R. Art.
Webb, *Sir* J. *MD*. Direct. Gen. Ord. Med. Department.
Whitmore, Maj.-Gen. *Sir* George, from R. Eng.
Whittingham, Lt.-Gen. *Sir* S. Ford, *KCB*. 71 Ft.
Wilson, Lt.-Gen. *Sir* Wiltshire .... R. Art.
☗ Woodford, Maj.-Gen. *Sir* J. G. *KCB*.
Ximenes, Maj.-Gen. *Sir* David

KNIGHTS. (KH.)

Abernethie, Col. Thomas ....late of R. Mar.
A'Court, Col. C. Ashe, *CB*............h. p.
Anderson, Maj. Joseph............... 50 F.
☗ Anderson, Lt.-Col. Robert ...... 91 F.
Angelo, Lt.-Col. E. A. .... Unatt.
Arnaud, Maj. J...................... do.
Arnold, Col. Jas. Robertson........ R. Eng.
Austen, Lt.-Col. John............... Unatt.
Badcock, Lt.-Col. Lovell B. ......15 Huss.
Balneavis, Col. Henry, *CMG*. ...... Unatt.
☗ Barton, Lt.-Col. Alex........... 12 Dr.
Bayly, Maj. *Sir* Henry .... Unatt.
☗ Baynes, Lt.-Col. Henry ..h. p. R. Art.
☗ Beckwith, Lt.-Col. Wm............ Unatt.
Benne, Capt. Lewis ....h. p. Ger. Leg.
☗ Bishop, Maj. Peter............ Unatt.
Booth, Lt.-Col. Henry .... 43 F.
Bossett, Col. Chas. P. de, *CB*........h. p.
Bradshawe, Lt.-Col. Geo. Paris ...... 77 F.
☗ Brereton, Lt.-Col. William, *CB*. R. Art.
Briggs, Lt.-Col. John F...............h. p.
Brock, Lt.-Col Saumarez ....do.
Brown, Col. George, *CB*. ...... Rifle Brig.
☗ Bruce, Maj. William .... Unatt.
☗ Bulow, Lt.-Col. J. *Baron*, *CB*. late G. L.
Bunbury, Col. Thos. .... 67 F.
☗ Burney, Maj. W. Cape Mounted Riflemen
Burrowes, Maj. Robt. Edw. .... Unatt.
Burslem, Col. Nath. ....late of 67 F.
Bush, Lt.-Col. William ......1 W. I. Regt.
Butler, Maj. James................ Unatt.
☗ Cadell, Lt.-Col. Charles.......... do.
Cairncross, Lt.-Col. Alex. ....96 Ft.
Cairnes, Lt.-Col. J. E. .... Unatt.
Campbell, Lt.-Col. Alexander........9 Dr.
Campbell, Col. James ....95 Ft.
Campbell, Lt.-Col. James .... Unatt.
☗ Carey, Lieut. Thos. h. p. 2 Line Ger. Leg.
Carter, Col. John ....1 Bt.
☗ Chalmers, Lt.-Col. Wm. *CB*. .....h. p.
Charleton, Lt.-Col. Edward, Unatt. *Dep.-Adj.-Gen., Ceylon.*
☗ Chatterton, Lt.-Col. Jas. Cha. 4 Dr. Gds.
☗ Clark, Maj. John ....54 Ft.
Clarke, Lt.-Col. Andrew............46 Ft.
Clarke, Dep.-Insp.-Gen. John, *MD*. ..h. p.
Clerke, Lt.-Col. St. John Aug. ...... Unatt.
Clerke, Maj. Thos. Hen. Shadwell ....h. p.
Cloete, Lt.-Col. A. J.................h. p.
Colebroke, Lt.-Col. *Sir* W. M. G. .. R. Art.
Considine, Lt.-Col. James .... Unatt.
Couper, Col. George, *CB*.......... Unatt.
☗ Cox, Lt.-Col. John................do.
☗ Cox, Lt.-Col. William...... Part. Serv.
Crabbe, Maj. Eyre J. ....74 Ft.
Creagh, Lt.-Col. *Sir* Michael........86 Ft.
☗ Cross, Lt.-Col. John ....68 Ft.
☗ Crowe, Lt.-Col. John........... Unatt.
Dales, Lt.-Col. Samuel ....h. p.
☗ Dance, Lt.-Col. *Sir* C. Webb ......do.

Royal Hanoverian Guelphic Order.

KNIGHTS—Continued.

Daubeney, Col. Henry..............do.
Davison, Lt.-Col. *Sir* William.........do.
Deane, Maj. Charles..............1 Ft.
🎖 Decken, Maj. Wm. *Baron*,late Ger.Leg.
Derinzy, Maj. B. Vigors.............11 Ft.
🎖 Diggle, Lt.-Col. Charles ..R. Mil. Coll.
Du Plat, Maj. Gustavus Cha........R. Eng.
Durie, Ass.-Insp. Wm. h. p. Ord. Med. Dep.
Edwards, Maj. R. Bidwell............Unatt.
Elliot, Lt.-Col. Wm................do.
🎖 Elliot, Lt.-Col. Wm. Hen......51 Ft.
England, Col. Richard.............41 Ft.
Eustace, Lt.-Col. *Sir* J. R......Gren. Gds.
Everard, Lt.-Col. Mathias, *CB*.....14 Ft.
Falconar, Col. C.Grant, *Ins.Fd.Off.Rec.Dist.*
Findlay, Lt.-Col. Alex. ....h. p.
🎖 Fitz Gerald, Lt.-Col. Edw.Thos......do.
🎖 Fitz Maurice, Maj. J. ....Unatt.
Forbes, Dep.-Insp.-Gen. Chas. F.*MD.& KC.*
🎖 Forlong, Maj. James ....43 Ft.
Forster, Maj. W. F................Unatt.
Fraser, Lt.-Col. Rob. ..*Fort-Major, Jersey.*
Freeth, Lt.-Col. Jas. Assist.-Qua.-Mast.-Gen.
French, Lt.-Col. Cudbert............28 Ft.
Fulton, Lt.-Col. Jas. Forrest late of 92 Ft.
Gabriel, Col. Rob. Burd, *CB*........h. p.
🎖 Garland, Lt.-Col. J. ....Unatt.
🎖 Gawler, Lt.-Col. George ....do.
Garrett, Maj. Robert ....46 Ft.
Geddes, Lt.-Col. John ....Unatt.
🎖 Goodman, Col. Step. Arthur, *CB*. h. p.
🎖 Gore, Col. *Hon.* Charles, *CB. Dep.-Qua.-Mast.-Gen. in Canada.*
Gorrequer, Col. Gideon........late of 4 Ft.
🎖 Grant, Maj. Alex...............Unatt.
🎖 Grant, Insp. *Sir* Jas. Rob. *MD.* ..h. p.
Graydon, Lt.-Col. George ....R. Eng.
Greame, Capt. J. D. ....late Ger. Leg.
Green, Lt.-Col. William ....Unatt.
Hamilton, Col. J. Potter,lateof Sco.Fus.Gds.
Hamilton, Col.Nicholas, *Insp.F.O.Rec.Dist.*
🎖 Hardinge, Maj. Richard......R. Art.
🎖 Hare, Col. John, *CB*..........27 Ft.
Harris, Col. H. Bulteel.
🎖 Harty, Maj. Jos. Mark.........33 Ft.
Harvey, Lt.-Col. Bissell,*Insp. F. O. Rec. Dt.*
Harvey, Lt.-Col. James ....h. p.
🎖 Havelock, Maj. William ....4 Dr.
Hely, Maj. Jas. Price.............Unatt.
Henderson, Col. Geo. Aug. ....h. p.
🎖 Henderson, Maj. James ....Unatt.
Henderson, Maj. John Wm...........h. p.
Higgins, Lt.-Col. Wm. W..........Unatt.
Hogge, Lt.-Col. John..............do.
🎖 Hope, Lt.-Col. John Cha.......Rif. Br.
Howard, Col. Thos. Phipps ....h. p.
Howden, Lt.-Col. J. H. *Lord* ....Unatt.
Irwin, Maj. F. C. 63 Ft. *Commandant of the Troops in Western Australia.*
Jackson, Lt.-Col. Edward ....Unatt.
🎖 Jackson, Lt.-Col. James ....6 Dr. Gds.
Jervois, Col. William ....h. p.
Jones, Lt.-Col. George E. ....57 Ft.
Jones, Lt.-Col. James...............h. p.

Jones, Lt.-Col. Rice ....R. Eng.
🎖 Kennedy, Lt.-Col. Alex. Kennedy Clark
CB. ....7 Dr. Gds.
Kerr, Lt.-Col. *Lord* Robert ....h. p.
🎖 King, Lt.-Col. Cha. *Insp. F.O. Rec. Dt.*
Kronenfeldt, Maj. Cha. von ..late Ger. Leg.
🎖 Lamont, Maj. Norman ....91 Ft.
🎖 Lautour, Col. P. A. *CB*..........h. p.
🎖 Law, Maj. Robert ..R. Newf. Vet. Cos.
Leslie, Lt.-Col. Charles ....Unatt.
Leslie, Lt.-Col. John ....4 Ft.
🎖 Lindham, Lt. Ole........late Ger. Leg.
Lockyer, Maj. Hen. Fred. ....97 Ft.
🎖 Love, Col. James Fred. *CB*. ....73 Ft.
Lowen, Maj. Pearce,Cape Mounted Riflemen.
M'Adam, Lt.-Col. William..........Unatt.
M'Caskill, Col. John ....9 F.
Mac Bean, Lt.-Col. Fred ....84 F.
🎖 Macdonald, Lt.-Col. Ranald, *CB. Dep. Adj. Gen. Bombay*.................4 F.
Macintosh, Col. A. F.............Unatt.
🎖 Mackworth, Lt.-Col. *Sir* Digby, *Bt.* do.
🎖 Macleod, Col. *Sir* Hen. Geo. ......do.
Macpherson, Col. R. B. *CB*. ....h. p.
🎖 Madox, Lt.-Col. Henry ....Unatt.
Manners, Lt.-Col. Henry Herbert ....37 F.
Mansel, Lt.-Col. Robt. Christ......Unatt.
Marshall, Lt.-Col. George ....82 F.
🎖 Marten, Lt.-Col. Thomas ....1 Dr.
Maxwell, Lt.-Col. Arch. Montgomery 36 F.
Meade, Maj. Roche, Unatt. Dep.As.Adj. Gen.
Meade, *Sir* John, *MD*. h. p. *Dep.Ins.of Hos.*
Menzies, Lt.-Col. Charles ....R. Mar. Art.
Michell, Maj. Chas. Cornwallis ...... h p.
Miller, Lt.-Col. William ......h. p. R. Art.
Moore, Lt.-Col. John ....Unatt.
Moriee, Maj. T. H. ....late of R. Mar.
Mullen, Maj. R................1 F.
🎖 Muller, Lt.-Col. George *CB*. late G. Leg.
Munro, Lt.-Col. Alex. ....R. Art.
Newton, Lt.-Col. Wm. Hen. ......Unatt.
Nicholson, Lt.-Col. Thos. W. ....do.
Nickle, Col. Robt............Part. Serv.
Norcliffe, Lt.-Col. Norcliffe ....h. p.
Oates, Lt.-Col. Jas. Poole ....do.
🎖 Oldfield, Lt.-Col. John ....R. Eng.
Onslow, Maj. Wm. ....Unatt.
Owen, Col. John, *CB*. ..Dep. Adj. R. Mar.
Parry, Maj.-Gen. Parry Jones
Paty, Col. Geo. Wm. *CB*...........94 F.
Pearce, Lt.-Col. William ....Unatt.
Peddie, Lt.-Col. John ....90 F.
Pennycuick, Lt.-Col. John ....17 F.
Pipon, Maj. George ....Unatt.
Pitt, Col. Geo. Dean, *Insp.Fd.Off.Rec.Dist.*
Power, Col. Wm. G. *CB*...........R. Art.
Rainey, Col. Henry, *CB*. ....Unatt.
Ratcliffe, Lt.-Col. John ....6 Dr.
Reeves, Maj.-Gen. Geo. Jas. *CB. Lt.-Gov. of Placentia.*
Rice, Col. Samuel, *CB*............Unatt.
Riddall, Col. Wm................do.
Riddell, Col. Hen. Jas...Ass.-Qr.-Mast.-Gen.
Roberts, Col. Rich...............Unatt.

471

Officers permitted to wear Foreign Orders.

KNIGHTS—*Continued.*
Robyns, Maj. John ....late of R. Mar.
🕮 Ross, Maj. Jas. Kerr ....Unatt.
Ryan, Maj. Thos....................50 Ft.
Sall, Lt.-Col. William....R. Newf. Vet. Cos.
St. Clair, Col. T. Staunton, *CB.* ....Unatt.
Sherlock, Col. Francis....late of 4 Dr. Gds.
Simson, Lt.-Col. Robert ....h. p.
Singleton, Major John..............90 Ft.
Slyfield, Maj. J. Clavell S...........60 Ft.
Smith, Lt.-Col. *Sir* J. M. F....... R. Eng.
Smith, Lt.-Col. C. Hamilton..........h.p.
Somerset, Col. Henry....Cape Mounted Rif.
Sorell, Lt.-Col. *Sir* T. S.
Southwell, Capt. *Hon.* Cha...late 12 R. V. B.
Spink, Lt.-Col. John ....Unatt.
Stack, Maj. Geo. Fitz Gerald.......24 Ft.
Stephens, Maj. Hen. Sykes..........86 Ft.
Stisted, Lt.-Col. Charles ....Unatt.
Taylor, Maj. Abraham B.............9 Ft.
Taylor, Lt.-Col. Pringle............Unatt.
🕮 Thackwell, *Sir* Jos. *KCB*.......3 Dr.
Thorn, Col. Nathan. *CB.* Ass.-Qr.-Mas.-Gen.
Thorn, Lt.-Col. William.......late of 25 Dr.
Thorne, Maj. Per. Fra. ....Unatt.
Thornhill, Maj. Jas. Badham ....do.
Thorpe, Maj. Samuel..................do.
Tremenheere, Col. Walter ..late of R. Mar.
🕮 Trevor, Maj. A. H.............Unatt.
Turner, Lt.-Col. Chas. Barker....Part. Serv.
🕮 Tyler, Lt.-Col. John ....Unatt.
Valiant, Col. Thomas ....40 Ft.
Walker, Maj.-Gen. Edward.
🕮 Walker, Lt.-Col. Leslie, *CB.* late of 25 F.
Wallace, Col. *Sir* J. M. ....5 Dr. Gds.
🕮 Wallace, Lt.-Col. Robert.........Unatt.
Weare, Lt.-Col. Thomas ....Prov. Bat.
Wetherall, Col. Geo. Aug. *CB.*.........1 F.
🕮 Whinyates, Maj. E. C. *CB.*.....R. Art.
Wilding, Lieut. Ernest ....late Ger. Leg.
🕮 Wildman, Col. Edward ....h. p.
🕮 Wilkins, Lt.-Col. *C. CB.* late of R. Brig.
Wilcocks, Maj. Rob. Hen. ....81 F.
Williams-Molyneux, Maj. Thos......Unatt.
Williams, Lt.-Col. W. F. ......Part. Serv.
Wilson, Col. J. M. *CB. Adj. to Chelsea Hosp.*
Wilson, Lt.-Col. Nathan............Unatt.
Wilson, Maj. Nicholas ....77 F.
🕮 Winchester, Lt.-Col. Rob........92 F.
Wood, Col. William, *CB.* ....h. p.
Wood, Lt.-Col. Wm. Leighton..........do.
Wooldridge, Col. Tho. T................do.
Wright, Lt.-Col. Charles ......R. Mil. Col.
Wright, Col. John................R. Mar.
Young, Lt.-Col. Plomer ....Part. Serv.

OTHER FOREIGN ORDERS.

🕮 Abercromby, Col. *Hon.* Alex. *CB.* late of Coldstream Gds. ....
- Knight Tower and Sword
- Knight Maria Theresa
- Fourth Class St. George

A'Court, Col. Cha. A. *CB. KH.* h. p. 1 Greek Lt. Inf. ....
- Commander St. Ferdinand and Merit
- Knight St. Maurice and Lazaro

🕮 Adam, Lt.-Gen. *Rt. Hon. Sir* Fred. *KCB. GCMG.* 57 F. ....
- Knight Maria Theresa
- First Class St. Anne

Alexander, Capt. Jas. Edw. Unatt............. Third Class Lion and Sun

🕮 Alten Maj.-Gen. Cha. *Count, GCB. GCH.* late Ger. Leg. ....
- First Class St. Anne
- Third Class Wilhelm
- Commander of Tower and Sword

Anderson, Col. *Sir* Alex. *CB.* Unatt.........
- Commander St. Bento d'Avis
- Knight Tower and Sword
- Second Class St. Anne
- Third Class Wilhelm

🕮 Anglesey, Gen. H. W. *Marq. of, KG. GCB.* & *GCH.* 7 Dr. ....
- Commander Maria Theresa
- Second Class St. George

🕮 Ansley, Col. Benj. ... late of Sco. Fus. Gds. Second Class of Crescent
Anson, Gen. *Sir* Geo. *GCB.* 4 Dr. Gds. ...... Commander of Tower and Sword
Arburthnot, Maj.-Gen. *Sir* R. *KCB*.......... do. do.
Arentsschildt, Maj. *Sir* V. von, *CB. KCH.* late G. L.................................... Knight do.
Armstrong, Col. *Sir* Rich. *CB.* Unatt......... do. do.
Arnold, Col. J. R. *KH.* R. Eng.............. Second Class of Crescent
Aubin, Capt. Tho. h. p. 8 Gar. Bn. .... Knight St. Joseph
🕮 Baring, Lt.-Col. G. *Bar.* von, *CB. KCH.* h. p. Ger. Leg. .... Fourth Class Wilhelm
🕮 Barnard, Lt.-Gen. *Sir* A. F. *KCB. GCH.* Rifle B. ....
- Knight Maria Theresa
- Fourth Class St. George

Barns, Lt.-Gen. *Sir* James S. *KCB.* Rif. Br. .. Knight Tower and Sword
Basset, Capt. Rich. R. Art. ....
- First Class St. Fernando
- Knight Isabella the Catholic

Officers permitted to wear Foreign Orders.

Beckwith, Col. Charles, *CB.* h. p. Rifle Brig...	Second Class St. Anne
Beresford, Gen. W. C. *Visc. GCB. GCH.* 16 F.	Grand Cross Tower and Sword ———— St. Ferdinand and **Merit** ———— of St. Hermenigilde ———— Charles the Third ———— St. Fernando
※ Berkeley, M. Gen. *Sir* G. H. F. *KCB.*	Knight Tower and Sword Fourth Class of St. Wladimir ———— Wilhelm
Blakeney, Lt.-Gen. *Rt. Hon. Sir* E. *KCB. GCH.* 7 F.	Knight Tower and Sword
Blunt, Lt.-Gen. Richard, 66 F.	Commander Tower and Sword
Brackenbury, Lt.-Col. *Sir* Edward, Unatt.	Commander St. Bento D'Avis Knight Tower and Sword ———— St. Fernando
Bradshaw, Maj.-Gen. Lawrence, late of 1 Life Gds.	Second Class of Crescent
Brown, Maj.-Gen. *Sir* John, *KCH.* from 13 Dr.	Knight Tower and Sword ———— Charles the Third
Buchan, Maj.-Gen. *Sir* John, *KCB.* 95 F.	Commander Tower and Sword
Burghersh, Lt.-Gen. J. *Lord, KCB. GCH.* from 63 F.	Knight Maria Theresa Grand Cross St. Ferdinand and Merit ———— St. Joseph
Burgoyne, M. Gen. *Sir* J. F. *KCB.* from R. Eng.	Knight Tower and Sword
Camac, Col. Burges, Unatt.	Knight Charles the Third
※ Cameron, Maj.-Gen. *Sir* A. *KCB.* Dep.-Gov. of St. Mawes.	Second Class St. Anne
※ Campbell, Lt.-Gen. *Sir* Colin, *KCB.* 72 F...	Knight Maria Theresa Fourth Class St. George Knight Maximilian Joseph Commander Tower and Sword
Campbell, Lt.-Gen. *Sir* Arch. *Bt. GCB.* 77 F.	Commander Tower and Sword
※ Campbell, Lt.-Col. Patrick, *CB.* h. p. 52 F.	Knight Charles the Third
※ Campbell, Col. Wm. *CB.* h. p. 23 F.	Second Class St. Anne
Carrol, Maj.-Gen. *CB. Sir* W. P. *KCH.* from 18 F.	Knight Charles the Third
Cathcart, Gen. W. *Earl, KT.* 2 Life Gds.	St. Andrew Fourth Class St. George
Cathcart, Col. *Hon.* Fred. h. p. 92 F.	Second Class St. Anne
※ Cathcart, Lt.-Col. *Hon.* George, 1 Dr. Gds.	Fourth Class St. Wladimir
Chichester, Lt.-Col. Cha. 81 F.	Knight Charles the Third Commander Isabella the Catholic First Class St. Fernando Third Class do
Church, Lt.-Col. *Sir* Richard, *CB. GCH.* late of Greek Lt. Inf.	Grand Cross St. George and Reunion of Naples Commander St. Ferdinand and Merit
Clay, Lt.-Gen John Granby	Second Class of Cresent
Clayton, Gen. R. B. 12 Dr.	do. do.
※ Clifton, Maj.-Gen. *Sir* A. B. *KCB.* 17 Dr.	Fourth Class Wilhelm Second Class St. Anne
※ Colville, Gen. *Hon. Sir* C. *GCB. GCH.* 5 Ft.	Commander Tower and Sword
Combermere, Gen. S. *Visc. GCB. GCH.* 3 Dr.	Grand Cross Tower and Sword ———— Charles the Third ———— St. Fernando
※ Cooke, Lt.-Col. R. Harvey, *CB.* late of Gr. Gds.	Fourth Class St. Wladimir
Considine, Capt. Wm. 69 F.	Second Class San Fernando
Cox, Col. *Sir* William, late of Port. Serv.	Knight Tower and Sword
Crofton, Lieut. Edw. Walter, R. Art.	First Class St. Fernando
Crosse, Lt.-Col. Joshua, Unatt.	Knight St. Fernando
D'Arcy, Lt.-Col. Joseph, late of R. Art.	Second Class Lion and Sun
※ Dick, Maj.-Gen. *Sir* R. H. *KCB. KCH.*	Knight Maria Theresa Fourth Class St. Wladimir
Douglas, Lt.-Gen. *Sir* Howard, *CB. Bt. GCMG.*	Knight Charles the Third
※ Douglas, Maj.-Gen. *Sir* N. *CB. KCB. KCH.*	Knight Maria Theresa Fourth Class St. Wladimir

Officers permitted to wear Foreign Orders.

Downes, Maj.-Gen. U. *Lord, KCB.*	Commander Tower and Sword
Doyle, Lt.-Gen. *Sir* C. W. *CB. GCH.*	⎧ Knight Legion of Honour ⎨ Knight Charles the Third ⎩ Second Class of Crescent
Doyle, Col. *Sir* J. M. *KCB.* late of 12 Gar. Bn.	Knight Tower and Sword
Dundas, Maj.-Gen. *Hon. Sir* R. L. *KCB.*	do. do.
D'Urban, Lt.-Gen. *Sir* B. *KCB. KCH.* 51 F....	Commander Tower and Sword
Effingham, Gen. K. A. *Earl of, GCB.* 3 F.	do. do.
※ Elphinstone, Maj.-Gen. W. K. *CB.*	⎰ Second Class St. Anne ⎱ Fourth Class Wilhelm
※ Evans, Col. *Sir* De Lacy, *KCB.* h. p. 5W.I.R.	⎧ Grand Cross St. Fernando ⎪ Third Class do. ⎨ Fifth Class do. ⎩ Grand Cross Charles the Third
Farrant, Lieut. Fra. E. I. Comp. Serv.	Second class Lion and Sun
Fitzgerald, Lt. Lionel Cha. Wm. Hen. 2 W. I Reg.	Knight Tower and Sword
Forbes, Gen. J. *Lord*, 21 F.	St. Januarius
Forbes, Cha. F. *MD. KH.* Dep. Insp. Gen.	Second Class of Crescent
※ Fremantle, Col. John, *CB.* Unatt.	Knight Maximilian Joseph
Gardiner, Col. *Sir* Robert, *KCB. KCH.* R. Art.	Second Class St. Anne
Giles, Capt. Stephen, R. Mar.	Knight Tower and Sword
※ Gomm, Maj.-Gen. *Sir* W. M. *KCB.* late of Coldst. Gds.	Second Class St. Anne
Gorrequer, Col. Gideon, *KH.* late of 4 F.	⎧ Commander St. Ferdinand and Merit ⎨ Second Class of Crescent ⎩ Commander St. Maurice and St. Lazare
Gosset, Col. *Sir* William, *CB. KCH.* R. Eng.	Commander St. Ferdinand and Merit
Gough, Maj.-Gen. *Sir* Hugh, *KCB.* 99 F.	Knight Charles the Third
Grant, Lt.-Gen. *Sir* Wm. Keir, *KCB. GCH.* 2 Dr.	⎰ First Class Lion and Sun ⎱ Knight Maria Theresa
※ Grant, *Sir* Jas. Rob. *MD. KH.* Med. Dep.	Second Class St. Anne
Gray, Maj.-Gen. Wm.	Second Class of Crescent
※ Greenock, Maj.-Gen. C. M. *Lord, KCB.* from R. Staff C.	⎰ Fourth Class St. Wladimir ⎱ ———Wilhelm
Grey, Maj.-Gen. John *CB.*	⎰ Knight Tower and Sword ⎱ Commander St. Bento d'Avis
※ Halkett, Lt.-Gen. *Sir* C. *KCB. GCH.* 31 F.	⎧ Commander Maximilian Joseph ⎨ Third Class Wilhelm ⎩ Knight Tower and Sword
※ Hare, Col. John, *CB. KH.* 27 F.	Fourth Class St. Wladimir
Harvey, Col. *Sir* Rob. J. *CB.* h. p. Port. Serv.	⎰ Commander St. Bento d'Avis ⎱ Knight Tower and Sword
Henderson, Col. G. A. *KH.* h. p.	Second Class of Crescent
※ Hill, Gen. R. *Lord, GCB. GCH.* R. H. Gds. Gen. Comm. in Chief	⎧ Grand Cross Tower and Sword ⎪ Commander Maria Theresa ⎨ Second Class St. George ⎪ Second Class of Crescent ⎩ Third Class Wilhelm
※ Hill, Col. *Sir* R. C. *CB.* late of R. H. Gds.	⎰ Knight Maria Theresa ⎱ Fourth Class St. George
Hill, Col. *Sir* Dudley, St. L. *CB.* Unatt.	⎰ Commander St. Bento d'Avis ⎱ Knight Tower and Sword
※ Hoste, Col. *Sir* G. C. *CB.* R. Eng........	Knight St. Ferdinand and Merit
Houstoun, Gen. *Sir* Wm. *Bt. GCB. GCH.* 20 F.	Second Class of Crescent
Howden, Lt. Col. J. H. *Lord, KH.* Unatt.	⎧ Second Class St. Anne ⎪ Commander Legion of Honour ⎨ Knight Charles the Third ⎪ Third Class Leopold ⎩ Commander Saviour
Imhoff, Lt. Gen. *Sir* Charles	Grand Commander St. Joachim
Jackson, Capt. *Sir* Keith Alex. *Bt.* 4 Dr......	Second Class Lion and Sun
Johnson, Lt.-Col. Cha. C. h. p. 10 F...........	do
Johnson, Surg. Edward, *MD.* h. p. 32 F.	Knight Charles the Third
Jones, Lt.-Col. James, *KH.* h. p. 15 Dr.	do
Jones, Lt.-Col. B. O. Unatt..................	Knight Tower and Sword

Officers permitted to wear Foreign Orders.

⚔ Kempt, Lt.-Gen. *Right Hon. Sir J. GCB.* *GCH.* 2 F..................................	Knight Maria Theresa Third Class St. George ———— Wilhelm
Kennedy *Sir* Robert Hugh, *KCH.* Comm. Dep.	Commander Tower and Sword Knight Charles the Third Second Class of Crescent
⚔ Lambert, Lt.-Gen. *Sir* John, *GCB.* 10 F...	Third Class St. Wladimir Commander Maximilian Joseph
Laughten, Lieut. John, E. I. Comp. Serv......	Second Class Lion and Sun
Lee, Lt.-Col. *Sir* F. G. G. Royal Marines......	Knight Charles the Third
Le Marchant, Lt.-Col. *Sir* John G. 99 F.......	Third Class San Fernando Knight Charles the Third
Logan Lt. George, Royal Marines............	Knight Legion of Honour
Londonderry, Gen. C. W. *Marq. of, GCB. GCH.* 10 Dr...................................	Commander Tower and Sword Fourth Class St. George Black Eagle Grand Cross Red Eagle ———— Sword Russian Medal in Commemoration of the Capture of Paris
⚔ Lygon Maj.-Gen. *Hon.* E. P. *CB.* from 2 Life Gds..............................	Fourth Class St. Wladimir
⚔ Lyon, Lt.-Gen. *Sir* J. *KCB. GCH.* 24 F..	Commander Maximilian Joseph ———— of Sword
M'Grigor, *Sir* J. *Bt. MD.* Dir.-Gen. of Med. Dep.	Commander Tower and Sword
Macbean, Maj.-Gen. *Sir* Wm. *KCB*..........	Knight Tower and Sword
⚔ Macdonald, Maj.-Gen. Alex. *CB.* from R. Art.	Second Class St. Anne
⚔ Macdonald, Col. Alex. *CB.* R. Art........	do
⚔ Macdonald, Lt.-Col. Robt. *CB.* late of 35 F.	do
⚔ Macdonell, Maj.-Gen. *Sir* James, *KCB. KCH.* from Coldst. Gds.........................	Knight Maria Theresa Fourth Class St. Wladimir
Macfarlane, Gen. *Sir* Rob. *KCB. GCH.* 32 F.	Grand Cross St. Ferdinand and Merit
Mackenzie, Gen. *Sir* Alex. *Bt. GCH.* from 36 F.	St. Januarius
Maclachlan, Lt.-Col. Alexander, R. Art......	Knight St. Maurice and St. Lazare
Maclaine, Col. *Sir* Arch. *CB.* Unatt.........	Knight Charles the Third
Maclean, Lt.-Gen. *Sir* John, *KCB.* 60 F......	Knight Tower and Sword
⚔ Macleod, Col. *Sir* H. G. *KH.* Unatt.......	Fourth Class St. Wladimir
⚔ Maitland, Lt.-Gen. *Sir* P. *KCB.* 76 F.....	Third Class St. Wladimir ———— Wilhelm
⚔ May, Maj.-Gen. *Sir* John, *KCB. KCH.* from R. Art....................................	Knight Tower and Sword Second Class St. Anne
Meade, Major Roche, *KH.* Unatt............	Knight of the Sword
Menzies, Lt.-Col. Cha. *KH.* R. Mar. Art......	Knight Charles the Third
Miles, Col. *Sir* Edward, *CB.* late of 89 F......	Knight Tower and Sword
⚔ Money, Col. Arch. *CB.* h. p. 60 F........	Second Class of Crescent
⚔ Montagu, Capt. Willoughby, h. p. R. Art...	Fourth Class St. Wladimir
Montresor, Lt.-Gen. *Sir* T. Gage, *KCH.* 2 Dr. Gds.	Second Class of Crescent
Moody, Lt.-Col. Thomas, R. Eng............	Knight Military Merit of France
Murray, Lt.-Gen. *Right Hon. Sir* Geo. *GCB. GCH.* 42 F................................	Grand Cross Leopold ———— St. Alexander Newski ———— Red Eagle Commander Tower and Sword ———— Maximilian Joseph ———— St. Henry Second Class of Crescent
⚔ Muttlebury, Lt.-Col. G. *CB.* late of 69 F...	Fourth Class Wilhelm
Otway, Lt.-Gen. *Sir* L. W. *CB.* from 26 F.....	Knight Charles the Third
Paget, Gen. *Hon. Sir* Edw. *GCB.* 28 F.....	Grand Cross Tower and Sword
Parker, Lieut. Edw. Aug. R. Mar............	Knight Tower and Sword
Paty, Col. Geo. Wm. *CB. KH.* 94 F.........	Commander St. Bento d'Avis Knight Tower and Sword
Peacocke, Gen. *Sir* W. M. *KCH.*............	Commander Tower and Sword Second Class of Crescent
Peacocke, Lt.-Col. Thomas, h. p. Port. Serv....	Knight Tower and Sword
Phillips, Lt.-Gen. *Sir* Charles, from 44 F......	St. Januarius

Officers permitted to wear Foreign Orders.

Pynn, Lt.-Col. *Sir* Henry, *CB.* la*t*e of Port Serv.	Commander Tower and Sword Knight St. Fernando —— Charles the Third
Reade, Col. *Sir* Thomas, *CB.* h. p. 24 F.	Knight St. Ferdinand and Merit
Reeves, Maj.-Gen. Geo. Jas. *CB.KH. Lt.- Gov. of* Placentia	Second Class of Crescent
👑 Reynell, Lt.-Gen. *Sir* T. *Bt. KCB.* 87 F.	Knight Maria Theresa Fourth Class St. George
Rivarola, Maj.-Gen. *Count* F. *KCH.* R. Malta F.	Commander St. Maurice and St. Lazare
Roberts, Col. Richard, *KH.* Unatt.	Knight do
Robertson, Maj.-Gen. George D. *CB.* late of 89 F.	Knight of Leopold
Rolt, Col. John, *CB.* Unatt.	Knight Tower and Sword
👑 Ross, Col. *Sir* H. D. *KCB.* R. Art.	Knight Tower and Sword Second Class St. Anne
St. Clair, Col. Thos. Staunton, *CB. KH.* Unatt.	Knight Tower and Sword
👑 Saltoun, Maj.-Gen. Alex. *Lord*, *CB. GCH.* from Gr. Gds.	Knight Maria Theresa Fourth Class St. George
👑 Scovell, Maj.-Gen. *Sir* G. *KCB.* Gov. R. Mil. Coll.	Fourth Class St. Wladimir
👑 Seaton, Lt.-Gen. John *Lord*, *GCB. GCH.* 26 F.	Knight Maria Theresa Fourth Class St. George
👑 Shaw, Lieut. *Sir* Chas. h. p. 90 F.	Commander Tower and Sword Third Class St. Fernando
Shearman, Capt. John, h. p. 7 F.	Knight St. Maurice and St. Lazare
Shee, Capt. Benj. B., E. I. Comp. Serv.	First Class Lion and Sun
Smith, Col. *Sir* C. F. *CB.* R. Eng.	Knight Charles the Third
Smith, Lt.-Col. Chas. Hamilton, *KH.* h. p. 15 F.	Fourth Class Wilhelm
👑 Somerset, Lt.-Gen. *Lord*, R. E. H. *GCB.* 1 Dr.	Knight Maria Theresa —— Tower and Sword Third Class St. Wladimir
👑 Somerset, Lt.-Gen, *Lord* Fitz Roy J. H. *KCB.* 53 F. Mil. Sec. to the Gen. Comm.-in-Chief.	Knight Maria Theresa Fourth Class St. George Knight Maxilian Joseph Commander Tower and Sword
Sorell, Lt.-Col. *Sir* Thos. S. *KH.*	Second Class St. Bento d'Avis
Stanhope, Col. *Hon.* Leicester, *CB.* Unatt.	Commander of Saviour
Steele, Lt. *Sir* Robert, h. p. R. Mar.	Knight Charles the Third
Stopford, Lt.-Gen. *Hon. Sir* E. *GCB.* 41 F.	Commander Tower and Sword
👑 Strafford, Lt.-Gen. John, *Lord*, *GCB. GCH.* 29 F.	Knight Maria Theresa Second Class St. Wladimir
👑 Straton, Lt.-Gen. *Sir* Jos. *CB. KCH.* 8 Dr.	Fourth Class St. Wladimir
Swan, Capt. Graves C. Part. Serv.	Second Class St. Fernando
Thompson, Lieut. Chas. Wm. 81 F.	First Class St. Fernando
Thornhill, Lt.-Col. Geo. *CB.* late of 14 F.	Second Class of Crescent
👑 Torrens, Col. Rob. *CB.* h. p. 38 F.	Second Class of St. Anne
Turner, Gen. *Sir* Hilgrove, *GCH.* 19 F.	Second Class of Crescent St. Anne
—— Lieut. Geo. Edw. R. Art.	First Class St. Ferdinand Knight Charles the Third Commander Isabella the Catholic
Upton, Lt.-Gen. *Hon.* A. P. *CB.* from Gren. Gds.	Knight Maxilian Joseph
👑 Vandeleur, Gen. *Sir* J. O. *GCB.* 16 Dr.	Second Class St. Wladimir Commander Maximilian Joseph
👑 Vere, Maj.-Gen. *Sir* Chas. Broke, *KCB.*	Knight Tower and Sword Fourth Class St. Wladimir —— Wilhelm
👑 Vivian, Lt.-Gen. *Right Hon. Sir* R. H. Bart. *GCB. GCH.* 1 Dr.	Third Class St. Wladimir Knight Maria Theresa
Walker, Gen. *Sir* Geo. T. *Bart. GCB.* 50 F.	Commander Tower and Sword
Warburton, Lieut. G. D. R. Art.	First Class St. Fernando
Warre, Col. *Sir* William, *CB.* Unatt.	Knight Tower and Sword Commander St. Bento d'Avis
👑 Waters, Maj.-Gen. *Sir* J. *KCB.*	Second Class St. Anne
Watson, Lt.-Col. *Sir* Fred. h. p. Port. Serv.	Commander St. Bento d'Avis
Watson, Maj.-Gen. *Sir* Henry, *CB.*	Commander Tower and Sword

Officers permitted to wear Foreign Orders.

Way, Maj.-Gen. *Sir* G. Holman B. *CB.* ...... Knight Commander and Sword
⛨ Webster, Lt.-Col. Henry, Unatt. .... Commander and Sword
⛨ Wellington, Field Marshal Arthur, *Duke* of, *KG. GCB. GCH.* Col. of Gren. Gds. and of the Rifle Brigade, Constable of the Tower of London, and Lord Warden of the Cinque Ports *First and highest Class of nearly every Order in Europe.*
West, *Sir* Aug. *MD.* h. p. Dep. Insp. Gen. .... Knight Tower and Sword
Whittingham, Lt.-Gen. *Sir* S. F. *KCB. KCH.* 71 F. .... Grand Cross St. Fernando
Williams, Col. *Sir* E. K. *KCB.* 9 F. .... Knight Tower and Sword
Wilson, Lt.-Gen. *Sir* John, *KCB.* 82 F. ...... { St. Bento d'Avis / Commander Tower and Sword
⛨ Wood, Lt.-Col. Charles, Unatt. .... Knight Military Merit of Prussia
⛨ Woodford, Lt.-Gen. *Sir* A. *KCB. GCMG.* from Coldst. Gds. .... { Knight Maria Theresa / Fourth Class of St. George
Wylde, Lt.-Col. William, R. Art. .... { Knight Charles the Third / Second Class St. Fernando / Commander Isabella the Catholic.

477

INDEX.

Name	page
Abbey, Robert	116
Abbott, James	234
——— Thomas	259
——— William Ward	187
Abercromby, Hon. Alex.	32
——— Hon. George	
——— Ralph	58
Aberdour, Sholto John Lord	223
Abernethie, Thomas, *KH*.	36
Ackland, Robert Dudley	122
Ackroyd, Robert	307
A'Court, Chas. Ashe, *KH*.	34
Acton, Francis, *Baron*	436
Adair, Charles William	296
——— James	86
——— Richard Bratton	272
——— Thomas	42, 292
——— Thomas James	99, 219
——— William Robert	219
Adam, Frederick, *KCB*.	12, 115, 208
——— William	224
Adams, Edward	240
——— Frank	179
——— George Pownoll, *KCH*.	13
——— Hen. Benj. Briscoe	263
——— Henry Balthazar	263
——— Henry Williams	102, 169
——— Mich. Goold	129
——— Samuel Goold	161
——— Septimus	240
——— Thomas	130
——— William Henry	161
Adamson, James	191
——— Joseph Samuel	189
Addison, Thomas	153
——— Thomas Fenn	37
Adolphus, Edwin, *MD*.	250
Adye, John Miller	272
Affleck, Duncan	247
Agnew, Andrew	245
——— Robert Vans	253
Ahmuty, John	208
——— James	115
——— Warren	208
Ainslie, Charles P.	128
——— Frederick George	172
——— Henry Francis	235
——— Wm. Bernard	245

Name	page
Ainsworth, Oliver D.	202
Airey, Dyonisius	271
Airey, James Talbot	154
——— Richard	70, 185
Aitcheson, Andrew	115
Aitchison, John	37, 149
——— Geo. Brooks	116
Aiten, Victor Von	433
Aitken, Alex.	229
Alcock, Thos. St. Leger	247
——— William	174
Alderson, Ralph Carr	101, 116, 284
Aldred, John Williams	41
Aldrich, Edward	285
Aldridge, Job	159
——— Robert	212
Aldworth, Robert	246
Alen, Luke	53
Alessi, M. de Marchesi	262
Alexander, Alexander	83
——— Archibald	179
——— Caledon DuPre	118
——— Chas. Carson	284
——— Geo. Gardiner	296
——— James	115
——— John	273
——— Thomas	311
Algeo, John	157
——— James	99, 229
Allan, A. T.	208
——— George	88
——— James	208
——— James	37, 208
——— John	197
——— Robert	311
Allard, Richard	255
Allen, Charles Davers	157
——— Edward	91
——— Hans	37
——— James	116
——— James	256
——— Ralph Shuttleworth	272
——— Seymour Phillips	118
——— William	119
——— Wm. Warner	140
Alleyne, James Holder	203
Alley, John H.	204
Allix, Charles	39
——— Frederick William	146
Allman, George	310
——— Wm. Hutchinson, *MD*.	155

Name	page
Alston, Hen. Frederick	251
——— Horace George	272
Alten, Chas. *Count, GCB. GCH*.	16, 434
Alves, John	226
——— Wm. Gemmell	180
Ambrose, John Annah	173
Ames, Lionel	143
Amiel, George	216
Amiens, Benj. O'Neale, *Viscount*	121
Amsinck, William	178
Anbury, Thomas, *Bt*.	115
Anderdon, Hobart Grant	174
Anderson, Abraham Collis	155
——— Alexander	294
——— Alexander	39
——— Andrew	152
——— Arthur, *MD*.	234
——— David	235
——— David D.	116
——— George	173
——— George	227
——— Henry	*114
——— James	92, 257
——— John	87, 256
——— Joseph, *KH*.	85, 201
——— Paul	13, 230
——— Robert, *KH*.	62, 243
——— Samuel Baxter Douglas	200
——— Thomas	189
——— William	256
——— Wm. Cochrane	268
——— William H. H.	192
Anderton, William	118
Andrews, Alfred	172
——— Augustus	115
——— Charles	116
——— John	124
——— Mottram	179
——— Robert	99, 267
——— Robert Alex.	181
Angelo, Edward Anthony, *KH*.	60
——— John	116
——— Wm. St. Leger	259
Angerstein, John Julius	
——— William	63, 144
Anglesey, H. W. *Mar. of, KG.GCB.GCH*.	6, 133
Anglin, Philip, *MD*.	218
Annesley, Hon. Ar r	11

Index.

	page		page		page
Annesley, Francis Chas.	213	Armstrong, Nenon	127	Autran, Alexander	436
———— Marcus	85	———— Richard	191	Axford, Richard	116
———— Stephen Fra.		———— Sir Richard	35	Ayles, John George Aug.	295
Chas.	215	———— Richard Say	268	Aylmer, Frederick Chas.	241
Ansell, Augustus Fra.	226	———— Thomas	54	———— George Edward	245
———— Edward Clarges	226	———— William	132	———— Henry	271
Ansley, Benjamin, KC.	33	———— William	198	———— Matthew, Lord,	
Anson, George, GCB.	9, 124	———— Wm. Henry	172	GCB.	11, 169
———— Hon. George	43	———— Wm. Cairnes	196	———— Thomas Brab.	34
———— John W. Hamilton	120	Armytage, Henry	58	Ayre, Thomas Eames	182
———— Octavius, H. St. G.	154	———— Henry	147		
———— William, Bt. KCB.		Arnaud, John, KH.	86	Babington, John	66
	9, 198	Arney, Chas. Augustus	209	Baby, Daniel	67
Anstruther, Rob. Lindsay	116	Arnold, Henry	296	Bace, Henry William	172
Anthony, J. A. Christian	436	———— Jas. Robertson,		———— Wm. Godfrey, MD.	177
Anton, James	67	KH.	36, 282	Bachellé, George de	434
Aplin, Andrew Snape Ham.		Arthur, Fred. Leopold	155	———— Lewis de, Baron	
	99, 241	———— Geo. KCH.	38, 115	Von Dem Brinck	435
———— John Guise Rogers	179	———— John	94, 245	Bacchaus, Arnold Erich	437
———— W. J. D. C.	241	———— Thomas	102, 123	———— Franz Fred.	437
Appleton, Edward	294	Arthure, Wm. Henry	100, 207	Bacmeister, Arnold	437
Appuhn, Arnold	436	Ash, Henry	125	———— Christian	435
———— Charles Ernest	438	Ashburnham, Hon. Thos.		———— Julius	436
———— George	435		64, 147	———— Lewis	435
Arabin, Frederick	70, 266	Ashe, Benjamin	116	Bacon, Hen. Hickman	123
Arbuthnot, Chas. George		———— St. George	115	———— William	116
James	44, 224	Ashhurst, John Henry	166	Badcock, Lovell Benja-	
———— Robt. KCB.	17	Ashmore, Charles	187	min, KH.	58, 141
———— Thos. KCB.	15,	———— John	293	Baddeley, Fred. Henry	284
	203	———— William	167	———— Wm. Clinton	115
———— Hon. Walter	203	Ashpitel, Felix	107	———— Wm. H. Clinton	200
———— Hon. Wm.	95, 267	Ashton, Thos. Hen.	246	Baertling, Frederick	433
Arbuthnott, Hon. Hugh	17	Ashworth, Frederick	40	Bagenall, William	258
Archdall, Edward	165	Askew, Henry	14	Bagot, Charles	145
———— John	203	Askwith, Wm. Harrison	270	———— Edward	211
———— Mervyn	132	Aslett, John Thompson	295	———— George	202
Archdeacon, Edw. Mon-		———— Thompson	44, 292	Bagwell, Edward	123
tagu	307	———— Wm. Stratton	296	Bailey, Charles	285
Archer, Clement Robt.	124	Astell, Rich. Wm.	71, 145	———— Morris William	54
———— Edw. Caulfield	88	———— Charles Edward	166	———— William	305
———— Fran. Bisset	307	Astier, Henry	214	Bailie, James	234
———— George, MD.	230	Aston, Joseph	150	Baillie, Frederick	312
———— William Henry	140	Astuto, Antonio	439	———— Geo. Clement	286
———— Wm. Spearman	307	———— Pierre	440	———— Hugh	32
Arentsschildt, Adol. Von		Atcherley, Wm. Sharp		———— Robert	224
	434	Lang	295	———— Robert	229
———— Sir Victor		Atchison, Henry Alex.	257	Bain, William, MD.	185
Von, KCH.	83, 437	Atherley, Mark Kerr	244	Bainbrigge, John Hankey	94
Arguimbau, Law	38	Atkins, Geo. Martin	197	———— Philip	39
Arkwright, Eustace	135	Atkins, Henry Martin	204	———— Philip J.	286
———— Ferd. Wm.	124	———— Robert	211	———— Thomas	208
———— William	132	———— Thomas	85	Baines, Cuthbert A.	183
Armstrong, Abraham	310	Atkinson, Edward D.	188	Baird, Sir Jas. Gardiner,	
———— Alexander	14	———— James S.	190	Bart.	136
———— Alex. Boswell		———— Thomas, MD.	234	———— John	296
	101, 260	Atty, Wm. Fred. Willes	182	———— John William	222
———— Anth. W. S. F.	169	Aubin, Philip	90, 208	———— Peter, M.D.	196
———— Charles	138	Auchmuty, Sam. Benj.	36	———— Wm. Dunlop	168
———— Daniel	236	Audain, John Willett P.	167	Baker, George	116
———— David Edw.	208	Austen, Henry Edmund	223	———— George	65
———— David Thos.	165	———— John, KH.	65	———— Geo. Granville	186
———— Elliott	92, 196	———— John Wentworth	198	———— Geo. Spenser Per.	296
———— James	42, 265	Austin, Chas. Wilson	235	———— Hugh Percy	156
———— John	251	———— George Isaac	154	———— James Swayne	286
———— John	254	———— William	202	———— John	169
———— John James	251	———— William, MD.	249	———— Narborough	69, 232

479

Index.

Name	page
Baker, Richard D.	202
——— Thomas	7
——— Thomas Richard	102, 158
——— Wellington Cha. C.	174
——— William	293
——— William L Y.	225
Balchild, Geo. Elliot	293
Balders, Cha.Wm.Morley	130
Baldwin, George	182
Baldwyn, Edward James	155
Baldy, William	307
Balfour, Arthur Lowry	224
——— Charles Anthony	272
——— Robert William	240
——— Thomas Graham, MD.	311
——— William	195
——— Wm. Stewart	69, 147
——— William	231
Balinhard, John Allan De	139
Ball, Thomas Gerrard	64, 159
——— Wm. Hawkins	90
Ballantine, Fretcheville D.	115
——— Stevenson	255
Ballard, Volant Vashon	160
Ballinghall, David James	293
Balneavis, Henry, *KH*	40
——— Henry Colin	209
Balvaird, William	39
Bambrick, Robert	137
Bamford, Rob. Carter	225
Bampfield, William	183
Bampton, Wm. Wright	86
Bannatine, Richard	312
Banner, Robt. Murray	245
Barbauld, Montague	206
Barbor, Robert Douglas	132
Barckhausen, Augustus	442
Barclay, Edward	248
——— George	310
——— Henry Bruce	207
——— John	116
Bardin, Michael	204
Barfoot, William	243
Baring, Ernest	436
——— Geo. *Baron* Von, *KCH*.	54, 434
——— George	438
——— Lewis Charles	434
——— William	171
Barker, Alexander	273
——— George	116
——— George Robert	271
——— John Cricklow	311
Barlow, Cuthbert	205
——— Frederick	213
——— Fred. Contart	171
——— Geo. Edw. Pratt	55
——— James, *MD.*	125
——— Maurice	87, 165
——— Robert Hilaro	220
Barnard, Andrew Fran. *KCB*. *GCH*.	13, 252
——— Hen. Clapton	116
——— Henry Wm.	61, 144

Name	page
Barnes, Andr. Armstrong	176
——— Caleb	294
——— George Adam	243
——— Geo. West, *MD.*	164
——— Rich. Knowles	294
——— Samuel	273
——— William	192
——— William English	
Fitz. Edw.	130
Barnett, Edward	129
——— William	125
Barney, George	94, 283
——— John Edward	243
Barns, Jas. Stevenson, *KCB.*	13, 252
Barnwell, Charles	94, 160
Baron, Richard John	97, 284
Barr, Marcus	154
Barrallier, Fra. Louis	88
Barrell, Frederick William Edward	206
Barrett, Richard	170
Barrow, Wallace	143
Barry, Charles	101, 225
——— James, *MD.*	309
——— John Richard	166
——— Philip	95, 283
——— Philip John Staple	286
——— Robt. Hugh Smith	140
——— St. Leger	217
Bartlett, Thomas	202
Bartley, George	201
——— George Francis	200
——— John Cowell	155
——— John Metge, *MD.*	128
——— Robert	57, 200
——— Walter Tyler	200
Bartoli, Joseph	441
Barton, Alexander, *KH.*	67, 138
——— Charles	98, 140
——— Hen. Cha. Benyon	243
——— Hugh William	58
——— Robert, *KCH*.	13
——— Wm. Hugh	228
Barttelot, Walter B.	128
Basden, Jas. Lewis	60, 241
——— Samuel Taylor	236
Bassano, Fran. Matthias	310
Basset, Richard	269, 273
Bastard, James Stokes	64, 266
——— John P. P. Wade	120
Bate, William	208
Bateman, Robert	199
——— Robert	68
Bates, Henry	234
——— Robert	196
Bateson, Thomas	212
Bathe, Wm. Percival	150
Bathurst, Benjamin	272
——— Henry	150
——— James, *KCB.*	13
——— Peter James	148
——— Tho. Harvey	204
Battersbee, Thomas	284

Name	page
Battersby, Robert	198
Battley, D'Oyly William	216
Battye, Edward	174
Bauermeister, Geo. Lewis	433
Baumgardt, John Gregory	44, 153
Baumgartner, Rob. Julian	179
Baxter, James	220
Bayldon, Richard	116
Baylee, Pery	90, 215
Bayley, Charles, *CMG.*	116
——— Chas. Andrews, *CMG.*	89
——— Edward	240
——— Hen. Addington	306
——— Jas. Twisleton	205
Baylie, Thos. Hewitt	95, 218
Bayly, Fra. Brownrigg	258
——— Frederick J.	243
——— George	186
——— Geo. Augustus	223
——— Henry, *GCH.*	10, 159
——— Henry, *KH.*	86
——— John	286
——— Paget	181
——— William	159
——— Wm. Prittie	244
——— Zachary Clutterbuck	94, 267
Baynes, Henry, *KH.*	67
——— O'Hara	95
——— Simcoe	93, 159
Bazalgette, Duncan	217
——— John	67
——— Louis	175
Beadon, Valentine	294
Beale, Walter Yonge	220
Beales, William	193
Beamish, Charles	186
Bean, Nathaniel	65
Beatson, Roger Stuart	285
——— Geo. Stewart	312
Beatty, Andrew	286
——— David	251
——— Edward	251
——— George	42, 292
Beauchamp, Richard	58
Beauclerk, Aubrey Fred.	158
——— *Lord* Charles	151
——— *Lord* Geo. Aug.	136
Beaufoy, Benjamin	175
Beaulieu, Adolphus de	434
Beausire, Joseph	83
Beavan, Thomas	133
Becher, Robert	116
Becker, Augustus	436
——— Ernest de	437
——— John	440
Beckham, Thomas	170
Beckwith, Charles	38
——— Hen. Ferdinand	252
——— Sidney	252
——— William, *KH.*	63
——— William Henry	16
Bedford, Wm. Fanshaw	212
——— James	116

Index.

	page		page		page
Bedford, Wm. Devaynes	137	Beresford, *Lord* James	242	Bingham, Henry	212
Bedingfield, John George	192	——— James D.	228	Birch, Jas. Hunter Blair	218
Beebee, Robert Morris	157	——— Marcus	57, 154	——John	88
Beere, George	165	——— *Lord* William	118	——John Francis	19, 282
Beers, Philip Grove	154	——— William Carr,		——Robert Henry	42, 265
Beete, John Picton	99, 172	*Visc. GCB. GCH.*	7, 167	Bird, Henry Charles	258
Beetham, William	85, 205	——— William Henry	253	—— Lawrence	134
Beevor, Robert	17, 264	Bergeon, Nich. Julien de	440	—— Louis Saunders	116
Begbie, Thos. Stirling	89	Berger, Charles	436	Birrell, William, *MD.*	228
Behne, Chas. Aug. Jacob	434	Berkeley, Cha. A. F. H.	150	Birtwhistle, John	99, 183
Behrens, Hen. Christopher	433	——— G. H. F., *KCB.*	18	Biscoe, Geo. Grattan	218
Bell, Edward Wells	59	——— Sackville Hamil.	18	——— Vincent, Joseph	284
—— George	102, 151	Bernal, Ralph	158	Bishop, Chas. Thos. Geo.	115
—— John	36	Bernard, Arthur	201	—— Francis	312
—— Robert	125	——— Scrope	169	—— R.	133
—— Robert	115	——— Thomas	138	—— Peter, *KH.*	87
—— Thomas	57, 199	——— William	170	—— William	305
—— William	163	——— William	83	Bisset, Thomas, *MD.*	141
—— William	167	——— Wm. Boran	190	Bissett, Daniel	68, 266
—— William, *MD.*	177	Berner, Carl Ernest	439	—— John T.	260
—— William	194	Berners, William	269	Bisshopp, Cecil	55, 162
—— William	241	Bernewitz, E. A. Wm. de	439	Blachford, Aug. George	175
—— William	246	Berry, James Parsons	261	——— Wm. Henry	115
—— William	95, 267	——— Richard	227	Blachley, Charles	89, 267
Bellasis, Edward H.	115	Bersy, Amedée Rodolph		——— Henry	95, 267
Bellingham, Wm.	183	de	441	Black, George	232
Belsher, Fred. Joseph	218	Bertie, *Hon.* Montague		——James	258
Belshes, John Murray	66	Per.	145	——John Lewis	100, 204
Belson, Frederick	253	Bertles, Henry Beckett	185	——Alex.	*114
——— George John	95, 267	Berwick, Thompson	259	Blackall, John	190
Bender, Benoit	234	Best, Abel Dottin Wm.	232	——Newcombe Edw.	136
Benn, Anthony	271	—— Gustavus, George	434	——Robert	200
——- Piercy	269	—— James John	185	——Robert	116
Benne, Lewis, *KH.*	438	—— *Hon.* John Charles	201	Blackburn, John	237
Bennett, Alex. Maxwell	116	—— Rich. Mordesley	158	Blackburne, Isaac	168
———Charles Luxmore	238	—— William	434	——— John Ireland	125
———Francis Levett	164	Bethune, Alexander	16	——— William	221
———George	256	—— Duncan Munro	160	Blackett, Charles	174
———George A.	285	—— Henry, *Bart.*	115	Blacklin, Richard	151
———Henry	294, 297	——— John Drinkwater	53	Blackmore, John	65
———Lewis Moore	97, 216	Betson, William	141	Blackwell, Thomas Eden	243
———Richard	97, 151	Bett, James	119	Blackwood, *Hon.* Hen.	
———Richard Baylis	238	Betts, William Thomas	177	Stephen	143
———William	67	Bevan, Howe Curtis	270	——— Richard	272
———Wm. Rob. Lyon	167	Beverhoudt, Adam	209	Blair, Augustus	156
Benson, Hen. Roxby	143	Beverley, Chas. Wm.	305	—— Edward Hunter	245
—— George Thomas	179	Bevians, James Montagu	42	—— Harry	154
—— Wm. Welbore H.	208	Bewes, Cecil Edward	237	—— James Hunter	150
Bent, George	286	Bibra, Frederick, *Baron*	440	—— Thomas Hunter	38
—— John	287	Bicknell, Philip Blundell	197	Blake, Fred. Rudolph	184
—— William Henry	268	———Thos. Barnacle	227	——George	116
Bentinck, Cha. Ant. Ferd.		Biddle, Thomas	116	——Henry	65
	43, 147	Biddulph, Tho. Middleton	118	——Isidore Anthony	159
——— Arth. Cavendish	236	Bigge, William Matthew	222	——John Brice	198
——— Hen. John Wm.		Biggs, Arthur Wm.	98, 133	——Matthew Gregory	43
	58, 147	——John Andrew	115	——Patrick Francis	239
Bentley, Alex. C. Downing	201	Bigland, Geo. Selsey	197	——Robert Dudley	8
—— Charles	169	Bill, Charles	141	——Stephen	217
Berbie, *Hon.* Brownlow C.	135	Billeb, Chas. Augustus		——William Williams	33
Berdmore, Scrope Reynett	171	Lewis	435	Blakeman, John	157
—— Vesey	215	Bindon, William	100, 261	Blakeney, *Rt. Hon.* Edw.	
Bere, Edw. Baker	142	Bingham, Charles	271	*KCB. GCH.*	14, 115, 158
Beresford, George John	270	—— Edm. Hayter	254	—— Edward Hugh	219
—— Henry Robert	212	—— George Wm.	269	Blamire, Charles	251
—— Hen. Tristram	223	—— Geo. Wm. Pow-		Blanckley, Edward Jas.	157
—— H. W. de la Poer	156	lett	247	Bland, John	305

Index.

Bland, William 272
Blane, Charles Collins 62
———— Robert 119
Blanshard, Thomas 66, 283
Blantyre, Charles, *Lord* 146
Blaquiere, *Hon.* Wm. de 11
———— John de 192
Blenkins, Geo. Eleazor 146
Blenkinsop, William 161
———— George Ant. Leaton 196
Blennerhasset, Barry 223
Bligh, *Hon.* Edward 7
———— John Thomas 213
Blois, William 72, 203
Blomefield, George 86
Blommart, Daniel Francis 14
Blood, John 91
Bloomfield, Benjamin, *Lord GCB. GCH.* 12, 264
———— Hen. Keane 99. 162
———— John 268
———— John Caldwell 163
Blosse, Edward Lynch 162
Blottnitz, Charles Von 437
Blount, Herbert 220
Bluett, Frederic Buckland 296
Blundell, Frederick 116
———— William 165
Blundstone, John 438
Blunt, Richard 10, 218
Bluntish, Robert 160
———— Archibald 160
Blyth, Alexander 297
———— David 296
———— Samuel 94, 200
Blythe, John David 254
Boalth, James 139
Boardman, Edward 115
Boddam, Alexander 209
Boggis, James Edward 256
Boidin, Jean Baptiste 441
Boileau, Sam. Brendram 94, 173
Boland, Robert Spencer 210
Boldero, Lonsdale 61, 144
Boles, Thomas 115
Bolton, Abraham 125
———— Daniel 100, 284
———— George 95
———— John 93, 127
———— John 227
———— Richard Nassau 236
———— Samuel 64, 182
———— Theophilus 116
Bonamy, John 99, 157
Bonavita, Vicenza 262
Bond, Adolphus Fred. 204
———— Edward 204
———— Frederick 116
———— Henry 99, 130
———— Wadham Wyndham 155
Bone, Hugh, *MD.* 309
Bonham, Henry Fred. 136
———— George William 116
———— John Brathwaite 201

Bonham, Pinson 142
———— Pinson 9
Bonner, John George 116
Bonnor, Thomas 100, 257
Bonnycastle, Rich. Hen. 94, 283
Booth, Henry, *KH.* 59, 194
———— John 163
———— William 69, 192
Borchers, Johann Daniel 433
Bordes, Geo. Fra. Wm. 284
Borton, Arther 160
Boscawen, Evelyn Spencer 191
Bosset, Chas. Philip de
Bosset, *KH.* 37
Bostlemann, Henry 438
Boteler, Robert 285
Both, Caspar Von 435
Bothe, Frederick 441
Bothmer, Bernard Von 432
———— Ferdinand de 438
Boucherett, Hen. Robert 143
Boughey, Geo. F. Fletcher 210
———— Anchitel, F. F. 233
Bourchier, Jas. Claud. 38
———— John 233
———— Legendre C. 168
———— Thomas 250
Bourdillon, Alfred Jas. 187
Bourke, Aylmer Lambert 123
———— Oliver Paget 168
———— Richd. *KCB.* 13, 216
———— Theophilus John 182
———— Thomas 195
———— Thomas 185
Bourne, Johnson 258
Boussingault, Pierre F. L. 439
Bouverie, Everard Wm. 62, 120
———— Hen. F. *KCB.* 15
———— James Wm. 88, 238
Bovill, John William 307
Bowater, Edward, *KCH.* 20
Bowdler, Henry 115
Bowdoin, James Temple 170
Bowen, Henry 116
———— Henry 83
———— Herbert 115
———— Hugh Thomas 238
Bower, George James 214
Bowers, Arth. M. Alex. 188
———— Chas. Robert 86
———— Henry 305
Bowes, Frederick 115
———— James 92, 239
Bowles, Charles 130
———— Francis Wm. 246
———— George 41, 147
———— Henry Oldfield 253
Bowling, John 150
Bowman, Wm. Flockhart 305
Bowyer, Edward 233
———— Geo. Douglas 242
Boxer, Edw. Mourrier 272
Boyce, Henry George 119
Boyd, Alexander 162
———— Charles 96

Boyd, James 163
———— Lewis Alexander 162
———— Mossem 115
———— R. Browne Tho. 162
———— Uriah 205
———— Walter 249
———— William 239
Boyer, Laurent 440
Boyes. Charles Rob. *MD.* 132
———— John Monson 116
Boyle, Cavendish Spencer 199
———— *Hon.* Hen. Chas. 158
———— *Hon* Robert Edw. 148
———— William 166
———— William St. John 312
Boylesve, Charles de 440
Boys, Edward French 62, 196
———— Henry 122
———— John Hen. Hartley 227
Brabazon, Chas. Geo. 172
———— Jas. Dupre 229
Brackenbury, *Sir* Edward 66
———— Langley 306
Brackmeyer, Henry 442
Braddell, Edw. Benj. 222
Bradford, Edward 207
———— John Yule 116
———— Thomas, *GCB. GCH.* 11, 181
———— Wilmot Henry 253
Bradfute, Robert 185
Bradish, John 60
Bradshaw, George Paris, *KH.* 55, 229
———— Hugh Hilton 130
———— Joseph 94, 188
———— Lawrence, *KC.* 16
———— Paris W. Aug. 229
Bragge, William 85
Braham, Augustus Fred. 163
Braimer, Jas. Louttet 296
Brand, Henry 148
———— James 125
———— James 167
Brandenstein, Henry Von 439
Brander, Thos. Coventry 141
Brandis, Augustus Von 434
———— Charles Von 436
———— Eberhard de 436
———— Edward Von 436
———— Ferdinand de 437
———— Frederick 435
Brandling, John J. 272
———— Ralph Thos. 158
Brandon, John 116
Brandreth, Frederick 150
———— Hen. Rowland 284
———— Thos. Alston 59, 265
Braman, John 212
Braun, George 432
———— William 437
Brauns, Charles 435
Bray, Edward Wm. 96, 182
———— William 182
Braybrooke, Samuel 93, 257

482

Index.

	page
Bredin, Andrew	36, 265
Breedon, John	212
Brem, Nich. Philibert de	84, 439
Bremer, Henry	295
Bremmer, William Thos.	197
Brenchley, Algernon G.	131
Brennan, John	173
Brereton, Robt. Edw. Per.	228
——— Wm. *KH*.	67, 267
——— Wm. Robert	222
Breslin, William Irwin	135
Breton, Henry William	63, 155
Brett, Charles	138
——— Henry	141
——— John	141
——— John Davy	143
——— Richard Rich. W.	87
Brewster, Henry	228
——— Cardinal	152
Breymann, Frederick	432
——— George	434
Brice, George Tito	116
Brickenden, R. T. W. L.	223
Bridge, Cyprian	209
——— Cyprian	65, 266
——— George	154
——— Robert Onslow	294
——— Thomas	236
Bridgeman, Cha. Orlando	220
——— Edm. Hen.	62
——— Fra. Ort. Hen.	196
Bridgen, Charles	306
Bridger, James Paul	54
Bridges, Edward Jacob	268
——— Henry	198
Briggs, John	115
——— John Falconer, *KH*.	66
Brinckmann, Ernest	435
——— Frederick	437
——— Julius	435
Bringhurst, John Henry	242
Brisbane, Chas. Baillie	100, 185
——— Thos. Makdougall, *Bt. GCB. GCH.*	11, 185
Briscoe, Hylton	122
Bristow, Frederick	157
——— Henry	60
——— Skeffington	176
Brittain, Joseph Francis	295
Broadhead, Brinkman	62, 147
——— John Richard	32
Broadley, Edw. Osborne	183
——— John Bourryan	143
Brock, Eugene	171
——— Saumarez, *KH*.	59
Brockman, James	200
Broderick, Edward	185
Brodie, Patrick	162
Brodribb, Samuel	140
Brodrick, *Hon.* John	7

	page
Broembsen, Adol. Otto Von	439
Broke, Horatio George	59
——— Charles Acton	286
Brome, Joseph Frederick	197
Bromet, William, *MD*.	118
Bromley, Henry	199
——— Robert	118
Bromwich, Arch. Edm.	131
Bronner, Charles de	440
Brooke, Arth. *KCB.*	12, 238
——— Arthur Beresford	174
——— Charles Aug.	247
——— Edw. Basil	90, 219
——— George	116
——— Gustavus Travers	206
——— Henry Vaughan	183
——— James Croft	182
——— Richard	118
——— Thomas	163
——— Thomas	39
——— William	10
Brooker, Henry Wm.	296
Brookes, Robert	90, 221
——— William	227
Brooks, George B.	115
Brooksbank, Joseph	85
Broom, Saville	94, 161
Broome, Henry	181
——— Louis, G. F.	181
Brotherton, Thos. Wm. *CB.*	36, 142
——— John Wm.	137
Brough, Rich. Secker	36, 265
——— Richard	235
——— Redmond Wm.	93, 153
Broughton, J. Delves, *Bt.*	7
——— Wm. E. Delves	285
Brown, Alexander	69, 283
——— Andrew	98, 231
——— Benjamin	225
——— Benj. Handley	235
——— Edw. John Vesey	212
——— George	134
——— George	146
——— George, *KH.*	36, 252
——— George	180
——— Gustavus	54
——— Henry	205
——— Henry	116
——— James	208
——— Jas. Dudgeon	91
——— James D.	116
——— Jas. Montagu	245
——— John	222
——— John	243
——— John Tatton	294
——— Nicholas R.	185
——— Peter	38
——— Robert Boyd	227
——— Samuel	14
——— Wm. Gustavus	175
Browne, Abraham Wm.	230
——— Alexander	162
——— Alexander, *MD.*	188
——— Benj. Chapman	59

	page
Browne, Barton Parker	99
——— Denis	139
——— Edward Stanley	295
——— Fielding	38
——— George	98, 183
——— George	86
——— *Hon.* Geo. Aug.	98, 216
——— Gore	92, 192
——— Gore	9, 195
——— Henry Sabine	237
——— *Hon.* John	116
——— John	17
——— John	67
——— John Frederick	33
——— Joseph Deane	126
——— Joseph Steere	306
——— Melville G. B.	225
——— Percival	192
——— Peter	154
——— *Hon.* Rich. Howe	134
——— Robert	100, 167
——— Rob. Fra. Melv.	56
——— St. John Thomas	271
——— Salwey	220
——— Stephenson	159
——— Thomas	126
——— Thomas, *KCH.*	11
——— Thomas	83
——— Thomas Gore	65, 266
——— Tho. Hen. *KCH.*	40
——— William P. K.	200
——— William R.	213
Brownrigg, Hen. Moore	203
——— Studholme	160
Brownson, Wm. Henry, *MD.*	216
Bruce, Eyre Evans	116
——— John	167
——— *Hon.* Robert	145
——— Robert	246
——— Robert Cairnes	187
——— William, *KH.*	87
——— Wm. Tyrrell	169
Bruere, Henry	194
——— Albert Sadlier	194
Brumell, William	227
Brunker, James Robert	166
Brunt, Thomas	120
Brunton, Richard	61, 139
Brydges, John Geo. Wm.	123
Buchan, Alexander	102
——— John, *KCB.*	16, 247
Buchanan, Alexander	231
——— Colin	214
——— Gilbert J. Lane	270
——— James	294
——— Neil Snodgrass	245
——— Phillips	126
Buck, Thomas	67
Buckley, Edward Pery	56
Budd, Ralph	165
——— Richard	116
——— William Sidney	296
Budgen, Thomas	284
Buhse, Geo. Aug. Hen.	436

Index.

Name	page
Buhse, John Fred. Wm.	434
Bulkeley, Lempster	220
—— Thomas	118
—— Thomas, *MD.*	223
—— Thomas	182
Bull, Frederick G.	203
—— John Edward N.	230
—— John James	161
Buller, Frederick William	11
—— Frederick Thomas	58
—— George	103, 252
—— Henry George	246
Bullock, Hen. Robert	90
Bulman, George	211
Bulow, Christian von	432
—— John, *Baron, KH.*	53, 432
—— O. W. F. J. C. von	432
Bunbury, Hen. E. *Bt.* *KCB.*	12
—— Henry William	184
—— Stonehouse Geo.	154
—— Thomas	212
—— Thos, *KH.*	41, 219
—— Thomas	92, 232
Bunce, Benjamin	293
—— Richard	60
—— Richard Searle	296
Burchell, Basil Herne	154
Burdett, Francis	143
—— Charles Sedley	212
—— Robert	61
Burer, Gabriel	55
Burgh, James Florence de	116
—— John	102, 245
—— Thomas	192
—— Thomas Hussey	251
—— William	115
Burghersh, J. *Lord, GCH.*	15
Burgmann, George	285
Burgoyne, John Mont. *Bt.*	64, 145
—— John Fox, *KCB.*	20, 282
Burke, John, *Bt.*	32
—— Joseph	312
—— John Hardman	240
—— Patrick	41
—— Thomas	246
—— Thomas	60
—— Thomas John	128
—— William	254
Burleigh, John	257
Burlton, William	116
Burmester, Arnold E.	210
—— John Claridge	286
Burn, James	155
—— Robert	268
Burnaby, Chas. Herrick,	270, 273
—— John Dick	32
—— Richard	286
—— Rich. Beaumont	268, 273
Burne, Cornwall	90, 243
Burnes, *Sir* Alexander	116

Name	page
Burnett, Francis, *MD.*	197
Burney, Hugh Somerv. S.	224
—— William, *KH.*	87, 260
—— William James	296
Burns, David	170
—— John,	230
—— William	192
Burnside, Henry	96, 213
Burrell, George,	34, 169
—— Graham	272
—— Henry Duncan	169
—— Wm. Henry, *MD.*	229
Burriss, Simpson Nelson	257
Burroughs, George	269
Burrowes, Rob. Edw. *KH.*	90
—— Wm. Nesbitt	62
Burrows, Arthur George	271
—— Montagu	14
Burslem, Nathaniel, *KH.*	33
—— Rollo Gillespie	164
Burt, Charles	284
—— James	230
—— James	273
Burton, Alfred	293
—— Edw. John, *MD.*	259
—— Edward William	311
—— Fowler	249
—— Wm. Moulden	72, 292
Bury, George Batt	293
Bush, Robert	248
—— Seddon Wm. Sutton	254
—— William, *KH.*	58, 254
Bushe, Gervase Parker	133
Bussiett, Francisco	97, 262
Butcher, John Alexander	259
—— Wm. Dickson	163
Butler, Edward Charles	187
—— Edw. Kent Strat.	65, 186
—— Gerald Villiers	248
—— Henry	178
—— *Hon.* Hen. Edw.	39
—— Henry Thomas	206
—— *Lord* James	158
—— James, *KH.*	91
—— James Arthur	71
—— Percy Archer	179
—— Robert	192
—— Robert	116
—— Thomas	158
—— Thomas	71
—— Thomas Lewis	231
—— Walter	178
—— Webbe	212
—— William Henry	196
Butt, John Wells	152
Butts, Augustus de, *KCH.*	13, 282
—— Jas. Witshed de	226
—— William M. de	213
Butze, Wilhelm	438
Byam, Edward	56
Byers, Patrick	115
Byles, Arthur William	207
Byng, *Hon.* Wm. Fredk.	180

Name	page
Byrne, Arthur	155
—— Arthur	178
—— John	131
—— John	93, 182
—— Stanhope Rich. M.	188
—— Thomas	183
—— Thomas	219
—— Tyrrel Matthias	152
—— William Gibson	251
Byron, *Hon.* Geo. Anson	150
—— James	159
—— Rich. Willoughby	185
Caddy, John Herbert	270
Cadell, Charles, *KH.*	63
Cadett, Henry	195
Cadogan, *Hon.* Edw.	66
—— *Hon.* George	145
—— Wm. Hodgson	86
Caffin, Wm. Geo. Chart	270
Cahill, David	225
—— John Campbell	243
Cain, William	177
Cairncross, Alex. *KH.*	63, 248
Cairnes, George	91, 187
—— John Elliott, *KH.*	57
Calamy, William	293
Calder, Benj. George, *MD.*	287
—— Fran. Wm. Grant	119
—— Patrick Doull	64, 283
—— Thomas	183
Caldwell, Charles Benj.	243
—— Clarke Maries	208
—— Frederick Edm.	230
—— Jas. Lillyman, *KCB.*	115
—— Vere	242
—— William	257
—— Wm. Bletterman	244
—— Wm. Charles	198
Caley, Henry Francis	116
Caledon, Jas. D. P. *Earl of*	148
Call, Geo. Frederick	169
—— George Isaac	169
Calleja, Salvatori	262
Callendar, Campbell	9
Calley, Henry	170
Calvert, Felix	38
Camac, Burgess	35
Cambridge, A. F. *Duke of, KG. GCB. GCH.*	147
—— Geo. W. F. C. *Prince of*	42
Cameron, Alexander	193
—— Alex. *KCB.*	20
—— Alex. John	154
—— Archibald	66
—— Charles	177
—— Donald Meeut	154
—— Duncan	193
—— Dun. Alex.	103, 193
—— Ewen	231
—— Geo. Paulet	116
—— Hugh John	59
—— James Allan	139

Index.

	page		page		page
Cameron, John, *KCB*.	14, 160	Campbell, James	213	Carden, John Cravan	134
———— John	155	———— James	239	Cardew, Christopher B.	226
———— John	286	———— James, *KH*.	62	———— George	39, 282
———— John Cha. *MD*.	311	———— James F. Glen-		———— Henry Clare	246
———— Kenneth	306	cairn	243	Cardigan, Jas. T. Earl of,	61,
———— Patrick	115	———— John	72		137
———— Robert Fulton	215	———— John	91	Carew, Harry	164
Camilleri, Mich. P. *MD*.	262	———— John	127	———— Robert	222
———— Paolo	262	———— John	129	———— Robt. Hallowell	187
Camm, John Philip	307	———— John	98, 189	———— William, Marcus	215
Campbell, Adam Gordon		———— John	226	Carey, Francis	202
	63, 167	———— John	70, 249	———— Le Marchant	218
———— Adam	246	———— John	38	———— Octavius, *KCH*.	19
———— Alexander	180	———— John, *MD*.	245	———— Peter	12
———— Alex. *KH*.	59, 135	———— John Charles	160	———— Robert	191
———— Alexander	255	———— John Cameron	139	———— Tupper	305
———— Alexander	311	———— John L.	219	Carfrae, John	115
———— Alexander	91	———— Morris R.	248	Carline, Henry	126
———— Alex. E. *MD*.	118	———— Neil Stewart,		Carlyon, Edward	59
———— Andr. Mitchell	116	*MD*.	207	Carmichael, Hum. H.	187
———— Archibald	173	———— Niel	116	———— Lewis	72
———— Archibald, *Bt*.		———— Patrick	54	Carnac, John Rivett	172
GCB.	15, 214	———— Patrick	59	Carncross, Joseph Hugh	
———— Archibald	193	———— Patrick F. W.	71,	*KCB*.	19, 264
———— Archibald	36		149	Carnegy, Chas. Hay, *MD*.	125
———— Arch. Colin	193	———— Patrick Scott	270	———— Thomas	204
———— Arch. James	174	———— Robert	183	Carney, John	153
———— Arch. Neil	244	———— Robert	197	Carnie, George	186
———— Arthur Wel-		———— Robert	200	Carpenter, George	101, 192
lington	165	———— Rob. Dennis-		———— George	115
———— Charles	190	town	131	Carr, George	311
———— Charles	213	———— Robert Edgar	174	———— George Kirwan	253
———— Charles	60	———— Rob. Parker	225	———— John	37
———— Charles F.	236	———— Thos. Edmund	133	———— Ralph	294
———— Charles Stuart	57	———— William	122	———— Robert	189
———— Colin, *KCB*.	15, 224	———— William	38	———— Samuel	306
———— Collin	206	———— William	83	———— Stephen	239
———— Colin	243	———— Wm. Cha. Jas.	123	Carrol, John Egerton	197
———— Colin,	62, 250	———— Wm. Huntley	171	———— Wm. Hutchinson	186
———— Colin Alex.	226	———— Wm. John	156	———— William Parker,	
———— David	33	———— William Mark	155	*KCH*.	18
———— Donald	293	———— Wm. Rich. New-		Carroll, James	169
———— Donald	60	port	244	Carruthers, Richard	72, 153
———— Dugald	58	Campion, Geo. Edw.	131	———— William	227
———— Duncan	235	Campsie, George Richard	152	Carson, William, *MD*.	237
———— Sir Edw. Alex.	116	Canavan, John	216	Carstens, Rudolph	436
———— E. S. Norman	256	Canch, Thomas	156	Cart, Robert	215
———— Farquhar, M.	155	Cane, Arthur Beresford	161	Carter, Charles Jeffries	167
———— Farquhard	193	———— Maurice	171	———— Henry	116
———— Fielding Alex.	295	———— Maurice	224	———— John, *KH*.	43, 151
———— Francis	66	———— Stopford	84	———— John	310
———— Frederick	260	Cannon, George Edward	260	———— John Chilton L.	195
———— Frederick	42, 265	———— William	100, 249	———— John Collis, *MD*.	220
———— Fred. Alex.	272	Cantilupe, Geo. J. F. *Visc*.	146	———— John Money	151
———— George	203	Capadose, Henry	159	———— S. G.	92, 167
———— Geo. Her. Fred.	145	———— Henry	64, 254	———— Wm. George	148
———— Guy, *Bart*.	35	Capel, Henry	252	———— Wm. Frederick	215
———— Henry Fred.,		———— Daniel	166	———— Wm. Scott	167
KCB. GCH.	8, 176	———— Sydney Aug.	138	———— Willoughby Har.	250
———— Hen. Dundas	71	———— *Hon*. Thomas Edw.	12	Cartmail, J.	166
———— Hugh, Mont.	129	Capelle, Augustus	438	Cartwright, Edmund	115
———— Hugh A. B.	272	Capron, John Shuckburgh	174	———— Henry	145
———— Hugh J. M.	170	Carabelli, Jean Baptiste	489	———— John	116
———— James	179	Carden, Andrew	192	———— William	70
———— James	192	———— Cha. Wilson	187	Carwick, Thomas Mayor	230
———— James, *KH*.	43, 247	———— Frederick	203	Cary, Septimus Alph. F.	235

Index.

	page		page		page
Carysfort, John, *Earl of*	12	Chaproniere, Aug. Hen.	206	Claremont, Edw. Stopford	152
Case, William	183	Charleton Edward, *KH.*	69	Clark, Fred. Hobson	247
Casement, W. *KCB.*	115	——— George	268	——— John, *KH.*	88, 205
Cash, Hen. Christmas	238	——— Thomas R.	9	——— John, *MD.*	139
Cassan, Matthew	236	Charlewood, John	207	——— Walter F.	162
——— Thomas	251	Charleton, Hen. Wilmot	103,	Clarke, Andrew, *KH.*	71, 197
Cassidy, Francis	167		122	——— Charles	294
——— Loftus	208	——— John Sam.	215	——— Cha. Anthony	305
Cassilis, Archibald, *Earl of*	143	Charretie, Thomas	37	——— Eric Mackay	168
Castieau, John Buckley	293	Charters, Samuel	96	——— Francis	83
Castle, John	33	——— Roberts	306	——— George Calvert	241
——— Slodden	307	Chatterton, J. C. *KH*	57, 124	——— Geo. Herbert	214
——— Wm.	*114	——— Oliver, Nicolls	186	——— Guy	229
Cater, Thomas Hicks	294	——— Thomas	154	——— Henry	307
——— Thomas Orlando	268	——— Thos. Justly G.	186	——— Henry Bourke	236
Cathcart, Andrew	136	Claytor, John	285	——— James	198
——— *Hon.* Frederick	41	Cheape, Peter	102, 243	——— James	254
——— *Hon.* Geo.	55, 121	Chearnley, William	159	——— James	293
——— Martin	127	Cheetham, Charles	270	——— John	99, 218
——— William, *Earl*, *KT.*	6, 115, 119	Cheney, Edward	38	——— John Fred. *MD.*	309
		——— Ralph	223	——— John F. Sales	98, 129
Cathrey, Werner	139	Chermside, Sam. Wm. *MD.*	174	——— Joseph	72, 228
Cator, John Farnaby	272			——— Philip Haughton	135
——— William	60, 266	Cherry, Fred. Clifford	*114	——— Robert	268
Caulfield, Henry	191	Chesney, Fran. Rawdon	70, 115, 267	——— Thomas	224
Cavallace, Chas. Felix	441			——— Thomas	306
Cavan, Philip Charles	181	Chesse, Jean de	440	——— Tredway	115
Cavarra, Guiseppe	262	Chester, Chas. Montagu	242	——— William	140
Cavendish, Geo. Henry	150	——— Harry George	174	——— W. H. F.	167
——— *Hon.* Henry F. C.	41, 118	——— John	62	——— William	213
——— Wm. George	136	Chetwode, Frederick	175	Clarkson, James Oran	116
Caw, John, *MD.*	311	——— Richard	155	Clavell, Richard King	296
Cecil, *Lord* Thomas	63	Chichester, *Lord* Arthur	239	Clavering, Hen. Mordaunt	32
Chabot, L. W. *Visc.* de, *KCH.*	16	——— Arthur Charles	167	Clay, John Granby	11
		——— Charles	62, 233	——— J. Herbert	210
Chads, John Cornell	93, 254	——— John Octav.	167	——— William	188
Chalk, John Brett	205	——— *Lord* John	239	Clayton, Rob. Browne, *KC.*	9, 138
Chalmer, Jas. Arch.	95, 267	——— *Lord* Stephen A.	242		
Chalmers, John	173	Child, William	197	——— Wm. Capel	148
——— William	38	Childe, Jonathan	138	——— Wm. Rob. *Bart.*	55
Chamberlain, Henry, *Bt.*	269	Childers, Michael	38	Cleaveland, Fred. Darby	271
——— HallPlumer	154	Childs, Joseph	294	——— Rich. Fran.	44, 265
——— John	128	Chisholm, John	116	——— Samuel	272
Chamberlayne, Wm.	56	——— Stewart	287	Cleaver, James Peach	121
Chambers, Courteney	61, 176	Cholmeley, Henry D.	178	Cleiland, Wm. Douglas	115
——— David Francis	155	——— Jas. Harrison	134	Cleland, Alex. B.	312
——— Edw. Tho. Harley	141	Cholmondeley, *Hon.* T. G.	194	Clements, Henry	94, 167
——— Jas. Walker	312	Christie, Arch. *KCH.*	32, 33	——— Henry St. John	255
——— John	141	——— Frederick Gordon	164	Clendon, William	294
Chambre, James	248	——— Gustavus Logie	154	Clephane, Rob. Douglas	231
——— William	97, 162	——— Henry Paget	272	Clerihew, George, *MD.*	152
Champagné, Josiah, *GCH.*		——— James	243	Clerk, Henry	272
	168	——— Sam. Tolfrey	232	——— Mildmay	124
——— Forbes	85	Chuden, William	83, 437	Clerke, St. John Aug. *KH.*	58
Champain Agnew	87	Church, Richard, *GCH.*	54	——— Tho. H. Shadwell, *KH.*	89
Champeaux, Cæsar Aug.	441	Churchill, Cha. Horace	38, 182		
Champion, John G.	247	——— Edward Wm.	294	——— Wm. Jonathan	229
Chandler, George	143	Chute, Thomas	173	Cleve, Carl. Died. U. O. F.	433
Chaplin, Thomas	56, 147	——— Trevor	222	——— Urban	433
Chapman, Frederick E.	286	Ciavaldini, Peter Fran.	439	——— Hen. Anth. Fred.	432
——— Frederick Wm.	247	Clanchy, Cassius M.	66	Clibborn, Wm. G. M.	188
——— George	116	Clapham, William	115	Clifford, Rob. Cav. Spen.	146
——— John Strange	142	Clapp, William Henry	312	Clifton, Arthur Benj. *KCH.*	17, 143
——— Stephen, R. *KCH.*	19, 115, 282	Clapperton, John P. N. F.	295, 297	——— John Talbot	118
		Clare, Louis	257	——— Thomas Henry	138

486

Index.

Name	page
Clinton, *Lord* Cha. Pelham Pelham	118
——— Frederick	70, 145
——— Henry	93
——— *Lord* Thos. Cha. Pel.	118
——— Wm. Hen. *GCB*.	8, 206
Clitherow, John	18
——— John Christie	148
Clive, Edward	56, 144
Cloete, Abra. Josias, *KH*.	68
——— Peter L. Graham	243
Close, John Marjoram	83
——— Maxwell	59
Cloudt, Morrice de	432
Clough, Howell H. L.	222
Clowes, Thomas	159
Clune, William	156
——— P.	203
Clunie, Jas. Oliphant	98, 154
Clyde, James	248
Coape, Arthur	236
——— Capel	219
Coates, Cha. Aylmer	226
——— William	160
Coats, John	206
Cobban, Geo. Geddes Mack.	201
Cobbe, George	64, 266
——— Charles A.	258
——— Henry C.	256
Cochran, James	192
Cochrane, Cha. Stewart	158
——— George	257
——— *Hon.* Horace, B. W.	244
——— James	170
——— Jas. Johnstone	33
——— John	160
——— Robert	252
——— Thomas B. *Lord*	218
——— William	43, 117
Cock, James	115
Cockburn, Alexander	162
——— Cha. Vansittart	270
——— Francis	37, 115, 256
——— George, *GCH*.	6
——— *Rt. Hon.* George, *GCB*.	292
——— James	181
——— James	231
——— Jas. Pattison	42, 265
——— Weymiss Tho.	87, 211
——— Wm. Peter	169
Cockcraft, Wm. Wild Jos.	228
Cocke, James	116
Cockell, William	174
Cocks, C. Lygon	148
——— Philip Reginald	271
——— John	141
Cocksedge, Henry Leheup	126
Codd, Augustus Fred.	215
——— John Edward	130
——— William	199
Coddington, FitzHerbert	191
——— Joshua	285
Codrington, Cha. Bethel	142
——— Edward	127
——— Wm. John	65, 147
Coffin, Edward Pine	305
——— Guy Carleton	64
Coghlan, John	238
——— Thos. John, *MD*.	312
Coker, Lewis	180
Colborne, *Hon.* James	176
——— *Hon.* Francis	166
Colby, Charles	250
——— Thomas	42, 282
——— Stephen Edward	250
Colchester, Thomas	287
Colclough, Anth. Cæsar	135
Cole, Arthur Lowry	194
——— *Hon.* Galbraith, L. *GCB*.	8, 178
——— *Hon.* Henry	133
——— John	85
——— John A.	166
——— Pennel	96, 284
——— Richard	67
——— Richard Sweet	157
——— Robert	199
——— William W. T.	224
Colebrooke, *Sir* W. M. G. *KH*.	59, 266
——— James Rob.	97, 267
Coles, Geo. Richard	173
——— Robert Bartlett	56
——— Josias Rogers John	131
——— William Cowper	61
Collett, John H.	115
Collette, Henry	219
Colley, Alexander Dick	167
Collings, John E.	184
Collington, John Wheeler	269
Collins, Francis	137
——— James Wood	230
——— Thomas	195
Collinson, Cha. John Russ.	169
——— Hen. Redfearn	216
——— Thos. Bernard	286
Collis, Charles	67
Colliss, John	294
Colman, George Denis	95, 166
——— Henry Scott	166
——— William Thomas	206
Colnett, Jas. Richard	116
Colomb, Geo. Thomas	87
Colquhoun, Daniel	18
——— Jas. N.	94, 116, 268
——— Robert	235
Colquitt, Goodwin Cha.	125
——— John Wallace	156
Columba, Pietro Santa	439
Colvile, Henry	59, 149
Colvill, Robert	249
——— Thomas, H.	223
Colville, *Hon.* Charles, *GCB. GCH*.	8, 156
——— Charles John	237
Combe, Charles William	225
Combermere, S. *Ld. Visc. GCB. GCH*	7, 115, 118
Combremont, A. la T. de	439
Comper, John Richard	306
Compton, *Ld.* Spencer S.	237
——— Henry C.	145
Comyn, William	115
Congdon, Geo. Walkup	295
Congreve, George	180
Connell, Abr. J. N., *MD*.	240
——— James	174
Connolly, Richard Geo.	296
——— William	42, 292
Connon, John	186
Connop, Richard	86
Connor, Alexander	187
——— Frederick	153
Conolly, James	125
——— Patrick	171
——— Thomas Rich.	176
Conran, Lewis Charles	207
——— Wm. Adam	207
Conroy, Henry George	145
——— Stephen Rowley	148
Considine, William	221
——— James, *KH*.	58, 115
——— James	236
Constant, John	125
Conway, Thos. Sydenham	173
Conyers, Cha. Edward	37
Conyngham, Francis, *Marq. of*, *GCH. KP*.	87
Coode, Cha. Penrose	296
Cook, Francis Augustus	188
——— Wm. Surtees	217
Cooke, John George	204
——— John Henry	99, 176
——— Richard Harvey	53
——— Robert	135
——— Rob. Wilton	222
Cookes, George	130
Cookson, William	232
Cooper, David	168
——— David Siritt	151
——— George	115
——— Henry	94, 186
——— Henry	196
——— Hen. Litellus Gilbert	272
——— Isaac Rhodes	209
——— Leonard Morse	103
——— Wm. Henry	134
Coote, Charles James	221
——— Henry J.	173
——— John Chidley	194
Copland, Francis	65
Copeland, George	150
Copinger, Henry	167
Coppon, Joseph	440
Corbet, Vincent	120
Corbett, Edward	202
——— Stuart	116
——— William	203
Corcoran, Alexis	199
Cordemann, Albert	435

487

Index.

Name	page
Cork, Edmund, *Earl of*, KP.	7
Cormick, Edward	130
—— Edward Henry	168
—— Wm. George	179
Cornelius Rich. Longfield	269
Cornock, Isaac	140
Cornwall, George	247
—— Wm. Henry	62, 147
Corry, Savage Hall	168
Corsellis, Thomas, *KCB.*	115
Coryton, George Edward	213
—— George Hunt	293
—— John Rawlins	293
Cosser, Walter	295
Coster, Tho. Oliver Watts	124
Costley, John	95
Costobadie, Jas. Palliser	222
Cother, Charles	53
Cotton, Corbet	246
—— Ed. Row. Jos.	34
—— Hugh Cotton	116
—— Sidney	179
—— Sydney, John	87, 179
—— Thomas F.	163
—— *Hon.* Wellington H. S.	133
—— Willoughby, *GCB. KCH.*	18, 250
—— Willoughby	195
Coulson, Forster	20
—— Rob. Blenkinsopp	145
Coultman, Humphrey W.	215
Couper, George, *KH.*	41
Courant, Antoine	440
Court, John	225
—— Major H.	116
Courten, Pierre P. Auguste de	440
—— Amand de	83, 441
Courtenay, George Henry	212
—— John Garnett	311
—— Wm. Hayley	152
Courtis, John Cha. Grey	295
Courtney, Jonathan	310
Coventry, Frederick	180
Cowan, Edw. Alphonso Fred.	305
Cowell, Henry C.	93
—— James	130
—— Lambert	251
—— William	54
Cowen, Augustus Henry	197
—— Charles	169
Cowley, Norman	125
Cowling, William	297
Cowper, Hen. Douglas	250
—— Geo. Alex. *MD.*	180
—— Jeremiah	99, 169
—— William	286
Cowslade, John	116
Cox, Augustus	145
—— Fran. Hawtrey	190
—— Henry	153
—— James	244
—— John, *KH.*	69

Name	page
Cox, John Gaggin	256
—— John Hamilton	227
—— John William	164
—— Lindsey Zachariah	126
—— Samuel Symes	162
—— William, *KH.*	64
—— William	96, 205
—— *Sir* William	32
Coxe, Edward Jones	216
—— James Thring	178
—— Rich. Lovelocke	236
Coxen, Edward	212
Coxworthy, Ferguson Th.	306
Crabbe, Eyre J. *KH.*	87, 226
Craig, Fran. Edw. Lascelles	295
—— Henry	58
—— Ninian	254
Craigie, Anth. David	286
—— David	249
—— Peter Edmonstone	64, 206
—— Robt. Collins	247
Cramer, Andrew Philip	442
Crampton, Philip Henry	171
Craufurd, Jas. Robertson	69, 145
—— Peter	172
—— Robert	253
Crause, Cha. B.	260
—— Henry	94, 260
Craven, Charles	129
—— Charles	11
Crawford, Adam Fife	68, 266
—— Francis H.	245
—— George	36, 265
—— Henry	241
—— Robert	17
—— Robt. Fitzgerald	270
—— William	129
—— Wm. Thomas	271
Crawfurd, Gavin Ralston	116
—— John	97, 157
—— Thos. Macknight	245
Crawley, Henry	171
—— Henry Owen	285
—— Thomas R.	141
—— Rich.	233
—— William	155
—— Wm. White	97, 226
Creagh, Andrew	36
—— Charles Myers	160
—— Giles, Vandel.	92, 233
—— James	100, 238
—— Jasper Byng	205
—— *Sir* Michael, *KH.*	61, 238
—— Thomas Miller	203
Creighton, Henry	132
—— Joseph	60
Cremer, James Smith	269
Crespigny, Geo. Blicke C.	171
—— Henry Otho de	171
Crespin, Henry	295
Crewe, John Frederick	57
Crispin, George	219

Name	page
Croad, Frederick	171
—— George Henry	131
Crocicchia Louis	439
Croft, Jonathan	312
—— John Thomas	116
—— Robert Manners	128
Crofton, Edw. Hen. L.	229
—— Edw. Walter	270
—— Hugh Dennis	171
—— John	157
—— Peter	91, 235
—— Richard Henry	272
—— Walter Frederic	271
Crofts, John	127
Crokat, William	68
Croker, Edward	143
—— Edward	168
—— Edward	190
—— Hen. Braddel	208
—— John L.	168
—— John Rees	157
—— Richard	66
—— William	64, 168
Croly, Henry	215
Crombie, Thomas	211
Crompton, Henry Thos.	215
—— Wm. Joshua	218
Crone, George	438
Crookshank, Blackm. C.	172
Croon, Bernard	436
Crosbie, John Gustavus, *GCH.*	7
—— John Talbot	186
—— William	252
Crosdill, John	116
Cross, John, *KH.*	61, 220
—— John William	225
—— William	220
Crosse, Joshua	67
—— William	35
Crouwell, Nicholas	441
Crowder, Edw. F.	157
Crowdy, James William	198
Crowe, John, *KH.*	67
—— Timothy	206
Croxton, Thomas	116
—— William	115
Cruice, Edmund John	247
Cruickshank, William	245
—— Alexander	231
Crusius, David	442
Crutchley, Charles	174
Cruttenden, Edwin	24, 267
—— Courtenay	71, 266
Cubitt, Edward George	225
—— George	160
—— Thomas	64, 266
—— William	116
Cuddy, Alexander Daniel	207
—— William, H. L. D.	206
Culpeper, John Bishop	140
Cumberland, Bentinck H.	248
—— Chas. B.	92, 248
—— Edw. Sandford	195
—— Geo. Burrell	193
Cumberlege, Chas. Lush.	131

Index.

	page		page		page
Cumberlege, Harry Altham	216	Dalgety, James W.	247	D'Arcy, Thomas, *MD*.	311
		Dallas, Charles	115	——— Thos. Dopping B.	241
Cuming, Henry H.	242	——— Robt. Wm.	122	Dardel, Geo. Alexander	440
Cummin, Geo. Robert	251	Dallwig, Conrad	432	Darell, *Sir* Harry, *Bt*.	169
Cumming, Alexander	226	Dalmer, Francis	38	——— Henry John	237
——— Alex. P. Gordon	223	——— Thomas	20	D'Arley, Wm. Wallace	260
——— Hen. John, *KCH*.	12, 138	Dalrymple, *Sir* Adolph. J. *Bt*.	36	Darley, Edward	20
				——— Henry	250
——— Hen. Wedderburn	210	——— Geo. Hadington	243	——— John	168
——— Jas. Slator	160	——— *Sir* Hew, *Bt*.	223	Darling, Henry Charles	306
——— John	177	——— John	150	——— Henry Charles	16
——— Robt. Octavius	203	——— John H. E.	150	——— Ralph, *GCH*.	11, 192
Cuninghame, Hen. Montgomery	180	——— John Fitz Roy	190	——— William James	215
		——— *Sir* John Hamilton, *Bt*.	9, 244	——— Wm. Lindsay	40
——— John	115			Darlington, Hen. *Earl of*	43
Cunliffe, Robt. Hen. *Bt*.	115	——— Wm. Henry	307	Darrah, Nicholas L.	70, 249
Cunningham, John	137	Dalton, Charles	97, 267	Darroch, Duncan	10
——— John	115	——— Charles James	270	——— Don. G. Angus	152
——— Thomas	42, 282	——— George	284	Dartnell, Geo. Russell	152
Cunnynghame, Augustus Thurlow	212	——— John	128	——— Nelson	131
		——— Thomas N.	213	Dashwood, Alex. W.	86
——— David, *Bt*.	32	D'Alton, Edward	235	——— Geo. A. C.	223
——— Geo. Aug. F.	127	Daly, Charles	241	Dassauville, Wm. A. *MD*.	287
Cuppage, Alexander	115	——— Denis	56	Dassel, Conrad Von	433
——— Burke	268	——— Fran. Dermot	72, 131	Daubeney, Hen. C. Barnston	206
——— Stephen	68	——— Robert	165		
Cureton, Chas. Robt.	72, 142	——— Robert	171	——— Henry, *KH*.	35
——— Edward B.	164	Dalyell, Melville	97	Daunt, William, *MD*.	132
Currer, Richard R.	248	——— Robert	41	Davenport, E. Montagu	218
Currie, George Alfred	219	Dalzell, *Hon*. Arth. Alex.	199	——— Hen. Wayet	190
——— John Robert	247	——— John	101, 167	——— Trevor	151
——— Robt. Hamilton	190	——— *Hon*. Rob. Alex. G.	233	——— John Salusb.	307
——— Samuel, *MD*.	154	——— William	244	——— Wm. Davenport	246
Curry, Robt. Murray	295	Damer, *Hon*.Geo.Lionel D.	54	Daveney, Burton	151
Curtayne, Denis Aloysius	155	Dames, Geo. Longworth	218	Davidson, Alexander	116
Curteis, William	187	——— Wm. Longworth	218	——— James	132
——— Henry John	188	Dammers, Hen. Wm.	84, 434	——— James	172
Curtin, Joseph	191	Dance, *Sir* Chas. Webb, *KH*.	39	——— James Batchelor	256
Curtis, Charles	152			——— John	305
——— Henry Charles	237	——— George	223	——— Patrick, *MD*.	222
Curzon, *Hon*. Rich. W. Penn	146	——— Dane Rich. *MD*.	242	Davie, Cha. Christopher	219
		——— John	214	Davies, Delmé Sey.	150
Cust, *Hon*. Chas. Henry	120	D'Angelo, Gaetano	441	——— Fra. John	57, 144
——— *Hon*. Edw. *KCH*.	56	Daniel, Alexander	65	——— John	225
——— Henry Francis	176	——— Lewis	437	——— John	312
Custance, Holman	56, 161	——— Peter Fane Edge	296	——— Joseph	197
——— Wm. Neville	197	——— Samuel	154	——— Richard	226
Cutajar, Carlo	262	Daniell, Chas. Augustus	206	——— Thomas Henry Hastings	39
Cuthbert, Robt. Alex.	166	——— Cyrus	206		
Cuyler, Henry	32	——— Edwin Gream	206	——— Thos. Williams	244
——— Jacob Glen	34	——— Francis A.	116	——— Timothy	85
		——— Henry	148	——— Wm. Hanbury	68
Dachenhausen, Hen. *Baron*	436	——— John	33	Davis, Charles Edward	116
		——— John Hinton	200	——— Geo. Lennox	98, 160
Dacres, Richard James	269	——— John M.	177	——— George William	169
Dacosta, Aug. Fred. Hippolito	286	——— Ralph, Allen Cha.	218	——— Hen. Samuel	103, 203
		Dansey, Cha. Cornwallis	68, 266	——— John Atkins	287
D'Aguilar, Geo. Charles	34			Davison, Hugh Percy	39
——— Chas. Lawrence	272	——— Richard Ingram	212	——— Thomas	236
——— Hen. Torrens	146	Danvers, Geo. Aug. Fred.	295	——— William, *KH*.	68
Dagg, Thomas	263	Darby, Charles	153	Davy, John, *MD*.	309
Dalbiac, Jas.Chas.*KCH*.	15, 123	Darby, Joseph	68, 266	——— Wm. Gabriel, *KCH*.	17
		D'Arcy, Oliver Barker	225	Dawes, Thos. Hath.	40
——— Geo. Charles	131	D'Arcy, Geo. Abbas Kooli	246	——— William Lewis	293
Dales, Samuel, *KH*.	53	——— Joseph	116	Dawkins, Francis Henry	55
Dalgety, Fred. Henry	221	——— Peter	34	——— Henry	37

489

Index.

	page		page		page
Dawn, James	122	Dennis, Morley S. T.	228	Diddep, John	192
Dawson, Charles	312	——— Maurice Griffin	157	Diebitsch, Frederick Von	437
——— Cha. Massey	156	Denniss, Geo. Gladwin	116	Diestelhorst, Frederick	435
——— Fra. R. M'G.	240	Denny, H. J.	132	Digby, Dunlop	67
——— George	225	——— Richard	209	——— Henry Robert	149
——— George Beresford	253	——— William	98, 223	Diggle, Charles, *KH*.	66
——— Geo. K. Massy	140	——— William	311	——— Fred. William	234
——— Henry	219	Dent, Thomas	116	Dighton, John	115
——— Rob. Kearsley	285	Denys, Montagu	229	Dilkes, Wm. Thomas	9
——— Robert Peel	146	Deppee, Frederick	433	Dill, Marcus	286
——— *Hon.* T. Vesey	148	Dering, Cholmeley Edw.	237	Dillon, Arthur Richard	10
——— William, *MD*.	310	Derinzy, Bartholomew V.		——— *Hon.* Constantine	
Day, Henry James	251	*KH*.	91, 162	A.	127
——— Matthew	171	——— Geo. Aug. Fred.	271	——— Francis Wm.	100, 169
——— Rob. Ladbroke	215	——— Thomas Rich.	235	——— John	183
Daykin, Wm. Bowes	146	De Ros, Wm. *Lord*	62	——— Martin M.	241
Deacon, Charles	139	Desborough, Lawrence	154	——— Robert	246
——— Charles, *KCB*.	115	Desbrisay, Theophilus	269	——— *Hon.* Theo. D. G.	212
——— Cha. Clement	213	Deschamps, John	269	——— William	170
——— Frederick	170	Deshon, Charles John	97, 168	Disney, Moore, *KCB*.	8, 166
Deakins, John	174	——— Fred. Geo. Tho.	207	Dix, Frederick	246
Dean, William	176	Despard, Henry	59, 263	Dixon, Charles	68
Deane, Charles, *KH*.	93, 151	——— Philip Henry	263	——— Cha. Cranston	65
——— Charles	156	D'Este, Aug. Fred. *KCH*.	43	——— George	64, 149
Deare, George	71, 172	Detmer, Frederick	432	——— George	229
——— George	172	Deverell, Wm. Devonish	254	——— Henry	233
Debenham, Thomas	207	——— Tho. Josephus	219	——— John	145
Debnam, Rob. Joseph	88, 164	Deverill, Gervas Stanford	242	——— Manley	62
Debs, Fra. Matthias	436	Devereux, *Hon.* Geo. Tal-		——— Matthew Cha.	272
Decken, Benedix, *Baron*	432	bot	272	——— Matthew Cha.	64, 283
——— Cha. Von der	432	D'Eyncourt, Eustace A. T.	197	——— William	269
——— Fred. *Count* Von		D'Holbreuse, Henry	440	——— Wm. Manley Hall	272
der, *GCH*.	10, 437	D'Homboldt, John Hen.	433	Dobbie, David	158
——— Frederick Von der	433	Dias, Isaac	297	Dobbin, Thomas	55
——— George, *Count*		Dicenta, Francis	441	Dobson, Thomas James	247
Von der	433	Dick, Francis	270	——— William	166
——— Wm. *Baron, KH*.		——— George	115	Dodd, John Beach	205
	84, 435	——— Hope	116	Dodgin, Wm. Henry	195
De Courcy, John F. R.	198	——— Rob. Henry, *KCH*.	19	D'Odiardi, Antonio	439
Deedes, Henry	98, 185	——— William, *Bt*.	116	Dods, George	116
——— George	168	——— William, *MD*.	311	——— George	65
Deere, Joseph Eyles	192	Dickens, Sam. Trevor,		——— Geo. Douglas, *MD*.	240
Deering, Rupert Barber	251	*KCH*.	13, 282	Doebell, Henrich von	439
Dehnel, Henry	435	Dickenson, Cha. F. B. G.	159	Doherty, Cha. Edmond	140
Deichmann, Carl. Fred.	433	Dickinson, Douglas John	153	——— Henry Edward	140
Delacombe, Henry Ivatt	293	——— Henry B. F.	166	——— Richard	56, 259
——— Henry Edw.	296	——— Jas. Esten	238	Dolphin, James	115, 252
Delafosse, Hen.	116	——— Richard	14, 264	Domvile, John Russell	272
De Lacy, John	187	Dickson, Alex. *GCB*.		——— William	172
Delancey, James	66	*KCH*.	19, 264, 273	Domville, Compton Cha.	237
——— Peter	227	——— Alex. Stephen	271	——— James Wm.	271
Delius, George	437	——— Archibald	168	Donald, John	312
Delmege, Colin C. John,		——— Cha. Sheffield	222	Donaldson, Robert	192
MD.	178	——— Collingwood	272	——— Thos. Hislop J.	259
Dely, William Alexander	172	——— David	247	——— Vance Young	94, 208
Dempster, John, *MD*.	214	——— Edw. John	227	Donelan, Anthony	199
——— William	192	——— Francis	192	Donkin, Geo. David	158
Dempsy, Charles	287	——— Geo. Cochrane	237	——— Rufane Shawe,	
Denison, Cha. Albert	203	——— James Henry	126	*KCB. GCH*.	9, 162
——— William Thomas	285	——— John Henry	152	Donnelly, John	160
Denman, Lewis W. R.	296	——— Jeremiah, *KCB*.	18	Donop, Geo. Cha. von	433
Dennie, William H.	62, 164	——— Sam. Auchmuty	183	Donovan, Cha. Henry	
Dennis, James	43, 154	——— William	257	Douglas	139
——— James Benjamin	272	——— William	115	——— Thomas	260
——— John Fitz Thomas	247	——— William F.	214	Doran, William	254
——— John Leslie	200	——— Wm. Ranaldson	95	Dore, Peter	154

Index.

Name	page	Name	page	Name	page
Dore, William Henry	246	Dresing, Charles	209	Dundas, *Hon.* Robert L. *KCB.*	17
Dores, Richard	239	Dreves, Lewis de	84, 435	——— Thos.	231
Dorehill, Wm. John	154	Drew, Rich. Robinson	268	——— Wm. Bolden	67, 266
——— George	249	Driberg, William	257	Dundee, Edward	198
Doring, William	434	Drought, John Alexander	217	Dunlevie, Gerald Geo.	162
Dornberg, Frederick	439	——— Thomas A.	90, 166	Dunlop, Franklin	270
Dorndorf, Frederick	437	Drumlanrig, Arch. Wm.		Dunn, George	174
Dorratt, Douglas Adam	295	*Viscount*	119	——— Duckworth	122
Dorville, Philip	54	Drummond, Berkeley	56, 149	——— William	94, 267
Douglas, Charles	100, 160	——— Charles Home	119	Dunne, Charles	169
——— Charles Pye	9	——— Edward	32	——— Edward	6
——— *Hon.* Edw. Gordon	63	——— Geo. Duncan	116	——— Francis	161
——— George	165	Drummond, Gordon,*GCB.*	7, 200	——— Francis	33
——— George	245	——— Gordon	148	——— James	160
——— Henry N.	69, 230	——— Henry, *MD.*	165	——— William	163
——— Hen. Sholto	193	——— Hen. Maurice	193	Dunsmure, Charles	193
——— Howard, *Bt.*	14	——— Jas. Walker	145	Du Plat, Gustavus C. *KH.*	102, 284
——— James	212	——— John	56		
——— James, *KCB.*	18	——— John Gavin	116	Dupuis, John Edward	269
——— Jas. William	116	——— Mortimer Percy	150	Durant, James	115
——— John	137	——— Percy	20, 264	D'Urban Benj. *KCB.*	
——— John	231	——— Thomas	285	*KCH.*	13, 202
——— John	231	——— William	39, 149	——— Wm. James	93, 176
——— Lynedoch	223	Drury, Henry	296	Durbin, Edmund	180
——— Neil, *KCH.*	19	——— Thomas	239	Durham, James	7
——— Robert	57	Drysdale, Jas. Murray	175	——— Patrick Fran.	188
——— Robert	167	——— William	131	Durie, Charles	156
——— Rob. Andrews,*Bt.*163		Duberley, George	216	During, Christ. Henry Von.	434
——— Rob. Percy	180	Duberly, Henry	183	——— Lewis Alex.	92
——— William	165	Du Bourdieu, Arthur	182	Durnford, Edward W.	285
——— William	43	——— John	156	——— Elias Walker	18, 282
——— Wm. Cunningham	143	Ducat, Dugald	243	——— George	222
Douro, Arthur, *Marq.*	63	Duckett, Geo. Floyd	239	——— George	97, 267
Doveton, *Sir* John,*GCB.*	115	Dudgeon, Peter	68	——— Geo. Anthony	178
——— John, *KCB.*	115	Duff, *Hon.* Alex.*GCH.*	9, 188	——— Geo, Augustus	190
——— Fra. Crossman	202	——— Alex. Tho. Wharton	244	Dury, Alexander	219
Dowdall, Aylmer	205	——— Folliott	185	Du Sage, Pierre	440
——— George James	247	——— George	97, 245	Dusautoy, Peter John J.	294
Dowman, James	294	——— James	220	Dutton, Charles	221
——— John	191	——— James	226	——— Thomas	223
Downes, Charles	84	——— Patrick	229	——— Wm. Holmes	87
——— George B. G.	286	——— Robert George	163	Du Vernet, Henry	258
——— Henry	192	Duffy, John	35	——— Henry	58
——— Henry	253	Duflef, Armand C. G.	439	——— John	234
———Ulysses,*Lord*,*KCB.*19		Duke, Jones	185	Dwyer, Henry	57
Downie, Hector	254	Dukes, James	241	——— John	165
Downing, Adam Giffard	66	Dumas, Peter	42	——— John James	257
Downman, John Thomas	235	Dunbar, Charles	169	——— Thomas Peard	294, 297
——— Thomas,*KCH.* 19,264		——— Edward	173		
Dowse, Lloyd	95,267	——— Frederick	190	Dyce, David, *MD.*	311
——— Richard	165	——— Jas. C. Alex.	250	——— Thomas Rose	312
Doxat, John J.	242	——— John P.	115	Dyer, Hen. Chas. Penrose	296
Doyle, Carlo Joseph	37	Duncan, Alexander	115	——— John Edward	130
——— Cha. Hastings	100, 175	——— Edward	96, 199	Dyneley, Thomas	66, 266
——— Cha. Wm. *KCH.*	13	——— *Hon.* Hew H. H.	223	Dynon, Patrick	142
——— John	94, 224	——— John Æneas	182	Dyott, Richard	204
——— John Milley, *KCB.*	33	——— William	312	——— William	7, 215
D'Oyly, Henry	20	Duncanson, James, *MD.*	255	Dyson, Edward	123
Drake, John J. C.	244	Duncombe,*Hon.*Octavius	118	——— Jerry Francis	115
——— Thomas, *CMG.*	56	Dundas, George	253	——— John	269
——— William Henry	307	——— *Hon.* Henry	59, 235	——— John Daniel	123
——— William Wickham	180	——— Jas. Fullarton	115		
Draper, Thomas	309	——— John Hamilton	237		
——— James	216	——— Philip	90, 198	Eagar, Edward Hungerford	191
Drawwater,Augustus Cha.	124	——— Philip	62		
Drechsler, Frederick	438				

491

Index.

Name	page	Name	page	Name	page
Eagar, Henry Yielding	242	Elgin, Thos. *Earl of, KC.*	8	English, Frederick	186
—— Robert John	182	Eliot, Francis B.	116	—— Frederick	69, 283
Earle, William Henry	116	—— Granville Heyw.	124	—— John Thos. Joseph	214
Eason, Peter	213	Elkington, Jas. Goodall	143	—— Nathaniel H.	60
Eaton, Christopher Edw.	180	—— James	214	Enoch, John	117, 174
Ebell, Charles	441	Ellary, William	210	—— James John	201
Eccles, William	234	Ellerman, Edward John	170	Eppes, Wm. Randolph	305
Eddie, Wm. Cruickshank	243	Ellice, Robert	16	Erdmann, Frederick	435
Eddington, Smollett, M.	230	Ellicombe, Cha. Grene	35,	Erichson, Alexander Von	438
Eddy, George Henry	227		282, 286	Errington, Arnold Chas.	202
Ede, George Arthur	122	Elliot, Edmund James	231	—— Fred. Arthur	216
Eden, George Morton 64,	149	—— Henry	13	Erskine, Archibald	196
—— John	61	—— James	309	—— *Hon.* David	202
—— William	9	—— Lempster R.	167	—— George	184
—— Wm. Hassall 72,	207	—— Richard, Coffin	287	—— George Pott	224
Edgar, Henry	177	—— Theodore Henry	87	—— Henry David	296
—— Jas. Handasyde	221	—— William, *KH.*	62	—— Henry Knight	184
Edgecombe, Chas. Yorke	152	—— Wm. Hamilton	271	—— Jas. Augustus	307
Edie, William	250	Elliott, George	295	—— John	168
Edleston, Joshua	294	—— George Henry	122	—— Wm. Howe K.	34
Edlin, George	130	—— John Perry	191	Erythropel, Frederick	437
Edmonds, Edward	263	—— Richard	256	Espinasse, Hen. William	116
—— Robert Joseph	160	—— William	188	—— James	180
Edmondson, Joseph	181	—— William	240	Estcourt, James B. B. 72,	194
Edmonstone, Cha. Hen.	233	—— W. Christ. Parkin	296	Esten, John Hamilton	252
Edmunds, Henry	241	—— Wm. Hen. *KH.*	70,	Estwick, Fred.	246
Edwardes, David J. B.	181		202	Eugene, John Mitchell	253
Edwards, Alexander	307	Ellis, *Hon.* Aug. Fred.	58,	Eustace, Henry	12
—— Cadwallader	180		211	—— John R. *KH.* 56,	144
—— Clement Alex.	179	—— Charles Parker	55	—— Wm. Cornwallis,	
—— David	169	—— Fran. Joyner	214	*KCH.*	17
—— Edward	181	—— Henry William	212	Evans, Charles S. S.	228
—— Edward	115	—— Powrie	270	—— De Lacy, *KCB.*	39
—— Edw. Freeman	222	—— Robert	139	—— Edward	189
—— George	208	—— Samuel Burdon	293	—— Francis Edw.	249
—— George	237	—— Thomas	174	—— George Thomas	226
—— Hume	206	Ellison, Christopher	240	—— Hen. Andr. Grant	228
—— Joseph	238	—— Robert	42, 144	—— Henry Roe	189
—— Michael Charles	439	Ellson, Robert	201	—— Hugh	294
—— Peter	70	Ellul, Paolo	262	—— Mark	268
—— Richard	293	Elmhirst, Charles	160	—— Thomas	20
—— Robert Bidwell,		Elmslie, Graham	220	—— Thomas Owen	192
KH.	92	Elphinstone, Howard, *Bt.*,	18	—— Thomas Williams	226
—— Thos. Maitland	250		282	—— William	195
—— William	238	—— Wm. Keith	19	Evatt, George	214
—— Wm. Gamuel	189	Elrington, Fred. Robt.	253	—— George	222
Effingham, Kenneth A.		—— Geo. Esdaile	83	—— George	39
Earl of, GCB.	9, 154	—— Jas. Loftus	148	—— Henry	15, 282
Egan, Hen. John White	206	—— R. Goodall	34, 198	—— Hen. Ashmore	242
Egar, John Francis	214	—— Richard John	198	Evelegh, Geo. Carter	271
Egerton, Caledon Rich.	241	—— Thomas Wm.	198	—— Frederick Cha.	171
—— Charles Bulkeley,		—— William Fred.	150	—— Henry	20, 264
KCH.	12, 241	Elsey, William	116	—— John Henry	183
—— Charles Du Pre	252	Elton, Arthur H.	165	Everard, Benjamin	90, 128
—— Richard 38,	117	Elwes, Lincoln Carey	220	—— John Mathias	34
—— Thos. Graham	229	Elwin, Fountain	59	—— Mathias, *KH.* 55,	165
—— Wilbraham	194	Elwyn, Thomas	271	—— Rich. Houstoun,	
Eichhorn, Christian Fred.	437	Eman, James	192	*MD.*	205
Eicke, Frederick	433	Emmett, Anthony 68,	283	—— Richard Nugent	238
Eidmann Frederick	433	—— Maurice	199	—— Walling	212
Einem J. Godf. de	438	Emslie, John	235	Everest, Henry Bennett 91,	157
—— Diederich de	434	England, James	69	Ewart, John A.	186
Einthoven, S. Jurdan	436	—— James Henry	227	—— John Frederick 37,	263
Eld, Frederick	242	—— Poole, V.	96, 267	Ewing, David	258
Elderhorst, Charles	432	—— Richard, *KH.* 44,	192	—— Joseph	247
Elgee, William	268	—— Richard	163	Eyles, Tho. Woodw. 103,	242

Index.

	page		page		page
Eyre, Annesley	226	Faunce, Bonham	172	Firebrace, William	94, 209
—— Giles	215	—— Thomas	155	Firman, Brooke	64
—— Henry	97, 250	—— Walter, Beresford	225	Fischer, Augustus	432
—— John	268	Faunt, Clareveaulx	200	—— Frederick	441
—— Vincent Edw.	41	—— Henry P.	239	—— F. L. Constantine	441
—— William	103, 225	Fawcett, David Lynar	103,206	—— John Christ. Fred.	442
Eyres, George William	65,145	—— William	59	—— Jean Albert	441
Eyton, Wm. Archibald	248	Fawkes, Richard	178	Fishbourne,Tho. M.,*MD.*	311
		Fead, George	54	Fisher, Alfred	130
Faber, William	140	Fearon, John Hodson	215	—— Andr. Sandilands	224
—— Wm. Raikes	200	—— Robert Brice	40, 191	—— Edw. Henry	272
Fabricius, George	435	Fegan, Charles	293	—— Henry, *MD.*	311
Faddy, Peter	72, 266	Feilde, Fulford Bastard	306	—— Robert Roe	270
—— Peter Pickmore	271	Felix, Orlando	86	—— Samuel	130
Fagan, Christopher	115	Fellowes, Edward	204	—— Seth Nuttall	202
——— Christ. Sullivan	115	—— James	286	—— William	246
——— James	250	—— Jas. Butler	196	—— William	247
Fahle, William	441	—— Peregrine Daniel	116	FitzClarence, *Lord* Fred.	
Fair, William	204	—— Peregrine Hen.	296	*GCH.*	36, 117
—— Alexander	115	Fendall, William	62, 131	Fitz Gerald, Cha. Lionel	67
Fairfax, Henry, *Bt.*	57	Feneran, Francis	247	—— David	211
Fairholme, William	223	Fenning, Daniel Alex.	116	—— Edward Tho.*KH.*	60
Fairtlough, Francis	167	Fenwick, Collingwood	228	—— *Lord,* Gerald	150
——— Charles Edw.	215	—— Horatio	238	—— Gerald Step.	163
——— James W.	63, 215	—— James H.	164	—— John	190
——— Wm. Haviland	206	—— Nicholas	258	—— John Forster,*KCB.*	17
Faithfull, Henry	115	—— Percival	221	—— John Forster,	131
Falconar, Chesb. Grant,		—— Percival Clen.	213	—— Lionel Charles Wm.	
KH.	44, 263	—— Robert	285	Hen.	256
Falconer, Robert	118	—— Thomas	286	—— Thomas George	116
Falla, Daniel	44	—— Tho. Howard	99, 284	—— Wm. Hervey	225
Falls, Thomas	65	—— William	161	Fitzgerald, Cha. Lionel	271
Fane, Henry, *GCB.*	9,115,121	—— Wm. Young	269	—— Crofton, Ham.	167
—— Henry	168	Fenton, Cha. Hamilton	204	—— John	116
—— Henry	69	Ferguson, George	212	—— William	197
—— *Hon.* Hen. Sutton	63	—— Hen. Rob.	58, 144	—— William Henry	212
—— Mildmay	42, 205	—— James	231	Fitz Gibbon, Jas. Gerald	175
Fanshawe, Charles	286	—— John	196	Fitz Herbert, Rich. Hen.	252
——— Edward	41, 282	—— Robert	64, 231	Fitzhugh, Thomas Lloyd	146
——— Hew Dalrymple	163	—— Robert	231	Fitz Maurice, John, *KH.*	91
Faris, Theophilus	186	—— Ronald C., *GCB.*		—— *Hon.* W. E.	119
—— William	284		7, 231	Fitzmayer, Jas. Wm.	270
Farmar, Edw. Sterling	162	Fergusson, Andrew	310	Fitzpatrick, Fred. C. W.	208
——— Richard	296	—— Andrew	174	Fitz Roy, Aug. Charles	
——— Tho. M. L.	192	—— George	174	Lennox	272
Farndon, Joseph	310	—— James	36	—— *Hon.* A. C. L.	212
Farquharson, Fred.	62, 158	—— Rob. Duncan	253	—— Hugh	145
——— Fred. Tho.	133	—— William	69, 292	Flack, John Stuart	209
——— John	116	—— William	310	Flamank, John	94
——— Peter	91, 217	Ferns, John Gore	228	Flanagan,John Bickerton	124
Farr, George	287	Ferrier, Geo. Abercromby	175	—— John B.	228
Farran, Charles	115	Ferris, George Thomas	287	Fleeming, John Elph.	223
Farrant, Augustus D. L.	296	Ferryman, Aug. Halifax	195	Fleming, Arthur Cecil	
——— Francis	116	Ffrench, Thomas	177	Crewe	121
——— Henry	233	Field, Charles	128	—— Edward	39, 263
——— Wm. Broom	160	—— John Frederick	160	—— Edw. J. Ingleby,	175
Farrell, James	236	Fife, James	273	—— Hamilton	295
——— John Sidney	209	Filder, William	305	—— James	56
Farren, Richard T.	198	Finch, *Hon.* Edward	6, 173	—— Julius	95
Farrer, James	34	—— *Hon.* John	43	—— Robert Crowe	234
——— John	118	Fincke, Frederick Von	441	Flemyng, Augustus	295
Farrington,John James	116	Findlay, Alexander, *KH.*		Fletcher, Edw. Cha.	117, 118
Fast, John Wells	115		58, 115	—— John	261
Faulkner, Henry Cole	153	—— Alexander	259	—— Thomas	64, 257
Faunce, Alured Dodsworth		—— James	256	—— William	306
	36, 263	Finlay, George	157	Fleury, John	187

Index.

Name	page	Name	page	Name	page
Flood, Nicholas Hen.	154	Forster, Wm. Fred., *KH.*	85	Fraser, John	57
Floyd, Charles	139	Forsyth, Thomas	183	―― John, *GCH.*	7
―― Henry, *Bt.*	55	Fortescue, *Hon.* John Wm.	158	―― John Wing, S.	148
Floyer, Richard	210	Fortune, Alexander	273	―― Leopold S. C.	222
Flude, Thomas Peters	269	Fortye, Fred. J. Campbell	195	―― Peter	159
Fludyer, William	65, 145	Fosbrooke, Edmund	207	―― Robert, *KH.*	70
Flyter, Campbell	200	―― Tho. Dudley	296	―― Robert W. M'L.	157
Foaker, Geo. Northon	194	Foss, Christoph. Vaughan	169	―― Simon	232
―― Frederick	312	―― Thomas	189	―― Thomas	295
Fogarty, Michael	216	Fossi, Thomas de	441	―― Thomas	306
Fogo, James	95, 267	Foster, Charles John	142	―― Thos. Wallace	207
―― Tho. Macm., *MD.*	287	―― *Hon.* Chich. T. S.	178	―― William	99, 194
Foley, *Hon.* Aug. Fred.	145	―― Col. Ly. Lucas	38	―― William	269
―― *Hon.* St. George Gerald	204	―― John, *MD.*	225	―― William	61
		―― Thomas	102, 284	―― William Charles	115
Follows, William	204	―― Thomas	17	―― William Kingston	131
Foote, Francis Robert	305	―― *Hon.* Tho. C. S.	254	Frazer, Augustus Henry	270
―― William Francis	296	―― *Hon.* W. Anth. S.	232	―― Daniel	102, 193
Foquett, William	116	Fothergill, William	201	―― Simon	295
Forbes, Alexander	93	Fotheringham, Robert H.	116	Fredrichs, Rudolph	433
―― Charles	71, 213	Foulis, Andrew	171	Frederick, Edward	115
―― David	243	―― David, *KCB.*	115	―― Thomas	53
―― David	37	―― William	210	Freeling, Arthur Henry	286
―― George	130	Foulston, John	215	Freeman, Edw. Deane	123
―― James	162	Fountaine, Chas. George	203	Freer, Daniel Gardner	194
―― James, *Lord*	6, 172	Foveaux, Joseph	11	―― John Harbridge	267
―― John	116	Fowle, John	215	Freese, John Noble Arb.	271
―― John	148	Fowler, James M.	240	Freeth, Jas. *KH.*	56, 117
―― John	244	Fownes, Edward Curtis	216	―― James Edw.	69, 216
―― John Alex.	102, 244	Fox, Charles Rich.	42	―― James H.	286
―― Jonathan	98, 230	―― Samuel	67, 248	―― Sampson	285
―― Nathaniel	115	―― Thomas, *MD.*	198	Freke, Fenton John Evans	119
―― Thomas John	42, 265	Foy, Edward	223	―― Henry	35
―― William	229	France, Hen. Hayhurst	126	―― Percy Aug. Evans	145
―― William Cameron	284	―― Richard	146	Freemantle, John, *CB.*	35
―― William Henry	270	Francis, Tho. John	131	French, Cudbert, *KH.*	64, 179
Ford, Cha. Erskine	285	Francklin, Thomas	32	―― Henry John	93, 237
―― Edmund T.	285	Francklyn, John Henry	270	―― James, *MD.*	200
―― John Randle	247	Frank, George	434	―― Richard	103, 203
―― Johnson	194	Frankland, Wm. Henry	253	Frend, Albert	246
―― Robert	293	Franklin, Henry	166	―― George	182
―― William	293	―― Henry	310	―― John	206
―― William Henry	285	―― Richard A. M.	170	―― John William	228
―― William Michael	224	Franklyn, Charles	102, 236	Frere, Richard Edward	164
Forde, Francis Charles	129	―― Gilbert William	188	Fresmoy, Frederick de	433
―― Matthew Thomas	123	Franks, Thomas Harte	161	Freudeuthal, Siegesmund	433
Fordyce, George William	226	Fraser, Æneas William	190	Freuller, Fridolin de	439
―― Charles F.	197	―― Adolphus	238	Frith, Cockayne	189
―― John	162	―― Alexander	86	―― Edm. Bentley	176
Forester, *Hon.* Cha. Rt.W.	138	―― Alexander	158	―― John	224
―― Cecil, William	203	―― Alex. Maclean	69	―― John Wharton	65, 209
―― *Hon.* Æmilius J.W.	164	―― Duncan	226	―― William	171
―― *Hon.* Geo. C. Weld	120	―― Fran. Michael	171	Frome, Edward	285
―― *Hon.* Hen. Town.	146	―― Fred. Alex. Mack.	85	Frost, Langford	208
Forlong, James, *KH.*	87, 194	―― Geo. Brodie	96, 267	Fry, Geo. Barlow	178
―― Robert Stein	129	―― Geo. Rob. *MD.*	208	―― John	252
Forman, Edward	202	―― Hastings	12, 235	―― Richard	215
Formin, Justus	435	―― Hugh, *KCB.*	115	Fryer, George	116
Forrest, John, *MD.*	311	―― Hugh	212	Fugion, Edward	209
―― John Henry	137	―― Hugh Andrew	88	Fulford, William	271
―― William Charles	137	―― James	186	Fuller, Burrell	121
Forster, Hugh Percy	263	―― Jas. Wm. Lovat	256	―― Francis	7, 256
―― Fran. Rowland	124	―― Jas. Alex.	312	―― Francis	55
―― John Burton	214	―― James S.	115	―― Francis	63, 210
―― Tho. Watkin	40	―― John	243	―― George	116
―― Rob. Matthew	234	―― John	294	―― Joseph, *GCH.*	11, 227

Index

	page		page		page
Fuller, William	210	Garforth, William	249	Gibsone, David And.	293, 297
—— Wm. Walter	286	Garland, Edmund	221	—— John Hope	127
Fullerton, David	199	—— John, *KH.*	70	Gichard, Wm. Rob.	272
—— Geo. Main	140	Garmston, Samuel	293	Giffard, Edward Carter	211
—— James Alex.	135	Garner, Thomas	115	Gifford, Rob. Francis, *Ld.*	126
Fulton, Geo. James	214	Garratt, Francis	123	Gilbert, Edm. Pomeroy	177
—— Jas. Forrest, *KH.*	116	—— Thomas	167	—— Walter Raleigh	270
—— William	210	Garrett, Rich. Hump. *MD.*	200	—— Walter Raleigh	115
Fumetti, Joan. Just. von	432	—— Robert, *KH.*	86, 197	—— William	115
Furer, Philip de	439	Garsford, John Wm.	224	Gilchrist, James	238
Furlong, Rich. Tasker	232	Garstin, Christophilus	258	Gildea, Stanhope Mason	176
Furneaux, William,	268, 273	—— Rob. Longmore	268	Gilder, Frederick	148
Fyers, Henry Tho.	270	Garstin, William	235	—— John	233
—— Peter	20, 264	Garthwaite, Edw. Hancock	116	Giles, Stephen	293
—— Robert Morse	271	Garvens, Henry	435	Gilland, J. Goodday Strutt	153
—— Thomas	41, 282	Garvock, John	161	Gillespie, Henry James	293
—— William Augustus	191	Gascoigne, Ernest Fr.	58	—— Hugh Rollo	268
Fyfe, Lawrence	168	—— John Hawkins	295	—— John	261
Fyffe, David	197	Gascoyne, Charles	73, 246	—— Robt. Rollo	141
Fyler, Lawrence	142	—— Isaac	6, 205	Gilley, Thomas	158
Fynmore, James	293	Gason, Charles Henry	214	Gillice, John	311
—— Thomas	294	Gates, James	202	Gillkrest, James, *MD.*	309
		—— William	273	Gillman, Bennett Watkins	163
Gabriel, Rob. B. *KH.*	40	Gatt, Salveiro	262	—— William Henry	220
Gage, Edward	102, 150	—— William	262	Gilmour, Dugald Little,	
—— *Hon.* H. Edw. Hall	253	Gaulter, Tho. Coke, *MD.*	134	*KCB.*	18
—— *Hon.* Wm.	235	Gauntlett, George	33	—— Charles	62
Gahan, Henry	208	Gausson, Wm. Aug.	210	Gilsa, Frederick de	434
—— Rob. Beresford	311	Gavin, Geo. O'Halloran	142	Gipps, *Sir* George	95, 283
Gaisford, Thomas	173	—— Michael	250	Girdlestone, Wm. Bolton	116
Galeani, Michael, *MD.*	197	Gawler, George, *KH.*	63	Girsewald, Gustavus C.	
Galiffe, John	54	Gaynor, Cha. Spencer	160	A. Von	438
—— John Fred.	227	Geale, Marcus	242	Giveen, Rob. Beauchamp	249
Gall, Richard Herbert	154	Geary, Henry	270	—— Nicholas Pelham	184
—— Isaac Hindley, H.	251	Gebser, Wm. Theodore	433	Gladstone, George	130
Galland, George	311	Geddes, Alexander	256	Glamis, *Lord,* Tho. Geo.	221
—— James	262	—— John, *KH.*	62	Glasgow, Geo. Mark	269
Gallenberg, Theodore	436	—— John Gordon	181	Glazbrook, John Hales	155
Gallie, John Lockhart	84	Gehse, Henry	433	Glegg, Baskerville	138
Galloway, Thomas James	184	Geils, Andrew	116	—— Edw Holt	252
—— Thomas L. L.	100, 161	—— Thomas William	131	—— Berkenhead	12
Gallwey, Philip P.	242	Geissmann, Lewis de	436	—— Hen. Vibart	116
—— Melbourne B.	287	Gemmellaro, Charles	440	Gleichen, Fred. von Uslar	432
—— Thomas Lionel J.	286	Gentzkow, Adolphus von	434	—— Geo. von Uslar	432
—— Wm. Payne, *Bt.*		George, Fred. Darley	173	—— Hans von Uslar	435
	103, 240	—— Geo. Thorne	227	—— Ferd. von Uslar	435
Galway, William	229	Gerard, Tho. Alexander	180	—— Thilo von Uslar	435
Gambier, Gloucester	270	Gerson, Geo. Hartog	436	Glen, Edward Southouse	259
Gammie, Patrick	232	Gerstlacher, Eberhard	433	Glenie, Melville	70, 211
Gannes, J. J. Chevalier de	441	Gethin, *Sir* Richard, *Bt.*	171	Glenlyon, George Aug.	
Garden, R. J.	196	Gib, John Binney	213	Frederick John, *Lord*	129
Gardiner, Alexander	183	Gibb, Chas. John	286	Gloag, John	136
—— David	159	Gibbes, J. Geo. Nathaniel	67	Gloster, Richard	213
—— Hen. Lynedoch	272	Gibbons, Richard	211	—— Thomas	90
—— Jas. Ballard	67	—— Thomas	200	Glover, Stirling Freeman	163
—— John, *KCB.*	16, 117	—— Tho. Ponsonby	200	Glubb, Fred. Philip	185
—— Nathan Smith	173	Gibbs, Edward	19	—— John Warren	256
—— John Ballard	221	—— Hen. Durham	167	Glutz, Amanz	440
—— Richard	228	—— John	202	Glynn, Richard Henry	146
—— Rob. *KCB.KCH.*		Gibson, Charles Fred.	222	Goate, Edward	89, 186
	35, 265	—— Edgar	103	Godby, Charles Henry	218
—— William	235	—— George	89	—— Dennis	226
Gardner, Richard	116	—— Geo. Washington	116	Goddard, John Hesketh	140
—— Wm. Bethell	271	—— Jas. Brown, *MD.*	143	—— Samuel	165
—— *Hon.* W. H.	20, 264	—— John	253	Godwin, Charles, *MD.*	312
Gardnor, Thomas	119	—— Thomas	155	—— Henry	41

405

Index.

Name	page
Goeben, Christian, *Baron*	441
—— Fred., *Baron*	434
—— George, *Baron*	434
—— Quintus, *Baron*	433
—— William de	438
Going, Richard	151
Gold, Charles	33
—— Cha. Emilius	217
—— William George	204
Goldfinch, Henry	35, 282
Goldfrapp, Geo. Alfred	222
Goldie, Alexander John	9
—— Andrew	116
—— George Leigh	41, 162
—— Mark Wilkes	173
—— Thomas Leigh	102, 218
Goldsmid, Albert	85
Goldsmith, Oliver	306
Goldsworthy, John	287
Gomm, Wm. M., *KCB.*	20
Gooch, Henry	62, 147
Good, Samuel	150
Goodall, George	151
Goode, William Henry	161
Goodenough, Arthur Cyril	185
—— Henry Philip	272
Goodfellow, Joseph	177
—— Samuel	115
Goodman, Charles A.	187
—— Stephen Arthur, *KH.*	35
—— Samuel E.	178
Goodrich, Wm. Bridger	208
Goodsir, James Tod	306
Goodsman, David	71
Goodwin, Hugh	83
Goodwyn, Henry Wm.	227
Goold, James	162
Gordon, Abraham Hen.	72, 292
—— *Hon.* Alexander	146
—— Alexander	152
—— Alexander	284
—— Archibald, *MD.*	186
—— Arthur Helsham	54
—— Benjamin	11
—— Bertie E. M.	243
—— *Lord* Cecil	193
—— Charles	245
—— Charles Edw.	73, 266
—— Charles E. P.	227
—— Charles Hen.	245
—— Cosmo	16
—— Duncan	92, 210
—— *Lord* Francis A.	118
—— Gabriel	11, 243
—— George Alex.	157
—— Geo. Hamilton	37
—— George James	231
—— Hamilton Douglas	230
—— Henry W.	210
—— Henry Wm.	68, 266
—— James	185
—— James	186
—— James	70, 283
—— Jas. Caulfield	244
—— Jas. Charles	244

Name	page
Gordon, Jas. Willoughby, *Bt. GCB. GCH.*	11, 117, 174
—— John	186
—— John	98, 198
—— John	96, 267
—— John	116
—— John W.	286
—— Lachlan Duff	171
—— Patrick Robert	215
—— Robert	293
—— Stephen Blaney	256
—— Theodore, *MD.*	309
—— William	168
—— William	218
—— William	294
—— Wm. Alex.	35
Gore, Arthur	70
—— *Hon.* Charles, *KH.*	41
—— Charles William	238
—— Henry Ross	84
—— Henry Wm. Knox	221
—— Jas. Pollock	152
—— John	269
—— Owen Arth. Ormsby	194
—— St. John Thos.	227
—— Wm. Rich. Ormsby	204
Gorgon, Stephen B.	196
Gorman Owen	232
Gorrequer, Gideon, *KH.*	40
Goslin, Samuel John	236
Gosselin, Gerrard	10
Gosset, Arthur	269
—— James Wm.	286
—— Wm., *KCH.*	39, 282
—— Wm. Matthew	100, 284
Gostling, Charles	269
Gotze, Henry	433
Gouder, Giovanni	99, 262
—— Guiseppe	262
Gough, Harry	176
—— *Sir* Hugh, *KCB.*	16
—— John Bloomfield	130
—— Tho. Bunbury	184
Goulbourn, Edward	145
Gossencourt, Jos. Ignace	439
Gowan, Edward Parry	116
—— Geo. Mauleverer	249
Gowdie, John	88
Grady, Robert Spread	165
Grame, Lawrence	100
Graffenried, Antoine Fred. de	440
—— Francis de	440
Graham, Allan Hamilton	272
—— Charles	305
—— Cha. Mackenzie	116
—— David	70
—— Edw. Smith, *MD.*	227
—— Fortescue	294
—— George	90
—— Henry Hope	210
—— Hen. Wm. Hartley	259
—— James	241
—— James John	222
—— *Lord* Mont. Wm.	148
—— Oliver Thos.	172

Name	page
Graham, Sandford	146
—— Thomas	151
—— Thomas	307
—— Thos. Campbell	116
—— William	100, 210
—— William	224
—— William	263
—— William	61
Grahn, Frederick	433
Granet, Charles	168
Grange, Richard George	116
Grant, Alexander, *KH.*	93
—— Alexander	306
—— Alexander G.	237
—— Bernard	234
—— Cath. Campbell Ham.	223
—— Chas. Lennox	312
—— Charles St. John	116
—— Colquhoun	310
—— Duncan	65, 266
—— Duncan Trevor	195
—— Edw. Fitzherbert	270
—— Edward John	181
—— Eyre Coote	179
—— *Hon.* Francis Wm.	32
—— Francis W. *MD.*	312
—— James	193
—— James	38
—— John	214
—— John	311
—— John Donald	311
—— John Francis	254
—— John Henry	161
—— John James	189
—— J. Hope	135
—— John Thornton	200
—— Joseph Jeffries	162
—— Lewis, *KCH.*	12, 248
—— Peter Cha. Stuart	220
—— Robert	306
—— Rob. Joynt Gord.	173
—— Thomas John	209
—— Turner	39, 144
—— William Charles	121
—— William Edward	209
—— Wm. Keir, *KCB. GCH.*	11, 129
—— William Lewis	212
Grantham, Francis	250
—— Thomas	96, 267
Granville, Frederick	174
Grasett, William	133
Grattan, Albert O'Donnel	286
—— Copeland, *MD.*	217
—— John	169
Gravatt, George	179
—— Thomas	153
—— William	33
Graves, *Hon.* Adolphus E. P.	148
—— Benjamin	55
—— Chas. Twisleton	239
—— *Hon.* Geo. A. F. C.	181
—— James William	169
—— John Steward	131

496

Index.

	page		page		page
Graves, Samuel Wood	214	Grierson, Henry	166	Haberland, Charles	439
Gray, Alured William	195	Grieve, Patrick	61, 227	Hacket, John George	243
—— Alured William	195	Griffin, Francis John	183	—— William, *MD.*	309
—— Arthur	152	—— George	183	Hackett, Adam	190
—— Basil	227	—— George	237	—— James	115
—— Charles	293	—— George	294	—— John	222
—— Charles Gordon	286	—— John Hungerford	268	—— Pierce	255
—— Edward William	233	Griffis, Charles Tindal	140	—— Wellington	168
—— Francis Delaval	138	Griffith, George Darby	242	Hadaway, Sam. Maitland	311
—— Humphrey	190	—— Henry Darby	129	Hadden, Wm. Cha.	285
—— James	94, 267	—— Henry Downe	229	Hadfield, Cha. Joseph	296
—— John	191	—— John	254	—— Wm. Howe	130
—— John Hamilton	141	—— Moses	171	Hadley, Henry, *MD.*	191
—— Owen Wynne	190	—— William Glynne	188	—— William, H. S.	153
—— Thos. Browne	294, 297	Griffiths, Edwin	248	Hagart, Charles	133
—— William	20	—— Frederick	33	—— Jas. Macaul	133
Graydon, Alex. *MD.*	201	—— Fred. Augustus	269,	Hageman, Lewis	438
—— George	272		273	—— John George	436
—— George, *KH.*	58, 283	—— Fred. Charles	72	Hague, Cha. Barnard	219
Greathed, Edw. Harris	159	—— Henry T.	190	Hailes, John	116
Greatly, Thomas	85	—— John Charles	95	Haines, Edw. Eldridge	244
Greatrex, Edward	148	—— John Thomas	157	—— F. Paul	155
Greaves, Richard	69	Grignon, James	188	Haining, James	217
Green, Andrew	199	Grigg, James Wm.	206	Hair, Archibald, *MD.*	120
—— Charles	201	Grimes, Charles Robert	201	Hake, William	102, 139
—— Charles William	154	—— Joseph John	201	Halahan, J. Wallon, *MD.*	287
—— David	152	Grimston, *Hon.* Charles	148	—— Rd. Robertus	195
—— George	215	Grindley, Edw. Thos.	307	Haldane, Robert	217
—— William	305	Grogan, George	158	Hale, Edw. Blagden	234
—— William, *KH.*	67	—— George	33	—— Hen. Grimstone	137
Greene, John	127	—— John	256	—— John Rich. Blagden	130
—— Thomas	172	Groskopff, Charles	442	—— Richard	233
Greenhill, James David	115	Grosvenor, Thomas	6, 217	—— William	253
Greenock, Chas. M., *Lord,*		Grote, William Henry	90	—— Wm. Amherst	203
KCB.	17	Grove, Robert	242	Halfhide, Benjamin	88, 195
Greenstreet, John	115	Groves, Stephen Percy	121	—— Cha. Alex.	200
Greenville, William	96, 153	Groyune, Fred. Ximenes	246	—— James	188
Greenwell, Leonard, *KCH.*	19	Grubbe, John Heneage	102,	Haliburton, John Fowden	230
Greenwood, George	42, 119		228	Haliday, Wm. Robert	245
—— Joseph	182	Gruttemann, Augustus	439	Halkett, Alex. *KCH.*	11
—— William	63, 144	Grylls, Rich. Gervys	181	—— Colin, *KCB.GCH.*	
—— William	268	—— Jas. Willyams	177		12, 182
Greer, Alex. *MD.*	312	Guanter, Jacques	439	—— Frederick	148
Gregg, Charles Francis	201	Guard, William	158	—— Henry	191
—— Edward Regan	177	Gubbins, Robert	214	—— Hugh, *KCH.*	53
Gregory, Arthur Cha.	90, 250	Guille, John Andros	176	—— Hugh	153
—— Charles	94, 200	Gnise, Jo. Wright, *Bt.*		—— James	180
—— William	284	*KCB.*	13	—— J. Tho. Douglas	131
Grehan, Peter	153	Gulliver, George	120	Hall, Charles	101, 118
Greig, John James	175	Gulston, Alan James	198	—— Gage, John	11, 222
—— William Isaac	306	—— Horatio Rob. M.	232	—— George	203
Greisheim, Albert von	439	Gumoens, Charles de	440	—— George	85
Greville, Fulke	118	Gunn, William	260	—— George Dry	91
Grey, *Hon.* Charles	62, 223	Gunton, Henry	201	—— Jasper Taylor	86
—— George	235	Gurtler, Joseph	440	—— John	70, 118
—— *Hon.* Harry Cavend.	203	Gurwood, John	57	—— John	184
—— *Hon.* Henry Geo.,		Guthrie, William	193	—— John	116
GCB. GCH.	7, 139	Guy, Lewis	233	—— John Edward	199
—— John	20	—— Philip M. Nelson	156	—— John Peter	165
—— John	44	—— William	214	—— Lewis Alexander	99, 284
—— John	53	Gwilt, John	185	—— Manley G. Dwarris	165
—— John William	237	—— Rich. Brandram	258	—— Morris	157
—— Warburton	207	Gwynne, Marmaduke	142	—— Sam. Madden Fra.	98, 227
Grier, John Joseph	245	—— Wm. Augustus	169	—— Thomas	156
Grierson, Alexander	230			—— Thomas	70, 168
—— Crighton	97, 284	Haardt, Lewis	438	—— Thomas	116

497

Index.

	page		page		page
Hall, William	143	Hammill, Robert	89, 169	Harriott, Thos. Geo.	90
—— William	311	Hammond, Frederick	88	Harris, Arthur, Miller	202
—— William T.	157	—— Fra. Thos. *GCH*.	8	—— Augustus	214
Hallen, Herbert	132	—— Wm. Oxenden	143	—— Chas. Robison	175
Hallewell, Edm. Gilling	171	Hamond, Philip	185	—— Harry Bulteel,	
Halliday, Francis Aug.	295	Hampton, Robert	115	*KH*.	40
—— Lewis	238	Hanbury, John, *KCH*.	18	—— Henry William	175
—— Geo. Edm.	234	Hancock, F. H. W. L.	226	—— John	175
Hallifax, Rob. Dampier		Handcock, *Hon*. Henry		—— John Crichton	224
	93, 227	Robert	249	—— Robert Russell	239
Haly, Standish	169	—— Richard	96, 197	—— Walter	99
—— Wm. O'Grady	198	—— *Hon*. Rob. French	270	—— William	287
Hambly, And. John Buck	296	Handfield, John C.	154	—— Wm. Thos.	186
Hamerton, W. Meadows	84	—— Carey	216	—— Wm. Geo. *Lord*,	
—— John Millet	18	Hankey, *Sir* Frederick,		*KCH*.	13, 225
Hames, Charles	116	*GCMG*.	33	Harrison, Anth. Robinson	
—— Weston	116	—— Hen. Aitchison	72		268
Hamilton, Alex. Duke	91	Hanley, Roderick John	236	—— Broadley	137
—— Abraham	143	Hanmer, Wyndham Edw.	120	—— Geo. Francis	236
—— Alex. Gra. W.	271	Hanna, Joseph Alex.	255	—— Gustavus Nicolls	215
—— Alex. Mark K.	16	Hanson, Denis	263	—— James Hull	94
—— Arch. Rowan	125	Hansord, Solomon Ed-		—— John	131
—— Aug. Terrick	223	man	307	—— John	146
—— Benj. Usher, *MD*.	312	Hanwell, Joseph	99, 267	—— John Bacon	53
—— Chas. John James	150	Harbord, *Hon*. Alfred A.	130	—— Nathaniel Evan-	
—— Charles P.	247	Harcourt, Fra. Venables	63,	son	270
—— Charles Thos.	190		144	—— Robt. Steppings	296
—— Christopher	20	—— John	195	—— Septimus	250
—— Digby St. Vincent	230	Hardie, John	215	Hart, Charles, *MD*.	312
—— Fra. Seymour	270	Harding, George Judd	44,	—— Henry, *MD*.	182
—— Fra. Smith	294		283	—— Henry George	200
—— Fred. Wm.	145	—— Francis Pym	173	—— Robert	84
—— Fred. Wm.	211	—— Jas. Augustus	224	—— Shepherd	116
—— George	206	—— Thomas Goldie	186	—— Thomas Frederick	246
—— Geo. Rowan	240	—— William	86	Harthill, Robert	160
—— Geo. Vallancy	153	Hardinge, *Rt. Hon*. Hen.		Hartle, John F. A.	245
—— Henry	139	*KCB*.	18, 249	Hartley, Bartholomew	199
—— Henry	230	—— Rich. *KH*.	99, 267	——Henry Winch.	101,159
—— Hen. Meade	214	—— William	190	—— Humph. Rob.	61
—— Jas. John, *Bt*.	92	Hardisty, William	258	Hartman, Wm. Henry	90,
—— John	33	Hardy, Jonas Paisley	209		160
—— John Jas.	227	—— Simeon Hen. *MD*.		—— Edmund F. A.	160
—— John Potter, *KH*.	32		312	Hartmann, Augustus C.	
—— Louis H.	156	Hare, *Hon*. Chas. Luke	158	F.	435
—— Nicholas, *KH*.	43,	—— John, *KH*.	38, 178	—— Gustavus F. W.	435
	263	—— Loftus	165	—— Henry	438
—— Richard	188	—— Rich. Goddard	35	—— Julius, *KCB*.	
—— Robert Charles	199	—— Thomas	178	*KCH*.	54, 437
—— Robert Georges	285	—— William Henry	202	Hartstonge, Rich. Weld	70
—— Samuel B.	176	Harenc, Neil Hulse	176	Hartwell, John Loftus	311
—— Thomas	165	Harford, Charles	161	Hartwig, Gottlieb de	437
—— Thomas	71, 170	Harger, John	256	Harty, Joseph M. *KH*.	87,
—— Thos. M. M'N.	237	Harker, Robert	173		184
—— Walter	230	Harlessem, Philip A. Von,		Harvest, Hector	249
—— Walter	235		442	—— Aug. Hamilton	250
—— William	188	Harling, Augustus de	433	Harvey, Bissell, *KH*.	66, 116,
—— William Digby	139	Harness, Henry D.	285		263
—— William James	154	Harold, John Casimer	95, 226	—— Edward	140
—— William J.	213	Harper, William Hosken	124	—— Edw. Warwick	187
Hamley, Chas. Ogilvy	296	Harpour, Geo. Cosby	96, 219	—— Francis Charles	185
—— Fran. Gilbert	163	Harpur, John	256	—— Henry B.	239
—— Wm. George	286	Harries, Thomas	215	—— James, *KH*.	60
Hammersley, Frederick	121	Harrington, Chas. *Earl of*		—— James, C.	190
Hammerstein, A. *Baron*	433		32	—— John	188
—— Otto Von	432	—— Christopher D.	296	—— John, *KCH*.	19
Hammill, Joseph	160	Harriott, George	142	—— John	217

Index.

Name	page	Name	page	Name	page
Harvey, John	272	Head, Charles	91	Herbert, Dennis	14
—— Richard	271	—— Henry Bond	166	—— Dennis	229
—— *Sir* Rob. John	34	Healey, Thomas	183	—— Henry Loftus	240
—— William	160	Heard, George Nares	210	Herford, William Lewis	54
—— William Fred.	168	—— William Hodder	181	Heriot, Frederick George	35
Harward, Geo. Netherton	210	Hearle, Edward	294	—— John, *M.D.*	126
Harzig, Frederick	434	Heathcote, Eustace	185	—— Tho. Ancrum	206
Haslewood, Dickens Mark	165	—— Wm. Samuel	115	—— Wm. Mackay 295,	297
Hassard, John	239	Heatley, Charles Fade	205	Heron, Basil Robinson 97,	267
—— Ross	287	—— John	200	—— Peter	7
Hassell, William de	433	Heaton, John R.	127	Herries, W. Lewis, *KCH.*	40
Hatton, Geo. Aug.	214	Hebert, Abraham Louis	441	—— William Robert	194
Hattorf, Hans Von	432	Hecker, Charles Higgin.		Herring, John	116
—— Hen. Geo. Von	432	Teush	141	—— Edmund	116
Haultain, Francis 96,	267	Heckscher, Cha. Martin		Hervey, Charles F.	185
—— Fred. Wm.	272	A.	434	Hesse, Adolphus	435
—— Theodore M.	215	Hegler, Charles	441	Hessing, Geo. Wm.	192
Hausler, Frederick	439	Heimburg, F. C. *Baron*	438	Heuer, Ludolph	432
Havelock, Cha. Fred.	142	—— Ernest, *Baron*	436	Heugel, William de	434
—— Henry	104	—— Lewis A. T.	439	Hewes, John	293
—— Wm., *KH.* 90,	131	Heise, Adolphus	434	Hewetson, William	305
Haviland, Francis	122	—— Arnold William	434	Hewett, *Rt. Hon.* G. *Bt.*	
—— John	122	—— Christopher	434	*GCB.* 6,	213
Havilland, Charles de	84	—— Joh. Christ. Ulrich	433	—— George Henry	43
—— Thomas de	206	—— Lawrence	435	Hewgill, Percy William	271
Hawker, Charles	167	—— Lewis	438	Hewitt, Cha. Coleman	295
—— Ernest Augustus	123	—— Wm. Augustus	186	—— Isaac Henry	169
—— Francis	84	Heitland, Wm. Emerton	270	Hewson, John Milliquet	241
—— Peter Wm. Lanoe	226	Hellen, D. W. von der	433	Hext, Cha. Staniforth	155
—— Thomas, *KCH.* 15,	126	—— C. A. von der	434	—— Francis John	235
Hawkes, Robert	155	Helmich, Augustus	437	Heyde, Fred. J. A. von der	439
—— John Blackburne	121	Hely, Jas. Price, *KH.*	86	Heydenreich, William	435
—— Robert	116	—— Joseph	200	Heyland, Alfred Thomas	247
Hawkey, Henry Charles		Helyar, Albert	133	—— John Rowley	186
Moorh.	296	Hemmans, Tho. Hinton	230	Heyman, Henry	131
—— John, *M.D.*	310	Hemphill, Andrew T.	180	Heyn, William	440
Hawkins, Arthur Cæsar	152	—— Edward	221	Hibbert, George 93,	191
—— John P.	54	—— William	226	—— John Gray, *M.D.*	210
—— John S.	286	Henderson, Alexander	284	Hickey, Edward	230
—— Samuel	294	—— Duncan, *M.D.*	156	Hickin, Tho. Bennett 96,	180
—— Thomas Scott	152	—— Edmund, Y. W.	286	Hickman, John Penn	141
Hawkshaw, Edward	116	—— G. Aug., *KH.*	37	Hicks, George	116
—— John	284	—— Hen. Barkley	116	—— John	116
—— John Stewart	116	—— James, *M.D.*	130	—— George Allen	212
Hawley, Robert B.	241	—— James, *KH.*	88	Hickson, John Annesley	225
Hay, Alex. Sebast. Leith	245	—— John	140	Hiern, John	187
—— Alexander Macleod	209	—— John	167	Higginbotham, Charles	215
—— Archibald	238	—— J. W. *KH.*	85	Higgins, Charles O'Conor	207
—— Cha. Craufurd 98,	170	—— J. Alexander	252	—— Henry	127
—— Chas. Murray 62,	147	—— William	271	—— Hugh Brabazon	141
—— David 96,	126	—— William	116	—— James Lewis	116
—— David	240	Hendley, Thomas	273	—— Sam. Gordon,	
—— Edward	116	Henley, J.	125	*KCH.*	33
—— *Lord,* Edward	61	Hennessey, Patrick	171	—— Thos. Gordon 101,	267
—— Humphrey	116	Henniker, *Hon.* Major	119	—— Warner, Westen-	
—— *Lord,* James	40	Hennis, William Howe	269	ra, *KH.*	55
—— James	166	Henry, Clifford Felix	199	Higginson, Alexander 39,	144
—— James	34	—— Frederick Hugh	186	—— Geo. Powell 41,	117
—— John Chas.	232	—— Rich. Francis	180	Hill, Alfred Edward 117,	220
—— Philip	37	—— Robert	294	—— Charles	205
—— Tho. Rob. Drum.	193	—— Walter	310	—— Charles John	63
—— William	55	Hepburn, Francis J. S.	213	—— Clement	20
Hayes, Frederick	232	—— David	116	—— Dudley Clarges	174
—— George James	295	Herbert, Arthur	190	—— *Sir* Dudley St. Ledger	34
—— Samuel Baker	188	—— Arthur Maynard	214	—— Edward	248
Haythorne, Edmund	250	—— Charles	227	—— Edward Roley	233

Index.

Name	page	Name	page	Name	page
Hill, Frederick William	161	Holden, William	253	Hope, William	223
——— Henry	208	Holder, Frederick	164	Hopegood, Fra. Vere	222
——— Hugh	159	——— Coulthurst	159	Hopkins, Geo. Robt.	228
——— John	270	Holdham, John Field	84	——— Richard Northey	10
——— John Thomas	183	Holdsworth, Samuel	234	——— Wm. Friend	295
——— Joseph	256	——— Tho. Weston E.	153	Hopper, William	115
——— Moore	209	Hole, Alfred Robert	139	——— Wm. Henry	232
——— Percy	220	Holford, James P. G.	86	Hopson, Wm. Hopson	258
——— Philip	93, 204	Holgate, Bennett	84	Hopton, John	123
——— Richard Fred.	64, 204	Holland, George Freer	116	Hopwood, Hervey	146
——— Sir Robt. Chambre	32	——— Frederick	172	Hore, James Ryves	88
——— Rowland, Lord, GCB. GCH. KC.	7, 117, 120	——— John	238	——— Thomas	284
		——— John	295	Horn, Frederick	171
		——— Launcelot	32	Hornbrook, Fred. Hillman	226
——— Stephen John	256	Holle, Lewis von	434	——— Richard Lyde	293
——— Lord Wm. F. A. M.	129	——— Fred. A. Baron	435	Hornby, Edw. Carter	42
——— Wm. Noel	93, 221	Hollingworth, George	295	——— Phipps, John	286
——— Wm. Noel Algernon	125	Hollinsworth, Hen. And.	232	——— Stanley Bing	271
Hilliard, Edw. Dav. Crosier	136	——— Henry	207	——— Thomas Wynn	234
		Hollis, John J.	88, 176	——— William	218
——— George	169	——— James	221	Horne, Arthur	195
Hillier, George	58, 214	——— Richard	121	——— Fran. Woodley	141
——— George E.	214	Holloway, Thomas	295, 297	——— George	141
Hilmer, John Frederick	438	——— Wm. C. E.	57, 283	——— James	191
Hilton, James	286	Holmes, Fra. Saunderson	159	Horner, John	206
——— John	155	——— Griffiths	116	——— William W.	220
——— Thomas	170	——— James Gustavus		Hornsby, John Romaine	268
——— William	142	Ham.	186	——— William Wilson	243
——— William Duncan	154	——— John Kent Eger.	239	Horrocks, Charles	166
Hind, Charles	196	——— Rob. Pattison	90, 174	——— George	230
Hinde, John	159	——— Tho. Edmonds	165	——— John	237
Hine, John	196	Holscher, Achatz Wm.	433	Horsburgh, James	161
Hingston, Clayton S. H.	259	Holt, George	205	Horsford, Alfred H.	253
Hirst, Simeon	120	Holtzermann, Frederick	433	——— George	11
Hislop, Thos. Bt. GCB.	8, 199	Holworthy, Edw. John	258	——— George Fahie	254
Hitchens, Benj. Robertson	116	Home, Alex. Geo. MD.	122	Horsley, Nicholas	248
Hobart, George	129	——— James	32	Hort, Richard	101, 233
Hobhouse, John Byron	164	——— James Murray	187	Horton, Christ. Wilmot	148
Hobson, Samuel	248	——— John	57, 144	——— George Wm.	56
Hocker, Edward	295	——— John Belshes	157	——— James	60
Hockin, Charles Francis	296	——— Rodham, C. D.	219	——— Sydney Lloyd	200
Hockings, Robert	296	——— William, MD.	311	Hosken, John	160
Hodenberg, Augustus von	437	Honeyman, John Ord	61, 144	Hosmer, Charles	116
——— Ernest, Baron	434	Honeywood, Edward	153	Hoste, Sir Geo. Cha.	44, 283
——— Hans, Baron	433	Honstedt, Barth. Geo. von	436	Hotham, Augustus Tho.	227
——— Ivan, G. F. Baron	433	Hood, Hon. Alex. Nelson	150	——— Beau. Lord	44
Hodge, Edw. Cooper	124	——— Alex. Bate. Periam	120	——— Henry	270
Hodges, Thomas Eardley	257	——— Hon. Fr. Grosvenor	145	Hotzen, Geo. Lewis Otto	437
Hodgson, Christopher	115	——— George	194	Hough, William	116
——— Henry	115	Hook, Archibald	88, 192	——— Harry Wainw.	201
——— John	8, 155	——— Charles Campbell	246	Houstoun, Alexander	131
——— Studholme J.	102, 170	——— Lionel	160	——— Geo. Aug. Fred.	145
Hodson, Chas. Robt. Geo.	116	Hookey, Geo.	297	——— Robert, KCB.	115
——— Henry Fred.	131	Hooper, Rich. Wheeler	95, 221	——— Wm. Bt. GCB.	
Hoey, William Francis	213	Hope, Archibald White	267	GCH.	8, 171
Hogarth, George	102, 177	——— Hon. Adrian	212	Hovenden, Fran. Parnell	125
Hogg, Arthur	195	——— Charles Reid	154	——— Nicholas	92, 210
——— Adam	115	——— Frederick	92, 224	Howard, Charles	306
——— William	127	——— Hon. James	69, 147	——— Hon. Fulke Grev.	32
Hogge, John, KH.	56	——— Jas. Arch., KCB.	34	——— Robert	66
Hohnhorst, Geo. Baron	435	——— James	263	——— Tho. Phipps, KH.	40
Holbech, Henry	212	——— John Cha., KH.	64, 252	Howden, Lord J. Hobart, KH.	57, 116
Holcombe, Alex. Essex F.	164	——— John Isaac	284		
——— Harcourt Fort	53	——— John Thomas	224	Howe, Rich. Uniacke	233
——— Francis	269	——— Hon. Louis	148	——— William	306
Holden, Charles	202	——— William	158	Howell, George	213

Index.

Name	page	Name	page	Name	page
Howes, James	216	Hutchinson, Bru. Æ. S.	256	James, William E.	185
Howison, John	116	——— Edw. Hely	186	——— William John	216
Howorth, Richard	285	——— Fred. J. T.	209	Jameson, Lawrence, *MD*.	311
Hoyer, Anthony Fred.	433	——— George	116	——— Thos. Ross, *MD*.	311
Huband, George J.	134	——— George	172	Janvrin, Francis Frederick	131
Hudson, Joseph Henry	145	——— Geo. Rowan	285		
——— Tho. Wright	213	——— *Hon.* Hen. Hely	43	Jardine, Alexander	227
Huey, Richardson W.	102, 220	——— James	100	Jarvis, Geo. R. Payne	55
Hughes, Charles	64, 175	——— Marley	204	——— John George	203
——— James	39	——— Timothy	241	——— James	189
——— J. W. M. G.	140	——— Wm. *KCH*.	11	Jasper, Lewis	437
——— Mar. Collingwood	221	——— Wm. Nelson	91, 171	Jauncey, Alex. S. G.	162
——— Robert	254	Hutchison, George	249	——— John Knight	161
——— Robert	255	——— John	152	——— Henry John	251
——— Robert George	164	Huthwaite, Fra. Cornelius	146	Ibbetson, Chas. Parke	124
——— Speer	236	——— Edward	116	——— Denzil	305
Hugo, Ludolph de	432	——— Henry	115	——— Fred. James	122
Hugonin, Fran. James	248	Hutton, Geo. Davis	192	Jean, Philip	172
Hull, William	115	——— Henry John	185	Jebb, Charles William	212
Hulme, William	66, 248	——— James	166	——— Joshua	284
Hulse, Richard Samuel	148	——— John	249	——— Richard	89, 191
Humbley, Wm. Wellington Waterloo	131	——— Robert	209	Jeffares, Harman	101, 261
		——— Thomas	85	Jefferson, Richard	258
Hume. Geo. Ponsonby	209	Hyde, George Hooton	269	Jeffery, John Uniacke	233
——— Henry	247	Hyder, William Augustus	131	——— John Morton	250
——— Thomas David	194	Hynes, N.	187	Jeffrey, George	255
——— William	224			Jeffreys, Edmund Rich.	240
Humfrays, Samuel P. C.	116	Jackson, Adam Thomson	311	——— Fred. Augustus	170
Humfrey, William Chas.	237	——— Basil	92	Jeinsen, Henry von	442
——— Rich. Morgan	219	——— Edward, *KH*.	56	Jekyll, William Frederick	157
Humphrys, Henry	133	——— Frederick Hall	208	Jellicoe, Richard	263
Hunt, Arthur	62, 266	——— George	115	Jenkin, James	285
——— George Evans	295	——— Geo. Wm. C.	121	Jenkins, Frederick	195
——— George Henry	208	——— Henry	214	——— John	92, 137
——— John	961	——— Hen. Augustus	125	——— Richard	176
——— John Philip	53	——— Henry Geo.	72, 267	——— Theophilus	156
——— Rich. Burgess	89	——— James, *MD*.	157	——— William	261
——— Robert	88, 208	——— James	100, 208	Jenkinson, Geo. Samuel	253
——— Thos. Bloomfield	232	——— James	259	Jenner, Augustus Fred.	162
——— William Thomas	100, 237,	——— James, *KH*.	55, 126	Jennings, Edmund Wm.	187
		——— John Napper	87, 251	——— John	306
Hunter, David	8	——— John R.	189	——— Peter Raymond	164
——— James	193	——— Joseph Reid	295	——— William	305
——— James	93	——— Keith, Alex. *Bt*.	131	Jennyns, Jos. Clayton	141
——— James William	127	——— Oliver	237	Jephson, Henry	239
——— Martin, *GCH*.	7	——— Richard Downes		——— Robert Geo.	220
——— Robert Francis	223	*KCB*.	15, 233	——— Stanhope Wm.	153
——— Rob. Hope Alston	153	——— Rob. Hen. Stuart	249	Jerningham, James Edw.	173
——— Thomas, *MD*.	138	——— Thomas Brooke	141	Jerome, Joseph	238
——— William, *MD*.	148	——— Wm. Ernest	97, 267	Jerrand, Joseph	60
——— William	179	Jacob, George Thomson	124	Jervis, Henry	224
——— William James	297	——— Henry Hutton	94	——— Thomas Best	116
Huntley, Wm. Warburton	97, 123	Jacson, Simon Fitzh.	162	Jervois, William, *KH*.	37
		Jaenicke, Lewis	436	——— Wm. Fra. Drummond	286
Hupeden, Richard	435	James, Abraham	116		
Hurdle, Thomas	294, 297	——— Charles	236	Jex, Thomas	129
Hurford, Rich. John Gedaliah	142	——— Charles Hugh	182	Jeyes, Samuel, *MD*.	310
		——— Cha. Woodcock	219	Ilderton, Chas. Richard	250
——— Thomas	141	——— Demetrius W. G.	153	Imhoff, *Sir* Charles	11
Hurtzig, Frederick	436	——— Edward Sims	175	Imlach, Alexander	152
Huskisson, John	296	——— George	268	Impett, John	223
——— Samuel	14	——— Geo. H. M.	180	Imray, Robert	235
Hussey, Wm. Hayter	219	——— Henry	285	Ince, Ralph Pigott	207
Hutchesson, Thomas	61, 265	——— John Kingston	132	Ingall, Frederick Lenox	166
Hutchins, Henry Thos.	214	——— Robert	133	Inge, Charles	204
——— William James	215	——— William	64, 177	——— Edward	131

501

Index.

Name	page
Ingham, Cha. Tho. *MD*.	180
Ingilby, William Bates	268
Ingleby, William	116
Inglefield, Samuel Hood Stovin	272
Inglis, Jas. Gordon, *MD*.	239
—— Jos. Eardley Wil.	183
—— Richard	306
—— Thos. Cochrane	221
—— William	155
Ingram, Fra. Edw. Winnington	132
—— Samuel	167
—— Tho. Ons. Winning.	249
Inman, John	226
Innes, Francis Wm. *MD*.	236
—— George	270
—— Joseph Long	190
—— William	115
Jocelyn, *Hon.* A. G. Fred.	126
—— Robert, *Viscount*	141
Joddrell, Henry Edm.	37
—— Francis Chas.	145
Jodrell, Edward	169
Johns, Richard	295
Johnson, Chas. Chris.	68
—— Dav. England	89, 156
—— George	133
—— George John	148
—— Henry, F. F.	156
—— Hen. Milham	157
—— James	146
—— John	116
—— John Brooke	240
—— Warner West	192
—— Wm. Augustus	17
Johnston, Arthur Lake	172
—— Frederick	85
—— Geo. Jos. Bidmead	116
—— James	159
—— James	191
—— James	89, 195
—— James, *MD*.	312
—— James T. O. *MD*.	199
—— John	184
—— John	218
—— John	220
—— John	222
—— Patrick	251
—— Peter	116
—— Robt. Gudgeon	168
—— Thos. Henry	71, 218
—— Wm. *KCB*.	14, 220
—— William	126
—— William	200
—— Wm. Fred.	69, 145
Johnstone, Fra. Jas. Tho.	115
—— Francis W.	244
—— George	72, 193
—— George G. Hope	244
—— John William	177
—— Mont. Cholm.	102, 178
—— William?	96, 177
—— Wm. Jas. Hope	193
Jolliffe, William	293
—— William	296

Name	page
Jones, Archibald Jas.	174
—— Benj. Orlando	66
—— Chas. Tyrwhitt	150
—— Douglas	225
—— Edward	85
—— George	42, 292
—— George E. *KH*.	63, 208
—— Griffin	439
—— Harry David	94, 283
—— Henry Richmond	126
—— James, *KH*.	59
—— Inigo	137
—— John	212
—— John Edw.	58, 265, 273
—— John Francis	168
—— John Landon	116
—— John Lloyd	116
—— John Tho. *Bt.*	19, 282
—— John Thos. Wm.	194
—— Joseph	64, 163
—— Loftus Francis	248
—— Meyrick	130
—— Mortimer	257
—— Peter	68
—— Rhys	183
—— Rice, *KH*.	59, 283
—— Richard	58, 265, 273
—— Richard	83
—— Robert Parker	272
—— Thomas	167
—— Thomas	213
—— Thomas	246
—— Thomas	67
—— William	208
—— William	213
—— Wm. Daniel	68, 266
—— Wm. Frederick	307
—— Wm. Fred. Foxcroft	203
—— William Prime	156
—— William Wynn	271
Jopp, James, *MD*.	153
—— Wm. Baillie	216
Irby, Augustus Henry	202
Ireland, Rich. Plunkett	259
Iremonger, Pen. Athelwold	159
Irton, Richard	103, 252
Irvine, Archibald	116
—— Charles	189
—— Charles	116
—— John	305
Irving, Alexander	271
—— Charles	220
—— George	20
—— Hen. Houghton	98, 209
—— James	37
Irwin, Fred. Chidley, *KH*.	93, 215
—— James Napper	221
—— John Henry	116
—— Lewis Chamberlain	178
—— William	96, 179
—— William	240
Isaac John Matcham	210
—— Cha. Tho. Vesey	234

Name	page
Isacke, Fred. James	135
Isham, Edmund	202
—— Thomas	231
Judd, William Henry	150
Juliani, Jean	440
Julien, Etienne Epiphane	439
Julius, Wm. Mavor	139
Junor, Elphington	208
Juxon, Geo. Plastow	84
Iveson, William	197
Ivey, William	312
Kains, Thomas	154
Kamptz, Louis de	439
Kander, Francis	439
Kay, Arthur	284
—— Robert	222
Kaye, Geo. Lister Lister	136
—— Robert	222
—— Wilkinson Lister	269
Keane, Benj. Bloomfield	258
—— Edward	55
—— Edw. Arthur Wellington	153
—— Edw. Vivian	152
—— Giles	238
—— Hussey Fane	286
—— John	158
—— John, *Lord, GCB. GCH.*	12, 194
Kearney, Charles	69, 122
—— Daniel	305
—— James, *KCH*.	17
—— Thomas J.	221
Keate, Wm. Augustus	33
Keating, Henry Sheehy, *KCB*.	12, 242
—— James	155
—— Roger	239
Kebbel, Wm. Henry	156
Kelly, Edward Henry	202
—— Edw. Hen. Moore	246
—— John	191
—— Luke, *MD*.	311
—— Richard D.	185
—— Robert	88
—— Thomas	89
—— Tho. Conyngham	182
—— Tho. Daniel	183
—— Thomas Edwin	97, 252
—— Waldron Barrs	173
—— William	287
—— William Henry	236
Kels, Henry	438
Kelsall, Edward	222
—— John	235
—— Joseph	71, 222
—— Roger	95, 284
Kelso, Edw. John Fran.	224
Kelson, Charles	257
Kemble, Hen. Jas. Vincent	219
Kemlo, William, *MD*.	222
Kemp, Philip	131
—— George Rees	115
—— William	97, 232

502

Index.

	page		page		page
Kempland, Geo. Arthur	116	King, Anthony Singleton	116	Knowles, William	201
Kempt, *Right Hon.* Jas.		—— Charles, *KH.*	57, 263	Knox, Alexander, *MD.*	152
GCB. GCH.	10, 115, 153	—— Edward	164	—— Brownlow William	
—— John Francis	163	—— Edward R.	187		73, 149
Kenah, Thomas	35	—— Finlay	193	—— Edward	66
Kendall, Richard	268	—— Frederick	178	—— George	130
Kennedy, Alex. K. Clark,		—— George	155	—— George	71, 147
KH.	59, 127	—— George	164	—— John Chichester	122
—— Arthur	66	—— George	206	—— Richard	141
—— Arthur	162	—— Henry, *KCH.*	19	—— Robert John	126
—— George	155	—— James	119	—— Thomas	272
—— Geo. Rob. Harry	270	—— James	132	—— Thos. Edmond	237
—— Hugh	296	—— John Wallace	125	—— William	138
—— James Shaw	40	—— John Wingfield	156	Koester, Adolphus	434
—— *Hon.* John	194	—— Michael	209	Korchann, Joseph	436
—— John Clark	127	—— Rich. Thomas	68, 266	Krauchenberg, G. *Baron*	
—— John Mackenzie	173	—— William James	88	von, *KCH.*	54, 433
—— Simson	89	—— William John	172	—— Louis	433
—— Thomas	43	Kingscote, Robert Arth.		Krause, Lewis	433
—— Vans	115	Fitzh.	143	Krönenfeldt, Charles von,	
—— Walter Crauford	256	Kingsley, James Bell	250	*KH.*	84, 434
Kennelly, James	239	—— John	260	——Ernest de	438
Kennett, Brackley	115	Kingston, Strickland	115	Kropp, John Albert	442
Kenny, David Courtney	115	Kington, Wm. Miles	90	Kruger, John Chas.	436
—— Edward	241	Kinloch, Arthur	187	Kuckuck, Augustus	435
—— Eyre Evans	66	—— Thomas	193	—— Augustus	84, 436
—— Michael Wm.	310	Kinnersley, Isaac	115	—— Aug. William	435
—— William	215	Kinnis, John, *MD.*	242	—— Henry Edward	435
—— William	202	Kinsman, And.	83, 297	Kuhls, Augustus	432
—— Wm. Henry	225	Kipling, Robert	195	—— Ferd. Carl Edm.	432
Kent, *Sir* Chas. Wm. *Bt.*	118	Kippen, Geo. A. Crooks	256	Kulemann, William	435
—— John	307	—— John Hardie	153	Kumme, Ludolph	434
—— Robert	116	Kirby, John	226	Kunoth, Godlove	437
Kenyon, Abra. Parkinson	256	—— Joshua Henry	185	Kuntze, John Frederick	434
—— Thomas	159	—— Stephen	63, 266	—— Eberhard	436
Keogh, Thos. Molyneux	188	—— Thomas Cox	67	Kuster, Ferdinand	432
Keown, Henry	121	—— Walter	202	Kyffin, Jas. Willington	168
Keppel, Edw. Geo. W.	91	—— Walter	296	—— Robert Willington	173
—— *Hon.* Geo. Tho.	87	—— William H.	246	Kyle, Hallam D'Arcy	196
Ker, James	170	Kirch, William	436	Kynoch, Robert Keith	216
Kerr, Charles Hope	233	Kirchner, Lewis	432		
—— *Lord* Chas. Lennox	193	Kirk, Wm. Alphonso	167	Labalmondiere, Douglas	
—— Henry Alexander	151	—— William John	258	W. P.	235
—— John Manners	7	Kirkland, John Ag. Vesey	148	Lacy, Henry Dacre	154
—— *Lord* Mark	171	Kirwan, Martin	131	—— Hen. Hearne	228
—— *Lord* Rob. *KH.*	60	Kitchener, Hen. Horatio	139	—— Joseph Dacre	65
—— Walter Foster	160	Kitson, John	89, 195	—— Rich. John Jas.	42, 265
—— William	179	Klingsöhr, George	436	—— Rich. Walter	207
Kerrison, *Sir* Edw. *Bt.*		—— Lewis	436	—— Thomas E.	224
CB. & GCH.	13, 140	Knatchbull, Thomas	269	—— William	197
Kershaw, James	103, 164	Kneebone, Thomas	180	Laffan, Robert M.	286
Kersteman, W. Brewse	66	Knight, Brook John	126	—— Joseph de Courcy	240
—— John Brewse	258	—— Charles	61, 184	Laing, James	60
Kersting, Joseph	436	—— Charles R.	176	Lake, Henry Halsey	179
—— Frederick	434	—— Edward	66	—— Noel Thomas	269
Kessler Charles	434	—— Henry	135	Lamb, Samuel Burges	172
Keszler, Frederick	435	—— James	184	Lambard, Multon	188
Kettlewell, John Wilson	64	—— Thomas Davis	306	Lambart, *Hon.* Edw. A.	
Key, George William	141	Knipe, Geo. Marshall	218	F. H.	218
—— Charles Hugh	141	—— Wm. Beaumaris	125	Lambert, John, *GCB.*	11, 161
Kidd, John M'Mahon	173	Knollys, Edward	227	—— John Arthur	146
—— Thomas, *MD.*	309	—— Wm. Thomas	57, 149	—— Robert	194
Kift, Arthur	297	Knop, Henry Augustus	434	—— Samuel	35, 144
Killeen, Arth. Jas. *Lord.*	134	Knowles, Francis Edw.	305	—— Thomas	234
Kilvington, Fran. Henry	216	—— Frederick	137	Lambrick, George	296
Kinderley, John	249	—— John	269	Lamert, Joseph Richard	230

503

Index.

	page		page		page
Lamond, Peter, *MD*	212	Lawrie, Fra. Raw. Hastings	231	Le Marchant, Thomas	127
Lamont, Norman, *KH*.	91, 243			Le Mesurier, Frederick	286
—— Wm. Alex. Robt.	307	Lawson, Jos. Ambrose, *MD*.	287	—— John	17
Lance, William Henry	231			Lemoine, William	268
Lancey, William	285	—— Robert	311	Lemon, Thomas	295
Land, John	294	—— Stephen	167	—— Thomas	89
Landels, George	273	—— Stephen	239	Lempriere, Charles	204
Landers, James	134	Layard, Bernard Gran.	190	—— Henry	272
Lane, Ambrose	65	—— Brownlow Ed.	257	—— Thomas James	307
—— Chas. Hen. John	214	—— Wm. Twisleton	257	Lennox, *Lord* Arthur	102, 223
—— Frederick Wm.	249	Laye, Joseph Henry	209	—— *Lord* Fitzroy G.	
—— Henry	43	Layton, Frederick	293	C. G.	194
—— James	84	Lea, Samuel Percy	239	Leonard, Daniel	162
—— John	238	—— William Percy	239	—— Robert	293
—— John	305	Leach, Geo. Archibald	286	Leonhart, Harry	434
—— Richard	215	—— Jonathan	54	Le Page, Felix	439
Lang, Frederick H.	185	Leader, Thomas Leonard	222	Lepper, Francis	233
Langeheineken, Philip	434	Leadbeater, Wm. Edw.		—— James	83
Langford, James E.	208	Blair	116	Leschen, Hannach Bogusl.	432
—— Wm. Bookey	295	Leake, Robert Martin	68	Leslie, Alexander	220
Langlands, George	83	Leatham, James Birley	215	—— Arthur	159
Langley, George Colt	295	Leathart, John	116	—— Charles, *KH*.	63
—— George Richard	170	Le Blanc, Francis	56	—— Charles Henry	232
—— Wm. Leslie, *MD*.	312	—— Henry	53	—— James	87
Langton, Bennett	218	—— Thomas Edm.	188	—— John, *KH*.	56, 155
Langwerth, Adolphus von	436	Lecky, Alexander	238	—— Lewis Xavier	224
Lapslie, Anthony Hart	256	—— Henry	96, 187	—— Nicholas	175
Larcom, Thos. Aiskew	285	—— Henry	242	L'Estrange, Arthur	172
Lardner, John	198	—— John Gage	189	—— Ant. Robert	223
—— William	256	Le Couteur, Philip	182	—— Geo. Guy Carleton	17
Lardy, Christian Fred.	90	Ledergerw, Pancrace	441	—— Harry Piesley	180
La Roche, Francis	435	Ledingham, George, *MD*.	175	—— Thomas	100, 187
Lascelles, Chas. F. R.	57, 144	Ledsam, John	158	—— Thomas	11
—— Edmund Wm.	196	Lee, Charles	229	Lethbridge, Thos. A.	268, 273
Lasperg, Frederick von	435	—— Edward	191	—— Tho. Christopher	
Last, Edward	103, 251	—— *Sir* Fra. Geary Gard.		Mytton	237
Latter, Robert James	115		69, 292	Le Touzel, Francis T.	260
Laughten, John	116	—— George	116	Lettsom, Samuel	103, 232
Laurence, Thos. Wm.	272	—— Henry	142	Leventhorpe, Collett	165
Laurie, Henry	305	—— John	162	Levett, Richard Byrd	212
—— John	116	—— Michael White	33	Levick, John	210
—— William	293	—— Robert	306	Levinge, Geo. Charles	
Lautour, Peter Aug., *KH*.	38	—— Thomas	148	Rawdon	271
—— Wm. Fra. Joseph	145	—— William	294	—— Rich. Geo. Aug.	194
Lavens, Patrick Henry	140	Leech, Francis Edw.	263	Lewes, John	178
Lavie, Ernest	159	—— Robert	116	Lewin, Hen. Pritchard	295
Law, Charles Edm.	253	Lees, Geo. Cholmondeley	186	Lewis, Cha. Algernon	145
—— Charles Fred.	221	—— George	215	—— George	42
—— James Smith	268	Le Fort, August. *Baron*	434	—— Geo. Cha. Degen	284
—— John	294	Lefroy, John Henry	271	—— Griffith, Geo.	44, 283
—— Robert, *KH*.	92, 261	Leggatt, John	305	—— Harry Percival	36
—— William Henry	101, 235	Legge, *Hon.* A. Chas.	97	—— John Edward	229
Lawe, Alexander	116	Legrew, John	139	—— John Owen	188
Lawley, Rob. Neville	119	Leicester, *Hon.* William	145	—— Richard	246
Lawrell, Digby Henry	216	Leigh, Edm. C.	249	—— Robert	241
Lawrence, Arth. Johnstone	252	—— Egerton	122	—— Thomas, *MD*.	121
		—— John de V., *MD*.	228	—— William Robert	163
		Leighton, David, *KCB*.	115	Ley, James	122
—— Elias	42, 292	—— For. Owen	93, 207	—— John Morgan	116
—— George	188	—— Tho. Richard	195	Liddell, *Hon.* Geo. A. F.	150
—— John	297	Leith, Alexander, *KCB*.	17	—— Henry	116
—— Jos. Edw. Wilson	296	—— George, *Bt.*	16	Light, Alex. Whalley	33
—— Thos. Lewis	88	—— William Forbes	249	—— Henry	116
—— Walter	192	Leman, Charles Orgell	211	Lightbody, John	232
—— Wm. Hudson	268	Le Marchant John Gaspard	72, 251	—— John	310
Lawrenson, John	101, 149			Lightfoot, Thomas	236

Index.

	page		page		page
Lightfoot, Thomas	36	Logan, George	294	Lucas, Arthur Hyde	168
Lilley, John	146	—— Joseph	59, 215	—— David	312
Lillicrap, Walter Welsford	296	—— Tho. Galbr. *MD.*	204	—— Edward	254
Lillie, *Sir* John Scott	66	Logie, Chas. Arnold	188	—— Francis	157
—— Thomas	257	Loinsworth, Fred. Albert	309	—— Henry	258
Limond, *Sir* James	115	—— Fred. Lussan	157	—— John Owen	180
Lindham, James Oliver	434	Lomax, James	16	—— Richard	119
Lindesay, Patrick	215	Londonderry, C.W. *Marq.*		—— William	227
Lindsay, Alexander	115	of *GCB. GCH.*	8, 136	—— William	258
—— Alex. Cruikshank	134	Long, George Frederick	205	—— William Russell	159
—— *Hon.* Chas. Hugh	194	—— John	136	Luderitz, Frederick	437
—— Effingham	17	—— William	97	Ludewig, Adolphus	435
—— George Topp	97, 246	Longden, Cha. Scudamore	272	—— Frederick	435
—— *Hon.* James	145	—— Henry E.	161	—— George	435
—— James	43	Longfield, John	159	Ludlow, George James,	
—— Martin	35	—— William	163	*Earl, GCB.*	6, 149
—— Martin, G. T.	97, 230	Longford, Edw. M. *Earl*		Ludowig, Chas. Herman	438
—— Thomas	143	*of*	119	Lugard, Edward	182
Lindsell, Rob. Henry	176	Longmore, Chas. Joseph	134	—— Hen. Williamson	285
Lindsey, Robert	305	Longworth, Dav. Fitz		Lukis, John	154
Linsingen, Charles, *Baron*	436	Gerald	246	Lumley, Fred. Douglas	159
Linton, John	61	Löning, Michael	433	—— Jas. Rutherford	115
—— William, *MD.*	218	Lonsdale, Charles	172	—— John	157
Lisle, Robert	249	—— Jas. Faunce	178	—— *Hon.* Wm. *GCB.*	8,
—— Robert	55	—— William, *Earl of,*			132
Lister, Amos	306	*KG.*	53	Lumsden, Alex. John H.	181
—— David	123	Looker, William	306	—— Thomas	116
—— Frederick D.	160	Lorimer, William	175	Lunde, Geo. Fred. Godfrey	437
—— Frederick George	116	Loriol, Augustus de	440	Luning, William	435
Liston, John Terry	159	Lorton, Robert, *Viscount*	8	—— Augustus	435
Little, James Somerville	287	Losack, George	221	Lushington, Franklin	160
—— Archibald	135	Louis, Charles	296	—— Jas. Law, *GCB.*	115
—— Robert John	297	—— Matthew	96, 267	Lutman, John Adrian	175
—— Tho. Sarjent	190	Love, Edw. Missenden	179	Lutterman, John	438
Littledale, Edward	128	—— James Fred. *KH.*	43,	Lutwidge, Skeffington	116
Littlehales, Charles	225		225	Lutyens, Benjamin	116
Lloyd, Arthur	18	Lovell, Fran. Fred.	118	Luxmoore, Tho. Coryndon	284
—— Edward Thomas	285	Loveday, Lambert	115	—— Robert	167
—— Evan, *KCH.*	10, 127	Lovelace, Robert	170	Lye, Richard Leigh	171
—— Evans Garnons	253	Lovett, Thos. Heaton	250	Lygon, *Hon.* Edw. Pyndar	18
—— Evan Herbert	128	Low, Alexander	131		
—— Henry	235	—— John	270	—— *Hon.* Hen. Beauch	18
—— Mount Stoughton		—— Rich. Butler	204	Lyle, Thomas Cromie	272
Heyliger	153	—— Robert	307	Lynch, Christopher	259
—— Richard	253	—— Sieg, C. G. *Baron,*		—— Edw. Alex. Thos.	208
—— Rob. Clifford	228	*KCB. KCH.*	16, 435	—— Edw. Pat.	116
—— Thomas	131	—— William	306	—— John Blake	66
—— William, *MD.*	187	Lowder, Sam. Netterville	296	—— Martin Crean	165
Lluellyn, Richard	38	Lowe, Arthur Charles	103,	—— Robert Blake	65
Lock, Walter Elph.	101, 267		142	—— Thomas	249
Locke, John Thomas	219	—— Edward W. D.	183	Lynedoch, Thomas *Lord,*	
Lockhart, Archibald	168	—— Hudson, *KCB.*	12, 115,	*GCB.*	7, 115, 151
—— Arch. Inglis	244		207	Lynn, James	285
—— Graeme Alex.	230	Lowen, Pearce, *KH.*	89,	Lyon, Jas. *KCB. GCH.*	
—— Robert Alex.	232		260		12, 115, 175
Lockwood, George	227	—— Wellington,	260	Lys, George Mowbray	199
—— George Henry	102, 130	Lowndes, Thos. Wm. Selby		—— William Henry	216
Lockyer, Edmond	208		134	Lysaght, Jas. Richard	215
—— Hen. Fred. *KH.*		Lowrie, Charles	86	Lysons, Daniel	152
	93, 249	Lowth, John Jackson	189	Lyster, Anthony	65
Lodder, Wm. Wynne	210	—— Robert Henry	238	—— John	62, 144
Lodwick, Peter	115	Luard, George	85	—— St. George L.	285
Loesecke, Geo. C. A. Von	436	—— John	71, 172	—— Septimus	246
Loftus, Ferrars	63, 144	—— Robert	269	—— Thomas	116
—— Wm. Fra. Bent.	34	Lubeck, William Von	438	—— Thomas Rice	286
—— William James	189	Lucan, George, *Earl of*	56		

Index.

	page		page		page
Lyster, William Martin	153	M'Gregor, James	312	Mac Andrew, David	200
Lyttleton, *Hon.* Spencer	150	M'Grigor, Alexander	183	——— Jas. Duncan	191
——— Westcote Whitchurch	216	——— Jas. *Bt. MD.*	309	——— John, *MD.*	191
		M'Haffie, James	65	——— John Lennox	155
		M'Illree, John Drope	229	Macann, Fra. Arth., *MD.*	310
M'Adam, David	200	M'Ilveen, Dalway	182	Mac Arthur, Alexander	116
——— David	293	M'Innes, John	115	Macartney, James Nixon	135
M'Alpin, Wm. Bain	246	M'Intosh, Thos. Graham	259	——— John	141
M'Alpine, James	57	M'Intyre, Archibald	84	——— J. Inglis	272
M'Arthur, Edward	85	——— Colin Campbell	230	Macbean, Archibald	268
——— John	294	——— James	238	——— Fred., *KH.*	71, 236
M'Bean, Jas. Arch. Duncan	156	M'Iver, Edward	199	——— Forbes	72, 267
		M'Kay, Manners	123	——— George Fred.	236
M'Beath, George	220	M'Kellar, Peter Martin	294, 297	——— Wm. *KCB.*	18
——— Robert	258			——— William Forbes	238
M'Bride, Michael	312	M'Kenzie, Boyce	191	Macbreedy, John Kenneth	305
M'Call, George	236	——— Charles Finch	192	Mac Call, James	103, 134
M'Callum, John	69, 292	——— John	8	Mac Carthy, James	254
——— Henry Atkins	296	——— Kenneth	154	——— Wm. Justin	208
M'Carthy, Hen. Hotham	296	M'Kerlie, John Graham	285	Macdiarmid, John Duncan	223
M'Carty, Charles	133	M'Kie, Patrick	154	Macdonald, Alexander	181
M'Caskill, Hector	206	M'Killop, Robert John	295	——— Alexander	251
——— John, *KH.*	43, 160	M'Kinlay, Donald, *MD.*	169	——— Alexander	20, 264
——— John	249	M'Kinnon, George	145	——— Alexander	40, 115, 267
——— Kenneth	214	——— Alexander	116	——— Sir A. K., *Bt,*	150
M'Causland, Conolly	286	——— William	294	——— Atholl Wentworth	193
M'Clellan, Jas. Creighton	136	M'Kirdy, David Elliot	209	——— George	68, 167
M'Cleverty, Robert	246	M'Lachlan, Lachlan Nicoll	208	——— George	245
——— William A.	199	M'Laren, George, *MD.*	243	——— Jas. Mitchell	258
M'Clintock, Hen. Stanley	270	M'Leod, Alexander	102, 213	——— Jas. Robert	241
M'Clure, Geo.	241	——— Charles	115	——— *Hon.* Jas. W. Bosville	118
M'Court, John	152	——— Donald, *MD.*	309		
M'Coy, Daniel	206	M'Lerie, John	209	——— John, *KCB.*	14, 117, 219
——— John	270	M'Mahon, Edmond John	307		
M'Crae, Alexander	236	——— John	60	——— John	167
——— Robert Bradford	195	——— Tho. *Bt.KCB.*	15, 246	——— John Angus	153
M'Credie, Wm. Scott	311	——— Tho. Westropp	132	——— John Duntze	241
M'Cumming, Rich. Hen. John Beaumont	166	M'Manus, Henry	167	——— Peter John	259
		M'Munn, Rob. And., *MD.*	173	——— Ranald, *KH.*	71, 155
M'Curdy, Daniel	226			——— Robert	55
M'Dermott, Michael, *MD.*	241	M'Murdo, Wm. M. G.	159	——— Robert	59
M'Donald, Alexander	177	M'Nair, John	12	——— Roderick Cha.	181
——— Donald	205	——— Robert	263	——— Ronald	232
——— Dun. Don. M'Cay	176	——— William	214	——— William	84
——— John	40, 244	M'Nally, Henry	198	——— William Peter	440
——— John M'Cay	184	M'Namee, John	208	Macdonell, Alex. Sheriff	179
——— William	176	M'Neill, Dugald	230	——— Alexander	253
——— William	245	——— Thomas G. B.	207	——— George	54
M'Donough, Matthew	136	M'Nicol, Dugald	98, 151	——— James, *KCH.*	16
M'Douall, James	101, 119	M'Niven, Tho. Wm. Ogilvy	91	——— James Fraser	214
——— Robert	35			Macdonnell, Rob. Harkness	207
M'Dougall, Patrick L.	187	M'Phee, Donald	179		
M'Dowell, Frederick	132	M'Pherson, Alexander	273	Macdougall, James	93, 193
——— Geo. James	72, 142	——— Alex. John	229	Mac Dougall, Duncan	231
M'Duff, John	191	——— Duncan	92, 178	——— Patrick	86, 199
M'Farlan, John	306	——— Duncan	115	Macdowall, Day Hort	86, 195
M'Farlane, Henry	202	——— Ewan	230	Macfarlane, Robert, *KCB. GCH.*	7, 183
M'Ghee, Holland Leckey	182	——— Louis J.	153		
M'Gibbon, Benj. W.	83	——— Mungo	116	Macfarpuhar, Hugh	116
M'Grath, Patrick	184	——— Philip	168	Mac Gregor, Donald	116
M'Gregor, Duncan	183	——— Thomas	92, 256	——— Evan J. Murray, *Bt.KCB. KCH.*	19
——— Duncan	43	M'Queen, James	101, 141		
——— Donald	179	Maberly, Evan	272	——— Malcolm	172
——— Hugh	67	——— Wm. Leader	56	——— Robert	166
——— James	190	Macan, C. K.	195	Macgregor, Malcolm	89
——— James	193	Macadam, Wm. *KH.*	55	——— John Alex. Paul	115

Index.

	page		page		page
Macgregor, William, *Bt.*	169	Maclean, Hen. Dundas	91, 247	Manwaring, John Montagu	12
Macintire, John	196	—— John	102, 171	Mair, John, *MD.*	210
Macintosh, Alex. Fisher	44	—— John	178	—— Philip	87
—— Alexander	116	—— John, *KCB.*	15, 211	—— William	251
Mackay, Alexander	257	—— Lachlan Hector		Maister, John	14
—— Angus William	172	Gilbert	200	Maitland, Alex. Chas.	231
—— Colin Campbell	66	—— Norman	206	—— Frederick	7, 209
—— Donald	116	—— Peter	271	—— Fred. Thomas	175
—— George	214	Macleod, Alexander	214	—— John, *MD.*	235
—— Henry Fowler	132	—— Donald, *KCB.*	115	—— Peregrine, *KCB.*	
—— Honeyman	90	—— Donald B.	160		12, 115, 228
—— John F.	91, 234	—— Donald John M.	129	—— *Hon.* Wm. Mord.	8
—— William	67	—— George Francis	55	Major, Francis Wm. A. C.	305
Mackenzie, Alex., *Bt.GCH.*	7	—— Hen. Geo. *KH.*	44	Makepeace, Charles	93, 124
—— Alexander	219	—— John, *KCH.*	13, 229	Malassez, Maximilian	307
—— Alexander	248	—— William	116	Malcolm, George Alex.	103,
—— Alexander	230	MacMahon, Bernard	139		130
—— Alexander Wm.	254	—— William	195	—— James, *KCB.*	54
—— Benjamin	254	MacNeal, Hector	231	—— James	224
—— Colin	284	Macneil, Roderick	41	Malet, Alfred Augustus	159
—— John	116	Macnicol, Anthony Alex.	151	—— Chas. St. Lo	98, 159
—— John Kenneth	212	Macnish, Arth. Colquhoun	232	Maling, Thomas	67, 117, 256
—— Keith, Wm. Stewart		Macphail, John	95, 250	—— William Eyles	89
	242	MacPherson, Wm.	151	Maltby, Frederick	295
—— Kenneth Doug.	244	Macpherson, Alexander	207	Maltei, Antonio	262
—— Roderick	248	—— Duncan	116	Malton, James	116
—— William Ord.	312	—— Evan	220	Man, Garnet	205
Mackey, Hugh	311	—— Evan Duncan	245	Manders, Thomas	126
Mackie, Edmund Phipps	254	—— Gillies	89, 251	Mandeville, Charles	116
—— Otto Bayer	272	—— James	64, 257	Manfredi, Adrian	439
—— William	240	—— James	307	Manly, John Sam.	178
Mackinlay, John Houston	116	—— John	89	Mann, Cornelius	19, 282
Mac Kinnon, Daniel Hen.	142	—— John Cameron	193	—— Frederick Wm.	58
—— Edm. Vernon	119	—— Rob. Barclay, *KH.*	37	—— Gother Frederick	286
Mackinnon, Donald Hen.		Macquarie, George W.	193	—— John Blaquiere	242
Aylmer	220	—— Lachlan	129	Manners, Charles	268
Mackintosh, Alex., *MD.*	311	Macqueen, Thos. Richard	116	—— *Lord* Charles	
—— Donald	249	MacQueen, Alex. *MD.*	154	Somerset, *KCB.*	15, 130
—— John, *MD.*	287	—— John Arch.	228	—— George	139
Macknight, William	172	Macra, John, *KCH.*	41	—— Henry Edward	188
Mackrell, Thomas	59, 195	Macready, Edw. Nevil	103	—— Henry Herbert,	
Mackworth, Digby, *Bt.*		—— Geo. Wm.	203	*KH.*	71, 188
KH.	67	Mactier, William	116	—— Herbert Russell	188
—— Digby Francis	242	Madigan, Jas. Alex.	155	—— Richard	99, 210
Macky, Thomas	85	Madocks, John Edward	135	—— Robert	231
Maclachlan, Arch.	40	Madox, Henry, *KH.*	55	—— Russell	53
—— Alexander	62, 267	Magee, Henry Wemyss	196	Mannin, John	192
—— Daniel, *MD.*	231	Magenis, Hen. Arthur	87, 239	Manning, John Spencer	121
—— Jas. Campbell	234	Maguis, Ernest, *Baron*	436	Mannsbach, James	435
Maclaine, *Sir* Archibald	34	Magnay, Alexander	221	Mansel, George	142
—— Hector	43	Magrath, Dennis Jos. *MD.*	184	—— George Pleydell	204
—— Murdoch	158	—— Jos. Rogers	206	—— Herbert	132
Maclaurin, David Scott		—— Rich. Nicholson	154	—— John	53
Kin.	121	Maguire, John	263	—— Rob. Christ, *KH.*	55
Maclean, Alexander	246	Maharg, John, *MD.*	222	Mansergh, John Craven	157
—— Alexander	96, 238	Mahon, Gilbert	246	—— Rob. John South-	
—— Allan, T.	63, 139	—— Luke	229	cote	170
—— Andrew, *MD.*	137	—— Matthew	34	Mansfield, William R.	204
—— Charles, *MD.*	204	—— Maurice Hartland	238	Manson, James	116
—— Charles Fitzroy	62	—— *Sir* Ross, *Bt.*	212	Manuel, Albert	441
—— Chas. Maxwell	87, 224	—— William Gun	296	Mapleton, Henry	214
—— Fitzroy Jeffries		Mahony, Montague Mar-		Marburg, Frederick	437
Grafton, *Bt.*	8, 236	tin, *MD.*	309	March, Chas. H. Gordon	
—— George	270	Mainwaring, Arthur	220	Lennox, *Earl of*	120
—— George	305	—— Fred.	99, 202	—— Leonard Geo.	
—— Hector, *KCB.*	115	—— George	239	Fred.	296

Index.

	page		page		page
March, William Henry	295	Masterson, Henry Wilkes	171	Mayow, George Wynell	124
Marcon, John	163	Matheson, Thomas	98, 174	Meacham, William Geo.	154
Marecheaux, C. H.	181	Mathews, Joseph Henry	185	Meade, Augustus	116
Margary, Alfred Robert	177	—— William Joseph	116	—— Frederick	85
Marindin, Henry Rich.	152	Mathewson, Peter	66	—— Hon. John	12
Markham, Charles	91, 211	Mathias, William	214	—— John	194
—— Frederick	103, 183	Matson, Edward	97, 284, 286	—— Hon. Robert	8, 163
—— Osborne	183	Matthew, Robert	189	—— Robert	125
Markland, George	270	Matthews, John Henry	182	—— Roche, KH.	94, 117
Marlay, David	293	—— Mark	255	Meaden, David	257
Marley, Bennet	115	—— William	273	Meason, Magnus Gilbert	
Marlow, Wm. Biddlecomb	285	Matthey, Frederick	440	Laing	134
		Maturin, William Henry	307	—— Malcolm Ronald	
Marriott, Charles	116	Maude, George Ashley	271	Laing	191
—— Hayes	296	—— Hon. Cornwallis	212	Mee, Charles Henry	269
—— Thomas	115	—— Warren	184	Meech, Giles	293
—— Tho. Beckett Fielding	271	Maule, John	177	Meehan, Geo. Waller	254
		—— Hon. Lauderdale	103, 231	Mehux, Rich. Williams	295
Marschalk, Charles Baron	432			Meik, Alexander Crie	246
—— Gustav. Baron	434	Mauleverer, James Thos.	168	—— Fras. Thomas	142
—— Otto de	434	—— William	187	—— James Patrick	200
—— Theodore Von	433	Maunsell, Frederick	64, 237	Meiklejohn, J. H. Johnstone	244
Marsden, John Long	159	—— George	71, 123		
Marsh, Francis	163	—— George	246	Mein, Frederick R.	152
—— Robert	175	—— John Borlase	121	—— George	164
Marshall, Anthony	94, 283	—— Nicholas	263	—— John Alex.	42, 226
—— George	64	—— Richard	158	Meinecke, George Fred.	438
—— George, KH.	71, 234	—— William Wray	237	Meier, Carl Peter Arnold	436
—— Geo. Cuthbert	182	Mawby, Sebright	12	—— Ern. Theo. Chr.	432
—— Henry	127	Maxwell, Alexander	197	Mejer, George	435
—— John	99, 243	—— Archibald M. KH.		—— Phil. Hen. Fred.	84, 436
—— John	311		58, 187	—— William	436
—— John Samuel	116	—— Charles Francis	234	Meldrum, Thomas	153
—— John Williams	217	—— Chas. Robbins	189	Mellish, William Leigh	253
—— Josiah	115	—— Chas. Wm. KCH.	17	Mello, Majens	196
Marshall, Wm. Clutton	197	—— Colin	245	Mellows, John	121
Marston, Hen. F.	192	—— Edw. Herbert	240	Melvin, Alexander	310
—— Molyneux Chas.	271	—— George	218	Melville, Geo. John White	245
Marten, Thomas, KH.	64, 128	—— George	240	Mends, Herbert	256
Martin, George, MD.	225	—— George Vaughan	240	—— Herbert Bowen	293
—— Henry William	172	—— Hon. Jas. Pierce	210	—— Hugh Bowen	296
—— James	130	—— James Robert	259	—— Jas. Delamain	256
—— James	252	—— Richard	212	—— William Fisher	307
—— John	123	—— Wm. Alex. Bart.	70	Mendibus, Antoine Louis de	441
—— John	42	—— William Craig	231		
—— Richard	121	—— William Robert	296	Mensing, Ernest	436
—— Robert	96, 197	May, Charles	156	Menzies, Allan	154
—— Robert Fanshawe	103, 228	—— Charles	441	—— Charles, KH.	69, 292, 297
		—— Chas. Emanuel	83, 440		
—— Samuel Yorke	219	—— Edward Stephen	132	—— Charles Fred.	296
—— Thomas	254	—— Frederick	258	—— Duncan	167
Martyn, Fran. Mountjoy	119	—— John, KCB. KCH.	20, 264	—— James Stewart	246
—— Peter	240			—— William Collier	286
Mason, James	96, 229	—— Joseph Mignon	83	Mercer, Alex. Cavalie	64, 266
—— James	306	—— Rodolphe, de	53, 441	—— Douglas	35
—— John Monck	175	—— Rudolph Amedée de	440	—— Edward Smith	246
—— William	261	May, William	192	—— Edw. Smith	69, 292
Massy, Hon. John	86	Maycock, Dottin	142	—— John Henry	296
—— Hon. Nath. Hen. Cha.	88	Mayers, John Perkins	209	—— Robert	293
		Maynard, Hon. Charles Hen.	120	Merckhel, Elias	440
—— John	199			Meredith, James	9
Master, Harcourt	101, 131	Mayne, Charles Frederick Hutchinson	213	—— Richard M.	164
—— Chas. Chester	209			Meriton, Rich. Ogilvie	116
—— Henry Orlando Chester	247	—— Henry	200	Mermet, Joseph	441
		—— John	151	Messiter, Geo. Hughes	157
—— Wm. Chester	156	—— John	115	—— John	92, 179

Index.

	page		page		page
Metcalfe, Studholme Hen.	160	Mills, William Maxwell	254	Money, Jas. Kyrle, *Bt.*	18
Methuen, *Hon.* Fred.		Milman, Edward Aug.	184	——— John Ernle	183
——— Hen. Paul	120	——— Egerton Cha. W.		——— William Bayley	185
Metrovich, Nicola	262	Miles	148	Monins, Eaton	64, 221
Meuron, Chas. Cæsar de	440	——— Fra. Miles	35	——— Wm. Godfrey	
——— Philip Fred. de	248	——— Geo. Bryan	156	Clerke	174
Meyer, Charles	434	Milne, William	84	Monke, Henry	116
——— Frederick	442	Milner, Charles	59	Monkland, George	226
——— Fred. Herman	433	——— Henry Robert	91, 246	Monro, Archibald Hale	244
——— George	433	Milnes, Colin James	53	——— Alexander	253
——— George Julius	433	Minchin, John	199	——— William	231
——— Gustavus	433	Miniussir, Nicholas de	434	Montagu, George	101, 193
Meynell, Francis	124	Minster, Henry Francis	192	——— *Hon.* Henry	62, 149
Meyrick, George	10	Minter, George	179	Montanaro, John	262
——— Wm. Henry	41	Minto, Jas. Clephane	311	Montenach, Ch. Theodore de	166
Michel, Charles Edward	218	Misani, Johan Theo. de	440		
——— John	154	Misset, Joseph	121	Montgomerie, Duncan	116
——— John	8	Mitchell, Alexander	198	——— Frederick	251
Michelet, Cha. Fred. Edw.	438	——— George	230	——— John	228
Michell, Chas. C. *KH.*	85	——— Hugh	293	Montgomery, Alex. Barry	151
——— Edward Tho.	60, 115, 266	——— Hugh And. Rob.	145	——— Francis Oct.	103, 196
——— George	8	——— John, *MD.*	311	——— Fred. Campbell	100, 201
——— H. Seymour	200	——— John	295	——— James	259
——— John	61, 265	——— John	68	——— John Myers	200
Micklethwaite, Nathaniel	150	——— John Wray	270	——— Lamb. Lyons	232
Middlemore, George	16	——— Livingston	248	——— Richard Tho.	130
——— Robert Fred.	243	——— Thomas	212	——— Robert Giles, *MD.*	255
Middleton, Charles	44	——— Thomas	89	Montizambert, Geo. Sheaffe	192
——— John	253	——— *Sir* Tho. Livingstone	86	Montresor, Auchmuty	257
——— Wm. Alex.	272	——— William	152	——— Henry William	272
Midgley, Benjamin	178	——— William	90	——— John	250
Mielmann, Henry	437	——— Wm. Murray	236	——— Tho. Gage, *KCH.*	11, 122
Milbank, Fred. Acclom	231	——— Wm. Simpson	142		
——— Mark Wm. Vane	129	Mitchelson, Walter	152	Moody, Hampden Clement Blamire	286
Mildmay, Henry St. John	122	Mitchison, Tho. Robinson	306	——— Rich. Clement	285
Miles, Edward, *Kt.*	34	Mitford, Bert. Charles	162	——— Stephen	116
——— Geo. Fred. Wm.	133	——— Henry George	294	——— Thomas	61, 283
Mill, James	85	——— John Philip	169	Moor, Hassell Rich.	90, 267
Millar, John	194	Moberley, Henry	116	——— Frederick	152
Miller, Alex. Penrose	244	Mockler, Edward	205	Moore, Edward	162
——— Archibald Robert	140	——— James	210	——— Edwin Colville	168
——— Charles	295, 297	——— John	208	——— Francis	8
——— Charles Robinson	294	Moeller, Frederick	438	——— Garrett	174
——— Charles Stuart	286	Moffatt, Rich. Jas. Hamilton	254	——— George	183
——— Colin	306			——— Geo. Fred.	182
——— Croker	168	——— Bowland	205	——— George Ogle	234
——— Fiennes S.	54	——— Eust J. Douglas	197	——— George Samuel	183
——— George	38	Moffitt, James, *MD.*	138	——— Henry	239
——— Geo. Cumming	205	Molesworth, Arthur	115	——— James	153
——— John, *MD.*	218	——— Arthur John	295	——— James	186
——— John	256	——— St. Aubyn	285	——— James Guy Piers	246
——— John	295	——— Edw. Nassau	178	——— James T.	99, 239
——— Thomas	191	——— Rich. Carr	95, 267	——— Isaac	249
——— William	305	Molle, George	180	——— John	181
——— William, *KH.*	70	Molyneux, *Hon.* Geo. Berkeley	57, 134	——— John, *KH.*	59
Milligan, William, *MD.*	168			——— John Wardrop	188
Milliken, William	306	——— *Hon.* Hen. Rich	58, 211	——— J. Hildebrand Oakes	186
Millingen, John Crispign	244	——— Thomas, *Bt.*	11		
Mills, Charles	184	Monck, John Winnington	236	——— Joseph	168
——— Cha. Jas. Conway	203	Monckton, *Hon.* Edm. Gambier	253	——— Joseph	201
——— Frederic	236			——— Nicholas	296
——— Robert William	40	——— Henry	14	——— Richard A.	130
——— Thomas	240	Moncrieffe, George	73, 149	——— *Hon.* Robert	55
——— Thomas Richard	121	——— Robert	32	——— Thomas	160
——— Wm. Maxwell	87, 254	Money, Archibald	37		

509

Index.

	page		page		page
Moore, Thomas	254	Moultrie, Geo. Bligh	227	Murray, Charles	228
—— Thomas	297	Mounsey, William Henry	155	—— *Hon.* Charles	83
—— Tho. Cha. Cotton	295	Mountain, Armine Simcoe		—— *Hon.* David Hen.	150
—— Tho· Lansdowne		Hen.	87, 177	—— Denis, *MD.*	164
Parr	173	—— Robt. Fred.	272	—— Freeman	211
—— William	66	Mountsteven, Hender	199	—— George	203
—— Wm. George	43	—— Tho. Wm. Blewett	231	—— *Hon.* George	14
—— Wm. Jas. Bury		Moylan, Charles	224	—— *Rt. Hon.* George,	
M'Leod	221	Moyle, Thomas	169	*GCB. GCH.* 10, 115, 193	
—— William Yorke	205	Moysey, Henry Gorges	137	—— Geo. Freeman	217
—— Willoughby	132	Mudge, Rich. Zach.	68, 283	—— *Hon.* Henry	20
Moorhead, Alex. Gordon	177	Mudie, Charles	167	—— Henry	271
Moorsom, Robert	150	Mulcaster, Fred. Wm.		—— Hugh Robertson	116
Morant, Edward	138	*KCH.*	15, 282	—— James	175
Mordaunt, Henry	197	Mulgrave, George Aug.		—— James	116
Moreau, William de	437	Constan., *Earl of*	150	—— *Hon.* Jas. Cha.	
Morewood, Cha. Roland		Mullen, Edward Cowell	152	Plantagenet	150
Palmer	120	—— Robert, *KH.*	88, 151	—— Jas. Florence	225
Morgan, Alex. Braith-		—— John	152	—— John	10
waite	208	Muller, Edw. A. G.	151	—— John, *MD.*	309
—— Charles	306	—— Fred. Augustus	434	—— Peter Daly, *MD.*	311
—— Evan	268	—— Frederick Bree	157	—— Rob. Sherbourne	171
—— Herbert	141	—— Frederick Henry	437	—— Samuel Hood	201
—— Hugh	268	—— George de	84, 433	—— Virginius	246
—— Nathaniel	243	—— Hen. William	442	—— Walter	172
—— Richard Gibbons	160	—— Jost	440	—— William	249
—— Thomas Charles	155	—— Lewis	440	—— William M'Carthy	256
Morice, David, *MD.*	212	—— Ludewig von	432	Murtagh, John, *MD.*	157
—— Tho. Henry, *KH.*	116	—— Nicholas	84, 440	Murton, Hen. John	69, 292
Morison, James	241	—— William	438	Mushet, John Hunter	255
Morley, Fra. B.	242	Mulock, Tho: Edmund	229	Mutio, John Geo. Leop. de	437
Morphett, Mars.	208	Mundell, Frederick	221	Muttlebury, George	54
Morrice, Fred. Fran. Jas.	253	—— St. John	221	Myers, Arthur	99, 173
Morris, Arthur	61	Munderloh, George	437	—— William James	223
—— Edmund	65, 200	Mundy, George V.	148	Mylius, George	177
—— Edward	246	—— Godfrey Basil	12	—— Rodney	257
—— Henry Joseph	270	—— Godfrey Charles	103	Mylrea, Frederick Thos.	307
—— James Deaves	232	—— Pierrepont Hen.	271		
—— John William	115	—— Robert Miller	271	Nagel, John Thomas	168
—— Jonas	128	Munns, Edward C.	226	Nagle, Michael	198
—— Rob. Caldecott	256	Munro, Alex. *KH.*	42, 265	Nanne, John Christ. Fred.	433
Morrish, Henry George	294	—— Alexander	167	—— Henry	432
Morrison, Arthur	293	—— Alex. Thompson	120	Napier, Chas. Jas. *KCB.*	18
—— Edward	6, 164	—— Arthur	138	—— Chas. Frederick	252
—— Wm. Mansfield	59	—— George	173	—— Edw. H. D. E.	103, 197
Morritt, Henry Edward	271	—— Hector	261	—— Geo. Thos. *KCB.*	19
—— Rob. Ambrose	229	—— James, *MD.*	129	—— Geo. Thos. Conolly	260
Morse, William	148	—— James St. John	211	—— John Moore	220
—— James	115	—— John	209	—— Mark	17
Morshead, Cha. Anderson	192	—— John	115	——Rob. John Milliken	231
—— Pentyre Anderson	272	—— Thomas, *Bt.*	253	—— Thos. Erskine	40
Mortimer, John Lewis	172	—— William	190	—— *Hon.* Wm.	286
——, Tho. Bythesea	172	—— William	309	—— William C. E.	176
Mosley, Tonman	132	—— William	115	—— W. Fran. Pat.	35
Mostyn, Edward	134	Munster, Geo. *Earl of*	36	Nash, Francis, Rowland	230
—— Hen. Thornton,		Munter, Frederick	437	Natermann, Frederick	432
MD.	198	Munton, John Oliver	186	Naylor, Charles Scarlin	191
—— Thomas	178	Murchison, Kenneth	180	—— Thomas	119
—— Thomas	205	Mure, John, *MD.*	158	Neale, Melville	244
Mothe, Peter James de la	441	Murphy,Geo.Hen.Edw.	95, 157	Nedham, William	16
Motte, Peter de la	115	Murray, Adam Walker	248	—— Wm. Robert	270
Mouart, James, *MD.*	139	—— Alexander	169	Need, Arthur	142
—— James	155	—— Arth. Stormont	253	Needham, *Hon.* Fran.	
Moubray, Rich. Yates		—— Augustus Wm.	225	Hen.	61, 144
Stuart	296	—— Charles	107	—— Henry	201
Mould, Thomas R.	285	—— Charles	193	—— *Hon.* Robert	138

Index.

Name	page	Name	page	Name	page
Neil, James Bruce	184	Nicolay, Edmund George	180	Nurg, John	441
Neill, John Martin Bladen	191	——— William, *KCH.*	13, 254		
——— Matthew	207			Oakeley, Soulden	207
——— Robert	307	Nicoll, John Edward	217	Oakley, Fred. W.	241
Neilson, James	245	——— Sam. John Luke	181	——— Jocelyn Ingram	196
Nelley, John Peter	103, 229	Nicolle, François	439	Oates, James Poole, *KH.*	60
Nelson, Alex. Abercromby	191	Nicolls, Edward	55	Obert, Marc. A.	200
——— Michael	129	——— Edward Elmore	207	Obins, Acheson Eyre	226
——— Richard J.	285	——— Geo. Green	86	——— Hamlet	60
——— Richard Thomas	8	——— Gustavus	19, 282	O'Brien, Bartholomew	256
——— Thomas L. K.	191	——— Gustavus Wm.	172	——— Cha. Donatus Corbet	215
——— Wm. Frederick	287	——— Jasper, *KCB.*	14, 115, 245	——— Donough	224
Nepean, Edmund	294	——— Oliver	217	——— Edward James	17
——— Molyneux Hyde	229	——— Robert Murphy	256	——— Francis	221
——— William	86	——— Wm. Burke	64, 256	——— Henry	269
Nesbitt, Alexander	17	——— Willoughby Haloran	256	——— John	158
——— Cosby Lewis	211	Nicolson, Patrick	37	——— John	190
——— Wm. Geo. Downing	161	——— Patrick, *MD.*	139	——— John Doyle	222
Nesham, Thomas W.	218	——— Malcolm	116	——— Oliver Creagh	241
Nethercote, Maximil. Art.	204	Nivison, Jas. Finlayson	176	——— Rich. Serrell	239
——— Wm. Charles	120	Nixon, Edward John	250	——— Terence	239
Neuschaffer, Cha. Ernest F.	437	——— Marmaduke Geo.	190	——— William	204
Nevett, Charles Henry	268	——— Murray Octavius	272	O'Bryen, Edward	259
Neville, Henry Draper	152	——— Robert	116	O'Callaghan, Patrick	124
——— Park Percy	215	——— William T.	184	——— Hon. Rob. Wm. *GCB.*	12, 190
——— Hon. Rich. Cornwallis	146	Noble, Wm. Woollett	296	O'Connell, Daniel	189
——— Robert Henry	208	Noel, Stephen	89, 244	——— Edw. Maurice	251
Newbery, Francis	14	Nokes, James	217	——— Maurice Cha. *KCH.*	16
Newbury, John	241	Nolan, Lewis Edw.	141	——— Maurice, Chas.	179
Newcome, George	198	Nolloth, Peter Braines	295	——— Maurice Chas.	225
Newcomen, Arthur	271	Nooth, Henry	65	——— Rickard	217
Newenham, Richard	217	Norcliffe, Norcliffe, *KH.*	68	——— Wm. B. J.	225
Newhouse, Charles	54	Norcott, W. Sher. Ramsay	253	O'Connor, John Ross	142
Newland, Arthur	152	Norman, John	182	——— Luke Smyth	254
Newland, Bingham	121	——— John	205	——— Nicholas, *MD.*	312
——— William	242	——— Henry Radford	185	——— William	176
Newman, Benjamin	171	——— Peter Shadwell	88, 207	Odell, William	311
——— Charles Rayner	165	Norris, Charles	216	O'Donnell, *Sir* Cha. Routledge	56
Newport, Christopher	116	——— John Style	185		
Newton, George	130	North, Charles Napier	157	O'Donoghue, Charles	228
——— John	312	——— John North Ouvry	239	——— Daniel	60
——— Thomas	115	Northey, Augustus J. W.	202	——— Edw. Algernon	254
——— Wm. Henry, *KH.*	70	——— Lewis Augustus	116	——— John William	55
——— William Samuel	148	——— Stewart	176	Oehlkers, Christian	433
Neynoe, Rawdon, S. C.	178	Norton, James Roy	166	Offen, Augustus de	437
Nicholas, Griffin	214	——— Eardley	207	O'Flaherty, Richard James	235
Nicholetts, Charles Hen.	179	——— Edward	240	——— Thomas Henry	312
Nicholl, William	116	——— John (alias Teyoninkoharawen)	116	Ogilby, David	157
Nicholls, George	68			Ogilvie, Alexander, *MD.*	287
——— Geo. Russell	234	Nott, Francis Percy	196	——— James	34
——— Henry	246	——— William	115	——— William	116
——— John	261	Nottidge, Jeremiah Brock	116	——— W. H. Middleton	155
Nicholson, Brinsley	309	Nugent, Andrew	187	Ogilvy, George	100, 182
——— Christ. Hamp.	145	——— Cha. Lavallin	209	——— James	176
——— Frederick	152	——— Eyre, T. J. R.	210	——— Thomas	119
——— Gilbert Thos.	135	——— George, Bt. *GCB.*	6, 157	——— Walter	159
——— Jaffray	251	——— Geo. Edm. N.	225	——— Walter	93
——— Joseph	236	——— James	187	Oglander, Henry	39, 177
——— Robert	172	——— John	123	Ogle, Arthur	160
——— Thos. Wm. *KH.*	72	——— Michael	311	——— Bertram Newton	131
——— William Smith	248	Nunn, James Winniett	89, 232	——— Edmund	286
Nickle, Robert, *KH.*	44			O'Grady, Robert Dring	181
Nickoll, Thomas	100, 151			——— Hon. Standish	58
Nicol, Charles	18				

511

Index.

	page		page		page
O'Grady, Hon. Thomas	226	Ormsby, Anthony	232	Palmer, Charles	305
——— William Stamer	212	——— August. Howard	152	——— Charles	16
O'Halloran, Henry Dunn	221	——— James	116	——— Chas. Quartley	244
——— Joseph, *KCB.*	115	——— John William	270	——— Francis Roger	212
——— Wm. Littlejohn	189	——— Owen Lloyd	240	——— Geo. Gayton	98, 268
O'Hara, Henry, *MD.*	310	——— Thomas	244	——— Henry W.	187
——— Robert	69, 240	——— Thos. Charles	250	——— James	254
Ohlen, Frederick von	438	Osborn, Charles Davers	156	——— John Roger	143
Oke, George	183	——— Hon. Wm. Go-		——— Joseph	155
Oldershausen, Franz. Geo. von	433	dolphin	177	——— Nicholas	100, 207
Oldershaw, Henry	184	Osborne, Hugh Stacey	115	——— Reynolds	268
——— Charles	285	Ossorio, Baldassare	441	——— Samuel	182
Oldfield, Anthony	272	Ostheyden, Frederick	258	Palmes, Bryan	203
——— John, *KH.*	62, 283	Oswald, John, *GCB.*	9, 186	Panattieri, Joseph	439
Oldwright, John	233	——— Jas. Townsend	146	Pannach, Charles	440
O'Leary, Arthur	206	——— Robert	54	Pape, William	435
Oliphant, James	116	O'Toole, John Arthur	163	Papillon, Alex. Fred. Wm.	271
Oliver, Joseph Boyer	191	——— John M'Culloch	200	Pardey, John Quin	204
——— Nathaniel Wilmot	42, 265	——— William Henry	169	Pardoe, Henry	251
——— Richard Silver	120	Otter, Charles J.	155	——— Edward	166
——— Robert	120	Ottley, Benjamin Wynne	32	Parish, Henry W.	196
Olivier, Hen. Stephen	86	Otto, Frederick	435	Park, Thomas	294
O'Loghlin, Terence	10	Otway, Arthur S.	202	——— Walter Brisbane	177
Olphert, John	271	——— Charles	268	Parke, George Thomas	257
Olpherts, Geo. Edward	214	——— Sir Loftus Wm.	13	——— Hamnett	295, 297
——— Richard	191	Ouvry, Henry Aime	220	——— Henry Wm.	294, 297
O'Malley, George	34	Ovens, John	208	——— Roger	37
——— George Patrick	240	Owen, Edward Barry	168	——— Tho. Adams	42, 292
——— *Sir* William, *Bt.*	158	——— Francis Mostyn	215	Parker, Ambrose Barcroft	216
O'Meara, Daniel	196	——— Hen. Mostyn	179	——— Charles Allan	295
O'Molony, H. Anthony	167	——— Hen. Cha. Cunliffe	286	——— Edward	202
Ompteda, Christ. Lewis von	436	——— John, *KH.*	44, 292, 297	——— Edw. Augustus	294
——— L. Albrecht von	436	——— Loftus	71	——— Fred. W. Priestly	179
O'Neill, Charles	97, 195	——— Robert	242	——— Hyde, Popham	272
——— Charlton	249	——— Robert	17	——— John	218
——— Henry Arthur	93, 163	——— Stephen	307	——— John Boteler	38, 266
——— Hon. John Bruce Rich.	14	——— William Mostyn	128	——— John Fleming	201
——— Robert	155	Oxenden, Wm. Dixwell	209	——— Richard	118
Onslow, Arthur Edw.	150	Oxley, Thomas	164	——— Rob. S.	164
——— Henry	161	Pack, Arthur John	158	——— Thomas James	152
——— Pitcairn	296	——— Denis William	272	——— Thomas John	139
——— Rich. Cranley	243	——— Richard Percy	256	——— William	216
——— Thomas P.	219	Padley, Alfred	249	Parkin, Henry	297
——— William, *KH.*	83	Pagans, Raphael	439	Parkinson, Cha. Augustus	188
Orange, John Edward	233	Page, George Curry	284	——— Cha. Fred.	225
——— Wm. Fred. Henry, *Prince of, GCB.*	6	Paget, *Lord,* Alfred	120	——— Edward	38
——— Wm. Nesbitt	92, 219	——— Catesby	158	——— Jas. Benners	220
Ord, Harry Gough	268	——— *Hon.* Edward, *GCB.*	7, 115, 179	——— John	146
——— Harry St. George	286	——— Frederick	73, 147	Parlby, Brook Bridges	115
——— Wm. Redman	95, 283	——— *Lord* Geo. Aug. Fred.	118	——— William	131
Orde, James	12	——— Henry W.	194	Parr, Frederick	205
Ordon, John	441	——— Patrick L. C.	205	——— James	307
Ore, James Alexander	231	Paine, William Staines	270	——— Robert	205
O'Reilly, Anth. Alex.	89	Pakenham, *Hon.* Cha. R.	224	Parratt, Evelyn Latimer	237
——— Duval Knox	221	——— *Hon.* Hercules R., *KCB.*	19	——— James	287
——— John	139	——— Edward Wm.	146	——— Jas. Edw. Thos.	287
——— John Robert	260	——— *Hon.* William	158	Parrott, William	260
——— Walter Fred.	57	Palairet, Septimus Hen.	180	Parry, Parry Jones, *KH.*	18
Oriel, Henry Francis	306	Paley, John Green	161	——— Richard	88
Ormond Harry Smith	87, 181	Palk, Lawrence	128	——— Spencer Claudius	13, 264
——— George	238	Palliser, George Hugh	294	——— William	155
		——— Henry	268	Parsons, John Whitehill	85
				Partridge, John	128
				Pascoe, John	268
				——— Richard Wm.	293

3 E

Index.

	page		page		page
Pasley, Charles William	34, 282, 286	Peck, John James	256	Petley, Patrick M'Leod	244
——— Gilbert	200	Peddie, Jas. Wm. B.	242	——— Robert	244
——— Richard	234	Peddie, John Crofton	102, 172	Pettit, Guglielmo	202
Paterson, James, *MD*.	193	——— John, *KH*.	57, 242	Pettingal, Francis Wm.	285
——— Joseph	44	Peebles, Adam John Laing	210	——— Edward	116
——— Peter Hay	244	——— Thomas	210	Peyton, Jos. John Wakehurst	119
——— Thomas	133	——— Thomas	70, 292	Pfannkuche, Augustus	438
——— Thomas,	42, 265	Peel, Edmund	184	Phelan, Richard	257
——— Wm. *KCH*.	13	——— Jonathan	57	Phibbs, Ormsby	98, 240
Patience, James	217	——— Robert Moore	253	——— Owen	238
Paton, John	243	——— William	128	Philpps, Courtenay,	91, 141
Patrickson, Christ. C.	33	Peile, Robt. Moore, *MD*.	309	——— John George	213
Patten, Edward Bullock	284	Peirse, Chas. Hen.	167	——— Rich. John. Allen	163
Pattenson, Wm. Hodges T.	176	Pelly, Raymond	53	Philips, Charles	191
Patterson, Alexander	237	Pender, Thomas	182	——— Frederick	129
——— Chas. Doyle	241	——— Wm. Ambrose	214	——— Henry	273
——— James	177	Pengelly, Wm. Jenny	296	——— James George	140
——— James	233	Penleaze, Henry	145	——— John	84
——— John	97	Penley, George Frederick	116	——— John Alex.	293
——— William T. L.	243	Penn, William	141	——— Joseph	138
Pattinson, Richard	142	Pennefather, John Lysaght	72, 173	Phillips, *Sir* Charles	12
Pattison, Charles	230	Pennell, Lovell	305	——— Grismond Fred.	296
——— John Rob. Graham	258	Pennington, Jas. Masterson	156	——— Harry Shakespear	102, 204
Pattison, Robert	164	——— Jas. Masterson	243	——— John	170
Pattle, Thomas	142	Penny, R. Nicholas	116	——— John	295
Patton, John	92, 103	——— Gabriel Richard	115	——— John Lort	174
——— Walter Douglas Phillipps	198	——— Henry	164	——— Owen	116
Pattoun, Rich. Tyrrell Rob.	205	Pennycuick, John, *KH*.	72, 168	——— Robert Newton	204
Patey, Geo. Wm.	207	Penrose, Charles Penrose	296	——— William S.	126
Paty, Geo. Wm. *KH*.	40, 246	——— Jas. Wm. Edw.	161	Phillott, Frederick J.	174
Patzinsky, Ernest von	439	Pepper, Charles	67	——— Joseph	59
Paul, Thomas	217	Perceval, Geo. Ramsay	224	Phillpotts, Arthur Thos.	271
Paulet, *Lord* Fred.	148	——— John Maxwell	163	——— George	72, 284
——— Hen. Chas. *Bt*.	122	——— John Pennefather	168	——— Henry	180
——— *Lord* William	90, 220	——— Philip, Joshua	69, 145	Philpot, Philip	17, 137
Pawsey, Edmond Wm. Wilton	207	——— Spencer	148	Phipps, *Hon.* C. Beaumont	69, 149
Paxton, Jas. Llewellyn	221	Percival, Philip	120	——— George William	13
Payler, James	55	Percivall, Charles	273	——— Henry B.	167
Payne, Chas. Wm. Meadows	224	——— William	118	——— Rich. Leckonby	220
——— Gallway Byng	295	Percy, *Hon.* Hen. Hugh Manvers	146	——— William	116
——— John	146	——— Hugh Josceline	133	Pickard, George Percy	228
——— Peter Trant	295	Pereira, Manasseh Lopez	115	——— James	296
——— Wm. Aug. Townshend	169	Peretti, Dominico Antonio	439	Pickering, John, *MD*.	310
Paynter, David William	271	Perkins, William Hill	115	——— William Henry	269
——— Howell	175	Perrott, Henry	210	Pidgeon, Joseph Tho.	63
——— Joshua	212	——— Octavius George	141	Pierce, Thos. Estwick	312
Peacock, William	197	Perry, Francis	98, 259	——— Frederick	248
Peacocke, Loftus Warren	203	——— Thos. Sarsfield	233	Piercy, Godfrey	153
——— Stephen Ponsonby	176	Persse, Henry D.	163	——— Henry	153
——— Thomas	66	——— William	122	Piers, Henry	90
——— Warren Marmaduke, *KCH. KC.*	9	——— William, *CB*.	63, 142	——— James	296
——— Warren Wm. Rd.	238	Perston, David, *MD*.	131	Pieters, Charles	152
Pearce, Charles Wm.	294	Pery, *Hon.* John Hartstonge	181	Piggott, James	177
Pearse, Walter	92, 241	Peshall, Charles	260	Pigot, Brooke	221
——— William G.	115	Pester, Henry	268, 273	——— George, *Bt.*	7
Pearson, Hugh	200	Peters, William Henry	127	——— *Sir* Henry	6, 189
——— Rich. Arth. *MD*.	239	Petit, Peter John	201	——— Richard	13
——— Thos. *KCH*.	17	Petley, John Cade	65, 266	Pigott, Arthur	241
——— Thos. Aylmer	194	——— John Alex. Chas.	209	——— Henry	165
Pearson, Thomas Hooke	142			——— John P.	183
				Pilcher, John Montresor	293
				Pilfold, Medwin R.	153
				Pilgrim, John Bunce	141

Index.

Name	page
Pilkington, And. *KCB*.	16
—— Edward	172
Pilleau, Henry	215
Pilling, Oswald	222
—— Oswold	96
Pilsworth, Edwin Godwin	181
—— William	219
Pinckney, Fred. Geo. Aug.	225
—— George	90, 234
Pinder, George	166
—— Henry	176
—— William Charles	206
Pine, Chilley	177
Pink, John Freeborn	261
Piper, Hugh	62, 189
—— John	189
—— Rob. Sloper	94, 283
—— Sam. Ayrault, *MD*.	261
—— William Donald	189
Pipon, Frederick	131
—— George, *KH*	85
—— Geo. Tho. Widdrington	142
—— James Kennard	237
—— John Hodges	286
—— Manaton	121
—— Thomas	116
—— Tho. Ommanney	121
Piro, *Marq*. Guis. de	70, 262
Pitcairn, David Charles	311
—— Geo. Kincaird, *MD*.	209
—— *Sir* James, *MD*.	309
—— Robert	244
Pitman, Robert	115
—— Edmund	206
Pitt, George Deane, *KH*.	41, 263
—— Geo. Dean	199
—— *Hon*. Horace	120
—— Wm. Grey	137
Place, Lionel	124
—— Thomas	156
Planta, Etienne de	439
Plasket, Thomas Henry	182
Plenderleath, Charles	54
Pleydell, Thomas Baker	296
Plowden, Francis	116
Plunkett, *Hon*. C. Dawson	152
—— *Hon*. Edw. Sidney	238
—— *Hon*. Elias R.	212
—— Francis	53
—— Thomas	184
Pocklington, Evelyn Hen. Fred.	203
Podmore, Richard	115
Poett, Matthew	128
Pogson, Fran, Milward Waskett	254
—— Henry Jenkins	181
—— Robert W.	116
Polnton, Michael	177
Pole, Arthur Cunliffe	98, 215
—— Edward	138

Name	page
Pole, George Robert	245
—— Mundy	241
Polkinghorne, Fra. James	296
Pollard, Thomas E.	224
Pollen, Chas. Hungerford	253
Pollock, Rob. Carlile	86
—— George	115
—— Thomas	115
Polwhele, Rich. Graves	116
Ponchalon, J. N. de	439
Ponsonby, Wm. Brabazon	158
Poole, Cha. Evered	152
—— Henry	269
—— John H.	103, 173
Pooley, Henry	285
Poore, Richard Francis	131
Pope, Patrick, *MD*.	234
Popham, Edw. Wm. Leyb.	8
—— Harcourt	270
Poppleton, Wm. Alex.	241
Portal, Robert	168
Portarlington, John *Earl of*	32
Porter, Henry Edward	63
—— John	219
—— William	273
Portlock, Joseph Ellison	284
Postlethwaite, Hen. J. W.	177
Poten, Augustus	432
—— Charles	437
—— Charles	437
—— Conrad	432
—— Conrad	433
—— Fred. *Baron* von	433
Potter, John	155
Pottinger, William	157
Potts, Charles Highmore	102, 170
—— John	176
—— John	256
Poulden, Rich. Mathews	270
Poulett, George	205
Powell, Charles Thomas	173
—— Cornelius	121
—— Geo. W. *MD*.	312
—— Hen. Buckworth	146
—— Hen. Claringbold	161
—— John	233
—— Scott	174
—— Stratford	116
Powell, Thos. Folliott	142
—— Thos. Harcourt	150
—— Thos. Sidney	103, 157
—— Walter	71, 292
—— Wm. Wellington	160
Power, Edmund James	121
—— Gervas	93, 161
—— James	36, 265
—— John	180
—— Kingsmill Manley	135
—— Manley	100, 237
—— William John	202
—— Wm. Greenshields, *KH*	39, 266
Powys, *Hon*. Charles	130

Name	page
Powys, *Hon*. Henry Littleton	212
Poyntz, Edward Henry	210
—— James	181
Pratt, Charles	60
—— Charles Compton	293
—— Edward	251
—— Edward Berens	218
—— Edward James	142
—— George	312
—— George Brookes	215
—— Henry	72, 169
—— John	187
—— Percy	86
—— Richard	247
—— Robert	192
—— Thomas Simson	93, 177
Pratt, Walter Caulfield	219
Precorbin, Silvain de	439
Prendergast, C. O'Neil	56
—— *Sir* Jeffery,	115
—— Jos. Sam. *MD*.	229
—— Robert K.	242
—— Thomas	196
Prescott, William	116
Preston, *Hon*. Charles	175
—— John William	228
—— Robert	85
—— Thomas Henry	133
—— William R.	173
Prettejohn, Rich. Buckley	131
Preussner, Victor	437
Price, Edward	271
—— Francis	170
—— James	115
—— John Banner	305
—— Richard	192
—— Spencer Cosby	251
—— Thos. Donaldson	214
—— William	258
—— Wm. Phillips	115
Prichard, Charles John	189
Priest, Phineas	295
Priestley, Edward R.	176
—— Frederick, J. B.	176
Prime, Cha. Edward	213
—— Arthur	125
Primrose, James M.	194
—— Wm. *MD*.	195
Pringle, Colin	60
—— George	97
—— John	18
—— John Henry	148
—— Wm. Hen. *KCB*.	10, 196
Prior, Lodge Morris Murray	138
Pritchard, Edward	16, 264
—— Sam. Dilman	91
Prittie, Fran. Sadlier	228
Procter, George	98
—— John	88, 181
Proctor, Hen. Adolphus	37
—— Thos. Beauchamp	120
Prosser, Geo. Walter	85
Prothero, Edward	165

Index.

	page		page		page
Prott, Victor, *KCH*.	438	Randolph, John W.	246	Reinecke, Cha. Augustus	433
Prower, John Elton Mervyn	219	Ranken, Robert	253	Remmett, Henry Gibbs	258
		Raper, Felix Vincent	115	Renny, George, *MD*.	309
Pryse, Edward Lewis	126	Ratcliffe, Jeremiah, *KH*. 70, 132		——— Henry	233
——— John Edw. Harryman	179	——— Edgar	203	——— William, *MD*.	128
Puddicombe, Geo. Bruce	293	Rattray, David	164	Renwick, Wm. Turnbull	285
——— Rob. Bruce	296	——— William	224	Rettberg, Charles de	437
Pugh, Charles Vaughan	242	Rautenberg, Geo. Fred. And.	441	——— Leopold von	434
Puleston, John Philip Bowyer	234	Rawdon, John Dawson	63, 147	Reuss, Henry Prince	116
				Reynard, Robert	253
——— Richard Price	227			Reynardson, Edw. Birch	145
——— Wm. Roger	235	Rawlins, John	116	——— Thomas Birch	12
Purnell, William P.	242	Rawlinson, H. C.	116	Reyne, Peter Bennet	257
Pursloe, James	248	Rawnsley, Rich. Burne 99, 267		Reynell, Tho., *Bt. KCB*. 13, 239	
Purves, John Home	145	Rawstone, John George	214	Reynett, J. H. *KCH*. 36, 115	
Purvis, Charles	55	Rawson, Samuel	179	Reynolds, Cha. Wm.	142
——— Rob. B. Arthur	203	Ray, Philip	41	——— Edward	286
Pym, Robert	36, 265	Raymond, Henry P.	151	——— George	222
Pyner, Francis Richard	156	——— Victor	178	——— Henry	153
Pynn, Henry, *Kt. CB*.	54	Rayner, Thomas	305	——— John Williams	137
		Raynes, Wm. Augustus	99, 267	——— Rich. Ant.	137
Quarrier, Daniel	297			——— Thomas Vincent	
Quentin, George A. *KCH*.	15	Rayson, John	235	——— Edgar	259
——— Geo. Aug. Fred.	136	Rea, Edward	294	Rhatigan, Christopher	217
Quigley, Thomas Haswell	287	Read, Blackwood Moutray	141	Rhodes, William	220
Quill, Gerrard	68			Rhys, Thomas	311
		——— Edward Rudston	139	Riach, John, *MD*.	219
Raban, William	173	Reade, George Hume	310	——— William A.	100, 231
——— William G.	195	——— Henry Cooper	141	Riall, Phineas, *KCH*. 10, 226	
Radcliff, William	239	——— Thomas, *Kt*.	39	Ricard, Edward	227
Radcliffe, Rob. Parker	272	——— William Ch. De B.		Rice, Augustus Thomas	202
Rae, Thomas	305		254	——— George Watkins	174
——— William	297	Ready, Charles	223	——— Henry	155
Rahlwes, Fred. Jacob	433	——— John	34	——— Percy	202
Raikes, George W.	233	——— William	139	——— Samuel, *KH*.	35
——— Fred. Thornton	208	Rebow, Francis Slater	10	Rich Robert Edwin	239
——— William Henly	33	Rechtern, Adolphus	438	Richards, Alfred	115
Raines, Joseph Rob.	100, 247	Reed, Archibald William	251	——— William, *KCB*.	115
Rainey, Henry, *KH*.	41	——— James Wm.	306	——— William H.	116
——— Henry Garner	200	——— John	59, 205	Richardson, Arthur	87
——— John	116	——— Matthew Benj. Geo.	236	——— Henry	55
Rainier, Daniel	250			——— Isaac	100, 162
Rainsford, James	124	——— Samuel	163	——— James	152
——— Thomas	218	——— Samuel	66	——— Jas. Earlsman	199
Raitt, Charles Robert	232	——— Thomas	58, 214	——— Jas. Wm.	180
——— Geo. Dalhousie Jolliffe	153	——— Thomas	94, 222	——— John	235
		——— William	157	——— John	256
——— Hen. Alexander	258	Rees, David	233	——— John George	293
Ralph, Joseph	157	Reeve, John	35	——— John Henry	56
——— William Nicol	153	——— John Henry	187	——— John Luther	115
Ralston, John	216	——— Thos. John	231	——— Johnstone Thomson, *MD*.	212
Rambke, Frederick	438	Reeves, Geo. Jas. *KH*.	20		
Ramdohr, George de	432	——— Geo. Marmaduke	251	——— Robert	127
Ramsay, Alexander	296	Regan, John	161	——— Thomas	150
——— Francis	271	Reid, George	129	——— Thomas Fred.	208
——— James	200	——— Geo. Alexander	62, 119	——— William	287
——— John	7	——— Henry	97	——— William	41, 120
——— *Hon.* John	17	——— John	201	Richmond, Mathew	248
——— Rob. Williamson	193	——— Thomas	95, 184	Richter, Ern. Fer. Cha. Bern.	440
——— Wm. Burnet	253	——— William	66, 283		
Ramsbottom, Richard	251	Reignolds, Thomas Scott	200	Reckets, Aubrey	128
Ramsey, William	116	Reilly, Gustavus Handcock	254	Ricketts, St. Vincent Wm.	129
Rand, George	200			Riddall, William, *KH*.	37
——— Samuel	194	——— Joseph	134	Riddell, Cha. Jas. Buchanan	271
Randolph, Archibald	286	Reind'l John	439		

Index.

	page		page		page
Riddell, Hen. Jas. *KH.*	34	Robertson, Robert	270	Romer, Robert William	165
Riddle, William	442	—— Wm. von, *KCH.*		Romhild, John Aug.	440
Riddlesden, John Buck	56		54, 434	Romilly, Frederick	150
Rideout, Goring	238	—— William	163	Romney, George Jas.	93
Rider, Wm. Barnham		Robeson, George	254	Roney, Richard	248
—— Thomas	296	Robinson, Charles	293	Rooke, Alex. B.	229
Ridley, Charles William	145	—— Fred. Philipse,		—— Hen. Willoughby,	
—— John Hen. Ellis	212	*GCB.*	10, 210	*KCH.*	18
—— William John	150	—— Fred. Adolphus	156	—— William W.	198
Riky, Benjamin	199	—— George Henry	116	Roome, Henry	115
Riley, Daniel	175	—— Henry Edw.	63, 181	—— William	115
—— Alexander Wm.	232	—— James	219	Rooper, Bonfoy	185
Rimington, Tho. Hosmer	285	—— John George	69, 149	—— Edward	253
Ring, William Francis	172	—— John Stephen	212	—— John	252
Rishton, James Neil	260	—— John Watson	160	Roper, Hen. Welladvice	159
—— Thomas	157	—— Oliver	153	Roquefeuil, Gustave de	441
Ritherdon, Peter	116	—— Peter Tooke	142	Rose, Alexander	83
Ritter, Herman Hen. Con.	432	—— Thomas	195	—— Cowper	284
Rivarola, Count Fra.		—— William	203	—— George B.	221
KCH.	17, 262	—— William	285	—— Hugh Henry	72
—— Francis	441	—— William Henry	224	—— John, *KCB.*	115
Rivers, Charles	101, 284	—— William Henry	305	—— John Baillie	206
Rizzo, Felice	262	—— Wm. Tho. Christ.	148	—— John Rose Holden	130
—— Vincenzo	262	Robson, Alex. Hamilton	154	Ross, Archibald P. G.	286
Robbins, Tho. Wm.	41	—— George Lloyd	125	—— Charles	260
Robe, Alex. Watt	101, 284	Robyns, John, *KH.*	84	—— Charles	311
—— Frederick Holt	239	—— Thomas	183	—— Gilliam Maclaine	167
—— Thos. Congreve	269	Roche, Charles Boyse	185	—— Hew Dalrymple,	
Roberts, Charles	210	—— Edmund	130	*KCB.*	34, 265
—— Frederick	210	—— John	119	—— Hew Graham	272
—— Henry	116	Rochfort, Gerald	87, 154	—— James	67
—— Peter	306	—— Gustavus	124	—— James Hamilton	162
—— Richard, *KH.*	37	—— Gustavus	41	—— Jas. Kerr, *KH.*	90
—— Roderick	116	Roddy, Charles Hamilton	257	—— John	14, 197
—— William	57	Rodgers, John	177	—— John	65
—— William	250	Rodney, George Brydges	296	—— John Moore	199
—— William	251	—— Robert Dennett	150	—— Kenneth Tolmie	218
—— William Henry	286	Rodon, John	123	—— Murdoch John Mac-	
Robertson, Alex. Cunning-		Rodwell, Edward Wm.	272	laine	142
ham	185	Roe, Peter Fitzrobert	137	—— Patrick, *KCH.*	16
—— Archibald	184	—— Samuel Crozier,		—— Pat. Wm. Sydenham	237
—— Archibald	254	*MD.*	310	—— Robert	187
—— Archibald	115	Roebuck, Fran. Algernon		—— Thomas	242
—— Chas. Duesberry	286	Disney	174	—— William	69, 174
—— David	116	Rofe, Samuel	140	—— William	306
—— Donald	177	Rogers, Charles	247	Rosser, George	142
—— Duncan, Stew.	182	—— Charles	116	—— Thomas	139
—— Edward, *MD.*	221	—— George	269	Rossing, Frederick von	434
—— Edw. Lovett	122	—— Geo. Jackmann	65	Rosslyn, Jas. Alex. *Earl*	
—— Geo. Abercrombie	141	—— Henry	272	*of*	57, 135
—— Geo. Duncan	193	—— Hen. Blanckley		Rothard, Adolphus	436
—— Geo. Duncan	16	Harrington	162	Rothe, Lorenzo	187
—— Geo. Gordon, *MD.*		—— Thomas William	257	Röttiger, Augustus	32
	152	—— Thos. Oldham G.	206	—— Franz	438
—— James	135	—— William	56	Rotton, James Rich.	88, 137
—— James	8	—— Wm. Armstrong	247	Rous, George Grey	146
—— Jas. Alexander	234	—— William Henry	209	Rouse, James Charles	154
—— Jas. Elphinston	157	—— William Henry	247	Routh, Henry	141
—— Jas. H. C.	223	—— William Reynolds	136	—— Randolph	142
—— Jas. Macdonald	63	Rolland, Stewart Erskine	250	—— Randolph	307
—— John, *MD.*	164	Rolles, Harry	202	—— Randolph Isham	305
—— John, *MD.*	309	Rollo, *Hon.* Robert	193	Rowan, Charles	53
—— Lewis Shuldham		Rolt, John	39	—— Hen. Sebastian	271
Barrington	101	Romer, John Charles		—— William	40
—— Peter	311	—— Robt. Frank	95, 267	Rowland, Geo. Tempest	268
—— Peter	311	—— Robert Corcyra	272	Rowles, Henry	134

Index.

	page		page		page
Rowley, Charles	61	St. Quintin, Fras. John	237	Savile, Albany Bourchier	133
—— John	136	—— Matthew Chitty		—— Hon. Frederick	272
Rubenz, William	434	Downes	73, 143	—— Henry Bourchier	
Rudyerd, Samuel	68, 266	Salamone, Paolo	262	Osborne	272
Rumann, Geo. Augustus	442	Sale, Robert Henry, *KCB.*		Sawbridge, Wanley Elias	179
Rumbold, Carlo Arth. Hen.			43, 115, 164	Sawers, Campbell	221
	202	Salinger, Otto Henry	440	Sawrey, Hen. Beckwith	240
Rumley, Charles	115	Salis, Hector de	440	Sawyer, Charles	154
—— George, *MD.*	258	—— Charles de	150	Say, William	32
—— Randall	211	—— Rodolph de	134	Sayer, Wm. Lawrence	296
Rummell, William	438	Sall, William, *KH.*	60, 261	Sayers, Richard Talbot	232
Rumpler, Anthony	116	—— William	261	Scarlett, *Hon.* Jas. Yorke	88,
Rush, Alfred	239	—— Henry	259		125
Rushbrooke, Cha. Davers	183	Salmon, George	14, 264	Schade, William de	437
—— R. F. Brownlow	150	Salter, Henry Fisher	116	Schaedtler, J. Phil. Anth.	436
Rushout, George	118	—— James F.	115	Schaefer, Augustus Hen.	442
Russell, Henry Charles	68, 266	Saltoun, Alexander, *Lord*	19	Schaeffer, Carl	432
—— *Lord* Alex. G.	253	Salvatelli, Francis	439	Schalch, And. Orcher W.	268
—— Andrew Hamilton	173	Salvatori, Pietro Antonio	440	Scharnhorst, Adolphus	436
—— *Lord* Cha. Jas.		Salvin, Anthony	14	—— Ferdinand	436
Fox	92	Salwey, Henry	56	—— Lewis	438
—— *Lord* Cosmo. Geo.	245	Sampson, John	151	—— William de	438
—— David	236	Sande, Henry Van	442	Schaumann, Christian	432
—— Francis Hastings	150	Sandeman, Thos. Fraser	225	—— Gustavus	433
—— Fred. Browne	179	Sander, Ernest	437	—— Henry Fred.	434
—— Fred. Tho. Lech-		Sanders, Frederick Paris	194	—— Otto	436
mere Graves	191	—— Robert	170	Schauroth, Geo. F. C. von	436
—— *Lord* Geo. Wm.		Sanderson, Arch. Christie	152	Schaw, George	206
GCB.	36, 115	Sandes, Charles	241	Scheberras, Rinaldo	232
—— Henshaw	249	Sandham, Back. L. *MD.*	137	Schembri, Joseph	310
—— James	201	—— Charles F.	84	Schlaeger, Charles	436
—— James, *KCB.*	115	—— George	270	Schlichthorst, John Fred.	438
—— John Ambrose	245	—— Henry	284, 286	Schlütter, Fred. von	435
—— John James	225	Sandilands, *Hon.* Jas.	134	Schmid, Patricio	440
—— Samuel William	250	—— Philip	101, 267	Schmidt, Augustus Fred.	435
—— William	179	—— William	127	Schmiedern, Ern. *Baron* de,	
—— William Lloyd	179	Sands, Hastings David	121	*KH.*	116
Rutherfoord, Archibald	228	—— William Robert	128	Schmitt, Alexander	441
Rutherford, Jas. Hunter	284	Sandwith, William	115	Schnath, Frederick	434
—— Wm. Henry	103	Sandys, Arthur W. M.		Schnehen, William von	433
Ruttledge, Thos. Ormsby	168	*Lord*	40	Schneider, Fred. Bern.	435
Ruxton, George	98, 185	—— Fred. Henry	116	Schoedde, Jas. Holmes	58, 206
—— George Aug. Fred.	241	Sanford, George Charles	306	Schonfeldt, Detlif. Sigfrid	260
—— John Hen. Hay	155	Sankey, Samuel	116	Schonswar, Henry	127
Ryall, Isaac	297	Sargeant, James	139	—— Jas. Smith	121
Ryan, Michael, *MD.*	311	Sargent, John James	169	Schooles, Henry James,	
—— Thomas, *KH.*	90, 201	Sarson, John	168	*MD.*	233
Ryhiner, Beniot	440	Saum, Julius Cæsar	440	Schot, Johannas Corn.	439
Ryneweld, Horatius Van	260	Saumarez, *Hon.* John St.		Schoveller, Wm. Ring	295
		Vincent	252	Schrader, Ernest von	438
Sabine, Edward	94, 267	—— S. F. de	226	Schrieber, Chas. Alfred	185
Sadlier, William	98, 155	—— *Sir* Thomas	9	—— Jas. Alfred	71
—— Anthony	192	Saunders, Henry Fred.	206	Schroder, William	434
Sage, William	116	—— John Stratford	9	Schroeder, John	127
St. Aubyn, Thos. John	235	—— John Wm.	209	Schuchardt, Henry	437
St. Clair, Thos. Staunton,		—— Richard	261	Schultze, Frederick	442
KH.	40	—— William John	208	—— Leopold Sigis-	
St. George, Howard John	138	—— Wm. Nonus	247	mond	433
—— John	270	Saunderson, Hardress Rob.	70	Schulze, Augustus	435
St. John, *Hon.* Frederick	6	Savage, And. Roger	296	Schwarzemberg, J. D. W.	
—— Charles	309	—— Henry	294, 297	L. von	439
—— Jas. Humphrey	269	—— Henry J.	243	Schweitzer, Augustus	438
St. Maur, *Lord* Alg. Percy		—— Henry John	96, 284	Schwencke, Herman	436
Banks	120	—— Johnson, *MD.*	287	Scobell, Edward Calvert	143
—— Edward	98, 202	—— John Boscawen	19	—— Frederick Edw.	214
St. Paul, Horace, *Bt.*	33	—— John Morris	269, 273	—— Thomas	305

517

Index

Name	page
Scott, Alexander	170
—— Alfred	121
—— Charles, *MD*.	187
—— Hon. Cha. Grantham	150
—— Daniel	310
—— Edward	131
—— Edward	16
—— Francis G.	223
—— Geo. Fred. Cooper	228
—— Henry Alex.	65, 266
—— Henry Arthur	138
—— Hen. Lockman Gordon	218
—— Hopetoun Stratford, *KCB*.	115
—— John	61, 131
—— John Snowden	182
—— Joseph	160
—— Matthew Rob.	273
—— Rob.	189
—— Robert Thomas	228
—— Thomas	293
—— T. F. P. C.	164
—— Thomas	7
—— Thomas Knox	214
—— Walter, *Bt*.	72, 141
—— William	126
—— William Douglas	202
—— Wm. Glendonwyn	243
—— William Henry	39, 149
—— William Boxell	195
Scovell, Edward W.	248
—————— George, *KCB*.	19
Scroggs, Wm. Seymour	156
Scudamore, Arthur	131
Seagram, Charles	196
Seale, Thomas Fownes	246
Sealy, Francis	216
—— Benj. Wm. Dowden	115
—— John	217
—— Thomas	153
Searle, Richard	294
—— William Ramsay	296
Seaton, John, *Lord*, *GCB*. *GCH*.	15, 115, 177
—— Thomas	287
Sebisch, Theo. von.	437
Seccombe, Thomas	177
Seeger, William	432
Seelhorst, Christian Geo.	436
Seffers, Henry	437
Segrave, O'Neal	127
Seinecke, Frederick	438
Selwyn, Chas. Jasper	100, 284
Semple, John	170
Senhouse, Wm. Wood	228
Senior, Henry	63, 217
Serjeantson, James H.	99, 201
Servaise, Antoine	439
Servanté, Henry	285
Servantes, Wm. Thornton	188
Sesino, Guiseppe	262
Seton, Alexander	172
Seton, David	245
—— George	245
—— Richard Somner	116
—— William Cardon	43
—— William Carden	246
Seward, Eliot Tho.	188
—— Mark Pattison	159
—— Thomas	87
—— William	91
Sewell, Alger. Robinson	166
—— Wm. Henry	40, 157
Sexton, Samuel	155
Seymour, Cha. Francis	150
—— Charles F.	236
—— Francis	170
—— Fra. Hug. Geo.	150
—— Henry	174
—— Henry	191
—— Henry R.	215
—— Wm. Hobart	224
Shadforth, Henry	18
—— Thomas	208
Shadwell, Taylor	253
Shakespear, Arthur Rob.	200
—— Geo. Bucknall	272
Shanks, Archibald, *MD*.	206
Shanly, Edward	161
Sharp, John Edward	152
—— Richard Palmer	177
—— William Granville	152
Sharpe, James B.	171
—— Matthew	10
Sharpin, Archdale	206
Sharrock, Alexander	103, 180
Shaw, Charles	182
—— Frederick Beckett	259
—— Geo. Bainbridge	182
—— Geo. Gar.	131
—— Henry John	196
—— Thomas	116
—— William	259
Shawe, Arthur George	172
—— Cha. Augustus	42, 147
—— Meyrick	54
Sheaffe, Roger Hale, *Bt*.	9, 187
—— William	201
Sheahan, John	157
Shean, Robert, *MD*.	158
Shearman, Robert	214
—— William	239
Shedden, John	34
Shee, Charles	61
—— Benjamin Bazil	116
Sheil, Justin	116
Sheils, James, *MD*.	187
Shelton, John	57, 195
—— William	160
Shepheard, George	307
Shepherd, Richard	269
—— Robert	228
Sheppard, Edmund	99, 267
—— Thomas	83, 297
—— Wm. Charles	155
Sherer, Moyle	89
Sheridan, Mark	164
Sherlock, Francis, *KH*.	32
Sherlock, Fra. George	234
Sherson, Alex. Nowell	224
Sherwin, Peter	119
Shewell, Frederick Geo.	134
Shewen, Edw. Thornbrough Parker	296
Shields, Richard	230
—— Thomas	263
Shirley, Arthur	133
—— Horatio	240
Shirrefs, James	256
Shone, Thomas Ackers	269
Shore, Bohun	33
Shorland, James	248
Shortall, James	17
Short, James Symington	155
—— John, *MD*.	309
—— William T.	214
Showers, Edw. Millian Gullifer	115
Shrapnell, Henry	12, 264
Shuckburgh, Cha. Rob.	184
Shuldham, Edmund W.	115
Shum, Henry	181
—— Charles Francis	188
—— John	177
Shute, Charles Cameron	139
—— James	293
Shuttleworth, Ashton Ashton	269, 273
Sibbald, Hugh	116
Sibley, E. W.	177
Sibthorp, Rich. F. Waldo	212
Sibthorpe, Cha. Coningsby Waldo	128
Sichart, Charles Lewis de	435
—— Lewis Henry de	435
Siddall, John	120
Sidey, James, *MD*.	176
Sidley, Anth. Gardiner	215
—— H. Edm. de Burgh	238
Sievwright, Francis, *MD*.	160
Sillery, Charles	181
—— Robert, *MD*.	186
Simeon, Charles	196
Simmie, James David	297
Simmonds, Henry	94, 213
—— John Henry	116
Simmons, Alfred A.	225
—— George	98
—— Jas. Egbert	153
—— John Linton Arabin	286
—— Joseph	98, 192
—— Thomas Fred.	224
—— Wm. Hen. More	228
Simonds, William	116
Simpson, Edward	287
—— Edward H.	115
—— James	43
—— James Woolley	310
—— John	185
—— John Duke	170
Sims, George	214
Simson, Robert, *KH*.	66

518

Index.

	page		page		page
Sinclair, Alexander, *MD.*	310	Smith, Cha. Fer. Hamilton,	179	Smith, Thomas Johnes	207
—— Charles	116	—— Charles George	176	—— Thomas Paterson	115
—— Charles Alex.	141	—— Cha. Ham. *KH.*	60	—— Thomas William	139
—— James	94, 267	—— Charles Hervy	70	—— Thomas William	253
—— *Hon.* James	87	—— C. H. Montresor	173	—— William	196
—— John, *Bt.*	115	—— Charles Thomas	258	—— William	88
—— John Hartley, *MD.*	206	—— David Rea	173	—— William Mein	269
—— Rob. Bligh	193	—— Edgar Steadman	213	—— Wm. Nepean	255
—— Robert Charles	189	—— Francis	178	—— William Sidney, *GCB.*	292
—— William Alex.	164	—— Frederick William,	191	—— Wm. Robt. Brudenell	103, 166
Singleton, John, *KH.*	87, 242	—— George	71, 120	—— Wordsworth	190
—— John	162	—— George Haddon	195	Smyly, Philip	251
Sinnott, John	198	—— George Hankey	225	Smyth, George	217
Sitwell, Rich. Staunton	85	—— George Roche	217	—— Geo. Brunswick	232
Sivewright, Edward	'138	—— Haskett	231	—— Harry	220
Skelly, Francis	188	—— Henry	228	—— Henry	220
Skelton, John	115	—— Henry	294	—— Henry Montagu	208
Skene, Charles	,231	—— Hen. Geo.	38	—— Henry C. W.	116
Skerrett, Jos. Marcus A.	116	—— Henry L.	234	—— James Dutton	216
Skey, Joseph, *MD.*	309	—— James, *MD.*	213	—— James Griffith	201
Skinner, Fred. Nepean	261	—— James Lewis	217	—— J. D. Carmichael	182
—— Samuel James	269	—— James Webber	199	—— Jas. Robt. Carmichael, *Bt.*	254
—— Thomas	93, 182	—— James Webber	35, 265	—— John	284
—— Thomas	257	—— John	166	—— John Rowland	126
Skipton, George Henry	195	—— John Carrington	116	—— John Stewart	231
Skipwith, Henry	194	—— John Charles	65	—— Robt. Carmichael	245
—— William	198	—— John Josiah	307	—— Robt. Donkin	311
Skurray, Francis Chas.	202	—— John Lewis	268	—— Stephen Henry	216
—— John Arthur	205	—— John Mark Fred. *KH.*	59, 283	Smythe, Carrington	134
Skyrme, James	306	—— John Nicholas	115	—— Frederick	247
Skrine, Clare	230	—— John Percy	142	—— William James	271
Skyring, Chas. Francis	285	—— John Stewart, *MD.*	206	Snell, Charles	116
Sladden, William	84	—— John William	307	—— Wm. Frederick	73, 149
Slade, Henry	268	—— John W. S.	189	Snodgrass, John	155
—— John Henry	87, 121	—— Joseph	165	—— John Jas.	56
—— John, *Bt. GCH.*	8, 125	—— Joshua Simmons	92, 156	—— Kenneth	39
—— Marcus John	73	—— Leicester Viney	285	Snow, William	102, 217
—— William Henry,	68, 283	—— Leonard	208	Snowe, Edw. Pownell	295
Slater, John James	103, 234	—— Lionel, *Bt. KCB. GCH.*	13, 191	—— William	259
—— William	234	—— Lucius Horton	116	Soden, Christian de	435
Sleator, Joseph	249	—— M. MacNaughten	236	—— Edward Charles	256
—— William	178	—— Matthew	160	—— Lewis von	436
Sleeman, George	190	—— Matthew	272	Soest, Ernest	433
Sleigh, James Wallace, *CB.*	16, 135	—— Michael Edward	216	Somerset, Arth. Wm. Fitz-Roy	145
Slessor, John	37	—— Michael William	141	—— Charles Henry	260
Slyfield, Joseph Clav. Slad., *KH.*	90, 211	—— Opie	137	Somerset, Edward A.	253
Smales, Thomas	259	—— Peter	310	—— *Lord* Fitzroy J. H. *KCB.*	15, 117, 204
Smart, Henry Dalton	179	—— Ramsay Hankey	216	—— Aug. Chas. Stapleton	272
—— Thomas	204	—— Robert	172	—— Henry, *KH.*	43, 260
Smedley, Thomas	229	—— Robert Algernon	130	—— Hen. Chas. Capel	202
Smelt, William	36, 188	—— Rob. Wm.	181	—— *Lord* John Thos. Hen.	41
Smidt, Johannes de	307	—— Seton Lionel	205	—— P. G. H.	184
Smith, Alexander	185	—— Thomas	126	—— *Lord* Robt. Edw. Hen. *GCB.*	11, 131
—— Alexander, *MD.*	121	—— Thomas	210	Somerville, Hen. Erskine	116
—— Andrew, *MD.*	310	—— Thomas, *MD.*	310	—— James	178
—— Archibald	89	—— Thomas	95, 249	—— John	268, 273
—— Arthur W.	192	—— Thomas Chaloner	137	—— William	173
—— Bellingham, John	58	—— Thomas Charlton	178	Sorell, Fred. Edward	233
—— Charles	271	—— Thomas Hatcher	115		
—— Charles	102, 171	—— Thomas Jacob	184		
—— *Sir* Cha. Felix	35, 282				

Index.

	page		page		page
Sorell, George	286	Stack, Nathaniel Massey	223	Stephenson, Fred. C. A.	150
——— Henry Edward	233	——— Richard	103, 196	——— George Alex.	123
——— Sir Thos. Stephen, KH.	116	Staff, W. B.	177	——— Robert	153
		Stafford, John	18	——— Tho. Gordon, MD.	205
Sorgenfrey, John Peter	440	Standen, Geo. Doug.	57, 149	Stepney, Arth. St. George H.	180
Sotheby, C. W. Hamilton	212	Standish, Henry	41		
——— Fred. Samuel	116	Stanhope, Hon. Sir Fran. Cha.	85	Sterling, Ant. Coningham	225
Souter, Richard	124			Steuart, Charles	232
——— Thos. Alexander	195	——— Hon. Lincoln	20	——— Cha. Erskine	141
South, Charles	171	——— Hon. Leicester	39	Stevelly, Jones Butler	258
——— Samuel	55	——— Philip Spencer,	62, 144	——— Robert Butler	258
Southall, Thomas	189			Stevens, Alex. Humphrey	295
Southwell, Hon. Arth. F.	87	Stanley, Hon. Cha. Jas. Fox	145	——— John Harvey	293, 297
Spalding, Richard Carr	296			——— John Philip	296
Spark, Robert	71, 245	——— Charles Edward	286	——— Thomas	293
Sparks, James Pattoun	189	——— Edward	208	——— William	306
——— Mitchell George	200	——— George Adamson	170	Stevenson, Geo. Milne	92, 252
——— Robt. Manners	154	——— James Talbot	162	——— George R.	127
Spearman, William	33	Stannus, Ephraim G.	115	——— Robert, MD.	154
Spedding, Carlisle	67	——— William Trevor	249	Stewart, Alexander, MD.	309
Speedy, James	154	Stanton, William	307	——— Alexander	192
——— Thos. Beckwith	164	Stanway, Henry	268	——— Alexander	84
Speer, Wilhelm	223	Stapleton, Henry	201	——— And. D. Alaton	172
Spence, Charles Howe	212	——— Herman	43	——— Archibald	244
——— Frederick	182	Stapylton, G. G. C.	104	——— Archibald	311
——— James	99, 182	——— Herman	178	——— Arthur, MD.	309
——— John	156	Stark, Robert, MD.	190	——— Charles	311
——— John	165	Starkie, Edmund	310	——— Charles	93
——— John	241	Staunton, Cha. Fred. MD.	287	——— Donald	154
——— Thomas	310			——— Donald	244
Spencer, Hon. Aug. Almoric	194	——— And. Ayler	287	——— George	211
		——— Edward	157	——— Grigor	311
——— Hon. Geo. Augustus	211	——— George	161	——— James	162
		——— John	83	——— James	257
——— Hon. Rob. Cha. Hen.	272	Staveley, Cha. Wm. Dunbar	239	——— James	287
				——— James Ainslie	296
Sperling, Wm. Henry	92	——— William	39	——— John	311
Spicer, John Wm. Gooch	135	Stawell, John Robert	189	——— John Hamilton	233
Spiel, Augustus	437	——— Jonas	196	——— John Henry	296
Spier, John	215	——— Sampson	44, 138	——— Matthew	39
Spiller, George	268	Stean, Joseph	200	——— Peter Desbrisay	95, 267
——— William	246	Stedman, Methuen	175		
Spink, John, KH.	55	Steel, James	116	——— Robert	116
Spinluff, Geo. Lovell	84	Steele, Edward	235	——— Thomas	115
Spitz, Francis Joseph	439	——— Henry	218	——— Thomas	97
Splaine, Abraham	233	——— Richard Chas.	293, 297	——— Wellington	204
Spong, Ambrose	99, 211			——— William	136
Spooner, William D.	116	——— Robert	218	——— William	269
Spottiswoode, Andrew	135	——— Thomas	37	——— William	17
——— George	60	——— Tho. Montagu	148	——— William	32
——— John	145	——— William	167	——— William Little	152
Spring, Robert	204	——— Wm. Armstrong	181	Stickney, Thomas	306
——— Thomas	175	Steer, William Frederick	116	Still, John Tryon	185
——— William	175	Steevens, George	171	Stirke, Henry M. F.	165
Spry, Frederick	293	Steffen, Augustus	437	——— Julius Henry	163
Spurin, George	293	Stehelin, Benj. Spicer	285	Stirling, Alex. Graham	8
Squair, John, MD.	134	——— Fran. William	164	——— George	153
Squire, Tristram Charnley	97, 164	Steiglitz, Adolphus W.	436	——— Geo. Claudius Beresford	216
		Steiger, Albert	116, 441		
——— William	123	Steinwehr, F. F. F. von	439	——— James	153
Stace, William	285	Stephens, Fran. Hearle	140	——— John	170
——— Henry Cope	270	——— Francis John	213	——— Thomas	216
Stack, Fred. Rich.	196	——— Henry Sykes	100, 238	Stisted, Charles, KH.	61
——— Geo. FitzGerald, KH.	93, 175	——— John Morse	268	——— Henry	56
		——— Thomas	91, 200	——— Henry William	153
——— John Massey	175	——— Thomas	294, 297	Stock, John Cassidy	182

3 F

520

Index.

	page		page		page
Stock, St. George Henry	153	Strutt, Wm. Goodday	16	Swan, Tho. Geo. Sanden	306
Stockley, William	273	Stuart, Hon. Archibald		Swayne, Thomas	195
Stockman, Henry	438	——— Geo.	219	Sweeny, George	177
Stoddard, John	205	——— Charles	145	Sweeting, Hen. Lewis	96, 267
——— Samuel George	192	——— Hon. Charles	224	Sweetman, Walter	88
Stoddart, Charles	102, 116	——— Donald	197	Sweny, John Paget	85
Stoeber, Jean Nepomu	439	——— Francesco	441	Swetenham, Clement	248
Stokes, Henry Francis	190	——— George	89, 229	——— Hen. Donithorne	142
——— Francis Fraser	243	——— Geo. Wm. Conyngham	227	Swift, B.	163
——— Patrick Day	217			Swinburn, John	88, 183
——— William John	269	——— George Francis	240	Swinburne, Francis	169
Stokoe, William	116	——— Henry	441	——— Joseph	101, 235
Stolte, William	434	——— Hugh Lindsay	189	——— Tho. Rob.	71
Stolzenberg, Ferdinand von	432	——— James	311	Swiney, George	115
		——— John	93, 158	Swinton, Edw. George	130
——— Theodor von	433	——— John	184	——— Samuel	195
Stone, Bayntun	60	——— John Ramsay	172	——— William	272
——— Edw. Wm. MD.	199	——— Patrick	172	Swyny, Exham S. T.	215
Stones, Henry	93, 139	——— Hon. Patrick	13, 211	——— Henry Joseph	215
Stoney, Henry Butler	170	——— Robert	158	Sykes, Francis Wm.	249
——— George	167	——— William	187	Symkath, John Ernest	441
Stopford, Cha. Philip Jos.	173	——— William	238	Symonds, Julian Fr. Anth.	285
——— James	191	Stubbeman, Denis		——— Jermyn Charles	296
——— Wm. Henry	95, 267	M'Carthy	235	——— Tho. George	124
Storey, Charles Robert	163	Stubbs, John	235	——— Wm. Cornwallis	248
——— Robert	139	Studd, Edward	57	Symons, Charles Bertie	269
Storks, Henry Knight	189	Studdert, George	245	Synge, Charles Edward	250
Storren, Frederick de	435	Stumpa, Ignatius	439		
Story, David	59, 265	Stuntz, Lewis	435	Tait, Alexander Duncan	124
——— Edmund Rich.	61	Sturler, Charles Louis	441	——— George	284
——— Robert William	268	Sturt, Cavendish	33	Talbot, Edw. Plantagenet Airey	185
——— Valentine Fred.	162	Stutzer, John Ernest	437		
Stotherd, Richard John	284	——— Jean Baptiste Phil.	440	——— George	194
Stourton, Hon. John	248	——— Nicholas	440	——— George	164
Stovin, Fred. KCB.	35	Suckling, Horace	99, 242	——— Robert	272
Stow, Benjamin	306	Suckow, Gottlieb von	437	——— Hon. Wellington, P. M.	158
——— Harry	269	Sulivan, Geo. Aug. Filmer	129		
Stoyte, John	99, 175	Sullivan, Henry, CB.	35, 157	Tallan, Lawrence	192
Stracey, Edward John	150	——— Henry Augustus	157	Tappe, Charles Fred.	432
Strachan, Henry A.	190	——— Henry Frederick	197	Tate, Henry Carr	295, 297
Strafford, John, Lord, GCB. GCH.	11, 180	——— John	130	Tathwell, Hen. Churchill	247
		——— William	252	Tatnall, Arch. Hamilton	244
Strange, Henry Francis	177	Sullock, Thomas	293	Tatter, John William	441
Strangways, Thos. Fox	267	Surman, John	141	Tattersall, Geo. Bulkeley	258
Stransham, Anth. Blaxland	294	Surtees, Henry Edward	136	Tatton, Richard	100, 229
Stratford, Hon. Cha. Hen.	160	Susini, Jean de	439	Taubman, J. T. Goldie	73, 150
Strath, John	238	——— Joseph	439	Taylor, Abra. Beresford,	91, 160
Straton, Joseph, CB. KCH.	14, 134	Suther, William Grigor	296		
		Sutherland, Geo. Burgoyne	207	——— Alex. Douglas	311
——— Francis	116	——— Sir James	115	——— Arthur Joseph	270
——— Robert Jocelyn	229	——— John	135	——— Brook	237
Stratton, Rob. Edm.	157	——— Peter	96, 224	——— Chas. Cyril	69
Straubenzee, Charles T. Van	190	——— Robt. Macleod	244	——— Edward James	210
		——— William	41, 156	——— George	245
——— Fred. Van	164	——— William	164	——— George A.	218
Streatfield, Charles Ogle	284	——— Wm. James	96, 172	——— Hen. Geo. Andrew	115
——— Henry C.	63, 239	Sutton, Chas. Wm.		——— Herbert Edward	237
Streng, Philip D'O. von	141	——— Francis	156	——— James	197
Stretton, Sempronius	39	——— Frederick	137	——— Jeremiah	57
——— S. W. Lynam,	91, 216	——— Henry John	133	——— John, KCB.	13, 232
Street, John Alfred	250	——— John	198	——— John Geo. Dalhousie	164
Strickland, Chris. Limebear	161	——— Richard	249		
		——— William	227	——— John Robert	311
Strode, Jas. Cranborne	132	Swain, Charles	306	——— Mascie Domville	220
Strong, Clement W.	199	Swaine, William W.	116	——— Monkhouse Graham	230
——— Richard Henry	177	Swale, Richard	70, 292		

521

Index.

	page		page		page
Taylor, Phillpotts Wright	248	Thompson, Arnold	272	Thursby, John Harvey	238
—— Pringle, *KH.*	71	—— Charles A.	154	Thwaites, Geo. Saunders	60
—— Richard	253	—— Charles Fred.	167	Thynne, *Lord* William	71
—— Richard	259	—— Charles Wm.	233	Tice, John Cha. Graham	159
—— Richard C. H.	231	—— Charles Wm.	209	Tickell, Edw. Lawrence	196
—— Robert Mascie	176	—— Childers Hen.	127	Tidy, Francis Grey	163
—— Thomas Edward	126	—— Edward	247	—— Gordon Skelly	199
—— Thomas John	230	—— Frederick	132	—— Thomas Holmes	165
—— Thomas Wm.	38	—— George	178	Tiensch, Godfrey	435
—— William	222	—— George Ashe	237	Tierney, Matthew Edward	148
—— William	293	—— Geo. Forbes	94, 283	Tighe, James Lowrie	202
—— William	89	—— Henry Hewett	226	—— Richard Hen.	157
—— Wm. Peregrine	206	—— Jacob	116	Tiller, William	156
Taynton, Wm. Henry	59	—— James	305	Tilt, Andrew	116
Teale, Charles Shipley	155	—— John Vaughan	309	Timbrell, Richard	209
Tedlie, James	186	—— Richard	177	—— Thomas	116
Teesdale, Christopher	123	—— Tho. Perronet	58	Timins, Thomas Charles	222
—— Henry George	269	—— Wm. *MD.*	157	Timm, Isaac	123
Teevan, Stephenson, *MD.*	161	—— William John	116	Timpson, Henry	296
Telfer, John Thomson	165	Thomson, Alexander	35	Tinklar, Roger Sawry	293
Telford, William	207	—— Arth. Saunders,		Tinley, Robert Newport	190
Tempest, Thos. Rich.		*MD.*	168	—— Wm. Newport	259
Plumbe	90	—— Francis Ringler		Tinling, Geo. Vaughan	284
Temple, Grenville Temple,			101, 284	—— Wm. Fred.	71
Bt.	86	—— Geo. Latham	178	Tinseau, Arthur Leon de	441
—— John	211	—— Harry	115	Tipping, Alfred	220
Templer, Francis Butler	258	—— James	68	Tireman, Hen. Stephen	270
Templeton, Robert, *MD.*	287	—— John Anstruther	135	Tisdall, Thomas	59
Tench, Donald Wm.	196	—— John Bathurst	168	Tobin, Geo. Edw. Alex.	162
—— John	305	—— Patrick	116	—— Henry Wilhelm	199
Tennant, Aralander	92, 186	—— Robert	59, 283	—— John	162
—— George	237	—— Tannatt Houston	305	—— Jos. Webbe	20, 264
Tennent, James	306	—— William	116	Tobing, Christian	437
Terraneau, Wm. Henry	116	Thoreau, John	95, 128	Toby, Isaac	294
Terry, Robert	60	Thoresby, Charles	116	Tod, Alexander	60
Tessier, Jas. Fitz Herbert de	168	Thorman, Charles	441	Todd, Elliott D.	116
		Thorn, Nathaniel, *KH.*	40	—— Francis	184
Teulon, Charles	85	—— William, *KH.*	116	—— George	63
—— George	61	Thorndike, Cha. Faunce	272	—— James	191
—— Thomas	186	—— Daniel	269	—— John Augustus	131
Tew, Geo. M'Leod	201	Thorne, Pereg. Fras. *KH.*	84	—— Suetonius Henry	115
—— Joseph M'Leod	173	Thornhill, George	57	—— William	237
Thackeray, Fred. Rennell		—— Jas. Badham, *KH.*	90	Tollemache, William Aug.	119
	19, 282	—— John	243	Tolson, Richard Henry	83
Thackwell, Jos. *KCB.*		—— William	116	Tombs, John	115
KCH.	40, 130	Thornton, Cha. Wade,		Tomkins, Alexander	229
—— Joseph Edwin	246	*KCH.*	19	Tomkinson, William	67
Thain, William	102, 172	—— Godfrey	61, 144	Tomkyns, Richard	268
Thiel, Chas. Zehender De	441	—— Henry	33	Tomline, John	210
Thistlethwayte, Alex.	187	—— John	85	—— William	136
Tholon, Joseph	434	—— Perrott	163	Tomlinson, James	99, 137
—— Joseph	442	—— Samuel Lewis	116	—— Nicholas R.	169
—— Louis	441	—— William, *KCB.*		Tonge, John Henry	140
Thom, Alexander	311		14, 237	Tongue, John	89, 181
Thomas, Edmund Stephen	221	—— William	145	—— John	181
—— George John	161	—— William	10	Tonson, Jacob	35
—— Henry	40, 171	—— William Henry	241	Toole, Archer	213
—— Henry John	272	Thorold, George Edw.	244	Torkington, Hen. Theodore	232
—— James	184	Thorp, Edward	101, 241	Torrens, Arth. Wellesley	145
—— John Barry	213	—— John	215	—— Charles John	271
—— John W.	191	Thorpe, Samuel, *KH.*	89	—— Frederick	174
—— Morgan	287	Thurlow, Henry Robert	242	—— Robert	37
—— Robert Lloyd	161	—— *Hon.* John Edm.		—— Rob. Samuel	198
—— Thomas Rees	293	Hovel	212	Tothill, John	294
—— William	10	—— *Hon.* Tho. Hugh		Tottenham, Charles J.	119
Thompson, Arnold	233	Hovel	158	—— W. Heathcote	138

522

Index.

	page		page		page
Touzel, Helier	18	Tucker, John Goulston		Udney, John Augustus	146
———— Thomas Percival	178	Price	32	———— John Robert	116
Tovey, Alexander	175	Tuckey, Cha. Timothy	192	Ulmenstein, J. W. de 53, 436	
———— George	60	Tudor, Frederick	189	Underwood, Wm. Henry	247
———— James Dunbar	58	———— Henry Bridger	221	———— John J.	116
Towers, Frederick	86	———— Wm. Langley	201	Unett, Thomas	219
Towesland, Samuel Jos.	306	Tugginer, Edmund de	440	———— Walter	130
Townsend, Edward	234	———— Edward de	440	Unger, William	438
———— John	58, 140	———— Joseph	440	Uniacke, James	293
———— John Gore	141	Tuite, George	170	———— Redmond Rochfort	
———— Samuel Philip	270	———— George Gustavus	69		223
———— Thomas	212	———— Hugh Manley	270	———— Richard	20
Townshend, Henry	240	———— Mark Anth. Hen.	170	———— Robert	161
———— *Hon.* Hor. G.		Tulloch, Alex. Murray	102	Upton, *Hon.* Arthur Percy	14
Powys, *KCH.*	33	———— Jas. Dundas Gre-		———— *Hon.* Arthur	73, 147
———— Hen. Dive	72, 175	gorie	242	———— *Hon.* George	98, 214
Trafford, Charles Guy	217	———— Thomas	193	Urmston, Lambert Bra-	
———— Robert	253	Tulloh, Alexander	269	bazon	182
———— Tho. Sam.	60	Tunnard, Bartholomew	178	Urquhart, Donald	70, 190
———— Tho. William	129	Tuper, Cha. W.	221	———— Francis Gregor	151
Tranchell, Geo. Adolphus	257	Turnbull, Robert	232	———— John	295
Tranter, William	208	———— William, *MD.*	246	Ussher, Edw. Pellew Ha-	
Trapaud, Cyrus Plaistow	159	Turner, Charles	34	mett	296
Travers, Boyle	11	———— Cha. Barker, *KH.*	61	Utterton, John	116
———— Fred. John	272	———— Charles Ernest	105	Uxbridge, Henry, *Earl of,*	43
———— James	259	———— Edmund John	124		
———— John	272	———— Frederick Henry	149	Vale, John	172
———— Joseph Oates	295	———— George	44, 265	Valiant, Hen. Fancourt	191
———— Julius Brockman	258	———— George Edward	271	———— Thomas, *KH.*	44, 191
———— Robert Otho	186	———— Henry Austin	271	———— Thomas James	191
———— Robert William	175	———— Henry John	218	Vance, James Young	191
———— Thomas Otho	116	———— Herbert	120	Van Cortlandt, Henry C.	
———— Thomas Robert	170	———— *Sir* Hilgrove,			95, 182
Trelawny, Hamelin	61, 265	*GCH. KC.*	8, 170	Vandeleur, Edward	138
———— Harry Brereton	146	———— James	269	———— John	57, 136
Tremenheere, Walter, *KH.*	36	———— John	207	———— John Ormsby,	
Trench, Fred. Wm. *KCH.*	19	———— John	272	*GCB.*	9, 142
———— Frederick Charles	218	———— Philip	307	———— Robert	86
———— Power le Poer	122	———— William	96, 201	Vander Meulen, C. Jowett	
———— *Hon.* Rich. le Poer		Turnor, Henry Martin	121		97, 225
	203	———— William	65	Vanderspar, Wm. Charles	258
———— William le Poer	177	Tuson, Geo. Baily	273	Vansittart, Robert	148
Trent, John Constantine	120	Tuthill, Jackson Villiers	122	Varlo, Berney	296
Trevelyan, Harrington	211	———— Richard, *MD.*	256	———— Henry	296
———— Walter	91, 211	Tuyll, Wm., *KCH.*	18	———— George	297
———— William Pitt	245	Tweddell, Rob. Wharton	306	Vassall, Rawdon J. Pop.	230
Trevor, Arth. Hill, *KH.*	86	Tweeddale, G. *Marq. of,*		Vaughan, Benj. Hutche-	
———— Edward	268	*KT.*	19	son	101, 267
———— *Hon.* Hen. Otway	13	Twiss, John	285	———— Eugene Jas.	192
Trew, Thomas Eggar	306	Twopeny, Edward	101, 230	———— Herbert	86
Trick, Frederick John	218	Tydd, Thomas	228	Vavasour, Henry Wm.	58, 283
Trigance, Joseph	181	Tylden, Wm. Burton	66, 283	———— Henry Felix	169
Trimmer, John	307	———— Richard	286	———— Mervin	286
Tripp, Peter	67, 250	———— John	269	Veetch, Thomas George	236
Trittau, Edward	432	Tylee, Alfred	270	Venour, Walter	247
Tritton, John	130	———— David William	286	Vere, Chas. Broke., *KCB.*	10
Trollope, Charles	187	Tyler, Henry Crickitt	191	Vereker, Charles	178
Tronson, Edward T.	72, 164	———— John, *KH.*	63	Verfenstein, Joseph	305
Trotman, Philip Phipps	254	———— Lennard Barrett	214	Verling, James, *MD.*	287
Trott, Charles Crato	440	Tynte, Cha. Kemeys Ke-		Verner, Robert Norris	213
Troubridge, Tho. St. Vin-		meys	237	———— William	116
cent, H. C.	158	———— Melbourne Kemeys	124	———— William J.	204
Trower, Fred. Courtney	142	Tyrell, Walter Robert	120	Vernon, George Augustus	184
Truscott, John	115	Tyssen, William Hough-		Vernon, George James	198
Trydell, Botet	88, 235	man	232	———— Henry Cha. Edw.	34
Tryon, Samuel	194	Tytler, Alexander	270	———— Justinian	141
Tucker, Henry	285	Tytler, George Alexander	160	———— William Fred.	189

Index.

Vesey, Arthur George 197
Vialls, Henry Thomas 196
Vicars, Edward 285
—— Henry 213
—— Robert Shafto 207
Victor, James Conway 97, 284
Vieusseau, Andrew 441
Vignoles, Francis Durell 179
Vigors, Cha. Hen. Fitz Roy 239
—— Horatio Nelson 164
—— John Urban 258
—— Joshua Allen 203
Vigoureux, Cha. Albert 34
Ville Ferdinand, Compte de la 440
Villiers, Hon. Fran. John Rob. 174
——Hon. Fred. Wm. C. 148
Vincent, John 11, 221
Vincenti, Giovanni Ant. 439
Viney, James, KCH. 16, 264
Vinicombe, Geo. Elliott 16
Virtu, Georgio 262
Vivian, Cha. Crespigny 92
—— John Cranck Walker 171
—— Rt. Hon. Rich. Hussey, Bt. GCB. GCH. 12, 128
Vogelsang, Charles de 53, 440
Volborth, Philip 433
Volger, Christ. Arnold 436
—— Henry William 437
Voss, Ernest Von 432
Vyse, George Howard 119
—— R. W. How. Howard 40
—— Rich. Hen. Rich. Howard 120

Wachholtz, Fred. Lewis de 439
Waddell, James 207
Waddington, Hen. Spencer 253
—— Charles 116
Waddy, Richard 201
Wade, Fran. Montresor 195
—— Claude Martine 116
—— George 164
—— Hamlet 164
—— John 295
—— Thomas Fra. 193
—— Thomas Fra. 38
—— Walter, John Plunkett 272
Wadeson, James 163
Wahab, George 115
—— Charles 116
—— George L. 115
Wahrendorff, Augustus 434
Waite, Thomas 246
Wakefield, Henry Furey 191
—— Joseph 69, 190
—— William 223
Walch, James W. Henry 95
Walcott, Edm. Yeamans 68, 266

Wale, Charles, KCB. 9, 184
—— Robert Gregory 184
Walhouse, Edward 163
Walker, Archibald 68, 283
—— Charles 166
—— Charles A. 115
—— Charles J. 190
—— Charles Montagu 241
—— Cha. Pynder Beauchamp 184
—— David 16
—— Edward, KH. 20
—— Edward Walter 150
—— Fitz William 166
—— Frederick 20, 264
—— George James 139
—— Geo. Townsend, Bt. GCB. 9, 201
—— Geo. Warren 40, 172
—— Hen. Torrens 258
—— James 240
—— John 226
—— John Geddes 270
—— Joseph 70, 292
—— Joseph 11
—— Leslie, KH. 54
—— Philip Warren 89, 267
—— Robert 53
—— Samuel 92, 217
—— Thomas 306
—— Thomas George 227
—— William 221
—— William 69, 292
—— Wm. Jas. Tyrwhitt 213
Wall, John Binns 150
Wallace, George Harris 167
—— James Maxwell, KH. 43, 125
—— John 192
—— John Alex. Bt. KCB. 12, 240
—— Peter Margetson 58, 265
—— Robert, KH. 58
—— William 250
—— William, MD. 166
Wallett, Charles 95, 257
Wallington, J. C. 91, 136
—— John Williams 235
Wallis, Lewis Bayly 8
Wallnutt, Thomas 226
Walmoden, Count, KCB. 115
Walmsley, Benjamin 207
Walond, Rich. Fallowes 204
Walpole, Arthur 284
—— Horatio, 98, 190
—— John 285
—— Hon. John 116
—— Robert 252
Walsh, Arth. Sandys Stawell 295
—— Lewis Edward 269
—— Philip 53
—— Robert 226
Walshe, Anthony 170
—— Blayney 160
Walter, Edgar 296

Walter, John 90, 247
—— John MacNeale 180
Walters, Edwin 196
Walther, William 436
Walton, Wm. Lovelace 41, 147
Warburton, Cosby 257
—— Geo. Drought 271
—— Geo. Edw. Egerton 202
—— Hen. Wm. Egerton 198
—— Richard 240
—— Robert 199
—— William White 219
Ward, Fra. Beckford 272
——Hunter 101, 199
——James 233
——John 181
——John 243
——John 116
——John Richard 33
——Robert Edward 136
——William 186
——William 213
——Wm. Cuthbert 70, 283
Warde, Edward Charles 270
—— Francis 268
—— J. H. T. 131
—— Walter 226
Wardell, George 179
—— Wm. Henry 245
Warden, Henry D. 260
Wardlaw, Gerald 225
—— John 17
—— Robert 128
Ware, Robert 200
Waring, Francis Robert 311
Warner, Charles 312
—— Edward 43
—— Isaac Redston 123
Warre, William 34
—— Henry J. 205
Warren, Augustus 251
—— Charles 92, 506
—— Chas. Edw. Dawson 204
—— Edward 206
—— Hen. Hyacinth 206
—— Jas. Low, MD. 133
—— Samuel Robinson 73, 217
—— William 252
—— William Shipley 253
Warriner, Ernle 126
Warrington, Osman F. 229
Wasey, Willoughby Clement 307
Waterfield, Wm. Hill 116
Waterhouse, Alan 212
Waters, Frederick 89
—— John, KCB. 18
—— Marcus, Antonius 96, 284
—— Thomas 293
Wathen, Augustus 103, 141
Watkins, George Green 189
Watson, Albert 258
—— Alexander 19, 264

Index.

Name	page
Watson, Andrew Vincent	178
——— Archibald	115
——— David	234
——— Sir Frederick	66
——— George	294, 297
——— Sir Henry	20
——— Jacob	65
——— James, KCB.	13, 165
——— James	103, 165
——— John	165
——— John	172
——— John Wm. MD.	215
——— John Willis	110
——— Richard Luther	253
——— Robert	258
——— William L.	116
Watt, Francis	123
——— James Duff	305
Watteville, Rodolphe de	441
Waugh, William Petrie	142
——— Gilbert	115
Way, Sir Greg. Holman B.	18
——— Gregory Lewis	180
Waymouth, Samuel	101, 181
Wayth, Charles	116
Weare, Thomas, KH.	59, 261
Wearing, Thomas	293
——— John William	296
Webb, George	136
——— John, KCH.	287
——— Rob. Smith	71
——— Theodosius	286
——— Thomas	242
Webber, Edward	11
——— William	67
Webster, Henry	62
——— Arthur Charles	192
——— George Murray	312
——— Joseph	230
——— Robert	251
——— Thomas	115
——— William	142
——— William	152
——— William	228
Wedderburn, J. K.	119
——— James	148
Wedderburne, Cha. Fra.	203
Wadekind, Charles	438
Wegener, John Henry	442
Wegg, John	207
Weguelin, Tho. Mat. Luz.	137
Wehsarg, Charles	439
Weir, James	201
——— John George	180
——— Thomas Christie	305
Weissen, Wilh. von	438
Weller, Francis	269
Wellesley, Lord Cha.	70, 166
——— Edward	176
——— Jas. F. H. Long	138
——— Wm. Hen. Co.	233
Wellington, Arthur, Duke of, KG. GCB. GCH.	144, 252
Wells, Edward	205
——— Crenville G.	152
——— Henry	214
——— John Neave	67, 283
Wells, Samuel	136
——— Samuel	176
——— William	118
Welman, Harvey	88, 208
——— Harvey Wellesley Pole	168
——— Hercules Atkin	232
Welford, Augustus Fred.	249
Welsh, James	115
Wemyss, Charles	306
——— David Douglas	230
——— Francis	263
——— Francis	83
——— John Maurice	296, 297
——— Thos. Jas.	40
——— William	36
Wend, Jas. Douglas de	195
Wentworth, D'Arcey	98
——— Samuel Hen.	285
Werge, Hen. Reynolds	176
——— Robert Dean	190
——— Wernham William	122
Wesley, Samuel Robert	294
West, Arthur, MD.	191
——— Chas. Aug.	53
——— Hon. Cha. Rich	166
——— Desaguilliers	198
——— James Alexander	236
——— John Elridge	159
——— John Temple	146
——— Osborne	234
——— Richard	115
——— William	83
Westenra, Francis	102, 125
——— Hon. J. Craven	63, 149
Western, Maximilian Jas.	216
——— Thos. Halifax	166
Westfeld, Herman	433
Westlake, John	91
Westmacott, Spencer	286
Westmore, Richard	100, 184
Weston, George	139
——— John Sam. Hen.	116
——— Thomas	33
Westropp, John Parson	251
——— Edward Hen.	219
——— John Thomas	217
——— Michael Lionel	209
Wetenhall, Wm. Marsden	161
Wetherall, Edw. Rob.	152
Wetherall, Fred. Aug. GCH.	8, 168
——— Fred. Aug.	168
——— George Aug. KH.	43, 151
——— John	192
Weyhe, Charles von	434
——— Ferdinand von	437
——— George W. F. von	435
——— Weyland, John Thorne	217
Weyssen, Jean Christian	441
Whalley, George Briscoe	188
——— Henry Charles	222
Whalley, Thos. Palmer	135
Whannell, George	101, 184
Wharton, Anthony	7
——— Geo. Heneage Lawrence	197
Wheatley, Henry, GCH.	116
——— John	193
Wheatstone, Henry	186
——— John Butler	204
Wheeler, Fra. Hugh Massey	116
——— Henry	199
——— James A.	229
——— John Ross	205
——— Thomas	179
——— Thomas Honer	219
Whelan, John Thomas	61
Wheeler, Trevor, Bt.	87
Whetham, John	41
Whichcote, George	71
Whimper, Fred. Amelius	250
Whinyates, Edw. Charles, KH.	61, 265
——— Fran. Frankland	186
——— Fred. Wm.	101, 284
Whish, Richard	115
Whitaker, John Gibson	134
Whitcomb, James	294
White, Charles H.	148
——— Edward James	19, 222
——— Edward Philip	97
——— Edward Rich.	161
——— Ferdinand	191
——— Frederick Charles	9
——— Frederick John	296
——— George Fra.	182
——— George Mathias	191
——— Henry Arthur	286
——— Hen. Dalrymple	132
——— Henry Jarvis	229
——— James	130
——— James	263
——— Lawrence Luke Esmond	236
——— Martin	115
——— Michael	73, 130
——— Moses, MD.	253
——— Raymond	98, 132
——— Robert	88
——— Thomas	190
——— Walter	100
White, William	83
——— William	130
——— William George	195
——— William Grove	54
——— William Ramsay	142
Whitehead, Thos, KCB.	115
Whitelaw, Thomas	287
Whitfeild, Henry Wase	256
Whitefield, Chas.Tomlins	287
Whiting, George Wm.	296
Whitmore, Fran. Locker	152
——— Geo. St. Vincent	285
——— Geo. KCH.	18, 282
——— Mortimer R. S.	158
Whitter, William Wood	228

Index.

Name	page
Whittingham, Ferdinand	219
——— H. B.	197
——— Paul, Bernard	286
——— Sam. Ford, *KCB*.	
KCH.	15, 115, 223
Whittuck, Wm. Jas.	234
Whitty, Irwine	97, 267
Whylock, James	293
Whyte, Charles	310
——— John James	69, 133
——— Samuel	222
Wichmann, George	434
Wicke, John Henry	436
Wickham, Rich. Straker	254
Widdrington, Adol. Lat.	225
Wieboldt, Dav. Cha. Corn.	433
Wieburg, John Andrew	255
Wieler, John William	433
Wiering, George	437
Wight, Arthur	116
Wightman, James	273
Wigram, Ely Duodecimus	69, 147
——— Jas. Richard	148
Wigston, Francis	169
Wilbraham, Chas. Philip	148
——— *Hon.* Edw. Bootle	148
——— Richard	116, 158
——— Thos. Edw.	180
Wilby, William	155
Wilder, George	272
Wilding, Ernest, *KH.*	434
Wildman, Edward, *KH.*	43
——— John	85
——— Thomas	41
Wilford, Edmund Neal	269
——— John Sutton	211
Wilkie, Fletcher	116
——— John	136
Wilkieson, William	223
Wilkins, George, *KH.*	54
——— George Hughes	253
——— Thomas	271
——— Wm. Mortimer	192
Wilkinson, Arth. Philip Savage	164
——— Charles C.	285
——— Christopher	84
——— James Allix	166
——— John	143
——— Joseph	253
Wilkinson, Rich. Steele	89
——— Thomas	116
——— Tho. Wm.	181
——— Wm. *Sir, GCMG.*	8
——— William	71, 200
——— Wm.	121
Willan, Tho. Wm. Douglas	138
——— Wm. Moffat Douglas	272
Willats, Peter John	95, 199
Willcocks, Rob. Hen. *KH.*	91, 233
Willes, James Irwin	293
——— William Gibson	182
Willett, Augustus Saltren	143
Williams, Arthur Charles	135
Williams, Arth. Wellesley	136
——— Charles	306
——— David	37
——— Edm. Keynton, *KCB.*	35, 160
——— Harry	154
——— Henry	268
——— Henry	7
——— Henry David	205
——— James E.	287
——— John	285
——— John	83
——— Joseph	89
——— Lewis Duncan	119
——— Montgomery	284
——— Norton Tho.	216
——— Robert Griffith	175
——— Sherburne	68
——— Thomas	155
——— Thomas	116
——— Thomas, *MD.*	170
——— Thomas Molyneux	86
——— Walter	143
——— William	142
——— William	164
——— William	251
——— Wm. Fenwick	270
——— Wm. Freke, *KH.*	70
Williamson, Cha. Cartwright	294
——— James	54
——— John	184
——— John Clark	135
——— Thomas Paul	245
——— Usher	178
Willington, Richard	102, 236
——— Ormsby	226
Willis, Browne	101, 267
——— Browne	272
——— Richard A.	115
Willoughby, Wm. Lemos	174
——— Fran. Digby	135
Willox, James	205
Willshire, Thomas, *KCB.*	39, 153
Willson, Selwyn	248
Wilmer, William	142
——— Wilmer	150
Wilmot, Eardley	90
——— Fred. Eardley	270
Wilmot, Hen. Rob. Eardley	271
——— John	161
Wilson, Arthur	169
——— Benjamin F.	
——— Dalton	93, 186
——— Charles	272
——— Cha. Townsend	210
——— Fleetwood, Tho. Hugh	134
——— Francis W.	115
——— Fred. J.	203
——— George	9
——— George A.	165
——— George Davis	54
——— James, *KCB.*	20
——— James	306
——— James, *MD.*	310
Wilson, James Kennett	294
——— James Wm.	84
——— John	203
——— John	242
——— John, *KCB.*	15, 234
——— John	293, 297
——— John Morillyon, *KH.*	39
——— John	116
——— John	116
——— John Alexander	268
——— John Gray	157
——— J. Rich. Sheppard	188
——— Joshua	86
——— Mackenzie	206
——— Nathan, *KH.*	55
——— Nicholas, *KH.*	87, 229
——— Rich. Gasden	
Bowen	268
——— *Sir* Robert Tho.	11, 141
——— Thomas	307
——— Thomas	115
——— Thomas	84
——— Tho. Maitland	248
——— Wiltshire, *KCH.*	13, 264
Wilton, John	206
Wily, Henry Williams	254
Winchester, Rob. *KH.*	71, 244
Winckler, Augustus	436
——— Charles	436
Windham, Cha. Ash	148
——— Jos. Doughty	152
Wingate, Thomas	153
Wingfield, Cha. Wm.	269, 273
——— Clopton Lewis	98, 218
——— John Hope	166
——— Tho. Hen.	72, 183
Wingrove, Geo. Prescott	36
Winne, John James	295
Winnington, Edward	184
——— John Taylor	162
Wint, Wm. Shute	139
Winter, Charles	228
——— Ludwig Aug.	440
Winterbottom, Robert	118
Winterscale, John	129
Winton, Cha. Lorenzo de	167
——— Rich. Davies de	203
——— Rob. Hen. de	251
Wisch, Hieronimus von der	433
Wischmann, George	436
Wise, Charles	217
——— Francis	217
——— William	198
Wissell, Lewis de	438
Witham, George	220
Witte, George de	441
Witte, Hen. Fred. Theo. de	435
——— John Fred. Cha. de	436
Witzendorff, Hartwig von	432
Witzleben, Cha. *Baron*	437

Index.

	page		page		page
Wodehouse, Edmond	175	Wordsworth, John	312	Wynyard, Septimus Barty	
——— Edwin	271	Workman, Samuel	88	Whitmore	168
——— Frederick	270	Wornum, John Robson	116		
——— Nicholas	43, 201	Worsley, Edw. Vaughan		Ximenes, David, *KCH.*	18
——— Philip	41		19, 264	——— Hen. Cockburne	
——— Wm. Thos.	128	——— Henry, *GCB.*	115	Milne	167
Wohler, Henry	438	Wortham, Hale Young	101, 284		
Wolfe, George	83	Worthy, John	116	Yale, Wm. Parry	70
——— Peter	217	Woulfe, John	115	Yarborough, Chas. Cooke	243
——— Wm. Clarges	190	Wragge, Alf. Romaine	272	Yarde, Henry	116
Wolff, Frederick	439	Wreford, Matthew	312	Yates, Edm. Rob. Wm.	
——— William	434	Wright, Amherst	101, 267	Wingfield	234
Wolffradt Frederick von	439	——— Charles, *KH.*	68	——— John Wildman	234
Wollaston, Frederick	132	——— Charles	101, 284	——— Jonathan	17
Wolley, Edward Lionel	162	——— Charles James	271	——— Richard H.	115
Wolrige, John	63	——— Cha. Ravenhill	194	——— William Charles	128
——— Ambrose A. R.	297	——— Daniel	68	Yea, Lacy Walter	158
Wolseley, Garnet Joseph	116	——— Edward W. C.	243	——— Raleigh Henry	250
Wombwell, Arthur	197	——— Frederick	96, 267	Yelverton, *Hon.* Geo. Fred.	
Wood, Arthur, *MD.*	130	——— George	161	Wm.	216
——— Charles	156	——— George	282	Yerbury, John William	130
——— C. W. A. H.	194	——— Henry Rich.	268	Yolland, William	285
——— David Edward	270	——— James Dennis	146	Yonge, Gustavus Nigel	
——— Edward	83	——— John, *KH.*	44, 292	K. A.	153
——— Edward Robert	138	——— John Hoskin	295	——— William James	197
——— Henry	130	——— John Ross	44, 283	Yorke, Fred. Augustus	285
——— Henry John	116	——— Robert	294	——— Charles	56
——— Henry Owen	94, 188	——— Robert	294	——— James Charles	125
——— James	294	——— Thomas	88	——— John	128
——— James	71	——— Thomas	72, 190	——— Philip James	64, 149
——— Jas. Humphreys		——— Wm. Alfred G.	296	Young, Augustus H. S.	206
	96, 267	Wrixon, Nicholas	172	——— Charles Allen	199
——— John	247	Wrottesley, *Hon.* Chas.		——— Charles	214
——— John Gillespie	312	——— Alex.	72, 180	——— Charles	287
——— John Joseph	109	Wulff, George	13, 264	——— Charles Colville	271
——— John Sulivan	8	——— Henry Powell	284	——— Dobson	177
——— John Stewart	164	Wulffen, William de	438	——— George	92, 189
——— Launcelot Edward	205	Wyatt, Alfred Fras. W.	217	——— Geo. Augustus	159
——— Peter Valentine	165	——— George John	272	——— George Dobson	182
——— Robert	311	——— Hen. Robartes	57	——— Henry	175
——— Robert Blucher	136	Wybault, Joseph Wm.	306	——— James, *MD.*	170
——— Thomas	72, 145	Wyld, John	130	——— James Robert	92, 176
——— Wm. *KH.*	34	Wylde, William	65, 115, 266	Young, John Crawford	92
——— William	190	Wynch, John	116	——— J. D.	195
——— William	294, 297	Wyndham, Charles	70, 129	——— Keith Wellington	253
——— Wm. Mark	212	——— Charles	43	——— Plomer, *KH.*	72
——— Wm. Leighton, *KH.*	67	Wyndham, Charles Henry	133	Young, Plomer J.	240
Woodd, Geo. Leslie	256	——— George	34	——— William Baird	270
Woodfall, George	116	——— Henry	19	——— William Henry	153
Woodford, Alex. *KCB.*	15	Wyneken, Frederick	441	——— William Pym	217
——— Adolphus F. A.	148	Wynn, Arth. Watkin Williams	174	Younghusband, Chas.	36, 265
——— John Geo. *KCH.*	18			——— Cha. Wright	272
Woodgate, Frederick	242	——— Herb. Wat. Wms.	161	——— Thos.	41
——— John	263	——— Watkin Williams, *Bt.*	118	Yule, Geo. Wm. Roper	295
——— William	156			——— Patrick	100, 284
——— William	33	Wynne, Charles Robert	271	——— Robert Abercromby	142
Woodhouse, Joseph Rob.	116	——— George	285		
——— Robert	189	——— Heneage Griffith	220	Zehupfenning, Chas. Jos.	440
——— William	115	——— Lowry Wm. Montgomery	271	Zeil Augustus Ferdinand	435
Woodman, William	122			Zerbi, Paul	439
Woodrooffe, George H.	116	Wynniatt, Wenman	235	Zerbi, Jean Baptiste	439
Woods, James	233	Wynter, Robert	270	Ziermann, Frederick	437
Woodward, John	156	Wynyard, Edward	36	Zimmermann, Fred. Adol	433
Woolridge, Thos. T. *KH.*	41	——— Edward G.	146	Zugiani, Marino	441
Woolhouse, Edward	195	——— Henry	237	Zuhlcke, George Henry	40
Woollard, Gilbert	240	——— Robert Henry	209	——— Charles W.	197

www.ingramcontent.com/pod-product-compliance
Lightning Source LLC
Chambersburg PA
CBHW021824220426
43663CB00005B/123